MODERN PROVERBS
AND
PROVERBIAL SAYINGS

MODERN PROVERBS
AND
PROVERBIAL SAYINGS

BARTLETT JERE WHITING

HARVARD UNIVERSITY PRESS

Cambridge, Massachusetts

and London, England

1989

This volume was prepared for the printer by Joseph Harris,
Susan Deskis, and Maud Wilcox.

Publication of the book has been aided by a grant from the
Hyder Edward Rollins Fund of Harvard University.

This book is printed on acid-free paper, and its binding materials
have been chosen for strength and durability.

Library of Congress Cataloging-in-Publication Data

Whiting, Bartlett Jere, 1904–
Modern proverbs and proverbial sayings / Bartlett Jere Whiting.
p.   cm.
Bibliography: p.
ISBN 0-674-58053-2
1. Proverbs.   2. Proverbs, English—Dictionaries.   I. Title.
PN6403.W48   1989   89-31520
398.9′21—dc20   CIP

FOREWORD

by Larry D. Benson

Around Harvard Yard one used to hear the story of how President Lowell, motoring down a back road in the countryside near Belfast, Maine, in the late summer of 1921, espied a boy sitting beneath a tree intent upon a book. Pleased and puzzled at this display of literacy in so unexpected a setting, he stopped his automobile and asked the lad, "What are you reading?" "Aristophanes, sir." "In Greek?" "Why, yes sir." "Get in this car, boy. You are going to Cambridge with me." That, students assured one another, is how Professor Whiting first came to Harvard.

Of course, even those who repeated the story knew it was apocryphal; the young Bartlett J. Whiting applied to and was accepted as a freshman by Harvard College in the usual prosaic manner. But the story persisted because it contained three of the most important facts about him—his close association with his native Maine, his long relationship with Harvard, and his lifelong devotion to reading. He began reading as a boy in the house in which he was born in East Northport, near Belfast; he continued during his more than a half century at Harvard; and when he became emeritus he returned to Maine to carry on his reading in that same house in which a lifetime of reading began. He was and is an insatiable reader, even now when the failing sight of his one usable eye (the other was blinded in boyhood) makes it possible only with bright illumination and a magnifying glass.

His taste in reading is and was broad; he read the classics, and he read the medieval literatures that he professed, but he also read widely and deeply in later English and American literature and in modern authors, from the works of established standard writers (such as James Joyce, one of his favorites for citation in this volume) to the most ephemeral varieties of fiction and nonfiction. He especially enjoyed historical novels, and for some years he wrote a regular (and regularly amusing) review of the year's output of historical fiction set in the Middle Ages—all of it, whether good or bad—which was published in the learned journal *Speculum*. One of that journal's learned subscribers objected to what he considered a waste of space on ephemera and he wrote with some asperity to the editor, suggesting in effect that this annual review be dropped, so that the footnotes in the other articles could be longer. Mr. Whiting was delighted at the opportunity to defend his interest in the genre, and in his next review of the year's output he effectively silenced his critic with a long history of attacks on historical fiction, beginning with the unsympathetic reviewers of Sir Walter Scott's *Waverley* novels. The critic was silenced but probably unsatisfied, since not many readers have Mr. Whiting's breadth of literary sympathies. That breadth was shown when the editor of his Festschrift some years ago was casting about for a photograph of him to adorn the collection of scholarly essays to be published in his honor. There were few to choose from and those few rather more solemn than he customarily appeared. The problem was solved by a candid snapshot, taken when Mr. Whiting was reading the Sunday comics in the *Boston Globe*. Suitably cropped, it admirably served the purpose.

Throughout his years of reading Mr. Whiting took notes, most especially notes on the proverbs and proverbial sayings that appeared in his reading. He had been interested in proverbs since his undergraduate days, and his doctoral thesis, which was directed by George Lyman Kittredge, concerned that topic. One chapter of the thesis formed the nucleus of his first book, *Chaucer's Use of Proverbs* (1934), and this was followed by other studies of proverbs in early literature, *Proverbs in the Earlier English Drama* (1938) and *Proverbs and Proverbial Sayings From Scottish Writers Before 1600* (1949). But from the beginning he had also been interested in the proverbs in later literature, and he was already reading systematically for *A Dictionary of American Proverbs and Proverbial Phrases, 1820 to 1880* (1958), compiled in collaboration with Archer Taylor, and for the three works that crown his career: *Proverbs, Sentences, and Proverbial Phrases from English Writings Mainly Before 1500*, prepared in collaboration with his wife, Helen Wescott Whiting (1968), *Early American Proverbs and Proverbial Phrases* (1977), and the present volume.

That he produced all three of these basic reference works entirely by his own efforts, with the assistance of his wife, Helen, is a remarkable fact in these days when such works are ordinarily undertaken by teams of scholars, backed by banks of computers, troops of research assistants, and funded by large grants from the federal government or private foundations.

For all three volumes his working method was the same. From the time he began teaching, Mr. Whiting made a practice of removing, after he had graded the examinations, any unused pages from his students' bluebooks. The torn pages served very well for note paper, and they saved the cost of buying notebooks. As he read through a book, he would write the title and necessary bibliographical information at the top of a recycled bluebook page and then jot down the page numbers and quotations for any proverbs, sentences, or proverbial sayings that he came across. A book particularly rich in proverbial materials might yield two or three pages of such notes, in which case they were carefully clipped together before being stacked, along with others, on open shelves in his study, weighted down with a variety of curious artifacts.

At regular intervals, as he was reading for *Proverbs, Sentences, and Proverbial Phrases*, Mr. Whiting would copy each of the citations intended for use in this work from bluebook pages to 3″ × 5″ pieces of paper. Occasionally a cardboard index card would be used, but slips of paper, more economical than cards, were the preferred form. The slips were then stored in an oak file cabinet salvaged from the Widener catalogue room and, when that was full, in shoe boxes of varying brands and dimensions. The file cabinet was discarded when he retired and moved back to his house in Maine, where he turned his principal attention to *Early American Proverbs*. It was perhaps more efficient to work with shoe boxes alone; they were spread on shelves in the pantry and on tables in his study, the tops off, so that he could easily insert new slips. They seemed somewhat precariously balanced to a visitor, especially one who had enjoyed his hospitality (his frugality affected only himself and he was a generous host) and who would customarily remain well on the other side of the room lest he lurch into and upset the filing system.

A good deal of editing was involved in the transcription of the material from the bluebook pages onto the slips; a preliminary selection was made, and by no means were all quotations in the bluebooks transcribed. The next step was filing the slips in the shoe boxes; as categories became apparent, headings were established or altered, a more nearly final selection of quotations was made, references and cross-references were inserted, and slips of accepted readings were paperclipped together. The final step in editing was the typing of the entries for submission to the press, which he did on his ancient Remington manual. It would have been hard to involve anyone else, for not only was his handwriting difficult to decipher—a postcard from Mr. Whiting would provide an hour's occupation for the most skilled paleographer—the typing was a crucial stage of editing, when he made his final decisions on classifications and the final selection of quotations.

This was the practice followed in preparing his *Proverbs, Sentences, and Proverbial Phrases from English Writings Mainly Before 1500*. The same procedure was used for his *Early American Proverbs and Proverbial Phrases*. The recycled bluebook pages for this work had been accumulating in other stacks on the shelves (since he did much of the reading for all three of these works concurrently). Since the slips of paper and index cards used for the previous work were no longer needed but it would have been wasteful to throw them away, he merely turned them over and wrote the quotations for *Early American Proverbs* on the backs. He had to be careful in typing them to make sure he was looking at the correct side. But the system worked. For the present volume, the same frugal recycling was employed. This time the cards were turned upside down; on many of the slips the quotation for the present volume is at the top, an unrelated one for *Early American Proverbs* is upside down at the bottom, and on the back is a citation for *Proverbs, Sentences, and Proverbial Phrases*. An occasional slip contains a fourth citation for one of his earlier works, a Scots proverb or a line from an Elizabethan play, for this thrifty practice began early. The newly transcribed slips were then tightly packed into the same thirty shoe boxes that had served so well for the previous volumes. "Waste not, want not" is still a common proverb (W31), but it is said more often than done (D193), and even in our ecologically enlightened times it is doubtful that this triumph of Maine frugality will soon be matched.

The list of books that had to be read for *Proverbs, Sentences, and Proverbial Phrases from English Writings Mainly Before 1500* was pretty well established by the period that was to be covered, since Old and Middle English are fairly self-contained bodies of literature, with some leakage at the end (hence the *Mainly* of the title). The list of books to be read for *Early American Proverbs* was a good deal more difficult to specify; though the period of time to be covered was shorter, the amount and range of printed materials was much greater. Nevertheless principles of selection were defined and a list of books to be included was established.

The present volume presented a very different problem, for Mr. Whiting was reading many of the materials—books, magazines, newspapers—as or shortly after they appeared from around 1930 to the early 1980s, and the corpus was continually expanding. He decided simply to record what he read in his leisure hours; that worked, since his own reading was so wide and various in scope. He recorded proverbs and proverbial sayings from well over six thousand books for the present volume, in addition to the magazines and newspapers he regularly read—the Boston papers, mainly the *Boston Globe* and the *Herald*, the *New York Times*, and the *Daily News* of Bangor, Maine. The bluebook pages that record his reading of books published in 1960 (those that proved useful for the proverbs they contained—his other reading recorded in other notes or left unrecorded) show that for this year alone he read 157 books in the odd hours when he was not teaching his popular undergraduate course on Chaucer, holding seminars, directing theses, serving on the Widener Library Committee, ordering acquisitions for the Child Library, serving as a Councillor of the Mediaeval Academy of America, reviewing scholarly books, writing his witty reports as the Mediaeval Academy's delegate to the American Council of Learned Societies, and fulfilling a variety of other professional and institutional responsibilities, including the chairmanship of his department.

Not all the cited books dated 1960 were read in or immediately after that year. When he finished *Early American Proverbs* in 1977, he was able to turn his full attention to the present project and catch up on his reading, filling in lacunae—such as the *New Yorker* magazine, most issues of which he had not had time to read but every one of which he had saved. Visitors to Northport in the late 1970s would find Mr. Whiting fully abreast of the news of the presidential campaigns of 1940 and 1944 or the progress of the Second World War, as chronicled in "The Talk of the Town" in that magazine.

The books cited for the year 1960 are a fair example of the books culled for this volume. There are "serious" novels (by writers such as John O'Hara, Muriel Spark, Elizabeth Bowen), comic novels (Nathaniel Benchley, P. G. Wodehouse, one of his favorites), mysteries (Rex Stout, Agatha Christie, Erle Stanley Gardner, and others), plays (Tennessee Williams), biographies, autobiographies, collections of letters, and histories of contemporary events (such as Theodore H. White's *Making of the President, 1960*). It is a generous sampling of what was published that year.

It is also a necessarily idiosyncratic list, reflecting Mr. Whiting's own tastes. There is, for example, a heavy component of murder mysteries, shocking to some who might expect a Harvard Professor of English to spend his evenings with more uplifting forms of modern literature. In this Mr. Whiting had the precedent of his seniors on the Harvard faculty, such as the famous Egyptologist who left the Widener Library his collection of over 1900 mystery novels—each carefully graded from A to D−—and, most notably, his teacher George Lyman Kittredge, who gave the Widener Library his own extensive collection of murder mysteries, including one volume, *The White Circle* by the now justly forgotten Carroll J. Day (1926), on the last page of which Mr. Kittredge jotted down the proverbs he had encountered in that book.

Poetry is scarcely represented at all in the quotations in this volume, and light reading clearly predominates. This is hardly surprising: formal literature since at least the eighteenth century has generally avoided the use of proverbs, which, as Mr. Whiting noted in the Introduction to *Early American Proverbs*, are more often found in works cast in the "easy and unbuttoned style." It is inevitable that those literary forms that favor the colloquial style should be most heavily represented.

It is inevitable too, and fortunate, that the works read reflect Mr. Whiting's own taste. This volume is the product of the reading of one man, and of the one man better qualified than any other in our time to recognize a proverbial usage when he saw one—no mean trick, for the proverb, sentence, and proverbial phrase are notoriously resistant to exact definition. "Finally," Mr. Whiting wrote in his introduction to *Proverbs, Sentences, and Proverbial Phrases*, "the collector relies on his own judgment . . . . There comes to be a sense of recognition, a pricking of the thumbs, which says that a statement is proverbial." Mr. Whiting's thumbs pricked more accurately than will anyone else's for many years to come.

In the past few years, Mr. Whiting has suffered from a deterioration of vision in his one usable eye. Reading became increasingly difficult in the early 1980s, and he turned his attention mainly to the editing of the entries in the shoe boxes. He completed this task before his failing eyesight made further work impossible, but he had not begun to transfer the quotations from the slips to a typed final form. Had it not been for the determination of the staff of the Harvard University Press, most notably Maud Wilcox, and the selfless devotion of his friend and former student, Professor Joseph Harris, this volume would never have appeared and the thirty shoe boxes would still be sitting on the pantry shelves and desk in Northport.

INTRODUCTORY NOTE

This book is patterned after B. J. Whiting's previous collections of proverbs and is similar in format to his *Early American Proverbs and Proverbial Phrases*.

Headings. Each numbered entry in the book gives twentieth-century instances of a proverb or proverbial phrase. The heading, or lemma, gives the usual wording of the saying, with variations indicated in parentheses. Where there are many or extensive variations the notation (*varied*) follows the lemma. Longer proverbs are sometimes curtailed in the heading, as in A32, When Adam delved and Eve span *etc.* In every lemma a key word, ordinarily the first important noun or verb, is capitalized and set in boldface type.

Alphabetization. The entries are alphabetized by their key words. Sayings with the same key word are arranged in alphabetical order, reading from left to right but ignoring initial A, An, and The. Substantive and verbal uses of the same key word are separated, however (*work* the noun precedes *work* the verb); and the few occurrences of homonyms (such as *hide*, skin, and *hide*, conceal) are separated as well. Plural and possessive nouns are grouped under the singular form, and verbs are normally alphabetized under the infinitive.

Quotations. Within each entry the quotations are arranged in chronological order, with the dates given in boldface. The source is identified by the author's first initial(s) and surname and the first word or words of the title; thus Gerald Durrell, *My Family and Other Animals* appears as GDurrell *My Family*, Wyndham Lewis, *The Apes of God* as WLewis *Apes*. Pseudonyms (such as Doctor X, Bryher, FRS, Xantippe) are given as they appear on the title page of the book; anonymous works are so labeled or appear without an author's name preceding the title. Biographies and critical studies of well-known figures are usually cited by the subject's surname, with or without initials. The place of publication is given in parentheses; New York, London, Boston, Chicago, Indianapolis, Los Angeles, and Philadelphia are abbreviated to initial letters: NY, L, and so forth. In the case of editions of diaries or collections of letters, the boldface date is the date of the diary entry or letter and the publication date of the volume is included in parentheses along with the place. After the parenthesis comes the page reference and then the quotation. A semicolon and page number at the end of a quotation indicate a second occurrence of the same saying in the same book.

Introductory Note

References. Following the quotations, there are references (in most entries) to compilations in which earlier examples of the saying can be found; full titles of the works are given in the list of abbreviations. Readers interested in looking into the origin or prior history of a proverb can find a helpful starting point in these works. The books most frequently cited are Whiting's previous collections (especially EAP, TW, and Whiting) and *The Oxford Dictionary of English Proverbs.* Further references in those books are ordinarily not repeated.

Cross-references. At the end of the entry there may be cross-references to more or less parallel sayings within this volume. Such references are easy to multiply, as Mr. Whiting points out, and he has not attempted to be systematic or exhaustive in his cross-referencing.

Collections and so-called dictionaries of proverbs do not as a rule provide definitions, and for good reason. Proverbial expressions, drawing on folk wisdom and shared experience, convey their message (if not a strict "meaning") more effectively than a definition could. And many proverbs are not susceptible of definition. A standard exercise in folklore classes demonstrates that many familiar proverbs are understood in contradictory ways. "A rolling stone gathers no moss" is none the less cogent because half its users regard moss as good, half as bad.

Sprinkled among the 5,567 proverbial sayings in this book are terms that may be unfamiliar to some readers (*galley-west* or *pot-valiant*, for example). Such terms are not glossed in the lemmas but the quotations generally make them clear enough, and almost all of them can be found in an unabridged dictionary. Within an entry there is occasionally a brief gloss giving the context of quotation, sometimes to highlight different ways in which a saying is used.

There is no bibliography. Mr. Whiting decided long ago that an alphabetical list of the sources—numbering some six thousand—from which the quotations are drawn would be of little use and would increase the size and price of the book inordinately. As it is, the book is long, longer no doubt than it would have been if the author's eyesight had not failed. Earlier he weeded out a great number of quotations in the process of copying them onto entry slips (transcribing them from the sheets on which he had originally recorded them) and then grouping them under their lemmas. Had he been able to prepare a typescript, he would have done further pruning of repetitive examples of many of the sayings. Most readers will not be bothered, we trust, by an occasional overabundance of quotations, or fret over minor inconsistencies of styling in headings and titles. The book was typeset directly from the handwritten entry slips, and changes in proof other than corrections of printer's errors had to be kept to a minimum.

J. H.
S. D.
M.W.

ABBREVIATIONS

Apperson: G. L. Apperson, *English Proverbs and Proverbial Phrases: A Historical Dictionary* (London: Dent, 1929).

Barbour: Frances M. Barbour, *Proverbs and Proverbial Phrases of Illinois* (Carbondale: Southern Illinois University Press, 1965).

Bartlett: John Bartlett, *Familiar Quotations: A Collection of Passages, Phrases and Proverbs Traced to Their Sources in Ancient and Modern Literature*, 14th ed., rev. Emily Morison Beck (Boston: Little, Brown, 1968).

Berrey: Lester V. Berrey and Melvin Van den Bark, *The American Thesaurus of Slang: A Complete Reference Book of Colloquial Speech* (New York: Crowell, 1942).

Bradley: F. W. Bradley, "South Carolina Proverbs," *Southern Folklore Quarterly* 1 (1937), 57–101.

Brunvand: Jan Harold Brunvand, *A Dictionary of Proverbs and Proverbial Phrases from Books Published by Indiana Authors before 1890* (Bloomington: Indiana University Press, 1961).

Champion: Selwyn G. Champion, *Racial Proverbs: A Selection of the World's Proverbs Arranged Linguistically*, 2nd ed. (New York: Barnes and Noble, 1950).

Clark: J. D. Clark, "Similes from the Folk Speech of the South: A Supplement to Wilstach's Compilation," *Southern Folklore Quarterly* 4 (1940), 205–26.

Colcord: Joanna C. Colcord, *Sea Language Comes Ashore* (New York: Cornell Maritime Press, 1945).

Cole: Arthur H. Cole, "The Social Significance of New England Idiomatic Phrases," *Proceedings of the American Antiquarian Society* n.s. 70 (1960), 21–68.

DA: *A Dictionary of Americanisms on Historical Principles*, ed. Mitford M. Mathews (Chicago: University of Chicago Press, 1951).

DARE: Frederic G. Cassidy, ed., *Dictionary of American Regional English* (Cambridge, Mass.: Belknap Press of Harvard University Press, 1985–).

DBC: Detective Book Club.

Dunwoody: H. H. C. Dunwoody, *Weather Proverbs* (Washington, D.C.: Government Printing Office, 1883).

EAP: Bartlett Jere Whiting, *Early American Proverbs and Proverbial Phrases* (Cambridge, Mass.: Belknap Press of Harvard University Press, 1977).

Hand: Wayland D. Hand, *Popular Beliefs and Superstitions from North Carolina*, in *The Frank C. Brown Collection of North Carolina Folklore*, 7 vols. (Durham, N.C.: Duke University Press, 1952–1964), vols. 6–7.

Abbreviations

Hislop: Alexander Hislop, *The Proverbs of Scotland* (Edinburgh: E. and S. Livingstone, 1868).

JAFL: *Journal of American Folklore.*

Janson: Horst W. Janson, *Apes and Ape Lore in the Middle Ages and the Renaissance* (London: Warburg Institute, University of London, 1952).

Leach: Maria Leach, ed., *Dictionary of Folklore, Mythology, and Legend*, 2 vols. (New York: Funk and Wagnalls, 1949–1950).

Lean: Vincent S. Lean, *Lean's Collectanea*, 4 vols. in 5 (Bristol, Eng.: J. W. Arrowsmith, 1902–1904).

NADS: *Newsletter of the American Dialect Society.*

NED: *A New English Dictionary on Historical Principles*, 1884–1928, reissued, with Supplement, as *The Oxford English Dictionary*, 13 vols. (Oxford: Clarendon Press, 1933).

Oxford: The Oxford Dictionary of English Proverbs, 3rd ed., rev. F. P. Wilson (Oxford: Clarendon Press, 1970).

Oxford *DQ: The Oxford Dictionary of Quotations*, 2nd ed. (London: Oxford University Press, 1966).

Partridge: Eric Partridge, *A Dictionary of Slang and Unconventional English*, 5th ed. (London: Routledge, 1961).

Spears: Richard A. Spears, *Slang and Euphemism: A Dictionary of Oaths, Curses, Insults, Sexual Slang and Metaphor, Racial Slurs, Drug Talk, Homosexual Lingo, and Related Matters* (Middle Village, N.Y.: Jonathan David, 1981).

Taylor *Index*: Archer Taylor, *An Index to "The Proverb,"* FF Communications, 113 (Helsinki: Suomalainen Tiedeakatemia, 1934).

Taylor *Prov. Comp.*: Archer Taylor, *Proverbial Comparisons and Similes from California*, Folklore Studies, 3 (Berkeley: University of California Press, 1954).

Taylor *Proverb*: Archer Taylor, *The Proverb* (Cambridge, Mass.: Harvard University Press, 1931).

Taylor *Western Folklore*: Archer Taylor, "More Proverbial Comparisons from California," *Western Folklore* 17 (1958), 12–20.

Tilley: Morris P. Tilley, *A Dictionary of the Proverbs in England in the Sixteenth and Seventeenth Centuries* (Ann Arbor: University of Michigan Press, 1950).

TW: Archer Taylor and Bartlett Jere Whiting, *A Dictionary of American Proverbs and Proverbial Phrases, 1820–1880* (Cambridge, Mass.: Belknap Press of Harvard University Press, 1967).

Wentworth: Harold Wentworth and Stuart B. Flexner, *Dictionary of American Slang* (New York: Crowell, 1960).

Whiting: Bartlett Jere Whiting, with Helen Wescott Whiting, *Proverbs, Sentences, and Proverbial Phrases from English Writings Mainly before 1500* (Cambridge, Mass.: Belknap Press of Harvard University Press, 1968).

Whiting *Chaucer*: Bartlett Jere Whiting, *Chaucer's Use of Proverbs*, Harvard Studies in Comparative Literature, 11 (Cambridge, Mass.: Harvard University Press, 1934).

Whiting *Devil*: Bartlett Jere Whiting, "The Devil and Hell in Current English Literary Idiom," *Harvard Studies and Notes in Philology and Literature* 20 (1938), 201–47.

Whiting *Drama*: Bartlett Jere Whiting, *Proverbs in the Earlier English Drama, with Illustrations from Contemporary French Plays*, Harvard Studies in Comparative Literature, 14 (Cambridge, Mass.: Harvard University Press, 1938).

Whiting *NC*: B. J. Whiting, ed., "Proverbs and Proverbial Sayings," in *The Frank C. Brown Collection of North Carolina Folklore*, vol. 1 (Durham, N.C.: Duke University Press, 1952), pp. 331–501.

Whiting *Scots*: B. J. Whiting, "Proverbs and Proverbial Sayings from Scottish Writings before 1600," *Mediaeval Studies* 11 (1949), 123–205; 13 (1951), 87–164.

Wilstach: Frank Jenners Wilstach, *A Dictionary of Similes* (Hildesheim: Georg Olms, 1973).

A

A1 From **A** to izzard

1931 HSKeeler *Matilda* (NY) 329: He's lying from A to Izzard. **1937** CBClason *Blind* (NY) 125: We went over the whole district from A to Izzard. TW 1; Brunvand 1.

A2 From **A** to Z

1903 ADMcFaul *Ike Glidden* (B) 21: I know horses from A to Z. **1914** JLondon *Letters* ed KHendrick (NY 1965) 421: Frank Norris from A to Z. **1936** FWCrofts *Man Overboard* (NY) 233: The case was discussed from A to Z. **1950** RStout *In the Best* (NY) 32: I know him from A to Z. **1955** FCrane *Death* (NY) 141: Go over the premises from a to z. **1960** MSpark *Ballad* (L) 166: To go through the factory from A to Z. **1971** JCreasey *Murder* (NY) 151: [He] fixed it from A to Z. **1974** PGWodehouse *Cat-Nappers* (NY) 11: He knows his spots from A to Z. EAP A1; TW 1.

A3 Not to know **A** from Adam's off ox

1967 JFDobie *Some Part* (B) 78: He doesn't know A from Adam's off ox. Cf. Whiting *NC* 360: From a bull's foot. Cf. Not to know one from Adam *below*.

A4 To give (get) **A** for effort

1941 VWMason *Rio Casino* (NY) 60: We'll give that lad A for effort. **1947** VWMason *Saigon* (NY) 228: But you get A for effort. **1954** JPotts *Go* (NY) 113: You had to give him an A for Effort. **1960** TPowell *Man-killer* (NY) 119: I'll give you an A for effort. Wentworth 2.

A5 As clear as **A B C**

1931 MMagill *Murder* (P) 312: It's as clear as ABC. EAP A4.

A6 As easy as **A B C**

1930 DDeane *Mystery* (L) 137: Easy as A.B.C. **1932** GCollins *Channel* (L) 68: No harder than ABC. EAP A5; Taylor *Western Folklore* 17(1958) 13.

A7 As plain as **A B C**

1906 JCLincoln *Mr. Pratt* (NY) 14: As plain as A B C. **1934** KLivingston *Dodd* (NY) 258: As plain as ABC. **1953** CBKelland *Sinister* (NY DBC) 144: That's plain as A B C. EAP A7; Brunvand 1.

A8 As simple as **A B C**

1916 WLewis *Letters* ed WKRose (L 1963) 79: As simple as A.B.C. **1931** RKeverne *Fleet* (NY) 238: It's as simple as ABC. **1937** JRhode *Hop Fields* (L) 208: It's as simple as ABC. **1957** AAmos *Fatal* (NY) 163: Simple as ABC. Taylor *Prov. Comp.* 73.

A9 To learn (know, teach) one's **A B C**

1903 EChilders *Riddle* (NY 1940) 109: To learn their ABC. **1929** SMartyn *Recluse* (NY) 108: You don't even know the a b c of the thing. **1946** HHowe *We Happy* (NY) 197: A man who knew his worldly ABC. **1962** JCreasey *Death* (NY DBC) 92: Your chaps don't need teaching their ABC. **1972** MInnes *Open* (NY) 162: You're drawing me into teaching you your own A.B.C. EAP A3.

1

A10   To be **A 1** (A Number 1)

1905 MLPeabody *To Be Young* (B 1967) 314: We have an A. 1. brother-in-law. **1906** JCLincoln *Mr. Pratt* (NY) 53: That was A No. 1. **1910** JCLincoln *Depot Master* (NY) 96: An A1, gold-plated saint. **1918** BMalinowski *Diary* (NY 1967) 259: Health is A1. **1922** VBridges *Greensea* (NY) 64: An A1 lunch. **1922** JJoyce *Ulysses* (NY 1934) 104: Everything went off A1. **1932** APowell *Venusberg* (L 1955) 154: He may be an A1 lad. **1933** PATaylor *Mystery* (NY) 63: She's an a-number-one cook. **1940** HAshbrook *Murder Comes* (NY) 65: A regular little A. no. 1 son of a bitch. **1948** ESherry *Sudden* (NY) 47: He ended up an A one souse. **1955** PDennis *Auntie* (NY) 73: She's an A number one bitch. **1965** AGilbert *Voice* (NY) 121: It had been A-1. **1966** HWaugh *Pure* (NY) 26: The A-number-one suspect. **1970** GBagby *Killer* (NY) 10: She's . . . in A-1 shape. TW 1.

A11   In **Abraham's** bosom

1931 LHollingworth *Death* (L) 190: No Father Abraham to take them to his bosom. **1935** JRhode *Mystery* (L) 127: Look down from Abraham's bosom. **1939** FBeeding *Ten Holy* (NY) 33: Abraham's Bosom [*a cocktail*]. **1947** RDavies *Diary* (Toronto) 135: Making its way toward Abraham's bosom. **1954** ADuggan *Leopards* (L) 203: King John, now in Abraham's bosom. **1966** NBlake *Morning* (NY) 208: To the shelter of Abraham's bosom. **1969** RNye *Tales* (L) 155: "I'll soon be lying in Beelzebub's bosom." I corrected her. "Surely you mean Abraham's." **1975** MButterworth *Man in* (NY) 7: Gone to Abraham's bosom. EAP A8; TW 2.

A12   **Absence** makes the heart grow fonder (*varied*)

1929 TCobb *Crime* (L) 133: It was impossible for absence or anything else to make her heart grow fonder. **1930** IWray *Vye* (L) 133: That proverb about absence making the heart grow fonder, is quite untrue. **1933** HAdams *Woman* (L) 255: Not absence makes the heart grow fonder, and that sort of rot. **1935** RCWoodthorpe *Shadow* (NY) 162: Distance makes the heart grow fonder. **1937** WETurpin *These Low* (NY) 317: Absence makes the heart grow fonder. **1943** AAMacGregor *Auld Reekie* (L) 17: Contrary to the popular adage, his absence from the home was making his heart grow the more bitter. **1948** HActon *Memoirs* (L) 352: Absence had not made my heart grow fonder of Europe. **1952** DGBrowne *Scalpel* (NY) 410: There is another proverb about absence to the effect that it inflames violent passions. **1958** RHutton *Of Those* (L) 66: On the principle that absence makes the heart grow fonder. **1960** TCurley *It's a Wise* (NY) 51: Absence makes the hard grow harder [*sexual*]. **1960** RFraser *Trout's* (L) 140: It's absence makes the heart grow fonder. **1961** WCooper *Scenes* (NY) 50: Absence had not lived up to its reputation. **1975** FHHall *In the Lamb* (I) 63: If absence makes the heart grow fonder. EAP A11.

A13   The **Absent** is always wrong

1912 HHMunro *Unbearable* (NY 1928) 41: The absent may be always wrong. **1927** H Ashton-Wolfe *Outlaws* (L) 116: The absent one is always wrong. EAP A13.

A14   Out of the [**Abundance**] of the heart the mouth speaks (*varied*)

1936 SFowles *Hand in Print* (L) 103: Out of the fullness of the heart the mouth speaketh. **1944** LAGStrong *All Fall* (NY) 190: Out of the heart the mouth speaketh. EAP A15; TW 2.

A15   An **Accent** (*etc.*) that one could cut with a knife (*varied*)

1929 FDGrierson *Murder* (L) 238: A common Cockney accent you could cut with a knife. **1932** IGreig *Baxter's* (L) 37: An accent that could be cut with a knife. **1937** JBentley *Whitney* (L) 88: An Oxford accent so pronounced that one could almost cut it with a knife. **1938** DHume *Corpses* (L) 42: The atmosphere had changed. It could have been cut with the proverbial knife. **1941** PWilde *Design* (NY) 34: The pause was so thick that you could have cut it with a knife. **1947** MCarleton *Swan* (NY) 66: A down-east accent that could be cut with a knife. **1948** PCheyney *Dance* (NY DBC) 11: One of those silences that you could cut with a knife. **1950** ESGardner *Musical* (NY) 17: There's a pall hanging over this place which you can cut with a knife. **1953** JFleming *Good* (L) 158: A Cockney accent you could cut with a knife. **1959** EMButler *Paper* (L) 150: A silence you could cut with a knife. **1959** HReilly *Not Me* (NY DBC) 137: You could have cut the tension in the house with a knife. **1964** GSimenon *Maigret's* (NY DBC) 64: An accent you could cut with a knife. **1967** LPDavies *Artificial* (NY) 145: The air was thick enough to cut with a knife. **1969** HLiggett *Murder* (L) 111: The silence was thick enough to cut with a knife. **1973** JSymons *Plot* (NY) 51: The atmosphere is one you could cut with a knife [*angry*]. Taylor *Prov. Comp.* 81: So thick.

A16 Accidents (mistakes) will happen

1922 JSFletcher *Herapath* (NY) 110: Accidents will happen. **1924** JSFletcher *Time-Worn* (NY) 134: Mistakes will happen. **1932** NKlein *No! No!* (NY) 148: Mistakes will happen to anybody. **1943** CEVulliamy *Polderoy* (L) 151: Accidents will happen, even to the most expert. **1950** BCarey *Man Who* (NY) 186: Accidents can happen. **1957** DJEnright *Heaven* (L) 156: Accidents will happen. **1957** AWilson *Bit* (L) 134: Accidents may happen to anyone. **1965** KLaumer *Galactic* (NY) 143: Accidents will happen, you know. **1975** MDelving *Bored* (NY) 45: Of course, accidents will happen. EAP A16; TW 247: Mistakes (3).

A17 Accidents happen in the best regulated families (*varied*)

1928 WRoughead *Malice* (L) 47: Accidents will happen in the best regulated families. **1930** KCStrahan *Death* (NY) 26: Accidents happen in the best regulated families. **1932** NKlein *No! No!* (NY) 203: Murder can happen in the best of families. **1935** MBurton *Devereux* (L) 169: Accidents will happen, even to the best regulated policemen. **1941** AChristie *Evil under* (NY) 78: Accidents happen in the best-regulated households. **1950** RStout *In the Best Families* (NY). **1951** DBOlsen *Cat* (NY) 19: Accidents happen in the best, and so on. **1961** ZHenderson *Pilgrimage* (NY) 127: These things happen in the best of families. **1972** JMcClure *Cat-*erpillar* (NY) 219: Accidents happen in the best regulated families. EAP A17.

A18 There is no **Accounting** for tastes (*varied*)

1922 JSFletcher *Ravensdene* (NY) 118: No accounting for tastes. **1922** JJoyce *Ulysses* (NY 1934) 151: No accounting for tastes. **1933** CBint *Three Strangers* (L) 190: There is no accounting for tastes. **1935** JRhode *Shot at Dawn* (NY) 27: There's no accounting for likes and dislikes. **1937** PGWodehouse *Laughing* (NY) 120: No accounting for tastes. **1943** PATaylor *Going* (NY) 22: Jeanne was always saying that there was no accounting for some people's taste, and adding some pungent comment about the old lady who insisted on kissing her pig. **1954** EWBarnes *Lady* (NY) 50: There was no accounting for tastes. **1964** WJovanovich *Now* (NY) 11: There is no accounting for people's tastes. **1971** CAird *Late* (NY) 28: There's no accounting for habit. **1971** DFJones *Denver* (NY) 202: There's no accounting for some people's tastes. EAP A18. Cf. Tastes *below*.

A19 As black (bald) as the **Ace** of spades (*varied*)

1929 CBarry *Clue* (NY) 214: He's as black as the ace of spades. **1930** HFootner *Viper* (L) 223: Black as the Knave of Spades. **1932** VWilliams *Fog* (B) 225: You could be as bald as the ace of spades. **1936** PGWodehouse *Young Men* (NY) 224: He was as black as the ace of spades. **1948** AHandley *Kiss* (P) 149: They were as black as the ace of spades. **1959** ASillitoe *Saturday* (NY) 45: As black as the ace of spades. **1965** LHWhitten *Progeny* (NY) 80: As black as spades. **1967** JPurdy *Eustace* (NY) 70: Black as the ace of spades and twice as baleful. **1973** APrice *Colonel* (NY) 32: She was black as the ace of spades. **1977** LBlock *Burglars* (NY) 35: The thing turned as black as the deuce of spades. TW 3(2).

A20 To be **Ace** high

1938 VWMason *Cairo* (NY) 125: I guess I rate ace high with her. **1940** DHume *Five Aces* (L) 26: You're ace high. Wentworth 2.

A21 To be within an **Ace**

1932 PHerring *Murder* (L) 289: We had our man within an ace. EAP A21.

A22 To have an **Ace** in the hole

1921 ERBurroughs *Mucker* (NY) 271: I have an ace-in-the-hole; 280, 291. **1930** MBDix *Murder* (L) 176: Keep him as an ace in the hole. **1937** CFGregg *Wrong House* (L) 251: That's merely the ace in the hole. **1947** MCarleton *Swan* (NY) 92: Iris was an ace in the hole. **1957** IWallace *Square* (NY) 58: His ace in the hole was a large ranch. **1969** JBoyd *Pollinators* (NY) 55: I have a true ace in a real hole. Wentworth 2.

A23 **Achilles** heel

1919 HFAshurst *Diary* ed GFSparks (Tucson 1962) 92: The Achilles heel to the United States. **1922** JJoyce *Ulysses* (NY 1934) 642: The vulnerable point too of tender Achilles; 644. **1930** AGilbert *Mystery* (NY) 159: We all have a heel of Achilles; 55, 140. **1941** RAldington *Life* (NY) 252: Achilles had his vulnerable heel. **1949** JBonett *Dead Lion* (L 1953) 76: She had an Achilles heel. **1951** LFord *Murder Is* (NY) 73: Even Achilles probably never went around bragging about his heel. **1953** IFleming *Casino* (L) 18: His gross physical habits . . . are an Achilles heel. **1958** *TLS* 1/24 38: The status of the Negro is the Achilles heel of the United States. **1958** *BHerald* 2/6 6: Taxation strikes at the Achilles heel of the racketeer. **1958** CI Blackstone *Dewey* (L 1965) 54: A flair for baring the Achilles heel and sticking a dagger into it. **1964** LLRue *World* (P) 109: Another Achilles heel is the racoon's insatiable curiosity. **1966** DRMason *From Carthage* (NY) 159: Even the professional psychologist had an Achilles' heel of *amour propre*. **1970** LKronenberger *No Whippings* (B) 147: To put its Achilles' heel inside a policeman's boot. **1977** DWilliams *Treasure* (NY) 41: His uncanny knack for exposing the Achilles' heel that left clay feet unprotected. EAP A23.

A24 **Actions** speak louder than words (*varied*)

1919 JBCabell *Jurgen* (NY 1922) 85: My actions often speak more unmistakably than my words. 182: Actions speak louder than words. **1926** CFJenkins *Button Gwinnett* (NY) 184: It is a trite saying that actions speak louder than words. **1934** NChild *Diamond* (L) 77: Actions speak louder than results. **1936** *New Yorker* 9/19 59: Actions speak louder than words. **1937** PGWodehouse *Laughing* (NY) 120: Actions speak louder than words. **1939** JJFarjeon *Seven Dead* (I) 314: It's actions that speak, not words. **1956** JDunbar *Golden* (B) 161: Her actions would speak louder than words. **1958** BKendrick *Clear* (NY) 31: My actions may shout out louder than words. **1964** PKinsley *Three* (L) 123: Actions speak louder than words. EAP A28.

A25 As dead as **Adam**

1924 JSFletcher *Mazaroff* (NY) 31: Dead as Adam. TW 3(2).

A26 As naked as **Adam**

1952 RMarshall *Jane* (NY) 147: Naked as Adam. **1959** CDBowen *Adventures* (B) 175: Naked as Adam. **1959** EWeeks *In Friendly* (B) 154: Pygmies . . . as naked as Adam. Wilstach 542.

A27 As old as **Adam**

1934 JJFarjeon *Sinister* (NY) 191: It was as old as Adam. **1937** GGoodchild *Call McLean* (L) 25: Many of them were as old as Adam. **1957** *TLS* 4/19 242: Such an attitude . . . is . . . well-nigh as old as Adam. Tilley A28.

A28 **Adam's** ale

1933 NBell *Lord* (B) 159: Adam's ale [*water*]. **1953** JRMacdonald *Meet* (NY) 68: Adam's ale, my mother called it. **1960** JLodwick *Moon* (L) 166: Adam's ale. EAP A29; DARE i 10.

A29 Not to know one (something) from **Adam** (Eve) (*varied*)

1909 JCLincoln *Keziah* (NY) 289: A strange critter that I didn't know from Adam's cat. **1910** EPhillpotts *Tales* (NY) 333: We didn't know from Adam where we was to. **1911** JCLincoln *Woman-haters* (NY) 149: Folks you . . . don't know from Adam. **1913** JSFletcher *Secret* (L 1918) 41: Would not have known Killingley from Adam. **1916**

SLeacock *Behind* (Toronto 1969) 54: I didn't know him from Adam. **1921** JSFletcher *Chestermarke* (NY) 198: "Don't know it!" "From Adam's writing." **1922** JJoyce *Ulysses* (NY 1934) 764: Not knowing me from Adam. **1927** OFJerome *Hand* (NY) 68: I don't know you from Adam except that you seem to wear more clothes. **1929** JJConnington *Grim* (B) 110: Know him from Adam by his costume, of course, but otherwise not. **1929** BFlynn *Billiard* (P) 145: I can't tell no more than Adam. **1930** HCBailey *Garston* (NY) 83: "I don't know her from Adam." "She isn't Adam." **1932** CAndrews *Butterfly* (NY) 79: I won't know her from Eve. **1932** RThorndike *Devil* (NY) 139: I couldn't tell you from Adam what make of car he was driving. **1933** GDHCole *Death* (NY) 6: Didn't know from Adam where I was. **1933** JGollomb *Curtain* (NY) 176: He didn't know you from Mother Eve. **1933** NBMavity *Fate* (NY) 75: Somebody I don't know from Adam's off ox. **1935** JStagge *Murder* (L) 240: I didn't know her from Adam. **1938** PMacDonald *Warrant* (NY 1957) 5: Neither knew of the other from Adam or even Eve. **1938** MTeagle *Murders* (NY) 119: He doesn't know me from Adam's off ox. **1940** LFord *Old Lover's* (NY) 89: Steve . . . didn't know me [*a woman*] from Adam. **1940** SMSchley *Who'd Shoot* (NY) 208: I don't think Westcott knew her from Eve. **1950** FO'Malley *Best* (NY) 119: What it was I didn't know from Adam, but this old man had a story. **1955** AChristie *So Many* (NY) 207: I don't know Thomas Betterton's wife from Adam. **1958** *BangorDN* 8/8 21: I don't know that woman from Adam. **1958** MAllingham *Tether's* (NY) 54: I don't know what 'e does from Adam. **1959** AHocking *Victim* (NY) 143: He didn't know the woman from Eve. **1960** LFletcher *Blindfold* (NY) 157: They don't know who Gloria King is from Adam. **1964** MWiddemer *Golden* (NY) 140: I didn't know him from Adam's house cat. **1967** RFulford *Trial* (L) 24: She did not know Lady Stuart from Eve. **1968** ESRussell *She Should* (NY) 177: [He] doesn't know this bug [*an automobile*] from Adam. **1969** DARandall *Dukedome* (NY) 301: The American public . . . wouldn't have recognized him

from Adam's off-ox. **1971** MScherf *Beautiful* (NY) 135: I don't know you from Adam's off ox. **1974** MInnes *Appleby's Other* (NY) 36: I can't see how you know me from Adam. EAP A30; Brunvand 2: Adam (1,2); DARE i 9: Adam 1; 11: Adam's off-ox 1. Cf. Not to know A *above*.

A30 The old **Adam**

c1923 ACrowley *Confessions* ed JSymonds (L 1969) 159: The chief mark of old Adam. **1924** EWallace *Green* (B) 121: The old Adam had not disappeared. **1929** LBrock *Stokes Silver* (NY) 247: The old Adam still survives. **1930** EBlunden *Leigh Hunt* (L) 317: The old Adam, male or female. **1931** SLeacock *Sunshine* (Toronto 1960) 107: The old Adam still needs further tanning. **1937** CBush *Eight O'Clock* (NY) 256: It was the old Adam in him coming out. **1952** EHahn *Love* (NY) 207: The old Adam rose up in the demoiselle. **1954** MMcCarthy *Charmed* (NY) 199: The old Adam in him sat up and took notice. **1962** ACraig *Banned* (L) 30: The Old Adam was . . . hard of dying. **1962** EGrierson *Massingham* (L) 238: The old Adam of honesty at work in him. **1968** MHolroyd *Strachey* (L) 2.68: To help banish the old Adam of loneliness. **1970** JRoss *Deadest* (NY) 42: A dark and dangerous streak of Old Adam in him. **1977** VCanning *Doomsday* (NY) 99: When the old Adam in you trapped you with your trousers down. EAP A31; TW 3(4); Brunvand 2: Adam (3).

A31 We are all **Adam's** children

1964 ABurgess *Eve* (L) 78: We're all Adam's children and Eve's too. *Oxford* 3.

A32 When **Adam** delved and Eve span *etc.*

1928 WRoughead *Malice* (L) 157: The Mulbrie Murder; or, When Adam Delved [*chapter title*]. **1929** BFlynn *Invisible* (L) 138: A spade . . . one of the kind that dear old Adam delved with when Eve span. **1930** PFGaye *Good Sir John* (L) 175: John Ball asked when Adam delved and Eve span who was then the gentleman. **1931** VMeik *People* (L) 190: I had seen Adam delve and Eve weave . . . **1939** TScudder *Jane Welsh Carlyle* (NY) 189: While Adam toiled, Eve spun. **1955** LBromfield *Passion* (C) 51: She's not only doing the spinning for Eve's part but the delving for Adam's as well. **1962** NMarsh *Hand* (B) 38: *When Adam delved,* you know. **1966** NMonsarrat *Life (I)* (L) 417: When Adam delved and Eve span, Who was then the gentleman. EAP A32; TW 4(5).

A33 As hard as **Adamant**

1927 CWells *Where's Smily* (NY) 234: She was like adamant. **1927** FLPackard *Two* (NY) 188: She was as hard as adamant. **1957** LBrackett *Tiger* (NY) 65: Faces . . . hard as adamant. EAP A34.

A34 As deaf as an **Adder**

1910 EPhillpotts *Tales* (NY) 158: He's deaf as an adder. **1927** TFPowys *Mr. Weston's* (L) 61: As deaf as adders. **1933** DLSayers *Murder* (NY) 219: Deaf as an adder. **1937** CHCurran *Snakes* (NY) 10: The old saying, "as deaf as an adder," is based upon fact, and not upon hearsay. **1957** MSharp *Eye* (L) 260: Ears as deaf as adders. **1969** AGilbert *Mr. Crook* (NY DBC) 124: She seemed as deaf as the proverbial adder that laid one ear to the sand and put the tip of its tail in the other. EAP A35; Brunvand 2; DARE i 12: Adder 2.

A35 As dumb as an **Adder**

1931 EPhillpotts *Ghostwater* (NY) 107: Dumb as an adder. **1936** EPhillpotts *Close Call* (L) 108: Dumb as an adder. Whiting NC 360.

A36 Much **Ado** about nothing

1922 JJoyce *Ulysses* (NY 1934) 199: Without more ado about nothing. **1930** ABCox *Vane* (L) 305: Much ado about nothing. **1947** PWentworth *Wicked* (NY) 106: Much ado about nothing. **1956** FAllen *Much Ado About Me* (B). **1966** HBrown *Prose Styles* (Minneapolis) 28: Much ado about a small matter. **1976** MRReno *Final* (NY) 45: It's all much ado about nothing. EAP A37.

A37 As handsome as **Adonis**

1937 ASoutar *One Page* (L) 20: Handsome as Adonis. **1967** COSkinner *Madame* (B) 208: Handsome as Adonis. EAP A10; Wilstach 15: Beautiful.

A38 **Adventures** are to the adventurous

1914 HHMunro *Beasts* (NY 1928) 203: Adventures, according to the proverb, are to the adventurous. *Oxford* 4.

A39 Not to know if one is **Afoot** or on horseback

1920 GBMcCutcheon *Anderson Crow* (NY) 191: Crow didn't know whether he was afoot or horseback. **1952** KMKnight *Vale* (NY) 93: They don't know whether they're afoot or on horseback. DARE i 15: Afoot or (a)horseback. Cf. NED Afoot 1.

A40 Out of **Africa** comes everything new

1936 NLofts *I Met* (NY) 37: The proverb: "Out of Africa comes every new thing." *Oxford* 5.

A41 To keep the **Afterbirth**

[In the early 1920's a family summering in Northport (Maine) had among its servants a German chauffeur and a Lithuanian maid. The German was the first any of us had seen fresh from Germany after the war. He and the maid hated each other with vigor. Once Karl remarked: "When she was born they buried the baby and brought up the afterbirth." As his English was not idiomatic I always regarded that as peculiarly German. BJW] **1970** RNeely *Walter* (NY) 40: I think your mother took one look at you and kept the afterbirth. Cf. MLeach *Dict. of Folklore* I 24–25.

A42 As hard as **Agate**

1928 AEApple *Mr. Chang's* (NY) 165: Eyes as hard as agate. **1936** LRGribble *Malverne* (L) 21: Agate-hard eyes. **1938** AWUpfield *Bone* (L 1966) 115: Eyes . . . became agate-hard. **1939** CMWills *Death at* (L) 89: Eyes . . . hard as agates. **1959** JBlish *Clash* (L) 153: His eyes turned as hard as agate. Cf. Adamant *above.*

A43 **Age** before beauty (*varied*)

1936 ESGardner *Stuttering* (NY) 117: Age before beauty. **1941** ESGardner *Haunted Husband* (NY) 225: Age before beauty. **1957** DJEnright *Heaven* (L) 203: Age before beauty. **1966** EPangborn *Judgment* (NY) 54: Youth before beauty. **1971** PDennis *Paradise* (NY) 317: Age before beauty.

1973 JPorter *It's Murder* (NY) 13: Age before beauty. TW 4(1,2).

A44 To act one's **Age**

1935 JGEdwards *Private* (NY) 216: Act your ugly age! Berrey 151.7, 12.

A45 To pile on (up) the **Agony**

1929 ABCox *Poisoned* (NY) 154: Bradley went on to pile up the agony. **1936** JJFarjeon *Detective* (L) 208: He was doing his best to pile on the agony. **1947** CBrand *Suddenly* (L) 74: He bitterly piled on the agony. **1957** STruss *Truth* (NY) 139: I don't want to pile on the agony. **1969** DMorris *Human* (NY) 126: It is a story of piling on the agony. TW 4(1); DARE i 23: Agony 1.

A46 As free as (the) **Air**

1910 EPhillpotts *Tales* (NY) 226: I was free as air. **1926** MKSanders *Dorothy Thompson* (B 1973) 102: You're free as air. **1938** AChristie *Death on the Nile* (NY) 38: The air is free to all. **1938** PGWodehouse *Code* (NY) 289: I'm as free as the air, as the expression is. **1944** VWBrooks *Washington Irving* (NY 1946) 313: Free as air. **1954** DMDisney *Last* (NY) 16: He was free as air. **1959** *BHerald* 9/15 1: Free as the air. **1959** GDEssart *Cry* (NY) 65: Free as air, free as a bird. **1962** JWoodford *Autobiography* (NY) 32: As free as air. EAP A53.

A47 As light as **Air**

1928 RAFreeman *As a Thief* (L) 213: Trifles light as air. **1940** GStockwell *Candy* (NY) 99: She felt light as air. **1952** DMDisney *Heavy* (NY) 194: He felt as light as air. **1972** RMaugham *Escape* (L) 171: I felt light as air. EAP A55.

A48 To beat the **Air** (wind)

1929 BFlynn *Case* (P) 246: He was merely beating the air. **1933** VLoder *Suspicion* (L) 191: I may be beating the air. **1953** JRhode *Mysterious* (NY DBC) 129: All this beating the wind [*futile*]. **1966** TLang *Darling* (NY) 176: You're only beating the air. EAP A58; Whiting *NC* 497: Wind(7); *Oxford* 36. Cf. To fight the Wind *below*.

A49 To curse until the **Air** is blue

1968 EBuckler *Ox Bells* (NY) 164: Cuss "until the air was blue." Partridge 69: Blue, make the air.

A50 To dance on **Air**

1940 RDarby *Death Conducts* (NY) 187: I would relish seeing the lady dance on air [*be hanged*]. Wentworth 139: Dance on air.

A51 To give one the **Air**

1959 GMitchell *Man Who* (L) 122: She gave me the air. Wentworth 2.

A52 To vanish (*etc.*) into thin **Air**

1920 ACrabb *Samuel* (NY) 94: Disappeared into thin air. **1924** RAFreeman *Blue* (NY) 215: Vanished into thin air. **1931** FDGrierson *Mystery* (L) 82: Vanished into thin air, as the saying is. **1933** GBegbie *Sudden* (L) 209: Disappeared into thin air. **1937** CBush *Hanging Rope* (L) 27: He vanished, as they say, into thin air. **1940** FWCrofts *Golden Ashes* (NY) 150: He had vanished . . . into thin air . . . the *cliché*. **1940** CRice *Corpse Steps* (NY) 9: She had vanished into the very thinnest of air. **1945** PATaylor *Proof* (NY) 30: Melt away into thin air. **1949** AAFair *Bedrooms* (NY 1958) 217: They might as well have been swallowed into thin air. **1952** AAFair *Top* (NY) 58: He had . . . vanished into thin air. **1961** ESGardner *Spurious* (NY) 66: Vanish into thin air. **1964** FArcher *Out of the Blue* (NY) 26: Vanished . . . Into thin air, as the cliché has it. **1970** JAGraham *Aldeburg* (B) 86: [He] had vanished into thin air. **1973** HPentecost *Beautiful* (NY) 101: She just disappeared into thin air. EAP A60.

A53 To walk on **Air**

1928 ABCox *Amateur* (NY) 217: I shall be walking on air. **1931** WWJacobs *Snug* (NY) 280: Sam walked back to his lodgings on air, as the saying is. **1940** GDHCole *Murder at* (NY) 173: I'll be walking on air and good riddance to him. **1951** AMachen *Autobiography* (L) 267: I . . . suddenly recollected the old proverb: "walking on air." **1965** JMaclaren-Ross *Memoirs* (L) 11: I walked away, as the saying goes, on air. **1972** DDevine *Three* (NY) 92: Lesley trod on air. NED Walk *v.* 6 l.

A54 As smooth as **Alabaster**

1912 HFAshurst *Diary* ed GFSparks (Tucson 1962) 17: Everything was smooth as alabaster [*a political convention*]. Wilstach 366: Monumental alabaster.

A55 As white as **Alabaster**

1923 VWilliams *Orange* (B) 48: White as a larst, he was [*the speaker is a Cockney*]. **1928** JAFerguson *Man in the Dark* (NY) 95: White as alabaster. **1941** RHLindsay *Fowl Murder* (B) 93: It's white like alabaster. **1965** HActon *Old Lamps* (L) 278: Her forehead was white as alabaster. EAP A62.

A56 As sure (true) as one is **Alive** (*varied*)

1900 CFPidgin *Quincy A. Sawyer* (B) 277: True as I live. **1904** JCLincoln *Cap'n Eri* (NY) 46: Sure's you're a livin' woman. **1917** JCLincoln *Extricating* (NY) 325: So sure as I live and breathe. **1922** JSFletcher *Ravensdene* (NY) 114: As sure as we're living men. **1932** FWCrofts *Double* (NY) 278: I'm as sure as that I'm alive. **1970** RNeely *Walter* (NY) 112: Sure as I was alive. EAP A68; Brunvand 2, 88: Live(1).

A57 To be **Alive** and kicking

1922 JJoyce *Ulysses* (NY 1934) 265: Is she alive? And kicking. **1926** EWallace *Terrible* (NY) 1: Still alive . . . and kicking. **1936** LBrock *Stoat* (L) 246: Bonzo was still alive and kicking. **1947** TKyd *Blood* (P) 242: I turned up alive and kicking. **1957** AArmstrong *Strange* (NY) 123: He is alive and kicking, to use the common phrase. **1968** LPDavies *Grave* (NY) 183: Alive and kicking. **1970** NMonsarrat *Breaking* (L) 203: Alive and frenziedly kicking. TW 5(1).

A58 All in good time

1928 EWallace *Sinister* (NY) 258: All in good time. **1936** ECRLorac *Death* (L) 291: All in good time is a good motto. EAP A71.

A59 All in the day's work

1903 EChilders *Riddle* (NY 1940) 135: All in the day's work. **1909** MRRinehart *Man in Lower Ten* (NY 1947) 248: All in the day's work. **1932** CAndrews *Butterfly* (NY) 299: All in the day's work. **1938** JLatimer *Dead Don't* (L) 214: It's all in the day's work. **1948** JFHutton *Too Good* (NY) 19: All in the day's work. **1957** SRansome *So Deadly* (NY) 188: It's all in the day's work. **1965** RVanGulick *Willow* (NY) 84: It was all in the day's work. **1976** WMarshall *Hatchet* (NY) 3: All in a day's work. **1977** JThomson *Death* (NY) 32: All part of his day's work. *Oxford* 9.

A60 All is fair in love and war (*varied*)

1912 JCLincoln *Postmaster* (NY) 266: All's fair in love and war, they say. **1919** KHoward *Peculiar* (NY) 77: All's fair in love, if not in war. **1930** WLewis *Apes* (NY 1932) 156: All's fair in love and war; 157. **1938** BGraeme *Mystery* (P) 290: All is fair in love and war. **1957** *Cambridge Chronicle* 5/16 14: An old saying tells us that all is fair in love and war. **1957** AArmstrong *Strange* (NY) 110: All is fair in love and business. **1961** CBeaton *Wandering* (L) 344: All's fair in love and war. **1975** EGundy *Naked* (NY) 27: All's fair in love and whoring. **1980** MInnes *Going* (NY) 70: I never believed that's all fair in love, but it damned well is in war. **1981** PDeVries *Sauce* (B) 104: Meaning all's fair in love and war. TW 5(3); Brunvand 2(2). Cf. EAP A72.

A61 All is fish that comes to net (*varied*)

1908 HMSylvester *Olde Pemaquid* (B) 77: It is all fish that comes to basket. **1923** *Horn Book* (L) 36: All is fish that comes to the female frigging net. **1924** LThayer *Key* (NY) 167: All is not fish that comes to my net. **1931** HKWebster *Who Is* (I) 294: Anything might be fish that came to his net. **1933** OMartyn *Body* (L) 192: All was fish that came to his net. **1947** RHichens *Yesterday* (L) 31: All were fish for which he cast his . . . nets. EAP F141; TW 135(1); Whiting F221.

A62 All is gas and gaiters

1923 MRJames *Letters* ed GMcBryde (L 1956) 124: All was gas and gaiters. **1932** HCBailey *Case* (NY) 306: All gas and gaiters? Sayin' it with flowers? **1940** HCBailey *Mr. Fortune Here* (NY) 65: All is gas and gaiters. **1947** JDCarr *Sleeping* (NY) 182: The sun shines again; and all is gas and gaiters. **1957** PGWodehouse *Over* (L) 189: All is gas and gaiters, not to mention joy and jollity. **1961** JDCarr *Witch* (L) 122: It's not all gas and gaiters. **1973** AGilbert *Nice* (NY) 55: All gas and gaiters. Partridge 317.

A63 **All** is (to bring) grist to one's mill (*varied*)

1913 TDreiser *Traveler* (NY 1923) 60: All . . . was . . . grist for my mill. **1918** F.W Emerson *Early Years* (B) 53: He needed men . . . as grist for his mill. 420: Natural philosophy did not afford much grist to his mill. **1920** JBCabell *Letters* ed PColum (NY 1962) 171: All is grist for your mill. **1922** JJoyce *Ulysses* (NY 1934) 616: With the object of bringing more grist to her mill. **1932** JJConnington *Sweepstake* (B) 5: All that sort of thing's grist to my mill. **1935** BFlynn *Sussex* (L) 257: More grisly grist to your murder mill. **1937** DRussell *Furtive* (L) 97: All was grist that came to his mill. **1946** FLockridge *Murder Within* (NY) 47: The grist was coming in. **1949** MColes *Diamonds* (NY) 178: All is grist . . . as comes to his mill. **1950** MCarleton *Bride* (NY) 96: You'll find grist for your mill even here. **1956** RLongrigg *High-pitched* (L) 164: All of it grist to J. and J.'s rickety mill. **1957** *Punch* 2/13 238: Grist to the mills of those who seek to undermine our way of life. **1959** *NYTimes Book Review* 9/13 1: Everything was grist to his mill. **1963** JBroderick *Don* (NY) 179: It was all grist to the mill. **1969** DShannon *Crime* (NY) 45: All grist that comes to his mill. **1970** RDAltick *Victorian* (NY) 119: The . . . sensation . . . continued to serve as grist for Lamb's epistolary mill. **1970** HCarmichael *Death* (NY) 117: As they say, all is grist that comes to the mill. **1971** JPope-Hennessy *Trollope* (B) 195: All this was grist to the novelist's mill. **1971** SKrim *Shake* (L) 260: All is sausage for the economic grinder. **1974** DMDisney *Don't Go* (NY) 177: The grist that had come to his mill. EAP G178.

A64 **All** (is) over bar (but) the shouting (*varied*)

1923 HGartland *Globe* (NY) 235: It's all over but the shouting. **1925** HHext *Monster* (NY) 16: It's not all over bar shouting yet. **1933** AAllen *Loose* (NY) 61: All over bar the shouting. **1938** CBarry *Case Dead* (L) 231: As the saying goes, to be all over but

the shouting. **1940** AGilbert *Dear Dead* (L) 228: It's all over bar the shouting. **1940** MRRinehart *Great Mistake* (NY) 164: It's all over but the shouting. **1961** EPeters *Death* (NY) 96: It's all over bar the shouting. **1962** ESGardner *Ice-cold* (NY DBC) 150: It's all over now—all except the shouting. **1962** STruss *Time* (NY) 43: It was all over bar the screaming. **1965** ESitwell *Taken Care* (NY) 230: Then it will be all over, bar the shouting and the worms. **1970** DMDevine *Illegal* (NY) 176: All over bar the shouting, as the saying goes. *Oxford* 10.

A65 **All** is vanity

1932 HCBailey *Mr. Fortune, Please* (NY) 165: Vanity of vanities, all is vanity. EAP A75.

A66 **All** is well that ends well (*varied*)

1914 PGWodehouse *Little Nugget* (NY 1929) 291: All's well that ends well. **1924** LO'Flaherty *Thy Neighbour's* (L) 12: All's well that ends well. **1930** AAustin *Murder* (NY) 187: All's swell that ends swell. **1934** LKink *Whispering* (NY) 86: All's well that ends well. **1937** HCBeck *Murder* (NY) 272: All's well that ends badly. **1945** HGreen *Loving* (L) 36: All's well that ends well as they say. **1950** SSmith *Man with* (NY) 90: All's well that ends well. **1959** *BHerald* 9/24 18: All's well that ends well. **1959** *NYTimes Book Review* 9/20 48: All's well that ends well. **1965** HPearson *By Himself* (L) 82: All's well that ends respectable. **1972** HHarrison *Montezuma* (NY) 170: All's well that ends well, as the quote goes. EAP A76; TW 6(5); Brunvand 3(4).

A67 **All** or nothing

1940 HReilly *Dead Can* (NY) 7: It was all or nothing. **1944** AEVanVogt *Winged Man* (NY 1966) 178: It's all or nothing. **1961** GFowler *Skyline* (NY) 14: An all-or-nothing player, as the saying goes. **1963** MErskine *No. 9* (NY) 4: All or nothing. Take it or leave it. **1971** CPlatt *Planet* (NY) 121: It was all or nothing. Cf. Whiting A109: Win all or lose all.

A68 **All** that glitters is not gold (*varied*)

1913 TDreiser *Traveler* (NY 1923) 327: All is not gold that glitters. **1928** WBeebe *Be-*

neath *Tropic Seas* (NY) 171: All is not pigment that glitters. **1931** GPahlow *Murder* (NY) 179: All is not gilt that glitters. **1935** MBurton *Devereux* (L) 75: The old proverb . . . All that glitters is not gold. **1939** DHume *Head* (L) 48: He found that all that glitters is not gold. **1941** CLittle *Black* (NY) 189: All that glitters is not gold. **1956** *BangorDN* 10/16 20: All that glitters . . . is not Goldwater. **1957** *BHerald* 3/7 39: All gold ain't what glitters. **1957** *New Yorker* 8/10 72: Q. Are *all* stocks good investments? *A. All that glisters is not gold.* **1958** *BangorDN* 9/13 24: All is not Goldfine that glitters in the Democratic campaign machinery in Maine. **1962** MCarleton *Dread* (NY) 46: Young doctors discover that all that glitters is generally that brass plate. **1966** DMDisney *At Some* (NY) 88: All that glitters is not gold—or, is it, All is not gold that glitters. **1970** AMontagu *Ignorance* (NY) 105: All that glisters is not gold. EAP G102; TW 154(1); Brunvand 59: Gold(1).

A69   Hear **All,** say nothing

1922 JSFletcher *Herapath* (NY) 293: I'm a Yorkshire man . . . We've a good old proverb . . . "Hear all—say naught"! **1926** JSFletcher *Massingham* (B) 140: The old North Country proverb which advises the wise man to hear all and say naught. **1968** ASilitoe *Guzman* (L) 117: Hear all, see all, say nowt. **1972** JRipley *Davis* (NY) 134: "See all, hear all, say now't"—the first line of the tyke's motto . . . the second line ("Eat all, sup all, pay now't") is a joke. *Oxford* 362: Hear and see . . . ; Hear much. . . .

A70   One cannot win them **All** (*varied*)

1956 GHCoxe *Suddenly* (NY) 169: Well, you can't win 'em all. **1965** RSPrather *Dead Man's* (NY) 28: You can't win 'em all. **1969** RStark *Dame* (NY) 93: You win a few, you lose a few. **1970** DDunnett *Murder* (B) 156: You can't win all the time. **1974** ARoss *If I Knew* (NY) 146: You win some, you lose some.

A71   To know (understand) **All** is to forgive (excuse) all (*varied*)

1930 BFlynn *Creeping* (L) 72: Tout comprendre c'est tout pardonner. **1934**

HCBailey *Shadow* (NY) 2: To understand all is to forgive all. **1936** HAdams *Death* (L) 271: "To understand is to forgive." The old proverb ran in Roger's mind. **1936** AR Clark *High Wall* (NY) 190: To understand is to pardon. **1941** DVanDeusen *Garden Club* (I) 41: To understand all is to forgive all. **1945** EPhillpotts *They Were Seven* (NY) 370: Where all's known, all's forgiven. **1951** JCollier *Fancies* (NY) 185: To know all is to excuse all. **1952** KFuller *Silken* (L) 175: After all, to know all is to forgive all, as my poor dear father used to say. **1959** HCarmichael *Marked* (NY) 111: They say "to know all is to forgive all." **1974** HCarmichael *Most* (NY) 221: They say to know all is to forgive all. Champion (French) 144:222: To understand everything etc.; Bartlett (14th ed) 502b: Attributed to Madame de Staël.

A72   When **All** is said and done

1908 JLondon *Letters* ed KHendricks (NY 1965) 276: When all is said and done. **1919** JSFletcher *Middle Temple* (NY) 272: When all's said and done. **1933** EBailey *Death* (L) 170: When all is said and done. **1956** RILee *Happy* (B) 191: When all is said and done. **1962** EHuxley *Mottled* (L) 325: When all's said and done. **1975** AChristie *Curtain* (NY) 44: When all was said and done. EAP A69.

A73   To be up (down) one's **Alley**

1932 BRoss *Tragedy of Y* (NY) 270: Right up our alley. **1934** LFord *Strangled* (NY) 65: Something straight up your alley. **1942** VCaspary *Laura* (NY 1957) 119: He was shooting right up my alley. **1951** DWMeredith *Christmas* (NY) 210: We're up the same old blind alley. **1955** KMKnight *They're* (NY) 12: It's not down my alley. **1961** JSStrange *Eye* (NY) 66: Right up Nellie's alley. **1970** STerkel *Hard* (NY) 131: This was right down our alley. NED Alley 4.

A74   **Alpha** and Omega

1929 SMElam *Borrow* (L) 102: He knew the Gipses from alpha to omega. **1933** DMorrah *Mummy* (NY) 124: Know the whole process from alpha to omega. **1936** BFlynn *Horn* (L) 108: He knows his hobbies from

Alpha to Omega. **1940** DCCameron *Grave* (NY) 262: They were the alpha and omega of his plan. **1941** KRoos *If the Shroud* (NY) 128: A fellow who knows managing . . . from Alpha to Omega. **1957** ECaldwell *Certain* (B) 213: [We] have talked the matters over from alpha to izzard. **1977** JLHensley *Rivertown* (NY) 44: To him it's alpha and omega. EAP A82, 83; TW 6; Brunvand 3. Cf. From A to Z *above*.

A75 All good **Americans** when they die, go to Paris

1928 WCWilliams *Voyage* (NY) 22: You know, dear, all good Americans go to Paris when they die. **1932** TSmith *Topper Takes* (NY) 299: We are those good Americans who go to Paris when they die; 309. **1936** HFootner *Kidnapping* (L) 20: I want to change the ancient wheeze to read: When Americans die they rise up in Monte Carlo. **1938** SLeslie *Film* (L) 213: The legend that good Americans go to Paris when they die. **1958** *NYTimes Book Review* 3/9 12: Good Americans when they die, go to Paris (as Oliver Wendell Holmes reported). *Oxford* 13.

A76 To run **Amuck** (amok)

1924 HCBailey *Mr. Fortune's Practice* (NY) 36: The man runs amuck; 117. **1933** AB Cox *Jumping* (L) 58: Run amok. **1933** WCBrown *Murder* (P) 276: Deduction gone wild, runing amuck. **1936** BFlynn *Horn* (L) 52: Your ideas run amuck with your common sense. **1940** HReilly *Murder in* (NY) 108: A banker had run amuck with a knife. **1952** BKendrick *You Die* (NY) 19: The blinded veteran ran amuck or blew his top. **1954** CBeaton *Glass* (NY) 58: Her taste ran amok in a jungle of flowers. **1957** *Punch* 4/ 10 475: Francophilia . . . has run a trifle amok. **1961** CBeaton *Wandering* (L) 188: Allowed to run amok with their whimsey. **1964** FArcher *Malabang* (NY DBC) 49: His sweetheart runs amok in the big city [*has a good time*]. **1968** JGFuller *Day* (NY) 108: Emile, naked, was running amok in the yard. **1969** HKubly *Goda* (NY) 87: He runs amok every evening [*sexual*]. **1972** LIsrael *Tallulah* (NY) 274: Tallulah was . . . drunk, but not running amok. **1975** GBlack *Big*

Wind (NY) 205: The lover goes amok with passion. **1975** ABrodsky *Madame* (NY) 34: It bloomed like an aspidistra run amok. EAP A85.

A77 To have an **Anchor** to windward

1909 JCLincoln *Keziah* (NY) 261: You're my anchor to windward, as they say down here. **1936** AFielding *Mystery* (L) 270: This was her anchor to windward. **1949** FLockridge *Dishonest* (P) 135: Anchor to windward. **1953** KMKnight *Akin* (NY) 33: We'll put it in the savings bank as an anchor to windward, as the fishermen say. **1968** ELathen *Stitch* (NY) 85: There can never be too many anchors to windward in the money market. EAP A86.

A78 To slip one's **Anchor**

1960 AWUpfield *Mystery* (L) 165: He slipped his anchor [*died*]. Partridge 783: Slip. Cf. TW 6(1).

A79 An **Angel** is passing overhead

1934 LKirk *Whispering* (NY) 135: The conversation began to dwindle . . . "An angel passing overhead." **1961** JBlish *So Close* (NY) 58: You know the old saw—when everybody in a party falls silent at once, an angel is passing over the house.

A80 As beautiful (*etc.*) as an **Angel**

1934 HCBailey *Shadow* (NY) 8: She was as pretty as an angel. **1951** JCollier *Fancies* (NY) 284: Beautiful as an angel. **1961** WEHuntsberry *Oscar* (NY DBC) 86: She looked bright as an angel. **1966** JAiken *Beware* (NY) 18: She's as beautiful as an angel. EAP A88, 93; Brunvand 3(1).

A81 Like **Angel** visits *etc.*

1958 DGBrowne *Death* (L) 135: My visits . . . are like angels', brief but short. TW 6(8); *Oxford* 13.

A82 Talk (speak) of **Angels** *etc.*

1917 JCLincoln *Extricating* (NY) 293: The old "Speak of angels" proverb. **1929** WScott *Mask* (P) 253: Talk of the—angels! **1929** LRGribble *Gillespie* (L) 310: Bruce muttered something . . . about talking of angels. **1933** RAJWalling *Prove It* (NY) 173: The warning that if you talk of an angel you'll see his wings. **1952** PHBonner *SPQR* (NY) 13: Speaking of angels, I thought to myself. **1957** THWhite *Master* (L) 78: Talk of an angel and we hear the rustling of his wings. **1972** HCarmichael *Naked* (NY) 190: Talk of angels and you hear the clump of their number tens. Brunvand 3(7); *Oxford* 804: Talk. Cf. Talk of the Devil *below*.

A83 To write (*etc.*) like an **Angel**

1950 MRHodgkin *Student* (L) 82: Char could write like an angel. **1959** CDBowen *Adventures* (B) 133: Talking, as the phrase goes, like an angel. **1964** HBTaylor *Duplicate* (NY) 95: He could sing like an angel. Brunvand 3(6): Sings; *Oxford* 923: Write.

A84 A soft **Answer** turns away wrath (*varied*)

1922 JJoyce *Ulysses* (NY 1934) 627: A soft answer turns away wrath. **1925** TRMarshall *Recollections* (I) 257: A soft answer turneth away wrath. **1935** CWells *Wooden* (P) 110: A soft answer turns away the wrath. **1942** HCBailey *Nobody's* (NY) 147: Clunk answered softly and failed to turn away wrath. **1949** JStagge *Three* (NY) 109: Given the soft word that turned away wrath. **1968** NBenchley *Welcome* (NY) 110: A soft answer turned away wrath. **1970** MJArlen *Exiles* (NY) 55: A soft answer turneth away harsh words. EAP A97.

A85 To give a civil **Answer** to a civil question

1935 EGreenwood *Pins* (L) 214: A civil answer to a civil question. TW 6(1).

A86 To know all the **Answers**

1958 AWUpfield *Bachelors* (L) 164: An ex-barmaid who knows all the answers, as the saying goes. Wentworth 6–7.

A87 As busy (restless) as an **Ant**

1933 WMarch *Company K* (NY) 177: As busy as ants. **1939** HFootner *Murder that* (L) 45: As restless as an ant. **1951** EPaul *Murder on* (NY) 310: Ulysses, now, as busy as an ant. Taylor *Prov. Comp.* 22: Busy.

A88 To have **Ants** in one's pants (*varied*)

1935 JLatimer *Headed* (NY 1957) 77: The butler's got ants in his pants. **1938** PGWodehouse *Code* (NY) 101: Ants in the pants for Bertram. **1940** RAvery *Murder a Day* (NY) 117: He had been acting like a man with ants in his pantry. **1954** LCochran *Row's End* (NY) 42: He's got ants in his pants and it won't hurt him to scratch a little. **1957** CWilliams *Big Bite* (L) 124: She was troubled with ants in the pants [*sexually excited*]. **1959** EMcBain *King's* (NY) 171: We laymen call it ants in the pants. **1963** HWaugh *Death* (NY) 98: What's she got, ants in her goddam pants? **1965** HActon *Old Lamps* (L) 235: The Trustees fidgeted as if they had ants in their pants, to borrow a Translantic expression. **1973** JCashman *Gentleman* (NY) 249: [They] started to get red ants in their pants. Wentworth 7.

A89 **Anticipation** is better than realization

1928 HCMcNeile *Female* (NY) 62: Anticipation . . . they say . . . is better than realization. **1962** DGillon *Unsleep* (NY) 113: Anticipation may be the better part of realization. **1964** BWilliams *Stranger* (NY) 25: The old saying that the anticipation was much greater than the realization. **1969** ELathen *When* (NY) 11: Anticipation had proved a great deal more gratifying than reality. Cf. Chase *below*.

A90 **Anything** for a quiet life

1922 JJoyce *Ulysses* (NY 1934) 347: Anything for a quiet life. **1928** JGoodwin *When Dead* (NY) 204: Anything for a quiet life. **1936** TBurke *Night-Pieces* (NY) 284: Anything for a quiet life. **1951** NMitford *Blessing* (NY) 149: Anything for a quiet life is their motto. **1969** RCook *Private* (NY) 12: Anything for a quiet life. **1975** ARoudybush *Suddenly* (NY) 10: Anything for a quiet life. Apperson 12; *Oxford* 15.

A91 **Anything** is better than nothing

1949 FLockridge *Dishonest* (P) 130: Anything is better than nothing. **1970** JLeasor *They Don't* (NY) 44: Anything is better than nothing. Cf. TW 7(1).

A92   Anything is possible

1936 GCBestor *Prelude* (L) 286: Anything's possible. **1942** BBloch *Bach* (NY) 190: Anything is possible. Cf. Nothing is impossible *below.*

A93   One should try **Anything** (everything) once (*varied*)

1929 RJCasey *Secret* (I) 80: I'll try anything once. **1929** HFootner *Self-Made* (NY) 258: They say a man ought to try everything once. **1932** HCBailey *Mr. Fortune, Please* (NY) 85: It's a principle of his that one ought to try everything. **1932** AFielding *Wedding-Chest* (NY) 57: Everything once, was his motto. **1936** LWMeynell *On the Night* (NY) 43: Willing to try anything once. **1939** EMarsh *Number* (NY) 56: A tendency, as the saying is, to try anything once. **1955** JCreasey *Murder* (NY DBC) 61: I'll try anything once. **1955** PGWodehouse *French* (L) 193: Try everything once . . . That's my motto. **1961** PGWodehouse *Ice* (NY) 121: "Try anything once" is always a good motto. **1970** DClark *Deadly* (NY) 118: I'll try anything once.

A94   To take (steal) **Anything** that isn't nailed down

1958 HReilly *Ding* (NY DBC) 78: Thay girl would take anything that wasn't niled down. **1959** WMiller *Cool* (B) 44: Steal anything that ain't nailed down. Cf. Heavy *below.*

A95   As drunk as an **Ape**

1959 RVanGulik *Chinese* (NY) 121: You were drunk as an ape. Whiting A140.

A96   As vain as an **Ape** with a mirror

1941 CCoffin *Mare's Nest* (NY) 120: As vain as an ape with a mirror. Cf. HWJanson *Apes and Ape Lore* (L 1952) 210ff.

A97   To grin like an **Ape**

1940 CBDawson *Lady Wept* (NY) 213: Hammond grinning like an ape. Wilstach 188: Enchanted apes.

A98   Not even **Apollo** can keep his bow always at stretch

1957 MColes *Death* (NY) 139: It is also said that not even Apollo can keep his bow always at stretch. Cf. *Oxford* 927: (The) Young are not always with their bows bent.

A99   Appearances (looks) are deceitful (*varied*)

1912 JCLincoln *Postmaster* (NY) 66: Appearances are deceitful. **1919** WLewis *Letters* ed WKRose (L 1963) 114: Appearances are deceptive. **1919** JBCabell *Jurgen* (NY 1922) 115: Appearances are proverbially deceitful. **1919** LMenick *Chain* (L) 346: I wish that appearances were not deceitful. **1925** FPitt *Waterside* (L) 127: In that case appearances are not deceptive. **1933** MBurton *Fate* (L) 144: Appearances are notoriously deceptive. **1935** VWMason *Budapest* (NY) 6: Looks are generally deceiving. **1937** RPenny *Policeman in* (L) 255: Appearances are not always deceptive. **1940** MArmstrong *Man with* (NY) 104: Appearances are deceitful. **1952** HCecil *Ways* (L) 259: Appearances are sometimes deceptive. **1957** *BHerald* 3/1 5: But appearances are deceiving. **1958** CCockburn *Crossing* (L) 137: Appearances are very rarely deceptive. **1958** *New Yorker* 8/9 59: Appearances at sea are very deceiving. **1961** RVanGulik *Chinese Lake* (L) 85: Appearances are often deceptive. **1968** MHolroyd *Strachey* (L) 2.187: Appearances and early impressions were deceptive. **1969** RSGallagher *If I Had* (NY) 18: Appearances are deceiving. **1973** EXFerrars *Small* (NY) 74: Appearances . . . are a bit deceptive. **1974** DCory *Bit* (NY) 91: And appearances don't deceive. **1974** THeald *Blue* (NY) 161: Remember looks are deceptive. EAP A103; Brunvand 4. Cf. Things are not always *below.*

A100   Appearances cannot be trusted (*varied*)

1928 JJConnington *Mystery* (B) 109: The implied warning against trusting too much in appearances. **1928** AGilbert *Mrs. Davenport* (NY) 259: You couldn't trust appearances. **1937** HAustin *Murder* (L) 166: But, as with fruit, appearances were sometimes untrustworthy. **1941** PWilde *Design* (NY) 212: Shows appearances ain't always what they look like. **1959** FCrane *Buttercup* (NY DBC) 54: Appearances lie. EAP A103; TW 7(5). Cf. Impressions *below.*

A101 Never judge from **Appearances** (*varied*)

1921 JSFletcher *Orange–Yellow* (NY) 290: The old saying that you should never judge by appearances. **1921** JCLincoln *Galusha* (NY) 406: You can't never tell by a person's looks. **1931** JJFarjeon *House* (NY) 146: Never judge by faces. **1933** EECummings *Eimi* (NY) 95: One should never judge by appearances. **1964** CWilson *Necessary* (NY 1966) 71: I suppose you can't really judge by appearances. **1967** AJToynbee *Acquaintances* (L) 52: You must not judge by outward appearances. **1970** HCarmichael *Death* (NY) 137: Shows how easy it is to jump to wrong conclusions . . . just because he judged by appearances. **1972** LIsrael *Tallulah* (NY) 42: You can't always tell by looks. EAP A103; TW 7(4). Cf. Never judge a Book *below.*

A102 **Appetite** grows by what it feeds on
1958 BNichols *Rich* (NY) 252: *L'appetit vient en mangeant.* **1963** PDJames *Mind* (L) 183: The appetite had grown by what it fed on. TW 7(2).

A103 An **Apple** a day keeps the doctor away (*varied*)
1927 GJNathan *Land* (NY) 208: An apple a day keeps the doctor away. **1930** GFairlie *Suspect* (NY) 236: Early rising better than an apple a day. **1935** SWilliams *Murder* (NY) 231: The saying, "An apple a day keeps the doctor away." **1939** BCobb *Inspector Burmann* (L) 66: They [apples] are supposed to keep the doctor away. **1943** WMcCully *Doctors* (NY) 155: "A murder a day keeps the doctor away," she quoted flippantly. **1957** PGWodehouse *Butler* (NY) 170: A snail a day keeps the doctor away. **1959** *BangorDN* 8/27 30: That old saying, "An apple a day keeps the doctor away." **1964** WHayward *It Never* (L) 15: An apple a day keeps the doctor away. **1972** EXFer-

rars *Foot* (NY) 127: A murder a day keeps boredom away. Whiting *NC* 362(1).

A104 An **Apple** does not fall far from the tree
1981 PDeVries *Sauce* (B) 183: You know the old expression about heredity. The apple doesn't fall far from the tree. TW 8(10).

A105 The **Apple** of one's eye
1906 JCLincoln *Mr. Pratt* (NY) 203: The apple of her eye. **1920** GBMcCutcheon *Anderson Crow* (NY) 60: The apple of [his] eye. **1924** EWallace *Green* (B) 210: The apple of his eye. **1933** FWCrofts *Hog's Back* (L) 28: It's the apple of his eye. **1937** DRussell *Furtive* (L) 20: He was the apple of Miss Pemberton's eye. **1940** MBoniface *Murder as* (NY) 18: The very apple of his father's eye. **1945** JRhode *Shadow of a Crime* (NY) 91: The apple of his father's eye. **1953** PGWodehouse *Ring* (L) 105: The apple of Biggar's eye. **1956** *New Yorker* 9/22 45: Why should we despise the apples of others' eyes? **1966** KMartin *Father* (L) 172: This was the apple of his eye. **1969** PCraig *Gate* (NY) 39: The apple of his professional eye. **1974** FWatson *Year* (NY) 153: The apple of his father's eye. EAP A105; Brunvand 4.

A106 As red (rosy) as an **Apple**; Apple-red
1940 JPPhilips *Murder in Marble* (NY) 97: Her cheeks red as apples. **1953** SBellow *Adventures* (NY) 75: Rosy as an apple. **1954** FCDavis *Another* (NY) 165: [His] cheeks turned apple-red. **1971** NBogner *Making* (NY) 139: Apple-red cheek. TW 7(3); Wilstach 327: Rosy-cheeked as a winter apple.

A107 How do you like those (them) **Apples**?
1940 JPPhilips *Murder in Marble* (NY) 155: How do you like those for apples! **1966** HWaugh *Pure* (NY) 135: How do you like those apples? **1970** DHarper *Hijacked* (NY DBC) 57: How do you like them apples? **1980** PDeVries *Consenting* (B) 89: How do you like them apples? saith the Lord. **1982** JLivingston *Piece* (NY) 64: How do you like them apples, Crazy Horse? **1983** PDeVries *Slouching* (B) 83: How do you like them apples? Berrey 158.9: Them, 282.7: Them.

A108 How we **Apples** swim!

1940 RStout *Where There's* (NY) 36: How we apples swim! EAP A106.

A109 Not (do something) for sour (little) **Apples** (*varied*)

1941 MHolbrook *Suitable* (NY) 251: You can't write copy for sour apples. **1942** ABMaurice *Riddle* (NY) 192: Graves . . . is crazy about her, but she won't see him for little apples. **1943** WMcCully *Doctors* (NY) 60: Imogene can't see him for a row of sour apples. **1954** JRMacdonald *Find* (NY) 43: She couldn't see him for sour apples. **1961** RFoley *It's Murder* (NY DBC) 153: He couldn't ride for sour apples. Wentworth 504–5.

A110 One rotten **Apple** can spoil the whole barrel (*varied*)

1928 DMarquis *When the Turtles* (NY) 3: Evil contaminations will spoil a whole barrel of good apples. **1928** HdeVStackpoole *Mystery* (NY) 59: He's like a bad apple in a barrel, . . . he's turning the others. **1937** CRCooper *Here's to Crime* (B) 45: A rotten officer is like a rotten apple: he spoils the whole barrel. **1938** WNMacartney *Fifty Years* (NY) 292: One rotten apple will spoil a barrel of good ones. **1944** LLariar *Man . . . Lumpy Nose* (NY) 224: One rotten apple can wreck a dump like this. **1955** KMKnight *Robineau* (NY) 186: One rotten apple does not spoil the barrel. **1956** *BHerald* 7/13 5: But, like the old story, one or two bad apples can ruin a whole barrel of apples. **1960** ADean *Bullet* (NY) 91: It would take but one rotten apple to spoil the whole barrel. **1960** LLevine *Great* (L) 342: Oh, well, a single bad apple. Won't spoil the barrel. **1964** RAHeinlein *Farnham's* (NY 1965) 231: One bad apple rots the rest, as my uncle was fond of saying. **1968** DSkirrow *I Was* (NY) 246: I know that one schmacky swallow doesn't have to spoil the barrel. **1970** DJOlivy *Never* (NY) 95: Rotten breeds rotten, an' that's a fact. **1973** JWhitehead *Solemn* (L) 106: He was a rotten apple that could easily have turned the whole barrel bad. EAP A107.

A111 A prize **Apple** can have a worm inside (*varied*)

1933 NKlein *Destroying* (NY) 137: Even a prize apple can be rotten inside. **1935** TDavis *Terror* (NY) 111: The best-looking apples have worms in 'em. **1940** PATaylor *Criminal* (NY) 286: What's all this about . . . nice looking red apples with worms? **1954** HWRosenhaupt *True* (NY) 326: Rosy apple with a worm inside. **1954** JSymons *Narrowing* (NY) 31: You're a sham, a rosy apple rotten at the core. **1956** UCurtiss *Widow's* (NY) 122: A worm in the apple, a thorn on the rose. **1972** SNBehrman *People* (B) 42: Women . . . they're fair to the eye an' rotten to the core. Whiting A155.

A112 There is at least one rotten **Apple** in every barrel (*varied*)

1960 WMasterson *Hammer* (NY DBC) 60: There can be a bad apple in any barrel. **1961** HPentecost *Deadly* (NY DBC) 73: There's at least one rotten apple in every barrel. **1973** HPentecost *Beautiful* (NY) 54: There's always a rotten apple in every barrel. **1977** MKirk *Dragonship* (NY) 161: I'll bet even the old-time Vikings had an occasional rotten apple in the barrel. Cf. A black Sheep *below*.

A113 To polish a (the) **Apple**(s)

1941 DKent *Jason* (NY) 135: You polish the apple with him until he writes a codicil. **1956** DMDisney *Unappointed* (NY) 168: Don't start polishing apples for me until you're sure I'm going to be Teacher. **1957** WMorris *Love* (NY) 107: Now they all polish his apple. Their big job is to applaud. Wentworth 7, 8.

A114 To upset the **Apple-cart** (*varied*)

1913 JSFletcher *Secret* (L 1918) 121: They usually upset a man's applecart. **1920** GDilnot *Suspected* (NY) 21: Upset the cart. **1922** JJoyce *Ulysses* (NY 1934) 636: Upsetting the applecart with a vengeance. **1932** MBurton *Death* (L) 163: That upset his apple-cart a bit. **1932** GDyer *Fire* (B) 244: Kicking over the applecart. **1933** CDickson *Bowstring* (NY) 273: Complete chance upset all the apples. **1938** WChambers *Dog* (NY) 55: I'll dump over the whole applecart. **1942** JDCarr *Emperor's* (NY) 289: The apple-cart had been upset again. **1953** VPJohns *Murder* (NY 1962) 136: Upset that Lady's applecart to a fare-thee-well. **1958** SBedford *Best* (L 1961) 71: It did not only shake the prosecution's apple cart, it put the cart before the horse. **1959** *NYTimes* 2/15 31: Don't rock the applecart. **1965** MAllingham *Mind* (NY) 252: It'll kick over a dozen applecarts. **1967** CMackenzie *Octave Six* (L) 50: We talk of upsetting the applecart. How many people have literally upset an apple-cart? **1971** JBlish *And All* (NY) 57: I may upset their pushcart for them. EAP A108.

A115   Apple-pie order

1913 TDreiser *Traveler* (NY 1923) 205: In apple-pie order. **1922** JJoyce *Ulysses* (NY 1934) 388: All in apple pie order. **1929** CWells *Tapestry* (P) 299: In apple-pie trim. **1932** VWilliams *Death* (B) 227: In apple-pie order, as the saying is. **1943** DGoldring *South Lodge* (L) xiv: In apple-pie order. **1955** JBCabell *As I* (NY) 41: In far more than apple pie order. **1968** JUpdike *Couples* (NY 1969) 79: Arranged in apple-pie order. **1976** JRLAnderson *Death* (NY) 12: In apple-pie order. TW 8.

A116   As American as Apple pie (*varied*)

1959 DThompson in VSheean *Dorothy* (B) 346: He was as American as ham and eggs and strawberry shortcake. **1965** DCLunt *Woods* (NY) 51: Names—as American as apple-pie. **1971** ELathen *Longer* (NY) 160: Puerto Rico was as American as apple pie. **1972** SAngus *Arson* (NY) 99: An idea as American as apple pie. **1974** RRosenblum *Good* (NY) 157: Something as American as apple-pie and baseball. **1982** *Harvard Gazette* 2/5 3: Harvard is as American as apple-pie and ice cream. Everyone wants to come here. Cf. Wilstach 493.

A117   April showers bring May flowers (*varied*)

1973 EMcBain *Let's Hear* (NY) 92: It was coming down in buckets; he was willing to forsake the goddamn May flowers. EAP A111.

A118   As fickle as April

1963 MPHood *Sin* (NY) 176: That little woman's fickle's April. Cf. EAP A112; Whiting A172.

A119   To be tied to Apron-strings (*varied*)

1911 JSHay *Amazing Emperor* (L) 145: Brought up at his mother's apron-strings. **1913** JCLincoln *Mr. Pratt's Patients* (NY) 115: The old lady never let her out of reach of her apron-strings. **1929** HHolt *Mayfair* (L) 10: Getting away from their apron-strings. **1932** DLSayers *Have* (NY) 56: Tied to that young woman's apron-strings. **1939** DBowers *Shadows* (L) 53: You wanted her tied to your starchy old apron-strings. **1948** JWKrutch *Thoreau* (NY) 20: He never cut his mother's apron-strings. **1949** JSymons *Bland* (L) 17: We don't want to be tied to anybody's purse strings. **1950** FO'Malley *Best* (NY) 98: Tied to Liza's apron strings. **1956** GMetalious *Peyton* (NY) 207: Apron strings are for women. **1957** NWYates *WT Porter* (Baton Rouge) 90: [They] did break away . . . from the apron strings of the genteel school of fiction. **1963** CMackworth *Apollinaire* (NY) 18: [Her] apron-strings were rough, and her son was securely tied to them. **1973** MGEberhart *Murder* (NY) 33: Tied to his mother's apron strings. **1974** JWain *SJohnson* (NY) 284: Tied to the apron strings of England. EAP A113.

A120   Argus and his eyes

1939 RAJWalling *Blistered Hand* (NY) 199: If we had more eyes than Argus. **1960** ASinclair *Project* (L) 113: One should always have a hundred eyes like Argus. EAP A114; TW 9; Brunvand 4.

A121   As long as one's Arm

1923 EWallace *Clue of the New Pin* (B) 182: A guarantee as long as your arm. **1932** VWilliams *Mystery* (B) 32: A criminal record as long as your arm. **1934** EJepson *Grinning* (L) 246: A list of orders as long as my arm. **1940** AGilbert *Dear Dead* (L) 64: A list . . . as long as your arm. **1955** AHocking *Poison* (NY) 156: A list . . . as long as your arm. **1959** MErskine *Graveyard* (NY) 148: She has a police record as long as my arm. **1964** JPhilips *Laughter* (NY DBC) 84: A list as long as my arm. **1974** CWilson *Schoolgirl* (NY) 13: A list . . . as long as your arm. EAP A115.

A122   The long **Arm** of coincidence
1917 GRSims *My Life* (L) 15: The long arm of coincidence; 228. **1929** SSVanDine *Bishop* (NY) 12: The proverbial long arm of coincidence. **1930** SHorler *Curse* (NY) 98: Old Man Coincidence gets his arm twisted. **1939** MDalman *Missing* (L) 121: Stretch the long arm of coincidence. **1941** ELFelta *Dressed* (NY) 283: The long arm of circumstance is taboo. **1948** JFHutton *Too Good* (NY) 42: In no mood for long-armed coincidence. **1955** VNabokov *Lolita* (Paris) I 140: The long hairy arm of coincidence. **1958** AMacKinnon *Summons* (NY) 39: The long arm of coincidence was practically dislocating itself. **1967** JAxelrad *Freneau* (Austin) 198: The long and withered arm of coincidence. **1970** DClark *Deadly* (NY) 32: Stretching the long arm of coincidence from here to Vladivostok and back. **1975** HCarvic *Odds On* (NY) 39: That would be stretching coincidence's arm a little far. Oxford *DQ* (2nd ed) 135.11 [*CHChambers*].

A123   Strong in the **Arm** (back) and weak (thin) in the head
1930 WLewis *Apes* (NY 1932) 127: *Strong i' the arm and weak i' the head*, as they say in Liverpool. **1934** WGore *There's Death* (L) 233: Thick i' th' arm and thin i' th' head, as they say up North. **1956** HCahill *Shadow* (NY) 35: Strong in the back and weak in the head.

A124   To chance one's **Arm** (*varied*)
1928 RAJWalling *That Dinner* (NY) 289: [He] would have chanced his arm. **1933** NBrady *Fair Murder* (L) 217: I'll have to chance my arm—a phrase in the vernacular meaning take some risk. **1940** GDHCole *Murder at* (NY) 22: I shall have to arrest Pearson and chance my arm. **1957** JBrooks *Water* (L) 28: No one's going to risk his arm. **1959** *TLS* 3/6 130: The young British poet is not ready enough to chance his arm. **1966** HRFKeating *Death* (NY) 130: They were chancing their arm a bit. **1972** SCloete *Victorian* (L) 317: Chance your arm and blow your own trumpet. Partridge 139.

A125   To cost an **Arm** and a leg
1970 TKenrick *Only* (NY) 39: It cost an arm and a leg to stay there [*a hotel*]. **1981** WLDeAndrea *Killed* (NY) 18: Cost us an arm and a leg.

A126   To twist someone's **Arm**
1950 RMacDonald *Drowning* (NY 1951) 36: You've twisted my arm. **1965** AGilbert *Voice* (NY) 141: It could be his arm was twisted a little. **1967** RRendell *New Lease* (NY) 31: All right, if you twist my arm.

A127   An **Army** marches on its stomach
1930 FBeeding *League* (B) 137: An army marches on its stomach. **1935** AChristie *Death* (L) 116: They say that an army marches on its stomach. **1936** VLoder *Deaf-Mute* (L) 75: Nap said an army marches on its stomach. **1947** GMWilliams *Silk* (L) 177: How true it is that an army marches on its stomach. **1959** DMDisney *Did She Fall* (NY) 181: "You and your stomach." "Army marches on it." **1963** SForbes *Grieve* (NY) 124: Like they say—an army can't travel on an empty stomach. *Oxford* 18.

A128   As straight as an **Arrow**; Arrow-straight
1912 ERBurroughs *Princess of Mars* (NY 1963) 152: Straight as an arrow. **1924** ADHSmith *Porto* (NY) 31: Straight as an arrow. **1930** GCollins *Horror* (L) 229: Arrow-straight. **1936** TAPlummer *Dumb* (NY) 277: As straight as an arrow from a bow. **1943** EWTeale *Dune Boy* (NY 1957) 28: Straight-as-an-arrow posture. **1952** JDrummond *Naughty* (L) 278: Straight as an arrow [*responsible*]. **1957** *New Yorker* 11/2 43: She had been straight as an arrow. **1957** VWMason *Gracious* (NY) 19: This arrow-straight-standing young woman. **1958** JBarth *End* (NY 1960) 51: He thinks as straight as an arrow. **1961** AAFair *Bachelors* (NY DBC) 37: Walked straight as an arrow. **1961** GGFickling *Blood* (NY) 9: Legs arrow-straight. **1965** PAnderson *Corridors* (NY) 22: Arrow straight it ran. **1971** DFJones *Denver* (NY) 212: State Highway 99,

straight as an arrow. EAP A117; Brunvand 4(1).

A129   As swift as an **Arrow**

1932 VWilliams *Death* (B) 135: Swift as an arrow. **1933** JJFarjeon *Ben* (NY) 136: Swift as the proverbial arrow, Ben darted to the sink. EAP A118.

A130   As upright as an **Arrow**

1932 PMacDonald *Escape* (NY) 15: She stood upright as an arrow. **1968** EWilliams *Beyond* (NY) 310: Upright as an arrow [*honest*]. Cf. Whiting B432.

A131   To have more than one **Arrow** to one's bow

1938 AGilbert *Treason* (L) 219: No harm having more than one arrow to your bow. EAP A120. Cf. To have two Strings *below*.

A132   **Arse** (*etc.*) over (this or that)

1929 CBush *Perfect* (NY) 244: Richardson knocked him tail over tip. **1935** BGraeme *Body* (L) 126: The ruddy taxi nearly turned arse over tip. **1940** KSteel *Dead of Night* (B) 148: Lit out ass-over-applecart. **1956** *BangorDN* 7/24 11: People who land on their dignity when taking a fall go "heels over bandbox." **1957** COLocke *Hell Bent* (NY) 211: The shot's impact . . . cartwheeled Tom Boyd ass over teakettle into the clear. **1957** CThompson *Halfway* (NY) 165: [He] had . . . fallen ass over teakettle in love. **1959** JLatimer *Black* (NY) 169: Knocked me ass over tea kettle. **1961** SSterling *Too Hot* (NY) 115: Knocked me tail over tea-kettle. **1963** HPentecost *Tarnished* (NY DBC) 33: He fell head over teakettle for a young girl. **1964** EPangborn *Davy* (NY) 81: He went flying ass over brisket. **1966** NMonsarrat *Life (I)* (L) 305: He went arse over tip into the river. **1968** RWClark *JBS* (NY) 87: He went arse over tip. **1968** KTopkins *Passing* (B) 3: Histology notes slung ass over teacup into my duffel bag. **1969** ADavidson *Phoenix* (NY) 110: The . . . helmsman . . . went tumbling arse over ale mug. **1969** CWatson *Just What* (NY) 52: Then over 'e went, arse over tit! I never seen the like. **1970** STerkel *Hard* (NY) 33: He just went arse over Tecumseh. **1972** HDPerry *Chair* (NY) 30: Rushed through their training

ass-over-bandbox. **1973** TWells *Brenda's* (NY) 82: She went down the stairs, ass over teakettle. **1980** RHFrancis *Daggerman* (NY) 134: One tread on them and he was arse over tip. **1981** NFreeling *Arlette* (NY) 170: Saul . . . got knocked arse over tip into the ditch. DARE i 100: Ass-over-teakettle; Partridge 18. Cf. Stern *below*.

A133   As soon (*etc.*) as kiss my **Arse** (*varied*)

1952 WClapham *Night* (L) 228: Politely as kiss your bottom. **1961** RJWhite *Smartest* (L) 239: I'd as soon put them [*bullets*] into you as kiss my arse. **1962** ABurgess *Clockwork* (NY 1965) 19: Everything as easy as kiss-my-sharries [*buttocks*]. Cf. As easy . . . Hand *below*.

A134   Not to know one's **Arse** from (whatever, esp. a hole in the ground [wall]) (*varied*) [But note that "hole in the ground" has frequently been preserved with a substitute for "arse."]

1933 BRoss *Tragedy of Z* (NY) 166: We don't know you from a hole in the wall. **1934** JTFarrell *Young Manhood* (NY 1935) 393: You don't know your fanny from a hole in the ground. **1936** JTFarrell *World* (NY) 123: You don't know your arse from a hole in the ground. **1937** ATilton *Beginning* (NY) 96: I don't know . . . McInnis from the well-known hole in the wall. **1941** MBardon *Murder Does* (NY) 207: She wouldn't know a poison from a hole in the ground. **1952** RMacdonald *Ivory* (NY 1965) 145: I didn't know Lucy from a hole in the ground. **1955** DParry *Sea* (L) 179: I do not know my fanny from my fingertips—as you are always saying. **1956** EMcBain *Cop* (NY 1959) 60: Don't know him from a hole in the wall. **1961** HReilly *Certain* (NY DBC) 12: Charles didn't . . . know Hester . . . from a hole in the ground. **1964** EMcBain *Ax* (NY) 179: He didn't know Lasser from a hole in the wall. **1965** ASharp *Green Tree* (NY 1966) 162: Gerda knows her arse from a hole in the ground. **1966** AEHotchner *Papa* (NY) 85: [He] does not know his ass from Adam. **1969** CBaker *Ernest* (NY) 357: You did not know Marx from your ass. **1969** JBurke *Firefly* (L) 96: Still don't know your arse from a hole in the ground. **1973**

WMasterson *Undertaker* (NY) 166: You don't know your ass from a hole in the ground. **1973** EMcBain *Hail* (NY) 39: He hardly knew [him] from a hole in the wall. **1975** HLawrenson *Stranger* (NY) 223: He don't know his ass from the Fourth of July. **1982** RBParker *Ceremony* (NY) 50: They don't know their ass from a hole in the ground. Berrey 148.4: Hole in the ground.

A135 Not to know one's **Arse** from his elbow (*varied*)

1949 RFinnegan *Bandaged* (L 1952) 20: He doesn't know his hind end from his elbow. **1950** DMDisney *Fire* (NY) 91: He was one guy who knew his—uh—elbow from third base. **1951** JDSalinger *Catcher* (NY) 12: He was a nice old guy that didn't know his ass from his elbow. **1952** EPaul *Black* (NY) 36: I don't think he knows his pratt from his elbow. **1954** EPangborn *Mirror* (NY 1958) 112: I sometimes wonder if he knows his aspirations from his elbow. **1956** EMcBain *Cop* (NY 1959) 77: The kid . . . didn't know his ass from his elbow. **1957** WHHarris *Golden* (NY) 192: You don't know your elbow from your anus. **1958** BKendrick *Clear* (NY) 154: I happen to think you know your ass from your elbow. **1964** BKaufman *Up the Down* (NY 1966) 178: They don't know their ass from—I beg your pardon. **1966** AEHotchner *Papa* (NY) 261: Some . . . flunky who doesn't know his ass from his elbow. **1969** AGilbert *Missing* (NY) 14: She hardly knows her arse from her elbow. **1970** DClark *Deadly* (NY) 30: They've not known whether they've been on their arses or elbows this last year. **1971** PDennis *Paradise* (NY) 221: Liz . . . knows her ass from her elbow. **1975** GHousehold *Red* (B) 251: "You don't know your ass from your elbow." "Ass, Mrs. Hilliard?" "Willie, my upbringing as a young lady in Connecticut prevents me to this day from pronouncing that word as it should be. Ass it is and ass it will remain. And don't you talk to me about Chaucer!" **1976** EKennedy *St. Patrick's Day* (NY) 30: The liberals don't know their ass from their elbow. **1982** BBronzini *Scattershot* (NY) 106: You don't know your ass from your elbow. **1982** EVCunningham *Kidnapped Angel* (NY) 103: If [it] knew its

ass from its elbow. Partridge 18; DARE i 99: Ass from.

A136 To have one's **Arse** hanging in the wind

1965 DoctorX *Intern* (NY) 309: Left with his bare ass hanging out in the wind.

A137 To have one's **Arse** in a sling (*varied*)

1950 WLGresham *Limbo* (L) 52: If the boss finds an unmade bed it'll be my neck in a sling. **1951** CWillingham *Reach* (NY) 121: Her arse is in a sling up there [*not a free agent*]. **1955** JO'Hara *Ten* (NY) 362: Before he gets his ass in a sling. **1956** JHoward *Blow* (Toronto) 129: If you're off on a drunken bender I'll really have my butt in a sling [*be in trouble*]. **1960** RPrice *Upright Ape* (NY) 76: Your backside is going to be in a sling. **1961** RAKnowlton *Court* (L 1967) 68: Don't get your ass in a bind. **1966** RHardwick *Season* (NY) 169: Every now and then you hear about some dumb cop getting his ass in the crack. **1969** SFisher *Saxon's* (LA) 132: If we found . . . any . . . irregularity, his ass was in a sling. **1974** EMcBain *Bread* (NY) 19: Or his ass'll be in a sling. **1975** RForrest *Child's* (I) 44: If he had died my ass would be in a sling. Wentworth 10: Ass.

A138 To work one's **Arse** off

1970 WANolen *Making* (NY) 22: You'll work your ass off. **1972** COverstreet *Boar* (NY) 9: He worked his black ass off with those hogs. Berrey 245.12: Tail; Partridge 18: Arse off, tear one's.

A139 The **Arse-end** (arsehole) of wherever

1966 HHarrison *Make Room* (NY) 120: I was stationed at the ass-end of Texas. **1972** JMangione *Dream* (B) 89: Who in the hell wants a guide to North Little Rock? Don't you know it's the asshole of the world? **1974** SKrim *YOU* (NY) 37: Stuck out at the ass-end of town. Cf. To be at the End of nowhere *below*.

A140 **Arsehole** or (to) breakfast time

1971 BWAldiss *Soldier* (L) 141: You don't know—as the poetical phrase has it—whether it's arsehole or breakfast time.

1971 RFDelderfield *For My* (NY) 311: Chivvied from arsehole-to-breakfast-time.

A141   Art is long and life is short (*varied*)
1924 RAFreeman *Blue* (NY) 211: Art is long but life is short. **1927** RAFreeman *Cat's Eye* (NY) 56: Life is short but Art is long. **1930** SBHustvedt *Ballad Books* (Cambridge, Mass.) 178: The truism that art is long and time is fleeting. **1931** GPahlow *Murder* (NY) 64: Art is long. **1938** RAFreeman *Stoneware* (L) 156: Art is long but life is short. **1953** SRansome *Shroud* (NY) 192: Ars longa, vita brevis. **1959** *NYTimes Book Review* 4/19 10: But, if Art is fleeting, Time is long. **1963** HMacInnes *Venetian* (NY) 137: Life is short; art is long. **1968** AMStein *Snare* (NY) 192: Art is long. Life? Short. EAP A122.

A142   As dry as Ashes
1946 JStagge *Death's Old* (NY) 158: Her voice was dry as ashes. **1949** JStagge *Three* (NY) 182: My mouth was dry as ash. EAP A123.

A143   As gray as Ashes
1928 RHWatkins *Master* (NY) 300: His face . . . gray as ashes. **1947** LFord *Woman* (NY) 237: His face gray as ashes. **1957** *Time* 10/14 85: A grey-as-ashes England. Whiting *NC* 362.

A144   As pale as Ashes; Ash-pale
1927 CRogers *Colonel Bob* (NY) 35: Pale as ashes. **1937** GBruce *Claim* (NY) 104: [Her] face was pale as ashes. **1958** ESGardner *Foot-loose* (NY) 141: His face became as pale as ashes. **1966** HPentecost *Hide* (NY) 17: An ash-pale man. EAP A124.

A145   As white as Ashes; Ash-white
1932 VLoder *Red Stain* (NY) 243: Boles was white as ashes. **1937** CBClason *Purple* (NY) 27: Her face was ash-white. **1940** RKing *Holiday* (NY) 190: Turning an ash-white. **1953** CBKelland *Sinister* (NY DBC) 163: Ash-white. **1970** CBrookhouse *Running* (B) 67: Her face is white as ash. EAP A125; TW 10(3).

A146   To have one's Ashes hauled
1955 ELacy *Best* (NY) 73: There's a pro down the street who was hauling Frankie's ashes. Wentworth 9.

A147   To quiver (shake, shiver, tremble) like an Aspen
1927 WBFoster *From Six* (NY) 62: Shaking now like an aspen. **1929** KCStrahan *Footprints* (NY) 150: She is as shakey as an aspen. **1930** WLewis *Apes* (NY 1932) 127: It would tremble like an aspen. **1931** PGWodehouse *Big Money* (NY) 87: I'm just quivering like an aspen. **1938** GDHCole *Mrs. Warrender's* (L) 100: The young poet, shivering like an aspen. **1941** ISCobb *Exit* (I) 368: He quivers like an aspen. **1945** MInnes *Appleby's End* (NY) 87: The maid was trembling like an aspen. **1951** TDubois *Solution* (NY) 14: You're all shivering like an aspen. **1958** CLBlackstone *Woman* (NY) 104: His very umbrella quivered like an aspen. **1958** FDuncombe *Death* (NY) 83: I felt as quivery as an aspen. **1965** CBeaton *Years* (L) 278: His hands trembled like aspen. EAP A128; TW 10(1,2); Brunvand 4.

A148   To quiver (shake, tremble) like an Aspen leaf
1921 RLardner *Big Town* (NY 1925) 70: The ladies was shaking like an aspirin leaf. **1927** JTaine *Quayle's* (NY) 318: Trembling like an aspen leaf. **1930** AChristie *Mysterious* (NY) 289: He began suddenly to quiver all over like an aspen leaf. **1932** GLane *Hotel* (L) 130: She trembled like an aspen tree. **1940** DWheelock *Murder at Montauk* (NY) 136: Jim was trembling like an aspen leaf. **1948** ELipsky *Murder One* (NY) 74: His fingers shook like an aspen leaf. **1954** HGardiner *Murder* (L) 161: I was quivering like an aspen leaf. **1960** EWolf *Rosenbach* (Cleveland) 61: I was shaking like the proverbial aspen leaf. **1968** JPorter *Dover Goes* (NY) 8: Shaking like an aspen leaf. **1974** LBlanch *Pavilions* (NY) 26: Trembling like aspen leaves. EAP A128; TW 10; Brunvand 5.

A149   Shy but willing, like an Ass pissing
1922 JJoyce *Ulysses* (NY 1934) 540: Shy but willing, like an ass pissing.

A150   Attack is the best defense (*varied*)
1930 RGBrowne *By Way* (NY) 57: The professional strategists say that attack is the best defence. **1931** PBaron *Round* (NY) 23: The best method of attack was defense. **1931** FDGrierson *Jackdaw* (L) 201: The best method of defending oneself is often to attack. **1931** JHRYardley *Before the Mayflower* (NY) 27: The old-age military axiom that attack is the best defence. **1933** GBegbie *Sudden* (L) 182: The good old army slogan of "Attack is the best method of defence." **1952** PGWodehouse *Pigs* (NY) 105: Attack is the best form of defence. **1961** JDavey *Touch* (L 1963) 113: Defence was the best attack. **1964** JWCampbell *Analog II* (NY) 207: The best form of defence is attack. **1970** GBagby *Killer* (NY) 43: The best defence is a good attack. **1971** RLFish *Rub* (NY) 147: Attack, he knew from long experience, was by far the best defence. **1974** CMartin *Whiskey* (NY) 33: A spirited attack is the best defence. EAP D100. Cf. Offense *below.*

A151   To cleanse the Augean stables
1952 MInnes *One-man* (NY) 109: The Augean stables will be cleansed. **1970** RFoley *Calculated* (NY) 23: The cleaning of Augean stables. EAP A137.

A152   Auntie's ruin
1953 NBlake *Dreadful* (L) 110: Have a drop of auntie's ruin [*cider*]. Partridge 535: Mother's ruin [*gin*].

A153   To see Aunt Sally
1957 HPBeck *Folklore of Maine* (P) 168: Go see Aunt Sally [*the privy*]. Partridge 20: Aunt.

A154   Avarice is the old man's sin
1971 JLord *Maharajahs* (NY) 6: Avarice, the old man's vice. EAP A140.

A155   To leave no Avenue unexplored (or stone unturned) (*varied*)
1931 CBush *Dead Man's* (L) 203: Every possible avenue had been explored. **1936** TAPlummer *Dumb* (NY) 145: A man who never left any avenue unexplored. **1947**
DBowers *Bell* (NY) 107: No stone unturned, no avenue unexplored. **1956** MGilbert *Be Shot* (L) 87: He has left no stone unturned and no avenue unexplored. **1967** DShannon *Rain* (NY) 202: We have to explore every avenue, as the old saw goes. **1970** RQuest *Cerberus* (NY) 134: You're prepared to leave stones unturned and avenues unexplored. **1976** JPorter *Package* (NY) 176: To leave no avenue unexplored or stone unturned. **1981** AMorice *Men* (NY) 164: There are still a few stones and avenues we haven't explored. Cf. To leave no Stone *below.*

A156   The Ax is at the root (of the tree)
1974 JWain *Samuel Johnson* (NY) 357: Now the axe was at the root. EAP A144.

A157   To have an Ax to grind (*varied*)
1903 EChilders *Riddle* (NY 1940) 287: She had . . . but one axe to grind. **1915** WLewis *Letters* ed WKRose (L 1963) 73: No political axe to grind. **1922** JJoyce *Ulysses* (NY 1934) 624: With an axe to grind. **1933** MBurton *Death* (L) 36: He's got an axe to grind. **1940** FWBronson *Nice People* (NY) 123: Had he an ax to grind? **1944** MLong *Bury* (NY) 47: She was effusive with Gordon (spitting on the axe before grinding it). **1945** ACampbell *With Bated* (NY) 110: I had some personal axe to grind. **1950** CLittle *Black* (NY) 143: She had an ax to grind, and she wanted to grind it right. **1957** *NYTimes Book Review* 3/17 10: So, while Clay could grind an axe, he could also bury one. **1960** LHale *Blood* (L) 32: A cunning man with a dirty axe to grind. **1963** RLhombreaud *ASymons* (L) 167: The critic has . . . his own axe to grind. **1968** GHCoxe *Candid* (NY) 158: You had an ax to grind with Arnold [*disliked him*]. **1974** MInnes *Appleby's Other* (NY) 18: I have no axe to grind. **1980** HPentecost *Death* (NY) 91: In walks Mr. X with some other axe to grind. EAP A143.

A158   To say Aye, yes or no
1935 KMKnight *Death* (NY) 179: Without sayin' aye, yes or no. **1941** CLClifford *While*

the Bells (NY) 209: Without any aye, yes or no from you. **1957** JPotts *Man with* (NY 1964) 37: A chance to say ay, yes or no. **1960** TCurley *It's a Wise* (NY) 94: It won't be safe for yours truly to say ay yes or no. DARE i 110: Aye.

B

B1 Not to know **B** from a bull's foot

1900 CFPidgin *Quincy A. Sawyer* (B) 6: One of those city chaps who know B from a bull's foot. **1929** RAJWalling *Murder* (NY) 54: People . . . who can tell B from a bull's foot. **1932** ERPunshon *Cottage* (B) 171: He didn't know Buluwago from a bull's foot. **1935** HHolt *Tiger* (L) 244: I don't know a plantation from a bull's foot. **1953** OAtkinson *Golden* (I) 235: He doesn't know B from a bull's foot. **1967** JDCarr *Dark* (NY) 127: He doesn't know B from a bull's foot. EAP B1; TW 12; Brunvand 6; DARE i 227: B from (a) bull's foot, 200: Beef from, Bee from, 203: Beeswax from.

B2 As helpless as a **Babe** (baby)

1921 P&MThorne *Sheridan* (NY) 231: You're helpless as a babe. **1929** CGLDuCann *Secret* (L) 186: Helpless as a baby. **1935** AChristie *Death* (L) 198: Helpless as a babe in arms. **1936** EBQuinn *One Man's* (L) 134: Helpless as a baby. **1940** AMChase *No Outlet* (NY) 58: I'm as helpless as a baby. **1952** PLoraine *Dublin* (L) 45: He'd be as helpless as a newborn babe without his mother. **1954** SDeLima *Carnival* (NY) 27: She is helpless as a babe almost. TW 12(3); Taylor *Western Folklore* 17(1958) 13.

B3 As innocent (clean) as a **Babe** (infant) (*varied*)

1920 EWallace *Three-Oaks* (L) 228: As innocent as a babe. **1923** EWallace *Clue* (B) 151: As innocent as a babe unborn. **1928** ABCox *Amateur* (NY) 278: [He] looked as innocent as a new-born infant. **1929** MAl-lingham *Crime* (L 1950) 69: I was as innocent as a new-born babe. **1930** EWallace *Green Ribbon* (NY) 168: I was as innocent as a baby. **1931** HHolt *Midnight* (NY) 160: Sam was as innocent as an unborn baby. **1936** VMcHugh *Caleb* (NY) 94: Innocent as babes. **1937** GGoodchild *Having No* (L) 38: Innocent as a new-born babe. **1939** GBagby *Bird* (NY) 187: You're as innocent as a baby. **1947** FCDavis *Thursday's* (NY) 38: Mel's as innocent as a newborn babe. **1950** CDickson *Night* (NY) 74: You're as innocent as a baby. **1950** ERPunshon *So Many* (NY) 84: Innocent as a babe. **1951** JCollier *Fancies* (NY) 291: She's as clean as a new-born babe. **1959** RMacdonald *Galton* (NY) 149: He's as innocent as an unborn babe. **1955** LWhite *To Find* (NY) 132: She looked as innocent as a newborn baby. **1974** DMarlowe *Somebody's* (NY) 96: As innocent as a babe in limbo. **1975** MDelving *Bored* (NY) 167: You're as innocent as a baby. EAP C142; TW 12(5), 13(9); Taylor *Western Folklore* 17(1958) 13; Tilley B4, I41; Wilstach 216: New-born babe, infant. Cf. As innocent as a Child *below*.

B4 As quiet as a **Babe**

1963 NBenchley *Catch* (NY) 73: You were quiet as a babe. Whiting B2: Still.

B5 **Babes** in the wood

1928 JJConnington *Mystery* (B) 149: Quite like the Babes in the Wood. **1931** LEppley *Murder* (NY) 160: We are as alone as the babes in the wood. **1938** ESGardner *Shoplifter's Shoe* (NY) 123: A babe in the woods.

1943 MCarpenter *Experiment* (B) 172: Babes in the woods. **1954** MHastings *Cork* (NY) 47: "I lost my way." "Like a babe in the wood." **1957** *Punch* 2/13 240: You poor little frightened babe in the woodshed. **1959** DMDisney *No Next* (NY) 33: A novice, a babe in the woods. **1960** RLDuffus *Tower* (NY) 119: We were babes in the woods, some with whiskers. **1965** HCarlisle *Ilyitch* (NY) 18: This babe-in-the-woods attitude. **1974** SForbes *Some* (NY) 76: Babes-in-the-wood. EAP B3.

B6 To know no more than (As ignorant as) a **Babe** unborn

1929 HHolt *Mayfair* (L) 258: She knows no more . . . than a babe unborn. **1932** FWCrofts *Double* (NY) 97: "You've no idea?" "No more than the babe unborn." **1970** JPorter *Dover Strikes* (NY) 184: As pig-ignorant as a new-born babe. TW 12(7). Cf. To know no more than a Child *below*.

B7 To sleep (slumber) like a **Babe**

1911 JLondon *Letters* ed KHendricks (NY 1965) 332: I sleep like a babe. **1925** JSFletcher *Wolves* (NY) 126: She slept like an innocent child. **1929** FDaingerfield *Linden* (NY) 157: Sleeping as peacefully as a baby. **1930** MAllingham *Mystery* (NY) 265: I shall slumber like a babe. **1931** KTrask *Murder* (NY) 167: He was sleeping like a baby. **1937** WMartyn *Old Manor* (L) 85: I shall sleep like a child. **1958** *NYTimes* 7/20 35: He was sleeping like a baby. **1970** DMDisney *Do Not* (NY) 11: You'd sleep like . . . a baby. **1970** PMoyes *Many* (NY) 203: She's sleeping like a little child. **1976** MGilbert *Night* (NY) 90: You'll sleep like a baby. **1977** VCanning *Doomsday* (NY) 130: Sleepin' like a babe. TW 13(11): Baby; Taylor *Prov. Comp.* 14: Baby; Wilstach 358: Sleep . . . babe. Cf. Infant *below*.

B8 As bare as a new-born **Baby**

1960 LSdeCamp *Bronze* (NY) 202: As bare as a new-born baby. Taylor *Prov. Comp.* 15: Babe.

B9 As harmless as a **Baby**

1957 JMerrill *Seraglio* (NY) 306: He's harmless as a baby and hairless as a French whore. Taylor *Western Folklore* 17(1958) 13.

B10 As naked as a **Baby**; Baby-naked

1940 GDHCole *Wilson* (L) 238: The parson was left naked as a new-born child. **1954** THoward *Blood* (NY) 201: He was naked as a baby. **1957** BVanorden *309 East* (NY) 48: She stood before me naked as a babe. **1965** RLPike *Police* (NY) 66: They're baby-naked. **1969** SMays *Fall Out* (L) 158: Naked as a baby. **1973** HPentecost *Beautiful* (NY) 3: They were both as naked as babes. **1977** SKaminsky *Bullet* (NY) 21: They were both baby naked.

B11 To cry like a **Baby**

1925 FSFitzgerald *Great Gatsby* (NY) 216: I . . . cried like a baby. **1949** EQueen *Cat* (B) 14: He cried like a baby. **1961** MErskine *Woman* (NY) 55: Cry like a baby. TW 13(10); Brunvand 6(2).

B12 To leave (be left) holding the **Baby** (*varied*)

1927 GDilnot *Lazy* (B) 80: Leaving you to hold the baby. **1932** EWallace *When the Gangs* (NY) 285: Leaving me to hold the baby. **1933** VWilliams *Clock* (L) 182: I certainly seem to be holding the baby. **1940** GHCoxe *Lady Is Afraid* (NY) 272: This is his baby now. **1947** KMKnight *Blue* (NY) 108: This is your baby. I'm afraid you'll have to hold it. **1951** SJepson *Man Dead* (NY) 133: He'd gone off after the bitch and left her to hold the baby. **1959** DMDouglass *Many* (L) 97: He said it was your baby. **1960** HSDavies *Papers* (L) 233: To leave me holding the baby. **1971** EPeters *Knocker* (NY) 172: Left the others holding the baby. Partridge 397: Holding. Cf. To be left . . . Bag *below*.

B13 To throw out the **Baby** with the bath (water) (*varied*)

1925 HWNevinson *More Changes* (L) 123: Lest, as the Germans say, we throw away the child with the bath-water. **1943** GGCoulton *Fourscore* (Cambridge, Eng.) 170: Throwing out the baby with the bath. **1950** ECrispin *Sudden* (NY DBC) 124: No bath water is ever thrown out without some species of baby goes down the plug-hole with it. **1955** DParry *Sea* (L) 211: You know the proverb about the baby and the bath-water. **1958** *NYTimes* 3/16 10E: That ancient maxim of common sense, not to throw the baby out with the bath. **1958** *NYTimes* 3/23 61: A ruthless approach which . . . throws out the baby with the bath. **1960** PO'Connor *Lower* (L) 93: The baby was well on the way out with the bath-water. **1967** RHKuh *Foolish* (NY) 228: We are not forced to throw out the baby with the bath water. **1971** TRosebury *Microbes* (NY) 60: Or, as the English like to say, to throw out the baby with the bathwater. *Oxford* 220: Empty.

B14 As bald (clear, innocent, pink) as a **Baby's** bottom

1936 NBlake *Thou Shell* (L) 35: As innocent as a baby's bottom. **1954** EForbes *Rainbow* (B) 142: Bald as a baby's bottom. **1957** VWMason *Gracious* (NY) 51: His . . . scalp shone pink as a baby's bottom. **1959** *Time* 6/15 61: His face as clear as a baby's bottom. **1960** PJFarmer *Strange* (NY) 150: As pink as a baby's bottom.

B15 As smooth as a **Baby's** (child's) bottom

1936 JMetcalfe *Sally* (NY) 465: Smooth as a baby's bottom. **1939** EQueen *Dragon's* (NY) 22: The set-up is as smooth as a baby's --- [*presumably bottom*]. **1942** RAHeinlein *Waldo* (NY 1965) 260: The road was . . . smooth as a baby's fanny. **1961** JBlofeld *City* (L) 189: My chin is as smooth as a child's bottom. **1964** BWilliams *Stranger* (NY) 204: The girl . . . has a stomach as smooth as a baby's ass. **1968** WTenn *Seven* (NY) 12: As smooth as a baby's bottom. Taylor *Western Folklore* 17(1958) 13: Arse, bottom.

B16 **Bachelor** Hall

1951 LFord *Murder Is* (NY) 35: Bachelor Hall stuff. EAP B9.

B17 The **Back** of beyond (*varied*)

1931 JSFletcher *Malvery* (L) 13: A sort of nowhere place—back of beyond. **1935** HHolt *Unknown* (L) 255: A one-horse hotel at the back of beyond. **1938** SLeslie *Film* (L) 236: One of those parishes which lie, as the Irish say, very comfortably at the back of God's Beyond. **1945** HCBailey *Wrong Man* (NY) 55: In his office here, back of

beyond. **1949** JReach *Late* (NY) 24: Brooklyn . . . it's just the back end of the world. **1959** AWUpfield *Journey* (NY) 68: The blacks are way in the back of beyond. **1961** SClayton *Crystal* (L) 69: Shut up at the back of beyond. **1972** DLees *Rainbow* (NY) 153: Round about here at the back of bloody beyond. NED Beyond C1b, Suppl. Back o' Beyond.

B18 To be glad to see one's **Back**

1925 JSFletcher *False* (NY) 281: What on earth does [she] want to see your back for? **1932** ACampbell *Murder* (NY) 141: The vicar's glad to see the back of her. **1955** DParry *Sea* (L) 208: You'll be glad to see the back of me. **1962** MGEberhart *Enemy* (NY) 43: I was glad to see their backs. **1970** RRendell *Best Man* (NY) 42: She was glad to see the back of them.

B19 To have one's **Back** to the wall

1957 *NYTimes* 11/10 25: With its back to the wall. Partridge 24.

B20 To have (put) one's **Back** up

1920 EWallace *Three-Oak* (L) 65: Put his back up. **1931** DAldin *Murder in a Haystack* (NY) 10: They both got their silly backs up. **1937** DAllan *Brandon* (L) 152: You'll just put her back up. **1940** CSaxby *Death Joins* (NY) 140: You seem to have got her back up. **1947** HLawrence *Death of* (NY) 123: I've got that woman's back up. **1957** HE Bates *Summer* (B) 200: [He] put my back up. **1961** PMoyes *Down Among* (NY) 52: He does put people's backs up. EAP B13; TW 13(3).

B21 To put one's **Back** into something

1929 JJConnington *Case* (B) 85: You seem to have been fairly putting your back into it. **1938** JRhode *Invisible* (L) 57: He puts his back into it [*work*]. NED Suppl. Back *sb.* 24h.

B22 You scratch my **Back** and I'll scratch yours

1929 EBYoung *Dancing* (P) 45: You scratch my back and I'll scratch yours. **1936** CMRussell *Death* (NY) 44: You scratch my back and I'll scratch yours. **1950** THoward *Shriek* (NY) 229: You scratch my back and

I scratch yours. **1959** MErskine *Graveyard* (NY) 147: A case of you scratch my back and I'll scratch yours. **1962** RLockridge *First* (P) 162: Could be I've scratched your back, as the saying goes. **1965** HWaugh *End* (NY) 94: I see no reason why we can't scratch each other's backs. **1971** RLWolff *Strange* (B) 234: A case of one brother's scratching another brother's back. **1975** HLawrenson *Stranger* (NY) 142: [He] operates . . . on a you-scratch-my-back-and-I'll-scratch-yours principle. TW 13(2). Cf. Whiting K1.

B23 As bald (bare, nude) as the **Back** of one's hand

1937 EGreenwood *Under the Fig* (NY) 173: Nude as the back of my hand. **1940** PWentworth *Rolling* (P) 236: It was as bare as the back of his hand. **1941** PWentworth *Weekend* (P) 110: Bald as the back of your hand. Tilley B18: Bare; Wilstach 12: Palm.

B24 As familiar (plain) as the **Back** of one's hand

1934 CBush *100% Alibis* (L) 138: It's as plain as the back of your hand. **1936** NMorland *Clue* (L) 88: As familiar as the back of her hand. **1970** RLPike *Reardon* (NY) 171: As familiar to him . . . as the back of his hand. Cf. To know like the Back *below.*

B25 To give the **Back** of one's hand (tongue)

1931 LEppley *Murder* (NY) 304: The back of my hand to you. **1939** CMWills *Death at* (L) 119: The back o' me hand to the . . . swine. **1964** JHillas *Today* (NY) 97: They'll give Tommy the back of their hand. **1965** ADerleth *Casebook* (Sauk City, Wisc.) 75: My uncle can do no worse than give me the back of his tongue. EAP B12.

B26 To know like the **Back** of one's hand (*varied*)

1928 AWUpfield *Lure* (NY 1965) 99: I know more about 'em than I do the back of me 'and. **1938** WJMakin *Queer Mr. Quell* (NY) 231: I asked him if he could remember the place. "Like the back of my hand." **1956** EMcBain *Mugger* (NY 1963) 133: I know the commissioner the way I know the back of my own hand. **1960** NWilliams

Knaves (NY) 21: She knew London like the back of her hand. **1972** KCampbell *Thunder* (I) 45: He knows this place like the back of his hand. Cf. As familiar as the Back *above.*

B27 To talk out of the **Back** of one's neck

1951 SJepson *Man Dead* (NY) 148: You're talking out of the back of your neck. **1973** JCashman *Gentleman* (NY) 249: He's talking through the back of his neck. Partridge 24.

B28 To save one's **Bacon**

1924 LO'Flaherty *Spring* (L) 133: Just saved my bacon. **1932** LCharterin *White* (NY) 28: Save the family bacon. **1948** JTey *Franchise* (NY 1955) 203: You have saved our bacon. **1950** NFlower *Just* (NY) 77: Here Rider Haggard saved his bacon. **1958** MHastings *Cork* (NY) 210: Who saved your bacon? **1964** JPorter *Dover One* (NY 1966) 130: Dover's bacon had been saved. **1976** JPorter *Package* (NY) 165: Saved their bacon. EAP B19.

B29 To make **Bad** worse (*varied*)

1933 VLoder *Suspicion* (L) 42: We mustn't make bad worse. **1941** MPRea *Compare* (NY) 93: Are you going from bed to hearse. EAP B21; Brunvand 6.

B30 As calm (*etc.*) as a **Badger**

1929 RRodd *Secret* (NY) 119: Surly as a badger. **1960** LLee *Edge* (NY) 18: I was sick as a badger. **1962** AMorton *If Anything* (L) 26: I've been as calm as a badger. **1971** SBerlin *Dromengro* (L) 121: I feel as daft as a badger.

B31 As grey as a **Badger**; Badger-grey

1932 VWilliams *Fog* (B) 36: A head as grey as a badger's. **1934** CBush *Dead Shepherd* (L) 14: [He] was badger-grey. **1946** AE Martin *Death in the Limelight* (NY) 27: Gray as a badger. EAP B22; Taylor *Prov. Comp.* 45.

B32 To stink like a **Badger**

1960 JBell *Fall* (NY) 136: Stink like a badger. Whiting B559: Brock; *Oxford* 715: Stink . . . brock.

B33   To work like a **Badger**

1934 JCameron *Body* (L) 73: Works like a badger. **1966** NMonsarrat *Life (I)* (L) 187: I began to work like a badger.

B34   As rough as **Bags**

1938 NMarsh *Artists* (L 1941) 204: He looks as rough as bags. **1958** JLindsay *Life* (L) 60: The rough-as-bags lad. Partridge 27.

B35   **Bag** and baggage (*varied*)

1923 DFox *Doom* (NY) 235: Bag and baggage. **1942** ESHolding *Kill Joy* (NY) 9: The day she came, bag and baggage. **1954** JRMacdonald *Find* (NY) 123: Kicked him out bag and baggage. **1966** JAiken *Beware* (NY) 97: To send her packing . . . back to Italy, bag and bastard. **1974** DMDisney *Don't Go* (NY) 59: Out she goes, bag and baggage. EAP B24; Brunvand 6.

B36   A **Bag** of bones

1954 CBeaton *Glass* (NY) 133: An incredibly tall, thin woman, the proverbial "Bag of bones." Partridge 26.

B37   A different **Bag** of tricks

1935 ECRLorac *Affair* (L) 141: Quite a different bag of tricks. Whiting B10: Wiles; NED Bag 17: Tricks; Partridge 26.

B38   To be in the **Bag**

1933 NBMavity *Fate* (NY) 245: That'll give me the story in the bag. **1940** NBlake *Malice* (L) 175: He's got it in the bag. **1955** PGWodehouse *French* (L) 103: The thing was in the bag. **1960** RFraser *Trout's* (L) 176: It's in the bag. **1972** LBlack *Ransom* (NY) 91: It's in the bag. Wentworth 15.

B39   To be left holding the **Bag** (*varied*)

1921 ERBurroughs *Mucker* (NY) 101: While we hold the bag. **1922** VThompson *Pointed* (NY) 250: Leave me to hold the bag. **1929** CFGregg *Three Daggers* (NY) 278: Left you holding the sack. **1937** DQBurleigh *Kristiana* (NY) 221: Leave us holding an empty bag. **1952** EPaul *Black* (NY) 107: He leaves you holding the bag. **1954** KMKnight *High* (NY) 18: Left me holding the bag—or the baby, to be more exact. **1965** ESGardner *Troubled* (NY) 246: I've held the bag on your snipe hunting this far.

1975 JLangton *Dark* (NY) 48: Left us holding the bag. EAP B28. Cf. To leave . . . Baby *above*; Sack *below*.

B40   A **Baker's** dozen (*varied*)

1900 CFPidgin *Quincy A. Sawyer* (B) 234: A baker's dozen he called it. **1923** JSFletcher *Markenmore* (NY) 11: Baker's dozen. **1936** VMcHugh *Caleb* (NY) 322: A baker's dozen. **1941** DBHughes *Bamboo* (NY) 252: A baker's dozen. **1948** KBercovici *Savage* (NY) 118: Men like him don't come thirteen to the dozen. **1952** JWKrutch *Desert* (NY) 239: In the good old days it took thirteen to make a baker's dozen. **1962** GMaxwell *Ring* (NY) 152: A baker's dozen of small . . . birds. EAP B30; Brunvand 6.

B41   To hang in the **Balance**

1957 *BHerald* 3/31 3A: Many things will be hanging in the balance, as the old saying goes. NED Balance *sb.* 9.

B42   To go for something **Baldheaded**

1922 JJoyce *Ulysses* (NY 1934) 124: Go for one another baldheaded in the papers. **1927** JMWalsh *Silver* (L) 189: He goes for it baldheaded. **1935** EJepson *Murder* (L) 127: Gone for them bald-headed. **1981** JSScott *View* (NY) 114: The utter baldheaded bane of every working policeman's life. TW 15; DARE i 136: Bald-headed.

B43   As round as a **Ball**

1945 CEVulliamy *Edwin* (L) 79: Head as bald and as round as an ivory ball. EAP B32.

B44   To be a **Ball** of fire

1933 CPenfield *After the Deacon* (NY) 177: Outwardly calm, but inwardly the proverbial ball of fire. **1940** MArmstrong *Man with* (NY) 147: He's a ball of fire compared to Pricie. **1954** JPotts *Go* (NY) 114: Greg's not a ball of fire. Wentworth 16–17.

B45   To have something on the **Ball**

1941 IMontgomery *Death Won* (NY) 69: You must have something on the ball yourself. **1948** NMailer *Naked* (NY) 464: [He] had more on the ball than Brown. **1965** JBell *No Escape* (NY) 148: The professor was very much on the ball. Wentworth 16.

B46 To have the **Ball** (world) at one's feet
1925 JSFletcher *Wolves* (NY) 41: The ball of Life was at his feet for him to kick as high as he pleased. **1957** EMButler *Heine* (NY) 131: The ball would have been at Heine's feet. **1965** VPurcell *Memoirs* (L) 359: I now "had the ball at my feet." **1972** DDevine *Three* (NY) 167: The world's at your feet. EAP B34.

B47 To play **Ball** with someone
1935 HMcCoy *They Shout* (NY) 38: You play ball with us and we'll play ball with you. **1958** RMarsten *Even* (NY) 58: Play ball with us. **1959** ASillitoe *Loneliness* (L) 9: If you play ball with us we'll play ball with you. DA Ball *n.* 3e.

B48 To start the **Ball** rolling
1923 DFox *Doom* (NY) 181: Started the ball rolling. **1933** JCMasterman *Oxford* (L) 138: Doyne started the ball rolling at once. **1938** LAnson *Such Natural* (L) 188: Carol started the ball rolling. EAP B35; TW 15(3); Brunvand 7(2).

B49 To be cold enough to freeze the **Balls** off a brass monkey (*varied*)
1869 TBAldrich *Story* (Boston 1897) 130: It was cold enough to freeze the tail off a brass monkey. **1920** ZFitzgerald in NMilford *Zelda* (NY 1970) 85: The place is 18 below zero and I go around thanking God that, anatomically and proverbially speaking, I am safe from the awful fate of the monkey. **1931** GFowler *Great* (NY) 140: Fire Island is so cold it would freeze the whatzis off a brass monkey. **1932** ARolls *Lobelia* (L) 11: Cold enough to freeze the bloody old brass monkey on the town hall. **1933** RAFreeman *Dr. Thorndyke Intervenes* (L) 72: The wind was enough to nip the nose off a brass monkey. **1938** EGilligan *Boundary* (NY) 99: The snow that high and the wind enough to freeze them off a brass monkey. **1949** GFowler *Beau* (NY) 120: Even a brass monkey would complain if he lost his pants in this weather. **1955** DParry *Sea* (L) 97: When it's cold here . . . it would take the nose off a brass monkey. **1957** ECaldwell *Certain* (B) 165: This is the kind of weather that'll freeze the balls off a brass

monkey. **1959** HCarmichael *Marked* (NY) 12: It's cold enough to freeze the balls off a pawnbroker's sign. **1961** MHHood *Drown* (NY) 80: Water's cold enough to freeze a brass monkey. **1964** EMcBain *Ax* (NY) 72: It's cold enough to freeze the balls off a brass monkey. **1966** HHarrison *Make Room* (NY) 183: It's cold enough to freeze a brass monkey in here. **1967** JFDobie *Some Part* (B) 253: It was cold enough to freeze the horns off a brass billygoat. **1978** SAngus *Dead to Rites* (NY) 84: "It is enough to freeze the ba . . . to freeze the blood." "Or the balls off a brass monkey." **1978** JSymons *Blackheath* (NY) 190: The look she gave me would have frozen the appendages off a brass monkey, if you'll pardon the expression. **1982** CMacLeod *Wrack* (NY) 32: A look that would o' froze the tail off a brass monkey. Taylor *Prov. Comp.* 28; Partridge 528: Monkey.

B50 To have more **Balls** than brains
1971 BWAldiss *Soldier* (L) 87: Your sergeant's got more balls than brains.

B51 To have someone by the **Balls**
1963 JMUllman *Neon* (NY) 77: I thought I had him by the balls. Wentworth 17.

B52 To go over like a lead **Balloon**
1962 ITRoss *Old* (NY DBC) 81: It [*a joke*] went over like a lead balloon. Taylor *Prov. Comp.* 15: Steel balloon; *Western Folklore* 17(1958) 13: Lead.

B53 To sag (drop) like a pricked **Balloon**
1935 HAdams *Fate Laughs* (L) 170: He sagged like a pricked balloon. **1939** HReilly *All Concerned* (NY) 178: Munn dropped into his chair like a pricked balloon. TW 15(1). Cf. Bladder, Bubble *below*.

B54 When the **Balloon** goes up (*varied*)
1929 TLDavidson *Murder* (L) 208: The balloon is about ready to go up. **1934** CBush *Dead Shepherd* (L) 163: The balloon failed to go up. Mr. Grey remained calm. **1938** LAnson *Such Natural* (L) 93: I'll not stick up for you when the balloon goes up. **1945** GBellairs *Calamity* (NY) 183: Will the balloon go up on the whole scheme? **1955** MGilbert *Country-house* (NY) 63: [He] was

in his bed when the balloon went up [*bomb exploded*]. **1961** LPayne *Nose* (NY) 248: I'll be all right when the balloon goes up. **1964** AMacKinnon *Report* (NY) 96: He wanted to be in top form if and when the balloon went up. **1973** AMorice *Death* (NY) 51: Before the balloon went up. **1975** HCarvic *Odds One* (NY) 148: The balloon would have gone up. Partridge 29. Cf. The Penny drops, The Shit hits *below*.

B55   Balm in Gilead

1929 BFlynn *Invisible* (L) 134: Balm in Gilead. **1932** HCBailey *Case* (NY) 85: There is no balm in Gilead. **1934** HCBailey *Bishop's* (NY) 164: But there is balm in Gilead. **1947** GLGower *Mixed* (L) 66: Balm in Gilead. **1955** DMDisney *Room* (NY) 125: It was balm and gilead to Aggie. **1964** JHIllas *Today* (NY) 148: There was balm in Gilead. **1974** DCavett *Cavett* (NY) 339: Was there balm in Gilead? EAP B36; Brunvand 7.

B56   No matter how you slice it, it's still Baloney (bologna)

1931 PATaylor *Cape Cod* (NY 1971) 196: No matter how you slice it, it's still bologna. **1935** AHobhouse *Hangover* (NY) 46: I don't care how thin you slice it, it's still baloney. **1936** PGWodehouse *Young Men* (NY) 20: Slice him where you like, he was still baloney. **1940** STowne *Death out* (NY) 207: Any way you slice it, it's still baloney. **1958** RMacdonald *Doomsters* (NY) 77: Baloney, no matter how you slice it. Wentworth 51: Boloney; Berrey 151.6,11; Partridge 76: Boloney.

B57   That beats (bangs) Banagher

1922 JSFletcher *Herapath* (NY) 290: This beats Banagher. **1930** JGBrandon *Murder* (L) 110: That beats Bannagher and he beat the devil. **1932** VWilliams *Mystery* (B) 35: This beats Banagher. **1937** NBell *Crocus* (NY) 208: As a bowyer he beats Banaghan. A bowyer's a chap who spins the tale, draws the long bow; but don't ask me who's Banaghan, for I don't know; king of sprucers if you like. **1960** RWatters *Murder* (Dublin) 111: That bates Banagher. **1973** JFleming *Alas* (NY) 136: It bangs bannacker! TW 15.

B58   To beat the Band

1904 JCLincoln *Cap'n Eri* (NY) 247: Blow to beat the band. **1924** LTracy *Token* (NY) 21: Beat the band. **1938** MBurton *Platinum* (L) 45: If that don't beat the band! **1951** SJepson *Man Dead* (NY) 105: Isn't that fit to beat the band! **1972** JBonett *No Time* (NY) 120: That fair beats the band. **1975** EMcBain *Where* (NY) 66: He started barking to beat the band. Whiting *NC* 365.

B59   As if out of a Bandbox (*varied*)

1923 JSFletcher *Markenmore* (NY) 47: Looking . . . as if he had just come out of a bandbox. **1929** GHWilkins *Undiscovered* (NY) 245: Clean as from a band-box. **1932** LFord *By the Watchman's* (NY) 12: Fresh as if they'd just come out of the customary bandbox. **1933** VMacClure *Crying Pig* (L) 205: Looked as if he had been turned, as they say, out of a bandbox. **1947** LFord *Woman* (NY) 19: She looked as if she'd just stepped out of an air-conditioned bandbox. **1957** JHJackson *Girl* (NY) 97: Neatly dressed, as if he had come out of a bandbox. **1970** RRendell *Best Man* (NY) 26: Lillian . . . looked as if she'd just stepped out of a bandbox. EAP B38; TW 15–6.

B60   To climb on the Bandwagon (*varied*)

1929 HFootner *Doctor* (L) 93: A form of climbing on the band wagon. **1938** KMKnight *Acts* (NY) 132: Climb aboard somebody else's band wagon. **1942** BBloch *Bach* (NY) 7: Everybody climbing aboard the bandwagon like sheep. **1957** *NYTimes* 5/19 1E: Most of the Democrats . . . have hopped on the economy bandwagon. **1959** PGraaf *Sapphire* (NY) 92: Climbing aboard her bandwagon. **1962** MClifton *When They* (NY) 152: Jump on the band wagon. **1969** TBesterman *Voltaire* (NY) 349: Rousseau now jumped on the band wagon. **1969** CIrving *Fake* (NY) 73: Everybody's going to jump on the bandwagon. **1973** HThomas *Strachey* (NY) 133: Here is the bandwagon: jump on it now or you'll be too late. Wentworth 18.

B61   As safe (right) as a Bank

1931 MMagill *Murder* (P) 271: You're as safe as a bank. **1949** RFoley *Girl* (NY) 48:

This place . . . as safe as a bank. **1966** HRFKeating *Death* (NY) 104: As safe as the bank. **1966** NMarsh *Killer* (B) 97: It'll all be right as a bank. Clark 219. Cf. EAP B39; TW 16(1). Cf. Vault *below*.

B62   As safe (*etc.*) as the **Bank** of England (*varied*)

1930 LThayer *They Tell* (NY) 200: As safe as the Bank of England. **1930** EWallace *Silver Key* (NY) 199: They're as solid as the Bank of England. **1931** HCBailey *Fortune Explains* (NY) 98: Sound as the Bank. **1937** JBentley *Landor* (L) 256: He was safe as the Bank of England. **1944** RAJWalling *Corpse Without* (NY) 101: She's as safe as the Bank. **1948** CDickson *Skeleton* (NY 1967) 77: Ruth's as honest as the Bank of England. **1957** *New Yorker* 10/12 38: Safe as the Bank of England. **1958** MCair *Burning* (NY) 31: Safe as the Bank of England, as we used to say. **1960** NWilliams *Knaves* (NY) 21: The Bank's proverbial security. **1970** GSmith *Shattered* (NY) 62: The remark "safe as the Bank of England" no longer had any meaning. Wilstach 333. Cf. EAP B39.

B63   To keep **Banker's** hours

[Heard in Northport, Maine as early as 1935. BJW] **1952** RFenisong *Deadlock* (NY) 147: We can't say you keep banker's hours. **1959** PGreen *KGrahame* (L) 77: Bankers' short hours are proverbial. **1970** RRood *Wild* (NY) 112: They [*crows*] keep bankers' hours.

B64   To howl like a **Banshee**

1952 AGilbert *Mr. Crook* (NY DBC) 70: It was howling like a banshee. **1958** SDean *Dishonor* (NY) 48: Howling like a banshee. Taylor *Western Folklore* 17(1958) 13; NED Banshee.

B65   As cocky as a **Bantam** rooster

1931 WBSeabrook *Jungle* (L) 138: As cocky as a bantam rooster. **1938** JGEdwards *Odor* (NY) 183: No bantam half so cocky as an old bantam. Whiting *NC* 365(1); TW 16(1).

B66   To strut like a **Bantam** rooster

1965 HPentecost *Sniper* (NY DBC) 63: He strutted around like a bantam rooster. TW 16 (2).

B67   Not to know someone from a **Bar** of soap

1925 JGBrandon *Cork* (L) 109: People . . . that I don't know from the . . . well-known bar of soap. **1931** GHolt *Green* (I) 32: I don't know him from a bar of soap. **1967** HRigsby *Calliope* (NY) 22: I don't know you from a bar of soap.

B68   A **Bargain** is a bargain

1950 STruss *Never* (NY) 235: A bargain's a bargain. EAP B42; Brunvand 7.

B69   To curse like a **Bargee**

1936 LAKnight *Night* (L) 193: He cursed like a bargee. NED Bargee (quote 1861).

B70   As close (tight) as the **Bark** on a tree (*varied*)

1900 CFPidgin *Quincy A. Sawyer* (B) 276: They hang to it [*money*] tighter'n the bark to a tree. **1903** ADMcFaul *Ike Glidden* (B) 218: She's as close as the bark ter a tree. **1904** JCLincoln *Cap'n Eri* (NY) 268: Closer'n the bark of a tree [*mean*]. **1941** FCrane *Turquoise* (P) 31: McClure is tighter'n the bark of a tree [*mean*]. **1953** RBissell *7½ Cents* (B) 5: He was tighter than the bark on a tree. **1957** LBeam *Maine* (NY) 60: He was a little mite close to the bark [*miserly*]. **1958** *BangorDN* 7/22 17: He's tight as the bark on a tree [*mean*]. **1959** DMDisney *Did She Fall* (NY) 35: [She] was as tight as the bark on a tree. EAP B43; TW 16(1,2,3); Brunvand 7.

B71   With the **Bark** on

1957 *BHerald* 11/25 29: Nobody in the Administration . . . seems willing to give us the truth with the bark on. **1959** *BHerald* 9/17 37: He wanted questions "with the bark on." **1959** *Time* 3/23 14: He intended to "get the truth with the bark off." TW 17(6).

B72   More **Bark** than bite

1928 ALivingston *Monk* (NY) 200: More bark than bite. **1932** PMacDonald *Mystery* (NY) 302: Don't be misled by his bark. No bite at all. **1956** WMankowitz *Old* (B) 125: You're all bark and no bite. **1974** EGertz *To Life* (NY) 52: He would bark more often than he would bite. Whiting *NC* 365: Bark 2(4).

B73 One's **Bark** is worse than his bite (*varied*)

1919 LTracy *Bartlett* (NY) 33: [Her] bark is worse than her bite. **1930** NDouglas *Three* (L) 49: Fear not . . . the bark of a certain wrathful Lamb. It is worse than his bite. **1933** VWilliams *Fog* (B) 93: His bark was worse than his bite, as the saying goes. **1946** LAllen *Murder . . . Rough* (NY) 42: His bark was worse than his bite. **1953** KMKnight *Three* (NY) 15: Her bark's worse than her bite. **1956** *BangorDN* 6/21 34: His bark is deadlier than his bite. **1959** *Time* 3/23 15: The bite was louder than the bark. **1966** LBiggle *Watchers* (NY) 110: My bark is worse than my bite. **1971** JPope-Hennessy *Trollope* (B) 85: Trollope's bow-wow bark was always worse than his bite. **1971** WHWalling *No One* (NY) 115: His bite is much worse than his bark. **1972** TWells *Die* (NY) 136: Her bite is even worse than her bark. EAP B45.

B74 **Barkis** is willing

1930 RAFreeman *Mystery* (NY) 79: Barkis himself was not more willing than I. **1930** EMarjoribanks *E.M.Hall* (L) 86: The proverbial "Barkis is willin'." **1940** HCBailey *Mr. Fortune Here* (NY) 51: Barkis is willin'. **1957** CASmart *At Home* (NY) 174: Barkis is still willin'. **1959** RMacdonald *Galton* (NY) 188: Barkis was willing. **1961** HPentecost *Deadly* (NY DBC) 35: Barkis is willing. **1966** DMDisney *At Some* (NY) 245: If you change your mind, "Barkis is willin'." Partridge 34 [*David Copperfield*].

B75 As big as a **Barn**

1962 KKesey *One Flew* (NY) 58: She's big as a damn barn. Taylor *Prov. Comp.* 16.

B76 As cold as a **Barn**

1930 MGEberhart *While* (NY) 99: My room is cold as a barn. **1953** BCClough *Grandma* (Portland, Me.) 17: The rooms were as cold as barns. Taylor *Western Folklore* 17(1958) 13(1).

B77 To burn a **Barn** to kill the rats (*varied*)

1938 WNMacartney *Fifty Years* (NY) 375: The man who burned down his barn to destroy the rats. **1956** *NYPost* 10/23 34: Like burning down the barn to kill a rat.

1958 *BHerald* 1/15 11: There were mice in the pantry so the house was burned down; the dog had fleas so the dog was chloroformed. **1958** *BHerald* 6/3 14: It is senseless to burn down the barn just to kill a couple of rats. **1967** RJackson *Occupied* (L) 231: It smacks too much, perhaps, of blowing up the house to get rid of the rats. EAP B48; TW 17: Barnburners; Whiting B49.

B78 To be born in a **Barn**

1964 JWCampbell *Analog II* (NY) 57: Were you born in a barn? [*a door left open*]. Berrey 147.7; DARE i 342: Born in, i 392: Brought up.

B79 As big (broad) as a **Barn** door (*varied*)

1927 BAtkey *Man* (NY) 174: A hint as broad as the side of a barn. **1937** JFerguson *Death* (L) 205: A smile as broad as any open door. **1940** AMcRoyd *Death in Costume* (NY) 20: The foolish heart—big as a barn door. **1941** CBClason *Green Shiver* (NY) 222: Can't see the truth when it's big as a barn door. **1958** MProcter *Man in* (NY) 64: A man . . . as broad as a door. **1961** RJWhite *Smartest* (L) 97: As broad as a barn door. **1962** ITRoss *Old* (NY DBC) 56: He was as big, as solid and as rural as the proverbial barn door. **1963** KAmis *Spectrum III* (L) 82: Kelly ran . . . feeling as big as a barn door. **1965** LBiggle *All the Colors* (NY) 174: Broad as a barn door. TW 17(1); Whiting B51. Cf. Taylor *Western Folklore* 17(1958) 13(2): Wide.

B80 To cling like a **Barnacle**

1903 EChilders *Riddle* (NY 1940) 113: Clinging like a barnacle. **1958** *NYTimes Book Review* 3/9 8: Having clung like a barnacle. **1958** EQueen *Finishing* (NY) 226: Clings to life like a barnacle. Wilstach 59. Cf. NED Barnacle *sb.*² 3.

B81 **Barney's** bull

1937 NBell *Crocus* (NY) 35: Tell that to Barney's Bull. Partridge 35.

B82 As big as a **Barrel**

1949 MAllingham *More Work* (NY) 181: She's big as a barrel. Whiting *NC* 366(1); Taylor *Prov. Comp.* 16.

B83 As round (tubby) as a **Barrel**

1930 AMuir *Silent* (I) 147: He's as tubby as a barrel. **1936** JBude *Sussex* (L) 222: Tom was as round as a barrel. Taylor *Prov. Comp.* 69.

B84 To be over a **Barrel**

1939 DBOlsen *Cat Saw* (NY) 47: They've got me over a barrel. **1941** JKVedder *Last Doorbell* (NY) 285: She's got me across a barrel. **1952** MHBradley *Nice* (NY) 198: She had you, in fact, over a barrel. **1959** PDeVries *Through* (B) 110: Having me over a barrel, as they say. **1968** SPalmer *Rook* (NY) 71: You got us over a barrel. **1971** HPentecost *Deadly* (NY) 85: That put Maxwell over a barrel. **1974** NWebster *Burial* (NY) 3: Preston had us over the proverbial barrel. Wentworth 21.

B85 Not to get to first **Base**

1939 GHCoxe *Four Frightened* (NY) 70: He hadn't got to first base. **1941** DVanDeusen *Garden Club* (I) 78: He never got to first base. **1951** MHead *Congo* (NY) 30: He didn't even get to first base. **1959** ESGardner *Mythical* (NY) 216: He hung up before I could get to first base. **1961** ESGardner *Spurious* (NY) 137: I couldn't get to first base. **1981** GMitchell *Death-Cap* (NY) 153: She didn't make first base, as the Americans say. Wentworth 21 [*sexual*].

B86 As polite (*etc.*) as a **Basket** of chips (*varied*)

1930 JFDobie *Coronado* (Dallas) 114: He was as perlite as a basket of chips. **1932** PATaylor *Death* (I) 52: He was happy an' cheerful as a basket of chips. **1943** EW Teale *Dune Boy* (NY 1957) 245: Polite ez a basket o' chips. **1956** *BangorDN* 5/28 23: We're friendly as a basket of kittens. **1968** EBuckler *Ox Bells* (NY) 144: He'd be pleasant as a basket of chips. **1969** APHannum *Look* (NY) 153: His wife had been as sweet and pretty as a basket of speckled pups when he courted her. TW 17(1,2); DARE i 164.

B87 Off one's own **Bat**

1928 ABerkeley *Silk* (NY) 73: Solve the case off his own bat. **1938** HHolt *Whispering* (L)

184: Doing the thing neatly off his own bat. Partridge 37.

B88 Right off the **Bat**

1929 EAPowell *Last Home* (NY) 121: He invites you right off the bat. **1971** DPryde *Nunaga* (NY) 140: Right off the bat. DA Bat *n.*² 3(4).

B89 As blind as a **Bat**; Bat-blind

1903 ADMcFaul *Ike Glidden* (B) 72: He's as blind as a bat. **1910** PGWodehouse *Leave It to Psmith* (L) 8: Blind, to use his own neat simile, as a bat. **1924** LTracy *Token* (NY) 72: Blind as a bat. **1931** CWells *Horror* (P) 237: Those bat-blind guards. **1937** CBush *Hanging Rope* (L) 14: As blind as a bat. **1943** MCarpenter *Experiment* (B) 304: She's blind as a bat. **1951** JDSalinger *Catcher* (B) 180: His mother's blind as a bat. **1959** KBulmer *Changeling* (NY) 30: Molly was drunk—as blind as a bat. **1973** EMcBain *Let's Hear* (NY) 204: Blind as a bat. EAP B54; Brunvand 7(1).

B90 As crazy as a **Bat**

1929 AKreymborg *New American* (NY) 217: You're crazy as a bat. **1935** WSeabrook *Asylum* (NY) 47: As crazy as bats. **1940** EQueen *New Adventures* (NY) 45: You're crazy as a bat. **1952** MGreenberg *Five* (NY) 16: Crazy as a bat. **1957** GWJohnson *Lunatic* (P) 210: [He] was probably as crazy as a bat. Whiting NC 366(2).

B91 Like a **Bat** (cat) out of hell (*varied*)

1928 SQuinn *Phantom* (Sauk City, Wisc. 1966) 178: He came outer here like a bat outer hell. **1936** HWeiner *Crime on the Cuff* (NY) 48: The Doll drove like a bat out of hell. **1945** BKendrick *Death Knell* (NY) 52: Quick as a bat out of hell. **1945** MWalsh *Nine Strings* (P) 77: He would make for cover like a cat out of hell. **1952** JWKrutch *Desert* (NY) 140: "Like a bat out of hell" is not, for me, an especially expressive metaphor. **1959** WHMurray *Appointment* (NY) 242: Snowing like cats out of hell. **1961** DLoovis *Last* (NY) 77: He drove the boat like the proverbial bat out of hell. **1965** PAnderson *Star* (NY) 252: She can move like a hellbat. **1966** MWorthington *Strange* (NY) 46: Gertrude Stein drove a car . . .

like a bat out of hell. **1971** HCarvig *Witch* (NY) 154: Drive like a bat out of hell. **1975** ELathen *By Hook* (NY) 206: He took off like a bat out of hell. Whiting *NC* 366(4,5).

B92 To have **Bats** in the belfry (*varied*)
1925 EPhillpotts *Voice* (NY) 45: Bats in the belfry. **1928** BAtkey *Midnight* (NY) 132: Bats! Belfries! **1937** ECRLorac *Bats in the Belfry* (L). **1944** MFitt *Clues* (NY) 44: In spite of the bats in the top storey. **1959** DMDisney *Did She Fall* (NY) 146: It's just a bat she let out of her belfry. **1963** MMcCarthy *Group* (NY) 207: A few bats in the belfry. **1965** AGilbert *Voice* (NY) 113: Bats are flying in his belfry, in his bonnet hums a bee. **1974** ELathen *Sweet* (NY) 114: He's got bats in the belfry. *Oxford* 32.

B93 In the **Batting** of an eye
1929 JSStrange *Clue* (NY) 60: Take him to the station in the batting of an eye. Cf. NED Bat *v.*² 2. Cf. Wink *below*.

B94 A **Battle** (game) is never lost until it is won
1927 FDGrierson *Smiling* (NY) 164: A battle is never lost until it is won. **1930** FDGrierson *Blue Bucket* (NY) 246: He remembered the boxing adage that a match is never lost until it is won. **1935** BFlynn *Sussex* (L) 189: A game's never won till it's lost. **1959** JABrussel *Just* (NY) 128: The sophomoric adage that "the game isn't over until the last whistle is blown." Whiting B65; Brunvand 56: Game (1).

B95 To be over the **Bay** [*drunk*]
1978 JGould *Trifling* (B) 177: The camp cook . . . was over the bay. EAP B56; TW 18.

B96 To flourish like the green **Bay** tree (*varied*)
1921 SMEllis *Solitary Horseman* (Kensington) 270: The wicked ones . . . flourish like the green bay-tree. **1928** EKRand *Founders* (Cambridge, Mass.) 167: Wicked men flourish like the green bay-tree. **1930** HHolt *Ace* (L) 152: She had blossomed like the green bay tree. **1935** CRyland *Twelfth Night* (L) 12: Such things flourish like the proverbial green bay tree. **1939** DCDisney

Golden Swan (NY) 235: Where screwballs flourish like the green bay tree. **1944** VWBrooks *Washington Irving* (NY 1946) 112: He throve . . . like the green bay tree. **1951** ACalder-Marshall *Magic* (L) 74: Eccentricity . . . flourishes like the green bay tree. **1957** VWMason *Gracious* (NY) 33: Flourishing like the green bay tree of Holy Writ. **1960** ADuggan *Cunning* (NY) 31: The wicked flourish like a green bay tree. **1967** CDrummond *Death* (NY) 91: The old Dad flourishes like that biblical tree. **1971** NMarsh *When* (NY) 74: May she flourish like the Green Bay Tree. **1973** KCampbell *Wheel* (I) 163: Bay trees. What the wicked flourish like. EAP B59.

B97 To be off the **Beam**
1959 SDean *Price* (NY) 73: You're a little off the beam. Wentworth 23.

B98 To be on one's **Beam-ends**
1904 JCLincoln *Cap'n Eri* (NY) 75: Don't go on your beam ends. **1909** JCLincoln *Keziah* (NY) 122: You've got me on my beam ends. **1933** CBarry *Murder* (L) 131: Somebody who . . . was on his beam ends. **1936** GDHCole *Last Will* (NY) 228: He's on his beam-ends again. **1937** JPMarquand *Late George* (B) 289: A bit on our beam ends [*drunk*]. **1939** VWilliams *Fox Prowls* (B) 72: I find him as the English say on his beam ends. **1949** NBlake *Head* (NY) 97: He's on his beam-ends and desperate. **1953** AChristie *Funerals* (NY) 19: On our beam-ends. **1966** MErskine *Family* (NY) 13: He was pretty well on his beam ends. **1973** MInnes *Appleby's Answer* (NY) 124: He must have been on his beamends. EAP B62; Partridge 39.

B99 Not to care (matter) a **Bean**
1929 GMWhite *Square* (L) 197: I don't see that it matters a bean. **1935** TThayer *Cluck* (NY) 154: She could not believe the Mexican girl cared a bean for him. DA Bean 4a.

B100 Not to give two **Beans**
1969 HFosburgh *Clearing* (NY) xvi: He just didn't give two beans for me. Whiting B86.

B101 Not worth a **Bean**

1930 CBush *Death* (NY) 237: Worth three thousand if it's worth a bean. **1930** JRhode *Dr. Priestly* (NY) 36: There isn't a stick in the place worth a bean. **1956** WTenn *Human* (NY) 50: He isn't worth beans as a shepherd. Partridge 39; Tilley B118.

B102 To be full of **Beans**

1927 GDilnot *Lazy* (B) 304: He'll be as full of beans as ever. **1937** ECRLorac *Bats* (L) 38: I woke up full of beans. **1947** JDCarr *Sleeping* (NY) 109: "In excellent health?" "Yes. Full of beans." **1956** SPalmer *Unhappy* (NY 1957) 20: He was a man still full of beans and business, as the saying goes. **1959** DCushman *Goodbye* (NY) 125: The sheriff came very full of beans. **1967** RPeterson *Another View* (NY) 203: Full of beans and twice as sassy. Partridge 39; Wentworth 205.

B103 To give someone **Beans**

1926 AMarshall *Mote* (NY) 160: She will give you beans [*a scolding*]. TW 19(4); DA Bean 4c; Partridge 39.

B104 To know (Not to know) **Beans** (*varied*)

1930 HSKeeler *Fourth* (NY) 103: He knows beans. **1935** CGBooth *Cat* (NY) 114: I know beans when I see them. **1950** MScherf *Curious* (NY) 73: He didn't know beans with the bag untied. **1954** EQueen *Glass* (B) 37: She doesn't know beans about art. **1954** EWalter *Untidy* (P) 161: Even people that didn't know beans from boathooks. **1968** MBorgenicht *Margin* (NY) 22: I didn't know beans about discipline. TW 18(3); DA Bean 4a; Wentworth 24; DARE i 183.

B105 To know how many **Beans** make five

1934 AGilbert *Man in Button* (L) 40: He knows how many beans make five. **1936** TAPlummer *Dumb* (NY) 48: I see you know how many beans make five. **1959** JFleming *Malice* (NY) 131: Doesn't know how many beans make five. **1962** MAllingham *China* (NY) 213: He might be bright enough to see how many beans make five. **1969** AGilbert *Missing* (NY) 70: Charlie knows how many beans make five. **1970** VCHall *Outback* (Adelaide) 130: Can't beat the old

Chinaman . . . He knew how many soya beans make five. **1971** RFDelderfield *For My* (NY) 169: The great majority know precisely how many beans make five. *Oxford* 437: Knows.

B106 To spill the **Beans**

1921 P&MThorne *Sheridan* (NY) 84: Spilled the beans. **1932** MThynne *Murder* (NY) 266: I went on spilling the beans. **1939** RStout *Some Buried* (L) 125: The bag was open now and most of the beans gone. **1940** DHume *Invitation* (L) 51: Somebody spilled a whole row of beans. **1941** MColes *Drink* (NY) 137: It's no good crying over unspilt beans. **1958** JSStrange *Night* (NY) 271: Without spilling the beans. **1959** NMarsh *False* (B) 130: I'm going to spill the beans and unbag cats galore. **1964** LMJanifer *Wonder* (NY) 64: I'll . . . spill every last little God damn bean. **1965** PAnderson *Corridors* (NY) 161: Spilled the whole beanpot. **1966** SGCrawford *Gascoyne* (L) 125: Talk, sing, spill the beans, let the cat out of the bag, 'fess up. **1970** RQuest *Cerberus* (NY) 72: Spill beans by the bushel. DA Bean 4b; Partridge 809: Spill; Wentworth 509. Cf. TW 18(1).

B107 As thin (lean, skinny) as a **Beanpole**

1936 HAsbury *French* (NY) 340: He . . . was as thin as the proverbial beanpole. **1947** PBennett *Varmints* (NY) 237: Tall as a beanpole and about as thin. **1955** SRansome *Frazer* (NY) 131: He's tall and as thin as a bean pole. **1959** *Time* 9/14 69: As lean as a beanpole. **1965** Doctor X *Intern* (NY) 29: Skinny as a beanpole. **1966** MErskine *Family* (NY) 103: My husband remains as thin as a beanpole. **1970** HBlyth *Skittles* (L) 147: Thin as a bean pole. Whiting *NC* 366(1,4); Taylor *Western Folklore* 17(1958) 13. Cf. Pole *below*.

B108 Always behind like a **Bear's** nuts

1968 EBuckler *Ox Bells* (NY) 161: Always behind like a bear's nuts. Cf. All behind, like a Cow's tail *below*.

B109 As cross (grouchy, grumpy) as a **Bear** (*varied*)

1903 ADMcFaul *Ike Glidden* (B) 79: She's as cross as an old she-bear. **1927** GDHCole

Murder at Croune House (NY) 60: Cross as a bear. **1938** ABoutell *Death* (NY) 66: Looking as cross as a bear. **1939** IJones *Hungry Corpse* (NY) 173: Miriam is as grump [*sic*] as a burnt bear. **1941** CFAdams *Decoy* (NY) 96: He's as grouchy as a bear. **1954** VYentzen *Feast* (NY) 27: Cross as two bears. **1959** *BangorDN* 8/17 18: Grandma is as cross as a bear. EAP B67; TW 19(5); Brunvand 7(2).

B110 As fierce as a she-**Bear** that has lost its cubs (*varied*)

1935 SVertal *Wine Room* (B) 155: She's as fierce as a she-bear that has lost its cub. **1940** CSaxby *Death Joins* (NY) 225: Don't get between a she-bear and her cubs. EAP B73; TW 19(1,8); Whiting B103.

B111 As hungry as a **Bear** (*varied*)

1900 CFPidgin *Quincy A. Sawyer* (B) 423: I'm hungry as a bear. **1923** DFox *Doom* (NY) 165: Hungry as a bear. **1928** GFairlie *Scissors* (NY) 143: As hungry as a starving bear. **1937** WETarpin *These Low* (NY) 184: Ah'm hungry as a bear. **1940** RLGoldman *Snatch* (NY) 126: I was hungry as a bear. **1958** *BangorDN* 8/11 19: I'm hungry as a bear. **1963** MPHood *Sin* (NY) 59: Hungrier'n a pair of black bears in April. TW 19(11); Whiting *NC* 366(3); Brunvand 8(3).

B112 As rude as a **Bear**

1903 EChilders *Riddle* (NY 1940) 81: As rude as a bear. **1947** GLGower *Mixed* (L) 194: She was as rude as a bear. Wilstach 329.

B113 As sleepy as a **Bear** (*varied*)

1952 RMacauley *Disguises* (NY) 36: Sleepy as a bear. **1959** FSmith *Harry* (B) 133: I sleep like a bear. Brunvand 8(7).

B114 As sore as a **Bear**

1952 AAFair *Some Women* (NY DBC) 72: Sore as a bear. Cf. Whiting *NC* 366(4).

B115 As strong as a **Bear**

1971 WTeller *Cape Cod* (Englewood Cliffs, NJ) 75: Strong as a bear. TW 20(22).

B116 As sulky (surly) as a **Bear** (*varied*)

1933 ATSheppard *Rose* (L) 9: Sulky as a bear. **1938** AEFielding *Black Cats* (NY) 100:

As sulky as a bear. **1966** MFagyas *Widow* (NY) 201: You're surly as a bear. TW 20(23).

B117 As ugly (mean) as a **Bear**

1956 *BangorDN* 7/17 5: Ugly as a bear. **1965** VRandolph *Hot Springs* (Hatboro, Pa.) 132: He was mean as a bear. Whiting *NC* 366(10).

B118 **Bears** suck their paws in winter (*varied*)

1951 JCFurnas *Voyage* (NY) 38: He was living off books, sucking his own paws. EAP B72.

B119 If it had been a **Bear** (snake, dog) it would have bitten you (*varied*)

1933 CPenfield *After the Deacon* (NY) 92: If they'd been bears, they'd have bitten you. **1934** HBaker *Cartwright* (B) 164: It was right where if it had been a dog, it would 'a bit her. **1934** ACampbell *Desire* (NY) 53: If it had been a snake, I should have been bitten. **1936** SWilliams *Aconite* (NY) 79: As they used to say in Pecquia, "If it had been a bear, it would have bitten you." **1943** EW Teale *Dune Boy* (NY 1957) 193: If it'd been a snake it'd a bit me. **1948** AHandley *Kiss* (P) 79: If it had been a snake it would have bit me. **1956** MPHood *Scarlet* (NY) 102: Be a bear they'd bite you. *Oxford* 34.

B120 Like a little **Bear** with all his troubles before him

1933 GRichards *Memoirs* (NY) 346: I am like the little bear who had all his troubles before him. EAP B76; TW 20(28).

B121 To be hungry enough to eat a **Bear**

1906 RLDuffus *Waterbury* (NY 1959) 241: Hungry enough, as we used to say, to eat a bear. Cf. Berrey 95.6.

B122 To be like (as . . . as) a **Bear** with a sore head (paw, tail) (*varied*)

1922 JJoyce *Ulysses* (NY 1934) 180: Bear with a sore paw. **1928** EBYoung *Murder* (P) 122: The red man is like a bear with a sore head. **1930** HAdams *Crime* (P) 319: As to Bill—the sore-headed bear was by comparison a docile pet. **1931** LMcFarlane *Murder* (NY) 221: He growled at me like a bear with a sore paw. **1933** REast *Murder* (L) 80: Simmy's as grumpy as a bear with a sore bottom. **1933** GYoung *Devil's* (NY) 16: Look like a sore-tailed bear. **1938** KMKnight *Arts* (NY) 226: As cranky as a bear with a sore head. **1940** HAshbrook *Murder Comes* (NY) 212: You're like a bear with sore paws. **1952** PLoraine *Dublin* (L) 100: He was like the proverbial bear with a sore head. **1962** JJMarric *Gideon's March* (NY) 28: I've been like a bear with a sore head. **1964** JAshford *Suprintendent* (NY) 27: He can be like a bear with two sore heads. **1965** JPorter *Dover Two* (NY 1968) 150: Sulk about all day like a bear with a sore ear. **1967** HBorland *Hill Country* (P) 281: Mean as bears with sore paws. **1973** KAmis *Riverside* (NY) 130: Talk about a bear with a sore head. TW 19–20(5,9,24,31); Apperson 123: Cross; *Oxford* 35.

B123 To be loaded for **Bear**

1940 CSaxby *Death Joins* (NY) 31: All loaded for bear. **1956** ESGardner *Terrified* (NY) 89: The D.A. is supposed to be loaded for bear. **1964** JKieran *Not Under* (B) 134: The "innocent victim" turned out to be loaded for bear. **1965** DCLunt *Woods* (NY) 287: And, man dear, was she loaded for bear? [*angry*]. **1970** DLippincott *E Pluribus* (NY) 95: His questions . . . would be loaded for bear. Wentworth 322: Loaded.

B124 We killed the **Bear**

1942 EWTeale *Dune Boy* (NY 1957) 160: Gran would say: "Yes, *we* killed the bear." Whiting *NC* 367(14). Cf. DARE i 224; DA Betsy 1: A . . . colloquial name for a favorite gun [*Betsy and me killed the bear*].

B125 Sell not your **Bearskin** till you have the bear (*varied*)

1941 LSdeCamp *Incomplete* (NY 1962) 71: Do not sell your bearskin till you have caught the animal. EAP B81. Cf. To count one's Chickens *below*.

B126 To make the **Beast** with two backs (*varied*)

1922 JJoyce *Ulysses* (NY 1934) 138: Or the other story, beast with two backs. 546: The beast that has two backs at midnight. **1930** WLewis *Apes* (NY 1932) 163: The double

backed beast. **1954** MMcCarthy *Charmed* (NY) 197: Playing the beast with two backs. **1954** EQueen *Glass* (B) 6: Infanticide by a seventeen-year-old girl who'd made the two-backed animal with a deacon of the church. **1961** NBogner *In Spells* (L) 42: We were about to "make the beast with two backs." **1963** MMcCarthy *Group* (NY) 376: I played the beast with two backs with her. **1965** MJones *Set* (L) 230: They rolled over and became a single writhing form, the beast with two backs. **1971** RSilverberg *World* (NY) 95: It was only the old two-backed beast. *Oxford* 36.

B127 **Beauty** draws more than oxen

1945 RLHines *Confessions* (L) 91: The old adage . . . that "beauty draws more than oxen." *Oxford* 37.

B128 **Beauty** is in the eye of the beholder

1939 AGilbert *Clock* (L) 65: Evil, like beauty, is in the eye of the beholder. **1957** AArmstrong *Strange* (NY) 57: Beauty . . . is in the eye of the beholder. **1966** WTrevor *Love* (L) 121: Beauty's in the eye of the beholder. **1970** HActon *Memoirs* (NY) 229: The old adage that one must suffer to be beautiful and that beauty is in the eye of the beholder. **1977** STWarner *Kingdoms* (NY) 176: Beauty is in the eye of the beholder. Bartlett 729 [*LWallace*], 831 [*MW Hungerford*].

B129 **Beauty** is only skin deep

1908 LFBaum *American Fairy Tales* (I) 76: The beauty will be only skin deep. **1923** LThayer *Sinister* (NY) 139: Beauty isn't always skin deep. **1926** VWilliams *Key* (NY) 90: Beauty's only skin-deep. **1939** JRonald *This Way Out* (P) 71: They say beauty's only skin deep. **1952** GBagby *Scared* (NY) 86: "Beauty," said the inspector a touch sententiously, "is only skin deep." **1956** HRoth *Crimson* (NY) 133: An old platitude: beauty is skin deep. **1960** IWallace *Chapman* (NY 1961) 295: The cliché: But beauty's only skin deep. **1962** GMalcolm-Smith *Lady* (NY DBC) 50: Beauty . . . can be sin [*sic*] deep. **1965** PGWodehouse *Galahad* (L) 19: "And what is beauty, after all?" "Exactly. Skin deep I often say." EAP B89; Brunvand 8.

B130   As busy as a **Beaver**; Beaver-busy

1947 LFord *Woman* (NY) 9: Busy as a beaver. **1949** EQueen *Cat* (B) 123: Everybody's busy as little beavers. **1952** FCDavis *Tread* (NY) 44: Speare was beaver-busy. **1953** FCDavis *Drag* (NY) 108: He was as beaver-busy and tireless as always. **1958** *New Yorker* 1/25 39: He was as busy as a beaver. **1970** ELathen *Pick* (NY) 73: Busy as a beaver. TW 21(1).

B131   As industrious as a **Beaver**

1934 ECRLorac *Greenwell* (L) 195: He's as industrious as a beaver. EAP B91.

B132   To sweat like a **Beaver**

1936 SLBradbury *Hiram* (Rutland, Vt.) 252: Sweatin' like a beaver. TW 21(5).

B133   To work like a **Beaver**

1928 JGoodwin *When Dead Men* (NY) 216: Innes is working like a beaver. **1932** JStevens *Saginaw* (NY) 249: "He works like a beaver" is the highest praise a boss logger can speak about a woodsman. **1937** EB White *Letters* (NY 1976) 151: Working like beavers. **1940** IMontgomery *Golden* (NY) 271: He worked like a beaver all morning. **1954** CCarnac *Policeman* (NY) 187: I'll work like a beaver. **1958** *BHerald* 10/12 34: Working like a beaver. **1960** *BHerald* 10/16 26: The Russians may be working like beavers. **1966** JAiken *Beware* (NY) 66: I worked like a beaver. **1971** EXFerrars *Stranger* (NY) 144: She worked like a beaver. EAP B94.

B134   **Because** is a woman's reason (*varied*)

1913 ERBurroughs *Thuvia* (NY 1963) 22: The age-old universal answer of the woman: Because! **1922** JJoyce *Ulysses* (NY 1934) 493: It is because it is. Woman's reason. **1923** JSFletcher *Lost Mr. Linthwaite* (NY) 141: "Why do you think so?" . . . "Because I do!" . . . "Good feminine reasons." *Oxford* 38.

B135   Early to **Bed** and early to rise *etc.* (*varied*)

1905 GDEldridge *Millbank Case* (NY) 8: "Early to bed and early to rise" was its motto. **1920** GDilnot *Suspected* (NY) 153: Early to bed and early to rise. **1922** JSFletcher *Ravensdene* (NY) 42: The old saw

. . . Get to your pillow early and leave it early. **1923** JSFletcher *Markenmore* (NY) 47: The old saying—"Early to bed and early to rise makes a man healthy, wealthy, and wise." **1933** HAdams *Golf House* (P) 276: Early to bed and early to rise was still a maxim generally observed in that part of England. **1934** VGielgud *Ruse* (NY) 155: The old adage of early to bed. **1940** EHealy *Mr. Sandeman* (NY) 23: Early to bed and early to rise makes Jack a dull boy. **1941** RPKuehler *Sing a Song* (NY) 204: The old saw about early to bed. **1947** RDavies *Diary* (Toronto) 75: The . . . hand of Puritanism, eager to push people into bed earlier, and get them up earlier, to make them healthy, wealthy and wise in spite of themselves. **1952** CAmory *Last* (NY) 475: Early to bed, and early to rise . . . and you meet few prominent people. **1954** HNearing *Sinister* (NY) 188: An early-to-bed-early-to-rise bug. **1956** MScherf *Cautious* (NY) 29: You know how Harvey is—early to bed and early to rise gets the worm. **1959** *BHerald* 1/2 16: Early to bed and early to rise or the boss'll promote the other guys. **1959** GMarx *Groucho* (NY) 9: "Early to bed, early to rise, make a man you-know-what." This is a lot of hoopla. **1965** SVizinczey *In Praise* (L) 107: The old saying, "Early to bed and early to rise." **1971** RLFish *Rub* (NY) 41: Early to bed and early to rise, has some salubrious effect on a man, if I recall my Franklin correctly. **1975** HCarmichael *Too Late* (NY) 175: "I was up early this morning. And it only succeeded in disproving the old adage." "Which one?" "About early to bed and early to rise. With me it works in reverse. I feel lousy, I'm flat broke—and I'm no wiser." EAP B98; TW 21(1).

B136   One has made his **Bed** and must lie on it (*varied*)

1908 JCLincoln *Cy Whittaker* (NY) 13: You've made your bed; now lay in it. **1910** JCLincoln *Depot Master* (NY) 303: She'd made her nest; now let her roost on it. **1921** APHerbert *House* (NY) 105: If you make your bed you must lie on it. **1922** JJoyce *Ulysses* (NY 1934) 531: You have made your second best bed and others must lie on it. **1928** SChalmers *House* (NY) 357: He made his bed, poor fool! Now he can sleep in it. **1931** MAllingham *Gyrth* (NY) 72: I have buttered my bun and now I must lie on it. **1935** BFlynn *Padded* (L) 164: The bed is made and I made it. Therefore, I'll lie on it. **1937** LFord *Simple Way* (NY) 120: Martin has made his bed and doesn't want to lie in it. **1937** NMarsh *Vintage* (B 1972) 219: As you made your apple-pie bed so you must lie on it. **1940** IMontgomery *Golden* (NY) 177: If my bed's a little hard . . . well, I made it. **1947** RBax *Disposing* (NY) 243: She's buttered her bread and now she's got to lie on it, that's what I say. **1949** JMMyers *Silverlock* (NY) 167: She had made her bed, and I shall lie in it. **1955** BCarey *Fatal* (NY) 152: A kind of a "I've made my bed, now I have to lay in it" attitude. **1957** *New Yorker* 11/23 72: This is my bed, as they say. I made it and I'll lie in it. **1957** *Time* 4/29 106: She makes convalescent Gerry's bed and eventually lies in it. **1958** *Time* 5/12 8: He made his Baedeker now let him sleep in it. **1959** EHuxley *Flame* (L) 219: You have buttered your bed, and now you must lie on it, as the babu said. **1960** COliver *Unearthly* (NY) 70: As the man said, you buttered your bread—now lie in it. **1965** JPhilips *Black* (NY DBC) 139: What are the clichés? . . . Make your own bed and lie in it? Chickens come home to roost? **1973** BPronzini *Undercurrent* (NY) 75: I've made my own bed most of the time—literally as well as figuratively. **1975** MHolroyd *Augustus* (NY) 134: She had made her bed, as it were, and sometimes she would have to lie in it alone. Brunvand 8; *Oxford* 302.

B137 To get out of **Bed** on the wrong side

1922 JJoyce *Ulysses* (NY 1934) 61: Got up wrong side of the bed. **1930** MKennedy *Corpse* (NY) 114: The lawyer evidently got out of bed very much the right side. **1934** FOursler *Joshua* (NY) 133: Papa was in a bad humor this morning. I guess he put the wrong foot out of the bed. **1938** JRice *Man Who* (NY) 153: He got out of the wrong side of the bed. **1942** MColes *They Tell* (NY) 44: Grogan had got out of bed the wrong side that morning. **1950** LKaufman *Jubel's* (NY) 187: The difference between getting out of bed on the right or

the wrong foot. **1956** *New Yorker* 6/16 100: She got out of the wrong side of bed this morning. **1964** PMoyes *Falling* (NY 1966) 22: He got out of bed on the wrong side this morning. **1970** RRendell *Guilty* (NY) 72: You got out of bed the wrong side this morning. EAP B100; TW 21(2).

B138 As bright (*etc.*) as **Bedamned**

1932 VWilliams *Death* (B) 193: Sitting up in bed as bright as be damned. **1933** NGordon *Shakespeare* (NY) 252: He works away, cool as bedamned. **1939** CSaxby *Death Cuts* (NY) 155: All as ugly as bedam. **1956** *Punch* 11/7 561: Smug as be damned. Cf. Billy-bedamned *below*.

B139 As crazy (*etc.*) as a **Bedbug** (bug) (*varied*)

1927 JTaine *Quayle's* (NY) 124: You're crazy as a bedbug. **1931** VStarrett *Dead Man* (NY) 264: He's crazy as a bug. **1937** JYDane *Cabana* (NY) 158: Crazier than a bedbug. **1937** WDickimon *Dead Man* (P) 293: He's batty as a bug. **1940** DCCameron *Grave* (NY) 213: He's loony as a bedbug. **1940** DWheelock *Murder at Montauk* (NY) 252: The Captain was screwy as a bedbug. **1951** TDubois *Foul* (NY) 49: The old girl was crazy as a bug. **1952** CDickson *Cavalier's* (NY) 89: She's crazy as a bedbug. **1957** The Gordons *Big* (NY) 123: Crazy as two bugs in a sewer. **1959** CCornish *Dead* (NY) 19: They must be as queer as bedbugs. **1964** NBenchley *Winter's* (NY) 204: Crazy as a bedbug. **1970** LKronenberger *No Whippings* (B) 38: She's crazy as a bedbug. **1975** EMcBain *Where* (NY) 91: The lady's a bedbug. She thinks she's Cleopatra. **1976** EMcBain *So Long* (NY) 162: You're crazier'n a fuckin' bedbug. TW 22; Brunvand 8.

B140 To go to **Bedfordshire**

1955 AWest *Heritage* (NY) 147: Who's for Bedfordshire? *Oxford* 38–9.

B141 As crazy as a **Bedlamite**

1909 JCLincoln *Keziah* (NY) 191: As crazy as a Bedlamite. NED Bedlamite A.

B142   Between you and me and the **Bed-post** (bed pan)
1932 VWilliams *Death* (B) 208: Between you and me and the bedpost. **1937** JDCarr *Four False* (NY) 124: Between you and me and the bedpost. **1954** NBlake *Whisper* (L) 148: Between you and me and the bed-pan. EAP B103. Cf. Gate-post *below*.

B143   As brisk as a **Bee**
1958 WDHassett *Off the Record* (New Brunswick, NJ) 179: Brisk as a bee. EAP B105.

B144   As busy as a **Bee** (*varied*)
1909 JCLincoln *Keziah* (NY) 335: Busy as a bee. **1910** JCLincoln *Depot Master* (NY) 86: Busy as the proverbial bee. **1916** NDouglas *London Street Games* (L) 78: Busy as a bee. **1932** MPlum *Murder* (NY) 260: Busy as a whole hive of bees. **1938** PMacDonald *Warrant* (NY 1957) 169: Busy . . . Quite the bee! **1944** PATaylor *Dead Ernest* (NY) 141: Busy as little bees. **1953** AJLiebling *Honest* (NY) 88: Busy as the proverbial bees. **1959** EMarshall *Pagan* (NY) 18: Busy as bees in a swarm. **1960** DHayles *Comedy* (L) 329: Busy as a bee in clover. **1965** BGrebanier *Great Shakespeare* (NY) 11: Stratford was as busy as a hive. **1974** GPaley *Enormous* (NY) 38: They were busy as bees. EAP B106; TW 22(2); Brunvand 8(2).

B145   As happy as a **Bee** (*varied*)
1940 EBenjamin *Murder Without* (NY) 208: The child went off as happy as a bee. **1977** JLHensley *Rivertown* (NY) 121: He . . . acted like he was as happy as a bee in the puddin'. TW 22(5).

B146   As mad as a **Bee**
1948 NMailer *Naked* (NY) 543: Croft was mad as a goosed bee. Taylor *Prov. Comp.* 56: Hornet, etc.

B147   As thick as **Bees** (*varied*)
1936 VMcHugh *Caleb* (NY) 298: Thick as bees in a honeycomb. **1940** CWoolrich *Bride* (NY) 203: They always were as thick as bees out there. **1961** EPeters *Death* (NY) 121: As thick as bees. EAP B112; TW 22(7).

B148   To have a **Bee** in one's bonnet (*varied*)
1910 EPhillpotts *Tales* (NY) 245: A bee in his bonnet. **1920** AChristie *Mysterious Affair* (NY) 52: A bee in his bonnet. **1933** MBeckett *Murder* (L) 183: Got some silly bee in his bonnet. **1937** ESGardner *D.A. Calls* (NY) 67: I put a bee in his bonnet. **1940** KSteel *Dead of Night* (B) 315: She had this bee in her head. **1945** RLockridge *Death in the Mind* (NY) 111: He put a bee in Johnny's bonnet. **1949** EQueen *Cat* (B) 91: I think you put a bee in his buzzer. **1955** AHunter *Gently Does* (L) 182: Gently had a bee in his bonnet. **1956** *New Yorker* 10/13 141: College presidents have perpetual bees in their bonnets. **1956** *Punch* 10/24 504: A little bee in his belfry. **1967** KLauner *Planet* (NY) 23: The Senator had a bug in his bonnet. **1972** JBonett *No Time* (NY) 122: Had a proper bee in his bonnet. **1975** DDurrant *With My Little Eye* (NY) 44: My bonnet positively sings with the hum of bees. Whiting *NC* 368(5); Brunvand 8(1), 17: Bumble bee (1); *Oxford* 40.

B149   To put the **Bee** on someone
1931 GFowler *Great* (NY) 186: We had put the bee on him. **1938** WChambers *Dog* (NY) 115: Put the bee on her—to pay up, or else. **1940** WReed *No Sign* (NY) 117: She put the bee on him for five grand. **1949** JLane *Murder Spoils* (NY) 145: Long had put the bee on Mrs. Bridgeman. **1959** SDean *Merchant* (NY) 187: She did try to put the B[ee] on Jefferson. Wentworth 28.

B150   To swarm like **Bees** (*varied*)
1934 JRhode *Poison* (NY) 51: They'll be swarming around here like bees. **1937** JO'Hanlon *Murder* (NY) 25: People swarmed like bees before a hive. **1945** GBellairs *Calamity* (NY) 183: All over Harwood Hall like bees round a honey-pot. **1968** MRowell *Below* (L) 115: Olive . . . used to collect boy-friends like bees round the proverbial honey pot. EAP B117–8; TW 23(10,14–15); Brunvand 137: Swarm (1,2).

B151   Where there are **Bees** there is honey
1931 PATaylor *Cape Cod* (NY 1971) 144: There's bees where's honey. EAP B120.

B152   As busy (active) as a **Bee-hive**
1931 JSFletcher *Malvery* (L) 213: As busy as a bee-hive. **1937** GGoodchild *Operator* (L) 252: The quay was as busy as a beehive. **1940** JBentley *Mr. Marlow Stops* (B) 104: The flat was active as a beehive. Taylor *Prov. Comp.* 22.

B153   As big as a **Bee's knee** (*varied*)
1930 VLoder *Shop* (L) 218: They are no bigger than a bee's knee. **1932** VLoder *Red Stain* (NY) 165: Since he was no higher than a bee's knee. **1933** HHolt *Scarlet* (L) 31: Auriel was only as big as a bee's knee. **1936** HHolt *There Has Been* (L) 204: A . . . hope about as big as a bee's knee. **1939** HHolt *Smiling Doll* (L) 93: Since he was the height of a bee's knee. Partridge 43–44. Cf. TW 210: Knee-high; Wentworth 28.

B154   **Bee line**
1922 VBridges *Greensea* (NY) 325: He made a bee line. **1922** JJoyce *Ulysses* (NY 1934) 599: They made a bee line across the back of the Customhouse. **1936** PGWodehouse *Laughing* (NY) 81: Made a bee-line for it. TW 23; Brunvand 9.

B155   **Beef** to the heels
1922 JJoyce *Ulysses* (NY 1934) 65: Fair day and all the beef to the heels were in. 366: Beef to the heels. *Oxford* 39; DARE i 201.

B156   **Beer** on whiskey, very risky *etc.*
1957 JCheever *Wapshot* (NY) 306: Beer on whiskey, very risky. Whiskey on beer, never fear. Apperson 100: Cider on beer etc. Cf. Taylor *Proverb* 123–24, *Index* 87.

B157   He that drinks **Beer** thinks beer
1930 RAFreeman *Mystery* (NY) 84: He that drinks beer thinks beer. **1958** DGBrowne *Death* (L) 134: "He who drinks beer, thinks beer," was one of his favorite aphorisms. TW 23(1).

B158   Not all **Beer** and skittles
1929 FBeeding *Pretty* (B) 148: Then it will be "all beer and skittles," as the English say. **1931** AChristie *Murder* (NY) 255: Life can't be all beer and skittles. **1938** ECRLorac *Slippery* (L) 42: Looking after a pack of old ladies can't be all beer and skittles. **1941**

HLMencken *Newspaper Days, 1899–1906* (NY) 36: His days . . . were not all beer and skittles. **1950** JCannan *Murder* (L 1958) 63: Life wasn't all beer and skittles to a woman. **1955** JLatimer *Sinners* (NY) 136: And not exactly, as the English were supposed to say, all beer and skittles. **1966** EFuller *Successful* (NY) 32: It is not all beer and skittles. *Oxford* 462: Life.

B159   To be small **Beer** (*varied*)
1921 CSLewis *Letters* ed WHLewis (NY 1966) 62: Very small beer. **1930** HCBailey *Garston* (NY) 188: He made very small beer of Mr. Wisberry. **1939** FWCrofts *Antidote* (NY) 165: His employer's death became pretty small beer to her. **1948** CDickson *Skeleton* (NY 1967) 145: They were pretty small beer. **1955** AHocking *Poison* (NY) 130: Rather small beer, I fancy. **1961** ALee *Miss Hogg* (L) 9: Authors are reckoned very small beer. **1968** JHaythorne *None of Us* (NY) 103: She considered me pretty small beer. EAP B121.

B160   To cry in one's **Beer** (*varied*)
1941 SFisher *I Wake Up* (NY 1960) 12: You should've heard him crying in his beer. **1961** MNelson *When the Bed* (L) 21: Let's all weep into our beer. **1966** DHitchens *Man Who Cried* (NY) 177: [He] bent over his beer as if about to shed tears into it. **1984** JDentinger *First Hit* (NY) 107: Despite its common usage in the English language, I don't think I've ever, in all my years of vast and varied experience, actually *seen* someone cry into their beer . . . before now . . . I think you'd better have another. That one's going to be too salty to finish.

B161   As red as a **Beet** (beetroot); Beet-red (beetroot-red)
1900 CFPidgin *Quincy A. Sawyer* (B) 28: His face as red as a beet; 63. **1924** CVan Vechten *Tattooed* (NY) 23: Red as a beet. **1936** CGGivens *Jig-Time* (I) 122: His face was red as a beet. **1942** CFAdams *What Price* (NY) 78: His face was beet-red. **1943** PATaylor *Going* (NY) 23: Still beet-red and breathless. **1950** CDickson *Night* (NY) 82: Bull's face was as red as beetroot. **1952** RMarshall *Jane* (NY) 53: Redder than a

beet. **1955** DMDisney *Room* (NY) 65: His face was as red as a beet. **1959** PMoyes *Dead Men* (L) 79: Rossati, as red as a beetroot. **1960** JSymonds *Only Thing* (L) 12: She had blushed beetroot red. **1966** NMonsarrat *Life (I)* (L) 125: Scarlet as beetroot. **1973** PMoyes *Curious* (NY) 205: You've gone as red as a beetroot. TW 24(2).

B162 **Beggars** cannot be choosers (*varied*)

1911 HHMunro *Chronicles* (L 1927) 98: Beggars can't be choosers. **1924** JJFarjeon *Master* (NY) 29: Tramps can't be choosers. 200: Beggars can't be choosers. **1930** W Lewis *Apes* (NY 1932) 180: Beggars can't be choosers. **1937** LRCribble *Who Killed* (L) 24: Paupers can't be fussy. **1940** PMcGuire *Spanish* (L) 106: Beggars can't be choosers. **1951** AEVanVogt *Slan* (NY) 47: Beggars can't be choosers, you know. **1957** *New Yorker* 11/2 46: Beggars couldn't be choosers. **1957** LDelRay *Robots* (NY) 11: But beggars made ill choosers. **1962** FLockridge *And Left* (P) 145: Thieves can't be choosers. **1963** MMcCarthy *Group* (NY) 155: "Beggars can't be choosers." . . . Hatton . . . was fond of a proverb. **1972** JGreenway *Down* (B) 139: Out here the beggars were the choosers. **1975** HLawrenson *Stranger* (NY) 53: The butler! Oh, well, buggers can't be choosers. **1977** CWatson *Fourth* (B) 91: Beggars shouldn't be choosers. EAP B126; TW 24(1); Brunvand 9(1).

B163 Set a **Beggar** on horseback *etc.*

1911 HHMunro *Chronicles* (L 1927) 177: Talk of beggars on horseback. **1923** CWells *Affair at Flower Acres* (NY) 29: There's an old proverb—"Set a beggar on horseback." **1934** LO'Flaherty *Shame* (L) 173: Put a beggar on horseback and he's sure to overstep the mark, or whatever the saying is. **1956** EDillon *Death* (L) 82: An upstart, sir. A beggar on horseback. **1961** WHLewis *Scandalous* (NY) 198: He had a good deal of the vulgarity and insolence of the beggar on horseback. EAP B127; Brunvand 9(2).

B164 Sue a **Beggar** and catch a louse

1937 RWWinston *It's a Far Cry* (NY) 129: The old one of suing a beggar and catching a louse. EAP B128; *Oxford* 784.

B165 Good to **Begin** well, better to end well

1957 LBeam *Maine* (NY) 54: Good to begin well, better to end well. *Oxford* 42.

B166 Sooner **Begun** sooner done (*varied*)

1955 MBorowsky *Queen's* (NY) 46: Sooner task's begun, sooner task is done—so 'tis said. **1958** LSdeCamp *Elephant* (NY) 45: Sooner begun, sooner done, as we say in Thessalia. *Oxford* 753: Sooner.

B167 Well **Begun** is half done

1931 PATaylor *Cape Cod* (NY 1971) 140: An' well begun's half done, as the feller said. **1933** PGWodehouse *Heavy* (B) 299: A thing well begun is half done. **1936** VMcHugh *Coleb* (NY) 322: Well begun is half done. **1959** *BangorDN* 7/29 9: A job well dreaded is half done. **1963** MErskine *No. 9* (NY) 28: The English had a saying that well begun was half done. *Oxford* 877–78; Whiting *NC* 369(2).

B168 **Beginner's** luck (*varied*)

1926 AFielding *Footsteps* (L) 13: A stroke of beginner's luck. **1939** GDHCole *Double* (NY) 91: They say beginner's luck goes. **1947** NMarsh *Final* (B) 88: Her own run of beginner's luck. **1954** CIsherwood *World* (L) 86: A big piece of beginner's luck. **1961** PDennis *Little* (NY) 48: Proverbial beginner's luck. **1975** JPearson *Edward* (NY) 3: [He] had the most terrible beginner's luck. Cf. A Fool for luck *below*.

B169 A bad **Beginning** makes a bad ending

1958 LSdeCamp *Elephant* (NY) 40: A bad beginning makes a bad ending. Cf. EAP B132.

B170 A bad **Beginning** may make a good ending (*varied*)

1962 *BangorDN* 6/25 22: A bad beginning makes a good ending. **1967** SForbes *Encounter* (NY) 47: Bad beginning, good ending. **1972** VTrefusis *From Dusk* (L) 111: Bad beginnings sometimes make good ends. EAP B130; Brunvand 9.

B171 **Beginnings** are (not) easy

1930 IGoldberg *Tin Pan* (NY) 10: Beginnings, here, contrary to the proverb, are easy. EAP B129.

B172 Of a good **Beginning** comes a good ending

1934 KGWeston *His First* (NY) 265: Of a good beginning cometh a good ending. EAP B131.

B173 To scare the **Bejesus** out of someone

1964 RBraddon *Year* (L 1967) 29: Scare the bejusus out of them. Wentworth 29.

B174 One **Believes** what he wants to believe

1967 RRendell *New Lease* (NY) 50: People believe what they want to believe. EAP B134.

B175 One must not **Believe** all he hears (*varied*)

1932 AGask *Murder* (NY) 91: You mustn't believe all you hear. **1938** WEHayes *Black* (NY) 125: You don't believe everything you hear, do you? **1961** RFoley *It's Murder* (NY DBC) 32: Don't believe more than half you hear. **1961** WEHuntsberry *Oscar* (NY DBC) 79: You can't believe everything you hear. **1975** HCarmichael *Too Late* (NY) 143: They say you can't believe all you hear. Whiting *NC* 369(2); *Oxford* 43.

B176 To **Believe** when one sees

1959 KWaterhouse *Billy* (L) 51: I'll believe it when I see it. EAP B135. Cf. Seeing *below*.

B177 As clear as a **Bell**; Bell-clear

1910 JCLincoln *Depot Master* (NY) 41: A fine day, clear as a bell. **1919** SLeacock *Frenzied* (Toronto 1971) 110: His head as clear as a bell for work. **1930** FAWinder *Behind* (L) 210: His own face was as clear as a bell. **1931** HSKeeler *Matilda* (NY) 171: It was all as clear now as a crystal bell. **1932** RKing *Murder* (L) 145: Her record is as clear as a bell. **1932** STruss *Coroner* (NY) 244: Marcia's voice, clear as a bell. **1940** MBurton *Mr. Westerby* (NY) 243: Clear as a bell [*weather*]. **1943** AAbbott *Shudders* (NY) 100: A . . . voice, clear as a silver bell. **1950** BBird *Death* (NY) 40: The stuff in the foreground was clear as a bell. **1953** CLittle *Black* (NY) 157: Clear as a bell [*a footprint*]. **1958** HReilly *Ding* (NY DBC) 159: Her quiet voice was bell-clear. **1970** ELathen *Pick* (NY) 29: The sky is as clear as a bell. **1972**

JDMacDonald *Long* (P) 173: There I was, clear as a bell [*in a photograph*]. EAP B136.

B178 As sound (true) as a **Bell**

1922 JJoyce *Ulysses* (NY 1934) 271: Sound as a bell. **1931** MAllingham *Police* (NY) 165: William's heart was as sound as a bell. **1931** LMcFarlane *Murder* (NY) 55: Her story rings true as a bell. **1935** LCharteris *Saint Goes On* (NY) 154: His constitution is as sound as a bell. **1945** MRRinehart *Yellow Room* (NY) 192: Good girl . . . Sound as a bell. **1953** JDolph *Dead Angel* (NY) 27: As sound as a bell o' brass [*a horse*]. **1970** A Christie *Passenger* (NY) 48: Sound as a bell [*honest*]. **1974** ELathen *Sweet* (NY) 101: He looks sound as a bell. *Oxford* 755.

B179 **Bell,** book and candle

1930 BReynolds *Stranglehold* (NY) 208: With bell, book and candle. **1931** RAJWalling *Stroke* (NY) 57: He'd have cursed Bob all over the parish if he'd had bell, book and candle handy. **1932** RThorndike *Devil* (NY) 93: It was forbidden [*by the Church*] with bell, book and candle. **1933** HHDunn *Crimson* (NY) 145: The bandit brothers could have taken his daughters without formality of bell, book or candle. **1934** AFielding *Cantley* (L) 185: He cursed me by book and by candle. **1937** WSMasterman *Border* (NY) 78: Exorcise the spirit with bell, book, and candle. **1940** HReilly *Murder in* (NY) 5: Where had she [*a dead girl in a bridal gown*] come from, without bridegroom or attendants or bell, book and candle? **1941** TDuBois *McNeills Chase* (B) 141: Sayres would read me out of town with bell, book, and candle. **1950** ECrispin *Sudden* (NY DBC) 71: Mrs. Flanders was . . . not . . . at all zealous to regularize the granting of her favours with bell and book. **1953** GRHEllis *Lesser* (L) 79: Every side can prove its correctness by bell, book and candle. **1958** PDeVries *Mackerel* (B) 38: It's damned well going to be with bell, book and candle [*marriage*]. **1961** JSStrange *Eye* (NY) 30: This was the disaster she'd been half expecting . . . the thing that must be warded off with bell, book, and candle, with crossed fingers, with knock on wood. **1962** HReilly *Day* (NY DBC) 79: Becoming my lawfully wedded wife with bell, book and candle and a white veil. **1969** DARandall *Dukedom* (NY) 321: Hogan was buried from Washington Cathedral with bell, book and candle. **1973** NMacKenzie *HGWells* (NY) 348: Belloc was the only popular writer to denounce him with bell, book and candle. **1979** GBagby *I Could* (NY) 89: We're already married . . . Bell, book, and candle, not to speak of license and blood tests. EAP B137; TW 25(4).

B180   To ring a **Bell**

1952 MMillar *Vanish* (NY) 148: Does that ring a bell? **1957** ESGardner *Screaming* (NY) 22: It's been ringing a bell with me all day. **1962** RMacdonald *Zebra* (NY) 60: The name . . . rings no bell. **1966** MMcShane *Night's* (NY) 66: Does that ring a bell? **1976** MGilbert *Night* (NY) 164: The name certainly rings a bell. Wentworth 29.

B181   With **Bells** on

1929 FDaingerfield *Linden* (NY) 212: I'll be there wid bells on. **1933** NChild *Murder* (L) 137: This is a murder with bells on. **1958** HMasur *Murder* (NY 1959) 171: "Can you be in the lobby at seven?" "With bells on." Wentworth 29–30.

B182   The **Belly** and the members

1925 HWNevinson *More Changes* (L) 145: It is bad for all when the members refuse to feed the belly, but worse still when the belly runs away from the members. EAP B141.

B183   Better **Belly** burst than good victuals wasted

1934 JHHoulson *Blue Blazes* (L) 139: The old saying among the darkies in Jamaica . . . "Better belly bust than good wittles waste." Damn good saying, that. *Oxford* 52.

B184   An empty **Belly** is no epicure

1959 HCarmichael *Marked* (NY) 19: An empty belly is no epicure. Cf. Whiting *NC* 369(2). Cf. Hunger *below*.

B185   A full **Belly** does not understand an empty one

1950 THoward *Shriek* (NY) 111: He adds that it is hard for a man with a full belly to understand the psychology of a man with an empty one. *Oxford* 45, 293.

B186   To starve the **Belly** to clothe the back

1969 SMays *Reuben's* (L) 152: Starve yer belly ter clothe yer back. EAP B145.

B187   To have a **Bellyful** (skinful)

1923 HWNevinson *Changes* (NY) 130: We have had our bellyful. **1937** NBell *Crocus* (NY) 249: I can promise you your bellyful. **1940** CMWills *R.E.Pipe* (L) 24: I've had a bellyful of your sort. **1952** WClapham *Night* (L) 32: I've had a bellyful of this. **1953** RChandler *Long* (L) 183: I had had a skinful of the Wade family. **1962** BRoss *Scrolls* (NY) 141: Arcadia has had a bellyful of Spartan rule. **1966** VSiller *Mood* (NY) 75: I had a bellyful of religion. **1975** MErskine *Harriet* (NY) 22: I've had a bellyful of the lions. EAP B147; TW 25.

B188   To hit below the **Belt**

1925 GBeasley *My First* (Paris) 296: Hitting below the belt. **1935** GBullett *Jury* (L 1947) 122: That's what I call hitting below the belt. **1956** *NY Post* 9/27 5: Dick "never hits below the belt." **1958** ESMorgan *Puritan* (B) 106: A blow below the belt. *Oxford* 374: Hit.

B189   To be around the **Bend**

1959 HCarmichael *Marked* (NY) 54: Unless I'm clear round the bend [*out of my mind*]. **1960** AGilbert *Out for* (NY 1965) 125: The woman was more than half round the bend. **1966** EXFerrars *No Peace* (NY) 86: She's a bit deranged, a bit round the bend. Cf. NED Suppl. Bend *sb.*⁴ 10c.

B190   **Bend** or break

1931 LCArlington *Through* (L) 31: We "break before we bend." **1934** LKink *Whispering* (NY) 219: She neither bent nor broke. **1936** CMRussell *Death* (NY) 119: She'd break before she'd bend. **1948** HReilly *Staircase* (NY) 28: If people don't bend, they break. **1970** PMoyes *Many* (NY) 3: Like the proverbial reed, she would bend but not break. EAP B148; *Oxford* 52: Better bend (bow).

B191   To give the **Benefit** of the doubt

1930 VLoder *Essex* (L) 75: I'll give you the benefit of the doubt. **1939** RStout *Crime on* (L) 167: To give you the benefit of all doubts. **1959** AWUpfield *Journey* (NY) 90: We have to give everyone the benefit of doubt. TW 25.

B192   As black as a **Berry**; Berry-black

1963 JGBallard *Passport* (NY) 67: Black as a berry. **1964** JGBallard *Terminal* (L) 13: Black as a berry. **1976** MButterworth *Remains* (NY) 26: Berry-black eyes. Whiting B257.

B193   As brown as a **Berry**; Berry-brown

1900 CFPidgin *Quincy A. Sawyer* (B) 469: You're as brown as a berry. **1924** AChristie *Man* (NY) 275: As brown as a berry. **1936** RTMScott *Murder Stalks* (NY) 1: As brown as a berry. **1940** ECRLorac *Tryst* (L) 141: The berry-brown face. **1941** RHLindsay *Fowl Murder* (B) 21: Brown as a berry with nicotine. **1954** EWalter *Untidy* (P) 145: Uncle Acis was brown, that old expression "brown as a berry" would have new meaning for you if you'd seen him, though in all my life I've never figured what berries are brown. **1957** MSharp *Eye* (L) 67: Her berry-brown eyes. **1960** GAshe *Man who Laughed* (NY) 110: Jeremy looked berry-brown. **1965** JJMarric *Gideon's Badge* (NY) 154: He had a berry-brown face. **1970** SGBoswell *Book* (L) 18: Brown as berries and fit as fiddles. Whiting B259, 259a; Whiting *NC* 369(1); Taylor *Prov. Comp.* 21: Brown.

B194   As red as a **Berry**

1932 PMcGuire *Three* (NY) 228: Mr. Horner, red as a berry. **1950** CDickson *Night* (NY) 253: Face red, red as a berry. **1967** VSPritchett *Cab* (NY) 46: She was as red as a berry. Cf. Wilstach 316: Mountain-ash berries.

B195   To give something a wide **Berth**

1934 CFGregg *Execution* (L) 173: Give the place a wide berth. TW 26.

B196   Do your **Best,** angels can do no more (*varied*)

1924 VLWhitechurch *Templeton* (NY) 299: You've done your best . . . And no man can do more. **1929** AFielding *Cluny* (NY) 55: My grandmother used to say: Do your best and leave the rest, angels can't do better. **1958** SBarr *Purely* (NY) 218: I can but do my best. The angels can do no more. TW 26(1); Brunvand 10(1).

B197   Hope for the **Best** and expect the worst

1940 JCLincoln *Out of the Fog* (NY) 16: We must hope for the best and more or less expect the worst. EAP B157.

B198   Save the **Best** until last

1972 JDMacDonald *Long* (P) 245: Save the best until last. Whiting *NC* 501: Worst.

B199   To make the **Best** of a bargain (business, job, *etc.*) (*varied*)

1919 HRHaggard *She and Allan* (NY 1921) 113: They made the best of a bad business. **1922** VBridges *Greensea* (NY) 133: To make the best of it. **1923** ACrowley *Confessions* ed JSymonds (L 1969) 893: I made the best of a bad job. **1928** JJConnington *Tragedy* (B) 21: Make the best of a business. **1928** JGoodwin *When Dead* (NY) 329: I'm always one for making the best of things. **1932** FBeeding *Murder* (B) 24: To make the best of a thoroughly bad business. **1933** FWCrofts *Hog's Back* (L) 68: To make the best of a bad bargain. **1933** FHShaw *Atlantic* (NY) 97: Make the best of a bad job. **1946** GBellairs *Death in the Night* (NY) 73: She got the best of a bad bargain. **1952** RMacdonald *Ivory* (NY 1965) 180: I made the best of a bad job. **1960** SRaven *Doctors* (L) 203: To make the best of a bad job. **1966** HTreece *Green* (L) 23: We . . . must make the best of a bad job. **1970** JPorter *Dover Strikes* (NY) 120: Dover . . . made the worst of a bad job. **1973** BHowar *Laughing* (NY) 37: Make the best of a bad situation. **1972** NMarsh *Tied* (B) 168: Make what you can of a bad job. EAP B159.

B200   To make (*etc.*) the **Best** of both worlds

1932 JJConnington *Castleford* (B) 93: He managed to make the best of both worlds. **1956** DWheatley *Ka* (L) 113: To have the best of both worlds. **1961** BKnox *In at* (NY) 42: I get the best of both worlds. **1963**

PMHubbard *Flush* (L 1964) 146: To want the best of both worlds. *Oxford* 48.

B201 To be no **Better** than one should be

1928 GDHCole *Man* (NY) 155: Mrs. Meston was no better than she should be. **1937** EGreenwood *Under the Fig* (NY) 100: She was no better than she should be. **1941** FWCrofts *Circumstantial* (NY) 47: He was supposed to be no better than he should be. **1946** CBush *Second Chance* (L) 105: She was no better—as they say—than she might be. **1956** JJMarric *Gideon's Week* (L) 148: [His] wife, in the common phrase, had been no better than she ought to be. **1960** FCrane *Death-wish* (NY DBC) 53: Maybe she was no better than she should be. **1965** AChristie *At Bertram's* (L) 153: A lot of girls who were no better than they should be. **1970** BWAldiss *Hand-reared* (L) 141: I heard Mother telling Father that she was no better than she should be. EAP B161.

B202 To be **Bewitched** and bewildered

1945 HGreen *Loving* (L) 165: I'm bewitched and bewildered. Berrey 106.7, s.v.

B203 To be cut on the **Bias**

1957 LBeam *Maine* (NY) 88: Single men were said to be "cut on the bias." Cf. DA Bias; NED Bias *sb.* B1,C1.

B204 One's best **Bib** and tucker

1909 JCLincoln *Keziah* (NY) 19: In his best bib and tucker. **1930** JGBrandon *McCarthy* (L) 63: Crime puts on its best bib and tucker. **1936** HFootner *Kidnapping* (L) 250: This is my best bib and tucker. **1957** MBGarrett *Horse* (University, Ala.) 203: Everybody in the community put on his bib and tucker. **1974** CMartin *Whiskey* (NY) 40: His best bib and tucker. EAP B166.

B205 When they are **Big** enough they are old enough

1935 HLDavis *Honey* (NY) 331: When they're big enough they're old enough. **1960** AHLewis *Worlds* (NY) 40: "If they're big enough, they're old enough." **1969** SMays *Reuben's* (NY) 176: When they're big enough, they're old enough. **1982** RAHeinlein *Friday* (NY) 181: "When they're big enough, they're old enough," as the old saw goes.

B206 The **Bigger** they are the harder they fall (*varied*)

1927 NMartin *Mosaic* (NY) 4: The bigger they are, the harder they fall. **1928** WA Wolff *Trial* (NY) 300: The wiser they are the harder they fall. **1930** GBMeans *Strange Death* (NY) 173: Using the parlance of the street, I reflected: "The bigger the man, the harder he falls." **1932** JTFarrell *Young Lonigan* (NY 1935) 83: The old adage . . . the bigger they are, the harder they fall. **1933** EDTorgerson *Cold Finger* (L) 105: The richer they are, the harder they fall. **1940** NMorland *Gun* (NY) 160: The older they are, the harder they fall. **1943** FScully *Rogues* (Hollywood) 252: The bigger you are the harder you fall. **1947** LFord *Woman* (NY) 225: The bigger they come the harder they fall. **1958** CCockburn *Crossing* (L) 15: The American saying to the effect that the bigger they come the harder they fall. **1960** JJMarric *Gideon's Risk* (NY) 3: Bigger the man, harder the fall. **1963** RAusting *I Went* (NY) 44: The bigger they come—the harder they fall. **1966** BNaughton *Alfie* (L) 116: The bigger they are the harder they fall. **1971** VScannell *Tiger* (L) 61: The bigger they are, the harder they fall. Cf. *Oxford* 59: Bigger, 372: Higher standing, Higher the fool, 373: Highest tree.

B207 As queer as a three-dollar **Bill** (*varied*)

1950 SPalmer *Green* (NY) 43: The act sounds queerer than a three-dollar bill. **1950** BSpicer *Blues* (NY) 47: Everything in here is just as honest as a six-dollar bill. **1952** RGHam *Gifted* (NY) 84: Queer as a seven-dollar bill. **1957** VWMason *Gracious* (NY) 84: Wrong as a nine-dollar bill. **1957** *BHerald* 4/7 19A: That premise is as phony as a three dollar bill. **1959** *NYTimes* 7/19 4E: As phony as a $7. bill. **1961** DLMathews *Very Welcome* (NY DBC) 23: As queer as a three-dollar bill. **1975** MDelving *Bored* (NY) 9: He's funny all right, like a three-pound note. **1975** HLawrenson *Stranger* (NY) 217: That faker's as phoney as a nine-dollar bill. **1983** PMoyes *Six-Letter* (NY) 138: Harry's as queer as a three-dollar bill—but don't quote me. He keeps his nose clean. Taylor *Western Folklore* 17(1958) 13(2,3); Wentworth 542–3.

B208 To sell (be sold) a **Bill** of goods
1947 HCahill *Look* (NY) 69: Somebody's sold a bill of goods somewhere. **1955** WSloane *Stories* (L) 418: We sold them a bill of goods. **1960** IWallace *Chapman* (NY 1961) 181: He hasn't sold you a bill of goods, has he? **1965** WRBurkett *Sleeping* (NY) 140: He'd sold them a bill of goods from the word go. Cf. Packet *below*.

B209 As bald as a **Billiard** ball
1925 RAFreeman *Red Thumb* (L) 139: As bald as a billiard ball. **1939** CBarry *Nicholas* (L) 25: A head as bald as the proverbial billiard ball. **1972** TWells *Die* (NY) 79: Bald as a billiard. TW 27(1).

B210 As smooth and round as a **Billiard** ball
1926 JTully *Beggars* (NY) 29: His head . . . was smooth . . . and round as a billiard ball. TW 27(2).

B211 As cold as **Billy-be-damned**
1926 JTully *Beggars* (NY) 28: She's colder'n Billy-be-damned outside. **1934** DGardiner *Drink* (NY) 101: It's colder than Billy-be-damned. Cf. Whiting *Devil* 243 III 1; DARE i 238.

B212 As stubborn as **Billy-be-damned**
1927 FLPackard *Devil's* (NY) 90: Stubborn as Billy-be-damned. Whiting *Devil* 243 III 1. Cf. DARE i 238.

B213 To blaze (bleed) like **Billy-be-damned**
1949 FBrown *Bloody* (NY) 92: [The fire] was blazing like Billy-be-damned. **1965** Doctor X *Intern* (NY) 249: Bleeding like Billy-be-damned. Cf. Whiting *Devil* 243 III 1; DARE i 238.

B214 As mad as all **Billy hell**
1966 JCraig *Case* (NY) 138: They were madder'n all Billy hell. Berrey 20.5; Spears 29; DARE i 238.

B215 As tough as **Billy Whitlam's bulldog**
1970 DClark *Deadly* (NY) 121: As tough as Billy Whitlam's bulldog.

B216 Safe **Bind,** safe find (*varied*)
1922 VSutphen *In Jeopardy* (NY) 171: Safe find, safe bind. **1928** JAFerguson *Man in the Dark* (NY) 27: Safe bind, safe find. **1937** DLSayers *Busman's* (NY) 107: Safe bind, safe find. **1952** HFMPrescott *Man on* (NY) 440: Safe bind, safe find. **1959** *New Yorker* 8/15 26: Safe bind, safe find. EAP B168; TW 27.

B217 As bare as a **Bird**
1965 FPohl *Plague* (NY) 138: I ran bare as a bird into a plane. **1968** EBuckler *Ox Bells* (NY) 162: A bald head was "bare as a bird's ass in fly time." Whiting B317.

B218 As blithe as a **Bird**
1923 DCScott *Witching* (Toronto) 31: As blythe as a bird. **1930** JFarnol *Over the Hills* (B) 184: Barbara laughs as blithe as any bird on bough. **1958** MRenault *King* (NY 1960) 229: The Corinthian, blithe as a bird. **1961** PGWodehouse *Ice* (NY) 6: As blithe as a bird. **1969** NHale *Life* (B) 106: She was as blithe as a bird, but the bird was Job's turkey. **1969** SMays *Reuben's* (L) 210: I was blithesome as a bird. EAP B169; TW 27(4).

B219 As bright as a **Bird**
1952 PQuentin *Black* (NY) 125: As bright as a bird. **1960** MColes *Concrete* (NY) 28: He'll be as bright as a bird. **1964** EFerrars *Legal* (L) 103: She may be bright as a bird tomorrow. **1975** JDaniels *White* (NY) 189: He is still bright as a bird. TW 27(5).

B220 As brisk as a **Bird**
1941 GWYates *If a Body* (NY) 277: He was brisk as a bird. TW 27(6).

B221 As free as a **Bird** (lark) (*varied*)
1937 GFowler *Salute* (NY) 274: You're as free as the birds. **1939** HMiller *Capricorn* (NY 1961) I am free as a bird. **1952** JWKrutch *Desert* (NY) 230: "As free as the birds in the air" is an inevitable simile. But it is only a simile. **1955** DMDisney *Room* (NY) 166: Walking the streets as free as a bird. **1958** *BangorDN* 6/18 24: Free as the

birds. **1963** EXFerrars *Doubly* (NY) 186: Send him home as free as a bird. **1966** DMDisney *At Some* (NY) 110: A son that's now as free as the birds in the air to marry again. **1967** WTucker *Warlock* (NY) 50: He's free as a lark. TW 27(9).

B222   As gay as a **Bird**
1966 MSteen *Looking* (L) 167: I was as gay as a bird. EAP B170.

B223   As happy as a **Bird** (*varied*)
1923 TFPowys *Left Leg* (L) 173: As happy as young birds. **1936** JCLenehan *Deadly* (L) 106: It's as happy as a bird in a golden cage she always seemed to be. **1938** ECRLorac *Slippery* (L) 56: She was as happy as a bird. **1940** WCClark *Murder Goes* (B) 79: She was as happy as a bird, singing all day long. **1945** CEVulliamy *Edwin* (L) 224: I'm as happy as a bird. **1961** RJWhite *Smartest* (L) 124: As happy as birds in a tree. **1970** SGBoswell *Book* (L) 67: Happy as the birds in the air. **1972** RHGreenan *Queen* (NY) 151: She was as happy as a bird. TW 28(11); Brunvand 10(3). Cf. As happy as a Lark *below*.

B224   As innocent as a **Bird**
1932 EDBiggers *Keeper* (L) 95: Innocent as a bird. **1964** SJay *Death* (NY) 113: Innocent as a bird and minding my own business.

B225   As light as a **Bird**
1934 HMiller *Tropic of Cancer* (NY 1962) 66: Light as a bird. **1952** MMillar *Vanish* (NY) 118: She was light as a bird. **1965** RNathan *Mallot* (NY) 131: My heart is light as a bird. TW 28(12).

B226   A **Bird** can't fly on one wing (*varied*)
1937 WMartyn *Blue Ridge* (L) 184: A bird can't fly far on one wing [*i.e., one drink*]. **1943** VSiller *Echo* (NY) 105: A bird . . . can't fly on one wing [*i.e., have a second drink*]. **1948** CLLeonard *Fourth* (NY) 96: How about another little drink? Can't fly on one wing. **1953** RFMirvish *Eternal* (NY) 177: You can't fly on one wing. **1957** JPotts *Man with* (NY 1964) 54: Birds can't fly on one wing. **1959** FLockridge *Murder* (P) 29: The old saying—can't fly on one wing. **1966** NMonsarrat *Life (I)* (L) 435: Can't fly on

one wing. **1974** JWalker *Self-Portrait* (B) 174: A bird can't fly on one wing. *Oxford* 60: Bird must.

B227   The **Bird** has flown (*varied*)
1905 JBCabell *Line* (NY 1926) 223: Always finding the bird flown, the nest yet warm. **1910** EWallace *Nine Bears* (L 1928) 114: Find the cage empty and the bird flown. **1923** DFox *Doom* (NY) 227: You've found the nest . . . but the birds have flown. **1928** AGMacleod *Marloe* (NY) 194: The bird had flown—but the nest was still warm. **1937** JRhode *Hop Fields* (L) 72: The bird had flown. **1938** ESGardner *Substitute Face* (NY) 169: The birds have flown the nest. **1940** ISShriber *Head over Heels* (NY) 302: Your bird had flown the coop. **1941** HReilly *Three Women* (NY) 184: The nesting bird had flown. **1955** CMWills *Death* (L) 100: The birds had flown. **1956** NFitzgerald *Imagine* (L) 184: [He] assumed that his own bird had taken wing. **1960** HReilly *Follow* (NY DBC) 24: When they did finally arrive the nest was empty. **1965** ESGardner *Troubled* (NY) 71: The bird had flown from the coop. **1969** A Roudybush *Capital* (NY) 176: Your birds have flown. **1972** HHarrison *Montezuma* (NY) 20: Has the bird flown the coop again? **1975** HCarvic *Odds On* (NY) 136: An empty nest from which the birds had flown. EAP B171; TW 29(20); Brunvand 99: Nest. Cf. Coop *below*.

B228   A **Bird** in a gilded cage
1970 AAFair *All Grass* (NY DBC) 120: I'd be sitting there—I won't say a bird in a gilded cage because it's too damn much of a cliché. EAP B173. Cf. Brunvand 10(5).

B229   A **Bird** in the hand is worth two in the bush (*varied*)
1902 D'AStJohn *Madge Buford* (NY) 60: I lay there with two birds in my hand and sure of having them both in my bush, also. **1904** HGarland *Companions on the Trail* (NY 1931) 257: He [*Henry James*] had a curious habit of repeating the word in hand while vaguely feeling about for another in the bush. **1922** JJoyce *Ulysses* (NY 1934) 389: A certain whore . . . whose name, she said, is Bird-in-the-Hand and she lay at him so

flatteringly that she had him in her grot which is named Two-in-the-Bush. **1923** JSFletcher *Lynne Court* (NY) 187: Even half a bird in the hand is worth a dozen in the bush. **1927** HAdams *Queen's* (P) 109: No one knew better than he did about the truth of that old saying about the bird in the hand. There might be no bird in the bush at all—only some nasty reptile with a vicious sting. **1927** HHBashford *Behind* (NY) 62: It may be the wrong thing to let the bird in the hand go. **1931** GDyer *Three-Cornered* (B) 108: A bootlegger in the hand is worth two in the bush. **1937** WHMack *Mr. Birdsall* (NY) 26: On the subject of wives, he alledged [*sic*] that a bird in the bush was worth five in the hand. And Chester, bless his soul, stayed out of the bushes. **1939** FWCrofts *Antidote* (NY) 17: A monkey in the zoo was worth two in the hand. **1939** CMWills *Calabar Bean* (L) 152: But I believe a bird in the hand's worth two in the bush. **1952** RMarshall *Jane* (NY) 254: I lean to the old proverb, a bird in the hand is worth two in the bush. **1952** CRand *Hongkong* (NY) 226: A bird in the bush was worth something there, a bird in the hand was not. **1953** LBaker *Snips* (NY) 76: A mouse in the hand is worth a snake in the grass any day. **1954** ESGardner *Restless* (NY) 76: The theory that a bird in the hand is worth two in the bush. **1957** *Boston Traveler* 7/3 20: A dam in the hand was worth a whole flock of flood insurance in the bushes. **1957** *BHerald* 7/14 comic sect., 9: Birds in the hand is nastier than two in the gravy. **1961** FLockridge *Drill* (P) 89: The bird in hand has flown . . . I am mixing metaphors. **1962** EFRussell *Great* (NY) 63: "A bird in the hand is worth two on the bust." "In the bush," corrected Harrison. **1967** GHousehold *Courtesy* (B) 100: A bird in the hand—if I may permit the vernacular to simplify my argument—is worth two in the bush. **1970** EWTeale *Springtime* (NY) 6: The living bird in the bush instead of the dead bird in the hand. **1972** HDPerry *Chair* (NY) 74: What an attractive bird-in-the-hand he was. **1972** GSchmitt *Godforgotten* (NY) 23: Two birds in the hand. **1973** EJKahn *Fraud* (NY) 60: Better to capture three birds in the hand. **1973** JSymons *Plot* (NY) 26: I've

got a date with a bird. You know the old saying, never keep a bird in the hand waiting if you want to end up in her bush. **1975** HBlack *My Father* (NY) 71: The old maxim that a bird in the hand is worth two in the bush. **1975** DMDisney *Cry* (NY) 111: [He] figured he'd better settle for a bird in the hand, half a loaf. Whatever you want to call it. EAP B174; TW 27(1); Brunvand 10(1).

B230 A **Bird** is known by its note, *etc.*
1929 EWallace *Ringer* (NY) 26: "As a bird is known by his note, so is a man by his conversation." It is a classy proverb, believed by many to be in the Bible. **1930** EWallace *India* (NY) 10: The Good Book says: "As a bird is known by his note, so is a man by the company he keeps." **1935** BFlynn *Sussex* (L) 196: You can tell a bird by its note, they say. *Oxford* 59–60.

B231 A **Bird** of a different feather (*varied*)
1927 GELocke *Golden* (NY) 81: Birds of another feather. **1929** NATemple-Ellis *Inconsistent* (NY) 3: A bird of very different plumage. **1930** JJFarjeon *Following* (NY) 77: It was a bird of quite a different feather. **1931** MAllingham *Gyrth* (NY) 148: You were a bird of a very different feather. **1940** EHealy *Mr. Sandeman* (NY) 80: Here were two birds of a different color. **1946** MInnes *What Happened* (NY) 62: Young Tommy was a fowl of a different feather. **1950** EA Mathew *Horse* (Belfast) 58: We have in this article a "bird of another color." Cf. To be a Horse *below.*

B232 A **Bird** of passage
1930 PMacDonald *Rynox* (L) 184: Birds of passage. **1935** CBarry *Death Overseas* (L) 102: People who are, as you might say, birds of passage. **1943** PCheyney *Dark Dust* (NY) 113: [He] was a bird of passage. **1961** EWilliams *George* (NY) 83: Such birds of passage. **1968** EPHoyt *Alexander Woollcott* (NY) 197: His friends were birds of passage. **1972** MGilbert *Body* (NY) 97: She was a bird of passage. **1974** JRichardson *Stendhal* (NY) 244: He was always to be a bird of passage. EAP B175.

B233 A **Bird** who can sing *etc.* *(varied)*

1952 JKnox *Little* (P) 18: A body who *can* sing and *won't* sing ought to be *made* to sing. EAP B176.

B234 The **Bird** that fouls its own nest *(varied)*

1927 EWallace *Serpent* (NY) 220: Avoids fouling his own nest. **1932** RCWoodthorpe *Public* (L) 284: We all know the proverb about the bird that fouls its own nest. **1935** RGraves *Claudius the God* (NY) 304: Wise birds do not foul their own nests. **1937** RWWinston *It's a Far Cry* (NY) 156: It's an evil bird . . . that befouls its own nest. **1943** FScully *Rogues* (Hollywood) 116: Dreiser freely befouls his own nest. **1954** JSymons *Narrowing* (NY) 83: It's a dirty bird that fouls its own nest. **1959** *BangorDN* 8/1 16: A four-footed hog, given a fair chance, will not foul its own nest. **1959** *Time* 8/17 74: And it's a dirty bird that fouls its own nest. **1960** BBenson *Huntress* (NY) 191: An animal usually doesn't soil his own nest. **1963** HMiller *Black* (NY) 198: The bird is definitely not obscene and has never been known to foul its nest. **1967** EHahn *Romantic* (B) 50: He was fouling his own nest and biting the hand that fed him. **1971** JHBPeel *Along* (L) 124: Having fouled his nest in England, and feathered it in America [*of T. Paine*]. **1976** JSScott *Poor* (NY) 73: Never evacuate in your own nest. **1978** AJLerner *Street* (NY) 247: You are a funny little boy. You build a nest and then shit in it. **1982** CMacLeod *Wrack* (NY) 60: It's a poor bird that fouls its own nest, as my mother used to say. EAP B180; TW 28(17). Cf. To be sick in one's Hat, Doorstep *below.*

B235 **Birds** of a feather flock together *(varied)*

1913 JSFletcher *Secret* (L 1918) 93: Birds of a feather—you know the old saying. **1917** JCLincoln *Extricating* (NY) 34: Birds of a feather gather no moss. **1919** SRohmer *Quest* (NY) 182: Birds of a feather—. **1922** JSFletcher *Ravensdene* (NY) 243: Made us still more birds of a feather. **1922** JJoyce *Ulysses* (NY 1934) 402: Birds of a feather laugh together. **1926** HSKeeler *Spectacles* (NY 1929) 230: It seems that birds of a phobia as well as birds of a feather herded together. **1926** CWTyler *Blue Jean* (NY) 91: Birds of a feather have a great habit of seeking their level, as a noted cliff dweller once observed. **1930** WLewis *Apes* (NY 1932) 563: He is an old bird of the same feather. **1937** MBurton *Clue* (NY) 269: There's a lot of truth in the proverb that birds of a feather flock together. **1939** LRGribble *Arsenal* (L) 110: They say birds of a feather are drawn together. **1941** EL Fetta *Dressed* (NY) 101: [They] were certainly two birds of the same color. **1949** MBurton *Disappearing* (NY) 66: Birds of a feather flocked together. **1952** EPaul *Black* (NY) 206: They looked around the lot for birds of a feather to help foul the nest, and found this Hungarian weasel. **1957** *Punch* 9/4 259: She's killing two birds of a feather. **1958** JCoates *Widow's* (NY) 122: Birds of a feather and all that. **1958** PBranch *Murder's* (L 1963) 132: As birds of a feather, let's get together. **1964** FArcher *Malabang* (NY DBC) 4: If birds of a feather flocked together. **1970** DMDisney *Do Not* (NY) 63: Snobs, smart-assed birds of a feather. **1970** TWells *Dinky* (NY) 96: I got no time to spend with birds of her feather. EAP B177.

B236 The early **Bird** catches the worm *(varied)*

1909 MRRinehart *Man in Lower Ten* (NY 1947) 261: McKnight is always a sympathizer with the early worm. It was late when he appeared. **1913** JSFletcher *Secret* (L 1918) 230: We all know the old proverb about the early worm. **1919** LTracy *Bartlett* (NY) 72: "You rose early." . . . "Yes, but worms are coy this morning." **1923** HGartland *Globe* (NY) 56: You're an early bird. **1923** VWilliams *Orange* (B) 90: It looks . . . as though the early bird was going to catch the worm. **1924** LO'Flaherty *Thy Neighbour's Wife* (L) 112: The early bird . . . catches the heavenly worm. **1928** JJFarjeon *Underground* (NY) 115: It was the *late* bird who caught the worm this time. **1929** AB Cox *Layton* (NY) 2: The early morning worm . . . refusing to act as provender for the early bird. **1930** RGBrowne *By Way* (NY) 110: "You're an early bird!" . . . "Worm day!" **1933** AWynne *Cotswold* (P)

263: It's the early bird gets the early worm, so never be an early worm. **1935** PGWodehouse *Blandings* (NY) 158: So might the early bird have howled if the worms earmarked for its breakfast had suddenly turned and snapped at it. **1940** FGruber *Talking Clock* (NY) 133: The early birds are getting all the worms. **1943** FMcDermid *Ghost Wanted* (NY 1945) 123: How are you going to get any worms, lying around in bed all day? **1947** WMoore *Greener* (NY 1961) 139: The proverb about the early bird. **1948** EKGoldthwaite *Root* (NY DBC) 56: The early morning caller proved to be the worm-catching Sterling. **1949** RMLaurenson *Six Bullets* (NY) 122: The early birds were put busily selecting the fat worms. **1951** CLittle *Blackout* (NY) 44: You're an early bird, ain't you? Although, what I always say, who wants to catch a worm, anyways? **1956** *New Yorker* 12/8 46: That bird caught early by the Worm of Sin. **1957** *This Week* 6/16 39: Early birds get worm. Late bird finds worm turned. **1957** *TLS* 8/16 494: Worms surface during the night in order to mate: which is why "the early bird catches the worm." **1965** HPearson *By Himself* (L) 83: The late bird gathers no moss. **1970** SKilpatrick *Wake* (NY) 54: Those early birds are too busy catching worms to see him coming. **1970** RRood *Wild* (NY) 29: Even though he may be here to get the first worm that dares to poke up through the matted grass under that tree, the robin is really no early bird. TW 28(19); Brunvand 10(8); *Oxford* 211: Early.

B237 A little **Bird** told me (*varied*)

1906 CPearl *Morrison of Peking* (Sydney 1967) 170: A small . . . bird has sung . . . in my ear. **1910** EPhillpotts *Tales* (NY) 293: A little bird told us. **1928** CFraser-Simson *Swinging* (NY) 48: "Who told you that?" "The proverbial bird." **1929** GFairlie *Yellow* (B) 215: A little bird told me—it was much engaged with an early worm. **1932** GMitchell *Saltmarsh* (L) 132: Nobody seemed to have encountered the proverbial little bird. Meg's secret is still a secret. **1938** NShepherd *Death Walks* (L) 120: A little bird whispered a song. **1939** DHume *Death Before* (L) 90: Maybe that famous little bird has been

working overtime. **1941** JBentley *Mr. Marlow Chooses* (B) 39: "Who told you?" "A little dicky bird." **1945** AChristie *Remembered* (NY) 131: "A little bird told me"—was a saying of my friends. **1951** DWMeredith *Christmas* (NY) 126: A little birdie told me . . . but after what's happened it seems that the salt was on my tail and not the bird's. **1954** MMcCarthy *Charmed* (NY) 57: A little bird must have told her. **1959** RCFrazer *Mark* (NY) 122: Some little bird must have talked. **1964** HPentecost *Shape* (NY DBC) 26: One of Chambrun's little birds whispered in his ear. **1967** ARose *Memoirs* (NY) 225: I didn't hear it from a birdie. **1973** HDoldon *Dying* (P) 32: A big bird told me. **1973** PMoyes *Curious* (NY) 126: A little bird has been whispering . . . Your little bird is twittering up the wrong tree. EAP B181; TW 27(2); Brunvand 10(2).

B238 Not to eat enough to keep a **Bird** alive

1930 FRyerson *Seven* (L) 234: You never eat enough to keep a bird alive. **1931** CWells *Umbrella* (NY) 108: She never did eat enough to keep a bird alive. **1941** IAlexander *Revenge* (NY) 105: That boy hardly ever showed up to eat what would keep a bird alive. **1958** *New Yorker* 7/19 22: I don't eat enough to keep a bird alive. **1966** DMDisney *At Some* (NY) 265: You haven't eaten enough to keep a bird alive. **1971** CAird *Late* (NY) 109: I don't eat enough to keep a bird alive. Cf. To eat like a Bird *below*.

B239 To be something for the **Birds**

1952 BKendrick *You Diet* (NY) 27: This was one for the birds. **1959** ADean *Something* (NY) 72: That is something for the birds. **1963** HCalvin *It's Different* (NY) 72: That was strictly for the birds. **1968** EWilliams *Beyond* (NY) 151: Dirty pictures is for the birds. Spears 30.

B240 To be too old a **Bird** to be caught with chaff (*varied*)

1929 FDGrierson *Murder* (L) 132: Like the bird in the story, he was too old a hand to be caught with chaff. **1929** HFootner *Doctor* (L) 125: He was too old a bird to be caught with such chaff. **1933** FWCrofts *Hog's Back* (L) 308: We're too old birds to be caught with that sort of chaff. **1937** JEsteven *While Murder* (NY) 218: He might be too old a fox to be tempted by such obvious bait. **1938** FWCrofts *End* (L) 57: He's not the bird to be caught with chaff. **1952** GKcrsh *Brazen* (L) 174: I'm too old a bird to be caught with chaff. EAP B188; TW 29(22).

B241   To be too old a **Bird** to learn a new tune

1916 EClodd *Memories* (L) 214: Too old a bird to learn a new tune. EAP B183.

B242   To be up with the **Birds** (*varied*)

1946 ABCunningham *Death Rides* (NY) 48: I have to be up with the birds. **1951** EQueen *Origin* (B) 101: Delia's father was invariably up with the birds. **1958** *New Yorker* 4/12 43: I was up with the birds. **1968** JRoffman *Grave* (NY) 141: I'm up with the birds. Cf. *Oxford* 38: Bed with the lamb . . . rise with the lark. Cf. To go to bed with the Chickens, To be up with the Lark *below*.

B243   To charm a **Bird** out of a tree (*very varied*)

1927 GDilnot *Lazy* (B) 27: He could charm a bird from a tree. **1929** LBrock *Murder* (NY) 18: A voice that . . . might have coaxed the birds off the bushes. **1930** AFielding *Murder* (NY) 96: Ann could charm a bird off a bough. **1939** WMartyn *Noonday* (L) 108: Ruth can charm a bird off a tree. **1949** RFoley *Girl* (NY) 36: He has a warmth of manner that would charm a bird off a tree. **1955** PDennis *Auntie* (NY) 276: She could charm the birds off the trees. **1955** STroy *Half-way* (L) 70: You could always charm the ducks off the water. **1956** *BHerald* 11/28 3: He can talk a bird out of a tree. **1958** ADuggab *Three's* (L) 31: Caesar's smile could charm a bird from a bush. **1960** RMacdonald *Ferguson* (NY) 145: One of those people who can talk birds out of trees. **1964** HBourne *In the Event* (NY) 105: She could charm a bird off a tree. **1965** JSUntermeyer *Private* (NY) 81: She could, as the saying goes, "Charm a bird off a bush." **1966** EPangborn *Judgment* (NY) 126: At his best he could charm the brass knocker off

a door. **1971** EPeters *Knocker* (NY) 56: A smile that could fetch the birds out of the bushes. **1974** JQuintero *If You* (B) 203: He has a smile that can charm a bird out of a tree. Cf. Brunvand 10(4).

B244   To do something or other like a **Bird**

1933 VLoder *Death* (L) 36: Clare was off like a bird. **1933** DMorrah *Mummy* (NY) 106: He took it like a bird [*nicely*]. **1937** MAllingham *Dancers* (NY) 235: She [*a bicycle*] runs like a bird. **1968** GWagner *Elegy* (L) 50: The stuff went through Customs like the proverbial bird. **1969** RCook *Private* (NY) 131: He'll sleep like a bird. **1973** JBrooks *Go-Go* (NY) 281: The enterprise took off like a bird. Cf. Brunvand 10(6): Sing, 7: Go; Partridge 483: Like a . . .

B245   To eat like a **Bird** (*varied*)

1930 BRoss *Drury Lane's* (NY) 269: She ate like a bird, slept little. **1952** RMacdonald *Ivory* (NY 1965) 109: Picked at her food like a bird. **1954** EStreeter *Mr. Hobbs'* (NY) 166: She picks at her food like a bird. **1957** *BHerald* 4/7 47: Those who "eat like a bird." **1969** RLockridge *Risky* (P) 63: Robert says I eat like a bird. Taylor *Prov. Comp.* 16; DARE i 241: Bird eater. Cf. Not to eat *above*.

B246   To kill two **Birds** with one stone (*varied*)

c1910 EWallace *Nine Bears* (L 1928) 135: Bringing down two birds with one stone. **1914** PGWodehouse *Little Nugget* (NY 1929) 4: Kill two birds with one stone. **1922** JJoyce *Ulysses* (NY 1934) 214: Two birds with one stone. **1925** TFPowys *Mr. Tasker* (L) 284: Unless . . . the good Bishop wished to kill two birds with one pat on the head [*i.e., confirm a pregnant girl*]. **1931** HWade *No Friendly* (L) 104: The subject thought it necessary to use two stones to kill the bird. **1937** DAllan *Brandon* (L) 151: Let's kill two birds with one stone. **1940** RAvery *Murder a Day* (NY) 240: You'd be killing two birds—or two women, if you will—with one dose of poison. **1942** MVHeberden *Murder Makes* (NY) 279: Killing a whole covey of birds with one stone. **1944** RAJWalling *Corpse Without* (NY) 194: Two birds with one barrel. **1950** HGreen *Nothing* (NY) 58: I was killing two birds with one stone. **1956** *Punch* 6/6 684: An ingenious and economic way of killing three birds with one stone. **1958** MInnes *Long* (NY) 215: He was going to kill two birds with one stone—and feather his own nest on the proceeds. **1959** *Republican Journal* 3/19 9: Why waste time trying to kill two birds with one stone—the stones are more plentiful. **1963** JJMarric *Gideon's Ride* (NY) 21: I'll kill the old two birds with one stone. **1966** LPDavies *Who Is* (NY) 178: Four birds with one stone would really be something. **1969** MGilbert *Etruscan* (L) 246: A plot . . . to kill two birds, if I may so express it, with one motor car. **1973** JWhitehead *Solemn* (L) 122: Wise had killed two birds with one stone. EAP B186; Brunvand 10–11(9).

B247 To give (be given) the **Bird**

1933 MKennedy *Bull's Eye* (L) 237: They've been given the bird. **1955** EWSmith *One Eyed* (NY) 240: Wilse gave me the bird. Wentworth 38: Bird (6).

B248 To pull a likely **Bird**

1977 PGWinslow *Witch* (NY) 130: "First I gave 'im some tips on 'ow to pull a likely bird and then he was eating out of my hand." Capricorn quickly translated "pull a likely bird" to attract a probably willing female. Cf. Whiting F148.

B249 As busy as a **Bird dog**

1930 NBMavity *Case* (NY) 336: Busy as a bird dog. **1939** NMorland *Knife* (L) 96: She's as busy as a bird-dog. **1940** LFord *Old Lover's* (NY) 164: He was . . . busy as a bird dog. **1948** JLeslie *Shoes* (NY) 76: You been busy as a bird dog. **1956** *BangorDN* 8/17 8: An active candidate busy as a bird dog. **1957** *BHerald* 1/21 7: As busy as a bird-dog with a covey of quail. **1963** MGEberhart *Run* (NY) 44: Busy as a bird dog. Taylor *Prov. Comp.* 22.

B250 To hold like **Birdlime**

1922 JJoyce *Ulysses* (NY 1934) 279: That holds them like birdlime. EAP B189.

B251 To sell one's **Birthright**

1972 PMHubbard *Whisper* (NY) 35: He sold his birthright for a mess of pottage. EAP B191.

B252 To take the **Biscuit**

1922 VBridger *Greensea* (NY) 106: [He] takes the biscuit. **1939** AMuir *Death Comes* (L) 104: My precious brother takes the biscuit for . . . nerve. **1954** MHastings *Cork* (NY) 48: You take the blooming biscuit. **1964** JCreasey *Hang* (NY DBC) 20: He takes the biscuit. **1970** JPorter *Dover Strikes* (NY) 71: [He] took the biscuit. Partridge 862: Take.

B253 As sober as a **Bishop**

1960 *FFrankfurter Reminisces* ed HBPhillips (NY) 124: I'm as sober as a Bishop. Cf. Wilstach 368: Vicar. Cf. Judge *below*.

B254 To get a **Bit** (*etc.*) of one's own back (*varied*)

1926 JJConnington *Death* (NY) 236: I was going to get a little of my own back. **1928** WRoughead *Murderer's* (NY 1968) 341: The time had come when, in the vulgar phrase, they could get some of their own back. **1931** HCBailey *Fortune Explains* (NY) 126: I'm going to get some of my own back. **1935** HCBailey *Mr. Fortune Objects* (L) 86: He wanted to get a bit of his own back. **1939** JDonavan *Coloured Wind* (L) 242: I wanted to get my own back, as they say. **1959** JBell *Easy* (NY) 168: To get a bit of my own back. **1972** SWoods *They Love* (NY) 116: Getting a bit of his own back. Cf. NED Own *a.* 3b.

B255 To take the **Bit** between one's teeth

1920 GDilnot *Suspected* (NY) 86: His girl had . . . the bit between her teeth. **1922** JJoyce *Ulysses* (NY 1934) 392: He took the bit between his teeth like a raw colt. **1933** ESnell *And Then* (L) 53: Craig . . . had taken the bit in his teeth. **1939** JJConnington *Counsellor* (L) 38: Apt to take the bit in his teeth. **1944** HReilly *Opening Door* (NY) 80: They take the bit in their teeth. **1948** JErskine *My Life* (P) 116: The Trustees took the bit in their teeth. **1954** DCecil *Melbourne* (I) 362: She had got the bit between her teeth. **1961** WHLewis *Scandalous* (NY) 111:

[He] took the bit between his teeth. **1965** ASharp *Green Tree* (NY 1966) 301: Lest Maureen take the bit in her teeth and describe her sex acts. **1968** MGibbon *Inglorious* (L) 52: Took the bit between its teeth and ran amok. **1971** CAird *Late* (NY) 121: Once they get the bit between their teeth. **1975** DRussell *Tamarisk* (NY) 47: I had begun to take the bit between my teeth. EAP B193; Brunvand 11.

B256 As busy as a **Bitch** with one tit
1965 NBenchley *Visitors* (NY) 7: I'm busier than a bitch with one tit.

B257 To put the **Bite** on someone
1947 GGallagher *I Found* (NY DBC) 52: Was he putting the bite on Sylvia? Wentworth 40.

B258 To take (make) two **Bites** at a cherry
1927 JSFletcher *Bartenstein* (NY) 153: You delight in making as many bites at a cherry as ever you can. **1933** LCharteris *Brighter* (NY) 221: I never take two bites at a cherry. **1936** JVTurner *Below the Clock* (L) 123: It wouldn't surprise me if Paling wanted another bite at the cherry. **1951** HSaunders *Sleeping* (L) 64: Why take two bites at the cherry? **1961** ADuggan *King* (L) 55: No sense in taking two bites at a cherry. **1963** FHoyle *Fifth* (L 1965) 95: You only get one bite at the cherry. **1964** JJMarric *Gideon's Lot* (NY) 200: He won't take a second bite at the cherry. EAP B195.

B259 The **Biter** bit (*varied*)
1906 JCLincoln *Mr. Pratt* (NY) 11: The biter's being bit. **1919** LTracy *Bartlett* (NY) 293: The Biter Bit. **1923** ACrowley *Confessions* ed JSymonds (L 1969) 306: The biter bit. **1939** JDonavan *Coloured Wind* (L) 175: It howls as though the biters are being bit. **1941** MHolbrook *Suitable* (NY) 244: The biter bit. **1951** EQueen *Origin* (B) 242: So that the biter would be bitten. **1956** CArmstrong *Dram* (NY 1958) 159: The biter bit. A bitter bite. **1960** JBell *Fall* (NY) 187: The biter had been bit. **1968** EQueen *House* (NY) 6: She . . . kept throwing the biter-bit bit in his teeth. **1970** RDAltick *Victorian* (NY) 39: The familiar case of the cheater cheated. **1970** TCoe *Wax* (NY) 158: A sim-

ple matter of biter bit. **1981** AAndrews *Pig* (NY) 98: Biters were bit. EAP B196. Cf. Pit *below.*

B260 Once **Bitten,** twice shy (*varied*)
1915 JBuchan *Thirty-Nine* (NY) 73: Once-bitten-twice-shy. **1924** RFirbank *Prancing* (Works 5, L 1929) 39: Once bit twice shy. **1928** AHuxley *Point* (L) 195: Once bitten, twice shy. **1930** WLewis *Apes* (NY 1932) 200: *Once bitten twice shy* is what they say. **1936** *New Yorker* 1/11 19: Once bitten, twice shy, goes the old saw. **1948** JRhode *Death* (NY) 13: Once bitten twice shy. **1957** *Punch* 9/11 298: Pardorn said he was twice shy as a result of having been once bitten. **1957** *NYTimes Book Review* 11/17 35: Once warned, however, there is no reason for the reader to be twice shy. **1959** *New Yorker* 8/15 31: Once bit, twice shy. **1966** GBagby *Dirty* (NY) 73: Once bitten and twice shy. **1970** JLeasor *They Don't* (NY) 38: Once bitten and so on. **1975** JFoxx *Dead Run* (I) 40: Once bitten, twice shy. *Oxford* 594. Cf. Once Burned *below.*

B261 To take the **Bitter** with the sweet
1934 AWynne *Death* (P) 16: One takes the bitter with the sweet. **1938** KMKnight *Acts* (NY) 5: You've got to take the bitter with the sweet. That's life. **1960** NBenchley *Sail* (NY) 75: Any guy . . . has gotta take the bitter with the sweet. EAP B197; Brunvand 11. Cf. Brunvand 137: Sweet. Cf. To take the Good, Rough *below.*

B262 To boom like a **Bittern**
1935 VGielgud *Death* (L) 32: [He] boomed like a bittern. NED Bittern *sb.*[1]

B263 As plain as **Black** and white
1961 BAldiss *Primal* (NY) 140: It's as plain as black and white. Whiting *NC* 372. Cf. *Oxford* 63: Black and white.

B264 As opposed as **Black** to white
1949 WLewis *Letters* cd WKRose (L 1963) 516: My own views are opposed to this as black to white. EAP B198.

B265 **Black** for beauty
1932 *Hot-Cha* (L) 30: Black for Beauty—you know. **1933** ERPunshon *Genius* (B) 190:

Black for beauty, as they say. Partridge 329: Ginger (4).

B266 Every **Black** has its white

1961 ESeeman *In the Arms* (NY) 31: The old saying: "Every black hath its white." Cf. *Oxford* 885: White has its black.

B267 In **Black** and white

1911 JLondon *Letters* ed KHendricks (NY 1965) 339: In black and white. **1922** JJoyce *Ulysses* (NY 1934) 175: Nothing is black and white. **1932** JJConnington *Castleford* (B) 48: It was down in black and white. **1937** RStout *Red Box* (L) 119: Having it down in black and white and signed. **1941** NMarsh *Death in Ecstasy* (NY) 178: He didn't exactly like to mention it in black and white. **1942** MGEberhart *Wolf* (NY) 114: Outlining their case [*orally*] . . . in black and white. **1953** SRansome *Hear* (NY) 59: It's down there in plain black and white. **1958** VSiller *Widower* (NY) 135: Every word . . . was there in black and white. **1964** HBTaylor *Duplicate* (NY) 78: He had the papers. All in black and white. **1970** JRoss *Deadest* (NY) 124: It says so in black and white. **1975** RStout *Family* (NY) 149: I prefer not to put it in black and white. EAP B199; TW 30(4).

B268 To curse (swear) **Black** and white

1933 CWells *Clue* (NY) 269: He used to curse them black and white. **1934** ERPunshon *Crossword* (L) 228: She swears black and blue there was nothing to it. **1935** MKennedy *Poison* (L) 73: He swears black and blue that he was told nothing. TW 30(1).

B269 To have everything **Black** and (or) white

1956 SWTaylor *I Have* (NY) 141: Everything had to be black or white. **1958** A Christie *Ordeal* (NY DBC) 137: Everything's black and white to you . . . No half-tones.

B270 To make **Black** white (*varied*)

1929 LBrock *Murder* (NY) 154: He'd convince you that black was white. **1931** HLandon *Back-seat* (NY) 149: He had convinced him that black was white and that white was black. **1948** DCDisney *Explosion* (NY DBC) 138: Some women will swear up and down that black is white. **1954** HCecil *According* (L) 123: You cannot make black white or white black. **1956** BJFarmer *Death* (L) 128: She will swear black is white. **1956** JJMarric *Gideon's Week* (L) 135: He swears black's blue that she didn't have anyone with her. **1961** AMorton *Double* (NY) 81: You could always make black sound white. **1963** NFitzgerald *Echo* (NY) 160: She wasn't the sort to say black was white, just to please you. **1970** WMasterson *Death* (NY) 43: He'd just lie . . . turn black into white. EAP B200; TW 30(5); Brunvand 11(2).

B271 Two **Blacks** don't make a white

1922 FPitt *Woodland* (L) 246: Two blacks don't make a white. **1929** GFairlie *Stone* (B) 65: The old saying that two blacks do not make a white. **1936** AHuxley *Eyeless* (NY) 68: Two blacks don't make a white. **1964** RConquest *World* (NY) 34: Two blacks don't make a white. *Oxford* 849. Cf. Wrongs *below*.

B272 To work like a **Black**

1916 MGibbon *Inglorious* (L 1968) 124: I am working like a black. **1931** MAHamilton *Murder* (L) 212: Work like blacks. **1939** RHull *And Death* (L) 86: He worked like a black with his own hands. **1953** RPostgate *Ledger* (L) 115: Work like a black. **1957** *Punch* 6/19 775: He worked like a black (if that phrase is still permissible). **1960** DHolman-Hunt *My Grandmothers* (L) 124: Hunt worked like a black. **1969** RBlythe *Akenfield* (NY) 95: They were expected to work like blacks. **1970** PDickinson *Sinful* (NY) 170: He worked like a black for that. Cf. EAP S247: Slave. Cf. Nigger, Slave *below*.

B273 As common as **Blackberries** (blueberries)

1928 GDHCole *Man* (NY) 9: As common as blackberries. **1936** ECRLorac *Death* (L) 225: Dunlop tykes are about as common as blackberries. **1940** NBlake *Malice* (L) 24: Common as blackberries. **1960** EWolf *Rosenbach* (Cleveland) 220: Common as blackberries. **1961** HReilly *Certain* (NY DBC) 102: They were as common as blueberries in August.

B274 As plentiful (plenty) as **Blackberries**

1936 RLehmann *Weather* (NY) 91: Museums plentiful as blackberries. **1946** WPartington *T.J.Wise* (L) 24: Plenty as blackberries. **1952** DWecter *Sam Clemens* (B) 221: Such tales are as plentiful as June blackberries. **1955** CPearl *Girl* (L) 34: Common brothels are as plentiful as blackberries. **1961** JDavey *Touch* (NY 1963) 149: The clams were as plentiful as blackberries. EAP B202; Brunvand 12.

B275 As thick as **Blackberries** (gooseberries)

1924 JSFletcher *Safety* (NY) 72: Gentlefolk . . . as thick as blackberries. **1934** BThomson *Richardson Scores* (L) 195: These little poultry farms are as thick as gooseberries. **1940** MCharlton *Death of* (L) 67: Automatics of that type were as thick as blackberries in May. **1957** *BHerald* 3/3 52: Historical novels are as thick as blackberries this season. TW 31(2).

B276 As common as **Blackbirds**

1954 MHastings *Cork* (NY) 139: Feuds . . . were as common as blackbirds. Cf. Taylor *Prov. Comp.* 81: Thick . . . in the spring. Cf. Blackberries *above.*

B277 As rare as a white **Blackbird** (crow)

1934 EPhillpotts *Mr. Digweed* (L) 164: Rarer than a white blackbird. **1934** ECVivian *Accessory* (L) 86: They're about as plentiful as white blackbirds. **1938** WNMacartney *Fifty Years* (NY) 373: Rare as white blackbirds. **1939** TStevenson *Silver Arrow* (L) 145: It's like the white sparrow in the old proverb. You've got to get up very early in the morning to see it and when you do see it you don't recognize it. **1955** DMDisney *Room* (NY) 60: There'll be white blackbirds flying when it happens. **1957** HPBeck *Folklore of Maine* (P) 168: Like seeing white blackbirds [*something unusual*]. **1970** AWRaitt *Prosper* (L) 272: I placed all my happiness in finding a white crow, far too rare a bird. TW 86(9): Crow. Cf. Swan *below.*

B278 To collapse like a stuck **Bladder**

1930 WAStowell *Marston* (NY) 271: He collapsed like a stuck bladder. Wilstach 62: Collapse. Cf. Balloon *above,* Bubble *below.*

B279 To be a wet **Blanket**

1927 AWynne *Sinners* (P) 143: 'Aving a wet blanket always in the house. **1939** JJConnington *Counsellor* (L) 144: Wet blankets don't damp me. **1955** KMKnight *Robineau* (NY) 67: I hate to be a wet blanket. **1958** ADuggan *Three's* (L) 160: At any party he was a wet blanket. **1965** GHolden *Don't Go* (NY) 42: I don't want to be a wet blanket. **1967** ARose *Memoirs* (NY) 175: I'm traveling with a wet blanket. **1975** MVonnegut *Eden* (NY) 68: I had to play the wet blanket. TW 31(2); Wentworth 572.

B280 As cold as **Blazes**

1930 JDosPassos *42nd* (NY) 21: It was cold as blazes. TW 32(5).

B281 One's **Blessings** are not known until lost

1929 GMWhite *Square* (L) 3: It has been said that one never knows one's blessings until one has lost them. Apperson 54(1).

B282 To count one's **Blessings**

1948 WMiller *Fatal* (NY) 88: Well, count your blessings. **1951** CBush *Sapphire* (NY) 25: Count your blessings. That's what I always say. **1971** JAiken *World* (NY) 171: Let's . . . count our blessings. **1975** NGuild *Lost* (NY) 2: Best to count your blessings.

B283 The **Blind** leading the blind (*varied*)

1908 HMSylvester *Olde Pemaquid* (B) 12: If the blind lead the blind, the ditch is but a little way on. **1920** N&JOakley *Clevedon* (P) 18: Another instance of the blind leading the blind. **1927** JTaine *Quayle's* (NY) 73: Blind leaders of the blind. **1931** PBaron *Round* (NY) 130: When the blind lead the blind, they're liable to get run over. **1940** NChambers *Dry* (NY) 69: The blind leading the blind. **1955** MWheeler *Still* (L) 184: A case of the blind leading the blind. **1958** *New Yorker* 1/11 22: An adage he deems mistaken, mischievous, and far too commonly accepted—the one that goes "When the blind lead the blind, they all fall into the ditch." **1960** CDLewis *Buried* (L) 215: A . . . signal instance of the blind leading the short sighted. **1967** JWCampbell *Analog 5* (NY) 30: Asking the blind to lead the blind.

1973 KCampbell *Wheel* (I) 28: The blind leading the blind. EAP B205; TW 33(2).

B284 None so **Blind** as those who will not see

1922 JJoyce *Ulysses* (NY 1934) 320: There's no-one so blind as the fellow that won't see. **1933** MBeckett *Murder* (L) 254: There's none so blind as those who won't see. **1946** LAllen *Murder . . . Rough* (NY) 39: There's none so blind as those who will not see. **1953** DMDisney *Prescription* (NY) 105: None so blind as those who will not see. **1965** HKane *Midnight* (NY) 131: None so blind as those that will not see. **1969** RPearsall *Worm* (L) 357: There was none so blind as Ruskin when he would not see. EAP B206; TW 32(1).

B285 "I see," said the **Blindman**

1962 WMorris *North* (B) 59: "I see," said the blindman. Cf. EAP H353.

B286 As quick as a **Blink**

1940 STowne *Death out* (NY) 203: As quick as a blink. Cf. Partridge 64: Like a blink. Cf. Wink *below.*

B287 In the **Blink(ing)** of an eye

1971 DWeeks *Corve* (NY) 4: In the blinking of an eye. **1974** JBrunner *Total* (NY) 102: The blink of an eye. NED Blink *sb.*² 3.

B288 To fit like a **Blister**

1928 JGoodwin *When Dead* (NY) 257: I think the name fits him like a blister. TW 33(1).

B289 As red as **Blood**; Blood-red

1911 CKSteele *Mansion* (NY) 90: Blood red. **1932** VWilliams *Death* (B) 61: Blood-red nails. **1933** JBCarr *Death* (NY) 8: Red as blood. **1954** EFrankland *Foster* (NY) 277: Gunnar had turned red as blood. **1959** MPHood *Bell* (NY) 44: Red as blood. **1963** AWUpfield *Body* (NY) 158: She'll be as red as blood. **1971** JLord *Maharajahs* (NY) 108: Blood-red parasol. EAP B213, 213a; TW 33(1).

B290 **Blood** is blood

1945 CEVulliamy *Edwin* (L) 146: Blood is blood. **1955** STroy *Half-way* (L) 64: Blood's blood. TW 33(4).

B291 **Blood** is thicker than water (*varied*)

1913 MRRinehart *Jennie Brice* (NY 1947) 385: Blood is thicker even than floodwater. **1920** CSLewis *Letters* ed WHLewis (NY 1966) 49: Blood is thicker than water, "and a good deal nastier," as someone added. **1922** EPower *Medieval English Nunneries* (Cambridge, Eng.) 376: Blood was thicker than holy water. **1924** JSFletcher *Mazaroff* (NY) 222: Blood is thicker than water. **1928** AB Cox *Amateur* (NY) 86: The river was all right, but blood is well known to be thicker. **1929** RAldington *Death* (L) 159: "Blood is thicker than water," they say sententiously . . . I hate proverbs—don't you? I've always noticed that anything absurd or tyrannical or fatuous can always be supported by a proverb—the collective stupidity of the ages. **1936** JRhode *In Face* (L) 187: I'm not sure that blood is always thicker than water. **1937** EGreenwood *Under the Fig* (NY) 87: This blood-thicker-than-water stuff. **1941** CCoffin *Mare's Nest* (NY) 10: Blood is thicker than water, after all. **1947** PWentworth *Wicked* (NY) 3: Blood's thicker than water. **1952** KMKnight *Death Goes* (NY) 18: I always say blood runs thicker than water. **1956** MSteen *Unquiet* (NY) 26: Blood being traditionally thicker than water. **1957** BGill *Day* (NY) 158: Blood may be thicker than water, but money is thicker than blood. **1958** *New Yorker* 4/5 95: The old adage that blood is thicker than water. **1958** *Time* 9/8 100: Blood is thicker than firewater. **1958** *TLS* 10/10 574: Nowhere more than in Montenegro is blood thicker than water. **1958** JByrom *Or Be* (L 1964) 36: Blood being thicker than mud. **1959** *NYTimes Book Review* 8/16 26: There used to be a saying mouthed by the old mothers among the mountain ridges of West Virginia that, "Blood is thicker than water." **1963** EQueen *Player* (NY) 32: Those bloody blood-is-thicker-than-water sessions. **1965** PAydemars *Fair* (NY) 25: Blue blood was thicker than glue. **1966** JRoffman *Ashes* (NY) 28:

Truth had a way of containing itself in old saws. Blood was thicker than water. **1972** JCreasey *Gallows* (NY) 195: I suppose that blood is thicker than water. **1973** WJBurley *Death* (NY) 140: Blood is thicker than water—at least, that's what they say. **1974** JFlaherty *Chez* (NY) 149: The stain of blood is thicker than not only water, but also well-meaning words. EAP B214; Brunvand 13(3).

B292 The **Blood** of the martyrs is the seed of the Church

1958 PDeVries *Mackerel* (B) 168: The blood of the martyrs is the seed of the church. EAP B215.

B293 **Blood** speaks to blood

1970 MStewart *Crystal* (NY) 441: Blood speaks to blood, they say. Whiting B359.

B294 **Blood** will have blood (*very varied*)

1936 JStagge *Murder Gone* (L) 86: "Blood will have blood," I quoted gloomily. **1945** BKendrick *Death Knell* (NY) 109: He had heard the saying that blood begets blood and murder is the child of murder. **1956** NMarsh *Death* (B) 119: Blood axes for blood. **1962** MStewart *Moon* (NY 1965) 32: Blood will always have blood. EAP B216; TW 33(2); Brunvand 12(2).

B295 **Blood** will tell (out) (*varied*)

c1923 ACrowley *Confessions* ed JSymonds (L 1969) 447: The aphorism "Blood will tell." **1935** EGreenwood *Deadly* (NY) 136: Blood will tell. **1935** CStJSprigg *Perfect* (NY) 227: What's in the blood must come out. **1937** GStockwell *Death* (NY) 243: Blood will tell. **1939** DBowers *Shadows* (L) 188: Bad blood will out. **1939** MPropper *Cheating Bride* (L) 171: Class will tell. **1942** QMario *Murder Meets* (NY) 34: Good blood—it's like murder—it always will out. **1956** WTenn *Human* (NY) 5: Blood will tell. **1957** JLodwick *Equator* (L) 174: As perhaps you say in English, also, blood will tell. **1963** RAHeinlein *Podkayne* (NY) 76: Blood will tell—bad blood or good blood—blood will always tell. **1966** HJBoyle *With a Pinch* (NY) 93: Others said that blood will tell. **1973** AWest *Mortal* (NY) 239: The old saying is

that blood will tell. **1974** THeald *Blue Blood Will Out* (NY). **1975** MKWren *Multitude* (NY) 27: Blood always tells. **1976** DWilliams *Unholy* (NY) 49: There's quality there; blood will out no matter what they say. TW 33(5); Brunvand 13(4). Cf. Breed(ing) *below*.

B296 To have one's **Blood** on his own head

1928 FBeeding *House* (NY) 62: His blood on his own head. **1937** WMartyn *Old Manor* (L) 89: Your blood be upon your own head. TW 34(8).

B297 To have one's **Blood** up

1939 FBeeding *Ten Holy* (NY) 235: My blood, as the saying is, was up. TW 34(9); Brunvand 13(5).

B298 You cannot get **Blood** out of a stone (*varied*)

1925 JSFletcher *False* (NY) 105: You can't get blood out of a stone. **1931** LEppley *Murder* (NY) 174: You can't get blood out of a stone. **1932** AGibbs *Murder* (NY) 111: He knew the old adage about blood and a stone. **1932** WSMasterman *Flying* (NY) 165: You can't get money out of a stone. **1932** RCWoodthorpe *Public* (L) 313: You try to draw blood from a stone. **1939** RStout *Mountain Cat* (NY 1958) 20: You can't get blood out of a brick. **1952** MInnes *One-man* (NY) 35: They say that blood is one thing that you can't get out of a stone. **1957** *BHerald* 6/23 11: You can't get blood out of a stone, as the old saying goes. **1959** *BHerald* 4/7 16: Continued efforts to squeeze blood from a stone. **1965** SWoods *Though I* (NY) 130: Blood will not come from a rock. **1970** JPorter *Dover Strikes* (NY) 110: You can't get blood out of a stone. **1975** DEWestlake *Two* (NY) 33: You can't get blood from a stone. EAP B218. Cf. To get Water *below*.

B299 You cannot get **Blood** out of a turnip (*varied*)

1925 GBeasley *My First* (Paris) 278: You couldn't squeeze blood out of a turnip. **1935** ESGardner *Counterfeit Eye* (NY) 45: He'll get blood out of a turnip. **1935** DOgburn *Will* (NY) 143: They say you can't get blood out of a turnip. **1939** DBOlsen *Cat*

Saw (NY) 134: They weren't getting any blood, so to speak, because Lily was financially a turnip. **1947** AAFair *Fools* (NY 1957) 49: I've put in my whole life getting blood out of a turnip. **1952** MRRinehart *Swimming* (NY) 172: You can't get blood out of a turnip. **1957** *Republican Journal* 4/18 4: You can't squeeze blood out of a turnip. **1957** CRice *My Kingdom* (NY) 43: A creditor chasing me . . . would be like a bloodhound chasing a turnip. **1968** PSBeagle *Last Unicorn* (NY) 53: You can't squeeze blood out of a turnip. **1968** AMStein *Snare* (NY) 168: Jaime is the well-known turnip that even Aristide can't get any blood out of. **1974** WSnow *Codline* (Middletown, Conn.) 348: To extract blood out of a turnip. **1978** JLangton *Memorial* (NY) 72: Getting blood from turnips. EAP B218.

B300   A **Blot** on the escutcheon

1930 LRGriddle *Case* (NY) 196: We want to go with no blot on the 'escutcheon. **1931** PATaylor *Cape Cod* (NY 1971) 193: No one talks about escutcheons till there's a blot on them. **1943** MVHeberden *Murder Goes* (NY) 66: The blot on the escutcheon. **1962** DTaylor *Blood* (NY) 127: That blot on his escutcheon. **1966** PGWodehouse *Plum* (L) 129: Blotted the escutcheon, that's what you've done. **1968** JHaythorne *None of Us* (NY) 132: I regret . . . that this blot should have occurred on the scutcheon of our friendship. **1973** JPorter *It's Murder* (NY) 92: One more blot on the Dover escutcheon. EAP B222.

B301   The first **Blow** is half the battle (*varied*)

1930 AFielding *Murder* (NY) 23: That's half the battle. **1938** SHAdams *World* (B) 164: There's a proverbial advantage in getting the first punch. **1938** EHuxley *Murder* (NY) 12: It's the first shot that counts. **1957** *Time* 3/11 23: "Once blest is he whose cause is just," goes the old American saying. "Twice blest is he who gets his blows in first." **1957** *BangorDN* 1/14 6: An old proverb says: "He who strikes the first blow loses the argument." **1964** JJMarric *Gideon's Vote* (NY) 86: Good start's half the battle. EAP B224.

B302   To **Blow** hot and cold (*varied*)

1922 JJoyce *Ulysses* (NY 1934) 124: Hot and cold in the same breath. 523: No more blow hot and cold. **1929** APryde *Secret* (NY) 31: Always blowing first hot and then cold. **1930** GDHCole *Corpse* (L) 252: He blew hot and cold on alternate days. **1932** JJConnington *Castleford* (B) 27: A sort of blow-hot, blow-cold attitude. **1936** AMChase *Twenty Minutes* (NY) 131: He was just the kind to blow hot one minute and cold the next. **1941** EL Fetta *Dressed* (NY) 12: Prunella had played hot and cold with him. **1944** PATaylor *Dead Ernest* (NY) 13: Nothin' to blow hot and cold about. **1947** HCahill *Look* (NY) 94: Blows hot one day and cold the next. **1956** *Punch* 10/31 537: He blows hot and cold with disturbing regularity. **1956** EBigland *Lord Byron* (L) 4: Gamba . . . was a blow-hot, blow-cold sort of fellow. **1960** STruss *One Man's* (NY) 43: The way you blow hot and cold. **1967** JDCarr *Dark* (NY) 57: Blow hot, blow cold. **1973** JFleming *Alas* (NY) 41: Blow hot, blow cold. EAP B225.

B303   Into the **Blue**

1924 HCBailey *Mr. Fortune's Practice* (NY) 204: She's off into the blue. **1924** AChristie *Man* (NY) 121: Vanished into the blue; 220. **1933** RAJWalling *Follow* (L) 137: Vanished into the blue. **1938** DHume *Corpses* (L) 76: Both men had vanished into the proverbial blue. **1962** AGarve *Prisoner's* (NY DBC) 70: Gone off into the blue. Partridge 69: In the blue. Cf. NED Vanish v. 2b(c).

B304   Out of the **Blue** (*varied*)

1924 HCBailey *Mr. Fortune's Practice* (NY) 224: An then this—out of the blue. **1929** EDBiggers *Black* (I) 264: Out of a blue sky—my moment came. **1933** RAFreeman *Dr. Thorndike Intervenes* (L) 90: Appeared out of the blue. **1938** HAdams *Bluff* (L) 55: And then, out of the blue, as the saying is, I got a note from her. **1939** DFrome *Mr. Pinkerton and the Old* (L) 10: People dropping in out of the blue, as they say. **1943** EDaly *Evidence* (NY) 146: He's the original bolt from the blue. **1949** RLTaylor *W.C.Fields* (NY) 336: Once, out of a blue sky, he sang . . . a . . . love song. **1950**

HReilly *Murder* (NY) 96: [He] had appeared out of the blue. **1956** MG Eberhart *Postmark* (NY) 58: He dropped out of the blue. **1960** HQMasur *Send Another* (NY) 36: She walked in out of a clear blue sky. **1964** FArcher *Out of the Blue* (NY). **1968** PGallico *Manxmouse* (NY) 15: Out of the blue something happened. **1972** EXFerrars *Foot* (NY) 76: Someone turns up out of the blue. **1974** MButterworth *Villa* (NY) 25: Right out of the blue. Cf. Bolt *below*.

B305   Till all is **Blue**

1929 GMWhite *Square* (L) 90: [She] stuck to it till all was blue. **1930** GDHCole *Corpse* (L) 193: He's prepared to swear . . . until all's blue. **1931** HCBailey *Fortune Explains* (NY) 67: You can spin theories till all's blue. EAP B226.

B306   To be true **Blue**

1927 EWallace *Feathered* (NY) 291: The only true-blue family retainer left. **1934** LRGribble *Riddle* (L) 18: Like the true-blue socialist he was. **1936** ECRLorac *Crime* (L) 27: The "true blue" of the Tory. **1953** ECrandall *White* (B) 124: True-blue Howard . . . a friend of a friend in need. **1956** JChristopher *Death* (L) 57: We're true-blue Englishmen and we play cricket. **1957** *NY Times* 5/5 1E: A true-blue Republican. **1959** JCross *Dark* (NY) 83: True-blue Communists. **1968** RBissell *How Many* (B) 140: A typical true-blue New Yorker. **1970** AHalper *Good-bye* (C) 194: I was true blue to you. EAP B227.

B307   To have the **Blues**

1928 JGoodwin *When Dead* (NY) 286: They only gave Mr. Leiter the blues. EAP B232; Brunvand 13.

B308   At the first **Blush**

1929 PRShore *Bolt* (NY) 102: At the first blush. **1936** CFGregg *Henry* (L) 86: At first blush. **1947** AAFair *Fools* (NY 1957) 124: At first blush. **1975** DDurrant *With My Little Eye* (NY) 84: You would agree, at first blush. EAP B233.

B309   After the **Boar** the leech *etc.*

1935 LBarringer *Kay* (NY) 282: *After the boar the leech,* they said, *and after the hart the bier.* Whiting B386.

B310   As bare as a **Board**

1934 VGielgud *Death* (L) 23: Their room's as bare as a board. Whiting B408.

B311   As flat as a **Board**

1906 JCLincoln *Mr. Pratt* (NY) 35: Flat as a board. **1939** RKing *Murder Masks* (NY) 118: His belly . . . was flat as a board. **1952** MColes *Alias* (NY) 106: It's as flat as a board for miles. **1955** HRoth *Sleeper* (NY) 4: [His] belly was . . . as flat as a board. **1956** *This Week* 11/18 10: I've always felt flat as a board. Taylor *Prov. Comp.* 41.

B312   As hard as a **Board**

1933 RAJWalling *Prove It* (NY) 133: The lawn was baked as hard as a board. **1963** EXFerrars *Doubly* (NY) 1: It would be as hard as a board. **1975** MButterworth *Man in* (NY) 41: As hard as a board. EAP B234.

B313   As stiff (rigid) as a **Board**

1931 GFowler *Great* (NY) 292: You were stiff as a board. **1932** BRoss *Tragedy of X* (NY) 247: Stiff as a board. **1937** MWGlidden *Long Island* (NY) 238: My face felt as stiff as a board. **1941** ISCobb *Exit* (I) 445: Stiff as a board. **1953** AJLiebling *Honest* (NY) 14: We would all get as stiff as boards [*drunk*]. **1959** BHitchens *Man Who* (NY) 26: He's stiffer'n a board [*dead*]. **1960** WMasterson *Hammer* (NY DBC) 116: He may be as stiff as a board [*drunk*]. **1962** IFleming *Spy* (NY) 191: Frightened stiff, as stiff as a board. **1971** LRhinehart *Dice* (NY) 92: I . . . lay as rigid as a board. **1975** MVonnegut *Eden* (NY) 138: You get rigid as a board. **1975** MErskine *Harriet* (NY) 93: She just stood, stiff as a board. TW 35(1); Taylor *Prov. Comp.* 77. Cf. Cardboard *below*.

B314   As straight as a **Board**

1952 MMillar *Vanish* (NY) 104: His back is straight as a board. **1961** CWillock *Death* (L 1963) 64: Straight as a board in his seat. TW 35(1).

B315   To be all above **Board** (*varied*)

1925 FWCrofts *French's Greatest* (NY) 282: All . . . straight and above board. **1927** CBStilson *Seven* (NY) 15: All square and above board. **1928** JJConnington *Tragedy* (NY) 251: All plain and above board. **1928**

JAFerguson *Man in the Dark* (NY) 297: It all seemed open and above-board. **1930** HAdams *Golden* (L) 72: Everything must be above board, is my motto. **1931** AChristie *Murder* (NY) 45: Perfectly clear and above board. **1932** WLHay *Who Cut* (L) 52: All fair and above board. **1935** MBurton *Milk-Churn* (L) 85: Perfectly honest and above-board. **1940** AChristie *Patriotic* (NY) 42: They're all square and aboveboard. **1954** HCecil *According* (L) 96: All fair and above board. **1956** HReilly *Canvas* (NY 1959) 117: All . . . open and aboveboard. **1961** LPayne *Nose* (NY) 54: It was all fair and square and above board. **1964** HKemelman *Friday* (NY 1965) 118: All open and above-board. **1970** JPorter *Dover Strikes* (NY) 193: Innocent and above board. **1970** RRendell *Best Man* (NY) 147: All open and above board. **1971** DClark *Sick* (NY) 109: All square and above board. **1973** EMcBain *Let's Hear* (NY) 60: All fair and above board. TW 35(1); Brunvand 13.

B316   To go by the **Board**

1929 EWallace *Girl* (NY) 104: All her theories must go by the board. TW 35(3).

B317   To be in the same **Boat**

1913 EDBiggers *Seven Keys* (I) 66: In the same boat. **1922** JSFletcher *Middle of Things* (NY) 86: All in the same boat. **1922** JJoyce *Ulysses* (NY 1934) 75: In the same boat. **1933** AAllen *Loose* (NY) 104: Both in the same boat. **1937** FBeeding *Hell* (L) 211: We are all in the same boat. **1941** JJConnington *Twenty-one* (B) 193: You and I are in the same boat. **1951** ECrispin *Long* (L 1958) 139: [He's] in the same boat. **1957** LDelRay *Robots* (NY) 109: We're all pretty much in the same boat. **1964** NBenchley *Winter's* (NY) 205: We're all in the same boat. **1966** BNaughton *Alfie* (L) 134: They all want to be in the same boat. **1970** MDelving *Die Like* (NY) 71: We were all in the same boat. TW 35(1); Brunvand 13.

B318   To burn one's **Boats**

1914 HHMunro *Beasts* (NY 1928) 9: Leonard had burned the boat. **1924** LO'Flaherty *Thy Neighbour's* (L) 179: And burn his boats. **1934** FNHart *Crooked* (NY) 275: He must burn his boats and prepare for flight. **1937** RAFreeman *Felo* (L) 307: He had burned his boats. **1950** CEVulliamy *Henry* (L) 147: The boats are burnt and the die is cast. **1956** *TLS* 5/25 311: The hot-headed revolutionary who burns his own boats as a preliminary to setting the torch to the enemy citadel. **1960** CDLewis *Buried* (L) 182: A grand burning-the-boats gesture. **1969** MGilbert *Etruscan* (L) 108: We've burned our boats. **1975** DRussell *Tamarisk* (NY) 82: I was still not ready to burn my boats. *Oxford* 91: Burn. Cf. Bridges *below*.

B319   To miss the **Boat** (train)

1901 JCLincoln *Mr. Pratt* (NY) 12: I'd missed the train. **1931** STWarner *T.H.White* (NY) 189: He had missed the boat. **1939** CRawson *Footprints* (L) 223: I wasn't going to miss that boat. **1940** JPPhilips *Murder in Marble* (NY) 78: I have—er—missed the boat, as the saying goes. **1951** DMDisney *Look* (NY) 62: He had missed the boat twice. **1956** *NYPost* 11/2 42: They missed the boat by appeasing the Arab nation. **1958** *BangorDN* 9/8 8: Governor Muskie completely missed the boat. **1958** AWUpfield *Bachelors* (L) 73: We're all in the same ship. **1968** JTMcIntosh *Take a Pair* (NY) 121: We don't want to miss the boat. **1971** JBlake *Joint* (NY) 86: I've missed a boat somewhere. **1972** DWalker *Lord's* (B) 48: Those Holy Romans have missed the boat. TW 35(3); Wentworth 340. Cf. Bus *below*.

B320   To rock the **Boat**

1921 JCLincoln *Galusha* (NY) 299: Those "spirits" . . . are rocking the boat. **1945** FAllan *First Come* (NY) 75: No need to rock the boat. **1952** HWaugh *Last Seen* (NY) 171: I'm not going to rock the boat. **1956** GHolden *Velvet* (NY) 187: The boat was certainly rocking. **1961** JSStrange *Eye* (NY) 71: If nobody rocked the boat.

B321   And **Bob's** your uncle

1936 JBude *Death* (L) 76: And Bob's your uncle. **1937** JBentley *Whitsey* (L) 68: One more round like the last and Bob's your uncle, as they say. **1945** CDickson *Curse* (NY) 59: He'll run for his news editor and Bob's-your-uncle. **1948** CDickson *Skeleton*

(NY 1967) 24: Just one little nip and Bob's-your-uncle. **1956** BJFarmer *Death* (L) 32: And Bob's your uncle, as someone said [*the thing is fixed*]. **1961** CBush *Sapphire* (NY) 132: Get yourself in with him and Bob's your uncle. **1961** JWelcome *Beware* (L) 209: A third world war and Bob's your uncle. **1970** RRendell *Best Man* (NY) 51: Put in your powder . . . and Bob's your uncle. **1973** JFleming *Alas* (NY) 179: Light the fuse, and Bob is no longer your uncle. **1974** PHighsmith *Ripley's* (NY) 56: And Bob's your uncle, as the English say.

B322   To lose a **Bob** and find a tanner (sixpence)

1922 JJoyce *Ulysses* (NY 1934) 319: You look like a fellow that had lost a bob and found a tanner. **1959** KWaterhouse *Billy* (L) 93: Don't look as if tha's lost a bob and found sixpence. NED Bob *sb.*⁸ (shilling), Tanner 2.

B323   To keep **Body** and soul together

1929 EWallace *Murder Book* (NY) 241: Sufficient food to keep body and soul together. **1952** GBullett *Trouble* (L) 121: She doesn't eat enough to keep body and soul together. **1958** MProcter *Three* (NY) 190: Enough to keep body and soul together. **1962** MJosephson *Life* (NY) 83: She earned barely enough to keep body and soul together. **1972** BLillie *Every* (NY) 315: Enough fresh air . . . to keep body and soul together. EAP B243; Brunvand 13(1).

B324   To know where the **Bodies** are buried

1966 HPentecost *Hide* (NY) 142: Boys . . . who know where more bodies are buried than most of us dream of. **1971** PTabor *Pauline's* (Louisville) 192: I had a reputation as a gal who knew where all the bodies were buried, a bad woman to tangle with.

B325   To own someone **Body** and soul

1959 ESGardner *Deadly* (NY) 182: He owned Barton . . . body and soul. Wentworth 49.

B326   As sore (mad) as a **Boil**

1930 JDosPassos *42nd* (NY) 102: Sore as a boil. **1937** HAshbrook *Murder* (NY) 186: Sore as boils. **1937** RStout *Red Box* (L) 80: Cramer's as sore as a boil on your nose. **1947** JIams *Body* (NY) 171: He was sore as a boil. **1955** ELacy *Best* (NY) 78: Mad as a boil. **1957** *BangorDN* 3/19 14: Beck has been sore as a boil. **1958** *New Yorker* 10/4 62: Looking sore as a boil. **1969** BCole *Funco* (NY) 183: Sore as a boil. EAP B247.

B327   A **Bolt** from the blue (*varied*)

1917 GRSims *My Life* (L) 268: A bolt from the blue. **1927** OFJerome *Hand* (NY) 105: Like a bolt from a clear sky. **1931** RScarlett *Cat's* (NY) 256: Then the bolt fell . . . lightning from a clear blue sky. **1933** BSKeirstead *Brownsville* (NY) 257: Then, like the proverbial bolt from the blue, the police descended on us. **1935** VRSmall *I Knew* (NY) 159: And then, striking like the proverbial lightning from a cloudless sky, it came. **1940** PMcGuire *Spanish* (L) 7: Like a bolt from the blue. **1957** WGHardy *City* (NY) 57: It was a bolt of lightning from a smiling sky. **1959** HWaugh *Sleep* (NY) 132: Like a bolt out of the blue. **1964** RMeinertztragen *Diary* (L) 358: The news came like a bolt from a clear sky. **1964** AStratton *Great Red* (NY) 346: It came to me like a bolt out of the blue. **1974** AGarve *Case* (NY) 92: A bolt from the blue. Taylor *Prov. Comp.* 20; Apperson 59(1); *Oxford* 73. Cf. Blue *above*.

B328   **Bolt** upright

1922 JJoyce *Ulysses* (NY 1934) 163: Bolt upright like surgeon M'Ardle. **1924** RO Chipperfield *Bright* (NY) 34: Bolt upright. **1938** JFarnol *Crooked* (NY) 114: Sitting bolt upright. **1954** JBingham *Third* (NY) 148: She was sitting bolt upright. EAP B249; TW 36.

B329   To be cut out of the same **Bolt** of cloth (*varied*)

1937 GFowler *Salute* (NY) 79: A cut of the same cloth. **1960** BAskwith *Tangled* (L) 47: Mrs Crawford's cut out of the same bolt of cloth. **1971** ELinington *Practice* (NY) 136: The nephew cut out of the same cloth. Cf. NED Cut *sb.*² 24.

B330   To shoot one's **Bolt**

1905 FMWhite *Crimson Blind* (NY) 296: He's shot his bolt. **1922** JJoyce *Ulysses* (NY 1934) 529: He shot his bolt. **1924** HSKeeler *Voice* (NY) 61: Your bolt is shot; 164. **1936** LCharteris *Saint Overboard* (NY) 101: Vogel had shot his bolt. **1951** PATaylor *Diplomatic* (NY) 16: The rowdy element has shot its bolt. **1956** HRoth *Crimson* (NY) 14: She seemed to have shot her bolt. **1966** HBlyth *Pocket* (L) 50: He had, so to speak, shot his academic bolt. **1967** JDetre *Happy* (NY) 153: He'd shot his bolt, so to speak. **1970** MStocks *My Commonplace* (L) 78: It had shot its bolt. EAP B250.

B331   To drop a **Bombshell**

1934 JCLenehan *Carnival* (L) 229: Got a bombshell to drop, as the saying is. TW 36. Cf. Brunvand 14.

B332   As bare as a **Bone**

1937 SPalmer *No Flowers* (L) 187: They're bare as a bone. **1939** CMRussell *Topaz Flowers* (NY) 70: The tenth floor was bare as a bone. **1958** RMacdonald *Doomsters* (NY) 208: His face was bare as bone. Whiting B440.

B333   As clean as a **Bone**

1931 WWJacobs *Snug* (NY) 353: As clean as a bone. **1931** JMWalsh *Company* (NY) 192: Pick the place as clean as a bone. Whiting B442; Taylor *Western Folklore* 17(1958) 13(1).

B334   As dry as a **Bone**; Bone-dry

1915 JBuchan *Thirty-Nine* (NY) 87: My mind was as dry as a bone. **1919** JSClouston *Simon* (NY) 299: Dry as a damned bone. **1924** TFPowys *Mark Only* (L) 90: As dry as bare bones. **1928** HAdams *Empty* (P) 251: The tank . . . was bone dry. **1930** JBude *Loss* (L) 173: The ground was bone-dry. **1932** JHWallis *Capital* (NY) 269: It's as dry and hard as bone. **1937** FProkosch *Seven* (NY) 3: It was as dry as bone. **1944** MVenning *Jethro* (NY) 38: His eyes dry as old bones. **1953** PGWodehouse *Ring* (L) 200: Dry as a bone. **1956** *Arizona Highways* Sept. 36: A bone-dry rule which forbade any whiskey to be sold. **1957** ESGardner *Screaming* (NY) 9: Absolutely bone dry.

1958 *New Yorker* 2/22 38: His mouth felt dry as a bone. **1961** RJWhite *Smartest* (L) 43: As dry as a bone. **1966** DMarlowe *Dandy* (NY) 135: The floor was as dry as a bone. **1974** SForbes *Some* (NY) 87: Dry as a bone. TW 36(3).

B335   As white (pale) as **Bone**; Bone-white

1929 FMPettee *Palgrave* (NY) 203: White as bones. **1933** ESnell *And Then* (L) 137: [His] face went bone-white. **1940** JDCarr *Man Who* (NY) 127: Bone-white beaches. **1956** ALernet-Holenia *Count* (NY) 190: Bone-white towers. **1958** PBrooke *Under* (NY) 56: You're white as a bone. **1962** RMacdonald *Zebra* (NY) 149: He was pale as bone. **1966** HTreece *Green* (L) 18: Her face went as white as a bone. Whiting B443.

B336   A **Bone** of contention

1924 JSFletcher *Safety* (NY) 119: The main bone of contention. **1926** AEHousman *Letters* ed HMaas (Cambridge, Mass. 1971) 242: The famous bone of contention. **1937** CFGregg *Wrong House* (L) 188: He choked at a bone of contention. **1941** LSdeCamp *Incomplete* (NY 1962) 130: The fair bone of this knightly contention. **1958** HMasur *Murder* (NY 1959) 165: This was . . . the bone of contention between them. **1963** RCroft-Cooke *Bosie* (L) 146: A bone of contention still gnawed over. **1973** JPorter *It's Murder* (NY) 82: A well-chewed bone of domestic contention. EAP B253; Brunvand 14(1).

B337   Not to have a funny (*etc.*) **Bone** in one's body

1909 JCLincoln *Keziah* (NY) 107: Elkanah ain't got a funny bone. **1932** BRoss *Tragedy of X* (NY) 70: There isn't a mean . . . bone in his body. **1943** GGCoulton *Fourscore* (Cambridge, Eng.) 48: There isn't one lazy bone in her whole body. **1949** KMKnight *Bass* (NY) 119: They ain't a mean bone in his body. **1951** JCFurnas *Voyage* (NY) 35: There was no lazy bone in his strange body. **1956** HRoth *Crimson* (NY) 2: She didn't have a superstitious bone in her body. **1962** HWaugh *That Night* (L) 57: Vic didn't have a mean bone in his body. **1966** LEGoss *Afterglow* (Portland, Me.) 104: [He] never had a lazy bone in his body. **1970** CEWerkley *Mister* (NY) 9: There wasn't a crooked bone in his body. TW 37(8).

B338 (Not) to make old **Bones**

1923 JSFletcher *Charing Cross* (NY) 5: Likely . . . to make old bones. **1935** LBlow *Bournewick* (L) 58: I doubt very much if he'll ever make old bones. **1939** MElwin *Old Gods* (NY) 94: George Moor made old bones. **1954** ADuggan *Leopards* (L) 18: They . . . don't expect the boy to make old bones. **1957** RStandish *Prince* (L) 31: He did not live to make old bones. **1961** CBlackstone *House* (L 1965) 17: He did not look as if he would make old bones. **1968** AChristie *By the Pricking* (NY) 160: People who may . . . make old bones. **1971** AChristie *Nemesis* (NY) 4: Nobody had expected her to make old bones. EAP B256.

B339 The nearer the **Bone** the sweeter the meat

1935 HNFreeman *Hester* (NY) 280: The nearer the bone, the sweeter the meat. **1937** VLoder *Choose* (L) 23: "The fact is that it looks dashed near the bone." "The sweeter the meat." **1957** DErskine *Pink* (NY) 27: That business about the sweetest meat being next to the bone was all in your hat in the ocean. **1957** CThompson *Halfway* (NY) 105: The closer the bone, the sweeter the meat. EAP B255. Cf. Meat *below*.

B340 To be close to the **Bone** (varied)

1937 JFerguson *Death* (L) 118: Going too near the bone, that would be. **1945** GBellairs *Calamity* (NY) 97: A few jokes as near the bone as possible [off-color]. **1954** HWade *Too Soon* (NY) 94: We must cut a bit closer to the bone. **1970** DStuart *Very* (NY) 51: A joke that came very close to the bone. **1972** ERCBrinkworth *Shakespeare* (L) 13: It went very near the bone. **1974** ELathen *Sweet* (NY) 127: This bit too close to the bone. Cf. Knuckle *below*.

B341 To feel in one's **Bones** (varied)

1920 ACrabb *Samuel* (NY) 91: I have a feeling in my old bones. **1920** EWallace *Three-Oaks* (L) 38: Soc knew in his bones. **c1923** ACrowley *Confessions* ed JSymonds (L 1969) 606: I felt it in the marrow of my bones. **1933** NBrady *Week-end* (L) 234: I could feel it in my bones. **1940** AGilbert *Dear Dead* (L) 41: I knew in my bones. **1941** HNicolson *Diaries* ed NNicolson (NY 1967) 2.149: I know in the marrow of my bones. **1941** EPhillpotts *Ghostwater* (NY) 95: I've got it in my bones, as they say, that he done the deed. **1952** JFleming *Man Who* (NY) 103: I feel it in my bones, as they say. **1955** RHarling *Enormous* (NY) 28: I knew in my bones. **1960** JPudney *Home* (L) 40: In my bones I had feared. **1961** WVanAtta *Shock* (NY) 111: I can feel it in every bone of my body. **1966** DHitchens *Man Who Cried* (NY) 136: I just feel it in my bones. **1969** RAirth *Snatch* (NY) 19: I've got a feeling in my bones. **1972** EPeters *Seventh* (NY) 42: You can feel it in your bones. EAP B258.

B342 To have a **Bone** in one's leg (teeth)

1957 HPBeck *Folklore of Maine* (P) 167: He has a bone in his teeth [is hurrying]. **1966** NMonsarrat *Life* (I) (L) 42: I've got a bone in my leg [grownup's excuse for not playing with children]. Oxford 73.

B343 To have a **Bone** to pick

1911 FRS *Way of a Man With a Maid* (L) 209: A certain bone to pick with her Ladyship. **1924** WBMFerguson *Black* (NY) 243: I've a bone to pick with [you]. **1952** KFCrossen *Future* (NY) 41: Jamie had a bigger bone to pick. **1956** SSmith *Shrew* (NY 1959) 25: The . . . tones of a wife with a bone to pick. **1957** PKDick *Eye* (NY) 117: The seven of us have a bone to pick. And you're on the other end. **1961** CDBurton *Long* (NY) 180: I have no bones to pick with age. **1975** EPeters *Crocodile* (NY) 273: I have a bone to pick with him. EAP B254; TW 37(7).

B344 To live close to the **Bone**

1962 LEgan *Borrowed* (NY DBC) 39: He's had to live pretty damn close to the bone. **1964** JHillas *Today* (NY) 154: He lived pretty close to the bone. **1969** DShannon *Crime* (NY) 11: She was living pretty close to the bone.

B345 To make no **Bones** of

1915 JBuchan *Thirty-Nine* (NY) 184: The butler made no bones about admitting the new visitor. **1920** GBMcCutcheon *Anderson Crow* (NY) 94: He don't make any bones about it; 169. **1922** JJoyce *Ulysses* (NY 1934) 639: He . . . didn't make the smallest bones about saying so. **1932** HBurnham *Telltale* (NY) 111: Chiquita made no bones of the fact. **1936** ECRLorac *Crime* (L) 85: We made no bones about it. **1940** CBush *Climbing Rat* (L) 218: He . . . made no bones . . . about going back. **1942** MGEberhart *Wolf* (NY) 128: I'm an old maid and make no bones about it. **1951** JCollier *Fancies* (NY) 52: I'd make no bones about going upstairs. **1956** *BangorDN* 8/28 1: All concerned made no bones of the fact. **1959** DMarkson *Epitaph* (NY) 95: I didn't make any bones about the kind of life Cathy had been leading. **1962** JLindsay *Fanfrolico* (L) 135: She made no bones about going with others. **1968** RWClark *JBS* (NY) 118: She made no bones about her feelings. **1971** JPope-Hennessy *Trollope* (B) 18: Trollope made no bones about his moralistic aims. **1974** MMcCarthy *Mask* (NY) 47: He was making no bones about his willingness. EAP B260; Brunvand 14(2).

B346 What is bred in the **Bone** will not out of the flesh (*varied*)

1906 JCLincoln *Mr. Pratt* (NY) 241: A proverb . . . concerning what is bred in the bone. **1908** WHHudson *Land's End* (L) 151: It's in the bone, and we can't help it. **1922** JJoyce *Ulysses* (NY 1934) 21: What's bred in the bone cannot fail me to fly. 634: What's bred in the bone. **1924** HHBashford *Augustus* (L 1966) 193: For what is bred in the bone could never be cast down. **1927** ELWhite *Lukundoo* (NY) 26: What's soaked into the bone won't come out of the flesh, any more than what's bred there. **1931** LCArlington *Through* (L) 47: It is so bred in the bone that it is difficult to eradicate. **1937** GGoodwin *White Farm* (L) 250: What's born in the bone is out in the blood. **1958** ECRLorac *People* (NY) 75: What's bred in the bone comes out in the blood. **1959** NMarsh *False* (B) 162: What's bred in the child comes out in the woman. **1969** EInglis-Jones *Augustus* (L) 179: What's bred in the bone . . . nothing will ever eradicate. **1981** AAndrews *Pig* (NY) 96: What's bred

in the bone will out in the flesh. EAP B262; TW 37(5); Brunvand 14(3).

B347 To throw one's **Bonnet** (cap, hat) over the windmill (*varied*)

1929 HFergusson *In Those Days* (NY) 147: It was also whispered that she had thrown her hat over the windmill. **1930** AGilbert *Mystery* (NY) 238: Refuse to throw her cap wholly over the windmill. **1934** DLSayers *Nine Taylors* (NY) 176: Suzanne had already thrown her bonnet over the windmill [*taken a lover*]. **1937** CDickson *Ten Teacups* (L) 96: She is the last woman in the world who would throw her bonnet over the windmill [*commit adultery*]. **1938** AGlanville *Body* (L) 253: I can't go chucking my bonnet over the windmills [*do anything unconventional*]. **1938** RAJWalling *Coroner* (L) 54: Looks as if she'd thrown her hat over the house [*eloped with another man—adultery*]. **1941** HReilly *Three Women* (NY) 264: Irene had thrown her cap over the windmill [*adultery*]. **1950** SJepson *Hungry* (NY) 161: To throw his hat over the nearest windmill [*marry without parental consent*]. **1951** JSStrange *Reasonable* (NY) 163: But she'd be careful. That's her nature. No throwing her bonnet over the wall. **1952** DBOlsen *Enrollment* (NY) 52: "But she's much too sensible to toss her bonnet over the windmill." "That expression sounds out of date." "Probably it is. I think my grandmother used to be fond of it. It made naughtiness sound sort of genteel." **1958** JSStrange *Night* (NY) 141: Celia was no girl to throw her cap over the windmill. **1959** AGilbert *Prelude* (NY DBC) 17: I would have to throw my heart over a windmill. **1962** AWaugh *Early* (L) 183: A flinging of many bonnets over windmills [*being seduced*]. **1965** HWaugh *Girl* (NY) 205: The little lady you tossed your cap over the windmill for. **1969** LHellman *Unfinished* (NY) 224: That was very hat-over-the-windmill stuff in a sick lady of seventy-four [*D.Parker not cashing checks when hard up*]. **1973** AWest *Mortal* (NY) 191: She could afford to throw her bonnet over the windmill. **1975** HLawrenson *Stranger* (NY) 138: Tossing my bonnet over the windmill [*refusing a good job*]. **1979** CMacLeod *Luck* (NY) 61: Wouldn't she, figuratively speaking, have thrown her mohair stole over the windmill and gone? [*off in the dark with a man*]. Cf. Broom(stick) *below.*

B348 Not to say **Boo**

1930 WLewis *Apes* (NY 1932) 249: Otherwise he certainly could not say Bo. **1959** DMDisney *Did She Fall* (NY) 24: He didn't dare say boo without consulting his uncle. TW 37(1).

B349 Not to say **Boo** to a goose (*varied*)

1905 JBCabell *Line* (NY 1926) 219: A lisping lad that cannot boo at a goose. **1908** JCLincoln *Cy Whittaker* (NY) 29: He don't dast say "boo" to a chicken. **1921** CTorr *Small Talk 2nd Series* (Cambridge, Eng.) 52: I have heard her say Bo to a goose. **1934** PGWodehouse *Brinkley* (B) 197: The sort of chap who can't say "boo" to a goose. **1939** HCBailey *Great Game* (L) 51: I always say bo to a goose. **1939** EHuxley *African Poison* (NY) 8: Say boo to a wild goose. **1940** CE Vulliamy *Calico Pie* (L) 69: I doubt if you will now find . . . a clergyman who dares to say bo! to the meekest of his parochial geese. **1941** CRice *Trial by Fury* (NY 1957) 17: Before anyone can say "Boo." **1950** ER Punshon *So Many* (NY) 57: A timid little thing you would hardly think dare say "Boo" to a goose. **1956** *Punch* 10/10 419: No boo to a Goose-step. **1958** JByrom *Or Be* (L 1964) 57: You wouldn't think an old man like me had ever been capable of saying boo to a goose. **1961** PGWodehouse *Ice* (NY) 102: Just a rabbit who couldn't say "Boo!" to a goose. **1970** PMoyes *Many* (NY) 1: She would not venture to say "Boo" to a sparrow, let alone a goose. **1970** JPorter *Dover Strikes* (NY) 143: [She] wouldn't say boo to a gander. **1975** SJPerelman *Vinegar* (NY) 61: Before you could say "bo" to a goose. **1980** CHough *Bassington* (NY) 115: You couldn't say boo to a mouse. TW 37(2); *Oxford* 701: Say bo.

B350 As clear as a **Book**

1932 MBurton *Death* (L) 67: Clear as a book. Wilstach 56: Open book.

B351 Never judge a **Book** by its cover

1946 ERolfe *Murder . . . Glass Room* (NY 1948) 10: You can never tell a book by its

cover. **1954** HGardiner *Murder* (L) 105: Never judge a book by its cover. **1959** SSterling *Body* (NY) 165: You can't tell a book by its cover. **1965** SForbes *Relative* (NY) 107: Never judge a book by its cover. **1968** ERHutchinson *Tropic* (NY) 17: The old saying, "You can't tell a book by its cover." **1973** AGilbert *Nice* (NY) 155: Never judge a book by its cover—don't they say that? Cf. Appearances *above.*

B352 To be in someone's black (bad) **Books**

1920 AChristie *Mysterious Affair* (NY) 181: I am in her black books. **1931** JSFletcher *Malvery* (L) 194: You're in his black books. **1966** MErskine *Family* (NY) 50: You are in her bad books. EAP B264.

B353 To know someone (something) like a **Book**

1924 WBMFerguson *Black* (NY) 277: I know you like a book. **1925** BAtkey *Pyramid* (NY) 186: He knows it like a book. **1933** WBlair *Mike Fink* (NY) 46: He knows the river like a book. **1939** GBagby *Bind* (NY) 74: I know her like a book. **1947** FCrane *Murder on* (NY) 57: I know him like a book. **1951** DFontaine *Sugar* (NY) 122: I know myself like a book. **1972** HPentecost *Champagne* (NY) 103: We know you like a book. TW 37(4); Brunvand 14.

B354 To read someone (something) like a **Book**

1909 MRRinehart *Man in Lower Ten* (NY 1947) 314: The kind of girl you . . . can read like a book. **1912** ERBurroughs *Princess of Mars* (NY 1963) 97: I could read his thoughts as if they were an open book. **1919** JBCabell *Jurgen* (NY 1922) 355: I can read you like a book. **1936** CBush *Monday Murders* (L) 40: I can read your mind like a book. **1941** GBagby *Red Is* (NY) 15: He can read it [*a corpse*] like a book. **1956** RMacdonald *Barbarous* (NY) 125: I can read him like a book. **1959** JJMarric *Gideon's Staff* (NY) 69: You can really read me like a book. **1968** RDuncan *How to Make* (L) 283: She could read me like a book. **1971** JFraser *Death* (NY) 91: Whose face he could read like an open book. TW 37(6).

B355   To suit someone's **Book**

1922 JJoyce *Ulysses* (NY 1934) 502: That suits your book. **1927** VWilliams *Eye* (B) 188: That would suit your book. **1937** HCBailey *Clunk's* (L) 27: It suited his book. **1958** NBlake *Penknife* (L) 187: It suited my book. **1972** SBrooke *Queen* (NY) 139: This suited his book very well. Partridge 79.

B356   To talk (lie) like a **Book**

1936 GCollins *Haven* (L) 319: He does talk rather like a book. **1940** NMarsh *Death of a Peer* (B) 190: She may have lied like a book. **1955** VNabokov *Lolita* (Paris) I 152: You talk like a book. **1958** ESchiddel *Devil* (NY) 202: You talk like a book. EAP B266.

B357   To throw the **Book** at someone

1942 GHCoxe *Silent* (NY) 231: The judge would've thrown the book at you. **1952** AA Fair *Top* (NY) 45: He'll have the book thrown at him. **1957** *BangorDN* 4/3 16: They "threw the book"—the Constitution— at the President. **1959** RMacdonald *Galton* (NY) 205: They'll throw the book at me. **1961** JWelcome *Beware* (L) 24: They threw the book at me. **1973** EJBurford *Queen* (L) 39: In modern police parlance, "they threw the whole book at her." Wentworth 544.

B358   To lower the **Boom** on someone

1957 ESGardner *Screaming* (NY) 152: I can lower the boom on you any time. **1962** ES Gardner *Blonde* (NY DBC) 163: Any time he chooses to lower the boom. Wentworth 327.

B359   As black (brown) as a **Boot**

1927 VBridges *Girl* (P) 66: You're as brown as a boot. **1937** WGore *Murder Most* (L) 1964: Mac's as black as a boot. **1968** PDickinson *Skin* (L) 46: His face was as black as a boot. **1971** MErskine *Brood* (NY) 54: Black as an old boot. Brunvand 14(1).

B360   As tough (stiff) as old **Boots**

1944 CBrand *Green for Danger* (B 1965) 81: I'm as tough as old boots. **1953** MMKaye *Death Walked* (L) 39: I'm as stiff as an old boot. **1959** EHuxley *Flame* (L) 62: She . . . is probably as tough as old boots. **1958** CLBlackstone *Foggy* (NY) 138: Tough as old boots. **1961** ALee *Miss Hogg* (L) 100:

The steak is as tough as an old boot. **1961** JWelcome *Beware* (L) 56: You are as tough as old boots. **1969** ELathen *When* (NY) 148: Everett had always been as tough as old boots. **1970** RCowper *Twilight* (NY) 175: He's tough as old boots. **1978** JCash *Gold* (NY) 77: He's tough as old boots. NED Boot *sb.*[3] 1b (quote 1870).

B361   The **Boot** (shoe) was on the other leg (foot) (*varied*)

1909 JCLincoln *Keziah* (NY) 86: The boot was on the other leg. **1923** ABlackwood *Episodes* (L) 152: The boot was on the other leg. **1928** AYoung *On My Way* (NY) 258: The shoe is on the other foot. **1928** ABerkeley *Silk* (NY) 44: The boot is on the other foot. **1930** FDBurdett *Odyssey* (L) 31: It was a case of putting the shoe on the other foot with a vengeance. **1932** RAJWalling *Fatal* (NY) 273: Put the boot on the other leg. **1933** BReynolds *Very Private* (NY) 21: The boot—to be really elegant—is on the other leg. **1933** HHolt *Gallows* (L) 36: The shoe's on the other foot. **1934** SHonler *Prince* (B) 65: It was more likely for the boot to be on the other foot. **1941** CLClifford *While the Bells* (NY) 34: She put the shoe on the other foot. **1950** MGEberhart *Hunt* (NY) 184: The shoe was on the other foot. **1951** A Christie *They Came* (NY) 178: The boot is on the other leg. **1954** OAnderson *Thorn* (L) 196: The boot is now on the other foot, as the saying goes. **1956** *BangorDN* 6/21 14: You boys from Mississippi should recollect when the shoe was on the other foot. **1957** *Punch* 9/11 305: The boot would be on the other foot. **1958** *NYTimes* 1/12 10E: The shoe is on the other foot. **1960** HSDavies *Papers* (L) 39: The boot was on the other foot. **1962** DMDisney *Find* (NY DBC) 97: The shoe would have been on the other foot. **1963** BWAldiss *Airs* (L) 132: The boot's on the other foot by a long chalk. **1968** DSkirrow *I Was* (NY) 224: The boot was . . . on another, cleaner foot. **1970** RDAltick *Victorian* (NY) 229: The shoe was on the other foot. **1973** AMorice *Death* (NY) 30: That boot's on the other foot. **1975** ABrodsky *Madame* (NY) 133: The slipper was now on the other foot. EAP B267; Brunvand 126(2): Shoe on the wrong foot.

B362   To be too big for one's **Boots**

1929 JBPriestley *Good* (NY) 13: He's got too big for his boots. **1937** MAllingham *Late Pig* (L 1940) 133: Getting too big for his boots. **1940** ELWhite *While She* (NY) 37: She's lazy and too big for her boots. **1950** ECRLorac *Accident* (NY DBC) 87: A bit too big for their boots. **1957** *Time* 4/1 22: Nasser was getting too big for its boots. **1961** JBPriestley *Thirty-first* (L) 16: Too big for his boots. **1969** DClark *Nobody's* (NY) 1: Masters had grown too big for his boots. **1972** JSymons *Players* (NY) 11: Somebody is getting too big for his boots. **1974** BWAldiss *Eighty* (NY) 22: [She] is getting too precocious for her own boots. TW 38(9). Cf. Breeches *below.*

B363   To bet one's **Boots**

1922 JJoyce *Ulysses* (NY 1934) 418: Bet your boots on. **1923** HGartland *Globe* (NY) 186: You can bet your boots. **1939** GDHCole *Off with* (NY) 27: You bet your boots he doesn't. **1952** HReilly *Velvet* (NY) 174: You can bet your boots. **1974** JMcClure *Caterpillar* (NY) 216: You can bet your boots. TW 38(6).

B364   To die with one's **Boots** on

1946 ESedgwick *Happy* (B) 201: She meant to die with her boots on. **1961** GFowler *Skyline* (NY) 160: Most of them had died with their boots on, as the saying was. **1965** JTurner *Blue* (L 1967) 112: Die . . . with both boots on. Cf. DARE i 339: Boot hill; Partridge 81: In one's.

B365   To give the (order of) the **Boot**

1922 JJoyce *Ulysses* (NY 1934) 309: Joe Cuffe gave him the order of the boot. **1933** VLoder *Suspicion* (L) 134: She gave French the boot. Partridge 80.

B366   To lie like old **Boots**

1922 JJoyce *Ulysses* (NY 1934) 619: He could . . . lie like old boots. Partridge 81.

B367   To pull oneself up by his **Bootstraps** (bootlaces)

1922 JJoyce *Ulysses* (NY 1934) 630: Others who had forced their way to the top . . . by the aid of their bootstraps. **1932** HFAnhurst *Diary* (Tucson 1962) 312: An attempt to lift ourselves by our own bootstraps. **1943** MRRinehart *Episode* (NY) 26: He had pulled himself up by his bootstraps. **1948** ESherry *Sudden* (NY) 26: This nobody who had pulled himself up by his own bootstraps. **1950** DMathews *Mango* (L) 207: There was a degrading element in all slang . . . to pull oneself up by one's bootstraps. **1956** SWTaylor *I Have* (NY) 127: Pulling themselves up by their boot straps. **1957** *NYTimes Book Review* 5/5 6: Jackson would have pulled himself up a long way by his bootstraps. **1957** *TLS* 11/8 677: Linguistics hauls itself up by its own bootlaces. **1958** MCair *Burning* (NY) 179: You can kind of pull yourself up by your bootlaces. **1962** AMStein *Home* (NY) 178: Pulling themselves up by their bootstraps. **1967** SMorrow *Insiders* (NY) 140: The up-by-your-own-bootstraps philosophy. **1970** RCowper *Twilight* (NY) 74: The cliché . . . about pulling ourselves up by our own bootstraps. **1974** WBridges *Gathering* (NY) 465: Lifting a handicapped aquarium by its boot straps. Brunvand 14.

B368   As sure as one was **Born**

1906 JCLincoln *Mr. Pratt* (NY) 173: Sure's you're born. **1920** GBMcCutcheon *Anderson Crow* (NY) 4: Sure as you're born. **1934** JGBrandon *Murder* (L) 72: Sure as you're born. **1947** HLawrence *Death of* (NY) 51: Sure's you're born. **1959** HWaugh *Sleep* (NY) 153: As sure as I'm born. EAP B273; Brunvand 14(1).

B369   Better to be **Born** lucky than (whatever) (*varied*)

1932 CAndrews *Butterfly* (NY) 75: It's a far better thing to be born lucky than with brains. **1934** JGBrandon *Murder* (L) 279: It bears out what I've always said—that it's better to be born lucky than beautiful. **1937** GDilnot *Murder* (L) 178: It's better to be born lucky than clever. **1956** DWheatley *Ka* (L) 220: They say that it is better to be born lucky than rich. **1963** JNHarris *Weird* (NY DBC) 91: I've always heard that it's better to be born lucky than rich. **1969** RHofstadter *Idea* (Berkeley) 182: If one is lucky enough, it is better to be lucky than clever. EAP B275.

B370 He that is **Born** to be hanged will never be drowned (*varied*)

1926 Anonymous *Great American Ass* (NY) 202: Howe was born to be hanged and nothing else would kill him. **1928** JGoodwin *When Dead* (NY) 129: I knew ye were never born to be drooned. **1931** EWallace *Devil* (L) 38: A man who's born to be hung can never be drowned. 246: An old saying and a true one—a man who is born to be hanged will never be drowned. **1932** DSharp *Code-Letter* (B) 59: Orford might be one of those persons known to proverbial philosophy, who, having been born to be hanged, cannot be killed by any other method. **1932** BABotkin ed *Land Is Ours* (Norman, Okla.) 265: Given a man borned to be drowned can't be hung. **1950** JChristopher *Death* (L 1958) 10: It looks like you were born for a hanging [*had escaped drowning*]. **1952** DWecter *Sam Clemens* (B) 58: People who are born to be hanged are safe in the water. **1958** PDWestbrook *Biography* (NY) 160: After a narrow escape a fisherman will say: "A man who is being saved to be hanged won't drown." **1971** DFJones *Denver* (NY) 51: One can only assume . . . you're destined to be hanged [*he had escaped drowning*]. EAP B276.

B371 If you never go to **Boston** you'll die a fool

1950 FFGould *Maine Man* (NY) 182: "If you never go to Boston you'll die a fool," is one of the maxims that is part of the education of a State-of-Mainer.

B372 To scrape the **Bottom** of the barrel

1958 NBlake *Penknife* (L) 148: [He's] scraping the bottom of the barrel. **1960** DHolman-Hunt *My Grandmothers* (L) 71: That would be scraping the bottom of the bin. **1962** EFRussell *Great* (NY) 97: When they inducted you two dopes, they were scraping the bottom of the barrel. Wentworth 450: Scrape.

B373 The bent **Bow** must be unstrung

1967 OLancaster *With an Eye* (L) 16: You know . . . that the bent bow must be unstrung. EAP B287.

B374 To draw a **Bow** at a venture (*varied*)

1903 EChilders *Riddle* (NY 1940) 310: This was drawing a bow at a venture. **1914** PJBrebner *Christopher* (NY) 99: A bow drawn at a venture. **1929** AGilbert *Death* (NY) 276: That had been a bolt drawn at a venture. **1930** EWoodward *House* (NY) 34: A shot at a venture. **1930** AWynne *Room* (P) 97: Dr. Haley drew a venturesome bow. **1934** HReilly *McKee* (NY) 172: He drew a bow at a venture and hit the bull's-eye. **1946** GBellairs *Death in the Night* (NY) 169: He drew a bow at a venture. **1947** AGilbert *Death in* (L) 167: Bill drew a bow at a venture. **1951** MColes *Now* (NY) 184: That was an arrow at a venture, but it sank to the feather. **1954** ECRLorac *Shroud* (NY) 167: Drawing a bow at a venture. **1955** MInnes *Man from* (L) 204: This was a bow drawn decidedly at a venture. **1960** NFitzgerald *Candles* (L) 66: Russell drew his bow at a venture. **1961** AGilbert *After* (NY DBC) 7: He saw his bow at a venture had found an unexpected target. **1974** MButterworth *Villa* (NY) 172: I was, as you [*English*] say, drawing a bow at a venture. EAP B289.

B375 To draw the (a) long **Bow** (*varied*)

1900 CFPidgin *Quincy A. Sawyer* (B) 256: Abner often drew the long bow. **1903** HGarland *Companions on the Trail* (NY 1931) 205: Pulling a long bow. **1904** HGarland *Companions* (NY 1931) 224: He pulls too long a bow. **1917** GRSims *My Life* (L) 220: Drawing the long bow. **1922** JJoyce *Ulysses* (NY 1934) 620: [It] would tempt any ancient mariner to draw the long bow. **1926** Anonymous *Great American Ass* (NY) 310: Charlestonian drawers-of-the-long-bow. **1930** SEMorison *Builders* (B) 8: Stretching the long bow was an old English custom. **1934** VGielgud *Death* (L) 130: Drawing the long bow of coincidence a bit too far. **1967** MErskine *Case with* (NY) 52: You're drawing a pretty long bow. EAP B290.

B376 As taut as a **Bowstring** (arrow, drawn bow)

1939 DBOlsen *Death Cuts* (NY) 17: Margaret, taut as a drawn bow. **1941** IMontgomery *Death Won* (NY) 127: Julie stood taut as an arrow. **1941** IMontgomery *Death Won* (NY) 143: Slim, taut as a bowstring. **1947** PWentworth *Wicked* (NY) 254: [Nerves] as taut as bowstrings. **1956** LBrackett *Tiger* (NY) 121: My insides were tight as a bowstring. **1959** PMacDonald *List* (NY) 17: You're taut as a bow-string. **1961** HNielsen *Sing Me* (NY DBC) 152: Alex's nerves as taut as a bowstring. **1971** DCWilson *Big-Little* (NY) 3: Taut as a bowstring. Cf. EAP B293; Wilstach 416: Fiddle-string.

B377 To be in a **Box** (*varied*)

1929 JJConnington *Case* (B) 7: I'm in a worse box. **1929** HFootner *Doctor* (L) 134: We had him in a box. **1930** DDeane *Mystery* (L) 23: You and me's in the same box. **1936** MBurton *Where Is* (L) 228: We're both in the same box. **1954** JRMacdonald *Find* (NY) 195: You're in a box. **1965** MGEberhart *R.S.V.P.* (NY) 29: You're in rather a box. EAP B294–5.

B378 As busy (happy) as a **Boy** killing snakes

1939 VHansom *Casual* (NY) 143: I'll be as busy as a boy killing snakes. **1939** JJones *Murder al Fresco* (NY) 81: They were as happy as a boy killing snakes. Wilstach 40.

B379 **Boys** will be boys

1922 JJoyce *Ulysses* (NY 1934) 341: Boys will be boys. **1924** WBMFerguson *Black* (NY) 212: Boys will be boys. **1931** WFaulkner *Sanctuary* (NY) 248: Boys will be boys. **1937** VGielgud *Death in Budapest* (L) 177: Boys will be boys. **1940** NBlake *Malice* (L) 44: The boys-will-be-boys attitude. **1951** KFarrell *Mistletoe* (L) 42: Boys will be boys. **1955** PDennis *Auntie* (NY) 166: Boys will be boys, like the fella says. **1960** FPohl *Drunkard's* (NY) 92: Boys will be boys. **1968** EWilliams *Beyond* (NY) 104: Kids will be kids. **1973** AMStein *Finger* (NY) 128: Boys will be boys. TW 40(4); Brunvand 15(2); *Oxford* 79. Cf. Girls, People *below*.

B380 To be the blue-eyed **Boy**

1930 ABCox *Second* (NY) 256: She looks on you as her own blue-eyed boy. **1937** MBurton *Clue* (NY) 229: The judge had treated him like his own blue-eyed boy. **1941** AChristie *Evil under* (NY) 178: Her own blue-eyed boy. **1953** JRhode *Mysterious* (NY DBC) 10: Hilary has always been his daddy's blue-eyed baby. **1956** RLongrigg *High-pitched* (L) 26: I', everybody's blue-eyed boy just now. **1961** SClayton *Crystal* (L) 138: You must be a blue-eyed boy. That never happened to me. **1964** RBlythe *Age* (B) 39: Goddard was the bluest-eyed boy in the vice squad. **1970** DMDevine *Illegal* (NY) 6: The blue-eyed boy, the paragon. **1972** RMaugham *Escape* (L) 182: The blue-eyed boy of the Foreign Office. Wentworth 47.

B381 To be the fair-haired **Boy**

1928 EDBiggers *Behind* (NY) 148: I'm the fair-haired boy. **1940** RDarby *Death Conducts* (NY) 36: There goes your fair-haired boy. **1954** JTey *Shilling* (NY) 168: He's the prior's fair-haired boy at the moment. **1955** LWhite *To Find* (NY) 104: I'll be the fair-haired boy all over again. **1960** EWolf *Rosenbach* (Cleveland) 56: The fair-haired boy of the family. Wentworth 176.

B382 To be the golden-haired **Boy**

1935 BThomson *Richardson Solves* (L) 209: Peter . . . was her golden-haired boy. **1940** HSKeeler *Crimson Box* (L) 36: He's the golden-haired boy. **1968** ASilitoe *Guzman* (L) 125: The gaffer's golden-haired boy. Wentworth 176: Fair-haired.

B383 To be the white-haired **Boy**

1924 HCBailey *Mr. Fortune's Practice* (NY) 43: His mother's white-haired boy. **1938** ECRLorac *John Brown's* (L) 20: His white-haired boy. **1954** LFord *Invitation* (NY) 152: I'd been Art's white-haired boy. **1954** EQueen *Bureau* (B) 107: The whitehaired boy of Center Street. **1962** FCrane *Amber* (NY) 146: He's the white-haired boy around here. **1963** EVCunningham *Alice* (L 1965) 52: Mr. Montez's white-haired number-one boy. **1974** WSnow *Codline* (Middletown, Conn.) 91: The white-haired boy of the intellectual world. Wentworth 576.

B384 To be the white-headed **Boy**

1931 VWilliams *Masks* (L) 68: I'm not precisely the white-headed boy round here. **1935** *New Yorker* 11/2 80: Red Russia's white-headed boy novelist. **1938** JSStrange *Silent* (NY) 5: The white-headed boy on whom fortune smiled. **1940** GDHCole *Murder at* (NY) 32: He's her white-headed boy. **1947** VWBrooks *Times of Melville* (NY) 27: The white-headed boy of the new generation. **1958** JByrom *Or Be* (L 1964) 11: The white-headed boy of the party. *Oxford* 884–5; Wentworth 576.

B385 To send a **Boy** to do a man's work (*varied*)

1931 GFowler *Great* (NY) 176: The People shouldn't send boys on men's errands. **1932** CDawes *Lawless* (L) 50: They sent a boy to do a man's work. **1938** RTorrey *42 Days* (NY) 261: Why fool around and expect a boy to do a man's work. **1941** TChanslor *Our Second* (NY) 299: Never send a boy to do a man's work. **1948** DCDisney *Explosion* (NY DBC) 15: Hunted up a boy to do a man's work. **1951** LLariar *You Can't* (NY) 18: Do you send a boy out on a man's job? **1956** *Time* 12/10 56: They had sent a boy on a man's errand. **1958** DRMcCoy *Angry* (Lawrence, Kan.) 7: The League was akin to the proverbial boy sent to do a man's job. **1971** ADavidson *Peregrine* (NY) 128: Well . . . set a boy to do a man's job, if you want a thing done right do it yourself. **1971** WTeller *Cape Cod* (Englewood Cliffs, NJ) 42: The electric heater turned out to be a boy trying to do a man's job.

B386 **Brag** is a good dog, but Holdfast is better

1937 RWWinston *It's a Far Cry* (NY) 276: To quote a Southern saying, "Brag is a good dog, but Holdfast is better." **1967** JFDobie *Some Part* (B) 95: An old proverb: "Brag's a good dog, but Hold Fast is a better." *Oxford* 80.

B387 An idle **Brain** is the devil's workshop

1930 EDBiggers *Charlie* (NY 1943) 261: An idle brain is the devil's workshop. **1971** JBlake *Joint* (NY) 234: An idle workshop is the devil's mind. Whiting *NC* 374; *Oxford* 395: Idle.

B388 As bold (confident) as **Brass**

1910 EPhillpotts *Tales* (NY) 67: As bold as brass. **1922** JJoyce *Ulysses* (NY 1934) 349: As bold as brass. **1932** HCBailey *Mr. Fortune, Please* (NY) 29: As bold as brass; 55.

1939 MStuart *Dead Men* (L) 84: Those bold-as-brass fellows. **1957** *BHerald* 9/23 27: Just as bold as brass. **1961** EPeters *Death* (NY) 25: A voice . . . confident as brass. **1963** HWaugh *Prisoner's* (NY DBC) 176: He talked to her, bold as brass. **1968** JJMarric *Gideon's Ride* (NY) 97: She's . . . as bold as brass. **1976** JSScott *Poor* (NY) 101: Bold as brass. TW 41.

B389 As brazen as **Brass**

1946 GBellairs *Death in the Night* (NY) 193: And says Bartlett, as brazen as brass. Whiting *NC* 374(2).

B390 As cool as **Brass**

1935 ECRLorac *Murder* (L) 275: As cool as brass. **1952** ECRLorac *Dog* (NY) 148: Cool as brass. **1954** CCarnac *Policeman* (NY) 76: Walked out . . . cool as brass.

B391 As hard as **Brass**

1922 JJoyce *Ulysses* (NY 1934) 624: The biscuits was as hard as brass. Whiting B511.

B392 To double in **Brass**

1954 DAlexander *Terror* (NY) 7: A character who doubled in brass. **1965** ALogan *Man who Robbed* (NY) 227: Many of its editors doubled in brass. **1967** RFenisong *Villainous* (NY) 139: In a pinch might be willing to double in brass. Wentworth 158.

B393 To get down to **Brass** tacks (*varied*)

1912 JCLincoln *Postmaster* (NY) 34: Get down to brass tacks. **1913** JLondon *Letters* ed KHendricks (NY 1965) 412: Getting down to brass tacks. **1917** JCLincoln *Extricating* (NY) 325: Gettin' down to tacks. **1927** HFAnhurst *Diary* ed GFSparks (Tucson 1962) 252: Our realistic, brass-tack world. **1930** VLoder *Shop* (L) 147: To get down to tin tacks. **1934** RKing *Lesser Antilles* (NY) 178: Get down to the well-known brass tacks. **1938** VLoder *Wolf* (L) 56: When they got down to tin-tacks. **1945** EPhillpotts *They Were Seven* (NY) 271: Now we'll come to brass tacks, as they say. **1948** CBush *Curious* (NY) 22: To get down to brass tacks, as they say. **1957** *BHerald* 7/14 9: Let's get down to brass talks. **1959** NMarsh *False* (B) 240: Get down to tin-tacks (*why tin-tacks, one wonders?*). **1969** TBesterman *Voltaire* (NY) 270:

Voltaire . . . got down to brass tacks. **1975** ELathen *By Hook* (NY) 87: Get down to brass tacks. Wentworth 61.

B394   To part Brass rags
1930 FDGrierson *Mysterious* (L) 124: No reason why we should part brass rags. **1938** NBlake *Beast* (NY 1958) 165: She and George had parted brass-rags. **1955** NMarsh *Scales* (B) 262: "We parted brass rags." "You had a row about it?" **1961** PGWodehouse *Ice* (L) 158: Have you really parted brass rags? *American Speech* 51(1979) 44; Partridge 607: Part.

B395   As good as Bread
1956 *NYTimes Book Review* 12/9 1: Good as bread [*a boy*]. Wilstach 183. Cf. Wheat *below*.

B396   Bread is the staff of life
1913 HTFinck *Food* (NY) 286: Bread is regarded as the staff of life. **1937** WGore *Murder Most* (L) 139: You know quite well that bread is the staff of life. **1968** JGFuller *Day* (NY) 7: Bread in France is more than the staff of life. **1971** WHMarnell *Once Upon* (NY) 104: Bread was indeed the staff of life. EAP B301; Brunvand 133: Staff.

B397   To be one's Bread and butter
1929 BFlynn *Billiard* (P) 226: My job—my bread and butter depends on it. **1931** HAdams *Paulton* (P) 103: I had my bread and butter to earn. **1942** ABMaurice *Riddle* (NY) 202: The job's my bread and butter. **1957** MPHood *In the Dark* (NY) 31: Ain't none of our bread 'n butter what Crie's doing. **1959** EHNisot *Sleepless* (NY) 12: We've all got our bread and butter to earn. **1961** FSinclair *But the Patient* (NY) 99: To earn our bread and butter. **1964** NFreeling *Because* (NY 1965) 177: I'm a policeman; whores are my bread and butter. **1974** CBerkin *Sewall* (NY) 17: The bread and butter of a colonial legal practice. Cf. EAP B310.

B398   To butter one's Bread on both sides
1930 DFrome *In at the Death* (NY) 222: He tried to butter his bread on both sides. EAP B307.

B399   To cast one's Bread upon the waters
1925 RAFreeman *Red Thumb* (L) 2: Thrown up . . . like the proverbial bread cast upon the waters. **1936** ECRLorac *Crime* (L) 28: I cast my bread upon the waters. **1937** ECRLorac *Bats* (L) 40: It might be bread cast upon the waters. **1957** *Punch* 9/4 269: She may be casting her bread upon swine. **1957** CRice *Knocked* (NY) 29: It wasn't always true that bread cast upon the waters came back all wet. Brunvand 15–16(3).

B400   To have one's Bread fall butter down
1929 AGray *Dead* (L) 189: Didn't her bread and butter *always* fall butter downwards? **1972** PDJames *Unsuitable* (NY) 10: The bread he dropped invariably fell buttered side downward. TW 41(4).

B401   To quarrel with one's Bread and butter
1928 CDane *Enter* (L) 249: He's no fool to quarrel with his bread and butter. **1932** AWynne *Green Knife* (P) 235: He's not the man to quarrel with his bread and butter. **1938** HAdams *Damned* (L) 87: He could not afford to quarrel with his bread and butter. **1955** CMWills *Death* (L) 180: No good quarreling with your bread and butter. **1956** HReilly (NY 1959) 56: It was his bread and butter and he had no quarrel with it. **1957** *New Yorker* 4/13 40: Who am I to argue with our bread and butter? EAP B311.

B402   To take the Bread out of one's mouth
1939 TPolsky *Curtains* (NY) 110: He tries to take the bread right out of my mouth. EAP B309.

B403   Sing before Breakfast, cry before night (*varied*)
1935 LFord *Burn* (NY) 133: Whistle afore breakfast, cry afore supper. **1940** TChanslor *Our First* (NY) 168: "You remember the saying, 'Sing before breakfast—'" "Oh dear—'Cry before night.'" **1957** HPBeck *Folklore of Maine* (P) 67: Sing before breakfast, cry before noon. **1965** JSUntermeyer *Private* (NY) 127: Sing befo' breakfas', cry befo' night. Whiting *NC* 375; *Oxford* 736.

B404 To eat someone for **Breakfast**

1962 CWatson *Hopjoy* (NY) 118: [He] would have three of him for breakfast. **1964** DBagley *Golden* (NY) 199: He'd eat you for breakfast. **1968** ELathen *Stitch* (NY) 183: He could eat Edmund Knox for breakfast. **1968** JPorter *Dover Goes* (NY) 139: I could eat two of him before breakfast and never notice. **1973** BKnox *Storm* (NY) 102: Maggie . . . could eat you for breakfast. EAP B313.

B405 Save one's **Breath** to cool one's porridge (*varied*)

1919 RFirbank *Valmouth* (Works 3, L 1929) 107: I should keep my breath to cool my porridge. **1936** ECRLorac *Pall* (L) 215: Keep your breath to blaw your parritch. **1937** KMKnight *Seven* (NY) 209: You might's well save your breath to cool your porridge. **1940** TChanslor *Our First* (NY) 277: So save your breath to cool your porridge. **1944** FLockridge *Killing* (P) 37: Might have saved my breath to cool my porridge. **1949** KMKnight *Bass* (NY) 109: He'd better have saved his breath to cool his porridge. **1954** NBlake *Whisper* (L) 127: You might as well save your breath to cool your porridge. **1957** *New Yorker* 6/1 26: So I can keep my breath to cool my porridge. **1976** JPorter *Package* (NY) 97: Con was saving her breath to cool her porridge with. EAP B314.

B406 To waste one's **Breath**

1970 KLaumer *World* (NY) 61: You're wasting your wind. NED Waste *v.* 9d.

B407 To be too big (smart) for one's **Breeches** (pants, britches) (*varied*)

1931 WFaulkner *Sanctuary* (NY) 224: He gits too big for his pants right away. **1934** HCorey *Crime* (NY) 191: I got too big for my breeches. **1935** CRawson *Footprints* (L) 127: Someone has been too smart for his pants. **1939** IJones *Hungry Bear* (NY) 198: Got too big for his breeches. **1940** GBagby *Corpse Wore* (NY) 117: He's too smart for his pants. **1946** RFinnegan *Lying* (NY) 113: Just a little too smart for his britches. **1948** RFoley *No Tears* (NY DBC) 7: Grown too big for his pants. **1952** EGCarey *Jumping* (NY) 28: Even if you talk too big for your britches. **1955** LCochran *Hallelujah* (NY) 14: Got too big for my britches. **1962** MClifton *When They* (NY) 147: Scientists were getting too big for their britches. **1965** HBevington *Charley* (NY) 148: She was too big for her pants. **1969** CBaker *Ernest* (NY) 115: He decided . . . that Hemingway was too big for his breeches and needed taking down a peg or two. **1970** JVizzard *See* (NY) 227: The Legion getting too big for its pants. **1972** ARoudybush *Sybaritic* (NY) 50: You're getting mighty big for your britches. **1976** LEgan *Scenes* (NY) 38: These damn punks are gettin too big for their britches. TW 42(1); DARE i 383: Britches 2b. Cf. To be too big for one's Boots *above*.

B408 To take the **Breeches** off a Highlandman

1926 JBlaikie *Egyptian Papyri* (L) 292: There is an old Scotch proverb about taking the unmentionables off a Highlandman. **1956** *Time* 11/12 95: You canna tak the breeks off a Hielan' mon. Cf. *Oxford* 84.

B409 To wear the **Breeches** (pants, trousers) (*varied*)

1921 JBCabell *Figures* (NY 1925) 272: [I] have learned who it is that wears the breeches in most marriages. **1922** JJoyce *Ulysses* (NY 1934) 374: Wore the breeches. Suppose she does. **1928** JGoodwin *When Dead* (NY) 136: As long as Delia wears the breeks. **1930** ACampbell *Murder* (NY) 141: It is she who wears the trousers. **1931** AC Edington *Monk's Hood* (NY) 121: They [*women*] simply will not let us put on the pants. **1934** SPalmer *Silver Persian* (NY) 244: *I'm going to wear the trousers.* **1935** JTFarrell *Judgment* (NY) 13: Let his wife wear the pants for him. **1940** ELWhite *While She* (NY) 38: The major wore the trousers. **1945** HCBailey *Wrong Man* (NY) 139: "Which of the Afflocks wears the breeches?" . . . "I back her." **1953** AWUpfield *Murder Must* (NY) 185: In vulgar parlance, his wife wore the trousers. **1954** MBodenheim *My Life* (NY) 111: A domineering wife who "wore the pants." **1957** *NYTimes* 11/17 63: The feminine gender loves to wear pants, not THE pants, but panties. **1957** M-CRoberts *Little* (NY 1963) 171: My wife wears the pants. **1958** SBarr *Purely* (NY) 144: You have been wearing the trousers in this household. **1961** RA Heinlein *6XH* (NY) 177: Who wears the pants in your family? **1962** AGarve *Prisoner's* (NY DBC) 65: Mrs. Winter wore the trousers. **1964** AStratton *Great Red* (NY) 181: She wore the pants of her tribal family. **1972** DDevine *Three* (NY) 5: His wife wore the trousers. EAP B319; DARE i 383: Britches 2.

B410 To be a different **Breed** of cats (*varied*)

1906 JCLincoln *Mr. Pratt* (NY) 112: The Hartleys was another breed of cats. **1908** JCLincoln *Cy Whittaker* (NY) 4: Her ma was the same breed of cats. **1912** JCLincoln *Postmaster* (NY) 93: A different breed of cats. **1955** PDennis *Auntie* (NY) 207: They're a different breed of cats. **1957** *BHerald* 9/11 18: The ordinary Lake vessel and the seagoing ships are two different breed of cats. **1958** FLockridge *Long* (P) 30: Same breed—of cats. **1961** FLockridge *Drill* (P) 147: He and Grant are the same breed of cats. **1967** WTucker *Warlock* (NY) 55: [They] are a different breed of cats. **1971** TPace *Fisherman's* (NY) 39: There's a different breed of cats. **1971** PTabor *Pauline's* (Louisville) 52: A whore and a prostitute are two completely different breeds of pussycats. DARE i 376: Breed of cat; Berrey 17.2: Order.

B411 **Breed(ing)** will tell

1956 BWAldiss *Saliva* (L) 150: It just shows how breeding will tell. **1957** MPHood *In the Dark* (NY) 20: The breed always tells. Cf. *Oxford* 61: Birth. Cf. Blood will tell *above*.

B412 As free as the (a) **Breeze**

1954 THoward *Blood* (NY) 108: Free as the breeze. **1957** *Time* 7/1 64: Free as a breeze. Whiting *NC* 375(1). Cf. As free as the Wind *below*.

B413 As gentle as a **Breeze**

1955 ESGardner *Sun* (NY) 40: I'm gentle as a summer breeze. Whiting *NC* 375(2).

B414 Light as a **Breeze**

1964 HBourne *In the Event* (NY) 126: Jacky said, light as a breeze. Wilstach 233: Light.

B415 To run (go) like a **Breeze**

1940 HFootner *Murderer's* (NY) 194: Ran like a breeze [*a car*]. **1973** PMoyes *Curious* (NY) 167: It went like a breeze. Cf. Wentworth 62: Breeze.

B416 To shoot (fan) the **Breeze** (with someone)

1937 CCrow *Four Hundred* (NY) 162: While I was, as the saying goes, fanning the breeze with the farmer. **1945** PATaylor *Proof* (NY) 67: While you're busy shooting the breeze. **1947** GGallagher *I Found* (NY DBC) 95: You came down to shoot the breeze with me. **1958** JAHoward *Murder* (NY 1959) 15: We shot the breeze for quite a little while. **1961** BJames *Night* (NY DBC) 59: Shooting the breeze with Herman. **1976** EFoote-Smith *Gentle* (NY) 94: Chewing tobacco and shooting the breeze. Wentworth 178, 470.

B417 As one **Brews** so let him drink

1937 EForbes *Paradise* (NY) 29: Let him drink his own sour ale. He had brewed it! *Oxford* 85.

B418 As hard as a **Brick**

1900 CFPidgin *Quincy A. Sawyer* (B) 493: As hard as a brick. **1931** GDHCole *Dead Man's* (L) 104: An egg . . . as hard as a brick. EAP B322; Brunvand 16(2).

B419 As red as a **Brick**; Brick-red

1933 VWilliams *Fog* (B) 68: Her face was brick red. **1941** GEGiles *Three Died* (NY) 210: Maloney was brick red. **1961** CBlackstone *House* (L 1965) 16: His face as red as a brick. **1975** HPentecost *Time* (NY) 29: Brick-red hair. EAP B323.

B420 As square as a **Brick**

1913 JCLincoln *Mr. Pratt's Patients* (NY) 262: Square as a brick [*honest*]. TW 42(2).

B421 To drop a **Brick**

1928 EHamilton *Four* (L) 64: We should have you dropping some appalling brick. **1931** MDalton *Night* (NY) 83: Don't drop too many bricks. **1933** JCMasterman *Oxford* (L) 45: "What's your odd expression for making a mistake?" "Dropped a brick." **1956** *Punch* 7/25 85: It's certainly both when it comes to dropping bricks. **1962** EHuxley *Mottled* (L) 185: My fear of dropping social bricks. **1974** JCreasey *As Merry* (NY) 3: [He] appeared to have dropped a brick. Wentworth 163: Drop.

B422 To drop someone like a hot **Brick**

1927 OFJerome *Hand* (NY) 77: Drop him like a hot brick. **1934** GVerner *Con Man* (L) 240: He'd drop 'em [*girls*] like hot bricks. **1952** GKersh *Brazen* (L) 229: She dropped you like a hot brick. **1961** MColes *Search* (NY DBC) 134: They'd drop him like a hot brick. **1969** RPearsall *Worm* (L) 387: Payne . . . dropped him like a hot brick. **1972** HCarmichael *Naked* (NY) 148: I'll drop him like a hot brick. Cf. To drop . . . Chestnut, Coal, Potato *below.*

B423 To make **Bricks** without straw

1913 CPearl *Morrison of Peking* (Sydney 1967) 278: One cannot build bricks without straw. **1925** JICClarke *My Life* (NY) 216: The man to make bricks without straw. **1926** RAFreeman *Puzzle* (NY) 162: One of those craftsmen who can make bricks, not only without straw, but without clay. **1928** RGore-Browne *In Search* (NY) 213: It's only a straw . . . but it may help to make a brick. **1934** FWCrofts *12:30* (L) 328: "Can't make bricks without straw." . . . "Can't make them without clay, at all events." **1937** ERPunshon *Mystery* (NY) 51: Told him to make bricks without straw. **1947** NBlake *Minute* (L) 81: A classical case of bricks without straw. **1956** *Punch* 10/3 397: I was about to ask Liberace if he expected a profile-writer to make bricks without clay or a kiln, not to mention straw. **1961** WHLewis *Scandalous* (NY) 47: A case of making bricks without straw. **1962** HNGibson *Shakespeare* (L) 207: Titherley also attempts the feat of trying to make bricks not only without straw, but without clay as well. **1965** SWoods *Though I* (NY) 44: No one can make bricks without straw. **1970** DShannon *Unexpected* (NY) 19: It's part of the job to make bricks without straw. **1972** ELathen *Murder* (NY) 184: He had provided straw

enough for an experienced brick maker. EAP B324; Brunvand 16(3).

B424 Happy is the **Bride** that the sun shines on *etc.*

1926 PWentworth *Black Cabinet* (NY) 288: "Happy's the bride that the sun shines on," is how the proverb goes. **1930** WFClark *Shetland* (Edinburgh) 35: Happy is the bride that the sun shines on. **1931** JDBeresford *Innocent* (NY) 215: The sun shone on our wedding day, and if I had little faith in the old saw, I was thankful that we shouldn't have to go to church in the rain. **1932** TThayer *Three Sheet* (NY) 251: You know the old saying, Blessed are the dead that the rain falls on. **1942** HReilly *Name Your Poison* (NY) 4: Happy is the bride that the sun shines on. **1959** PCurtis *No Question* (NY) 39: Lucky is the bride whom the sun shines on. **1966** MFagyas *Widow* (NY) 57: Sun for the wedding, rain for the funeral. **1970** RRendell *Best Man* (NY) 12: Happy is the bride that the sun shines on. **1976** CLarson *Muir's* (NY) 138: "'Happy is the corpse that the sun shines on today.' My mother always said that." "Bride?" *Oxford* 85.

B425 Often a **Bridesmaid** but never a bride

1954 AWBarkley *That Reminds* (NY) 149: In any event, I had been often a bride's maid but never a bride, as the old saying goes. **1955** LCochran *Hallelujah* (NY) 73: Though she was often a bridesmaid she was never a bride. Cf. Brunvand 81: Maiden.

B426 One should not cross a **Bridge** until he gets to it (*varied*)

1926 JTully *Beggars* (NY) 225: We . . . worried about a bridge before we had crossed it. **1927** JCaine *Quayle's* (NY) 260: Why cross our bridges before we come to them? **1930** RAJWalling *Squeaky Voice* (NY) 20: We won't cross the river before we get there. **1937** JBentley *Landor* (L) 145: I refuse to cross any bridges before I come to them. **1941** KMKnight *Exit a Star* (NY) 231: We're crossing bridges that we may never come to. **1942** CRice *Big Midget* (NY 1948) 27: Never cross your bridges until the horse is stolen. **1953** KMKnight *Three* (NY) 86: Let us not cross any bridges till we come to them. **1959** *BHerald* 6/2 8: I don't cross bridges that I can't even see before I get to them. **1959** DMDouglass *Many* (L) 108: In the words of your Abraham Lincoln, we'll cross that bridge when we come to it. **1960** RWilson *30 Day* (NY) 19: We'll jump off that bridge when we come to it. **1965** RStout *Doorbell* (NY) 44: I would have to dive off that bridge when I came to it. **1969** SWilson *Away* (NY) 187: It was best not to cross these bridges until I found them burning under me. Whiting *NC* 375; *Oxford* 156: Cross. Cf. To jump a Fence *below*.

B427 To build someone a Golden **Bridge**

1932 VWilliams *Death* (B) 214: His Lordship builded him a Golden Bridge by giving a fistful of guineas to the catchpoll. **1954** HWRosenhaupt *True* (NY) 325: I just built him a golden bridge [*gave an excuse for action*]. EAP B325; TW 43(1).

B428 To burn one's **Bridges**

1923 ACrowley *Confessions* ed JSymonds (L 1969) 775: She wouldn't burn her bridges. **1924** TMundy *Om* (NY) 92: If I burn all my bridges. **1933** HDavis *Islands* (NY) 54: New bridges to burn. **1935** AHobhouse *Hangover* (NY) 128: You're burning your bridges before you come to them. **1939** RKing *Murder Masks* (NY) 169: "I've burned my bridge." "What bridge?" "I don't know. Just talking." **1957** MShulman *Rally* (NY) 233: Her bridges were burned, her back was against the wall, her clock was running out, and her canoe was up the well-known creek. **1959** BHecht *Sensualists* (NY) 146: Burn all my bridges. **1965** Doctor X *Intern* (NY) 226: This was like trying to unburn a burnt bridge. **1972** SNBehrman *People* (B) 196: To allow her to burn her own bridges. **1974** EPHoyt *Horatio's* (Radnor, Pa.) 6: He had burned every bridge to his past. **1975** DEWestlake *Two* (NY) 217: Go ahead . . . Burn your bridges while you're standing on them. Cf. Boats *above*.

B429 The **Brink** of the grave

1972 PKruger *Cold* (NY) 9: Tottering on the brink of the grave. EAP B329.

B430 As **Broad** as it is long

1922 JJoyce *Ulysses* (NY 1934) 91: As broad as it's long. **1925** JGBrandon *Cork* (L) 89: It's as broad as it is long. **1931** CBrooks *Ghost* (NY) 235: It was as broad as long. EAP B332.

B431 To pull a **Brodie**

1958 *BHerald* 5/15 47: They're trying to pull a Brodie and commit suicide. Wentworth 64. Cf. DARE i 386: Brodie.

B432 New **Brooms** sweep clean (*varied*)

1908 JCLincoln *Cy Whittaker* (NY) 142: A new broom sweeps fine. **1923** ABlackwood *Episodes* (L) 282: A proverbial new broom. **1928** RCullum *Mystery* (NY) 205: We all have to be new brooms sometimes. **1930** CWalsh *Crime in India* (L) 75: Dalt was a new broom, and he began to sweep vigorously. **1931** TFPowys *Unclay* (L) 274: A man be like a new broom that do want to sweep in all the corners. **1933** "Diplomat" *Death* (NY) 93: One new broom doesn't make a clean sweep. **1937** JRhode *Death on the Board* (L) 44: New brooms sweep clean was a very apt proverb, especially in the mouth of an iron monger. **1937** WETurpin *These Low* (NY) 13: For two days, like the proverbial new broom that sweeps so clean, she did admirably. **1952** PGosse *Dr. Viper* (L) 95: The new broom at once set about raising a cloud of dust and trouble. **1956** *Punch* 5/30 649: For a day or two a Minister may see himself as a new broom, sweeping out the dirty corners . . . But the broom will be snatched away . . . Least of all in this great Department is a new broom likely to achieve more than a momentary whisk in an unimportant corner. **1956** *BangorDN* 7/17 5: A new broom sweeps clean but it takes the old one to know where the dirt lies. **1957** *NYTimes* 4/14 3F: A new broom in an old house. **1957** *New Yorker* 8/24 79: The . . . type of young new broom in public life. **1959** FWakeman *Verginia* (L) 142: You know that old saying: New feathers brush out the old dust. **1961** PDennis *Little* (NY) 179: "A new broom," they say, "sweeps clean." **1967** FSwinnerton *Sanctuary* (NY) 83: New brooms bring their own dirt. **1968** EBuckler *Ox Bells* (NY) 72: This new man was as prying as a new broom. **1974** LKronenberger *Wilkes* (NY) 21: As an ignorant new broom faced with so much to sweep away, he couldn't possibly sweep clean but could decidedly raise dust. EAP B334; TW 44; Brunvand 16.

B433   To jump the **Broom**(stick) (*varied*)

1919 JBCabell *Jurgen* (NY 1922) 274: A broomstick was laid before them and they stepped over it. **1938** AGilbert *Treason* (L) 76: If you call jumping over a pair of tongs being married? **1960** VWilliams *Walk* (NY) 48: We jumped the broom [*got married*]. **1972** HCarmichael *Naked* (NY) 76: Who's married and who's living over the brush. EAP B335. Cf. Bonnet *above*.

B434   To love one as a **Brother**

1906 JCLincoln *Mr. Pratt* (NY) 101: To love you like a brother. **1928** ABCox *Amateur* (NY) 168: The Inspector loves me like a brother. **1936** PGWodehouse *Laughing* (NY) 37: I love him like a brother. **1941** HCBailey *Bishop's* (NY) 24: He loves me like a brother. **1960** HInnes *Doomed* (NY) 170: I love him like my own brother. **1975** EMcBain *Where* (NY) 115: I love you like a brother. EAP B336; TW 44(3). Cf. Brunvand 17(1): Nursed.

B435   To stick (cling) closer than a **Brother**

1927 PBNoyes *Pallid* (NY) 183: [He] stuck to me like a brother. **1930** ECVivian *Double* (L) 100: It's sticking to me closer than a brother. **1936** RAJWalling *Floating Foot* (NY) 294: He'd stick to him closer than a brother. **1943** AAFair *Bats Fly* (NY) 147: I'm going to stick closer than a brother. **1958** NMonkman *From Queensland* (NY) 75: It clings closer than a brother. EAP B337.

B436   **Brown,** Smith or Robinson (*varied*)

1922 JSFletcher *Ravensdene* (NY) 123: Whether they were . . . Brown, or Smith, or Robinson. **1922** JJoyce *Ulysses* (NY 1934) 611: The average man, i.e. Brown, Robinson and Co. **1925** JGBrandon *Cork* (L) 74: The name might be Brown, Smith, Jones or Robinson, as the old song or whatever it was says. **1931** JSFletcher *Solution* (NY) 125: Credit that should be given to Smith or Brown or Robinson. **1932** VLoder *Red*

Stain (NY) 61: Brown . . . It might equally well have been Jones or Robinson. **1933** PMacDonald *Mystery* (NY 1958) 169: Not a John Brown, Tom Smith, and Harry Robinson. **1933** RAJWalling *Prove It* (NY) 232: Jones, Brown or Robinson. **1934** VLoder *Two Dead* (L) 21: Smith, Jones, and Robinson. All common names. **1938** ECRLorac *John Brown's* (L) 191: Smith, Brown or Robinson. **1940** ELWhite *While She* (NY) 9: Brown, Smith and Robinson. **1959** ECRLorac *Last* (NY) 68: The name given is Brown, Jones, or Robinson. **1964** AChristie *Caribbean* (NY) 10: Mr. Jones or Robinson covered his tracks. **1965** AGilbert *Voice* (NY) 124: Smith, Brown or Robinson. Cf. Tom *below*.

B437   To do someone **Brown**

1926 JSFletcher *Marringham* (B) 199: [He] did him brown, as the saying was in those days [*tricked him*]. TW 44(1).

B438   To be tarred with the same **Brush** (stick)

1922 JJoyce *Ulysses* (NY 1934) 366: All tarred with the same brush. **c1923** ACrowley *Confessions* ed JSymonds (L 1969) 92: To be tarred with the same brush. **1925** BBLindsay *Revolt* (NY) 34: Don't let the stick that has tarred you disfigure them. **1927** SSVanDine *Canary* (NY) 208: All tarred with the same stick. **1932** WLHay *Who Cut* (L) 264: Both Annette and the secretary were literally tarred with the same stick. **1939** RCSherriff *Hopkins* (NY) 109: All "experts" were tarred with the same brush. **1944** MFilt *Clues* (NY) 186: You're all tarred with the same brush. **1951** ECRLorac *I Could* (NY) 68: All tarred with the same brush. **1956** *NYPost* 9/26 47: Tarred his own party with the same business-influence brush. **1957** *Punch* 2/6 220: Those untarred by the brush of a classical education. **1962** HReilly *Day* (NY DBC) 79: Tarred with the same brush as that sister of yours. **1969** LPDavies *Stranger* (NY) 186: We are all tarred with the same brush. **1970** KGiles *Death* (L) 27: Tarred with the same brush. **1976** HPentecost *Fourteenth* (NY) 183: They force us to tar ourselves with the same brush. EAP B338.

B439 To spread (run) like a **Brushfire**

1961 WMasterson *Evil* (NY) 47: Word . . . spread through the crowd like brushfire. **1975** PMoyes *Black* (NY) 12: Gossip runs like a brush fire. Cf. DA Brush *n.* 4(7). Cf. Wildfire *below.*

B440 To collapse like a pricked **Bubble**

1926 FWCrofts *Cheyne* (NY) 82: He collapsed like a pricked bubble. **1933** HHolt *Scarlet* (L) 12: He must have collapsed like a pricked bubble. Cf. Balloon, Bladder *above.*

B441 As wild as a **Buck**

1936 ISCobb *Judge Priest* (I) 150: Good family but wild as a buck. **1950** MLong *Louisville* (NY) 175: He went wild as a buck when he was growin' up. **1969** APHannum *Look* (NY) 153: I was wild as a buck [*liked the girls*]. EAP B343.

B442 To pass the **Buck** (*varied*)

1920 ACrabb *Samuel* (NY) 46: Passed the buck. **1926** EMillay *Letters* ed ARMacdougall (NY 1952) 207: I pass the buck to you. **1934** VMacClure *Counterfeit* (L) 25: It would be a relief to me to pass the buck, as the Yanks say. **1939** TPolsky *Curtains* (NY) 193: I'm passing the buck to you. **1948** PCheyney *Dance* (NY DBC) 9: He passed the buck to me. **1955** NFitzgerald *House* (L) 160: Someone passed the buck to me. **1963** MMcCarthy *Group* (NY) 326: He wants to pass the buck to Harold. **1971** RFDelderfield *For My* (NY) 320: At the rank of corporal the buck, as the Americans say, stops. **1972** LIsrael *Tallulah* (NY) 48: The buck passed from hand to hand. TW 45; DARE i 407: Buck *n.*³ 2a.

B443 Like **Buckets** in a well

1937 EMillay *Letters* ed ARMacdougall (NY 1952) 293: We seem always to be going in opposite directions, like the two buckets in the well. **1957** MSharp *Eye* (L) 91: As though they were two buckets in a well, as soon as [her] fortunes rose a little, so [his] sank. Whiting B575.

B444 To kick the **Bucket** (pail)

1922 JJoyce *Ulysses* (NY 1934) 565: She kicked the bucket. **1926** HAdams *Crooked* (L) 96: He ought to kick the bucket once and for all. **1932** BRoss *Tragedy of Y* (NY) 274: He's kicked the bucket himself. **1947** AAFair *Fools* (NY 1957) 143: Baldwin would have kicked the bucket. **1954** EDillon *Sent* (L) 204: The bold Captain is about to kick the bucket. **1969** BCole *Joseph* (NY) 185: I may kick the bucket tomorrow. **1970** TWells *Dinky* (NY) 122: I . . . damn near kicked the bucket. **1974** DCavett *Cavett* (NY) 323: To kick the proverbial pail [*die*]. EAP B345.

B445 Like **Buckle** to thong

1952 HFMPrescott *Man On* (NY) 364: He and Haughton were no stranger to each other than buckle is to thong. EAP B346.

B446 To nip in the **Bud**

1928 GGardiner *At the House* (NY) 299: Nipped any question of a trial in the bud. **1933** WCBrown *Murder* (P) 21: Those things have to be nipped in the bud. **1936** PATaylor *Out of Order* (NY) 102: To nip him in the bud. **1938** WMartyn *Murder Walks* (L) 70: I nipped him in the bud. **1951** TDubois *Foul* (NY) 13: To be nipped off even before the bud. **1960** NFitzgerald *Candles* (L) 54: Crime should be nipped in the bud. **1961** CWillock *Death* (L 1963) 162: Before he could bud, . . . Howard nipped him. **1971** CAird *Late* (NY) 126: He nipped his own train of thought in the bud. EAP B348; Brunvand 17.

B447 As comfortable as a **Bug** in a rug

1940 HSKeeler *Cleopatra's* (L) 114: As comfortable as a bug in a rug. **1959** *Atlantic Monthly* Nov. 62: Then I worked out the caption for the drawing of a bug in a rug. It is saying to another bug, "I can't get comfortable." **1978** JLangton *Memorial* (NY) 203: As comfortable as a bug in a rug. TW 45–6(4).

B448 As cozy as **Bugs** (in a rug)

1958 WKelly *Pogo* 2/1: "You ever hear the maxim 'Cozy as a bug in a rug'?" [*A mouse speaks and a flea replies.*] "That's cozy? How'd you like to be working in a rug? Nobody to talk to but them brainless moths and a few cigaret ashes. Did you ever try to put the bite on a carpet!" **1969** JTrahey *Pecked* (Englewood, NJ) 107: Just the two of us, cozy as bugs. Cf. Whiting *NC* 376(2): Warm.

B449   As cute as a **Bug** (bug's ear)

1944 MBramhall *Murder Solves* (NY) 142: He's cute as a bug. **1947** HLawrence *Death of* (NY) 295: Cute as a bug. **1957** *New Yorker* 9/7 32: Cute as a bug. **1968** TMcGuane *Sporting* (NY) 130: You're cute as a bug. **1971** JBlake *Joint* (NY) 178: Cute as a bug's ear. **1971** PDennis *Paradise* (NY) 242: Cute as a bug's ear. Taylor *Prov. Comp.* 31: Cute as a bug's ear; Berrey 37.12.

B450   As happy as a **Bug** (in a rug)

1926 WWadsworth *Paul Bunyan* (NY) 45: As happy and contented as two bugs in a rug. **1955** SRansome *Frazer* (NY) 34: I'm happy as a bug. TW 45–6(1,4).

B451   As snug as a **Bug** in a rug

1900 CFPidgin *Quincy A. Sawyer* (B) 9: As snug as a bug in a rug. **1929** LBrock *Murder* (NY) 230: He was snug as a bug in Mrs. T.'s empty flat. **1937** LPendleton *Down East* (NY) 24: As snug as a bug in a rug. **1938** HMcCloy *Dance* (NY) 188: I'd be snug as a bug in a rug at the Waldorf bar. **1948** CBush *Curious* (NY) 143: Snug as bugs in a rug. **1953** BCClough *Grandma* (Portland, Me.) 25: As snug as a bug in a rug. **1957** *BHerald* 11/10 5A: The only thing snugger than the proverbial bug in a rug is a stick-tight in a woolen sock. **1958** *New Yorker* 8/23 32: As snug as a carpet beetle. **1960** *Portland Press Herald* 2/7 sec. C: Just as snug as three bugs in a rug. **1966** PGWodehouse *Plum* (L) 44: As snug as two bugs in a rug. **1968** WTenn *Seven* (NY) 14: Everything was as snug as a bug in a bughouse. **1973** RCondon *And Then* (NY) 299: Snug as bugs in a rug. EAP B350. Cf. As snug as a Cricket, Pea *below*.

B452   Like a **Bug** in a rug

1940 HSKeeler *Cleopatra's* (L) 237: Where I shall be as a bug in a rug—as a needle in a haystack. Taylor *Prov. Comp.* 20.

B453   To put a **Bug** in someone's ear (*varied*)

1930 MMPropper *Ticker-tape* (NY) 10: This fellow seems to have a bug in his ear. **1930**

KCStrahan *Death* (NY) 141: Gerald put a bug in his ear. **1938** EQueen *Devil* (NY) 222: If we can somehow plant the proverbial bug in her ear that little Anatole was lying. **1940** DTeilhet *Broken Face* (NY) 232: I . . . put a bug in her ear how lonely you might be. **1953** CBKelland *Sinister* (NY DBC) 62: I was dismissed with a bug in my ear. **1957** *NYTimes* 11/3 8E: Brownell . . . put the bug in President Eisenhower's ear about sending troops to Little Rock. **1959** DTracy *Big* (NY DBC) 61: Wondering what kind of a bug Doc had in his ears. **1964** HWaugh *Missing* (NY) 82: Something put the bug in your ear. Whiting *NC* 376(3); DARE i 433, 434: Bug 14[d,h]; Wentworth 70.

B454   Not to give a **Bugger**

1975 GBlack *Big Wind* (NY) 68: [He] don't give a bugger. **1982** RBarnard *Death and the Princess* (NY) 56: He didn't give a bugger.

B455   Thanks for the **Buggy** ride

1935 EGreenwood *Pins* (L) 69: Thanks for the buggy-ride. **1967** GBaxt *Swing* (NY) 42: Thanks for the buggy ride. Cf. next entry.

B456   To be taken for a **Buggy** ride

1938 HAustin *Lilies* (NY) 28: He is being taken for a buggy ride. **1940** NMorland *Gun* (L) 41: She took you for the biggest buggy ride in your . . . life. Berrey 118.1.

B457   As mad as a **Bull**

1936 JTFarrell *World* (NY) 229: He was mad as a bull. TW 46(2).

B458   As red as a **Bull**

1929 SGluck *Shadow* (NY) 105: He was as red as a bull. Cf. TW 46(3); Wilstach 316: Bull's blood.

B459   As strong as a **Bull**(ock)

1920 JSFletcher *Dead Men's* (NY) 17: Strong as a bull. **1930** WSMasterman *Yellow* (NY) 19: Heart strong as a bull. **1931** LCharteris *Wanted* (NY) 130: He was strong as a bull. **1934** HCBailey *Shadow* (NY) 271: He must be as strong as a bull. **1937** GDilnot *Murder* (L) 106: Strong as a bullock. **1939** LBrock *Riddle* (L) 243: He was as strong as a bull. **1940** AGaines *While the*

Wind (NY) 46: Heart . . . strong as a bull's. **1941** PWentworth *Weekend* (P) 167: He looked as strong as a bull. **1952** MVHeberden *Tragic* (NY) 18: He's as strong as a bull. **1959** FSmith *Harry* (B) 100: I'm strong as a bull. **1965** RLPike *Police* (NY) 130: The man was strong as a bull. **1961** SDean *Credit* (NY) 75: Strong as a bull. TW 46(4).

B460 As tight as a **Bull's** arse in August (flytime)

1969 SMays *Fall Out* (L) 27: They're as tight as a bull's arse in August [*of trousers*]. **1969** SMays *Fall Out* (L) 210: He's a mean bastard, tight as a bull's arse in August [*stingy, unpleasant*]. **1978** JGould *Trifling* (B) 106: The . . . Maine expression is "Tight as a bull's [arse] in fly-time" [*drunk*].

B461 As ugly (jumpy) as a **Bull** in fly time

1911 JCLincoln *Woman-haters* (NY) 167: As ugly as a bull in fly time. **1973** JCashman *Gentleman* (NY) 79: As jumpy as a stump-tailed bull in fly time. EAP B356; TW 46(2,7).

B462 A **Bull** in a china shop (*varied*)

1922 JJoyce *Ulysses* (NY 1934) 393: An Irish bull in an English chinashop. **1923** OR Cohen *Jim Hanvey* (NY) 207: A veritable china-shop bull. **1923** EMPoate *Behind* (NY) 208: Like a bull in a china shop. **1930** W Lewis *Apes* (NY 1932) 69: A bull in its own china-shop; 438. **1935** RHull *Murder* (NY) 141: She says what she wishes to say like the proverbial bull in a china shop. **1938** JTDonning *Last Trumpet* (L) 203: You and your methods would produce the results of the proverbial bull in a china closet. **1939** AMuir *Death Comes* (L) 16: Rampaging about his room like a Bull of Basin in a china-shop. **1945** GBellairs *Calamity* (NY) 52: It looked like a china-shop ravaged by a bull. **1948** JTey *Franchise* (NY 1955) 66: The bull-in-the-china-shop type. **1954** DAlexander *Terror* (NY) 90: You blundered in like a bull in the china shop. **1955** AChristie *Hickory* (NY) 172: The Sergeant . . . looked as out of place as the traditional bull in a china shop. **1957** CWThayer *Unquiet* (NY) 249: Built like an ox with a bull's predeliction for china shops. **1959** MNeville *Sweet*

(L) 153: Bulls in china shops are proverbially inapposite. **1960** TFurlong *Time* (NY) 167: His teeth are very white and straight and artificial (like a china-shop in a bull, as Tom Blair once remarked). **1963** HWaugh *Prisoner's* (NY DBC) 99: In a china shop you should be a pussy cat, not a bull. **1963** HPentecost *Only* (NY DBC) 14: He's like a mortally wounded old bull crashing about in a china-shop of a world. **1966** BHDeal *Fancy's* (NY) 63: I'm beginning to feel like an elephant tiptoeing through a china closet. **1970** JAGraham *Aldeburg* (B) 15: Kind of a bull-in-a-china-shop type. TW 46(5); Brunvand 17(1); *Oxford* 90.

B463 To roar (bellow) like a **Bull**

1930 JRhode *Venner* (NY) 95: Bellowing like a bull. **1956** NMarsh *Death* (B) 272: He was roaring like a bull, but you couldn't make head or tail of it. **1959** ASillitoe *Saturday* (NY) 121: He roared like a bull. **1963** NMarsh *Dead* (B 1964) 27: You'll . . . roar like a bull. **1972** NMarsh *Tied* (B) 77: Blore roared like a bull. EAP B357; TW 46(9); Brunvand 17(2).

B464 To roar (bellow) like the **Bull** (bulls) of Bashan (*varied*)

1900 CFPidgin *Quincy A. Sawyer* (B) 341: With a roar like the bull of Bashan. **1910** JCLincoln *Depot Master* (NY) 241: He roars, like the bull of Bashan. **1917** JCLincoln *Extricating* (NY) 297: Bellowing . . . like a bull of Bashan. **1932** RAFreeman *When Rogues* (L) 159: Bargees . . . bellowing like bulls of Bashan. **1934** JGBrandon *Murder* (L) 39: Barkin' at him like the bull of Bashan. **1936** NMorland *Clue* (L) 158: You always burst in on me like the Bull of Bashan. **1936** FBeeding *Nine Waxed* (NY) 50: I howled after them like the Bull of Bashan. **1968** LSdeCamp *Great Monkey* (NY) 36: Roar like all the bulls of Bashan. EAP B355.

B465 To take the **Bull** by the horns

1903 EChilders *Riddle* (NY 1940) 168: I took the bull by the horns. **1911** JSHay *Amazing Emperor* (L) 67: Taken the bull by the horns. **1922** JJoyce *Ulysses* (NY 1934) 34: Take the bull by the horns. 199: Took the cow by the horns. **1923** HGartland

Globe (NY) 25: Take the bull by the horns. **1935** RGarnett *Starr* (L) 139: We ought to take the bull by the proverbial horns. **1939** HReilly *All Concerned* (NY) 11: We have got hold of the bull by the tail instead of by the horns. **1949** AMStein *Days* (NY) 160: Tim took the bull by the horns. **1957** *Punch* 9/4 259: But I think she's hitting the bull on the horns. **1957** *BHerald* 12/22 3A: To see who finally takes the bull by the horns. **1963** BFarwell *Burton* (L) 353: Took the bull, by the horns. **1963** EFerber *Kind* (NY) 200: You must—to paraphrase an old saying—take the bully by the horns. **1969** ELe Comte *Notorious* (L) 112: The hale and hearty take-the-bull-by-the-horns type. **1974** DCavett *Cavett* (NY) 78: To seize the bull by the horns. **1975** BNByfield *Solemn* (NY) 99: Took the bull by the horns. EAP B358.

B466 As big as **Bull-beef**
1938 BFlynn *Ebony* (L) 168: 'E's as big as bull beef. EAP B359.

B467 To hang on (hold) like a **Bulldog**
1934 GVerner *Con Man* (L) 178: He would hang on like a bulldog. **1934** ECRLorac *Greenwell* (NY) 55: He'd have held on to it like a bull-dog. **1937** MBurton *Clue* (NY) 247: He always hangs on to a thing like a bulldog. TW 47(3).

B468 To hit the **Bull's eye**
1939 DHume *Death Before* (L) 171: He knew he had hit the bull's eye. **1946** DWilson *Make with the Brains* (NY) 167: This dart hit the bull's eye. Wentworth 73.

B469 As swift as a **Bullet**
1959 ADean *Something* (NY) 103: Swift as a bullet. Whiting *NC* 377(2).

B470 Every **Bullet** has (finds) its billet
1922 JJoyce *Ulysses* (NY 1934) 366: Every bullet has its billet. **1926** HHMunro *Toys* (L) 221: Every bullet finds a billet, according to a rather optimistic proverb. **1932** RCWoodthorpe *Public* (L) 237: It is said that every bullet finds its billet. **1938** BFlynn *Five Red* (NY) 92: Bullets find strange billets upon occasion. TW 47(3); *Oxford* 90.

B471 No two **Bullets** hit the same spot
1934 DGBrowne *Plan XVI* (NY) 139: No two bullets hit the same spot. EAP B361. Cf. Lightning never strikes *below*.

B472 To bite (on) the **Bullet**
1931 GCollins *Phantom* (L) 252: Bite on the bullet, lady, and don't miss a syllable. **1938** NMarsh *Death* (NY) 187: We've got to bite on the bullet. **1964** NFreeling *Because* (NY 1965) 175: The court will make you bite the bullet. **1968** WTenn *Wooden* (NY) 200: Bite the bullet. **1973** DDelman *He Who* (NY) 152: Bite the bullet, he told himself.

B473 **Bullies** are always cowards
1974 KAmis *Ending* (NY) 171: Bullies are always cowards. *Oxford* 90–91.

B474 To give someone the **Bum's** rush
1939 WChambers *You Can't* (NY) 122: Giving me the bum's rush. DARE i 458: Bum's; Wentworth 75.

B475 To sit (*etc.*) like a **Bump** (knot) on a log
1927 CWells *Where's Emily* (NY) 127: Sit here like a bump on a log. **1932** TSmith *Bishop's* (NY) 31: Let's sit like a couple of bumps on a log. **1936** KMKnight *Wheel* (NY) 34: Don't stand there like a bump on a log. **1937** KCKempton *Monday* (NY) 1: You set there like a bump on a log. **1951** EPaul *Murder On* (NY) 243: Stood around like a bump on log. **1956** *BangorDN* 10/6 25: Don't stand there like a knot on a log. **1957** BHitchens *End* (NY) 112: Waiting like a bump on a log. **1959** *BGlobe* 6/30 20: I'd feel like a bump on a log in the new format. **1962** LDRich *Natural* (NY) 94: Sitting there like a bump on a log. **1967** BStoltzfus *Eye* (NY) 57: You just lay there on top of me. Like a bump on a log. TW 47.

B476 Quick like a **Bunny**
1959 GBagby *Real* (NY) 57: Then quick like a bunny. **1970** RNeely *Walter* (NY) 87: Some guys . . . are quicker than bunnies [*sexual intercourse*]. **1970** EQueen *Last* (NY) 111: I can answer that quick like a bunny. **1977** LBlock *Burglars* (NY) 83: Get in and get out, quick as a bunny. Taylor *Prov.*

Comp. 65. Cf. Spears 55: Bunny-fuck. Cf. Rabbit *below.*

B477   As sore as a **Bur** under the saddle
1929 JSStrange *Clue* (NY) 3: I'm as sore as a burr under the saddle. Cf. next entry.

B478   To have a **Bur** under one's tail (*varied*)
1958 WDHassett *Off the Record* (New Brunswick, NJ) 197: They need a burr under their tails. **1964** MEChaber *Six* (NY DBC) 123: It certainly had put a burr in [his] pants [*stirred him up*]. Cf. preceding entry.

B479   To stick (cling) like a **Bur** (*varied*)
1928 WBeebe *Beneath Tropic Seas* (NY) 96: Cling as closely as the proverbial burr. **1929** HFootner *Doctors* (L) 41: The idea was sticking in his mind like a burr. **1930** HBedford-Jones *Shadow* (NY) 266: That there Chink stuck tighter'n a bur. **1930** RAFreeman *Mystery* (NY) 190: That good lady stuck to me like a burr. **1937** RCWoodthorpe *Death in* (NY) 254: He clung to them like a burr. **1941** KSecrist *Murder Makes* (NY) 154: He's been stickin' to my tail like a bur. **1953** AAFair *Some Women* (NY DBC) 169: [He] stuck to me like a burr on a blanket. **1957** JBlish *Frozen* (NY) 46: I'm going to stick to you like a burdock. **1957** CRice *Knocked* (NY) 151: You stuck to me like a chestnut burr. **1958** NBlake *Penknife* (L) 46: She's as faithful as a burr. **1967** FMBrodie *Devil* (NY) 26: The contrast . . . stuck like a burr in Burton's memory. **1968** RBissell *How Many* (B) 202: Shipboard acquaintances who stick like sandburs. **1974** SKrim *You* (NY) 13: [They] will stick like burrs. EAP B364: Stick; TW 48(3): Stick; Brunvand 18: Hold on. Cf. Cockle-bur *below.*

B480   The **Burden** of the song
1932 ABCox *Murder* (L) 148: The burden of Amy's song. EAP B365.

B481   As bare as **Burkey**
1958 *NYTimes Book Review* 10/12 39: My Scotch grandmother used to say "as bare as Burkey."

B482   Once **Burned** twice shy (*varied*)
1949 SSterling *Dead Sure* (NY) 123: Once burned, twice shy, you know. **1960** HLivingston *Climacticon* (NY) 189: Once burned is twice learned. **1973** CJackson *Kicked* (NY) 13: Once burned, twice shy. Cf. Bitten *above;* A burnt Child *below.*

B483   To miss the **Bus**
1926 AJArnold *Murder!* (L) 291: We must drop on him tonight or we shall miss the 'bus. **1934** HCBailey *Shadow* (NY) 74: Osmond's missed the bus. **1939** CSLewis *Letters* (NY 1966) 164: You have missed the bus. **1957** *Punch* 8/28 227: The bus that Hitler missed. **1962** LDavidson *Rose* (NY) 23: He had somehow missed the bus. **1970** VCClinton-Baddeley *No Case* (NY) 156: The author had missed the bus by about ten years. Partridge 112; NED Suppl. Bus 1b. Cf. Boat *above.*

B484   To be drawn through a **Bush** (hedge) backwards
1963 MPHood *Sin* (NY) 186: Lookin' as if he'd been drawn through a bush backward. **1980** PDeVries *Consenting* (B) 40: He hath been pulled through a hedge backwards. Cf. Knothole *below.*

B485   To beat about (around) the **Bush**
1904 JCLincoln *Cap'n Eri* (NY) 224: No beating about the bush. **1905** JLondon *Letters* ed KHendricks (NY 1965) 185–6: Beating about the bush. **1923** EMPoate *Behind* (NY) 88: Beating about the bush. **1932** LFrost *Murder* (NY) 145: Beating around the bush. **1937** CGGivens *All Cats* (I) 74: You always could beat further around a bush than any man I know. **1950** BCarey *Man who* (NY) 99: I won't beat about the bush. **1954** JBingham *Third* (NY) 120: I won't beat about the bush, as the saying is. **1954** JRMacdonald *Find* (NY) 188: We won't beat around the bush. **1966** BHDeal *Fancy's* (NY) 85: Let's stop beating around the well-known bush. **1968** CDSimak *Goblin* (NY) 125: All this beating amongst the bushes. **1975** ELathen *By Hook* (NY) 53: No use beating around the bush. EAP B368; TW 48(3); Brunvand 18. Cf. Mulberry bush *below.*

B486 To beat the **Bush**

1922 VSutphen *In Jeopardy* (NY) 261: Enough of this bush beating. **1952** CEVulliamy *Don* (L) 109: We can't go on indefinitely beating these empty bushes. **1958** MAllingham *Tether's* (NY) 19: A considerable display of bush-beating. **1971** MCollins *Walk* (NY) 81: Don't come here and beat bushes for straws. **1971** WHWalling *No One* (NY) 200: You're beating the bush to death but I think I see what you mean. EAP B369.

B487 A **Bushel** of March dust is worth a king's ransom

1936 HCBailey *Clue* (L) 36: Bushel of March dust worth a king's ransom . . . I've never believed that. *Oxford* 511: March dust.

B488 **Business** (duty) before pleasure (*varied*)

1908 JCLincoln *Cy Whittaker* (NY) 337: Pleasure first and business afterwards. **1920** ACrabb *Samuel* (NY) 90: Business comes before pleasure. **1924** HCBailey *Mr. Fortune's Practice* (NY) 30: Pleasure before business. **1931** LCharteris *Wanted* (NY) 55: We can't let pleasure interfere with business. **1933** GBeaton *Jack* (L) 284: Business before pleasure. **1934** SPalmer *Silver Persian* (NY) 178: Duty before pleasure. **1935** *New Yorker* 9/21 22: Business before pleasure, like they say. **1938** JJConnington *For Murder* (L) 224: "Business before pleasure," as the man said when he kissed his wife before calling on his sweetheart. **1939** GGoodchild *We Shot* (L) 229: Duty before pleasure. **1949** AA Fair *Bedrooms* (NY 1958) 151: You never let pleasure interfere with business. **1958** CSibley *Malignant* (NY) 129: Business before pleasure, I always say. **1959** CBrown *Terror* (NY) 23: Business before pleasure, as the actress said to the producer when he wanted her to read a script before she relaxed on his couch. **1960** TWBurgess *Now I* (B) 60: The old saw . . . "Business first, pleasure afterwards." **1961** NBlake *Worm* (L) 104: Duty before pleasure. **1963** HMacInnes *Venetian* (NY) 194: Duty before pleasure. EAP B374; Brunvand 18(1).

B489 **Business** is business

1904 JCLincoln *Cap'n Eri* (NY) 220: Business is business. **1923** ORCohen *Jim Hanvey* (NY) 100: Business is business. **1930** EWallace *Green Ribbon* (NY) 128: Business is business, love is love, and they don't mix. **1950** SJepson *Hungry* (NY) 112: Business was business. **1957** *BangorDN* 8/29 34: But—like they say—business is business. **1959** HSlesar *Grey* (L 1963) 43: But business is business, as the fella says. **1968** ELustgarten *Business* (NY) 133: Business is business; what gets by gets by. **1970** JWechsberg *First* (B) 176: *Les affaires* were still *les affaires,* business is business. TW 48(2); Brunvand 18(2); *Oxford* 93. Cf. Duty is, Orders are, Rules are, Work is *below.*

B490 Do not mix **Business** with pleasure

1913 JSFletcher *Secret* (L 1918) 118: I don't believe in mixing up pleasure and business. **1931** RWhitfield *Death* (NY) 54: Business is business . . . And pleasure is pleasure. **1935** MJFreeman *Case* (NY) 118: Business and love don't mix—any more than gasoline and gin. **1939** HWPriwen *Inspector* (L) 188: Business and pleasure don't mix. **1957** *New Yorker* 8/10 20: It is not in my nature to mix business with pleasure, as the saying goes. **1960** HWaugh *Road* (NY DBC) 12: Business and pleasure don't mix. **1968** RVanGulik *Poets* (NY) 26: I never mix business with pleasure. **1970** JLeasor *They Don't* (NY) 185: There's an old family motto: Never mix business with pleasure. **1972** NWebster *Killing* (NY) 74: I never mix business with pleasure. **1976** EFoote-Smith *Gentle* (NY) 163: To mix business with pleasure. Cf. Work is work *below.*

B491 To combine **Business** with pleasure (*varied*)

1922 JJoyce *Ulysses* (NY 1934) 83: Combine business with pleasure. **1926** JJConnington *Death* (NY) 182: Combining business with pleasure. **1933** LRGribble *Yellow* (L) 24: Business and pleasure combined. **1937** NBlake *There's Trouble* (L) 123: Combine business with pleasure. **1945** GBellairs *Calamity* (NY) 23: Refusing to mingle business with pleasure. **1970** KGiles *Death* (L) 19: We might combine business with pleasure.

B492 A **Busman's** holiday

1916 SRohmer *Tales* (NY 1922) 319: Busman's holiday; 335. **1927** CBarry *Witness* (NY) 167: A busman's holiday. **1937** DLSayers *Busman's* (NY) 134: A kind of busman's holiday for you . . . busman's honeymoon. **1941** TDowning *Lazy Lawrence* (NY) 44: A busman's holiday. **1954** MMainwaring *Murder* (NY) 110: This voyage is a busman's holiday for him. **1957** *BangorDN* 7/31 1: Busman's holiday. **1960** NFitzgerald *Candles* (L) 153: They're like busmen—they [*psychiatrists*] analyse each other. **1964** CChaplin *Autobiography* (NY 1966) 144: I took a cook's holiday. **1971** RLockridge *Inspector's Holiday* (P). **1972** NMarsh *Tied* (B) 139: No holiday like a Busman's. **1973** AGilbert *Nice* (NY) 12: "That is a busman's holiday. What is a busman's holiday?" "Sort of out of the frying pan into the fire." NED Suppl. Bus *sb.*[2] 3. Cf. Postman, Sailor *below.*

B493 The **Butcher,** the baker and the candlestick maker

1925 TRMarshall *Recollections* (I) 164: Butchers and bakers and candle-stick makers. **1927** JHawk *Serpent* (NY) 77: A butcher, a baker, a candlestick maker. **1932** JCLenehan *Mansfield* (L) 120: The butcher and the baker and the candle-stick-maker. **1937** GBarrett *I Knew* (L) 230: He might be the local baker, or butcher, or candlestick maker. **1950** ECRLorac *And Then* (NY) 23: The butcher, the baker, and the candlestick maker. **1958** *Time* 11/10 8: You include the butcher, the baker, the candlestick maker. **1960** JO'Hara *Ourselves* (NY) 53: The butcher, the baker, the candlestick-maker. **1966** NMitford *Sun King* (L) 126: He was charming to the butcher, the baker and the candlestickmaker. **1972** CTurney *Byron's* (NY) 55: The butcher, the baker, the candlestickmaker. TW 49(2).

B494 As bland as **Butter**

1941 CFAdams *Decoy* (NY) 178: [His] voice was as bland as butter. **1948** PClark *Flight* (NY) 41: A glance as bland as butter. **1958**

BWAldiss *Starship* (NY 1960) 99: Marapper was as bland as butter in return. **1968** KChristie *Child's* (L) 138: Looking bland as butter. **1973** HCarvic *Miss Seeton Sings* (NY) 102: As bland as butter [*a woman*].

B495 As easy as cutting **Butter** (*varied*)

1931 EWallace *Device* (L) 30: As easy as cutting butter. **1932** HCBailey *Red Castle* (NY) 247: Easy as cutting butter. **1959** AGilbert *Death* (NY) 93: It went as easy as butter from a hot knife. **1968** JAiken *Crystal* (NY) 148: Easy as butter one minute and slap your face . . . the next. Cf. To go like a Knife *below.*

B496 As fat as **Butter**

1930 MAllingham *Take Two* (L 1959) 42: Fat as butter. **1957** *New Yorker* 6/8 72: The zebras . . . are always as fat as butter. **1961** MMillar *How Like* (NY DBC) 159: She's a frisky one, fat as butter. **1962** EHuxley *Mottled* (L) 234: Loam . . . fat as butter. **1968** IPetite *Life* (NY) 26: Fat as butter. EAP B384; Taylor *Western Folklore* 17(1958) 14(1).

B497 As slick as **Butter**

1927 LTracy *Mysterious* (NY) 317: Slick as butter. **1963** MPHood *Sin* (NY) 31: Things were smoothed over slick as butter.

B498 As smooth as **Butter** (lard); Butter-smooth

1923 ORCohen *Jim Hanvey* (NY) 84: Smooth as butter. **1933** WADarlington *Mr. Cronk's* (L) 153: Smooth as butter, but they'd skin you alive without turning a hair. **1934** MDavis *Murder* (NY) 168: Slick as lard in February. And as smooth. **1948** HReilly *Staircase* (NY) 161: He was as smooth as butter. **1959** HPentecost *Lonely* (NY) 207: Smooth as sweet butter, he was. **1959** *Time* 8/3 82: Outwardly butter-smooth. **1971** MScherf *Beautiful* (NY) 20: It will all be as smooth as butter. NED Suppl. Butter *sb.*[1] 4: Butter-smooth.

B499 As soft as **Butter**

1926 EWallace *Terrible* (NY) 302: She was born that way—soft as butter. **1932** CDawes *Lawless* (L) 42: Soft as butter. **1945** PWentworth *She Came* (NY) 202: He had a heart as soft as butter. **1955** PWentworth *Gazebo* (L 1965) 25: A heart as soft as butter. **1956** PWentworth *Fingerprint* (NY) 231: As soft as butter [*of a woman*]. **1963** NFitzgerald *Echo* (NY) 249: She was as soft as butter. **1969** AGilbert *Mr. Crook* (NY DBC) 172: Soft as butter. **1970** GMFraser *Royal* (L) 27: Morally as soft as butter. EAP B385; Taylor *Western Folklore* 17(1958) 14(2).

B500 As thick as **Butter**

1926 JTully *Beggars* (NY) 93: A brogue as thick as butter. Brunvand 18.

B501 As yellow as **Butter;** Butter-yellow

1948 HReilly *Staircase* (NY) 87: Hair as yellow as butter. **1953** EWTeale *Circle* (NY) 48: They turn butter yellow. Whiting *NC* 378(2).

B502 To get **Butter** from a dog's mouth (*varied*)

1919 JSFletcher *Middle Temple* (NY) 171: He'd have coaxed butter out of a dog's throat. **1923** JSFletcher *Markenmore* (NY) 283: You might as well try to get butter out of a dog's mouth. **1937** SFowler *Post-Mortem* (L) 95: A proverb concerning butter in a dog's mouth came to his mind. Apperson 75(9). Cf. *Oxford* 94.

B503 To look as if **Butter** would not melt in one's mouth (*varied*)

1908 JCLincoln *Cy Whittaker* (NY) 197: Butter wouldn't melt in your mouth. **1910** EPhillpotts *Tales* (NY) 186: Butter wouldn't have melted in his mouth, as they say. **1913** ECBentley *Trent's* (NY 1930) 70: Butter might possibly melt in his mouth. **1927** WJohnston *Affair* (NY) 235: So sweet that butter would melt in their mouths. **1932** JJConnington *Castleford* (B) 203: Girls . . . looked as though butter wouldn't freeze in their mouths. **1936** GHeyer *Behold* (NY) 74: Butter wouldn't have melted in her mouth. **1937** GStockwell *Death* (NY) 184: In a tone that wouldn't melt butter. **1941** ESGardner *Haunted Husband* (NY) 220: A butter-wouldn't-melt-in-my-mouth manner. **1950** CDickson *Night* (NY) 143: As polite as butter. **1951** EMarshall *Viking* (NY) 163: You'd think that butter wouldn't melt in her prim mouth. **1955** NFitzgerald *House* (L) 193: It's all very well to say that sugar wouldn't melt in that one's mouth. **1959** THWhite *Godstone* (NY) 215: The holy, innocent Irish that butter wouldn't melt in the mouth of. **1963** NFreeling *Question* (NY 1965) 76: Butter wouldn't melt in his mouth or under his armpit. **1964** ABoucher *Best Detective* (NY) 146: A tortoni wouldn't have melted in his mouth. **1969** PAnderson *Satan's* (NY) 42: I sat meek like my mouth wouldn't smelt [*sic*] butter. **1972** SCloete *Victorian* (L) 55: No one could have imagined that butter could melt in those lovely unpainted mouths. **1975** HCarvic *Odds On* (NY) 114: That butter-wouldn't-melt-in-the-mouth little schoolmarm. **1975** SJPerelman *Vinegar* (NY) 35: So pure that marzipan wouldn't melt in their mouths. **1979** OPritchett *Prize* (NY) 19: Sarah looked demure . . . as a bride, as if wedding cake would not melt in her mouth. TW 49(3); *Oxford* 177: Demure.

B504 To melt like **Butter**

1945 JTRogers *Red Right* (NY 1957) 60: He might melt like butter. Whiting *NC* 378(3).

B505 To put **Butter** on one's bread (*varied*)

1926 JArnold *Murder!* (L) 247: That won't put any butter on my bread. **1928** GYoung *Treasure* (NY) 13: I've got to keep butter on my bread. **1932** CDawes *Lawless* (L) 105: Knew how to butter their bread. **1954** NBlake *Whisper* (L) 156: Little boys should keep their buts to butter their bread with. **1969** PMcGerr *For Richer* (NY) 71: She knows who puts the butter on her bread. **1970** BWAldiss *Hand-reared* (L) 182: In her modest way she was expert; and expertise is really the butter on the bread of sex. EAP B306: Butter one's bread.

B506 As fat as a **Butterball**

1951 JCollier *Fancies* (NY) 264: A small mouse, fat as a butter-ball. **1962** LDRich *Natural* (NY) 166: Fat as a butterball. **1971** DCWilson *Big-Little* (NY) 111: Fat as a butter ball. Taylor *Prov. Comp.* 40.

B507 As fresh as a **Buttercup**

1946 MBennett *Time to Change* (NY) 215: She'll wake up fresh as a buttercup. TW 50(1).

B508 As fleeting as a **Butterfly's** fart
1951 MZolotow *No People* (NY) 275: Every thing on radio is as fleeting as a butterfly's f—t [*ascribed to Fred Allen*]. Cf. Sparrow-fart *below.*

B509 As gay as a **Butterfly**
1944 MFitt *Clues* (NY) 92: Gay as a butterfly. Whiting *NC* 378.

B510 To break a **Butterfly** on the wheel
1959 ESherry *Defense* (NY) 133: It would be breaking a butterfly on a wheel. EAP B388.

B511 To have **Butterflies** in one's stomach
1938 LAnson *Such Natural* (L) 114: I have butterflies in the stomach today. **1943** FMcDermid *Ghost Wanted* (NY 1945) 49: Hogan had butterflies in his stomach. **1951** PATaylor *Diplomatic* (NY) 41: [He] felt butterflies work in his stomach. **1955** STruss *False* (NY) 129: I had butterflies in my tummy when they wouldn't let me go. **1958** MUnderwood *Lawful* (NY) 43: His stomach full of butterflies. **1962** DMDisney *Should Auld* (NY) 22: She had butterflies in her stomach. **1964** JPhilips *Laughter* (NY DBC) 54: Now the agitated butterflies in his belly. **1968** TBarman *Diplomatic* (L) 198: To appear natural when the butterflies are hammering away at your stomach. **1975** A Roudybush *Suddenly* (NY) 93: My stomach . . . is full of butterflies. Wentworth 81.

B512 As bright as a **Button;** Button-bright
1924 AEHousman *Letters* ed HMaas (Cambridge, Mass. 1971) 224: As bright as a button. **1930** JRussell *Cops* (NY) 250: Button-bright eyes. **1934** CRourke *Davy Crockett* (NY) 154: [He] looked . . . bright as a pewter button. **1940** AMcRoyd *Crime in Costume* (NY) 253: Bright as a button. **1947** FCDavis *Thursday's* (NY) 137: Button-bright restless eyes. **1948** EDaly *Book* (NY) 209: Bright as a button. **1959** *BHerald* 4/1 1: Bright as a new button. **1961** HKuttner *Bypass* (NY) 89: Absalom as bright as a button. **1969** EBagnold *Autobiography* (B) 22: As bright as a button [*a memory*]. **1971** CAird *Late* (NY) 148: A shrimp of a man, bright as a button. **1977** PDJames *Death* (NY) 91: The button-bright eyes. EAP B390.

B513 As cute as a **Button** (pin)
1940 MBoniface *Murder as* (NY) 153: Cute as a button. **1954** HStone *Man Who* (NY 1957) 22: She was as cute as a button. **1958** *New Yorker* 5/31 50: Oxford's women students look as cute as pins. **1958** *Time* 5/26 45: He's cute as a button. **1970** AALewis *Carnival* (NY) 307: Cute as a button. Taylor *Prov. Comp.* 31.

B514 As round as **Buttons**
1939 EHuxley *African Poison* (NY) 74: Eyes . . . round as buttons. Whiting *NC* 378(3).

B515 Not to care a **Button** (*varied*)
1910 EPhillpotts *Tales* (NY) 275: Don't care a button. **1922** JSFletcher *Middle of Things* (NY) 261: Not care the value of a brass button. **1922** JJoyce *Ulysses* (NY 1934) 191: I don't care a button. **1926** HHext *Monster* (NY) 29: I don't care a brass button. **1933** GDHCole *Lesson* (L) 262: I don't believe you care a button. **1934** AFielding *Paper Chase* (L) 91: Starr doesn't care a brass button. **1936** LRGribble *Malverne* (L) 95: He doesn't care a broken button for her money. **1947** ELustgarten *One More* (NY 1959) 221: Not that I care a button. **1958** HRobertson *Crystal Gazers* (NY) 51: I don't care a brass button. **1966** HRFKeating *Death* (NY) 155: Not to care a button. **1970** AFreemantle *Three-cornered* (NY) 255: I don't care a button. **1977** VCanning *Doomsday* (NY) 190: Not really caring a button. EAP B391.

B516 Not to give a **Button** (*varied*)
1930 WLewis *Apes* (NY 1932) 18: For survival she did not give a button. **1956** DWheatley *Ka* (L) 17: Didn't give a button. **1972** MGilbert *Body* (NY) 138: You didn't give a brass button for her. EAP B392; TW 50(4).

B517 Not to matter a **Button**
1921 JBCabell *Figures* (NY 1925) 346: I cannot see that these doings matter a button's worth. **1929** HMSmith *Jigsaw* (NY) 176: It doesn't matter a button. **1939** NMarsh *Overture* (NY) 65: It doesn't matter a tupenny button. **1949** EPhillpotts *Address* (L) 201: [It] doesn't matter a button. Cf. Whiting B634.

B518   Not to mind (signify) a **Button**
1941 EPhillpotts *Ghostwater* (NY) 226: It doesn't signify a button. **1969** GMFraser *Flashman* (NY) 14: I didn't mind a button. Whiting B632.

B519   Not worth a **Button**
1939 TStevenson *Silver Dollar* (L) 221: Ain't worth a button. **1965** AGilbert *Voice* (NY) 62: Ain't worth a button. EAP B395; TW 50(9); Brunvand 18(2).

B520   To lose (have) one's **Buttons**
1919 LMenick *Chain* (L) 317: The young woman had all her buttons on [*was clever*]. **1932** MTurnbull *Return* (P) 85: I don't know that Bet's got all her buttons. **1955** GBagby *Dirty* (NY) 94: [He] doesn't have all his buttons. He's crazy. **1960** DMDisney *Dark* (NY) 59: Old Milt lost all his buttons years ago. **1969** LEGoss *Knight* (NY) 22: The old lady had lost her buttons [*insane*]. Partridge 115.

B521   To **Buy** and sell (be bought and sold)
1936 HCBailey *Clue* (L) 238: Bought and sold—aren't you? **1940** DWheelock *Murder at Montauk* (NY) 190: He had enough money to buy and sell Mrs. Jessup. **1948** WMiller *Fatal* (NY) 42: I can buy and sell guys like you. **1952** RMacdonald *Ivory* (NY 1965) 49: I can buy and sell you twenty times over. **1960** JO'Hara *Ourselves* (NY) 37: He could buy and sell us. **1962** DHonig *No Song* (L) 43: I could have bought and sold the lot of them. **1974** AChurchill *Splendid* (NY) 9: He could buy and sell nearly every husband. EAP B397.

B522   Let the **Buyer** beware
1932 WMartyn *Murder* (NY) 118: Let the buyer beware. **1937** SPalmer *Blue Banderella* (NY) 68: Let the buyer beware. **1952** EPaul *Black* (NY) 206: The buyer had better beware. **1966** EFuller *Successful* (NY) 68: The old time let-the-buyer-beware tradition. EAP B399.

B523   As bald (drunk) as a **Buzzard**
1953 GRHEllis *Lesser* (L) 112: Drunk as a buzzard. **1961** ESeeman *In the Arms* (NY) 37: He is bald as a buzzard. Cf. Coot *below*.

B524   To puke like a **Buzzard**
1967 JFDobie *Some Part* (B) 18: "Puke like a buzzard" was a common expression. Whiting *NC* 378(4).

B525   Let **Bygones** be bygones
1900 CFPidgin *Quincy A. Sawyer* (B) 398: To let bygones be bygones. **1905** JBCabell *Line* (NY 1926) 20: Bygones are bygones. **1908** JCLincoln *Cy Whittaker* (NY) 291: I'm willing to let bygones be past. **1908** LDYoung *Climbing Doom* (NY) 214: Let bygones be bygones, as the saying is. **1929** WFaulkner *Sound* (NY) 134: Let bygones be bygones. **1930** FDBurdett *Odyssey* (L) 96: We let bygones be bygones as the old saying has it. **1937** HAustin *Murder* (L) 80: Ready to let bygones be by. **1942** PGWodehouse *Money* (NY) 225: The let-bygones-be-bygones spirit. **1955** DMDisney *Trick* (NY) 123: Let bygones be bygones. **1959** *Time* 5/4 21: Let bygones be bygones. **1964** SRansome *One-Man* (NY DBC) 73: In a spirit of let bygones be bygones. **1969** CBaker *E Hemingway* (NY) 141: Bygones were now gone by. **1977** JLHensley *Rivertown* (NY) 186: To let bygones be bygones. EAP B401.

C

C1 To be not as green as one is **Cabbage** looking

1922 JJoyce *Ulysses* (NY 1934) 307: He's not as green as he's cabbage looking. **1962** MAllingham *China* (NY) 202: I'm not as green as I'm cabbage looking. **1980** RBarnard *Death* (NY) 30: You're not so green as you're cabbage looking. Partridge 352: Green.

C2 To chew (boil) one's **Cabbage** (fat) twice (*varied*)

1955 DMDisney *Room* (NY) 42: I don't chew my cabbage twice. **1959** PDeVries *Through* (B) 127: Chew mah cabbage twice. Ah will not. **1966** NMonsarrat *Life (I)* (L) 66: I don't boil cabbage twice. **1971** GBaxt *Affair* (NY) 124: I don't chew my fat twice. **1981** PDeVries *Sauce* (B) 203: Even Daisy had sometimes had to chew her cabbage twice, when her Hoosier twang had met with a "Beg pardon?" DARE i 609: Chew; DA Cabbage b: Boil; Wentworth 97: Chew one's cabbage, 98: Chew one's tobacco twice. Cf. *Oxford* 97.

C3 To find (*a baby*) under a **Cabbage** leaf

1937 HAshbrook *Murder* (NY) 222: Her mother didn't find her under a cabbage leaf, you know. MLeach *Dict. of Folklore* I 101: Babies.

C4 To slip (cut) one's **Cable**

1906 JCLincoln *Mr. Pratt* (NY) 47: Pack up and cut your cable. **1909** JCLincoln *Keziah* (NY) 297: He's slipped his cable [*died*]. **1933** HWade *Policeman's* (L) 225: Slipped his cable. TW 52.

C5 To cut the **Cackle** and come to the horses (*varied*)

1926 AMarshall *Mote* (NY) 193: Cut a lot of cackle. **1927** RAFreeman *Magic* (NY) 112: Cut the cackle and get to the hosses. **1934** JVTurner *Murder* (L) 12: Let's cut the cackle and get down to the facts. **1937** DHume *Halfway* (L) 110: Cut the cackle and get down to brass tacks. **1941** NMarsh *Death and the* (B) 85: It was time to cut the cackle and get to the horses. **1956** WMankowitz *Old* (B) 149: Cutting the cackle, it's a bloody washout in which the baby is thrown out with the bath-water and devil take all. **1956** *Punch* 9/26 363: I "cut the cackle and come to the horses." **1962** AWUpfield *Death* (NY) 238: I think it was a gentleman named Sam Weller who used to say: "Cut the cackle and get to the horses." Partridge 119.

C6 As dead as (Julius) **Caesar**

1928 HVO'Brien *Four-and-Twenty* (NY) 175: As dead and historical as Julius Caesar. **1930** VLoder *Essex* (L) 11: Dead as Caesar. **1946** ESedgwick *Happy* (B) 45: Dead as Caesar. **1958** WDHassett *Off the Record* (New Brunswick, NJ) 193: It is as dead as Julius Caesar or a door nail. TW 52(3).

C7 **Caesar's** wife must be above suspicion (*varied*)

1925 JSFletcher *Wrychester* (L) 140: Cæsar's wife, and all that sort of thing. **1930** HGHutchinson *Lost Golfer* (L) 246: I can hardly believe that all the politicians . . . come up to the standard of Caesar's wives even now. **1930** EDTorgerson *Murderer* (NY) 128: Not a woman whom Caesar would have prized as a wife. Not above suspicion. **1931** LEppley *Murder* (NY) 209: "Caesar's wife." . . . "She who was above suspicion." **1938** NMarsh *Death* (NY) 89: The well known position of Caesar's wife . . . She did not appear in the gossip columns. **1942** JDCarr *Emperor's* (NY) 163: And Caesar's wife and all that. **1955** MAllingham *Estate* (NY) 185: [He] is absolutely Caesar's wife. **1956** AMWells *Night* (NY) 78: Being above reproach, like Caesar's wife, was all very well. **1960** EWolf *Rosenbach* (Cleveland) 376: He owns a set as chaste as Caesar's wife. **1967** LPDavies *Artificial* (NY) 39: No reason why [he] should be as inviolate as Caesar's wife. **1971** TCatledge *My Life* (NY) 268: Like Caesar's wife, it must keep its reputation above reproach. **1975** NGuild *Lost* (NY) 68: Teaching is a sensitive profession—you have to be Cæsar's wife. **1982** JRoss *Rattling* (NY) 65: She was a bitch. And a promiscuous bitch at that. Like Caesar's wife or whoever it was: all things to all men. EAP C4.

C8 Render unto **Caesar** the things that are Caesar's

1939 RStout *Mountain Cat* (NY 1958) 103: I . . . must render unto Caesar the things that are Caesar's. Whiting C1; *Oxford* 671: Render. Cf. EAP C5.

C9 To be in **Cahoots** with

1932 NTrott *Monkey* (NY) 260: He was in cahoots with Brainerd. **1958** FLockridge *Long* (P) 154: They could have been in cahoots. TW 52; DARE i 506: Cahoot.

C10 To raise **Cain**

1922 JJoyce *Ulysses* (NY 1934) 155: Raise Cain. **1931** CHTowne *This New York* (NY) 107: They . . . raised Cain, as the saying went. **1938** SLeslie *Film* (L) 174: We raised heavenly Cain all day. **1944** CWoolrich *Black Path* (NY) 180: She's been raising Cain. **1956** DWheatley *Ka* (L) 21: Certain to raise Cain. **1969** HLiggett *Murder* (L) 166: [He] raised Cain. TW 52(2).

C11 One cannot have his **Cake** and eat it (*varied*)

1922 JJoyce *Ulysses* (NY 1934) 202: You cannot eat your cake and have it. **c1923** ACrowley *Confessions* ed JSymonds (L 1969) 775: She wanted to have her cake and eat it as well. **1927** DYates *Blind* (NY) 27: Where a man may eat his cake and have it too. **1931** PWynnton *Ten* (P) 143: I'm going to have my cake, and I'm going to eat it. **1934** VLincoln *February Hill* (NY) 293: You can't have everything and eat it too, as the sayin' is. **1941** ISShriber *Murder Well Done* (NY) 26: He's planning to have his cake and you too. **1948** HReilly *Staircase* (NY) 7: I'd rather have my cake and not eat it. **1951** KBennett *Wink* (L) 96: You appear to wish to have your cake and eat it, as they say in England. **1952** JMFox *Shroud* (B) 155: What do you want? . . . Eat your cake and have the crumbs in bed with you. **1956** *NY Times Book Review* 11/25 5: Santayana was able to eat his cake and yet not eat it at the same time. **1956** *PMLA* 71 604: Twain . . . hoped to have his cake and eat it too. **1957** *Punch* 2/6 225: We cannot eat our cake and export it. **1957** *Time* 4/22 10: We can have our quake and read it too. **1957** *Punch* 7/11 137: Labour must realize that it cannot have its Stock Exchange and eat it. **1958** *TLS* 2/7 73: Hodgins wants to have his cake, and enough money to buy more when he has eaten it. **1958** *NYTimes Book Review* 6/1 20: In theory . . . we can have our high production cake and eat it without the problems of inflation. **1959** *BHerald* 4/13 10: A better instance of having one's cake and eating it, too, could hardly be imagined. **1960** CBrossard *Double* (NY) 129: In a way, eat her cake and throw it up too. **1964** RO'Connor *Jack* (B) 166: There was no reason he couldn't have his marital cake and his illicit frosting. **1970** RFBanks *Maine* (Middletown, Conn.) 202: One could, so to speak, have his cake and eat it too. **1973** GWheeler *Pierpont* (Englewood Cliffs, NJ) 23: [They] were having their cake and eating it, too. EAP C8; TW 52(1).

C12 To be a **Cake** walk

1952 GKersh *Brazen* (L) 14: It seems to be a Cake Walk, as you say in America, or, as they say in England, money for jam. DA Cake walk 1b.

C13   To take the Cake

1929 GLimnelius *Medbury* (NY) 260: That taikes the caike. **1933** WMarch *Company K* (NY) 34: This one takes the cake. **1940** CBDawson *Lady Wept* (NY) 156: This seemed to take the cake. **1956** EMcBain *Cop* (NY 1959) 157: If that don't take the cake. **1961** DLoovis *Last* (NY) 294: That takes the cake. **1971** ELathen *Longer* (NY) 85: Take the cake. TW 53(6).

C14   To groan like a dying Calf

1961 RFoley *It's Murder* (NY DBC) 21: He's groaning like a dying calf. EAP C12.

C15   To kill the fatted Calf

1943 AAMacGregor *Auld Reekie* (L) 156: Every autumn she sacrificed to hospitality, not the proverbial fatted calf, but an ox. **1972** CDSimak *Choice* (NY) 161: "We'll kill the fatted calf" . . . "You'll do what?" . . . "Just a saying." EAP C13; Brunvand 19(1).

C16   To take the Calf to get the heifer

1961 FPohl *Turn Left* (NY) 26: I'll take the calf to get the heifer [*be nice to daughter to get mother*]. EAP C10. Cf. Whiting *NC* 379(3). Cf. Way to the daughter *below*.

C17   A California widow

1935 *New Yorker* 12/21 69: A "California widow"; i.e., a lady whose husband's long absence in the gold fields had made the birth of a child biologically amazing. DA California 2 (17, quote 1877).

C18   As weak as Cambric tea

1954 EForbes *Rainbow* (B) 195: Still weak as cambric tea. DA Cambric tea.

C19   The Camel and the needle's eye

1928 JArnold *Surrey* (L) 143: Talk about getting a camel through the eye of a needle! **1928** CDane *Enter* (L) 267: Talk about looking for a camel in a needle's eye, you'd lose a bloody elephant in this 'er roundabout. **1945** CEVulliamy *Edwin* (L) 175: How difficult it is for a rich man to pass through the eye of a needle! **1959** FHoyle *Ossian's* (NY) 75: It were easier for a camel to pass through the eye of a needle . . . **1960** ADug-

gan *Cunning* (NY) 65: Can you find a very small camel, small enough to go through the eye of a needle? **1965** AGilbert *Voice* (NY) 81: Talk about an elephant going through the eye of a needle. **1965** RHardwick *Plotters* (NY) 94: Getting a candle [*sic*] through the eye of a needle would be easy compared to getting him into the Riverside Club. EAP C15; TW 54(3); Brunvand 20(2).

C20   The Camel's nose in the Arab's tent

1958 *NYTimes* 5/18 10: The gift horse we have accepted is permanently installed in our stable . . . and threatening to kick us off the island. 13E: Any national grant . . . is a camel's nose in education's tent. **1965** ESGardner *Beautiful* (NY) 34: Relatives can act like the proverbial camel in the tent. **1966** LGreenbaum *Hound* (The Hague) 39: Pound . . . accepted the invitation like the proverbial camel outside the Arab's tent. **1967** PMcGerr *Murder* (NY) 146: It's the old nose-under-the-tent routine. **1983** *BGlobe* 12/13 15: [In] the 60's . . . the camel's nose of trendy leftist politics was poking its way into the suburban tent. Cf. Champion 330(68).

C21   Enough to choke a Camel

1957 WRBurdett *Underdog* (NY) 122: A roll that would choke a camel. TW 54(1). Cf. Enough to choke a Horse *below*.

C22   A Can of worms

1969 RMacdonald *Goodbye* (NY) 49: I'm sorry I ever opened this can of worms [*trouble*]. **1970** KLaumer *World* (NY) 183: We won't reopen that can of worms for a while. **1971** MScherf *Beautiful* (NY) 119: This opens up a whole new can of worms. **1972** TWells *Die* (NY) 167: I don't need this can of worms [*trouble*]. **1974** TWells *Have Mercy* (NY) 91: That opened a whole new can of worms [*skulduggery*]. 147: Sounds like Dover's got a can of worms [*trouble*]. **1975** JFraser *Wreath* (NY) 39: When you lift the lid off these old families you often find a can of worms. **1976** RBDominic *Murder* (NY) 156: It's pretty much the same can of worms to me. We can't prove anything about the weapon. **1981** PLauben *Nice* (NY)

72: You've managed to really tangle up an already messy can of worms. Wentworth 88.

C23 To tie a **Can** to someone

1930 CSHammock *Why Murder* (NY) 124: I'll be lucky if they don't tie a can to me this time. Wentworth 545: Tie.

C24 Those who **Can** do, those who can't teach

1933 PStong *Strangers* (NY) 109: Those who can, do, those who can't, teach. **1956** RILee *Happy* (B) 16: The old cliché: "Those who can do; those who can't teach." **1964** BKaufman *Up the Down* (NY 1966) 66: "Those who can, do; those who can't teach." Like most sayings, this is only half true. **1969** ACGreene *Personal* (NY) 295: Them as can does, them as can't teaches. Bartlett 836b [*GBShaw*].

C25 Not able to hold a **Candle** to

1919 JBCabell *Jurgen* (NY 1922) 188: She cannot hold a candle to you. **1922** JJoyce *Ulysses* (NY 1934) 620: The lies . . . couldn't probably hold a proverbial candle to the wholesale whoppers other fellows coined. **1932** JCLenehan *Mansfield* (L) 244: The Black Boy . . . couldn't hold a candle to Albert for wickedness. **1953** DCushman *Stay Away* (NY) 193: He couldn't hold a candle to my great-uncle. **1959** LWibberly *Quest* (NY) 115: They got coeds at UCLA that she couldn't hold a candle to. **1964** JWiles *March* (L) 192: Richard . . . could not hold a candle to Barbarossa. **1965** HPearson *By Himself* (L) 194: Sancho Panza could not hold a candle to Falstaff. **1968** EBuckler *Ox Bells* (NY) 66: The Reformation couldn't hold a candle to the Gunpowder Plot. **1975** JFoxx *Dead Run* (I) 115: Ideology couldn't hold a candle to . . . greed. EAP C20.

C26 To be snuffed out like a **Candle**

1931 EQueen *Dutch* (NY) 112: Snuffed out like a candle. **1937** DQBurleigh *Kristiana* (NY) 209: I snuffed out like a candle. **1938** CWitting *Michaelmas Goose* (L) 94: Poor young fellow! . . . Snuffed out like a candle. NED Snuff *v.*[1] 2. Cf. Partridge 796: Snuff out; *Oxford* 307: Go out.

C27 To burn one's **Candle** at both ends

1925 JRhode *Paddington* (L) 197: It doesn't do to burn the candle and both ends. **1928** JAGade *Christian* (NY) 255: [He] was consuming his candle by burning at both ends. **1932** RWhitfield *Virgin* (NY) 9: My candle burns at both ends . . . I gotta hunch it'll be out before morning. **1933** GDHCole *Death* (NY) 199: Don't burn the candle at both ends. **1939** LRGribble *Arsenal* (L) 74: You can't burn the candle and both ends and still live to blow it out. **1947** VWMason *Saigon* (NY) 60: Like burning the candle at both ends. **1957** WGHardy *City* (NY) 56: "Burning the candle at both ends and in the middle too," Lycisca scolded, quoting a proverb from Verona. **1961** GGFickling *Blood* (NY) 42: You're lit at both ends and the middle. You'd better go home before you wind up working in some candle shop as a salesgirl. **1965** AHeckstall-Smith *Consort* (NY) 42: His mother-in-law didn't burn her candle in the middle as well as at both ends. **1970** JVizzard *See* (NY) 303: It wanted to burn the candle from both ends. **1975** JDaniels *White* (NY) 173: He had been burning the candle. EAP C21.

C28 To go out like a **Candle**

1939 JJFarjeon *Seven Dead* (I) 241: I went out like a candle. **1945** MWalsh *Nine Strings* (P) 174: Out like a candle [*dead*]. **1958** VCanning *Dragon* (NY) 62: Went out like a candle [*fainted*]. Cf. *Oxford* 307: Go out.

C29 To hold a **Candle** to the devil

1934 GDilnot *Crook's* (L) 159: There are times when one has to hold a candle to the devil. EAP C22.

C30 Like taking **Candy** from a baby (*varied*)

1914 PGWodehouse *Little Nugget* (NY 1929) 291: Like taking candy from a kid. **1921** ERBurroughs *Mucker* (NY) 343: Like taking candy from a baby. **1933** FLPackard *Hidden* (L) 60: It's like taking candy from a kid. **1957** *BangorDN* 2/11 20: That must be like taking candy from a baby. **1967** JDetre *Happy* (NY) 114: It was like taking candy from a baby. **1975** ELathen *By Hook* (NY) 78: Like taking candy away from a baby. Taylor *Prov. Comp.* 23.

C31 To paddle one's own **Canoe**

1902 WJames *Letters* ed TFlournoy (Madison, Wisc. 1966) 134: Everyone must paddle his own canoe. **1933** AChristie *Tuesday* (NY) 188: You must paddle your own canoe. **1935** LAKnight *Super-Cinema* (L) 62: You can paddle your own damned canoe. **1950** ESGardner *Musical* (NY) 154: I'll paddle my own canoe. **1956** *BangorDN* 8/25 10: They have their own canoes to paddle. **1963** HPentecost *Only* (NY DBC) 61: You're going to have to paddle your own canoe. **1970** JLeasor *They Don't* (NY) 66: You have to paddle your own canoe, to coin a phrase. EAP C27; Brunvand 20.

C32 If the **Cap** fits wear it (*varied*)

1923 ACrowley *Confessions* ed JSymonds (L 1969) 768: Lest Washington should think the cap fitted. **1927** AGilbert *Tragedy* (NY) 45: There's only one man here whom the cap fits. **1928** LTracy *Women* (NY) 67: If the cap fits, I'll wear it. **1930** AFielding *Craig* (NY) 198: Prejudice is not evidence, and the cap must fit the head. **1930** MKennedy *Half Mast* (NY) 234: "If the cap fits . . ." "Loathsome proverb." **1941** KRoos *If the Shroud Fits* (NY). **1953** GRHEllis *Lesser* (L) 103: If the cap seems to fit it would be seemly to wear it. **1958** WGraham *Wreck* (NY) 112: If the cap fits, wear it. **1973** JMann *Troublecross* (NY) 163: If the cap fits, put it on. EAP C29. Cf. If the Shoe fits *below.*

C33 To put on one's thinking **Cap**

1924 JSFletcher *Safety* (NY) 285: Bartlett assumed his thinking cap. **1934** JVTurner *Murder* (L) 179: Put your thinking cap on. **1945** GBellairs *Calamity* (NY) 47: Put on your thinking-cap. **1956** *BangorDN* 8/28 17: Put on yore thinkin' cap. **1956** AGilbert *Riddle* (NY) 193: Bring your thinking cap with you. **1966** JDCarr *Panic* (NY) 133: Your thinking cap becomes you. **1970** CDrummond *Stab* (NY) 169: I put my Thinkin' Cap on. EAP C32.

C34 To set one's **Cap** at (for) someone (*varied*)

1909 JCLincoln *Keziah* (NY) 103: Settin' your cap to be a parson's wife. **1922** JJoyce

Ulysses (NY 1934) 356: I can throw my cap at who I like because its leap year. **1924** CWells *Furthest* (P) 300: All the women set their caps for him. **1933** HCBailey *Mr. Fortune Wonders* (NY) 28: She has set her cap at you. **1933** GWeston *Murder* (NY) 62: She's been throwing her cap at Mr. Mallory. **1947** AGilbert *Death in* (L) 19: Every woman sets her cap at a bachelor. **1958** HCarmichael *Or Be* (NY) 80: To set her cap at the boss. **1966** LEGoss *Afterglow* (Portland, Me.) 10: Ed had set his cap for Molly. **1973** NNicolson *Portrait* (NY) 153: Violet set her cap at him. **1974** EPHoyt *Horatio's* (Radnor, Penn.) 97: With her cap set for anything in pants. EAP C31; Brunvand 20.

C35 **Cape** Cod turkey

1957 MPHood *In the Dark* (NY) 90: Nothing better than Cape Cod turkey. **1958** *BHerald* 2/12 13: To many, salt cod is "Cape Cod Turkey." DARE i 538–9; DA Cape Cod; Wentworth 88. Cf. DARE i 32–3: Alaska turkey.

C36 To cut **Capers**

1903 ADMcFaul *Ike Glidden* (B) 3: Cut up any more capers. **1930** HHolt *Ace* (L) 63: Gloria did cut some pretty capers. **1935** DMagarshack *Death Cuts a Caper* (NY). **1939** WTarg *Mr. Cassidy* (NY) 41: She's been cutting capers with the chauffeur. **1940** NMarsh *Death of a Peer* (B) 371: We must use our cunning and cut our capers according to our cloth. **1946** RHuggins *Double Tale* (NY 1959) 104: I think somebody's cutting capers out of school. **1953** CBKelland *Sinister* (NY DBC) 35: She cut up capers. **1965** ESGardner *Beautiful* (NY) 167: Cut any more capers. EAP C33.

C37 Where the **Carcass** is there will the vultures (*etc.*) be gathered

1908 JCLincoln *Cy Whittaker* (NY) 238: Where the carcass is the vultures are on deck, or words similar. **1917** JCLincoln *Extricating* (NY) 92: Where the carcass is the-er-er-dogfish are gathered together. **1919** LTracy *Bartlett* (NY) 4: Where the carcass is there the vultures gather. **1932** CBush *Unfortunate* (L) 247: "Where the carcass is . . ." "there's nothing of the eagle about me." **1933** MPlum *Murder* (NY) 212: Where the booty is, there do the jackals gather. **1935** CBrooks *Three Yards* (L) 67: Where the carcass is, there the kites gather. **1958** CHare *He Should* (L) 93: Where the carcass is, there shall the eagles be gathered together. **1962** AGilbert *Uncertain* (NY DBC) 74: Where the body is, there shall the vultures be gathered together. **1965** RESt-Leger-Gordon *Witchcraft* (L) 108: Where the carcass is there will the ravens be gathered together on Dartmoor. **1969** JDrummond *People* (NY) 26: It looks as if the eagles are beginning to gather. EAP C36; TW 56; Brunvand 20.

C38 To be on (in) the **Cards**

1929 TCobb *Crime* (L) 131: It's quite on the cards. **1937** GBarnett *I Knew* (L) 178: It's on the cards. **1956** MGEberhart *Postmark* (NY) 193: It was in the cards. EAP C38.

C39 To give **Cards** and spades

1927 NMartin *Mosaic* (NY) 1: [It] would have given cards and spades to any trunk. **1933** CWells *Clue* (NY) 134: He could give cards and spades to . . . the young people. **1936** CMRussell *Death* (NY) 265: Parker could give me cards and spades and still win. **1959** JBlish *Clash* (L) 61: You . . . could . . . give all the rest of us cards and spades. **1969** PAnderson *Beyond* (NY) 179: We can give him cards and spades and still defeat him. DA Card n.² 6b.

C40 To have the **Cards** stacked against one

1928 WAWolff *Trial* (NY) 160: The cards were stacked against Mary. **1936** LRGribble *Malverne* (L) 121: The cards are stacked against me. DA Stack v. 1; Partridge 821: Stack.

C41 To put (lay) one's **Cards** on the table

1921 P&MThorne *Sheridan* (NY) 91: I have laid my cards on the table; 92. **1923** LThayer *Sinister* (NY) 104: Put my cards on the table. **1933** MBeckett *Murder* (L) 254: I've put my cards on the table. **1937** A Christie *Cards on the Table* (NY). **1940** CKnight *Death Valley* (NY) 204: All my cards are on the table. **1941** TFuller *Reunion* (B) 162: Put all his cards on the table, as the saying went. **1955** CMWills *Death* (L)

74: I'll put my cards right on the table. **1956** *BHerald* 8/17 18: Mr. Starsen laid his cards on the table and called a spade a spade, regardless of whose political toes he stepped upon. **1961** WMasterson *Evil* (NY) 76: Let's put all the cards on the table. **1974** DMarlowe *Somebody's* (NY) 122: To put his cards on the table. NED Suppl. Card *sb.*² 2d.

C42 Unlucky at **Cards,** lucky in love (*varied*)

1927 FEverton *Dalehouse* (NY) 225: Unlucky at cards, lucky in love. **1928** HCrosby *Shadows* (Paris) 5: Lucky in cards, unlucky in love. **1928** AFielding *Net* (NY) 111: Judging by his cards, he must be the luckiest man in love in the world. **1931** GHolt *Green* (I) 251: Lucky at boule, unlucky at—what? **1931** HCrooker *Crime* (NY) 34: Doubly lucky—in love and at the race track. **1931** MDalton *Night* (NY) 198: I should think . . . that Hugh Darrow must be phenomenally unlucky at cards [*lucky in love*]. **1936** JDosPassos *Big Money* (NY) 299: Lucky at cards, unlucky at love. **1937** JDCarr *Four False* (NY) 227: Unlucky in love, lucky at cards. **1938** BGraeme *Mystery* (P) 182: Unlucky at cards, lucky at love. **1940** MRRinehart *Great Mistake* (NY) 67: I've held rotten cards . . . maybe I'm lucky in love. **1943** WMcCully *Doctors* (NY) 20: Lucky in golf, unlucky in love. **1947** PMcGerr *Pick* (NY) 91: You know what they say about people who are unlucky at cards. **1949** GFowler *Beau* (NY) 52: Lucky at horses and lucky at love. **1954** EBox *Death* (NY 1955) 112: Lucky in love, unlucky in crime. **1957** WHHarris *Golden* (NY) 101: The old saying: lucky at cards, unlucky in love. **1960** NFitzgerald *Candles* (L) 58: I'm dead out of luck [*at cards*] . . . It must be my night for love. **1973** JSymons *Plot* (NY) 131: It must be love I'm lucky at [*he had lost a card game*]. **1974** CMartin *Whiskey* (NY) 219: The old saying, "Lucky at cards, unlucky at love." **1977** JThomson *Death* (NY) 76: Unlucky at cards, lucky in love. EAP C37.

C43 As stiff as **Cardboard**

1934 SPalmer *Murder* (L) 231: The girl was stiff as cardboard. **1959** EWeeks *In Friendly*

(B) 126: Stories . . . stiff as cardboard. Cf. As stiff as a Board *above.*

C44 Care killed a (the) cat

1904 LFBaum *Marvelous Land of Oz* (NY) 113: Care once killed a cat. **1929** BFlynn *Case* (P) 71: Care may have killed the cat. **1935** RCWoodthorpe *Shadow* (NY) 184: Care killed the cat. **1942** HReilly *Name Your Poison* (NY) 29: Care killed a cat. **1953** OAtkinson *Golden* (I) 24: Care killed a cat. **1973** AGilbert *Nice* (NY) 74: Care killed the cat. EAP C41; Brunvand 20. Cf. Curiosity *below.*

C45 To be on the **Carpet**

1931 JJFarjeon *House* (NY) 228: What was on the carpet. **1940** HCBailey *Mr. Fortune Here* (NY) 206: His women are on the carpet. **1946** MInnes *What Happened* (NY) 55: Whatever had been on the carpet. **1960** MColes *Concrete* (NY) 170: The matter which we have now upon our carpet. EAP C44. Cf. Tapis *below.*

C46 To have someone (be put) on the **Carpet**

1926 CJDutton *Flying* (NY) 224: I had him on the carpet. **1932** JVTurner *Who Spoke* (L) 143: We'll both be hauled on the carpet. **1936** NMorland *Street* (L) 159: She would be called on the carpet. **1953** JWyndham *Kraken* (L 1955) 17: I don't want to find myself on the carpet. **1959** BHerald 3/22 23: I will not be called on the carpet. **1970** RLPike *Reardon* (NY) 70: Has Captain Tower had you on the carpet? Wentworth 89.

C47 The **Carrot** and the stick

1953 VPJohns *Murder* (NY 1962) 36: The carrot dangled before a plodding donkey's nose. **1957** *NYTimes* 4/28 5E: Satellites seeing carrot and stick. **1957** IFleming *From Russia* (NY 1958) 29: The stick and then the carrot. **1958** BHerald 3/23 16 IV: The residuals are the carrots (in front of the donkey) that keep us going. **1963** JLeCarré *Spy Who* (NY) 170: With the carrot in front and the stick behind, Mundt was recruited. **1966** PAnderson *Trouble* (NY) 187: The carrot of trade and the stick of war. **1967** SMorrow *Insiders* (NY) 127: "I dangled a carrot just before I left him." . . . "First the carrot and then the stick." NED Suppl. Carrot 2a: To dangle a carrot.

C48 To put the **Cart** before the horse (*varied*)

1928 EKRand *Founders* (Cambridge, Mass.) 82: The horse follows the cart. **1929** AFielding *Mysterious* (NY) 220: If we haven't got the cart before the horse. **1935** MKennedy *Poison* (L) 14: I am putting the cart before the horse. **1937** MFAshley-Montagu *Coming Into Being* (L) 2: A very neat example of the manner in which the cart should not be put in relation to the horse. **1941** CRice *Right Murder* (NY) 155: You mean like putting the horse before the barn door after the cart has been stolen? **1949** ESGardner *Dubious* (NY 1954) 117: You're getting the cart and horse all mixed up. **1957** *Punch* 1/9 86: This cart-before-the-horse thing. **1958** *TLS* 3/28 170: The cart, one feels, is in front of the horse. **1961** AGilbert *After* (NY DBC) 124: Putting the cart before the horse. **1967** LWoolf *Downhill* (L) 241: The real question . . . is: which was the cart and which the horse? **1972** CBeaton *Memoirs* (NY) 28: Putting the cart before the horse. EAP C48; TW 56(2).

C49 To be in the **Cart**

1922 JJoyce *Ulysses* (NY 1934) 320: We're all in a cart [*unlucky*]. **1927** GDilnot *Lazy* (B) 257: If we're in the cart, we're in it. **1930** AGilbert *Mystery* (NY) 214: That rather puts our young man in the cart. **1936** JMWalsh *Crimes* (L) 182: We'll be in the cart together, to put it quite vulgarly. **1945** MColes *Green Hazard* (NY) 146: You're in the cart, not me. **1948** JRhode *Death* (NY) 169: He'll be properly in the cart. **1960** MSpark *Bachelors* (L) 182: If Patrick gets convicted, she'll be in the cart. **1971** CAird *Late* (NY) 15: He'd be properly in the cart. Partridge 130.

C50 As many as **Carter** has pills

1957 WGoldman *Temple* (NY) 134: He had more excuses than Carter has pills. Taylor *Prov. Comp.* 57.

93

C51 As stubborn as **Carter's** mule

1965 AGilbert *Voice* (NY) 55: He's as stubborn as Carter's mule—whoever that remarkable beast may have been. Cf. As stubborn as a Mule *below*.

C52 The **Case** is altered

1928 RTGould *Oddities* (L) 124: The case is altered. **1933** DGBrowne *Cotfold* (L) 79: "The case is altered, as some one said." "Plowden." **1938** ABCox *Not To Be* (L) 73: The case is altered. **1959** GCarr *Swing* (NY) 232: The case is altered. **1969** AGilbert *Mr. Crook* (NY DBC) 31: The Case is Altered. **1970** DJacobson *Rape* (L) 107: The case is altered. EAP C51; TW 57(4).

C53 Hard **Cases** make hard (bad) law

c**1923** ACrowley *Confessions* ed JSymonds (L 1969) 119: Hard cases make hard law. **1966** LNizer *Jury* (NY) 87: An old saying, "Hard cases make hard law." **1978** NFreeling *Night Lords* (NY) 109: Hard cases make bad law. *Oxford* 352–3.

C54 To build **Castles** in Spain

1904 SArmitage-Smith *John of Gaunt* (L) 272: Building castles in Spain; 301. **1912** HHMunro *Unbearable* (NY 1928) 165: Not a castle in Spain. **1925** BAtkey *Pyramid* (NY) 208: I have several [*castles*] already—some in Spain and some in the air. **1925** JSFletcher *Wolves* (NY) 205: The castles in Spain . . . had fallen into dust and fragments. **1934** REast *Bell* (L) 171: He was building his castles in Spain. **1942** MG Eberhart *Wolf* (NY) 159: My castles in Spain. **1952** HFMPrescott *Man on* (NY) 362: When her castles in Spain had been a house in London. **1959** EHuxley *Flame* (L) 84: I mean to have a castle in Spain when my ship comes home. **1971** WHMarnell *Once upon* (NY) 115: Our castles of cheese went the way of castles in Spain. **1974** ELathen *Sweet* (NY) 101: [He] was not building castles in Spain. TW 57(2).

C55 To build **Castles** in the air

1925 HHext *Monster* (NY) 25: Built castles in the air. **1930** LCharteris *Enter* (NY) 171: It was a fantastic castle to build in the air. **1932** JJConnington *Sweepstake* (B) 201: That brief visit to the castle in the air. **1933** CWells *Clue* (NY) 308: My air castle is in ruins. **1936** PGWodehouse *Luck* (B) 223: When all the castles he had been building in the air . . . come tumbling about his ears. **1950** DMDisney *Fire* (NY) 80: The little air castles she had built. **1956** SWTaylor *I Have* (NY) 179: [Her] shining castles in the air had crashed about her ears. **1958** MAMusmanno *Verdict* (NY) 142: The castle in the clouds. **1964** JPorter *Dover One* (NY 1966) 106: Don't lets build too many castles on thin air. **1970** JWechsberg *First* (B) 323: Building castles in the sky. **1978** HFleetwood *Roman* (NY) 81: Build his marvellous gothic castles in the air. EAP C56; Brunvand 21(2).

C56 As agile as a **Cat**

1913 ERBurroughs *Warlord* (NY 1963) 21: Agile as a cat. Whiting *NC* 381(4).

C57 As busy as a **Cat** on a tin roof

1942 CFAdams *What Price* (NY) 22: You've been busier than a cat on a tin roof. Taylor *Prov. Comp.* 22; *Western Folklore* 17(1958) 14(1).

C58 As curious as a **Cat** (kitten)

1934 CCranston *Murder* (P) 53: As curious as a cat. **1938** VWMason *Cairo* (NY) 92: You are as curious . . . as Mother McGinty's cat. **1941** MGEberhart *With This Ring* (NY) 185: He's curious as a cat. **1961** AMorton *Double* (NY) 138: Curious as any kitten. **1962** LEgan *Against* (NY DBC) 3: And they say cats are curious. **1970** RFoley *Calculated* (NY) 16: He's as curious as a cat. Whiting *NC* 381(6).

C59 As dark as a black **Cat** (*varied*)

1930 HAdams *Crime* (P) 76: Two Morrises in the dark are as much alike as black cats. **1930** MPlum *Killing* (NY) 141: It's all dark as a black cat. **1931** EABlake *Jade* (NY) 114: It's dark out as seven black cats. **1931** AC Edington *Monk's Hood* (NY) 150: The place was as dark as an alley cat's back. **1948** IFletcher *Roanoke* (I) 269: As dark as two black cats. **1952** DBOlsen *Enrollment* (NY) 154: It was as dark as a barrelful of black cats in that grove. TW 58(8).

C60   As dry as a **Cat's** arse

1964 NBenchley *Winter's* (NY) 2: They're dry as a cat's ass.

C61   As fast as a (scalded) **Cat**

1929 GFairlie *Yellow* (B) 197: Move as fast as a scalded cat. **1939** NMarsh *Overture* (NY) 195: She was off like a scalded cat. **1958** ELacy *Be Careful* (NY) 162: Doc sat up fast as a cat. **1958** MProcter *Three* (NY) 134: He ran like a scalded cat. **1969** AGilbert *Mr. Crook* (NY DBC) 125: As fast as a cat. Taylor *Prov. Comp.* 39.

C62   As jealous as a **Cat**

1939 EHuxley *African Poison* (NY) 160: He was jealous as a cat. **1942** SHAdams *Tambay* (NY) 88: She was jealous as a mother cat. **1966** HTracy *Men* (L) 12: He was as jealous as a cat. Taylor *Prov. Comp.* 52.

C63   As jumpy (edgy) as a **Cat** (kitten) (*varied*)

c1910 PGWodehouse *Leave It to Psmith* (L n.d.) 140: As jumpy as a cat. **1931** MAllingham *Gyrth* (NY) 71: You're as jumpy as a cat. **1933** CDickson *Bowstring* (NY) 217: I was as jumpy as a cat. **1937** CKnight *Heavenly Voice* (NY) 37: Those two women are as jumpy as cats on a hot stove. **1948** A Derleth *Strange* (NY) 230: I'm jumpy as a cat today. **1957** LBrackett *Tiger* (NY) 137: We were all jumpy as cats. **1958** SDean *Dishonor* (NY) 23: She's jumpy as a cat on a hot griddle. **1961** HKuttner *Bypass* (NY) 39: I'm as jumpy as a cat. **1962** JHSchmitz *Tale* (NY) 60: You're as edgy as a cat. **1976** SBrett *So Much* (NY) 92: She was as jumpy as a kitten. **1977** PMoyes *Coconut* (NY) 34: He was as jumpy as a cat. Wilstach 222.

C64   As light as a **Cat** on its feet (*varied*)

1900 CFPidgin *Quincy A. Sawyer* (B) 67: As light and agile on his feet as a cat. **1925** BAtkey *Pyramid* (NY) 47: He came light-footed as a cat. **1939** ECRLorac *Black Beadle* (L) 192: Reeves, light as a cat on his toes. **1942** CHare *Tragedy at Law* (L 1953) 106: He moved as lightly as a cat. Cf. A Cat lands *below.*

C65   As mad (angry) as a wet (scalded) **Cat**

1929 RPeckham *Murder* (NY) 49: He was mad as a wet cat. **1933** SHPage *Fool's Gold* (NY) 123: Madder'n a wet cat. **1934** CKendrake *Clew* (NY) 146: He was mad as a wet cat. **1935** LAKnight *Super-Cinema* (L) 92: Wild as a scald cat she was! **1966** WTrevor *Love* (L) 219: As angry as a cat. Wilstach 249. Cf. As mad as a wet Hen *below.*

C66   As mean as **Cat's** meat

1957 *New Yorker* 1/5 22: Susan . . . could be as mean as cat's meat. **1962** WHaggard *Unquiet* (NY DBC) 111: Looking like cat's meat [*in bad shape*]. **1963** JBroderick *Don* (NY) 29: She's as mean as cat's meat [*miserly*]. Cf. Partridge 134.

C67   As melancholy as a gib **Cat**

1941 RAldington *Life* (NY) 177: As melancholy as a gib cat. EAP C61.

C68   As nervous (jittery) as a **Cat** (kitten) (*varied*)

1911 RAFreeman *Eye of Osiris* (NY 1929) 17: As nervous as a cat. **1928** EHamilton *Four* (L) 272: I am . . . as nervous as a kitten. **1931** LEppley *Murder* (NY) 298: I'm nervous as a cat. **1931** SMartin *Hangman's* (NY) 254: As nervous as a kitten. **1935** MBurton *Milk-Churn* (L) 159: She was as nervous as a kitten. **1939** JJones *Murder al Fresco* (NY) 159: I'm nervous as a cat in a strange garret. **1945** AChristie *Remembered* (NY) 127: Just as nervous as a cat on wires. **1947** RKing *Lethal* (NY DBC) 84: She was nervous as a cat. **1948** PHastings *Autobiography* (L) 84: I was as nervous as the proverbial kitten. **1949** MGilbert *He Didn't* (NY DBC) 78: He'll be as nervous as a scalded kitten. **1953** CMRussell *Market* (NY) 98: He was nervous as a scalded cat. **1955** JCreasey *Gelignite* (NY) 153: I'm as nervous as a kitten. **1958** RHiscock *Last* (NY) 141: As nervy as a kitten. **1961** RKirk *Old House* (NY DBC) 66: As nervous as pregnant cats. **1965** ESGardner *Beautiful* (NY) 201: I'm jittery as a cat in a thunderstorm. **1970** NMilford *Zelda* (NY) 84: Scott, as nervous as a cat. **1971** PMoyes *Season* (NY) 142: She's as nervous as a kitten. **1977** PMoyes *Coconut* (NY) 64: He's nervous as a kitten. **1980** MInnes

Going (NY) 22: I'm as nervous as a cat. Taylor *Prov. Comp.* 59.

C69   As nimble as a **Cat**
1936 *New Yorker* 5/16 49: We're as nimble as a cat. **1962** JDCarr *Demoniacs* (NY) 148: Nimble as a cat. TW 59(16).

C70   As pleased as a **Cat** with nine cocks
1970 GEEvans *Where* (L) 266: The old lady I was a-staying with was as pleased as a cat with nine cocks. Cf. As pleased as a Cow with six tits *below*.

C71   As quick as a **Cat**
1903 EChilders *Riddle* (NY 1940) 65: He is . . . quick as a cat. **1925** BAtkey *Pyramid* (NY) 88: As quick as a cat; 139. **1934** GCronyn *Fool* (NY) 262: He's quick as a cat. **1934** BAWilliams *Hostile* (NY) 86: Quick as a tomcat. **1936** VMcHugh *Caleb* (NY) 33: Quicker'n a cat can jump. **1938** ECRLorac *Devil* (L) 60: As quick as a cat on his feet . . . and as quiet. **1956** MStewart *Wildfire* (NY) 33: As quick as a cat. **1960** SRaven *Doctors* (L) 28: As quick and clever as a cat. **1966** EYates *Is There* (NY) 38: Quick as a cat. EAP C62; Brunvand 21(3).

C72   As quiet as a **Cat**
1903 EChilders *Riddle* (NY 1940) 249: Quiet as a cat. **1929** HMSmith *Jigsaw* (NY) 265: Brown came in as quiet as a cat. **1952** RVickers *Sole* (L 1965) 32: The man was as quiet as a cat. TW 59(18); Taylor *Prov. Comp.* 67. Cf. As quiet as a Kitten *below*.

C73   As restless as a **Cat** on a hot stove-lid
1947 VWMason *Saigon* (NY) 178: She was as restless as a cat on a hot stove-lid. **1960** HRobertson *Swan* (NY) 28: Restless as a cat. Cf. To act like a Cat *below*.

C74   As sick as a **Cat**
1915 JBuchan *Thirty-Nine* (NY) 149: I . . . felt as sick as a cat. **1931** HMSmith *Waverdale Fire* (L) 180: He was as sick as a cat. **1936** VMcHugh *Caleb* (NY) 236: Looking sicker'n a dead cat. **1941** GDHCole *Counterpoint* (NY) 62: Sick as a cat. **1966** JBell *Catalyst* (NY) 68: You'd have been as sick as a cat. Cf. Wilstach 351: Sick as a cat with eating rat. Cf. As sick as a Dog *below*.

C75   As silent as a **Cat**
1934 GDilnot *Crook's* (L) 185: He was as silent as a cat. **1950** ECRLorac *And Then* (NY) 186: As silent as a cat. TW 59(21).

C76   As softly as a **Cat**
1973 MGEberhart *Murder* (NY) 98: He acts and moves as softly as a cat. TW 59(23).

C77   As sore as a scalded **Cat**
1912 JCLincoln *Postmaster* (NY) 288: Sore as a scalded cat. **1920** EWallace *Three-Oak* (L) 21: As sore as a scalded cat. Cf. Taylor *Western Folklore* 17(1958) 14(3): To sound like a scalded cat.

C78   As spry as a **Cat**
1982 CMacLeod *Wrack* (NY) 65: He stepped around them roosts spry as a cat. EAP C64. Cf. As spry as a Kitten *below*.

C79   As still as a **Cat** (at a mouse hole)
1960 MGEberhart *Jury* (NY DBC) 59: Clare . . . as still as a cat at a mouse hole. **1963** CArmstrong *Little Less* (NY) 36: Justin was still as a cat. **1973** MGEberhart *Murder* (NY) 125: As still as a cat at a mouse hole. TW 59(25); Brunvand 21(4).

C80   As tidy (neat) as a **Cat**
1934 VParadise *Girl Died* (NY) 67: Tidy as a cat. **1949** JDCarr *Below* (NY) 195: [He] was neat as a cat.

C81   As weak as a **Cat**
1932 TThayer *Thirteen* (NY) 215: I'm weak as a cat. **1956** *BangorDN* 8/23 34: I am weak as a cat. **1959** FCrane *Buttercup* (NY DBC) 59: I felt weak as a cat. Whoever was it said cats were weak. EAP C65. Cf. As weak as a Kitten *below*.

C82   A **Cat** has nine lives (*varied*)
1904 LFBaum *Marvelous Land of Oz* (NY) 154: Tailors, having like cats, nine lives. **1908** LFBaum *Dorothy and the Wizard of Oz* (I) 33: "I have nine lives," said the kitten. **1919** JBCabell *Jurgen* (NY 1922) 271: The nine lives of the cat. **1922** JJoyce *Ulysses* (NY 1934) 392: As many times as a cat has lives.

1928 HAsbury *Gangs* (NY) xii: Has more lives than the proverbial cat. **1930** WLewis *Apes* (NY 1932) 598: They say a cat has nine lives. **1934** EQueen *Adventures* (NY) 322: He'd need the nine living with Cheshire Cat. **1938** NBlake *Beast* (NY 1958) 108: How many lives has a cat o' nine tails? **1949** EQueen *Cat* (B) 234: The old saying, *A woman hath nine lives like a cat.* **1957** *Punch* 7/10 43: Risking those nine lives with which nature has . . . endowed them. **1957** CE Maine *Isotope* (L) 41: The guy's got more lives than a cat. **1964** TPowell *Corpus* (NY) 85: I'll need the total lives of half a dozen cats. **1970** CArmstrong *Protege* (NY DBC) 100: Mrs. Calabash [*a cat*] got married . . . and had nine children, one for each life. **1975** JBland *Death* (NY) 161: You've got more lives than the Persian cat. EAP C71. Cf. Brunvand 22: Catamount . . . nineteen lives.

C83 The **Cat** has someone's tongue

1921 RLardner *Big Town* (NY 1925) 8: At first the cat had everybody's tongue; 240. **1927** WBFoster *From Six* (NY) 194: He wanted to know if the cat had got Peter's tongue. **1933** PStong *Strangers* (NY) 246: You'd think the cat had got his tongue. **1939** JDCarr *Black Spectacles* (L) 23: Has the cat got your tongue? **1941** GBagby *Here Comes* (NY) 52: The cat's got Harvey's tongue. **1950** MCarleton *Bride* (NY) 126: The cat has my husband's tongue. **1956** BJChute *Greenwillow* (NY) 57: Speak up . . . Devil got your tongue? **1962** EAmbler *Light* (L) 152: Has the cat got your tongue? **1968** RMStern *Merry* (NY) 88: The cat has got his tongue. **1970** RFenisong *Drop* (NY) 199: The cliché of "Has the cat got your tongue?" TW 62(59).

C84 A **Cat** lands (falls) on its feet (*varied*)

1928 WRoughead *Murderer's* (NY 1968) 6: The lady had indeed, as the phrase is, fallen on her feet. **1931** ACEdington *Monk's Hood* (NY) 125: I can land like a cat [*on his feet*]. **1935** GDilnot *Murder* (L) 32: You've fallen on your feet. **1935** LThayer *Dead* (NY) 272: I'm a kind of cat for falling on my feet. **1938** HAdams *Bluff* (L) 224:

Sure to fall on her feet, as a good dancer should. **1940** EPaul *Mayhem* (NY) 184: [He] landed safely on his feet, like a cat. **1947** JDCarr *Sleeping* (NY) 198: Landed on his feet like a cat. **1948** CBush *Curious* (NY) 67: Trust Sid to drop on his feet. **1957** JStevenson *Weep* (NY) 106: The proverbial cat that always lands on his feet. **1958** PBranch *Murder's* (L 1963) 32: Landing slap on your feet like a ruddy cat. Well, eight lives to go. **1965** SForbes *Relative* (NY) 145: It's not true, you know that cats always land on their feet. They don't if they fall far enough. **1965** CGaskin *File* (NY) 27: She's the type who lands on her feet. **1968** JMyrdal *Confessions* (NY) 188: You are like a cat. You always land on your feet. **1970** STerkel *Hard* (NY) 283: I was always able to fall on my feet like a cat. **1975** HBlack *My Father* (NY) 48: He's like a cat. Always lands on his feet. EAP C70; TW 58(2). Cf. As light as a Cat *above*.

C85 The **Cat** loves fish but hates water

1908 LDYoung *Climbing Doom* (NY) 37: The cat, which loves to eat fish, but hates water. **1934** JCLenehan *Carnival* (L) 240: You remind me of the funny old cat in the adage . . . letting "I dare not wait upon I would." *Oxford* 109.

C86 A **Cat** may look at a king (*varied*)

1918 ERPunshon *Solitary* (NY) 9: A cat may look at a king. **1924** LO'Flaherty *Informer* (L) 112: A cat can look at a king. **1928** RThorndike *Slype* (NY) 76: A cat may shake hands with a king, as they say. **1929** EHope *Alice* (NY) 258: A Wildcat may look at an Oil King. **1937** DHume *Halfway* (L) 106: A cat, she had been told, could laugh at a king. **1938** EGilligan *Boundary* (NY) 363: To prove that a cat may not look at a queen. **1941** SFisher *I Wake Up* (NY 1960) 2: A cat can look at heaven, of course. **1952** BWolfe *Limbo* (L) 97: A cat can only look at a king but a bedbug can dine on him for weeks. **1956** *Punch* 5/2 519: Thus instructed a cat may write to a Queen. 10/3 407: A king may now look at a cat. **1960** KCrichton *Total* (NY) 218: Even a cat may look at a king. **1969** RPearsall *Worm* (NY) 272: A cat could, indeed, not look at a king. **1970** RFenisong *Drop* (NY) 204: Even kings have been known to look at beautiful cats. EAP C74; TW 58(5).

C87 Enough to make a **Cat** laugh

1922 JJoyce *Ulysses* (NY 1934) 524: Wouldn't it make a Siamese cat laugh? **1929** JBPriestly *Good* (NY) 190: Make a cat laugh; 551. **1932** RThorndike *Devil* (NY) 121: That's funny enough to make a cat laugh. **1939** LBlack *Mr. Preed* (L) 97: Some of those big noises would have made a cat laugh. **1951** MInnes *Paper* (NY) 34: It would have made a cat laugh. **1956** *Punch* 6/20 745: It is enough to make Lord Beaverbrook's cat laugh. **1964** JPorter *Dover One* (NY 1966) 176: It's enough to make a cat laugh. TW 60(40). Cf. To be enough . . . Dog; Enough to . . . Horse *below.*

C88 Enough to make a **Cat** sick

1930 RAFreeman *Savant's* (L) 203: It's enough to make a cat sick. **1950** DMathew *Mango* (L) 78: To see that old booby . . . was enough to make a cat sick. **1960** HRFKeating *Zen* (L 1963) 203: And the smell of rice pudding's enough to make a cat sick. TW 60(40).

C89 Not a (celluloid) **Cat's** (dog's) chance (in hell)

1914 PGWodehouse *Little Nugget* (NY 1929) 246: You don't stand a dog's chance. **1921** JSFletcher *Orange-Yellow* (NY) 307: You ain't [got] a cat's chance. **1924** VBridges *Red* (NY) 242: He hasn't a dog's chance. **1929** RJCasey *Secret* (I) 215: He'll not have the chance of a celluloid collar in hell. **1932** EPOppenheim *Man* (B) 43: I wouldn't have a dog's chance. **1938** BFlynn *Tread* (L) 8: You're like that celluloid cat in Hades. **1948** CDickson *Skeleton* (NY 1967) 221: He hadn't the chance of a celluloid cat in hell. **1950** NFlower *Just* (NY) 115: Not the chance of a snowball in hell. **1955** AHunter *Gently Does* (L) 72: I don't think you stand a dog's chance. **1958** MProcter *Man in* (NY) 11: He hasn't a cat-in-hell chance. **1961** EPeters *Death* (NY) 13: You won't have a dog's chance. **1962** HCarmichael *Of Unsound* (NY) 158: So don't think

you've got a cat-in-hell chance of bluffing your way out of this. **1972** DEmrich *Folklore* (B) 23: There's no more peace here than for a cat in hell without claws. **1973** KAmis *Riverside* (NY) 63: Not a celluloid cat's chance in hell. **1974** HCarmichael *Most* (NY) 122: I haven't a cat's chance in hell. **1976** SWoods *My Life* (NY) 23: I wouldn't stand a dog's chance. Taylor *Prov. Comp.* 24.

C90 A scalded **Cat** fears hot (cold) water

1936 FBeeding *No Fury* (L) 94: The scalded cat fears hot water. EAP C80.

C91 Since the **Cat** (father) died

1934 JJConnington *Ha-Ha* (L) 51: I haven't laughed so much since the cat died. **1954** CCarnac *Policeman* (NY) 149: I haven't talked so much since father died, as they say.

C92 That **Cat** won't fight

1927 JMWalsh *Silver* (L) 51: That cat won't fight. **1933** LThayer *Hell-Gate* (NY) 11: That cat won't fight. TW 60(37). Cf. Cock *below.*

C93 That **Cat** won't jump

1927 JRhode *Ellerby* (NY) 8: That cat won't jump. **1928** RAFreeman *A Certain* (NY) 300: That cat didn't jump. **1934** JRhode *Shot* (L) 227: That cat won't jump! **1942** JDCarr *Emperor's* (NY) 194: That cat won't jump. TW 60(38). Cf. That Horse *below.*

C94 To act like a **Cat** on hot bricks (*varied*)

c1910 PGWodehouse *Leave it to Psmith* (L n.d.) 191: Dancing about like a cat on hot bricks. **c1923** ACrowley *Confessions* ed JSymonds (L 1969) 879: He was like a cat on hot bricks. **1928** AChristie *Mystery of the Blue Train* (NY) 289: I am like a cat upon the hot tiles. **1928** JGollomb *Portrait* (NY) 157: He was like a cat on a hot griddle. **1932** HLandon *Owl's* (L) 12: Act as skittish as a kitten on a hot brick. **1932** PMacDonald *Rope* (L) 93: To feel as if one were an ill-used cat sitting upon a white-hot brick. **1934** FNHart *Crooked* (NY) 232: She's been like a kitten on hot coals all evening. **1940** DBillany *It Takes* (NY) 35: You've been like a cat on hot coals. **1940** CKnight *Death Val-*

ley (NY) 100: You're all at once like a cat on a hot stove. **1956** *Punch* 9/5 282: It made a sound like a cat on a hot tin roof. **1959** SFarrar *Snake* (NY) 19: Daddy's like a cat on hot bricks. **1961** CBeatons *Wandering* (L) 97: Jumping about like cats on hot bricks. **1963** HEEvans *Wasp* (NY) 76: The males hop simply because the sand surface is too hot for them to sit still . . . the proverbial cat on a hot tin roof. **1971** HCarvig *Witch* (NY) 155: That'd make her foot a caper or two—like a cat on hot bricks. **1976** MButterworth *Remains* (NY) 142: He's been like a cat on hot bricks. *Oxford* 109. Cf. As restless as a Cat *above*.

C95 To be (made) a **Cat's** paw

1911 JSHay *Amazing Emperor* (L) 43: He was the cat's paw. **1921** IOstrunter *Crimson* (NY) 289: Making a cat's paw of her. **1923** JGollomb *Girl* (NY) 19: We're pulling out chestnuts for somebody who'll shove us into the fire. **1927** EHBall *Scarlet* (NY) 66: The monkey to pull the chestnut out of the fire for the—Fox! **1927** ORCohen *Outer* (NY) 130: And you're going to let him rake your chestnuts out of the fire? **1928** AWynne *Horseman* (P) 60: I . . . must pull . . . your chestnuts out of the fire. **1929** FBeeding *Pretty* (B) 309: I've pulled hotter chestnuts out of the fire. **1930** ECVivian *Double* (L) 122: The cat that raked out the chestnuts. **1931** Roger Scarlett *Cat's Paw* (NY). **1932** CFGregg *Body* (L) 77: Dobell did not eat chestnuts which someone else had pulled out of the fire. **1937** GGoodchild *Murder Will* (L) 100: He only uses him as a cat's paw to pull his own chestnuts out of the fire. **1939** RAJWalling *Blistered Hand* (NY) 168: Abbot is the monkey and Samuel the cat's paw. **1947** FCDavis *Thursday's* (NY) 35: Somebody's got another chestnut to be yanked out of the fire. **1955** DParry *Sea* (L) 137: Willing to pull the chestnuts out of the fire. **1959** RStout *Plot* (NY) 36: If those four were merely the cat's-paws, where is the monkey? **1960** TBDewey *Girl* (NY DBC) 136: You may be using us to pull your chestnuts out of the fire. **1962** FGruber *Brothers* (NY DBC) 96: A cat's paw I fish the chestnuts out of the fire and the monkey eats them. **1965** RJWhite *Dr. Bentley* (L)

166: Grigg had been made a cat's paw by Bentley. **1975** SJPerelman *Vinegar* (NY) 116: He could pull the chestnuts out of the fire. EAP C97; TW 66: Chestnut(3), 277: Paw; DARE i 570: Cat's paw.

C96 To be like a **Cat** in a strange garret (*varied*)

1925 RAFreeman *Red Thumb* (L) 163: Wandering in and out . . . like a cat in a new house. **1928** RAFreeman *As a Thief* (L) 166: Feeling a little like a cat in a strange house. **1934** RPTCoffin *Lost Paradise* (NY) 63: He was like a cat in a strange garret. **1936** JSStrange *Bell* (NY) 254: I'm a cat in a strange garret—I'm scared. **1956** ACLewis *Jenny* (NY) 388: He kept looking around again, like a cat in a strange garret. **1956** BCClough *More* (Portland, Me.) 17: They felt like cats in a strange garret. **1971** KLaumer *Deadfall* (NY) 194: Ellen came into the room, moving stiffly, like a cat in a strange kitchen. EAP C76; Brunvand 21(5).

C97 To be like a singed **Cat**

1943 EWTeale *Dune Boy* (NY 1957) 114: Some things are like a singed cat: they taste better'n they look. EAP C81; TW 60(36).

C98 To be the **Cat's** whiskers (pajamas)

1932 PMacDonald *Rope* (L) 234: I might be the cat's whiskers. **1938** CAlington *Crime* (L) 106: His sister was the cat's whiskers. **1951** AChristie *They Came* (NY) 61: He's absolutely the cat's whiskers. **1954** EWalter *Untidy* (P) 50: People will think you are the cat's pajamas. **1956** *BangorDN* 9/6 2: He carried several of them by the proverbial cat's whiskers. **1961** RJWhite *Smartest* (L) 194: He thinks you're the cat's whiskers. **1965** MFrayn *Tin* (B) 110: You're the real cat's pajamas. **1971** AChristie *Nemesis* (NY) 30: She thinks she's the cat's whiskers. **1982** CMacLeod *Wrack* (NY) 74: [She] thought he was the cat's whiskers. DARE i 571: Cat's whisker(s); Wentworth 92.

C99 To bell the **Cat**

1918 JBCabell *Letters* ed PColum (NY 1962) 26: Who is going to bell the cat? **1927** VWilliams *Eye* (B) 9: They want me to bell the cat. **1932** TCobb *Death* (L) 15: Did Mrs. Maybury bell the cat? **1941** RAldington *Life*

(NY) 120: A group of very little mice planning to put bells on an extremely large . . . cat. **1954** MBodenheim *My Life* (NY) 159: As at the convention of mice, the vital question arose, who is going to bell the cat? **1959** DMDisney *Did She Fall* (NY) 89: It was like the problem of who should bell the cat. **1960** BBenson *Huntress* (NY) 76: The old fable of asking which mouse would bell the cat. **1961** JBTownsend *John* (New Haven) 157: Proposing that Davidson be the elder mouse to bell the young tom. **1968** WTenn *Wooden* (NY) 99: A gigantic cat that the mice had belled again and again. **1971** JGreen *Mind* (NY) 31: And just who is going to bell the cat? **1974** CSweeney *Naturalist* (NY) 180: The problem now was that of the mice in the fable, who was going to bell the cat? EAP C82; TW 60(41).

C100 To fight like **Cats** (*varied*)

1930 GDHCole *Corpse* (L) 9: They get along about as well as two cats in a shoe-box. **1931** HSimpson *Prime* (NY) 125: We fought like cats. **1933** DGBrowne *Cotfold* (L) 211: He and his sister quarrel like cats. **1954** MErskine *Dead by* (NY) 74: He spoke of the two women . . . as being like "two cats in a sack." **1956** BJFarmer *Death* (L) 50: Husband and wife were fighting like the proverbial cats. **1971** MPolland *Package* (NY) 47: They were fighting like cats. Whiting *NC* 381(17). Cf. Kilkenny *below.*

C101 To fight (*etc.*) like **Cat(s)** and dog(s) (*varied*)

1929 WScott *Mask* (P) 138: Like a cat hates a dog. **1931** LCArlington *Through* (L) 138: Each watched the other like cat and dog. **1932** CFitzsimmons *No Witness* (NY) 177: Fight like cats and dogs. **1937** HCBailey *Black Land* (NY) 11: Hating like cat and dog. **1940** MCharlton *Death of* (L) 104: Fought like cat and dog. **1953** JRMacdonald *Meet* (NY) 101: They fought like cats and dogs. **1963** MPHood *Sin* (NY) 96: Vinnie and her mother were cat and dog, oil and water. **1969** ADavidson *Phoenix* (NY) 73: They fought like cats and dogs. **1970** JCreasey *Part* (NY) 108: Fighting like cat and dog. EAP C87.

C102 To hate as a **Cat** hates water

1930 MGEberhart *While* (NY) 121: A fellow who hates trouble like a cat hates water. **1935** TDowning *Murder* (NY) 120: I imagine she'll take to it like the proverbial cat to water [*i.e. not at all*]. **1939** CMRussell *Topaz Flowers* (NY) 243: He hated her like a cat hates water. Cf. TW 60(39). Cf. The Devil hates *below.*

C103 To lead a **Cat** and dog life

1912 JCLincoln *Postmaster* (NY) 85: The pair lived a cat and dog life. **1922** JSFletcher *Herapath* (NY) 132: They led a sort of cat-and-dog life. **1940** AMChase *No Outlet* (NY) 122: He and his wife led a cat and dog life. TW 61(58); Brunvand 22(10).

C104 To let the **Cat** out of the bag (*varied*)

1900 CFPidgin *Quincy A. Sawyer* (B) 116: I've let the cat out of the bag; 291, 404. **1904** JCLincoln *Cap'n Eri* (NY) 75: You can't sell her a cat in a bag. **1918** JBCabell *Letters* ed PColum (NY 1962) 49: The cat of natural taste is out of the bag of culture. **1922** JJoyce *Ulysses* (NY 1934) 413: Once a woman has let the cat into the bag . . . she must let it out again or give it life. **1928** DHLawrence *Lady* ("Allemagne") 325: The cat is out of the bag along with various other pussies. **1934** RCWoodthorpe *Death Wears* (NY) 245: I have done my best to keep the cat in the bag, but it has got out and spilled the milk, and there is no use crying over it. **1936** RAFreeman *Penrose* (NY) 203 Lets the cat out of the bag. **1940** MInnes *There Came* (L 1958) 119: The cat is still in the bag. **1949** AAFair *Bedrooms* (NY 1958) 30: Let the cat out of the bag. **1955** SNGhose *Flame* (L) 140: The cat was out of the bag. **1957** *TLS* 3/15 157: The children's aunts let all the family cats out of the bag. **1970** AEHotchner *Treasure* (NY) 246: Julietta . . . unbagged that cat. **1970** AJMarshall *Darwin* (Sydney) 76: Once the cat was out. **1971** HCarvig *Witch* (NY) 136: Letting the cat out of the bag that she's spent a night on the tiles. **1971** TZinkin *Odious* (L) 214: The cat lept out of the bag. **1977** CAlverson *Not Sleeping* (B) 179: The cat that Rachel had just let out of the bag. EAP C85; Brunvand 21–2(7).

C105 To look for a black **Cat** (hat)

1950 ERPunshon *So Many* (NY) 88: The proverbial black cat in a coal cellar at midnight, and not sure whether there is either a cat or a coal cellar. **1957** *NYTimes Book Review* 9/22 42: They are unwilling to look for the black hat in the dark cellar unless they believe that it may just possibly be there. Cf. Whiting *NC* 381(7). Cf. A blind Man in a dark room *below*.

C106 To look like a (the) **Cat** that has swallowed a (the) canary (*varied*)

1930 CFitzsimmons *Manville* (NY) 218: You look like the cat who swallowed the gold fish. **1930** WSMaugham *Cakes* (L 1948) 151: You look like a cat that's swallowed a canary. **1932** ACampbell *Murder* (NY) 93: The cat that had eaten the canary occurred to him as the correct comparison. **1932** RKing *Murder* (L) 150: She seemed like any cat on the point of swallowing any canary. **1939** JRonald *This Way Out* (P) 66: You've the smug look of the cat that swallowed the canary. **1944** RAJWalling *Corpse Without* (NY) 195: You look like the cat who's about to swallow the canary. **1947** RBradbury *Dark Carnival* (Sauk City, Wisc.) 230: Stop looking like the cat that ate the bird. **1950** SPalmer *Green* (NY) 88: You look like the canary that ate the cat. **1951** EPaul *Murder on* (NY) 216: You look like the canary who has swallowed the milk punch. **1957** *Time* 4/8 6–8: Grin like Cheshire cats who have just swallowed the canary. **1958** MAMusmanno *Verdict* (NY) 35: The cat-canary expression. **1964** RAHeinlein *Farnham's* (NY 1965) 168: A secret smile . . . He called it "canary that ate the cat." **1970** RLPike *Reardon* (NY) 135: You look like the canary that swallowed the cat. **1972** JRipley *Davis* (NY) 20: He has a canary-swallowing-cat expression on his face. DA Cat *n.* 9i.

C107 To look like the **Cat** that swallowed the cream (*varied*)

1906 JCLincoln *Mr. Pratt* (NY) 154: As innocent and easy as the cat with the cream on its whiskers. **1938** DCDisney *Strawstack* (NY) 173: His expression was as smug as the cat's who has swallowed the last of the cream. **1951** FCrane *Murder in* (NY) 239:

He hung up, looking like the cat who got the cream. **1955** AChristie *Hickory* (NY) 82: Looking as smug as a cat that's swallowed cream. **1959** NCoulehan *Quadrantus* (L) 287: Don't stand there like a cat which has stolen the milk. **1965** CBeaton *Years* (L) 316: I felt like the cat that had swallowed the Devonshire cream. **1968** NBowen *Hear* (NY) 132: A cat in the cream smile. **1971** DCWilson *Big-Little* (NY) 242: He looked like the proverbial cat licking cream from its whiskers. **1976** MRReno *Final* (NY) 28: He looked like the cat that swallowed the cream. TW 59(14); Brunvand 21(2).

C108 To need as much as a **Cat** needs two tails

1936 SPalmer *Briar Pipe* (L) 201: Gregg needed a nurse about as much as a cat needs two tails. **1953** KMKnight *Three* (NY) 161: Need me about as much as a cat needs two tails. TW 61(53).

C109 To play **Cat**-and-mouse (*varied*)

1921 ERBurroughs *Mucker* (NY) 194: As a cat might play with a mouse. **1928** ABerkeley *Silk* (NY) 226: My little cat-and-mouse act. **1928** ESnell *Kontrol* (P) 256: It's just the old story of the cat and the mouse. **1932** CFGregg *Body* (L) 87: A sort of cat and mouse affair. **1937** HAustin *Murder* (L) 179: It's not necessary to play with me like a cat with a mouse. **1940** LTreat *B as in Banshee* (NY) 204: Riggman was cat-and-mousing his dinner guests. **1950** SJepson *Hungry* (NY) 211: Don't play cat and mouse any more. **1953** HBPiper *Murder* (NY) 217: He realizes that I'm cat-and-mousing him. **1957** *NYTimes* 3/31 10E: This cat-and-mouse game of freeing one victim at a time. **1957** *BHerald* 11/10 V 6: A cat-and-mouse game. **1957** ESGardner *Screaming* (NY) 118: Playing with you as a cat plays with a mouse. **1962** DBickerton *Murders* (L) 40: Playing with him as a cat plays with a mouse. **1964** LSDeCamp *Ancient* (NY) 108: The game of cat and mouse continued. **1972** AGarve *Case* (NY) 159: I've no wish to go on playing cat-and-mouse. **1972** MWilliams *Inside* (NY) 60: It really is a kind of cat and mouse game with a bit of carrot and stick as well. EAP C86; TW 61(56); Brunvand 22(8).

C110 To put the **Cat** among the pigeons (*varied*)

c1923 ACrowley *Confessions* ed JSymonds (L 1969) 196: My arrival . . . put the cat among the chickens. **1932** EWallace *When the Gangs* (NY) 87: This is going to put the cat among the pigeons. **1932** RCWoodthorpe *Public* (L) 116: The cat is out of the bag and among the pigeons. **1946** GBellairs *Death in the Night* (NY) 12: [He] put the cat properly among the pigeons. **1950** STruss *Never* (NY) 249: Without putting the Scotland Yard cat among the fraternal pigeons. **1961** CWillock *Death in* (L 1963) 142: [He] had certainly put the fox among the pheasants. **1965** JPorter *Dover Two* (NY 1968) 52: Rex's father put the cat among the pigeons. **1970** AChristie *Passenger* (NY) 39: Put the cat among the pigeons. **1975** HCarvic *Odds On* (NY) 121: That's fairly put the pigeon amongst the cats. *Oxford* 107.

C111 To rain (*etc.*) **Cats** and dogs

1927 EWallace *Traitor's* (NY) 50: Pouring cats and dogs. **1932** JStevens *Saginaw* (NY) 97: She's rainin' mud cats and mud dogs. **1938** ECRLorac *Slippery* (L) 210: It was pelting cats and dogs. **1953** PChadburn *Treble* (L) 57: Seemed to be seeing half of a proverbial phenomenon: it was raining cats. **1957** *Punch* 7/10 43: When it rains cats and dogs we may be sure a cat started it. **1962** DTaylor *Blood* (NY) 142: It was pelting cats and dogs. **1964** HBourne *In the Event* (NY) 46: It's raining! Cats and dogs! **1974** JFleming *How To* (NY) 91: It was raining cats and dogs . . . to describe it as "raining rats and mice" would be merely absurd. EAP C88; Brunvand 22(11).

C112 To sleep like a **Cat** (kitten)

1934 ABCox *Mr. Pidgeon's* (NY) 144: Sleep like a cat. **1938** KMKnight *Acts* (NY) 144: He slept like a cat. **1955** RFenisong *Widows* (NY) 130: "Did you sleep?" . . . "Like a—like a cat." **1959** GMalcolm-Smith *If a Body* (NY) 128: I sleep . . . like a kitten. Taylor *Prov. Comp.* 52: Kitten.

C113 To smell a dead **Cat**

[My maternal grandfather (died 1930) used to say of one of our neighbors, "Ada is a good woman and a kind woman and I don't suppose she can help always looking as if she smelled a turd." In the presence of woman or strangers he might substitute "dead mouse" for "turd." BJW] **1964** SJay *Death* (NY) 153: I hate those bastards . . . with their lips stuck together like they smelt a dead cat.

C114 To watch as a **Cat** watches a mouse(hole)

1921 JSFletcher *Orange-Yellow* (NY) 244: Watching . . . like a cat watches a mousehole. **1924** JSFletcher *King* (NY) 296: Watch like cats at the hole of a mouse. **1926** JArnold *Murder!* (L) 160: Bowen watched us like a cat. **1929** JSFletcher *Ransom* (NY) 295: As sharp a look-out . . . as a cat keeps on a mouse-hole. **1930** JSFletcher *Heavensent* (NY) 21: He proceeded to watch as closely—to use a well worn but highly convenient simile—as a cat watches a mouse. **1932** WCBrown *Laughing* (P) 114: A cat-at-the-mousehole situation. **1936** JGBrandon *Pawnshop* (L) 255: His two grim-looking companions were watching him like the proverbial cat and mouse. **1940** JBentley *Mr. Marlow Stops* (B) 12: She was watching them like a cat watches a mouse. **1972** JRipley *Davis* (NY) 112: Watching me like a cat watching a new mousehole. EAP C91; Brunvand 22(8).

C115 When the **Cat's** away the mice will play

1917 JCLincoln *Extricating* (NY) 234: When the cat's away the mice'll play. **1922** JJoyce *Ulysses* (NY 1934) 367: Cat's away the mice will play. **c1923** ACrowley *Confessions* ed JSymonds (L 1969) 542: While the cat was away the mice had been extremely busy. 893: The moment the cat was away the mice began to play. **1926** BNiles *Black Haiti* (NY) 24: "When the cat's away," their proverb runs, "the rats dance the *calinda*." **1928** RByron *Station* (L) 30: But the minister was on leave, and his mice were at play. **1931** LEppley *Murder* (NY) 296: When the cat was away the mouse would play with the cat's catnip. **1937** CBush *Hanging Rope* (L) 201: With the cat away the mice were playing. **1956** *BangorDN* 8/20 19: When the cat's away the mice will play. **1960** *BHerald* 4/23 4: If any . . . should try to assemble the playful mice while the cat is overseas. **1962** FBrown *Five-day* (NY DBC) 90: A wild weekend while the cat's away. **1966** DMDisney *At Some* (NY) 222: When the cat's away the mice will play. **1970** CArmstrong *Protege* (NY DBC) 86: As busy as mice when the cat's away. **1972** HCarmichael *Naked* (NY) 140: There's an old saying that when the cat's away the mice will play. **1973** TWells *Brenda's* (NY) 79: While the cat's away, happy days. **1974** WCAnderson *Damp* (NY) 64: When the cat's away, the mice will play . . . an old adage. **1975** DEWestlake *Two* (NY) 102: "When the cat's away, you know." "The rats will play." "I don't think that's quite the way that goes." EAP C93.

C116 You can have no more of a **Cat** than her skin

1952 HFMPrescott *Man on* (NY) 482: A man can have no more of a cat than to have its skin. *Oxford* 572.

C117 Catch-as-catch-can

1911 HHMunro *Chronicles* (L 1927) 240: In a catch-as-catch-can progress across the floor. **1926** AMarshall *Mote* (NY) 207: In the general catch-as-catch-can scramble. **1930** WLewis *Apes* (NY 1932) 546: A catch-as-catch-can rude win. **1940** VRath *Death of a Lucky* (NY) 109: The service is catch-as-catch-can. **1951** LSdeCamp *Rogue* (NY) 17: Do they go about it catch-as-catch-can, like the beasts? **1959** BCushman *Goodbye* (NY) 259: Doc's boys received their toilet training catch-as-catch-can. **1962** JWoodford *Autobiography* (NY) 11: He slept catch-as-catch-can. **1963** EMCottman *Out-Island* (NY) 77: The rest of the passengers slept catch-as-catch-can. **1964** RO'Connor *Jack* (B) 66: A number of catch-as-catch-can romances. **1970** STerkel *Hard* (NY) 80: It was catch as catch can. EAP C95; Brunvand 22.

C118 Catching comes before hanging

1961 ESeeman *In the Arms* (NY) 60: Ketchin' comes before hangin', I always say. EAP C96.

C119 To turn **Cat-in-pan**

1930 JFarnol *Over the Hills* (B) 269: My noble lord hath turned cat-in-pan. EAP C90.

C120 Hurry no man's **Cattle**

1922 JSFletcher *Ravensdene* (NY) 110: One of those old men who won't allow their cattle to be hurried. **1932** JSFletcher *Ninth Baronet* (NY) 225: The old adage: Hurry no man's cattle. *Oxford* 394. Cf. Brunvand 23: Fret the cattle.

C121 To be a **Caution** to rattlesnakes

1922 JJoyce *Ulysses* (NY 1934) 155: He's a caution to rattlesnakes. TW 63.

C122 To throw **Caution** to the winds

1965 BGrebanier *Great Shakespeare* (NY) 89: Thrown all caution to the winds. **1965** SWoods *Though I* (NY) 65: He was symbolically throwing caution to the winds. **1970** RWMacKelworth *Tiltangle* (NY) 87: She had thrown caution to the winds.

C123 To hit the **Ceiling**

1933 PATaylor *Mystery* (NY) 64: Red just hit the ceiling. **1961** GHCoxe *Last* (NY) 128: He hit the ceiling. Wentworth 92.

C124 As quiet as a **Cemetery**

1934 RAJWalling *Eight* (L) 47: Quiet as a cemetery. Whiting *NC* 382. Cf. Taylor *Prov. Comp.* 67: Grave, graveyard.

C125 Not care two **Cents**

1917 JCLincoln *Extricating* (NY) 303: [She] did not care two cents. **1929** CWells *Tapestry* (P) 143: Gay did care two cents for her. EAP C103; Brunvand 23(1).

C126 To look (feel) like thirty (*etc.*) **Cents**

1904 MLPeabody *To Be Young* (B 1967) 308: Made all the other men look like thirty cents. **1924** JJFarjeon *Master* (NY) 236: She made me feel like thirty cents, as you say in America. **1932** NKlein *No! No!* (NY) 231: You make them look like nine cents. **1934** MHBradley *Unconfessed* (NY) 279: She made the lot of you look like thirty cents. **1940** AAFair *Gold Comes* (NY) 22: Made him look like thirty cents. **1966** JDosPassos *Best* (NY) 177: Made Freud look like thirty cents. **1970** AAFair *All Grass* (NY DBC) 67: He feels like ten cents. DA Thirty 2(1).

C127 To stick (put) in (add) one's two **Cents** worth (*varied*)

1930 BRoss *Drury Lane's* (NY) 168: That'll teach you to stick your two cents in. **1940** RAvery *Murder a Day* (NY) 45: Put in his two cents worth. **1941** ARLong *Four Feet* (NY) 212: Templeton had to put in his two cents worth. **1950** LKaufman *Jubel's* (NY) 155: Ella stuck in her two cents' worth. **1957** *BostonDN* 3/29 14: I would like to put in my two cents' worth. **1962** MGair *Snow Job* (NY) 158: To put in your two cents worth. **1967** TWells *Dead by* (NY) 132: Mahoney put in his two cents' worth. **1970** STerkel *Hard* (NY) 207: If I could just add my two cents worth. **1972** MKaye *Lively* (NY) 140: Adding his two-cents-worth. **1972** BLillie *Every* (NY) 11: She put in her two bits. **1972** JRipley *Davis* (NY) 15: The wife pushes her four-penny-worth in. Wentworth 414.

C128 It takes three **Centuries** to make a gentleman

1930 LTracy *Manning* (NY) 170: They say it takes three centuries to make a gentleman. *Oxford* 298: Generations.

C129 A **Chain** is as strong as its weakest link

1930 JGBrandon *McCarthy* (L) 12: The strength of a chain was its weakest link. **1934** AGilbert *Man in Button* (L) 105: A chain's as strong as its weakest link. **1958** *BangorDN* 7/3 13: There's an old saying that a chain is no stronger than its weakest link. **1958** JSymons *Pipe* (NY) 150: It is said that the strength of a chain is the strength of its weakest link. **1959** WHMurray *Appointment* (NY) 155: The strength of a chain is its weakest link. **1969** AGilbert *Missing* (NY) 168: A chain's only as strong as its weakest link. **1976** EXFerrars *Cup* (NY) 169: She had always been the weak link in the chain. *Oxford* 113.

C130 As different as **Chalk** and (from) cheese (*varied*)

1929 JBPriestley *Good* (NY) 24: Places as different as chalk and cheese. **1931** STWarner *T.H.White* (NY) 332: A chalk and cheese

difference. **1932** AGilbert *Body* (NY) 27: As different from this as chalk from cheese. **1937** MBurton *Clue* (NY) 127: As unlike as chalk and cheese. **1940** CBush *Climbing Rat* (L) 159: He was as different as chalk is from cheese. **1949** JCreasey *Here Comes* (NY 1967) 75: As different from Phyllis as the proverbial chalk from cheese. **1949** SJepson *Golden* (NY) 153: Chalks and cheeses could not be more unlike. **1951** JCFurnas *Voyage* (NY) 542: There is always a difference between the best chalk and the worst cheese. **1962** AGilbert *Uncertain* (NY DBC) 10: As different as chalk from cheese. **1966** LPDavies *Paper* (NY) 9: There was a chalk and cheese difference. **1973** PMoyes *Curious* (NY) 189: You're as different as chalk from cheese. **1976** JPorter *Package* (NY) 3: It was a matter of chalk and cheese. **1980** MFredman *You Can* (NY) 15: We were as different as chalk from cheese. EAP C113; TW 64(7). Cf. Chalk and cheese *below*.

C131 As pale as **Chalk**; Chalk-pale

1929 RConnell *Murder* (NY) 19: He was a chalk-pale man. **1935** REast *Twenty-five* (L) 157: His face as pale as chalk. **1970** RRendell *Best Man* (NY) 29: [He] went as pale as chalk. TW 63(2).

C132 As white as **Chalk**; Chalk-white

1908 MRRinehart *Circular Staircase* (NY 1947) 62: Face as white as chalk. **1919** EWallace *Secret House* (NY) 289: Face . . . chalk white. **1920** AChristie *Mysterious Affair* (NY) 45: White as chalk. **1924** TFPowys *Mark Only* (L) 26: As white as any chalk stone. **1932** RKing *Murder* (L) 203: Her chalk-white face. **1937** GBarnett *I Knew* (L) 189: He was as white as chalk. **1941** DCCameron *And So He* (NY) 31: The girl's face was white as chalk. **1957** CWilliams *Big Bite* (L) 97: Her face was white as chalk. **1976** EFoote-Smith *Gentle* (NY) 115: Her face was chalk white. EAP C112.

C133 **Chalk** and cheese (*varied*)

1917 AEHousman *Letters* ed HMaas (Cambridge, Mass. 1971) 149: Someone who knows chalk from cheese. **1927** EPhillpotts *Jury* (NY) 204: He returns chalk for her cheese. **1955** MBorowsky *Queen's* (NY) 24:

He'd sell you chalk for cheese. **1959** CHassall *E.Marsh* (L) 519: He will recognize that it was cheese and not chalk. **1960** HInnes *Doomed* (NY) 37: You can't make chalk cheese by a legal declaration. EAP C113. Cf. As different as Chalk and cheese *above*.

C134 Not by a long **Chalk** (long chalks)
1910 EPhillpotts *Tales* (NY) 220: [Not] by long chalks. **1922** JJoyce *Ulysses* (NY 1934) 158: Best papers by long chalks for a small ad. **1928** DHLawrence *Lady* ("Allemagne") 122: Not by a long chalk. **1937** MAllingham *Dancers* (NY) 167: Not . . . by a long chalk. **1952** JBingham *My Name* (L 1958) 39: Not good enough by a long chalk. **1959** KWaterhouse *Billy* (L) 142: Not by a long chalk. **1968** JPorter *Dover Goes* (NY) 112: Not by a long piece of chalk. **1975** HCarvic *Odds On* (NY) 27: Not by a long chalk. TW 64(5).

C135 The **Chameleon** lives on air
1929 HMSmith *Jigsaw* (NY) 15: I don't live on air. **1933** VMarkham *Inspector* (L) 31: Brush could not live on air. **1937** BThomson *Milliner's* (L) 152: He can't live on air. **1961** MErskine *Woman* (NY) 105: She can't live on air. **1964** EHuxley *Forks* (L) 168: Shelley believed chameleons to feed on light and air. EAP C114.

C136 To change like a **Chameleon**
1935 FErskine *Naked* (L) 25: She changes a lover as quickly as a chameleon changes colour. **1939** WChambers *You Can't* (NY) 214: You can change color faster than a chameleon. **1943** FScully *Rogues* (Hollywood) 25: More changeable than a chameleon. **1958** NMarsh *Singing* (B) 151: You keep changing colour like a chameleon. EAP C115.

C137 A **Change** is as good as a rest (*varied*)
1938 FDGrierson *Covenant* (L) 115: Change is good for everyone. **1940** CFGregg *Fatal Error* (L) 189: The proverb that a change of occupation was as good as a rest. **1945** GBellairs *Calamity* (NY) 211: It's been a rest and a change. **1951** MColes *Now* (NY) 32: The principle that a change of work is a rest. **1957** GDurrell *My Family* (NY) 174: "After all a change is as good as a feast." So, bearing that novel proverb in mind, we

moved. **1961** GLangford *Richard* (NY) 207: Seeking rest through a change of scene. **1961** FLockridge *Murder* (P) 61: Change is pleasant. **1965** DAcheson *Morning* (B) 155: Justice Brandeis used to get off a Puritan maxim that I never much believed in . . . "the best vacation is a change of work." **1966** BNaughton *Alfie* (L) 123: Whoever said a change was as good as a rest must have had birds [*women*] in mind. **1972** RRendell *Murder* (NY) 198: They say a change is as good as a rest. Cf. Tilley C230, C235, M831.

C138 Not to get much **Change** out of someone (*varied*)
1922 JJoyce *Ulysses* (NY 1934) 614: He was not likely to get a great deal of change out of such a wily old customer. **1929** GDHCole *Poison* (NY) 80: Not that I'm likely to get much change in that quarter. **1937** AChristie *Cards* (NY) 45: Didn't get any extra change out of her. **1940** ACampbell *They Hunted* (NY) 112: He got no change out of me. **1952** MGilbert *Death* (NY 1964) 34: I don't think you'd get much change out of him. **1965** HPearson *By Himself* (L) 237: I haven't got much change out of you. NED Suppl. Change 7c; Partridge 139.

C139 As black as **Charcoal**
1931 ELoban *Calloused* (NY) 240: Everything was as black as charcoal. EAP C118. Cf. Coal *below*.

C140 As cold as **Charity**
1936 AGlanville *Death* (L) 153: It [*weather*] was as cold as charity. **1937** GGoodchild *Call McLean* (L) 201: It's as cold as charity. **1950** ECRLorac *Accident* (NY DBC) 133: It's as cold as charity. **1955** RChurch *Over the* (L) 8: Cold as charity. **1968** JPorter *Dover Goes* (NY) 184: It's as cold as charity. EAP C119; TW 65(1).

C141 **Charity** begins at home (*varied*)
1908 JCLincoln *Cy Whittaker* (NY) 21: Charity . . . begins at home. **1925** RAFreeman *Red Thumb* (NY) 167: Charity begins at home. **1925** HHext *Monster* (NY) 41: She'll leave it all to charity, and that won't begin at home. **1933** LCharteris *Brighter* (NY) 267: My charity begins at home. **1936** EC

Bentley *Trent's Own* (NY) 95: The charity that doesn't begin at home. **1937** JBentley *Landor* (L) 37: Charity does begin at home, sometimes. **1937** CFGregg *Wrong House* (L) 236: "Clarity begins at home." . . . "I'll lay a hundred to six you got that out of a book." **1946** FLockridge *Murder Within* (NY) 41: Sympathy . . . began at home. **1950** JChristopher *Death* (L 1958) 48: Charity still begins at home. **1955** HMHyde *United* (L) 191: Delinquency, like charity, begins at home. **1956** *BHerald* 7/7 6: Their motto is "Charity begins abroad." **1956** FAllen *Much* (B) 152: Sin as well as charity often begins at home. **1957** *Time* 7/22 4: Agonizing reappraisals, like charity, should begin at home. **1959** *BHerald* 3/18 3: Brevity, like charity, should start at home. **1961** BPym *No Fond* (L) 146: The old saying, "Charity begins at home." **1963** EQueen *Player* (NY) 22: The ancient edict that charity should begin at home. **1964** RMacdonald *Chill* (NY) 101: Welfare begins at home. **1968** CWatson *Charity Ends at Home* (NY). **1972** CMaclean *Island* (NY 1980) 127: Charity, as well as being the voice of the world, begins at home. **1974** JWalker *Self-Portrait* (B) 100: For him attribution, unlike charity, did not begin at home. **1980** MFredman *You Can* (NY) 11: Only in this case charity began and ended at home. EAP C120; TW 65(2).

C142 Charity covers a multitude of sins
1909 JCLincoln *Keziah* (NY) 30: This fog's like charity, it'll cover a heap of sins. **1925** EBChancellor *Old Q* (L) 101: Music covers a multitude of sins. **1925** FWCrofts *Grootie* (NY) 39: Prompt payment covered a greater multitude of sins than charity. **1938** WNMacartney *Fifty Years* (NY) 84: Charity covers a multitude of sins. **1971** SWoods *Serpent's* (NY) 175: Because of charity covering a multitude of sins. **1974** RHelms *Tolkien's* (B) 64: Victory covers a multitude of sins. **1975** MKWren *A Multitude of Sins* (NY). EAP C121.

C143 As dry as a **Charity sermon** (charity)
1957 VWMason *Gracious* (NY) 179: I'm dry as a charity sermon. **1957** *Punch* 2/27 309:

The bottom of the pit looks as dry as charity. TW 65.

C144 A good-time **Charlie**
1947 HCahill *Look* (NY) 190: Too much of a good-time Charlie. **1952** CLittle *Black* (NY) 67: What about your sister? Was she a good-time Charlie too? **1962** HWaugh *That Night* (L) 54: One of those good-time Charlies. DARE i 594: Charlie 1; Berrey 438.1.

C145 To work like a **Charm**
1915 PGWodehouse *Something Fresh* (L 1935) 157: It worked like a charm. **1923** JSFletcher *Markenmore* (NY) 242: Worked like a charm. **1937** NGayle *Death* (NY) 10: It's working like a charm. **1950** ECRLorac *And Then* (NY) 187: Worked like a charm. **1958** JSymons *Pipe* (NY) 23: The whole thing went like a charm. **1964** SJay *Death* (NY) 239: "Did it work?" "Like a charm." **1967** DMorris *Naked* (NY) 195: It works like a charm. **1976** MRReno *Final* (NY) 89: It worked like a charm. EAP C124. Cf. To work like a Dream, Magic; Third Time *below*.

C146 The **Chase** is more than the kill
1965 DMDisney *Shadow* (NY) 56: The chase meant more to her husband than the kill. Cf. EAP C126. Cf. Anticipation *above*.

C147 A stern **Chase** is a long chase
1908 SHAdams *Flying Death* (NY) 129: A stern chase which developed into a long chase. **1934** ECVivian *Accessory* (L) 300: Stern chase, long chase. **1956** *BangorDN* 11/7 12: A stern chase is a long chase. **1960** PAnderson *Guardians* (NY) 101: A stern chase is a long chase. **1962** ACClarke *Tales* (NY) 72: A stern chase always takes a long time. TW 65(1).

C148 A wild-goose **Chase**
1908 AEHousman *Letters* ed HMaas (Cambridge, Mass. 1971) 97: His wild goose chase. **1922** JJoyce *Ulysses* (NY 1934) 444: Wildgoose chase. **1924** HCBailey *Mr. Fortune's Practice* (NY) 97: You were hunting the wild, wild goose. **1928** DBWLewis *Villon* (NY) 124: Into such frantic chasings of wild geese through bogs and fogs. **1932** RJCasey

News (I) 155: Wild goose hunt. **1932** MC Johnson *Damning* (NY) 91: A wildcat chase. **1932** PMcGuire *Black Rose* (NY) 195: It was a wild chase, but it led to the goose. **1937** ERPunshon *Mystery* (NY) 259: Talk about a wild-goose chase—there's not even a wild goose. **1947** GGallagher *I Found* (NY DBC) 92: Sending you on a wild-goose chase. **1952** AAFair *Top* (NY) 16: It's all a wild-goose chase . . . Let's start looking. We might even find the golden egg. **1958** PBranch *Murder's* (L 1963) 65: Look, you're wild-goosing. **1959** MInnes *Hare* (NY 1964) 110: Another wild-goose chase . . . The quintessential red herrings. The perfect turn round Robin Hood's barn. **1964** FLockridge *Quest* (P) 100: Chase of a wild goose. **1970** KLaumer *World* (NY) 75: A wild-duck chase. **1975** HCarmichael *Too Late* (NY) 180: "A wild goose chase." . . . "Wild gooses are for wild ganders." EAP C127; Brunvand 23.

C149 As drunk as **Chaucer's** ape
1950 EQueen *Double* (NY) 13: Even drunk as Chaucer's ape. Whiting A147 (quote c1390). Cf. *Oxford* 16.

C150 To be **Cheap** and nasty
1932 GLane *Hotel* (L) 125: They looked cheap and nasty. **1938** VLoder *Wolf* (L) 12: They're cheap, without being nasty. **1956** PWentworth *Fingerprint* (NY) 111: Cheap and nasty. **1964** WTrevor *Old Boys* (NY) 157: Cheap and nasty. TW 65(1); *Oxford* 116.

C151 To hand (*etc.*) in one's **Checks**
1915 JBuchan *Thirty-Nine* (NY) 75: He . . . was to hand in his checks. **1928** ACampbell *Juggernaut* (NY) 92: I was about to "pass in my checks," as your Yankee friends say. **1930** PMacDonald *Rynox* (L) 210: Carruthers was cashing in his checks. **1941** NMarsh *Death in Ecstasy* (NY) 115: Passing in her checks. **1955** DMDisney *Room* (NY) 144: Before I cash in my checks. TW 66; Brunvand 23; DARE i 601: Checks, cash in.

C152 **Cheek** by jowl
1922 JJoyce *Ulysses* (NY 1934) 389: Cheek by Jowl. **1923** EWallace *Clue of the New Pin* (B) 87: Living cheek by jowl with a man of millions. **1933** HNicolson *Diaries* ed NNicolson (NY 1966) 138: Second-hand cars standing cheek by jowl. **1940** ECBentley *Those Days* (L) 34: Lying cheek by jowl with the beer-bottles. **1946** ESedgwick *Happy* (B) 132: Cheek by jowl with respectable . . . residences. **1953** PGWodehouse *Ring* (L) 186: We're all here together, cheek by jowl as it were. **1957** NBlake *End* (L) 251: Living cheek by jowl with a woman. **1964** AHunter *Gently* (NY) 123: Five of them [*church bells*] hung cheek-by-jowl. **1972** GSchmitt *Godforgotten* (NY) 75: Eating cheek by jowl. **1973** AMStein *Finger* (NY) 159: The two big trucks riding along cheek by jowl. EAP C131; Brunvand 24.

C153 To turn the other **Cheek**
1936 JGCrandon *Pawnshop* (L) 100: And offer the other cheek. **1937** NForrest *Greek God* (L) 73: I refuse to turn the other cheek for anybody. **1941** CBClason *Green Sliver* (NY) 147: She's one of the turn-the-other-cheek-when-slapped kind. **1953** ACClarke *Expedition* (NY) 71: Turning the other cheek. **1959** AGilbert *Death* (NY) 155: She's not the kind to turn the other cheek. **1967** SMorrow *Insiders* (NY) 89: I am definitely not of the other-cheek school. **1972** JDMacDonald *Long* (P) 97: Like turning the other cheek. **1973** WMasterson *Undertaker* (NY) 134: He keeps turning the other cheek. Matthew 5:39.

C154 As pale as **Cheese**
1961 ANeame *Adventures* (NY) 26: The unhappy woman turned as pale as cheese. Wilstach 282: A new cheese.

C155 To be hard **Cheese** for someone
1934 VLoder *Murder* (L) 188: It seems hard cheese for him [*bad*]. **1946** MInnes *Unsuspected* (NY) 158: This had been hard cheese on Duncan [*bad luck*]. **1951** KFarrell *Mistletoe* (L) 50: It's hard cheese . . . to be called back. **1970** NMonsarrat *Breaking* (L) 357: It was just bad luck, hard cheese, tough tits on the loser. *Oxford* 353: Hard.

C156 To make the **Cheese** more binding
1935 HMcCoy *They Shoot* (NY) 34: The cheese is beginning to bind. **1937** DQBurleigh *Kristiana* (NY) 282: That makes the

cheese more binding. **1940** DWheelock *Murder at Montauk* (NY) 73: That would make the cheese more binding. **1948** BSBallinger *Body* (NY) 135: You could make the cheese in your story more binding. **1960** NBenchley *Sail* (NY) 48: It doesn't make the cheese any the less binding. **1968** ESRussell *She Should* (NY) 158: [It] might only make the cheese more binding.

C157 As dead as **Chelsea**

1933 VWMason *Shanghai* (NY) 29: He's sure deader'n Chelsea. Apperson 137: Dead (6).

C158 As red as a **Cherry**; Cherry-red

1929 FAPottle *Stretchers* (NY) 262: His nose as red as a cherry. **1931** PWylie *Murderer* (NY) 3: Sparks that went cherry red. **1932** APowell *Venusberg* (L 1955) 90: My cheeks used to be as red as cherries. **1936** SPalmer *Briar Pipe* (L) 33: His face had turned a deep cherry-red. **1937** WGore *Murder Most* (L) 21: It's as red as a cherry. **1940** GCKlingel *Anagua* (NY) 210: The sun turned cherry red. **1952** FPratt *Blue* (NY 1969) 86: Face . . . cherry-red. **1971** PAlding *Despite* (NY) 66: Cherry-red lips. EAP C133; TW 66(1).

C159 Not worth a **Cherry** stone

1931 MElwin *L.Powys* (L 1946) 205: Not worth a . . . cherry stone. Whiting C187.

C160 To grin like a **Cheshire** cat (*varied*)

1912 JCLincoln *Postmaster* (NY) 118: A grin on him like a Chessy cat. **1924** VBridges *Red Lodge* (NY) 40: Grinning like a Cheshire cat. **1930** FAWinder *Behind* (L) 246: The Major smiled like a satisfied cat. **1933** JWVandercook *Murder* (NY) 155: Lynch was grinning like a Cheshire cat. **1938** CWitting *Michaelmas Goose* (L) 15: You can smile like a Cheshire cat. **1940** SMSchley *Who'd Shoot* (NY) 120: Toby was grinning like a cat. **1940** LTreat *B as in Banshee* (NY) 173: I did me a Cheshire cat. Just faded away to nothin'. **1951** DSDavis *Gentle* (NY 1959) 29: You just sat there grinning like a cat. **1953** BMcMillion *Lot* (P) 243: Grinning like a Cheshire cat. **1960** LFielden *Natural* (L) 72: Smiling like a Cheshire cat. **1960** LLee *Edge* (NY) 186: They were Cheshire-cat smiles. **1961** AGilbert *After* (NY DBC) 137: Miss West . . . seemed to vanish like a Cheshire cat's grin. **1972** SAngus *Arson* (NY) 130: His face rounded and lit up like a Cheshire cat's. **1974** JFleming *How To* (NY) 50: Vanished, faded out like the Cheshire cat, well not quite like that, the Cheshire cat slowly dissolved. **1975** NGuild *Lost* (NY) 27: [He] grinned like a neurotic Cheshire cat. TW 66; *Oxford* 339: Grin.

C161 To get (something) off one's **Chest**

1934 CBush *100% Alibis* (L) 177: Get it off my chest. Partridge 145.

C162 To drop something like a hot **Chestnut**

1935 LAKnight *Super-Cinema* (L) 184: Colby dropped his confidential attitude like a hot chestnut. TW 66(2). Cf. To drop . . . Brick *above*; Potato *below*.

C163 To have neither **Chick** nor child

1912 JCLincoln *Postmaster* (NY) 186: Without chick nor child. **1936** CBush *Body* (NY) 207: The poor gentleman was alone in the world; neither chick nor child as the saying is. **1939** ECRLorac *Black Beadle* (L) 55: I've neither chick nor child . . . neither kith nor kin. **1942** PGWodehouse *Money* (NY) 99: I have neither chick nor child. **1948** DCDisney *Explosion* (NY DBC) 32: She was without chick or child. **1956** *New Yorker* 7/14 25: Without chick or child of her own color. **1966** JDosPassos *Best* (NY) 204: Having neither chick nor child, as the saying was. **1970** SGraham *Garden* (NY) 137: I've no chick, I've no child. EAP C136.

C164 **Chickens** (curses) come home to roost (*varied*)

1908 MDPost *Corrector of Destinies* (NY) 61: The chicken is come home to roost. **1921** JBCabell *Letters* ed PColum (NY 1962) 183: Rash words are now coming home to roost. **1928** EHBierstadt *Curious Trials* (NY) 347: His chickens now came home to roost. **1928** JJConnington *Tragedy* (B) 10: The family curse would come home to roost. **1929** AFielding *Mysterious* (NY) 229: Threats always seem to come home to roost—like curses. **1930** FIAnderson *Book* (NY) 207: Sooner or later all chickens come home to roost. **1931** HSKeeler *Matilda* (NY) 497: So felines come home to roost? **1931** JMWalsh *Company* (NY) 87: There are such things as curses coming home to roost. **1935** AWynne *Toll House* (P) 201: The crows were coming home to roost. **1936** JTFarrell *World* (NY) 47: Your curses will all come to roost on your own head. **1941** ISCobb *Exit* (I) 145: Too often the chickens hatched of bribery come cackling home to roost. **1949** DKeene *Framed* (NY) 61: His chickens have come home to roost. **1956** *BHerald* 6/6 23: Capitol's Birds of Ill-Omen Sure to Come Home to Roost. **1957** *New Yorker* 1/12 70: When the Suez birds will be coming home to roost. **1958** *TLS* 9/12 518: Dickens coming home to Proust. **1958** CCarnac *Affair* (NY) 137: It's possible that his past came home to roost. **1959** *BHerald* 2/26 21: Our socialist inspired chickens are coming home to roost. 12/12 4: Chickens eventually come home to roost. **1961** RGordon *Doctor* (NY) 175: The flutter of chickens coming home to roost. **1961** HKlinger *Wanton* (NY) 108: Two of our pigeons have come home to roost. **1964** RMacdonald *Chill* (NY) 231: His sky was black with pigeons coming home to roost. **1970** LGrafftey-Smith *Bright* (L) 146: The flocks of chickens coming home to roost. **1974** MMcCarthy *Mask* (NY) 163: Nearly all of Nixon's chickens have come home to roost. TW 67(5); Whiting D342; *Oxford* 162: Curses.

C165 To be no spring **Chicken**
1930 CClausen *Gloyne* (NY) 212: She wasn't no spring chicken. **1930** KCStrahan *Death* (NY) 11: Rhoda is no spring chicken. **1933** QPatrick *S.S. Murder* (NY) 228: Neither of them is what you might vulgarly describe as a spring chicken. **1939** IOellrichs *Man Who* (NY) 51: He's no spring chicken. **1954** EForbes *Rainbow* (B) 88: She was no spring chicken, but youngish yet. **1959** HShaw *Crime* (NY) 36: She was, as they say, no spring chicken. **1965** RHardwick *Plotters* (NY) 168: That's not exactly a spring chicken. **1966** SGCrawford *Gascoyne* (L)

173: I'm no spring chicken any more. EAP C137; Brunvand 24(3).

C166 To count one's **Chickens** before they are hatched (*varied*)
1924 RAFreeman *Blue* (NY) 18: Counting your chickens in pretty good time. **1926** EPhillpotts *Jig-Saw* (NY) 125: Counting my chickens before they're hatched. **1929** JMWalsh *Mystery* (L) 194: We're counting the chickens before the eggs are laid. **1935** JDCarr *Death-Watch* (L) 184: Do not count your chickens before they are hatched. **1937** DScott *Five Fatal* (NY) 74: That is what is known as counting your bridges [*chickens*] before you have eaten them. **1939** AWebb *Thank You* (L) 238: But I'm not going to count chickens before the eggs are so much as laid. **1941** RHLindsay *Fowl Murder* (B) 16: This gin is making me count my chickens too soon. **1948** ECrispin *Buried* (L 1958) 65: No good counting our chickens before they're hatched. **1956** *BangorDN* 6/20 14: The Democrats, in a way, have been counting their chickens too early. 10/12 29: Don't count your eggs—we're not there yet. **1958** *New Yorker* 3/1 61: Don't count your chickens. **1958** *BHerald* 5/8 11: Democrats gleefully counting their November chickens. **1958** DMDisney *Black* (NY) 164: Nothing like having a drink to chickens that aren't hatched yet. **1958** EStarkie *Baudelaire* (NY) 127: Counting chickens long before they were hatched—indeed often before the eggs were even laid. **1964** RAHeinlein *Farnham's* (NY 1965) 78: You're counting your chickens before the cows come home. **1973** ARoudybush *Gastronomic* (NY) 82: No good ever comes of counting chickens before they're hatched. EAP C138; Brunvand 24(2).

C167 To get it where the **Chicken** got the axe
1912 JCLincoln *Postmaster* (NY) 101: I've got it where the chicken got his. **1924** CVanVechten *Tattooed* (NY) 25: That boy'll get it in the neck where the chicken got the ax. **1929** FBeeding *Pretty* (B) 227: He's copped it good and proper, where the chicken got the axe. **1936** JMWalsh *Crimes*

(L) 92: He'll get it where the chicken got the axe. **1954** JSymons *Narrowing* (NY) 112: It's the man who sticks his neck out who catches it where the chicken caught the chopper. Partridge 146. Cf. To get . . . Neck *below.*

C168 To go to bed with the **Chickens** (*varied*)

1913 JCLincoln *Mr. Pratt's Patients* (NY) 245: Does she go to bed with the chickens? **1931** DAldis *Murder in a Haystack* (NY) 21: Going to bed with the birds. **1961** CDBurton *Long* (NY) 269: I turn in with the chickens. Cf. Brunvand 11(10): Slept with the birds; *Oxford* 38: Bed with the lamb. Cf. To be up with the Lark *below.*

C169 To run around like a **Chicken** (hen) with its head cut off

1915 JLondon *Letters* ed KHendricks (NY 1965) 461: Running around like a chicken with its head cut off. **1939** LFord *Mr. Cromwell* (L) 68: Stop dashing about like a chicken with its head off. **1958** JSStrange *Night* (NY) 163: Running around like a chicken with its head cut off. **1964** CSSumner *Withdraw* (NY) 159: I am familiar with the country expression "flying around like a chicken with its head cut off." **1965** RLPike *Police* (NY) 139: We're running around like a chicken with its head cut off. **1966** SMarlowe *Search* (NY) 244: I have been running around like a chicken that never had a head. **1969** EStewart *Heads* (NY) 192: She was running around like a headless hen. TW 181: Hen (15).

C170 To be **Chicken feed**

1950 ERPunshon *So Many* (NY) 129: That's not chicken feed. **1960** CAshe *Man Who Laughed* (NY) 98: This one is chicken feed [*easy*]. DARE i 615: Chicken feed 2; Wentworth 98–99.

C171 Too many **Chiefs,** not enough Indians

1974 NWebster *Burial* (NY) 131: It's that kind of a world—too many chiefs and a shortage of Indians. **1976** JPorter *Package* (NY) 54: Too many chiefs and not enough Indians.

C172 As happy as a **Child** (*etc.*) with a new toy (*varied*)

1912 JCLincoln *Postmaster* (NY) 101: As tickled as a youngster with a new tin whistle. **1928** TFPowys *House* (L) 193: She was . . . as happy as a child. **1930** FWCrofts *Sir John* (NY) 56: He was like a child with a new toy. **1939** CFGregg *Danger* (L) 7: He was like a kid with a new toy. **1939** JJones *Murder al Fresco* (NY) 150: Looking as happy as a baby with a nice new rattle. **1951** GHCoxe *Widow* (NY) 107: Crane sounded as pleased as a small boy with a new toy. **1959** ESchiddel *Devil* (NY) 273: Happy as a child. **1967** ESGardner *Queenly* (NY) 47: As happy as a kid with a new toy. **1967** ATurnbull *T.Wolfe* (NY) 213: He was happy as a child. TW 40: Boy (1,2); Brunvand 24(2).

C173 As innocent as a **Child**

1919 JSFletcher *Middle Temple* (NY) 307: As innocent as a child. **1929** AHayes *Crime* (L) 276: As innocent as a child unborn. **1930** GCollins *Horror* (L) 187: He was innocent as a child. **1935** LBlow *Bournewick* (L) 187: I am as innocent of the crime as a newborn child. **1950** MRHodgkin *Student* (L) 203: Eyes that were innocent as a child's. **1955** DMDisney *Trick* (NY) 78: As innocent as a child. **1964** RMacdonald *Chill* (NY) 196: I'm as innocent as a little child. EAP C142. Cf. As innocent as a Babe *above.*

C174 A burnt **Child** dreads the fire (*varied*)

1913 TDreiser *Traveler* (NY 1923) 339: As a burned child would recoil from fire. **1919** JCLincoln *Extricating* (NY) 34: A burnt child dreads the— **1922** RFirbank *Flower* (Works 4, L 1929) 87: One does not burn one's fingers twice. **1935** ESGardner *Caretaker's Cat* (NY) 98: He's a burnt child who dreads the fire. **1935** HEStearns *Street* (NY) 177: A burned child proverbially dreads the fire. **1950** RMacDonald *Drowning* (NY 1951) 171: The burnt child can't stay away from the fire. **1957** *PMLA* 72 382: A burnt child dreads the fire. **1968** DBagley *Vivero* (NY) 4: The proverb of the burnt child fearing the fire. **1975** DRussell *Tamarisk* (NY) 262: A burnt child dreads the fire.

EAP C145; TW 68(17); Brunvand 24(4). Cf. Burned *above*.

C175 The **Child** (boy) is father to the man

1921 SMEllis *Solitary Horseman* (Kensington) 29: It is both the tritest and truest of sayings that the boy is father of the man. **1925** EBChancellor *Hell Fire* (L) 141: The child is father to the man, as we have poetic authority for stating. **1931** MKennedy *Death to the Rescue* (L) 199: The boy is father to the man. **1933** RCurle *Corruption* (I) 15: Is it correct what the proverb says about the boy being father to the man? **1934** PGWodehouse *Brinkley* (B) 173: The boy is the father of the man. **1938** JCLenehan *Guilty* (L) 182: The child is father to the man. **1943** GGCoulton *Fourscore* (Cambridge, Eng.) 303: The child had been father of the man. **1952** JLeslie *Intimate* (NY) 128: The child is father to the man. **1962** HBaker *W.Hazlitt* (Cambridge, Mass.) 3: The child is father to the man. **1964** JHillas *Today* (NY) 265: There is no greater truism than that the child is father to the man. **1966** SMarcus *Other* (NY 1967) 17: The child is father of the man—and with a vengeance. **1969** EInglis-Jones *Augustus* (L) 27: The old saying has it the child is father to the man. **1974** JWain *Johnson* (NY) 27: The child was very clearly the father of the man. TW 68(18); Brunvand 24(5); *Oxford* 119.

C176 It's a wise **Child** that knows its own father (*varied*)

1922 JJoyce *Ulysses* (NY 1934) 87: The wise child that knows her own father. 406: The wise father knows his own child. **1928** VMarkham *Death* (NY) 378: It's a wise egg that knows its own rooster. **1928** EO'Neill *Strange* (NY) 205: It's a wise father who knows his own child. **1954** SDeLima *Carnival* (NY) 10: It's a wise father who knows his own children. **1955** RGraves *Homer's* (NY) 127: It is a wise child that knows its own father. **1956** AWUpfield *Man of* (NY) 27: I never knew my father, and in any case it's a wise man who does, according to someone. **1957** *NYTimes* 8/18 9E: It's a wise father that'll know his own child. **1959** JA Brussel *Just* (NY) 86: Is it too trite to say it is a wise child that knows her father? **1960**

TCurley *It's a Wise Child* (NY). **1968** JGould *Europe* (B) 210: It's a wise parent who knows his own child, in any language. **1970** RRendell *Best Man* (NY) 121: It's a wise father that knows his own child. **1974** A Menen *Fonthill* (NY) 135: It's a wise child who knows his own father. EAP C149.

C177 To be **Child's** play

1912 ERBurroughs *Princess of Mars* (NY 1963) 108: Child's play to me. **1913** JSFletcher *Secret* (L 1918) 101: This is a mere child's game. **1922** AAMilne *Red House* (NY 1959) 111: Child's play. **1932** JDCarr *Corpse* (NY) 113: Child's play. **1941** CMRussell *Dreadful* (NY) 18: Child's play to get rid of them. **1942** CFAdams *What Price* (NY) 81: This was no longer a children's game. **1957** MLBarnes *Isabel* (P) 208: It would be child's play to him. **1958** FLockridge *Long* (P) 66: One or two more would be child's play. **1965** FPohl *Plague* (NY) 155: It was child's play. **1968** AChristie *Child's Play* (L). EAP C151; TW 68(19); Brunvand 24(6).

C178 To know no more than a **Child** unborn

1919 JSFletcher *Middle Temple* (NY) 197: He knows no more than a child unborn. TW 68(11). Cf. To know . . . Babe *above*.

C179 **Children** and fools speak the truth

1921 JCLincoln *Galusha* (NY) 83: You know what they say about children. **1930** GGoodchild *Monster* (NY) 157: It's astonishing what truths come from the mouths of children. **1936** ARClark *High Wall* (NY) 190: Children and fools speak the truth. **1945** FBunnamy *King Is Dead* (NY) 98: Children and fools . . . almost never tell the truth. **1969** DShannon *Crime* (NY) 105: What was that bone about children and fools speaking the truth? **1972** DShannon *Murder* (NY) 38: Children and fools speak the truth. EAP C157; *Oxford* 119.

C180 **Children** (boys, girls, women) should be seen and not heard (*varied*)

1929 RRodd *Secret* (NY) 65: A decent telephoner, like a well-trained child, should be seen, not heard. **1929** GMitchell *Speedy* (NY) 114: Let little girls be seen and not heard. **1930** WLewis *Apes* (NY 1932) 195: Little boys should be seen and not heard. **1930** HLofting *Twilight* (NY) 11: In those days children were supposed to be seen and not heard. **1930** SSassoon *Memoirs* (L) 108: He wasn't good at being "seen but not heard." **1931** APryde *Emerald* (NY) 265: Little girls should be seen and not heard. **1935** TRoscoe *Murder* (NY) 59: The dictum about children being seen and not heard. **1937** MBenney *Angels* (NY) 73: Little boys should be seen and not heard. **1952** C Amory *Last* (NY) 224: Children should be seen and not heard. **1955** WSloane *Stories* (L) 194: Children should be seen and not heard, as the good old-fashioned saying is. **1962** Bryher *Heart* (NY) 104: A child should be seen and not heard. **1964** I Morris *World* (L) 228: Women were normally heard but not seen. **1969** RGMartin *Jennie* (NY) 110: Victorian children were seldom seen and almost never heard. **1971** MErskine *Brood* (NY) 125: Little girls must remember to be seen and not heard. **1975** MHolroyd *Augustus* (NY) 225: Women must be seen and not heard. EAP C156; TW 68(13); Brunvand 15: Boy(1), 58: Girl(4).

C181   One's second **Childhood**

1920 AChristie *Mysterious Affair* (NY) 257: I am not in my second childhood. **1932** RCWoodthorpe *Public* (L) 100: In his second childhood. **1936** NMorland *Clue* (L) 23: Grown men in their second childhood. **1940** LMacNeice *Strings* (L 1965) 105: Their second childhood having come too early. **1952** AChristie *Mrs. McGinty* (NY) 221: I'm in my second childhood. **1963** WMorris *Cause* (NY) 143: A second childhood is the climax of his life. **1969** BCole *Joseph* (NY) 11: He was heading for second childhood. EAP C152.

C182   To smoke like a **Chimney**

1936 RLehmann *Weather* (NY) 39: Smoking like a chimney. **1958** *New Yorker* 6/28 24: I smoked like a chimney. **1958** JByrom *Or Be* (L 1964) 72: My husband smoked like a chimney. **1961** JBingham *Night's* (L 1965) 126: Personally, I smoke like a chimney. **1963** GMaxwell *Rocks* (NY) 190: Everybody

smoked like chimneys. **1976** JPorter *Package* (NY) 4: The chap smoked like a blessed chimney. TW 68.

C183   To drag one's **Chin**

1949 EQueen *Cat* (B) 21: She really was dragging her chin [*very depressed*]. See next entry.

C184   To keep one's **Chin** up

1931 VWilliams *Masks* (L) 244: Keep your chin up. **1935** TWilder *Heaven's* (NY) 253: Keep your chin up. **1941** DCCameron *And So He* (NY) 80: She kept her chin up. **1955** KMKnight *Robineau* (NY) 148: Keep your chin up. **1960** RWilson *30 Day* (NY) 18: Keeping the old chin up. **1963** JMUllman *Neon* (NY) 235: She's trying hard to keep her chin up. Berrey 299.3.

C185   To lead with one's **Chin** (*varied*)

1950 ESGardner *Musical* (NY) 147: You're certainly leading with your chin. **1956** ES Gardner *Demure* (NY) 149: I'm going to lead with my chin. **1961** SDean *Credit* (NY) 101: I stuck out my chin. **1970** AAFair *All Grass* (NY DBC) 157: You led with your chin. **1972** MGilbert *Body* (NY) 159: You led with your chin on that one. Berrey 701.12.

C186   Not a **Chinaman's** chance (*varied*)

1928 WAWolff *Trial* (NY) 41: [Not a] Chinaman's chance. **1933** HAsbury *Barbary* (NY) 207: He hadn't even the proverbial Chinaman's chance of regaining his liberty. **1936** PQuentin *Puzzle* (NY) 59: There wasn't a Chinaman's chance of that. **1937** JBentley *Whitney* (L) 53: Vardon hasn't a Chinaman's hope. **1940** CRice *Corpse Steps* (NY) 197: It would be easy as pie to break into the building, and not a Chinaman's chance that anyone would blunder in and discover it. **1941** GBenedict *Deadly Drops* (NY) 213: Not a Chink's chance. **1947** HCahill *Look* (NY) 184: Give me a Chinaman's chance. **1956** *BHerald* 8/5 63: Here is . . . not a Chinaman's chance that he can be defeated. **1958** *BHerald* 2/2 42: He hasn't a Chinaman's chance of hitting a bull's-eye. **1962** ESherry *Girl* (NY DBC) 101: He hadn't a Chinaman's chance. **1975** FMNivens *Publish* (NY) 157: There's not a Chinaman's chance in hell that that body is Graham Dillaway. Wentworth 100.

C187 As dry as a **Chip**

1906 JCLincoln *Mr. Pratt* (NY) 182: Says she, dry as a chip. **1935** JYDane *Murder Cum Laude* (NY) 245: Every shoe . . . was as dry as a chip. **1937** DQBurleigh *Kristiana* (NY) 16: Dry as chips. **1953** CMRussell *Market* (NY) 41: Dry as chips. **1955** NMarsh *Scales* (B) 94: The ground was as dry as a chip. EAP C164.

C188 The **Chips** are down

1959 BBenson *Seven* (NY) 181: Now the chips were down. **1960** SDean *Murder* (NY DBC) 49: When the chips are down. Wentworth 101–2.

C189 A **Chip** in the porridge

1968 EBuckler *Ox Bells* (NY) 164: One who had no mind of his own but agreed with everyone was "a chip in the porridge." EAP C166.

C190 A **Chip** of (off) the old block (*varied*)

1900 CFPidgin *Quincy A. Sawyer* (B) 71: A chip of the old block. **1907** CMGayley *Plays of Our Forefathers* (NY) 173: The Herod of the latter is a chip of the York block. **1922** JJoyce *Ulysses* (NY 1934) 142: Chip of the old block. **1927** NMartin *Mosaic* (NY) 2: Kenneth had wanted, as any young chip might, to cut loose from the old block. **1928** DHLawrence *Lady* ("Allemagne") 341: Chip of the old block. **1938** NMorland *Rope* (L) 89: He's a chip of his dad all right. **1940** TChanslor *Our First* (NY) 241: Another chip off the old block. **1941** HCBailey *Orphan Ann* (NY) 19: His son has been called a block of the old chip. **1941** CMRussell *Dreadful* (NY) 4: Poston . . . was a chip off another block. **1944** MBramhall *Murder Solves* (NY) 106: A chip off my block. **1956** *BangorDN* 11/15 35: You're a chip off the old block, son. **1957** *Time* 3/11 28: A flinty chip off the old block. **1966** NBlake *Morning* (NY) 108: A chip—a very small chip— off the old block. **1966** LLafore *Nine* (NY) 83: A chip off the old blockhead. **1970** CDrummond *Stab* (NY) 84: The brighter chips off the block. **1971** EHCohen *Made-*

moiselle (B) 133: His sisters were evidently chippies off the old block. **1974** JFlaherty *Chez* (NY) 61: Sort of a chip off the old chip [*sic*]. **1974** THeald *Blue* (NY) 23: Knock some chips off the old blocks. **1981** AAndrews *Pig* (NY) 96: Chip off the old block. EAP C165; Brunvand 24–5(1).

C191 To have a **Chip** on one's shoulder (*varied*)

1917 JCLincoln *Extricating* (NY) 31: I had a chip on each shoulder [*was confident*]. **1932** LFrost *Murder* (NY) 109: Forgetting the chip on his shoulder. **1936** *New Yorker* 3/28 34: Heads may be in the clouds, but chips are on every shoulder. **1938** PATaylor *Banbury* (NY 1964) 64: They're knockin' the chip off for me. **1941** KRoos *If the Shroud* (NY) 116: Blew away the chip that was forming on my shoulder. **1942** WIrish *Phantom* (NY 1957) 8: With that chip-on-the-shoulder look. **1946** HHowe *We Happy* (NY) 117: A chip on his shoulder so big he can't see straight. **1950** BSpicer *Blues* (NY) 83: I've had my chip knocked off enough to learn to carry it in my pocket. **1954** RKLeavitt *The Chip on Grandma's Shoulder* (P). **1956** *BHerald* 12/22 4: Mr. Thompson should take the chip off his shoulder. **1957** *BangorDN* 3/27 14: All the chips having slipped quietly off my shoulder. **1957** *NY Times Book Review* 5/5 29: A chip-on-the-shoulder attitude about air power. **1957** *Time* 7/8 10: Putting chips on their shoulders for the Supreme Court to knock off. **1957** *NYTimes Book Review* 11/3 50: Just had the chip taken off Lucky Jim's shoulder. **1958** *TLS* 2/7 73: For "snob" and "chip on the shoulder" are only different facets of the same thing. **1960** AHLewis *Worlds* (NY) 66: The theoretical chip . . . was knocked off the shoulder. **1967** ANLMunby *Portrait* (L) 86: Maddan . . . carried a chip on his shoulder. **1971** RMStern *Murder* (NY) 17: You have a chip on your shoulder . . . Are you asking me to knock it off? **1972** AGarve *Case* (NY) 73: A chip on his shoulder as big as a tree. **1972** HTeichmann *Kaufman* (NY) 71: He's in the chips now, but most of them seem to have stayed on his shoulders. **1975** HDolson *Please* (P) 35:

Wearing chips on both shoulders. EAP C167; Brunvand 25(2).

C192 As crazy (cute) as a **Chipmunk**
1940 GBagby *Corpse Wore* (NY) 142: Women . . . are . . . as crazy as chipmunks. **1956** *New Yorker* 12/22 31: She was a small blonde, cute as a chipmunk and bright as a dollar.

C193 As drunk as **Chloe**
1948 AWUpfield *Author* (Sydney 1967) 132: He was as drunk as Chloe. **1956** AWUpfield *Man of* (NY) 34: Drunk as Chloe. *Oxford* 206: Drunk.

C194 Small **Choice** in (of) rotten apples
1931 CWells *Umbrella* (NY) 63: Small choice in rotten apples. **1944** MLong *Bury* (NY) 55: Small choice of rotten apples. **1958** SDean *Dishonor* (NY) 157: It's a choice of rotten apples. Taylor *Proverb* 152, *Index* 21.

C195 To **Chop** and change
1929 STruss *Living* (NY) 221: He hated his plan to be chopped and changed about. **1930** AGilbert *Night* (NY) 32: Life's over short for changin' and choppin'. **1938** SLeslie *Film* (L) 351: It is strange how literary values chop and change. **1956** AMoorehead *Gallipoli* (NY) 47: He chops and changes. **1964** RRendell *From Doom* (B 1966) 50: People are always chopping and changing their cars. **1969** PDickinson *Old English* (NY) 92: To go chopping and changing your way of talking from sunup to cattle-calling time. **1970** NMonsarrat *Breaking* (L) 215: Years of trial and error, of chopping and changing. **1973** VSPritchett *Balzac* (NY) 166: The chopping and changing of governments. EAP C171.

C196 **Christ** (death) on a crutch! (*varied*)
1949 BSBallinger *Body* (NY) 31: Keerist on a crutch! **1965** Doctor X *Intern* (NY) 255: He looked like death on crutches. Berrey 194.6: Christ.

C197 As cool (cold) as **Christmas**
1934 MBurton *Chasabanc* (L) 79: The scent will be as cold as Christmas. **1935** *New Yorker* 12/21 50: Cold as Christmas. **1936** ECBentley *Trent's Own* (NY) 281: As cool as Christmas. **1950** ECBentley *Chill* (NY) 60: He is as cool as Christmas. **1965** MMcShane *Girl* (NY) 121: "And Oz's trail stayed cold, eh?" "Cold as Christmas." EAP C174; Taylor *Western Folklore* 17(1958) 14.

C198 As sure as **Christmas**
1915 JBuchan *Thirty-Nine* (NY) 75: As sure as Christmas. **1952** MAllingham *Tiger* (NY) 235: As sure as Christmas. **1963** DGardiner *Lion* (NY) 134: Sure as Christmas. Wilstach 402: Comes.

C199 **Christmas** comes but once a year
1932 FIles *Before* (NY 1958) 171: Christmas comes but once a year. **1937** SPalmer *No Flowers* (L) 75: Christmas only comes once a year. **1957** *Punch* 3/27 404: It [*Christmas*] comes but once a year. **1958** JLindsay *Life* (L) 41: [New Year] only comes once a year. **1960** DHayles *Comedy* (L) 143: Christmas comes but once a year. **1971** PTabor *Pauline's* (Louisville) 231: As the good ole Yuletide saying goes, Christmas comes but once a year, and when it does it brings good cheer. TW 69(1).

C200 **Christmas** is coming
1939 HMiller *Capricorn* (NY 1961) 255: The bastard trying to pretend she was coming and not coming any more than Christmas was coming. **1946** FWCrofts *Death of a Train* (L) 55: There's a train coming all right—like Christmas. EAP C175.

C201 A green **Christmas** (winter) makes a fat (full) churchyard (*varied*)
1934 VLincoln *February Hill* (NY) 330: Green Christmas means a full churchyard, as the saying is. **1934** DLSayers *Nine Tailors* (NY) 313: They say a green winter makes a fat churchyard. **1937** KPKempton *Monday* (NY) 145: A green Christmas makes a fat graveyard. **1953** EBGarside *Man from* (NY) 173: They've always said a black Christmas fills the graveyards full. **1956** BJChute *Greenwillow* (NY) 87: Green Christmas was a full churchyard. **1956** MPHood *Scarlet* (NY) 15: Green winter, full churchyard. **1967** RDavies *Marchbank's* (Toronto) 148: A green Christmas makes a fat graveyard. EAP C176. Cf. *Oxford* 337: Green Winter (Yule).

C202 Till **Christmas**

1959 HStone *Man Who* (NY) 169: You can tell him from here to Christmas. **1969** GBabby *Honest* (NY) 130: References? She had them from here to Christmas. **1972** JAnderson *Alpha* (NY) 114: You can talk till Christmas. EAP C177; TW 69(2).

C203 To be dressed up like a **Christmas** tree

1941 KSecrist *Murder Makes* (NY) 149: She was dolled up like a Christmas tree. **1952** MMillar *Vanish* (NY) 219: All dressed up like a Christmas tree. **1957** WRBurdett *Underdog* (NY) 36: All dressed up like a Christmas tree.

C204 To be trussed up like a **Christmas** turkey (goose)

1935 HHolt *Unknown* (L) 85: Trussed up after the manner of a Christmas turkey. **1939** HReilly *All Concerned* (NY) 112: I was trussed up like a fowl. **1975** HPentecost *Time* (NY) 173: He will be trussed up like the proverbial Christmas goose. DARE i 656–7: Christmas tree 1. Cf NED Truss, *v.* 8, Trussed 1c.

C205 To light (be lit) up like a **Christmas** tree

1939 MGEberhart *Chiffon* (NY) 291: Her face used to light up like a Christmas tree. **1940** CSaxby *Death Joins* (NY) 46: All lit up like a Christmas tree [*drunk*]. **1944** CBrand *Green for Danger* (NY 1965) 111: She really did look perfectly lovely that night, all lit up like a Christmas tree. **1952** JBClayton *Wait* (NY) 127: He was all lit up like a Christmas tree [*drunk*]. **1957** *CSMonitor* 1/3 2: Its switchboard has been lighted up like the proverbial Christmas tree. **1957** WGoldman *Temple* (NY) 251: Terry's face lit up like a Christmas tree. **1969** EPetaja *Nets* (NY) 21: I can just see his round face lighting up like a Christmas tree. **1973** DShannon *No Holiday* (NY) 144: All lit up like a Christmas tree [*excited*]. Taylor *Western Folklore* 17(1958) 14; DARE i 657: Christmas tree 2; Berrey 97.11.

C206 As dead as a **Church** on Monday

1955 ESGardner *Sun* (NY) 99: Dead as a church on Monday. Taylor *Western Folklore* 17(1958) 14(1): Empty.

C207 As quiet as a **Church**

1923 VWilliams *Orange* (B) 87: As quiet as a church. **1934** HBaker *Cartwright* (B) 209: Quiet as a church. **1973** WJBurley *Death* (NY) 131: It was quiet as a church. Whiting *NC* 384; Taylor *Western Folklore* 17(1958) 14(2).

C208 As safe (sound) as a **Church**

1922 DFox *Ethel* (NY) 236: Safe as a church. **1924** WBMFerguson *Black* (NY) 310: Safe as a church. **1932** ACampbell *Murder* (NY) 84: Drop asleep sound as a church. **1947** MCarleton *Swan* (NY) 102: Safe as a church. **1952** PHBonner *S.P.Q.R.* (NY) 191: I'm as safe as a church. **1959** AMStein *Never* (NY) 121: We'd be safe as churches. **1961** GBagby *Evil* (NY) 20: Safe as churches. **1961** PDennis *Little* (NY) 94: All is safe as a church. **1976** GBagby *Two* (NY) 98: I'm safe as churches.

C209 As silent as a **Church**

1969 HPentecost *Girl with* (NY) 108: The woods were silent as a church. TW 70(2).

C210 As steady as a **Church**

1937 KPKempton *Monday* (NY) 14: Steady as a church. **1956** JDunbar *Golden* (B) 21: The *Jupiter* went flying along as steady as a church. EAP C178.

C211 As still as a **Church**

1932 VWilliams *Death* (B) 159: The house is as still as a church. **1974** MGEberhart *Danger* (NY) 126: As still . . . and solemn as a church.

C212 The nearer the **Church,** the farther from God (*varied*)

1939 MHealy *Old Munster* (L) 26: The nearer the church, the farther from God. **1943** AAMacGregor *Auld Reekie* (L) 84: That trite adage, the newer the kirk, the farther frae grace. **1952** MColes *Night* (NY) 137: Following the proverb "The nearer the church the further from God," there are some of the liveliest quarters of Paris in the immediate neighborhood of Notre Dame. **1957** RGraves *They Hanged* (NY) 20: "The nearer the church, the farther from God," is a proverb of doubtful truth. **1978** PMcGinley *Bogmail* (NY 1981) 113: For the benefit of those who were nearest the church and farthest from God. EAP C180.

C213 See you in **Church**

1938 MJohnson *Comets* (NY) 247: See you in church. **1949** FCrane *Flying* (NY) 142: Well, be seeing you folks in church. **1964** WHayward *It Never* (L) 118: See you in church. Berrey 350.8. Cf. Funny papers, Jail *below*.

C214 As poor (dead) as a **Church mouse** (rat)

c1910 PGWodehouse *Leave it to Psmith* (L n.d.) 50: As poor as a church mouse. **1911** RAFreeman *Eye of Osiris* (NY 1929) 25: As poor as church mice. **1924** JSFletcher *Time-Worn* (NY) 59: Poor as a church-mouse. **1928** AGilbert *Mrs. Davenport* (NY) 46: As poor as church rats. **1929** HAdams *Caroline* (P) 225: Poor as a mouse. **1930** DLSayers *Strong* (NY) 86: We're quite the proverbial church mice. **1934** EWaugh *Handful* (NY) 232: Poor as church mice . . . but stinking proud. **1938** LBarret *Rough Young* (NY) 64: Down in the basement lived church mice, notoriously poor. **1941** ISShriber *Murder Well Done* (NY) 67: We lived like the proverbial church mice. **1945** RLHines *Confessions* (L) 227: As poor as a church mouse . . . as poor as a Methodist mouse, which is twice as poor. **1953** JMorris *Man and Two* (L) 30: He was as poor as a mouse. **1954** CIsherwood *World* (L) 50: Poor as a mouse. **1957** *BangorDN* 3/23 5: About as poor as a mouse in a church steeple. **1957** *NYTimes* 11/10 55: As long as the South was church-rat poor. **1959** THWhite *Godstone* (NY) 38: He was as poor as a church mouse. **1963** JLudwig *Confusions* (Greenwich, Conn.) 39: Poor as temple mice. **1969** JTrahey *Pecked* (Englewood, NJ) 49: It's as dead as a church mouse. **1970** STerkel *Hard* (NY) 95: Poor as church mice. **1970** EQueen *Last* (NY) 119: I've been church mouse poor. **1974** WSnow *Codline* (Middletown, Conn.) 454: "As poor as a church mouse." (I could never understand why a church mouse who delighted in the leavings of all the church suppers . . . should be considered more underprivileged than other mice!) **1982** JLangton *Natural* (NY) 53: "Poor as a

church-mouse—that wasn't fair to Mus musculus, who probably had better sense than to hole up in a church anyway," thought John scornfully. EAP C181; Brunvand 25. Cf. DARE i 665: Church mouse preacher. Cf. As poor as a Rat *below*.

C215 As quiet as a **Churchyard**

1938 MECurne *Death* (NY) 235: This place is as quiet as a churchyard. Cf. Wilstach 309: Quiet . . . graveyard.

C216 As silent as a **Churchyard**

1958 MAllingham *Tether's* (NY) 128: The whole place was as silent as a churchyard. Wilstach 353: Country churchyard.

C217 As dry as **Cinders**

1964 HRFKeating *Perfect* (NY 1966) 73: His mouth felt as dry as cinders. Wilstach 105: A cinder.

C218 **Circumstances** alter cases (*varied*)

1922 JSFletcher *Herapath* (NY) 89: An old saying that circumstances alter cases. **1922** JJoyce *Ulysses* (NY 1934) 537: Circumstances alter cases. **1929** EDBiggers *Black* (I) 203: Circumstances . . . upset cases. **1932** FIles *Before* (NY 1958) 141: Circumstances alter women. **1932** EPartridge *Literary* (L) 124: The "circumstances" which, proverbially, alter cases. **1940** RPenny *Sweet Poison* (L) 85: Circumstances alter cases, as they say in the copy-books. **1948** HAustin *Drink* (NY) 39: The cliché circumstances alter cases. **1952** MAllingham *Tiger* (NY) 185: But, as Mother always said, circumstances alter cases. **1953** JTrench *Docken* (L 1960) 184: Circumstances alter cases, I always say. **1962** SRansome *Without* (NY) 129: Circumstances alter cases. **1967** VSPritchett *Cab* (NY) 44: Circumstances alter cases. **1968** RLockridge *Plate* (P) 185: Circumstances alter tastes. **1975** BNByfield *Solemn* (NY) 138: Do circumstances alter cases? EAP C188; Brunvand 25.

C219 As good as a **Circus**

1900 CFPidgin *Quincy A. Sawyer* (B) 437: Strout was as good as a circus. **1930** MCKeaton *Eyes* (NY) 118: As good as a circus. **1957** *BangorDN* 4/1 21: He's gooder-'n a three-ring circus. **1957** JCheever

Wapshot (NY) 44: She's better than a three-ring circus. Taylor *Western Folklore* 17(1958) 14.

C220   You can't fight **City Hall**

1964 RAHeinlein *Farnham's* (NY 1965) 147: You can't fight City Hall. **1966** PFHealy *Cissy* (NY) 356: The old saw that "you can't fight City hall."

C221   As calm as a **Clam**

1936 GDyer *Catalyst* (NY) 81: He was calm as a clam. **1939** ADemarest *Murder on* (NY) 67: He sat there as calm as a clam. Cf. Wilstach 41: Clam shells.

C222   As close(mouthed) as a **Clam**

1928 JGoodwin *When Dead* (NY) 662: He's as close as a clam. **1935** ECRLorac *Murder* (L) 3: This door fits—close as a clam. **1935** JYDane *Murder Cum Laude* (NY) 65: He's close mouthed as a clam. **1936** FWCrofts *Man Overboard!* (NY) 75: As close as a clam. **1940** CRawson *Headless* (NY) 278: The man is as close-mouthed as a clam. Whiting *NC* 384(1); Taylor *Western Folklore* 17(1958) 14(1); NED Clam *sb.*² 2. Cf. As close as an Oyster *below.*

C223   As cold as a **Clam** (oyster)

1933 CFitzsimmons *Red Rhapsody* (NY) 272: She was as cold as the proverbial clam. **1937** GBruce *Claim* (NY) 143: She was as cold as an oyster. **1941** CRice *Right Murder* (NY) 103: He was as cold as a clam [*dead drunk*]. **1943** MVenning *Murder through* (NY) 114: The home made hootch knocked him out, cold as a oyster. **1946** RFinnegan *Lying* (NY) 143: I knocked two of them cold as clams. **1959** MScherf *Never Turn* (NY) 73: You're as cold as a clam. TW 71(1).

C224   As happy as a **Clam** (at high tide) (*varied*)

1923 LThayer *Sinister* (NY) 157: As happy as a clam at high tide. **1935** LThayer *Sudden* (NY) 213: Happy as a clam. **1937** HFootner *Dark Ships* (L) 201: As happy as a pair of clams at high water. **1951** PATaylor *Diplomatic* (NY) 84: [He's] going to be as happy as a clam at high tide. **1954** IFleming *Live* (NY 1959) 84: Looking as happy as a clam. **1957** *BHerald* 3/4 1: She's happy as a clam.

1959 *BHerald* 10/26 12: She was as happy as a clam at high tide. **1961** MHHood *Drown* (NY) 105: Contented as a clam at high water, as the natives say [*Maine*]. **1965** PDeVries *Let Me* (NY 1966) 77: Art was happy as a clam. **1968** MMannes *They* (NY) 112: "I know people with strange habits who're as happy as clams." "An astonishing phrase, I have always thought. How can clams be happy?" **1970** TWells *Dinky* (NY) 24: Happy as clams at high tide. **1971** BDennis *Paradise* (NY) 98: Happy as clams—however happy clams were supposed to be. **1973** JDMacDonald *Turquoise* (P) 197: Happy as a fat clam. **1981** PDeVries *Sauce* (B) 183: But Mother's happy as a clam. TW 71(4); Brunvand 25; Taylor *Western Folklore* 17(1958) 14(2).

C225   As silent as a **Clam**; Clam-silent

1929 WKSmith *Bowery* (NY) 101: [He] was as silent as the proverbial clam. **1956** DKnight *In Search* (C) 16: Clam-silent and snake-sinister. **1978** JLHensley *Killing* (NY) 59: He could be silent as an antisocial clam. Taylor *Prov. Comp.* 73.

C226   As talkative (gabby) as a **Clam**

1937 DQBurleigh *Kristiana* (NY) 116: As gabby as a clam. **1938** DCDisney *Strawstack* (NY) 183: She's about as talkative as a clam. Whiting *NC* 384(2).

C227   As tight as a **Clam** (*varied*)

1928 RCullum *Mystery* (NY) 170: He was as tight shut as a clam. **1929** CRJones *King* (NY) 151: Shut up tighter 'an a clam. **1937** PHaggard *Dead Is* (P) 210: Everybody is tighter than a clam. **1939** AMuir *Death Comes* (L) 135: Tight as a clam [*closed*]. **1970** CDrummond *Stab* (NY) 153: Ambrose was as tight as a clam as far as advance money is concerned. Whiting *NC* 384(3); Taylor *Prov. Comp.* 82.

C228   To shut up like a **Clam** (*varied*)

1906 JCLincoln *Mr. Pratt* (NY) 53: Shut up like a clam. **1921** IOstranter *Crimson* (NY) 124: Shut up like a clam. **1930** ACampbell *Murder* (NY): He had shut up like a clam. **1950** STruss *Never* (NY) 163: She shut up like a clam. **1953** BCClough *Grandma* (Portland, Me.) 6: The common expression "he shut up like a clam." **1958** *New Yorker* 1/11 90: The town was shut up like a clam. **1960** BAskwith *Tangled* (L) 115: He shut up like a clam. **1964** CSSumner *Withdraw* (NY) 62: The clams he had eaten . . . had infected him with their own proverbial uncommunicativeness. **1966** ELinington *Date* (NY) 189: He's shut up like the proverbial clam. Cf. Berrey 205.4: Make a noise like a clam and shut up. Cf. To shut up like an Oyster *below.*

C229 The **Clap** is no worse than a bad cold

1934 JO'Hara *Appointment* (NY) 49: The clap was no worse than a bad cold. 165: No worse than a bad cold . . . you're not a man till you had it once. **1964** SBecker *Covenant* (NY) 45: It's [*the clap*] no worse than a bad cold. 79: My classic little joke is now obsolete; a clap may be cured in two or three days, but a bad cold lingers for a week. Whiting *NC* 384.

C230 To go like the **Clatter** bone of a goose's arse

1925 GBeasley *My First* (Paris) 160: Their tongues would go . . . like the clatter bone of a goose's ass. DARE i 679: Clatterbones [Scots]. Cf NED Clatter *sb.*[1] 3.

C231 As pale as **Clay**

1960 GAshe *Man Who Laughed* (NY) 185: Her face as pale as clay. *Oxford* 132: Cold.

C232 As white as **Clay**

1950 MRHodgkin *Student* (L) 209: A face as white as clay. Wilstach 473.

C233 **Clay**-cold

1968 JRoffman *Grave* (NY) 181: The flesh . . . had been clay-cold. EAP C191a.

C234 To be (as) **Clay** in someone's hands

1932 GLane *Hotel* (L) 222: I was as clay in her hands. **1933** CBush *Three Strange* (L) 186: He was as clay in his hands. **1935** GWeston *Murder in Haste* (NY) 97: She had been clay in his hands. **1974** DMDisney *Don't Go* (NY) 160: Clay in that girl's hands. NED Clay *sb.* 1b (quote 1797). Cf. To be Putty, Wax *below.*

C235 To take someone to the **Cleaners**

1938 WMartyn *Murder Walks* (L) 43: They take me to the cleaners every time. **1941** JPhilips *Odds on* (NY) 200: He was all set to take us to the cleaners. **1954** LFord *Invitation* (NY) 27: The family took him to the cleaners. **1962** NFreeling *Death* (NY 1964) 34: [He] will take you to the cleaners. **1966** VSiller *Mood* (NY) 8: Cynthia had taken him to the cleaners. Wentworth 108.

C236 **Cleanliness** is next to godliness (*varied*)

1909 JCLincoln *Keziah* (NY) 63: Cleanliness is next to godliness. **1913** HTFinck *Food* (NY) 91: Cleanliness is next to godliness. **1924** WBMFerguson *Black* (NY) 240: Cleanliness is next to godliness. **1928** HVMorton *In Search* (NY) 189: I would like to know when the proximity of cleanliness to Godliness was defined. **1933** EJepson *Memoirs* (L) 28: St. Paul had written . . . that Cleanliness was next to Godliness. **1939** TStevenson *Silver Arrow* (L) 86: Cleanliness is next to godliness. **1940** EL White *While She* (NY) 14: [He] ran neck-to-neck with cleanliness, to come in second to Godliness. **1946** MInnes *Unsuspected* (NY) 208: Godliness came next to cleanliness. **1948** HActon *Memoirs* (L) 301: The Dutch had at least taught that cleanliness was next to godliness. **1952** GBullett *Trouble* (L) 62: Cleanliness is next to godliness, as the proverb tells us. **1955** MGilbert *Country-House* (NY) 2: Cleanliness [is] furthest from godliness, really. **1955** MO'Brine *Passport* (L) 142: Cleanliness and ungodliness hand in hand. **1956** *BHerald* 10/31 24: There's an old saying, "Cleanliness is next to Godliness." Personally, I am ignorant as to how this became a part of American folklore. **1963** MBourke-White *Portrait* (NY) 167: If we can't have godliness, at least we can have cleanliness. **1964** SGelder *Timely* (L) 31: Cleanliness had no connection with godliness. **1968** DSkirrow *I Was* (NY) 10: [He] knows that godliness comes a very poor second to cleanliness. **1970** RQuest *Cerberus* (NY) 113: Cleanliness was evidently not next to ancient godliness. **1971** TRosebury *Microbes* (NY) 53: The aphorism attributed to John Wesley, "cleanliness is near akin to godliness." **1973** CAird *His Burial* (NY) 164: Justice being . . . only a very short head behind godliness and rather ahead of cleanliness. **1974** WSnow *Codline* (Middletown, Conn.) 79: That group of New England women known as "nasty neat." They do not believe that "cleanliness is next to godliness;" they go further and give cleanliness the place of honor. EAP C193. Cf. Brunvand 25.

C237   As **Clear** as clear
1928 JJConnington *Tragedy* (B) 193: My own tracks showed up . . . as clear as clear. **1936** EPhillpotts *Close Call* (L) 91: All is clear as clear. **1951** HMcCloy *Through* (L 1961) 63: I saw her mouth . . . as clear as clear. **1956** RParker *Harm* (NY) 186: I can remember her clear as clear. Cf. Plain *below.*

C238   To tower like a **Cliff**
1939 FWCrofts *Fatal* (L 1959) 59: She [*a ship*] seemed to tower above him like the proverbial cliff. Wilstach 430: An ocean-cliff [*Keats*].

C239   To cap the **Climax**
1941 PWilde *Design* (NY) 158: To cap the climax. TW 71.

C240   The higher one **Climbs** (soars, flies) the farther one falls (*varied*)
1928 AJSmall *Master* (NY) 94: The higher you climb the further you flop. **1929** AThomas *Death* (P) 289: The higher he soars, the greater his fall. **1931** SChalmers *Whispering* (NY) 4: The higher they fly—you know! Whiting C296.

C241   As calm as a **Clock**
1940 MArmstrong *Man with* (NY) 245: I feel as calm as a clock. EAP C199.

C242   As regular as the (a) **Clock**
1922 JJoyce *Ulysses* (NY 1934) 727: As regular as the clock. **1928** CBarry *Smaller* (NY) 14: As reg'lar as the clock; 93. **1934** HFootner *Dangerous* (L) 197: Just as regular as a clock. **1937** RVercel *Lena* (NY) 161: She was as regular as a clock. **1952** MColes *Night* (NY) 173: He was always so regular . . . you could set the clock by him, as the saying is.

1964 JVance *Future* (NY) 87: I am regular as a clock. EAP C201. Cf. As regular as Clockwork *below.*

C243   As steady as a **Clock**
1962 FCrane *Amber* (NY) 82: Steady as a clock [*pulse*]. **1970** VCClinton-Baddeley *No Case* (NY) 145: You're as steady as a clock. Whiting *NC* 385(2).

C244   To fix (stop, wind up) someone's **Clock**
1938 VWMason *Cairo* (NY) 158: She was laying to fix your clock, maybe. 296: Zara and me would have wound up your clock for keeps. **1941** GBenedict *Deadly Drops* (NY) 9: We'll stop his clock for you. **1956** SDean *Marked* (NY) 112: They'll try to stop her clock. **1961** MHHood *Drown* (NY) 71: He bragged how he'd fix Andy's clock [*beat him*]. DA Fix *v.* 3b. Cf. Partridge 960: Wind up [*quite different sense*].

C245   To put the **Clock** back
1952 EPempleton *Proper* (B) 125: You can't put the clock back. EAP C204.

C246   To run like a **Clock**
1930 HBedford-Jones *Shadow* (NY) 96: Everything runs like a clock. **1938** NShepherd *Death Walks* (L) 172: The whole organization runs like a clock. **1976** GEklund *Grayspace* (NY) 180: Everything running as smooth as a clock. Cf. To go like Clockwork *below.*

C247   As punctual as **Clockwork** (a clock)
1928 RAJWalling *That Dinner* (NY) 221: Punctual as a clock. **1932** VLoder *Red Stain* (NY) 9: Punctual as clockwork. **1938** GDHCole *Mrs. Warrender's* (L) 273: As punctual as clockwork. **1953** AChristie *Funerals* (NY) 2: Punctual as clockwork.

C248   As regular as **Clockwork**
1904 JCLincoln *Cap'n Eri* (NY) 143: Reg'lar as clockwork. **1922** DFox *Ethel* (NY) 206: Regular as clock-work. **1932** JDCarr *Poison* (NY) 41: Regular as clockwork. **1937** MBurton *Murder* (L) 29: As regular as clockwork. **1946** MBennett *Time to Change* (NY) 16: [He] eats like clockwork at eight. **1957** *Punch* 5/1 552: As regular as clock-

work. **1959** EHNisot *Sleepless* (NY) 61: As regular as clockwork. **1970** JFrazer *Deadly* (NY) 44: Twice a week, regular as clockwork. TW 72(2); Taylor *Western Folklore* 17(1958) 14. Cf. As regular as a Clock *above*.

C249   As smooth as **Clockwork**

1949 MGilbert *He Didn't* (NY DBC) 93: Smooth as clockwork. **1961** TWalsh *Eye* (NY DBC) 27: Smooth as clockwork. Whiting *NC* 385(1).

C250   To go like **Clockwork** (*varied*)

1905 HRHaggard *Ayesha* (NY) 61: Things were "going like clockwork." **1913** EDBiggers *Seven Keys* (I) 398: Breakfast passed off like clockwork. **1938** NMarsh *Artists* (L 1941) 109: All will go like clockwork. **1940** CWoolrich *Bride* (NY) 289: Everything went like clockwork. **1963** JNHarris *Weird* (NY DBC) 173: It went like clockwork, to coin a phrase. **1968** PMoyes *Death* (NY) 209: The inquest went like clockwork. **1970** AEHotchner *Treasure* (NY) 244: My bowels . . . operate like clockwork. **1971** TCatledge *My Life* (NY) 23: The two job presses ran like clockwork. **1972** FFarmer *Will There* (NY) 163: He still showed up like clockwork. EAP C205; Brunvand 25. Cf. To run like a Clock *above*.

C251   From **Clogs** to clogs in three generations (*varied*)

1932 VWilliams *Death* (B) 167: From clogs to clogs, they say in Lancashire, four generations. **1948** PHastings *Autobiography* (L) 59: It takes three generations to get back to the clogs, and even that period of time may be an exaggeration. **1955** DParry *Sea* (L) 201: His father made the money and according to the "clogs-to-clogs" rule it'll last another generation. **1960** DHayles *Comedy* (L) 299: Clogs to clogs in three generations. **1967** DBloodworth *Chinese* (NY) 149: The same depressing clogs-to-clogs course. *Oxford* 849. Cf. Shirtsleeves *below*.

C252   To be made out of whole **Cloth**

1928 RHFuller *Jubilee* (NY) 81: Jim's story was made up of whole cloth. **1932** CAndrews *Butterfly* (NY) 60: A lie out of whole cloth. **1934** JGregory *Emerald* (NY) 271:

Lying . . . out of whole cloth a good yard wide. **1942** HReilly *Name Your Poison* (NY) 170: A lie out of whole cloth. **1950** HReilly *Murder* (NY) 121: It was a lie out of whole cloth. **1957** MPHood *In the Dark* (NY) 130: Made a story up out of whole cloth. **1972** JLDillard *Black* (NY) 13: Created out of whole cloth. **1975** ARoudybush *Suddenly* (NY) 159: You made the wedding up out of whole cloth. EAP C208.

C253   To cut the **Cloth** to fit the pattern (*varied*)

1957 *BangorDN* 3/28 4: If they cut the cloth to fit the pattern. **1957** *Time* 4/22 67: [Britain] is trying to cut the cloth to what it has, not to what it would like to have. **1959** *BGlobe* 2/17 43: We've just got to cut the pattern to meet the cloth. **1959** *BHerald* 2/21 2: Cut your garment to fit your cloth. **1959** *Republican Journal* 11/19 2: The railroad would have to "cut the cloth to fit the suit." Whiting *NC* 385: Cut your coat; Partridge 161: Cut one's coat. Cf. Coat *below*.

C254   **Clothes** do not make the man (*varied*)

1921 JBCabell *Figures* (NY 1925) 53: The coat does not make the man. **1926** BHecht *Count* (NY) 133: Clothes . . . evidently do not make the gentleman. **1928** HVO'Brien *Four-and-Twenty* (NY) 21: Clothes did not make a man. **1930** APHerbert *Water* (NY) 116: Clothes do not Make the Gentleman. **1931** ABCox *Top* (NY) 111: Clothes never did unmake a gentleman and never would. **1933** GFowler *Timber* (NY) 252: In Bonfil's instance, clothes did not unmake the man. **1937** WHMack *Mr. Birdsall* (NY) 215: Clothes make the coxcomb, but meals make the man. **1941** SHHolbrook *Murder Out* (NY) 231: The old saw about "clothes do not make the man." **1968** HWaugh *"30"* (NY) 145: It's not just clothes that make the man. **1970** MZuckerman *Peaceable* (NY) 73: If clothes do not make the man, they do mark social [distinctions]. TW 72(1). Cf. EAP C209.

C255   **Clothes** make the man (*varied*)
1928 PThorne *Spiderweb* (P) 226: Clothes certainly make the man. **1937** VWilliams

Mr. Treadgold (L) 13: It's clothes, not manners, that makyth man. **1940** NBlake *Malice* (L) 133: For whom clothes did very much make the man. **1941** GBagby *Here Comes* (NY) 210: The old saw about clothes making the man. **1945** CDickson *Curse* (NY) 190: Clothes . . . do make the woman. **1946** MColes *Fifth Man* (NY) 71: The truth of the saying that clothes make the man. **1950** IFletcher *Bennett's* (I) 424: The clothes do make the man. **1954** SDeLima *Carnival* (NY) 136: Fine clothes make the man . . . That is, handsome does as handsome is, things are always what they seem, all that glitters *is* gold, my golden girl. **1957** *Republican Journal* 11/28 1: The old saying about clothes making the man does have merit. **1966** JRothenstein *Brave Day* (L) 325: Clothes make the man. **1969** HWaugh *Run* (NY) 6: Looks might not make the man. EAP C209; TW 73(2).

C256 Clothes might make the man

1962 PDennis *Genius* (NY) 197: Clothes might make the man. **1970** ELathen *Pick* (NY) 193: Clothes might make the man. Cf. Whiting C313, 314.

C257 Every **Cloud** has a silver lining (*varied*)

1906 JCLincoln *Mr. Pratt* (NY) 91–2: To see a silver lining to any cloud. **c1910** PGWodehouse *Leave it to Psmith* (L n.d.) 201: Every stomach has a silver lining. **1912** HHMunro *Unbearable* (NY 1928) 47: It is the silver lining to their cloud. **1914** HHMunro *Beasts* (NY 1928) 225: The cloud has a silver-fox lining. **1918** AE Housman *Letters* ed HMaas (Cambridge, Mass. 1971) 155: The cloud has a silver lining. **1928** JGoodwin *When Dead* (NY) 323: There's always a silver lining, if you looks for it. **1931** FWCrofts *Mystery* (NY) 226: A faint silver lining became apparent at the edge of the cloud. **1932** JStevens *Saginaw* (NY) 98: The blackest clouds have silver linings. **1933** EECummings *Eimi* (NY) 27: Every cloud has a silver lining. **1934** JJConnington *Ha-Ha* (L) 310: There's always something in the way of a silver lining. **1934** WGore *There's Death* (L) 54: Every bright cloud must have a darker lining.

1940 RStout *Where There's* (NY) 105: You can't have a silver lining without a cloud. **1942** CFAdams *What Price* (NY) 197: The proverbial silver lining. **1943** CEVulliamy *Polderoy* (L) 85: Woman . . . was the silver lining that gilded the cloud of man's existence. **1945** EPhillpotts *They Were Seven* (NY) 36: His clouds never have a silver lining. **1952** AGilbert *Mr. Crook* (NY DBC) 6: If there is no cloud without a silver lining, equally there is no rose without a thorn. **1956** BHerald 11/20 46: Every silver lining has its cloud, eh? **1959** *NYTimes* 11/15 27: The proverbial silver lining appeared in the om'nous sky. **1961** GFowler *Skyline* (NY) 181: We applies silver polish to the lining of all our clouds. **1963** AWUpfield *Body* (NY) 103: Every cloud has a silver lining. **1964** WBlunt *Cockerell* (L) 118: There had been a silver lining to his melancholy journey. **1967** DTylden-Wright *A.France* (L) 115: Every silver lining had its cloud. **1970** TAWaters *Probability* (NY) 35: Every silver lining, as the other song goes, has a cloud. **1971** PAlding *Despite* (NY) 71: There wasn't a silver cloud that didn't have a dirty lining for him. **1972** MGilbert *Body* (NY) 127: There is a silver lining to every cloud. **1972** JMcClure *Caterpillar* (NY) 60: Every silver lining has its cloud. **1975** PDickinson *Lively* (NY) 69: Some clouds do have silver linings. **1981** PDeVries *Sauce* (B) 104: There was a silver lining to this cloud on which Daisy swiftly seized. TW 73(2,3).

C258 To be on **Cloud** nine

1969 DARandall *Dukedome* (NY) 352: I descended suddenly from cloud nine. **1973** OSela *Portuguese* (NY) 161: Walking on cloud nine. Cf. EAP C212; Wentworth 110–111: Cloud seven.

C259 To live (*etc.*) in **Clover**

1905 FMWhite *Crimson Blind* (NY) 239: To live in clover. **1913** JSFletcher *Secret* (L 1918) 36: Thieves in clover. **1922** JJoyce *Ulysses* (NY 1934) 530: Living there in clover. **1933** HCBailey *Mr. Fortune Wonders* (NY) 216: We're in clover. **1936** CBarry *Poison* (L) 204: You're in clover. **1940** DHume *Five Aces* (L) 91: I think we're sitting on clover [*in good luck*]. **1956** *BHerald*

7/16 1: I'll be in clover the first of the month. **1959** DMDisney *No Next* (NY) 49: He'd have been in clover, yes, ass-high in clover. **1966** JAiken *Beware* (NY) 213: Cara would be in clover. **1974** MGEberhart *Danger* (NY) 211: Keep him in clover. EAP C215.

C260   To be able to drive a **Coach** through (*varied*)

1929 ABCox *Poisoned* (NY) 85: There were gaps in Sir Charles's case that counsel . . . could have driven a coach-and-six through. **1945** GBellairs *Calamity* (NY) 158: You could drive a carriage and pair through the sky theory. **1964** EHuxley *Incident* (NY) 18: You could drive a coach and horses through them. *Oxford* 129.

C261   As black as **Coal**; Coal-black

1908 MRRinehart *Circular Staircase* (NY 1947) 16: Coal black. **1922** JJoyce *Ulysses* (NY 1934) 511: A coal black throat. **1925** GBeasley *My First* (Paris) 295: As black as coal. **1926** JTully *Beggars* (NY) 247: The night was as black as coal. **1932** CFGregg *Body* (L) 17: A coal-black negro. **1932** A Sand *Señor Bum* (NY) 263: Black as coal. **1936** RKing *Constant God* (NY) 123: Coal-dark eyes. **1939** LFord *Town* (NY) 205: Her eyes were black as coals. **1944** BFischer *Hornet's* (NY) 79: Eyes as black as two coals. **1957** DJEnright *Heaven* (L) 43: Black as coal. **1963** IGlackens *Yankee* (NY) 14: Land black as coal. **1971** PTabor *Pauline's* (Louisville) 155: Coal-black pubic hair. EAP C218, 218a; TW 73(1); Brunvand 26(1). Cf. Charcoal *above*.

C262   As hot as a **Coal**

1954 EPangborn *Mirror* (NY 1958) 210: She was hot as a coal. EAP C219.

C263   As red as **Coals** of fire

1929 CvonHoffman *Jungle* (L) 53: Her eyes were red as coals of fire. **1972** COverstreet *Boar* (NY) 2: His eyes were as red as coals of fire. EAP C220.

C264   To carry **Coals** to Newcastle (*varied*)

1908 HMSylvester *Olde Pemaquid* (B) 9: Carrying coals to Newcastle. **1922** JJoyce *Ulysses* (NY 1934) 396: To carry coals to Newcastle. **1935** AFielding *Tragedy* (L) 41: Like taking coals to Newcastle. **1937** BHarvey *Growing Pains* (NY) 135: He would sell coals to Newcastle. **1939** VWilliams *Fox Prowls* (B) 38: Rather like taking coals to Newcastle. **1949** JReach *Late* (NY) 159: Carrying coals to Newcastle. **1952** RFenisong *Deadlock* (NY) 75: Perhaps I'm bringing coals to Newcastle. **1956** *Punch* 5/16 592: Carrying coals to Newcastle, Herrings to Yarmouth and New Forest timber to Southampton. **1956** *BangorDN* 9/24 9: The old joke about coal delivered to Newcastle. **1957** *Punch* 9/4 259: So why carry coals when Scotland is burning? **1958** *JAFL* 71 81: I would be carrying coals to Newcastle. **1959** *Time* 5/11 48: A coals-to-Newcastle gesture. **1962** WMorris *North* (B) 349: That was like bringing combustible coal to Newcastle. **1965** JBell *Murder* (NY) 160: Coals from Newcastle. **1970** MInnes *Death* (L) 164: This is the Newcastle to which . . . Ashmore brought his coal. **1973** THeald *Unbecoming* (NY) 179: It smacked of coals to Newcastle. EAP C225.

C265   To drop like a hot **Coal**

1929 TCobb *Crime* (L) 128: He would drop her as if she were a hot coal. **1935** HHolt *Unknown* (L) 158: Drop him like a hot coal. **1940** PWentworth *Rolling* (P) 281: They dropped it like a hot coal. **1959** RVickers *Girl* (NY DBC) 116: Dropped like a hot coal. **1961** PGWodehouse *Ice* (NY) 119: They drop her like a hot coal. **1976** MWarner *Medium* (NY) 15: Cissie dropped her like a hot coal. Cf. To drop . . . Brick, Chestnut *above*; Potato *below*.

C266   To haul (rake) over the **Coals**

1904 JCLincoln *Cap'n Eri* (NY) 239: She raked me over the coals. **1926** LBrock *Colonel Gore* (NY) 110: To haul him over the coals. **1932** AGilbert *Body* (L) 73: Hauled over the coals. **1937** TStevenson *Nudist* (L) 112: I may get called over the coals. **1938** CWells *Minning* (P) 215: She raked me over the coals. **1954** HWRosenhaupt *True* (NY) 324: They hauled me over the coals. **1968** JHaythorne *None of Us* (NY) 109: To haul me over the coals. **1971** MPanter-Downes *At the Pines* (L) 139: He hauled her over the coals severely. EAP C227; TW 74(2); Brunvand 26(3): Draw; DARE i 700: Coals (rake).

C267 To heap **Coals** of fire on the head
1900 CFPidgin *Quincy A. Sawyer* (B) 585: Heaped coals of fire on my head. **1922** JJoyce *Ulysses* (NY 1934) 635–6: Heaping coals of fire on his head. **1924** LSpringfield *Some Piquant* (L) 55: I was heaping coals of fire on his distinguished head. **1932** VLoder *Red Stain* (NY) 162: I don't like coals of fire on my head. **1936** REast *Detectives* (L) 43: I might even heap extra coals to the fire upon your head. **1937** RAJWalling *Bury Him* (L) 310: I'll heap coals on your head. **1940** EBenjamin *Murder Without* (NY) 192: Don't heap coals of fire on my head. **1943** AAFair *Bats Fly* (NY) 192: You heap coals of fire on my head. **1956** DWheatley *Ka* (L) 151: Heaping coals of fire upon my head. **1958** KDGuinness *Fisherman's* (L) 109: He has heaped the coals of fire on my unloving head. **1971** WHMarnell *Once upon* (NY) 67: [He] would heap on further coals of fire. **1974** AMorice *Killing* (NY) 28: I shall be burned under your coals of fire. EAP C228; TW 74(4); Brunvand 26(4).

C268 As black as a **Coal hole**
1964 NFreeling *Because* (NY 1965) 111: Black as a coal hole. TW 74. Cf. Wilstach 81: Dark.

C269 As dark as a **Coal-pit**
1957 JBlish *Frozen* (NY) 53: It was still as dark as a coal-pit there. Cf. TW 74: Coal mine.

C270 As black as **Coaley's** (Coalie's) cellar (arse)
1957 *BHerald* 1/13 Comics Section 10: It's as black as Coaley's cellar out here. **1968** RBissell *How Many* (B) 185: The Carnegie Institute itself is as black as Coalie's ass.

C271 The **Coast** is clear
1905 GDEldridge *Millbank Case* (NY) 286: The coast was clear. **1922** JJoyce *Ulysses* (NY 1934) 126: Seeing the coast clear. **1923** TFPowys *Black* (L) 169: Finding the coast clear. **1936** ESGardner *Sleepwalker's* (NY)

131: The coast is clear. **1937** DQBurleigh *Kristiana* (NY) 282: Until the coast is clearer. **1940** JRhode *Murder at* (L) 233: The coast was clear. **1948** EQueen *Ten* (B) 242: In the phrase which has served similar purposes since it was first used in 1590 . . . the coast was clear. **1966** ELathen *Murder* (NY) 152: The coast was clear. **1969** RBlythe *Akenfield* (NY) 196: "The coast is clear," she says, and comes down on me like a ton of bricks [*his first sex*]. **1973** JWhitehead *Solemn* (L) 18: The coast had been clear. EAP C231; TW 74; Brunvand 26.

C272 To cut one's **Coat** according to his cloth (*varied*)
1930 WLewis *Apes* (NY 1932) 181: Trim her sails according to her cloth. **1932** AWynne *White Arrow* (P) 36: One cuts one's coat according to one's cloth. **1933** AWynne *Cotswold* (P) 257: You've got to cut your coat according to your cloth. **1951** KFarrell *Mistletoe* (L) 48: Bess must cut her coat according to her cloth. **1954** EMarriner *Kennebec* (Waterville, Me.) 303: This cutting the garment to the cloth. **1967** MBlunden *Countess* (L) 135: Lady Warwick [had] failed to cut her coat according to her cloth. **1970** IOrigo *Images* (NY) 22: I cut my coat according to my cloth. **1976** LEgan *Scenes* (NY) 143: Cut the coat according to the cloth. EAP C235; TW 74(4). Cf. Cloth *above*.

C273 To measure one's **Coat** on another's body
1956 ABurgess *Time* (L) 39: But do not measure another's coat on your own body. Cf. TW 74(3). Cf. Corn *below*.

C274 To turn (change) one's **Coat**
1938 AGlanville *Body* (L) 130: Before I definitely turn my coat. **1949** FLockridge *Dishonest* (P) 220: [He was] killed before he had a chance to turn his coat. **1956** *BHerald* 8/10 10: He has not turned his coat. **1957** *NYTimes Book Review* 3/24 45: He changed his political coat. **1961** JBlish *So Close* (NY) 20: Who would turn his coat next. **1968** MGibbon *Inglorious* (L) 104: Soldiers willing to turn their coat. **1973** VSPritchett *Balzac* (NY) 18: Turn his coat. EAP C234.

C275 Let the **Cobbler** stick to his last (*varied*)

1920 ACrabb *Samuel* (NY) 86: It's a wise shoemaker that sticks to his last. **1925** RA Freeman *Red Thumb* (L) 165: *Ne sutor ultra crepidam,* sure is an excellent motto: let the medical cobbler stick to his medical last. **1928** AHuxley *Point* (L) 216: I do think that the cobbler should stick to his last. **1928** EBYoung *Murder* (P) 92: That particular cobbler knew all about this particular last. **1930** RGBrowne *By Way* (NY) 38: *Ne sutor ultra crepidam.* **1932** PMcGuire *Three* (NY) 177: A crook sticks to his last. **1932** RAJWalling *Fatal* (NY) 36: Let the shoemaker stick to his last, you know. **1945** RLHines *Confessions* (L) 169: The cobbler should stick to his last. **1953** BCarey *Their Nearest* (NY) 88: There's an old saying: The shoemaker should stick to his last. **1956** MInnes *Appleby* (L) 96: *Ne sutor ultra crepidam.* That's Latin for "Backroom boys should stay put." **1959** *TLS* 8/14 471: Mr. Dudley Edwards . . . should, like the cobbler in the Gaelic proverb, stick to his last. **1961** RKirk *Old House* (NY DBC) 92: Every man to his last. **1963** AWUpfield *Body* (NY) 77: Every man to his own last. **1964** HMHyde *Norman* (L) 320: Let the cobbler stick to his last. **1973** JBrooks *Go-Go* (NY) 154: The shoemaker should stick to his last. EAP C239.

C276 **Cock** of the walk (*varied*)

1925 CGBowers *Jefferson* (NY) 371: The Federalists . . . were cocks of the walk. **1927** WGerhardi *Pretty* (L) 55: Her Otto cock of the walk! **1939** AChristie *Murder Is* (L) 175: Strutting about as cock of the walk. **1948** ESherry *Sudden* (NY) 18: She had to be cock of the walk or else. **1950** IFletcher *Bennett's* (I) 400: Mister Cock-of-the-walk. **1959** ASillitoe *Saturday* (NY) 227: You think you're the cock of the walk. **1968** E Sprigge *Cocteau* (NY) 29: He was cock of the walk. **1970** SGraham *Garden* (NY) 18: Chaplin, cock of the walk. EAP C245.

C277 A **Cock** on its own dunghill (*varied*)

1925 HHext *Monster* (NY) 88: The unknown was on his own dunghill. **1929** BFlynn *Invisible* (L) 253: The cock crows,

does it? But I fear only upon his own dunghill. Like most cocks. **1930** ATrain *Adventures* (NY) 377: A strutting little cock on his own particular dunghill. **1935** FDGrierson *Murder* (L) 16: Cock of his own dunghill. **1936** LRobinson *General* (NY) 147: Thinks he's cock of his own dung-heap. **1936** DLSayers *Gaudy* (NY) 399: Every cock will crow upon his own dung-hill. **1951** GPettuloo *Always* (NY) 156: In our own backyards and on our own dunghills, we can crow. **1957** *NYTimes* 2/3 2E: "This is not my dunghill" [*Charles E. Wilson*] . . . the reference was to an ancient proverb: the version credited to the Roman philosopher Seneca is that "Every cock is at his best on his own dunghill." **1960** LFielden *Natural* (L) 193: I was a king of my growing dunghill. **1966** NBlake *Deadly* (L) 55: Content to be cock on his own medieval midden. EAP C243.

C278 The **Cock** who goes to bed crowing will rise with a watery head

1956 *BangorDN* 9/13 11: The cock who goes crowing to bed will surely rise with a watery head. **1957** HPBeck *Folklore of Maine* (P) 81: If a rooster crows before going to bed he will rise with a wet head. Dunwoody 39: Rooster. Cf. Hand in FCBrown *Collection* 7.6686, 6687, 6689, 6690, 6691.

C279 That **Cock** won't fight (*varied*)

1926 AFielding *Footsteps* (L) 70: That cock won't fight. **1927** LTracy *Mysterious* (NY) 254: That bird won't fight. He's dead. **1930** EWallace *Silver Key* (NY) 318: That dog doesn't fight. **1933** CBush *April Fools* (L) 274: That cock won't fight. **1937** JJConnington *Minor* (L) 191: That cock won't fight. **1955** JBingham *Paton* (L 1964) 80: The cock won't fight. **1956** EGrierson *Second* (NY) 242: Your cocks won't fight. **1962** EGrierson *Massingham* (L) 41: That cock won't fight. TW 75(4). Cf. That Cat *above*.

C280 To be **Cock-a-hoop** (whoop)

1922 JJoyce *Ulysses* (NY 1934) 315: And she with her nose cockahoop after she married him. c**1923** ACrowley *Confessions* ed JSymonds (L 1969) 500: He was absolutely cock-a-whoop over this. **1928** JGoodwin *When Dead* (NY) 152: He's getting quite cock-a-hoop enough as it is. **1930** WLewis *Apes* (NY 1932) 87: Once the body is cock-a-hoop. **1933** KCStrahan *Meriwether* (NY) 119: Cock-a-hoopish from her recent success. **1934** VLoder *Murder* (L) 222: That's what made them all so cock-a-whoop. **1940** PWentworth *Rolling* (P) 225: Very cock-a-hoop . . . aren't you? **1957** *Time* 2/25 28: The Laborites, cock-a-hoop with the victory. **1959** AHocking *Victim* (NY) 188: He was cock-a-hoop with success. **1964** JJMarric *Gideon's Vote* (NY) 57: Lemaitre was so cock-a-hoop. **1973** ARoudybush *Gastronomic* (NY) 57: Jean is cock-a-hoop as all hell. **1976** JPorter *Package* (NY) 156: Cock-a-hoop with . . . success. EAP C246.

C281   A Cock-and-bull story
1905 FMWhite *Crimson Blind* (NY) 60: That cock-and-bull story; 226. **1912** CPearl *Morrison of Peking* (Sydney 1967) 247: These cock-and-bull yarns. **1922** JJoyce *Ulysses* (NY 1934) 440: Humbugging . . . with your cock and bull story. **1931** JDCarr *Lost* (L) 15: A cock-and-bull tale. **1932** EDBiggers *Keeper* (L) 56: Cock-and-bull story. **1932** RAJWalling *Fatal* (NY) 185: A cock-and-bull yarn. **1938** EBWhite *Letters* ed DLGuth (NY 1976) 183: A cock-and-bull story. **1945** MInnes *Appleby's End* (NY) 127: A regular tale of a cock and a bull. **1950** FO'Malley *Best* (NY) 69: A big cock-and-bull story. **1961** LSdeCamp *Dragon* (NY 1968) 102: The story . . . was a lot of cock and bull. **1965** NFreeling *Criminal* (L) 21: Damned complicated cock and bull story. EAP C242.

C282   According to Cocker
1928 RAJWalling *That Dinner* (NY) 26: Every thing went according to Cocker. **1938** PMacDonald *Warrant* (NY 1957) 166: It's all according to Cocker. **1944** LAGStrong *All Fall* (NY) 103: Not cricket. Not according to Cocker. **1950** ECLorac *And Then* (NY) 105: It's all according to Cocker. **1952** AChristie *Mrs. McGinty* (NY) 108: It's probably all according to Cocker. **1958** DGBrowne *Death* (L) 57: Some . . . deal . . . that isn't . . . according to Cocker. **1969** AGilbert *Missing* (NY) 53: All according to Cocker. *Oxford* 131.

C283   To beat Cock-fighting
1936 CBush *Monday Murders* (L) 280: Well, if that doesn't beat cock-fighting! **1960** MProcter *Devil's* (NY DBC) 12: That beats cockfighting. Partridge 165.

C284   To warm the Cockles of one's heart
1932 JCLenehan *Mansfield* (L) 32: Warm the cockles of your heart. **1935** BFlynn *Edge* (L) 189: It warms the cockles of my heart. **1954** HGardiner *Murder* (L) 62: It warmed the cockles of my heart. **1959** AGilbert *Prelude* (NY DBC) 95: Warmed the cockles of his heart. **1961** LPayne *Nose* (NY) 147: She was a daughter fit to warm the cockles of anyone's heart. TW 76.

C285   To stick like a Cockle-bur
1932 GLane *Hotel* (L) 174: It will stick like a cockle-burr. Cf. TW 75–6; Brunvand 30: Cuckle-bur; Wilstach 388: To a sheep's coat. Cf. Bur *above*.

C286   Cockneys are born within sound of Bow bells
1911 HFAshurst *Diary* ed GFSparks (Tucson 1962) 5: A Cockney . . . one who was reared within range of the sound of the bells of Bow Church, London. **1922** JSFletcher *Rayner-Slade* (NY) 142: I was born within sound of Bow Bells . . . I'm a Cockney. **1930** EDBiggers *Charlie* (NY 1943) 136: A little cockney born within sound of Bow-bells. **1936** AGlanville *Death* (L) 166: Cockney—born within sound of Bow Bells. **1964** SCooper *Mandrake* (L 1966) 39: He was a real Cockney, you know—born in the sound of Bow Bells. **1967** FSwinnerton *Sanctuary* (NY) 51: Mrs. Badcock must have been born within the sound of Bow Bells. **1969** SMays *Fall Out* (L) 85: Gough, who lived about eighteen inches from Bow Bells. EAP C247.

C287   Coffee strong enough to float (something) (varied)
1953 MPHood *Silent* (NY) 12: Stout enough to float an anchor [coffee]. **1956** MPHood *Scarlet* (NY) 6: Coffee . . . black as tar and strong enough to float a battleship. **1960** VWilliams *Walk* (NY) 89: Coffee strong enough to float a wedge edgewise. **1964** FArcher *Malabang* (NY DBC) 52: Cof-

fee, strong and black enough to float an anvil. **1971** DCWilson *Big-Little* (NY) 59: "Tea" strong enough to float an ox. **1975** HLawrenson *Stranger* (NY) 134: Some coffee in which, as the saying goes, you could float an ax. Cf. Whiting *NC* 480: Strong enough to stand alone.

C288   To slip a **Cog**

1955 KMKnight *Robineau* (NY) 127: I sure slipped a cog there. Berrey 152.4, 170.6.

C289   To pay one back in his own **Coin**

1903 ADMcFaul *Ike Glidden* (B) 76: You are getting paid in your own coin. **1922** JJoyce *Ulysses* (NY 1934) 355: Gerdy could pay them back in their own coin. **1922** AAMilne *Red House* (NY 1959) 209: Paid her back in her own coin. **1933** FLPackard *Hidden* (L) 245: A repayment in Dollaire's own coin. **1938** CBush *Tudor Queen* (L) 88: Paying back her husband in his own coin. **1949** ESGardner *Dubious* (NY 1954) 40: He gets paid back in exactly his own coin. **1952** HHunter *Bengal* (NY) 230: Enough to pay your husband back in his own coin. **1962** HMirrlees *Fly* (L) 339: She was paying him in his own coin. **1967** FWeldon *And the Wife* (NY) 102: You'd pay Alan out in his own coin. EAP C250.

C290   As full of holes as a **Colander**

1956 JFStraker *Ginger* (L) 122: It's as full of lies as a colander is of holes. **1962** AGilbert *Uncertain* (NY DBC) 91: It can be as full of holes as a colander. TW 76. Cf. Sieve *below*.

C291   Feed a **Cold** and starve a fever (*varied*)

1934 SHAdams *Gorgeous* (B) 535: Feed a cold and starve a fever. **1950** IFletcher *Bennett's* (I) 172: Feed a fever, the butler tells me. **1959** *BHerald* 10/11 II 11: Remember the adage, "Feed a cold and starve a fever"? **1959** MPHood *Bell* (NY) 132: Feed a cold, starve a fever. **1961** LPayne *Nose* (NY) 54: Feed cold, starve a fever. **1961** CBeaton *Wandering* (L) 5: I fed my rotten cold according to the old wives' rule. TW 76(3); *Oxford* 783: Stuff.

C292   To be left out in the **Cold**

1924 LTracy *Token* (NY) 271: Left out in the cold. TW 76(2).

C293   To be hot under the **Collar**

1929 SMElam *Borrow* (L) 25: George would get hot under the collar. **1929** SGluck *Shadow* (NY) 213: I'm hot under the collar. **1941** MTYates *Midway* (NY) 307: Oscar got hot under the collar. **1953** DMDisney *Prescription* (NY) 29: Why are you getting so hot under the collar? **1957** MPHood *In the Dark* (NY) 175: He'd be some old hot 'round the collar. **1962** LDavidson *Rose* (NY) 138: No need to get hot under the collar. **1971** ELathen *Longer* (NY) 114: Harry can get pretty hot under the collar. Wentworth 275.

C294   To pass with flying **Colors**

1939 CFGregg *Danger* (L) 39: Had passed with flying colours. EAP C256.

C295   To sail under false **Colors**

1933 FDGrierson *Mystery* (L) 44: Richard . . . would sail under no false colours; 207. **1936** RCWoodthorpe *Silence* (L) 254: She sails under fake colours. **1954** MColes *Brief* (NY) 122: I will not sail under false colors. **1959** DCushman *Goodbye* (NY) 43: Sailing under false colors. **1962** FHoyle *A for Andromeda* (NY 1964) 48: She was sailing under false colors. TW 77(5); Brunvand 27(2).

C296   To see the **Color** of someone's money

1930 JSFletcher *Matheson* (L) 224: There ain't nobody seen the colour of his money. **1948** CRBoxer *Fidalgos* (Oxford 1968) 62: He never saw the color of his money. **1951** MInnes *Paper* (NY) 108: Asking to see the color of his money first. Partridge 171: Colour.

C297   As nervous as a **Colt**

1941 TFuller *Reunion* (B) 226: You're as nervous as a colt. Cf. TW 77(3); Taylor *Western Folklore* 17(1958) 14: Frisky.

C298   To rave like a **Comanche**

1931 DOgburn *Death* (B) 90: "He been ravin' all day like a Comanchee." Stephen knew Simon had no idea what a Comanche was; it was just a saying. Brunvand 75: Indian (3); DA Comanche 3: Comanche yell.

C299   To cut one's **Comb**

1934 JGBrandon *One-Minute* (L) 20: I will very soon cut his comb. EAP C262; DARE i 897: Cut one's comb.

C300   To go through something with a **Comb** (*very varied*)

c1910 PGWodehouse *Leave it to Psmith* (L n.d.) 200: Go through that room . . . with a fine-tooth comb. **1915** JBuchan *Thirty-nine* (NY) 34: I went over the flat with a small-tooth comb. **1919** JBCabell *Letters* ed PColum (NY 1962) 109: You have been through [it] with a fine-tooth comb. **1920** JBCabell *Letters* ed PColum (NY 1962) 164: We have fine-tooth combed the book. **1923** JSFletcher *Charing Cross* (NY) 59: Raked London with a comb for her. **1925** JGBrandon *Cork* (L) 253: The place has been fine-combed. **1931** LCharteris *Wanted* (NY) 276: Went through the bungalow with a small-toothed comb. **1931** HCBailey *Fortune Explains* (NY) 304: I go through Bourges with a small-tooth comb. **1931** GDyer *Three-Cornered* (B) 286: I went over the Podesta hallway with a fine tooth comb. **1931** MAHamilton *Murder* (L) 217: I've been through them all with a tooth-comb. **1931** HReilly *Painted Head* (NY) 75: We've been over each room with a fine-toothed comb. **1933** NGordon *Shakespeare* (NY) 66: They've gone through the place with a pocket comb. **1934** VGielgud *Purse* (NY) 190: I went over it with a toothcomb, as they say in the stories. **1940** STowne *Death out* (NY) 217: [He] had gone over it with as fine-toothed a comb as had ever been made. **1941** MHolbrook *Suitable* (NY) 110: I went through that desk with the proverbial fine-tooth comb. **1944** PATaylor *Dead Ernest* (NY) 68: They were at the fine-tooth-combing stage. **1952** MO'Brine *Corpse* (L) 82: We'll take a tooth-comb through your cabin. **1956** SPalmer *Unhappy* (NY 1957) 90: They went through the room . . . with the proverbial fine-toothed comb. **1956** *New Yorker* 8/4 25: I'm goin' over the entire situation with a fine tooth. **1957** *BangorDN* 7/27 2: [The] police had been through Adams' life "with

the proverbial fine tooth comb." **1957** *Punch* 9/11 292: Go through everything with a fine tooth-comb. **1959** FMcDermid *See* (NY) 165: I'd be searching that house with a comb. **1961** ALee *Miss Hogg* (L) 54: You've been over it with the proverbial small-tooth comb. **1964** CBrown *Never-Was* (NY) 27: He fine-combed his way through a client's contract. **1964** LPaybe *Deep* (L) 32: All over the place with a small tooth-comb. **1966** DGilman *Unexpected* (NY) 66: We have gone through these books with what you Americans call a fine-toothed comb. **1970** AEHotchner *Treasure* (NY) 45: The police . . . had fine-combed the place. **1971** DClark *Sick* (NY) 16: The locals will have been over it with a flea comb. **1974** HCarmichael *Most* (NY) 42: Go through [his] life with a fine tooth-comb. TW 77; Brunvand 27.

C301   As pretty (brave) as they **Come**

1960 FSWees *Country* (NY) 23: She was as pretty as they come. **1981** RHLewis *Cracking* (NY) 119: Billy was as brave as they come. Cf. As . . . they Make them *below*.

C302   Easy **Come,** easy go (*varied*)

1924 LO'Flaherty *Thy Neighbour's Wife* (L) 93: Money that was easily got was easily spent. **1925** HCWitwer *Bill* (NY) 179: Easy come, easy go. **1932** TSmith *Topper Takes* (NY) 215: Easy come easy go. **1934** SHAdams *Gorgeous* (B) 120: Come-light—go-light's his name. **1937** GGoodwin *White Farm* (L) 283: Quick come, quick go. **1937** GHeyer *They Found* (L) 79: Light come light go. **1938** BGraeme *Mystery* (P) 83: Easy come, easy go. **1940** LTreat *B as in Banshee* (NY) 148: Carl had summed up his artistic career in an epigram. "Easel come, easel go." **1954** AWUpfield *Sinister* (NY) 15: Easy come, easy go. **1957** *Time* 9/2 17: Easy-come, easy-go Paraguayan passports. **1960** JLodwick *Moon* (L) 23: It's easy come, but it's easier go. **1964** RStewart *Professor* (NY) 228: Easy come, easy go. **1965** JMBrown *Worlds* (NY) 258: A case of easy go no matter how hard come. **1966** NMonsarrat *Life (I)* (L) 346: Oh well—easy come, as the girl said to the bishop. **1970** AALewis *Carnival* (NY) 280: It's easy come, easy go. **1971**

NMarsh *When* (NY) 111: One of the easy-come easy-go sort [*sexually loose*]. **1972** VTrefusis *From Dusk* (L) 51: A world of easy-come and easy-go. **1974** GWheeler *Easy Come* (NY). EAP C263; TW 77(1,4).

C303 First **Come**, first served (*varied*)

1912 JCLincoln *Postmaster* (NY) 241: First come first served. **1925** FPitt *Waterride* (L) 186: First come, first served. **1937** NBell *Crocus* (NY) 14: First come, first served. **1943** EDaly *Nothing Can Rescue* (NY 1963) 129: First come first served. **1945** FAllan *First Come, First Kill* (NY). **1947** CCaldwell *Speak the Sin* (L) 15: Then it will be first come, first served—and the devil wait on the hindmost. **1957** *NYTimes* 5/5 16: A case of first come, first served. **1958** *NYTimes* 12/7 59: A first-come, first-served basis. **1959** BHecht *Sensualists* (NY) 117: First come, first served was . . . her love motto. **1962** RLockridge *First Come, First Kill* (P). **1970** NMilford *Zelda* (NY) 15: It was first come, first served. EAP C264; TW 77(2).

C304 Not to know if one is **Coming** or going

1930 JGBrandon *Murder* (L) 189: I don't know whether I'm coming or going. **1948** AWUpfield *Author* (Sydney 1967) 168: I don't know whether I'm coming or going. **1957** *Punch* 4/17 499: I don't know whether I'm coming or going. **1960** MSpark *Ballad* (L) 161: I don't know whether I'm coming or going. **1962** HPentecost *Cannibal* (NY DBC) 116: I don't know whether I'm coming or going. Cf. NED Come *v.* 26.

C305 To have someone **Coming** and going

1928 CWood *Shadow* (NY) 269: We get 'em comin' an' goin'. **1937** ATilton *Beginning* (NY) 51: I had him comin' and goin'. **1958** RPHansen *Deadly* (NY DBC) 88: We've got Jazzman coming and going. **1958** HPentecost *Obituary* (NY 1960) 100: They had her, coming and going. Cf. NED Come *v.* 26.

C306 To get a **Comeuppance**

1938 CCMunz *Land* (NY) 282: [He] done got his come-uppance fer once. **1946** KMKnight *Trouble* (NY) 15: She's heading for a comeuppance. **1951** DWMeredith *Christmas* (NY) 41: [They] deserved this come-uppance. **1954** RKLeavitt *Chip* (P) 77: She got a . . . comeuppance. **1961** HPentecost *Deadly* (NY DBC) 13: Simon would get his comeuppance in spades. DARE i 739; NED Suppl. Comeuppance; Wentworth 117.

C307 Cold **Comfort**

1930 MBDix *Murder* (L) 239: "I hope so," was Gordon's cold comfort. **1932** FIles *Before* (NY 1956) 162: She found it cold comfort. **1947** DBowers *Bells* (NY) 35: It's cold comfort. **1958** HRobertson *Crystal-gazers* (NY) 32: Cold comfort farm. **1962** HWaugh *Late* (NY) 111: Letters are such cold comfort. **1969** JSteinbeck IV *In Touch* (NY) 177: It was cold comfort. **1972** RBernard *Illegal* (NY) 124: How cold her comfort was. EAP C267.

C308 To **Command** one must learn to obey

1972 SCloete *Victorian* (L) 122: I knew I must learn to obey before I could command. TW 78; *Oxford* (2nd ed.) 467: Obedience.

C309 The eleventh **Commandment**: Thou shalt not be found out

1933 ECVivian *Girl* (L) 74: I broke the eleventh commandment—got found out. **1959** JABrussel *Just* (NY) 20: The eleventh commandment: Thou shalt not be caught. **1961** GHCoxe *The Last Commandment* (NY). **1962** HCarmichael *Of Unsound* (NY) 106: The Eleventh [Commandment]: Thou shalt not be found out. **1970** EQueen *Last* (NY) 164: Do you know what the first commandment in the gay life is? "Thou shalt not be found out?" *Oxford* 137.

C310 Evil **Communications** corrupt good manners

1930 WSMaugham *Cakes* (L 1948) 36: Evil communications corrupt good manners; 91. **1933** MBurton *Death* (L) 187: Evil communications corrupt good manners, you know. **1945** JRhode *Shadow of a Crime* (NY) 90: On the principle that evil communications corrupt good manners. **1960** MInnes *New Sonia* (L) 58: Evil communications, you know. **1964** HMHyde *Norman* (L) 331: Evil communications corrupt good manners. EAP C270; TW 78.

C311 Present **Company** excepted

1928 ESnell *Kontrol* (P) 251: Present company always excepted; 252. **1938** CFGregg *Brazen* (L) 272: Present company excepted, of course. **1954** GScott *Sound* (NY) 194: Present company excepted. **1961** NBlake *Worm* (L) 119: Present company excepted.

C312 **Comparisons** are odious (*varied*)

1903 MLPeabody *To Be Young* (B 1967) 280: Comparisons are odious. **1928** BNewman *Round About Andorra* (L) 201: But I make odious comparisons **1934** EWaugh *Handful* (NY) 33: Comparisons are odious. **1935** JHWallis *Politician* (NY) 280: Comparisons are odious, according to the old saying. **1936** ECRLorac *Death* (L) 206: Comparisons are "odorous." **1954** SDeLima *Carnival* (NY) 50: Comparisons are odious. **1956** *TLS* 6/8 340: Comparisons are said to be odious. **1957** *NYTimes Book Review* 11/10 34: Comparisons may be odious, but they are fun. **1959** *TLS* 2/13 83: If comparisons are odious, generalizations are dangerous. **1959** *BHerald* 3/15 1: Comparisons are . . . odious. **1963** ADuggan *Elephants* (L) 268: I am making odious comparisons. **1968** JGould *Europe* (B) 115: As odious as comparisons are. EAP C272; TW 78.

C313 **Competition** is the life of trade

1903 ADMcFaul *Ike Glidden* (B) 94: The old saw that "competition is the life of trade." Brunvand 27.

C314 Never **Complain** (apologize), never explain (*varied*)

1937 JDCarr *Four False* (NY) 107: "Never complain, never explain," is an excellent motto. **1943** HNicolson *Diaries II* ed NNicolson (NY 1967) 307: Never complain and never explain. **1954** MMcCarthy *Charmed* (NY) 167: Never apologize, never explain. **1955** RDavies *Leaven* (L) 293: Never deny; never explain. That's my guiding rule of life. **1957** *BHerald* 10/20 3A: The old proverb, "He who explains is damned." **1961** JMaclaren-Ross *Doomsday* (L) 112: The old adage, "Never apologize, never explain." **1967** FDonaldson *E.Waugh* (L) 83: He [*Evelyn Waugh*] approved of the adage "never apologize, never explain." **1972** RRendell *Murder* (NY) 22: Never apologize, never explain. Oxford *DQ* (2nd ed.) 181.25 [*BDisraeli*].

C315 A left-handed (back-handed) **Compliment**

1937 WDickinson *Dead Man* (P) 189: That's a left-handed compliment! **1940** JCreasey *Here Comes* (NY 1967) 10: You've paid me a compliment. Even then it was backhanded. **1941** PWilde *Design* (NY) 163: That's a left-handed compliment. **1965** ADavidson *Rork!* (NY) 8: The faintest and most left-handed of compliments. **1970** RFoley *Calculated* (NY) 18: Of all the left-handed compliments! **1973** DLeitch *God* (L) 135: This was a back handed compliment. NED Left-handed 3; Partridge 23: Backhanded.

C316 To jump to **Conclusions**

1938 EQueen *Devil* (NY) 123: Don't jump to conclusions. **1940** JLBonny *Death by* (NY) 105: You're leaping to unwarranted conclusions. **1968** JPorter *Dover Goes* (NY) 33: Here you are, jumping to conclusions, like a cat on hot bricks. NED Jump *v*. 3b.

C317 **Confess** and be hanged

1966 MFagyas *Widow* (NY) 205: The fools who confess will hang and the smart ones who kept their mouths shut will go free. *Oxford* 139.

C318 **Confession** is good for the soul (*varied*)

1900 CFPidgin *Quincy A. Sawyer* (B) 526: Confession, they say, is good for the soul; 583. **1930** MMPropper *Ticker-Tape* (NY) 225: Confession is good for the soul. **1930** KCStrahan *Death* (NY) 70: Honest confession is good for the soul. **1936** BFlynn *Horn* (L) 121: Open confession has the reputation of benefitting our immortal souls. **1936** VMcHugh *Caleb* (NY) 224: Confession's good for the soul, as the old sayin' goes. **1939** MMGoldsmith *Detour* (L) 100: That old gag about confession being good for the soul. **1942** MGEberhart *Wolf* (NY) 17: Honest confession is good for the soul. **1953** SRansome *Shroud* (NY) 143: Not an instance when confession is good for the

Conniption

soul. **1956** FWinwar *Wingless* (NY) 47: Confession, even if devious, is beneficial to the soul. **1959** GMitchell *Man Who* (L) 45: Confession is said to be good for the soul. **1966** JStuart *My Land* (NY) 154: Open confessions are good for the soul. **1967** RTraver *Jealous* (B) 21: Confession is good for the soul. **1970** AEVanVogt *Quest* (NY) 165: Confession is good for the soul. **1971** LBiggle *World* (NY) 16: Confession is said to be healthful. **1975** DMDisney *Cry* (NY) 119: Confession's supposed to be good for the soul. TW 78.

C319 To throw a **Conniption** fit

1960 SDean *Murder* (NY DBC) 10: She would throw a conniption fit. Berrey 284.2. Cf. Wentworth 543: Throw a fit.

C320 A guilty **Conscience** needs no accuser (*varied*)

1927 PBNoyes *Pallid* (NY) 204: Bad consciences make cowards. **1937** CKnight *Heavenly Voice* (NY) 106: The theory that a guilty conscience makes an itching foot; 246. **1943** HLMencken *Heathen Days* (NY) 33: A guilty conscience needs no accuser. **1957** EXFerrars *Count* (NY) 166: See what a guilty conscience he's got. Justifying himself before anyone's accused him of anything. **1962** GHCoxe *Mission* (NY) 137: It just goes to show what a guilty conscience can do to a guy. EAP C279; Brunvand 27. Cf. Guilty *below.*

C321 Not care a **Continental**

1910 JCLincoln *Depot Master* (NY) 150: Don't care a continental. **1922** JJoyce *Ulysses* (NY 1934) 630: Not caring a continental. **1929** HFootner *Self-made* (NY) 138: I don't give a continental. **1931** FWCrofts *Mystery* (NY) 93: Nor did he care a blanked Continental if he ever did see them. **1959** PFrank *Alas* (NY 1964) 108: The shilling of the Continental Congress hadn't been worth, in the British phrase, a Continental damn. TW 79; DARE i 756–757.

C322 Chief (head) **Cook** and bottle washer

1900 CFPidgin *Quincy A. Sawyer* (B) 107: I should be chief cook and bottle washer. **1912** JCLincoln *Postmaster* (NY) 216: A chief cook and bottle washer. **1930** LThayer

They Tell (NY) 63: Chief cook and bottle washer. **1934** CBush *100% Alibis* (L) 159: Sort of head cook and bottle-washer. **1936** SGibbons *Miss Linsey* (NY) 287: The unlikely position of head muck-and-bottle washer. **1940** JBentley *Mr. Marlow Stops* (B) 192: I'm head cook and bottle-washer. **1950** VSReid *New Day* (L) 172: Davie what was head cook and bottle-washer. **1956** UCurtiss *Widow's* (NY) 55: They turned Miss Blair into chief cook and bottle-washer. **1962** RMacdonald *Zebra-* (NY) 132: Chief cook and bottlewasher. EAP C283; TW 79(2); DARE i 621: Chief cook.

C323 Too many **Cooks** spoil the broth (*varied*)

1906 JCLincoln *Mr. Pratt* (NY) 34: Case of too many cooks spoiling the soup. **1914** PGWodehouse *Little Nugget* (NY 1929) 167: Too many cooks spoil the broth. **1922** JJoyce *Ulysses* (NY 1934) 173: Too many drugs spoil the broth. **1928** ABerkeley *Silk* (NY) 135: Roger was very anxious that a superfluity of cooks should not spoil this particular broth. **1929** POldfield *Alchemy* (L) 231: Haven't you a proverb: "Too many cooks spoil the broth"? **1930** MKennedy *Death* (L) 262: The proverbial dangers of a surfeit of chefs. **1930** PMacDonald *Noose* (NY) 256: Two extra cooks won't spoil this potage. **1931** HJForman *Rembrant* (NY) 241: Where there are so many cooks, the broth is bound to be eclectic. **1932** PMacDonald *Mystery* (NY) 168: Another cook might improve the broth. **1939** LBrock *Fourfingers* (L) 117: His present dish of broth was in danger from too many cooks. **1952** GKersh *Brazen* (L) 80: Too many cooks spoil the broth. **1956** *BangorDN* 12/17 13: Case of too many cooks spoiling broth. **1957** *BHerald* 3/13 39: Unlike cooks and the broth, I find that my interviews are more productive when someone else is present. **1960** NWilliams *Knaves* (NY) 100: A case of too many cooks spoiling the broth. **1966** BKnox *Ghost* (NY) 92: As my old mother always said, too many cooks spoil the broth. **1969** JAGraham *Arthur* (NY) 137: Her husband . . . worked alone. Others spoiled the broth for him. **1970** MMcGrady *Stranger* (NY) 192: You have twenty-five cooks and you're going to have . . . rancid broth. **1973** ARoudybush *Gastronomic* (NY) 137: The proverb "Too many cooks spoil the broth." **1974** LKronenberger *Wilkes* (NY) 137: It was a matter of too many cliques spoiling the brotherhood. **1977** DWilliams *Treasure* (NY) 151: There were too many cooks stirring the broth. **1981** RRendell *Death* (NY) 94: Ames murmured that it would be unwise to spoil the ship with too many cooks. EAP C285.

C324 All **Coons** look alike to me

1929 FMPettee *Palgrave* (NY) 104: It's just another slant to the old saying, "All coons look alike to me." **1936** MMPropper *Murder* (L) 115: All coons look alike to me.

C325 As curious as a **Coon**

1970 RRood *Wild* (NY) 56: "As curious as a coon" is an old expression.

C326 In a **Coon's** age

1934 HVines *This Green* (B) 118: I ain't seed you in a coon's age. **1936** ISCobb *Judge Priest* (I) 61: Once't in a coon's age. **1947** VWMason *Saigon* (NY) 40: Best I've tasted in a coon's age. **1950** RMacDonald *Drowning* (NY 1951) 140: It seems a coon's age. **1963** MMcCarthy *Group* (NY) 336: We hadn't had sex together for a coon's age. **1972** FVWMason *Brimstone* (L) 89: In a 'coons age. TW 79(1); Brunvand 28(1). Cf. In a Dog's *below*.

C327 To be a gone **Coon**

1930 GDHCole *Berkshire* (NY) 279: I knew I was a gone coon. **1933** TSmith *Turnabout* (NY) 249: She's a gone coon. **1936** GDHCole *Brothers* (L) 249: We'd be gone coons. TW 79(7); Brunvand 28(2).

C328 To have all one's **Coons** up one tree

1938 MKRawlings *Yearling* (NY) 70: You cain't git all your 'coons up one tree. Bradley 67.

C329 To fly the **Coop**

1934 CFGregg *Execution* (L) 121: Williams flew the coop. **1940** EBenjamin *Murder Without* (NY) 35: Frank's flown the coop. **1958** VCanning *Dragon* (NY) 59: We don't want them flying the coop. **1959** PDeVries

Through (B) 129: He's flown the coop. **1963** HWaugh *Death* (NY) 173: The bastard's flown the coop. Wentworth 195. Cf. Bird has flown *above*.

C330 As bald as a **Coot**

1930 ABCox *Piccadilly* (NY) 101: As bald as a coot. **1930** AMuir *Silent* (I) 147: He's as bald as a coot. **1957** *Punch* 7/10 43: Coots, always bald and often mad. **1964** EHuxley *Incident* (NY) Bald as a coot. **1969** SMays *Reuben's* (L) 189: He was bald as a coot. Whiting C419; Taylor *Western Folklore* 17(1958) 14; *Oxford* 28: Bald.

C331 As batty as a **Coot**

1933 MAllingham *Sweet* (L 1950) 207: He's as batty as a coot. See NED Coot *sb.*[1] 4 [*silly person, simpleton*].

C332 As crazy (loony, screwy) as a **Coot**

1909 JCLincoln *Keziah* (NY) 307: Crazy as a coot. **1924** AOFriel *Mountains* (NY) 139: Crazy as a coot. **1935** *New Yorker* 9/14 36: Loony as a coot. **1951** JSStrange *Reasonable* (NY) 83: They were both as crazy as coots. **1953** KMKnight *Three* (NY) 74: She was screwy as a coot. **1954** EWalter *Untidy* (P) 87: Crazy as a cootie-bug. **1960** PGWodehouse *Jeeves* (L) 73: The man is as loony as a coot. **1969** JGould *Jonesport* (B) 151: "Crazy as a coot" is therefore standard Maine judgment, and those who best know the bird, often add . . . "in a south wind." EAP C287.

C333 As daffy (daft) as a **Coot**

1968 JAiken *Crystal* (NY) 203: As daffy as a coot. **1973** CAird *His Burial* (NY) 167: Daft as coots the pair of 'em.

C334 As deaf as a **Coot**

1933 MAllingham *Sweet* (L 1950) 163: Deaf as the proverbial coot.

C335 As drunk as a **Coot**

1933 TSmith *Turnabout* (NY) 147: As drunk as coots. **1936** JDosPassos *Big Money* (NY) 68: Drunk as coots. **1939** GHCoxe *Four Frightened* (NY) 143: I'm as drunk as a coot. **1951** GPettullo *Always* (NY) 212: She's as drunk as a coot. **1958** HReilly *Ding*

(NY DBC) 96: As drunk as a coot. Whiting *NC* 387(2).

C336   As mad as a **Coot**

1928 PGWodehouse *Money* (NY) 124: Mad as a coot. **1938** CDickson *Judas* (L) 65: Mad as a coot. **1938** PWTaylor *Murder in* (NY) 177: He's as mad as a coot. **1947** JDCarr *Sleeping* (NY) 94: The little devils as mad as a coot. **1955** MAllingham *Estate* (NY) 214: You're mad as a coot. Cf. Whiting C421.

C337   As queer as a **Coot**

1934 MDavis *Murder* (NY) 167: Queer as coots. **1965** JBrooks *Smith* (L) 224: I'm queer as a coot. **1967** JBrunner *Quicksand* (NY) 211: The poor guy is as queer as a coot [homosexual]. **1970** BWAldiss *Hand-Reared* (L) 98: [He] is as queer as a coot [homosexual]. **1974** THeald *Blue* (NY) 173: He's as queer as a coot [homosexual].

C338   To blot one's **Copybook**

1927 EWallace *Law* (NY 1931) 50: She blotted her copybook. **1937** FBeeding *Hell* (L) 237: You will both be regarded as having blotted your copybooks. **1940** NBlake *Malice* (L) 217: His copy-book appeared to be unblotted. **1956** JFStraker *Ginger* (L) 194: Without blotting his copybook with Diane. **1958** RHutton *Of Those* (L) 165: I had blotted my copybook with Mrs. Currie. **1962** Bryher *Heart* (NY) 80: I blotted my copybook badly. **1969** SMays *Fall Out* (L) 22: I blotted my copy book. **1972** DDevine *Three* (NY) 174: I'd better not blot my copybook. **1976** CLarson *Muir's* (NY) 101: I blotted my copybook. Partridge 67: Blot.

C339   Not every one can get to **Corinth**

1931 PATaylor *Cape Cod* (NY 1971) 82: Every one can't get to Corinth; but you can read the signposts, as the feller said. *Oxford* 143.

C340   As crooked as a **Corkscrew**

1935 DHume *Call in* (L) 15: You're as crooked as a corkscrew. **1940** GPatten *Autobiography* ed HHinsdale (Norman, Okla. 1964) 133: Many [judges] were as crooked as corkscrews. **1956** GMetalious *Peyton* (NY) 21: Crooked as a corkscrew. **1965** AGilbert

Voice (NY) 162: The chap's as crooked as a corkscrew. **1974** SChance *Septimus* (Nashville) 51: She was as crooked as a corkscrew. TW 80(1). Cf. Taylor *Western Folklore* 17(1958) 14: Straight.

C341   As greedy as a **Cormorant**

1935 VLoder *Death* (L) 15: As greedy as a cormorant. Wilstach 187. Cf. EAP C295.

C342   To measure another's **Corn** by one's bushel

1935 VLoder *Dead Doctor* (L) 164: The father measuring her corn by his own bushel. EAP C297. Cf. Coat *above*.

C343   To tread on another's **Corns**

1930 GDHCole *Berkshire* (NY) 51: Don't tread on his corns. **1937** RHull *Ghost* (NY) 153: There was no need to tread on quite so many corns. **1937** RVercel *Lena* (NY) 22: I suppose you trod on a pet corn. **1938** PMcGuire *Burial* (L) 158: You are trampling on my corns. **1945** EQueen *Murderer* (NY) 60: Ellery's not going to step on anybody's corns. **1955** IFleming *Moonraker* (NY 1960) 62: I don't want to tread on Five's corns. **1965** RJWhite *Dr. Bentley* (L) 238: He trod on other people's corns. EAP C299.

C344   In a **Corner**

1923 JSFletcher *Markenmore* (NY) 155: Done in a corner. EAP C300.

C345   As cold as a **Corpse**

1925 HWNevinson *More Changes* (L) 128: Cold as a corpse. EAP C303.

C346   As pallid as a **Corpse**

1924 RAFreeman *Blue* (NY) 120: Pallid as a corpse. Wilstach 284. Cf. Brunvand 28(1): Pale.

C347   As white as a **Corpse**; Corpse-white

1939 CMWills *Death at* (L) 94: She was as white as a corpse. **1943** AAbbott *Shudders* (NY) 57: His skin was corpse-white. **1946** FBLong *Hounds* (NY 1963) 7: His face corpse-white. TW 81(1).

C348   As dry as **Cotton**
1966 DHitchens *Man Who Cried* (NY) 20: Her throat and mouth were dry as cotton. Cf. To spit Cotton *below*.

C349   As white as **Cotton**
1941 CLClifford *While the Bells* (NY) 267: His face was white as cotton. **1954** EForbes *Rainbow* (B) 52: Hair white as cotton. Whiting *NC* 387(1).

C350   To chop in tall **Cotton**
1966 LNizer *Jury* (NY) 239: "Chopping in tall cotton" was his way of saying that the going was tough. Cf. DA Chop *v.* 3.

C351   To spit **Cotton**
1940 RDarby *Death Conducts* (NY) 67: I'm so thirsty I could spit cotton. **1941** SHHolbrook *Murder out* (NY) 81: The man's mouth was notably dry. He was "spitting cotton." **1953** BMcMillion *Lot* (P) 82: I was so thirsty I'se spitting cotton. TW 81(2). Cf. As dry as Cotton *above*.

C352   A churchyard **Cough**
1910 EPhillpotts *Tales* (NY) 112: That churchyard cough. EAP C306.

C353   Another **Country** heard from (*varied*)
1932 JTFarrell *Young Lonigan* (NY 1935) 50: Another lost country heard from. **1956** RBloomfield *When* (NY) 81: Another country heard from. **1959** DMDouglass *Many* (L) 38: A new country had been heard from. **1960** DKarp *Enter* (NY) 157: Another country heard from.

C354   Different **Countries**, different customs (*varied*)
1927 GELocke *Golden* (NY) 34: Different countries, different customs. **1930** ALivingston *Trackless* (I) 42: Other countries, other customs. **1930** LPowys *Apples* (L) 202: Other countries, other manners. **1932** CRyland *Notting* (L) 178: Different nations, different customs. **1951** RKing *Duenna* (NY) 203: Different climes, different customs. **1951** AMStein *Shoot* (NY) 38: Different countries, different laws. **1955** JCreasey *Gelignite* (NY) 144: Different people, different ideas. **1961** WMasterson *Evil* (NY) 104: Different people, different methods. **1963**

NFreeling *Question* (NY 1965) 17: Other countries, other tastes. **1963** RAHeinlein *Glory* (NY) 118: Other countries, other customs. **1965** FHerbert *Dune* (NY) 65: Different people, different customs. Whiting T63; *Oxford* 147. Cf. EAP C312.

C355   It's a free **Country**
1909 JCLincoln *Keziah* (NY) 315: It was a free country. **1923** JSFletcher *Exterior* (NY) 206: This is a free country. **1923** JSFletcher *Markenmore* (NY) 256: This is a free country. **1932** CAndrews *Butterfly* (NY) 163: She said this was a free country. **1939** AWebb *Mr. Pendlebury Makes* (L) 164: This is a free country. **1948** TKyd *Blood* (P) 211: It's a free country, they say. **1951** EQueen *Origin* (B) 117: It's a free country. **1959** EHNisot *Sleepless* (NY) 15: It's a free country—or so we are assured. **1973** PMoyes *Curious* (NY) 68: It's a free country, isn't it? TW 82(2).

C356   **Courage** breeds courage
1931 TFPowys *Unclay* (L) 11: Courage breeds courage.

C357   The **Courage** of one's convictions
1928 RHWatkins *Master* (NY) 157: A lad with the courage of his convictions. **1970** LGrafftey-Smith *Bright* (L) 76: He seemed to lack the courage of his own convictions. NED Courage *sb.* 4d.

C358   To screw one's **Courage** to the sticking point (*varied*)
1932 DFrome *Man* (NY) 90: Screwed his courage to the sticking point. **1937** JDCarr *To Wake* (L) 154: I got my courage to the sticking point. **1939** HReilly *All Concerned* (NY) 16: He watched her screw her courage to the sticking point. **1966** DSlavitt *Rochelle* (L) 9: I poured another round of drinks to stick my courage to the screwing point. TW 82(1); Brunvand 28.

C359   To whistle to keep one's **Courage** up (*varied*)
1925 CGBowers *Jefferson* (NY) 275: Whistling the while to keep up courage. **1932** AFielding *Wedding-Chest* (NY) 174: We speak of whistling to keep up one's courage. **1935** ASPier *God's Secret* (NY) 166: Whistling to keep up his courage. **1942** EB

White *Letters* ed DLGuth (NY 1976) 230: Whistling to keep her courage up. **1949** EPhillpotts *Address* (L) 13: As schoolboys alone on a dark night, they will whistle to keep up their courage. **1959** *BHerald* 8/21 33: They're just whistling to keep up their courage. **1963** IGlackens *Yankee* (NY) 104: Amanda was whistling to keep up her courage. **1967** HBorland *Hill Country* (P) 68: We whistle in the dark . . . We whistle up our courage . . . We whistle down the wind . . . We let the other fellow go whistle. **1970** DStuart *Very* (NY) 229: The President was whistling to keep up his courage. **1972** JBonett *No Time* (NY) 139: Over the evening air . . . came the sound of a whistled song. Was it the expression of a man trying to keep up his courage? Oxford *DQ* (2nd ed.) 191.25: Whistling to keep myself from being afraid [Dryden, *Amphitryon* III.1]. Cf. EAP D16: Dark (also *below*). Cf. Graveyard *below*.

C360 The **Course** of true love never did run smoothly (*varied*)

1928 AECoppard *Silver* (L) 264: The course of true love never did run smoothly. **1928** WRoughead *Murderer's* (NY 1968) 7: The path of true love presenting more of the customary obstacles. **1929** IBrown *Deep Song* (NY) 249: How much of literature merely illustrates the proverb on the course of true love! **1930** HCMcNeile *Tiny* (NY) 86: May the course of your young love run smooth. **1934** RAJWalling *Legacy* (NY) 106: The traditional roughness of the course of true love. **1936** AChristie *Murder* (L) 177: It's nice when the course of true love runs smoothly. **1939** CMWills *Calabar Bears* (L) 87: The course of true love had run smoothly enough. **1941** RAldington *Life* (NY) 122: Perhaps the course of true love runs all the truer for not being smooth. **1948** DCDisney *Explosion* (NY DBC) 46: Somewhat . . . as though the course of true love wasn't running smoothly. **1955** W Sloane *Stories* (L) 303: The course of true love always runs smooth. **1955** DMDisney *Trick* (NY) 141: I had to impede the course of true love. **1960** JBlish *Galactic* (L) 106: The course of true love always runs smooth. **1968** IPetite *Life* (NY) 178: The

path of true love or, let's face it, false love, never ran smoothly and never will. **1970** HBlyth *Skittles* (L) 65: The course of this affair . . . was by no means smooth. **1971** PMoyes *Season* (NY) 13: The course of their true love was running according to form. EAP C315; Brunvand 28–9.

C361 To be put through a **Course** of sprouts

1930 HFootner *Viper* (L) 73: He was being put through a course of sprouts. **1951** ES Gardner *Angry* (NY DBC) 95: Put her through a course of sprouts. TW 349: Sprouts.

C362 To send (be sent) to **Coventry** (*varied*)

1923 ABlackwood *Episodes* (L) 254: Sent to Coventry for three days. **1933** HDuffy *Seven* (NY) 190: Send her to Coventry. **1936** WMartyn *House* (L) 190: She'd put him—coventry. **1939** RPhilmore *Death in* (L) 148: We seem to be in coventry. **1943** DGoldring *South Lodge* (L) 207: They "sent him to Coventry." **1955** VWMason *Two* (NY) 188: You're still in Coventry. **1956** *NYTimes Magazine* 8/19 10: Senator Johnson could have sent Senator Daniel to a very chilly Coventry. **1960** KCrichton *Total* (NY) 70: Placing the antiwar people in a state of coventry. **1962** RO'Connor *Scandalous* (NY) 32: She had married her way into Coventry. **1967** VThomson *V.Thomson* (L) 183: I was in coventry exactly a week. **1972** JSymons *Players* (NY) 213: They sent him to Coventry. **1975** SJPerelman *Vinegar* (NY) 146: Put me in Coventry. EAP C319.

C363 All behind, like a **Cow's** tail (*varied*)

1935 HEBates *Cut and Come* (L) 230: All behind, like the cow's tail. **1939** HMiller *Capricorn* (NY 1961) 61: Always dragging behind, like a cow's tail. **1952** WClapham *Night* (L) 210: We're all behind like a cow's arse. **1957** LBeam *Maine* (NY) 81: Tardiness was "like the cow's tail—always behind." **1970** WBreem *Eagle* (NY) 129: Small wonder then that Rome grew downwards like a cow's tail. **1972** NWebster *Killing* (NY) 158: The Maltese have a saying . . . when they feel gloomy they say the world grows downward like a cow's tail. EAP C327; DARE i 819: Cow's tail. Cf. Always behind like a Bear's nuts *above.*

C364 As awkward as a **Cow** on skates

1943 EWTeale *Dune Boy* (NY 1957) 232: As awkward as a cow on skates. Whiting *NC* 387(1): As awkward as a cow. Cf. Taylor *Prov. Comp.* 27: Clumsy as a cow on a bicycle, 44: Graceful.

C365 As busy as a **Cow's** tail in flytime

1950 SPalmer *Green* (NY) 184: Nemesis was busier . . . than a cow's tail in flytime. Wilstach 41 [*JFCooper*]. Cf. As tight as a Bull's, As ugly as a Bull *above.*

C366 As placid as a **Cow**

1933 RHare *Doctor's* (NY) 311: You're as placid as a cow. **1937** NBerrow *One Drilling* (L) 65: Cleopatra was placid as a cow. Taylor *Prov. Comp.* 62.

C367 As pleased as a **Cow** with six tits

1964 NFreeling *Because* (NY 1965) 145: [He] is as pleased as a cow with six tits. Cf. As pleased . . . Cat *above.*

C368 **Cows** in Connacht (far away) have long horns

1922 JJoyce *Ulysses* (NY 1934) 322: Cows in Connacht have long horns. **1934** VLincoln *February Hill* (NY) 72: Cows far away have long horns. **1956** EDillon *Death* (L) 101: I warned them when he was being appointed . . . but cows in Connacht have long horns and they insisted on having him. Whiting *NC* 388(7): Off yonder etc.

C369 Till the **Cows** come home

1925 JGBrandon *Bond* (L) 40: Keep goin' till the cows come home. **1932** TSmith *Topper Takes* (NY) 128: You can chew on that till the cows come home. **1939** AWebb *Thank You* (L) 137: Some people can drink beer till the cows come home. **1951** DMDisney *Straw* (NY) 32: They can blame Retail Credit till the cows come home. **1954** EQueen *Glass* (B) 257: We'll stay here till the cows dry up. **1957** *New Yorker* 3/23 27: They can sit on him till the cows come home. **1960** JSymonds *Only Thing* (L) 156: You can discuss this subject till the cows

come home. **1969** AMcCaffrey *Decision* (NY) 20: We can argue until the cows land. **1970** JBlackburn *Bury* (NY) 89: Till the cows come home. TW 83(6); *Oxford* 152.

C370 To swallow a **Cow** and choke on the tail

1935 CMRussell *Murder* (NY) 230: I'm not one to swallow a cow and choke on the tail. EAP C329. Cf. Gnat *below.*

C371 When **Cows** lie down it's a sign of rain

1957 *BHerald* 9/25 22: "When the cows lie down it's a sign of rain" (old American proverb). Dunwoody 31.

C372 Why keep a **Cow** when milk is so cheap (*varied*)

1927 TFPowys *Mr. Weston's* (L) 283: It is cheaper to buy the milk than to keep a cow. **1929** POldfield *Alchemy* (L) 139: It's cheaper to buy milk than to keep a cow, as the saying goes. **1931** JTully *Blood* (NY) 69: It's not wise to buy a cow when milk's so cheap. **1932** TThayer *Three Sheet* (NY) 200: The adage that *it is cheaper to buy milk than to keep a cow.* **1934** JJConnington *Ha-Ha* (L) 153: No use keepin' a cow when you can buy milk. **1938** JJConnington *Truth* (L) 68: Cheaper to buy milk than to keep a cow, they say. **1956** HCahill *Shadow* (NY) 316: Mandan says if I got the cow why do I keep buying the milk? **1966** HKane *Conceal* (NY) 26: McGregor recollected an ancient oriental proverb: "One who is provided with all the milk he can drink would be foolish to acquire a cow." **1971** KLaumer *Deadfall* (NY) 79: "Why haven't you married, Mianne?" . . . "Why buy a bull . . . when beef's so cheap?" *Oxford* 151; Partridge 450.

C373 Better be a live **Coward** than a dead hero

1940 MVHeberden *Fugitive* (NY) 9: It's much better to be a live coward than a dead hero. **1960** RWilson *30 Day* (NY) 118: Better to be a live coward than a dead hero . . . Old copy-desk maxim. **1966** WJSchoonmaker *World* (P) 82: It is wise enough to practice being a living coward rather than a dead hero. Whiting *NC* 388: Better a coward than a corpse. Cf. Tilley C776: It is better to be a coward than foolhardy.

C374 The **Cowl** (habit) does not make the monk

1931 PBaron *Round* (NY) 295: "Cucullus non facit monachum" . . . although I admit that this particular cowl fitted the monk well. **1931** RInce *When Joan* (L) 227: There is a proverb that the habit does not make the monk. **1957** *Punch* 5/29 665: *Cucullus non facit monachum.* EAP C333.

C375 As sore as a **Crab** (crustacean)

1925 WAStowell *Singing Walls* (NY) 102: The old man was sore as a crab. **1932** AMizair *Many* (NY) 239: As sore as a crab. **1936** JDosPassos *Big Money* (NY) 264: Sore as a crab. **1939** MArmstrong *Murder in* (NY) 137: Jake was as sore as a crab.

C376 As sour as a **Crab** apple

1936 LWMeynell *On the Night* (NY) 79: Sour as a crab apple. Whiting *NC* 388. Cf. TW 83(1); Berrey 283.6, 284.6: Sour.

C377 First **Crack** out of the box (barrel)

1944 CDickson *He Wouldn't* (NY) 104: Straight off and first crack out of the box. **1955** SRansome *Frazer* (NY) 147: First crack out of the box we nail the guy. **1961** SRansome *Some Must* (NY 1963) 68: First crack out of the box he'd found something. **1966** BHDeal *Fancy's* (NY) 69: They're all out to get married first crack out of the barrel. Berrey 9.1.

C378 Not what it's **Cracked** up to be

1930 JCournos *Grandmother* (NY) 75: Married life isn't what it's cracked up to be. TW 83(1).

C379 Rock the **Cradle** empty and you will rock it plenty

1957 HPBeck *Folklore of Maine* (P) 79: Rock the cradle empty and you will rock it plenty. Cf. Hand in Brown *Collection* 6.145.

C380 To rob the **Cradle**

1934 WSutherland *Death Rides* (L) 116: Takes too much interest in robbing the cradle. **1952** FKane *Bare* (NY 1960) 54: Kind of robbing the cradle. **1959** DTaylor *Joy*

(NY) 188: Been robbing the cradle again? **1969** RLockridge *Die* (P) 69: She robbed cradles. Wentworth 127, 430: Rob.

C381 **Craft** is better than muscle

1955 MBorowsky *Queen's* (NY) 184: Muscle is good but craft is better. Cf. *Oxford* 784: Subtlety is better than force.

C382 To meet **Craft** (cunning) with craft

1924 JSFletcher *Safety* (NY) 257: Let's meet craft with craft. **1932** RAJWalling *Fatal* (NY) 197: Let's meet craft with craft. **1933** FHShaw *Atlantic* (NY) 229: Cunning, I felt, must be met with cunning. **1936** WSMasterman *Rose* (NY) 104: It's meeting guile with guile. **1948** TKyd *Blood* (P) 182: We can meet craft with craft. Whiting G487: Guile, cf. F491: Force, F610: Fraud. Cf. Force *below.*

C383 As busy as a **Cranberry** merchant

1940 HAshbrook *Murder Comes* (NY) 172: The origin of the phrase "busier than a cranberry merchant" is obscure, and the phrase itself is not as good as it might be. Taylor *Prov. Comp.* 22: Busy.

C384 Not give a **Crap**

1974 PThomas *Seven* (NY) 104: I didn't give a crap. Wentworth 127–8.

C385 As smooth as **Cream**

1929 HFootner *Doctor* (L) 79: Smile was as smooth as cream. **1935** AGilbert *Man* (L) 162: He said, as smooth as cream. **1939** HFootner *Murder That* (L) 49: Lee's voice was as smooth as cream. **1950** CDickson *Night* (NY) 263: That sounds as smooth as cream. **1959** LGOfford *Walking* (NY DBC) 80: It went smooth as cream. **1962** IFleming *Spy* (NY) 38: Band as smooth as cream. **1964** EPangborn *Davy* (NY) 200: A contralto smooth as cream. **1966** DMDisney *Magic* (NY) 179: I remember every day of it smooth as cream. Cf. As smooth as Milk *below.*

C386 As sweet as **Cream**

1958 HPentecost *Obituary* (NY 1960) 157: He treats you sweet as cream. Whiting C537.

C387 The **Cream** of the crop

1960 FSWees *Country* (NY) 139: The cream of the crop. **1961** DMDisney *Mrs. Meeker's* (NY) 80: The cream of the crop. **1966** DHitchens *Man Who Cried* (NY) 146: The cream of the crop Cf. NED Cream *sb.*² 3.

C388 The **Cream** of the joke (jest)

1908 JCLincoln *Cy Whittaker* (NY) 16–7: The cream of the joke. **1922** JJoyce *Ulysses* (NY 1934) 601: The cream of the joke. **c1923** ACrowley *Confessions* ed JSymonds (L 1969) 355: The cream of the jest. **1934** CFGregg *Inspector* (L) 208: The cream of the joke. **1939** MInnes *Stop Press* (L) 93: The cream of the joke. **1948** PCheyney *Dance* (NY DBC) 101: The cream of the jest. **1948** PCheyney *Dance* (NY DBC) 149: The cream of the joke is you didn't do it. **1956** *NYTimes Book Review* 7/8 7: The cream of the jest. **1968** RCroft-Cooke *Feasting* (NY) 69: The cream of the jest. EAP C339.

C389 To get **Cream** from a pisspot

1961 CDBurton *Long Goodnight* (NY) 9: Never try to get cream from a pisspot.

C390 All **Creation** and part of Ostable Neck

1912 JCLincoln *Postmaster* (NY) 186: The view . . . took in all creation and part of Ostable Neck, as the sayin' is. ["You can see all over God's creation and part of Thorndike." Said of the view from the top of Richardson's Hill in Knox, Maine. Common half a century and more ago and sometimes heard now. BJW]

C391 To give **Credit** (*etc.*) where credit is due (*varied*)

1922 JJoyce *Ulysses* (NY 1934) 342: Honour where honour is due. **1922** VThompson *Pointed* (NY) 310: Credit where credit is due. **1928** EForbes *Mirror* (NY) 108: Always give thanks where thanks are due. **1934** BFlynn *Spiked* (P) 192: *Palmam qui meruit ferat.* Honor to whom honor is due. **1937** VMacClure *House* (L) 239: Honour where honour's due. **1940** NBlake *Malice* (L) 278: Give credit where credit is due. **1944** LAGStrong *All Fall* (NY) 21: Praise where praise is due. **1956** BCClough *More* (Portland, Me.) 91: Giving credit where credit is

due. **1957** *Time* 12/30 4: Credit is given where credit is due. **1959** HSlesar *Grey* (L 1963) 127: Credit where credit's due, my gramps always said. **1966** LPDavies *Who Is* (NY) 23: Give credit where it is due. **1968** LBlanch *Journey* (L) 48: Praise where praise is due. **1973** JFleming *Alas* (NY) 19: He was ready to give credit where credit was due. Cf. *Oxford* 303: Give everyone his due.

C392 To be up the **Creek** (shit creek) without a paddle (*varied*)

1930 JDosPassos *42nd* (NY) 70: We're up the creek now for fair. **1937** EGowen *Old Hell* (NY) 56: I didn't aim to be caught up the creek with my britches down, as a fellow says. **1938** LAnson *Such Natural* (L) 93: I'm up the creek myself. **1938** TDowning *Night* (L) 207: So there they were—up the creek without a paddle. **1938** EGilligan *Boundary* (NY) 200: I'm up the famous creek. **1940** BHalliday *Uncomplaining* (NY) 134: I'll be up a dirty creek without a paddle. **1941** TDowning *Lazy Lawrence* (NY) 131: You were scared of bein' left up the creek without a paddle. **1946** LBBaghmann *Kiss of Death* (NY) 130: We're permanently up a creek, to coin an old proverb. **1951** HQMasur *You Can't* (NY) 170: That leaves us up a creek. **1951** WCWilliams *Autobiography* (NY) 165: I'm up shit creek. **1952** RMacDonald *Ivory* (NY 1965) 160: I'm up the crick without a paddle. **1957** WFuller *Girl* (NY) 24: You're up the well-known creek without a paddle. **1959** PAnderson *Perish* (NY) 123: I'm on some kind of trail, but it might leave me up that famous tributary with no means of propulsion. **1959** IColeman *Sam* (NY) 144: She married me, so she's up Shit Creek. **1959** EMcBain *King's* (NY) 4: "[He] is going to be right up the proverbial creek." "Without the proverbial paddle." **1962** RBissell *You Can* (NY) 8: Definitely up the Charles River somewhere in the neighbourhood of Waltham, without a paddle. **1964** LPayne *Deep* (L) 174: We're not only up the creek but we're also round the bend. **1966** AEHotchner *Papa* (NY) 67: Up the creek without paddles or oar locks. **1967** NFreeling *Strike* (NY) 167: He would be up shit creek, and without a paddle. **1972** MGilbert *Body* (NY) 188: He's up shit creek without a paddle. **1973** KCampbell *Wheel* (I) 48: [The] captain is up you-know-what creek without a paddle. **1973** ELDoctorow *Ragtime* (NY 1976) 168: There goes your theory up shits creek. **1975** FMNivens *Publish* (NY) 88: Do you know where we'd be? Up the creek with no riparian rights. **1975** MKWren *Multitude* (NY) 90: "So where does that leave you?" "Up a creek." "And you want me to hand you a paddle." **1978** MKWren *Nothing's* (NY) 66: [It] put Tally even further up the creek. Wentworth 682: Up shit, up the.

C393 One must **Creep** before he walks *etc.* (*varied*)

1933 WCBrown *Murder* (P) 201: First we creep, then we walk, then we run. **1935** LAKnight *Super-Cinema* (L) 170: We must stumble before we run. **1939** DHume *Death Before* (L) 186: He tried to run before he learnt to walk. **1950** HGreen *Nothing* (NY) 99: The poor sweet mustn't be expected to fly before he is able to walk. **1950** VSReid *New Day* (L) 263: You are no' forgetting you must creep 'fore you walk? **1950** PWhelton *Pardon* (P) 167: Let's walk before we run. **1956** RFoley *Last* (NY DBC) 100: The novice soprano had learned to run before she had learned to walk. **1963** MRichler *Incomparable* (L) 147: We have to learn to walk before we can run. **1964** RAHeinlein *Orphans* (NY) 52: Don't expect him to run before he can crawl. **1964** EPangborn *Davy* (NY) 116: I gotta creep before I walk. **1964** HTreece *Oedipus* (L) 195: You think I ran before I could walk. **1972** DShannon *Murder* (NY) 92: It's like my granddad says—I think it's an old-country proverb—you got to learn to walk before you can run. EAP W7; Whiting C202: Child; *Oxford* 120: Children.

C394 **Cretans** are liars

1971 PDickinson *Sleep* (NY) 89: "Everybody is lying." "Not just Cretans." EAP C342.

C395 As brisk as a **Cricket**

1934 SHAdams *Gorgeous* (B) 534: Brisk as a cricket. **1970** JVizzard *See* (NY) Brisk as a cricket.

C396 As cheerful as a **Cricket**

1910 EPhillpotts *Tales* (NY) 184: Cheerful as a cricket. **1956** HCahill *Shadow* (NY) 251: Cheerful as crickets. **1963** BWAldiss *Airs* (L) 153: They were as cheerful as crickets. Taylor *Western Folklore* 17(1958) 14(1).

C397 As chipper as a **Cricket**

1961 MHHood *Drown* (NY) 9: Chipper as a cricket. **1971** DCWilson *Big-Little* (NY) 103: Chipper as a cricket.

C398 As cute as a **Cricket**

1944 EBWhite *Letters* ed DLGuth (NY 1976) 249: She is as cute as a cricket. **1965** PDeVries *Let Me* (NY 1966) 209: Cute as a cricket.

C399 As gay as a **Cricket**

1933 FHShaw *Atlantic* (NY) 31: He was gay as a cricket. **1956** AAtkinson *Exit* (NY) 123: Gay as a cricket. **1956** IFleming *Diamonds* (NY 1961) 134: I'm as happy as a cricket. **1958** RHutton *Of Those* (L) 87: As gay as crickets and as drunk as fiddler's bitches. EAP C343.

C400 As lively as a **Cricket**

1917 JCLincoln *Extricating* (NY) 98: Lively as a cricket. **1931** RAFreeman *Mr. Pottermack* (L) 58: As lively as a cricket. **1936** LAKnight *Night* (L) 54: Todfeather was as lively as a cricket. **1947** AGilbert *Death in* (L) 103: She was as lively as a cricket. **1954** JPotts *Go* (NY) 146: As lively as a cricket. **1964** JAiken *Silence* (NY) 182: Lively as a cricket. **1967** FSwinnerton *Sanctuary* (NY) 270: As lively as crickets. EAP C344.

C401 As merry as a **Cricket**

1934 AChristie *Mr. Parker* (NY) 210: Merry as a—a cricket. **1960** LLevine *Great* (L) 46: Merry as a cricket in December. **1969** HE Bates *Vanished* (L) 61: Joe was as merry as a boozy cricket. EAP C345; TW 84(5); Whiting C550; Taylor *Western Folklore* 17(1958) 14(2).

C402 As snug as a **Cricket**

1959 BHitchens *Man Who* (NY) 98: As snug as a cricket. Cf. As snug as a Bug *above*, Pea *below*.

C403 As spry as a **Cricket**

1947 JIams *Body* (NY) 13: Spry as a cricket. **1953** JBClayton *Wait* (NY) 227: Spry's a cricket. **1954** JPotts *Go* (NY) 1: Spry as a cricket. TW 84(7).

C404 **Crime** does not pay (*varied*)

1927 NMartin *Mosaic* (NY) 91: To prove the truth of the old adage that you can't get away with [crime]. **1928** RHWatkins *Master* (NY) 81: Who said crime didn't pay? **1930** JGBrandon *Murder* (L) 134: Crime doesn't pay. **1935** GDilnot *Murder* (L) 80: Sin does not pay. **1937** QPatrick *Death* (NY) 255: Crime does not pay. **1939** GHomes *No Hands* (NY) 148: It just goes to prove that crime doesn't pay. **1940** KRoos *Made up* (NY) 132: If you get caught, crime don't pay. **1941** STowne *Death out of* (NY) 221: Seems as if crime does pay after all. **1955** CMKornbluth *Mindworm* (L) 250: Crime pays only temporarily. **1957** *Punch* 6/5 703: Crime, it is axiomatic, does not pay. **1959** *TLS* 1/30 55: It was poor, so that crime could not pay—much. **1959** *TLS* 6/12 356: War, like crime, may not pay. **1961** RGordon *Doctor* (NY) 74: Crime doesn't pay in the end. **1964** CSimmons *Powdered* (NY) 142: Who says rhyme doesn't pay. **1971** PJFarmer *To Your* (NY) 85: Proving that crime *did* pay. **1971** LRhinehart *Dice* (NY) 266: Crime, even in the United States, does not pay. **1972** RLPike *Gremlin* (NY) 50: Who said crime doesn't pay, or that the wages of sin were dark?

C405 To seek whom the **Crime** benefits

1935 AChristie *Death* (L) 160: The old adage: seek whom the crime benefits. **1973** CAird *His Burial* (NY) 161: The old adage that crimes are usually committed by those who benefit from them.

C406 A **Criminal** (murderer) always makes one mistake (*varied*)

1926 CJDutton *Crooked* (NY) 130: Criminals . . . always make mistakes. **1927** VWilliams *Eye* (B) 179: The mistakes that every criminal makes, say, tryin' to cover up his tales. **1928** AWUpfield *Lure* (NY 1965) 155: In all great crimes that are found out the criminal makes one mistake that lays him

low. **1930** ABCox *Piccadilly* (NY) 36: They say every murderer makes some bad mistake. **1938** AWebb *Mr. P.'s Hat* (L) 265: It's a truism . . . that the criminal always trips upon some small point. **1947** ECrispin *Dead* (NY DBC) 148: It's the dreariest of platitudes to say that every murderer makes at least one mistake, but unlike most platitudes, that one happens to be true. **1952** KMKnight *Valse* (NY) 123: According to the detective stories, every murderer makes one mistake. **1962** AGarve *Prisoner's* (NY DBC) 102: They say murderers usually make a mistake.

C407 **Cripples** do not mock cripples

1934 RGraves *I, Claudius* (NY) 29: In the words of the proverb, cripples do not mock cripples. Whiting C551; Tilley C827.

C408 He who lives with a **Cripple** learns how to limp

1970 WMasterson *Death* (NY) 193: You remember the old saying: When you live with a cripple, you learn how to limp. *Oxford* 210: Dwells.

C409 **Crocodile** tears

1900 CFPidgin *Quincy A. Sawyer* (B) 363: Sheddin' crocodile's tears. **1922** JJoyce *Ulysses* (NY 1934) 532: Crybabby! Crocodile tears! **1930** RGoldman *Murder* (L) 212: Hers were no crocodile tears. **1936** CBush *Monday Murders* (L) 237: Wharton could weep like a crocodile. **1940** BHalliday *Private Practice* (NY 1965) 153: Weeping crocodile tears. **1941** ELFetta *Dressed* (NY) 99: There won't be many noncrocodile tears at her funeral. **1950** OAnderson *In for* (NY) 180: A tissue of crocodile tears. **1957** *Punch* 7/10 42: The crocodile weeps as he devours a man. **1960** NWilliams *Knaves* (NY) 229: Would he have wept? Only crocodile tears. **1962** DMDisney *Find* (NY DBC) 137: Salve his conscience with crocodile tears. **1966** NBlake *Morning* (NY) 58: The crocodile weeps no tears. **1968** NBenchley *Welcome* (NY) 39: I know what makes the crocodile weep and the leopard change its spots. **1973** KCampbell *Wheel* (I) 140: Weep no crocodiles for him. EAP C347; TW 85; Brunvand 29.

C410 As rich as **Croesus** (*varied*)

1900 CFPidgin *Quincy A. Sawyer* (B) 413: She's as rich as Creazers. **1920** GBMcCutcheon *Anderson Crow* (NY) 292: As rich as Crowsis. **1927** JSFletcher *Bartenstein* (NY) 145: The old man might be as rich as "what-dye-call-him." **1939** GBagby *Corpse* (NY) 123: A nickel richer than Croesus. **1951** JCollier *Fancies* (NY) 63: Rich as Croesus. **1956** PDeVries *Comfort* (B) 18: Sauces were rich as Crœsus. **1962** PDennis *Genius* (NY) 188: You're rich as creases [*sic*]. **1969** LPDavies *Stranger* (NY) 97: Rich as Crœsus. **1974** GMcDonald *Fletch* (I) 71: All as rich as Croesus. EAP C348: Wealthy; TW 85; Brunvand 29: Wealthy.

C411 To stick in one's **Crop**

1906 JCLincoln *Mr. Pratt* (NY) 195: It kind of stuck in Lys's craw. **1929** JSStrange *Clue* (NY) 2: Stoner sticks in my craw. **1931** AFielding *Upfold* (L) 203: It always has stuck in my crop. **1933** GDHCole *Death* (NY) 182: That's what sticks in the police gullet. **1937** WDickinson *Dead Man* (P) 24: It stuck in his craw. **1947** VWMason *Saigon* (NY) 221: It stuck in his craw. **1952** KMKnight *Death Goes* (NY) 164: One thing that sticks in my craw. **1959** PMacDonald *List* (L) 68: He's a little sticky in my craw. **1961** FSinclair *But the Patient* (NY) 13: Things that stick in the gullet. **1962** HWaugh *Born* (NY) 155: People like Jarold stick in my craw. **1965** HMiller *Quiet Days* (NY) 135: Two things he said . . . which stuck in my crop. **1967** JDCarr *Dark* (NY) 123: What sticks in my craw. **1973** JCashman *Gentleman* (NY) 35: They used to stick in my craw. EAP C349; TW 85; Amer. Herit. Dict.: Craw 2. Cf. Gizzard *below*.

C412 The greater the **Cross**, the higher the crown (*varied*)

1929 TKenyon *Witches* (NY) 60: The greater the Cross, the higher the Crown. **1934** AGilbert *An Old Lady* (L) 153: We are told no cross, no crown. EAP C351.

C413 As black as a **Crow** (crow's back, crow's wing)

1935 JLatimer *Headed* (NY 1957) 51: Her hair was as glistening black as a crow's wing. **1936** VMcHugh *Caleb* (NY) 59: Black's a crow. **1937** WBrewster *October* (Cambridge, Mass.) 261: As black as any crow. **1938** DBaker *Young Man* (B) 192: Black as a crow. **1950** FFGould *Maine Man* (NY) 124: His hair was as black as a crow's back. **1953** MPHood *Silent* (NY) 125: Her hair black as a crow's wing. **1956** AMMaughan *Harry* (NY) 263: Black as a crow. **1960** RHolles *Captain* (L) 26: Black as a tarred crow. **1964** EHemingway *Moveable* (NY) 5: Her hair was black as a crow's wing. **1965** RDSymons *Silton* (NY 1975) 38: Black as a crow. **1972** SCloete *Victorian* (L) 197: Hair . . . black as a crow's wing. EAP C352; TW 85(2); Brunvand 29(1,2); Taylor *Western Folklore* 17(1958) 14(1). Cf. Raven, Rook *below*.

C414 As hoarse as a **Crow**

1908 JCLincoln *Cy Whittaker* (NY) 68: Hoarse as a crow. **1932** RThorndike *Devil* (NY) 304: Made me hoarse as a crow. **1936** DLSayers *Gaudy* (NY) 25: I shall be as hoarse as a crow. **1955** Miss Read *Village* (L 1960) 85: As hoarse as a crow. **1957** LBeam *Maine* (NY) 193: People as hoarse as crows. TW 85(3).

C415 As hungry as a **Crow** in December

1946 RHuggins *Double Take* (NY 1959) 67: I was as hungry as a crow in December. Cf. Whiting *NC* 389(4): As poor as a winter crow.

C416 As poor as a **Crow**

1926 JSFletcher *Amaranth* (B) 64: As poor as a crow. **1927** BAtkey *Smiler* (NY) 168: As poor as a crow. Whiting *NC* 389(4); Brunvand 29(3).

C417 As the **Crow** flies (*varied*)

1903 EChilders *Riddle* (NY 1940) 88: As the crow flies . . . seventy miles. **1924** TMundy *Om* (NY) 287: The miles are reckoned as the crow flies. **1926** CFJenkins *Button Gwinnett* (NY) 34: Something less than ten miles as the proverbial crow would fly. **1937** BCobb *Fatal* (L) 187: It's only three miles as the crow flies—or as the fish swims. **1941** AAmos *Pray* (NY) 257: A couple of miles as the crow flies. **1954** HClement *Mission* (NY) 21: Thirty-odd thousand miles as the crow flies. **1955** JBCabell *As I* (NY) 211:

Rollins stood, as a crow flies in a cliché, some twenty-five miles from the St. John. **1960** RHeppenstall *Four* (L) 12: Two hundred and ten miles away from each other, as the crow flies (if a crow ever flies so far). **1961** LPayne *Nose* (NY) 158: As the crow flies . . . just a flutter of wings away. 281: As the crow flies, we're only a stone's throw from *chez moi*. **1965** MThomas *Such Men* (L) 26: As the crow flies . . . there was a more direct way. **1968** FLeiber *Swords* (NY) 188: Straight as the crow flies. **1968** EWilliams *Beyond* (NY) 19: Five crow miles from Ashton. **1969** SMays *Fall Out* (L) 197: Four hundred miles as the vulture flies. **1970** KLaumer *World* (NY) 25: Twenty miles . . . as the buzzard flies. **1971** RLockridge *Inspector's* (P) 152: Sixty miles . . . As a crow might fly. But all the many crows Heimrich had seen flew zigzag. **1977** JRLAnderson *Death* (NY) 68: As the crow flies, it wasn't much more than eighteen miles—but I wasn't a crow. TW 85(4); Brunvand 30(4); Taylor *Prov. Comp.* 31.

C418 Crow should not feed on crow
1943 FScully *Rogues* (Hollywood) 240: Crows shouldn't feed on crows. Cf. *Oxford* 359: Hawks (Crows). Cf. Tilley C856: One crow never pulls out another's eyes. Cf. Dog does not *below.*

C419 To eat Crow (*varied*)
1928 RBenchley *20,000 Leagues* (NY) 184: Or eat crow. 143: Not so long ago as the crow-eater flies. **1931** ACEdington *Monk's Hood* (NY) 221: I'll eat crow. **1932** HLandon *Owl's* (L) 77: "I'll make you eat craw." "Craw? Never tasted it." **1934** RStout *Fer-de-lance* (NY 1958) 197: But you caught the crow, now you can eat it. **1946** JKyd *Blood Is a Beggar* (P) 200: Just wouldn't eat crow. **1950** EQueen *Double* (B) 22: We made them eat crow. **1959** FBrown *Knock* (NY) 137: He'd have to eat a little crow. **1962** JBarry *Strange* (NY) 174: I'm eating crow. **1964** DDeJong *Whirligig* (NY) 30: How do you like your crow—under glass or just plain broiled? **1974** WCAnderson *Damp* (NY) 161: That stuff around my mouth is crow feathers. [*He's been "eating crow."*] **1975**

SJPerelman *Vinegar* (NY) 9: Eat crow . . . kiss and make up. DA Crow 4b; NED Crow *sb.*[1] 3.

C420 To have Crow's feet around one's eyes
1924 CVanVechten *Tattooed* (NY) 12: The crow's feet . . . around her eyes. **1932** BRoss *Tragedy of Y* (NY) 52: Crow's feet around her eyes. **1941** EPOppenheim *Man Who* (B) 20: With crow's feet about his eyes. **1947** VWMason *Saigon* (NY) 199: The crow's feet materialized at North's eye corners. **1953** ERuggles *Prince* (NY) 364: The crow's feet . . . would deepen and lift. **1954** JWMeagher *Through Midnight* (B) 169: A new line—another crease—an extra crow's foot. It's hell being a woman. **1955** VWMason *Two* (NY) 12: Good-humored crow's-feet showing at the corners of his eyes. **1970** JAGraham *Something* (B) 6: Crow's feet around the corners of his eyes. **1975** EGundy *Naked* (NY) 84: Crow's-feet on some men look like wisdom. TW 86(10); Whiting C578.

C421 To pick (pluck, pull) a Crow
1905 JBCabell *Line* (NY 1926) 123: There is a crow needs picking between us two. **1910** EPhillpotts *Tales* (NY) 93: What a crow he's got to pluck with you. **1923** ECVivian *City* (NY) 162: I think I'll take a hand in the plucking of this particular crow. **1926** JSFletcher *Kang-He* (NY) 159: I had a crow to pull with her. **1930** NBMavity *Case* (NY) 93: I have a crow to pick with you. **1937** FWCrofts *Found* (NY) 34: I have a crow to pluck with you. **1941** ABCunningham *Strange Death* (NY) 243: I've got a crow to pick with you. **1954** LCochran *Row's End* (NY) 96: I've got a crow to pick with you. **1955** NFitzgerald *House* (L) 43: He would have a crow to pluck with [him]. EAP C355; Brunvand 30(5); DARE i 867–8.

C422 As stiff as a Crowbar
1952 MScherf *Elk* (NY) 134: He was frozen as stiff as a crowbar. EAP C358.

C423 To pass in a Crowd
1934 DLSayers *Nine Tailors* (NY) 61: It'll pass in a crowd with a push, as they say. **1936** JMetcalfe *Sally* (NY) 287: She would

141

"pass in a crowd." **1941** VRath *Death Breaks* (NY) 20: She'll pass in a crowd [*pretty enough*]. **1959** HEBates *Watercress* (L) 173: You think I shall pass in a crowd. Partridge 194.

C424   From **Crown** to heels

1919 JSFletcher *Middle Temple* (NY) 399: [He] cursed him from crown to heels. **1933** CBush *April Fools* (L) 185: A sahib from crown to sole. Whiting C575: To the toe; Tilley C864, T436. Cf. From Top to toe *below*.

C425   Not matter a **Crumb**

1957 AECoppard *It's Me* (L) 85: That did not matter a crumb. Cf. NED Crumb *sb.* 2.

C426   As crazy as a **Crumpet**

1953 RChandler *Long* (L) 187: The whole thing was as crazy as a crumpet. Partridge 195.

C427   As funny (subtle) as a **Crutch**

1932 ORCohen *Star* (NY) 276: You're funny as a crutch. **1937** SPalmer *No Flowers* (L) 242: That was another funny joke, funny as a broken crutch. **1951** GBagby *Death* (NY) 20: You're funny as a crutch. **1951** GConklin *Possible* (NY) 253: [He] is about as subtle as a crutch. **1957** *New Yorker* 5/4 48: You're about as funny as a crutch. **1960** RMacdonald *Ferguson* (NY) 73: You're about as funny as a crutch. **1965** PDeVries *Let Me* (NY 1966) 10: Funny as a crutch. Whiting *NC* 389.

C428   Much **Cry** and little wool (*varied*)

1927 DYates *Blind* (NY) 199: Much cry, but little wool. **1928** AFielding *Net* (NY) 24: Big cry and little wool. **1930** GBaxter *Ainceworth* (NY) 256: All cry and no wool. **1934** GDHCole *Death* (NY) 189: More cry than wool there. **1935** AWynne *Toll House* (P) 288: Much cry and sma' wool, as the barber said when he shaved the sow. **1938** BFlynn *Tread* (L) 224: "Much cry" of examination with "little wool" of result. **1958** MRenault *King* (NY 1960) 57: Much cry and little wool, as the saying goes. **1959** *TLS* 10/9 579: His book is "much cry, little wool." **1967** JDCarr *Dark* (NY) 98: This disturbance . . . is all cry and no wool. **1971** HBev-ington *House* (NY) 35: All cry and no wool. EAP C362; TW 86.

C429   To **Cry** before one is hurt (*varied*)

1927 GDilnot *Lazy* (B) 267: Don't snivel till you're hurt. **1930** NBMavity *Other Bullet* (NY) 199: Don't cry before you're hurt. **1932** BABotkin ed *Land Is Ours* (Norman, Okla.) 258: Holler afore they're hurt. **1936** JMWalsh *Crimes* (L) 186: Don't scream before you're hit. **1939** AMcRoyd *Double Shadow* (NY) 19: Maybe I did kick before I was spurred. **1951** JCollier *Fancies* (NY) 144: The good old saying, "Never holler before you're hurt." **1952** AMenen *Duke* (NY) 74: Don't shout before you're hurt. **1961** RAHeinlein *6XH* (NY) 116: Don't cry till you're hurt. *Oxford* 158. Cf. Frightened *below*.

C430   As clean as **Crystal**

1967 EVCunningham *Samantha* (NY) 173: The air is as sharp and as clean as crystal. Whiting C588.

C431   As clear as **Crystal**; Crystal-clear

1901 MLPeabody *To Be Young* (B 1967) 202: Clear as crystal. **1903** EChilders *Riddle* (NY 1940) 224: It was clear as crystal. **1922** JJoyce *Ulysses* (NY 1934) 356: Her words rang out crystal clear. **1924** JJFarjeon *Master* (NY) 291: Clear as crystal. **1930** LRGribble *Case* (NY) 290: They [*glasses*] were already crystal-clear. **1935** SHPage *Tragic* (NY) 253: It's clear as crystal. **1937** GGoodchild *Operator* (L) 66: The air was clear as crystal. **1939** RCSherriff *Hopkins* (NY) 181: Every word came as clear as crystal. **1944** PATaylor *Dead Ernest* (NY) 135: The situation [is] clear as sparkling crystal. **1956** *New Yorker* 10/27 152: As clear as crystal. **1958** NMonkman *From Queensland* (NY) 171: Crystal-clear water. **1959** LDickson *Ante-room* (L) 202: Clear as crystal. **1961** SDean *Credit* (NY) 85: One thing was crystal-clear. **1965** AHeckstall-Smith *Consort* (NY) 148: "Do I make myself clear?" "As crystal." **1974** RSaltonstall *Maine* (B) 26: One thing is crystal clear. EAP C363; TW 86(1); Brunvand 30.

C432 As hard as **Crystal**

1954 MErskine *Dead by* (NY) 45: The eyes grew hard as crystal. Whiting C590.

C433 As white as **Crystal**

1958 MRenault *King* (NY 1960) 43: As white as crystal. Whiting C592.

C434 As crazy (barmy) as a **Cuckoo**

1935 GDilnot *Murder* (L) 173: Crazy as a cuckoo. **1950** LAGStrong *Which I* (L) 207: Barmy as a cuckoo. **1959** JPhilips *Killer* (NY) 201: Crazy as a cuckoo.

C435 As lousy as a **Cuckoo**

1930 FAWinter *Behind* (L) 85: You're as lousy as a cuckoo. Partridge 196.

C436 As calm as a **Cucumber**

1930 HAshbrook *Murder* (NY) 34: As calm as a cucumber. **1932** HBurnham *Telltale* (NY) 25: Calm's a cucumber. **1936** AA Carey *Memoirs* (NY) 39: As calm as a cucumber. Taylor *Prov. Comp.* 23: Calm.

C437 As cold as a **Cucumber**

1912 JCLincoln *Postmaster* (NY) 245: Cold as a fresh cucumber. **1960** LHale *Blood* (L) 67: As coold [*sic*] as the proverbial cucumber. EAP C370.

C438 As cool as a **Cucumber**; Cucumber-cool

1903 ADMcFaul *Ike Glidden* (B) 171: He was as cool as a cucumber. **1922** JJoyce *Ulysses* (NY 1934) 169: Cool as a cucumber. **1929** HWHaggard *Devils* (NY) 340: The common expression "cool as a cucumber" is derived from the therapeutic theory of Galen. **1932** JSFletcher *Four Degrees* (L) 214: As cool as the proverbial cucumber. **1933** LWMeynell *Paid* (L) 56: Cooler than most cucumbers I've seen. **1937** GBruce *Claim* (NY) 216: He was cooler than the proverbial cucumber. **1946** HNicolson *Diaries III* ed NNicolson (NY 1968) 68: Cool and clean as a cucumber. **1951** PCheyney *Ladies* (NY DBC) 33: She was cool as a cucumber, as wicked (if need be) as a snake. **1952** FCDavis *Tread* (NY) 145: Speare looked cucumber-cool. **1953** VPJohns *Murder* (NY 1962) 171: Althea, cucumber cool. **1957** *Time* 11/18 75: Cucumber-cool effi-ciency. **1957** *New Yorker* 10/5 37: Cool as little old cucumbers. **1957** GWJohnson *Lunatic* (B) 25: They are as cool as the proverbial cucumber. **1959** AGilbert *Prelude* (NY DBC) 71: Bennie was as cool as the proverbial cucumber. **1961** FLeiber *Silver* (NY) 96: He was cool and crafty as a cucumber. **1962** AGilbert *Uncertain* (NY DBC) 125: He could have attended a fancy dress ball just as he was, going as the proverbial cool cucumber. **1968** HCarvic *Picture* (NY) 13: Cool as a cold-blooded cucumber. **1973** AGilbert *Nice* (NY) 107: Out he came, cool as the proverbial cucumber. EAP C371; Brunvand 30.

C439 To chew the **Cud**

1933 CBush *April Fools* (L) 186: Chewing the cud on that. **1936** RAJWalling *Crimson Slipper* (L) 46: This conversation provided Tolefree with his cud to chew. **1937** CBush *Eight O'Clock* (NY) 47: Travers . . . chewed the cud of thought. **1958** WGraham *Wreck* (NY) 180: To chew the cud of her grievance. **1967** WGolding *Pyramid* (NY) 75: Chewing the cud of an idea. EAP C372; Brunvand 30.

C440 To take up the **Cudgels**

1922 JJoyce *Ulysses* (NY 1934) 635: By taking up the cudgels on their behalf. EAP C373.

C441 To be a different **Cup** (dish) of tea

1933 HDuffy *Seven* (NY) 40: He's a totally different cup of tea. **1939** VWilliams *Fox Prowls* (B) 122: The Baron's a very different cup of tea. **1957** *TLS* 4/19 234: They were a different cup of tea. **1959** DMDisney *No Next* (NY) 62: He . . . was going to be a very different cup of tea from his wife. **1965** AGilbert *Voice* (NY) 69: This one was a different cup of tea. **1972** JPotts *Troublemaker* (NY) 2: That's a different dish of tea.

C442 To be (not to be) one's **Cup** (dish) of tea

1938 VWMason *Cairo* (NY) 109: This sort of thing is just his dish. **1938** NMarsh *Death* (NY) 53: [Not] quite your cup of tea. **1941** NMarsh *Death in Ecstasy* (NY) 125: Not my cup of tea at all. **1943** GHCoxe *Murder in Havana* (NY) 131: Women were his dish.

1949 JBonett *Dead Lion* (L 1953) 73: His doings just aren't my cup of tea. **1952** JLeslie *Intimate* (NY) 56: Not everyone's dish of tea. **1954** ECRLorac *Shroud* (NY) 20: This is just his cup of tea. **1957** *Time* 10/28 80: The model . . . would not have been everybody's cup of tea. **1961** FDurbridge *Case* (NY) 196: Just your cup of tea. **1961** HCromwell *Dirty* (LA) 46: The couple . . . were not my dish of tea. **1964** DBagley *Golden* (NY) 15: This wasn't Tom's cup of tea. **1968** DDempsey *Triumphs* (NY) 250: Miss Hopper proved to be not quite her cup of tea. **1969** JBoyd *Rakehells* (NY 1971) 70: Jesus is more your cup of tea. **1970** EQueen *Last* (NY) 58: This sort of thing is your dish of blood. **1971** PDJames *Shroud* (L) 29: [He] wasn't everyone's cup of tea. **1972** MDelving *Shadow* (NY) 13: It's not my dish. Partridge 198; Wentworth 134.

C443 He that will to **Cupar** will to Cupar

1930 GBaxter *Ainceworth* (NY) 283: Weel, Weel, "Wha maun tae Cupar maunt tae Cupar" [*a Scot speaks*]. *Oxford* 161.

C444 **Cupboard** love

1935 CBarry *Shot* (NY) 222: Cupboard love. **1936** JCPowys *Maiden Castle* (NY) 202: Not for "cupboard-love." **1948** JTey *Franchise* (NY 1955) 72: A cup-board love kid. **1957** THWhite *Master* (L) 199: Cupboard love. **1977** VCanning *Doomsday* (NY) 128: Cupboard love. TW 87(1); *Oxford* 161.

C445 Like the **Curate's** egg, good in parts

1936 JBude *Sussex* (L) 72: A curate's egg . . . good in parts. *Oxford* 161.

C446 The **Cure** (remedy) is worse than the disease (*varied*)

1927 OWarner *Secret* (NY) 60: The cure was worse than the disease. **1929** KPreston *Pot Shots* (NY) 242: The remedy is more flagrant than the disease. **1936** JDKerruish *Undying* (NY) 90: To use a familiar simile: The remedy was worse than the disease. **1939** GGoodchild *We Shot* (L) 235: The cure seems worse than the disease. **1951** LBrown *Cleopatra* (NY) 134: The cure was worse than the disease. **1954** RKLeavitt *Chip* (P) 36: The cure was worse than the disease. **1961** JBTownsend *John* (New Ha-

ven) 153: The cure . . . to prove deadlier than the disease. **1966** DLMoore *E.Nesbit* (NY) 213: The medicine was rather worse than the disease. **1969** RHofstadter *Idea* (Berkeley) 65: The remedy is clearly far worse than the disease. **1970** RDAltick *Victorian* (NY) 255: The curative regimen was worse than the disease. **1973** ELopez *Seven* (NY) 145: The cure is worse than the ill. EAP R53: Remedy.

C447 There is no **Cure** for a fool

1931 LJVance *Lone Wolf's* (P) 77: They do say there's no cure for a fool. Cf. *Oxford* 369: No herb will cure love.

C448 What can't be **Cured** must be endured (*varied*)

1900 CFPidgin *Quincy A. Sawyer* (B) 4: What can't be cured must be endured. **1917** JCLincoln *Extricating* (NY) 203: What can't be cured must be endured. **1929** LBrock *Stoke Silver* (NY) 191: What couldn't be cured would have to be borne. **1936** SGibbons *Miss Linsey* (NY) 178: What can't be cured must be endured, as they say. **1939** JDCarr *Problem* (B 1948) 149: What can't be cured must be endured. **1953** AChristie *Pocket* (NY) 159: What can't be cured must be endured. **1955** WSloane *Stories* (L) 436: What can't be helped must be borne. **1960** DShannon *Case* (NY 1964) 25: What can't be cured must be endured. **1960** HSlesar *Enter* (NY 1967) 107: And if it can't be helped, it can't be helped. **1966** HTreece *Green* (L) 145: What can't be cured must be endured. **1977** SWoods *Law's Delay* (NY) 62: What can't be cured must be endured. EAP C376.

C449 **Curiosity** killed a (the) cat

1926 RASimon *Weekend* (NY) 38: Curiosity once killed a cat. **1931** ALivingston *In Cold* (I) 300: I differ from the famous cat; I'll never die of curiosity. **1932** LFrost *Murder* (NY) 7: Curiosity had killed more than cats. **1937** EGowen *Old Hell* (NY) 8: That woman has got enough curiosity to kill a nine-life cat. **1940** ECRLorac *Tryst* (L) 208: Worry killed the cat. **1948** EDaly *Book* (NY) 96: Curiosity killed the cat. **1950** HGreen *Nothing* (NY) 243: Curiosity never killed a cat in spite of all they say. **1953** JDolph *Dead Angel* (NY) 40: I'm curious as the killed cat. **1957** BHitchens *End* (NY) 37: Curiosity'll kill Amy someday, just like it did that mythical cat. **1959** *BangorDN* 6/9 9: How did curiosity kill the cat? And which cat was it? And who's curiosity? **1961** RFoley *It's Murder* (NY DBC) 114: Curiosity killed the cat. **1968** OLevant *Unimportance* (NY) 90: To . . . friend who had to get rid of a cat: "Have you tried curiosity?" **1970** RDAltick *Victorian* (NY) 215: Curiosity has been known to kill more than cats. **1971** ADavidson *Peregrine* (NY) 35: Curiosity killed the cat, and, says I, serve it right for letting "I dare not" wait upon "I will." **1980** HPentecost *Death* (NY) 160: "Curiosity killed the cat," my old lady used to say. Whiting *NC* 390. Cf. Care *above*.

C450   The **Curse** of Cromwell

1922 JJoyce *Ulysses* (NY 1934) 335: Cursing the curse of Cromwell on him, bell, book and candle in Irish. **1933** LO'Flaherty *Martyr* (NY) 122: The curse o' Cromwell on it for a story. **1935** DBennett *Murder* (NY) 214: The curse of Cromwell on him. **1955** NFitzgerald *House* (L) 28: I believe that was the real curse of Cromwell on this country [*Ireland*], puritanism. TW 88(7); *Oxford* 162.

C451   Not care a **Curse** (cuss)

1925 JGBrandon *Bond* (L) 13: Don't care a curse. **1928** HAdams *Empty* (P) 245: He doesn't care a cuss. **1933** FDGrierson *Empty* (L) 89: Without . . . caring a tupenny curse. **1951** EQueen *Origin* (B) 9: I don't care a curse. **1957** RStandish *Prince* (L) 91: They did not care a curse. EAP C378; Brunvand 31.

C452   Not give a **Curse** (cuss) (*varied*)

1929 WFaulkner *Sound* (NY) 23: I don't give a cuss. **1952** EFerrars *Alibi* (L 1967) 182: Why should I have given a curse. **1963** MPHood *Sin* (NY) 54: Don't give a continental cuss. **1974** LBlack *Life* (NY) 104: [Not] have given a tupenny cuss about it. EAP C379.

C453   Not matter a **Curse** (cuss)

1930 JRhode *Venner* (NY) 92: It doesn't matter a cuss. **1932** FDGrierson *Murder* (L) 132: They don't matter a curse to me.

C454   Not worth a **Curse**

1919 HRHaggard *She and Allan* (NY 1921) 57: Not worth a curse. **1931** EPhillpotts *Found* (L) 107: No gifts are worth a curse. EAP C380.

C455   A **Curtain** lecture

1916 EClodd *Memories* (L) 255: Fears of curtain lectures. **1931** CWells *Horror* (P) 37: A curtain lecture. **1939** TStevenson *Silver Arrow* (L) 146: I can't give him a curtain lecture. **1968** LDurrell *Tunc* (NY) 307: This sort of curtain lecture. EAP C381.

C456   The **Customer** is always right

1931 GFowler *Great* (NY) 309: The customer is always right. **1935** ERPunshon *Death* (L 1948) 76: A good tradesman whose motto has to be that the customer is always right. **1942** CRice *Big Midget* (NY 1948) 5: The customers are always right. **1949** FCrane *Flying* (NY) 120: The damned customer is always right. **1967** MZarubica *Scutari* (NY) 195: The customer isn't always right. **1969** RStark *Dame* (NY) 14: The customer's always right. **1970** JPorter *Dover Strikes* (NY) 60: The dictum that the customer is always right. Taylor *Western Folklore* 17 (1958) 54–5.

C457   The **Cut** of one's jib

1922 JJoyce *Ulysses* (NY 1934) 620: There was something spurious about the cut of his jib. **1932** TCobb *Who Closed* (L) 132: A foreigner by the cut of his jib. **1941** A Christie *Evil under* (NY) 46: I know the cut of a fellow's jib. **1948** JRhode *Death* (NY) 64: I didn't care very much for the cut of his jib. **1956** AMenen *Abode* (NY) 101: The cut of his jib was definitely Anglican. **1963** KVonnegut *Cat's* (NY) 159: I like the cut of your jib. EAP C391.

C458   Not have **Cut**, shuffle or deal to do with something

1954 EDillon *Sent* (L) 124: I wouldn't have cut, shuffle nor deal to do with it. Cf. NED Cut *sb.*² 8 (quote 1728).

C459   To be **Cut** and dried

1919 JSFletcher *Middle Temple* (NY) 53: The usual cut-and-dried account. **1932** JJConnington *Sweepstake* (B) 9: Ideas . . . all cut and dried. **1937** FBeeding *Hell* (L)

53: They had their arrangements cut and dried. **1940** DWheelock *Murder at Montauk* (NY) 72: It looked like a cut-and-dried suicide. **1949** FKane *Green* (NY) 190: A nice cut-and-dried suspect. **1953** HBPiper *Murder* (NY) 94: It's all cut and dried and in the bag now. **1958** HMasur *Murder* (NY 1959) 72: It was cut and dried. Open and shut. **1967** CAird *Most Contagious* (NY) 74: A real . . . cut and dried murder. **1969** RDavies *Print* (L) 92: John's . . . cut and dried lasciviousness. **1975** NFreeling *Bugles* (NY) 11: It should be cut and dried. EAP C392.

C460   To **Cut** (nip) and run

1903 EChilders *Riddle* (NY 1940) 216: The time to cut and run. **1928** GGardiner *At the House* (NY) 84: A case of nip and run. **1931** CBush *Dead Man's* (L) 279: He didn't cut and run. **1939** HWPriwen *Inspector* (L) 41: Have to cut and run. **1958** MInnes *Long* (NY) 132: Alice had decided to cut and run for it. **1965** DHitchens *Bank* (NY) 31: Unless he could cut and run. **1968** HWAllen *Genesis* (NY 1970) 98: Cut and run, save Number One. **1972** HDPerry *Chair* (NY) 3: The time to cut and run. EAP C390.

D

D1   To be at **Daggers** drawn

1922 JSFletcher *Middle of Things* (NY) 95: At daggers drawn. **1922** JJoyce *Ulysses* (NY 1934) 342: She was black out at daggers drawn with Gerty. **1937** DScott *Five Fatal* (NY) 58: My old cronies were at daggers drawn. **1939** AChristie *Murder Is* (L) 97: Him and Dr. Humbleby was daggers drawn, as the saying is. **1940** MBurton *Mr. Westerby* (NY) 16: At daggers drawn. **1952** JDrummond *Naughty* (L) 74: They looked at daggers-drawn. **1956** SDean *Marked* (NY) 172: The men were plainly at daggers' points. **1963** CBlackstock *Mr. Christopoulos* (NY 1965) 27: He and Jed are at daggers drawn. **1971** RLWolff *Strange* (B) 74: Their wives were at daggers drawn. **1975** JBland *Death* (NY) 27: He and Towzie are at daggers drawn. EAP D1.

D2   To look **Daggers** (*varied*)

1908 MRRinehart *Circular Staircase* (NY 1947) 149: He looked daggers at me. **1929** OSchingall *Barron* (NY) 57: Their smiles were as cutting as daggers. **1929** SSpewack *Murder* (NY) 29: Looking daggers at me; 87. **1955** DGarnett *Aspects* (L) 89: Rose looked daggers at him. **1961** ATCurtis *Poacher's* (L) 154: He looked daggers at me. TW 90(2); Brunvand 32.

D3   As bright as a **Daisy**

1934 ABliss *Murder* (P) 24: As bright as a daisy. **1939** EHuxley *African Poison* (NY) 45: He was bright as a daisy. **1952** AGilbert *Mr. Crook* (NY DBC) 98: As bright as a daisy and as fresh as paint. **1962** FCrane *Amber* (NY) 160: She was bright as a daisy this morning. Whiting D2.

D4   As common as **Daisies**

1931 APryde *Emerald* (NY) 7: White suits . . . were as common as daisies. Wilstach 64.

D5   As fresh as a **Daisy** (daffodil); Daisy-fresh (*varied*)

1917 GRSims *My Life* (L) 82: As fresh as a daisy. **1926** MRRinehart *Bat* (NY 1959) 153: As fresh as a daisy. **1930** LCharteris *Last Hero* (NY) 81: The proverbial morning daisy would have looked . . . haggard beside him. **1939** PATaylor *Spring* (L) 82: She wasn't by any means as fresh as the proverbial daisy. **1949** SJepson *Golden* (NY) 218: Looking as fresh to the day as a dew-kissed daisy. **1956** *New Yorker* 10/13 144: He's fresh as a daisy. **1956** RILee *Happy* (B) 9: As fresh as the proverbial daisy. **1960** NWoodin *Room* (L) 198: A roadman . . . is daisy-fresh first thing in the morning. **1961** EWilliams *George* (NY) 377: As fresh as a bisexual daisy. **1965** AGilbert *Voice* (NY) 174: There you are, fresh as a daisy, and willin' as Barkis. **1969** EAnderson *Miss* (B) 233: As fresh as a daffodil. **1974** PHighsmith *Ripley's* (NY) 221: Fresh as a daisy. **1977** HDolson *Beauty* (P) 200: [He] appeared, fresh as an unfolding daisy. Taylor *Prov. Comp.* 42. Cf. Morning glory *below*.

D6   As neat as a **Daisy**

1951 ECRLorac *I Could* (NY) 23: Neat as a daisy. **1959** AGilbert *Death* (NY) 272: Neat as a daisy.

D7   Daisy-white

1960 CWatson *Bump* (L 1963) 17: Daisy-white hair. Whiting D3: White as.

D8   To push up the **Daisies** (*varied*)

1933 HAdams *Woman* (L) 97: While I'm above the daisies. **1935** JStagge *Murder* (L) 73: I'll be pushing up daisies before the year's out. **1937** HCBailey *Clunk's* (L) 87: Here's the . . . fellow sent to push up the daisies. **1939** DHume *Heads* (L) 22: There are scores of people who'd like to see you pushing up daisies. **1959** DCushman *Good-bye* (NY) 243: He's pushing up daisies now. **1965** HActon *Old Lamps* (L) 12: I'll soon be pushing up the daisies. **1966** WTrevor *Love* (L) 115: He'll be pushing up the daisies. **1970** RCowper *Twilight* (NY) 125: All the other professors were pushing up the daisies. Partridge 205, 671; NED Suppl. Daisy 1c; Spears 318; Wentworth 413.

D9   As near (close) as **Dammit**

1919 KHoward *Peculiar* (NY) 50: As near as dammit. **1922** JJoyce *Ulysses* (NY 1934) 175: They're as close as damn it. **1939** CFGregg *Danger* (L) 151: As near as dammit. **1941** AWebb *Suicide Club* (L) 96: As near as damn it. **1953** RUsborne *Clubland* (L) 15: As near as dammit. **1966** MErskine *Family* (NY) 172: It was as near as dammit. **1970** HCarmichael *Death* (NY) 214: As near as dammit. **1976** JPorter *Package* (NY) 11: Near as damn it. Partridge 205.

D10   Not amount to a **Damn**

1931 GFowler *Great* (NY) 44: They'll never amount to a good God damn. **1947** FCrane *Murder on* (NY) 54: It didn't amount to a damn. **1971** PDennis *Paradise* (NY) 13: He hadn't amounted to a damn. Cf. Berrey 21.7.

D11   Not care a **Damn** (God damn) (*varied*)

1923 JSFletcher *Lost Mr. L* (NY) 102: Not care a two-penny damn. **1924** HHBashford *Augustus* (L 1966) 259: Not care a damn. **1929** STruss *Stolen* (L) 283: He didn't care two damns. **1930** JGBrandon *Death* (L) 154: I don't care a darn. **1933** MKennedy *Bull's Eye* (L) 80: Neither of them care a two-penny damn. **1933** ECRLorac *Case* (L) 150: I don't care a double damn. **1939** CMWills *Death at* (L) 236: He don't care a darn. **1959** KMKnight *Beauty* (NY) 14: I don't care one good god damn. **1965** JLeigh *What Can* (NY) 90: I wouldn't care a damn. **1968** JHaythorne *None of Us* (NY) 115: He did not care a twopenny damn. EAP D3. Cf. Not care a Tinker's dam(n) *below*.

D12   Not give a (good God) **Damn** (*varied*)

1912 JCLincoln *Postmaster* (NY) 269: I don't give a durn. **1931** KTKnoblock *There's Been* (NY) 39: I don't give a god-damn. **1932** CAndrews *Butterfly* (NY) 59: I don't give a damn. **1932** NKlein *No! No!* (NY) 196: I don't give a good God-damn about Aunt. **1933** GBegbie *Sudden* (L) 82: They don't give a tuppenny damn. **1935** LRGribble *Mystery* (L) 247: I don't give a penny damn. **1940** KMKnight *Death Came* (NY) 28: Liane doesn't give a continental damn. **1953** BCarey *Their Nearest* (NY) Just not give one good God damn. **1958** CL Blackstone *Dewey* (L 1965) 193: I don't give a damn. **1958** SEllin *Eighth* (NY 1959) 42: I don't give a goddam. **1961** GHCoxe *Moment* (NY) 9: A reckless, don't-give-a-damn attitude. **1968** ESRussell *She Should* (NY) 195: I don't give a goddam. **1969** JDrummond *People* (NY) 11: I don't give a darn. **1969** HWaugh *Run* (NY) 30: I don't give a good God damn. **1970** PAlding *Murder* (NY) 148: I don't give a single twopenny damn. **1975** HBHough *Mostly* (NY) 16: Not that I give a God damn. EAP D4. Cf. Not give a Tinker's dam(n) *below*.

D13   Not matter a **Damn** (*varied*)

1930 LBrock *Murder* (NY) 159: It mattered not a tuppenny damn. **1931** PMacDonald *Murder* (L) 83: It doesn't matter a damn. **1967** JWCampbell *Analog 5* (NY) 209: It won't matter a damn. Cf. Berrey 21.3. Cf. Not matter a Tinker's curse *below*.

D14   Not worth a **Damn**

1923 ORCohen *Jim Hanvey* (NY) 211: [Not] worth a damn. **1933** HAshbrook *Murder* (NY) 199: Not worth a damn. **1959** GHCoxe *Focus* (NY) 144: That guy's not worth a damn. **1970** HCarvic *Miss Seeton Draws* (NY) 12: Nothing . . . worth a damn.

EAP D5. Cf. Berrey 21.13. Cf. Not worth a Tinker's dam(n) *below.*

D15 Damn all (*varied*)

1922 JJoyce *Ulysses* (NY 1934) 268: Rhapsodies about damn all. **1931** LHollingworth *Death* (L) 253: And I know damn-all [*nothing*]. **1934** GDHCole *Death* (NY) 96: I think that's damn-all. **1953** JWyndham *Kraken* (L 1955) 210: A geographer who knows damn-all about oceans. **1958** CLBlackstock *Foggy* (NY) 74: And all I'm doing is sweet damn-all [*nothing*]. **1960** HRFKeating *Zen* (L 1963) 185: He probably knows damn all [*nothing*]. **1963** NFitzgerald *Echo* (NY) 232: And it's damn all I've done today. **1969** JMPatterson *Doubly* (NY) 23: I don't think the marriage amounts to damn all. **1970** RQuest *Cerberus* (NY) 42: They know damn-all [*nothing*]. **1976** LEgan *Scenes* (NY) 19: Come up with damn all. **1977** RThomas *Yellow-Dog* (NY) 67: You're gonna prove that I had fuck all to do with it. Partridge 206.

D16 From Dan to Beersheba

1908 JCLincoln *Cy Whittaker* (NY) 306: Blowed from Dan to Beersheby. **1921** JCLincoln *Galusha* (NY) 96: From Dan to Beersheba. **1935** BFlynn *Sussex* (L) 68: I ought to be kicked from Dan to Beersheba. **1938** EQueen *Four* (NY) 136: I've subpoenaed her from Dan to Beersheba. **1968** LSdeCamp *Great Monkey* (NY) 417: File it from Dan to Beersheba. EAP D6; TW 90; Whiting D7.

D17 To lead someone a Dance (*varied*)

1930 JCournos *Grandmother* (NY) 27: She's led him a merry dance. **1930** LRGribble *Case* (NY) 210: They're leading us a pretty fine dance. **1930** LMeynell *Mystery* (P) 186: Bache had led him the devil's own dance. **1933** LRGribble *Secret* (L) 146: He's leading us a pretty dance. EAP D8.

D18 To get (*etc.*) **one's Dander up**

1900 CFPidgin *Quincy A. Sawyer* (B) 265: When my dander's up. **1920** GBMcCutcheon *Anderson Crow* (NY) 166: Got her dander up. **1924** CWells *Furthest* (P) 157: Gets her dander up. **1930** HFootner *Mystery* (NY) 22: Keep your dander up! **1936**

ECRLorac *Pall* (L) 185: I got my dander up. **1940** MSScott *Crime Hound* (NY) 41: They got his dander up [*made him angry*]. **1947** JIams *Body* (NY) 198: While my dander's up. **1950** MGEberhart *Hunt* (NY) 30: Old Benny must have got his dander up. **1957** MPHood *In the Dark* (NY) 156: I felt my dander a'risin'. **1961** MGEberhart *Cup* (NY DBC) 62: Don't get your dander up. **1967** SEMorison *Old Bruin* (B) 30: He and the President began to get their dander up. TW 90(1); Brunvand 32.

D19 A Danger foreseen is half escaped

1937 GDefean *Who Killed* (L) 109: A danger foreseen is half escaped. Tilley D29. Cf. EAP D17: Darts.

D20 Darby and Joan

1931 HWade *No Friendly* (L) 80: He's a regular Darby, never away from his Joan. **1937** DLSayers *Busman's* (NY) 34: A pleasantly tottering, Darby and Joan pair. **1942** MColes *They Tell* (NY) 223: Don't go all Darby and Joan. **1946** CDickson *My Late* (NY) 111: A woman they live with . . . as cozy as Darby and Joan. **1956** AGilbert *Riddle* (NY) 88: I'm pinning my hopes on a Darby and Joan. **1966** BNaughton *Alfie* (L) 82: The Darby and Joan club. **1968** MRowell *Below* (L) 117: And [the privy] had one of those seats with two holes, the sort for Darby and Joan who couldn't bear to be separated. **1970** RRendell *Best Man* (NY) 99: There was a kind of Darby and Joan air about them. **1972** SBrooke *Queen* (NY) 180: No "Darby and Joan" finale for us in our old age. **1981** AMStein *Body* (NY) 133: It was Victorian, pure Darby and Joan. EAP D13.

D21 In the Dark all cats are gray (*varied*)

1908 JCLincoln *Cy Whittaker* (NY) 204: All cats are gray in the dark. **1928** CBarry *Corpse* (NY) 36: *La nuit tous les chats sont gris.* **1929** CWells *Tapestry* (P) 249: All cats are gray in the dark. **1930** AGilbert *Mystery* (NY) 127: The saying that in the dark all cats are grey. **1931** HCBailey *Fortune Speaking* (NY) 214: In the dark all cats are black. **1931** JTully *Blood* (NY) 258: They're all alike in the dark anyhow. **1932** EDBiggers

Keeper (L) 225: At night all cats are dark. **1936** VMcHugh *Caleb* (NY) 154: Sounds to me like the old Frog sayin' bout when the lights 're out all cats are gray. **1937** CGGivens *All Cats Are Gray* (I). **1937** CGGivens *All Cats* (I) 224: When candles Be out, all cats Be gray. **1939** MElwin *Old Godo* (NY) 21: The cynicism that all women are alike in the dark. **1948** IFletcher *Roanoke* (I) 133: All cats were grey in the night. **1951** EMarshall *Viking* (NY) 103: His face is a dire sight, but in the dark all cats are gray. **1952** IGordon *Night* (NY) 155: They're all men and in the dark I can't tell the difference—no one can. **1953** CBKelland *Sinister* (NY DBC) 160: All men are alike in the dark. **1954** ASeton *Katherine* (B) 259: To a determined man, all cats are gray at night. **1956** UCurtiss *Widow's* (NY) 128: All cars are gray in the dark. **1957** DErskine *Pink* (NY) 75: [Women] were all alike . . . Ben Franklin was right. A pillowslip covered the difference. **1959** *Time* 8/31 19: In the dark all men were the same color. **1959** CHenry *Hostage* (NY) 56: In the dark there ain't no such thing as a lady. **1960** HAlpert *Some Other* (NY) 209: They [*women*] all look alike in the dark. **1960** HRobertson *Swan* (NY) 91: At night all cats are grey. **1963** FSwinnerton *Figures* (L) 237: From outside, like cats at night, all best-sellers look alike. **1965** JLeigh *What Can* (NY) 148: Such bestial superstitions as "All cats are grey at night" and "If you stand 'em on their heads they all look like sisters." **1969** RPearsall *Worm* (L) 315: In the darkness, as one philosopher maintained, all cats are gray. **1971** RSilverberg *World* (NY) 95: In the dark all cats are gray: old twentieth-century proverb. **1975** GMacBeth *Samurai* (NY 1976) 18: They're all gray in the dark, as they say. **1977** PDJames *Death* (NY) 262: As Lord Chesterfield said, all cats are gray in the dark. **1981** SWoods *Cry* (NY) 169: All cats are grey at night. EAP C57.

D22 To whistle in the **Dark**

1940 EQueen *New Adventures* (NY) 43: A badly scared little boy whistling in the dark. **1953** JWyndham *Kraken* (L 1955) 223: Too many people were whistling the same tune in the dark. **1956** RStout *Might* (NY) 21:

You're just whistling in the dark. **1958** VSiller *Widower* (NY) 80: Whistling in the dark to make Irene feel better. **1966** MDuberman *J.R.Lowell* (B) 268: This might be whistling in the dark. **1969** TBesterman *Voltaire* (NY) 309: Voltaire was whistling in the dark. **1970** FSteegmuller *Cocteau* (B) 416: It was a whistling in the dark. **1972** SCloete *Victorian* (L) 251: A kind of whistling in the dark—the darkness of fear—like boys in a graveyard. EAP D16. Cf. Courage *above*; Graveyard *below*.

D23 As straight as a **Dart**

1919 JSFletcher *Middle Temple* (NY) 148: Straight as a dart. **1932** TCobb *Who Closed* (L) 127: She was as straight as a dart. **1933** MMagill *Murder* (P) 245: Go as the crow flies—straight as a dart. Wilstach 393.

D24 A **Daughter** is a daughter all the days of her life *etc.* (*varied*)

1942 ABMaurice *Riddle* (NY) 152: An old saying: "A daughter's a daughter all the days of her life, but a son is a son till he gets him a wife." **1952** NTyre *Mouse* (NY) 81: Never a word was spoken as true as the old saying, a daughter's a daughter all the days of her life, a son's a son till he gets him a wife. **1952** JFleming *Man Who* (NY) 22: A son's a son till he gets a wife, a daughter's a daughter all your life! **1953** OAtkinson *Golden* (I) 254: A daughter's a daughter all her life, A son's a son till he gets him a wife. **1955** DGarnett *Flowers* (L) 234: A daughter's a daughter all your life. A son is a son till he gets him a wife. **1963** UCurtiss *Wasp* (NY DBC) 56: You know the old saw about losing a son and gaining a daughter-in-law. EAP S319: Son.

D25 The **Daughters** of the horse leech

1926 HHMunro *Toys* (L) 115: The daughters of the horseleech were not more persistent. **1928** MSummers *Vampire* (L) 230: The horseleech has two daughters crying give, give. **1973** AGilbert *Nice* (NY) 30: Like the horse-leecher's daughters of old, crying for more. EAP D19; Brunvand 32.

D26 As drunk as **David's** sow

1923 EMPoate *Behind Locked Doors* (NY) 33: As drunk as Davy's sow. **1937** JDCarr *Four*

False (NY) 191: Drunk as Davy's sow. **1954** RAldington *Pindorman* (L) 206: Drunk as David's sow. EAP D21. Cf. Sow *below*.

D27 Davy Jones's locker (*varied*)

1922 JJoyce *Ulysses* (NY 1934) 372: Davy Jones' locker. **1928** WJerrold *Bulls* (L) 103: Gone to Davy's locker. **1930** FDBurdett *Odyssey* (L) 234: Davy Jones' locker. **1932** BRoss *Tragedy of X* (NY) 111: Dark as Davy's locker. **1938** NJones *Hanging Lady* (NY) 8: Clapped into Davy Jones' locker. **1945** GBellairs *Calamity* (NY) 33: There stood old Burt, like a drowned sailor from Davy Jones's locker. **1953** MPHood *Silent* (NY) 166: You're jerked overboard to Davy Jones' locker. **1956** MPHood *Scarlet* (NY) 163: I thought Davy Jones had us for sure. **1957** RChurch *Golden* (NY) 111: The lowest dregs of Davy Jones's locker. **1960** NWilliams *Knaves* (NY) 88: He died in Davy Jones's locker. **1962** AChristie *Pale* (NY DBC) 4: Davy Jones, arriving from his locker. **1969** RGrayson *Voyage* (L) 207: I signed the bill with the signature Davy Jones and instructed him to take it away and put it in his locker. **1974** JWain *Samuel Johnson* (NY) 312: To keep his mind off Davy Jones's locker. EAP D22.

D28 As bright as (the) Dawn

1957 LFord *Girl* (NY) 76: She was bright as dawn. **1957** MShulman *Rally* (NY) 225: Maggie Larkin, bright as the dawn. Cf. Whiting *NC* 390: Beautiful.

D29 As fresh as (the) Dawn

1933 TSmith *Rain* (NY) 237: They seemed as fresh as the dawn. **1957** LFord *Girl* (NY) 71: Voice . . . fresh as dawn. Wilstach 161.

D30 Another Day, another dollar (*varied*)

1957 DErskine *Pink* (NY) 10: Another Day, Another Dollar. **1963** NBenchley *Catch* (NY) 134: Another day, another dollar. **1968** GBagby *Another Day—Another Death* (NY). **1969** DDoolittle *Only in Maine* (Barre, Mass.) 273: Another day, another dollar.

D31 Any Day in the week and twice on Sunday

1919 SLeacock *Frenzied* (Toronto 1971) 39: Any day in the week and twice on Sunday.

Tilley D67: Every day in the week one shower of rain and on Sunday twain.

D32 As beautiful as the Day (is long)

1923 JSFletcher *Markenmore* (NY) 50: Beautiful as the day. **1957** IAsimov *Earth* (NY) 165: As beautiful as the day is long. TW 92(1).

D33 As big as Day

1948 ESGardner *Lonely* (NY DBC) 49: There it was, big as day. **1959** ESchiddel *Devil* (NY) 260: Big as day.

D34 As bright as Day

1932 TCobb *Death* (L) 124: Bright as day. Whiting D33; TW 92(2); Brunvand 33(1); Taylor *Western Folklore* 17(1958) 14(1).

D35 As certain as the Day

1926 JLomas *Man with the Scar* (B) 264: That is as certain as the day. EAP D28. Cf. As certain as Daylight *below*.

D36 As clear as (the) Day (is long)

1920 ACrabb *Samuel* (NY) 48: Clear as day. **1933** MBurton *Death* (L) 65: Lit up the place as clear as day. **1956** *New Yorker* 10/6 42: George was as clear as the day is long. **1969** BCole *Funco* (NY) 27: She heard the death watch clickin' . . . clear as day. EAP D27; TW 92(4); Brunvand 33(2); Whiting D34. Cf. Daylight, Noonday *below*.

D37 As different as Day (night) and night (day)

1930 CWells *Doorstep* (NY) 10: As different as day and night. **1939** FWCrofts *Fatal* (L 1959) 181: As different as day and night. **1942** QMario *Murder Meets* (NY) 20: They were as different as day and night. **1951** DSDavis *Gentle* (NY 1959) 33: There was the difference of night and day in their voices. **1951** WCWilliams *Autobiography* (NY) 93: As different as night and day. **1959** *BHerald* 9/29 7: Two cars . . . as different as night and day. **1959** MSarton *I Knew* (NY) 107: As different as night and day. **1962** BRoss *Scrolls* (NY) 180: As unlike as day and night. **1964** LLafore *Devil's* (NY) 63: As different as night from day. EAP D44; Whiting *NC* 390.

D38 As fresh as the **Day**

1941 IMontgomery *Death Won* (NY) 118: She looked as fresh as the day. Taylor *Western Folklore* 17(1958) 15(2).

D39 As happy as the **Day** is long

1905 JBailey *Letters and Diaries* (L 1935) 98: As happy as the day is long; 293. **1922** JJoyce *Ulysses* (NY 1934) 340: Happy as the day was long. **1928** ABerkeley *Silk* (NY) 18: As happy as the day is long. **1936** DWheatley *They Found* (P) 289: As happy as the day is long. **1940** NMarsh *Death of a Peer* (B) 168: Gabriel's as happy as the day's long. **1951** EMarshall *Viking* (NY) 228: He seemed as happy as the day was long. **1958** *BangorDN* 7/8 12: Happy as the day is long. EAP D29; Brunvand 33(3).

D40 As honest as the **Day** (is long)

1927 HEWortham *Victorian Eton* (L 1956) 304: Honest and upright as the day. **1930** The Aresbys *Murder* (NY) 157: As honest as the day is long. **1937** MAllingham *Dancers* (NY) 335: Honest as the day. **1952** AWUpfield *Venom* (NY) 141: He was always honest as the day. **1957** *BangorDN* 3/14 31: I'm as honest as the day is long. **1959** *Life* 8/3 16: He is as honest as the day is long. **1960** JPudney *Home* (L) 64: As honest as the day. **1971** EPeters *Knocker* (NY) 147: Honest as the day. **1973** HDoldon *Dying* (P) 58: He's as honest as the day is long. EAP D30. Cf. As honest as Daylight *below*.

D41 As innocent as (the) **Day** (one was born)

1932 DLSayers *Have* (NY) 352: Innocent as day. **1939** MArmstrong *Murder in* (NY) 139: Innocent as the day. **1960** AGilbert *Out for* (NY 1965) 113: Innocent as the day she was born. **1962** LEgan *Against* (NY DBC) 25: All innocent as day. **1962** MStewart *Moon-* (NY 1965) 121: Everything as innocent as the day. Cf. As innocent as Daylight *below*.

D42 As merry as the **Day** is long

1919 HRHaggard *She and Allan* (NY 1921) 372: She was merry as the day is long. Tilley D57.

D43 As naked as the **Day** one was born (*varied*)

1912 ERBurroughs *Princess of Mars* (NY 1963) 19: Naked as at the moment of my birth. **1927** AHaynes *Crow's* (L) 288: Naked as he came into the world. **1937** PKeenagh *Mosquito* (L) 230: Jet black and as naked as the day they were born. **1938** AGlanville *Body* (L) 99: As naked as the day he was born. **1948** RFoley *No Tears* (NY DBC) 50: As naked as the day she was born. **1951** GBagby *Death* (NY) 19: As naked as the day he was born. **1957** MBGarrett *Horse* (University, Ala.) 202: Naked as God made them. **1957** JCheever *Wapshot* (NY) 246: As bare as the day they were born. **1964** PKDick *Martian* (NY) 12: As naked as the day they were born. **1971** PDennis *Paradise* (NY) 194: Naked as the day he was born. EAP B272; TW 38(1); Taylor *Western Folklore* 17(1958) 15(3).

D44 As open as the **Day**

1928 HFootner *Velvet* (NY) 61: A life as open as the day. **1949** RKing *Redoubled* (NY) 49: His purpose . . . was as open as the day. **1959** PCurtin *No Question* (NY) 63: We were as open as the day. TW 92(13); Brunvand 33(4). Cf. As open as Daylight, Sun *below*.

D45 As plain (obvious) as **Day** (dawn)

1917 JCLincoln *Extricating* (NY) 343: 'Twas plain as day. **1920** GBMcCutcheon *Anderson Crow* (NY) 100: That feller's voice, plain as day. **1933** GYoung *Devil's* (NY) 159: Plain as dawn. **1938** WEHayes *Black* (NY) 168: I heard . . . Stack's voice plain as day. **1941** AAFair *Spill* (NY) 106: You could hear . . . just as plain as day. **1951** ESGardner *Angry* (NY DBC) 151: A scream that Nora heard as plain as day. **1951** RStout *Curtains* (NY) 237: It was plain as day. **1970** RByrne *Memories* (NY) 115: Labelled as plain as day. **1974** DMarlowe *Somebody's* (NY) 53: It was as obvious as the day. **1976** EMcBain *So Long* (NY) 148: You can see him plain as day. EAP D32; Brunvand 33(5). Cf. As plain as Daylight *below*.

D46 As straight as **Day**

1933 PHunt *Murder* (NY) 30: It's all straight as day. Taylor *Prov. Comp.* 78.

D47 As sure as **Day** (comes, is long)

1932 ECaldwell *Tobacco* (NY) 4: Sure as day comes. **1938** JTFarrell *No Star* (NY) 102: I'm as sure as the day is long. **1949** JLane *Murder Spoils* (NY) 102: Sure as day. TW 92(15). Cf. Whiting D39: Sicker.

D48 As white as **Day**

1964 AStratton *Great Red* (NY) 49: White as day. Wilstach 470.

D49 As the **Day** lengthens the cold strengthens

1965 RDSymons *Silton* (NY 1975) 149: We say of old: "As the days lengthen the cold will strengthen." TW 93(27); Tilley D58.

D50 Be the **Day** never so long *etc.*

1922 JJoyce *Ulysses* (NY 1934) 51: All days make their end. **1935** JJConnington *In Whose* (L) 243: "Be the day weary or be the day long, At last it ringeth to evensong," quoted the Chief Constable. **1969** NHale *Life* (B) 120: Be the day short or be the day long, At length it cometh to evensong. Whiting D40; *Oxford* 169.

D51 The better the **Day**, the better the deed

1923 EMPoate *Behind Locked Doors* (NY) 309: The better the day, the better the deed. **1933** ISCobb *Murder* (I) 215: They say, the better the day the better the deed. **1938** JSStrange *Silent* (NY) 62: And the better the day, the better the deed [*refers to weather*]. **1945** EPhillpotts *They Were Seven* (NY) 55: The better the day, the better the deed. **1950** JCannan *Murder* (L 1958) 139: The better the day, the better the deed. **1952** SSmith *Crooked* (NY) 125: He recalled a saw that seemed to him doubly applicable: "Better the day, better the deed." **1963** MPHood *Sin* (NY) 37: Better the day, better the deed, old Gram Crocket used to say. **1965** HBevington *Charley* (NY) 167: The better the day, the better the deed. **1973** RRendell *Some* (NY) 128: The better the day, the better the deed. EAP D33.

D52 Come **Day**, go day (God send Sunday)

1931 JTully *Blood* (NY) 105: It's come day, go day with you kids. **1937** WETurpin *These Low* (NY) 269: Come day, go day. **1947** DBowers *Bells* (NY) 117: Ravenchurch, with its come-day-go-day respectabilities. **1965** ADavidson *Rork!* (NY) 57: Come day, go day, God send Sunday. **1969** APHannum *Look* (NY) 83: Just come day, go day. *Oxford* 134: Come; DARE i 735: Come day.

D53 A **Day** after the fair (*varied*)

1924 HCBailey *Mr. Fortune's Practice* (NY) 59: We are rather after the fair. **1928** JJConnington *Mystery* (B) 191: He was a day after the fair. **1928** NGordon *Professor's* (NY) 11: They'll be late for the fair this time. **1931** MSadleir *Edward* (B) 23: A little behind the fair. **1932** BGQuin *Murder* (NY) 184: You're a bit late for the fair. **1936** RAJWalling *Dirty Face* (L) 243: You were a day behind the fair. **1940** RAFreeman *Mr. Pulton* (NY) 206: It is the day after the fair. **1950** ERPunshon *So Many* (NY) 183: You're a day behind the fair. **1952** HHunter *Bengal* (NY) 56: You were way behind the fair. EAP D35; TW 93(32).

D54 In a **Day's** march (*varied*)

1932 JRhode *Dead Men* (L) 90: As honest [a man] as you'll find in a long day's journey. **1933** NBrady *Fair Murder* (L) 85: As smart and pretty a woman as you'd see in a day's march or a month of Sundays. **1935** CBarry *Death Overseas* (L) 212: As nice an old boy as you'd meet in a day's walk. **1971** DClark *Sick* (NY) 114: We're as big a pair of scalp hunters as you could hope to find in a day's march. Cf. Summer's day *below*.

D55 It will be a cold **Day** in hell (July, June) before something happens

1953 ABoucher *Best from* (NY) 72: It will be a cold day in July before we see him again. **1959** *BHerald* 3/13 19: It will be a snowy day in June when you become a judge. **1961** CDBurton *Long* (NY) 129: It'll be a cold day in hell before I call you again. **1968** FHerbert *Santaroga* (NY) 22: It'll be a cold day in hell when I ever come back. **1982** CMacLeod *Wrack* (NY) 101: It'll be a cold day in hell before [that].

D56 One never knows what a **Day** may bring forth

1938 MSaltmarsh *Clouded* (NY) 292: One never knows what a day may bring forth. EAP D46; Whiting D57.

D57 Other **Days**, other ways

1936 VMcHugh *Caleb* (NY) 140: Other days, other ways. **1956** AWilson *Anglo-Saxon* (L) 386: Other days, other stays, they say. But you'd not remember the whalebone, dear. **1969** RBlythe *Akenfield* (NY) 123: Other days, other ways.

D58 Praise not the **Day** before evening

1971 CAird *Late* (NY) 105: Praise not the day before evening. *Oxford* 643: Praise a fair.

D59 A red letter **Day**

1929 HAdams *Oddways* (P) 225: A red-letter day. **1932** JMarsh *Murder* (L) 66: On red-letter days such as this. **1938** JStagge *Murder by* (NY) 207: This is a red-letter day. **1954** EQueen *Glass* (B) 34: A red-letter day in my life. **1965** SVizinczey *In Praise* (L) 103: It was a red-letter Friday for me. **1972** ELathen *Murder* (NY) 90: One red-letter day. EAP D39.

D60 Sufficient unto the **Day** is the evil thereof (*varied*)

1922 JJoyce *Ulysses* (NY 1934) 137: Sufficient for the day is the newspaper thereof. **1928** RAFreeman *As a Thief* (L) 38: Sufficient for the day is the evil thereof. **1931** HJForman *Rembrant* (NY) 324: Sufficient unto the day is the evil thereof. **1963** FHoyle *Fifth* (L 1965) 86: Sufficient unto the day is the evil thereof. **1972** RLPike *Gremlin* (NY) 160: Sufficient unto the day is the lousing-up thereof. **1975** SJPerelman *Vinegar* (NY) 81: An old maxim, "Sufficient unto the day are the rhetorical questions thereof." EAP D40.

D61 To be all **Day** with someone

1921 T&MThorne *Sheridan* (NY) 179: It would be all day with you. TW 93(28); DARE i 38: All day.

D62 To call it a **Day** (night)

1920 ACrabb *Samuel* (NY) 222: Ready to call it a day. **1930** CFitzsimmons *Bainbridge* (NY) 213: We may as well call it a night. **1932** RJCasey *News* (I) 51: We'll call it a night. **1932** DFrome *Man* (NY) 119: Pinkerton decided to call it a day. **1938** DLTeilhet *Journey* (NY) 281: How's for calling it a day? **1940** JLBonney *Death by* (NY) 195: Shall we call it a night? **1941** HCBailey *Orphan Ann* (NY) 215: I'm calling it a day. **1956** NFitzgerald *Imagine* (L) 40: We'd better call it a day. **1958** GMitcham *Man from* (NY) 27: I'm calling it a night. **1962** ES Gardner *Blonde* (NY DBC) 50: We may as well call it a day. **1962** JJMcPhaul *Deadlines* (NY) 79: Unwilling to call it a night. **1968** JCFurnas *Lightfoot* (NY) 125: We'd better call it a day. **1972** JDCarr *Hungry* (NY) 43: The superintendent decided to call it a night. **1972** JAnderson *Alpha* (NY) 15: We'll call it a day. TW 92(17).

D63 To leave between two **Days** (*varied*)

1903 ADMcFaul *Ike Glidden* (B) 12: He left town 'tween two days. **1956** SPalmer *Unhappy* (NY 1957) 161: Olaf . . . packed his trunk and skipped between two days, as the saying goes. **1957** GWJohnson *Lunatic* (P) 87: He disappeared between two days. TW 92(18).

D64 To look for **Day** with a candle

1928 WCWilliams *Voyage* (NY) 214: Looking for day with a candle. EAP S525.

D65 To put aside for a rainy **Day** (*varied*)

1900 CFPidgin *Quincy A. Sawyer* (B) 23: Put aside for a rainy day. **1923** ABlackwood *Episodes* (L) 288: Against another rainy day. **1927** BAtkey *Man* (NY) 170: A little nest of rainy day eggs. **1927** AGilbert *Tragedy* (NY) 255: Letters . . . he'll stick to in case of the proverbial rainy day. **1937** WMartyn *Blue Ridge* (L) 43: A store of money for rainy days. **1941** FWCrofts *Circumstantial* (NY) 12: Against the proverbial rainy day. **1948** ESGardner *Lonely* (NY DBC) 10: Put by for a rainy day. **1957** *New Yorker* 6/1 26: None of your damned putting by against a rainy day. **1960** MColes *Concrete* (NY) 75: A little nest egg I have laid away for a rainy

day. **1965** LBiggle *All the Colors* (NY) 79:
The Rainy Day Pawn Shop. **1970** GEEvans
Where (L) 272: A bottle of beer he'd put by
for a rainy day. **1975** AHOlmstead *Threshold* (NY) 10: Folklore suggests unpleasant
associations for rainy days, making them
something one ought to save money for.
EAP D45; Brunvand 33(7).

D66   As certain as **Daylight**
1928 AEWMason *Prisoner* (NY) 86: Make
that certain as daylight. **1933** MBeckett
Murder (L) 242: Certain as daylight. Cf. As
certain . . . Day *above*.

D67   As clear as **Daylight**
1903 EChilders *Riddle* (NY 1940) 208: It
had been clear as daylight. **1924** L
O'Flaherty *Informer* (L) 35: As clear as daylight. **1933** CBush *Three Strange* (L) 245:
Seems clear as daylight. **1949** SJepson
Golden (NY) 21: It was as clear as the bright
daylight. **1957** *Punch* 3/13 361: It is as clear
as daylight. **1969** EBagnold *Autobiography*
(B) 194: It was as clear as daylight it was
he. EAP D47.

D68   As honest as **Daylight**
1931 WWJacobs *Snug* (NY) 530: You're as
honest as daylight. **1934** VParadise *Girl
Died* (NY) 68: Honest as daylight. **1957**
AArmstrong *Strange* (NY) 33: As honest as
daylight. Cf. As honest as the Day *above*.

D69   As innocent as **Daylight**
1968 PMoyes *Death* (NY) 183: The two little
girls were as innocent as daylight. Cf. As
innocent as Day *above*.

D70   As open as **Daylight**
1936 LRGribble *Riley* (L) 64: He was as
simple and open as daylight. **1939** AChristie *Sad Cypress* (NY 1958) 174: Open and
aboveboard as daylight. **1963** NFreeling
Question (NY 1965) 7: It was open as daylight [*an incident*]. Cf. As open as the Day
above, Sun *below*.

D71   As plain as **Daylight**; Daylight plain
1913 EDBiggers *Seven Keys* (I) 355: Plain
as daylight. **1930** CClausen *Gloyne* (NY)
116: As plain as daylight. **1932** AWynne
White Arrow (P) 308: It's as plain as daylight.

1937 PATaylor *Octagon* (NY) 34: It's all
plain as daylight. **1937** CBush *Eight O'Clock*
(NY) 193: His course of action was daylight
plain. Cf. As plain as Day *above*.

D72   To let (put) **Daylight** through someone
1922 JJoyce *Ulysses* (NY 1934) 322: Looking for him to let daylight through him.
1936 RAJWalling *Floating Foot* (NY) 234:
I've got a mind to put daylight through
you. **1968** WTenn *Wooden* (NY) 194: I let
daylight through you. EAP D49; TW 94(3).

D73   To scare (*etc.*) the living **Daylights** out
of someone
1931 JWVandercook *Forty* (NY) 101: I'm
going to kick the living daylights out of
him. **1931** CCoffin *Mare's Nest* (NY) 160:
You . . . scared the daylights out of me.
1938 EHuxley *Murder* (NY) 95: Beat the
daylights out of Sir Gordon. **1948** PCheyney *Dance* (NY DBC) 90: Ricaud beat the
living daylights out of me. **1953** KMKnight
Three (NY) 135: Scared the daylights out of
him. **1957** CThompson *Halfway* (NY) 210:
She was getting the living daylights screwed
out of her. **1959** JGill *Dead* (NY) 95: She
can beat the daylights out of me. **1963** EX
Ferrars *Doubly* (NY) 36: I'll knock the living
daylights out of you. **1965** GBagby *Mysteriouser* (NY) 178: I'll kick the living daylights
out of you. **1975** ELathen *By Hook* (NY)
208: Paul scared the daylights out of Harriet. EAP D48; Wentworth 141.

D74   As sober as a **Deacon**
1912 JCLincoln *Postmaster* (NY) 245: As sober as a deacon. **1913** JCLincoln *Mr. Pratt's
Patients* (NY) 97: He was sober as a deacon.
EAP D50.

D75   As steady as a **Deacon**
1930 CSHammock *Why Murder* (NY) 163:
He's steady as a deacon now. EAP D51.

D76   Enough to wake the **Dead**
1911 JCLincoln *Woman-Haters* (NY) 182:
Enough to wake the dead. **1927** VBridges
Girl (P) 220: 'E was snorin' fit to waike the
dead. **1930** LMeynell *Mystery* (P) 167: The
damned animal will wake the dead. **1937**
KRoberts *Northwest* (NY) 165: The noise we

made seemed loud enough to wake the dead. **1938** GStockwell *Embarrassed* (NY) 138: It was loud enough to raise the dead . . . I learned that silly phrase from my nurse. **1960** ADean *Bullet* (NY) 55: A . . . cat . . . purring loud enough to waken the dead. **1967** FSwinnerton *Sanctuary* (NY) 260: Your voice . . . it's enough to wake the dead. **1970** JBlackburn *Bury* (NY) 182: His notes sounded loud enough to wake the dead . . . the cliché. EAP D53.

D77 Let the **Dead** bury their (the, its) dead
1924 CWells *Furthest* (P) 306: Let the dead bury the dead. **1925** HHext *Monster* (NY) 30: The dead past can bury its dead. **1929** JGSarasin *Fleur* (NY) 7: Let the dead bury their dead. **1935** ECRLorac *Affair* (L) 184: It's a case of the dead burying their dead with a vengeance. **1939** MStuart *Dead Men* (L) 29: Let the dead bury their dead. Isn't that *Hamlet* or something? **1942** MColes *They Tell* (NY) 255: Let the dead bury its dead. **1952** ECRLorac *Dog* (NY) 22: The old admonition about the dead bury their dead is not without wisdom. **1960** DMDisney *Dark* (NY) 140: Letting the dead past bury its dead has certain merits. **1970** ELathen *Pick* (NY) 196: Better let the dead bury their dead, and the living keep their secrets. EAP D54; Brunvand 34(3), 106: Past.

D78 Not willing to be seen **Dead** in (with) something or other (*varied*)
1927 LBamburg *Beads* (NY) 320: An ugly string of beads "our Ada wouldn't be seen dead in." **1931** GPahlow *Murder* (NY) 169: I wouldn't be found dead in it. **1940** DHume *Five Aces* (L) 177: I wouldn't be seen dead here. **1961** PMoyes *Down Among* (NY) 145: I wouldn't be seen dead in your dinghy. **1963** NFreeling *Question* (NY 1965) 107: The admirable English phrase that expresses hatred, ridicule and contempt: "I wouldn't be found dead in a ditch with you." **1967** LJBraun *Cat* (NY) 25: The . . . Taits wouldn't be caught dead in a place called Happy View. **1973** JSymons *Plot* (NY) 22: It was not the kind of place she would have expected him to be seen dead

in, to use the old phrase. Partridge 743: Seen dead.

D79 Speak well of the **Dead** (*varied*)
1908 MRRinehart *Circular Staircase* (NY 1947) 98: De mortuis, what's the rest of it? **1920** GBMcCutcheon *Anderson Crow* (NY) 352: Far be it from me . . . to speak ill of either the living or the dead. **1922** JJoyce *Ulysses* (NY 1934) 107: Daren't joke about the dead for two years at least. *De mortuis nil nisi prius.* **1927** HAdams *Queen's* (P) 95: You mean the *de mortuis* business. It's an old-fashioned maxim. **1928** CWells *Crime* (P) 95: It's too bad for me to knock a man who is dead. **1930** EFBenson *As We Were* (NY) 200: There comes a point when "*de mortuis nil nisi bonum*" merges into "*de mortuis nil nisi bunkum.*" **1930** JATyson *Rhododendron* (NY) 207: An old adage says "Of the dead all things are good." **1932** WMartyn *Trent* (NY) 219: That stupidest of sayings: "Concerning the dead speak no evil." **1933** ABCox *Jumping* (L) 143: *De mortuis nil nisi verum.* **1934** HSKeeler *Riddle* (NY) 190: *De mortuis nil nisi bones.* **1935** MKennedy *Poison* (L) 152: *De mortuis nil nisi malum.* **1937** MBurton *Murder* (L) 203: Isn't there some proverb or other about not speaking evil of the dead? **1940** HRutland *Poison Fly* (NY) 64: You know the old tag, "De mortuis, nil nisi bonum," vz "Don't call the dead names, they make good bones." **1941** CEVulliamy *Ghost History* (L) 225: *De Mortuis nil nisi Veritas.* **1944** ECrispin *Gilded Fly* (NY 1970) 109: *De mortuis nil nisi malum.* **1944** WBThomas *Way of a Countryman* (L) 167: The maxim *De Mortuis nil nisi Bunkum.* **1946** CBust *Second Chance* (L) 29: Concerning the dead nothing but good. **1951** HMcCloy *Through* (L 1961) 176: So was born that fear of the ghost that made Romans speak nothing but good of the dead. **1956** PMiller *Raven* (NY) 269: How foreign to his nature was the injunction of *de mortuis.* **1959** HCarmichael *Marked* (NY) 108: The old nonsense that one shouldn't speak ill of the dead. **1959** NFitzgerald *Midsummer* (NY) 178: That *de mortuis nil nisi bonum* nonsense. **1959** FLockridge *Murder Is* (P) 73: You're one of those speak-no-ill-of-the-dead people. **1963** PDunne *Mr.*

Dooley (B) 119: The old maxim *de mortuis nil nisi bonum* has of late been translated "about the dead say nothing but evil." **1968** JRoffman *Daze* (NY) 51: The old adage, never speak ill of the dead. **1971** RMStern *You Don't* (NY) 23: The admonition to say nothing but good of the dead. **1972** PWarner *Loose* (NY) 100: I don't like to say nothing about the dead that's bad. **1981** RDavies *Rebel* (NY) 322: *De mortuis nil nisi hokum.* EAP D55.

D80 To sleep like the **Dead**

1932 HFootner *Dead Man's* (NY) 10: Sleeps like the dead. **1938** GDHCole *Mrs. Warrender's* (L) 330: He slept like the dead. **1959** DMDisney *Did She Fall* (NY) 61: Sleeping like the dead. **1960** HInnes *Doomed* (NY) 295: I slept like the dead. **1966** PMHubbard *Holm* (NY DBC) 103: I slept like the dead. **1970** EQueen *Last* (NY) 44: Sleep like the dead. **1976** JSScott *Poor* (NY) 150: Slept like the dead. Taylor *Western Folklore* 17(1958) 15.

D81 None so **Deaf** as those who will not hear (*varied*)

1934 HAdams *Mystery* (P) 90: None so deaf as those who won't hear. **1938** MTeagle *Murders* (NY) 148: There are none so deaf as those who stop up their ears with impatience. **1952** AWilson *Hemlock* (L) 39: There's none so deaf as do not choose to hear. EAP D56.

D82 A "**Dear John**" letter

1956 GHCoxe *Man on* (NY 1958) 51: He had been familiar with the so-called "Dear John" letters that had come to acquaintances in Korea. **1958** HAlpert *Summer* (NY) 16: This is my big night. My "Dear John" night. Dear John, I have something very important to tell you. You know what I mean. **1959** CCornish *Dead* (NY) 106: He got a "Dear John" and that was that. End of engagement. **1964** JPhilips *Laughter* (NY DBC) 10: He had received a "Dear John" letter from Elizabeth, telling him that she was married. **1975** JFoxx *Dead Run* (I) 26: I had been Dear-Johned from my home in San Francisco. Wentworth 143.

D83 As bitter as **Death**

1930 AGilbert *Night* (NY) 242: Bitter as death. EAP D58.

D84 As black as **Death**

1936 VWBrooks *Flowering* (NY 1946) 93: An eye as black as death. EAP D59.

D85 As cold as **Death**

1928 ESnell *Kontrol* (P) 220: Hands as cold as death. **1937** GBarnett *I Know* (L) 7: Cold as death. **1953** PIWellman *Female* (NY) 68: Her mind was cold as death. **1969** BCole *Funco* (NY) 85: She was cold, cold as death. EAP D62; Brunvand 34(1).

D86 As cruel as **Death**

1956 AGilbert *Riddle* (NY) 60: The facts were as cruel as death. EAP D63.

D87 As dumb as **Death**

1938 HCBailey *This is Mr. Fortune* (L) 78: They're dumb as death. TW 95(6).

D88 As grim as **Death**

1956 AGilbert *Riddle* (NY) 176: With a courtesy as grim as death. Whiting *NC* 391(3); Taylor *Western Folklore* 17(1958) 15(2).

D89 As inevitable as **Death**

1952 WClapham *Night* (L) 251: It was inevitable as death. **1957** JKerr *Please* (NY) 94: As inevitable as death and taxes. EAP D65; TW 95(8).

D90 As pale as **Death**

1911 CKSteele *Mansion* (NY) 119: A face as pale as death itself. **1919** LMerrick *Chain* (L) 163: Pale as death. **1923** EWallace *Clue* (B) 185: As pale as death. **1933** EBBlack *Ravenelle* (NY) 110: His face was pale as death. **1958** *New Yorker* 1/4 53: Pale as death. **1964** SBecker *Covenant* (NY) 15: Pale as death. **1970** AKarmel *My Revolution* (NY) 307: She . . . turns pale as death. EAP D66. Cf. Brunvand 34(2).

D91 As quiet as **Death**

1923 LThayer *Sinister* (NY) 34: As quiet as death. **1974** HCrews *Gypsy's* (NY) 148: The . . . steps were quiet as death. Wilstach 309.

D92 As sick as **Death**

1935 NBlake *Question* (L) 281: He looked sick as death. **1939** GDHCole *Off with* (NY) 154: Feeling sick as death. EAP D68.

D93 As silent(ly) as **Death**

1932 THWhite *Darkness* (L) 176: He came . . . as silently as death. **1954** WGolding *Lord* (L) 60: The crowd was as silent as death. EAP D69.

D94 As still as **Death**; Death-still

1922 DLindsay *Haunted Woman* (L 1964) 25: As still as death. **1928** FDaingerfield *That Gay* (NY) 28: The house lay still as death. **1939** DDean *Emerald* (NY) 88: As still as death—stiller than death, in fact. **1960** PAnderson *Guardians* (NY) 65: Everard stood death-still. **1961** AMorton *Double* (NY) 102: He looked as still as death. EAP D71; TW 95(17); Brunvand 34(7); Taylor *Western Folklore* 17(1958) 15(4).

D95 As strong as **Death**

1970 RCowper *Twilight* (NY) 20: As strong as death. Whiting D84; Whiting *NC* 392(12).

D96 As sure as **Death** (and taxes) (*varied*)

1904 JCLincoln *Cap'n Eri* (NY) 61: Sure as death. **1919** KHoward *Peculiar* (NY) 21: As certain as death. **1928** JMBall *Sack-'Em-Up* (L) xxi: Death [and] taxes . . . are regarded by most people as facts beyond dispute. **1928** RCullum *Mystery* (NY) 106: Just as sure as death. **1929** VLoder *Between* (NY) 218: There is nothing sure in the world but death and taxes. **1933** EQueen *American* (NY) 116: There's nothing certain but death and taxes, they say. **1936** EPhillpotts *Close Call* (L) 95: Sure as death. **1937** TStevenson *Nudist* (L) 121: Nothing lasts but death and taxes. **1952** CMackenzie *Rival* (L) 14: Sure as death. **1955** PWentworth *Gazebo* (L 1965) 188: As sure as death he'll kill me. **1957** *BangorDN* 3/29 14: The old cliché: "There are only two safe bets, namely Death and Taxes." **1957** LBeam *Maine* (NY) 16: Cows, death, and taxes conquered all. **1958** TEDikty *Six from* (NY) 82: Nothing sure but Death and Taxes. **1961** RAKnowlton *Court* (L 1967) 211: Nothing is certain save death and taxes. **1963**

TBDewey *Sad Song* (NY DBC) 25: Only two things are certain in life . . . that's an old cliché . . . death and taxes. **1972** SAngus *Arson* (NY) 34: Jay is like death and taxes. A sure thing. **1977** VCanning *Doomsday* (NY) 179: Nothing more certain than death and taxes. **1978** MKWren *Nothing's Certain but Death* (NY). TW 95(18); Taylor *Western Folklore* 17(1958) 15(5); Brunvand 34(8). Cf. Taxes *below*.

D97 As tired as **Death**

1936 NBlake *Thou Shell* (L) 140: He felt tired as death. TW 95(19).

D98 As white as **Death**

1915 JBuchan *Thirty-Nine* (NY) 70: White as death. **1919** LMerrick *Chain* (L) 269: As white as death. **1928** ESnell *Kontrol* (P) 170: His face . . . was as white as death. **1952** TShy *Terror* (L) 82: His face was as white as death. **1961** JPhilips *Murder* (NY DBC) 61: Her face was white as death. TW 95(21).

D99 Better **Death** than dishonor

1931 PWylie *Murderer* (NY) 92: Life, contrary to the adage, is usually found to be dearer than honor in a crisis. **1932** CDawes *Lawless* (L) 49: Better death than dishonour. **1955** SNGhose *Flame* (L) 224: Death is better than disgrace. **1965** HWaugh *End* (NY) 143: Death before dishonor is our motto. EAP D73.

D100 **Death** pays all debts (*varied*)

1920 N&JOakley *Clevedon* (P) 280: Death ends all stories. **1927** VWilliams *Eye* (B) 304: Death wipes the slate clean. **1928** CDane *Enter* (L) 125: Death pays for all. **1929** JJConnington *Grim* (B) 55: Death settles most scores. **1930** JSFletcher *South Foreland* (NY) 146: Death . . . wipes out all scores—old saying. **1936** AGilbert *Courtier* (L) 188: Death absolves from vows. **1954** RStout *Three* (NY) 101: He that dies pays all debts. **1957** THWhite *Master* (L) 249: He that dies pays all debts. **1959** EMarshall *Pagan* (NY) 9: Death pays all debts. **1963** CKeith *Rich* (NY) 135: I figure his death cancels all debts. **1965** FPohl *Plague* (NY) 69: No debts are owed to the dead. EAP D75; *Oxford* 174.

D101 **Death** takes all (*very varied*)

1926 SQuinn *Phantom* (Sauk City, Wisc. 1966) 27: The axiom that death makes all men equal. **1935** BFlynn *Edge* (L) 21: Death's no respecter of persons. **1955** FCrane *Death* (NY) 125: Death comes to all. **1965** HActon *Old Lamps* (L) 286: Death is the grand leveller, as my old dad used to say. **1972** WJBurley *Guilt* (NY) 7: Death is no respecter of persons. **1972** ELathen *Murder* (NY) 182: Death may be the great leveller—but only in the better world beyond. EAP D79.

D102 To be at **Death's** door (*varied*)

1922 JJoyce *Ulysses* (NY 1934) 111: Near death's door. **1924** VLWhitechurch *Templeton* (NY) 283: [He] was at death's door. **1934** DFrome *Arsenic* (L) 83: Her mother was at death's door. **1937** GDejean *Who Killed* (L) 35: He was at death's door. **1941** CCoffin *Mare's Nest* (NY) 19: You were at death's door. **1951** JCreasey *Puzzle* (L 1962) 28: He's at death's door. **1959** GAshe *Pack* (NY) 142: You were at death's door. **1960** LHolton *Pact* (NY DBC) 117: You are at the door of death. **1965** Doctor X *Intern* (NY) 87: At death's doorstep. **1971** EPeters *The Knocker on Death's Door* (NY). **1977** EXFerrars *Pretty* (NY) 65: At death's door. EAP D82.

D103 To be in at the **Death**

1938 EQueen *Devil* (NY) 51: You're in at the death. NED Death 15.

D104 To be pecked to **Death** by goslings

1969 JTrahey *Pecked to Death by Goslings* (Englewood Cliffs, NJ). *Oxford* 618: Pecked; Tilley D156.

D105 To feel (look) like **Death** warmed up (over)

1933 JVTurner *Amos* (L) 91: I still feel like death warmed up. **1941** NMarsh *Death and the* (B) 40: I look like death warmed up. **1947** NMarsh *Final* (B) 84: It feels . . . like death warmed up. **1953** RBissell *7½ Cents* (B) 125: You look like death warmed over. **1957** VWMason *Gracious* (NY) 266: Feel like death warmed over. **1958** JYork *My Brother's* (NY DBC) 72: She looked like death warmed up. **1963** MGEberhart *Run* (NY) 141: You looked like death warmed over. **1964** JJMarric *Gideon's Vote* (NY) 21: He's been looking like death warmed up. **1965** JBrooks *Smith* (L) 37: I am Death, warmed up, as they say. **1968** HWaugh *"30"* (NY) 138: He looked, to use the old high school cliché, "like death warmed over." **1971** JMacNab *Education* (NY) 96: He looked like death not even warmed over. **1981** PDeVries *Sauce* (B) 107: He looked like death warmed over.

D106 To hang on (*etc.*) like grim **Death** (*varied*)

1913 JCLincoln *Mr. Pratt's Patients* (NY) 307: I hung onto it like grim death. **1920** GBMcCutcheon *Anderson Crow* (NY) 250: I hung on like grim death. **1927** JSFletcher *Lynne* (L) 175: They'll stick to it like grim death. **1928** DLSayers *Unpleasantness* (NY) 130: Freeze on to him like grim death. **1929** POldfield *Alchemy* (L) 60: He clung on . . . like grim death. **1932** DLSayers *Have* (NY) 238: She'll hang on like grim death. **1932** DSharp *Code-Letter* (B) 157: Holding on like grim death. **1935** VWMason *Budapest* (NY) 122: I'll stick to Br'er Crowell like death to a dead nigger. **1938** VWMason *Cairo* (NY) 147: He stuck to his word like death to a dead nigger. **1950** RFoley *Hundredth* (NY) 7: You stuck to your diet like grim death. **1957** HPBeck *Folklore of Maine* (P) 242: Cling to her perch like grim death. **1961** CBeaton *Wandering* (L) 98: I hung on for grim death. **1963** MPHood *Sin* (NY) 39: An old codger clings to life like death to a dead nigger. **1969** JCreasey *Baron* (NY) 130: We must hold on to her like grim death. **1975** DNott *List* (NY) 150: Hanging like grim death onto the single foot. EAP D86; TW 96(25–7).

D107 To pay the **Debt** to Nature

1927 HEWortham *Victorian Eton* (L 1956) 197: She paid the universal debt to Nature. EAP D88; TW 96.

D108 To clear the **Decks**

1930 CBush *Dead Man* (NY) 75: We're just getting the decks cleared. **1941** GMitchell *Hangman's* (L) 66: Cleared the decks for action. EAP D90.

D109 Deeds speak louder than words (*varied*)

1915 JFerguson *Stealthy* (L 1935) 29: The English say, "deeds not words"; 216. **1933** HAdams *Strange Murder* (P) 279: Deeds speak louder than words. **1939** MStuart *Dead Men* (L) 168: Deeds speak louder than words. **1948** CLLeonard *Fourth* (NY) 37: Something about deeds being better than words. **1951** HSaunders *Sleeping* (L) 130: Deeds, as you are saying in England, speak louder than words. **1955** MInnes *Man from* (L) 72: Deeds sometimes speak louder than words. **1962** DGillon *Unsleep* (NY) 100: Deeds count more than words. EAP D92, 95; *Oxford*, 175, 187. Cf. Words and deeds *below.*

D110 As swift as a **Deer**

1962 LDRich *Natural* (NY) 75: Swift as a deer. EAP D96.

D111 To run like a **Deer** (doe, stag)

1929 EWallace *Ringer* (NY) 216: Lesley ran like a deer. **1933** LWMeynell *Paid* (L) 211: I had to run like a stag. **1935** DGardiner *Translantic* (L) 203: She . . . ran like a deer. **1939** EQueen *Dragon's* (NY) 89: She ran like a doe. **1940** LTreat *B as in Banshee* (NY) 217: I ran like a deer. **1954** JRMacdonald *Find* (NY) 33: The broads run like a deer. **1964** HPentecost *Shape* (NY DBC) 145: I saw Juliet running like a deer. **1973** JDMacDonald *Turquoise* (P) 233: Ran like a deer. EAP D99; Brunvand 35(2).

D112 Delays are dangerous

1922 JSFletcher *Rayner-Slade* (NY) 170: Isn't delay dangerous? **1926** HAdams *Crooked* (L) 214: Delays are dangerous. **1932** BFlynn *Murder* (P) 263: Delays are proverbially dangerous. **1939** EPaul *Mysterious* (NY 1962) 102: Delay is fatal. **1941** IMontgomery *Death Won* (NY) 56: Delay was dangerous. **1957** *Republican Journal* 10/31 11: Delays are dangerous. **1959** WHMurray *Appointment* (NY) 116: Delay is too dangerous. **1960** JJMarric *Gideon's Fire* (NY) 80: I do not believe there is any danger in delay. **1964** JStoye *Siege* (L) 93: These delays became dangerous. EAP D101; TW 96–7; Brunvand 35.

D113 There is something rotten in **Denmark**

1934 LFord *Strangled* (NY) 130: There's something rotten in Denmark. **1941** EL Fetta *Dressed* (NY) 242: There's something screwy in Denmark. **1969** CMatthews *Dive* (LA) 111: Something's rotten in Denmark. **1971** NMarsh *When* (B) 122: Something is rotten in the state of Denmark. EAP D104; Brunvand 35.

D114 The **Descent** to Avernus is easy

1932 RAFreeman *When Rogues* (L) 12: The descent to Avernus is proverbially easy. **1934** RCWoodthorpe *Death Wears* (NY) 219: We will disprove the proverb about the descent of Avernus. *Oxford* 177.

D115 As busy as the **Devil** in a gale of wind (*varied*)

1927 EMillay *Letters* ed. ARMacdougall (NY 1952) 219: We are, as my mother says, busier than the devil in a gale of wind. **1929** AGilbert *Death* (NY) 290: At home [*in Ireland*] when we have a storm like this we say the devil's dancing on the roof trying to find some cranny where he can come in. TW 97(2).

D116 As dark as the **Devil's** dishrag

1944 LLariar *Man . . . Lumpy Nose* (NY) 85: It was dark as a devil's dishrag in that place. Cf. EAP D108, 109; Whiting *Devil* 211.

D117 As if the **Devil** were after one (*varied*)

1930 CBarry *Avenging* (NY) 177: The perfect stranger scuttled off as if the devil was at his heels. **1934** ESHolding *Death Wish* (NY) 37: He walked as if the devil were after him. **1939** MArmstrong *Murder in* (NY) 92: Made for the woods like Ole Nick was after him. **1940** HReilly *Murder in* (NY) 183: He dashed out . . . as if the devil were after him. **1947** JDCarr *Sleeping* (NY) 9: I hurried away . . . as though the devil were after me. **1951** MColes *Now* (NY) 204: A big car came down like the devil was after it. **1954** EWalter *Untidy* (P) 155: Go on, hurry up, the devil's after you with his long-handled spoon. **1971** JFraser *Death* (NY) 19: He came in here like the devil was chasing 'im. **1972** RRendell *No More* (NY)

98: She scooted off like all the devils in hell were after her. **1974** LBlanch *Pavilions* (NY) The coffin maker, planing and hammering as if the devil were after him. EAP D112; Taylor *Western Folklore* 17(1958) 15(2).

D118 Better the **Devil** you know than the devil you don't (*varied*)

1934 KLivingston *Dodd* (NY) 19: You prefer the devil you know to the devil you don't know. **1957** *New Yorker* 11/23 198: A preference for the devil they knew to the devil they didn't know. **1957** DJEnright *Heaven* (L) 181: A preference for the devil he didn't know. **1961** MColes *Search* (NY DBC) 6: Better the devil we don't know than the one we do. **1962** AMoorehead *Blue Nile* (NY) 99: The Mamelukes were the devil they knew, and Bonaparte was not. **1968** PHJohnson *Survival of the Fittest* (NY) 23: Better the devil he did know than the devil he didn't. **1970** CDrummond *Stab* (NY) 64: They might choose the devil they knew something of. **1971** EXFerrars *Stranger* (NY) 140: Better the devil you don't know than the devil you do. **1972** DDevine *Three* (NY) 16: Better the evil I knew than the evil I didn't. Whiting *Devil* 210(23); *Oxford* 55: Better.

D119 Between the **Devil** and the deep blue sea (*varied*)

1912 ERBurroughs *Gods of Mars* (NY 1963) 31: We are between the devil and the deep sca. **1919** KHoward *Peculiar* (NY) 143: The "devil" being Harriet and myself the "deep sea." **1922** JJoyce *Ulysses* (NY 1934) 185: Between the Saxon smile and the yankee yawp. The devil and the deep sea. **1930** RScarlett *Beacon Hill* (NY) 91: She preferred the devil to the deep blue sea. **1939** EFerber *Peculiar* (NY 1960) 245: Floundering thus between the devil of the short story and the deep sea of the unwritten novel. **1941** TDowning *Lazy Lawrence* (NY) 178: I'm between the devil and the deep. **1949** CDickson *Graveyard* (NY) 85: This poor devil . . . was between Satan and deep water. **1950** IFletcher *Bennett's* (I) 31: You've put him between the devil and the deep sea. **1956** HKubly *Easter* (NY) 188:

Life here is lived literally between the devil and the deep blue sea. **1958** *BHerald* 5/22 39: You're between the devil and the deep blue sky. **1960** RWilson *30 Day* (NY) 84: Between the devil and the deep blue tax collector. **1964** JPope-Hennessy *Verandah* (NY) 122: She was between the devil and the deep blue Sulu Sea. **1974** WCAnderson *Damp* (NY) 92: You are between the devil and the deep blue sea. **1978** EXFerrars *Murders Anonymous* (NY) 124: Between the devil and the deep. Whiting *Devil* 203(2); *Oxford* 179.

D120 The blue **Devils**

1934 VLoder *Two Dead* (L) 85: The blue devils got on her back. **1970** AWRaitt *Prosper* (L) 326: He kept the blue devils at bay. EAP D118; Whiting *Devil* 218(63); Brunvand 36(9).

D121 The **Devil** among the tailors

1961 CWillock *Death* (L 1963) 130: It [*a bomb*] exploded like a devil among the tailors. *Oxford* 179.

D122 The **Devil** and his dam

1955 MBorowsky *Queen's* (NY) 270: The Devil and his dam will not have them. EAP D119.

D123 The **Devil** can quote Scripture (*varied*)

1928 RGore-Browne *In Search* (NY) 60: The painter, like other disreputable characters, could quote Scripture. **1930** A Christie *Murder* (NY) 3: The example of the devil in quoting Scripture for his own ends. **1936** HCBailey *Clue* (L) 109: The devil . . . Using Scripture for his purpose. **1936** ECRLorac *Death* (L) 21: Like the devil on another occasion, you quoted Holy Writ. **1938** FDGrierson *Cabaret* (L) 172: The Devil can quote texts for his own ends. **1941** GMitchell *Hangman's* (L) 196: The devil . . . can cite Scripture for his purpose—especially . . . if a fairly free translation be allowed. **1948** EQueen *Ten* (B) 176: The Devil can quote Scripture to his purpose. **1957** *BHerald* 3/12 29: The devil can quote scripture for his purposes. **1958** EQueen *Finishing* (NY) 125: He remembered the Devil's gift for crooking Scripture. **1963** RNathan *Devil* (NY) 193: The Devil can quote Scriptures for his own purposes. **1970** JBlackburn *Bury* (NY) 17: The Devil can quote scripture to his own ends. EAP D120.

D124 The **Devil** (Satan) finds work for idle hands (*varied*)

1912 JCLincoln *Postmaster* (NY) 3: Satan finds some mischief still for idle hands. **1917** JCLincoln *Extricating* (NY) 30: The Old Harry finds some mischief still for lazy folks to run afoul of, as the Good Book says. **1928** EWallace *Sinister* (NY) 237: "Satan finds work for idle hands," as the Good Book says. **1935** CHaldane *Melusine* (L) 215: The Devil finds work for idle hands to do. **1936** VMcHugh *Caleb* (NY) 114: Devil finds work for idle hands. **1946** RPowell *Shoot If* (NY) 1: Arabella seems to think that the devil finds work for idle feet to do. **1948** IFletcher *Roanoke* (I) 187: The Devil dwells in idleness. **1957** LBeam *Maine* (NY) 90: Satan finds mischief for idle hands to do. **1959** MRuss *Half Moon* (NY) 48: The devil finds work for idle hands. **1964** MColes *Knife* (NY DBC) 46: The mischief Satan provided for idle hands. **1964** LLafore *Devil's* (NY) 68: The devil finds work for idle fingers. **1972** BLillie *Every* (NY) 242: The devil finds work for idle hands. **1976** LEgan *Scenes* (NY) 59: They do say, Satan finds work for idle hands. EAP D121; TW 318(1): Satan. Cf. Idleness *below*.

D125 The **Devil** hates holy water (*varied*)

1924 LO'Flaherty *Thy Neighbour's Wife* (L) 214: He hated England as the Devil is supposed to hate holy water. **1925** JGBrandon *Bond* (L) 61: He hated a crook . . . "as th' devil hates holy water." **1927** JTully *Circus* (NY) 178: You got to run like the Devil away from Holy Water. **1932** GCollins *Channel* (L) 252: It was a case of devil and holy water. **1934** RJCasey *Third Owl* (I) 243: She hates him like the devil does holy water. **1949** JSStrange *Unquiet* (NY) 32: He hated desk work . . . as the devil hates virtue. **1968** KDetzer *Myself* (NY) 18: Grandfather . . . hated the Devil and holy

water with equal vigor. EAP D122. Cf. To hate as a Cat *above*.

D126 The **Devil** is a gentleman

1926 BHecht *Count* (NY) 253: The devil was a honeyed and gallant gentleman. **1930** JFarnol *Over the Hills* (B) 204: It is the saying that the devil he is a gentleman. **1930** FDGrierson *Mysterious* (L) 64: The Devil is reputed to be a very polished gentleman. **1951** JCollier *Fancies* (NY) 150: I thought that you [*the Devil*] . . . were supposed to be a gentleman. **1951** HSaunders *Sleeping* (L) 87: The Prince of Darkness is a gentleman. **1957** *TLS* 10/18 622: The Prince of Darkness, however much a gentleman. TW 98(19).

D127 The **Devil** is beating his wife

1956 *New Yorker* 8/18 30: In Colorado, almost every afternoon in the summertime, the Devil briefly beats his wife; the skies never darken, but there is a short, prodigal fall of crystal rain. *Oxford* 663: Rains.

D128 The **Devil** is dead

1936 LThayer *Dead End* (NY) 247: You know the old saying, "The devil is dead." It's true in a sense. **1960** JBWest *Taste* (NY) 19: As quick as God could get the news the devil died. Whiting D187; *Oxford* 181.

D129 The **Devil** is not as black as he is painted (*varied*)

1919 HRHaggard *She and Allan* (NY 1921) 180: The devil is not so black as he is painted. **1924** WBMFerguson *Black* (NY) 197: They can't believe he's really so bad as he's painted. **1924** ADHSmith *Porto* (NY) 77: All is not so black as is painted. **1928** SHuddleston *Paris Salons* (NY) 158: If we are willing to admit that the devil is as black as he is painted. **1935** FYeager *Jungle* (NY) 1: The jungle wasn't so black as it had been painted. **1940** RPenny *Sweet Poison* (L) 223: He is not as bad as you painted him [*not the devil*]. **1953** AChristie *Pocket* (NY) 169: You don't believe the devil was as black as he was painted? **1956** *Punch* 7/18 74: Stalin wasn't as black as he's painted. **1958** HTreece *Red Queen* (L) 14: Rome was not as black as she had been painted. **1974** KAmis *Ending* (NY) 36: People not being so black as they were painted. EAP D126; TW 99(22).

D130   The **Devil** is the father of lies
1934 HAdams *Body* (L) 138: If the devil is the father of lies, who is the mother? EAP D127.

D131   The **Devil** looks after his own (*varied*)
1910 EPhillpotts *Tales* (NY) 177: The devil looks after his own, we all know. **1928** CBarry *Corpse* (NY) 237: The devil tykes care of his own, we all know. **1928** VL Whitechurch *Shot* (NY) 297: They say the devil protects his own. **1933** EBBlack *Ravenelle* (NY) 85: The devil looks after his own. **1938** VSwain *Hollow Skin* (NY) 17: The devil protects his own. **1940** HAdams *Chief Witness* (L) 64: The devil looks after his own. **1945** ADerleth *In Re* (Sauk City, Wisc.) 176: It is said the devil protects his own. **1955** MColes *Man in* (NY) 183: It seems that the devil fights for his own, as we [*English*] say. **1958** *New Yorker* 8/2 30: The devil looks after his own. **1960** PCurtis *The Devil's Own* (NY). **1960** RWatters *Murder* (Dublin) 268: The black devil always takes care of his own. **1961** JBingham *Night's* (L 1965) 177: The old trite remark about the Devil looking after his own. **1966** JGaskell *City* (NY 1968) 102: The mark was set on us to show the devil his own. **1967** MDolbier *Benjy* (NY) 3: The devil knows his own. **1969** AGilbert *Mr. Crook* (NY DBC) 14: The Lord looks after his own. **1969** GMaxwell *Raven* (NY) 21: They say the devil looks after his own. **1970** PDickinson *Sinful* (NY) 102: The Lord looks after his own. **1970** RRendell *Best Man* (NY) 109: They say the devil looks after his own. EAP D125; Brunvand 36(13).

D132   **Devil**-may-care
1925 CAndrews *Butterfly* (NY) 25: A . . . jovial devil-may-care sort of chap; 155. **1930** ECRLorac *Murder* (L) 276: His own devil-may-care fashion. **1944** MBramhall *Murder Solves* (NY) 45: A devil-may-care insouciance. **1965** JDavey *Killing* (L) 181: A devil-may-care kind of hat. **1968** RPer-

rott *Aristocrats* (NY) 173: Exponents of devil-may-care. TW 101(40).

D133   The **Devil** rebukes sin
1958 CCockburn *Crossing* (L) 99: This seemed to be indeed the Devil rebuking sin. *Oxford* 699: Satan.

D134   A **Devil's** advocate
1926 AMarshall *Mote* (NY) 278: Devil's Advocate. **1940** LFord *Old Lover's* (NY) 181: You're going to be devil's advocate. **1944** RAJWalling *Corpse Without* (NY) 13: I'm playing devil's advocate. **1960** IWallace *Chapman* (NY 1961) 76: He's our Devil's Advocate. **1969** SAngus *Death* (L) 137: Nobody needs to know the whole truth more than the devil's advocate. **1970** OFriedrich *Decline* (NY) 118: The devil's advocate. **1974** RSaltonstall *Maine* (B) 101: I was playing the devil's advocate. Whiting *Devil* 219(76); NED Devil 25b.

D135   The **Devil's** own luck (*bad*)
1923 DCScott *Witching* (Toronto) 162: The devil's luck. **1925** HAdams *By Order* (L) 218: The Devil's own luck. **1928** ESnell *Blue* (P) 156: That fellow had the luck of the deuce. **1938** KMKnight *Acts* (NY) 19: The devil's own luck. **1948** FWCrofts *Silence* (NY) 13: I had the devil's own luck. Whiting *Devil* 204(3b).

D136   The **Devil's** own luck (*good*)
1919 LTracy *Bartlett* (NY) 283: The fiend's luck. **1925** FBeeding *Seven* (B) 296: By the luck of the devil. **1938** ECRLorac *Devil* (L) 77: He had the devil's own luck. **1956** NFitsgerald *Imagine* (L) 186: [He] has the devil's own luck. **1958** RHutton *Of Those* (L) 25: The luck of the Devil. **1961** NBlake *Worm* (L) 213: James had the luck of the devil. **1963** HMacInnes *Venetian* (NY) 132: "You have the devil's own luck." "The trouble with the devil's luck is that it doesn't last long." **1966** JDosPassos *Best* (NY) 42: The devil's own good luck. **1972** DLees *Rainbow* (NY) 188: I had the luck of the devil. **1975** HCarmichael *Too Late* (NY) 91: You might call it the luck of the devil . . . to coin a phrase. **1977** VCanning *Doomsday* (NY) 134: The luck of the devil. Whiting *Devil* 204(3a).

Devil

D137   **Devil** take the hindmost
1939 HMiller *Capricorn* (NY 1961) 201: It was fuck and be fucked—and the devil take the hindmost. **1943** MCarpenter *Experiment* (B) 89: Devil take the hindmost means the biggest devil of all on top. **1947** PWentworth *Wicked* (NY) 111: Your proverb—"The devil take the hindmost." **1954** EPangborn *Mirror* (NY 1958) 77: It's all tooth and claw, devil take the hindmost. **1959** *Time* 3/23 81: One of the most outspokenly devil-take-the-hindmost editors in the U.S. **1959** *TLS* 7/17 419: The harsh devil-take-the-hindmost view of provincial life. **1963** AMoorhead *Cooper's* (NY 1965) 113: Leaving the devil to take the hindmost. **1970** JVizzard *See* (NY) 38: And the devil take the hindmost. **1972** SCloete *Victorian* (L) 27: A policy of *laissez-faire* in which the devil took the hindmost. **1975** JDaniels *White* (NY) 21: The mood of "devil take the hindmost." EAP D130; Whiting *Devil* 208(11). Cf. Every Man for *below.*

D138   The **Devil** (hell) to pay
1900 CFPidgin *Quincy A. Sawyer* (B) 205: There has been the devil to pay. **1909** MRRinehart *Man in Lower Ten* (NY 1947) 276: There's hell to pay. **1913** JCLincoln *Mr. Pratt's Patients* (NY) 195: There'll be the Old Harry to pay. **1923** ORCohen *Jim Hanvey* (NY) 227: There'd be thunder to pay. **1933** ABCox *Jumping* (L) 232: There is going to be the devil to pay. **1934** ABCox *Mr. Pidgeon's* (NY) 176: Hell to pay. **1938** EQueen *The Devil To Pay* (NY). **1941** MArmstrong *Blue Santo* (NY) 77: The devil and all to pay. **1949** MBurton *Disappearing* (NY) 109: There'll be the devil to pay. **1953** JRhode *Mysterious* (NY DBC) 149: There'll be the devil to pay. **1960** JMcGovern *Berlin* (NY DBC) 95: There would be the devil to pay. **1974** MGEberhart *Danger* (NY) 145: A certain amount of hell to pay. **1976** SWoods *My Life* (NY) 206: There'll be the devil to pay. EAP D131; TW 99(26). See next entry.

D139   The **Devil** (hell) to pay and no pitch hot
1927 WBFoster *From Six* (NY) 102: The very devil's to pay . . . and no pitch hot! **1931** KTrask *Murder* (NY) 170: Here is what you call hell to pay . . . And no pitch hot that I can see. **1933** CWells *Clue* (NY) 99: The Devil to pay, and no pitch hot. **1941** ISCobb *Exit* (I) 150: There was hell to pay and no pitch hot. **1956** MPHood *Scarlet* (NY) 74: The devil'd be to pay 'n no pitch hot. **1963** MPHood *Sin* (NY) 194: The devil'll be to pay 'n no pitch hot. **1971** RMStern *You Don't* (NY) 171: There would have been hell to pay and no pitch hot. EAP D132; *Oxford* 184; Colcord 99: Hell to pay.

D140   The **Devil** was sick, the devil a monk would be (*varied*)
1928 SChalmers *House* (NY) 117: When the devil isn't sick, he's a diplomat. **1929** TCobb *Crime* (L) 70: The devil was ill, the devil a monk would be. **1930** JHWade *Rambles in Devon* (L) 36: It was a case of "the devil a saint would be." **1931** MGEberhart *From This* (NY) 3: A "when-the-devil-was-sick" reform. **1933** EECummings *Eimi* (NY) 26: What is that proverb . . . the devil is sick, the devil a monk—. **1939** AGilbert *Clock* (L) 87: "When the devil was old, the devil a monk would be," Crook misquoted. **1943** HAdams *Victory* (L) 8: When the devil was sick. **1972** FVWMason *Brimstone* (L) 233: When the Devil was young, a devil was he, but when the Devil grew old, a saint he'd be. EAP D134.

D141   Do not greet the **Devil** until you meet him
1967 JFDobie *Some Part* (B) 125: Don't greet the devil until you meet him. Cf. To meet Trouble *below.*

D142   Fight the **Devil** with fire (*varied*)
1926 MMTaylor *Heart* (L) 28: He applied the ancient system of fighting the devil with fire. **1928** CWood *Shadow* (NY) 184: Fight the devil with brimstone. **1929** SQuinn *Phantom* (Sauk City, Wisc. 1966) 129: Have you heard of combatting the devil with flames? **1932** RKing *Murder* (L) 232: The tactical value of fighting the devil with evil, more modernly, of fighting fire with fire. **1933** AWilliams *Death* (NY) 165: One fights the Devil with fire. **1956** AAFair *Beware* (NY DBC) 134: You're going to have to fight

164

the devil with fire. TW 98(11); Brunvand 36(8). Cf. To fight Fire *below*.

D143 Go to the **Devil** for truth and to a lawyer for a lie

1930 JSFletcher *Investigators* (NY) 136: Go to the devil for truth and to a lawyer for a lie. Whiting *Devil* 210(21).

D144 He who sups with the **Devil** needs a long spoon (*varied*)

1928 RAJWalling *That Dinner* (NY) 21: On the principle that he who sups with the devil needs a long spoon. **1929** EBYoung *Dancing* (P) 46: You'd better bring a long spoon [*to eat with suspected people*]. **1930** FDBurdett *Odyssey* (L) 97: The old adage which prescribes the use of a spoon with a long handle when you sup with the devil. **1934** GMitchell *Death* (L) 156: Who sups with the devil must have a long spoon. **1936** AFielding *Two Pearl* (L) 225: You ought to have a long spoon . . . when supping with the devil. **1938** JTFarrell *No Star* (NY) 291: They used to say in the old country, "Sup with the devil and you need a long spoon." **1952** MAllingham *Tiger* (NY) 159: Who sups with the devil must use a long spoon. **1954** EDillon *Sent* (L) 162: She turned to stare, with a long spoon in her hand—like someone about to sup with the devil. **1959** IFleming *Goldfinger* (NY) 82: Talk of the devil! . . . And then go and sup with him. What was that about a long spoon? **1960** LLevine *Great* (L) 333: The devil's got a long spoon. **1964** LLafore *Devil's* (NY) 69: He who sups with the Devil should use a long spoon. **1970** RCowper *Twilight* (NY) 169: No spoon on earth is long enough to sup with the devil. **1973** CAird *His Burial* (NY) 22: If you happen to need someone to sup with the devil for you, he'd be just the man for the job. Whiting *Devil* 205(5); Brunvand 36(7); *Oxford* 480: Long.

D145 Like the **Devil** beating tanbark

1930 JFDobie *Coronado* (Dallas) 27: We rode like the devil beating tan bark. **1951** EWTeale *North* (NY) 110: When I've got her wide open . . . she goes like the devil beating tanbark. TW 97(8); Brunvand 35(3).

D146 Pull **Devil**, pull baker

1928 JAFerguson *Man in the Dark* (NY) 252: It was pull devil, pull baker. **1937** JDCarr *Burning* (NY) 286: It becomes pull-baker, pull-devil, pull-murderer. **1944** RAJWalling *Corpse Without* (NY) 205: A great game of pull-devil-pull-baker. **1950** ECRLorac *And Then* (NY) 73: Pull devil, pull baker. **1957** *New Yorker* 9/28 153: The pull-devil, pull-baker postwar world. EAP D140.

D147 Talk (speak) of the **Devil** and he will appear (*varied*)

1923 JSFletcher *Lost Mr. L* (NY) 143: And talk of the—there she is! **1926** HSKeeler *Spectacles* (NY 1929) 51: The old adage that when you speak of the devil the devil appears. **1927** JSFletcher *Scarhaven* (NY) 58: Talk of the—you know . . . Here's Addie Chatfield herself. **1930** HLandon *Three Brass* (NY) 220: Talk about the devil and he is sure to appear. **1934** SHAdams *Gorgeous* (B) 94: Talk of the devil, you see his shaddah in red. **1938** ERonns *Death* (NY) 180: Speak of the devil and he comes in person. **1941** ESHolding *Speak of the Devil* (NY). **1945** JSymons *Immaterial* (L 1954) 99: "Speak of the devil"—Wilson is rather fond of these tags. **1950** DAWollheim *Flight* (NY) 91: Speak of the Devil and his imps will appear. **1955** VWMason *Two* (NY) 191: Ah, there, Bruce! Speak of the Devil and his imps appear. **1955** JO'Hara *Ten* (NY) 63: Speaking of the devil, or I should say speaking of the angel. **1961** EPeters *Death* (NY) 25: Speak of the devil, and his bat wings rustle behind you. **1972** PWarner *Loose* (NY) 102: Thinking of the devil! "It's good to see you." **1976** CLarson *Muir's* (NY) 12: Speak of the goddamn devil. EAP D144; Brunvand 36(11,12). Cf. Talk of Angels *above*.

D148 To beat the **Devil** around the bush (*varied*)

1927 CDiehl *Byzantine* (NY) 110: Any one of the thousand ways of "beating the devil around the bush." **1928** RHFuller *Jubilee* (NY) 225: A neat way of chasing the devil round the stump. **1929** RJCasey *Secret* (I) 31: It's chasing the devil around Robin

Devil

Hood's barn to suggest that. **1933** WBlair *Mike Fink* (NY) 187: Whip the devil around the meeting-house. **1934** RJCasey *Third Owl* (I) 269: You're certainly beating the devil around Robin Hood's barn. **1936** JSStrange *Bell* (NY) 236: Beat the devil round the bush. **1938** WNMacartner *Fifty Years* (NY) 13: The present Age of Repudiation and whipping the devil around the stump. **1955** LCochran *Hallelujah* (NY) 51: A good rousing shouting revival in which the devil is whipped round and round the stump until he knows his proper place. EAP D159. Cf. Brunvand 35–36(5,16).

D149 To give the **Devil** his due (*varied*)
1922 JJoyce *Ulysses* (NY 1934) 175: Give the devil his due. **1924** GRFox *Fangs* (NY) 202: Maybe the old hellion should have his dues. **1925** GBeasley *My First* (Paris) 277: You've got the devil his dues. **1929** APryde *Secret* (NY) 30: Let us give our pious parent his due. **1934** GMitchell *Death* (L) 243: Even the devil likes to receive his due. **1938** PATaylor *Annulet* (NY) 81: Asey gave the devil her due. **1951** IChase *New York 22* (NY) 177: To give the devil his due. **1952** JKnox *Little* (P) 29: The Book says give the devil his due. **1958** MGilbert *Blood* (NY) 97: Give the devil no more than his due. **1960** MProcter *Devil's Due* (NY DBC). **1963** HMiller *Black* (NY) 22: I am a man of God and a man of the Devil. To each his due. **1975** ELathen *By Hook* (NY) 163: Gabler gave the devil his due. EAP D151.

D150 What goes over the **Devil's** back *etc.*
1952 NTyre *Mouse* (NY) 93: What goes over the devil's back is sure to come under his belly. **1958** *BHerald* 6/22 1: "Whatever goes over the devil's back has got to come under his belly. They [the GOP] put a lot over our backs during the Truman administration. Now it's coming under their belly mighty hard, and it's pretty hot" [*Sam Rayburn*]. EAP D160.

D151 As fresh as a **Dewdrop**
1965 CBeaton *Years* (L) 227: Edith was as fresh as a dewdrop. TW 101(1).

D152 As hard as a **Diamond**; Diamond-hard
1939 HHolt *Smiling Doll* (L) 31: As hard as a diamond. **1941** AAFair *Double* (NY) 3: Eyes, diamond-hard. **1949** AAFair *Bedrooms* (NY 1958) 8: Hard as a diamond. TW 101(4).

D153 **Diamond** cut diamond
1927 BNorman *Thousand* (NY) 281: Diamond cut diamond. **1928** EWallace *Sinister* (NY) 147: Diamond against diamond. **1932** RCWoodthorpe *Public* (L) 294: Diamond cut diamond. **1937** GGoodchild *Murder Will* (L) 215: A queer case of "diamond cut diamond." **1954** HRAngeli *Pre-Raphaelite* (L) 190: Diamond cut diamond. **1969** JDrummond *People* (NY) 114: A case of diamond cut diamond. EAP D167.

D154 A rough **Diamond**
1900 CFPidgin *Quincy A. Sawyer* (B) 205: A diamond in the rough; 399. **1906** JCLincoln *Mr. Pratt* (NY) 106: A rough diament. **1922** JJoyce *Ulysses* (NY 1924) 625: That rough diamond. **1932** PATaylor *Death* (I) 154: A diamond in the rough. **1940** TChanslor *Our First* (NY) 209: With . . . a heart like a rough diamond. [*A good sort, but odd.*] **1950** ECBentley *Chill* (NY) 57: He was a very rough diamond. **1951** SSpender *World* (L) 271: Suitable clichés such as that he was a "rough diamond" who had a "heart of gold." **1956** GHolden *Velvet* (NY) 29: A diamond in the rough. **1962** JJMcPhaul *Deadlines* (NY) 211: Diamond-in-the-rough characters. **1963** NFreeling *Question* (NY 1965) 42: There was some English metaphor about rough diamonds. **1967** DBloodworth *Chinese* (NY) 255: The integrity of a rough diamond and the morals of a monkey. **1970** EHahn *Times* (NY) 58: The diamond in the rough. EAP D169; Brunvand 36–7(2).

D155 As crazy (dark, plain, sharp) as **Dick's** hatband.
1953 MPHood *Silent* (NY) 14: Crazy as Dick's hatband. **1959** AAnderson *Lover* (NY) 51: Always dressed sharper'n Dick's hatband. **1967** VThomson *V.Thomson* (L) 384: My plain-as-Dick's-hatband harmony

[*music*]. **1979** GWest *Duke* (NY) 186: It was as dark as Dick's hatband in there. See next entries.

D156　As odd as **Dick's** hatband (*varied*)
1969 DClark *Nobody's* (NY) 124: It's as odd as old Nick's hatband. **1970** DClark *Deadly* (NY) 120: This case is as odd as Dick's hatband. **1971** DClark *Sick* (NY) 127: As odd as Dick's hatband. *Oxford* 185.

D157　As queer as **Dick's** hatband
1921 JCLincoln *Galusha* (NY) 384: As queer as Dick's hatband—whatever that is. **1931** LThayer *Last Shot* (NY) 123: The man acted as queer as Dick's hat band. **1934** KCStrahan *Hobgoblin* (I) 185: Queer as Dick's hatband. **1951** JCFurnas *Voyage* (NY) 54: Queer as Dick's hat band. **1953** RAldington *Pindorman* (L) 207: Queer as Dick's hat-band. **1959** ESchiddel *Devil* (NY) 359: He was as queer as Dick's hatband. *Oxford* 185.

D158　As lazy as old **Dick Mullet's** dog *etc.*
1933 GBeaton *Jack* (L) 125: He's as lazy as old Dick Mullet's dog, that leaned against the wall to bark. *Oxford* 448: Lazy . . . Ludlam's.

D159　To cut up **Didoes**
1931 GFowler *Great* (NY) 310: The sisters cut up didoes. **1935** DGardiner *Translantic* (L) 54: It's his ancestors that cut up the didoes. **1956** BCClough *More* (Portland, Me.) 22: Among the didos cut up. **1959** SDean *Price* (NY) 23: Her dido-cutting in café society. **1962** AMStein *Home* (NY) 74: Cutting up some kind of kid didoes. **1966** LEGoss *Afterglow* (Portland, Me.) 94: Cutting up his didos. TW 101–2.

D160　As square as a **Die**
1930 HHolt *Ace* (L) 273: She was as square as a die. Cf. Whiting D236: As square as dice [*literal*].

D161　As straight as a **Die**
c**1910** EWallace *Nine Bears* (L 1928) 33: Straight as a die. **1931** EQueen *Dutch* (NY) 177: The man is straight as a die. **1938** JJConnington *Truth* (L) 285: He wasn't as straight as a die. **1945** ACampbell *With*

Bated (NY) 34: Straight as a die [*a line*]. **1952** EPaul *Black* (NY) 91: With a face straight as a die. **1959** WGraham *Wreck* (NY) 29: Straight as a die. **1962** EHuxley *Mottled* (L) 281: Hair . . . straight as a die. **1964** PMoyes *Falling* (NY 1966) 176: Biddy is as straight as a die. **1970** HCarmichael *Death* (NY) 111: [He] was straight as a die. **1970** PMoyes *Many* (NY) 163: Straight as a dye. TW 102 *sb.* (1).

D162　The **Die** is cast
1912 ERBurroughs *Princess of Mars* (NY 1963) 136: The die was cast. **1924** AOFriel *Mountains* (NY) 181: The die was cast. **1932** DLSayers *Have* (NY) 394: The die was cast. **1938** DFrome *Guilt* (L) 189: The die was cast. *Alea facta erat.* **1941** FWCrofts *Circumstantial* (NY) 35: The die was cast. **1953** WBlunt *Pietro's* (L) 98: The die is cast. **1962** DGillon *Unsleep* (NY) 168: The die is cast, the Rubicon crossed, the boats burned. Why are there so many English metaphors for taking decisions? **1975** PDJames *Black* (NY) 250: The die was cast. EAP D174; Brunvand 37.

D163　All must **Die** (*varied*)
1930 Private 19022 *Her Privates* (L) 136: You've got to die some day. **1935** FGEberhard *Microbe* (NY) 202: We all die on our appointed day. **1938** RWhite *Run Masked* (NY) 190: How people do enjoy saying: "Well, we must all die some day." **1939** JJFarjeon *Seven Dead* (I) 301: We've all got to die once. **1955** EWSmith *One Eyed* (NY) 150: We all got to die sometime. **1957** *BHerald* 11/13 5: You got to die some time, Senator . . . You can't live forever. **1966** VSiller *Mood* (NY) 169: We all have to die some time. EAP D175; TW 102 *vb.* (1). Cf. Death takes *above*.

D164　Never say **Die**
1919 HRHaggard *She and Allan* (NY 1921) 119: Never say die. **1931** WWJacobs *Snug* (NY) 614: Never say "die." **1956** *New Yorker* 11/10 59: Never say die. **1957** *Time* 3/4 40: The never-say-die band. **1957** *Punch* 9/4 269: It's never too late to say die, she warns. **1958** RMacdonald *Doomsters* (NY) 81: With never-say-die eroticism. **1964** AMStein

Blood (NY) 119: I never say die. **1966** DMDisney *Magic* (NY) 59: An optimistic cliché, never say die, every cloud has a silver lining, tomorrow will be better. **1972** JMDobson *Politics* (NY) 24: The never-say-die Northern Democrats. EAP D176.

D165   One **Dies** but once (*varied*)

1905 JBCabell *Line* (NY 1926) 193: One can die but once. **1929** AKreymborg *New American* (NY) 255: You can only die once. **1933** LO'Flaherty *Martyr* (NY) 26: A man can only die once. **1937** NBlake *There's Trouble* (L) 246: One could only die once. **1941** AAmos *Pray* (NY) 258: We can only die once. **1947** GGallagher *I Found* (NY DBC) 72: He points out the obvious, a man can hang only once. **1948** NMailer *Naked* (NY) 12: You can only get killed once. **1953** JTrench *Docken* (L 1960) 110: One can only die once. **1958** CLBlackstone *Woman* (NY) 73: You can only hang once, as they say. **1959** *NYTimes Magazine* 8/16 85: You can only die once. **1964** JVance *Future* (NY) 85: No one dies more than once. **1970** CBrooke-Rose *Go When* (L) 28: One only dies once. EAP D178; TW 102 *vb.* (2). Cf. One only Lives once *below*.

D166   As near as makes no **Difference**

1928 AGilbert *Mrs. Davenport* (NY) 98: As near as makes no difference. **1937** NBell *Crocus* (NY) 108: As near fifty pounds as makes no difference. **1954** ECRLorac *Shroud* (NY) 64: As near as makes no difference. **1958** BAldiss *Starship* (NY 1960) 96: As near a mutant as made no difference. **1962** MCarleton *Dread* (NY) 204: As near . . . as doesn't make any difference. **1967** RLockridge *With Option* (P) 105: Dead, or as near as makes no difference. **1970** JPorter *Dover Strikes* (NY) 56: As near hysterical as makes no difference. Cf. Berrey 40.6: As no matter.

D167   There is a **Difference** between saying and doing

1940 ECRLorac *Tryst* (L) 104: There's a mort o' difference between saying and doing. **1963** JJMarric *Gideon's Ride* (NY) 138: There's a lot of difference between

saying and doing. *Oxford* 187: Between word and deed. Cf. Deeds *above*.

D168   A **Dime** (penny) a dozen

1939 MMGoldsmith *Detour* (L) 148: Actors out here you can get a dime a dozen. **1939** HHolt *Smiling Doll* (L) 16: One of those penny-a-dozen fellows. **1940** RDarby *Death Conducts* (NY) 8: Nick would be dear at a dime a dozen. **1940** JStagge *Turn* (NY) 109: One of those two-cents-a-dozen romances. **1951** MSpillane *Long* (NY) 110: A dime a dozen in the daytime. **1956** GHolden *Velvet* (NY) 58: Murderers were a dime a dozen in his business. **1959** JThurber *Years* (B) 5: Writers are a dime a dozen. **1963** AAFair *Fish* (NY DBC) 121: Good looking waitresses were a dime a dozen. **1966** EMcBain *Eighty* (NY) 71: Novelists are a dime a dozen. DA Dime 3b; Berrey 21.14 etc. [*see Index*]; Wentworth 148.

D169   After **Dinner** rest a while *etc.*

1922 JJoyce *Ulysses* (NY 1934) 369: After supper walk a mile. **1933** ERPunshon *Genius* (B) 70: "After dinner rest a while, after supper walk a mile," is the old saying. **1939** RAJWalling *Blistered Hand* (NY) 90: Pye said it was his daily contribution to the Keep Fit campaign to walk a mile after supper, [and] asked us to observe that the proverbs of England had anticipated the whole corpus of modern wisdom. *Oxford* 6: After.

D170   As cheap as **Dirt**; Dirt-cheap

1920 GBMcCutcheon *Anderson Crow* (NY) 284: Cheap as dirt. **1930** JWilliamson *American Hotel* (NY) 205: Dirt-cheap. **1939** EAmbler *Coffin* (NY 1957) 35: I'm dirt cheap. **1961** LDelRay *And Some* (NY) 69: Faith was dirt cheap. EAP D184; Brunvand 37(1,2); Berrey 21.14.

D171   As common as **Dirt**

1927 EWallace *Law* (NY 1931) 79: Common as the dirt of my boots. **1929** SWPierce *Layman* (NY) 43: They're as common as dirt. **1930** WLewis *Apes* (NY 1932) 409: Homosexuals are as common as dirt; 410. **1937** MMPropper *One Murdered* (L) 62: He was as common as dirt. **1945** FBonnamy *King Is Dead* (NY) 167: Common as dirt [*a* man]. **1961** CBlackstone (L 1965) 42: It's a name as common as dirt. **1963** MErskine *No. 9* (NY) 162: A . . . girl as common as dirt. **1973** DDelman *He Who* (NY) 43: [He] isn't common as dirt. **1977** VCanning *Doomsday* (NY) 200: Common as dirt. Whiting *NC* 395(2). Cf. Muck, Mud *below*.

D172 As easy as **Dirt**

1933 AGilbert *Musical* (L) 129: Easy as dirt. Whiting *NC* 395(3).

D173 As mean as **Dirt**

1912 JCLincoln *Postmaster* (NY) 195: Feelin' meaner'n dirt. **1935** DBennett *Murder* (NY) 117: Mean as dirt. **1940** EDean *Murder Is* (NY) 206: Meaner than dirt he was too. **1950** MHBradley *Murder* (NY DBC) 109: Mean as dirt. **1956** ABurgess *Time* (L) 100: Mean as dirt [*stingy*]. TW 103(3); Brunvand 37(3).

D174 As poor as **Dirt**; Dirt-poor

1935 TWilder *Heaven's* (NY) 61: We're as poor as dirt. **1958** CLBlackstone *Woman* (NY) 68: We were as poor as dirt. **1961** ESherry *Call* (NY DBC) 10: She was dirt-poor.

D175 To treat someone like **Dirt** (*varied*)

1922 JJoyce *Ulysses* (NY 1934) 763: They treat you like dirt. **1932** DLSayers *Have* (NY) 88: Treats us like dirt. **1935** JRhode *Corpse* (L) 121: He treated me like dirt beneath his feet. **1956** *Time* 8/13 23: They treat their women like dirt—worse than dirt. **1959** TWalsh *Dangerous* (B DBC) 101: You treat them like dirt. **1961** DMDisney *Mrs. Meeker's* (NY) 128: You'd think I was the dirt under his feet. Taylor *Prov. Comp.* 34. Cf. Sand *below*.

D176 **Discretion** is the better part of valor (*varied*)

1909 MRRinehart *Man in Lower Ten* (NY 1947) 229: Judging discretion the better part. **1911** JSHay *Amazing Emperor* (L) 66: Discretion being the better part of valour. **1923** HWNevinson *Changes* (NY) 146: The Better Part of Discretion is Valour. **1929** LBrock *Stoke Silver* (NY) 172: Pamela had judged discretion the better part of imprudence. **1932** JVTurner *Who Spoke* (L) 170: Silence was the better part of valour. **1933** MBurr *Fussicker* (L) 59: I decided prudence was the better course. **1935** HAustin *It Couldn't* (NY) 215: Discretion overcame valor. **1935** NGayle *Death* (NY) 267: An ounce of discretion is worth more than a ton of valor. **1936** REast *Detectives* (L) 248: I always say that discretion is the better part of married happiness. **1940** JRhode *Death on* (NY) 212: Discretion being the better part of friendship. **1948** KWilliamson *Atlantic* (L 1970) 131: A discreet retreat is the better part of valour. **1951** HSaunders *Sleeping* (L) 16: For him, too, the better part of valour was, on this occasion, discretion. **1954** DAlexander *Terror* (NY) 130: The old saying Discretion is Better Than Vallor. **1958** MAMusmanno *Verdict* (NY) 171: Valota exercised the better part of valor by remaining home. **1960** STruss *One Man's* (NY) 162: Discretion is the better part of knowledge. **1961** LSdeCamp *Dragon* (NY 1968) 117: Thinking valor the better part of discretion. **1962** PDJames *Cover* (NY 1976) 179: Discretion had long taken precedence of valour. **1964** LPayne *Deep* (L) 231: I didn't care for discretion any more and valour could go and jump in the lake. **1966** ALoos *Girl* (NY) 172: The better part of valor was to cut and run. **1968** MHolroyd *Strachey* (L) 2.243: Discretion was the better part of common sense. **1972** JGreenway *Down* (B) 67: [He] knew the better part of valor. **1975** JBurke *Rogue's* (NY) 247: Flight would have to be the better part of discretion, if not valor. **1975** JPearson *Edward* (NY) 85: Discretion was the better part of class survival. EAP D190; Brunvand 37.

D177 To throw **Discretion** to the wind(s)

1942 VCaspasy *Laura* (NY 1957) 46: I cast discretion to the wind. **1965** DAcheson *Morning* (B) 132: Discretion thrown to the winds. NED Wind 25b.

D178 Desperate **Diseases** require desperate remedies (*varied*)

1929 BFlynn *Case* (NY) 192: Desperate men have a habit of using desperate remedies. **1929** APryde *Secret* (NY) 235: Desperate ills need desperate remedies. **1929**

EWallace *Twister* (L) 247: Desperate diseases . . . **1930** WWoodrow *Moonhill* (NY) 272: Desperate cases require desperate remedies. **1933** FBeeding *Two Undertakers* (L) 285: Desperate stakes . . . and the means must also be desperate. **1933** JVTurner *Amos* (L) 216: Drastic cases . . . call for drastic remedies. **1935** FBeeding *Norwich* (NY) 124: Desperate situations required desperate remedies. **1935** BFlynn *Edge* (L) 98: Desperate diseases need desperate remedies. **1948** FWCrofts *Silence* (NY) 27: To meet a desperate situation you need a desperate remedy, as someone has said. **1951** LSdeCamp *Hand* (NY 1963) 34: Desperate conditions dictate desperate remedies. **1957** WGHardy *City* (NY) 27: Desperate cases demand desperate remedies. **1961** SBlanc *Green* (NY DBC) 42: Desperate cases, desperate measures. **1964** RBlythe *Age* (B) 150: Desperate ills require desperate remedies. **1970** MStewart *Crystal* (NY) 432: A desperate position . . . called for desperate measures. **1971** JGolden *Watermelon* (P) 113: Desperate times called for desperate action. EAP D191; TW 56(2): Case, 103.

D179 If one **Dishes** it out he should also take it (*varied*)

1936 DHume *Crime* (L) 188: I can take it as well as give it. **1936** PGWodehouse *Luck* (B) 283: He was a man who knew how to take it as well as dish it out. **1946** CTGardner *Bones* (NY) 19: You dish it out. I can take it. **1948** ESherry *Sudden* (NY) 112: Can you take it as well as dish it? **1953** JRKennedy *Prince* (NY) 53: She can dish it out, but she can't take it. **1956** *BHerald* 8/10 10: If you can't take it then don't dish it out. **1957** *New Yorker* 3/9 27: He can dish it out . . . but he can't take it. **1959** AWUpfield *Journey* (NY) 56: I can take it. And I can dish it out, too. **1960** KCrichton *Total* (NY) 16: The old adage holds true: if you hand it out, you must expect to take it. **1968** LTanner *All the Things* (NY) 52: He could take it as well as dish it out. **1970** RByrne *Memories* (NY) 172: We dished out as much as we took. Berrey 300.4.

D180 As limp as a **Dishrag**

1938 RAJWalling *Coroner* (L) 15: He was limp as a dish-rag. **1953** EBurns *Sex Life*

(NY) 228: As limp as a dish-rag. **1956** *BHerald* 11/4 26: His mother . . . described herself as "limp as a dishrag." **1963** CKeith *Rich* (NY) 103: I feel limp as a dishcloth. **1964** TPowell *Corpus* (NY) 135: "I feel limp." "I'm a little dishraggish myself." **1971** PTabor *Pauline's* (Louisville) 144: He's as limp as an old wet dishrag. Whiting *NC* 395: Limber; Taylor *Prov. Comp.* 54, *Western Folklore* 17(1958) 15. Cf. As limp as a Rag, Sack *below*.

D181 As weak as a **Dishrag**

1968 JGould *Europe* (NY) 220: Weak as a dishrag. Taylor *Prov. Comp.* 54: Limp.

D182 As dull as **Dishwater**

1931 WMorton *Mystery* (NY) 67: Dull as dishwater. **1937** PATaylor *Octagon* (NY) 33: Dull as dishwater. **1951** MHead *Congo* (NY) 136: She's duller than dishwater. **1957** *BHerald* 4/21 5: My shoes are as dull as dishwater. Partridge 224.

D183 As weak (pale) as **Dishwater**

1934 MDavis *Hospital* (NY) 221: Weak as dishwater. **1935** EGreenwood *Deadly* (NY) 127: Weak as dishwater. **1954** EForbes *Rainbow* (B) 79: She was pale as dishwater. **1961** MHHood *Drown* (NY) 71: Weak as dishwater. Cf. As weak as Ditchwater, Water *below*.

D184 There is no **Disputing** about tastes

1929 KPreston *Pot Shots* (NY) 204: *De gustibus non disputandum.* **1967** RDavies *Marchbank's* (Toronto) 110: "There is no disputing about tastes," says the old saw. In my experience there is little else. EAP D201.

D185 **Distance** lends enchantment

1925 EDBiggers *House* (NY) 139: Distance has lent enchantment. **1927** HHBashford *Behind* (NY) 248: Distance had lent its enchantment. **1951** ACalder-Marshall *Magic* (L) 95: It was distance that led enchantment. **1958** DGBrowne *Death* (L) 164: Distance lent enchantment. TW 103.

D186 To fight to the last **Ditch** (*varied*)

1928 PThorne *Spiderweb* (P) 21: Lowell is fighting to the last ditch. **1936** HAdams *Death* (L) 124: Fight to the last ditch. **1937**

WEHayes *Before the Cock* (NY) 159: Loyal to the last ditch. **1938** PPhilmore *Short List* (L) 38: He wasn't going to die in the last ditch for him. **1939** GBagby *Corpse* (NY) 218: A man I'd trust to the last ditch. **1958** EPargeter *Assize* (L) 33: He was set to fight to the last ditch. **1961** EPeters *Death* (NY) 76: I'd fight him to the last ditch. **1965** JPorter *Dover Two* (NY 1968) 96: Dover fought to the last ditch. EAP D205.

D187   As clear as Ditchwater

1933 PMcGuire *Death* (NY) 322: "Is it clear?" "As ditch water." **1935** VWilliams *Clue* (B) 210: As clear as ditch water [*not clear*]. Cf. Mud, Pea soup *below*.

D188   As dull as Ditchwater

1922 JSFletcher *Ravensdene* (NY) 249: As dull as ditch-water. **1924** AChristie *Man* (NY) 80: As dull as ditch water. **1941** CWells *Murder . . . Casino* (P) 64: She is dull as ditchwater. **1950** ELinklater *Mr. Bycula* (L) 151: They were dull as ditchwater. **1955** DMDisney *Room* (NY) 21: Someone that's dull as ditchwater. **1970** RBernard *Deadly* (NY) 170: He's dull as ditchwater. **1976** AChristie *Sleeping* (NY) 66: Dull as ditchwater. Taylor *Prov. Comp.* 37; Apperson 218: Flat.

D189   As flat as Ditchwater

1956 MColes *Far* (NY) 162: These scenes are as flat as ditchwater. Apperson 218: Flat.

D190   As weak as Ditchwater

1936 RHull *Keep It Quiet* (NY) 9: Weak as ditch water. Apperson 670: Weak. Cf. As weak as Dishwater *above*, Water *below*.

D191   Divide and rule (conquer)

1930 RAJWalling *Squeaky Voice* (NY) 220: Divide et impera. **1934** AMerritt *Creep* (NY) 244: Divide and rule. **1939** CSaxby *Death Cuts* (NY) 133: "Divide and conquer," as Lincoln or St. Paul or somebody had said. **1945** MColes *Green Hazard* (NY) 57: Divide and rule. **1953** BMcMillion *Lot* (P) 155: There's that old saying, divide and conquer. **1957** JLodwick *Equator* (L) 74: "Divide and rule" is . . . your motto. **1964** NFreeling *Because* (NY 1965) 174: Divide

and conquer. **1967** JAxelrad *Freneau* (Austin) 229: The old method of divide and conquer. **1968** HHarrison *Deathworld* (NY) 53: Those two ancient techniques known as "Divide and rule," and "If you can't lick 'em, join 'em." **1973** GSheehy *Hustling* (NY) 174: Divide and conquer. **1975** MKWren *Multitude* (NY) 162: Divide and conquer. EAP D207.

D192   Do as you would be done by (*varied*)

1928 JJConnington *Mystery* (B) 123: "Do unto others as you'd be done by" is my motto. **1930** JJFarjeon *Mystery* (L) 211: Do unto others as you have been done by! That is the law of the world. **1935** VLoder *Death* (L) 117: Do as you would be done by is my motto. **1937** PATaylor *Figure* (NY) 204: Do unto others as you're done by. **1952** DMDisney *Do Unto Others* (NY). **1957** *Time* 11/24 111: "Do unto others as they do unto you," is his motto. "Only do it first." **1964** BWAldiss *Dark* (L) 12: Do unto others as you would be dung [*sic*] by. **1970** PDickinson *Sinful* (NY) 117: As he has done to others, so shall he be done by. **1977** CA Goodrum *Dewey* (NY) 112: I'm a great believer in "do unto others as you would they do unto you." EAP D209; TW 104(2).

D193   Don't Do as I do but do as I say

1962 JJMcPhaul *Deadlines* (NY) 4: Don't do as I do; do as I say. **1965** HBevington *Charley* (NY) 171: Don't do as I do, but do as I say. **1965** JMaclaren-Ross *Memoirs* (L) 90: A case of "Don't do as I do, do as I tell you." EAP D208.

D194   Do or die

1928 ABCox *Amateur* (NY) 74: His but to do and die. **1933** MBurton *Mystery* (L) 53: Do or die. **1936** HAustin *Murder* (L) 220: A do-or-die chance. **1939** HMiller *Capricorn* (NY 1961) 72: Mine is to do or die, as Kipling says. **1954** EWBarnes *Lady* (NY) 183: Resolved to do or die. **1957** *Time* 4/15 34: The do-or-Dies Dallas *Morning News*. **1966** HTracy *Men* (L) 109: Resolved to do or die. **1970** RFBanks *Maine* (Middletown, Conn.) 91: Their "do or die" situation. EAP D210; TW 104(3).

D195 What is **Done** once can be done again (*varied*)

1936 MBeckett *Escape* (L) 15: What's done once can be done again. **1953** ECRLorac *Shepherd's* (NY) 148: We've a saying here-abouts—"You can do what you've always done." TW 104(6).

D196 What is **Done** cannot be undone (*varied*)

1927 JMWalsh *Silver* (L) 96: It's done now and it can't be undone. **1928** JArnold *Surrey* (L) 225: What was done, was done. **1928** CBarry *Corpse* (NY) 214: What's done is done. **1930** AChristie *Murder* (NY) 148: What is past is past and cannot be undone. **1936** JDKerruish *Undying* (NY) 104: What is done cannot be undone. **1937** ESGardner *Dangerous Dowager* (NY) 267: What's been done has been done. **1938** AChristie *Death on the Nile* (NY) 64: One can't alter the past. **1940** RPostgate *Verdict* (NY 1944) 148: What was done couldn't be undone. **1947** HLawrence *Death of* (NY) 87: What was done was done. **1950** MGEberhart *Hunt* (NY) 26: I always say what's done is done. **1954** JRRTolkien *Fellowship* (L) 179: What's done can't be undone. **1961** MKelly *Spoilt* (L) 210: Once it's done it's done. **1969** JBoyd *Pollinators* (NY) 103: What's done is done and cannot be undone. **1970** DLippincott *E Pluribus* (NY) 63: What's done is done. **1972** RRendell *No More* (NY) 87: What's done cannot be undone. **1973** DDelman *He Who* (NY) 155: What was done was done. Spilled milk was spilled milk. **1975** AMancini *Minnie* (NY) 17: What's past is past. EAP D215; TW 104(5,7).

D197 **Doctor** Diet and Doctor Quiet

1922 JJoyce *Ulysses* (NY 1934) 416: Doctor Diet and Doctor Quiet. EAP D220; Apperson 156.

D198 **Doctors** bury their mistakes

1931 ACEdington *Monk's Hood* (NY) 272: We fellows [*doctors*] . . . bury our mistakes. **1962** DMDisney *Find* (NY DBC) 102: There's an old saying that doctors bury their mistakes. **1970** WANolen *Making* (NY) 76: It's true that surgeons bury their mistakes. Apperson 492: Physicians; Tilley D424.

D199 To be just what the **Doctor** ordered

1931 PMacDonald *Murder* (L) 20: Just what the doctor ordered. **1936** AGlanville *Death* (L) 272: Just what the doctor ordered. **1941** CLClifford *While the Bells* (NY) 77: She was what the doctor ordered but forgot to leave a prescription for. **1953** BCClough *Grandma* (Portland, Me.) 21: As the saying goes, "She was just what the doctor ordered." **1957** *Punch* 8/14 178: This type of knowledge is about what the doctor ordered. **1961** FLockridge *Drill* (P) 112: A ball of heavy cord. What the doctor ordered. **1965** SRansome *Alias* (NY DBC) 100: Bless your heart, just what the doctor ordered. **1970** RCowper *Twilight* (NY) 122: Just what the doctor ordered. Partridge 448: Just what.

D200 When **Doctors** disagree *etc.*

1957 DJEnright *Heaven* (L) 192: When doctors disagree . . . Apperson 156.

D201 As dead as a (the) **Dodo**

1932 GLane *Hotel* (L) 282: As dead as a dodo. **1935** DHume *Murders* (L) 219: You'll be as dead as the proverbial dodo. **1947** MBurton *Will in the Way* (NY) 43: It's as dead as the dodo. **1947** LFord *Woman* (NY) 44: Dead as a dodo. **1954** EForbes *Rainbow* (B) 208: Dead as the dodo. **1956** *New Yorker* 6/20 41: The kitchen as we know it to-day is a dead dodo. **1959** RMacdonald *Galton* (NY) 152: That sort of thing is as dead as the proverbial dodo. **1970** JBlackburn *Bury* (NY) 53: As dead as a dodo. **1974** DCory *Bit* (NY) 112: Dead as the dodo. Whiting *NC* 396(1); Taylor *Western Folklore* 17(1958) 15.

D202 As extinct as the **Dodo**

1914 MAdams *In the Footsteps* (L) 72: As extinct as the dodo. **1926** EDBiggers *Chinese* (NY) 186: We'll be as extinct as the dodo. **1957** GWJohnson *Lunatic* (P) 36: Both are as extinct as the dodo. **1967** VPowell *Substantial* (L) 61: As extinct as the Dodo. Whiting *NC* 396(2).

D203 As busy as a three-legged **Dog** with fleas

1950 DHamilton *Murder Twice* (NY) 244: I've been busy as a three-legged dog with fleas. Cf. Wilstach 501: Busy.

D204 As crooked (weak) as a **Dog's** (goat's) hind leg

1931 ACEdington *Monk's Hood* (NY) 151: Weaker'n a dog's hind leg. **1934** NChild *Diamond* (L) 137: As crooked, people said, as a dog's hind leg. **1944** HReilly *Opening Door* (NY) 175: He was always as crooked as a dog's hind leg. **1952** EPaul *Black* (NY) 101: They're all as crooked as a dog's hind leg. **1962** PDennis *Genius* (NY) 275: Leander was as crooked as a dog's hind leg. **1964** RBraddon *Year* (L 1967) 134: Crooked as a dog's hind leg . . . Bloody old fake. **1976** JFoxx *Freebooty* (I) 9: A game . . . crooked as a goat's leg. TW 105(10); Brunvand 38(3). Cf. Donkey *below*.

D205 As drunk as a **Dog**; Dog drunk

1922 JJoyce *Ulysses* (NY 1934) 430: Drunk as a dog. **1938** WEHayes *Black* (NY) 91: You were dog drunk. EAP D227; TW 105(11): Dog drunk. Cf. DARE i 354: Bowdow, drunk as.

D206 As faithful as a **Dog**

1929 JSFletcher *Ransom* (NY) 56: As faithful as a dog. **1936** RTMScott *Murder Stalks* (NY) 84: He was as faithful as a dog and quite as alert. TW 105(13).

D207 As pleased (happy) as a **Dog** (cat) with two tails (*varied*)

1929 AGray *Dead* (L) 184: I'm as proud as a dog with two tails. **1930** ABCox *Wychford* (NY) 269: I'm as pleased as a dog with two tails. **1932** RKeverne *William* (L) 312: He's like a cat with two tails [*happy*]. **1933** JLilienthal *Gambler's* (B) 155: He was jes' as happy as a little dog with two tails. **1937** HCBailey *Black Land* (NY) 301: He's as pleased as a cat with two tails. **1940** CMWills *R.E.Pipe* (L) 75: I felt like a dog with two tails [*elated*]. **1944** CBrand *Green for Danger* (NY 1965) 166: As proud and pleased as a dog with seventeen tails. **1948** ECrispin *Buried* (L 1958) 140: As pleased as a dog with two tails. **1950** ECBentley

Chill (NY) 96: I felt . . . like a dog with two tails. **1951** JCreasey *Puzzle* (L 1962) 73: As pleased as a dog with two tails. **1959** ASillitoe *Loneliness* (L) 11: As happy as a dog with a tin tail. **1961** BKnox *In at* (NY) 83: As pleased as a dog with two tails. **1963** PDJames *Mind* (L) 223: He's as pleased as a dog with a new collar. **1963** JJMarric *Gideon's Ride* (NY) 39: He'll be like a dog with two tails and a pair of . . . **1976** DWilliams *Unholy* (NY) 68: He was like a dog with two tails [*pleased*]. Whiting *NC* 397(21).

D208 As sick as a **Dog**

1922 EMillay *Letters* ed ARMacdougall (NY 1952) 153: Sick as a dog. **1927** HHBashford *Behind* (NY) 225: To have made me as sick as the proverbial dog. **1936** GDHCole *Last Will* (NY) 234: I was sick as a dog. **1959** EMButler *Paper* (L) 53: He'll be as sick as a dog. **1970** NMonsarrat *Breaking* (L) 400: Sick as dogs. **1974** LBlack *Life* (NY) 192: Sick as a dog. EAP D229. Cf. As sick as a Cat *above*, Pup *below*.

D209 As tired as a **Dog**; Dog-tired

1905 FMWhite *Crimson Blind* (NY) 126: As tired as a dog. **1910** EPhillpotts *Tales* (NY) 130: Dog-tired. **1931** SHorler *Evil* (NY) 237: Tired as a dog. **1932** EMillay *Letters* ed ARMacdougall (NY 1952) 246: I was dog-tired (milk-wagon-dog-tired). **1936** PQuentin *Puzzle* (NY) 107: He was still as tired as a dog. **1952** BWolfe *Limbo* (L) 111: I was dog-tired, pooped. **1959** KWaterhouse *Billy* (L) 159: I was dog-tired. **1970** WMasterson *Death* (NY) 71: He was dog-tired. TW 105(19).

D210 Barking **Dogs** do not bite

1929 EHope *Alice* (NY) 48: Barking dogs do not bite. **1940** RDarby *Death Conducts* (NY) 52: The loud-barking dog seldom bites. **1956** *New Yorker* 9/1 71: Barking dogs never bite. **1956** GBagby *Cop* (NY) 107: There is an old, old story that says barking dogs don't bite. Cf. TW 104(1); Whiting *NC* 396(1); Brunvand 38(4). Cf. Silent Dog *below*.

D211 Betwixt **Dog** and wolf

1966 COgburn *Winter* (NY) 97: At the darker end of that hour known as "twixt dog and wolf." Cf. *Oxford* 359: Between hawk and buzzard.

D212 Dainty **Dogs** eat dirty puddings

1960 JLodwick *Moon* (L) 339: He means that dainty dogs eat dirty puddings, or look before you weep. EAP D239. Cf. TW 106(30): Hungry Dogs.

D213 Dead **Dogs** do not bite

1933 DGBrowne *Dead* (L) 49: "Dead dogs don't bite" or "The dead don't bite." Whiting *NC* 396(3). Cf. Dead Men *below*.

D214 The **Dog** barks but the caravan moves on

1935 LFord *Burn* (NY) 25: My granpappy used t' say, "The dog barks but the caravan moves on." **1959** CElliott *Unkind* (L) 176: An old Arab saying . . . The dog barks but the caravan passes. **1960** DHayles *Comedy* (L) 327: The dogs bark but the caravan goes on. Champion (Arabic) 330: 72.

D215 **Dog** does not eat dog (*varied*)

1913 JSFletcher *Secret* (L 1918) 74: Dog doesn't eat dog. **1919** HRHaggard *She and Allan* (NY 1921) 246: Dog does not eat dog. **1931** EWallace *Black* (NY) 152: Dog does not eat dog, nor thief eat thief. **1933** RAJWalling *Prove It* (NY) 108: You know, *canis canium,* dog doesn't eat dog. **1938** ECRLorac *John Brown's* (L) 24: Dog does not eat dog, likewise honour among thieves. **1940** RPostgate *Verdict* (NY 1944) 148: But dog does not eat dog. **1954** OAnderson *Thorn* (L) 131: Dog doesn't eat dog. **1957** *TLS* 4/5 203: The rule Dog Don't Eat Dog. **1962** WHaggard *Unquiet* (NY DBC) 21: Dog doesn't eat dog. **1967** LWoolf *Downhill* (L) 22: "Dog does not eat dog" and "a wolf does not make war on a wolf" are such ancient truths that they are proverbial. **1975** GHousehold *Red* (B) 80: Dog doesn't normally eat dog. EAP D235. Cf. Crow should not *above;* Wolf should not *below.*

D216 **Dog** eat dog (*varied*)

1921 ERBurroughs *Mucker* (NY) 319: Dog eat dog. **1926** JArnold *Murder!* (L) 247: Dog robbing dog. **1933** RAJWalling *Follow* (L) 104: Crook generally eats crook. **1937**

CGGivens *All Cats* (I) 347: It's dog-eat-dog in this Valley. **1938** WChambers *Dog Eat Dog* (NY). **1953** RBissell *7½ Cents* (B) 20: Dog-eat-dog business. **1957** WHHarris *Golden* (NY) 40: It's tiger eat tiger. **1958** *BHerald* 5/18 V 5: Dog-eat-dog faculty politics. **1961** RGordon *Doctor* (NY) 143: Some nasty remark about bitch eat bitch. **1966** HWaugh *Pure* (NY) 3: A real dog-eat-dog rat-race. **1967** CDrummond *Death* (NY) 189: Dog bite dog. **1970** KGiles *Death* (L) 115: A dog that ate dogs. **1975** HLawrenson *Stranger* (NY) 175: A dog-eat-dog industry. EAP D232.

D217 The **Dog** (sparrow) in the manger

1911 JLondon *Letters* ed KHendricks (NY 1965) 330: The part of a dog-in-the-manger. **1928** JJConnington *Tragedy* (B) 22: Damned dog-in-the-manger! **1932** HWade *No Friendly* (NY) 314: The point of view of the dog in the manger. **1939** IOellrichs *Man Who* (NY) 96: His dog-in-the-manger attitude. **1946** KMKnight *Trouble* (NY) 127: [He] can't be a dog in the manger. **1950** SSmith *Man Who* (NY) 189: All women are dog-in-the-mangerish about letting another woman have something they don't want themselves. **1957** *Punch* 9/4 259: But don't put all your dogs in one manger. **1959** DCCooke *Best Detective* (NY) 150: She was playing dog-in-the-manger. **1964** RMacdonald *Chill* (NY) 109: He killed her like a dog in the manger [*out of spite*]. **1965** RDSymons *Silton* (NY 1975) 28: His sparrow-in-the-manger procedure. **1967** GPorter *World* (P) 117: In the fashion of a "toad in the manger." [*The book is about frogs and toads.*] **1972** JDCarr *Hungry* (NY) 199: A dog in the manger. I might say a bitch in the manger. EAP D233; TW 106(28).

D218 A **Dog** is man's best friend (*varied*)

1927 VBridges *Girl* (P) 28: I have often heard it said that a dog is the best friend a man can have. **1935** DGardiner *Translantic* (L) 234: Truly, the dog was man's best friend. **1956** SDean *Marked* (NY) 108: Man's best friend. **1957** *Punch* 7/10 43: The Dog is man's best friend, after his mother. **1958** TEDikty *Six From* (NY) 82: A man's best friend is his mother. **1963** RAusting *I*

Went (NY) 124: Being "man's best friend" the canine generally fares rather well at man's hand. **1964** BKaufman *Up the Down* (NY 1966) 104: My best friend is my dog. A dog is man's best friend . . . through thick and thin. **1970** EWTeale *Springtime* (NY) 264: How curious it is . . . that the dog is "man's best friend," and yet nobody wants to be compared to him. **1975** EGundy *Naked* (NY) 142: A man is the dog's best friend. Whiting H566; Whiting NC 396(5).

D219 A **Dog's** life, hunger and ease

1962 AWUpfield *Death* (NY) 148: Lucy Meredith married him, married a merely lazy dog wanting only ease, even ease with hunger. EAP D236. Cf. To lead a Dog's life *below.*

D220 The **Dog** returns to his vomit

1929 JCPowys *Wolf* (NY) 2.728: You've gone back like a dog to's vomit. **1936** AGlanville *Death* (L) 248: A dog returns to his vomit. **1940** GDHCole *Wilson* (L) 83: A case of the dog returning to his vomit. **1947** WMoore *Greener* (NY 1961) 81: I could not say *canis revertit suam vomitem,* for it would invert a relationship—the puke had returned to the dog. **1954** HRAngeli *Pre-Raphaelite* (L) 223: The dogs return eagerly to their vomit. **1957** RAHeinlein *Door* (NY) 59: As surely as a cat returns to his vomit. **1962** JSymonds *Bezill* (L) 205: The dog that returned to its vomit. **1966** JRothenstein *Brave Day* (L) 188: It's bad enough for a dog to return to its vomit, but for the vomit to return to the dog—that's insupportable. EAP D234; TW 106(31).

D221 The **Dog** that brings a bone will pick a bone (*varied*)

1940 CBDawson *Lady Wept* (NY) 39: A dog that will bring a bone will pick a bone [*of a tale-bearer*]. **1959** ESchiddel *Devil* (NY) 147: The saw, the dog who brings a bone also will carry one away [*gossip-mongers*]. Cf. Whiting NC 398(47): Dog that fetches; Oxford 196: Dog that fetches.

D222 Every **Dog** has his day (*varied*)

1927 WGerhardi *Pretty* (L) 54: Every dog has his day. **1928** HAsbury *Gangs* (NY) 254:

Every dog has his day. **1937** NBlake *There's Trouble* (L) 9: Every dog, they say, has its day. **1938** DCDisney *Strawstack* (NY) 93: The oldest dog is entitled to his day. **1938** WNMacartney *Fifty Years* (NY) 464: As every dog has his flea, every boil has its hair. **1939** CSaxby *Death Cuts* (NY) 168: Every dog has his drink. **1951** CHare *English* (L) 47: Every dog has his day. **1957** *Time* 11/18 76: Every dognik has its daynik [*the sputnik fever*]. **1961** RAHeinlein *6XH* (NY) 119: Every dog has his day. **1964** ABurgess *Nothing* (L) 6: A dog shall have his day. EAP D243; TW 106(27); Brunvand 38(5).

D223 Every **Dog** is entitled to (allowed) one bite (*varied*)

1930 ATrain *Adventures* (NY) 510: Every dog is entitled to one bite. **1935** CJDaly *Murder* (NY) 117: A dog is only entitled to one bite. **1943** CWoolrich *Black Angel* (NY) 40: Everyone is entitled to be forgiven at least once. Even a dog; they give a dog three bites. **1945** RLHines *Confessions* (L) 93: To every dog one bite, to every bitch one—. **1949** JReach *Late* (NY) 154: They even allow a dog three bites, before they shoot him. **1950** SPalmer *Green* (NY) 179: As every dog is supposed to be allowed one bite. **1955** LWhite *Flight* (NY 1957) 77: Everyone is allowed to make one mistake. **1956** *Cambridge Chronicle* 7/26 1: It is a standing joke among [letter] carriers . . . that every dog is entitled to the first bite. After that, the carrier is entitled to take defensive measures. **1959** MScherf *Never Turn* (NY) 166: Every dog is entitled to one bite. **1959** RMStern *Bright* (NY) 77: The law says a dog is allowed one bite. **1965** AChristie *At Bertram's* (L) 255: Even the law seems to go on the principle of allowing a dog to have one bite. **1970** CDrummond *Stab* (NY) 85: A dog, or person, was allowed one bite. **1972** MWilliams *Inside* (NY) 187: Every dog was allowed one bite. *Oxford* 195.

D224 Give a **Dog** a bad name *etc.* (*varied*)

1908 SHAdams *Flying Death* (NY) 173: Give a dog a bad name! **1913** HTFinck *Food* (NY) 132: Give a dog a bad name, etc.! **1925** EBChancellor *Old Q* (L) 237: But like

the proverbial dog with a bad name, ru-
mour had chosen to hang him. **1928** EK
Rand *Founders* (Cambridge, Mass.) 73: The
Roman dogs have been given a bad name
and hanged. **1928** WRoughead *Murderer's*
(NY 1968) 246: It was the proverbial case
of a dog with a bad name. **1930** AHarbage
T.Killigrew (P) 127: The old saying about
giving a dog a bad name . . . **1930** JRhode
Peril (NY) 266: Give a cat a bad name and
swing her. **1936** PATaylor *Out of Order* (NY)
271: The Give-a-Dog-a-Bad-Name-Club.
1937 MBurton *Clue* (NY) 46: You'd rather
give a dog a bad name and let the jury hang
him. **1949** RLTaylor *W.C.Fields* (NY) 33:
He found dogs with bad names consistently
dangerous. **1950** SPalmer *Green* (NY) 39:
Give a dog a bad name . . . and he may
live. **1958** JCoates *Widow's* (NY) 35: Give a
dog a bad name and he will soon merit
hanging. **1968** MSteen *Pier* (L) 123: An example of "Give a dog a bad name and hang
it." **1982** CMacLeod *Wrack* (NY) 49: The
principle of "Give a dog a bad name and
hang him." EAP D245.

D225 He that lies down with **Dogs** *etc.*
1932 BABotkin ed *Land Is Ours* (Norman,
Okla.) 32: If you lie down with dogs, you'll
get up with fleas. **1937** SPalmer *Blue Banderilla* (NY) 165: He who lies down with
dogs gets up with fleas. **1940** EBQuinn
Death Is (L) 126: Them that lies down with
dogs gets up with fleas. **1953** SBellow *Adventures* (NY) 20: Sleep with dogs and rise
with fleas. **1959** MRuss *Half Moon* (NY)
150: He that lieth down with dogs riseth
up with fleas. **1965** JMitchell *Joe Gould* (NY)
125: If you lie down with dogs, you have
to expect to get up with fleas. EAP D246.

D226 In a **Dog's** age
1929 EBWhite *Letters* ed DLGuth (NY
1976) 87: [Not] in a dog's age. **1930** BRoss
Drury Lane's (NY) 171: Ain't seen you in a
dog's age. **1935** CDickson *Red Widow* (NY)
248: We haven't seen you in a dog's years.
1935 *New Yorker* 11/2 14: He only sees it
once in a dog's age. **1937** JDCarr *Burning*
(NY) 30: A dog's years ago. **1938**
KMKnight *Acts* (NY) 214: Once in a dog's
age. **1949** SSterling *Dead Sure* (NY) 35:

Once in a dog's age. **1961** AGilbert *After*
(NY DBC) 115: I had not seen him in—in a
dog's age, as I think the young people say
now. TW 105(3). Cf. In a Coon's *above.*

D227 It is a poor **Dog** that's not worth whistling for
1952 WSHoole *Simon Suggs* (University,
Ala.) 23: I was a poor dog indeed that
wasn't worth whistling for. *Oxford* 638: Poor
dog.

D228 Let sleeping **Dogs** lie (*varied*)
1919 LThayer *Mystery of the 13th Floor* (NY)
263: Dogs . . . believe in letting sleeping
dogs lie. **1928** DHLawrence *Lady* ("Allemagne") 105: She had wakened the sleeping dogs of old voracious anger. **1930** WLewis *Apes* (NY 1932) 621: Let sleeping dogs
lie. **1934** VLoder *Two Dead* (L) 7: Pity to
wake the sleeping lions of an obsession.
1935 AHobhouse *Hangover* (NY) 236: You
figured that a sleeping dog never bites.
1940 SMSchley *Who'd Shoot* (NY) 276: The
dog is asleep forever. Let's not do anything
. . . to wake him up. **1948** FWCrofts *Silence*
(NY) 167: In other words, if the dogs were
sleeping so satisfactorily, why not let them
lie? **1949** FLockridge *Dishonest* (P) 91: Let
sleeping murders lie. **1950** HGreen *Nothing*
(NY) 59: He said let sleeping dogs lie, don't
stir up mud, better not throw glass stones.
1956 *New Yorker* 6/30 61: I deduced that
the Messrs. Truman and Chinigo had decided to let sleeping squirrels lie. **1957**
BHerald 10/4 37: The New York Yankees
refused to let sleeping dogs lie—and they
had the teeth marks, in the end, to show
for it. **1960** CWatson *Bump* (L 1963) 150:
This communal conspiracy to let a dead
dog lie. **1962** RLockridge *First* (P) 107: It
is sometimes wise to let sleeping illegalities
lie. **1967** FSwinnerton *Sanctuary* (NY) 180:
They say "let sleeping dogs lie." I suppose
that's true of bitches, too. **1968** HCarvic
Picture (NY) 103: I'm all for letting sleeping
birds lie. **1969** PDickinson *Old English* (NY)
43: Otherwise let sleeping lions lie. **1973**
ELopez *Seven* (NY) 190: He said it was better to let sleeping dogs lie. He knew that
was an old cliché, but it was one of his
favorite proverbs. **1976** AChristie *Sleeping*

(NY) 42: I'd let sleeping murder die. Whiting H569; *Oxford* 456–7: Let. Cf. EAP L168: Lion.

D229 A live **Dog** (ass, donkey, horse) is better than a dead lion (*varied*)

1929 LBrock *Stoke Silver* (NY) 134: A live donkey is worth two dead heroes, any day. **1930** WSMaugham *Cakes* (L 1948) 185: They always prefer a live mouse to a dead lion. **1930** RAJWalling *Squeaky Voice* (NY) 191: Remember the Live Donkey and the Dead Lion. **1932** WBMFerguson *Murder* (NY) 177: I preferred . . . to be a live mouse rather than a dead lion. **1932** WSMasterman *Flying* (NY) 110: Hilda evidently thought that a live lawyer was better than a dead gentleman. **1935** ECRLorac *Affair* (L) 213: A live ass is more useful than a dead lion. **1935** WMartyn *Nightmare* (L) 222: You know the old proverb about a dead lion and a living dog. **1935** DYates *She Fell* (NY) 139: Living dogs have their uses, you know—especially when they're mistaken for lions that are dead. **1938** MSaltmarsh *Clouded* (NY) 168: Better a live dog than a dead lion. **1946** NGidding *End over End* (NY) 163: A living dog can talk more than a dead lion. **1958** *Time* 5/26 100: "It's better to be a live lion than a dead dog." **1961** AGilbert (NY DBC) 151: Live dog better than a dead lion. **1967** VPowell *Substantial* (L) 65: A willing donkey was a better proposition than a reluctant lion. **1970** JPorter *Dover Strikes* (NY) 158: I'd sooner be a live donkey than a dead sitting duck any old day of the week. **1970** JVizzard *See* (NY) 192: I'd rather be a live jackass than a dead lion. EAP D251; TW 105(5).

D230 Not turn a **Dog** out on a night like this (*varied*)

1923 JSFletcher *Copper* (NY) 18: You couldn't turn a dog out on a night like this. **1934** CBrackett *Entirely* (NY) 223: You couldn't have turned a dog away in that storm. **1937** ECVivian *38 Automatic* (L) 9: It's the sort of evening . . . when you wouldn't turn a dog out. **1949** JBonett *Dead Lion* (L 1953) 159: She couldn't turn him out like a dog. **1956** RILee *Happy* (B) 119:

I wouldn't send a dog out on a night like this. **1970** DClark *Deadly* (NY) 24: "It's not fit to send a fiddler's bitch out in, if you'll pardon the expression." "I'll pardon it all right. If you'll tell me why a fiddler's bitch." "They're the ones that always get drunk, aren't they?" **1976** JMcClure *Snake* (NY) 90: You can't throw a knight out on a dog like this. EAP D267.

D231 Only **Dogs** and Englishmen walk in the sun (*varied*)

1933 ESnell *And Then* (L) 230: Only dogs and Englishmen, it is said in Latin America, walk in the sun. **1973** OSela *Portuguese* (NY) 145: A lunatic Englishman running in what was still the noonday sun. EAP D252.

D232 The silent **Dog** is the first to bite

1962 *Bangor DN* 6/19 3: The silent dog is the first to bite. Whiting B323: Bitch. Cf. Barking Dogs *above*.

D233 To be (look like) a **Dog's** dinner (*varied*)

1954 EWalter *Untidy* (P) 214: They got poor Acis [*a corpse*] painted up like a dog's dinner. **1955** JTrench *Dishonoured* (NY) 57: Tarting up my house and the garden like a dog's dinner and letting the field walls fall down. **1957** MProcter *Midnight* (NY) 115: It was Martineau, done up like a dog's dinner. **1959** ASillitoe *Saturday* (NY) 201: You talk to me as if I was the dog's dinner. **1960** HRobertson *Swan* (NY) 121: You look like the dog's dinner [*hair style*]. **1966** NMarsh *Killer* (B) 109: You look . . . like the dog's dinner and you sound like nothing on earth. **1974** MInnes *Appleby's Other* (NY) 90: She looks like the cat's breakfast. **1980** RBarnard *Death* (NY) 29: One of them dressed up like the dog's dinner, the other looking like something the cat's brought in, but both of them as like as two peas underneath. Partridge 231.

D234 To be enough to make a **Dog** laugh (sick)

1936 JVTurner *Below the Clock* (L) 145: If it isn't enough to make a dog sick. **1968** EBuckler *Ox Bells* (NY) 164: The mimic could "make a dog laugh." Apperson

159(39). Cf. Enough to make a Cat *above*, Horse *below*.

D235   To be hanged like a **Dog**
1911 JSHay *Amazing Emperor* (L) 70: To be hanged like dogs. **1939** EAmbler *Coffin* (NY 1957) 42: To be hanged like a dog. EAP D254.

D236   To be like a **Dog** baying at the moon
1956 MColes *Far* (NY) 101: Like a dog baying at the moon. EAP D231.

D237   To be top (bottom) **Dog**
1922 JJoyce *Ulysses* (NY 1934) 307: So the wife comes out top dog. **1929** JSFletcher *Ransom* (NY) 24: You are bottom dog. **1933** RHare *Doctor's* (NY) 271: You're the bottom dog. **1940** GDHCole *Murder at* (NY) 108: Which of them is top dog? Wentworth 551: Top dog.

D238   To die like a **Dog**
1959 FCrane *Buttercup* (NY DBC) 131: They let him die like a dog. **1972** SCloete *Victorian* (L) 247: Die like a dog in a ditch. EAP D257; TW 107(35); Brunvand 38(7).

D239   To follow like a **Dog**
1919 LThayer *Mystery of the 13th Floor* (NY) 135: Following me like a dog. **1956** NMarsh *Death* (B) 63: He follows me round like a dog. EAP D258.

D240   To go to the **Dogs**
1905 HRHaggard *Ayesha* (NY) 129: Going to the dogs. **1910** EPhillpotts *Tales* (NY) 28: Bringing England to the dogs. **1922** JJoyce *Ulysses* (NY 1934) 367: Chaps that would go to the dogs. **1930** WLewis *Apes* (NY 1932) 517: The country's going to the dogs. **1940** FWCrofts *Golden Ashes* (NY) 112: The place had gone to the dogs. **1944** VWBrooks *Washington Irving* (NY 1946) 317: The nation was going to the dogs. **1954** EDillon *Sent* (L) 33: The country is going to the dogs. **1959** BHecht *Sensualists* (NY) 32: Throwing Henry to the dogs. **1963** HMiller *Black* (NY) 22: The world is going to the dogs. **1967** RDavies *Marchbank's* (Toronto) 87: The world is going to the dogs. **1970** CEWerkley *Mister* (NY) 158: It was somehow akin to Going to the Dogs,

whatever *that* meant. **1974** THeald *Blue* (NY) 180: The entire country goes to the dogs. EAP D259; Brunvand 38(8).

D241   To have a black **Dog** on one's back (*varied*)
1932 JSFletcher *Squire's Pew* (NY) 164: As if she'd a black dog on her back. **1941** NMarsh *Death and the* (B) 168: Perhaps Bill might work off his black dog on the wireless. **1949** NMarsh *Wreath* (NY) 37: If I don't talk to somebody soon . . . I shall get a black dog on my back. **1952** AWilson *Hemlock* (L) 138: Somebody's got a little black dog on his back. **1956** SDean *Marked* (NY) 32: You mustn't wear it like a black dog on your back [*sense of guilt*]. **1976** AGilbert *Nice* (NY) 187: [He] seems to have the proverbial little black dog on his shoulder [*ill tempered*]. Partridge 59: Black dog. Cf. To have a Monkey *below*.

D242   To help a lame **Dog** over a stile (*varied*)
1920 FWCrofts *Starvel* (NY) 66: If he could help a lame dog over a stile, he did it. **1930** TCobb *Crime* (L) 77: He wouldn't hesitate to help a lame dog over a stile. **1931** JJoyce *Ulysses* (NY 1934) 314: The other gave him a leg over the stile. **1939** FWCrofts *Antidote* (NY) 198: He was using it to boost lame dogs over stiles. **1939** RPenny *She Had* (L) 70: I'm always willing to help a lame dog into the ditch. **1941** JJConnington *Twenty-one* (B) 153: He helped me over a stile. **1948** HActon *Memoirs* (L) 205: To help over stiles lame dogs that turned and bit her. **1953** NLangley *Rift* (NY) 5: Help a lame dog over a stile and he will defecate in your hand. **1957** *Punch* 7/31 120: Lame dogs willing to be assisted over stiles . . . don't grow on trees. **1961** FLockridge *Murder* (P) 114: Lame dogs over stiles. **1967** HBlyth *Old Q* (L) 6: His passion was for helping lame ducks. **1967** DBloodworth *Chinese* (NY) 129: To help the lame dog in the pack over the stile. **1971** RLockridge *Inspector's* (P) 43: No lame dogs over stiles. EAP D260.

D243   To keep a **Dog** and bark oneself
1929 RGraves *Good-bye* (L) 175: They did not . . . believe in "keeping a dog and bark-

Dog

ing themselves." **1931** FWCrofts *Mystery* (NY) 58: No use in keeping a dog etcetera. **1937** CFGregg *Wrong House* (L) 57: No good keeping a dog and barking yourself! **1940** MVHeberden *Fugitive* (NY) 36: A case of hire a dog and bark yourself. **1956** EDillon *Death* (L) 66: One should not hire a dog and bark oneself. **1965** AGilbert *Voice* (NY) 152: I've never understood the point of keeping a dog and barking yourself. **1970** DClark *Deadly* (NY) 13: There's no use in having a dog and barking yourself. EAP D261.

D244 To kill someone like a **Dog**

1927 LBamburg *Beads* (NY) 113: Kill him like a dog. **1930** SChalmers *Crime* (NY) 250: Kill you like a dog. EAP D263.

D245 To know as much as a **Dog** knows about Christmas

1960 JBWest *Taste* (NY) 65: Morris knew as much . . . as a dog knows about Christmas. Cf. TW 109: Donkey (2). Cf. To know as little as a Hog *below*.

D246 To lead a **Dog's** life

1908 LFBaum *American Fairy Tales* (I) 77: And led him a dog's life. **1922** VBridges *Greensea* (NY) 4: A dog's life. **1933** ABCox *Dead Mrs.* (NY) 56: A dog's life. **1939** AWebb *Thank You* (L) 54: It's a dog's life. **1956** *New Yorker* 10/20 23: A dog's life has become the life of Riley. **1956** EXFerrars *We Haven't* (NY) 65: She'd had a dog's life. **1968** BKellner *C.VanVechten* (Norman, Okla.) 56: Leading . . . a dog's life. **1973** AWest *Mortal* (NY) 34: To live a dog's life. EAP D264; TW 107(46). Cf. A Dog's life *above*.

D247 To play a **Dog's** trick

1922 VBridges *Greensea* (NY) 278: Played some dog's trick. EAP D237.

D248 To put on the **Dog**

1938 HReed *Swing Music* (NY) 111: Putting on the dog. **1939** EPaul *Mysterious* (NY 1962) 37: One who doesn't put on any dog. **1951** CLittle *Blackout* (NY) 21: Your ma sure likes to put on the dog. DA Dog 5b.

D249 To shoot someone (down) like a **Dog**

1923 JSFletcher *Markenmore* (NY) 87: Shoot him like a dog. **1924** VBridges *Red* (NY) 266: Shot him down like a dog. **1932** WSMasterman *Flying* (NY) 277: Shoot me down like a dog. **1938** ESHolding *Obstinate* (NY) 172: Shooting him down like a dog. **1954** JRMacdonald *Find* (NY) 30: Shoot like a dog. **1963** FHoyle *Fifth* (L 1965) 159: Shot down like a dog. **1974** MInnes *Appleby's Other* (NY) 137: This shooting of him like a dog. TW 108(53).

D250 To stick (hang on) like a **Dog** to a bone

1930 TCoff *Sark* (L) 231: He sticks to it like a dog to a bone. **1967** JAxelrad *Freneau* (Austin) 298: Hanging on to peace like a dog to a bone. Cf. TW 107(43), 108(55).

D251 To teach an old **Dog** new tricks (*varied*)

1906 JCLincoln *Mr. Pratt* (NY) 282: It's hard to teach old dogs new tricks. **1913** HTFinck *Food* (NY) 51: It is difficult to teach an old dog new tricks. **1928** SChalmers *House* (NY) 239: Being too old a dog to learn new tricks. **1930** MBDix *Murder* (L) 165: No use trying to teach an old dog new tricks. **1935** *New Yorker* 11/2 67: You can't teach an old dog new tricks. **1952** HHunter *Bengal* (NY) 193: I am too old a dog to learn new tricks. **1953** RFenisong *Wench* (NY) 18: You can't teach an old dog new tricks. **1956** *Time* 8/13 58: The old dog learned a pathetic array of new tricks. **1959** *BangorDN* 8/6 21: If you think you are going to teach your old dog new tricks— you are barking up the wrong tree. **1963** PDJames *Mind* (L) 141: He's getting an old dog now and too fond of his own tricks. **1966** GKanin *Remembering* (NY) 15: The old dog had learned some new tricks. **1969** HLiggett *Murder* (L) 21: I'm like the old dog whose habits can't be broken. **1972** AGarve *Case* (NY) 135: It's the old dog that knows the best tricks. EAP D272. Cf. To be too old a Bird *above*.

D252 To treat someone like a **Dog**

1930 GBMeans *Strange Death* (NY) 218: He treated me like a dog. **1932** MThynne *Mur-*

179

der (NY) 127: Treated her worse than a dog. **1940** RAvery *Murder a Day* (NY) 74: She treated him like a dog. **1944** MVenning *Jethro* (NY) 68: We treated Jethro like a dog. **1952** RFenisong *Deadlock* (NY) 53: His . . . brother treated him like a dog. **1970** RFoley *Calculated* (NY) 25: She treated him like a dog. TW 108(56); Brunvand 38(11).

D253 To try something on the **Dog**

1919 LMerrick *Chair* (L) 217: I am "trying it on the dog." **1922** JJoyce *Ulysses* (NY 1934) 172: Try it on the dog first. **1926** JJConnington *Death* (NY) 26: "Try it on the dog," as we used to say. **1928** SHuddleston *Paris Salons* (NY) 146: A vulgar English expression—trying it on the dog. **1929** JB Prestly *Good* (NY) 307: Trying it on the dog. **1930** VLoder *Essex* (L) 69: We'll try that on the dog. **1938** BCobb *Fatal* (L) 43: Not unless I can try it on the dog first. **1954** JSymons *Narrowing* (NY) 43: Something you're trying out on the dog. Partridge 913: Try.

D254 To work like a **Dog** (hound)

1925 EMillay *Letters* ed ARMacdougall (NY 1952) 194: Working like . . . dogs. **1925** GBeasley *My First* (Paris) 115: Working like a dog. **1932** PGWodehouse *Hot Water* (NY) 277: I worked like a dog. **1938** PMcGuire *Burial* (L) 107: To work like dogs in a treadmill. **1942** VCaspary *Laura* (NY 1957) 30: She worked like a dog. **1945** EDaly *Any Shape* (NY) 132: She . . . works like a dog over her face. **1948** LFord *Devil's* (NY) 55: She worked like a hound. **1950** MScherf *Curious* (NY) 21: Worked like a dog. **1956** MScherf *Cautious* (NY) 82: I've been working like a dog. **1963** HPentecost *Tarnished* (NY DBC) 80: I worked like a dog. **1964** RBraddon *Year* (L 1967) 14: Works like a drover's dog. **1973** CJackson *Kicked* (NY) 8: Working like a dog. EAP D268; Brunvand 38(12): Dogs in a meat-pot.

D255 Two **Dogs** over one bone

1934 RAJWalling *Eight* (L) 223: Like two dogs over a bone. **1954** KAmis *Lucky* (L) 110: They'll fight over her like dogs over a bone. EAP D270.

D256 Until the last **Dog** was hung

1931 TThayer *Greek* (NY) 258: Tertia, who had never before left any gathering until the last dog had been hung. **1957** *BHerald* 2/17 30: He always sticks around until the last dog is hung. **1959** DTaylor *Joy* (NY) 48: Remaining at a party until the last dog was hung. **1966** JDosPassos *Best* (NY) 155: He stuck to it till the last dog was hung. Whiting *NC* 397–8(35); DA Dog 3(8).

D257 It is **Dogged** that does it

1919 HRHaggard *She and Allan* (NY 1921) 119: It's dogged as does it. **1930** ECRLorac *Murder* (L) 137: Dogged does it. **1932** HWade *Hanging* (L) 283: As my chief says: "It's dogged as does it." **1941** NMarsh *Death and the* (B) 218: It's dogged as does it. **1975** MButterworth *Man in* (NY) 3: It's dogged as does it. *Oxford* 197.

D258 To lie **Doggo**

1958 RMacdonald *Doomsters* (NY) 174: He may be lying doggo. **1963** JKirkup *Tropic* (L) 157: Lying doggo and playing possum. Partridge 231.

D259 To be in the **Doghouse** (*varied*)

1937 ABCaldwell *No Tears* (NY) 194: Rudy is out building a doghouse to put me in. **1939** TPolsky *Curtains* (NY) 115: While I sit forlorn in my humble dwelling, the doghouse. (That quiet little shack out there behind the eight ball.) **1941** GBAgby *Here Comes* (NY) 233: I've been in the doghouse up here. **1951** IChase *New York 22* (NY) 7: I guess Pa's in the doghouse. **1957** DMDisney *My Neighbour's* (NY) 102: I wasn't in the doghouse. **1958** MHastings *Cork in the Doghouse* (NY). **1961** EPeters *Death* (NY) 176: Find himself in the doghouse. **1962** HWaugh *Late* (NY) 108: Waterhouse is in the doghouse. Wentworth: Doghouse (2).

D260 To be a **Dogsbody**

1929 ABCox *Layton* (NY) 12: A general dogsbody for the old man. **1930** ABCox *Piccadilly* (NY) 66: Unpaid companion, dogsbody, and whipping-post to the old lady. **1951** AChristie *They Came* (NY) 16: The old boy's personal Yesman and Dogsbody. **1968** AChristie *By the Pricking* (NY) 52: Wills [is] the dog's body of the firm.

1972 MGilbert *Body* (NY) 43: I'm just the dogsbody. Partridge 231.

D261   As big as a (silver) **Dollar**

1939 JNDarby *Murder in* (I) 65: Her eyes looking as big as silver dollars. **1940** CSaxby *Death Joins* (NY) 129: Their eyes big as dollars. Cf. Saucers *below.*

D262   As bright as a (new) **Dollar**

1924 CVanVechten *Tattooed* (NY) 64: She's bright as a dollar. **1929** KPreston *Pot Shots* (NY) 43: Bright as a new dollar. **1937** CBClason *Blind* (NY) 59: Cynthia's bright as a new dollar. **1938** DBaker *Young Man* (B) 11: Bright as a dollar. **1950** MLong *Louisville* (NY) 215: She's bright as a dollar. **1956** *New Yorker* 8/18 20: The sisters are Viennese, and bright as dollars. EAP D274.

D263   As sound (fit) as a **Dollar**

1925 SJohnson *Professor* (NY) 118: I'm sound as a dollar. **1932** NKlein *No! No!* (NY) 254: She's fit as a dollar. **1933** CPenfield *After the Deacon* (NY) 19: Sound as a dollar. **1938** LBarret *Though Young* (NY) 121: Um's advice rang as sound as a dollar. **1947** MCarleton *Swan* (NY) 91: He's sound as a dollar. **1950** MScherf *Curious* (NY) 62: Sound as a silver dollar and well rested. **1955** LCochran *Hallelujah* (NY) 194: The Bank . . . was as sound as a dollar. **1958** *BHerald* 12/15 35: I sleeps sound as a dollar. **1960** *BHerald* 5/15 28: His health "is as sound as a dollar used to be." **1961** WMasterson *Evil* (NY) 126: She's as sound as the dollar used to be. **1963** EMcBain *Ten* (NY) 102: Sound as a dollar [*honest*]. TW 109(5).

D264   **Dollars** to doughnuts (*varied*)

1926 JTully *Beggars* (NY) 116: It's dollars to doughnuts. **1932** BRoss *Tragedy of X* (NY) 318: I'll bet dollars to doughnuts. **1939** VHansom *Casual* (NY) 259: Dollars to Crullers, as the saying goes. **1948** GHJohnston *Death Takes* (L 1959) 183: It's doughnuts to dimes. **1955** FCrane *Death* (NY) 93: Dollars to doughnuts . . . she could do it. **1967** JDCarr *Dark* (NY) 169: Dollars to doughnuts. **1977** CAGoodrum *Dewey* (NY) 113: I'll bet you dollars to doughnuts. DA Dollar 2b(3); Partridge 232.

D265   No **Dollars**, no riders

1937 WMartyn *Blue Ridge* (L) 296: No dollar, no riders. Cf. *Oxford* 573: No penny. Cf. No Money *below.*

D266   To bet one's bottom **Dollar**

1926 JArnold *Murder!* (L) 292: You can bet your bottom dollar. **1940** DHume *Five Aces* (L) 116: You can bet your bottom dollar. **1952** RFenisong *Deadlock* (NY) 32: I'll bet my bottom dollar. **1959** MProcter *Killer* (NY) 173: You can bet your bottom dollar. **1962** KKesey *One Flew* (NY) 13: You can bet your bottom dollar. **1966** SMarlowe *Search* (NY) 62: You can bet your bottom old franc. **1982** CMacLeod *Wrack* (NY) 179: You can bet your bottom dollar on that. TW 109(8).

D267   To look like a million **Dollars** (*varied*)

1938 PGWodehouse *Code* (NY) 222: Feeling like a million dollars. **1940** KRoos *Made up* (NY) 172: And it looks like a million dollars on you! **1954** JPotts *Go* (NY) 27: She looks like a million dollars. **1959** FLockridge *Murder* (P) 165: They looked, as people said, "like a million dollars." **1966** MMcShane *Crimso* (NY) 99: She looks like a million dollars. **1967** VLincoln *Private* (NY) 235: Bridget came in looking like a million dollars. DA Dollar 2b(5).

D268   To squeeze a **Dollar** *etc.*

1929 FDaingerfield *Linden* (NY) 50: She'd squeeze a dollar closer than that coat's squeezin' you. **1952** MRRinehart *Swimming* (NY) 133: She'd squeeze a quarter until the eagle screamed. **1963** CKeith *Rich* (NY) 27: He did pinch every penny and dollar so hard . . . that the eagle screamed. DA Eagle 2b.

D269   As straight as a **Donkey's** hind leg

1948 CBush *Curious* (NY) 124: Sid's as straight as a donkey's hind leg. Wilstach 392: As a loon's leg.

D270   For **Donkey's** years

1927 RAFreeman *Cat's Eye* (NY) 78: I haven't seen you for donkey's years; **1930** WLewis *Apes* (NY 1932) 215: I have not seen him for a donkey's years; 286. **1931**

WMartyn *Scarlett* (L) 306: A mess you are not going to get rid of in a donkey's age. **1939** GDHCole *Double* (NY) 234: Dead for donkey's years. **1954** EWalter *Untidy* (P) 147: It's been donkey's years since I've seen them. **1964** SCooper *Mandrake* (L 1966) 34: Donkey's years ago. **1972** DLees *Rainbow* (NY) 53: Donkey's ages ago. Wentworth 155.

D271 Like a **Donkey** between two bundles of hay (*varied*)

1937 WGore *Murder Most* (L) 217: I am like Buridan's ass, between two piles of hay. **1938** LBrock *Silver Sickle* (L) 67: Nor a donkey between two carrots. **1941** EPhillpotts *Ghostwater* (NY) 270: Like a donkey between two bundles of hay. **1946** ABCunningham *One Man* (NY) 89: Did you ever hear of the mule that starved to death at equal distances between two bales of hay? *Oxford* 199.

D272 Till **Doomsday** (or after) (*varied*)

1930 WSMaugham *Cakes* (L 1948) 71: I'd have to wait till Doomsday. **1931** PATaylor *Cape Cod* (NY 1971) 129: We could sit here . . . till doomsday or the day after. **1937** DWhitelaw *Face* (L) 227: They could look till Doomsday. **1949** FCrane *Flying* (NY) 65: Iles would cover for her till doomsday. **1955** FCDavis *Night* (NY) 120: When these boys run out of resources it will be the week after Doomsday. EAP D276.

D273 To be behind the **Door** (*varied*)

1950 ECBentley *Chill* (NY) 29: And if it comes to faces, I know one that wasn't behind the door when ugly ones were given out. **1968** JGould *Europe* (B) 259: She was an unfortunate young thing who had been out of the room when looks were passed around. She had about as much glamour as a pail of whale manure. **1969** AGilbert *Mr. Crook* (NY DBC) 33: One of those hardworking men who always seems to be behind the door when promotion's handed around. TW 109(1). Cf. When it's raining Gold *below*.

D274 To lock the **Door** after the horse is stolen (*very varied*)

1920 AJRees *Hand in the Dark* (NY 1929) 62: The old proverb about locking doors after stolen steeds. **1924** HCBailey *Mr. Fortune's Practice* (NY) 90: Shutting the stable door after the horse's stolen; 124. **1928** PMacdonald *White* (NY) 5: It's shutting the stable door after the horse has gone. **1928** AEWMason *Prisoner* (NY) 183: We lock the door . . . after the horse has stolen the oats. **1930** WWoodrow *Moonhill* (NY) 129: We found the horse gone and the stable door unlocked. **1931** SFowler *Bell Street* (L) 170: Watch the stable-door when the horse is in the next county. **1932** MKennedy *Murderer* (L) 118: Lock the stable door when half the horse is stolen. **1932** JHWallis *Capital* (NY) 214: Locking the door after the horse had been stolen. **1936** CHarris *Going* (P) 201: A case of locking the barn after the horse is stolen. **1936** KCStrahan *Desert* (I) 280: The one [*adage*] about no use in locking the barn door after the horse has fled. **1937** EForbes *Paradise* (NY) 28: You can shut the door now—after the horse is stolen. **1940** RStout *Double for Death* (L) 143: Locking the door after the horse is stolen. **1948** JFHutton *Too Good* (NY) 52: He's the man who rushes up and slams barn doors on empty stalls. **1951** SJepson *Man Dead* (NY) 177: In the same continuity of compulsion to shut the stable door after the horse is stolen. **1956** *Punch* 6/20 742: They bolt the stable door after the horse has fled. **1957** *New Yorker* 3/30 121: This is one place where the barn door will be locked, before lightning strikes. **1958** *BHerald* 9/29 31: "Lockin' up the horse after the barn door is stole don't help." "It does if the horse is guilty." **1959** *BHerald* 5/12 18: This will be like closing the door after the Horse is gone. **1959** PMacDonald *List* (NY) 142: There must be a lot of empty stable doors in London that need shutting. **1960** HInnes *Doomed* (NY) 308: A matter of bolting the door after the horse has gone. **1962** HReilly *Day* (NY DBC) 104: McKee finished locking the closet door after two horses had been stolen. **1966** PGWodehouse *Plum* (L) 107: Just locking the stable door after the milk has been spilt, as you might say. **1970** STerkel *Hard* (NY) 140: You're too damn late. I've got the barn door locked. **1973** KAmis *Riverside* (NY) 39: Rather like locking the proverbial stable door. **1973** ARoudybush *Gastronomic* (NY)

9: He went over to lock the stable door before any other horses were stolen. **1975** GHousehold *Red* (B) 8: Shutting the stable door when the horse has bolted. **1981** ELathen *Going* (NY) 118: This was a case of locking the barn door with a vengeance. **1982** CMacLeod *Wrack* (NY) 120: That may be a case of locking the stable after the bull is thrown [*pun*]. EAP S419; TW 109(2). Cf. Brunvand 140: Thief (3).

D275 As bald as a **Doorknob**

1954 RStout *Three* (NY) 148: Bald as a doorknob. Whiting *NC* 399(1).

D276 As dead as a **Doorknob**

1932 PATaylor *Death* (I) 99: Dead as a door-knob. **1954** AStone *Harvard* (B) 213: Dead as a doorknob. **1956** *BangorDN* 5/21 23: Dead as a doorknob. **1957** *BHerald* 7/9 3: Kill the sales tax as dead as a doorknob. **1964** LPayne *Deep* (L) 131: Dead as a door-knob. Whiting *NC* 399(2).

D277 As deaf as a **Doorknob**

1965 HVanDyke *Ladies* (NY) 62: As deaf as a doorknob. **1976** EFoote-Smith *Gentle* (NY) 98: Ben's deaf as a doorknob. Whiting *NC* 399(3).

D278 As dead as a **Doornail** (bobnail, door knocker)

1900 CFPidgin *Quincy A. Sawyer* (B) 340: Deader'n a door nail. **1924** AChristie *Man* (NY) 22: Dead as a door-nail. **1930** CFGregg *Murder* (NY) 23: Dead as a door-knocker. **1932** PMacDonald *Escape* (NY) 301: Lionel is as dead as the proverbial doornail. **1933** HAsbury *Barbary* (NY) 313: The Barbary Coast was as dead as the proverbial doornail. **1937** PHaggard *Dead Is The Doornail* (P). **1939** JRWarren *Murder from* (NY) 119: As dead as a doornail, as the saying is. **1941** PWentworth *Weekend* (P) 33: Dead as a doornail, as the saying is. **1957** *New Yorker* 10/19 64: Miami'll be as dead as a doornail. **1958** *BHerald* 1/19 3A: Dead as a doornail. **1965** RSPrather *Dead Man's* (NY) 57: She was dead as a doornail. **1970** MInnes *Death* (L) 174: As dead as a doornail. **1974** DMDisney *Don't Go* (NY) 39: Dead as a doornail. **1976** JFoxx *Free-booty* (I) 117: Deader than a bobnail. EAP

D282; TW 109–10; Brunvand 39(1). Cf. Taylor *Prov. Comp.* 32: Doornail. Cf. As dead as a Nail *below*.

D279 As deaf as a **Doornail**

1961 LWhite *Grave* (NY DBC) 118: She's deaf as a doornail. Whiting *NC* 399(2); Brunvand 39(2).

D280 As dumb as a **Doornail**

1967 CDrummond *Death* (NY) 110: Dumb as a doornail. Taylor *Prov. Comp.* 37.

D281 As dead as a **Door post**

1930 HAdams *Golden* (L) 18: Dead as a door post, as my 'usband used to say. **1936** PKelway *Hedge Folk* (L) 28: Dead as a door-post. Cf. Whiting D352: Door-tree; Apperson 138–9; *Oxford* 132.

D282 Don't shit on your own **Doorstep**

1976 CDexter *Last Seen* (NY) 124: There's an old saying, isn't there—if you'll excuse the language—about not shitting on your own doorstep. Cf. Bird that fouls *above*; To Shit where *below*.

D283 To sleep like a **Dormouse**

1926 AMarshall *Mote* (NY) 22: I slept like a dormouse. **1940** RAFreeman *Mr. Polton* (NY) 129: Sleeping like a dormouse. **1957** NMitford *Voltaire* (L) 269: They were both sleeping like dormice. **1970** EHahn *Times* (NY) 101: I slept like a dormouse. **1977** STWarner *Kingdoms* (NY) 115: Slept like a dormouse. EAP D283.

D284 To go through like a **Dose** of salts (*varied*)

1929 JBPriestley *Good* (NY) 137: Going through the lot "like a dose of salts." **1933** DMarfield *Mystery* (NY) 251: I'm going through his office like Rochelle salts. **1938** EBell *Fish* (NY) 141: They'd go through you like salts through a widder womurn. **1941** GBenedict *Deadly Drops* (NY) 134: They went through you guys like a dose o' salts. **1945** HGreen *Loving* (L) 100: When they come through this tight little island like a dose of Epsom salts. **1949** MGilbert *He Didn't* (NY DBC) 141: They hauled it out, quick as a dose of salts. **1952** JDCarr *Nine Wrong* (NY) 208: General Grant will go through them Confederates like a dose of salts. **1953** OAtkinson *Golden* (I) 171: He's been through his women like a dose of oil. **1953** TWicker *Kingpin* (NY) 25: This feeling passed through Tucker like a dose of salts. **1956** RRobinson *Landscape* (L 1963) 169: In and out like a dose of salts. **1959** JFleming *Malice* (NY) 7: His patrimony having "run through him like a dose of salts." **1961** MNelson *When the Bed* (L) 13: Gone through her lovers like salts. **1962** NFreeling *Death* (NY 1964) 52: I can take time to go through that woman's past like a dose of salts. **1965** HActon *Old Lamps* (L) 215: She has been through Cubism . . . like a dose of salts. **1970** VCHall *Outback* (Adelaide) 42: The mare went through the timber like a dose of salts, as Patsy put it later. **1970** JLeasor *They Don't* (NY) 213: Then the car came through the last bend like a dose of salts through a man with dysentery. **1976** CLarson *Muir's* (NY) 111: "Have the police been through here?" "Like a dose of salts." **1976** JSScott *Bastard's* (NY) 94: We'll be up that fucking path like a dose of fucking salts. DA Dose 1; Partridge 236. Cf. Grease *below.*

D285 When in **Doubt**, don't *(varied)*

1925 JSFletcher *Annexation* (NY) 219: The old adage—"When in doubt, count twenty before you act or speak." **1927** ELWhite *Lukundoo* (NY) 199: There is a fine old proverb that says, "When in doubt, do nothing." **1936** PCheyney *This Man* (L) 99: [A] proverb which says "When in doubt don't." **1938** MJFreeman *Scarf* (NY) 153: His motto was, "When in doubt, do nothing." **1952** HCecil *Ways* (L) 109: The maxim: When in doubt, don't. *Oxford* 200.

D286 As white (pale) as **Dough**; Dough-white

1934 GFowler *Father Goose* (NY) 162: As pale as dough. **1940** LFord *Old Lover's* (NY) 230: His face was white as dough. **1946** JTShaw *Hard-Busted* (NY) 115: Face was as white as dough. **1965** JPotts *Only Good* (NY) 177: His face was dough-white. **1971** PMoyes *Season* (NY) 200: Claudet had gone as white as dough. **1976** CLarson *Muir's* (NY) 85: Face . . . white as dough.

D287 As gentle as a **Dove**

1931 RInce *When Joan* (L) 181: These old gods are as gentle as doves. **1940** JCLincoln *Out of the Fog* (NY) 62: As gentle as the cooing dove. **1941** ESHolding *Speak* (NY) 112: She answered, gentle as a dove. **1962** CDSimak *All the Traps* (NY) 285: Gentle as a dove. **1972** JCreasey *First* (NY) 77: He had been as gentle as a dove. EAP D285.

D288 As happy as a **Dove**

1931 WFaulkner *Sanctuary* (NY) 189: We was happy as two doves. Whiting *NC* 400(2); Taylor *Prov. Comp.* 35.

D289 As innocent as **Doves**

1954 EForbes *Rainbow* (B) 117: Innocent as two doves. EAP D286. Cf. Turtledoves *below.*

D290 As meek as **Doves**

1931 GDHCole *Dead Man's* (L) 127: They're all as meek as doves. TW 110(4).

D291 As soft as **Doves**

1956 NMarsh *Death* (B) 148: Soft as doves. TW 110(5).

D292 To bill and coo like **Doves**

1976 MLeister *Wildlings* (Owings Mills, Md.) 172: The clichéd billing and cooing of proverbial doves. Whiting *NC* 400(7): Coo.

D293 Young **Doves** do not hatch from ravens' eggs

1948 KWilliamson *Atlantic* (L 1970) 66: Seldom do young doves hatch from ravens' eggs—an old proverb. *Oxford* 211: Eagles don't breed doves.

D294 To be **Down** but not out

1946 ABCunningham *Death Rides* (NY) 122: She was down but she wasn't out. **1951** HSaunders *Sleeping* (L) 44: Though down . . . he was by no means out. **1968** RDuncan *How to Make* (L) 174: I was down but not yet out. Whiting *NC* 400.

D295 To talk (*etc.*) nineteen (*etc.*) to the **Dozen**

1919 KHoward *Peculiar* (NY) 83: Chattering away nineteen to the dozen. **1919**

LMerrick *Chain* (L) 350: Their tongues went nineteen to the dozen. **1928** ESnell *Blue* (P) 216: Talked nineteen to the dozen. **1929** VLoder *Between* (NY) 204: The others . . . were talking fourteen to the dozen. **1930** JSFletcher *Green Rope* (L) 187: They'll talk thirteen to the dozen. **1931** JDBeresford *Innocent* (NY) 125: With that tongue of hers clacking nineteen to the dozen. **1931** PGWodehouse *If I Were You* (NY) 104: Talking sixteen to the dozen. **1932** JJConnington *Castleford* (B) 26: My heart beating sixteen to the dozen. **1933** GHolt *Six Minutes* (L) 199: Talked forty to the dozen. **1933** RAJWalling *Follow* (L) 201: Lying thirteen to the dozen. **1935** VLoder *Death* (L) 92: Mercer began to talk twenty to the dozen. **1939** HCBailey *Great Game* (L) 74: Asking questions thirteen to the dozen. **1940** PATaylor *Deadly* (NY) 256: That fellow can talk sixty to the dozen. **1946** JDCarr *He Who Whimpers* (NY) 73: Marion had talked away twenty to the dozen. **1950** CDickson *Night* (NY) 239: These . . . women . . . talk twenty to the dozen. **1951** AChristie *They Came* (NY) 74: Talking nineteen to the dozen. **1952** CDickson *Behind* (NY) 12: Asking questions twenty to the dozen. **1953** ERuggles *Prince* (NY) 361: Talked ten to the dozen. **1956** AAtkinson *Exit* (NY) 178: Sneezing nineteen to the dozen. **1957** *Punch* 7/10 40: Talked nineteen to the dozen. **1958** *New Yorker* 1/11 27: They chattered away, thirteen to the dozen. **1958** WRoss *Immortal* (NY) 87: Chattering sixty to the dozen. **1959** FHoyle *Ossian's* (NY) 27: Talked away twenty to the dozen. **1960** COLocke *Taste* (NY) 71: Talking Spanish six to the dozen. **1960** FFrankfurter *Reminisces* (NY) 59: Now—what's the phrase? Thirteen to the dozen. **1966** LPDavies *Paper* (NY) 27: Chatting away twenty to the dozen. **1968** JFraser *Evergreen* (NY) 58: They'd be going twelve to the dozen [*talking*]. **1969** RRendell *Secret* (NY) 101: The editor's prim mouth was opening and shutting nineteen to the dozen. **1976** MGilbert *Night* (NY) 44: She talks nineteen to the dozen. **1976** BMooney *LBJ* (NY) 269: His old boss was talking thirteen to the dozen. *Oxford* 830: Tongue runs; Partridge 239: Nineteen, thirteen.

D296   To be (go) down the **Drain**

1931 MAHamilton *Murder* (L) 23: Down the drain. **1937** PWentworth *Case Is Closed* (L) 150: Gone down the drain, as you may say. **1948** CBush *Curious* (NY) 63: Just money down the drain. **1956** ABurgess *Time* (L) 128: Money thrown down the drain. **1959** BClifton *Murder* (NY) 76: Petersen's sold you down the drain. **1960** HQMasur *Send Another* (NY) 98: It was money down the drain. **1964** CBrown *Never-Was* (NY) 106: It would be money down the drain. **1967** CBush *Deadly* (NY) 95: Everything's gone down the drain. **1970** RRendell *Best Man* (NY) 160: Money down the drain.

D297   **Dreams** go by contraries (*varied*)

1922 JJoyce *Ulysses* (NY 1934) 557: Dreams go by contraries. **1932** JHWallis *Capital* (NY) 55: Dreams go by contraries. **1956** *BHerald* 10/26 58: Dreams always turn out just the opposite. EAP D298; TW 110–11; Brunvand 39.

D298   To vanish like a **Dream**

1971 BEnglish *War* (L) 133: So did the Persians vanish like a dream. EAP D299.

D299   To work like a **Dream**

1936 NMorland *Clue* (L) 194: It worked like a dream. **1950** HGreen *Nothing* (NY) 125: Every thing worked like a dream. **1961** IFleming *Thunderball* (NY DBC) 17: Worked like a dream. Cf. Charm *above*.

D300   To be all **Dressed** up and nowhere to go

1930 JGBrandon *McCarthy* (L) 24: All dressed up and nowhere to go, as the song says. **1930** GMitchell *Mystery* (NY) 29: All dressed up and nowhere to go. **1952** AWilson *Hemlock* (L) 44: All dressed up and nowhere to go. **1960** JSymons *Progress* (L) 67: All dressed up . . . nowhere to go. Partridge 88: All dressed-up; Bartlett 896 b [*William Allen White*].

D301   To be a long, tall (thin) **Drink** of water

1927 JTully *Circus* (NY) 210: He was a long tall drink o' water. **1940** AAFair *Gold Comes* (NY) 195: He looks like . . . a long, thin drink of water. Wentworth 324: Long drink.

D302   As pissed as a **Dromedary**

1981 JSScott *View* (NY) 82: Pissed as a dromedary [*drunk*].

D303   At the **Drop** of a hat

1905 Jack London *Letters* ed KHendricks (NY 1965) 175: He was groggy at the drop of a hat. **1930** HFootner *Mystery* (NY) 194: At the drop of a hat. **1935** VSheean *Personal History* (NY) 117: Write a book at the drop of a hat. **1937** LFord *Simple Way* (NY) 204: Women who go to pieces at the drop of a hat. **1944** MLong *Bury* (NY) 143: Rape a girl at the drop of a hat. **1951** WCWilliams *Autobiography* (NY) 30: Ready to fight at the drop of a hat. **1956** *Time* 10/1 24: In Texas—where observations are made at the drop of a Stetson. **1956** SBaron *Facts* (NY) 22: She could be seduced at the drop of a hat. **1966** TWells *Matter* (NY) 119: She lied at the drop of a hat. **1970** RFenisong *The Drop of a Hat* (NY). **1972** SNBehrman *People* (B) 270: I get a chill at the drop of a hat. DA Drop 4.

D304   A **Drop** in the bucket

1929 JJConnington *Case* (B) 174: A mere drop in the bucket, as you would say in English. **1939** CRawson *Footprints* (L) 148: Two hundred thousand is only a drop in the bucket. **1957** *BHerald* 12/29 56: Eighty-two and a half million dollars. A drop in the bucket . . . that proverbial drop. **1964** CChaplin *Autobiography* (NY 1966) 16: His contribution was less than a drop in the bucket. **1966** JLymington *Froomb!* (NY) 21: It is just a drop in the bucket. **1968** WTenn *Seven* (NY) 139: But 2119 is just a drop in the historical bucket. **1970** CEWerkley *Mister* (NY) 16: Not a drop in the bucket . . . not even a little drop in a great big bucket. **1973** GSheehy *Hustling* (NY) 147: [It] is a droplet in the bucket. EAP D303.

D305   A **Drop** in the ocean

1956 JChristopher *Death* (L) 19: We're sending food, but it's a drop in the ocean. **1958** CLBlackstone *Foggy* (NY) 100: But what's a little drop . . . in the ocean? **1965** AChristie *At Bertram's* (L) 246: That's only

a drop in the ocean. EAP D304. Cf. Ocean *below*.

D306   Constant **Dropping** wears away a stone (*varied*)

1927 EPhillpotts *Jury* (NY) 124: Running water wears out a stone. **1929** EWallace *Flying* (L) 155: Water constantly dripping wears away stone. **1931** CWells *Horror* (P) 30: The continual dropping that wears away a stone. **1933** PMacDonald *Mystery* (NY 1958) 170: Satisfied to wear away the stone by the repeated-drop-of-water process. **1935** PMacDonald *Death* (NY) 51: Enough drops of water falling in the same spot will wear away a rock. **1939** MBurton *Babbacombe* (L) 105: The old story of the water dripping on the stone. **1946** ESedgwick *Happy* (B) 165: If ever the famous drip wore down the granite underneath. **1947** MCarleton *Sway* (NY) 23: It's like wearing away stone with drops of water. **1958** WGraham *Wrack* (NY) 131: His best water-weareth-away-stone manner. **1961** LSde Camp (NY 1968) 381: As the drop of water wears away a stone. **1962** ESGardner *Mischievous* (NY DBC) 61: The constant dripping water . . . can wear away the toughest stone. **1963** UCurtiss *Wasp* (NY DBC) 42: Like water on stone, ceaseless and hollowing. **1964** DMDisney *Departure* (NY DBC) 111: A word here, a word there, water wearing away a stone. **1965** HKane *Midnight* (NY) 19: The falling drops at last will wear the stone . . . Lucretius. **1966** DMDisney *Magic* (NY) 119: She kept after him like water wearing away stone. **1970** RFoley *Calculated* (NY) 82: On the theory of constantly dripping, I suppose. EAP D306; TW 111(1).

D307   A **Dropping** (of water) on a rainy day and a contentious woman are alike

1966 HJBoyle *With a Pinch* (NY) 190: But according to the proverbs, a continual dropping on a very rainy day and a contentious woman are alike. Whiting T187; *Oxford* 817: Three things.

D308   A **Drug** on (in) the market

1900 CFPidgin *Quincy A. Sawyer* (B) 192: Poetry is a drug. **1911** HHMunro *Chronicles*

(L 1927) 108: It could scarcely be called a drug in the market; people bought drugs. **1922** JJoyce *Ulysses* (NY 1934) 192: Genius would be a drug in the market. **1929** HAdams *Oddways* (P) 209: His learning is a drug in the market. **1938** VLoder *Kill* (L) 88: Bottles were a drug in the market. **1940** VRath *Death of a Lucky* (NY) 66: It's a drug on the market [*a house*]. **1947** GGallagher *I Found* (NY DBC) 57: She was a drug on the marriage market. **1955** MGilbert *Country-house* (NY) 37: They're rather a drug on the market. **1957** *BHerald* 12/15 48: Asian flu vaccine . . . [is] literally and figuratively a drug on the market. **1963** MPUtzel *Man in the Mirror* (Cambridge, Mass.) 163: In 1900 Whitman admirers had become a drug on the market. **1969** CBaker *Ernest Hemingway* (NY) 158: Short stories were a drug on the market. **1973** DLeitch *God* (L) 14: Apple trees . . . were a drug on the market. **1975** PDJames *Black* (NY) 136: Large country houses were a drag on the market. EAP D307.

D309 As empty (toom) as a **Drum**

1929 JBPriestley *Good* (NY) 113: Empty as a drum. **1931** DLSayers *Suspicious* (NY) 71: His interior was as toom as a drum. **1939** HFootner *Murder That* (L) 97: Empty as drums . . . Only fit to make a noise. **1970** HCarmichael *Death* (NY) 131: His mind was as hollow as an empty drum. EAP D308.

D310 As tight as a **Drum**; Drum-tight

1922 JJoyce *Ulysses* (NY 1934) 266: Trousers tight as a drum on him. **1923** LThayer *Sinister* (NY) 96: He was tight as a drum about 'em all [*secretive*]. **1929** FDaingerfield *Linden* (NY) 30: "House locked?" "Tight as a drum"; 71. **1930** GCollins *Horror* (L) 219: The hole's packed tight as a drum. **1930** JRhode *Davidson* (L) 55: Tight as a drum [*drunk*]. **1932** COrr *Wailing* (NY) 63: Every other house is shut tight as a drum. **1935** VSheean *Personal History* (NY) 122: The blockade was, as they said, tighter than a drum. **1936** CBClason *Death Angel* (NY) 8: They're all of them sewed up tighter than a drum [*very busy*]. **1938** MPage *Fast Company* (NY) 14: Lapping up liquor and get-ting tight as a drum. **1943** ADerleth *Seven* (NY) 196: He's tight as a drum [*drunk*]. **1947** PMcGerr *Pick* (NY) 88: Shut up tight as a drum. **1950** RStout *In the Best* (NY) 202: It's tight as a drum [*foolproof*]. **1951** RStout *Curtains* (NY) 191: He had kept himself concealed, as tight as a drum. **1952** CLittle *Black* (NY) 167: She's tight as a drum [*tense*]. **1956** MProcter *Pub* (NY) 34: I'm as tight as a drum [*drunk*]. **1969** RStout *Death* (NY) 113: [His] alibi was tight as a drum. **1973** KAmis *Riverside* (NY) 167: As tight as a drum [*drunk*]. **1973** ELopez *Seven* (NY) 126: My lips sealed tight as a drum. **1976** CTrowbridge *Crow* (NY) 108: All secure. Tight as a drum. **1961** HNielsen *Sing Me* (NY DBC) 13: My nerves were drum-tight. TW 112(3).

D311 As tight as a **Drumhead**

1904 JCLincoln *Cap'n Eri* (NY) 388: Tight as a drumhead [*drunk*]. **1944** CDickson *He Wouldn't* (NY) 72: Every place is sealed up as tight as a drumhead. EAP D309.

D312 To have one's **Druthers**

1959 HSlesar *Grey* (L 1963) 128: If I had my druthers. **1967** LJBraun *Cat* (NY) 171: If I had my druthers. Whiting *NC* 400.

D313 As black (tight) as a **Duck's** arse

1974 DCory *Bit* (NY) 136: Black as a duck's arse [*a storm*]. **1982** RHill *Who Guards* (NY) 90: He'll have an alibi tighter than a Duck's arse. Cf. Wentworth 165: Duck's ass.

D314 As dead as a **Duck**

1936 HReilly *Mr. Smith's* (NY) 2: As dead as a duck. **1940** HReilly *Death Demands* (NY) 16: As dead as a duck. **1947** *BHerald* 4/14 42: If ever there were a pair of dead ducks, they were Molway and Berrett. **1957** *Time* 10/21 37: Everything has been as dead as duck. **1960** DMDisney *Dark* (NY) 149: Saxby was a dead duck. **1960** AGarve *Golden* (NY DBC) 60: He's dead as a duck. **1965** PAudemars *Fair* (NY) 84: This one . . . is a dead duck and a cooked goose. Cf. Wentworth 141: Dead duck.

D315 Could (would) a **Duck** swim?

1922 JJoyce *Ulysses* (NY 1934) 307: Could a duck swim? **1924** LTracy *Token* (NY) 219: Would a duck swim? *Oxford* 207.

D316 To be a sitting **Duck**

1947 FCDavis *Thursday's* (NY) 70: That guy was . . . a sitting duck. **1947** VWMason *Saigon* (NY) 26: They got knocked off like sitting ducks. **1953** FKane *Poisons* (NY 1960) 46: He doesn't want to shoot a sitting duck. **1960** RDahl *Kiss* (NY) 83: A Tory . . . always a sitting duck for Mr. Boggis. Wentworth 479: Siting.

D317 To have one's **Ducks** in a row

1952 BBloch *Mrs. Hulett* (NY) 65: I'll have all my ducks in a row. Whiting *NC* 401(4).

D318 To look like a dying **Duck** in a thunderstorm (*varied*)

1933 AChristie *Lord Edgware* (L) 183: You did look . . . like a dying duck in a thunderstorm. **1940** CFitzsimmons *One Man's* (NY) 5: He looks at her like a dying duck in a thunder storm. **1955** Miss Read *Village* (L 1960) 174: His famous dying-duck-in-a-thunderstorm act. **1957** CThomas *Leftover* (L) 23: My dying-duck-in-a-thunderstorm airs. **1966** NMonsarrat *Life(I)* (L) 384: A face . . . like a dying duck in a thunderstorm. **1970** AFreemantle *Three-Cornered* (NY) 202: That dying-duck-in-a-thunderstorm attitude. **1971** MErskine *Brood* (NY) 89: Your going about like a dying duck isn't doing anything to improve matters. EAP D311; Brunvand 40(4).

D319 To play (make) **Ducks** and drakes with (of) something

1906 JLondon *Letters* ed KHendricks (NY 1965) 225: Played ducks and drakes with the exposition. **1913** JSFletcher *Secret* (L 1918) 129: Having made ducks and drakes of everything. **1921** JSFletcher *Chestermarke* (NY) 42: Thousands to play ducks and drakes with. **1922** JJoyce *Ulysses* (NY 1934) 623: A fellow . . . proceeded to make general ducks and drakes of [his money]. **1924** ADHSmith *Porto* (NY) 194: Played ducks and drakes . . . with my plane. **1924** VLWhitechurch *Templeton* (NY) 226: She'll throw your money about like ducks and drakes. **1929** JJFarjeon *5:18 Mystery* (NY) 167: Plays ducks and drakes with time. **1930** CFitzsimmons *Bainbridge* (NY) 175: He could not go on playing ducks and drakes with them [*deceiving them*]. **1931** VLoder *Death* (NY) 46: Certainly not the kind of policeman to play ducks and drakes with. **1932** MTurnbull *Return* (P) 287: She was making ducks and drakes of his case. **1933** JWoodford *Five Fatal* (NY) 224: Playing ducks and drakes with his fellow men. **1934** CCDobie *Portrait* (NY) 265: Make ducks and drakes of poor, defenceless widow women. **1938** JDonovan *Talking Dust* (L) 99: You're playing ducks and drakes with me [*confusing him*]. **1942** HReilly *Name Your Poison* (NY) 220: Making ducks and drakes of Moore's life. **1947** GMWilliams *Silk* (L) 187: You've played ducks and drakes with your life. **1954** EForbes *Rainbow* (B) 125: Playing ducks and drakes with the Seventh and Eighth Commandments. **1956** *New Yorker* 12/22 27: All doubtless making ducks and drakes of the Doctor's farewell message [*making nonsense*]. **1961** FDurbridge *Case* (NY) 104: She's playing ducks and drakes with Goodman [*having another lover*]. **1963** EQueen *Player* (NY) 74: Let's play ducks and drakes and fat red herrings. TW 112(7); *Oxford* 207.

D320 To swim like a **Duck**

1922 VBridges *Greensea* (NY) 146: She can swim like a duck. **1957** JCreasey *Model* (L 1961) 178: Swim like a duck. TW 112(8); Brunvand 40(3).

D321 To take to something like a **Duck** (fish) to water (*varied*)

1908 SHAdams *Flying Death* (NY) 63: Everybody . . . takes to him like a duck to water. **1922** DFox *Ethel* (NY) 63: Take to it like a duck to water. **1930** The Aresbys *Murder* (NY) 245: He took to the sea like a duck. **1936** GDHCole *Last Will* (NY) 14: Rupert took to the City like a duck to water. **1940** MBurton *Murder in* (L) 245: Dick takes to drink like a duck to water. **1941** JBentley *Mr. Marlow Chooses* (B) 184: Lads . . . take to it like a fish to water. **1946** PQuentin *Puzzle for Fiends* (NY) 145: She seems to take to criminality like a duck to water. **1952** RMarshall *Jane* (NY) 127: Take to it like ducks to water. **1955** RDavies *Leaven* (L) 136: [He] had taken to gin as a duck takes to water. **1958** *TLS* 2/14 85: The wife and children take to their new surroundings . . . like ducks to water. **1960** DKarp *Enter* (NY) 130: Takes to the business like a fish to water. **1960** CDLewis *Buried* (L) 107: I had taken to vice like a duck to water, but it ran off me like water off a duck's back. **1970** CDBowen *Family* (B) 110: Ernesta . . . took to Europe like a duck to pond water. **1977** EPGreen *Rotten* (NY) 140: He took to it [*crime*] like the proverbial duck. TW 112(9).

D322 To be **Duck** soup

1938 WMartyn *Marrowby* (L) 98: The sort of thing that would be duck soup for him. **1947** KMKnight *Blue* (NY) 206: It would have been duck soup. Wentworth 165–6.

D323 Not give a **Dump**

1938 AGilbert *Treason* (L) 65: Most people don't give a dump for the truth. Partridge 248: Not care.

D324 To be down in the **Dumps**

1942 WABarber *Murder Enters* (NY) 266: Down in the dumps. **1970** RLPike *Reardon* (NY) 68: Don't look so down in the dumps. **1972** JBonett *No Time* (NY) 93: Millie was in the dumps. EAP D318.

D325 The **Dunmow** flitch

1930 JCournos *Grandmother* (NY) 267: I don't think either of them would have much chance for the Dunmow Flitch. **1933** VLoder *Suspicion* (L) 27: There were many calculated . . . to qualify for the Dunmow flitch. **1937** EJepson *Memories* (L) 41: We were qualified to receive the Dunmow flitch, though we never applied for it because we believed it to be Essex bacon, and we preferred Wiltshire. **1968** DEAllen *British* (L) 79: Despite the background of the . . . Dunmow flitch. **1971** SWoods *Serpent's* (NY) 53: He and Mrs. Baker would have qualified for the Dunmow flitch. **1973** AGilbert *Nice* (NY) 132: He brings home enough bacon to supply the Dunmow flitch. EAP F189: Flitch.

D326 As dry as **Dust**; Dust-dry

1908 SHAdams *Flying Death* (NY) 171: The dry-as-dust scientist. **1923** JSFletcher *Cop-*per* (NY) 43: A dry-as-dust antiquary. **1929** CReeve *Ginger* (NY) 110: As dry as dust. **1940** WChambers *Dry* (NY) 232: My mouth was as dry as dust. **1954** LFord *Invitation* (NY) 92: The familiar dust-dry tones. **1957** BHitchens *End* (NY) 158: Her throat was as dry as dust. **1958** *New Yorker* 5/31 27: Dry-as-dust cow dung. **1960** HLGold *Bodyguard* (NY) 99: Tomes as thick as sin and dry as dust. **1965** JTurner *Blue* (L 1967) 106: His tongue was dry as dust. **1970** AWRaitt *Prosper* (L) 158: A dry-as-dust old fogey. EAP D323; Brunvand 40(1).

D327 As low as **Dust**

1956 NMarsh *Death* (B) 23: Brought as low as dust. **1961** CWillock *Death* (L 1963) 24: You're lower than the dust.

D328 Not to see someone for **Dust**

1937 ECVivian *38 Automatic* (L) 13: You won't see me for dust. **1952** MAllingham *Tiger* (NY) 93: You couldn't see me for dust. **1956** *Punch* 9/12 291: Can't see us for dust. **1959** DMDisney *No Next* (NY) 129: I'd get out of here so fast you wouldn't see my dust. **1961** NBlake *Worm* (L) 154: [He] won't see you for dust. **1966** JDCarr *Panic* (NY) 193: He . . . went so fast you couldn't see him for dust. **1973** WJBurley *Death* (NY) 138: I wouldn't see him for dust.

D329 To bite the **Dust**

1930 HHolt *Ace* (L) 148: He had bitten the dust. **1939** CMRussell *Topaz Flower* (NY) 254: Clarinda bit the dust. **1958** RKing *Malice* (NY) 152: [They] had bit the dust. **1974** CMSmith *Reverend* (NY) 61: Bobbie bites the dust. **1975** JBurke *Rogue's* (NY) 138: One more white man bit the dust. EAP D325; Brunvand 40(2).

D330 To kick up a **Dust**

1959 LGOfford *Walking* (NY DBC) 109: My parents would kick up a dust. **1971** NMarsh *When* (NY) 168: Why are you kicking up such a dust now? EAP D326.

D331 To shake the **Dust** from one's feet

1903 EChilders *Riddle* (NY 1940) 13: I had shaken off the dust of London from my foot. **1913** JSFletcher *Secret* (L 1918) 8: Shake the dust of London off his feet. **1918**

BMalinowski *Diary* (NY 1967) 207: Desire to shake Anglo-Saxon dust off my sandals. **1931** HNicolson *Diaries 1930–39* (NY 1966) 131: As I leave the building, I shake my shoes symbolically. **1933** VLoder *Suspicion* (L) 251: French . . . shook the dust of Martley off his feet. **1941** GDHCole *Counterpoint* (NY) 104: In a desperate hurry to shake the mud of Essex off his shoes. **1946** HHowe *We Happy* (NY) 23: To shake the dust of the effete East off your neck. **1955** JO'Hara *Ten* (NY) 400: Shake the dust of Gibbsville from his heels. **1956** *TLS* 6/15 357: Simply for the pleasure of shaking the dust of Paris off one's shoes. **1959** FPohl *Tomorrow* (NY) 49: I'm about ready to shake the dust of this crummy planet off my feet. **1962** MJosephson *Life* (NY) 9: Stearn shook the dust of America from his feet. **1965** VStarrett *Born* (Norman, Okla.) 155: To shake the dust of journalism from my shoes and sink or swim as a free lance. EAP D328; TW 113–14(5).

D332 To throw **Dust** (sand) in someone's eyes

1919 JSFletcher *Middle Temple* (NY) 313: To throw the dust in the eyes of the police. **1924** CSLewis *Letters* ed WHLewis (NY 1966) 94: Throwing dust in the examiner's eye. **1929** JCameron *Seven* (L) 259: Throw sand in our eyes. **1930** MDalton *Body* (NY) 143: You can't throw sand in my eyes. **1933** HAshbrook *Murder* (NY) 132: She can . . . throw sand in our eyes. **1936** JBude *Sussex* (L) 252: To throw dust in our eyes. **1941** AWebb *Suicide Club* (L) 49: To . . . throw dust in her eyes. **1949** FLockridge *Dishonest* (P) 153: Dust in our eyes. **1954** JRRTolkien *Fellowship* (L) 113: You had thrown dust in all our eyes. **1959** PBoileau *Evil* (L) 49: You can't throw dust in my eyes. **1961** NBlake *Worm* (L) 184: To throw dust in the husband's eyes. **1967** JRichardson *Courtesans* (L) 125: She had always tried to throw dust in people's eyes. **1975** HPentecost *Time* (NY) 53: Throwing dust in our faces. EAP D329; TW 114(6); Brunvand 40(3).

D333 **Dutch** courage

1922 JJoyce *Ulysses* (NY 1934) 177: Dutch courage. **1926** JJConnington *Death* (NY)

67: Primed himself with Dutch courage. **1937** CBush *Hanging Rose* (L) 79: Taking the drug to give him Dutch courage. **1947** PMcGerr *Pick* (NY) 218: Dutch courage. **1954** HWade *Too Soon* (NY) 150: A spot of Dutch courage. **1959** DMDouglass *Many* (L) 146: I wondered where the phrase "Dutch courage" had come from. **1969** JBrunner *Jagged* (NY) 258: This is Dutch courage in a pill. **1970** JBlackburn *Bury* (NY) 7: A bit of Dutch courage. **1975** HCarmichael *Too Late* (NY) 52: What has often been called Dutch courage. EAP D333.

D334 A **Dutch** treat

1926 JArnold *Murder!* (L) 205: A Dutch treat. **1940** AAFain *Turn on* (NY) 114: It's Dutch treat. **1951** MGilbert *Death Has* (NY) 220: I was strictly a Dutch treat. **1972** JBonett *No Time* (NY) 106: Dutch treat. Partridge 251; Wentworth 168.

D335 To be double **Dutch** to one

1909 CPearl *Morrison of Peking* (Sydney 1967) 195: This was double-Dutch to me. **1920** AChristie *Mysterious Affair* (NY) 190: It's double Dutch to me. **1933** CBarry *Murder* (L) 206: That's all double Dutch to me. **1936** JRhode *Death Pays* (L) 222: It's double Dutch to me. **1940** LMacNeice *Strings* (L 1965) 66: [It] would have been Double Dutch to Carrickfergus. **1948** GHJohnston *Death Takes* (L 1959) 36: It's all double-Dutch to me. **1961** EPeters *Death* (NY) 104: Lectures that would be double Dutch to him. **1968** EHuxley *Love* (L) 94: All this was double Dutch to me. **1971** HCarvig *Witch* (NY) 119: Speech in double Dutch [*incomprehensible*]. EAP D331. Cf. Greek *below.*

D336 To beat the **Dutch**

1911 JCLincoln *Woman-haters* (NY) 88: That beats the Dutch. **1913** ECBentley *Trent's* (NY 1930) 84: He would fly off the handle to beat the Dutch. **1920** GBMcCutcheon *Anderson Crow* (NY) 47: Beats the Dutch; 294. **1936** JDosPassos *Big Money* (NY) 293: This beats the Dutch. **1939** TPolsky *Curtains* (NY) 268: Don't it beat the Dutch? **1958** SBarr *Purely* (NY) 250: If these eggheads don't beat the Dutch! EAP D335; Brunvand 40; DARE i 192: Beat the Dutch.

D337 To do the Dutch

1924 ROChipperfield *Bright Lights* (NY) 31: She's done the Dutch [*killed herself*]; 112. Wentworth 168: Dutch act.

D338 To get in Dutch

1966 JDosPassos *Best* (NY) Getting myself deeper in Dutch. Wentworth 168: Dutch.

D339 To talk like a Dutch uncle (aunt) (varied)

1904 JCLincoln *Cap'n Eri* (NY) 90: I talked to her like a Dutch uncle; 258. **1908** JCLincoln *Cy Whittaker* (NY) 146: Talk Dutch to her [*speak severely*]. **1913** JCLincoln *Mr. Pratt's Patients* (NY) 12: To talk Dutch to Nate. **1920** GBMcCutcheon *Anderson Crow* (NY) 64: Talk to 'em like a Dutch uncle. **1929** JLeonard *Back to Stay* (NY) 273: She talked to me like a Dutch aunt. **1932** VWilliams *Death* (B) 147: Talk to Rod like a Dutch uncle. **1936** CBush *Monday Murders* (L) 103: I'll talk to you like a Dutch uncle. **1945** HLawrence *Time to Die* (NY) 241: They wanted to elope, but I pulled the old Dutch uncle. **1949** JReach *Late* (NY) 185: Talk to you like a Dutch uncle. **1952** FCDavis *Tread* (NY) 132: Talk to her like a Dutch uncle. **1953** SBellow *Adventures of* (NY) 213: He dutch-uncled me. **1957** *BangorDN* 3/4 18: I'm going to talk to you like a Dutch aunt. **1957** *Time* 9/30 23: Volunteered a Dutch uncle's advice. **1960** FFrankfurter *Reminisces* (NY) 246: I am going to talk Dutch to you [*frankly*]. **1963** JLudwig *Confusions* (Greenwich, Conn.) 213: I was starting to sound like a horny Dutch uncle. **1968** JAiken *Crystal* (NY) 49: She talked to me like a Dutch aunt. **1970** CDrummond *Stab* (NY) 70: Somebody might have taken him aside for the Dutch uncle business. TW 114: Dutch uncle, Dutch(5).

D340 If . . . (or) I'm a Dutchman

1919 LTracy *Bartlett* (NY) 91: . . . or I'm a Dutchman. **1921** EWallace *Daffodil* (B) 227: If . . . I'm a Dutchman. **1933** GBegbie *Sudden* (L) 65: Or I'm a purple-faced Dutchman. **1933** MBurton *Mystery* (L) 107: If . . . I'm a Dutchman. **1940** ACampbell *They Hunted* (NY) 22: Or I'm a Dutchman. **1941** PWentworth *Weekend* (P) 245: If . . . I'm a Dutchman. **1947** HWade *New Graves* (L) 110: Whiskey, or I'm a Dutchman. **1955** AHocking *Poison* (NY) 90: But I'm a Dutchman if it isn't. **1961** AGilbert *After* (NY DBC) 151: Or he was a Dutchman. **1964** JAshford *Superintendent* (NY) 36: . . . or I'm a Dutchman. TW 114(3).

D341 Duty is duty

1928 CJDaly *Man* (NY) 37: But duty's duty. **1937** JRhode *Hop Fields* (L) 261: But duty's duty, you know. **1955** JBingham *Paton* (L 1964) 141: Duty is duty. **1959** AChristie *Ordeal* (NY) 33: Duty is duty. Cf. Business *above;* Orders, Rules *below.*

D342 A Dwarf on giant's shoulders (varied)

1957 CDBowen *Lion* (B) 510: Their longer vision is gained by standing on other men's shoulders. **1969** RWeiss *Renaissance* (Oxford) 47: Dwarves standing on the shoulders of giants who had come before them. **1979** MSecrest *Being Bernard Berenson* (NY) 371: "The words of the Chinese sage are recommended: 'When you stand on another man's shoulders, try not to spit on his head.'" EAP D338.

D343 To play with Dynamite

1942 FGruber *Buffalo Box* (NY) 250: You've been playing with dynamite. **1947** VSailler *Curtain* (NY) 107: You're fooling with dynamite. **1949** FKane *Green* (NY) 123: That's really playing with dynamite. **1955** ESGardner *Sun* (NY) 165: You're playing with dynamite. Cf. To play with Fire *below.*

E

E1 To Each his own

1955 BBenson *Silver* (NY) 122: To each his own. **1955** RNathan *Sir Henry* (NY) 64: Each to his own. **1960** IWallace *Chapman* (NY 1961) 114: Each to his own. **1970** JVizzard *See* (NY) 345: To each his own. **1971** MEChaber *Bonded* (NY) 57: Each to his own. **1972** SBrooke *Queen* (NY) 79: To each his own. EAP E1.

E2 An Eagle does not catch flies

1932 WMartyn *Trent* (NY) 29: *Aquila non captat muscas* . . . An eagle does not catch flies. **1942** HCBailey *Nobody's* (NY) 7: Eagles don't catch flies. **1951** EMarshall *Viking* (NY) 277: *Aquilla non captat muscas* . . . Eagles do not hawk at flies. EAP E4.

E3 To watch like an Eagle

1909 JCLincoln *Keziah* (NY) 11: She watched him with an eagle eye. **1958** CLBlackstone *Woman* (NY) 155: To watch Dr. Heslop like an eagle. TW 115(6). Cf. Brunvand 41(3).

E4 By the Ears

1915 JBuchan *Thirty-Nine* (NY) 16: To set Europe by the ears. **1924** TMundy *Om* (NY) 13: Set all Delhi by the ears. **1924** ADH Smith *Porto* (NY) 105: Set by the ears. **1932** AWynne *White Arrow* (P) 164: Setting . . . his partners . . . by the ears. **1939** A Christie *Murder for* (NY) 67: To set them all by the ears. **1943** GGCoulton *Fourscore* (Cambridge, Eng.) 96: After setting the Colleges by the ears. **1948** JTey *Franchise* (NY 1955)

198: Set the whole battalion by the ears. **1951** AThorne *Man Who* (L) 146: Enough to set the place by the ears. **1957** GWJohnson *Lunatic* (P) 102: The country really was set by the ears. **1964** JCreasey *Hang* (NY DBC) 29: A . . . job which had set the Yard by the ears. **1969** RDavies *Print* (L) 24: The whole district was set by the ears. **1973** HCarvic *Miss Seeton Sings* (NY) 57: Setting everybody by the ears. EAP E6; TW 115(5).

E5 In at one Ear and out at the other

1926 JSFletcher *Marringham* (B) 61: It all went in at one of Garning's ears and out at the other. **1932** GMitchell *Saltmarsh* (L) 170: Go in at one ear and out at the other. **1939** HMiller *Capricorn* (NY 1961) 95: In one ear and out the other. **1940** PWentworth *Rolling* (P) 139: Better go in at one ear and out of the other as the saying goes. **1949** MAllingham *More Work* (NY) 197: It went in one ear and out the other. **1953** CMRussell *Market* (NY) 16: I let it all in one ear and out the other. **1957** *BHerald* 3/12 31: It went right in one ear and out the other. **1958** *BangorDN* 8/19 9: It goes in one ear and out the other. **1962** DMDisney *Find* (NY DBC) 23: In at one ear and out the other. **1969** GBagby *Honest* (NY) 127: It was in one ear and right out the other. EAP E7.

E6 Over Ears in debt (varied)

1926 HWade *Verdict* (L) 168: Up to his ears in debt. **1937** JRhode *Death on the Board* (L) 150: He's up to his ears in debt. **1939** RStout *Some Buried* (L) 164: Bennett was in

192

up to his ears. **1941** DCCameron *And So He* (NY) 79: I'm up to my ears in work. **1950** RFoley *Hundredth* (NY) 125: Kim is in debt up to his ears. **1958** MHastings *Cork* (NY) 76: Up to his eyes and ears in debt. **1961** JPhilips *Murder* (NY DBC) 114: You're up to your ears in trouble. **1966** LPDavies *Paper* (NY) 124: Up to the ears in trouble. **1975** MButterworth *Man in* (NY) 112: Up to our ears in debt. EAP E8.

E7   To be (not to be) dry (wet) behind the **Ears**

1932 TThayer *Three Sheet* (NY) 114: He wasn't dry behind the ears yet. **1937** DQBurleigh *Kristiana* (NY) 158: You're not exactly wet behind the ears. **1938** MECorne *Death* (NY) 62: You aren't dry yet behind the ears. **1939** TPolsky *Curtains* (NY) 14: You're wet behind the ears. **1940** JLBonney *Death by* (NY) 74: Youngsters not quite dry behind the ears. **1952** MMurray *Doctor* (NY DBC) 112: They are still wet behind the ears. **1954** MMcCarthy *Charmed* (NY) 52: Not dry behind the ears yet, intellectually. **1959** NFitzgerald *This Won't* (L) 223: These girls aren't exactly wet behind the ears. **1962** DMDisney *Find* (NY DBC) 123: He ain't dry behind the ears yet. **1963** DGardiner *Lion* (NY) 2: Still wet behind the ears. Wentworth 358: Not dry; DA Ear *n.*[1] b(5).

E8   To be out on one's **Ear** (*varied*)

1941 TDuBois *McNeills Chase* (B) 74: The university would kick you out on your tin ear. **1954** EDillon *Sent* (L) 164: She was thrown out on her ear. **1957** BHitchens *End* (NY) 68: They could both be out on their ears. Partridge 252.

E9   To get (up) on one's **Ear**

1911 CKSteele *Mansion* (NY) 290: Don't get on your ear so quick. **1929** SGluck *Shadow* (NY) 200: I got up on my ear a bit. TW 115(1); Wentworth 169; DA Ear *n.*[1] b(1).

E10   To have big **Ears** and a small mouth

1960 JBWest *Taste* (NY) 34: I got big ears and a small mouth. Cf. *Oxford* 887: Wide ears and short tongue.

E11   To have (something) about one's **Ears** (*varied*)

1930 RScarlett *Beacon Hill* (NY) 213: She felt her small world crashing about her ears. **1932** DFrome *Man* (NY) 107: His world was crashing about his head. **1936** GHomes *Doctor* (NY) 295: He saw his world coming down around his ears and grasped at a straw to save himself. **1938** NMarsh *Death* (NY) 308: My house is falling about my ears. **1942** CFAdams *What Price* (NY) 173: His world . . . had finally crumpled about his ears. **1952** DMDisney *Heavy* (NY) 184: My world had come down around my ears. **1959** PDeVries *Through* (B) 238: Her whole world came tumbling down around her ears . . . collapsing like a house of cards. **1965** JPhilips *Black* (NY DBC) 35: The whole thing is going to come down around our ears. **1970** RFoley *Calculated* (NY) 33: You are going to pull the whole damned house around your ears. **1973** AMorice *Death* (NY) 88: Her case has tumbled about her ears. **1975** SJPerelman *Vinegar* (NY) 197: Bring down our world about our ears. EAP E12.

E12   To lug in by the **Ears**

1948 JWKrutch *Thoreau* (NY) 276: The essay on Persius, which is lugged by the ears into *A Week on the Concord and Merrimack Rivers*. Cf. NED Hair 80: "He will . . . tugge it in by the heare" (1584), Head 47a: By head and shoulders. Cf. Scruff *below*.

E13   To make (have) one's **Ears** tingle (burn)

1922 JJoyce *Ulysses* (NY 1934) 158: Her ears ought to have tingled for a few weeks after. **1924** JSFletcher *Time-Worn* (NY) 113: Your ears must have burned this dinner-time [*bad things being said*]. **1927** VBridges *Girl* (P) 119: Was your left ear tingling this morning [*praise*]? **1931** HSimpson *Prime* (NY) 149: We've just been talking about you; did your ears burn? **1931** JMWalsh *Company* (NY) 219: My ears were burning. What were you saying about me? **1940** EDean *Murder Is* (NY) 287: You're talking about me . . . My ears burn. **1941** PWilde *Design* (NY) 179: Do you believe that your ears tingle when people talk about you? If so, mine ought to be burning! **1965** HActon *Old Lamps* (L) 13: Your ears must have burned. EAP E14.

E14 To play it by **Ear**

1957 MLaswell *Far* (NY) 82: We've got to play it by ear. **1959** HPentecost *Lonely* (NY) 137: We'll just have to play it by ear from now on in. **1963** FHoyle *Fifth* (L 1965) 60: The crew would have to play it by ear. **1970** RQuest *Cerberus* (NY) 118: I shall play it by ear. **1972** JLHensley *Legislative* (NY) 20: We'll play it by ear.

E15 To pound one's **Ear**

1940 FGruber *Talking Clock* (NY) 134: We were pounding our ears here. **1944** MLong *Bury* (NY) 194: Vera was still pounding her ear in Ann's room. Wentworth 405: Pound.

E16 To set one on his **Ear**

1930 RGoldman *Murder* (L) 72: She'll answer it reasonably enough to set you right on your ear. Berrey 284.8.

E17 To talk one's **Ear** off

1934 PHunt *Murder* (NY) 103: She'll talk the ear off a couple of brass monkeys. **1940** STowne *Death out* (NY) 5: She talked my ear off. **1957** JPotts *Man with* (NY 1964) 27: She talked your ear off. **1973** TAWaters *Lost* (NY) 17: Susan can talk your ear off. Wentworth 536: Talk. Cf. To talk the Leg *below*.

E18 To turn a deaf **Ear**

1922 JJoyce *Ulysses* (NY 1934) 630: Which he pointedly turned a deaf ear to. **1933** CJDutton *Circle* (NY) 240: The suggestion fell upon deaf ears. **1937** PATaylor *Figure* (NY) 153: Should I turn a deaf ear to this entanglement? **1941** ABCunningham *Strange Death* (NY) 40: Square had turned a deaf ear to all suggestions. **1953** EBigland *Indomitable* (L) 96: She turned a deaf ear. **1966** DMDisney *Magic* (NY) 49: To turn a deaf ear to her. **1972** RRendell *Murder* (NY) 6: You can turn a deaf ear to your nephew. **1972** JMangione *Dream* (B) 43: Such scoldings fell mainly on deaf ears. **1975** MHolroyd *Augustus* (NY) 159: Ida turned a deaf ear to them. EAP E16.

E19 As black as the **Earl** of Hell's waistcoat (*varied*)

1925 BAtkey *Pyramid* (NY) 154: It's as black as the Earl of Hell's riding boots. **1933** VMacClure *Crying Pig* (L) 195: As dark as the Earl of Hell's waistcoat. **1962** MStewart *Moon* (NY 1965) 182: What my dear old father used to call a night for the Earl of Hell [*very dark*]. **1963** BKnox *Grey* (NY) 130: As black as the Earl of Hell's waistcoat. **1966** BKnox *Devilweed* (NY) 23: As black as the Earl o' Hell's waistcoat. **1968** BKnox *Figurehead* (NY) 23: It's dark as the Earl of Hell's waistcoat. Whiting *NC* 402.

E20 As if the **Earth** (ground) had swallowed one (*varied*)

c1910 EWallace *Nine Bears* (L 1928) 25: Disappeared as though the earth had swallowed him. **1913** EDBiggers *Seven Keys* (I) 92: As though the earth had swallowed me. **1921** EWallace *Daffodil* (B) 66: Disappeared as though the earth had swallowed her up. **1928** RThorndike *Slype* (NY) 208: The earth had opened and swallowed up Norris. **1930** GVenner *Embarkment* (L) 68: It was as if the ground had opened and swallowed him up. **1930** EWallace *India* (NY) 145: The well known ground had opened and swallowed him. **1932** WBMFerguson *Murder* (NY) 26: Young Mrs. Wilmerding had disappeared as though the proverbial ground had opened and swallowed her. **1933** AGMcLeon *Case* (NY) 236: Vanished with as little trace as if the earth had opened and swallowed him. **1946** KMKnight *Trouble* (NY) 91: Both . . . disappeared as if the earth had swallowed 'em. **1955** DMDisney *Room* (NY) 79: It was . . . as if the earth had swallowed him. **1963** MErskine *No. 9* (NY) 58: Marietta had disappeared as completely as if the ground had opened and swallowed her. Cf. To vanish off the Face *below*.

E21 **East**, west, home is best

1947 HLawrence *Death of* (NY) 272: East, West, home's best. **1961** BPym *No Fond* (L) 229: East or West, Home is best. **1974** WSnow *Codline* (Middletown, Conn.) 477: East, West, home is best. Whiting *NC* 402.

E22 If **Easter** falls in Lady Day's lap, *etc.*

1963 HMiller *Black* (NY) 116: If Easter falls in Lady Day's lap, beware old England of the clap. *Oxford* 213.

E23 **Easy** (gently, steady, *etc.*) does it

1908 LDYoung *Climbing Doom* (NY) 313: Easy does it. **1922** JJoyce *Ulysses* (NY 1934) 363: Gently does it. **1922** VThompson *Pointed* (NY) 171: Quiet does it. **1924** AO Friel *Mountains* (NY) 310: Slow and easy does it. **1929** GMitchell *Speedy* (NY) 234: Gently does it. **1930** WLewis *Apes* (NY 1932) 76: Gently does it. **1930** MAllingham *Mystery* (NY) 213: Gently does it; 215. **1931** SChalmers *Whispering* (NY) 111: Easy does it. **1931** ELoban *Calloused* (NY) 9: Steady does it. **1931** DLSayers *Suspicious* (NY) 368: Gently does it. **1931** LSteffens *Autobiography* (NY) 129: Easy does it. **1933** DFrome *Eel Pie* (NY) 108: Slow and steady does it. **1935** ECRLorac *Organ* (L) 205: "Careful does it" was always my motto. **1939** ECRLorac *Black Beadle* (L) 232: Steady does it. **1940** EDean *Murder Is* (NY) 202: Easy does it. **1945** A Christie *Remembered* (NY) 65: Steady does it. **1950** PMcGerr *Follow* (NY) 105: Slow and easy. **1951** HSaunders *Sleeping* (L) 192: Easy does it, as the girl said to the soldier. **1955** NMarsh *Scales* (B) 29: Steady does it. **1955** AHunter *Gently Does It* (L). **1956** NMarsh *Death* (B) 283: Gently does it. **1958** *BangorDN* 8/22 18: Easy does it. **1962** STruss *Time* (NY) 189: Easy does it. **1966** DGilman *Unexpected* (NY) 200: Easy does it. **1967** RFenisong *Villainous* (NY) 155: Softly does it. **1970** JBlackburn *Bury* (NY) 134: Bloody gently does it. **1971** RLockridge *Death* (P) 142: Easy does it, you know. Partridge 253: Easy.

E24 On **Easy** Street

1930 JGBrandon *Death* (L) 247: Put her upon what I understand you call "Easy Street." **1937** PGWodehouse *Laughing* (NY) 9: On Easy Street. **1950** RMacDonald *Drowning* (NY 1951) 109: Put you on easy street. **1962** AGarve *Prisoner's* (NY DBC) 118: Put them on Easy Street. **1966** LThayer *Dusty* (NY DBC) 16: He's sitting pretty in his big house on Easy Street. **1975** ARoudybush *Suddenly* (NY) 28: Life on Easy Street. Wentworth 170; NED Suppl. Easy 8b; DA Easy 2(4).

E25 **Eat**, drink, and be merry *etc.* (*varied*)

1913 EDBiggers *Seven Keys* (I) 225: Eat, drink, and be merry, for tomorrow the cook leaves, as the fellow says. **1913** JSFletcher *Secret* (L 1918) 36: To eat and drink and be merry. **1922** JJoyce *Ulysses* (NY 1934) 374: Love, lie and be handsome, for tomorrow we die. **1930** EWallace *Crimson Circle* (NY) 256: Eat, drink, and be merry, for tomorrow we die. **1932** JVTurner *Who Spoke* (L) 117: "Eat, laugh and be merry, for tomorrow you may die. What Socrates said is good enough for me." "Epicurus." **1943** GGCoulton *Fourscore* (Cambridge, Eng.) 199: Let us eat and drink; for tomorrow we die. **1956** RStout *Eat, Drink, and Be Buried* (NY). **1959** HLGold *World* (NY 1961) 253: Eat, drink, be merry . . . for you died yesterday. **1961** OManning *Great* (NY) 34: Eat, drink and be merry, for tomorrow we may be starving to death. **1964** JCreasey *Hang* (NY DBC) 39: You can eat, drink, be merry, and make love to whom you like. **1965** VPurcell *Memoirs* (L) 29: "To eat, drink, and be merry for tomorrow we die." **1970** PAlding *Murder* (NY) 83: Eat drink and be merry, for tomorrow we've had it. **1975** NGuild *Lost* (NY) 88: Eat, drink, and be merry, and all that crap. EAP E18; TW 116.

E26 **Eat** to live *etc.*

1940 GCKlingel *Anagua* (NY) 335: Most animals eat to live. Sharks live to eat. **1973** RRendell *Some* (NY) 56: She hated cooking and she used to say she ate to live. EAP E20.

E27 To set up one's **Ebenezer**

1900 CFPidgin *Quincy A. Sawyer* (B) 73: I sot up my Ebenezer. **1956** MPHood *Scarlet* (NY) 40: Joseph had set up his Ebenezer and refused. **1959** MPHood *Bell* (NY) 42: Settin' up her Ebenezer. **1963** MPHood *Sin* (NY) 155: Teach her not to set up her Ebenezer. TW 116(2).

E28 As black as **Ebony**

1905 JBCabell *Line* (NY 1926) 151: Black as ebony. **1912** ERBurroughs *Gods of Mars* (NY 1963) 13: As black as ebony. **1935**

HFootner *Whip-poor-will* (NY) 42: As black as ebony. **1957** GDurrell *My Family* (NY) 110: Black as ebony. **1958** TBrooke *Under* (NY) 264: Black as ebony. **1965** FRussell *Secret* (NY) 161: Water black as ebony. **1968** MAllingham *Cargo* (NY) 37: Hair . . . dark as polished ebony. EAP E24.

E29   As hard as **Ebony**

1929 EWallace *Door* (NY) 69: As hard as ebony. **1961** EPeters *Death* (NY) 112: Floor . . . as hard as ebony. **1963** NFreeling *Question* (NY 1965) 55: Wood, hard as ebony.

E30   The thin **Edge** (end) of the wedge

c**1923** ACrowley *Confessions* ed JSymonds (L 1969) 827: The thin edge of the wedge. **1931** HNicolson *Diaries 1930–31* (NY 1966) 180: We are to be the thin end of the wedge. **1938** JGloag *Documents* (L) 147: The thin edge of Rafferty's wedge of blackmail. **1947** AGilbert *Death in* (L) 178: The thin end of the wedge. **1950** SJepson *Hungry* (NY) 138: The thin end of a wedge to drive between us. **1954** CCarnac *Policeman* (NY) 117: It'd 've the thin end of the wedge, as they say. **1960** ASinclair *Project* (L) 93: The thin-edge-of-the-wedge argument. **1962** ABurgess *Clockwork* (NY 1965) 158: The thin end of the wedge. **1970** RAtkin *Revolution* (NY) 23: The thin edge of the wedge of discontent. **1970** JVizzard *See* (NY) 87: Scenes like these were the thin edge of the wedge. **1972** KCampbell *Thunder* (I) 18: It's the thin end of the wedge. **1974** RLGreen *Lewis* (NY) 280: The thin edge of the wedge. NED Wedge 2b.

E31   To hang on the little **Edge** of nothing

1904 JCLincoln *Cap'n Eri* (NY) 175: Hangin' on the little aidge of nothin'. TW 120: End(7).

E32   To sit on the **Edge** of a volcano (*varied*)

1931 ABCox *Second* (NY) 69: There is a trite metaphor about sitting on the edge of a volcano. **1936** TDowning *Murder* (L) 98: It's like sitting on top of a volcano. **1937** CBush *Eight O'Clock* (NY) 27: Like living on the edge of a volcano, as they say. **1970** RCarson *Golden* (B) 181: We're sitting on a volcano.

E33   As limber as an **Eel**

1962 *BangorDN* 6/25 22: Limber as an eel. TW 117(4).

E34   As quick (agile) as an **Eel**

1929 OSchisgall *Barron* (NY) 121: As agile as an eel. **1930** JGBrandon *McCarthy* (L) 52: He was as quick as an eel. **1935** MGEberhart *House* (L) 90: As quick as an eel. **1962** HEBates *Golden* (L) 77: Quick as an eel.

E35   As slick as an **Eel**

1912 JCLincoln *Postmaster* (NY) 14: As smooth and slick as an eel in a barrel of sweet ile. **1913** JCLincoln *Mr. Pratt's Patients* (NY) 54: Slick as a greased eel. **1938** TDowning *Last Trumpet* (L) 120: He's slick as an eel. **1960** BKendrick *Aluminum* (NY DBC) 67: He's as slick as an eel. **1974** SForbes *Some* (NY) 44: Slick as an eel. Whiting *NC* 402(1); Brunvand 42(1); Taylor *Prov. Comp.* 73.

E36   As slippery as an **Eel** (*varied*)

1927 BAtkey *Smiler* (NY) 84: Slippery as an eel. **1929** PGWodehouse *Fish* (NY) 75: The man's as slippery as a greased eel. **1938** MJohnston *Comets* (NY) 182: Every thing else is as slippery as a live eel. **1942** PGWodehouse *Money* (NY) 90: As slippery as an eel dipped in butter. **1956** *BangorDN* 7/17 5: As slippery as an eel. **1959** EHuxley *Flame* (L) 251: Slippery as eels. **1962** JTAppleby *Henry* (NY) 151: They found him as slippery as an eel. **1967** CDrummond *Death* (NY) 81: As slippery as an eel. **1973** DGilman *Palm* (NY) 178: She's slippery as an eel. **1977** BShaw *Wreath* (NY) 144: Snook is as slippery as an eel. EAP E28; TW 117(6).

E37   As supple (lithe) as an **Eel**

1930 LRGribble *Case* (NY) 9: The American, lithe as an eel. **1956** DWheatley *Ka* (L) 83: She was as supple as an eel. TW 117(8).

E38   To wriggle like an **Eel**

1961 RLockridge *With One* (P) 164: Wriggled like an eel, as they say. Cf. EAP E31; TW 117(12, 13); Brunvand 42(2).

E39   As bald as an **Egg**; Egg-bald

1912 ERBurroughs *Gods of Mars* (NY 1963) 48: As bald as an egg. **1924** VLWhitechurch

Templeton (NY) 31: Bald . . . like an egg. **1925** FBeeding *Seven* (B) 6: Bald as an egg. **1933** MAllingham *Sweet* (L 1950) 163: Bald as an egg. **1938** FBeeding *Big Fish* (NY) 301: A skull as bald as the proverbial egg. **1940** JPPhilips *Murder in Marble* (NY) 151: His head was as bald as an egg. **1941** PStong *Other Worlds* (NY) 172: Bald-headed as an egg. **1947** NMarsh *Final* (B) 294: As bald as eggs. **1949** RChandler *Little* (NY 1951) 52: The dead egg-bald head.**1952** ESHolding *Widow's* (NY DBC) 3: Bald as an egg. **1954** RJHealy *Tales* (NY) 242: Egg-bald head.**1955** EWSmith *One Eyed* (NY) 16: As bald as a loon's egg. **1977** HPentecost *Murder* (NY) 32: A wiry, dark little man, egg-bald. TW 117(1). Cf. Wentworth 171: Egg-head.

E40 As full as an **Egg** is of meat (*varied*)

1908 MRRinehart *Circular Staircase* (NY 1947) 100: He's as full of superstition as an egg is of meat. **1919** JSFletcher *Middle Temple* (NY) 221: Full of meat as an egg. **1932** JSFletcher *Man in the Fur Coat* (L) 237: This land of ours was as full of romance as a fresh egg is full of good meat. **1937** AGilbert *Murder* (L) 171: Full of apprehension as an egg of meat. **1946** ESedgwick *Happy* (B) 237: 'Tis full of Sedgwick as an egg is of meat. **1952** GKersh *Brazen* (L) 5: As full of information as an egg with meat. **1956** AGilbert *Riddle* (NY) 195: As full of prejudice as an egg's full of meat. **1969** ADavidson *Phoenix* (NY) 153: It is as full of good things as an egg is of meat. EAP E32. Cf. Brunvand 1: Acorn(1).

E41 As naked as an **Egg**

1964 EPangborn *Davy* (NY) 83: Naked as eggs. **1966** CMackenzie *Octave Five* (L) 247: As naked as an egg. Wilstach 542.

E42 As smooth as an **Egg**

1952 ETempleton *Proper* (B) 23: That face of yours is as smooth as an egg. **1954** A Seton *Katherine* (B) 411: Floors were polished smooth as an egg. **1960** HGold *Love* (NY) 89: His head was as smooth as an egg. **1969** GMFraser *Flashman* (NY) 120: His skull was as smooth as an egg. TW 117–18(4).

E43 As sure as **Eggs**

1932 GMitchell *Saltmarsh* (L) 72: Would have dropped it as sure as eggs. **1940** CFGregg *Fatal Error* (L) 67: As sure as eggs. TW 118(5).

E44 As sure as **Eggs** is eggs

1920 AChristie *Mysterious Affair* (NY) 164: As sure as eggs is eggs. **1932** DLSayers *Have* (NY) 423: As sure as eggs is eggs. **1937** PGWodehouse *Crime Wave* (NY) 258: As sure as eggs is eggs. **1940** LBruce *Ropes and Rings* (L) 8: As sure as eggs is eggs. **1951** NMitford *Blessing* (NY) 226: Sure as eggs is eggs. **1952** SSmith *Crooked* (L) 152: Sure as eggs were eggs. **1961** JBingham *Night's* (L 1965) 83: Sure as eggs are eggs. **1961** LPayne *Nose* (NY) 139: As sure as eggs is eggs. **1965** JPorter *Dover Two* (NY 1968) 84: Sure as eggs is eggs. **1971** BWAldiss *Soldier* (L) 106: As sure as eggs were eggs. TW 118(6). Cf. Eggs is eggs *below*.

E45 A bad **Egg** (*varied*)

1918 JWatson&AJRees *Mystery of the Downs* (NY) 243: He's a pretty bad egg. **1922** VBridges *Greensea* (NY) 341: A bad egg. **1928** LThomas *Raiders* (NY) 58: It was a case of a bad egg spoiling a good one. **1931** HKWebster *Who Is* (I) 289: He's the typical . . . bad egg of a good family. **1937** RPenny *Policeman's Holiday* (L) 186: Plenty of bad eggs have good shells. TW 118(10); Brunvand 42(3); NED Suppl. Egg 4a.

E46 **Eggs** is eggs

1924 HCBailey *Mr. Fortune's Practice* (NY) 112: Eggs is eggs. TW 118(7). Cf. As sure as Eggs *above*.

E47 Go lay (fry) an **Egg**

1934 CBrackett *Entirely* (NY) 206: Will you go lay an egg? **1949** JLane *Murder Spoils* (NY) 12: She told me to go fry an egg.

E48 One cannot unscramble **Eggs**

1928 AEApple *Mr. Chang's* (NY) 81: Eggs cannot be unscrambled. TW 118(18).

E49 To have **Egg** on one's face

1970 TKenrick *Only* (NY) 104: If the clerk was wrong they would have been left with egg on their face. **1971** RMacLeod *Path*

(NY) 101: Leaving the U.N. with egg on its face. **1974** GCEdmonston *T.H.E.M.* (NY) 148: They've just been trying to come up with some version to keep the egg off their own faces. **1975** SJPerelman *Vinegar* (NY) 18: My department was left with egg on its face. **1982** GHammond *Fair Game* (NY) 86: You'll end up with egg all over your face.

E50   To have one's **Eggs** cooked

1928 AWUpfield *Lure* (NY 1965) 158: To use an Australian aphorism, "Your eggs are cooked." Partridge 255: Eggs are.

E51   To lay an **Egg**

1938 TDavis *Murder on* (NY) 53: That lays an egg on our act if we don't move. **1939** RStout *Some Buried* (L) 233: You laid an egg, that's all. **1940** GStockwell *Candy* (NY) 188: His plan for Bart and me did lay an egg. **1951** JMFox *Aleutian* (B) 67: We laid an egg. **1958** PGWodehouse *Cocktail* (L) 27: It had laid an egg. **1963** MMcCarthy *Group* (NY) 98: The party . . . had laid an egg. **1971** TCatledge *My Life* (NY) 119: Taft laid an egg. Wentworth 313–4.

E52   To put all one's **Eggs** in one basket (*varied*)

c1910 EWallace *Nine Bears* (L 1928) 171: [It] does not put all its eggs into one basket. **1912** HHMunro *Unbearable* (NY 1928) 57: The sage precaution of not putting all one's eggs into one basket. **1918** EWEmerson *Early Years* (B) 285: His eggs were always in too many different baskets. **1924** AChristie *Man* (NY) 46: I would put all my eggs in one basket. **1926** AHuxley *Two or Three* (L) 105: She has put too many of her eggs in his basket. **1932** RKeverne *William* (L) 316: Bill had entrusted many eggs to one basket. **1936** DHume *Meet the Dragon* (L) 110: Never lay all your eggs in one basket. **1939** EMarsh *Number* (NY) 379: Don't put all your Basques in one exit. **1940** JCLincoln *Out of the Fog* (NY) 33: Having all your goods in one package must be pretty bad. **1946** FWCrofts *Death of a Train* (L) 71: All our eggs in one basket—bad catering. **1952** MMillar *Vanish* (NY) 163: A man putting all his eggs in one basket. **1954** SJepson *Black* (NY) 43: I took all my eggs and threw

them into the one basket which looked as if it would hold them. **1955** PGWodehouse *French* (L) 12: Don't put all your eggs in one basket . . . Oh, I beg your pardon. These proverbial expressions. **1957** *BHerald* 4/9 28: Survival requires Britain to put its eggs in the atomic basket. **1957** *Punch* 6/19 774: Those industrial units prudent enough to disperse their eggs among many baskets. **1957** *BHerald* 12/16 10: We cannot afford to put all our eggs in the military basket. **1957** NMitford *Voltaire* (L) 82: Voltaire never kept all his eggs in one basket. **1958** *NYTimes* 4/13 52: He was putting his strategic eggs in just two baskets. **1959** *BHerald* 4/7 21: The old saw about not putting all of your eggs in one basket. **1962** RUnekis *Chase* (NY DBC) 85: He risked putting all his eggs in one basket. **1965** SForbes *Relative* (NY) 54: Don't put all your eggs in one basket. **1970** RRendell *Guilty* (NY) 185: She was used to her two worlds, her eggs in two baskets. **1974** EGertz *To Life* (NY) 178: They had placed all their eggs in the Democratic basket. TW 118(17).

E53   To tread (walk) on **Eggs** (*varied*)

1930 BReynolds *Stranglehold* (NY) 70: Danbrag, who was treading on eggs, relaxed. **1930** DLSayers *Strong* (NY) 55: I'll walk on egg shells [*be careful*]. **1938** VLoder *Wolf* (L) 245: Luck had . . . been walking on thin-shelled eggs. **1940** CFGregg *Fatal Error* (L) 229: I was treading on eggs. **1944** MLong *Bury* (NY) 243: A long period of walking on eggs. **1949** PGWodehouse *Mating* (NY) 87: We shall be walking on eggshells. **1950** IKaufman *Jubel's* (NY) 213: They seemed to be walking on eggs—old eggs. **1951** JCFurnas *Voyage* (NY) 325: Off she went, treading on eggs, so to speak. **1955** CMKornbluth *Not This* (NY) 61: Life would be an unbearable round of walking on eggs. **1956** *New Yorker* 10/20 40: It's all dangerous ground. Treading on eggs. **1959** MPHood *Bell* (NY) 82: Walkin' soft like she's treadin' on eggs. **1961** LPayne *Nose* (NY) 26: I was walking on eggs. **1968** CDSimak *Goblin* (NY) 67: Arnold is walking on a crate of eggs. **1969** LThomas *Between* (B) 337: The Mexican officials were treading on eggshells. **1975** HPentecost *Time* (NY) 89:

We're walking on eggs. **1976** CTrowbridge *Crow* (NY) 66: Walking there as if on eggshells. **1980** HPentecost *Death* (NY) 82: It's been like walking on eggs with him for seven long years. EAP E33.

E54 As black (dark) as **Egypt**

1909 JCLincoln *Keziah* (NY) 113: A night as black as Pharaoh's Egypt. **1924** CWells *Furthest* (P) 197: As black as Egypt. **1929** CBush *Perfect* (NY) 75: I'm as dark as Egypt's night. **1936** SGibbons *Miss Linsey* (NY) 24: It's as dark as Egypt. EAP E40.

E55 To spoil the **Egyptians**

1928 RAJWalling *That Dinner* (NY) 23: Bent on spoiling the Egyptians. **1937** JDCarr *To Wake* (L) 103: A spoiler of the Egyptians. **1946** MColes *Fifth Man* (NY) 115: We will spoil the Egyptians. EAP E41.

E56 To be behind the **Eight** ball

1939 WChambers *You Can't* (NY) 227: You're right behind the eight ball. **1941** BDougall *I Don't Scare* (NY) 84: Behind the eight ball. **1942** SHAdams *Tambay* (NY) 57: The Civil War is their eight-ball, they do most of their thinking behind it. **1951** HQMasur *You Can't* (NY) 61: I was behind the eight ball. **1958** WRoss *Immortal* (NY) 48: The picture starts out with a big eight-ball in front of it. **1959** PMacDonald *List* (NY) 189: In latter-day American, the answer is "Behind the eight ball." **1965** HKane *Midnight* (NY) 77: He's so far behind the eight-ball, he needs a periscope to look over it. **1970** RFoley *Calculated* (NY) 11: It looks as though you were behind the eight-ball. Wentworth 171: Eight ball (3).

E57 **Elbow-grease**

1939 FLGreen *On the Night* (L) 225: Put some elbow-grease into it. **1947** WMoore *Greener* (NY 1961) 16: Can't beat the old elbow grease. **1956** *Time* 8/13 58: Advanced as much by elbow grease as by genius. **1957** WFuller *Girl* (NY) 7: Sweat and elbow grease. **1965** RDSymons *Silton* (NY 1975) 91: A little steel wool and elbow grease. EAP E42.

E58 **Elbow-room**

1962 EFRussell *Great* (NY) 175: They'd have more elbow-room. EAP E43.

E59 To lift (bend) one's **Elbow**

1933 GDHCole *Death* (NY) 169: He likes lifting his elbow. **1937** GDilnot *Murder* (L) 90: I have been lifting my elbow too much. **1942** MBurton *Death at Ash* (NY) 264: [He] was inclined to lift the elbow. **1954** HWade *Too Soon* (NY) 114: He hinted at a tendency to lift the elbow. **1959** HReilly *Not Me* (NY DBC) 24: He's probably bending his elbow somewhere. EAP E47; DARE i 220: Bend.

E60 An **Elephant** never forgets (*varied*)

1937 WMartyn *Blue Ridge* (L) 52: Like elephants, the Lowes never forget. **1938** JAllen *I Lost* (NY) 182: He is like an elephant who can't forget. **1940** JJFarjeon *Friday* (I) 266: Australians, like elephants, never forget an enemy. **1949** EPhillpotts *Address* (L) 29: [An elephant's] memory is proverbial. **1951** MSpillane *Long* (NY) 136: The guy had a memory like an elephant. **1952** AGarve *Hole* (NY 1959) 21: Aren't you ever going to forget that? Talk about an elephant. **1955** ELacy *Best* (NY) 127: That kid, what a memory—Grace must have been frightened by an elephant. **1957** RAHeinlein *Door* (NY) 55: Pete has an elephant's memory. **1958** *BTraveler* 11/14 15: Elephants may never forget—but they sure can be forgotten. **1960** JJMarric *Gideon's Risk* (NY) 91: It's no use telling me that you forgot; elephants don't. **1963** DHayes *12th* (NY DBC) 24: Elephants never forget. **1970** DStuart *Very* (NY) 271: Johnson whose memory was elephantine. **1971** CAird *Late* (NY) 41: Face like the back of a bus but a memory like an elephant. **1974** WBridges *Gathering* (NY) 255: An elephant's memory is proverbial. Whiting *NC* 403(4, 5); Taylor *Prov. Comp.* 38: Memory.

E61 To make an **Elephant** out of a flea

1936 EBQuinn *One Man's* (L) 62: Made an elephant out of a flea. *Oxford* 270-1: Fly into.

E62 To see the **Elephant**

1928 CRourke *Troupers of the Gold Coast* (NY) 29: To see the elephant, in the great popular phrase of the time, was to go to California expecting good luck at every turn, and to be monstrously lifted up and deceived by fortune. **1959** RIDuffus *Water-bury* (NY) 218: People said of him that he had been around. They also said that he had seen the elephant. TW 119(2); Brunvand 42(2); NED Suppl. Elephant 1d. Cf. Brunvand 3: See the "big animal."

E63   A white **Elephant** (*varied*)

1903 EChilders *Riddle* (NY 1940) 21: I sat down upon my white elephant [*portmanteau*]. **1918** JBCabell *Letters* ed PColum (NY 1962) 90: The white and indecorous elephant [*a manuscript*]. **1932** VWilliams *Death* (B) 264: A vast white elephant of a place in Scotland. **1933** AJRees *Aldringham* (NY) 244: That white elephant . . . the pearl necklace. **1942** FGruber *Buffalo Box* (NY) 131: How much is a white elephant worth? **1954** HRAngeli *Pre-Raphaelite* (L) 6: A white elephant, in the shape of a Portuguese cow. **1955** RChurch *Over the* (L) 228: A piano . . . picked up at a white-elephant price. **1956** *Punch* 11/14 595: House agents sell white elephants to buyers. **1959** *NY Times* 2/1 6E: The President's lap is the best place to dump a political white elephant. **1959** HMehling *Scandalous* (NY) 160: This green fluid is a white elephant. **1963** JIM Stewart *Last* (NY) 103: This monstrous white elephant [*an art collection*]. **1964** GSims *Terrible* (L 1967) 102: A white elephant in the form of an . . . oil painting. **1964** LWoolf *Beginning* (L) 239: His large rotary press was really a white elephant. **1969** RSGallagher *If I Had* (NY) 202: It was . . . a blue-and-white elephant [*a building*]. **1969** JBPriestley *Prince* (NY) 249: His architecture white elephant. **1974** JKaplan *Lincoln Steffens* (NY) 299: [His] book was going to be a white elephant. **1977** HDolson *Beauty* (P) 9: Her purple elephant of a house. NED Elephant 2.

E64   As green as an **Emerald**; Emerald-green

1932 FBeeding *Take It* (B) 88: A lake green as an emerald. **1937** VGielgud *Death in Budapest* (L) 203: Emerald-green lawn. **1956** EDillon *Death* (L) 45: Her eyes were emer-

ald green. **1957** DDuncan *Occam's* (NY) 43: Her eyes were green as emeralds. **1959** JBlish *Clash* (L) 57: An emerald-green world. **1968** HWaugh *Con* (NY) 24: Dawn . . . as green as an emerald. TW 119.

E65   The **End** crowns the work

1920 JBailey *Letters and Diaries* (L 1935) 202: *Finis coronat opus*. **1939** LBlack *Mr. Preed* (L) 149: The end would crown the work. **1961** JWebb *One for* (NY DBC) 85: The end should crown the work. EAP E50.

E66   The **End** justifies the means

1900 CFPidgin *Quincy A. Sawyer* (B) 584: Some writer has said the end justifies the means. **1929** STruss *Living* (NY) 171: The end justifies the means. **1930** CBarry *Avenging* (NY) 127: I am Jesuit. I say the end justifies the means. **1935** BGraeme *Disappearance* (L) 184: The end justifies the means. **1937** BCobb *Fatal* (L) 160: The end justifying the means. **1939** DCCameron *Murder's Coming* (NY) 91: The end . . . always justifies the means. **1948** MEChase *Jonathan* (NY) 195: The always simple conclusion that the end justifies the means. **1951** PCheyney *Ladies* (NY DBC) 54: The end is always worthy of the means. **1957** *Punch* 10/2 397: Emphasis on the means rather than the ends. **1957** CEMaine *High* (NY) 163: The end is all that matters. It justifies the means. **1968** CHaldane *Queen* (I) 147: Machiavelli's dictum that the end justified the means. **1973** AMStein *Finger* (NY) 110: The unprinciple that says the end justifies the means. **1976** EFoote-Smith *Gentle* (NY) 139: The credo that the end justifies the means. EAP E51; Brunvand 43(1).

E67   The **End** of an old song

1961 RKirk *Old House* (NY DBC) 39: The last of an old song. **1963** ADuggan *Elephants* (L) 235: It's the end of an old song. *Oxford* 220–1.

E68   (Not) to know which **End** (side) is up

1959 ADean *Something* (NY) 21: Until a guy didn't know which end was up. **1964** DDeJong *Whirligig* (NY) 157: You don't know which end is up. **1968** MBorgenicht *Margin* (NY) 148: Those nurses—they know which side is up. **1969** RLockridge *Die* (P) 18: The . . . district attorney . . . doesn't know which end is up. Berrey 148.4: Which way.

E69 Not to know which **End** one is on
1937 ATilton *Beginning* (NY) 53: Didn't know which end he was on. TW 120(3). Cf. Not to know . . . Head *below.*

E70 Not to see (beyond) the **End** of one's nose (*varied*)
1929 RAJWalling *Murder* (NY) 41: He can't see to the end of his nose. **1935** AGilbert *Man* (L) 37: You couldn't see as far as the end of your nose. **1947** PMcGerr *Pick* (NY) 164: They don't seem able to see past the end of their noses. **1967** RCowper *Phoenix* (NY) 167: I have to look beyond the end of my nose. **1972** RBernard *Illegal* (NY) 102: He can't see past the end of his nose. **1976** JJMarric *Gideon's Drive* (NY) 59: [He] saw no further than the end of his nose. **1977** AYork *Tallant* (NY) 145: I wasn't looking any further than the end of my nose. Whiting *NC* 403(1). Cf. To see no farther than one's Nose *below.*

E71 To be at a loose **End** (*varied*)
1927 HHBashford *Behind* (NY) 59: I was at a loose end. **1927** FLPackard *Devil's* (NY) 90: A bit at loose ends. **1929** JJConnington *Grins* (B) 296: I hate to leave loose ends. **1934** AChristie *Calais Coach* (NY) 58: I was at a lost end. **1941** RPKoehler *Sing a Song* (NY) 230: He was at loose ends. **1955** JEGill *House* (NY) 143: She was at loose ends. **1959** JWelcome *Run* (NY) 29: I'm quite at a loose end. **1960** SRaven *Brother* (NY) 65: You were at a loose end. **1972** PWarner *Loose Ends* (NY). TW 120(9).

E72 To be at the **End** of one's rope (row)
1909 MRRinehart *Man in Lower Ten* (NY 1947) 341: He was almost at the end of his rope. **1924** ROChipperfield *Bright* (NY) 143: At the end of my rope. **1952** MRRinehart *Swimming* (NY) 125: Reached the end of my rope. **1954** EWBarnes *Lady* (NY) 98: Tiffany was at his rope's end. **1957** GMalcolm-Smith *Trouble* (NY) 12: He'd reached the end of his rope, so he made a noose of it. **1960** FCrane *Death-wish* (NY DBC) 100:

She's at the end of her row. **1960** EWolf *Rosenbach* (Cleveland) 75: At the end of his financial rope. **1968** WGRogers *Ladies* (NY) 171: Joyce was at the end of his rope. **1972** FFarmer *Will There* (NY) 17: At the end of my rope. **1975** DMDisney *Cry* (NY) 4: About at the end of my rope. TW 120(5); Brunvand 120: Row(2).

E73 To be at the **End** of one's string
1926 LThayer *Poison* (NY) 21: Reached the end of his string. **1932** HFootner *Dead Man's* (NY) 220: I'm near the end of my string. **1939** JDCarr *Black Spectacles* (L) 188: I'm nearly at the end of my string. **1946** CDickson *My Late* (NY) 186: I was at the end of my string. Brunvand 43(2).

E74 To be at the **End** of one's tether
1908 MDPost *Corrector of Destinies* (NY) 6: Come to the end of his tether. **1922** JJoyce *Ulysses* (NY 1934) 649: Reached the end of his tether, so to speak. **1923** ABlackwood *Episodes* (L) 239: Come to the end of his tether. **1933** ABCox *Jumping* (NY) 35: At the end of my tether. **1937** NMarsh *Vintage* (B 1972) 205: He'd got to the end of his tether. **1944** MFitt *Clues* (NY) 72: She was at the end of her tether. **1953** JRhode *Mysterious* (NY DBC) 121: Pretty much at the end of his tether. **1958** MAllingham *Tether's End* (NY). **1961** FBiddle *Casual* (NY) 119: Coming to the end of their tether from overwork [*die*]. **1968** LDurrell *Tunc* (NY) 115: I have reached the end of my tether. **1973** WJBurley *Death* (NY) 80: The boy was near the end of his tether. EAP E55.

E75 To be at the little (west, ragged) **End** of nowhere (*varied*)
1906 JCLincoln *Mr. Pratt* (NY) 86: At the little end of nowhere. **1908** JCLincoln *Cy Whittaker* (NY) 378: In the west end of nowhere. **1940** DWheelock *Murder at Montauk* (NY) 61: The company was on the ragged edge of nowhere. CF. NED Nowhere 5. Cf. Arse-end *above.*

E76 To come out at the little **End** of the horn (*varied*)
1928 ALivingston *Monk* (NY) 92: Come out at the short end of the horn. **1931** DFrome *Strange* (NY) 226: They're always leaving

him with the little end of the horn. **1936** SLBradbury *Hiram* (Rutland, Vt.) 174: Hit gen'rally come out of the little end o' the horn. EAP E56.

E77   To get the right **End** of the stick

1932 JJConnington *Sweepstake* (B) 303: You had the right end of the stick. **1940** JJConnington *Four Defences* (B) 273: We'd got the right end of the stick. **1940** ECRLorac *Tryst* (L) 16: [He's] got hold of the right end of the stick. **1956** AMenen *Abode* (NY) 116: They seem always to get the right end of the stick when others get the wrong one. EAP E57.

E78   To get the wrong **End** of the stick (*varied—always bad*)

1920 GDilnot *Suspected* (NY) 130: You've got the wrong end of the stick. **1922** JSFletcher *Ravensdene* (NY) 225: Got hold of the wrong end of the stick. **1928** WMcFee *Pilgrims* (NY) 33: The foreman got the dirty end of the stick. **1932** AMizner *Many* (NY) 194: They had always had the dirty end of the stick. **1932** CRyland *Notting* (L) 47: They'd got the wrong end of the stick. **1935** GHCoxe *Murder* (NY) 222: I'm tired of getting the short end of the stick. **1936** RGDean *Sutton* (NY) 273: He gets the short end of the stick. **1938** VSwain *Hollow Skin* (NY) 220: You give us the dirty end of the stick just once more. **1939** RAJWalling *Blistered Hand* (NY) 30: Which would leave his father with the burnt end of the stick. **1941** LThayer *Hallowe'en* (NY) 56: I had the hard end of the stick. **1947** PMcGerr *Pick* (NY) 56: What do I get in return? The dirty end of the stick. **1948** DCDisney *Explosion* (NY DBC) 143: They sometimes get the short end of the stick. **1948** NMailer *Naked* (NY) 202: You're gonna get the shitty end of the stick. **1950** FO'Malley *Best* (NY) 143: I ended up with the short end of the stick. **1952** CJay *Beat* (NY) 89: He thinks he always gets the thin end of the stick. **1952** RPSmith *Time* (NY) 52: Touch a *verkackte* stick and on your hands it is *verkackte*, too. Shit, you know. **1953** GPhelps *Dry Stone* (L) 195: You've got hold of the wrong end of the stick. **1954** LCochran *Row's End* (NY) 39: Gets the dirty end of the stick. **1954**

EDillon *Sent* (L) 36: You've got the wrong end of the stick. **1955** KAmis *That Uncertain* (L) 76: He always seems to get the rough end of the stick. **1958** JAHoward *Murder* (NY 1959) 8: You're on the cruddy end of the stick. **1959** *NYTimes* 5/17 55: The long end of the country has been getting the short end of the stick. **1960** NFitzgerald *Candles* (L) 102: I may easily have had the wrong end of the stick. **1960** BMcKnight *Running* (NY) 6: This guy seemed to have the short and dirty end of the stick. **1960** JBWest *Taste* (NY) 57: Henning was getting the shitty end of a short stick. **1965** AGilbert *Voice* (NY) 135: Ted had got the dirty end of the stick. **1970** HCarvic *Miss Seeton Draws* (NY) 18: They always get hold of the wrong end of the stick. **1970** AEHotchner *Treasure* (NY) 254: What a shit-end of the stick you got. **1973** DShannon *No Holiday* (NY) 44: I get the short end of the stick. **1974** KAmis *Ending* (NY) 55: So that you could yet again get hold of the wrong end of the stick through the eye of a needle in a haystack. **1974** SKrim *You* (NY) 319: Each of his adolescents gets the shit end of the stick. EAP E57.

E79   To go off the deep **End**

1928 EBYoung *Murder* (P) 182: Go off the deep end, if the ladies will forgive the expression. **1933** GDHCole *End* (L) 109: Gregory would have gone off the deep end. **1947** VSiller *Curtain* (NY) 78: Women sometimes go off the deep end. **1950** MRHodgkin *Student* (L) 136: Candy would go off the deep end. **1955** MErskine *Old Mrs.* (NY) 164: Liable to go off the deep end. **1960** FSWees *Country* (NY) 163: Going off the dead end. **1972** JBonett *No Time* (NY) 87: No good going off the deep end. Partridge 257.

E80   To keep one's own **End** up

1948 JRhode *Death* (NY) 220: We want to keep our own end up. Partridge 257.

E81   To make (both) **Ends** meet

1906 JCLincoln *Mr. Pratt* (NY) 187: To make both ends meet. **1912** JCLincoln *Postmaster* (NY) 9: To make both ends meet. **1919** LMerrick *Chain* (L) 31: Difficult to make both ends meet. **1929** JSFletcher *Ransom* (NY) 223: All I can do to make ends meet this year. **1937** AFielding *Scarecrow* (L) 23: They're having a hard time to make ends meet, let alone lap. **1951** HSaunders *Sleeping* (L) 24: Striving to make both ends meet. **1957** MBGarrett *Horse* (University, Ala.) 90: To make both ends meet at the end of the crop season. **1970** REaston *Max* (Norman, Okla.) 229: To make ends meet on an income of $75,000 a year. **1976** SWoods *My Life* (NY) 184: Making ends meet grows harder. EAP E58; Brunvand 43(4).

E82 To play both **Ends** against the middle

1928 RMaury *Wars of the Godly* (NY) 74: Bennett played both ends of the religious fight against the middle. **1932** WFEberhardt *Dagger* (NY) 167: As long as you try to play both ends against a wobbly middle. **1936** RCarson *Revels* (NY) 320: Playing both ends against the middle. **1943** PCheyney *Dark Dust* (NY) 120: Playing both ends at once. **1949** GFowler *Beau* (NY) 104: He can play both ends against the middle. **1952** RPowell *Shot* (NY) 72: But you like to play both ends against the middle. **1957** AAmos *Fatal* (NY) 19: The little bitch seems to have been playing both ends against the middle. **1962** ESGardner *Mischievous* (NY DBC) 101: He was . . . playing both ends against the middle. **1965** ESGardner *Beautiful* (NY) 203: I'm playing both ends against the middle. **1971** DDaiches *Third* (Sussex, Eng.) 28: Some . . . played both ends against the middle. **1975** SMangeot *Manchurian* (NY) 175: This difficult art of playing both ends against the middle. DA End 3b.

E83 To make an **Enemy** lend a man money (*varied*)

1961 MErskine *Woman* (NY) 96: There's a saying, "Never do business with friends." **1969** NHale *Life* (B) 134: The way to make an enemy is to lend him money. **1970** CDrummond *Stab* (NY) 138: If you wish to make an enemy . . . lend or give 'em money. EAP M207: Lend money; *Oxford* 455: Lend your money; Tilley F725. Cf. Lend one's Money *below*.

E84 **England** is a paradise for women *etc.*

1931 ELinklater *Ben Jonson* (L) 111: England was a paradise for women and hell for horses. **1965** MStewart *Airs* (NY 1966) 71: "Who was it said that hell was a paradise of horses?" "Nobody . . . they said England was a paradise for horses and a hell for women." *Oxford* 222.

E85 Merry **England**

1952 AGilbert *Mr. Crook* (NY DBC) 134: England isn't Merry England any more. Whiting E102; *Oxford* 528.

E86 In plain **English** (*varied*)

1925 JSFletcher *Annexation* (NY) 224: Let's hear some plain English. **1934** EPhillpotts *Mr. Digweed* (L) 62: In plain English. **1940** ECameron *Malice* (NY) 120: I'll say it in plain English. **1941** MGEberhart *With This Ring* (NY) 20: Please to understand plain English. **1954** HCecil *According* (L) 124: Do you not understand plain English? **1956** *Republican Journal* 8/23 7: You are a fool, in plain English. **1967** PHighsmith *Those Who* (NY) 37: I'm talking plain American. **1970** JBlackburn *Bury* (NY) 156: A short sentence in plain English. **1972** GRDickson *Pritcher* (NY) 137: On the verge of telling him in plain Anglo-Saxon what he could do with himself, Chaz checked. EAP E63.

E87 An **Englishman** loves a lord (*varied*)

1964 JHillas *Today* (NY) 9: It is said that every Englishman loves a lord. **1967** MBerkeley *Winking* (B) 89: You know the saying that an English servant "dearly loves a lord." **1969** RPearsall *Worm* (L) 132: Everyone loves a lord, it has been mooted. *Oxford* 224.

E88 An italianate **Englishman** is a devil incarnate

1930 LMarkun *Mrs. Grundy* (NY) 69: An Italianate Englishman is an "incarnate devil" was a common saying in Italy as well as England; 103. **1933** JAston *First Lesson* (NY) 117: "Inglese italianato è il diavolo incarnato." *Oxford* 224.

E89 **Enough** is as good as a feast

1910 EPhillpotts *Tales* (NY) 251: Enough is as good as a feast. **1913** HTFinck *Food* (NY)

320: Enough is as good as a feast. **1930** WLewis *Apes* (NY 1932) 17: Enough's as good as a feast. **1938** SFowler *Jordans* (L) 182: Enough's as good as a feast. **1953** EBigland *Indomitable* (L) 108: Enough . . . was as good as a feast. **1953** EBGarside *Man from* (NY) 139: Enough's a feast. **1965** VPurcell *Memoirs* (L) 177: Enough is as good as a feast. **1968** JHaythorne *None of Us* (NY) 4: Enough is as good as a feast. EAP E65; TW 121(1).

E90   Enough is enough

1935 DFrome *Both in Bedford Square* (L) 105: Enough was enough. **1938** EBell *Fish* (NY) 144: Enough's enough and then it's too God-damn much. **1940** WChambers *Dry* (NY) 201: Enough is enough. **1941** MTYates *Midway* (NY) 264: Enough . . . is plenty. **1948** TKyd *Blood* (P) 87: He said that enough was enough. **1954** MKArgus *Rogue* (L) 207: But enough is enough. **1956** BCClough *More* (Portland, Me.) 87: He called enough aplenty. **1963** AChristie *Clocks* (NY) 251: Enough is enough. **1969** GSAlbee *By the Sea* (NY) 157: Enough is enough. **1972** RBraddon *Thirteenth* (NY) 15: Enough's enough. **1975** HCarvic *Odds On* (NY) 97: Enough was enough. TW 121(2).

E91   As black as Erebus

1948 IFletcher *Roanoke* (I) 461: A great cavern, black as Erebus. TW 121; Brunvand 43. Cf. EAP E69.

E92   A sleeveless Errand

1953 RUsborne *Clubland* (L) 47: Berry goes off on sleeveless errand. **1961** LSdeCamp *Dragon* (NY 1968) 211: On a sleeveless errand. **1968** WTenn *Square* (NY) 16: He sent me on sleeveless errands. EAP E71.

E93   As cold as an Eskimo's arse

1973 EMcBain *Hail* (NY) 10: It's colder'n an Eskimo's arse out here. Cf. Taylor *Prov. Comp.* 28–29.

E94   As naked as Eve

1943 AAbbott *Shudders* (NY) 154: Naked as Eve. Cf. EAP E76; Wilstach 542. Cf. As naked as Adam *above*.

E95   Coming Events cast their shadows before

1922 JJoyce *Ulysses* (NY 1934) 163: Coming events cast their shadows before. **1923** HGartland *Globe* (NY) 261: Coming events cast shadows. **1928** CJDaly *Man* (NY) 45: Coming events cast their shadows before. **1935** CBrooks *Three Yards* (L) 37: They do say that coming events cast a shadow afore 'em. **1936** RAFreeman *Penrose* (NY) 3: Coming events cast their shadows before. **1937** ABCaldwell *No Tears* (NY) 89: Coming events cast their shadows before. **1954** CBeaton *Glass* (NY) 164: Coming events cast their shadows before. **1964** AVaughan *Those Mysterious* (NY) 205: The proverb that coming events often cast their shadows before. **1966** HBlyth *Pocket* (L) 63: Coming events cast their shadows before them. **1971** EHCohen *Mademoiselle* (B) 134: Coming events, it is said, cast their shadow before. TW 122(1); Brunvand 43.

E96   Great Events from little causes spring (*varied*)

1929 GMWhite *Square* (L) 219: The somewhat hackneyed saying that "great events from trivial causes spring." **1932** BFlynn *Crime* (NY) 210: Great events from little causes spring. **1933** DGBrowne *Dead* (L) 57: Great events from little causes flow. **1961** PMoyes *Down Among* (NY) 3: The trifling causes that lead to great events. EAP E77. Cf. Oaks *below*.

E97   To be wise after the Event

1920 AJRees *Hand in the Dark* (NY 1929) 185: It is easy to be wise after the event. **1921** CTorr *Small Talk, 2nd Series* (Cambridge, Eng.) 7: The wisdom that comes after the event. **1930** FBeeding *League* (B) 123: My usual wisdom after the event. **1932** FWCrofts *Double* (NY) 206: Only a fool is wise after the event. **1932** RAFreeman *When Rogues* (L) 260: It is proverbially easy to be wise after the event. **1939** CFGregg *Danger* (L) 26: The wise-after-the-event reprimand. **1949** AMorton *Rope* (NY) 222: It is easy to be wise after the event. **1955** MGilbert *Country-house* (NY) 11: Trust a woman to be wise after the event. **1957** *TLS* 5/10 287: Pathetically wise after the event. **1961**

GBagby *Evil* (NY) 82: Wisdom after the fact. **1968** RGSherriff *No Leading* (L) 109: The easy old game of being wise after the event. **1971** CAird *Late* (NY) 164: Wise after the event. **1976** GBagby *Two* (NY) 90: We can all be wise after the fact. *Oxford* 898: Wise.

E98 Everybody and his brother (cousin)

1936 KMechem *Frame* (NY) 156: Everybody and his brother is out there. **1946** GHomes *Build* (NY) 179: Everybody and his brother showed up last night. **1956** BCClough *More* (Portland, Me.) 63: Everyone and his brother . . . invited himself to stay. **1970** RLPike *Reardon* (NY) 121: Everybody and his brother saw it. **1972** MKaye *Lively* (NY) 126: Everybody and his cousin is on the phone. Cf. All the World *below*.

E99 Everybody's business is nobody's business

1932 AMSullivan *Last Serjeant* (NY) 161: What was everybody's business was nobody's business. EAP B377.

E100 Everything but the kitchen sink (stove)

1929 HFootner *Doctor* (L) 197: [She] used to put on everything but the kitchen stove [*clothes*]. **1941** STowne *Death out of* (NY) 224: The Invisible Man got away with everything but the kitchen stove. **1947** NMarsh *Final* (B) 60: You've got everything on but the kitchen sink. **1949** FCrane *Flying* (NY) 80: We've already dragged in everything but the kitchen sink. **1957** *BHerald* 5/15 43: Everything but the kitchen sink is in it. **1957** WFuller *Girl* (NY) 62: "And she cleaned you out?" "Everything but the kitchen sink, as the saying goes." **1970** O Friedrich *Decline* (NY) 165: The group decided to throw in everything else, including the kitchen sink. Cf. Whiting H316: Too heavy.

E101 Everything comes to him who waits (*varied*)

1911 FRS *Way of a Man with a Maid* (L) 10: As the proverb says, everything comes to the man who can wait. **1913** JSFletcher *Secret* (L 1918) 131: All things come round to them who will wait. **1928** EWallace *Sinister* (NY) 258: Everything comes to her who waits. **1929** EJMillward *Copper* (NY) 122: The French say, "Everything comes to him who knows how to wait." **1940** DWheelock *Murder at Montauk* (NY) 131: All things come to him who waits. **1957** *BHerald* 6/24 11: Everything comes to him who waits . . . the old maxim. **1958** JYork *My Brother's* (NY DBC) 10: Everything came to those who knew how to wait. **1962** KAmis *Spectrum(1)* (L) 184: All good things come to him who waits. **1969** HEBates *Vanished* (L) 139: "Everything comes to him who waits" was an adage of great falsity. *Oxford* 231.

E102 Everything has a beginning (*varied*)

1914 PGWodehouse *Little Nugget* (NY 1929) 78: Everything's got to have a beginning. **1965** HPentecost *Sniper* (NY DBC) 95: There has to be a beginning for everything. EAP E90.

E103 Everything has an end and a piece of string has two

1971 CAird *Late* (NY) 151: But as I used to say to the wife—everything has an end and a piece of string has two. EAP E91: Pudding.

E104 You cannot have **Everything**

1930 Private 19022 *Her Privates* (L) 97: You can't 'ave everythink, so you've got to be content with what you can get. **1939** RAJWalling *Blistered Hand* (NY) 169: But you can't have everything. **1942** GHCoxe *Silent* (NY) 37: You couldn't have everything. **1972** EXFerrars *Foot* (NY) 159: You can't have everything.

E105 Not enough **Evidence** to hang a cat (*varied*)

c1923 ACrowley *Confessions* ed JSymonds (L 1969) 384: I wouldn't swing a cat on their dying oaths. **1927** GDilnot *Lazy* (B) 142: You'll never get evidence against me that would hang a cat. **1930** TCobb *Crime* (L) 239: You wouldn't hang a cat on the strength of it [*evidence*]. **1930** IWray *Vye* (L) 75: There was not enough evidence to hang a cat. **1930** DLSayers *Strong* (NY) 51: She wouldn't hang a dog on medical evidence. **1932** PHerring *Murder* (L) 143: What you have against me wouldn't hang a cat. **1932**

VLoder *Red Stain* (NY) 102: You couldn't hang a dog on all we've got. **1952** AGilbert *Mr. Crook* (NY DBC) 27: She hasn't enough evidence to hang a dog. **1958** MProcter *Man in* (NY) 16: I wouldn't swing a cat on your unsupported word. **1966** SWoods *Enter* (NY) 22: I wouldn't hang a dog on the evidence. **1971** PAlding *Despite* (NY) 150: Evidence that wouldn't hang a cat.

E106 Of two **Evils** choose the lesser

1903 EChilders *Riddle* (NY 1940) 257: The lesser of two evils. **1908** MRRinehart *Circular Staircase* (NY 1947) 99: He had to choose between two evils. **1932** ACampbell *Murder* (NY) 256: She . . . had chosen the lesser of two evils. **1936** ERBurroughs *Swords of Mars* (Tarzana, Calif.) 171: The poor girl was forced to choose between the lesser of two evils [*sic*]. **1939** FWCrofts *Antidote* (NY) 111: It was a choice of two evils. Which was the lesser? **1940** EBenjamin *Murder Without* (NY) 217: She turned the radio on as the lesser of two evils. **1948** PCheyney *Dance* (NY DBC) 44: You think of the two evils I should choose the lesser. **1949** SSterling *Dead Sure* (NY) 225: I guess you're the lesser of two weevils. **1952** AGilbert *Mr. Crook* (NY DBC) 126: It was a choice of two evils. **1956** *BHerald* 8/18 3: When they were confronted with what they regarded as two evils the pros simply took what appeared to them to be the lesser. **1959** GMitchell *Man Who* (L) 157: Of the two evils, we choose the lesser. **1960** JMcGovern *Berlin* (NY DBC) 137: To take the lesser of two evils. **1963** JKirkup *Tropic* (L) 101: The lesser of two not very distinguished evils. **1973** HDolson *Dying* (P) 122: [He] seized on Mario as the milder of two evils. **1976** JPorter *Package* (NY) 131: Jones chose the lesser of the two evils. EAP E102; TW 122(1); Brunvand 44(1).

E107 To do **Evil** that good may come (*varied*)

1938 AGlanville *Body* (L) 279: I do a little evil that great good may befall. **1958** CCockburn *Crossing* (L) 139: At this point somebody mutters something about doing evil that good may come, or the end justifying the means. EAP E103.

E108 **Example** is better than precept

1934 GHeyer *Why Shout* (L) 45: Example is better than precept. **1935** JRhode *Mystery* (L) 186: Example is better than precept. **1958** LSdeCamp *Elephant* (NY) 48: Example is better than precept. EAP E104.

E109 The **Exception** proves the rule (*varied*)

1922 FPitt *Woodland* (L) 167: The old saying, that "exceptions prove the rule." **1923** HGartland *Globe* (NY) 259: The exception that proves the rule. **1928** AWynne *Red* (P) 94: It is true of scientific work, isn't it, that a single exception disproves the rule. **1935** MKennedy *Poison* (L) 134: The exception proves the rule. **1936** JGBrandon *Pawnshop* (L) 150: They say it takes an exception to prove a rule. **1940** EBenjamin *Murder Without* (NY) 210: No rule's any good unless there's an exception to prove it. **1951** ADean *August* (NY) 125: Maggie was the exception that proved the rule. **1955** JBCabell *As I* (NY) 171: That axiomatic exception which proves every general rule. **1968** RHughes *Hong Kong* (NY) 65: Waley was the prodigious exception that tests this rule. **1969** PZiegler *Black* (L) 240: In medieval history . . . it is not the exception which proves the rule but the rule which generates the exception. **1974** MGAVale *Charles* (Berkeley) 95: The exception which proved the rule. EAP E105.

E110 There are **Exceptions** to all rules (*varied*)

1916 SLeacock *Behind* (Toronto 1969) 78: An exception to the rule. **1923** JSFletcher *Exterior* (NY) 57: There are always exceptions to every rule. **1924** ADHSmith *Porto* (NY) 20: There's an exception to every rule. **1933** DGBrowne *Dead* (L) 120: Here, at last, was the proverbial exception to the rule. **1938** MInnes *Lament* (L) 10: There are exceptions, maybe, to each rule. **1941** GBagby *Red Is* (NY) 126: There's an exception to every rule. **1955** MErskine *Old Mrs.* (NY) 115: Every rule has its exception. **1957** *TLS* 3/8 144: There is an obvious sense in which this rule is a valid one, but there are exceptions. **1965** AGilbert *Voice* (NY) 60: Still, there have to be exceptions, or there wouldn't be rules. **1967** JWCampbell *Analog 5* (NY) 48: All rules must have their exceptions. **1970** MCrichton *Five* (NY) 181: They are more the rule than the exception. **1970** WANolen *Making* (NY) 55: The rule rather than the exception. **1972** MBNorton *British-Americans* (B) 68: A few exceptions to the general rule. EAP E106; Brunvand 44. Cf. Rules *below.*

E111 (Fair) **Exchange** is no robbery

1923 ORCohen *Jim Hanvey* (NY) 200: Fair exchange . . . ain't always robbery. **1926** NSLincoln *Blue Car* (NY) 271: A fair exchange . . . and no robbery. **1928** EBarker *Cobra* (NY) 108: Fair exchange, you know. **1933** RAFreeman *Dr. Thorndyke Intervenes* (L) 10: I have heard it said that exchange is no robbery. **1938** MSaltmarsh *Clouded* (NY) 85: We have an English motto that says: "Fair exchange is no robbery." **1958** ECooper *Tomorrow's* (NY) 128: Fair exchange is no robbery. **1958** HReilly *Ding* (NY DBC) 116: Fair exchange is no robbery. **1963** RJStonesifer *W.H.Davies* (L) 151: Exchange is no robbery. **1965** HActon *Old Lamps* (L) 99: Exchange was no robbery. EAP E107.

E112 Any **Excuse** is better than none (*varied*)

1924 HHMunro *Square* (L 1929) 200: But one excuse is as good as another. **1931** PMacDonald *Polferry* (NY) 84: Any excuse . . . is better than none. **1969** CBush *Deadly* (NY) 61: Any excuse . . . is better than none. EAP E108.

E113 He who **Excuses** himself, accuses himself

1919 HRHaggard *She and Allan* (NY 1921) 264: *Qui s'excuse, s'accuse.* **1928** AWynne *Red* (P) 138: One of the best ways of accusing people . . . is to excuse them. **1936** JStagge *Murder Gone* (L) 59: The good old French proverb of "he who excuses, accuses himself." **1937** CBClason *Blind* (NY) 107: There's a French proverb . . . "Who excuses himself accuses himself." **1968** GWagner *Elegy* (L) 122: Who excuses himself accuses himself. **1970** WBlunt *Dream* (L) 55: The old adage, *Qui s'excuse, s'accuse.* Oxford 234.

E114 **Experience** is the best teacher (*varied*)

1928 EALehman *Zeppelins* (NY) 254: Experience is the best teacher. **1930** JSFletcher *Dressing Room* (L) 65: No doubt he learnt wisdom by experience. **1930** RA Freeman *Savant's* (L) 112: *Experientia docet.* **1934** JGBrandon *Murder* (L) 94: Experience teaches us many things. **1953** CSWebb *Wanderer* (L) 100: *Experientia docet* is a saying. **1959** CMKornbluth *Marching* (NY) 137: Experience is the best teacher. **1967** FSwinnerton *Sanctuary* (NY) 98: Experience is the only teacher, they say. **1972** A Friedman *Hermaphrodeity* (NY) 12: Experience is the best teacher. EAP E114; Brunvand 44.

E115 To buy **Experience**

1920 GDilnot *Suspected* (NY) 82: Dam buying experience. **1930** AChristie *Mysterious* (NY) 92: I've bought experience myself in my time. EAP E109.

E116 **Extremes** meet

1905 JBCabell *Line* (NY 1926) 181: It is a venerable saying that extremes meet. **1922** JJoyce *Ulysses* (NY 1934) 493: Extremes meet. **1953** RPostgate *Ledger* (L) 215: Extremes meet, so to speak. **1955** NLewis *Day* (L) 128: Extremes might easily meet. **1965** AChristie *At Bertram's* (L) 17: Extremes meet. EAP E116.

E117 Before one could bat (wink) an **Eye**

1931 HLandon *Back-seat* (NY) 91: Before you can bat an eye. **1933** JCLenehan *Death* (L) 114: In less time than it would take you to wink your eye. **1957** ESGardner *Screaming* (NY) 53: Before a man can wink his eye. TW 125(25). Cf. DARE i 166–7: Bat *v.*[2]

E118 An **Eye** for an eye *etc.*

1922 DFox *Ethel* (NY) 311: An eye for an eye and a life for a life. EAP E118.

E119 An **Eye** to the main chance (*varied*)

1916 MGibbon *Inglorious* (L 1968) 112: A keen eye to the main chance. **1933** DLSayers *Murder* (NY) 226: A very good eye for the main chance. **1938** NJones *Hanging Lady* (NY) 61: With always an eye to the main chance. **1940** JCLincoln *Out of the Fog* (NY) 302: She had one eye on the main chance. **1948** ECrispin *Buried* (L 1958) 34: An eye to the main chance. **1956** JFStraker *Ginger* (L) 41: An eye to the main chance. **1957** BWAldiss *Space* (L) 170: He had . . . only one eye, and that was on the main chance. **1960** JBarry *Malignant* (NY) 114: Perhaps she was only on the make. After the main chance. **1962** HBaker *W.Hazlitt* (Cambridge, Mass.) 108: An eye to the main chance. **1969** JHGrainger *Character* (Cambridge, Eng.) 149: Had . . . a good eye for the financial main chance. **1975** JPearson *Edward* (NY) 105: A keen eye for the main chance. EAP E121.

E120 Four **Eyes** are better than two (*varied*)

1929 AGray *Dead* (NY) 21: Two pairs of eyes are better than one. **1930** LMeynell *Mystery* (P) 69: Four eyes are better than two. **1935** MThomas *Inspector* (L) 44: Four eyes were better than two. **1941** FCrane *Turquoise* (P) 52: Two pair of eyes are better than one. **1958** AMacKinnon *Summons* (NY) 108: Four eyes are better than two. **1959** MInnes *Hare* (NY 1964) 66: It shows that two pair of eyes are better than one. **1962** HReilly *Day* (NY DBC) 66: Four eyes were better than two. **1968** LPDavies *Grave* (NY) 148: Two pair of eyes are better than one. EAP E125: Many. Cf. Two Heads *below*.

E121 No **Eye** like the master's eye

1933 RAFreeman *Dr. Thorndyke Intervenes* (L) 312: There is no eye like the master's eye. Cf. EAP E120,126; Whiting *NC* 404(7).

E122 Not see **Eye** to eye

1934 MThomas *Inspector Wilkins* (L) 80: They did not see exactly eye to eye, as you may say. **1946** VKelsey *Whisper Murder* (NY) 55: [He] and I don't always see eye to eye. **1956** DWheatley *Ka* (L) 252: Giff and young Harold never saw eye to eye. NED Eye 5.

E123 To be all (in) one's **Eye**

1904 HGarland *Companions on the Trail* (NY 1931) 265: I suspect [it] is all "in his eye," as the old slang phrase has it. **1931** ABCox *Top* (NY) 155: That magnanimous offer . . .

was all my eye. **1952** CDickson *Cavalier's* (NY) 41: He's all my eye. **1958** MProcter *Man in* (NY) 84: That smooth line of your's is all my eye. **1966** JBell *Death* (NY) 175: That about Mrs. Potter was all my eye and you knew it. EAP E127; TW 123–4(2,3); Brunvand 44(2).

E124 To be all my **Eye** and Betty Martin (*varied*)

1924 AEHousman *Letters* ed HMaas (Cambridge, Mass. 1971) 224: All my eye and Beatus Martinus. **1928** DHLawrence *Lady* ("Allemagne") 61: The my-eye-Betty-Martin sobstuff. 92: The rest all-my-eye-Betty-Martin. **1928** LTracy *Women* (NY) 264: [His] sudden change of heart is all my eye and Betty Martin. **1929** RRodd *Secret* (NY) 252: Bless my soul and Betty Martin. **1930** ECRLorac *Murder* (L) 27: You can bet my eye and Betty Martin. **1936** ECRLorac *Death* (L) 12: It's all my eye and Betty Martin. **1936** JWVandercook *Murder in Fiji* (NY) 199: Wriggles my eye and Mary Ann! **1937** ERPunshon *Mystery* (NY) 100: All my eye and Betty Martin. **1964** CMackenzie *Life III* (L) 223: All my eye and Betty Martin. **1970** AChristie *Passenger* (NY) 218: All my eye and Betty Martin. *Oxford* 10: All.

E125 To be blind in one **Eye** and not see out of the other (*varied*)

1937 RStout *Red Box* (L) 67: You're blind in one eye and can't see out of the other. **1940** HSKeeler *Cleopatra's* (L) 100: I could see 'ith one ey closed an' the other blinded. **1953** CMRussell *Market* (NY) 34: Blind in one eye and couldn't see out of the other.

E126 To be up to one's **Eyes**

1943 SShane *Lady . . . Millions* (NY) 110: You're into something up to your eyes. **1979** OPritchett *Prize* (NY) 43: We were up to the old proverbial eyes [*in work*]. NED Eye 2e.

E127 To do (be done) in the **Eye** (*varied*)

1932 FWCrofts *Sudden* (NY) 194: Grinsmead's done us in the eye. **1933** FDGrierson *Empty* (L) 81: This . . . girl has done you in the eye. **1935** HHolt *Unknown* (L) 52: That's one in the eye for the murderer. **1950** ERPunshon *So Many* (NY) 121: One in the eye for Shakespeare. **1962** STruss *Time* (NY) 48: It's one in the eye for Henry. **1972** MKaye *Lively* (NY) 167: I'm not trying to do you in the eye.

E128   To have come-hither (bedroom) **Eyes**
1936 LRGribble *Malverne* (L) 205: What they call come-hither eyes on the films. **1953** SBellow *Adventures* (NY) 222: He has a pair of bedroom eyes. **1964** AChristie *Caribbean* (NY) 159: Lacks come-hither in her eye. Berrey 224.1, 356.2, 5.

E129   To have **Eyes** bigger than one's belly (stomach) (*varied*)
1933 DHoldridge *Pindorama* (NY) 19: A little boy whose eyes were bigger than his belly. **1933** PStong *Strangers* (NY) 142: I guess my eyes was bigger than my stomach. **1938** MKRawlings *Yearling* (NY) 11: Your eyes is bigger'n your belly. **1952** FKane *Bare* (NY 1960) 19: I hope your eyes aren't bigger than your stomach. **1959** HEBates *Watercress* (L) 18: His eyes are bigger'n his belly. **1966** HTracy *Men* (L) 170: Nurse . . . always did say his eyes were too big for his tummy. **1968** EBuckler *Ox Bells* (NY) 163: His eyes were bigger than his belly. **1971** OZinkin *Odious* (L) 97: Papa . . . warned me against having eyes bigger than the stomach. EAP E131.

E130   To have **Eyes** like holes burned in a blanket
1924 WBMFerguson *Black* (NY) 23: [Eyes] resembled holes burned in a blanket. **1938** MECorne *Death* (NY) 87: His eyes like burned holes in a blanket. **1940** JCLincoln *Out of the Fog* (NY) 33: His eyes look like two burnt holes in a dish-towel, as my grandmother used to say. **1952** KMKnight *Death Goes* (NY) 178: Eyes like burnt holes in a blanket. **1956** SPalmer *Unhappy* (NY 1957) 87: Eyes . . . like two burnt holes in a blanket. **1962** FCrane *Amber* (NY) 48: People talk about eyes like holes in a blanket. **1963** MPHood *Sin* (NY) 175: Eyes like two burnt holes in a blanket. TW 185: Hole(4).

E131   To keep one's **Eye** on the ball
1947 TKyd *Blood* (P) 51: That's keeping your eye on the ball. **1958** WJLederer *Ugly* (NY) 76: He's a smart cookie with his eye on the ball. **1962** HPentecost *Cannibal* (NY DBC) 104: Keep your eye on the ball. Berrey 153.2, 245.15. Cf. NED Eye 6a.

E132   To keep one's **Eyes** peeled (skinned)
1908 JCLincoln *Cy Whittaker* (NY) 347: I should keep my eye peeled. **1913** JSFletcher *Secret* (L 1916) 90: Keep his eyes skinned. **1927** SHorler *Black* (L 1935) 77: I'll keep my eyes skinned. **1932** WLHay *Who Cut* (L) 7: This is where I keep my peepers skinned. **1934** DFrome *Arsenic* (L) 106: We'll keep our eyes peeled. **1955** CMWills *Death* (L) 59: Keep your eyes skinned. **1958** MColes *Come* (NY) 224: Keep your eyes skinned. **1970** JBlackburn *Bury* (NY) 55: Keep your eyes skinned. **1970** JFrazer *Deadly* (NY) 26: Keep your eyes peeled. TW 124(16,17); Brunvand 44(5).

E133   To put (something) in one's **Eye** and not feel it (*varied*)
1930 JJConnington *Two Tickets* (L) 148: Just about as big as you could put in your eye and not feel it tickle you. **1931** GFowler *Great* (NY) 396: What I got out of Nicky Arnstein, you could put in a gnat's eye. **1940** AAFair *Gold Comes* (NY) 154: Anything he missed you could put in your eye. **1945** HLawrence *Time to Die* (NY) 85: What they didn't know you could put in your eye. **1950** DMDisney *Fire* (NY) 57: The old girl didn't have enough money to put in your eye. **1956** *New Yorker* 8/4 26: What is left you can shove in your left eye without you should even blink yet. **1960** DMDisney *Dark* (NY) 52: You could put in your eye all I've done lately. **1963** FGruber *Bridge* (NY DBC) 68: What he knew about languages . . . you could stick in your eye. **1963** MPHood *Sin* (NY) 127: With no more help from you two than I could put in my eye without blinkin'. **1974** DMDisney *Don't Go* (NY) 22: The amount of cooking I'm going to do . . . you could put in your eye. EAP E137.

E134   To wipe (someone's) **Eye**
1928 JJConnington *Tragedy* (B) 247: We can wipe your eye this time [*beat you*]. **1931** APryde *Emerald* (NY) 83: Rudolph wouldn't like it if you wiped his eye. **1939**

TStevenson *Silver Arrow* (L) 31: He'd still be able to wipe everybody's eye. **1948** MColes *Among* (NY) 62: You have rather wiped his eye. **1960** JWyndham *Trouble* (NY) 12: She's wiped the old bastard's eye properly. Brunvand 44–45(6); Partridge 961: Wipe; NED Eye 2g.

E135 What the **Eye** cannot see the heart cannot grieve for (*varied*)

1922 JJoyce *Ulysses* (NY 1934) 490: What the eye can't see the heart can't grieve for. **1928** DHLawrence *Lady* ("Allemagne") 17: What the eye doesn't see and the mind doesn't know, doesn't exist. **1928** WMcFee *Pilgrims* (NY) 71: What the eye don't see the heart don't grieve for. **1931** CFGregg *Rutland* (NY) 196: What the eye does not see, the heart does not grieve. **1932** FIles *Before* (NY 1958) 70: What the mind doesn't know, the eyes don't cry over. **1937** WGore *Murder Most* (L) 125: The motto, "what the eyes don't see the mind needn't worry about." **1949** NBlake *Head* (NY) 29: What the eye don't see, the heart don't grieve for. **1950** VSReid *New Day* (L) 256: If eyes do no' see, hearts can no' speak o' shame. **1956** HCahill *Shadow* (NY) 295: Like the fella says, "What the ears don't hear the heart doesn't grieve." **1959** HEBates *Watercress* (L) 60: What they don't hear . . . they don't grieve over. **1960** CBrown *Dream* (NY) 71: What is it they always say? "What the eye doesn't see, the heart doesn't grieve." **1968** JAiken *Crystal* (NY) 102: What the ear didn't hear the heart didn't grieve over. **1971** NMarsh *When* (NY) 122: What they can't grieve about they won't see. **1975** GBlack *Big Wind* (NY) 28: What the eye doesn't see the mind doesn't worry about too much. EAP E140.

E136 To hang on by one's **Eyebrows** (eyelashes, eyelids)

1933 HHolt *Scarlet* (L) 160: Hanging on by his eyebrows. **1934** WSharp *Murder* (NY) 169: We're just hanging on by an eyebrow. **1942** HNicolson *Diaries II* ed NNicolson (NY 1967) 210: We are . . . hanging on by our eyelids in Singapore. **1956** MGilbert *Be*

Shot (L) 10: We hung on by our eyelashes. **1958** RHiscock *Last* (NY) 25: Holding on to this job by his eyelashes. **1959** GCarr *Swing* (NY) 131: The phrase *hanging on by my eyebrows*. **1975** HPentecost *Time* (NY) 114: She's hanging on by an eyelash [*emotionally*]. EAP E141.

E137 Not bat an **Eyelid** (eyelash)

1932 DHume *Bullets* (L) 29: He'd have done this man in without batting an eyelid. **1937** VLoder *Choose* (L) 98: Without batting an eyelash. **1942** JBell *Death . . . Medical Board* (NY) 81: Never batted an eyelid. **1952** BWolfe *Limbo* (L) 61: Without batting an eyelash. **1958** CCarnac *Affair* (NY) 127: And never batted an eyelid. **1970** ELathen *Pick* (NY) 103: Without batting an eyelash. Berrey 178.5: Eyelid, 266.6; DARE i 167 Bat *v.*[2] 1a: Not to bat.

E138 To cut one's **Eyeteeth**

1929 HFootner *Self-Made* (NY) 142: I've cut my eyeteeth. **1934** CFGregg *Execution* (L) 91: [He] had cut his eye-teeth. **1939** CBClason *Dragon's* (NY) 160: You should have cut your eyeteeth long ago. **1956** PDeVries *Comfort* (B) 83: Everybody has to cut his eyeteeth. EAP E143; Brunvand 45(1).

E139 To give one's **Eyeteeth**

1909 JCLincoln *Keziah* (NY) 42: Didama would have given her eyeteeth. **1961** EMcBain *Lady* (NY) 126: Meyer would have given his eyeteeth to have known. **1966** SMarlowe *Search* (NY) 221: Any journalist would give his eye-teeth . . . to be in my shoes. **1967** EWallach *Light* (NY) 205: Would give their eyeteeth to be back there. **1971** HVanDyke *Dead* (NY) 175: Dozens would give all sorts of eyeteeth to belong. Amer. Herit. Dict. Eyetooth.

E140 To trade one out of his **Eyeteeth** (*varied*)

1954 RJHealy *Tales* (NY) 187: They'll trade you out of your eyeteeth. **1957** LBeam *Maine* (NY) 178: His grandfather . . . would lift anybody's eyeteeth. **1965** KAmis *Spectrum IV* (L) 29: Sam swindled her out of her eyeteeth. TW 125(2).

F

F1 As plain as one's **Face**

1933 PHunt *Murder* (NY) 18: Plain as your face. **1934** RAJWalling *Legacy* (NY) 159: How it was done is plain as my face. **1940** CMWills *R.E.Pipe* (L) 62: Made it as plain as your face he didn't believe us. **1962** FCrane *Amber* (NY) 163: It's plain as your face he wants no truck with Audrey. TW 126(2).

F2 The **Face** is the index of the mind

1966 RStout *Death* (NY) 6: *Vultus est index animi* . . . A Latin proverb. The face is the index of the mind. EAP F2; Brunvand 28: Countenance, 46(1): To the heart.

F3 A **Face** that would sour milk (*varied*)

1908 MRRinehart *Circular Staircase* (NY 1947) 96: Your face would sour milk. **1933** ECRLorac *Murder* (L) 78: He'd curdle good milk . . . to even look at 'im. **1939** HCBailey *Veron* (L) 247: He looked sour enough to turn the milk. TW 244(9).

F4 A **Face** that would stop a clock (*varied*)

1906 JCLincoln *Mr. Pratt* (NY) 199: There ain't a female . . . that wouldn't stop a clock. **1913** JCLincoln *Mr. Pratt's Patients* (NY) 27: Her face mightn't have stopped a clock. **1928** HFootner *Velvet* (NY) 223: Enough to stop a clock [*a woman's face*]. **1935** DGardiner *Translantic* (L) 23: She can stop a clock unaided just by looking at it. **1939** JDCarr *Problem* (B 1948) 44: She had a face which . . . would stop a clock. **1955** PGWodehouse *French* (L) 80: Faces well calculated to stop any clock. **1957** PGWodehouse *Butler* (NY)

95: She had a face that would have stopped a clock. **1970** AHalper *Good-bye* (C) 54: She's got a face that could stop a clock. Whiting *NC* 405(1).

F5 Fair to one's **Face** and foul behind one's back

1934 RForsyth *Pleasure Cruise* (NY) 203: Fair to your face they are and foul behind your back. Cf. EAP F9; Whiting F4–6.

F6 One's **Face** is his fortune

1930 MPlum *Killing* (NY) 259: His face is our fortune. **1940** RDarby *Death Conducts* (NY) 221: Geraldine's face is her fortune. **1949** MGilbert *He Didn't* (NY DBC) 116: His face is his fortune. **1956** MColes *Far* (NY) 142: My poor face—it was never my fortune. **1970** VCClinton-Baddeley *No Case* (NY) 102: Jane's face is her fortune. Bartlett 1095a; Oxford *DQ* 369.15.

F7 To fly in the **Face** of Providence

1924 ROChipperfield *Bright* (NY) 75: Fly in the face of Providence. **1936** LThayer *Dark of the Moon* (NY) 71: Flying in the face of Providence. **1937** EJepson *Memories* (L) 20: Flying in the face of Providence. **1958** STruss *In Secret* (NY) 52: Nor do they fly in the face of a generous Providence. EAP F5; TW 126(5).

F8 To vanish off the **Face** of the earth (*varied*)

1930 MDalton *Body* (NY) 42: She . . . vanished off the face of the earth. **1975** DE Westlake *Two* (NY) 266: She had dropped, as the saying is, from the face of the earth. Cf. NED Face 11a. Cf. Earth *above*.

F9   Until one is black (blue) in the **Face**

1920 JSFletcher *Dead Men's* (NY) 121: Talk till you were black in the face. **1920** EWallace *Three-Oaks* (L) 200: If you cried till you was blue in the face. **1922** JJoyce *Ulysses* (NY 1934) 345–6: They could talk about her till they were blue in the face. 488: Talk away till you're black in the face. **1928** CKingston *Guilty* (L) 89: Arguing about it until they've got black in the face. **1930** TCobb *Sark* (L) 161: You may ask till you're blue in the face. **1930** TThayer *Thirteen Men* (NY) 125: He had talked her black in her face. **1931** AChristie *Murder* (NY) 230: It's been worrying my aunt blue in the face. **1940** PWentworth *Rolling* (P) 99: The telephone would ring itself black in the face. **1944** MLong *Bury* (NY) 101: You can kiss the damn woman until you are blue in the face. **1947** NBlake *Minute* (L) 160: You could work yourself black in the face. **1952** ESHolding *Widow's* (NY DBC) 53: Drink till they're blue in the face. **1955** AHunter *Gently Does* (L) 55: He was lying himself black in the face. **1958** NMarsh *Singing* (B) 240: You can resist till you're purple in the face. **1959** SDean *Merchant* (NY) 20: I'll sue you blue in the face. **1961** LPayne *Nose* (NY) 59: I've heard those wretched lines of hers until I'm blue in the face. **1963** WMasterson *Man on* (NY DBC) 48: Crow could cultivate the child until he was blue in the face. **1968** SPalmer *Rook* (NY) 48: I knocked until I was blue in the face. **1970** RFenisong *Drop* (NY) 150: Lie yourself blue in the face. **1973** RRendell *Some* (NY) 144: Lie themselves black in the face. TW 126(3); Brunvand 46(2); *Oxford* 792: Swear.

F10   **Facts** are chiels that winna ding

1932 AWynne *White Arrow* (P) 278: But "facts are chiels as winna ding." Hislop 92; *Oxford DQ* 105.11 [*Robert Burns*].

F11   **Facts** are facts

1930 MKennedy *Corpse* (NY) 269: Facts are facts. **1933** FDell *Homecoming* (NY) 119: Facts are facts, you can't get around that. **1938** RAJWalling *Coroner* (L) 264: Facts are facts. **1957** JYork *Come Here* (NY) 153: Facts are facts. **1960** IWallace *Chapman* (NY 1961) 274: Facts are facts. **1968** WTenn *Wooden* (NY) 86: Facts are facts and weakest people always go to the wall. Brunvand 46(1).

F12   **Facts** are stubborn things

1942 HCBailey *Nobody's* (NY) 262: Facts are stubborn things. EAP F12; Brunvand 46(2).

F13   **Facts** speak louder than opinions (*varied*)

1929 ABCox *Layton* (NY) 111: Facts speak louder than opinions. **1964** NFreeling *Because* (NY 1965) 173: Facts talk loud. **1965** HCarlisle *Ilyitch* (NY) 115: Facts don't lie. EAP F14.

F14   To face **Facts** (*varied*)

1930 JCournos *Grandmother* (NY) 94: We might as well face facts. **1932** FDGrierson *Murder* (L) 61: We must look facts in the face. **1937** ECRLorac *These Names* (L) 86: I prefer to look facts in the face. **1939** MBurton *Babbacombe* (L) 56: We've got to face the facts. **1958** HAlpert *Summer* (NY) 141: I'm perfectly willing to face facts. Amer. Herit. Dict. Face *v.* 3a.

F15   The **Fag-end**

1921 JCLincoln *Galusha* (NY) 6: 'Way out in the fag-end of nothin'. **1940** BHalliday *Uncomplaining* (NY) 188: You look like the fag-end of a misspent life. **1971** EDahlberg *Confessions* (NY) 32: He was in the fag-end of his forties. EAP F15.

F16   **Fair** and softly goes far

1937 EJepson *Memories* (L) 30: Fair and softly goes far in a day. EAP F16; TW 127(1).

F17   **Fair** do's

1928 RThorndike *Slype* (NY) 72: Fair do's. **1938** FDGrierson *Covenant* (L) 99: Fair do's, as they say in Ireland. If we help you, you've got to help us. **1951** SRattray *Knight* (L 1966) 138: Fair do's. **1973** AGilbert *Nice* (NY) 14: They don't know about fair do's. **1981** JSScott *View* (NY) 114: Fair do's. Partridge 263.

F18 Fair, fat and forty (*varied*)

1922 JJoyce *Ulysses* (NY 1934) 640: Married women getting on for fair and forty. **1931** CWells *Horror* (P) 27: All three stipulations of fair, fat and forty. **1939** CFGregg *Danger* (L) 82: Mrs. Murgatroyd was fair, fat and forty-five. **1951** PCheyney *Ladies* (NY) 34: Mrs. Vayne—fair, fat and forty. **1955** DMDisney *Trick* (NY) 44: Fat, fair and well over forty. **1959** EMButler *Paper* (L) 102: Fair, fat and fifty. Bartlett 276a [*John O'Keeffe*]; Oxford *DQ* 420.20.

F19 Fair is fair

1928 CBarry *Corpse* (NY) 261: Fair's fair. **1937** DWhitelaw *Face* (L) 5: Fair's fair. **1945** AChristie *Remembered* (NY) 193: Fair's fair. **1950** CDickson *Night* (NY) 117: Fair's fair. **1958** NMarsh *Singing* (B) 238: Fair's fair. **1960** GSAlbee *By the Sea* (NY) 40: Fair is fair. **1968** WTenn *Of Men* (NY) 248: Fair's fair. **1976** JMcClur *Snake* (NY) 22: Fair's fair. Apperson 201: Fair *sb.* 1.

F20 He that is down need fear no **Fall**

1938 ECRLorac *Devil* (L) 119: He that is down need fear no fall. *Oxford* 461: Lies upon the ground.

F21 To be riding for a **Fall**

1925 HCWitwer *Bill* (NY) 174: You are riding for a fall. **1933** DHoldridge *Pindorama* (NY) 61: The politicians were riding for a fall. **1936** HWeiner *Crime on the Cuff* (NY) 246: Don't be riding for another fall. **1951** ESGardner *Fiery* (NY) 71: He's riding for a fall. **1958** TEDikty *Six from* (NY) 83: He was riding for a fall, riding hell-for-leather. **1960** EMcBain *See Them* (NY) 43: He's been riding for a fall. Amer. Herit. Dict. ride *v.* 10.

F22 Common **Fame** is seldom to blame

1936 RAJWalling *Crimson Slippers* (L) 15: As the proverb says, common fame is seldom to blame. Apperson 109–10(8); *Oxford* 138: Common.

F23 Fame is better than fortune

1932 JMarsh *Murder* (L) 278: They say fame's better than fortune any day. Whiting N12: A good name. Cf. *Oxford* 319: Good fame.

F24 Familiarity breeds contempt (*varied*)

1911 JSHay *Amazing Emperor* (L) 31: Familiarity has bred contempt. **1920** ACrabb *Samuel* (NY) 159: For all the contempt that familiarity breeds. **1922** EPower *Medieval English Nunneries* (Cambridge, Eng.) 446: Familiarity with the bonds of religion possibly bred contempt. **1925** HWNevinson *More Changes* (L) 353: Perhaps familiarity breeds indifference. **1930** EDBiggers *Charlie* (NY 1943) 213: Familiarity had bred charity where he was concerned. **1930** WLewis *Apes* (NY 1932) 129: The contempt bred of familiarity. **1933** HDuffy *Seven* (NY) 39: The familiarity of marriage breeds little besides children and contempt. **1938** WNMacartney *Fifty Years* (NY) 165: Too much familiarity breeds contempt, and a prophet is not without honor save in his own country. I have a lot of other bromides available if desired. **1956** FAllen *Much* (B) 197: Familiarity breeds a variety of contempt. **1957** *Punch* 9/18 319: Familiarity bred. **1959** JABrussel *Just* (NY) 163: No one had told him that "familiarity breeds attempt." **1960** TWBurgess *Now I* (B) 235: It is an old and well-known saying that "Familiarity breeds contempt." **1968** ELathen *Stitch* (NY) 35: Familiarity . . . breeds compliance more often than it breeds contempt. **1968** JTMcIntosh *Six Gates* (NY) 43: Familiarity usually did breed, if not contempt, satiation. **1972** SCloete *Victorian* (L) 237: Their [*rats'*] familiarity with the dead having made them contemptuous of the living. **1976** JHerbers *No Thank You* (NY) 63: In the White House press corps, contrary to the popular belief, nothing breeds contempt like unfamiliarity with the President. **1978** MKWren *Nothing's* (NY) 90: Unfamiliarity inevitably breeds distrust. EAP F22; TW 127; Brunvand 47.

F25 All in the **Family**

1932 *Hot-cha* (L) 12: We are sisters you know, and they say it is all in the family. TW 127.

F26 Fanny Adams

1949 MGilbert *He Didn't* (NY DBC) 88: You didn't ask me here to talk about sweet Fanny Adams or drink tea. **1964** AHunter

Gently (NY) 66: He noticed Hamnet was missing and did Fanny Adams about it. **1969** AGilbert *Missing* (NY) 127: If he ain't it's sweet Fanny Adams so far as tonight's concerned. Partridge 266.

F27 So **Far** so good

1905 FMWhite *Crimson Blind* (NY) 13: So far so good; 184. **1915** JFerguson *Stealthy* (L 1935) 95: So far, so good. **1923** TFPowys *Left Leg* (L) So far so good. **1931** TSmith *Stray* (NY) 1: So far so good. **1941** ESGardner *Haunted Husband* (NY) 113: So far so good. **1952** MColes *Alias* (NY) 117: So far, so good. **1958** NMonkman *From Queensland* (NY) 33: So far, so good. **1967** ARose *Memoirs* (NY) 94: So far so good. **1970** JLeasor *They Don't* (NY) 91: So far so bad. **1974** WStegner *Uneasy* (NY) 75: So far, so good. EAP F24.

F28 To a **Fare-you-well**

1930 RWallace *Seven Men* (NY) 131: Drugged to a fare-you-well. **1932** MCJohnson *Damning* (NY) 4: Curse each other to a fare-you-well. **1935** LThayer *Sudden* (NY) 91: He was planning to work the old inheritance motive to a fare-you-well. **1940** CDickson *And So to Murder* (NY) 250: He misled you all to fare-ye-well. **1956** SDean *Marked* (NY) 87: We'll sue you to a fare-thee-well. **1971** WHMarnell *Once Upon* (NY) 128: The floor . . . was holystoned to a fare thee well. DA *s.v.*; NED Suppl. *s.v.*; Wentworth 178.

F29 Who wouldn't sell a **Farm** and go to sea? (*varied*)

1900 JLondon *Letters* ed KHendricks (NY 1965) 91: Who wouldn't sell a farm and go to writing? **1934** SHAdams *Gorgeous* (B) 154: You know the sailors' proverb: "Who wouldn't sell his farm and go to sea?" **1937** VGielgud *Death in Budapest* (L) 189: Why did I ever sell my little farm and go to Budapest! EAP F26.

F30 As effective as a **Fart** in a whirlwind

1971 RMStern *You Don't* (NY) 36: The advice was about as effective as a fart in a whirlwind. Whiting *NC* 405 Cf. Sneeze below.

F31 Like a **Fart** in a mitten

1975 HLawrenson *Stranger* (NY) 40: Don't rush around like a fart in a mitten.

F32 Like a **Fart** (hoot) in a windstorm (*varied*)

1932 SHPage *Resurrection* (NY) 87: He went like a hoot in a gale of wind. **1959** JLatimer *Black* (NY) 220: Would he have whizzed out of that theatre like a fart in a windstorm if he hadn't. Whiting *NC* 405: Whirlwind. Cf. Sneeze *below*.

F33 Not care a **Fart** (*varied*)

1964 EPangborn *Davy* (NY) 14: Nobody cares to the extent of a fart in a whirlwind. **1972** AFriedman *Hermaphrodeity* (NY) 53: I don't care a fart. **1981** JBHilton *Playground* (NY) 108: Not that Bielby cared a monkey's fart. EAP F28.

F34 Not give a **Fart** (*varied*)

1963 NFitzgerald *Echo* (NY) 225: I don't give a fart. **1964** ABurgess *Nothing* (L) 26: Not one fart do I give. **1966** SGCrawford *Gascoyne* (L) 91: She doesn't give a living fart. **1975** NFreeling *Bugles* (NY) 119: Nobody gives a fart. **1979** LRosten *Silkey* (NY) 112: I don't give a fart in a bottle. Whiting F60; Partridge 267(4).

F35 Not worth a **Fart** (*varied*)

1922 JJoyce *Ulysses* (NY 1934) 324: They were never worth a roasted fart to Ireland. **1928** MKSanders *D.Thompson* (B 1973) 129: This book as art Ain't worth a —. **1936** JTFarrell *World* (NY) 118: He wasn't worth a fart in bed. **1956** WMankowitz *Old* (B) 82: Not worth a fart. Whiting F62; Partridge 267(4). Cf. Sneeze *below*.

F36 Not care (amount to, give) a brass **Farthing**

1928 JArnold *Surrey* (L) 39: You don't care a brass farthing. **1933** DGBrown *Dead* (L) 81: He . . . didn't care a brass farthing. **1948** ECrispin *Buried* (L 1958) 103: I wouldn't give a brass farthing. **1951** ECrispin *Long* (L 1958) 70: I don't care a brass farthing. **1954** JTey *Shilling* (NY) 51: Not one of us cared a brass farthing for her. **1967** RJones *Three* (B) 175: Doesn't amount to a brass farthing. EAP F32.

F37 Not worth a (brass) **Farthing**

1928 EHamilton *Four* (L) 66: Isn't worth a brass farthing. **1938** NBlake *Smiler* (L) 130: Her . . . life . . . wouldn't be worth a farthing. **1971** GBaxt *Affair* (NY) 119: Her life might not be worth a farthing. EAP F35.

F38 To play **Fast** and loose

1921 JBCabell *Figures* (NY 1925) 54: Fast and loose is a mischancy game to play. **1927** NMartin *Mosaic* (NY) 218: He played fast and loose. **1938** NBlake *Beast* (NY 1958) 144: Playing fast and loose with the wife of this man. **1940** CEVulliamy *Calico Pie* (L) 242: To play fast and loose with every one of the Thirty-nine Articles. **1941** ARLong *4 Feet* (NY) 56: Playin' fast and loose with the family silver. **1953** KMKnight *Akin* (NY) 177: Playing fast and loose with the law. **1958** JAHoward *Murder* (NY 1959) 6: A wife who plays at fast and loose. **1964** LSDeCamp *Ancient* (NY) 149: Nennius . . . plays fast and loose with his source. **1970** JVizzard *See* (NY) 220: I was playing fast and loose. **1975** HCarmichael *Too Late* (NY) 104: Don't play fast and loose with me. EAP F37.

F39 The **Fat** is in the fire (*varied*)

1905 FMWhite *Crimson Blind* (NY) 158: The fat will be in the fire; 180. **1924** HSKeeler *Voice* (NY) 57: The fat would be in the fire. **1930** AChristie *Murder* (NY) 237: The fat would be in the fire, to use an old-fashioned expression. **1939** HReilly *All Concerned* (NY) 196: The fat's in the fire for sure. **1940** JDonavan *Plastic Man* (L) 66: The fat will be fairly in the fire. **1946** DDuncan *Shade of Time* (NY) 63: Are you building that fire to put the fat in? **1954** EForbes *Rainbow* (B) 115: The fat was in the fire. **1956** PDeVries *Comfort* (B) 146: Pulling the fat out of the fire. **1959** *BHerald* 4/13 10: To add "fat to the fire." **1961** WCooper *Scenes* (NY) 51: In common language, the fat was in the fire. **1967** RJones *Three* (B) 257: The fat was in the fire; the fur was flying; the claws were out—all the classic old clichés came true. **1968** RGSherriff *No Leading* (L) 140: I had pulled the fat out of the fire. **1970** ACross *Poetic* (NY) 78: The fat was in the fire or, as McQuire would have said, the four-let-ter-word-bathroom had hit the fan. **1970** KLaumer *World* (NY) 39: I guess the fat's on the hotplate now. EAP F38; TW 127(2); Brunvand 47.

F40 To chew the **Fat**

1922 JJoyce *Ulysses* (NY 1934) 300: Chewing the fat. **1931** CJDaly *Third* (NY) 45: Chewing the fat over a bottle. **1936** GHomes *Doctor* (NY) 65: I came back to chew the fat with pop here. **1954** EWalter *Untidy* (P) 73: Y'all can chew the fat at home. **1957** WFuller *Girl* (NY) 140: He's just chewing the fat. **1960** CWatson *Bump* (L 1963) 117: Men wished to chew the fat and swap yarns. **1964** JPhilips *Laughter* (NY DBC) 93: We chew the fat about the old days. **1970** WANolen *Making* (NY) 241: Chewing the fat with us. **1973** CJackson *Kicked* (NY) 131: To chew the fat with the guards. Wentworth 97: Chew.

F41 To live on (off) the **Fat** of the land

1908 LFBaum *Dorothy and the Wizard of Oz* (I) 199: I live on the fat of the land. **1922** JJoyce *Ulysses* (NY 1934) 149: Living on the fat of the land. **1931** GFowler *Great* (NY) 322: He lived on the fat of the land. **1936** PGWodehouse *Young Men* (NY) 148: Living off the fat of the land, as the saying is. **1940** RLGoldman *Snatch* (NY) 184: He lived off the fat of the land. **1953** JWyndham *Kraken* (L 1955) 224: Living on the fat of the land. **1970** SGBoswell *Book* (L) 170: Living off the "fat of the land," as the saying goes. EAP F39.

F42 To take the **Fat** with the lean (*varied*)

1924 RAFreeman *Blue* (NY) 244: We have to take the fat with the lean. **1928** DHLawrence *Lady* ("Allemagne") 206: T'ae the thick wi' th' thin. **1957** JCheever *Wapshot* (NY) 124: They take the fat with the lean. **1961** MHHood *Drown* (NY) 20: A man must take the lean with the fat in his morning bacon. **1962** HReilly *Day* (NY DBC) 133: Take the fat with the lean. *Oxford* 800: Take. Cf. To take the Good, Rough *below*.

F43 As sure as **Fate**

1904 JCLincoln *Cap'n Eri* (NY) 8: Sure as fate. **1924** JSFletcher *Mazaroff* (NY) 139: Sure as fate. **1938** ECRLorac *Devil* (L) 93:

As sure as fate's fate. **1946** FWCrofts *Death of a Train* (L) 143: Sure as fate. **1954** RJHealy *Tales* (NY) 19: Sure as fate. **1971** PAlding *Despite* (NY) 126: As sure as fate. TW 128(3). Cf. Brunvand 47.

F44 A **Fate** worse than death (*varied*)

1938 NMorland *Rope* (L) 131: To save her from a fate that is popularly supposed to be worse than death. **1939** RStout *Some Buried* (L) 51: She paid me two bucks to save her brother from a fate worse than death. **1940** NMorland *Sun* (L) 2: She was apparently warding off the fate which maiden ladies insist is far worse than death. **1953** GBagby *Big Hand* (NY DBC) 129: A fate worse than death [*arrest*]. **1956** MProcter *Ripper* (NY) 192: You want to save Elliott from a fate worse than death [*a bad marriage*]. **1958** CLBlackstone *Dewey* (L 1965) 189: You are at least saved from what they say is worse than death. I wonder if it is. **1962** EHuxley *Mottled* (L) 124: A damsel in distress, rescued from a fate worse than death. **1969** RGrayson *Voyage* (L) 149: She . . . had no fear of a fate worse than death. **1973** OSela *Portuguese* (NY) 225: She really believed in fates worse than death.

F45 The **Father** and mother of a beating (row)

1922 JJoyce *Ulysses* (NY 1934) 313: Handed him the father and mother of a beating. **1958** CCockburn *Crossing* (L) 56: There was the father and mother of a row. **1959** AGilbert *Death* (NY) 17: Kicked up the father and mother of a row. Partridge 268: Father of a.

F46 Like **Father** (parent), like child

1961 MErskine *Woman* (NY) 26: The saying, "Like father like child." **1961** RJWhite *Smartest* (L) 115: Like father, like child. **1975** ELathen *By Hook* (NY) 21: An old Armenian proverb—like parent, like child. TW 128(3).

F47 Like **Father**, like daughter (*varied*)

1924 GRFox *Fangs* (NY) 57: Like father, like son . . . like father, like daughter. **1937** RPenny *Policeman in* (L) 70: Like father, like daughter. **1945** FLockridge *Payoff* (P) 150: Like father, like daughter. **1958** NMacNeil *Death* (Greenwich, Conn.) 121: Like daughter, like father. **1961** RLockridge *With One* (P) 74: Like father, not like daughter. **1968** RLockridge *Murder* (P) 65: Like father, like daughter. **1972** CTurney *Byron's* (NY) 234: Like father, like daughter. Cf. Whiting M720; *Oxford* 546: Mother.

F48 Like **Father**, like son (*varied*)

1924 WBMFerguson *Black* (NY) 125: Like father, like son. **1933** TSmith *Rain* (NY) 255: Like father like son. **1939** HMiller *Capricorn* (NY 1961) 158: Like father like son was his motto. **1941** MVHeberden *Lobster Pick* (L) 38: Like father, like son. Sons of bitches, both. **1954** ASeton *Katherine* (B) 116: Like father, like son. **1955** JCreasey *Gelignite* (NY) 90: Like father, unlike son. **1968** EQueen *House* (NY) 154: Like son, like father. EAP F48.

F49 Small **Favors** are welcome (*very varied*)

1906 JCLincoln *Mr. Pratt* (NY) 158: Small favors thankfully received. **1931** ALivingston *In Cold* (I) 56: I'm grateful for small favors. **1934** KSteel *Murder for What?* (I) 333: Thanks for small favors. **1947** VWMason *Saigon* (NY) 57: Thank the Lord . . . for all small favors. **1956** RAHeinlein *Double* (NY 1957) 91: Thank God for small favors. **1958** BKendrick *Clear* (NY) 128: Thank God for small favors. **1965** JPhilips *Black* (NY DBC) 103: Thanks for small favors. **1965** Doctor X *Intern* (NY) 127: Thanking God for small favors. **1976** ACross *Question* (NY) 59: Thank heaven for small favors. **1982** CMacLeod *Wrack* (NY) 143: Thank God for small favors.

F50 To curry **Favor**

1926 FWCrofts *Cheyne* (NY) 199: To curry favor. **1936** JRhode *Murder* (NY) 196: To curry favour. **1937** GDejean *Who Killed* (L) 256: To curry favor with me. **1949** JBonett *Dead Lion* (L 1953) 126: He'd not curry your favor. **1959** EMButler *Paper* (L) 46: To curry favor with the Professor. **1963** AA Fair *Fish* (NY DBC) 127: Trying to curry favor. **1975** LBiggle *This Darkening* (NY) 61: To curry favor. EAP F53; TW 128(2).

F51 As shy as a **Fawn**

1964 AStratton *Great Red* (NY) 294: A girl, as shy as a fawn. TW 128(3). Cf. Brunvand 47: Wild.

F52 As timid as a **Fawn**

1927 BAtkey *Smiler* (NY) 78: Timid as a fawn. **1942** VCaspary *Laura* (NY 1957) 16: Timid as a fawn. TW 128(4).

F53 **Fear** lends wings

1930 ECVivian *Double* (L) 124: The old saying that fear lends wings. *Oxford* 249–50.

F54 The **Fear** of God is the beginning of wisdom

1930 AFielding *Murder* (NY) 125: The fear of God . . . is the beginning of wisdom. EAP F56.

F55 To put the **Fear** of God into someone

1926 HAdams *Crooked* (L) 232: Put the fear of God into him. **1928** ESnell *Kontrol* (P) 262: Put the fear of heaven into the rest. **1935** DHume *Murders* (L) 22: Put the fear of God into his subordinates. **1938** AGlanville *Body* (L) 228: Put the fear of God into him. **1949** JSStrange *Unquiet* (NY) 159: Put the fear of God into Loraine. **1955** DMDisney *Room* (NY) 120: Put the fear of God in her. **1962** EAmbler *Light* (L) 73: To put the fear of God into me. **1969** LPDavies *Stranger* (NY) 121: To put the fear of God into you. **1976** JSScott *Poor* (NY) 71: To put the fear of God into [him]. NED Fear *sb.* 3d: Fear of God.

F56 A **Feast** or a famine

1941 ISCobb *Exit* (I) 76: Either a feast or a famine. **1956** GMetalious *Peyton* (NY) 257: Feast or famine, that was the Witcher. **1960** ABudrys *Unexpected* (NY) 113: We were a feast-and-famine group. **1968** RLockridge *Murder* (P) 68: A feast-or-famine trade. EAP F57; Brunvand 47–8.

F57 As light as a **Feather**; Feather-light

1909 JCLincoln *Keziah* (NY) 276: Rides 's light as a feather. **1913** ERBurroughs *Warlord* (NY 1963) 92: Light and airy as a feather. **1932** CFGregg *Body* (L) 47: The girl, light as a feather. **1939** JNDarby *Murder in* (I) 60: Something as light as a feather.

1941 RAldington *Life* (NY) 202: My belt was feather-light. **1946** ESHolding *Innocent* (NY) 6: They're as light as feathers. **1958** NMarsh *Singing* (B) 170: She's as light as a feather on her pins. **1963** MMcCarthy *Group* (NY) 13: Light as a feather. **1976** JSScott *Poor* (NY) 133: The . . . body, light as a feather. EAP F59; TW 129(1); Brunvand 48(1).

F58 **Feathers** from a toad (horse)

1918 CTorr *Small Talk* (Cambridge, Eng.) 55: Us cannot pluck feathers from a toad [*Devon*]. **1929** RPeckham *Murder* (NY) 231: A guy can't grow feathers on a horse. Cf. Frog hair, To gather Goat feathers, To get Wool off a goat *below.*

F59 A **Feather** in one's cap

1905 FMWhite *Crimson Blind* (NY) 275: A feather in your sister's cap. **1923** ABlackwood *Episodes* (L) 292: A feather in my cap. **1928** DHLawrence *Lady* ("Allemagne") 84: Another feather in the family cap. **1936** JBude *Death* (L) 288: I've a feather for each of you—of the variety one proverbially sticks in a cap. **1941** BDougall *I Don't Scare* (NY) 173: You can take that feather out of your cap and knock me down with it. **1949** AAFair *Bedrooms* (NY 1958) 200: An opportunity to put a whole bevy of feathers in your cap. **1956** EBigland *Lord Byron* (L) 250: Its capture would be a large feather in his own cap. **1957** *BangorDN* 2/26 1: It would be a feather in his cap and a feather in our cap. **1960** NFitzgerald *Ghost* (L) 174: A great feather in the cap of any plain woman. **1970** DClark *Deadly* (NY) 1: Another feather . . . for his cap. **1975** AChristie *Curtain* (NY) 36: A feather in my cap. EAP F60; Brunvand 48(3).

F60 Fine **Feathers** make fine birds (*varied*)

1913 TDreiser *Traveler* (NY 1923) 253: Fine feathers make fine birds. **1927** FEverton *Dalehouse* (NY) 32: Fine feathers make fine birds. **1930** APHerbert *Water* (NY) 116: Fine feathers do not make fine birds. **1931** CBrooks *Ghost* (NY) 77: "Fine feathers make a fine bird, at night, when all cats are gray," said Rae, juggling his proverbs neatly enough. **1936** DWheatley *They Found* (P) 12:

Fine feathers make fine birds, they say. **1950** AWUpfield *Widows* (NY) 42: Fine feathers do not make fine birds. **1952** HFMPrescott *Man on* (NY) 57: If fine feathers'll make a fine bird. **1961** LSdeCamp *Dragon* (NY 1968) 180: It takes more than fine feathers to make fine birds. **1968** IPetite *Life* (NY) 135: Fine feathers make a fine bird. EAP F61; Brunvand 48(2).

F61 To be in high (fine) Feather

1913 TDreiser *Traveler* (NY 1923) 217: Barfleur was in fine feather. **1913** JSFletcher *Secret* (L 1918) 39: In apparent high feather. **1928** GGardiner *At the House* (NY) 107: In high feather; 287. **1941** NMarsh *Death in Ecstasy* (NY) 282: She went away in high feather. **1967** SEMorison *Old Bruin* (B) 101: They . . . departed in high feather. TW 129(12).

F62 To knock one down with a Feather (*varied*)

c1910 PGWodehouse *Leave it to Psmith* (L n.d.) 182: You could have knocked me down with a feather. **1920** JSFletcher *Dead Men's* (NY) 80: You could have knocked me down with a feather, as the saying is. **1934** JVTurner *Murder* (L) 137: You could have knocked me down with the proverbial feather. **1936** DHume *Crime* (L) 26: You could have knocked me down with the proverbial feather. **1938** DHume *Good-bye* (L) 139: You could have put me down for the full count with the proverbial feather. **1939** AMuir *Death Comes* (L) 147: You could have knocked me down without even a feather. **1940** MBoniface *Murder as* (NY) 133: You could have knocked Watkins over with the proverbial feather. **1945** HGreen *Loving* (L) 77: You could 'a' knocked me down with a leaf. **1951** HSaunders *Sleeping* (L) 28: The proverbial feather with which Bailey was so fond of telling me she could be successfully assaulted, would certainly have laid me low in a twinkling. **1959** AGoodman *Golden* (NY) 99: You could have knocked me over with a feather. **1964** CSSumner *Withdraw* (NY) 187: I have always heard of the feather that could knock a body over. **1970** RFoley *Calculated* (NY) 35: You could have knocked me over with a feather. **1974**

SForbes *Some* (NY) 35: You could have knocked me down with a feather. EAP F68; Brunvand 48(4).

F63 To show the white Feather

1915 JFerguson *Stealthy* (L 1935) 23: Showing nothing of the white feather. **1930** GBMeans *Strange Death* (NY) 222: He was showing the white feather. **1934** GFairlie *Copper* (L) 236: No hint of the white feather had . . . appeared. **1941** AAFair *Spill* (NY) 85: Show the white feather. **1952** GHHeinold *Burglar* (NY) 5: He never . . . shows the white feather. **1963** HWaugh *Death* (NY) 13: He could not show the white feather. **1968** WTenn *Wooden* (NY) 200: Don't show the white feather. EAP F70; Brunvand 48(5).

F64 February fill-dyke

1965 RDSymons *Silton* (NY 1975) 143: February fill-dyke, they say in England. *Oxford* 252.

F65 February Ground Hog Day, half your meat and half your hay

1957 LBeam *Maine* (NY) 195: February Ground Hog Day, Half your meat and half your hay. **1958** MKimmerle *Colorado Quarterly* 7:70: If the ground-hog sees his shadow today (Feb. 2) Save half your corn and half your hay. Cf. DA Ground hog 2(2); Hand in FCBrown *Collection* 7.209–10, 214–5.

F66 To be off one's Feed

1943 SShane *Lady . . . Million* (NY) 146: Them brats is off their feed tonight. TW 130.

F67 Feed them or amuse them

1951 JCollier *Fancies* (NY) 290: I heard an old proverb once, how to get on in the world. "Feed 'em or amuse 'em," it said. Cf. *Oxford* 81: Bread and circuses.

F68 Hail Fellow well met (*varied*)

1916 EClodd *Memories* (L) 73: Hail fellow well met. **1922** JJoyce *Ulysses* (NY 1934) 124: Hailfellow well met the next moment. **1928** GBHLogan *Rope* (L) 80: A hearty, hail-fellow-well-met kind of man. **1930** WLewis *Apes* (NY 1932) 187: A hail-fellow-well-met eye of understanding. **1937** NBlake *There's Trouble* (L) 40: The hail-fellow-well-met sort. **1952** MVHeberden *Tragic* (NY) 99: Nothing hail fellow well met about him. **1955** MHutchins *Memoirs* (NY) 158: Not hale fellow and not well met. **1961** LWoolf *Growing* (L) 136: The hail-fellow-well-met . . . formula. **1965** AHunter *Gently with* (NY 1974) 134: We're hail-bedfellows-well-met. **1970** PAnderson *Tau* (NY) 100: I never was hail-fellow-well-met. **1972** SBirmingham *Late John* (P) 159: Adelaide's hail-fellow-well-met quality. EAP F73.

F69 A **Fence** should be horse high *etc.*
1950 FFGould *Maine Man* (NY) 44: Father's fences were "horse high, bull strong and hog tight." **1956** *NYTimes Magazine* 8/12 26: The standard [*in Maine*] of a good rock wall was, "Horse high, hog tight, bull strong." DA Horse-high.

F70 Good **Fences** make good neighbors
1953 ELinklater *Year* (L) 19: Good fences make good neighbours. **1961** ADuggan *King* (L) 239: We have a saying: "Good fences make good neighbours." [*The story is set in Alfred's England.*] **1968** DCLunt *Taylor's* (NY) 270: The old saw that good fences make good neighbors. **1972** DWalker *Lord's* (B) 16: Good fences make good neighbors. EAP F74.

F71 One **Fence** at a time
1928 AFielding *Net* (NY) 283: One fence at a time or we'll never get home! **1934** VGielgud *Ruse* (NY) 69: We'll take our fences one at a time. Cf. Step *below.*

F72 To jump (cross) a **Fence** (hurdle) before one reaches it (*varied*)
1931 HReilly *Murder* (NY) 276: Don't jump your fences before you come to them. **1939** AChristie *Murder Is* (L) 72: You don't cross your fences till you get to them. **1939** NMarsh *Overture* (NY) 23: Aren't we jumping our fences before we meet them? **1940** RStout *Where There's* (NY) 32: Let's jump that fence when we get to it. **1946** CBush *Second Chance* (L) 41: There's no need to jump hurdles till we get to them. **1951** JCreasey *Puzzle* (L 1962) 10: Supposing we

jump that fence when we get to it. Cf. Bridge *above.*

F73 To mend (keep up) one's **Fences**
1932 TThayer *Thirteen* (NY) 113: They had better "mend their own fences," as my grandfather used to say. **1932** JHWallis *Capital* (NY) 31: Working on his political fences. **1934** TMundy *Tros* (NY) 640: Mend your fences! **1937** GGoodwin *White Farm* (L) 278: A young wife, and canna keep his fences up! **1956** ESGardner *Demure* (NY) 108: They were keepin' their fences up. **1958** *NYTimes* 5/11 4E: What can the United States do to mend fences? **1958** RFenisong *Death* (NY) 105: Mending his fences. **1960** MClifton *Eight* (NY) 150: He'd better mend some fences. DA Fence 3b(6); NED Suppl. Fence 5c.

F74 To rush one's **Fences**
1930 MPlum *Killing* (NY) 238: I'm not much given to rushing my fences. **1953** STruss *Doctor* (NY) 191: We English don't rush our fences. **1956** JFStraker *Ginger* (L) 145: I'm not rushing my fences. **1963** JLeCarré *Spy Who* (NY 1965) 63: They're rushing their fences. **1972** HCarmichael *Naked* (NY) 37: You're rushing your fences. Partridge 717: Rush.

F75 To sit on (straddle) the **Fence** (*varied*)
1919 JSFletcher *Middle Temple* (NY) 127: I'm going to sit on the fence. **1923** DFox *Doom* (NY) 317: I am on the fence. **1925** HAdams *By Order* (L) 103: I am sitting on the fence. **1926** AFielding *Footsteps* (L) 16: Other people can sit on both sides of the fence. **1930** HAdams *Crime* (P) 182: You can't be both sides of the hedge. **1930** KCStrahan *Death* (NY) 288: It's always a good thing to know which side of the fence a person is on. **1932** JJConnington *Castleford* (B) 267: Trying to sit on the fence. **1932** DSharp *Code-letter* (B) 119: Your friend is going to find himself on the wrong side of the fence. **1938** SHAdams *World* (B) 146: Fence-sitters and cat-jumpers. **1938** MJohnston *Comets* (NY) 122: He never had seen him straddling a fence before. **1946** FWCrofts *Death of a Train* (L) 81: When I can find a fence . . . I sit on it. **1959** JHChase

Shock (L) 155: I'm glad I'm sitting on the fence. **1963** MPHood *Sin* (NY) 157: I'm sorta straddlin' the fence. **1976** JPorter *Package* (NY) 79: A wishy-washy, sitting-on-the-fence . . . answer. **1981** EVCunningham *Sliding* (NY) 142: They say he plays both sides of the fence. EAP F75–6; TW 130(1); Brunvand 48(1); DA Fence 2b; NED Suppl. Fence 5c.

F76   As deaf as a **Fence pole**
1960 TWilliams *Three Players* (L) 92: As deaf, you might say, as a fence pole. Cf. Wilstach 84: Post. Cf. As deaf as a Post *below.*

F77   As quick as a **Ferret**
1930 VLoder *Essex* (L) 242: He seemed as quick as a ferret. **1941** DKent *Jason* (NY) 174: Quicker than a ferret.

F78   As sharp as a **Ferret**
1950 MLong *Louisville* (NY) 169: She was sharp as a ferret. Wilstach 343: At a field-rat's hole.

F79   **Few** but (and) fit
1934 ERathbone *Brass* (NY) 11: The company—few but fit. **1936** VWBrooks *Flowering* (NY 1946) 275: Persons fit and few.

F80   As fit as a **Fiddle**
1915 PGWodehouse *Something Fresh* (L 1935) 19: Feeling as fit as a fiddle. **1922** JJoyce *Ulysses* (NY 1934) 283: Fit as a fiddle. **1924** LO'Flaherty *Spring* (L) 46: As fit as a fiddle. **1933** HFootner *Ring* (NY) 259: Fit as a fiddle. **1938** BFlynn *Five Red* (NY) 23: As fit as the proverbial fiddle. **1942** MBurton *Death at Ash* (NY) 139: He's as fit as a fiddle. **1955** RFenisong *Widows* (NY) 171: Fit as a fiddle. **1959** AGilbert *Prelude* (NY DBC) 119: Fit as the proverbial fiddle. **1963** AChristie *Mirror* (NY) 223: You look as fit as a fiddle. **1967** JDetre *Happy* (NY) 13: You look fit as a fiddle . . . right as rain, good as gold. **1974** PGWodehouse *Cat Nappers* (NY) 29: As fit as ten fiddles. Cf. EAP F80; Fine; Whiting *NC* 406(1); Taylor *Prov. Comp.* 41.

F81   As long as a **Fiddle**
1933 JSFletcher *Mystery* (L) 222: Their faces as long as fiddles. **1934** CBarry *Death Overseas* (L) 65: With a face as long as a fiddle. **1939** HHolt *Smiling Doll* (L) 91: With a face as long as a fiddle. **1947** AGilbert *Death in* (L) 98: Faces as long as fiddles. **1968** JPorter *Dover Goes* (NY) 42: A face as long as a fiddle. *Oxford* 237: Face.

F82   As right as a **Fiddle**
1939 JNDarby *Murder in* (I) 136: She'll be as right as a fiddle. Lean II ii 867.

F83   The **Fiddle** cannot play without the bow
1938 MKRawlings *Yearling* (NY) 226: The fiddle can't play without the bow. TW 131(3).

F84   To play second **Fiddle**
1919 JSClouston *Man from the Clouds* (NY) 148: Playing second fiddle. **1924** ADH Smith *Porto* (NY) 221: Played second fiddle. **1933** TThayer *American* (NY) 209: Playing second fiddle. **1937** VMacClure *House* (L) 121: Playing second fiddle to him. **1946** MBlankfort *Widow-Makers* (NY) 149: I know it's not nice to play second fiddle. **1949** JMMyers *Silverlock* (NY) 155: Damned if she'd play second fiddle to a cow! **1952** HPearson *Whistle* (NY) 164: He was content to play second fiddle. **1958** *New Yorker* 5/31 21: Perhaps . . . the human race is not destined to play second fiddle to its own cleverness. **1965** RDrexler *I Am* (NY) 48: I'm second fiddle and bow and scrape. **1972** HCarmichael *Naked* (NY) 136: Her husband played second fiddle. **1980** AOliver *Pew* (NY) 147: I don't intend . . . to play second fiddle to a horse. TW 131(5).

F85   As drunk as a (blind) **Fiddler**
1928 DLSayers *Dawson* (NY) 292: Poor kid, as drunk as a blind fiddler. **1938** DBaker *Young Man* (B) 50: Drunk as a fiddler. TW 131(1). Cf. EAP F83.

F86   As drunk as a **Fiddler's** bitch (*varied*)
1928 RHFuller *Jubilee* (NY) 71: Drunker'n a fiddler's bitch. **1937** CGGivens *All Cats* (I)

338: Drunker than a fiddler's bitch. **1950** PFrischauer *So Great* (NY) 324: You are as drunk as a fiddler's bitch. **1959** LJLatimer *Black* (NY) 85: Drunk as a fiddler's bitch, Blake thought, and found himself inanely wondering what a fiddler's bitch was. Dog or lady friend? **1960** RHolles *Captain* (L) 150: Drunk? He must be as pissed as a fiddler's bitch. **1960** AWUpfield *Valley* (NY DBC) 154: He was drunk as a fiddler's dog. **1969** DARandall *Dukedome* (NY) 31: A gal . . . "handsome as a fiddler's bitch." **1972** FVWMason *Brimstone* (L) 258: He was as drunk as a fiddler's bitch. **1974** CCarpenter *Dead Head* (NY) 115: You were pissed as a fiddler's bitch [*drunk*]. **1978** JGould *Trifling* (B) 177: He was tighter'n a fiddler's bitch [*drunk*]. Whiting *NC* 407(2); Taylor *Western Folklore* 17(1958) 15.

F87 As fit as a **Fiddler** (*varied*)

1925 JSFletcher *Annexation* (NY) 18: As fit as a fiddler. **1931** CBrooks *Ghost* (NY) 112: As fit as a fiddler. **1938** EGilligan *Boundary* (NY) 35: Fit now as a fiddler's bi– hem! fit as a fiddle now. **1966** PGWodehouse *Plum* (L) 10: I found him in excellent shape— few fiddlers could have been fitter. Whiting *NC* 407(3).

F88 As thick as **Fiddlers** in hell

1930 JFDobie *Coronado* (Dallas) 125: Thicker'n fiddlers in hell. **1937** HCKittredge *Mooncussers* (B) 50: An old Provincetown saying that Doanes and Knowleses in Eastham are thicker than fiddlers in hell. **1959** TRoscoe *Only* (NY) 193: A village where liars are reputedly thicker than fiddlers in hell. Whiting *Devil* 222(6); Wilstach 564.

F89 Not give (care) a **Fiddler's** fuck (*varied*)

1933 DHoldridge *Pindorama* (NY) 91: They don't give a fiddler's fornication for the natives. **1970** JVizzard *See* (NY) 102: I don't give a fiddler's fuck. **1979** GWest *Duke* (NY) 236: I didn't care a fuddler's fuck where my father was. Cf. Spears 149: Fuck (10).

F90 As lean (straight, tight) as a **Fiddlestring**

1930 SMartin *Trial* (NY) 41: Straight as a fiddle-string. **1940** HReilly *Death Demands* (NY) 100: He was as tight as a fiddlestring [*taut*]. **1971** RFDelderfield *For My* (NY) 54: Lean as fiddlestrings.

F91 To worry (wear) oneself to **Fiddle-strings**

1926 AMarshall *Mote* (NY) 205: Worrying yourself to fiddle strings. **1928** MThynne *Draycott* (NY) 42: Don't wear yourself to fiddle-strings. **1952** EBIgland *Indomitable* (L) 161: Worn to fiddle-strings by the long strain. *Oxford* 287: Fret.

F92 A fair **Field** and no favor

1922 JJoyce *Ulysses* (NY 1934) 297: Open to all comers, fair field and no favour. **1928** JJConnington *Mystery* (B) 289: "A fair field and no favour," is the only motto. **1937** MBurton *Murder* (L) 97: A fair field and no favour. **1938** JRhode *Bloody* (L) 134: You've got a fair field and no favour. TW 131(1).

F93 A **Fig** for (whatever)

1919 LMerrick *Chair* (L) 259: A fig for the rule! **1928** CWells *Crime* (P) 265: A fig for your clever detectives. **1953** AChristie *Pocket* (NY) 82: And a fig for the aristocracy. **1959** PBoileau *Evil* (L) 176: A fig for that! **1964** SJay *Death* (NY) 58: A fig for the coroner. **1965** HActon *Old Lamps* (L) 245: A fig for art historians. EAP F88; TW 131(1).

F94 Not a **Fig** to choose

1962 PQuentin *Ordeal* (NY) 240: There wasn't a fig to choose between them. Cf. NED Fig *sb.*[1] 4.

F95 Not care a **Fig** (fig-leaf)

1925 RAFreeman *Red Thumb* (L) 112: He cared not a fig. **1937** RHull *Ghost* (NY) 65: I don't care a fig for your opinions. **1940** PATaylor *Deadly* (NY) 64: I don't care two figs. **1947** RDavies *Diary* (Toronto) 125: I do not care a fig. **1950** SSmith *Man with* (NY) 126: I don't care a fig for you. **1956** SBaron *Facts* (NY) 18: Didn't care a fig. **1963** EQueen *Player* (NY) 128: Jason didn't care a fig leaf. **1964** LComber *Strange* (Rutland, Vt.) 16: Did not care a fig. **1971** GBaxt *Affair* (NY) 61: She didn't care a fig. EAP F89; Brunvand 49(1).

F96 Not give a **Fig**

1927 FWCrofts *Ponson* (NY 1931) 280: I don't give a fig. **1932** JMarsh *Murder* (L) 216: I wouldn't give a fig for his alibi. **1939** FGerard *Red Rope* (NY) 229: I don't give a fig. **1957** PGreen *Sword* (L) 271: I don't give a fig. **1960** RLDuffus *Tower* (NY) 88: Did not give a fig. **1970** MStewart *Crystal* (NY) 114: I wouldn't give a fig. **1971** GBaxt *Affair* (NY) 128: She doesn't give two figs. EAP F90.

F97 Not matter a **Fig**

1930 JRhode *Venner* (L) 73: I don't see that it matters a fig. **1956** EDillon *Death* (L) 20: This was not worth a fig. **1957** CThomas *Leftover* (L) 164: The murder itself mattered not a fig. Cf. NED *Fig sb.*[1] 4.

F98 Not worth a **Fig**

1962 BRoss *Scrolls* (NY) 162: None of them was worth a fig. EAP F91; TW 132(5); Brunvand 49(2).

F99 To be in full **Fig**

1953 JFleming *Good* (L) 110: Ivy was in full fig. **1959** EHuxley *Flame* (L) 281: The young men came in full fig. **1972** SNBehrman *People* (B) 300: I dressed, full fig, and went . . . to the synagogue. **1974** JWain *Samuel Johnson* (NY) 81: Dressed in full fig. TW 132(4).

F100 He who **Fights** and runs away may live to fight another day (*varied*)

1932 WMartyn *Trent* (NY) 115: Your fate is to live and fight another day. **1933** GBegbie *Sudden* (L) 307: He who fights and runs away . . . **1937** SPalmer *No Flowers* (L) 123: A firm believer in the old adage that he who fights and runs away will live to fight another day. **1939** LBlack *Mr. Preed* (L) 245: He who fights and runs away lives to fight another day. **1952** AGilbert *Mr. Crook* (NY DBC) 63: He who fights and runs away lives to fight another day. **1955** MColes *Happy* (NY) 151: He that fights and runs away . . . will live to fight another day. **1956** *New Yorker* 9/1 22: He who hunts and turns away may live to hunt another day. **1962** ME Chaber *Jade* (NY DBC) 115: The man who fights and runs away lives to fight another day. **1966** The Gordons *Undercover Cat*

Prowls (NY) 64: [He] decided to retreat and live another day. **1971** DFJones *Denver* (NY) 128: You may live to fight another day. 217: He who fights and runs away . . . Okay, so another day has arrived. EAP F94; Brunvand 49.

F101 As game as a **Fighting cock**

1935 ECRLorac *Murder* (L) 168: He'll be as game as a fighting cock. Taylor *Prov. Comp.* 40: To feel.

F102 To live like **Fighting cocks** (*varied*)

1926 RAFreeman *Puzzle* (NY) 190: I live like a fighting cock. **1932** MBurton *Death* (L) 221: They are living like fighting cocks. **1933** CBush *Three Strange* (L) 260: He's got money enough to live like a fighting cock. **1956** WMankowitz *Old* (B) 52: Live like fighting cocks. **1957** *TLS* 3/15 163: And as the satisfied eater lays down his knife and fork, and compares his sense of well being with the life of a fighting cock we may be forgiven for supposing that after all . . . a game cock's existence was a short life but a merry one. **1963** FSwinnerton *Figures* (L) 167: All novelists live like fighting-cocks. **1968** KChristie *Child's* (L) 5: Feed us like fighting cocks. **1970** UO'Connor *Brendan* (L) 85: [They] were fed like fighting cocks. EAP F95.

F103 **Figures** don't lie

1956 *BHerald* 8/29 35: It reminds me of a proverb: "Figures don't lie when there's only one set of books—your's." **1958** *BGlobe* 9/18 3: Figures don't lie. **1965** JJMarric *Gideon's Badge* (NY) 88: Figures can't lie. EAP F96; Brunvand 49.

F104 **Figures** don't lie but liars can figure (*varied*)

1925 BBLindsay *Revolt* (NY) 81: There is a saying that figures don't lie, but that liars will figure. **1933** ECRLorac *Murder* (L) 314: Mathematics cannot lie . . . a statement which does not apply to mathematicians. **1936** JTMcIntyre *Steps* (NY) 98: The modern wisecrack that while figures can't lie, liars can figure. **1941** CBClason *Green Shiver* (NY) 15: Figures don't lie . . . though liars sometimes figure. **1952** ECRLorac *Dog* (NY) 169: Mathematics cannot lie. That is axiomatic, but the axiom does not always apply to mathematicians. **1960** MGEberhart *Jury* (NY DBC) 89: There's the old saying, figures don't lie but liars can figure.

F105 As gay as **Finches** (goldfinches, *etc.*)
1958 JLindsay *Life* (L) 86: I felt as gay as a flock of finches. Whiting G319: Goldfinch; Wilstach 168: Bullfinch, 169: Chaffinch.

F106 **Finders** are keepers (finding is keeping)
1928 RBenchley *20,000 Leagues* (NY) 88: Finders are keepers. **1928** SFWright *Deluge* (NY) 54: Findin's keepin's. **1931** GPahlow *Murder* (NY) 242: Findin's keepin's, as the Good Book says. **1931** TThayer *Illustrious* (NY) 302: Finders are keepers, you know. **1938** JRRTolkien *Hobbit* (B) 92: Finding's, keeping. **1940** GHomes *Finders Keepers* (NY). **1949** ILeighton *Aspirin* (NY) 329: Finders were keepers. **1956** *New Yorker* 7/28 23: Finders are not their brothers' keepers. **1957** BHerald 7/14 10: Finders keepers. **1958** PGWodehouse *Cocktail* (L) 64: Findings are keepings. **1962** ABoucher *Best from Fantasy* (B) 64: Findings are keepings. **1962** FGruber *Brothers* (NY DBC) 118: In America we have an old axiom, "Finders' keepers'." **1964** NBKubie *Road* (NY) 137: Finders were keepers. **1973** JMann *Troublecross* (NY) 77: Finder's keepers. **1978** MKWren *Nothing's* (NY) 114: You know, like they say, finders keepers. TW 133; Brunvand 49; *Oxford* 257.

F107 **Finders** are keepers, losers are weepers (*varied*)
1929 JCPowys *Wolf* (NY) 219: Finding's keepings, losing's seekings. **1930** ATrain *Adventures* (NY) 646: Finders keepers—loosers weepers. **1933** SPalmer *Pepper Tree* (NY) 216: Finders are keepers . . . And losers are weepers. **1940** ABCunningham *Murder at* (NY) 233: Finders keepers, losers weepers. **1956** *Time* 10/1 94: She played finders keepers, losers weepers. Taylor *Proverb* 90.

F108 At one's **Fingers'** ends (finger-tips)
1908 AEHousman *Letters* ed HMaas (Cambridge, Mass. 1971) 94: He has the vocab-ulary at his fingers' ends. **1928** RAFreeman *As a Thief* (L) 151: I had the case at my fingers' ends. **1940** MAllingham *Black Plumes* (L) 203: Every fact at her finger-tips. **1954** CHare *That Yew* (L) 148: I have them at my finger-tips. **1962** LEgan *Against* (NY DBC) 141: You've got it—as they say—at your fingers' ends. **1973** MInnes *Appleby's Answer* (NY) 61: [She] has all that at her finger-tips. EAP F99; Brunvand 49(1).

F109 **Fingers** were made before forks (*varied*)
1922 JJoyce *Ulysses* (NY 1934) 514: Fingers was made before forks. **1935** AChristie *Boomerang* (NY) 236: As they used to say to me in my youth . . . fingers were made before forks. **1948** KWilliamson *Atlantic* (L 1970) 146: The incontrovertible fact that fingers were made before forks. **1957** *New Yorker* 5/16 32: And she thought that the Gunpowder Plot involved poisoning the Parliament with toadstools because she had learned on a nature walk that fungus was made before Fawkes [*Ogden Nash*]. **1958** JBarth *End* (NY 1960) 108: Fingers were invented before forks. **1966** NMonsarrat *Life (I)* (L) 9: Fingers were made before forks. **1969** SMays *Fall Out* (L) 49: Fingers were made before forks. TW 133(1).

F110 To burn one's **Fingers**
1922 VThompson *Pointed* (NY) 324: She'll burn her fingers one of these days. **1925** JSFletcher *Wrychester* (NY) 227: He went to the fire too often, and got his fingers burned in the end. **1928** RHFuller *Jubilee* (NY) 93: He never burned his fingers twice at the same fire. **1932** BRoss *Tragedy of Y* (NY) 15: She had badly burnt her fingers in the fires of Wall Street. **1974** ROllard *Pepys* (NY) 251: Pepys had burnt his fingers. EAP F105.

F111 To have more in one's little **Finger** *etc.* (*varied*)
1955 RDavies *Heaven* (L) 187: I have more insight in my little finger than Puss Pottinger has in her whole body. **1964** HBourne *In the Event* (NY) 183: She had more sense in her little finger . . . than I had in the

whole of me. **1964** CChaplin *Autobiography* (NY 1966) 101: I have more talent in my arse than you have in your whole body! **1968** EBuckler *Ox Bells* (NY) 246: She's got more charity in her little finger than you've got in your whole carcass. **1972** KCampbell *Thunder* (I) 109: He's got more sense in his little finger than the rest put together. *Oxford* 903: Wit.

F112 To have one's **Finger** in the pie (*varied*)

1911 JSHay *Amazing Emperor* (L) 139: In the plots [she] had a considerable finger. **1913** JSFletcher *Secret* (L 1918) 121: They generally get to the bottom of every pie they put their fingers into. **1919** LTracy *Bartlett* (NY) 105: He had a finger in the pie. **1922** JJoyce *Ulysses* (NY 1934) 152: Have a finger in the pie. **1929** GMWhite *Square* (L) 142: Warning us to keep our fingers out of the pie. **1933** FDell *Homecoming* (NY) 135: Stick their fingers into all the creative art pies. **1935** TRoscoe *Murder* (NY) 137: It was my own voice putting a finger in the pie. **1939** RStout *Some Buried* (L) 116: Clyde always said it wasn't a pie if I didn't have my finger in it. **1942** FLockridge *Death . . . Aisle* (P) 22: Lots of fingers in lots of pies. **1953** RBloomfield *Stranger* (NY) 173: The late-lamented had many a finger in many a pie. **1955** PMatthiessen *Partisans* (NY) 83: He gets his fingers into all the soups. **1961** HActon *Last Bourbons* (L) 56: [He] kept a finger in every pie. **1965** MGEberhart *R.S.V.P.* (NY) 127: Benni . . . had his dirty fingers in a lot of dirty pies. **1970** LGrafftey-Smith *Bright* (L) 49: [He] had his . . . thumb in every . . . pie. **1972** SCloete *Victorian* (L) 34: He had a finger in a lot of very small pies. **1976** JMcClure *Snake* (NY) 69: A finger in a lot of pies. EAP F106.

F113 To have one's **Fingers** all thumbs (*varied*)

1926 AHuxley *Two or Three* (L) 34: Her fingers were all thumbs. **1932** HFootner *Casual* (L) 213: Our fingers are all thumbs. **1937** PCoffin *Search* (NY) 136: Fingers that seemed all thumbs. **1940** WCClark *Murder Goes* (B) 31: My hands are all thumbs. **1950** OAnderson *In for* (NY) 70: My fingers are all thumbs. **1956** MProcter *Pub* (NY) 9: My fingers were all thumbs. TW 133(2); Brunvand 49(2).

F114 To keep one's **Fingers** crossed

1927 FLPackard *Two* (NY) 47: We kept our fingers crossed. **1953** EQueen *Scarlet* (B) 32: Martha has her fingers crossed. **1960** JJMarric *Gideon's Risk* (NY) 111: Keep your fingers crossed. **1970** HCarmichael *Death* (NY) 33: Keep your fingers crossed . . . You never know your luck. Cf. WDHand in FC Brown *Collection* 7.5701, 5745, 5841, 5843.

F115 To twist (*etc.*) around one's little **Finger** (*varied*)

1906 JCLincoln *Mr. Pratt* (NY) 246: He can tie 'em [*women*] in bow knots round his finger. **1919** JSFletcher *Middle Temple* (NY) 278: He twisted your father round his little finger. **1922** JJoyce *Ulysses* (NY 1934) 114: Martin could wind a sappyhead like that round his little finger. **1932** JJConnington *Sweepstake* (B) 78: She could have twisted old Thursford round her finger. **1936** BCobb *Poisoner's* (L) 200: The old saying is that a wife can twist her husband round her finger. **1937** RAJWalling *Bury Him* (L) 70: Girls can twiddle you round their thumbs. **1939** DCCameron *Murder's Coming* (NY) 98: Carter was a man who could twist a dull-witted girl round his little finger. [*Get her pregnant.*] **1944** PATaylor *Dead Ernest* (NY) 154: They [*blonds*] just twist people around their little fingers. **1953** DMDisney *Prescription* (NY) 72: He had her wound right around his finger. **1959** AChristie *Ordeal* (NY) 94: His easy habit of twisting everyone round his finger. **1961** JPhilips *Murder* (NY DBC) 19: She could twist Jerome round her little finger. **1962** DMDisney *Find* (NY DBC) 143: She had him wound around her little finger. **1967** RFenisong *Villainous* (NY) 29: I can twist him around my pinky. **1970** CArmstrong *Protege* (NY DBC) 66: He's got her wrapped around his pinky. **1974** GWheeler *Easy* (NY) 34: He can twist you around his finger. EAP F117; TW 133(7,8,9); Brunvand 50(7–9).

F116 To work one's **Fingers** to the bone (*varied*)

1923 EWallace *Blue Hand* (B) 146: Works her fingers to the bone. **1935** GDHCole *Dr. Tancred* (L) 27: You had to work your fingers to the bone. **1939** JNDarby *Murder in* (I) 41: Mrs. Ragland "worked her fingers to the bone." **1939** HMiller *Capricorn* (NY 1961) 11: People . . . work themselves to the bone. **1945** PATaylor *Proof* (NY) 135: Worked her fingers to the bone. **1947** RKing *Lethal* (NY DBC) 67: Fingers . . . worked to the bone. **1952** AWUpfield *New Shoe* (L 1968) 199: And she workin' her fingers to the bone. **1959** RMacdonald *Galton* (NY) 195: I worked myself to the bone keeping our heads above water. **1962** RMacdonald *Zebra-* (NY) 50: I . . . work my fingers to the bone. **1964** BKaufman *Up the Down* (NY 1966) 176: You work yourself to the bone. **1973** ARoudybush *Gastronomic* (NY) 96: I worked my fingers to the bone. EAP F116.

F117 In again . . . **Finnegan** (*varied*)

1936 EBQuinn *One Man's* (L) 224: In again, out again, Finnagan, I am. **1937** PATaylor *Figure* (NY) 223: Off again, on again, gone again, Finnegan. **1943** WMcCully *Doctors* (NY) 197: On again, off again, home again, Finnigan. **1952** PQuentin *Black* (NY) 32: In again out again Finnegan. **1965** PDeVries *Let Me* (NY 1966) 171: With me its in-again-out-again-Finnegan. Bartlett 897b [*Strickland Gillilan*].

F118 As angry as **Fire**

1957 JDCarr *Fire* (NY) 208: Angry as fire. Whiting F161.

F119 As hot as **Fire**

1931 JTully *Blood* (NY) 73: Our tempers are hot as fire. **1937** JDCarr *Burning* (NY) 198: Her hand was as hot as fire. EAP F120; TW 134(2).

F120 As red as **Fire**

1933 MBurton *Fate* (L) 50: His face was as red as fire. **1952** HFMPrescott *Man On* (NY) 183: His face as red as fire. **1954** ASeton *Katherine* (B) 54: Katherine turned red as fire. **1974** JBrunner *Total* (NY) 53: His face

was red as fire. EAP F123; TW 134(6); Brunvand 50(1).

F121 Build a small **Fire** *etc.*

1950 FFGould *Maine Man* (NY) 10: "Build a small fire and warm yourself, build a big fire and freeze to death." Cf. Whiting F179: Better a small fire; *Oxford* 80.

F122 **Fire** in straw

1932 HFootner *Dead Man's* (NY) 196: The news had run . . . like fire in straw. EAP F125.

F123 **Fire** is a good servant *etc.*

1948 HBeston *Northern* (NY) 196: "Fire is a good servant but a bad master." So runs the proverb. I can remember hearing it said in the long ago. **1969** UKLeGuin *Left Hand* (NY) 164: Fire and fear, good servants, bad lords. **1973** JCaird *Murder* (NY) 201: Is not whiskey a wonderful thing? But like fire, a good servant but a bad master. EAP F124.

F124 To be caught between two **Fires**

1928 GFairlie *Scissors* (NY) 254: They're caught between two fires. **1934** SHAdams *Gorgeous* (B) 336: Between two fires. **1937** RVercel *Lena* (NY) 24: We're going to be caught between two fires. **1957** *NYTimes* 11/10 60: We were caught between three fires. **1972** RLaxalt *In a Hundred* (Reno) 110: Caught between two fires. EAP F131.

F125 To fight **Fire** with fire

c**1923** ACrowley *Confessions* ed JSymonds (L 1969) 79: Fighting fire with fire; 548. **1933** WMarch *Company K* (NY) 127: You've got to fight fire with fire. **1945** RLockridge *Death in the Mind* (NY) 225: Fire with fire. Or, if you prefer, sauce for the gander. **1948** ELipsky *Murder One* (NY) 99: We fought fire with fire. **1951** MHead *Congo* (NY) 167: The way to get at this woman is the fire-with-fire idea, or dose-of-her-own-medicine. **1958** MKenton *Candy* (NY 1965) 144: We must fight fire with fire. **1961** WMasterson *Evil* (NY) 107: You have to fight fire with fire. **1966** SRansome *Hidden* (NY) 80: Fight fire with fire. **1970** JAGraham *Something* (B) 113: Fighting fire with fire. **1976** HPentecost *Fourteenth* (NY) 116: Old adage . . . you fight fire with fire. TW

134(9); Brunvand 50(2). Cf. To meet Craft, Fight the Devil *above;* Force *below.*

F126   To go through **Fire** and water
1904 JCLincoln *Cap'n Eri* (NY) 301: To go through fire and water to win her. **1923** DFox *Doom* (NY) 257: I'd go through fire and water. **1924** CWells *Furthest* (P) 162: Go through fire and water for her. **1932** JCLenehan *Mansfield* (L) 160: Connor would go through the proverbial fire and water to help you. **1956** PWentworth *Fingerprint* (NY) 199: Jonathan would go through fire and water to get a really good specimen for his collection. **1962** DTaylor *Blood* (NY) 135: Through fire and water. **1970** AFreemantle *Three-Cornered* (NY) 72: She would have gone through fire and water for him. EAP F134; TW 134(13).

F127   To play with **Fire** (*varied*)
1913 HHMunro *When William* (L 1929) 11: Playing with fire. **1926** EWallace *Terrible* (NY) 267: You're playing with fire. **1928** EO'Neill *Strange* (NY) 160: Playing with fire is dangerous. **1930** MPShiel *Black Box* (NY) 221: Those that play with fire must expect to get burned. **1937** NBerrow *One Thrilling* (L) 317: If you play with fire, you're apt to get burnt. **1939** MPropper *Cheating Bride* (L) 58: You're playing with the wrong kind of fire. **1940** BHalliday *Uncomplaining* (NY) 53: You can't play with fire and not be burned. **1947** MAllingham *Look to* (L) 131: If you go on playing with fire . . . you'll get burnt one of these days. **1956** AGilbert *Riddle* (NY) 38: Warned you not to play with fire. **1957** BVanOrden *309 East* (NY) 123: She began to ponder how George-ish it was to put quotation marks around an old proverb like not playing with fire. "Don't play with fire," he had written. **1963** MGEberhart *Run* (NY) 209: When you play with fire you can expect to get singed. **1968** ELustgarten *Business* (NY) 195: Females often relish playing with fire. **1970** JAtkins *Sex* (L) 255: This is playing with fire. **1974** JWain *Johnson* (NY) 107: If he played with fire, it may have happened sooner or later that he burnt his fingers. Whiting F210; Brunvand 50(3); *Oxford* 632: Play. Cf. Dynamite *above.*

F128   First **Fire** (shoot), then enquire
1932 VWilliams *Mystery* (B) 62: The old cowboy saying, "First fire, then enquire." **1933** DWhitelaw *Roof* (L) 255: The old adage of shooting first and making enquiries afterwards. *Oxford* 345: Halifax, 459: Lidford law. Cf. Hang, Lydford Law *below.*

F129   As hot as a **Firecracker** (*varied*)
1942 CFAdams *What Price* (NY) 112: I'm hotter than a firecracker [*wanted by police*]. **1947** FCDavis *Thursday's* (NY) 157: One thing makes me hotter'n a firecracker. **1954** RKLeavitt *Chip* (P) 209: He was getting hotter than a firecracker [*writing a sermon*]. **1955** ESGardner *Sun* (NY) 111: You're hotter than a firecracker [*under suspicion*]. **1961** HCromwell *Dirty* (LA) 214: It's hotter than a goddamned firecracker [*a speakeasy often raided*]. **1963** ESGardner *Amorous* (NY DBC) 115: He got hotter than a firecracker [*lucky gambler*]. **1963** HWaugh *Death* (NY) 60: And hotter'n a firecracker [*of a woman*]. **1971** NBogner *Making* (NY) 131: I'm hotter than a firecracker [*sexually*]. Taylor *Prov. Comp.* 50. Cf. Wentworth 271–2 [*for meanings of "hot"*].

F130   As cold (chilly) as a **Fish** (*varied*)
1931 MGEberhart *From This* (NY) 236: Cold as a little fish. **1932** ORCohen *Star* (NY) 14: Chilly as a fish. **1935** WSeabrook *Asylum* (NY) 222: I've seen the old boy knock himself coldernafrozenfishesarsole. **1941** CRice *Right Murder* (NY) 222: Cold as a fish [*dead drunk*]. **1945** EDaly *Any Shape* (NY) 98: Cold as fishes. **1952** MGreenberg *Five* (NY) 268: He's cold as a fish's tail. **1959** THWhite *Godstone* (NY) 220: Joyce's heart was as cold as a dead fish. **1962** FCrane *Amber* (NY) 29: She was . . . cold as a fish. **1964** HBourne *In the Event* (NY) 45: Cold like a fish. **1981** JRoss *Dark* (NY) 90: I'm . . . cold as a wet fish. Whiting *NC* 408(1); Taylor *Western Folklore* 17(1958) 15(1). Cf. Haddock *below.*

F131   As cold-blooded as a **Fish**
1931 AWynne *Silver Scale* (P) 168: He's as cold blooded as a fish. **1933** NBrady *Weekend* (L) 71: You are as cold-blooded as a fish. **1940** CRice *Corpse Steps* (NY) 90: He's

cold-blooded as a fish. **1947** KMKnight *Blue* (NY) 128: She's as cold-blooded as a fish. Cf. preceding entry.

F132   As cool as a Fish
1933 DLSayers *Murder* (NY) 87: As cool as a fish. **1939** HCBailey *Veron* (L) 85: Tover, as cool as a fish. Cf. As cold as a Fish *above*.

F133   As dead as a Fish
1940 HRutland *Poison Fly* (NY) 121: She's dead, as dead as a—a fish. **1970** KGiles *Death* (L) 59: Dead as a fish. Cf. Wilstach 84: Smelts. Cf. Flounder, Haddock, Mackerel *below*.

F134   As dry as a Fish
1959 HEBates *Watercress* (L) 105: I'm as dry as a fish. Wilstach 515: Seasoned fish.

F135   As drunk as a Fish
1935 CCranston *Murder* (P) 118: Drunk as a fish. **1957** *BHerald* 9/15 6A: Drunk as a fish. Whiting *NC* 408(3).

F136   As dumb as a Fish
1929 VLoder *Between* (NY) 122: Dumb as a fish. **1956** AChristie *Dead Man's* (L) 21: Dumb as a fish. Whiting F222.

F137   As mute (mum) as a Fish
1934 VLoder *Murder* (L) 26: He was sitting mum as a fish. **1935** CMRussell *Murder* (NY) 110: As mute as a fish. **1959** AGilbert *Death* (NY) 103: [She] sat as mute as a fish. EAP F142.

F138   As naked as a Fish
1952 HFMPrescott *Man on* (NY) 10: Naked as a fish, between the sheets. Whiting F226.

F139   As nervous as a Fish
1930 The Aresbys *Murder* (NY) 288: I'm nervous as a fish. Taylor *Prov. Comp.* 59.

F140   As weak as a Fish
1939 LPowys in MElwin *Life* (L 1946) 256: I . . . am weak as a fish. **1954** MAllingham *No Love* (NY) 100: The patient was as weak as a fish.

F141   As wet as a Fish
1957 MPHood *In the Dark* (NY) 95: You're wet as a fish. Wilstach 468.

F142   A Fish stinks from the head
1930 ABrown *Green Lane* (L) 114: A fish stinks from his head, was what he always used to say. **1959** *TLS* 7/24 430: "Fish," runs the Oriental proverb, "begin to stink from the head." **1961** BAldiss *Primal* (NY) 124: As the Persian has it, . . . a rotten fish stinks from the head. **1970** JVizzard *See* (NY) 339: The homely Russian adage that "a fish stinks from the head." EAP F145.

F143   Like a Fish out of water (varied)
1922 EPower *Medieval English Nunneries* (Cambridge, Eng.) 341: Fish out of water. **1933** MBurton *Tragedy* (L) 11: Standing there like a fish out of water. **1935** Jde Meyer *Bailey's* (NY) 99: I was beginning to feel like a duck out of water. **1937** FDe Laguna *Arrow* (NY) 210: I'd be like a fish out of water, away from the Academy. **1943** DGoldring *South Lodge* (L) 124: Felt like a fish out of water. **1951** JCollier *Fancies* (NY) 249: In the society of men you would be like a fish out of water, a bull in a china shop or a round peg in a square hole. **1954** EQueen *Bureau* (B) 86: He was like a fish out of water. **1957** NMitford *Voltaire* (L) 184: The du Chalets would have been fish out of water in that homosexual society. **1962** JWoodford *Autobiography* (NY) 54: Feeling, to be very original, like a fish out of water. **1968** RSDominic *Murder* (NY) 167: She had been a fish out of water. **1970** WBlunt *Dream* (L) 75: He is a fish out of water among the generals. **1970** LWolfe *Journey* (NY) 97: When someone says "Like a fish out of water," it will mean a lot more to me. **1982** Feiffer in *BGlobe* 3/12 34: A fish out of water. EAP F149; TW 135(3); Brunvand 51(2); Taylor *Western Folklore* 17(1958) 15(2).

F144   Neither Fish, flesh, nor fowl, nor good red herring (varied)
1907 CMGayley *Plays of our Forefathers* (NY) 48: Neither fish, flesh, nor fowl, nor yet good red herring. **1916** JLondon *Letters* ed KHendricks (NY 1965) 477: Is it fish, flesh, or fowl? **1919** JBCabell *Jurgen* (NY 1922) 214: Neither fish nor beast nor poultry. **1922** JJoyce *Ulysses* (NY 1934) 315: A fellow that's neither fish nor flesh. Nor good red

herring. **1928** CDane *Enter* (L) 251: Half-caste, that what I am—neither fish, flesh, fowl nor—. **1928** HFootner *Velvet* (NY) 102: They're neither fish, flesh, nor good red herring. **1934** CSForester *Payment* (NY) 50: He would not be fish, flesh nor fowl, nor good red herring. **1936** LAKnight *Night* (L) 191: An old saw, to whit, "Tis neither fish nor fowl nor good red herring." **1939** GDHCole *Greek* (L) 93: He was neither fish, flesh, nor fowl, a pariah. **1941** MBardon *Murder Does* (NY) 115: Riley hadn't a notion whether it was fish, fowl or good red herring. **1948** CRBoxer *Fidalgos* (Oxford 1968) 261: Neither fish, fowl nor good red herring. **1958** BKendrick *Clear* (NY) 173: Tell us, is it fish, or fowl, or good red herring. **1960** DHolman-Hunt *My Grandmothers* (L) 159: You're . . . neither fish, fowl nor good red herring. **1963** RArnold *Orange* (L) 31: I was neither fish, fowl, nor good red herring. **1972** SCloete *Victorian* (L) 292: Neither fish, flesh, nor good red herring. EAP F150; TW 136(8).

F145   Old **Fish** and young flesh

1922 JJoyce *Ulysses* (NY 1934) 172: Was the oyster old fish at table. Perhaps he young flesh in bed. Whiting F236.

F146   There are other **Fish** in the sea (*varied*)

1909 JCLincoln *Keziah* (NY) 228: There's other fish in the sea. **1922** JJoyce *Ulysses* (NY 1934) 392: There's as good fish in this tin as ever came out of it. **1928** DHLawrence *Lady* ("Allemagne") 33: There's lots of good fish in the sea—maybe. **1929** LTracy *Lastingham* (L) 238: This is not a case of good fish being still in the sea. **1930** EQueen *French* (NY) 163: There were more fish in the sea than a faithless husband. **1930** EWallace *Mr. Reeder* (NY) 93: There's as good fish in the sea as ever came out. **1934** JCameron *Body* (L) 169: He wasn't the only fish in the sea. **1935** JRhode *Corpse* (L) 31: There are as good fish in the sea as ever came out of it. **1938** DFrome *Guilt* (L) 220: Just think about all the proverbs you know about fish left in the sea. **1940** NBlake *Malice* (L) 199: There are more fish in the sea than ever came out of it. **1950** MLong *Louis-*ville (NY) 78: There's plenty more fish in the ocean. **1951** CWillingham *Reach* (NY) 173: There's more than one oyster in the ocean. **1957** *BangorDN* 1/25 20: There's plenty fish in the sea. Play 'em, don't try to land 'em [*the girls*]. **1961** AAFair *Bachelors* (NY DBC) 33: There are as good fish in the sea as have ever been caught . . . think about the bird in the hand and the two in the bush. **1963** HWaugh *Prisoner's* (NY DBC) 116: There were too many easier fish in the sea. **1973** KCampbell *Wheel* (I) 99: There being more fish in the sea than ever came out. EAP F151; Brunvand 51(5).

F147   To cry stinking **Fish**

1931 EPhillpotts *Found* (L) 106: I put a bold face on it and didn't cry stinking fish. **1931** AWynne *Blue* (P) 132: Even fools don't cry "Stinking fish" about their business affairs. **1934** ERPunshon *Mystery* (L) 268: Cry stinking fish, I suppose you would. **1935** RGraves *Claudius the God* (NY) 251: You know the proverb "No man cries 'Stinking Fish.'" **1947** HWade *New Graves* (L) 241: Where it's a case of "stinkin' fish" . . . I'm not the man to cry it unless I know the facts for myself. EAP F153.

F148   To drink like a **Fish**

1914 HHMunro *Beasts* (NY 1928) 78: Drinks like a fish. **1931** AFielding *Upfold* (L) 8: Drinks like a fish. **1937** WSMasterman *Border* (NY) 242: She drinks like a fish. **1957** *Punch* 8/7 159: They drink like fish. **1961** CBush *Sapphire* (NY) 96: He drinks like a fish. **1966** MMcShane *Night's* (NY) 28: Drinks like a fish. **1973** HThomas *Strachey* (NY) 71: She drank like a fish. EAP F154.

F149   To have other **Fish** to fry (*varied*)

1905 FMWhite *Crimson Blind* (NY) 307: She had her little lot of fish to fry. **1906** JCLincoln *Mr. Pratt* (NY) 83: I had other fish to fry. **1919** JBCabell *Jurgen* (NY 1922) 355: My lord . . . had other fish to fry. **1927** FDGrierson *Smiling* (NY) 179: You've got better fish to fry. **1932** DLSayers *Have* (NY) 45: He seems to have better fish to fry. **1938** MBurton *Death* (L) 9: She's got other fish to fry. **1939** HWPriwen *Inspector* (L) 80: I've bigger fish to fry. **1941** MArmstrong *Blue*

Santo (NY) 301: I have more important fish to fry. **1951** LLariar *You Can't* (NY) 131: There were other fish for me to fry. **1957** DErskine *Pink* (NY) 196: You've probably got better fish to fry. **1970** LKronenberger *No Whippings* (B) 149: I had other fish to fry. **1975** HLawrenson *Stranger* (NY) 101: She had other fish to fry. EAP F155; Brunvand 51(4).

F150 To make **Fish** of one and flesh of another (*varied*)

1934 FWCrofts *12:30* (L) 85: He can't make fish of me and flesh of another. **1937** FWCrofts *Found* (NY) 32: I couldn't make flesh of one and fowl of the other. EAP F156.

F151 To peddle one's **Fish** (*varied*)

1934 RJCasey *Third Owl* (I) 55: Go peddle your fish! **1934** DHammett *Thin Man* (NY) 35: You're peddling your fish in the wrong market. **1941** GBagby *Here Comes* (NY) 252: You've got plenty of your own fish to peddle around here. **1949** KMKnight *Bass* (NY) 158: You just run along and peddle your fish. Berrey 217.3. Cf. Wentworth 380: Papers.

F152 To shoot **Fish** (ducks) in a barrel (*varied*)

1931 GFowler *Great* (NY) 87: It's like shooting fish in a barrel. **1939** HPentecost *Cancelled* (NY) 214: This is going to be like shooting fish in a barrel. **1948** ELipsky *Murder One* (NY) 106: I don't like shooting fish in a barrel. **1952** AAFair *Top* (NY) 19: It was like shooting fish in a barrel. **1952** EF Bleiber *Year's Best* (NY) 253: As easy as the proverbial shooting of ducks in a pond. **1957** *BangorDN* 4/27 28: Then they'll be like fish in a barrel [*easy to shoot*]. **1959** HNielsen *Fifth* (NY DBC) 18: It does seem a little like shooting fish in a barrel. **1962** VWMason *Trouble* (NY DBC) 200: Shootin' a guy like a fish in a barrel. **1965** HPentecost *Sniper* (NY DBC) 42: He could pick us off like fish in a barrel. **1966** SGCrawford *Gascoyne* (L) 58: Easy, ducks in a barrel. 87: Like shooting ducks in a barrel. **1969** HPentecost *Girl with* (NY) 121: Like shooting fish in a barrel. **1970** AALewis *Carnival* (NY) 90: It was like

shooting goldfish in a bowl. **1970** RLPike *Reardon* (NY) 150: It must have been like shooting carp in a rain barrel. **1971** RMStern *You Don't* (NY) 113: Shooting fish in a rain barrel. **1973** JDMacDonald *Turquoise* (P) 103: Like shooting fish in a barrel.

F153 To swim like a **Fish**

1930 JHawk *House* (NY) 244: Dorcas can swim like a fish. **1941** HCBranson *I'll Eat You* (NY) 191: She swims like a fish. **1960** MGEberhart *Jury* (NY DBC) 43: [He] swims like a fish. EAP F157.

F154 **Fish** or cut bait (*varied*)

1928 RHFuller *Jubilee* (NY) 70: We had to fish or cut bait. **1938** DHume *Good-bye* (L) 242: You can't catch old fish on bait like that. **1948** LFord *Devil's* (NY) 130: It's fish or cut bait. **1953** ESGardner *Hesitant* (NY) 93: Make her either fish or cut bait. **1958** *BangorDN* 8/21 23: Fish or cut bait. **1962** WMorris *North* (B) 186: A time to fish and a time to cut bait. **1963** AAFair *Fish or Cut Bait* (NY DBC). **1968** DBagley *Vivero* (NY) 251: Fish, or I'll cut you into bait. **1972** ELathen *Murder* (NY) 38: Fish or cut bait. **1976** RBDominic *Murder* (NY) 117: Fish or cut bait. DA Fish *v.* 3; Wentworth 185.

F155 **Fish** or fornicate

1966 COgburn *Winter* (NY) 294: He said the inhabitants [*of a Maine island*] were opposed to the bridge, having no other desire than "to be left alone to fish and fornicate," and the former only enough to permit them to indulge in the latter and take it easy.

F156 As white (pale) as a **Fish's belly;** Fish-belly-white (*varied*)

c**1923** ACrowley *Confessions* ed JSymonds (L 1969) 607: As white as a fish's belly. **1934** RJBlack *Killing* (NY) 181: His pasty face was even paler than usual, like a fish's belly. **1946** FBLong *Hounds* (NY 1963) 85: Face . . . as white as the belly of a dead fish. **1954** MMainwaring *Murder* (NY) 168: His fat face was as white as the belly of a dead fish. **1958** TBrooke *Under* (NY) 300: His skin was white as a fish's belly. **1962** NFreeling *Death* (NY 1964) 96: Pale like a dead fish's belly. **1963** HPentecost *Tarnished* (NY DBC) 18: His face was fish-belly white. **1971**

PDennis *Paradise* (NY) 58: Buttocks fish-belly white. **1972** GRDickson *Pritcher* (NY) 112: A fish-belly-white sky. **1975** MButterworth *Man in* (NY) 32: Breasts fish-belly white. Cf. Wilstach 470: Fish.

F157 Keep your ain **Fish gut** for your ain sea maws

1952 PPiper *Corpse* (NY) 118: [He] quoted lugubriously, "Keep your ain' fish guts for your ain' sea maws." *Oxford* 418: Keep.

F158 Not care a **Fish-tit**

1951 AThorne *Man Who* (L) 235: Uncle Nogo don't care a fish-tit.

F159 A **Fishing rod** is a stick *etc.*

1938 NBlake *Beast* (NY 1958) 138: A fishing-rod . . . is a stick with a hook at one end and a fool at the other. *Oxford* 266.

F160 As drunk as a **Fishwife**

1950 HGreen *Nothing* (NY) 92: I'll be drunk as a fish wife. Cf. NED Fishwife.

F161 To swear (*etc.*) like a **Fishwife** (*varied*)

1927 GDilnot *Lazy* (B) 239: She swore like a fish-wife. **1928** JJConnington *Tragedy* (B) 120: He abused me like a fish-wife. **1931** EQueen *Dutch* (NY) 142: Wrangling like fishwives. **1935** ECRLorac *Murder* (L) 19: We quarreled, or behaved like the proverbial fish wives. **1937** VMacClure *House* (L) 94: I scolded you like a fishwife. **1940** LFord *Old Lover's* (NY) 239: Leaving Pearl, yammering like a fishwife. **1941** FCrane *Turquoise* (P) 229: Mona cussed like a fishwife. **1945** MMillar *Iron Gates* (NY 1960) 32: We might rail at each other like fishwives. **1968** MAllingham *Cargo* (NY) 57: She curses like a fishwife. **1968** MRowell *Below* (L) 31: Swearing like Billingsgate. **1968** GWagner *Elegy* (L) 64: Her mother swore at her like a fishwife. **1974** MButterworth *Villa* (NY) 156: She screeched like a bloody fishwife. EAP F160.

F162 As bright as **Flame**

1959 ECRLorac *Last* (NY) 110: Hair that's as bright as flame. Wilstach 34: A flame.

F163 As red as **Flame**

1963 MPHood *Sin* (NY) 12: She turns red as flame. Wilstach 550: The flame *etc.*

F164 As flat as a **Flapjack**

1936 ISCobb *Judge Priest* (I) 132: This stretch, which lay as flat as a flapjack. **1956** HCahill *Shadow* (NY) 7: Flat like a flapjack. TW 137. Cf. Fritter, Pancake *below*.

F165 As quick as a **Flash**

1903 ADMcFaul *Ike Glidden* (B) 70: As quick as a flash. **1913** JCLincoln *Mr. Pratt's Patients* (NY) 90: Quick as a flash. **1932** MCJohnson *Damning* (NY) 18: Quick as a flash. **1953** RChandler *Long* (I) 104: He was as quick as a flash. **1953** PGWodehouse *Ring* (L) 194: As quick as a flash. **1970** TKenrick *Only* (NY) 225: Quick as a flash. **1970** JVizzard *See* (NY) 58: Quick as a flash. TW 137(1); Brunvand 51(1).

F166 As swift as a **Flash**

1930 RWallace *Seven Men* (NY) 170: Swift as a flash; 248. TW 137(2).

F167 A **Flash** in the pan

1925 EBChancellor *Hell Fire* (L) 256: It was but a flash in the pan. **1934** BOrwell *Burmese* (NY) 328: A mere flash in the pan. **1940** AAFair *Gold Comes* (NY) 192: It may be just a flash in the pan. **1947** KMKnight *Blue* (NY) 15: A flash in the pan. **1956** AWilson *Anglo-Saxon* (L) 211: Unsustained flashes in the pan. **1957** *BHerald* 12/27 10: Miss Bardot is no flash in the pan. **1961** BAldiss *Primal* (NY) 67: This isn't just a flash in the pan. **1968** RGSherriff *No Leading* (L) 38: Another flash in the pan. **1973** BHowar *Laughing* (NY) 183: I was a very tacky flash in the pan. **1976** EFoote-Smith *Gentle* (NY) 34: A flash in the brain pan. EAP F165.

F168 Like a **Flash**

1916 SLeacock *Behind* (Toronto 1969) 55: Like a flash. **1930** HCMcNeile *Guardians* (NY) 240: It was gone in a flash. **1971** VScannell *Tiger* (L) 56: I was over the side like a flash. EAP F166; TW 137(3); Brunvand 51(2).

Flea

F169 Flattery will get you nowhere (*varied*)
1954 EBox *Death* (NY 1955) 93: Flattery will get you nowhere. **1960** JBWest *Taste* (NY) 80: Flattery ain't gonna get you nowhere. **1961** LSdeCamp *Dragon* (NY 1968) 293: Flattery will get you nought. **1965** SForbes *Relative* (NY) 168: Flattery will get you anything. **1968** BBlack *Associate* (NY) 88: Flattery will get you everywhere. **1973** AGilbert *Nice* (NY) 4: Flattery will get you nowhere. **1975** GBlack *Golden* (NY) 136: Flattery gets you a long way. Cf. TW138; Tilley F349.

F170 As fit as a **Flea**
1930 EWallace *White Face* (NY) 39: Fit as a flea. **1936** ECBentley *Trent's Own* (NY) 293: In a short time you'll be as fit as the proverbial flea. **1944** LAGStrong *All Fall* (NY) 197: Fit as a flea. **1949** NMarsh *Wreath* (NY) 63: I'm fifty-five and as fit as a flea. **1957** NShute *On the Beach* (NY 1958) 223: I'm feeling as fit as a flea. **1959** THWhite *Godstone* (NY) 196: Jack, always as fit as a flea. **1960** NWoodin *Room* (L) 144: She's as fit as a flea. **1968** HCarvic *Picture* (NY) 33: You'll feel fit as a flea in the morning. **1970** GMFraser *Royal* (L) 34: He was still fit as a flea. Partridge 279: Fit.

F171 As restless (nervous) as a **Flea**
1936 DTeilhet *Crimson Hair* (NY) 248: Nervous as a flea with hives, if fleas do have hives. **1941** MArmstrong *Blue Santo* (NY) 91: Restless as the proverbial flea and a fly in a flue. Cf. Partridge 285: Jumpy.

F172 As snug as a **Flea** in a quilt
1934 MKing-Hall *Gay* (NY) 328: Snug as a flea in a quilt. EAP F173. Cf. Bug *above.*

F173 As thick as **Fleas**
1935 MJFreeman *Case* (NY) 220: As thick as fleas. **1939** ADemarest *Murder on* (NY) 29: Him and her was as thick as fleas. TW 138(5).

F174 A **Flea** in one's ear (*varied*)
1904 JCLincoln *Cap'n Eri* (NY) 106: He went away with a flea in his ear. **1913** JCLincoln *Mr. Pratt's Patients* (NY) 231: He'd dropped a flea in the ears of Greenbaum and the rest. **1920** AJRees *Hand in the Dark* (NY 1929) 277: I sent him . . . off with a

flea in his ear. **1928** GDHCole *Man* (NY) 24: Shut him up wi' a flea in his mouth, a did. **1928** VMarkham *Death* (NY) 151: Having a bit of a flea in his ear. **1932** ACampbell *Murder* (NY) 165: She flounced out . . . with a flea in her ear. **1933** AChristie *Lord Edgware* (L) 158: He . . . sent you away with a flea in the ear. **1951** NMitford *Blessing* (NY) 171: I'd send you off with a flea in your ear. **1956** AMenen *Abode* (NY) 142: Sent them back with, if you'll excuse the coarse expression, a flea in their ear. **1961** WH Lewis *Scandalous* (NY) 57: Come away with a flea in his ear. **1961** ESherry *Call* (NY DBC) 73: He left with a flea in his ear [*a suspicion*]. **1965** MEchard *I Met* (NY) 20: He had put the flea in the jury's ear. **1973** THeald *Unbecoming* (NY) 136: Sent him away with a flea in his ear. **1975** HCarmichael *Too Late* (NY) 68: Our . . . sergeant knows how to dish out the proverbial flea-in-the-ear. EAP F174; TW 138(7); Brunvand 52(1). Cf. To put a Bug *above.*

F175 Kill a **Flea** in March, kill a hundred
1969 BLehame *Compleat* (L) 29: If you kill one flea in March you will kill a hundred. *Oxford* 267.

F176 Not hurt (harm) a **Flea**
1929 TShannon *Catspaw* (NY) 202: You wouldn't hurt a flea. **1934** GHeyer *Unfinished* (L) 162: Her ladyship wouldn't hurt a flea. **1940** JFBonnell *Death over* (NY) 127: [He] wouldn't harm a flea. **1941** CRice *Trial by Fury* (NY 1957) 56: Phil Smith wouldn't murder a flea. **1956** RMacdonald *Barbarous* (NY) 175: He wouldn't hurt a flea, unless it was biting him. **1956** HRoth *Crimson* (NY) 28: "He wouldn't hurt a flea." The cliché gave no pause. **1961** RSPrather *Shell* (NY) 16: I wouldn't hurt a flea. **1973** HDolson *Dying* (P) 94: Mario wouldn't hurt a flea. Cf. Not hurt a Fly, Mouse *below.*

F177 To skin (flay) a **Flea** (louse) for its hide and tallow (*varied*)
1904 JCLincoln *Cap'n Eri* (NY) 269: He'd skin a flea for the hide and taller. **1927** JTully *Circus* (NY) 256: A man that'd do that ud skin a louse for its hide. **1928** GYoung *Treasure* (NY) 19: She would skin

a flea for hide and tallow. **1933** ISCobb *Murder* (I) 48: He'd skin a louse for its hide and tallow. **1935** LFord *Burn* (NY) 222: Turner'd skin a flea fer hits taller. **1936** CBarry *Poison* (L) 209: You'd skin a flea for the sake of its hide. **1969** BLehame *Compleat* (L) 18: To be mean . . . was "to flay a flea for hide and tallow." **1971** HBevington *House* (NY) 58: Why skin a flea for its hide and tallow? **1972** DEmrich *Folklore* (B) 27: So stingy he'd skin a flea for its hide and tallow. EAP F177. Cf. Flint *below*.

F178   A Flea-bite

1924 EWallace *Green* (B) 328: It is not going to hurt him any more than a flea-bite. **1927** AHaynes *Crow's* (L) 92: My legacy is a mere flea-bite. **1929** AHayes *Crime* (L) 166: Day's price would be a flea-bite to what I've heard. **1933** MKennedy *Bull's Eye* (L) 205: It was impossible to call £15,000 a mere flea-bite. **1938** JDonovan *Beckoning Dead* (L) 254: That's only a flea-bite—quite a side issue. **1945** CDickson *Curse* (NY) 150: It's a flea-bite—it's nothing at all. **1960** HReilly *Follow* (NY DBC) 132: The irritation was only a flea bite. EAP F178; TW 138.

F179   All Flesh is grass

1929 PGWodehouse *Fish* (NY) 288: All flesh is grass. **1934** PGWodehouse *Brinkley* (B) 219: All flesh is grass. **1938** RAJWalling *Grimy Glove* (NY) 59: All flesh is grass. **1952** PGWodehouse *Angel* (NY) 25: All flesh is grass. **1961** PGWodehouse *Ice* (NY) 112: "What is it they say all flesh is as?" "Grass, isn't it?" **1970** PMoyes *Many* (NY) 198: All flesh is grass. **1975** NFreeling *Bugles* (NY) 12: All that flesh was grass now. EAP F182; TW 138–9(1).

F180   (The spirit is willing but) the Flesh is weak

1920 AChristie *Mysterious Affair* (NY) 217: The flesh is weak. **1962** EGrierson *Massingham* (L) 92: The flesh is weak. **1967** VSNaipaul *Flag* (L) 48: Flesh is frail. **1971** HCarvig *Witch* (NY) 104: His spirit was willing but the flesh had betrayed him. **1977** VCanning *Doomsday* (NY) 46: The flesh is weak. EAP F183, S370.

F181   The Fleshpots of the south

1972 DDevine *Three* (NY) 55: The fleshpots of the south. EAP F184.

F182   Not care (give) a Flick (of the fingers)

1929 EJMillward *Copper* (NY) 121: He said he didn't care a flick. **1937** JMWalsh *White Mask* (L) 70: I do not care a flip of the fingers. **1964** JAshford *Superintendent* (NY) 183: I wouldn't give two flicks what the two of you did. Whiting F280: Not worth.

F183   As hard as Flint; Flint-hard

1915 LPowys in MElwin *Life* (L 1946) 127: As hard as flint. **1919** JSClouston *Simon* (NY) 303: Hard as flint. **1931** JSFletcher *Solution* (NY) 77: His face set as hard as flint. **1939** HFootner *Murder That* (L) 162: A face as hard as flint. **1941** KSecrist *Murder Makes* (NY) 20: He was hard as flint. **1953** PIWellman *Female* (NY) 202: His face hard as flint. **1956** RStout *Eat* (NY) 107: Flint-hard. **1961** JPhilips *Murder* (NY DBC) 134: Voice . . . hard as flint. **1968** JFraser *Evergreen* (NY) 113: His [*face*] was flint hard. EAP F185; TW 139(2); Taylor *Western Folklore* 17(1958) 15.

F184   To skin a Flint (stone)

1932 JSFletcher *Man in the Fur Coat* (L) 174: She'd skin a stone . . . if she could save a farthing by doing it. **1956** MLSettle *O Beulah* (NY) 153: He would skin a flint. EAP F188; TW 139(7). Cf. To skin a Flea *above*.

F185   As flat as a Floor

1931 RScarlett *Cat's* (NY) 12: It was flat as a floor. **1965** DCLunt *Woods* (NY) 228: The ocean was calm, as flat as a floor. Cf. EAP F192: Level.

F186   A Floor one could eat from (*varied*)

1926 LO'Flaherty *Mr. Gilhooley* (L) 165: As we say in the west: "Ye could eat yer dinner on the floor." **1929** ARMartin *Death* (NY) 121: You could eat your dinner off the floor, as the saying is. **1936** SPalmer *Briar Pike* (L) 279: You could eat offen the floor. **1939** TStevenson *Silver Arrow* (L) 86: As my grandmother used to say, you could eat your dinner off the floor. **1948** EQueen *Ten* (B) 122: She keeps it clean herself. You could eat off the floor. **1968** KDetzer *Myself*

(NY) 57: [Her] kitchen was so clean you could eat off the floor. **1969** APHannum *Look* (NY) 41: The floor "so clean you could eat off it." **1970** AALewis *Carnival* (NY) 116: It's so clean you could eat off the floors. TW 139(4).

F187   As dead as a **Flounder**

1939 JNDarby *Murder in* (I) 257: There lay old Hiram as dead as a flounder. **1956** MPHood *Scarlet* (NY) 13: You're still as dead as a split flounder. Cf. As dead as a Fish *above*; Mackerel *below*.

F188   As flat as a **Flounder**

1938 JFarnol *Crooked* (NY) 66: Flat as a flounder. **1940** GCKlingel *Anagua* (NY) 40: It was mashed as flat as a flounder. **1961** ANeame *Adventures* (NY) 97: As flat as a flounder. **1963** GMaxwell *Rocks* (NY) 201: Flat as a flounder. **1975** SJPerelman *Vinegar* (NY) 153: Flattened as neatly as a flounder. EAP F193.

F189   As white as **Flour**; Flour-white

1939 HMiller *Capricorn* (NY 1961) 60: She was as white as flour. **1949** WKrasner *Walk* (NY) 147: Her flour-white face appeared. **1962** JKnowles *Morning* (NY) 18: Her big flour-white face. NED Flour 1b.

F190   As fresh as **Flowers**

1941 GWYates *If a Body* (NY) 124: Fresh as a flower. **1968** MConnelly *Voices* (NY) 82: As fresh as flowers. EAP F195.

F191   As pretty as **Flowers** (in May)

1941 MArmstrong *Blue Santo* (NY) 193: Pretty as flowers in May. **1958** CLBlackstone *Foggy* (NY) 26: She's as pretty as a flower.

F192   As welcome as (the) **Flowers** (birds) in May

1921 JSFletcher *Orange-Yellow* (NY) 30: You're as welcome as the flowers in May. **1936** LThayer *Dark of the Moon* (NY) 182: You're as welcome as the birds in May. **1937** CGordon *Garden* (NY) 153: She made him as welcome as the flowers in May. **1940** JCreasey *Here Comes* (NY 1967) 38: Welcome as the flowers. **1946** ABCunningham *One Man* (NY) 17: You're as welcome as the

flowers in May. **1947** NMarsh *Final* (B) 39: You are as welcome as flowers in spring. **1951** MColes *Now* (NY) 210: [He] was as welcome as flowers in May. **1954** JPotts *Go* (NY) 78: You're welcome as the flowers of May. Whiting *NC* 409(3); Taylor *Prov. Comp.* 85; *Oxford* 270.

F193   To be up the **Flue**

1940 HSKeeler *Crimson Box* (L) 273: Then the whole case is up the flue. TW 140.

F194   As common as **Flies**

1930 SChalmers *Crime* (NY) 23: Detectives were as common as flies. **1933** NGordon *Shakespeare* (NY) 43: Common as flies. **1939** JRWarren *Murder from* (NY) 101: As common as flies.

F195   As mad as a **Fly** in a bottle

1957 RFuller *With My* (NY) 140: He's as mad as a fly in a bottle. Cf. TW 140(2); Apperson 220(10).

F196   As thick as **Flies** (*varied*)

1930 SChalmers *Crime* (NY) 227: West's as thick with the . . . man . . . as two flies in a jam-pot. **1930** EWallace *India* (NY) 204: Policemen are as thick as flies. **1935** Xantippe *Death* (NY) 206: Rumors were as thick as flies around a stable. **1947** FLockridge *Untidy* (NY) 216: The State cops were as thick as flies. **1959** DTaylor *Joy* (NY) 194: People were standing as thick as flies. **1965** JTurner *Blue* (L 1967) 134: They're coming in as thick as flies. EAP F199; TW 140(3); Taylor *Western Folklore* 17(1958) 15(1).

F197   **Flies** have their virtue

1936 JLindsay *Come Home* (L) 375: You know the proverb. Flies have their virtue. Cf. Apperson 220(2); *Oxford* 270.

F198   A **Fly** in the amber (*varied*)

1915 PGWodehouse *Something Fresh* (L 1935) 20: The only fly in the British . . . amber. **1919** LTracy *Bartlett* (NY) 89: She's the fly in the amber. **1930** LBrock *Murder* (NY) 265: [It] was but the most microscopic of flies in the rich and glowing amber of his superiors' commendation. **1931** HBurnham *Murder* (NY) 4: The bug in Corey's amber. **1938** RAJWalling *Coroner* (L) 67:

There's a fly in the amber. **1946** TKyd *Blood is a Beggar* (P) 94: Always a fly in the amber. **1947** HCahill *Look* (NY) 297: The only real fly in the lacquer was the guerrilla warfare. **1957** YBridges *How Charles* (L) 77: No fly was discernable in the amber of their friend's life. **1961** PDennis *Little* (NY) 183: Only one fly in the amber. **1962** HMirrlees *A Fly in Amber* (L). **1965** FPohl *Plague* (NY) 53: Chandler felt like a fly in amber, imprisoned in his own barinbox. **1974** TWells *Have Mercy* (NY) 116: That's the racket . . . the fly in the amber. *Oxford* 270.

F199 A **Fly** in the buttermilk (*etc.*)

1932 MCJohnson *Damning* (NY) 143: The sole lonely fly in his porridge. **1934** CStead *Salzburg* (NY) 175: What's the fly in the jampot? **1935** JEGrant *Green Shadow* (NY) 110: This racket outfit was the fly in the soup. **1953** FCDavis *Drag* (NY) 92: The only fly in the gravy. **1965** LGralapp *Boom!* (NY) 17: There's only one fly in the buttermilk. Whiting F352: Milk.

F200 The **Fly** in the ointment (*varied*)

1920 AChristie *Mysterious Affair* (NY) 29: The only fly in the ointment. **1920** GBMcCutcheon *Anderson Crow* (NY) 232: The fly avoided his ointment. **1927** MRJames *Letters to a Friend* ed GMcBryde (L 1956) 145: They were what you may fairly call fleabites in the ointment. **1932** QMario *Murder Meets* (NY) 227: He just had to put the fly in every ointment. **1937** JHunter *Three Die* (NY) 80: The large black fly in the juicy white ointment. **1956** *Punch* 10/10 434: Just as I have never been able to see what harm a fly does in the ointment. **1957** JBrooks *Water* (L) 98: He is the fly in the ointment. **1957** DJEnright *Heaven* (L) 20: That's the bloody snake in the ointment. **1959** *Atlantic Monthly* Nov. 62: When you were the fly in the ointment and I was the cat in the bag. **1961** BAldiss *Primal* (NY) 92: Every ointment has its fly. **1966** BHDeal *Fancy's* (NY) 116: But she hadn't *told* him. That, of course, was the fly in the ointment, the pig in the poke, the nigger in the woodpile. **1971** DFJones *Denver* (NY) 106: The only minor fly in the ointment. **1974** GWheeler *Easy* (NY) 18: There's a fly in the body lotion. **1974** PHWodehouse *Cat-Nappers* (NY) 143: That was a small flaw in the ointment. Or is it fly? EAP F201; Brunvand 52.

F201 Like **Flies** around a honey pot (*varied*)

1922 JJoyce *Ulysses* (NY 1934) 368: Women buzz around it like flies round treacle. **1928** GDHCole *Man* (NY) 88: This does look like flies to a honey pot. **1937** JBentley *Landor* (L) 277: He took to me like a fly does to honey. **1953** MPHood *Silent* (NY) 104: The men hanging around like flies around a honey pot. Cf. TW 141(5).

F202 More **Flies** are caught with honey than vinegar (*varied*)

1930 GBMeans *Strange Death* (NY) 80: More flies are caught with sugar than with vinegar. **1930** WWoodrow *Moonhill* (NY) 306: There's an old saying that it's easier to catch flies with honey than with vinegar. **1931** CJDaly *Third* (NY) 85: You catch more flies with molasses than with vinegar. **1934** SPalmer *Silver Persian* (NY) 89: Try trapping flies with honey instead of vinegar. **1937** RGDean *Three Lights* (NY) 126: Honey catches more flies than vinegar. **1941** VRath *Death Breaks* (NY) 258: Honey draws flies. **1953** CBKelland *Sinister* (NY DBC) 54: She is the kind of fly you're more apt to catch with vinegar than honey. **1956** BJChute *Greenwillow* (NY) 127: Honey, Gramma reflected suddenly, catches more flies than vinegar. **1959** *BangorDN* 9/1 9: You can catch more flies with sugar than you can with vinegar. **1963** SForbes *Grieve* (NY) 115: You can't catch flies with vinegar. **1964** BWilliams *Stranger* (NY) 135: You can catch more flies with honey. **1974** SForbes *Some* (NY) 102: His old grandma used to tell him, "You can't catch flies with vinegar." **1977** HDolson *Beauty* (P) 157: An old saying of her grandmother's: "You catch more flies with honey than vinegar." EAP F203.

F203 Not hurt (kill) a **Fly** (*etc.*) (*varied*)

1904 JCLincoln *Cap'n Eri* (NY) 298: Folks . . . that wouldn't hurt a fly. **1924** VLWhitechurch *Templeton* (NY) 255: He wouldn't hurt a fly. **1932** MThynne *Murder* (NY) 151:

He wouldn't, and couldn't, hurt a fly. **1941** RDAbrahams *Death after Lunch* (NY) 86: I wouldn't hurt a fly. **1946** JStagge *Death's Old* (NY) 98: He would not harm a fly except in self defence. **1950** LAGStrong *Which I* (L) 16: [He] wouldn't hurt a fly. **1952** PMacDonald *Something* (NY) 168: He couldn't even hurt a fly that was pestering him. **1963** DMDisney *Here Lies* (NY) 127: She wouldn't hurt a fly. **1963** The Gordons *Undercover* (NY DBC) 27: He wouldn't hurt a fly or a spider. **1963** EQueen *Player* (NY) 80: "You never hurt a fly." "A fly never hurt me." **1964** EMcBain *Ax* (NY) 126: I wouldn't even touch a fly . . . unless it was unzipped. **1971** MScherf *Beautiful* (NY) 164: Althea wouldn't kill a gnat. **1974** CMSmith *Reverend* (NY) 176: He couldn't harm a fly. **1977** LBlock *Burglars* (NY) 106: A nice boy who would never hurt a cockroach. NED Fly *sb.*[1] 1d. Cf. Not hurt a Flea *above*; Mouse *below*.

F204 There are no **Flies** on (someone)
1924 HCBailey *Mr. Fortune's Practice* (NY) 14: There were no flies on his chauffeur. **1924** JSFletcher *Safety* (NY) 82: I don't think you'll let the flies settle on you. **1932** HCBailey *Red Castle* (NY) 287: No flies on Josh. **1939** CMWills *Death at* (L) 68: That pair . . . have no flies on them. **1953** JTrench *Docken* (L 1960) 124: No flies on the Force. **1957** MSharp *Eye* (L) 63: There were no flies on old man Joyce. **1961** HCromwell *Dirty* (LA) 43: There were no flies on Adele's fast ass. **1967** NWollaston *Jupiter* (L) 118: No flies on Trotter's, if you'll pardon the indelicacy. **1973** JPorter *It's Murder* (NY) 39: There were no flies on him. Partridge 286; NED Suppl. Fly *sb.*[1] 1f; Wentworth 357: No flies.

F205 To die like **Flies**
1924 GRFox *Fangs* (NY) 140: Die like flies. **1926** AMarshall *Mote* (NY) 55: My men died like flies. **1936** HWeiner *Crime on the Cuff* (NY) 249: He'd kill us all like flies. **1937** RBriffault *Europa* (NY) 73: Dying like flies. **1953** CMRussell *Market* (NY) 146: They're dying like flies. **1958** VSiller *Widower* (NY) 21: The cattle died like flies. **1962** LWoolley *As I Seem* (L) 101: People were

dying like flies. **1963** EMcBain *Ten* (NY) 116: People dying like flies. **1971** SBerlin *Dromengro* (L) 248: The old uns are dying like flies. Cf. Whiting F350.

F206 In like **Flynn**
1953 GBagby *Big Hand* (NY DBC) 91: I'm in like Flynn. **1959** SDean *Merchant* (NY) 185: The manager . . . would be in like Flynn with the widow. **1964** HPentecost *Shape* (NY DBC) 70: If we knew that . . . we'd be in like Flynn. **1965** DKnight *Dark Side* (NY) 184: All of a sudden I was in like Flynn [*accepted*]. **1972** JGreenway *Down* (B) 152: He's in like Flynn. Wentworth 280: In.

F207 As white as **Foam**
1934 AMerritt *Creep* (NY) 295: Her face white as foam. **1959** EMarshall *Pagan* (NY) 125: Foam-white as any snow. EAP F206; TW 141.

F208 **Fog** on the hill, water for the mill
1956 *BangorDN* 9/13 11: Fog on the hill—water for the mill. Dunwoody 52: Fog and rain, 53: Weather.

F209 **Food** for thought (*varied*)
1913 ERBurroughs *Warlord* (NY 1963) 66: The incident gave me . . . food for speculation. **1925** FWCrofts *Pit-prop* (NY) 221: Willis had food for thought. **1935** BFlynn *Case* (L) 113: Food for subsequent thought. **1938** ECVivian *Rainbow* (L) 233: With that as food for thought. **1949** RFoley *Girl* (NY) 47: Food for thought. **1959** MInnes *Hare* (NY 1964) 72: There was food for thought in it. **1966** JHSchmitz *Witches* (NY) 146: To give [him] more food for thought. **1968** JPorter *Dover Goes* (NY) 119: Plenty of food for thought there, as they say. **1974** AChurchill *Splendid* (NY) 72: This gave Cornelius food for thought. **1974** AMorice *Killing* (NY) 68: [It] gave me food for reflection. NED Food 3b.

F210 Answer a **Fool** according to his folly
1929 RAJWalling *Murder* (NY) 6: Instead of answering him after his folly. **1931** CWells *Horrors* (P) 106: Answer a fool according to his folly. **1950** SSmith *Man with* (NY) 33: Answer a fool according to his folly. EAP F215.

F211 As drunk as a **Fool**

1930 EDTorgerson *Murderer* (NY) 208: He's drunk as a fool. **1930** ANewell *Who Killed* (NY) 264: He was drunk as a fool. **1939** JNDarby *Murder in* (I) 286: Drunk as two fools. TW 142(11).

F212 Bray a **Fool** in a mortar *etc.*

1943 CEVulliamy *Polderoy* (L) 244: Bray a fool in a mortar, says the proverb, and he remains a fool. EAP F247: To bray.

F213 A **Fool** and his money are soon parted (*varied*)

1911 JLondon *Letters* ed KHendricks (NY 1965) 350: The old adage . . . "A fool and his money are soon parted." **c1923** ACrowley *Confessions* ed JSymonds (L 1969) 208: The gentle art of parting a fool and his money. **1924** HHMunro *Square* (L 1929) 208: Isn't there a proverb, a fool and his hair are soon parted? **1925** HCWitwer *Bill* (NY) 3: A fool and his honey is soon parted. **1934** AChristie *Mr. Parker* (NY) 107: Fools and their money are soon parted, they say. **1938** RAFreeman *Stoneware* (L) 167: Which illustrates the proverbial lack of cohesion between a fool and his money. **1939** AMuir *Death Comes* (L) 203: The proverbial process of parting a fool and his money. **1954** AW Barkley *That Reminds* (NY) 32: A fool and his money are soon parted. **1958** *BangorDN* 9/15 19: You also told me that a fool and his money were soon parted. **1964** LCohen *New York* (P) 112: A fool and his money are soon parted. **1965** RBissell *Still* (NY) 192: A fool and his money soon part company. **1967** HBlyth *Old Q* (L) 60: He knew that a fool and his life are soon parted. **1970** HBlyth *Skittles* (L) 100: A fool and his money are soon parted. **1971** ADavidson *Peregrine* (NY) 107: A fool and his money are soon parted, as I believe Homer remarks somewhere, or is it the Proverbs of King Solomon? EAP F221.

F214 A **Fool** for luck (*varied*)

1910 JCLincoln *Depot Master* (NY) 160: A fool for luck. **1924** WBMFerguson *Black* (NY) 293: You always did play in fool's luck; 305. 318: Some fools have all the luck. **1928** JEsteven *Door* (NY) 238: Fool's luck. **1938** MTeagle *Murders* (NY) 150: We may thank Providence for the luck of fools. **1940** VRath *Death of a Lucky* (NY) 3: You're a fool for luck. **1947** LFord *Woman* (NY) 103: Playing into fool's luck. **1963** HCalvin *It's Different* (NY) 112: Fools are lucky. **1971** JMuir *Stranger* (NY) 24: Fool's luck and leg work. TW 142(1). Cf. Beginner's luck *above*.

F215 **Fools** build houses and wise men live in them

1933 EJepson *Memoirs* (L) 45: Fools build houses and wise men live in them. EAP F229. Cf. Brunvand 92: Man (7).

F216 A **Fool's** errand

1900 CFPidgin *Quincy A. Sawyer* (B) 469: On such a Tom fool's errand. **1924** ADH Smith *Porto* (NY) 87: A fool's errand. **1933** CJDutton *Circle* (NY) 256: A fool's errand. **1933** HHolt *Scarlet* (L) 156: On a fool's errand. **1948** DCDisney *Explosion* (NY DBC) 126: On a fool's errand. **1956** SWTaylor *I Have* (NY) 2: It was a fool's errand. **1958** RMacdonald *Doomsters* (NY) 238: Running on fool's errands. **1963** EXFerrars *Double* (NY) 14: On a fool's errand. **1977** PGWinslow *Witch* (NY) 226: A fool's errand. EAP F244; TW 142(5); Brunvand 53(3).

F217 **Fools'** names and fools' faces *etc.*

1951 JCFurnas *Voyage* (NY) 433: The remaining surface carried many fools' names in pencil. **1956** *BHerald* 10/7 10: Fools' names and fools' faces are always seen in public places. **1971** PDennis *Paradise* (NY) 202: "Fools' names and fools' faces . . ." she quoted. Whiting NC 410(5).

F218 **Fools** rush in where angels fear to tread (*varied*)

1927 FEverton *Dalehouse* (NY) 150: Fools rush in where angels fear to tread. **1928** TCobb *Who Opened* (L) 16: He was rushing in where a discreet angel might have feared to tread. **1931** LCArlington *Through* (L) 1: The saw "Fools rush in where angels fear to tread." **1935** EJepson *Murder* (L) 169: He might be one of the fools who rush in where angels fear to tread. **1940** DHume *Five Aces* (L) 40: Poking in your nose where angels fear to tread. **1941** NMarsh *Death in Ecstasy* (NY) 247: Fools step in where angels fear to tread. **1954** GFowler *Minutes* (NY) 171: Men who walked where not only angels, but devils feared to tread. **1956** *BHerald* 6/10 A49: Alma Andosca . . . adjusted an old proverb to "Fools drive on where angels keep their heads." **1958** *NYTimes Magazine* 9/28 28: [Broadway] Angels . . . rush in where even fools fear to tread. **1959** SDean *Merchant* (NY) 180: I would not rush in where angels might fear to tread; I don't expect to be an angel for some time yet. **1961** JWebb *One for* (NY DBC) 86: Fools rush . . . Haste makes waste . . . make haste slowly and all that sort of thing. **1964** EDahlberg *Alms* (Minneapolis) 14: He was not only the angel that foolishly rushed in where others feared to tread; he had no fear afterward of being mocked. **1965** JMBrown *Worlds* (NY) 37: She rushed in where Emily Post was never to dare to tread. **1968** DBagley *Vivero* (NY) 219: Fools may rush in where angels fear to tread, but there is also something called Fool's Luck. **1971** WHMarnell *Once Upon* (NY) 96: In total innocence and utter unawareness of the proverbial consequences of rushing in. **1973** WMasterson *Undertaker* (NY) 93: Pat was always rushing in where angels fear to tread. **1975** JBland *Death* (NY) 37: "Rush in where angels fear to tread." "I wouldn't have used quite that quotation . . . It refers to fools, doesn't it?" EAP F233.

F219 No **Fool** like a damn (big) fool
1930 CClausen *Gloyne* (NY) 178: No fool like a damn fool. **1936** MBeckett *Escape* (L) 69: There's nu sic a fule as a big fule. See following entries.

F220 No **Fool** like an old (young) fool
1908 JCLincoln *Cy Whittaker* (NY) 199: The fools ain't all dead, and there's none to beat an old one. **1920** AChristie *Mysterious Affair* (NY) 24: There's no fool like an old fool. **1922** JJoyce *Ulysses* (NY 1934) 724: No fool like an old fool. **1925** FWCrofts *French's Greatest* (NY) 186: A trite remark anent the folly of an old fool. **1927** DYates *Blind* (NY) 199: No fool like a young fool. **1940** EDean *Murder Is* (NY) 191: There was certainly no fool like an old fool, except a young one. **1953** CBKellend *Sinister* (NY DBC) 160:

There's no damn fool . . . like a young female damn fool. **1956** *New Yorker* 11/17 41: There is no fool like a poll fool. **1959** DTaylor *Joy* (NY) 99: There is no fool like a young fool. **1964** FArcher *Malabang* (NY DBC) 63: There's no fool like a young fool. **1970** VCClinton-Baddeley *No Case* (NY) 86: But old men grow foolish. **1975** GBlack *Golden* (NY) 149: No fool like an old fool. TW 142(8).

F221 Not such a **Fool** as one looks
1927 BAtkey *Man* (NY) 21: He's not such a fool as he looks. **1938** RAJWalling *Coroner* (L) 184: Ilka mon isna sae big a fule as he looks. **1939** JJFarjeon *Seven Dead* (I) 218: You're not quite the fool you look. *Oxford* 273.

F222 To live in a **Fool's** paradise
1908 WHHudson *Land's End* (L) 141: Living in a fool's paradise. **1912** HHMunro *Unbearable* (NY 1928) 172: In a fool's paradise. c**1923** ACrowley *Confessions* ed JSymonds (L 1969) 815: Living in a fool's paradise. **1933** FDell *Homecoming* (NY) 3: Fool's paradise. **1939** ATilton *Cold Steal* (NY) 105: Living in a fool's paradise. **1941** HReilly *Three Women* (NY) 211: She had been living in a fool's paradise. **1951** SRattray *Knight* (L 1966) 139: In a Paradise where only a fool would go. **1952** JLeslie *Intimate* (NY) 87: I lived in a fool's paradise. **1966** CMBowra *Memories* (L) 292: Live in a fool's paradise. **1977** PMoyes *Coconut* (NY) 119: Living in a fool's paradise. EAP F227.

F223 To suffer **Fools** gladly
1928 EHamilton *Four* (L) 123: You suffer fools anything but gladly. **1930** IWray *Vye* (L) 6: She's one of those who suffer fools gladly. **1931** MBurton *Menace* (L) 73: That recommendation to suffer fools gladly is a counsel of perfection. **1937** RCWoodthorpe *Death in* (NY) 55: Too old to suffer fools gladly. **1944** ECrispin *Gilded Fly* (NY 1970) 33: [An] inability to suffer fools gladly. **1952** AWUpfield *Venom* (NY) 21: Spender is unable to suffer fools gladly or otherwise. **1959** CDBowen *Adventures* (B) 57: She did not suffer fools gladly. **1965** HActon *Old Lamps* (L) 17: He was incapable of suffering

fools gladly. **1966** KMartin *Father* (L) 104: I doubt if he ever learnt to suffer fools gladly. **1973** SWoods *Yet She* (NY) 147: [He] wasn't one to suffer fools gladly. II Corinthians 11.19.

F224   As plain as one's **Foot**

1935 NBlake *Question* (L) 222: It's as plain as my feet. Cf. As plain as one's Hand *below*.

F225   As sure as one is a **Foot** high

1935 FGEberhard *Microbe* (NY) 108: Sure as you're a foot high. **1939** JPPhilips *Death Delivers* (NY) 180: Just as sure as you're a foot high. **1940** AGaines *While the Wind* (NY) 88: As sure as you're a foot high. **1957** *BHerald* 7/26 31: As sure as you're a foot high.

F226   To get cold **Feet**

1960 LFletcher *Blindfold* (NY) 75: Somebody has gotten cold feet. **1974** JPHennessy *Stevenson* (NY) 110: He began to get cold feet again. NED Suppl. Cold *a.* 19; Partridge 169; Wentworth 115: Cold.

F227   To get off on the wrong **Foot** (*varied*)

1925 TRMarshall *Recollections* (I) 222: I should have got off on the wrong foot. **1932** EDBiggers *Keeper* (L) 163: I sure got off on the wrong foot. **1932** MRRinehart *Miss Pinkerton* (NY) 261: They're off on the wrong foot. **1939** DHume *Make Way* (L) 163: You've got off with the wrong foot. **1942** HCBailey *Nobody's* (NY) 297: You have caught me on the wrong foot. **1947** ELustgarten *One More* (NY 1959) 74: The prosecution had clearly got off on the wrong foot. **1956** *Punch* 7/18 79: It's not that we've been caught on the wrong foot; we haven't got a leg left to stand on. **1956** WTenn *Of All* (L) 40: You are getting off on the wrong foot. **1959** PSomers *Shivering* (NY) 40: She started off on the wrong foot. **1964** JWhite *Deadly* (NY) 61: The voyage got off on the wrong foot. **1968** JCFurnas *Lightfoot* (NY) 98: Having got off on the wrong foot. **1970** EHahn *Times* (NY) 69: [He] had started me off on the wrong foot. **1970** KLouchheim *By the Political* (NY) 171: Any relationship can begin on the wrong foot. **1974** JCreasey *As Merry* (NY) 31: To

catch his subordinates on the wrong foot. EAP F258.

F228   To have **Feet** of clay

1935 AGilbert *Man* (L) 164: She must have known he had feet of clay. **1937** NForrest *Greek God* (L) 43: They've all got feet of clay. **1962** HWaugh *Late* (NY) 21: The doctor is revealed as having the same clay feet as their own husbands. **1963** JSutton *Apollo* (NY) 68: A hero never has feet of clay. Daniel 2.33.

F229   To have one **Foot** in the grave (*varied*)

1923 HGartland *Globe* (NY) 9: Him with one foot in the grave. **1934** EPhillpotts *Mr. Digweed* (L) 36: With a foot in the grave. **1936** JBude *Death* (L) 10: Standing on his own foot with one leg in the grave. **1938** CFGregg *Mystery* (L) 216: If that old reprobate hasn't got one foot in the grave and the other all butter. **1940** FGruber *Talking Clock* (NY) 10: He's got a millionaire father who already has one foot in the grave and the other on a fresh banana peel. **1943** GHCoxe *Murder for Two* (NY) 145: To hear him . . . he has both feet in the grave. **1957** MPHood *In the Dark* (NY) 172: [He] has one foot in the grave, and the other all butter. **1970** JFraser *Deadly* (NY) 54: Having one foot in the grave. **1970** RRendell *Best Man* (NY) 56: One foot in the grave and the other on a bar of soap. **1972** KCampbell *Thunder* (I) 163: He's got more'n one foot in t'grave hissen. **1972** EX Ferrars *Foot in the Grave* (NY). EAP F253; TW 143(3); Brunvand 53(1).

F230   To inherit one's six **Feet** of earth

1960 AGilbert *Out for* (NY 1965) 83: Before I inherit my six feet of earth and the conquering worm. EAP F254.

F231   To keep one's **Feet** on the ground

1931 CWells *Horrors* (P) 283: Keep your feet on the ground. **1938** ZPopkin *Death Wears* (P) 227: She . . . kept both her feet quite completely on the ground. **1939** LRGribble *Arsenal* (L) 180: She had her feet on the ground. **1946** FLockridge *Murder within* (P) 144: My feet are quite firmly on the ground. **1951** TDubois *Foul* (NY) 88:

He had his feet firmly planted on the ground and was not in the least excited. **1956** JFStraker *Ginger* (L) 55: A young woman with both feet on the ground. **1972** PKruger *Cold* (NY) 14: A likeable kid with both feet on the ground. Cf. NED Foot 27, 29c.

F232 To keep one's **Foot** under his own table

1982 RRendell *Master* (NY) 48: Keep your feet under your own table. Cf. *Oxford* 253: Under another man's table.

F233 To put one's best **Foot** forward

1930 JSFletcher *Heaven-sent* (NY) 223: Put your best foot forward. **1938** BFrancis *Death at* (L) 67: We'll have to put our best foot forwards. **1941** ISShriber *Murder Well Done* (NY) 12: I would like to put my best foot forward. **1947** FCDavis *Thursday's* (NY) 82: He was not putting his best . . . foot forward. **1951** JCFurnas *Voyage* (NY) 181: Fanny put her best foot forward. **1960** JO'Hara *Ourselves* (NY) 96: You can put your best foot forward. **1975** BNByfield *Solemn* (NY) 14: Best foot forward. EAP F257; TW 143(5); Brunvand 53(2).

F234 To put one's **Foot** in it

1919 JSClouston *Simon* (NY) 295: You've put your foot fairly in it. **1922** JJoyce *Ulysses* (NY 1934) 757: He puts his big foot in it. **1934** CBush *100% Alibis* (L) 199: Casey put his foot in it. **1955** AWest *Heritage* (NY) 28: You've put your foot in it. **1959** EFenwick *Long Way* (NY DBC) 98: I put my big foot in it. **1962** EXFerrars *Wandering* (NY) 52: Putting my big foot in it as usual. EAP F256.

F235 To stand on one's own **Feet**

1931 FDGrierson *Mystery* (L) 74: You'll have to stand on your own feet. EAP F259.

F236 To take one's **Foot** in one's hand

1937 CGordon *Garden* (NY) 57: He made 'em take their foot in their hand and walk. **1949** PGWodehouse *Mating* (NY) 110: Racing down to Deverill Hall with her foot in her hand. **1950** VSReid *New Day* (L) 54: Put foot in hand and go light [*make haste*]. TW 143(9).

F237 To meet **Force** with force (*varied*)

1936 NMorland *Street* (L) 211: She answers force with force. **1937** EGreenwood *Under the Fig* (NY) 11: We'll meet force by force. **1941** EPhillpotts *Ghostwater* (NY) 140: Force has to be met with force, cunning with equal cunning and craft with craft. **1966** KAmis *Spectrum V* (L) 67: You only lick force with force. **1968** RSDominic *Murder* (NY) 18: He could meet force with force. EAP F264. Cf. Craft, To fight Fire *above*.

F238 **Forewarned** is forearmed (*varied*)

1910 EPhillpotts *Tales* (NY) 82: 'Tis half the battle to be forewarned. **1922** JSFletcher *Ravensdene* (NY) 225: Forewarned is forearmed. **1932** BFlynn *Murder* (P) 203: Forewarned is forearmed, you know. **1938** CFGregg *Brazen* (L) 101: The old adage, "forewarned is forearmed." **1951** CHare *English* (L) 30: Forewarned is forearmed. **1955** SNGhose *Flame* (L) 193: To be forewarned is to be forearmed. **1958** TSouthern *Flash* (NY) 195: Forewarned is quite often, as they say, forearmed. **1961** TWalsy *Eye* (NY DBC) 15: Forewarned is forearmed. **1966** WTrevor *Love* (L) 110: Forearmed is forewarned. **1968** RMStern *Merry* (NY) *Præmonitus, præmunitus*—forewarned, forearmed. **1971** GBaxt *Affair* (NY) 89: Forewarned is forearmed. **1976** DWilliams *Unholy* (NY) 46: Forewarned . . . forearmed. EAP F265; TW 144; Brunvand 53.

F239 **Forgive** (forget) and forget (forgive)

1909 JCLincoln *Keziah* (NY) 240: Forget and forgive. **c1910** EWallace *Nine Bears* (L 1928) 28: Neither forgets nor forgives. **1913** EDBiggers *Seven Keys* (I) 43: To forgive and forget. **1920** AChristie *Mysterious Affair* (NY) 24: Forget or forgive. **1933** AAllen *Loose* (NY) 286: Forgive and forget. **1936** GDHCole *Sleeping* (NY) 293: She wants to forgive me and forget him. **1937** GGVanDeusen *Henry Clay* (B) 126: A man who never forgot and seldom forgave. **1940** RKing *Holiday* (NY) 165: All was forgiven and forgotten. **1950** SJepson *Hungry* (NY) 71: Forget it—and forgive me. **1956** *BHerald* 4/24 11: They will never forget or forgive. **1957** JMerrill *Seraglio* (NY) 295: All was forgiven, forgotten. **1960** EWolf *Rosen-*

bach (Cleveland) 553: Philip was not one to forget and forgive. **1963** DHayes *12th of Never* (NY DBC) 109: Forgive and forget. **1966** GKanin *Remembering* (NY) 247: Forgiving is one thing . . . forgetting is another. **1970** DStuart *Very* (NY) 50: Forgive and forget. **1975** NFreeling *Bugles* (NY) 42: Forgets and forgives nearly everything. EAP F266; TW 144.

F240   To hold the Fort
1932 JVTurner *Who Spoke* (L) 24: He's holding the fort. **1937** CBush *Eight O'Clock* (NY) 170: Carry can hold the fort here. **1941** VWMason *Rio Casino* (NY) 42: I'm holding the fort. **1950** RStout *In the Best* (NY) 105: So you're holding the fort. **1958** RFenisong *Death* (NY) 166: I'm leaving you here to hold the fort. Cole 53: To hold.

F241   Fortune and her wheel (*varied*)
1925 JSFletcher *Secret* (B) 233: Then a sudden turn of fortune came—the wheel spun his way. **1928** AGMacleod *Marloe* (NY) 20: A not altogether welcome turn of fortune's wheel. **1930** HFootner *Mystery* (NY) 40: A little different turn of fortune's wheel. **1932** VWilliams *Mystery* (B) 157: One of those unforeseen twists of fortune's wheel. **1936** RAFreeman *Penrose* (NY) 8: The turning of the wheel of fortune. **1947** VWBrooks *Times of Melville* (NY) 102: Prepared for any turn of the wheel of fate. **1947** WMoore *Greener* (NY 1961) 28: The wheel of Fortune had been a long time turning before stopping at the proper spot. **1962** MJosephson *Life* (NY) 276: Depending on how the wheel of fortune turned for them. **1969** ELeComte *Notorious* (L) 157: The wheel of fortune was deceptive in its lurchings up and down. **1971** HGregory *House* (NY) 257: The Wheel of Fortune was slowly turning toward disillusionment. **1973** KCampbell *Wheel of Fortune* (I). **1978** DNDurant *Bess* (NY) 203: Fate's wheel had turned full circle. EAP F269; TW 144(1).

F242   Fortune favors fools
1928 FGibbons *Red Knight* (NY) 39: The fortune that favours fools. **1961** OManning *Great* (NY) 68: Fortune favors fools. *Oxford* 281–2.

F243   Fortune favors the bold (brave) (*varied*)
1928 GDilnot *Great Detectives* (L) 190: Fortune favours the bold. **1930** APHerbert *Water* (NY) 77: Fortune favours the brave. **1934** AGilbert *Man in Button* (L) 282: Fortune and Love, they say, love the bold heart. **1934** HBrooke *Web* (NY) 118: The motto: *Audaces fortuna juvat.* **1942** SEMorison *Admiral* (B) 199: Fortune always favors the brave. **1951** JCollier *Fancies* (NY) 183: Fortune favors the brave. **1954** MColes *Brief* (NY) 113: Fortune favours the bold. **1964** RConquest *World* (NY) 59: The theory that fortune favours the brave. **1966** WTrevor *Love* (L) 250: He had heard of fortune favouring the brave. **1970** JVizzard *See* (NY) 66: Fortune favors the brave. **1973** DGilman *Palm* (NY) 45: *Fortes fortuna iuvat* or Fortune favors the bold. EAP F271; TW 144(2).

F244   Fortune is fickle
1938 WNMacartney *Fifty Years* (NY) 46: Fortune is an essentially feminine and fickle goddess. **1969** ABarton *Penny* (L) 38: Fortune . . . is fickle. EAP F273.

F245   The Fortunes of war
1914 PGWodehouse *Little Nugget* (NY 1929) 219: It's the fortune of war. **1936** LRGribble *Riley* (L) 207: The fortune of war favoured the detective. **1936** JMWalsh *Crimes* (L) 198: It's the fortunes of war. **1940** MBoniface *Murder as* (NY) 149: The fortunes of war. **1945** FLockridge *Payoff* (P) 128: It's the fortunes of—well, of war. **1953** WBlunt *Pietro's* (L) 173: The fortunes of war are ever changing. **1963** MInnes *Connoisseur's* (L) 115: The fortune of war. **1967** JAxelrad *Freneau* (Austin) 123: The fortunes of war were incalculable. **1971** RLFish *Rub* (NY) 79: The fortunes of war. EAP W25.

F246   Like Forty
1930 EDTorgerson *Murderer* (NY) 131: It was snowing like all forty. **1936** CMRussell *Death* (NY) 77: The forties, they say, are dangerous. TW 145; Brunvand 53.

F247   As cunning (artful) as a **Fox**

1920 GBMcCutcheon *Anderson Crow* (NY) 196: As cunning as a fox. **1931** FBeeding *Three* (B) 85: Mortimer was cunning as a fox. **1931** GTrevor *Murder* (L) 256: As cunning as an old fox. **1956** MProcter *Pub* (NY) 111: Gunner was as cunning as a whole family of foxes. **1958** HWeenolsen *To Keep* (NY) 510: Cunning as a fox. **1961** MErskine *Woman* (NY) 34: Artful as a dog fox. **1963** RWarner *Pericles* (L) 51: He was as cunning as a fox. **1972** SAngus *Arson* (NY) 24: Cunning as a fox. EAP F279. Cf. Brunvand 53(1).

F248   As cute (acute) as a **Fox**

1940 LBrock *Stoat* (L) 136: Two London smoothies—'cute as foxes. **1953** VPJohns *Murder* (NY 1962) 166: Althea was . . . cute as a fox [*sly*]. **1982** CMacLeod *Wrack* (NY) 64: Cute as a fox and twice as big a stinker. Cf. As cunning *above*; As sharp, shrewd, sly, wily *below*.

F249   As quick as a **Fox**

1932 SHPage *Resurrection* (NY) 84: He's quick as a fox. TW 145(6).

F250   As red as a **Fox** (tail)

1941 HCBailey *Orphan Ann* (NY) 109: Red as a fox. **1959** EHuxley *Flame* (L) 12: Soil red as a fox. **1968** JDHicks *My Life* (Lincoln, Neb.) 26: Red as a fox's tail. Whiting F589.

F251   As sharp as a **Fox**

1936 VMcHugh *Caleb* (NY) 82: Sharper'n an old dog fox. **1957** LBrackett *Tiger* (NY) 129: Quinn . . . looked as sharp as an old dog fox. **1960** MProcter *Devil's* (NY DBC) 77: He's as sharp as a fox.

F252   As shrewd as a **Fox**

1956 *NYTimes Book Review* 8/12 1: He [*Roosevelt*] was . . . as shrewd as a fox. **1966** ESGardner *Worried* (NY) 59: Shrewd like a fox. Brunvand 54(3).

F253   As sly (shifty, wary) as a **Fox**

1925 BAtkey *Pyramid* (NY) 88: As shifty as a fox. **1929** JSFletcher *Ransom* (NY) 56: As sly as a fox. **1931** HHolt *Necklace* (NY) 174: He's as wary as a fox. **1950** IFletcher *Bennett's* (I) 260: Looked sly as a fox. **1959** A

Sillitoe *Saturday* (NY) 28: Sly as a fox. **1964** SRansome *Meet* (NY DBC) 100: As sly and careful as an old fox. EAP F280; TW 145(7).

F254   As wily as a **Fox**

1935 LGolding *This Wanderer* (NY) 261: Wily as a fox. Apperson 688: Wily.

F255   The **Fox** changes his skin but not his habits

1936 EQueen *Halfway* (NY) 5: The fox changes his skin . . . but not his habits. EAP F284; *Oxford* 284–5.

F256   To be crazy (stupid) like a **Fox** (*varied*)

1934 ESGardner *Howling Dog* (NY) 59: He's crazy like a fox; 135. **1938** JAllen *I Lost* (NY) 197: He's crazy like a fox. **1947** HCahill *Look* (NY) 210: Stupid like a fox. **1953** BMcMillion *Lot* (P) 161: Crazy like a fox, she was. **1959** JLatimer *Black* (NY) 31: Crazy . . . like bitch fox. **1962** FCrane *Amber* (NY) 109: Crazy like a fox. **1966** MWorthington *Strange* (NY) 149: He's crazy as a fox. **1967** HStone *Funniest* (NY) 187: "The killer would have to be insane to think he could do it." "And he isn't?" . . . "Like the proverbial fox, a rabid fox perhaps, but still a fox." **1972** HHarrison *Montezuma* (NY) 139: He is stupid like a fox. Taylor *Prov. Comp.* 30; Berrey 148.9, 168.6, 257.11, 317.6.

F257   To put the **Fox** to guard the hen-house (*varied*)

1956 *NYTimes* 8/5 2E: A shocking case of putting the fox to guard the henhouse. **1956** *Time* 9/24 4: A picture of the proverbial fox guarding the chickens. *Oxford* 285: Fox to keep. Cf. TW 145(11).

F258   To smell a **Fox**

1927 RAFreeman *Cat's Eye* (NY) 156: I suspect Master Percy smells a fox. **1933** RA Freeman *Dr. Thorndyke Intervenes* (L) 241: Evidently he "smelt a fox." *Oxford* 745: Smell a rat (quote 1595).

F259   **Free**, gratis, and for nothing

1926 MLewis *Island* (L) 291: Free, gratis and for nothing. **1936** LBrock *Stoat* (L) 54:

Free gratis and for nothing. **1938** CFGregg *Brazen* (L) 36: Some advice, free, gratis and for nothing. **1955** PWentworth *Gazebo* (L 1965) 66: Get the house, free, gratis and for nothing. TW 145–6(1).

F260 **Free**, white and twenty-one (*varied*)
1932 CFGregg *Body* (L) 110: She's free, white, and twenty-one. **1933** BRoss *Drury Lane's* (NY) 13: Free, white, over twenty-one. **1940** CWorth *Trial* (NY) 93: I'm an American citizen, free, white and twenty-one. **1949** RChandler *Little* (NY 1951) 75: I'm free, white and twenty-one. **1955** A Christie *Hickory* (NY) 59: She's free, white, and twenty-one. **1959** JABrussel *Just* (NY) 164: I was, as the expression goes, free, white, and quite a bit over twenty-one. **1959** HReilly *Not Me* (NY DBC) 88: He was free, white and going on for forty. **1964** WTrevor *Old Boys* (NY) 58: We are free, white, and over twenty-one. **1971** CAird *Late* (NY) 24: Free, white, and not more than twenty-five. **1975** TWells *Hark* (NY) 113: He's free, white, and over twenty-one. Berrey 381.3.

F261 To take **French** leave (*varied*)
1905 JBCabell *Line* (NY 1926) 101: Taking French leave. **1925** GKnevels *Octagon* (NY) 257: Taken French leave. **1933** BGraeme *I'm Perfect* (P) 215: I have taken English leave. **1938** EPOppenheim *Curious* (B) 74: She was taking French leave. **1942** JDCarr *Emperor's* (NY) 69: I am not taking English leave. **1951** RLHine *Relics* (NY) 109: Some offenders took French leave. **1954** GFowler *Minutes* (NY) 174: He took French leave. **1959** SSterling *Body* (NY) 190: The General has taken Dutch leave. **1966** LPDavies *Who Is* (NY) 143: To take French leave. **1968** ERaymond *Story* (L) 147: They took a frequent French leave. **1972** RBernard *Illegal* (NY) 56: He took French leave. EAP F294.

F262 A **Friday** face
1968 RGoulart *Sword* (NY) 117: Why the Friday face? *Oxford* 288.

F263 On **Friday** the weather changes
1918 CTorr *Small Talk* (Cambridge, Eng.) 6: When the weather do change, it do gen-

erally change upon a Friday [*Devon*]. Whiting F622; *Oxford* 288. Cf. Dunwoody 101.

F264 Fair-weather **Friends**
1931 RAFreeman *Mr. Pottermack* (L) 167: These fair-weather friends. **1939** DCDisney *Golden Swan* (NY) 78: The loss of fair-weather friends. **1956** ADuggan *Winter* (L) 148: A friend for fair weather only. **1959** JFleming *Malice* (NY) 6: A fair-weather friend. **1962** AWaugh *Early* (L) 62: Friendship is a fair-weather business. **1964** DForbes-Robertson *My Aunt* (NY) 11: Fair-weather friends. **1970** RAtkin *Revolution* (NY) 267: A fair-weather friend. **1973** DLeitch *God* (L) 132: A lot of foul weather friends. **1975** DMDisney *Cry* (NY) 52: Fair-weather friend, fair-weather cousin. EAP F18.

F265 **Friends** are known in adversity (*varied*)
1933 DEMuir *In Muffled* (L) 171: It's the old platitude—Adversity shows your true friends. **1935** RCWoodthorpe *Shadow* (NY) 232: There is nothing better than misfortune for showing us who are our best friends. **1962** BWilliams *Well-dressed* (NY DBC) 116: It is said that a man didn't know his true friends until times of adversity. **1967** AWaugh *My Brother* (L) 15: No man knows who his friends are till he is in trouble. *Oxford* 289.

F266 A **Friend** in need is a friend indeed (*varied*)
1915 JBuchan *Thirty-Nine* (NY) 154: He was a true friend in need. **1929** HAdams *Caroline* (P) 247: She was a real pal in Judy's time of need. **1930** JGBrandon *McCarthy* (L) 188: Your English proverb: "A friend in need is a friend indeed." **1938** EBell *Fish* (NY) 87: I say a friend in need is a friend indeed. **1954** JWMeagher *Through Midnight* (B) 146: A friend in need is a friend indeed. **1957** *BHerald* 7/17 34: "I wish I could be somebody's friend. I'd even be glad to be a friend in need." "Indeed?" **1960** AWUpfield *Mystery* (L) 134: You are indeed a friend in need. **1966** PFHealy *Cissy* (NY) 157: A friend in need is a friend indeed. EAP F297; TW 146(2); Brunvand 54.

F267 Give and give back make the best **Friends**

1932 EFrankland *Huge* (L) 147: Give and give back make the best friends. Whiting G95: Give.

F268 Old **Friends** are best

1931 HReilly *Murder* (NY) 115: Old friends are best. **1932** EDBiggers *Keeper* (L) 270: Old friends are best friends. **1935** SVestal *Wine Room* (B) 4: There are no greater blessings on this earth than old friends and old wine. **1941** JPhilips *Oddson* (NY) 59: Old friends are the best friends, I guess. **1950** HGreen *Nothing* (NY) 106: No friend like an old friend. **1952** KFuller *Silken* (L) 10: No friends like old friends, you know, in spite of the years between. **1959** JWelcome *Run* (NY) 97: Old friends, after all, are best. EAP F303.

F269 To have a **Friend** at court

1917 GRSims *My Life* (L) 143: It is always well to have friends at court. **1922** JJoyce *Ulysses* (NY 1934) 308: He had a friend in court. **1924** JJFarjeon *Master* (NY) 301: There's nothing like a friend at court. **1930** LBrock *Murder* (NY) 17: Willing to act as friend at court; 112. **1934** SPalmer *Murder* (L) 243: You could use a friend at court, as the saying goes. **1947** AGilbert *Death in* (L) 30: You know what they say about a friend at court. **1959** GAshe *Pack* (NY) 37: He had no special friend at court. **1961** ESherry *Call* (NY DBC) 7: He had a friend at court. **1963** WMasterson *Man on* (NY DBC) 56: Always good to make a friend at court. **1973** AGilbert *Nice* (NY) 101: Never any harm having a friend in court. EAP F305.

F270 What a **Friend** gets is not lost

1933 NGordon *Shakespeare* (NY) 237: It isn't lost, what a friend gets. **1965** ASharp *Green Tree* (NY 1966) 167: No loss what a friend gets. *Oxford* 487: Lost.

F271 Not give a **Frig**

1954 MMcCarthy *Charmed* (NY) 66: I don't give a frig. **1959** FSmith *Harry* (B) 58: She does not give two frigs for what anybody thinks about her. Cf. Partridge 302; Spears 147.

F272 To be more **Frightened** than hurt (*varied*)

1908 LFBaum *Dorothy and the Wizard of Oz* (I) 24: More frightened than he was injured. **1928** WMcFee *Pilgrims* (NY) 377: More frightened than hurt, as you English say. **1929** RConnell *Murder* (NY) 74: She's more scared than hurt. **1932** NTrott *Monkey* (NY) 101: He was more scared than hurt. **1955** Miss Read *Village* (L 1960) 201: More scared than hurt. EAP A44; TW 147(1). Cf. Cry *above.*

F273 As flat as a **Fritter**

1928 RPThompson *Giant Horse* (C) 198: I'm flat as a fritter. Whiting *NC* 409: Flitter (for Fritter). Cf. Flapjack *above;* Pancake *below.*

F274 As naked as a **Frog**

1963 RAHeinlein *Glory* (NY) 180: Naked as a frog. Wilstach 271.

F275 A big **Frog** (toad, fish) in a small puddle (*varied*)

1930 RKing *Somewhere* (NY) 79: A big mental frog in a little mental puddle. **1931** EA Blake *Jade* (NY) 234: I prefer to be the big frog in the little pond. **1931** HBurnham *Murder* (NY) 181: Randall was the big frog in the small puddle of Vineville. **1934** EB Black *Crime* (NY) 245: The big frog of the puddle. **1937** ESGardner *D.A. Calls* (NY) 228: You may be a big toad in a small puddle. **1938** WNMacartney *Fifty Years* (NY) 104: It is all a choice between being a big toad in a little puddle or a little toad in a big puddle. **1946** HHowe *We Happy* (NY) 170: The big frog in the small puddle. **1948** CLLeonard *Fourth* (NY) 151: She likes being a big frog in a little puddle. **1954** TDuBois *Seeing* (NY) 20: A small fish in a very large and dirty pond. **1956** AAFair *Beware* (NY DBC) 142: He's a big toad in a small puddle. **1960** EWolf *Rosenbach* (Cleveland) 31: The big toad from the big pond back home in the little pond. **1962** AGilbert *Uncertain* (NY DBC) 27: I'd sooner be a big fish in the village pond than a minnow in the ocean. **1965** AGilbert *Voice* (NY) 88: Foreman was quite a big frog in a little pond. **1965** RJWhite *Dr. Bentley* (L) 48: A big fish in a little pond. **1966** JBell *Death*

(NY) 35: A large pebble on a small beach. **1968** RStout *Father* (NY) 166: He had always been a tadpole in a big frog pond as a public-relations counselor. **1969** DMorris *Human* (NY) 62: Being a big fish in a little pond cannot blot out dreams of a bigger pond. **1970** WMasterson *Death* (NY) 57: Better to be a big frog in a small puddle, et cetera. **1973** MSadler *Circle* (NY) 38: To be a big fish in a smaller pond. **1975** LSde Camp *Lovecraft* (NY) 442: [He] was a very large frog in a very small puddle. TW 376: Toad(4); Brunvand 51: Fish(3).

F276 To blow and puff like a **Frog**

1931 MAllingham *Police* (NY) 46: A slightly pathetic, overheated old gentleman, blowing and fuming like the proverbial frog. Taylor *Prov. Comp.* 65: Puffy as a Toad.

F277 As fine as **Frog hair** (*varied*)

1957 *BangorDN* 3/1 21: I feel fine as frog hair. **1958** *Time* 7/14 43: I feel fine as a frog hair split four ways—and you don't get no finer than that. **1959** *Time* 5/4 12: Wage increases are as useless as fuzz on a frog. **1960** VWilliams *Walk* (NY) 76: Fine as frog hair. **1974** WCAnderson *Damp* (NY) 45: Ah'm fine as frog hair. Whiting *NC* 412(4); Taylor *Prov. Comp.* 40. Cf. Tits *below*.

F278 As white as **Frost**

1958 WHCanaway *Ring-givers* (L) 44: As white as frost. TW 147(1): Frost-white.

F279 To put the **Frosting** on the cake

1966 PGWodehouse *Plum* (L) 134: This put the frosting on the cake. **1974** WCAnderson *Damp* (NY) 128: This really put the frosting on the cake.

F280 Stolen **Fruit** is sweet

1927 AWynne *Sinners* (P) 44: Stolen fruit, I suppose, is always sweet. **1943** PCheyney *Dark Dust* (NY) 63: All women believe that stolen fruit is sweetest. **1945** RLHines *Confessions* (L) 226: Stolen fruits and stolen holidays are sweetest. **1958** RHutton *Of Those* (L) 15: Stolen fruits may be the sweetest. **1971** EHCohen *Mademoiselle* (B) 22: Stolen fruits are sweeter. Whiting *NC* 413(1); Brunvand 54(2); *Oxford* 279–80.

F281 As nutty as a **Fruitcake** (*varied*)

1938 PHaggard *Death Talks* (NY) 22: He sounds as nutty as fruitcake. **1946** ABCunningham *Death Rides* (NY) 27: He must be nutty as a fruit cake. **1952** ESGardner *Grinning* (NY) 179: He was nutty as a fruit cake. **1954** DAlexander *Terror* (NY) 96: He's nutty as a Hershey bar. **1959** JLatimer *Black* (NY) 83: Nuttier than a Christmas fruit cake. **1960** RMacdonald *Ferguson* (NY) 262: He's nuttier than a fruitcake. **1963** RA Heinlein *Podkayne* (NY) 119: One of them [*children*] nutty as a Christmas cake. **1969** AGilbert *Missing* (NY) 93: Nutty as a fruit cake. **1970** HCarvic *Miss Seeton Draws* (NY) 142: Nutty as fruitcakes, both of them. **1975** MVonnegut *Eden* (NY) 163: I was nutty as a fruitcake. Wentworth 203: Fruitcake, 361.

F282 Out of the **Frying pan** into the fire (*varied*)

1900 CFPidgin *Quincy A. Sawyer* (B) 315: Jump out er the fryin'-pan inter the fire. **1922** JJoyce *Ulysses* (NY 1934) 109: Out of the frying pan of life into the fire of purgatory. **1927** RKing *Mystery* (NY) 90: A jumping out of the frying pan into the fire. **1927** SWilliams *Drury* (NY) 109: Out of the frying-pan, and into a far worse fire. **1933** ATorrance *Junglemania* (NY) 305: We had jumped from the frying pan into the fire. **1938** DHume *Corpses* (L) 194: I might easily jump from the proverbial fryingpan into the fire. **1939** DHume *Death Before* (L) 122: To take that famous leap out of the frying pan. **1945** ACampbell *With Bated* (NY) 193: Walking out of the frying-pan into the fire. **1945** LGay *Unspeakables* (NY) 19: From the skillet to the fire. **1951** IChase *New York 22* (NY) 15: I wouldn't hop out of the frying pan until the fire's lighted. **1951** KBennett *Wink* (L) 65: The fire was no less uncomfortable than the frying-pan. **1954** IFleming *Live* (NY 1959) 35: Better the frying pan you know than the fire you don't. **1957** *NYTimes Book Review* 4/28 42: Ross . . . struggles to keep the Cherokees from the frying pan of complete appeasement and the fire of total war. **1957** *BangorDN* 7/16 13: A Rockland man jumped out of the frying pan but landed in the proverbial fire this morning. **1960** KCrichton *Total* (NY)

46: I had leaped from the frying-pan into the fire. **1960** LFielden *Natural* (L) 36: Out of the fire into the frying-pan. **1973** APrice *Colonel* (NY) 27: Out of the fire into the frying pan. **1974** DMDisney *Don't Go* (NY) 172: Any chance of jumping out of the frying pan into the fire. EAP F315; TW 147–8; Brunvand 54–5.

F283 Not give (care) a **Fuck** (screw)

1934 HMiller *Tropic of Cancer* (NY 1962) 22: Nobody gives a fuck. **1939** HMiller *Capricorn* (NY 1961) 14: I didn't give a fuck. **1947** BDeVoto *Letters* ed WStegner (NY 1975) 292: He announced "I don't give a f—k for Harvard." **1949** JReach *Late* (NY) 38: I don't give a screw. **1968** JUpdike *Couples* (NY 1969) 128: What the fuck do I care? **1971** NBogner *Making* (NY) 226: I . . . don't give a fuck. **1972** RMaugham *Escape* (L) 228: You don't care a fuck about me. **1972** PWarner *Loose* (NY) 164: I really don't give a flying fuck. **1974** CWilson *Schoolgirl* (NY) 170: He didn't give a screw. **1976** JSScott *Bastard's* (NY) 7: I don't care a fuck. **1976** WMarshall *Hatchet* (NY) 105: I couldn't give a fuck. **1981** NFreeling *Arlette* (NY) 80: [He] don't care a fuck about the poor. Spears 149(10); Wentworth 204. For *screw* in this sense see Amer. Herit. Dict. screw *n.* 6.

F284 To add **Fuel** to the fire (*varied*)

1933 CWells *Clue* (NY) 206: Add fuel to the fire. **1940** DHume *Five Aces* (L) 230: He was anxious to add a little fuel to the fire. **1960** EWolf *Rosenbach* (Cleveland) 384: Adding fuel to the fire. **1963** RJStonesifer *W.H. Davies* (L) 112: Added coals to the fire. **1966** JAiken *Beware* (NY) 178: Added fuel to the fire. **1982** VWebb *Little* (NY) 53: You are the first to see the danger of heaping coals on the fire, or whatever the saying is. EAP F317.

F285 **Fun** and games (*varied*)

1932 PMacDonald *Maze* (L) 222: There had been fun and games [*sex*]. **1938** CRawson *Death from* (L) 40: Zelma and Sabbat were having fun and games behind Alfred's back. **1943** PCheyney *Dark Dust* (NY) 25: What she called "fun and games." **1950** STruss *Never* (NY) 147: In the middle of all the fun and games [*sex*]. **1955** AHunter *Gently Does* (L) 119: The fun and games were over with the arrest of Peter. **1959** HCarmichael *Marked* (NY) 131: He was having fun and games with a married woman. **1959** AGilbert *Death* (NY) 169: Let's stop all this fun and games [*nonsense*]. **1962** DGillon *Unsleep* (NY) 104: I'm too sleepy for fun and games. **1964** JHillas *Today* (NY) 256: A little old-fashioned fun and games seemed indicated [*trouble*]. **1964** RRendell *From Doon* (L 1966) 67: They've had their fun and games in the back of the car. **1965** RMacdonald *Far Side* (NY) 76: More fun and games [*fighting*]. **1970** ELathen *Pick* (NY) 176: This isn't just fun and games. **1971** JMuir *Stranger* (NY) 92: They just like fun and games [*sex*]. **1973** EMcBain *Let's Hear* (NY) 48: Police work is not all fun and games. Spears 151.

F286 **Fun** is fun

1939 GBagby *Corpse* (NY) 241: Fun's fun. **1942** CRice *Big Midget* (NY 1948) 156: Fun is fun . . . and all that. **1947** FCDavis *Thursday's* (NY) 131: Fun's fun. **1958** MKenton *Candy* (NY 1965) 132: Fun is fun. **1963** ABurgess *Enderby* (NY 1968) 43: Fun's fun, as the saying goes. TW 148(1). Cf. Joke *below*.

F287 As funny (glum) as a **Funeral**

1941 RStout *Alphabet* (NY) 180: You're as funny as a funeral. **1956** EDillon *Death* (L) 111: He looked as glum as a funeral. Wilstach 166: A funeral in a snowstorm.

F288 To be (not to be) one's **Funeral**

1906 JCLincoln *Mr. Pratt* (NY) 106: 'Twa'nt none of my funeral. **1931** SChalmers *Whispering* (NY) 14: Another thing that seems none of his funeral. **1932** JMarsh *Murder* (L) 159: It's more your funeral than ours. **1939** RPhilmore *Death in* (L) 114: That's his funeral. **1953** BCarcy *Their Nearest* (NY) 94: It was not her funeral. **1956** WTenn *Human* (NY) 33: It's your funeral. **1960** JO'Hara *Ourselves* (NY) 191: But as the fellow says, it's your funeral. **1963** HPentecost *Only* (NY DBC) 50: As the cliché goes . . . it's your own funeral. TW 148.

F289 To see one in the **Funny papers**
1954 EWalter *Untidy* (P) 175: Bye, toots, see you in the funny papers. **1960** JBWest *Taste* (NY) 23: See you . . . in the funny papers. Berrey 350.8. Cf. See you in Church *above*.

F290 The **Fur** will fly (*varied*)
1923 VWilliams *Orange* (B) 123: You'll see the fur fly. **1924** CWells *Furthest* (P) 157: The fur flies. **1932** FWCrofts *Sudden* (NY) 212: You should have heard the fur fly. **1935** HHolt *Tiger* (L) 72: There would have been fur and feathers flying if they had met. **1947** JDCarr *Sleeping* (NY) 154: You were going to make the fur fly. **1951** RStout *Curtains* (NY) 74: Fur was going to fly. **1956** RStout *Eat* (NY) 222: The fur began to fly. **1957** *NYTimes* 3/31 17: Much political fur will fly before the votes are counted. **1960** RStout *Too Many* (NY) 79: The fur would fly. **1967** JBrunner *Quicksand* (NY) 14: Feathers would fly. **1969** RStout *Death* (NY) 88: Now the fur will start to fly. **1973** A Roudybush *Gastronomic* (NY) 26: The fur began to fly. EAP F318.

F291 To rub the **Fur** the wrong way
1938 WNMacartney *Fifty Years* (NY) 381: You are rubbing the fur the wrong way. **1938** CRawson *Death from* (L) 28: That was the wrong way to rub the Colonel's fur. **1940** WReed *No Sign* (NY) 153: Madden was careful not to rub his fur the wrong way. NED Fur *sb.*[1] 2b: Stroke.

F292 As hot as a **Furnace**
1968 JMorris *Eating* (L) 25: As hot as a furnace. Cf. Whiting F704.

F293 To smoke like a **Furnace**
1934 ABliss *Murder* (P) 194: He smokes like a furnace. Clark *Similes* 221.

F294 As dark as old **Fury**
1932 EQueen *Egyptian* (NY) 27: Dark as old fury. Whiting *Devil* 246(7).

F295 To blow a **Fuse**
1956 SDean *Marked* (NY) 97: Celeste blew a fuse. **1973** WMasterson *Undertaker* (NY) 121: He blew the proverbial fuse. Wentworth 45.

F296 **Fuss** and feathers
1923 HGartland *Globe* (NY) 280: Married quietly without fuss or feathers. **1938** NJones *Hanging Lady* (NY) 86: Cleared up without fuss or feathers. **1940** TChanslor *Our First* (NY) 12: Not any fuss-and-feathers when they put me underground. **1949** CDickson *Graveyard* (NY) 87: He was all fuss and feathers. **1957** *BangorDN* 1/10 14: Why all the fuss and feathers about polio clinics? **1957** *New Yorker* 9/21 33: Without fuss and feathers. **1961** PGWodehouse *Ice* (NY) 221: All this fuss and feathers. **1966** AAHomans *Education* (B) 94: With a minimum of fuss and feathers. TW 148(1).

G

G1 **Gabriel's** horn (*varied*)

1900 CFPidgin *Quincy A. Sawyer* (B) 74: Ef angel Gabriel blew his horn now. **1926** AMerritt *Ship* (NY) 19: I don't want to be disturbed for anything less than Gabriel's trumpet. **1932** MRRinehart *Miss Pinkerton* (NY) 5: Nothing but Gabriel's horn would ever wake me again. **1937** DHume *Halfway* (L) 171: Stay here until they toot the last trumpet. **1949** JEvans *Halo* (NY) 173: A blackjack had spread his brains over a hotel rug and left him to wait for Gabriel's horn. **1962** JJMcPhaul *Deadlines* (NY) 232: When Gabriel blows his horn. **1969** EAnderson *Miss* (B) 146: A house that will last until Gabriel blows his horn. TW 149; Brunvand 56; *Oxford* 294.

G2 To blow the **Gaff**

1922 JJoyce *Ulysses* (NY 1934) 161: [He] blew the gaff on the invincibles. **1928** ABerkeley *Silk* (NY) 47: You'll blow the gaff. **1940** NMarsh *Death of a Peer* (L) 249: The gaff is blown, the cat out of the bag, and the balloon burst. **1946** CBush *Second Chance* (L) 155: I blew the gaff. **1962** FHoyle *A for Andromeda* (NY 1964) 53: He'll blow the gaff to anyone. **1968** HCarvic *Picture* (NY) 176: She might blow the gaff on him. **1971** AGarve *Late* (NY) 119: Blown the gaff. *Oxford* 70: Blow.

G3 To stand the **Gaff**

1940 HReilly *Death Demands* (NY) 78: You'll have to stand the gaff. **1960** JBarry *Malignant* (NY) 192: He couldn't stand the gaff. Berrey 270.3.

G4 No **Gains** without pains

1956 *NYPost* 9/26 5: No gains without pains. EAP G2.

G5 As bitter as **Gall**

1925 AJSmall *Death* (NY) 12: Bitter as gall. **1927** CRogers *Colonel Bob* (NY) 67: Bitter as gall. **1933** GBegbie *Sudden* (L) 128: Bitter as gall. **1941** CFAdams *Decoy* (NY) 20: The coffee was bitter as gall. **1948** DCDisney *Explosion* (NY DBC) 156: Sense as bitter as gall. **1957** EMButler *Heine* (NY) 237: As bitter as gall. **1967** JPurdy *Eustace* (NY) 92: He wept tears as bitter as gall. EAP G4; TW 149(1).

G6 To work like a **Galley** slave

1930 IWray *Vye* (L) 97: She works like a galley-slave. **1947** MBurton *Will in the Way* (NY) 166: He works like a galley slave. **1952** JSherwood *Ambush* (NY) 113: You have to work like a galley slave. EAP G9. Cf. Slave *below*.

G7 To knock (be knocked) **Galley-west**

1900 CFPidgin *Quincy A. Sawyer* (B) 342: Knocked it galley-west. **1921** JCLincoln *Galusha* (NY) 251: To knock another beetle galley-west. **1924** CWells *Furthest* (P) 163: Knocking me galley west. **1930** ALivingston *Murder* (I) 316: All our work had gone galley-west. **1934** PATaylor *Sandbar* (NY) 71: Enough to knock an average income galley-west for Sundays. **1940** TChanslor *Our First* (NY) 78: Knocked her galley-west. **1950** EQueen *Double* (B) 147: Knocked galley-west. **1953** SRansome *Hear* (NY) 108:

Something had knocked him galley-west emotionally. **1967** RLockridge *With Option* (P) 164: "A storm like that knocks everything galley-west. What does galley-west mean, by the way? Where does it come from?" "I haven't the faintest idea." TW 149.

G8   The **Game** is hardly worth the chase
1928 CJDutton *Clutching* (NY) 3: The game was hardly worthy of the chase. EAP G13.

G9   The **Game** is not (is) worth the candle (*varied*)
1914 PGWodehouse *Little Nugget* (NY 1929) 91: Find the game worth the candle. **1919** JBCabell *Jurgen* (NY 1922) 84: The game is well worth the candle. 175: Hardly worth the candle? **1932** TSmith *Night Life* (NY) 167: Whether the game is worth the candle remains to be seen. **1935** CFGregg *Danger* (L) 250: The game might be worth the candle. **1939** AGilbert *Clock* (L) 72: The game wouldn't be worth the candle. **1941** FWCrofts *Circumstantial* (NY) 123: The game wouldn't be worth the candle. **1949** RLTaylor *W.C.Fields* (NY) 247: The game was scarcely worth the candle. **1952** GBullett *Trouble* (L) 137: Finding (as they say) the game not quite worth the candle. **1956** *NYTimes* 11/11 IX: The game is worth the candle. **1956** EMcBain *Mugger* (L 1963) 102: She's making the game worth the candle. **1959** GMitchell *Man Who* (L) 154: The point is whether the stink is going to be worth the candle. **1962** WHaggard *Unquiet* (NY DBC) 49: The game would hardly be worth the candle. **1969** PAnderson *Satan's* (NY) 30: As the saying goes on earth, the game is not worth the lantern. **1970** DMDevine *Illegal* (NY) 99: The game's not worth the candle. **1972** SCloete *Victorian* (L) 54: On "a game being worth, or not worth, the candle" basis. **1976** CLarson *Muir's* (NY) 94: The game is worth the candle. **1976** JPorter *Package* (NY) 136: His job wouldn't be worth a candle. EAP G12.

G10   The **Game** is up
1920 BEStevenson *Gloved Hand* (NY) 294: The game was up. **1932** HFootner *Casual* (L) 81: The game was up. **1946** HRCamp-bell *Crime in Crystal* (NY) 229: She decided the game was up. **1953** JRhode *Mysterious* (NY DBC) 123: The game was up. **1957** CEMaine *Isotope* (L) 84: He knows the game's up. **1974** ROllard *Pepys* (NY) 146: The game was up. EAP G14; Brunvand 56(2).

G11   To beat (be beaten) at one's own **Game**
c1923 ACrowley *Confessions* ed JSymonds (L 1969) 548: To beat your mother at her own game. **1931** HFootner *Easy* (L) 32: They have beaten us at our own game. **1935** CRawson *Footprints* (L) 264: Anyone can be fooled at the other man's game. **1953** GPhelps *Dry Stone* (L) 156: Determined to beat them at their own game. **1956** RRobinson *Landscape* (L 1963) 190: One has to beat them at their own game. **1962** DHonig *No Song* (L) 154: You can't beat the rich at their own game. **1970** AALewis *Carnival* (NY) 282: Tried to beat me at my own game. EAP G17; TW 150(5). Cf. Brunvand 145: Trick.

G12   **Garbage** in, garbage out
1970 RRhodes *Inland* (NY) 109: The computer doesn't read the letters—"Garbage in, garbage out," as the saying goes. Cf. What Goes in *below.*

G13   As mean as **Garbroth**
1937 CGordon *Garden* (NY) 56: Mean as Garbroth. DA Gar 2(1).

G14   A common or **Garden** (this or that)
1927 VBridges *Girl* (P) 141: This is no ordinary common or garden burglary. **1927** AGilbert *Tragedy* (NY) 126: A common or garden murder. **1930** DDeane *Mystery* (L) 120: Not a common or garden rifle. **1938** CRawson *Death from* (L) 136: This isn't the usual garden variety of murder case. **1943** PCheyney *Dark Dust* (NY) 51: An ordinary common or garden bastard. **1951** ECrispin *Long* (L 1958) 29: Just common or garden snobs. **1959** PMacDonald *List* (NY) 180: This isn't any common-or-garden, four-for-a-shilling murderer. **1962** MInnes *Connoisseur's* (L) 89: A common-or-garden squalid crime. **1967** CAird *Most Contagious* (NY) 170: A common or gardener [*sic*] laborer. **1973** AGilbert *Nice* (NY) 130: The

murder might be a common or garden crime. **1976** MWarner *Medium* (NY) 91: Your common or garden variety villain. NED Garden *sb.* 5c.

G15 Every **Garden** has its weeds

1942 SEMorison *Admiral* (B) 518: Every garden has its weeds. *Oxford* 296.

G16 To go into the **Garden** and eat worms (*varied*)

1932 HCBailey *Case* (NY) 301: "Where are you going?" "Into the garden to eat worms." **1933** DLSayers *Hangman's* (NY) 99: Gone into the garden to eat worms. **1936** PATaylor *Crimson* (L) 136: Can I eat worms in your garden? No one loves me. **1942** HCBailey *Nobody's* (NY) 94: Come into the garden and eat worms. **1946** AE Martin *Death in the Limelight* (NY) 150: I'll go into the orchard and eat worms. **1967** JDCarr *Dark* (NY) 169: Go out and chew worms [*sulk*]. **1984** ACross *Sweet Death* (NY) 158: An I'll-go-into-the-garden-and-eat-worms kind of feeling.

G17 To lead (be led) up (down) the **Garden** (path)

1928 TKindon *Murder* (NY) 165: [He] led Mrs. Gaskel a very long way up the garden path. **1929** GMitchell *Speedy* (NY) 71: You are trying to lead me up the garden. **1930** WLewis *Apes* (NY 1932) 552: Led Cockeye up the garden. **1931** MMagill *Death* (P) 242: Perhaps I did lead poor John up the garden path. **1932** GKChesterton et al. *Floating* (NY) 162: Lead you up the garden. **1935** PMcGuire *Murder* (NY) 283: You're leading us right up the garden. **1936** DHume *Bring 'Em Back* (NY) 108: Lead a girl along the garden path of deceit. **1937** GGoodchild *Having No* (L) 118: He was leading us up the garden path. **1937** DInce *In Those* (L) 227: I've been leading him down the garden. **1940** RDarby *Death Conducts* (NY) 58: But I wasn't being led down the garden path by any such obvious red herring. **1948** CBush *Curious* (NY) 83: I led him up the garden a bit. **1954** HGardiner *Murder* (L) 129: He's been leading women up the garden path all his life. **1956** AGilbert *Riddle* (NY) 25: Led up the garden

path. **1959** AGilbert *Death* (NY) 187: He had led her straight up the garden—hanging was too good for him. **1964** RMeinertztragen *Diary* (L) 260: Accused of having led the girl down the garden path. **1965** HWaugh *End* (NY) 166: To lead her down the garden path. **1971** AChristie *Nemesis* (NY) 30: He was leading her up the garden path. **1974** JBrunner *Total* (NY) 44: He had been led a very long way up a very twisted garden path. Partridge 316.

G18 To cook with **Gas**

1950 ESGardner *Musical* (NY) 70: Now you're cooking with gas. **1962** FHoyle *A for Andromeda* (NY 1964) 57: We're cooking with gas. Wentworth 121: Cook.

G19 To blow a **Gasket**

1957 MScherf *Judicial* (NY) 55: He'd blow a gasket. **1959** HLGold *World* (NY 1961) 55: There's no use blowing a gasket. Wentworth 45: Blow.

G20 A creaking **Gate** lasts long (*varied*)

1928 RAFreeman *As a Thief* (L) 8: One repeats the old saying of "the creaking gate," and perhaps makes unduly light of habitual illness. **1932** FDGrierson *Murder* (L) 137: But creaking hinges last a long time. **1934** AChristie *Three Acts* (NY) 30: He was the sort of creaking gate that would have lived to be ninety. **1953** AChristie *Funerals* (NY) 183: Uncle Timothy will probably outlive us all. He's what is known as a creaking gate. **1960** HEBates *Aspidistra* (L) 37: Bertie's just a creaking gate. That sort that lasts for years. **1967** FSwinnerton *Sanctuary* (NY) 28: Creaking doors hang longest. *Oxford* 154: Creaking.

G21 To give the **Gate** to someone

1932 AGibbs *Murder* (NY) 89: I gave him the gate completely; 240. **1939** EDean *Murder Is* (NY) 263: Petty . . . gave her the gate. **1940** WCClark *Murder Goes* (B) 48: The girl who was given the gate by Jack. **1955** FCrane *Death* (NY) 138: He gave her the gate. **1958** HMasur *Murder* (NY 1959) 42: You gave Crawford the gate. **1961** LThayer *And One* (NY DBC) 22: She certainly had given him the gate. **1964** SBecker *Covenant*

(NY) 154: Rosemary gives me the gate. Wentworth 209.

G22 Between you and me and the **Gate-post** (*etc.*) (*varied*)

1924 JSFletcher *Mazaroff* (NY) 19: Between you and me and the post. **1925** AJSmall *Death* (NY) 187: Between you and me and that door-knob. **1925** JSFletcher *Wrychester* (L) 182: Just between you and me and the doorpost. **1926** LThayer *Poison* (NY) 236: Between you and me and the lamp post. 263: Between you and me and the gate post. **1928** AWynne *Red* (P) 73: Between you and me, haystack, and all that sort of thing. **1930** FWCrofts *Sir John* (NY) 164: Between you and me and the wall. **1932** LAdamic *Laughing* (NY) 86: Between you and me and that lamp-post. **1932** JSFletcher *Man in the Fur Coat* (L) 116: Between you and me and the post, as the saying is. **1934** FDGrierson *Murder* (L) 207: Betwixt you an' me an' the gatepost, as the sayin' is. **1936** JTFarrell *World* (NY) 232: Between you and me and the lamppost. **1937** JDonovan *Case* (L) 30: Between you and me and the gate-post. **1948** ESGardner *Lonely* (NY DBC) 51: Between you and me and the guide post. **1950** SPalmer *Green* (NY) 116: Between you and me and the lamppost. **1959** PSomers *Shivering* (NY) 32: Between you and me and the gatepost. **1963** JLudwig *Confusions* (Greenwich, Conn.) 13: Between you and me and the lamppost. **1975** HLawrenson *Stranger* (NY) 146: Between you and me and the lamp-post. **1975** EGundy *Naked* (NY) 3: Between you, me and this table. EAP P245: Post; TW 151(2); Brunvand 57; DARE i 226: Between . . . post; *Oxford* 57: Between. Cf. Bed-post *above*; Pump *below*.

G23 To talk with a **Gate-post**

1940 MArmstrong *Man with* (NY) 34: Might as well try to chat with a gate post. TW 213: Lamp post (1).

G24 Tell it not in **Gath** *etc.*

1935 BFlynn *Case* (L) 165: Publish his troubles . . . in the streets of both Gath and Ascalon. **1937** JMWalsh *White Mask* (L) 196: Whisper it not in Gath. Tell it not in

the streets of Ascalon. **1965** HActon *Old Lamps* (L) 241: Tell it not in Gath. **1966** EFuller *Successful* (NY) 7: When it was told in Gath and published in the streets of Ashkelon. EAP G26.

G25 To run the **Gauntlet**

1939 LFord *Mr. Cromwell* (L) 137: Running the gauntlet of a pack of jackals. **1941** PWilde *Design* (NY) 171: She should run the gauntlet first. EAP G27; TW 151.

G26 To throw down the **Gauntlet** (*varied*)

1949 JStagge *Three* (NY) 11: To throw down the gauntlet. **1969** SFisher *Saxon's* (LA) 169: I'm laying down the gauntlet. **1972** TCBhaduri *Chambal* (Delhi) 41: He . . . had thrown the gauntlet. **1974** TWells *Have Mercy* (NY) 109: Let them think . . . she had dropped the gauntlets or kicked over the traces or what cliché have you. EAP G28.

G27 It takes three **Generations** to make a gentleman (*varied*)

1955 KAmis *That Uncertain* (L) 13: It took three generations to make a gentleman. **1974** JCrowe *Bloodwater* (NY) 61: The English have a proverb . . . The first generation makes the money; the second goes into politics; the third is a dilettante. TW 151. Cf. Centuries *above*.

G28 **Gentlemen** prefer blonds (*varied*)

1925 ALoos *Gentlemen Prefer Blondes* (NY). **1938** ECVivian *Rainbow* (L) 134: Ages ago . . . it was laid down as an axiom of life . . . that gentlemen prefer blonds. **1945** MBurton *Not a Leg* (NY) 111: Gentlemen prefer blondes, we've been told. **1958** EMcBain *Lady* (NY 1964) 125: The age-old adage . . . that gentlemen prefer blonds. **1961** LNizer *My Life* (NY) 168: A man who is caught with the proverbial blonde is hardly in a position to take the offensive against his wife. **1964** AHunter *Gently* (NY) 23: Some gentlemen prefer blonds. **1968** NBowen *Hear* (NY) 106: I never did believe that stuff about men liking blonds.

G29 Let **George** do it

1930 JFDobie *Coronado* (Dallas) 111: A remarkable aptitude for letting George do it.

1931 PATaylor *Cape Cod* (NY 1971) 276: Let George do it. **1942** PGWodehouse *Money* (NY) 165: The fine old slogan, "Let George do it." **1957** *BangorDN* 3/9 22: The old time motto of "Let George do it." **1958** *BGlobe* 9/25 14: George just isn't doing it. **1958** *BHerald* 10/19 45: This . . . let-George-do-it-approach. **1966** HPentecost *Hide* (NY) 5: The phrase, "Let George do it." **1970** ELathen *Pick* (NY) 161: A let-George-do-it attitude. **1972** SCloete *Victorian* (L) 193: Let George do it. I'm OK, Jack . . . Wentworth 212.

G30 Soon **Got**, soon gone

1922 JJoyce *Ulysses* (NY 1934) 444: Soon got, soon gone. *Oxford* 752: Soon gotten.

G31 As crazy (*etc.*) as all **Get-out**

1906 JCLincoln *Mr. Pratt* (NY) 183: You was crazy as all get out. **1908** JCLincoln *Cy Whittaker* (NY) 13: Stubborn as all get-out. **1931** DAldis *Murder in a Haystack* (NY) 212: I ran like all get-out. **1932** PATaylor *Death* (I) 139: She was godly as all get-out. **1940** DCCameron *Grave* (NY) 47: Busy as all get out. **1951** RKing *Duenna* (NY) 108: A heart as big as all get out. **1960** JWelcome *Stop* (NY) 24: I felt as tired as all get out, and as tight strung as a violin string. **1967** GBrooks *If Strangers* (NY) 110: "Heavy as all get-out," a phrase of my father's. **1970** DShannon *Unexpected* (NY) 123: The living room's neat as all get-out. **1973** MGEberhart *Murder* (NY) 62: Calm as all get-out. Whiting *NC* 413; Taylor *Prov. Comp.* 43.

G32 As gray as a **Ghost**

1930 ATrain *Adventures* (NY) 337: Gray as a ghost. **1965** DoctorX *Intern* (NY) 64: Gray as a ghost. **1973** JBWest *Upstairs* (NY) 45: [He] looked gray as a ghost.

G33 As pale as a **Ghost**

1927 RAFreeman *Magic* (NY) 200: As pale as a ghost. **1963** BWAldiss *Airs* (L) 78: You're as pale as a ghost. **1967** MPeissel *Mustang* (NY) 300: He was as pale as a ghost. **1973** DGilman *Palm* (NY) 106: Pale as a ghost. EAP G37; TW 151(1); Brunvand 57(1).

G34 As silent as a **Ghost**

1934 GSinclair *Cannibal* (NY) 185: He was silent as a ghost. **1954** MAllingham *No Love* (NY) 209: As silent as ghosts. Whiting *NC* 413(2).

G35 As white as a **Ghost**; Ghost-white

1913 MRRinehart *Jennie Brice* (NY 1947) 355: He looked ghost-white. **1925** TFPowys *Mr. Tasker* (L) 128: She lay white as a ghost. **1940** CDickson *And so to Murder* (NY) 191: You're as white as a ghost. **1971** DPryde *Nunaga* (NY) 272: Face white as a ghost. **1972** LNiven *Ringworld* (L) 181: He was no longer ghost-white. EAP G38; Brunvand 57(2).

G36 The **Ghost** walks

1922 JJoyce *Ulysses* (NY 1934) 122: The ghost walks. **1970** JLeasor *They Don't* (NY) 7: The ghost walks every Friday if you're on someone's payroll. NED Ghost 8b; Partridge 327.

G37 To give up the **Ghost**

1932 JVTurner *Who Spoke* (L) 85: His colleagues gave up the ghost and said nothing. **1934** JVTurner *Murder* (L) 172: Naylor groaned and gave up the ghost. **1951** ADean *August* (NY) 7: The head light gave up the ghost. **1971** JFraser *Death* (NY) 44: The brass bell . . . gave up the ghost. EAP G39; TW 152(3); Brunvand 58(3).

G38 As firm (steady) as (the rock of) **Gibraltar**

1928 EDBiggers *Behind* (NY) 236: I am firm like well-known Gibraltar rock. **1935** WMartyn *Nightmare* (L) 250: My hands will be as steady as Gibraltar. **1937** MAllingham *Late Pig* (L 1940) 21: All firm as the Rock of Gibraltar. **1955** MHutchins *Memoirs* (NY) 63: As firm as the rock of Gibraltar. **1959** DCushman *Goodbye* (NY) 253: Firm as the rock of Gibralter. **1961** AGilbert *After* (NY DBC) 163: Their alibi was as firm as Gibraltar rock. **1963** EMCottman *Out-Island* (NY) 185: She was as steady as Gibraltar. **1974** DCavett *Cavett* (NY) 302: His cheek muscle was firm as Gibraltar rock. Whiting *NC* 414(1).

G39 As safe as (the rock of) **Gibraltar**

1938 SHAdams *World* (B) 17: Safe as the Rock of Gibraltar. **1941** GBenedict *Deadly Drops* (NY) 100: We're safe as Gibraltar. Cf. As safe as a Rock *below*.

G40 As solid as (the rock of) **Gibraltar**

1932 BRoss *Tragedy of Y* (NY) 169: The walls . . . are as solid as Gibraltar. **1956** MGilbert *Be Shot* (L) 118: He looked as solid and reliable as the Rock of Gibraltar. **1959** AGilbert *Prelude* (NY DBC) 103: Bessie . . . was as solid as the Rock of Gibraltar. **1968** KTopkins *Passing* (B) 39: Solid as the rock of Gibraltar. **1970** NMonsarrat *Breaking* (L) 412: The house, solid as Gibraltar. Whiting *NC* 414(2); Taylor *Western Folklore* 17(1958) 18: Rock.

G41 As strong (sound) as **Gibraltar**

1927 JTaine *Quayle's* (NY) 121: Our security was as strong as Gibraltar. **1972** MGilbert *Body* (NY) 149: Jack's as sound as the Rock of Gibraltar. EAP G40.

G42 The **Gift** of the gab

1903 MLPeabody *To Be Young* (B 1967) 269: A gift of gab. **1915** JBuchan *Thirty-Nine* (NY) 28: Gift of the gab. **1931** JDonavan *Talking Dust* (L) 237: A heaven-sent gift of the gab. **1941** HAshbrook *Purple Onions* (NY) 214: Your gift of the gab. **1956** BWAldiss *Saliva* (L) 162: You've no gift of the gab. **1959** JBell *Easy* (NY) 125: A gift of the gab. **1966** SHignett *Picture* (NY) 88: The great gift of the gab. **1970** KGiles *Death* (L) 141: Gift of the gab. **1974** ROllard *Pepys* (NY) 249: His gift of the gab. EAP G41.

G43 As high as **Gilderoy's** kite

1934 HCorey *Crime* (NY) 35: The colt threw him higher'n Gilderoy's kite. **1959** *CSMonitor* 3/5 22: She's higher than Gilroy's kite. Prancing in the stanchion, dancing on her tail, blatting and carrying on [*of a cow*]. TW 152.

G44 To look blue about the **Gills**

1932 GLane *Hotel* (L) 209: You look rather blue about the gills. **1941** MHolbrook *Suitable* (NY) 48: Looking blue around the gills. NED Gill 5b[1]. 3b.

G45 To look green about the **Gills**

1927 FWCrofts *Ponson* (NY 1931) 18: Green about the gills. **1938** JGBrandon *Cork Street* (L) 54: I've seen women go green about the gills with envy. **1949** JLane *Murder Spoils* (NY) 212: It's too bad you're so green around the gills. **1960** PGWodehouse *Jeeves* (L) 156: He was looking . . . fairly green about the gills. **1964** DDeJong *Whirligig* (NY) 56: You look kind of green around the gills. Amer. Herit. Dict. Gill 3; Wentworth 214–5.

G46 To look pale about the **Gills**

1932 GHeyer *Footsteps* (L) 202: Looking rather pale about the gills. **1965** WRBurkett *Sleeping* (NY) 207: A little pale around the gills. Brunvand 58(1).

G47 To look white about the **Gills**

1928 JJConnington *Tragedy* (B) 33: A bit white about the gills. **1934** VGielgud *Death* (L) 8: White as a sheet about the gills. **1947** HWade *New Graves* (L) 118: Rather white about the gills. **1955** CMWills *Death* (L) 97: Looking a bit white about the gills. **1960** SDean *Murder* (NY DBC) 77: He's white around the gills. **1968** RBusby *Main Line* (NY) 16: He had gone . . . white about the gills. EAP G46; TW 152.

G48 To take the **Gilt** off the gingerbread (*varied*)

1928 RHWatkins *Master* (NY) 61: That rather takes the gilt off the gingerbread. **1929** AHayes *Crime* (L) 204: Gilding the gingerbread, so to speak. **1930** DDeane *Mystery* (L) 58: The gilt is too thick for the quality of the gingerbread to matter. **1938** JJConnington *For Murder* (L) 209: The gilt was off the gingerbread. **1940** JJConnington *Four Defences* (B) 197: The gilt was off the gingerbread. **1943** NMarsh *Colour Scheme* (L 1960) 235: That takes the icing off old Ackrington's gingerbread. **1945** GBellairs *Calamity* (NY) 110: Being one of the family, the writer gilds the gingerbread a bit. **1951** JCollier *Fancies* (NY) 6: He had properly taken the gilt off all the gingerbread. **1960** HSDavies *Papers* (L) 117: The gilt was off the gingerbread. **1962** NFreeling *Death* (NY 1964) 83: And indeed the gilt wore off the gingerbread (he greatly enjoyed such phrases; what on earth did they mean?—English was a fascinating language) very quickly. **1968** MRowell *Below* (L) 160: That soon knocked the gilt off the gingerbread. **1969** RPearsall *Worm* (L) 66: Added gilt to the gingerbread. **1974** AMenen *Fonthill* (NY) 50: It quite took the gilt off the gingerbread. EAP G45.

G49 As dry (keen, smart) as **Ginger**

1936 NBlake *Thou Shell* (L) 138: It's made my mouth dry as ginger. **1936** WMartyn *House* (L) 125: As keen as ginger to find it out. **1963** MPHood *Sin* (NY) 43: Good youngster, smart's ginger.

G50 **Ginger** for pluck

1960 MProcter *Devil's* (NY DBC) 57: She's a smashin' little red head. Ginger for pluck, they always say. Partridge 329: Ginger 4. Cf. Wentworth 215.

G51 A **Girl's** first man *etc.*

1939 LBrock *Riddle* (L) 213: A girl's first affair is never quite forgotten. **1960** FSWees *Country* (NY) 154: But you know what they say—a girl's first man. **1963** MMcCarthy *Group* (NY) 172: Some women, they say, never get over their first man, especially if he were skillful. Whiting *NC* 414. Cf. First Love *below*.

G52 **Girls** will be girls

1922 AAMilne *Red House* (NY 1959) 72: Girls will be girls. **1934** ABinns *Lightship* (NY) 220: Girls would be girls. **1936** HCBailey *Clue* (L) 204: Girls would be girls. **1951** EPaul *Murder on* (NY) 277: Girls will be girls. **1967** RJackson *Occupied* (L) 226: Girls will be girls. **1971** PTabor *Pauline's* (Louisville) 119: Girls will be girls. TW 152(6). Cf. Boys will *above*; People *below*.

G53 **Give** and take

1940 MBurton *Murder in* (L) 97: A certain amount of give and take. **1941** MTYates *Midway* (NY) 209: Give and take is Jessie's motto . . . Also tit for tat. **1946** GBellairs *Death in the Night* (NY) 20: Give and take's my motto. **1954** EFrankland *Foster* (NY) 167: I know that give and give back make the best of friends. **1961** JBingham *Night's*

(L 1965) 127: A spirit of give and take, as the saying is. **1966** HHarrison *Make Room* (NY) 185: I believe in fair play, give and take. EAP G50; TW 152(3).

G54 He **Gives** twice who gives quickly

1932 ARolls *Lobelia* (L) 255: The old adage, *Bis dat qui cito dat.* **1941** EPhillpotts *Ghostwater* (NY) 182: He gives twice who gives at once. **1968** PDickinson *Skin* (L) 170: The only Latin he could remember, "*Bis dat qui cito dat.*" **1970** WBlunt *Dream* (L) 126: *Bis dat qui cito dat*—He gives twice who gives quickly. EAP G48.

G55 It is more blessed to **Give** than to receive

1973 JPorter *It's Murder* (NY) 143: It's more blessed to give than to receive, as the parsons say. EAP G47.

G56 To **Give** as good as one takes (*varied*)

1910 JCLincoln *Depot Master* (NY) 288: He gets as good as he sends. **1935** DHume *Murders* (L) 180: Always give as good as you take. **1938** FWCrofts *End* (L) 25: She gave him as good as she got. **1940** GBagby *Corpse Wore* (NY) 220: Lena was giving as good as she got. **1959** TWalsh *Dangerous* (B DBC) 123: Giving back as good as he got. **1967** HBlyth *Old Q* (L) 50: He would give back as much as he received. **1968** MGibbon *Inglorious* (L) 18: He gave as good as he got. **1970** CDrummond *Stab* (NY) 20: Giving as good as she got. **1973** BBehan *My Life* (LA) 141: She gave as good as she got. **1974** GNRay *H.G.Wells* (New Haven) 176: Rebecca . . . gave as good as she got. EAP G49, G113.

G57 To stick in one's **Gizzard**

1930 HCBailey *Garston* (NY) 161: What keeps sticking in my gizzard. **1930** JRhode *Venner* (L) 169: Those two documents . . . stick in your gizzard. **1936** JGBrandon *Pawnshop* (L) 128: One thing stuck in his gizzard. **1947** MBurton *Will in the Way* (NY) 29: It's that point . . . that sticks in my gizzard. **1958** ECRLorac *People* (NY) 85: That sticks in my gizzard. EAP G51. Cf. Brunvand 58(1): Fret. Cf. Crop *above*.

G58 Gladness follows sadness

1900 CFPidgin *Quincy A. Sawyer* (B) 377: How true it is . . . that gladness quickly follows sadness. *Oxford* 691: Sadness.

G59 As bright as **Glass**

1956 SSmith *Shrew* (NY 1959) 57: Eyes which became as bright as glass. Whiting G108.

G60 As brittle as **Glass**

1945 HQMasur *Bury Me* (NY 1948) 169: Her face was as brittle as glass. **1952** KMKnight *Valse* (NY) 134: The wood is as brittle as glass. **1959** RMartin *Key* (NY DBC) 80: Her voice was as brittle as glass. EAP G52; TW 153(1).

G61 As calm as **Glass**

1931 SLeacock *Sunshine* (Toronto 1960) 36: As calm as glass [*a lake*]. **1956** IFleming *Diamonds* (NY 1961) 144: Sea's as calm as glass. Wilstach 41. Cf. Mill pond, As still as Glass *below*.

G62 As clear as **Glass**

1929 EPOppenheim *Nicholas* (B) 104: A . . . stream . . . clear as polished glass. **1933** EO'Duffy *Bird Cage* (NY) 78: A clear-as-glass affair. **1937** JWVandercook *Dark Islands* (NY) 329: Water clear as glass. **1940** NMarsh *Death of a Peer* (B) 144: It's clear as glass. **1950** MMurray *Neat* (NY DBC) 140: The water is as clear as glass. **1953** TWicker *Kingpin* (NY) 11: It's all clear as glass. **1961** WMasterson *Evil* (NY) 89: Clear as glass. **1966** SGCrawford *Gascoyne* (L) 105: It's pretty clear, clear as glass, that he's following orders. **1975** TWells *Hark* (NY) 26: His eyes were clear as glass. EAP G53.

G63 As slick as **Glass**

1933 NBMavity *Fate* (NY) 182: That soil is slick as glass. **1954** MLSettle *Love* (L) 185: Now it [*a face*] was slick as glass. **1967** HBorland *Hill Country* (P) 14: Icy slush, slick as glass. **1972** RHGreenan *Queen* (NY) 113: He's slick as glass with the chicks. Taylor *Prov. Comp.* 73.

G64 As slippery as **Glass**

1930 JGBrandon *Murder* (L) 181: The tiles were as slippery as glass. **1932** TPerry *Never* (NY) 130: The man's tone was cool and slippery as glass. **1946** ECrispin *Holy Disorders* (NY) 93: They're slippery as glass. **1948** MColes *Among* (NY) 113: As slippery as glass. **1957** SDean *Murder* (NY) 176: Road's slippery as greased glass. **1962** FCrane *Amber* (NY) 86: She's slippery as greased glass. TW 153(2); Brunvand 58(1).

G65 As smooth as **Glass**

1927 WDSteele *Man Who* (NY) 274: Smooth as glass. **1930** FWCrofts *Sir John* (NY) 41: The sea . . . was like the proverbial glass. **1944** MVenning *Jethro* (NY) 129: Water as smooth as glass. **1952** EPaul *Black* (NY) 28: He was smooth as glass. **1956** RMacdonald *Barbarous* (NY) 141: Young and pretty and smooth as glass. **1961** RFoley *It's Murder* (NY DBC) 148: Hair . . . as smooth as glass. **1962** GMaxwell *Ring* (NY) 128: When the sea is really as smooth as glass—a much misused simile, for it rarely is. **1972** JMcClure *Caterpillar* (NY) 161: As smooth as glass. EAP G54; TW 153(3); Brunvand 59(2).

G66 As still as **Glass**

1903 EChilders *Riddle* (NY 1940) 21: The cove was still as glass. **1942** MColes *They Tell* (NY) 57: The water was still as glass. **1952** HFMPrescott *Man on* (NY) 86: It's as still as glass. **1966** GWBrace *Between Wind* (NY) 147: The night stayed as still as glass. Cf. As calm as Glass *above*.

G67 As transparent (open) as **Glass** (*varied*)

1929 HFootner *Doctor* (L) 61: Lads, as transparent as window glass. **1934** HFootner *Dangerous* (L) 249: Good-humoured, and apparently as open as window-glass. **1937** MBurton *Murder* (L) 212: Charley's as transparent as glass. **1943** SShane *Lady . . . Million* (NY) 108: We see through him like a glass. **1964** JJMarric *Gideon's Vote* (NY) 75: It's transparent as glass. **1965** HWaugh *Girl* (NY) 63: She was as transparent as glass. **1971** SHElgin *Furthest* (NY)

69: He was as transparent to her as a pane of glass. EAP G56.

G68 When the **Glass** falls low, prepare for a blow

1932 GDyer *Five* (B) 195: The old saying "When the glass falls low, prepare for a blow." Dunwoody 83: Barometer.

G69 Sic transit **Gloria** mundi

1948 LFord *Devil's* (NY) 34: Sic transit gloria mundi. **1968** WASwanberg *Rector* (NY) 152: *Sic transit gloria mundi.* EAP G61.

G70 As tight as a **Glove**

1960 JJMarric *Gideon's Risk* (NY) 119: You've got them as tight as a glove. Taylor *Prov. Comp.* 82: Tight.

G71 To cast away like an old **Glove** (*varied*)

1905 JBCabell *Line* (NY 1926) 130: To be cast away as though she were an old glove. **1932** CFGregg *Body* (L) 161: He chucks 'em away like an old glove. **1956** *Punch* 12/12 698: To cast aside like an old glove. **1965** JPorter *Dover Two* (NY 1968) 139: Tossed aside like an old glove. *Oxford* 725: Shoe.

G72 To fit like a **Glove**

1913 JSFletcher *Secret* (L 1918) 119: The door fits like a glove. **1922** JJoyce *Ulysses* (NY 1934) 153: Fitted her like a glove, shoulders and hips. **1923** JSFletcher *Copper* (NY) 218: It'll fit their tastes like a glove. **1932** CBush *Unfortunately* (L) 270: It fits like a glove. **1933** JVTurner *Amos* (L) 256: His overcoat fitted him with the snugness of the proverbial glove. **1941** IMontgomery *Death Won* (NY) 108: It fitted her like a glove. **1946** ABCunningham *Death Rides* (NY) 195: The facts began to fit like a glove fits the hand. **1954** IFleming *Live* (NY 1959) 126: It fitted like a glove. **1958** GMitcham *Man from* (NY) 92: This Kennedy business fits the situation like a glove. **1964** HWaugh *Missing* (NY) 162: Fits him like a glove. **1965** PAudemars *Fair* (NY) 73: These other crimes fit [him] like a glove. **1972** JAnderson *Alpha* (NY) 131: Everything fits . . . like a glove. **1973** TZinkin *Weeds* (L) 26: Her dresses fitted me like a glove. EAP G62.

G73 To handle with **Gloves** (kid gloves) (*varied*)

1921 IOstrander *Crimson* (NY) 126: Handled with gloves. **1933** CCNicole *Death* (L) 139: I've handled him with kid gloves long enough. **1938** HFootner *Murder* (L) 44: To be handled with gloves. **1939** GHCole *Murder for* (NY) 74: I got to handle 'em with kid gloves. **1941** MPRea *Compare* (NY) 34: Use your kid gloves on them. **1949** RLTaylor *W.C.Fields* (NY) 309: To handle him with kid gloves. **1956** ESGardner *Terrified* (NY) 50: You have to handle him with kid gloves. **1959** WMiller *Cool* (B) 92: I wouldn't touch them with kid gloves. **1964** TPowell *Corpus* (NY) 84: They'll handle you with kid gloves. **1970** PAlding *Guilt* (NY) 101: It's [he] whom we have to handle with kid gloves. **1971** PMoyes *Season* (NY) 98: Sylvie . . . had been treated with kid gloves. TW 153(4–5).

G74 (With) **Gloves** off

1930 FDGrierson *Blue Bucket* (NY) 151: It's gloves off now. TW 153(3).

G75 To stick (hang on) like **Glue**

1929 MMPropper *Strange* (NY) 269: They just hang on to it like glue. **1933** GDHCole *Death* (NY) 143: Stuck there like glue. **1937** KRoberts *Northwest* (NY) 372: All Scots stick together like glue. **1955** AWest *Heritage* (NY) 103: He'd stick like glue. **1956** *BangorDN* 11/9 26: That spook'll stick to him like glue. **1960** HReilly *Follow* (NY DBC) 74: I'd stick to the person . . . like glue. **1967** MGEberhart *Woman* (NY) 180: They hung on like glue. **1972** WJWatkins *Ecodeath* (NY) 68: Snyder made a mental note to stick to Ashley like glue. **1976** RBDominic *Murder* (NY) 103: She stuck to you like glue. Whiting *NC* 414(2); Taylor *Prov. Comp.* 44.

G76 To strain at a **Gnat** and swallow a camel (*varied*)

1914 CPearl *Morrison of Peking* (Sydney 1967) 305: Strain at a gnat and swallow a camel. **1917** GRSims *My Life* (L) 332: After swallowing the camel . . . why gape at the gnat? **1926** AFielding *Footsteps* (L) 51: No one could accuse you of swallowing camels, but you certainly do go for any gnat in sight. **1932** HWade *Hanging* (L) 231: It is absurd for me, having swallowed a camel, to strain at a gnat. **1937** SPalmer *No Flowers* (L) 221: Don't go swallowing camels or straining at gnats or whatever it is. **1938** ECRLorac *John Brown's* (L) 182: Neither straining at gnats, nor refusing to swallow camels. **1944** HTalbot *Rim* (NY 1965) 86: There's such a thing as snatching at a straw and swallowing a camel. **1946** VKelsey *Whisper Murder* (NY) 186: I may swallow a gnat now and then, but I draw the line at pianos. **1947** HCahill *Look* (NY) 310: An old policy of swallowing a few gnats to get a camel. **1954** MMcCarthy *Charmed* (NY) 197: Straining at a gnat and swallowing a camel. **1958** *BHerald* 6/15 sec. III 6: To strain at a gnat and swallow a camel. **1960** LFielden *Natural* (L) 281: We strain at gnats and swallow camels. **1966** CWMorton *It Has* (P) 232: If the Civil Service had been straining at a gnat in my case, it had certainly swallowed a few camels in some of the new colleagues. **1967** PMcGerr *Murder* (NY) 127: Or was he, in Biblical terms, straining at a gnat and swallowing a camel? **1974** FWatson *Year* (NY) 13: A year of straining at gnats and tilting at windmills. EAP G64; TW 153–4. Cf. To swallow a Cow *above*.

G77 One must **Go** back before he can go forward

1961 FSinclair *But the Patient* (NY) 151: We've got to go back before we can go forward. *Oxford* 667: Recoil; Tilley 369.

G78 To **Go** farther and fare worse (*varied*)

1928 SFWright *Deluge* (NY) 140: You might go further and fare worse. **1935** BFlynn *Padded* (L) 257: You'd go a long way and fare much worse. **1940** TChanslor *Our First* (NY) 170: I've seen plenty girls go farther and fare worse. **1954** MColes *Brief* (NY) 131: Nevertheless, we calculate we might go further and fare better, despite the proverb. **1959** MPHood *Bell* (NY) 190: You could go far 'n fare worse'n to marry him. **1970** CDBowen *Family* (B) 137: [He] could have sought farther and fared worse.

EAP G65; TW 154(1). Cf. To go through the Woods *below*.

G79 To **Go** west

1916 SRohmer *Tales* (NY 1922) 166: Gone west. **1926** EDBiggers *Chinese* (NY) 20: He may . . . have gone west—as they said in the war. **1930** MPlum *Killing* (NY) 243: Jim went west in the war. **1930** DLSayers *Strong* (L) 14: "To go west" is a well known metaphor for dying. **1931** HHolt *Midnight* (NY) 30: Another shilling goes west. **1932** ACampbell *Murder* (NY) 305: A holiday on the river gone west! **1947** RKing *Lethal* (NY DBC) 50: Mr. Watertown had gone west . . . in the sense that the expression had been used during World War I. **1953** RPostgate *Ledger* (L) 60: Your clue's gone west. **1955** AChristie *Hickory* (NY) 58: Another good man gone west. **1969** AChristie *Hallowe'en* (NY) 200: So that pretty story's gone west. **1976** SBrett *So Much* (NY) 63: Another good idea gone west. Partridge 337; Taylor *Proverb* 192.

G80 To **Go** while the going is good (*varied*)

1928 EWallace *Sinister* (NY) 19: Get out while the going's good. **1929** RJCasey *Secret* (I) 171: They're going to ease out gracefully while the going is good. **1930** HCBailey *Garston* (NY) 242: She'd better go while the going was good. **1931** LEppley *Murder* (NY) 200: I got out while the getting was good. **1937** JJConnington *Minor* (L) 235: It seemed best to go while the goin' was good. **1951** DMDisney *Straw* (NY) 219: Clear out now while the going's still good. **1955** NMarsh *Scales* (B) 82: Let's go while the going's good. **1960** SRaven *Brother* (NY) 17: To go while the going was good. **1969** DClark *Nobody's* (NY) 185: Get out . . . while the going's good. **1970** ELathen *Pick* (NY) 70: Got out while the going was good. Partridge 339: Going's.

G81 What **Goes** in must come out

1970 RLockridge *Twice* (P) 122: What goes in must come out. **1971** BCraig *September* (NY) 75: What goes in, has to come out. EAP G67. Cf. Garbage *above*; Where there is a Way . . . *below*.

G82 What **Goes** up must come down

1929 FAPottle *Stretchers* (NY) 168: What goes up must come down. **1935** FGEberhard *Microbe* (NY) 228: Whatever goes up, must come down, as the old saying goes. **1939** CMRussell *Topaz Flowers* (NY) 70: What goes up must come down. **1945** MColes *Green Hazard* (NY) 150: Everything that goes up . . . must come down. **1951** JBlish *So Close* (NY) 61: What goes up must come down. **1957** *BangorDN* 1/29 14: The old school-boy adage is that whatever goes up must come down. Whiting *NC* 414.

G83 What is **Gone** is gone

1934 AHalper *Foundry* (NY) 391: What's gone is gone. **1951** MGilbert *Death Has* (NY) 161: What's gone is gone. **1955** JBingham *Paton* (L 1964) 137: What's gone is gone. EAP G66.

G84 When you gotta **Go**, you gotta go

1962 JWoodford *Autobiography* (NY) 74: When you gotta go, you gotta go [*die*]. **1965** JPhilips *Black* (NY DBC) 25: When you gotta go, you gotta go [*die*]. **1970** AALewis *Carnival* (NY) 193: When you gotta go you gotta go [*bathroom*]. **1973** JPorter *It's Murder* (NY) 6: When you gotta go, you gotta go. Cf. Berrey 308.2.

G85 To knock (be knocked) for a **Goal**

1921 RLardner *Big Town* (NY) 16: A gal that knocked you for a goal. **1931** GFowler *Great* (NY) 403: I was knocked for a goal. Wentworth 308: Knock [someone] for 3; Berrey 22.3 etc. [*see Index*].

G86 As drunk (soused, stiff, tight) as a **Goat** (billy goat)

1937 JGEdwards *Murder* (NY) 107: "Drunk as a goat." "I've heard that expression all my life. . . . Before this goes any further I think that once and for all she should settle just how drunk is a drunk goat." **1938** CWhitcomb *In the Fine* (NY) 175: He's drunk as a billy-goat. **1938** VWMason *Cairo* (NY) 53: Soused as a billy goat. **1939** KSecrist *Murder Melody* (NY) 80: I've been drinkin'—almost as stiff as a goat. **1942** CRice *Big Midget* (NY 1948) 51: He was drunk as a goat. **1947** VWMason *Saigon* (NY) 70: I'd get tighter than a billy goat.

1948 WPMcGivern *But Death* (NY) 102: Drunker than billy goats. **1950** THoward *Shriek* (NY) 201: He's drunk as a goat. **1959** DMDisney *No Next* (NY) 116: He's drunk as a goat. **1960** ASeager *Death* (NY) 54: She stayed as drunk as a billy-goat. **1961** WVanAtta *Shock* (NY) 14: Drunk as a goat. **1966** CArmstrong *Dream* (NY DBC) 77: She was as drunk as eighteen goats. Spears 165: Goat-drunk, 394: Tight as.

G87 As full as a **Goat**

1920 GBMcCutcheon *Anderson Crow* (NY) 301: You're as full as a goat [*drunk*]. Wilstach 165.

G88 As sore as a **Goat**

1932 ORCohen *Star* (NY) 162: He's sore as a goat. **1942** CRice *Big Midget* (NY 1948) 163: Angela was sore as a goat. Cf. To get one's Goat *below*.

G89 To be made the **Goat**

1928 CJDaly *Man* (NY) 232: You can make me the goat. **1938** GHomes *Man Who* (NY) 258: He picked young Miller as the goat. **1951** DBOlsen *Cat* (NY) 131: She . . . made a goat of you, as the phrase goes. DA Goat 3b(1).

G90 To come to the **Goat's** house for wool

1969 JBoyd *Rakehells* (NY 1971) 143: [He] was coming to the goat's house for wool. TW 154(1). See next entry.

G91 To gather **Goat** feathers

1930 CClausen *Gloyne* (NY) 72: You'll go gathering goat feathers; 225. Cf. *Oxford* 307: Wool; Partridge 337: Goat's wool. Cf. Feathers from a toad *above*.

G92 To get one's **Goat**

1919 AMerritt *Moon Pool* (NY) 260: They get my goat. **1924** AOFriel *Mountains* (NY) 297: Got his goat. **1932** AMSullivan *Last Serjeant* (L) 225: He got Pether's goat, as the Yankees would say. **1936** KMKnight *Wheel* (NY) 49: It got my goat. **1948** CBush *Curious* (NY) 142: Used to get my goat. **1953** CLittle *Black* (NY) 23: That ought to get her goat. **1958** BNichols *Rich* (NY) 128: That young gentleman gets my goat. DA

Goat 3b(3); Partridge 337; Wentworth 218; NED Suppl. Goat 3c.

G93 As old as **God**

1932 RThorndike *Devil* (NY) 201: As old as God. **1948** EQueen *Ten* (NY) 222: His mother's older than God. **1954** DAlexander *Terror* (NY) 168: I'm old as Mrs. God. **1955** MErskine *Old Mrs.* (NY) 12: Looking as old as God's mother. **1963** SForbes *Grieve* (NY) 14: It's as old as God. **1970** RLPike *Reardon* (NY) 92: You've got to be older than God. **1971** PDennis *Paradise* (NY) 241: Rich as God an' even older. Taylor *Western Folklore* 17(1958) 16.

G94 As safe as in **God's** pocket

1934 VLincoln *February Hill* (NY) 208: Safe as God's pocket. **1939** CMRussell *Topaz Flowers* (NY) 168: You're as safe here as in God's pocket. **1943** VSiller *Echo* (NY) 104: The murderer's as safe as he'd be in God's pocket. **1968** WMuir *Belonging* (L) 101: He'll be as safe as if he were in God's pocket.

G95 As slow as **God's** off ox

1960 *BHerald* 2/7 16: I remember him [*father of St. Johnsbury, Vt.*] often referring to an extremely moderate person as being "slower than God's off ox." Cf. DA Off 1b(3).

G96 As sure as **God** made little apples (*varied*)

1928 SLewis *Man Who Knew* (NY) 231: Since God made little apples. **1928** AJSmall *Master* (NY) 321: Sure as God made little apples. **1932** MCJohnson *Damning* (NY) 259: She's coming as sure as the Lord made little apples. **1932** JVTurner *Who Spoke* (L) 198: As certainly as God made little apples. **1933** GDHCole *Death* (NY) 23: Sure as little apples. **1940** MArmstrong *Man with* (NY) 136: As sure as God made little apples. **1954** TDuBois *Seeing* (NY) 62: As sure as God made little apples. **1956** AAtkinson *Exit* (NY) 174: As sure as little apples. **1957** WGoldman *Temple* (NY) 7: As sure as God made green apples. **1958** RMacDonald *Doomstars* (NY) 177: Since God made little green apples. **1965** MFrayn *Tin* (B) 93: As sure as God made little apples. **1966** JStuart

My Land (NY) 57: As sure as God made little green apples. Whiting *NC* 415(3); Taylor *Prov. Comp.* 79: Sure; Wilstach 402. Cf. next entries.

G97 As sure as **God** made little fishes (*varied*)

1913 MRRinehart *Jennie Brice* (NY 1947) 405: As sure as God made little fishes. **1932** MRRinehart *Miss Pinkerton* (NY) 242: As sure as God made little fishes. **1940** HSKeeler *Cleopatra's* (L) 232: As sure as God made little fishes. **1949** KMKnight *Bass* (NY) 213: Sure as God made little fishes. **1952** KMKnight *Death Goes* (NY) 125: As sure as I knew God made little fishes. **1963** DGardiner *Lion* (NY) 141: It sure as little fishes wasn't what he was reading. **1968** ELathen *Stitch* (NY) 88: Sure as God made little fishes.

G98 As sure as **God** made Moses

1922 JJoyce *Ulysses* (NY 1934) 339: As sure as God made Moses. Wilstach 402.

G99 As sure as **God's** in Gloucestershire

1962 RSpeaight *W.Rothenstein* (L) 339: There was an old Gloucestershire saying: "As sure as God's in Gloucestershire." *Oxford* 789: Sure.

G100 As sure as **God's** in heaven (*varied*)

1930 JSFletcher *Matheson* (L) 157: As sure as there's a God in heaven. **1932** NBell *Disturbing* (NY) 14: As sure as God. **1955** JO'Hara *Ten* (NY) 351: As sure as the Lord's above. **1966** ARRandell *Sixty* (L) 45: True's God. EAP G70; TW 154(1).

G101 As tall (big) as **God**

1937 ESGardner *Dangerous Dowager* (NY) 60: He struts around that place ten inches taller than God. **1957** WGoldman *Temple* (NY) 55: Smiling, big as God. **1965** HVanDyke *Ladies* (NY) 9: She was as tall as God.

G102 **God** bless you!

1942 NMarsh *Enter Murderer* (NY) 181: He sneezed violently. "Bless you, Mr. Alleyn," he said piously. **1960** PSBeagle *Fine* (NY 1969) 187: She sneezed. "God bless you." **1969** DShannon *Crime* (NY) 61: Say God bless you when somebody sneezes. **1970** DShannon *Unexpected* (NY) 183: He sneezed . . . "God bless you." EAP G72.

G103   God's (own) country

1902 JLondon *Letters* ed KHendricks (NY 1965) 137: I have heard of God's country. **1913** JCLincoln *Mr. Pratt's Patients* (NY) 251: Going back to God's country. **1930** KCStrahan *Death* (NY) 197: Yakima— God's country. **1938** HHolt *Whispering* (L) 21: In the language of God's own country. **1939** AAbbot *Creeps* (NY) 10: California is God's country. **1941** NMarsh *Death in Ecstasy* (NY) 201: Back home in God's Own Country. **1962** VWMason *Trouble* (NY DBC) 45: Somebody from God's country. **1962** JWoodford *Autobiography* (NY) 6: The American way. The God's country way. **1970** SO'Toole *Confessions* (Minneapolis) 69: We got back to God's country. **1971** BWAldiss *Soldier* (L) 198: God's Own Country was the ironical Fourteenth Army name for Burma. DA God 4(1); NED Suppl. Country 2b.

G104   God deliver me from my friends *etc.* (*varied*)

1937 LFord *Simple Way* (NY) 193: An old saying of Lilac's: "It's you' friends that do you—you' enemies cain' get to you." **1941** FCharles *Vice Czar* (NY) 215: Deliver me from my friends! . . . You can take care of your enemies; but friends . . . are hell on wheels. **1958** *NYTimes* 9/28 4E: "God save me from my friends, I can take care of my enemies." This proverb must be much in the mind of Hugh Gaitskell. **1963** DHamilton *Ambushers* (NY) 7: The military gent, whoever he was, who said that he could deal with his enemies, but God would have to protect him from his allies. **1963** EJHughes *Ordeal* (NY) 136: The I-can-attend-to-my-enemies—but-God-protect-me-from-my-friends attitude. **1966** EConnell *I Had* (NY) 113: I don't know who first said: "My enemies I can handle, but God save me from my friends." **1970** WBlunt *Dream* (L) 50: God preserve me from my friends; my enemies I can look after myself. **1970** JWechsberg *First* (B) 172: A proverb ascribed to Hungarians, Rumanians, and

Bulgarians, all of whom decline to acknowledge authorship, says, "Lord, protect me against my friends, I can take care of my enemies." **1972** RRendell *Murder* (NY) 5: May God protect me from my friends. EAP G73.

G105   God fits the back to its burden (*varied*)

1955 DMDisney *Room* (NY) 131: God makes the back to fit the burden, they say. **1971** EHCohen *Mademoiselle* (B) 80: It is said that God fits the back to its burden. *Oxford* 312: God shapes.

G106   God (the Lord) giveth *etc.*

1972 KCampbell *Thunder* (I) 118: The Lord giveth and the Lord taketh away. EAP G75.

G107   God's help is nearer than the door

1924 LO'Flaherty *Thy Neighbour's Wife* (L) 109: God's help is nearer than the door. **1970** UO'Connor *Brendan* (L) 142: The Irish proverb . . . the help of God is nearer than the door. Whiting G231: Is ever near; *Oxford* 313: Than one fair even.

G108   God (Heaven, the Lord) helps those who help themselves

1929 AFielding *Mysterious* (NY) 257: Heaven helps those that help themselves. **1933** AFielding *Westwood* (NY) 19: Heaven helps those who help themselves. **1937** HCKittredge *Mooncursers* (B) 152: God was more likely to help those who helped themselves. **1940** ECRLorac *Tryst* (L) 117: Heaven helps those who help themselves. **1942** JShepherd *Demise* (NY 1962) 103: The Lord looks out for those who look out for themselves. **1952** HCecil *No Bail* (NY) 46: Heaven helps those who help themselves. **1955** MColes *Man in* (NY) 59: Does not the Scripture tell us that the good God helps those who help themselves? **1956** DWheatley *Ka* (L) 329: The old adage that "God helps those who help themselves." **1958** *TLS* 12/26 750: "God helps those who help themselves" is one of our [*British*] most popular sayings although not quite so popular today as it was one hundred years ago . . . before the advent of the welfare state. **1958** LSdeCamp *Elephant* (NY) 118: 'Tis an old and true saying that the gods help them that help themselves. **1961** SBlanc *Green* (NY DBC) 104: God helps those who help themselves. **1965** JPorter *Dover Two* (NY 1968) 43: [The Bible] also says—"The Lord helps those who help themselves." **1969** ACGraene *Personal* (NY) 295: God helped the man who helped himself. **1974** JWain *Samuel* (NY) 265: Johnson . . . believed firmly that God helped those who helped themselves. **1977** DWilliams *Treasure* (NY) 127: God helps those who help themselves. EAP G77; Brunvand 59(2).

G109 **God** is no respecter of persons (*varied*)

1911 JSHay *Amazing Emperor* (L) 263: Elagabalus was no respecter of persons. **1929** TLDavidson *Murder* (L) 6: Blythe . . . was no respecter of persons. **1935** ECRLorac *Organ* (L) 236: The law is no respecter of persons. **1940** GHCoxe *Lady is Afraid* (NY) 168: Murder was no respecter of persons. **1960** AGilbert *Out for* (NY 1965) 143: Crook, like the Lord God, was no respecter of persons. **1969** JBoyd *Pollinators* (NY) 18: God is no respecter of persons. **1969** DClark *Nobody's* (NY) 37: No disease is a respecter of persons. EAP G80.

G110 **God** knows and he won't tell (*varied*)

1928 RHFuller *Jubilee* (NY) 369: God alone knows and he won't tell; 392. **1938** PMacDonald *Warrant* (NY 1957) 267: God knows! And, as I'm fond of remarking, He won't split. **1955** PMacDonald *Guest* (NY) 114: Gawd knows . . . An' 'E won't split. Partridge 338: And he won't split.

G111 **God** made the country *etc.*

1922 JJoyce *Ulysses* (NY 1934) 280: God made the country, man the tune. **1972** BCatton *Waiting* (NY) 35: People . . . revised the saying: God made the country and man made the city, they said, but the devil himself made the small town. Brunvand 59(3), 92: Man(9); *Oxford* 311.

G112 **God's** plenty

1943 GGCoulton *Fourscore* (Cambridge, Eng.) 245: There was God's plenty. **1957** *Punch* 2/13 254: The riot of "God's plenty"

that awaited them. **1959** RPayne *Gold* (NY) 194: Here was God's plenty. Whiting G228.

G113 **God** sends meat and the devil cooks (*varied*)

1913 HTFinck *Food* (NY) 224: It has been said that God sent us our food and the devils our cooks. **1922** JJoyce *Ulysses* (NY 1934) 169: God made food, the devil the cooks. **1929** JCPowys *Wolf* (NY) 1.129: The Lord gives us beef, but we must go to the Devil for sauce, as my granddad used to murmur. **1969** RBlythe *Akenfield* (NY) 116: The lord sent the meat and the devil sent the cooks. **1973** RCondon *And Then* (NY) 108: God sends meat and the devil sends cooks. EAP G85.

G114 **God** speed the plough

1936 EMeynell *Sussex* (L) 111: "God speed the plough," as the old saying has it. EAP G86.

G115 **God** stone the crows (*varied*)

1956 *New Yorker* 12/8 140: God stone the crows, I don't know. **1956** WMankowitz *Old* (B) 58: Gord [*sic*] stone the crows. **1958** PGWodehouse *Cocktail* (L) 153: Cor lumme, stone the crows. **1966** NMonsarrat *Life(I)* (L) 365: Gawd stone the crows! **1970** KGiles *Death* (L) 8: Stone the crows. Partridge 834: Stone.

G116 **God** tempers the wind to the shorn lamb (*varied*)

1923 HWNevinson *Changes* (NY) 82: The wind was tempered to many a fleeced . . . lamb. **1927** RAFreeman *Magic* (NY) 33: You must temper the wind to the shorn lamb. **1928** SSVanDine *Greene* (NY) 167: The Lord tempers the wind—or is it something about an ill wind I'm trying to quote? **1930** SEMorison *Builders* (B) 306: Tempering the wind to the shorn lamb. **1938** FDGrierson *Cabaret* (L) 172: God tempers the wind to the shorn lamb. **1940** RAFreeman *Mr. Palton* (NY) 43: He frequently tempered the wind to the shorn lamb. **1953** EWTeale *Circle* (NY) 33: How many perversions of observable truth have been cherished in the sayings of past generations: "the wind is tempered to the shorn lamb." "God builds the nest of the blind bird." The wish is father of the thought; the wishful thought becomes the epigram. **1956** JChristopher *Death* (L) 116: Was the wind tempered to the shorn lamb? **1959** RMacDonald *Galton* (NY) 225: You have a reputation for tempering the wind to the shorn lamb. **1960** CDLewis *Buried* (L) 164: He could temper himself to the shorn lamb. **1960** NWilliams *Knaves* (NY) 195: He is the proverbial lamb just waiting to be shorn. **1967** JAxelrad *Freneau* (Austin) 396: The winds of all doctrine were tempered to the shorn lamb of business. **1970** JCreasey *Part* (NY) 97: You needn't temper the wind. **1977** RRendell *Judgment* (NY) 58: God tempers the wind to the shorn lamb. EAP G87; Brunvand 153: Wind(11).

G117 **God** willing and the creek don't rise
1982 *BGlobe* 5/29 10: The rest next week, God willing and the Creek don't rise. **1982** BRouché *Special* (B) 100: God willing and the creeks don't rise.

G118 Good **God**, good devil
1927 WBFoster *From Six* (NY) 132: "Good god, good devil," with a lot of those pagans. EAP G94.

G119 Out of **God's** blessing *etc.*
1962 MInnes *Connoisseur's* (L) 158: It might be seemly to get out of God's blessing and into the warm sun. EAP G93.

G120 Thank **God** (the Lord) for small blessings (mercies) (*varied*)
1922 JJoyce *Ulysses* (NY 1934) 362: Thankful for small mercies. **1928** TCobb *Who Opened* (L) 256: I have to be thankful for small mercies. **1928** AWUpfield *Lure* (NY 1965) 205: Let's be thankful for small mercies. **1930** ECRLorac *Murder* (L) 165: Thank God for small mercies. **1933** PA Taylor *Mystery* (NY) 206: Thank God . . . for small blessin's. **1940** RKing *Holiday* (NY) 17: He thanked God for that small mercy. **1948** DCDisney *Explosion* (NY DBC) 52: For small mercies . . . let us be thankful. **1952** PQuentin *Black* (NY) 61: Thank God for small mercies. **1958** TSouthern *Flash* (NY) 170: Thank the lord for small blessings. **1962** JLeCarré *Murder* (NY 1964) 41: Thank God for small mercies. **1968**

RSDominic *Murder* (NY) 46: Thank God for small blessings. **1970** KGiles *Death* (L) 156: Thank God for small mercies. **1970** PMoyes *Many* (NY) 24: Let's be thankful for small mercies. **1974** JFleming *How to* (NY) 28: You just thank Him for small mercies. **1975** NGuild *Lost* (NY) 187: Thank God for small mercies. **1980** MFredman *You Can* (NY) 92: I thanked God for small mercies. Cf. Favors *above*.

G121 To be **God's** gift to woman
1954 JHenry *Yield* (NY) 106: He was God's gift to women. **1958** DMDisney *Black* (NY) 56: He thinks he's God's gift to women. **1966** TWells *Matter* (NY) 145: If you think you're God's gift to woman, you've got another think coming. Berrey 445.6.

G122 To owe **God** a death
1929 TFPowys *Fables* (NY) 25: I do owe God a death. **1950** ECrispin *Sudden* (NY DBC) 35: We owe God a death. **1962** ABurgess *Wanting* (L) 258: Owing God a death. **1964** SBecker *Covenant* (NY) 162: Thou owest God a death. *Oxford* 603: Owe.

G123 We are as **God** made us (*varied*)
1938 LBrock *Silver Sickle* (L) 236: Making a bigger fool of him than God had already made him. **1939** JDonavan *Coloured Wind* (L) 62: We're all as God makes us, and none of us is perfect. **1954** TDuBois *Seeing* (NY) 162: We are all as God made us, and frequently much worse. **1962** NBenchley *Catch* (NY) 109: We're all as God made us, or whatever the saying is. *Oxford* 311: God made me.

G124 Where **God** goes the devil goes
1926 TFPowys *Innocent* (L) 75: Where God goes the Devil goes. Cf. *Oxford* 309: God has his church.

G125 Whom the **Gods** love die young
1969 LBruce *Death* (L) 113: Whom the Gods love die young. Brunvand 59(2); *Oxford* 314. Cf. Good die young *below*.

G126 Whom the **Gods** would destroy *etc.* (*varied*)
1913 HHMunro *When Williams* (L 1929) 84: Whom the gods wish to render harm-

less they first afflict with sanity. **1927** GDil-not *Lazy* (B) 308: Do you know Latin? *Quos Deus vult perdere prius dementat.* **1930** LTracy *Manning* (NY) 309: Those whom the gods wish to destroy they first make mad. **1937** GDilnot *Murder* (L) 272: There's an old tag that those whom the gods would destroy they first make mad. **1957** IFleming *From Russia* (NY 1958) 77: Those whom the Gods wish to destroy they first make bored. **1961** RJWhite *Smartest* (L) 146: Whom the gods intend to destroy they first make mad. *Quem deus vult perdere, prius dementat.* **1965** JSUntermeyer *Private* (NY) 126: "Quos Deus vult perdere prius dementat" ". . . they first make mad." **1970** WANolen *Making* (NY) 216: As Longfellow said, "Whom the Gods want to destroy they first make mad." **1970** RPowell *Whom the Gods Would Destroy* (NY). EAP G99; Brunvand 59(1).

G127 The **Godolphins** never lack wit *etc.*
1948 IFletcher *Roanoke* (I) 29: The old Devon saying goes "The Godolphins never lack wit, nor the Grenvilles loyalty." *Oxford* 561: Never a Granville.

G128 As good as **Gold**
1906 HNewbolt *Old Country* (L) 206: She is as good as gold. **1922** JJoyce *Ulysses* (NY 1934) 340: Baby was as good as gold. **1928** MRJames *Letters* ed GMcBryde (L 1956) 148: Good as gold. **1936** JDosPassos *Big Money* (NY) 390: He was as good as gold. **1944** CDickson *He Wouldn't* (NY) 110: As good as gold. **1958** NMarsh *Singing* (B) 116: Jourdain was . . . as good as gold. **1961** RStout *Final* (NY) 69: It's good as gold. **1963** PTaylor *Miss Leonora* (NY) 64: They were apt to be as good as gold. **1972** QBell *Virginia* (NY) 17: [She] was as good as gold. **1973** GSereny *Case* (NY) 64: She was . . . as good as gold. TW 155(5); Brunvand 60(2).

G129 As yellow as **Gold**
1926 JTully *Beggars* (NY) 314: Face, yellow as gold. **1970** RRhodes *Inland* (NY) 48: Butter . . . as yellow as gold. EAP G106; TW 155(6); Brunvand 60(3): Gold-yellow.

G130 The **Gold** (wealth) of Golconda (*etc.*)
1926 AFielding *Footsteps* (L) 98: Not the wealth of Golconda would make him deviate from the truth. **1929** PRShore *Bolt* (NY) 38: Not for the goold [*sic*] of India. **1934** JGBrandon *One-minute* (L) 164: I wouldn't have . . . for all the jewels of Asia. **1960** NFitzgerald *Ghost* (L) 123: I wouldn't go up for all the gold in Fort Knox. **1962** AGilbert *Uncertain* (NY DBC) 146: All the gold of Araby wouldn't be enough. EAP W83.

G131 When it's raining **Gold** (soup) to be caught with a leaky teaspoon (*varied*)
1943 AAFair *Bats Fly* (NY) 55: I'm mixed up in a case where it's raining gold, and I'm caught out with a leaky teaspoon. **1948** NMailer *Naked* (NY) 346: If 'twere rainin' soup, there Ay'd be stahndin' with a fork in me hand. Cf. TW 109(1): Behind the door; *Oxford* 662: Rain pottage. Cf. Door *above.*

G132 To sell someone a **Gold brick**
1955 WSloane *Stories* (L) 345: Sold them a load of gold bricks. NED Suppl. Goldbrick; Partridge 339.

G133 To live in a **Goldfish** bowl (*varied*)
1938 MJohnston *Comets* (NY) 154: About as private as goldfish. **1951** FCrane *Murder in* (NY) 98: You've got less privacy than a goldfish. **1952** PQuentin *Black* (NY) 60: I was a goldfish in a bowl. **1955** BBenson *Silver* (NY) 94: It's like living in a goldfish bowl. **1959** FMcDermid *See* (NY) 67: I was . . . trying to hide in a goldfish bowl. **1959** DTaylor *Joy* (NY) 238: I felt like the proverbial goldfish. **1960** PCurtis *Devil's* (NY) 155: It's like living in a goldfish bowl. **1972** KBooton *Quite* (NY) 31: We don't like living in a fish bowl. Whiting *NC* 416; Wentworth 219.

G134 As **Good** as good
1936 RCWoodthorpe *Silence* (L) 284: Good as good. Partridge 341.

G135 **Good** and quickly seldom meet
1927 SSVanDine *Canary* (NY) 165: Good and quickly seldom meet. *Oxford* 317.

G136 The **Good** die young (*varied*)

1928 EWallace *Sinister* (NY) 39: The good die young. **1934** HAdams *Knife* (L) 15: The good die young. **1939** JCreasey *Toff Goes On* (L) 192: Only the good die young. **1956** JBarlow *Protagonists* (L) 189: The good die young, as they say. **1956** RFenisong *Bite* (NY) 47: Besides, most saints die young. **1962** GBerriault *Conference* (NY) 34: The old saw about the good die young. **1970** RRendell *Guilty* (NY) 40: It's always the good as dies young. TW 155(2). Cf. Whom the Gods *above*.

G137 If you can't be **Good** be careful

c1923 ACrowley *Confessions* ed JSymonds (L 1969) 92: If he couldn't be good he should be careful. **1927** CMackenzie *Vestal* (NY) 201: If you can't be good be careful. **1930** HCBailey *Garston* (NY) 224: If you can't be good, be careful. **1932** HCBailey *Red Castle* (NY) 131: "I hope you're always careful." "Yes, when I can't be good." **1954** MHyman *No Time* (NY) 41: Be good, and if you can't be good, be careful. **1963** PDJames *Mind* (L) 14: If you can't be good be careful. **1968** EWilliams *Beyond* (NY) 25: If you can't be good, be careful. **1973** EJBurforn *Queen* (L) 16: "Si non caste tamen caute," which may be colloquially translated "if you can't be good, be careful." *Oxford* 116: Chastely.

G138 To take the **Good** with the bad

1931 LHollingworth *Death* (L) 189: Took the good with the bad. **1938** MPage *Fast Company* (NY) 80: You have to take the good with the bad. **1950** IFletcher *Bennett's* (I) 284: We can take the good with the bad. Cf. Fat *above*, Rough *below*.

G139 Too **Good** (true) to be true (good)

1909 MRRinehart *Man in Lower Ten* (NY 1947) 341: It seemed too good to be true. **1920** GBMcCutcheon *Anderson Crow* (NY) 148: Too good to be true. **1930** WLewis *Apes* (NY 1932) 550: That sounds too good to be true. **1931** HSimpson *Prime* (NY) 250: He was almost too true to be good. **1932** NTrott *Monkey* (NY) 245: Arnold looks a little too good to be true. **1943** MCarpenter *Experiment* (B) 32: It's too good to be true.

1948 JFHutton *Too Good to be True* (NY). **1951** MInnes *Paper* (NY) 224: It was all too true to be good. **1954** MMainwaring *Murder* (NY) 101: It's almost too good to be true. **1955** CMcCormac *You'll Die* (NY) 183: It was almost too good to be true. **1964** NFreeling *Because* (NY 1965) 137: Almost too good to be true. **1965** JRothenstein *Summer's* (L) 224: It all seemed, as the saying goes, too good to be true. **1973** AMorice *Death* (NY) 138: She was a little too goody-goody to be true. **1975** EXFerrars *Alive* (NY) 8: Much too good to be true. EAP G114.

G140 Ill gotten **Goods** never thrive

1937 DLSayers *Busman's* (NY) 184: Ill gotten goods never thrive. EAP G115.

G141 All one's **Geese** (ducks) are swans (*varied*)

1928 ESnell *Kontrol* (P) 33: All Lady Thorn's geese were swans. **1932** EVLucas *Reading* (L) 286: Too many of his swans were geese. **1932** PMacDonald *Rope* (L) 256: You may be chasing a swan which will turn into a wild goose. **1937** CBush *Eight O'Clock* (NY) 143: Carry's . . . ducks were always prize swans. **1937** RPEckert *Edward Thomas* (L) 60: None of his swans proved geese. **1943** DGoldring *South Lodge* (L) 33: His capacity for turning geese into swans. **1948** HActon *Memoirs* (L) 65: Mistaking several geese for swans. **1951** SSpender *World* (L) 88: A goose who became a swan. **1957** AECoppard *It's Me* (L) 16: My swans were indubitably geese. **1959** ESherry *Defense* (NY) 76: I'm not one to call a goose a swan. **1960** FFrankfurter *Reminisces* (NY) 36: Dean Pound, all of whose geese were swans. **1961** MHHood *Drown* (NY) 157: All your ducks are swans. **1968** JCleugh *History* (NY 1970) 223: Always ready to call a goose a swan. **1971** CBeaton *My Bolivian* (L) 45: Their swans turned into geese. **1973** KCampbell *Wheel* (I) 57: All his geese were swans. EAP G119.

G142 As giddy as a **Goose**

1937 LZugsmith *Home* (NY) 114: I'm giddy as a goose. Lean II ii 834.

Goose

G143 As loose as a **Goose**

1930 BABotkin ed *Folk-Say* (Norman, Okla.) 106: She's loose as a goose. **1960** KO'Farrell *I Made* (NY) 64: "I'm free. Loose as a goose." **1964** JLarner *Drive* (NY) 16: Loose as a goose [*free*]. Whiting *NC* 416(4).

G144 As silly as a **Goose**

1937 RWWinston *It's a Far Cry* (NY) 24: As silly as a goose. Whiting *NC* 416(5); Taylor *Prov. Comp.* 73.

G145 The **Goose** hangs high

1926 CWTyler *Blue Jean* (NY) 92: It was a great life, and the goose hung high. **1930** JFDobie *Coronado* (Dallas) 252: The goose was hanging high. **1936** SLBradbury *Hiram* (Rutland, Vt.) 222: Everything was lovely and the goose hung high. **1938** VWMason *Cairo* (NY) 276: Now be a good girl while I'm out and the goose will hang high. **1947** HTKane *Natchez* (NY) 14: The goose hung high; all looked right with the world, for another twelve months anyway. **1948** EQueen *Ten* (B) 94: The goose of commerce hangs high. **1957** CDBowen *Lion* (B) 126: The goose hung high. **1966** LNizer *Jury* (NY) 239: The goose hangs high. **1971** WTeller *Cape Cod* (Englewood Cliffs, NJ) 91: The goose hangs high. TW 156(5).

G146 A **Goose** is walking over one's grave (*varied*)

1920 AChristie *Mysterious Affair* (NY) 20: It makes me feel as if a goose were walking over my grave. **1927** CAiken *Blue Voyage* (NY) 111: A goose walked over my grave. **1930** WSMaugham *Cakes* (L 1948) 192: A shiver passed through me as though someone had walked over my grave. **1931** DAldis *Murder in a Haystack* (NY) 46: It was just one of those some-one-is-walking-over-your-grave feelings. **1931** LPowys *Pagan's* (NY) 17: We used to be told when we shivered in a particular way that a goose was walking over our graves; the adage . . . **1931** PMacDonald *Choice* (L) 52: Lucia suddenly shivered . . . "Somebody walking over my grave." **1933** KCStrahan *Meriwether* (NY) 229: Evadne gave that quick shiver which, in my childhood, we used to explain by saying that a goose had walked over our graves. **1938** EHuxley *Murder* (NY) 47: He shivered and goose-flesh rose on his arms. "A goose walking over my grave." **1949** JSymons *Bland* (L) 103: I felt all the time as if a goose was crawling over my grave. **1951** CArmstrong *Black-eyed* (NY) 6: He shivered . . . "cat walked over my grave, I guess." **1951** IChase *New York 22* (NY) 212: It was just one of those goose-flesh things. Someone walking on my grave. **1957** KFerrer *Gownsman's* (L) 197: "What a silence! . . . An angel passing, as we say." "In England, we say it's a goose walking over your grave." **1958** JByrom *Or Be* (L 1964) 90: Whatever has passed over our graves, I'm very sure it's not an angel. **1960** AGilbert *Out for* (NY 1965) 20: People presumably felt like this when geese walked over their grave—why geese? **1963** IFleming *On Her* (L) 57: He gave an involuntary shudder, as if someone had walked over his grave. **1966** TWells *Matter* (NY) 73: She shuddered and I thought of the old expression, somebody walked over my grave. **1967** AChristie *Endless* (NY) 166: "I felt as though someone were walking over my grave." "A goose is walking over your grave. That's the real saying, isn't it?" **1968** KChristie *Child's* (L) 56: I give a cold shudder. "Donkey walking over my grave." **1972** HPentecost *Champagne* (NY) 137: Ghost walked over my grave [*a premonition*]. **1972** WJWatkins *Ecodeath* (NY) 77: He sensed a slight tingling at the back of his neck. As the old wives' tale went, someone had just walked over his grave. *Oxford* 864: Walking over.

G147 To be a gone **Goose**

1927 NMartin *Mosaic* (NY) 25: I'm a gone goose. **1940** HReilly *Dead Can* (NY) 54: He would have been a gone goose. **1941** JKVedder *Last Doorbell* (NY) 216: I'm a gone goose. **1956** *BHerald* 7/7 4: His license is a dead goose. **1959** GBagby *The Real Gone Goose* (NY). **1970** TCoe *Wax* (NY) 138: The Brady girl is a gone goose. **1975** SJPerelman *Vinegar* (NY) 24: I was a gone gosling. TW 156(2). Cf. Brunvand 60: Gosling(1).

G148 To cook one's (someone's) **Goose** (*varied*)

1905 FMWhite *Crimson Blind* (NY) 304: That would cook Henson's goose. **1922** JJoyce *Ulysses* (NY 1934) 635: [It] very effectually cooked his matrimonial goose. **1924** WBMFerguson *Black* (NY) 157: Waiting to cook my goose. **1930** AEHousman *Letters* ed HMaas (Cambridge, Mass. 1971) 293: You have cooked your own goose. **1936** RAJWalling *Floating Foot* (NY) 246: I think he's cooked his matrimonial goose. **1941** JKVedder *Last Doorbell* (NY) 44: My goose is cooked. **1952** HReilly *Velvet* (NY) 181: His goose would be cooked. **1957** BVanOrden *309 East* (NY) 65: Henry's cooked his goose this time. **1959** BHitchens *Man Who* (NY) 179: His goose was cooked. **1963** EMcBain *Ten* (NY) 72: He just cooked his own goose. **1969** HPentecost *Girl Watcher* (NY) 39: You were a cooked goose without Christmas to go with it. **1971** JTMcIntosh *Coat* (NY) 141: He would have been a cooked goose. **1982** CMacLeod *Wrack* (NY) 100: [He's] cooked your goose good and proper. *Oxford* 143: Cook.

G149 To drive a **Goose** to market

1951 KFarrell *Mistletoe* (L) 47: She is a little ninny . . . who couldn't be trusted to drive a goose to market. Cf. TW 156(12).

G150 To kill the **Goose** that lays the golden eggs (*varied*)

1908 WHHudson *Land's End* (L) 315–6: The goose that lays the golden eggs. **1919** LTracy *Bartlett* (NY) 82: If you had killed me what other goose would lay golden eggs? **1929** LBrock *Stoke Silver* (NY) 59: Still the silliest goose may cackle if it's asked to lay too many golden eggs. **1930** NSLincoln *Marked* (NY) 218: Would she kill the goose that provided a home for herself? **1934** RJBlack *The Killing of the Golden Goose* (NY). **1937** PATaylor *Octagon* (NY) 168: The old adage about the goose and the golden eggs. **1940** LTreat *B as in Banshee* (NY) 98: The goose that laid the golden egg shall lay no more for thee. **1941** AA Fair *Spill* (NY) 199: Let you beware the goose that would lay his golden eggs. **1944** FLockridge *Killing the Goose* (P). **1954** HWade *Too Soon* (NY) 9: To kill the goose that laid the golden eggs. **1956** BHerald 6/7 24: To kill it is as witless as to kill the goose that lays the golden eggs because it has to be fed. **1956** NYTimes 12/2 3X: The old story of "killing the goose that laid the golden egg." **1957** DJEnright *Heaven* (L) 152: To kill the Mother Goose that laid the golden eggs. **1958** FLockridge *Long* (P) 156: Because it's a golden goose. I mean eggs. Nobody breaks golden eggs. **1959** BTraveler 8/21 20: City workers shouldn't try to kill the golden goose. **1960** TBDewey *Girl* (NY DBC) 120: Nobody will make trouble for you. You're the golden goose. **1964** DCecil *Max* (L) 339: The wish to escape was the goose that laid the golden eggs of art. **1968** BHays *Hotbed* (NY) 43: Senator, if we don't stop shearing the wool off the goose that lays the golden egg we are going to pump the well dry. **1971** PTabor *Pauline's* (Louisville) 82: I was reluctant to kill the goose that was laying all those beautiful dollar bills. **1974** OBleeck *Highbinders* (NY) 114: I was the goose that was supposed to lay their golden egg and if I didn't, well, they could always have roast goose for dinner. EAP G125; TW 156(6); Brunvand 60(1).

G151 To roast the **Goose** that pisses on someone's grave

1961 HCromwell *Dirty* (LA) 12: I'll be around to roast the goose that pisses on your grave. Whiting G383; *Oxford* 214: Eat of. Cf. TW 156(11).

G152 To play **Gooseberry** (*varied*)

1922 VSutphen *In Jeopardy* (NY) 274: I was reduced to playing gooseberry. **1933** RAJWalling *Follow* (L) 22: You aren't asking me to play gooseberry at an assignation. **1947** CBrand *Suddenly* (L) 95: To play gooseberry to my own husband would be a bit too much. **1959** NBlake *Widow's* (L) 44: She feels she must play gooseberry to me [*keep an eye on*]. **1961** RJWhite *Smartest* (L) 187: He could get somebody else to play gooseberry for him [*be his mistress*]. **1969** SMays *Reuben's* (L) 66: The absorbing game of playing gooseberry on courting couples. Partridge 344.

G153   As slick as **Goosegrease**

1951 GConklin *Possible* (NY) 93: Everything fell into place. Slick as goose grease. TW 157(2).

G154   To cut the **Gordian** knot

1928 AGilbert *Mrs Davenport* (NY) 251: It cuts one Gordian knot. **1929** RBInce *Calverley* (L) 209: The effort of untying or cutting those Gordian knots. **1931** GTrevor *Murder* (L) 194: Cut the Gordian knot that entangled his own miserable affairs. **1938** TDowning *Night* (L) 6: To cut a few Gordian knots. **1947** GGallagher *I Found* (NY DBC) 123: And didn't Alexander cut the Gordian knot? **1948** JErskine *My Life* (P) 52: A resolute cutter of Gordian knots. **1951** JCollier *Fancies* (NY) 260: I cut the Gordian knot, crossed the Rubicon, burned my boats. **1959** EMButler *Paper* (L) 96: All snarled together with red tape in grisly Gordian knots. **1960** JBlish *Galactic* (L) 196: Gordian knots fell asunder with magical suddenness. **1969** EPetaja *Nets* (NY) 100: Cutting through the Gordian knots of science. **1970** RDAltick *Victorian* (NY) 159: Sliced the Gordian knot. EAP G126.

G155   When **Gorse** is out of bloom kissing is out of season (*varied*)

1947 DBowers *Bells* (NY) 23: "Jane's sort's always in fashion." . . . "Like gorse and love." **1952** HFMPrescott *Man on* (NY) 546: When gorse is out of bloom . . . kissing's out of season. **1969** JMPatterson *Doubly* (NY) 186: On Jersey they say there'll be an end to kissing when the gorse stops blooming . . . Thank God it blooms all the year here. *Oxford* 329.

G156   As sure as **Gospel**

1952 OAtkinson *Golden* (I) 46: Sure as gospel. Wilstach 401: The gospel.

G157   As true (good) as **Gospel**

1900 CFPidgin *Quincy A. Sawyer* (B) 372: That's true as Gospel. **1924** ADHSmith *Porto* (NY) 143: True as gospel. **1932** ACampbell *Murder* (NY) 153: Natasha's story might be true as gospel. **1934** MKingHall *Gay* (NY) 139: True as the gospel. **1939** AWebb *Mr. Pendlebury Makes* (L) 40: Any report he makes is as good as Gospel. **1954** EForbes *Rainbow* (B) 37: If every word isn't truer than Gospel. **1958** JDCarr *Dead Man's* (NY) 183: That's as true as gospel. EAP G128; TW 157(2). Cf. Brunvand 60(2): Gospel truth.

G158   As fine as **Gossamer**

1930 AFielding *Murder* (NY) 64: A chain, fine as gossamer. Whiting *NC* 417; Taylor *Western Folklore* 17(1958) 16.

G159   As light as **Gossamer**

1955 GBagby *Dirty* (NY) 119: It was as light as gossamer. **1972** JDCarr *Hungry* (NY) 161: A passing fancy . . . as light as gossamer. EAP G130.

G160   The wise men of **Gotham**

1964 SJay *Death* (NY) 119: "Like the three wise men of Goshen." . . . "Probably a misquotation." EAP G132.

G161   To go against the **Grain**

1903 MLPeabody *To Be Young* (B 1967) 278: Went against my grain. **1919** JBCabell *Letters* ed PColum (NY 1962) 105: I wrote it against the grain. **1922** JJoyce *Ulysses* (NY 1934) 75: Against my grain somehow. **1932** JJConnington *Castleford* (B) 260: Wendover admitted, rather against the grain. **1939** ECRLorac *Black Beadle* (L) 111: It goes all against the grain. **1951** ECRLorac *I Could* (NY) 109: Goes all against the grain. **1955** WSloane *Stories* (L) 398: It goes against the grain. **1965** RMacdonald *Far Side* (NY) 174: It's very much against my New England grain. **1968** KChristie *Child's* (L) 104: You go against the grain. **1974** ROlland *Pepys* (NY) 111: Against the grain of his nature. EAP G134; Brunvand 60.

G162   To sift the **Grain** from the chaff (*varied*)

1931 AChristie *Murder* (NY) 203: To sift the grain from the chaff. **1932** JJConnington *Castleford* (B) 207: Sift the chaff from the grain. **1935** WMartyn *Nightmare* (L) 127: To sift the grain from the chaff. **1939**

EPhillpotts *Monkshood* (L) 115: Sifting the grain from the chaff. **1948** AWUpfield *Author* (Sydney 1967) 97: The grain should be winnowed from the chaff. **1971** TRosebury *Microbes* (NY) 44: Let me separate the grain from the chaff. EAP C107. Cf. Wheat *below*.

G163 To take with a **Grain** of salt (*varied*)

1907 WLewis *Letters* ed WKRose (L 1963) 38: Taken with a grain of salt. **1925** EB Chancellor *Hell Fire* (L) 140: To take with the proverbial amount of salt. **1928** RTGould *Oddities* (L) 116: Their story . . . requires a good deal of salt to make it palatable. **1928** AGMacleod *Marloe* (NY) 293: We are taking that with a considerable pinch of salt. **1929** WGreenleaves *Trout* (NY) 200: Take any good tale of his with a handful of salt. **1931** ACEdington *Monk's Hood* (NY) 131: Take what he tells us with a lot of salt. **1936** JBude *Death* (L) 203: We'll take . . . his evidence with a pinch of salt. **1937** MDavis *Chess* (NY) 232: I still take that woman with a grain of salt. **1939** RCSherriff *Hopkins* (NY) 349: His followers took it with a pinch of salt. **1940** JCreasey *Here Comes* (NY 1967) 7: Much that [he] says must be taken with the proverbial pinch of salt. **1941** CWells *Murder . . . Casino* (P) 229: He took the guaranty with a lump of salt. **1948** CRBoxer *Fidalgos* (Oxford 1968) 264: Be taken *cum grano salis*. **1952** AThorne *Young* (L) 181: She had taken his decision with a grain of salt. **1956** MPHood *Scarlet* (NY) 154: I've taken you with a grain of thought. **1957** CDBowen *Lion* (B) 118: A complaint to be taken . . . with three grains of salt. **1957** RStandish *Prince* (L) 198: All claims . . . must be taken with the proverbial pinch of salt. **1959** *TLS* 5/1 263: More than one grain of the proverbial salt. **1959** SDean *Price* (NY) 144: I took all that with a shaker full of salt. **1960** JPudney *Home* (L) 81: She took it, as he gave it, with a grain of salt. **1963** NBGerson *Golden* (NY) 334: His hero-worshiping biography must be taken with large doses of salt. **1969** P Ziegler *Black* (L) 142: All statistics . . . should be taken with a massive pinch of salt. **1972** ELathen *Murder* (NY) 118: Take Clemmie with a grain of salt. **1973** AGilbert

Nice (NY) 219: Take their evidence with a tinful of salt. **1981** MKWren *Seasons* (NY) 129: He accepted that with a grain or two of salt. EAP G136.

G164 To blow (puff, snore) like a **Grampus**

1930 GVennu *Next to Die* (L) 216: Puffing and blowing like a grampus. **1933** LWMeynell *Paid* (L) 25: You're puffing like a grampus. **1934** RAJWalling *Eight* (L) 59: Snoring like a grampus. **1953** ECRLorac *Shepherd's* (NY) 124: Puffing like a grampus. **1960** JJMarric *Gideon's Risk* (NY) 12: Stop blowing like a grampus. **1964** LPayne *Deep* (L) 135: Snoring like a grampus. EAP G137. Cf. Wilstach 367: Snore . . . porpoise. Cf. Walrus *below*.

G165 To teach one's **Grandmother** how to suck eggs (*varied*)

1922 JSFletcher *Rayner-Slade* (NY) 109: They'd show their grandmother how to suck eggs. **1922** JJoyce *Ulysses* (NY 1934) 309: Teach your grandmother how to milk ducks. **1926** LBrock *Colonel Gore* (NY) 25: "Have you ever ridden a motor-bike?" . . . "Has your grandmother ever sucked eggs?" **1932** HCBailey *Red Castle* (NY) 162: My grandmother knew how to suck eggs too. **1934** DFairfax *Masked Ball* (L) 226: You teach your grandmother to play poker. **1938** SHorler *Gentleman* (NY) 75: Are you trying . . . to teach your father to suck eggs? **1939** MElwin *Old Gods* (NY) 195: Irresponsible youth, who recklessly proposes to instruct his grandmother in sucking the proverbial egg. **1940** RAHeinlein *Puppet* (NY 1965) 209: Don't teach grandma to steal sheep. **1946** DDuncan *Shade of Time* (NY) 112: If I may be trite, aren't you trying to teach your grandmother to suck eggs? **1952** HHunter *Bengal* (NY) 19: Can your grandmother suck eggs? **1952** AMenen *Duke* (NY) 103: Do not try to teach your grandfather to suck eggs. **1961** WCooper *Scenes* (NY) 103: Tom could never resist the satisfaction of teaching his grandmother to suck eggs. **1970** PAlding *Guilt* (NY) 40: "That's trying to teach my grandmother to suck eggs. Now why suck eggs? Why should anyone want to suck an egg?" "I've no idea." **1972** JBonett *No Time* (NY) 102: If I had half a dozen grandmothers I'd be teaching the lot how to suck eggs. **1973** HCarvic *Miss Seeton Sings* (NY) 136: Talk about teaching your grandmother. **1976** JPorter *Package* (NY) 91: Don't try to teach your grandfather. TW 158(2).

G166   As firm as **Granite**

1954 ASeton *Katherine* (B) 408: Thinking it firm as granite. TW 158(1).

G167   As hard as **Granite**; Granite-hard

1926 EDBiggers *Chinese* (NY) 173: He's hard as granite. **1930** AGilbert *Mystery* (NY) 77: His face was granite-hard. **1938** MBrucker *Poison* (NY) 72: A face . . . hard as granite. **1946** JTShaw *Hard-Boiled* (NY) 394: Face . . . hard as granite. **1953** AWUpfield *Murder Must* (NY) 44: Eyes granite hard. **1958** ESGardner *Foot-loose* (NY) 184: Mason's face became granite-hard. **1975** NFreeling *Bugles* (NY) 107: Hard as granite. TW 158(2).

G168   To take as **Grant** took Richmond

1938 WChambers *Dog* (NY) 220: He could give you all the aces and take you as Grant took Richmond. **1938** EGilligan *Boundary* (NY) 77: I'll take him all right. Just like Grant took Richmond. **1952** FVWMason *Himalayan* (NY 1953) 253: She and Sam have taken me like Grant took Richmond. **1961** HPentecost *Deadly* (NY DBC) 35: I'll take you like Grant took Richmond. Taylor *Prov. Comp.* 44.

G169   The **Grapes** are sour (*varied*)

1922 JJoyce *Ulysses* (NY 1934) 540: The fox and the grapes. **1926** EDBiggers *Chinese* (NY) 251: Sour grapes. **1931** BGraeme *Murder* (P) 213: It was a case of sour grapes. **1935** RCWoodthorpe *Shadow* (NY) 37: We all know the proverb about sour grapes. **1940** VRath *Death of a Lucky* (NY) 207: The grapes are sour. **1956** FWinwar *Wingless* (NY) 160: There is a suggestion of the fox and the inaccessible grapes. **1957** NMitford *Voltaire* (L) 199: Only when out of reach did the grapes turn sour for him again. **1959** MFitzgerald *This Won't* (L) 79: It had an effect on him like that of the unreachable grapes on the fox. **1961** CJenkins *Mes-*

sage (L) 7: He'd better stop eating sour grapes. **1969** EStewart *Heads* (NY) 147: It's just sour grapes. EAP G140; TW 158(2); Brunvand 60–1(2).

G170   One cannot gather **Grapes** from thorns *etc.*

1929 CGBowers *Tragic* (NY) 320: Men do not grow grapes from thorns nor figs from thistles. **1931** RScarlett *Cat's* (NY) 83: Figs do not grow on thistles. **1957** NBlake *End* (L) 48: Then thistles can bear figs. EAP G141; Brunvand 60(1).

G171   As green as **Grass**

1917 BMalinowski *Diary* (NY 1967) 145: The waters green as grass. **1920** GBMcCutcheon *Anderson Crow* (NY) 185: As green as grass. **1927** JTaine *Quayles'* (NY) 428: You are still as green as virgin grass. **1934** AHalper *Foundry* (NY) 7: You're as green as grass. **1938** NJones *Hanging Lady* (NY) 119: [He] was green as grass. **1951** FCrane *Murder in* (NY) 52: This American girl, green as grass. **1953** EWTeale *Circle* (NY) 255: Similes. Green as grass. Quick as a squirrel. Hard as a rock. Slippery as an eel. Busy as a bee. All the truest similes of nature are clichés. Many people have been struck by the same comparison. **1959** WHaggard *Venetian* (NY DBC) 144: Green as grass [*inexperienced*]. **1969** SPalmer *Hildegarde* (NY) 73: She's a kid. Green as grass. EAP G143; TW 159(1).

G172   Go to **Grass**!

1904 JCLincoln *Cap'n Eri* (NY) 82: You go to grass! **1929** VStarrett *Murder* (NY) 42: You go to grass. EAP G150; Brunvand 61(1).

G173   The **Grass** is (looks) greener on the other side *etc.* (*varied*)

1957 BWAldiss *Space* (L) 90: Possibly you recall the old saying about the chlorophyll being greener on someone else's grass. **1959** *BangorDN* 6/16 9: Why does the grass always look greener on the other side of the fence? **1959** *NYTimes* 12/13 54: The grass always looks greener on the other side of the fence. **1960** HReilly *Follow* (NY DBC) 11: The grass was forever greener over the next hill. **1962** HCarmichael *Of Unsound*

(NY) 9: The grass always looks greener on the other side of the hill. **1964** LLRue *World* (P) 30: To a raccoon "the grass is always greener on the other side of the fence." **1966** EVCunningham *Helen* (NY) 161: It's just the other side of the fence here in San Verdo, and the cows are always fatter there. **1968** WGRogers *Ladies* (L) 22: She simply believed in the green grass on her side of the fence. **1969** JTrahey *Pecked* (Englewood Cliffs, NJ) 6: Could it be that the cement was not green on the other side? **1971** PRubenstein *Groupsex* (NY) 236: "The grass is greener . . ." [*of sex*]. **1973** RCondon *And Then* (NY) 301: The grass seems greener on the other side of the fence. Cf. *Oxford* 560: Neighbour's ground; Tilley N115: Neighbor's ground. Cf. Far-off Hills, Pastures *below*.

G174 Keep off the **Grass**

1922 JJoyce *Ulysses* (NY 1934) 368: Please keep off the grass. **1929** GFairlie *Yellow* (B) 69: I'm here to warn you to keep off the grass. **1940** NBlake *Malice* (L) 193: Warning me off the grass [*mind your own business*]. **1976** SWoods *My Life* (NY) 137: I was warning him off the grass. Partridge 450: Keep off.

G175 Not to let **Grass** grow under one's feet

1900 CFPidgin *Quincy A. Sawyer* (B) 349: You don't let no grass grow under yer feet. **1924** HSKeeler *Voice* (NY) 84: Never let the grass grow under your feet. **1933** WCBrown *Murder* (P) 145: He won't let any grass grow under his feet. **1937** AChristie *Cards* (NY) 110: I . . . shall not let the grass grow under my feet. **1938** CNGovan *Plantation* (B) 124: I'm not letting any daisies grow under my feet. **1940** EDean *Murder Is* (NY) 85: He don't let the grass grow under his feet none. **1941** MArmstrong *Blue Santo* (NY) 181: There don't much grass sprout under my feet. **1955** RFenisong *Widows* (NY) 190: [He] wouldn't let the grass grow under his feet. **1961** JSStrange *Eye* (NY) 172: [He] hasn't let the grass grow under his feet. **1964** CWilson *Necessary* (NY 1966) 137: That man . . . doesn't let the grass grow under his feet.

1970 JCreasey *Part* (NY) 66: I've let a lot of grass grow under my feet. **1973** JPorter *It's Murder* (NY) 95: I've hardly been letting the grass grow under my feet. EAP G147. Cf. Brunvand 61(4).

G176 While the **Grass** grows the horse starves

1950 VSReid *New Day* (L) 174: While the grass is growing, the horse can be starving. **1973** MInnes *Appleby's Answer* (NY) 25: While the grass grows the steed mustn't starve. EAP G152.

G177 As black as the **Grave**

1904 JCLincoln *Cap'n Eri* (NY) 116: As black as the grave. TW 160(2). Cf. Tomb *below*.

G178 As close as the **Grave**

1937 CBush *Eight O'Clock* (NY) 266: Hidden close as the grave itself. **1956** MSteen *Unquiet* (NY) 63: They're closer than the grave [*secretive*]. TW 160(3).

G179 As cold as the **Grave**

1924 JSFletcher *King* (NY) 103: As cold as the grave. EAP G155; Taylor *Western Folklore* 17(1958) 16. Cf. Tomb *below*.

G180 As dark as the **Grave**

1970 PMoyes *Many* (NY) 222: It was as dark as the grave. EAP G157. Cf. Tomb *below*.

G181 As deep as the **Grave**

1933 EPhillpotts *Captain's* (NY) 237: Such men are deep as the grave. Wilstach 87.

G182 As deserted as the **Grave**

1928 JArnold *Surrey* (L) 217: As deserted as the grave. **1969** JLunt *Bokhara* (L) 155: As deserted as the grave.

G183 As lonesome (lonely) as the **Grave**

1912 JCLincoln *Postmaster* (NY) 94: I'll be lonesomer than the grave. **1933** ECRLorac *Case* (L) 254: As lonely as the grave.

G184 As mute as the **Grave**

1936 WSMasterman *Rose* (NY) 140: Mute as the grave. TW 160(5).

G185 As quiet as the **Grave** (a mausoleum)

1924 JSFletcher *King* (NY) 190: As quiet as the grave. **1933** CWaye *Figure* (NY) 242:

The house was as quiet as the grave. **1938** BGraeme *Mystery* (P) 191: The house was as quiet as a mausoleum. **1938** CRawson *Death from* (L) 193: Place quiet as a graveyard. **1955** MGilbert *Country-house* (NY) 176: Quiet as the grave. **1970** JBlackburn *Bury* (NY) 55: Quiet as the grave. **1975** SJPerelman *Vinegar* (NY) 51: As quiet as the grave and equally somber. TW 160(6). Cf. Morgue, Tomb *below*.

G186 As safe as the **Grave**

1939 MStuart *Dead Men* (L) 193: Her alibi is as safe as—as the grave. **1956** DEden *Death* (L) 93: It was almost as safe as a grave. Cf. Tomb *below*.

G187 As secret (discrete) as the **Grave**

1924 JSFletcher *Time-Worn* (NY) 49: Secret as the grave. **1927** HHBashford *Behind* (NY) 19: He was discreter than the grave. EAP G158.

G188 As silent (mum) as the **Grave** (a graveyard, a mausoleum) (*varied*)

1910 EPhillpotts *Tales* (NY) 303: Silent as the grave. **1922** JJoyce *Ulysses* (NY 1934) 359: Silent as the grave. **1925** AJSmall *Death* (NY) 182: All was silent as a sepulchre. **1927** RAFreeman *Magic* (NY) 261: As silent as—not the grave; that is an unpleasant simile. **1935** ECRLorac *Affair* (L) 275: I'll be as mum as the grave. **1949** JEvans *Halo* (NY) 209: The room was as silent as a mausoleum. **1952** WSHoole *Simon Suggs* (University, Ala.) 120: Silent as a grave. **1957** MProcter *Midnight* (NY) 16: As silent as a graveyard. **1959** *NYTimes* 7/19 19: As silent as the grave. **1963** HWaugh *Prisoner's* (NY DBC) 172: I'll be as silent as the grave . . . and just about as grim. **1968** ELustgarten *Business* (NY) 149: But all was silent—and the metaphor is appropriate—as the grave. **1970** EWTeale *Springtime* (NY) 140: As silent as the grave. EAP G160; Brunvand 61(8). Cf. Tomb *below*.

G189 As still as the **Grave** (a mausoleum)

1910 EPhillpotts *Tales* (NY) 39: So still as the grave. **1920** ACrabb *Samuel* (NY) 26: As still as the grave. **1920** GBMcCutcheon *Anderson Crow* (NY) 98: As still as the grave. **1937** RAFreeman *Felo* (L) 91: The place

was as still as the grave. **1953** ECrandall *White* (B) 43: The house was as still as a mausoleum. TW 160(9). Cf. Tomb *below*.

G190 To dance on someone's **Grave**

1934 PGWodehouse *Brinkley* (B) 132: I shall want to dance on your grave. **1938** JTFarrell *No Star* (NY) 400: You witch, when you die I'll dance on your grave.

G191 To dig one's **Grave** with his teeth (*varied*)

1915 PGWodehouse *Something Fresh* (L 1935) 35: That man . . . is digging his grave with his teeth. **1928** MChideckel *Strictly* (NY) 113: He was digging his own grave with his teeth. **1934** DGardiner *Drink* (NY) 295: He dug his own grave with his teeth. **1937** CGordon *Garden* (NY) 111: All of 'em dig their graves with their teeth. **1945** PA Taylor *Proof* (NY) 151: You're practically digging your grave with your teeth [*talking too much*]. **1952** PGWodehouse *Angel* (NY) 64: Digging your grave with your teeth. **1970** JLeasor *They Don't* (NY) 234: Dr. Johnson once declared that we dig our graves with our tongues, our teeth, or our tails. **1973** AMStein *Finger* (NY) 61: He was digging his grave with his teeth. **1973** DMDisney *Only Couples* (NY) 98: She would eat herself into her grave. EAP G164.

G192 To turn in one's **Grave**

1930 JRhode *Davidson* (L) 22: It must make his father turn in his grave. *Oxford* 847.

G193 As quiet as a **Graveyard**

1930 AProcter *Murder* (NY) 68: Quiet as a graveyard. Whiting *NC* 417.

G194 To whistle in a **Graveyard**

1933 CDickson *Bowstring* (NY) 134: I'm whistling in a graveyard. **1935** JDCarr *Death-water* (L) 158: What's known as whistling in a graveyard. **1950** CDickson *Night* (NY) 173: You're all whistling in a graveyard. **1971** JBlake *Joint* (NY) 85: I didn't know that my graveyard whistling was so apparent. Cf. Courage, Dark *above*.

G195 To ride the **Gravy** train (*varied*)

1938 VWMason *Cairo* (NY) 231: So you're riding on the gravy train. **1948** WMiller

Fatal (NY) 125: He decided to get on the gravy train. **1957** *Time* 1/7 15: There are some who ride the Uncle-pays plan like a gravy train. **1964** JHillas *Today* (NY) 141: Found themselves on the gravy train. **1969** HPentecost *Girl Watcher* (NY) 13: I am on the gravy train. **1973** JBrooks *Go-Go* (NY) 144: The parlor cars of the new gravy train. **1974** WBridges *Gathering* (NY) 36: Penelope had been riding the gravy train. Whiting *NC* 417; Wentworth 228.

G196 As slick as **Grease**

1910 JCLincoln *Depot Master* (NY) 212: Slick as grease. **1932** MCJohnson *Damning* (NY) 215: Slick as grease. **1941** RStout *Alphabet* (NY) 265: That was slick as grease. EAP G165; Taylor *Western Folklore* 17 (1958) 16.

G197 As smooth as **Grease** (*varied*)

1937 LFord *Ill Met* (NY) 199: He was . . . as smooth as owl's grease. **1938** JGloag *Documents* (L) 151: A gunman's job was just about as smooth as grease. **1947** LFord *Woman* (NY) 53: Things were as smooth as owl's grease. **1959** CCornish *Dead* (NY) 45: His manner was as smooth as hog grease. TW 160(2).

G198 To go like **Grease** through a goose

1977 LBlock *Burglars* (NY) 34: You go through locks like grease through a goose. Cf. Dose *above.*

G199 **Greeks** bearing gifts (*varied*)

1922 DFox *Ethel* (NY) 136: Greeks bearing gifts. **1926** LTracy *Gleave* (NY) 58: There's a proverb, or something of the sort, about fearing certain persons who come with gifts. **1928** RAFreeman *As a Thief* (L) 168: Dealing with a "Greek gift" of some sort. **1934** GWLee *Beale* (NY) 272: Remembering that "Greeks often bear gifts." **1938** HMcCloy *Dance* (NY) 189: And you distrust Greeks bearing gifts. **1940** FGruber *Talking Clock* (NY) 224: The quotation . . . is, "Beware of Greeks bearing gifts." **1941** CRice *Trial by Fury* (NY 1957) 152: Never look a Greek in the mouth when he comes bearing a gift horse . . . I mean beware of the Greek when he comes bearing a horse in his mouth. **1956** *BHerald* 6/3 54: Beware

of the Trojan Horse! **1959** ESGardner *Deadly* (NY) 55: The D.A. gets suspicious of the Greeks when they bring gifts—of red herrings. **1966** AMStein *I Fear the Greeks* (NY). **1967** LWoolf *Downhill* (L) 81: *Timeo Danaos et dona ferentes,* I fear the Greeks especially when they offer me gifts. *Oxford* 250: Fear.

G200 The **Greek** calends

1923 ABlackwood *Episodes* (L) 48: Set down in the Greek calends. **1924** JSFletcher *King* (NY) 67: From now till the Greek calends. **1934** TMundy *Tros* (NY) 293: At about the time of the Greek calends. **1937** RBriffault *Europa* (NY) 26: Not to be disturbed until the Greek calends. **1953** ARhodes *Ball* (L) 28: Relegated it to the Greek Kalends. **1959** MInnes *Hare* (NY 1964) 40: He can be snug till the Greek Kalends. **1963** RAHeinlein *Glory* (NY) 142: "Someday" . . . "When the Greeks reckon time by the kalends." EAP G172.

G201 To be **Greek** to one (*varied*)

1903 EChilders *Riddle* (NY 1940) 31: An ignoramus to whom it would be Greek. **1910** JCLincoln *Depot Master* (NY) 262: It was hog Greek to me. **1913** ECBentley *Trent's* (NY 1930) 179: A vocabulary . . . that is simply Greek to the vast majority. **1920** JBCabell *Letters* ed PColum (NY 1962) 200: All this to me is Greek. **1935** WSMasterman *Perjured* (NY) 5: It was all so much Greek to me. **1939** FBeeding *Ten Holy* (NY) 294: In any case, Greek was Greek to me. **1940** EQueen *New Adventures* (NY) 160: This is all classical Greek to me. **1950** JCannan *Murder* (L 1958) 44: This was Greek to Price. **1958** PDeVries *Mackerel* (B) 92: That's all Greek to me [*bad Latin*]. **1962** ESherry *Girl* (NY DBC) 30: The whole set up's worse than Greek to me. **1964** BKaufman *Up the Down* (NY 1966) 57: It's Greek to us. **1975** MKWren *Multitude* (NY) 26: Cuneiform's Greek to me. EAP G169. Cf. Brunvand 25: Choctaw. Cf. To be double Dutch *above.*

G202 When **Greek** meets Greek *etc.* (*varied*)
1913 JSFletcher *Secret* (L 1918) 198: When Greek meets Greek. **1926** AHuxley *Two or*

Three (L) 175: When Greek meets Greek then comes, in this case, an exchange of anecdotes. **1935** CBrooks *Three Yards* (L) 61: When Greek meets Greek . . . then comes the tug of war. **1946** MInnes *What Happened* (NY) 193: It was a case of Greek meeting Greek. **1955** LCochran *Hallelujah* (NY) 187: It was a case of Greek meets Greek. **1957** RChurch *Golden* (NY) 17: That must have been Greek meeting Greek. **1963** BWAldiss *Yale* (L 1966) 36: Greek had met Greek. **1972** QBell *Virginia* (NY) II 152: A case of Greek meeting Greek. EAP G170.

G203 To see **Green** in one's eye

1922 JJoyce *Ulysses* (NY 1934) 316: Do you see any green in the white of my eye? **1927** WGerhardi *Pretty* (L) 85: Do you see any green in my eye? **1932** JTFarrell *Young Lonigan* (NY 1935) 119: She asked him if he saw anything green. **1936** RAJWalling *Floating Foot* (NY) 294: Practically asking him if he saw any green in the corner of his eye. **1956** MInnes *Appleby* (L) 75: Keenly progressive . . . No green in his eye. **1958** JSymons *Pipe* (NY) 87: "Do you see any green?" Jerry rolled up the corner of an eyelid and revealed the bloodshot egg of his eye. **1961** JDCarr *Witch* (L) 85: Do you see any green in my eye? **1968** KMartin *Editor* (L) 282: Do you see any green in my eye? TW 161(2).

G204 As cold as **Greenland**

1904 JCLincoln *Cap'n Eri* (NY) 191: Colder'n Greenland. **1936** JNDarby *Murder in* (I) 160: It was . . . as cold as Greenland. **1941** RPKoehler *Sing a Song* (NY) 92: It's cold as Greenland. TW 161.

G205 As cheerful (chipper, gay, happy) as a **Grig**

1933 FHShaw *Atlantic* (NY) 143: Both of them as happy as grigs. **1934** JSStrange *Chinese Jar* (L) 45: As chipper as a grig. **1953** ERuggles *Prince* (NY) 64: He was broke, but gay as a grig. **1961** MHHood *Drown* (NY) 146: Cheerful as a grig. Cf. next entry.

G206 As merry as a **Grig**

1929 FDGrierson *Murder* (L) 203: As merry as grigs. **1939** EFerber *Peculiar* (NY 1960) 26: We all were as merry as grigs. (A grig is a cricket, and it has the reputation for merriness when in reality it is only making a lot of noise.) **1953** OAtkinson *Golden* (I) 225: He was merry as a grig. **1953** MPHood *Silent* (NY) 129: Liv was merry as a grig. **1967** MErskine *Case with* (NY) 182: She was . . . merry as a grig. **1970** HActon *Memoirs* (NY) 130: As merry as a grig. **1975** HLawrenson *Stranger* (NY) 11: I was no merry grig. EAP G174.

G207 To **Grin** and bear it

1922 JJoyce *Ulysses* (NY 1934) 609: Grin and bear it. **1924** WBMFerguson *Black* (NY) 97: Grin and bear it. **1932** ASand *Señor Bum* (NY) 216: But I had to bear it—and I didn't even dare the proverbial grin. **1937** JJFarjeon *Holiday* (L) 107: Women have to grin and bear it. **1948** ESherry *Sudden* (NY) 153: She'd have to grin and bear it until she was sitting pretty. **1950** EAMathew *Horse* (Belfast) 104: The patient had to bear it without the grin. **1959** JABrussel *Just* (NY) 90: To grin and bear it. **1962** ADuggan *Lord* (L) 216: We must grin and bear it. **1964** HPentecost *Shape* (NY DBC) 49: A lot of silly phrases like "grin and bear it." **1976** CIsherwood *Christopher* (NY) 61: Her grin-and-bear-it grin. EAP G176.

G208 As plain as a **Grindstone**

1927 BAtkey *Smiler* (NY) 53: As plain as a grindstone. Cf. Wilstach 293: As a hole in a grindstone.

G209 To see through a **Grindstone**

1922 VSutphen *In Jeopardy* (NY) 160: He can see through a grindstone with a hole in it as quickly as the next man. EAP G177. Cf. Brunvand 95: Millstone. Cf. To see . . . Wall *below*.

G210 Patient **Griselda**

1933 GHolt *Six Minutes* (L) 124: That Griselda of chief constables. **1935** CWells *Wooden* (P) 35: A patient Griselda. **1959** PAnderson *Perish* (NY) 32: I'm no Griselda, you understand. **1961** JDCarr *Witch* (I) 60:

Two women . . . to sit . . . like patient Griseldas. Whiting G472; *Oxford* 613.

G211 To cut the **Ground** from under one's feet

1929 LO'Flaherty *House* (NY) 243: We'll cut the ground from under their feet; 244. **1934** MThomas *Inspector Wilkins* (L) 194: The ground will be cut from under our feet. *Oxford* 164.

G212 To stand one's **Ground**

1913 ERBurroughs *Warlord* (NY 1963) 53: Stand our ground. TW 163(2).

G213 To worship (hate) the **Ground** one walks on

1912 ERBurroughs *Prisoner of Mars* (NY 1963) v: Worshipped the ground he trod. 117: She walks upon. **1917** JCLincoln *Extricating* (NY) 127: He worships the ground you tread on. **1933** EPhillpotts *Captain's* (NY) 101: Worshipped the ground he went upon. **1937** ECVivian *38 Automatic* (L) 83: Worshipped the ground she walked on, as the saying is. **1941** AAFair *Spill* (NY) 82: I hate the ground you walk on. **1951** ES Gardner *Fiery* (NY) 15: He hates the ground you walk on. **1960** NFitzgerald *Ghost* (L) 106: Timm worships the ground you walk on. **1969** RMacDonald *Goodbye* (NY) 10: [He] still worships the ground his father walked on. **1973** AMorice *Death* (NY) 110: She . . . worships the ground he treads on. *Oxford* 493.

G214 To be in on the **Ground floor**

1914 PGWodehouse *Little Nugget* (NY 1929) 116: You're right in on the ground floor. **1930** GDHCole *Berkshire* (NY) 103: Let me in on the ground floor. **1936** ECRLorac *Crime* (L) 59: Letting me in on the ground floor. **1950** RMacDonald *Drowning* (NY 1951) 68: Get in on the ground floor. **1956** AAFair *Beware* (NY DBC) 85: To get in on the ground floor. **1965** LGralapp *Boom!* (NY) 114: Nothing like getting in on the ground floor. **1969** CBush *Deadly* (NY) 59: I'm beginning on the ground floor, so to speak. **1974** RLockridge *Death* (NY) 58: To be in on the

ground floor. DA Ground floor 2; Partridge 357.

G215 To take the **Gruel**

1935 FDGrierson *Death* (L) 72: I'll take the gruel [*punishment*]. **1939** GGoodchild *Mc Lean Excels* (L) 20: I'll take my gruel ["*medicine*"]. Partridge 358.

G216 Mrs. **Grundy**

1906 RLDuffus *Waterbury* (NY 1959) 59: Putting Nature ahead of Mother Grundy. **1906** JLondon *Letters* ed KHendricks (NY 1965) 225: Truckling to Mrs. Grundy. **1922** JJoyce *Ulysses* (NY 1934) 630: A thing good Mrs. Grundy . . . was terribly down on. **1939** JNDarby *Murder in* (I) 30: Regular old Mrs. Grundys. **1941** DKent *Jason* (NY) 211: Mrs. Grundy isn't entirely extinct. **1943** AAMacGregor *Auld Reekie* (L) v: That invisible *censor mori*, Mrs. Grundy. **1960** IWallace *Chapman* (NY 1961) 69: The moral voices of the Mrs. Grundys. **1962** MCarleton *Dread* (NY) 99: Her family name was Grundy. **1967** SMorrow *Insiders* (NY) 108: I hate to sound like a Mother Grundy. **1968** JCFurnas *Lightfoot* (NY) 216: All the best people are always named Grundy. TW 163; Brunvand 62; *Oxford* (1st ed.) 569: What will.

G217 By **Guess** and by God (*varied*)

1909 JCLincoln *Keziah* (NY) 122: Steered by guess and by Godfrey. **1917** JCLincoln *Extricating* (NY) 5: By guess and by godfreys. **1930** DHammett *Maltese* (NY) 101: You're fumbling along by guess and by God. **1934** BAWilliams *Hostile* (NY) 234: I don't know why, only by guess and by gorry. **1938** RTorrey *42 Days* (NY) 238: Works by guess and by God. **1949** MGilbert *He Didn't* (NY DBC) 3: To work by guess and by God. **1954** RJHealy *Tales* (NY) 60: We've been going by-guess-and-by-God. **1956** SWTaylor *I Have* (NY) 247: By guess and by God. **1958** PDWestbrook *Biography* (NY) 141: It never operated except "by guess and by damn." **1960** JWelcome *Stop* (NY) 70: One just has to go by guess and by God. **1965** DoctorX *Intern* (NY) 324: By guess and by God. **1970** DClark *Deadly* 48: Not bad for by guess and by God. **1972**

RHRamsay *No Longer* (NY) 109: Finding longitude was strictly by guess-and-by-God. DARE i 495: By guess etc.; DA God 5(3); Partridge 359.

G218 One('s) **Guess** is as good as another's

1930 EDTorgerson *Murderer* (NY) 179: One guess is as good as another. **1933** BRoss *Tragedy of Z* (NY) 35: Your guess is as good as mine. **1939** DHume *Death Before* (L) 203: One guess is as good as another. **1940** RPenny *Sweet Poison* (L) 109: Your guess is probably every bit as good as mine. **1949** JSymons *Bland* (L) 88: A guess . . . as good as the next man's. **1952** MColes *Alias* (NY) 173: Your guess is as good as mine. **1957** NShute *On the Beach* (NY 1958) 65: Your guess is as good as mine. **1963** HPentecost *Tarnished* (NY DBC) 127: Your guess is as good as mine. **1969** RStout *Death* (NY) 168: Their guess was as good as mine, or better. **1973** PMoyes *Curious* (NY) 50: Your guess is as good as mine.

G219 To have another **Guess** (think) coming

1924 EWallace *Green* (B) 23: You've got another guess coming. **1940** DHume *Five Aces* (L) 177: You've got another thought coming to you. **1940** HSKeeler *Cleopatra's* (L) 279: You may have another think coming. **1941** DVanDeusen *Garden Club* (I) 222: You've got another guess coming. **1952** STruss *Death* (NY) 115: You've got another think coming. **1954** RKLeavitt *Chip* (P) 134: He soon found that he had, as the feller said, another think coming. **1961** RAHeinlein *6XH* (NY) 62: He's got another think coming. **1966** JBall *Cool* (NY) 91: She had another guess coming. **1966** HWaugh *Pure* (NY) 184: You've got another think coming. **1972** JBonett *No Time* (NY) 26: You've got another think coming.

G220 **Guests** and fish stink after three days (*varied*)

1928 EDBiggers *Behind* (NY) 332: The guest who lingers too long deteriorates like unused fish. **1931** AAbbot *Night Club Lady* (NY) 66: You know what Benjamin Franklin says about house guests—they're like fish: after three days they begin to stink.

1939 CBClason *Dragon's* (NY) 13: Plautus, I believe, originally made the observation that even a welcome guest becomes a bore after three days. **1953** RFenisong *Wench* (NY) 7: The axiom that guests and fish stink after three days. **1962** EHuxley *Mottled* (L) 129: An old Chinese proverb . . . , "guests and fish stink after three days." **1964** CChaplin *Autobiography* (NY 1966) 46: As Mother said, guests were like cakes: if kept too long they became stale and impalatable. EAP F144.

G221 Welcome the coming, speed the parting **Guest** (*varied*)

1904 SArmitage-Smith *John of Gaunt* (L) 58–9: Hastened to speed the parting guest. **1918** CTorr *Small Talk* (Cambridge, Eng.) 71: It was not his interest to speed the parting guest. **1930** JWilliamson *American Hotel* (NY) 23: Welcome the coming and speed the parting. **1932** MCJohnson *Damning* (NY) 157: Welcome the coming, speed the parting guest. **1934** JFerguson *Grouse Moor* (NY) 255: Wanted to speed the parting guest, if you know what I mean. **1939** NBlake *Smiler* (L) 35: Don't want to speed the parting guest. **1968** JGould *Europe* (B) 176: He doesn't thus speed every departing guest. Bartlett 405b, 411b [APope].

G222 The **Guilty** (wicked) flee when no man pursueth (*varied*)

1929 SQuinn *Phantom* (Sauk City, Wisc. 1966) 107: The nonsense talked of the guilty who flee when no man pursueth. **1930** JSFletcher *Green Rope* (L) 216: It says in the Proverbs . . . *The wicked flee when no man pursueth!* **1938** MGEberhart *Hasty* (NY) 261: "The guilty flee," said Wait rather sententiously, "where a shadow pursues." **1939** MGEberhart *Chiffon* (NY) 295: It's a case of the wicked flee where no man pursueth. **1942** AMStein *Only the Guilty* (NY) 174: That old line . . . I think it's in the Bible. Something like "Only the guilty flee when no man pursueth." **1945** HCBailey *Wrong Man* (NY) 245: The wicked flee when no man pursueth. **1953** CDickson *Cavalier's* (NY) 160: The guilty flee when no man pursueth. **1954** EQueen *Glass* (B) 280: The wicked flee when no man pursueth. **1963**

LEgan *Run* (NY DBC) 99: What's that line from the Bible—*The wicked flee when no man pursueth.* **1967** AMStein *Deadly* (NY) 168: You know that jazz about the guilty man running even when he's got nobody on his tail? **1970** DShannon *Unexpected* (NY) 48: The guilty flee where no man—. EAP W144. Cf. Conscience *above.*

G223   As bright as a new **Guinea**

1935 VWMason *Budapest* (NY) 133: Bright as a new guinea. TW 163(1).

G224   As yellow as a **Guinea**

1929 EWallace *Flying* (L) 41: His face was as yellow as a guinea. **1957** RGraves *They Hanged* (NY) 46: A face as yellow as a guinea. Partridge 360.

G225   To be up a **Gum-tree** (tree)

1925 IOstrander *Neglected* (NY) 223: Both of them up a tree. **1928** ACBrown *Dr Glazebrook* (NY) 115: Your gang will be fairly up a gum-tree. **1933** LRGribble *Yellow* (L) 174: Up a tree for sure. **1936** LAKnight *Night* (L) 126: His finances are absolutely up a gum tree. **1939** EHuxley *African Poison* (NY) 63: Leave things a bit up a gum-tree. **1960** MProcter *Devil's* (NY DBC) 123: I'm up a gum tree. **1963** BKnox *Grey* (NY) 69: You're up a gum tree. **1970** CDrummond *Stab* (NY) 56: We are up the proverbial gum-tree. **1970** HCarvic *Miss Seeton Draws* (NY) 47: [She's] found herself a gum tree and chased herself up it. **1972** RBraddon *Thirteenth* (NY) 117: The Gifford boys 'd have him up a gum tree. TW 381: Tree (4); *Oxford* 837: Tree; NED Gum-tree 2, Suppl. *s.v.*

G226   As straight as a **Gun**

1971 SKrim *Shake* (L) 57: Straight (and stubborn) as a gun. TW 164(1).

G227   As sure as a **Gun** (guns)

1928 CBarry *Corpse* (NY) 17: As sure as a gun. **1934** GSinclair *Cannibal* (NY) 247: Sure as guns. **1939** JDCarr *Problem* (B 1948) 17: As sure as guns. **1946** CDickson *My Late* (NY) 279: As sure as guns. **1949** CDickson *Graveyard* (NY) 135: As sure as guns. **1961** JDCarr *Witch* (L) 208: As sure

as guns. EAP G189. Cf. Brunvand 63(2): Sure's gun's iron.

G228   To blow great **Guns**

c1923 ACrowley *Confessions* ed JSymonds (L 1969) 496: It blew great guns and poured blue cats all day. **1928** MThynne *Draycott* (NY) 146: Blowing big guns and bitterly cold. **1934** AWynne *Gold Coins* (P) 79: It was . . . blowing guns. **1937** RAJWalling *Bury Him* (L) 51: Still blowing great guns. **1948** HBeston *Northern* (NY) 29: Blowing great guns. **1969** EInglis-Jones *Augustus* (L) 69: The wind was blowing great guns. EAP G190.

G229   To go great **Guns**

1934 CRyland *Murder* (L) 26: It ought to go great guns. **1960** MGEberhart *Jury* (NY DBC) 30: I hear you're going great guns. **1962** SRansome *Night* (NY DBC) 102: Plantation Manor was going great guns. Berrey 243.3, 261.2, 644.10.

G230   To jump the **Gun**

1938 JGEdwards *Odor* (NY) 64: What is . . . known as jumping the gun. **1940** FWBronson *Nice People* (NY) 127: You're jumping the gun. **1952** KFCrossen *Future* (NY) 62: I don't want to jump the gun. **1958** CCockburn *Crossing* (L) 95: Somebody had, as the saying goes, jumped the gun. **1962** JBarry *Strange* (NY) 25: She jumped the gun. **1966** VSiller *Mood* (NY) 171: Conway was jumping the gun. **1970** DJOlivy *Never* (NY) 181: You may still be jumping the gun. **1972** KCampbell *Thunder* (I) 101: We may be jumping the gun. Wentworth 299: Jump.

G231   To spike someone's **Guns**

1909 JCLincoln *Keziah* (NY) 374: Daniels's guns was spiked. **1924** CWells *Furthest* (P) 190: Spiking his guns. **1939** TPolsky *Curtains* (NY) 82: Chester tried to spike your guns. **1946** CDickson *My Late* (NY) 70: I'll spike the gentleman's guns. **1957** KFarrer *Gownsman's* (L) 28: Spiking your adversary's guns. **1967** AJToynbee *Acquaintances* (L) 200: The . . . hecklers' guns were spiked. TW 164(8).

G232 To stick (stand) to one's **Guns**

1913 EDBiggers *Seven Keys* (I) 220: Stick to your guns. **1920** ACrabb *Samuel* (NY) 138: He stood to his guns. **1922** JJoyce *Ulysses* (NY 1934) 638: [He] stuck to his guns. **1930** WLewis *Apes* (NY 1932) 33: Guns must be stuck to. **1950** SJepson *Hungry* (NY) 26: He stuck to his guns. **1954** ESGardner *Restless* (NY) 246: Burger stuck to his guns. **1964** JPLash *Eleanor* (NY) 214: Mrs. Roosevelt stuck to her guns. TW 164(7): Stand; *Oxford* 770: Stand (quote 1912); NED Gun 6b: Stand *or* stick.

G233 As straight as a **Gun barrel**

1929 CBush *Perfect* (NY) 181: One of the best, and straight as a gun barrel [*honest*]. **1929** BFlynn *Invisible* (L) 168: He's as straight as a gun-barrel. **1933** DWhitelaw *Roof* (L) 51: Jimmy was as straight as a gun-barrel. **1939** JRWarren *Murder from* (NY) 272: [He's] as straight as a gun-barrel. **1948** CBush *Curious* (NY) 217: Bob's genuine, straight as a gun-barrel. **1954** AWBarkley *That Remains* (NY) 65: Able to look "straight as a gun barrel" at the law. TW 164.

G234 Not fit to carry **Guts** to a bear

1938 SLeslie *Film* (L) 70: He was not fit to carry guts to a bear. **1941** DKent *Jason* (NY) 82: There isn't a man . . . with enough brains to carry guts to a bear. **1952** MScherf *Elk* (NY) 97: He didn't have sense to pack guts to a bear. **1968** EBuckler *Ox Bells* (NY) 164: Didn't feel fit to carry guts to a bear. EAP G195; DARE i 550: Carry guts. Cf. To lead Pigs *below*.

G235 To hate someone's **Guts** (*varied*)

1925 FSFitzgerald *Great Gatsby* (NY) 9: Men . . . had hated his guts. **1935** CDKing *Ob-elists* (NY) 29: He probably hates our guts. **1937** JWVandercook *Dark Islands* (NY) 319: [He] hated the dear Bishop's guts. **1940** HAshbrook *Murder Comes* (NY) 12: She hates my guts. **1941** JKVedder *Last Doorbell* (NY) 22: They all hate my guts. **1944** LLariar *Man . . . Lumpy Nose* (NY) 164: Winters hates his gizzard. **1951** GHCoxe *Widow* (NY) 90: I hated his guts. **1957** LFord *Girl* (NY) 177: They hate each other's guts. **1962** JBarry *Strange* (NY) 208: I hate their guts, as the saying goes. **1962** RO'Connor *Scandalous* (NY) 8: Hated his tripes. **1968** DMDisney *Voice* (NY) 141: He hated her guts. **1970** RQuest *Cerberus* (NY) 148: I loathed his guts. **1971** BWAldiss *Soldier* (L) 143: [He] hates my fucking guts. **1976** JMcClure *Snake* (NY) 116: She despises his guts. Berrey 282.4, 351.4.

G236 To have someone's **Guts** for garters

1943 MVHeberten *Murder Goes* (NY) 105: I'll stick you like a pig and give you your guts for garters. **1952** GBullett *Trouble* (L) 23: She'll have my guts for garters, my mother will. **1962** LDavidson *Rose* (NY) 309: They'll have your guts for garters. **1966** PO'Donnell *Sabre-Tooth* (L) 77: She'll save my guts for garters. **1971** BWAldiss *Soldier* (L) 60: They would have had my guts for garters. **1975** JFraser *Wreath* (NY) 112: I'll have his guts for garters. Partridge 362.

G237 To strain a **Gut**

1972 MGilbert *Body* (NY) 187: The skipper doesn't strain a gut trying to be matey. Berrey 242.5. Cf. DARE i 480: Burst a gut.

H

H1 Habit is a cable (*very varied*)

1919 JBCabell *Jurgen* (NY 1922) 198: Custom is all. **1930** KCStrahan *Death* (NY) 102: Habit is a cable. **1931** ACEdington *Monk's Hood* (NY) 67: Habit is a mighty thing. **1932** BFlynn *Crime* (NY) 130: Habits are hard to break. **1933** EPhillpotts *Captain's* (NY) 136: Use reconciles to nearly everything. **1934** CFGregg *Execution* (L) 47: The axiom that a habit is hard to break. **1935** CFGregg *Danger* (L) 237: Habit is a strong master. **1938** JFarnol *Crooked* (NY) 171: Use is everything. **1940** RAFreeman *Mr. Polton* (NY) 3: Use is second nature, as a copy book once informed me. **1944** HTalbot *Rim* (NY 1965) 102: Old habits die hard. EAP H2,4; TW 166.

H2 To have one's **Hackles** up (*varied*)

1929 VLoder *Between* (NY) 28: Merton . . . had his hackles up like a fighting cock; 188. **1931** RAJWalling *Stroke* (L) 22: Which was what got Stephen's hackle up. **1939** GDHCole *Greek* (L) 89: He continued to put Philip's hackles up. **1958** WDHassett *Off the Record* (New Brunswick, NJ) 22: FDR's hackles were stirred. **1960** HRobertson *Swan* (NY) 163: Dynes felt his hackles rising. **1966** LThayer *Dusty* (NY DBC) 80: Don't get your hackles up! **1973** AMStein *Finger* (NY) 169: I felt my hackles rising [*frightened*]. NED Hackle *sb.*² 3b; Partridge 365.

H3 As cold as a **Haddock**

1938 JLatimer *Dead Don't* (L) 79: Cold as a haddock [*unconscious*]. **1954** RKLeavitt *Chip* (P) 126: A craving to be knocked cold as haddocks. Cf. As cold as a Fish *above*; Herring, Mackerel *below*.

H4 As dead as a **Haddock**

1946 ESedgwick *Happy* (B) 86: Dead as a haddock. **1954** KMKnight *High* (NY) 135: It's dead as a haddock. Cf. As dead as a Fish, Flounder *above*; Herring, Mackerel *below*.

H5 As deaf as a **Haddock**

1939 ATilton *Cold Steal* (NY) 117: He's the deafest old haddock. **1963** FWTolman *Mosquitobush* (Peterborough, NH) 42: I'm deefer'n a goddam haddock. **1966** AG Martin *True Maine* (Freeport, Me.) 105: As deaf as a dead haddock. **1978** CMacLeod *Rest You* (NY) 9: He was deaf as a haddock. EAP H6.

H6 As dumb as a **Haddock**

1959 KMKnight *Beauty* (NY) 174: Dumb as a haddock. Whiting *NC* 418.

H7 As thick as **Hail**

1952 HTreece *Dark* (L) 84: Arrows flew thick as hail. **1961** LSdeCamp *Dragon* (NY 1968) 158: Arrows flying thick as hail. EAP H8; TW 166(3); Whiting H13.

H8 To give (get) **Hail Columbia**

1909 JCLincoln *Keziah* (NY) 106: Givin' the young feller Hail Columby. **1930** MCKeator *Eyes* (NY) 26: I ought to get Hail Columbia. TW 166.

H9 As true as a **Hair**

1933 FHShaw *Atlantic* (NY) 195: Steering a course as true as a hair. TW 166–7(4).

H10 A **Hair** of the dog (*varied*)

1900 CFPidgin *Quincy A. Sawyer* (B) 150–1: They say a hair of the dog is good for its bite [*not liquor*]. **1920** JJWalsh *Medieval Medicine* (L) 52: Taking a hair of the dog that bit you was . . . a maxim with the Salernitans for the cure of potation headaches. **1925** RAFreeman *Red Thumb* (L) 190: A hair of the dog that bit him . . . on the principle that *similia similibus curantur*. **1927** LBamburg *Beads* (NY) 49: He had indulged in what is popularly known as "a hair of the dog." **1936** KMKnight *Clue* (NY) 162: How about a hair from the dog's tail? **1938** JLatimer *Dead Don't* (L) 82: A hair of the St. Bernard that bit you. **1940** EBenjamin *Murder Without* (NY) 118: I'd suggest a bit of the hair of the dog. **1948** JTey *Franchise* (NY 1955) 134: The only cure is a hair of the dog that bit us. **1954** MProcter *Somewhere* (NY) 203: A hair of the dog. A hair of the tail of the dog that bit you. **1957** COLocke *Hell Bent* (NY) 85: He had a drink he called doghair which was no different from the others. **1957** *Time* 1/8 23: Some hair-of-the-doggerel from my unregenerate youth: "Candy is dandy, but liquor is quicker" [*ONash*]. **1959** *BHerald* 4/3 51: I would like to see the Herr of the dog that bit me. **1960** HAlpert *Some Other* (NY) 211: Then I take some of the hair that bit me. I mean I get me another girl and I'm over it. **1968** PBarr *Deer Cry* (L) 28: A couple of whiskies . . . the hair of the proverbial dog. **1973** BPronzini *Undercurrent* (NY) 157: Unless you've got a little hair of the dog. **1981** AMStein *Body* (NY) 53: It's dog-hair time. **1981** JBrett *Who'd Hire* (NY) 96: I treated myself to a morning hair-of-the-hound. EAP H14; TW 166(1); Brunvand 64(1).

H11 Not harm (hurt) a **Hair** of one's head

1921 IOstrander *Crimson* (NY) 20: Harm a hair of his head. **1929** JRhode *House* (NY) 209: She wouldn't have hurt a hair of his head. **1937** GDHCole *Missing* (L) 232: Denys wouldn't hurt a hair of her head.

1938 CWells *Missing* (P) 251: He . . . wouldn't harm a hair of her head. **1943** PATaylor *Going* (NY) 154: We wouldn't hurt the hair on a fly's head. **1952** RMacdonald *Ivory* (NY 1965) 39: I wouldn't hurt a hair of Lucy's head. EAP H17; Brunvand 64: Hurt (5).

H12 Not turn a **Hair**

1926 RAFreeman *D'Arblay* (NY) 168: He did not turn a hair. **1932** MStDennis *Death Kiss* (NY) 37: Cardigan never turned a hair. **1940** ECRLorac *Tryst* (L) 183: Any one of them would have stood up to be fired at without turning the proverbial hair. **1967** RJones *Three* (NY) 156: No one, as the saying is, turned a hair. Cf. EAP H16: Change; NED Hair 8n.

H13 To a **Hair**

1931 EPhillpotts *Found* (L) 272: My sentiments to a hair. **1945** EPhillpotts *They Were Seven* (NY) 65: My opinion to a hair. **1957** AECoppard *It's Me* (L) 106: Fitted him to a hair. EAP H18.

H14 To comb one's **Hair** for him

1936 ECVivian *With Intent* (L) 131: Wait until your wife reads about this—she'll comb your hair for you! Partridge 171: Comb one's head; DARE i 731: Comb one's head(2).

H15 To get in one's **Hair**

1937 CKnight *Scarlet Crab* (NY) 43: This fellow . . . is beginning to get in my hair. **1938** NMorland *Case Without* (L) 57: What's got in your hair? **1955** ELacy *Best* (NY) 16: Kept getting in our hair. **1956** FDOmmanney *Isle* (P) 216: He got, as the Americans say, ever so slightly in my hair. **1960** FPohl *Drunkard's* (NY) 25: The son of a bitch is getting in my hair. Wentworth 239.

H16 To have by the short **Hairs** (where the hair [wool] is short)

1925 JGBrandon *Cork* (L) 137: To have [him] by the short hair. **1928** RHFuller *Jubilee* (NY) 108: He had them where the hair was short. **1932** MThynne *Murder* (NY) 199: He'd got Miller by the short hairs. **1934** HReilly *McKee* (NY) 144: You've got me where the wool is short. **1939** JRWarren *Murder from* (NY) 14: [He] had me by the short hairs. **1941** BHalliday *Bodies* (NY 1959) 87: He had you where the hair was short. **1948** ELipsky *Murder One* (NY) 53: We got you by the short hairs. **1955** PMacDonald *Guest* (NY) 113: 'E's got 'em by the short 'airs. **1957** CWilliams *Big Bite* (L) 127: If anybody had me where the wool was that short I'd be an eager beaver myself. **1959** AMStein *Never* (NY) 21: They'd have us by the short hairs. **1968** RDuncan *How to Make* (L) 43: [He] again had me by the short hairs. **1970** AEHotchner *Treasure* (NY) 275: [He] had us by the short hair. **1972** NWebster *Killing* (NY) 156: To use a phrase from my youth, they really had you by the short and curlies. **1981** LCutter *Murder* (NY) 122: JG doesn't let anybody lead him around by the short and curlies. TW 167(12).

H17 To keep (hold) one's **Hair** on
1917 JCLincoln *Extricating* (NY) 258: Set still and hold your hair on. **1923** VWilliams *Orange* (B) 50: Keep your hair on. **1933** GDHCole *End* (L) 76: Keep your hair on. **1954** AWUpfield *Death* (NY) 46: Keep your hair on. **1958** BNichols *Rich* (NY) 81: Keep your hair on. **1960** MSpark *Ballad* (L) 7: Keep your hair on. Partridge 366. Cf. Pants, Shirt, Wig, Wool *below*.

H18 To make one's **Hair** curl
1925 JICClarke *My Life* (NY) 76: See something that would "make my hair curl" [*with pleasure*]. **1938** BFrancis *Death at* (L) 39: News that'll make your hair curl. Partridge 199: Curl.

H19 To miss by a **Hair** (hair's breadth)
1922 JJoyce *Ulysses* (NY 1934) 238: Just missed that by a hair. **1926** EDBiggers *Chinese* (NY) 309: "You beat us to it" . . . "By a hair's width." **1930** SSVanDine *Scarab* (NY) 258: Escaped . . . by the proverbial hair's-breadth. **1935** TRoscoe *Murder* (NY) 188: Only missed finishing me by the proverbial hair. **1935** PATaylor *Deathblow* (NY) 130: Less than the proverbial hair's breadth away. **1937** NBell *Crocus* (NY) 215: One other of his posters missed a similar banning by the proverbial hair.

1937 LPendleton *Down East* (NY) 227: Missed . . . by the proverbial hair's breadth. **1949** RKing *Redoubled* (NY) 67: Cordova's voice sharpened a hair's breadth. **1956** FAllen *Much* (B) 337: A truck . . . missed hitting him by the proverbial hair. **1964** HBourne *In the Event* (NY) 151: I had missed the bus . . . by a hair's breadth. **1965** ECheesman *Who Stand* (L) 90: Not to deviate a hair's breadth. EAP H22; TW 167; Brunvand 64: Hair's breadth.

H20 To split **Hairs** (straws)
1921 P&MThorne *Sheridan* (NY) 203: It might be splitting hairs. **1928** RAFreeman *As a Thief* (L) 217: Set my learned friend splitting straws. **1932** MKennedy *Murderer* (L) 280: Don't bother to split hairs. **1933** DGBrowne *Dead* (L) 45: The curator could split a hair with any man. **1934** LRGribble *Death* (L) 242: Don't split straws. **1937** ASoutar *One Page* (L) 197: You are taking advantage—splitting straws. **1952** MMurray *Doctor* (NY DBC) 127: This was splitting hairs. **1957** WRBurdett *Underdog* (NY) 9: Always splitting hairs. **1961** JSStrange *Eye* (NY) 82: I wish you wouldn't split hairs. **1963** HPentecost *Tarnished* (NY DBC) 116: If you want to split hairs. **1972** HCarmichael *Naked* (NY) 28: Aren't you splitting hairs? **1975** PMoyes *Black* (NY) 110: I don't want to split hairs. EAP H21.

H21 To take (let) one's **Hair** down (*varied*)
1936 EQueen *Door* (Cleveland 1946) 233: You may take your hair down now. **1937** WDickinson *Dead Man* (P) 58: Suppose you take down your back hair, little girl, and explain this masquerade. **1938** MECorne *Death* (NY) 16: Mrs. Greeley was not a girl to let her hair down. **1938** NMorland *Rope* (L) 259: Are you going to take your hair down, as they say. **1940** DBurnham *Last Act* (NY) 19: [He] let down his hair. **1947** KMKnight *Blue* (NY) 189: We girls seem to be taking down our hair. **1950** PMcGerr *Follow* (NY) 75: Afraid you'll let your hair down? **1952** EHahn *Love* (NY) 162: In modern parlance, he really let down his hair. **1958** JByrom *Or Be* (L 1964) 121: I had caught her with her hair down. **1971** MHarrison *Fanfare* (L) 143: That relaxa-

tion . . . that women call "letting one's hair down." **1981** JSScott *View* (NY) 94: Nothing like letting your hair down in your free time. Wentworth 239.

H22 **Half** a loaf is better than none (*varied*)
1919 RFirbank *Valmouth* (Works 3, L 1929) 97: Half a loaf is better than no bread. **1919** LThayer *Mystery of the 13th Floor* (NY) 197: Half a loaf is better than no bread. **1925** CGBowers *Jefferson* (NY) 110: He never refused the half loaf he could get because of the whole loaf he could not have. **1928** EO'Neill *Strange* (NY) 232: Half a loaf is better—to a starving man. **1929** ABCox *Layton* (NY) 229: Half a bun was better than no cake. **1930** JBude *Loss* (L) 112: After all a crumb of cake is better than no cake at all. **1933** HDuffy *Seven* (NY) 241: Half a loaf is better than no bread. **1938** MPage *Fast Company* (NY) 103: Half a truth is better than none. **1940** RAFreeman *Mr. Polton* (NY) 260: A vulgar saying . . . has it that half a loaf is better than no bread. **1944** RShattuck *Said* (NY) 122: "On the theory that half a loaf was better than none?" "Yes, but it must have depended a great deal on the size of the loaf." **1952** PHBonner *SPQR* (NY) 288: "Half a cake is better than none." "Not this kind of cake. All the half will give us is indigestion." **1957** DJEnright *Heaven* (L) 26: Half a lie is better than no truth. **1958** NBlake *Penknife* (L) 222: Half a loaf is worse than no bread. **1959** *BHerald* 3/26 6: That half-loaf labor bill. **1962** EAmbler *Light* (L) 254: Even a crumb is better than no bread. **1964** TDubois *Shannon* (NY DBC) 163: Half a loaf? But it was a nice loaf, too, and in time she might find that it had become, not the half, but the whole. **1970** HCarmichael *Death* (NY) 203: Half a loaf is better than no bread. **1970** RWMackelworth *Tiltangle* (NY) 36: Half a victory was better than none. **1974** WSnow *Codline* (Middletown, Conn.) 427: The gospel of the half-loaf, the real gospel of democracy. EAP H23; TW 167–8(1). Cf. Brunvand 88: Loaf.

H23 Not to do things by **Halves** (*varied*)
1923 JSFletcher *Charing Cross* (NY) 151: Don't believe in half-measures. **1928**

EHamilton *Four* (L) 209: My little cousin sure didn't do things by halves. **1930** HCrooker *Hollywood* (NY) 64: Mr. Gilbert never did things half-way, as the saying goes. **1930** HFootner *Mystery* (NY) 156: Half measures are always fatal. **1972** AGarve *Case* (NY) 145: Robert never did do things by halves. *Oxford* 562: Never.

H24 One **Half** the world does not know how the other half lives (*varied*)
1919 LMerrick *Chair* (L) 114: How nearly it has been said, One half of the world does not know how the other half loves. **1930** HAdams *Crime* (P) 212: One half of the world doesn't know how the other half lives, but it suspects the worse. **1950** STruss *Never* (NY) 9: Half the . . . population . . . preferred not to know how the other half lived. **1953** BCarey *Their Nearest* (NY) 175: This sure has been our night for seeing how the other half lives. **1956** DWheatley *Ka* (L) 163: There's no truer saying than that "one half of the world does not know how the other half lives." **1962** ESGardner *Ice-Cold* (NY DBC) 14: It's wise to listen to how the other half lives. EAP H25; Brunvand 156: World(2).

H25 To be cheap at **Half** the price
1936 HFootner *Kidnapping* (L) 253: Cheap at half the price. Berrey 551.15.

H26 To be too clever by **Half**
1930 NGordon *Silent* (NY) 204: Too clever by half. **1952** PLoraine *Dublin* (L) 122: [He] was too clever by half. **1961** ADuggan *King* (L) 31: The King was too clever by half. **1969** DMDevine *Death* (L) 118: Too bloody clever by half. NED Half *sb.* 7e (quote 1858).

H27 To see with **Half** an eye
1928 GDHCole *Man* (NY) 41: The greatest mug could have seen it with half an eye. **1951** CHare *English* (L) 45: One can see with half an eye that you are well enough. **1958** CHare *He Should* (L) 30: Anyone can see with half an eye that you're married at the drop of a hat. **1972** JCreasey *Gallows* (NY) 98: That's obvious with half an eye. **1976** JPorter *Package* (NY) 50: Anybody can see that with half an eye. EAP H26.

H28 To go off **Half-cocked** (at half cock)

1912 JCLincoln *Postmaster* (NY) 193: Don't go off half-cocked. **1932** GDyer *Five* (B) 245: Go off at half-cock. **1939** HReilly *All Concerned* (NY) 79: Don't go off half cocked. **1940** DCCameron *Grave* (NY) 46: I hate to go off half-cocked. **1954** EQueen *Glass* (B) 279: We went off half-cocked. **1958** HMasur *Murder* (NY 1959) 88: Before going off half-cocked. **1960** KM Knight *Invitation* (NY DBC) 128: Let's not go off half-cocked. **1968** SPalmer *Rook* (NY) 88: Going off a little half-cocked. **1972** MGilbert *Body* (NY) 70: Go off at half cock. EAP H27.

H29 To be **Half-seas** over (*varied*)

1925 TRMarshall *Recollections* (I) 142: More than half-seas over. **1928** MPShiel *How the Old Woman* (L) 93: You are half-seas over. **1935** BGraeme *Body* (L) 210: A long way from being half seas over. **1940** BHalliday *Private Practice* (NY 1965) 98: The old boy was half-seas under. **1945** ABarber *Noose* (NY) 106: Pete [is] half-seas under. **1955** MHutchins *Memoirs* (NY) 128: Half seas over, three sheets in the wind . . . tipsy as David's sow. **1961** LThayer *And One* (NY DBC) 124: He was half-seas over at the time. **1962** MStewart *Moon-* (NY 1965) 49: I must have been half-seas-under [*delirious, but not drunk*]. EAP H30.

H30 It is merry in **Hall** when beards wag all

1930 RAFreeman *Mystery* (NY) 86: Such conversation as is possible "when beards wag all" over the festive board. **1933** CWells *Clue* (NY) 292: Sort of "Merry in hall, when beards wagged all." **1943** GGCoulton *Fourscore* (Cambridge, Eng.) 315: 'Tis merry in hall when beards wag all. EAP H32.

H31 To be like **Ham** and eggs (*varied*)

1934 WChambers *Murder* (NY) 137: They're tied as close together as ham and eggs. **1941** AAmos *Pray* (NY) 22: We get along like ham and eggs. **1947** GGallagher *I Found* (NY DBC) 102: Baxter and his wife went together as perfectly as ham and eggs.

H32 To hang as high as **Haman** (*varied*)

1905 JBCabell *Line* (NY 1926) 158: Hang the lad as high as Haman. **1920** AChristie *Mysterious Affair* (NY) 106: Hang him as high as Haman. **1921** JCLincoln *Galusha* (NY) 120: Curtains strung up higher'n Haman. **1937** VLoder *Choose* (L) 205: He wants to hang someone Haman-high. **1938** RAJWalling *Grimy Glove* (NY) 235: Jerked by the neck as high as Haman. **1947** DBowers *Bells* (NY) 16: You seem as high as Haman. **1947** ELustgarten *One More* (NY 1959) 217: Hanged high as Haman. **1951** ECRLorac *I Could* (NY) 167: It's as high as Haman [*smell*]. **1958** WDHassett *Off the Record* (New Brunswick, NJ) 183: Hanged high as Haman. **1963** NBlake *Deadly* (L) 245: The quotation about hanging as high as Haman. **1965** AGilbert *Voice* (NY) 52: I hope he hangs as high as Haman. EAP H33. Cf. Judas *below*.

H33 Like *Hamlet* without the Prince of Denmark (*varied*)

1928 GGardiner *At the House* (NY) 16: Like *Hamlet* without the Prince of Denmark, as the proverb goes. **1931** JSFletcher *Dressing* (NY) 112: Hamlet, with Hamlet left out. **1932** JJConnington *Sweepstake* (B) 302: *Hamlet* minus the Prince of Denmark. **1957** *Punch* 9/11 301: As dry as Hamlet without the Prince. EAP H34.

H34 As dead as a **Hammer**

1910 EPhillpotts *Tales* (NY) 72: He was dead as a hammer. **1933** JGregory *Case* (NY) 19: He was as dead as a hammer. **1949** EPhillpotts *Address* (L) 154: So dead as a hammer. **1960** MJones *Forest* (NY) 227: Dead as a hammer. EAP H35.

H35 At it **Hammer** and tongs (*varied*)

1905 JBCabell *Line* (NY 1926) 124: Fighting . . . hammer-and-tongs, as the saying is. **1910** JCLincoln *Depot Master* (NY) 57: Gabe went at it hammer and tongs [*worked rapidly*]. **1928** DHLawrence *Lady* ("Allemagne") 242: And I flew back hammer and tongs. **1930** WLewis *Apes* (NY 1932) 183: At it again hammer and tongs. **1937** LTWhite *Homicide* (NY) 233: He goes at Wallace hammer and ice-picks. **1941** EL

Fetta *Dressed* (NY) 105: "They were going at it hammer and tongs." "Coining phrases again, darling?" **1953** HBPiper *Murder* (NY) 178: Going at it, hammer-and-tongs. **1957** MPHood *In the Dark* (NY) 129: I can't go hammer and tongs after the fat woman. **1962** ESGardner *Ice-Cold* (NY DBC) 54: He's a hammer-and-tongs investigator. **1970** PAlding *Guilt* (NY) 178: We've been going hammer and tongs all day trying to tie up loose ends. **1976** LEgan *Scenes* (NY) 38: Going at each other hammer and tongs. EAP H36; Brunvand 64.

H36 To be between **Hammer** and anvil

1933 BRoss *Tragedy of Z* (NY) 117: In the unenviable position of being between the hammer and the anvil. **1958** WHCanaway *Ring-givers* (L) 169: We are between the hammer and the anvil. *Oxford* 346.

H37 To be **Hammer** or anvil

1961 CJenkins *Message* (L) 111: We must, as has been said, be either the hammer or the anvil. **1974** WStegner *Uneasy* (NY) 308: Like all who elect to be hammer, he found himself now and then an anvil. EAP H37.

H38 All **Hands** *etc.*

1912 JCLincoln *Postmaster* (NY) 207: It's a case for all hands and the ship's cook, workin' together. **1929** JJConnington *Case* (B) 66: It's a case of all hands to the pumps. **1939** JJones *Murder al Fresco* (NY) 39: With all hands on deck. DARE i 41: All hands; Colcord 93.

H39 As bare (naked) as one's **Hand**

1931 WMorton *Mystery* (NY) 144: That long white corridor, bare as one's hand. **1937** JFerguson *Death* (L) 82: The floor was as bare as my hand. Whiting H51: Bare.

H40 As easy (*etc.*) as kiss your **Hand**

1924 VBridges *Red Lodge* (NY) 76: Chatted away as friendly as kiss me 'and. **1929** HWilliamson *Beautiful* (NY) 248: As quick as kiss yer hand. **1929** JJConnington *Case* (B) 81: As easy as kiss-your-hand. **1931** WWJacobs *Snug* (NY) 203: It's as easy as kissing your fingers. **1934** WGore *There's Death* (L) 167: Cool as kiss me 'and. **1935** MBeckett *Teatime* (L) 274: As easy as kiss-

your-hand. **1936** MAllingham *Flowers* (NY) 155: Clean as kiss yer hand. **1938** JC Lanehan *Guilty* (L) 179: She'd as lief do it as kiss your hand. **1940** LBrock *Stoat* (L) 31: It's as simple as kiss-my-hand. **1940** JCreasey *Here Comes* (NY 1967) 38: Easy as kiss me. **1947** PWentworth *Wicked* (NY) 61: It's as easy as kissing your hand. **1954** JRRTolkien *Two* (L) 323: As gladly as kiss his hand. **1959** BWAldiss *Vanguard* (NY) 28: As easy as kiss your hand. **1962** NMarsh *Hand* (B) 140: It's all as sweet as kiss-your-hand. EAP H38. Cf. As soon as kiss my Arse *above*.

H41 As flat as one's **Hand**

1940 HCBailey *Mr. Fortune Here* (NY) 79: The sea was as flat as your hand. **1951** JCFurnas *Voyage* (NY) 127: The place was flat as your hand. **1959** GCarr *Swing* (NY) 222: It was as flat as me hand. TW 169(3). Cf. As flat as the Palm *below*.

H42 As plain as one's **Hand**

1953 MPHood *Silent* (NY) 54: Plain as the hand before my face. TW 169(4). Cf. As plain as one's Foot *above*; To know like the Palm *below*.

H43 Cold **Hand**, warm heart

1928 ESnell *Blue* (P) 246: They tell me folks with cold hands have warm hearts. **1971** PDickinson *Sleep* (NY) 3: Cold 'and, warm 'eart. *Oxford* 132: Cold.

H44 The **Hand** that rocks the cradle *etc.*

1922 JJoyce *Ulysses* (NY 1934) 283: Her hand that rocks the cradle rules the Ben Howth. That rules the world. 490: The hand that rocks the cradle. **1926** HHMunro *Toys* (L) 119: The hand that rocks the cradle rocks the world. **1958** *BTraveler* 11/28 46: It is axiomatic that the hand that rocks the cradle rules the world. *Oxford* 347.

H45 The iron **Hand** in the velvet glove (*varied*)

1903 EChilders *Riddle* (NY 1940) 55: The iron hand in the velvet glove. **1929** TShannon *Catspaw* (NY) 14: The iron hand in the velvet glove. **1930** JGBrandon *McCarthy* (L) 137: The iron hand was concealed beneath the silken glove. **1931** LHollingworth *Death* (L) 147: The velvet hand or the glove of iron. **1934** GFairlie *Copper* (L) 240: The steel hand in the velvet glove. **1941** GBagby *Red Is* (NY) 70: You've heard of the iron hand in the velvet glove. **1947** JIams *Body* (NY) 209: The mailed-fist-in-velvet-glove quality of the cocktails. **1952** GBagby *Corpse* (NY) 145: The iron hand in the velvet glove. **1953** LThompson *Time* (L) 19: The iron hand in the velvet glove. **1958** PBranch *Murder's* (L 1963) 42: Velvet-fist-in-iron-glove. **1967** CBush *Deadly* (NY) 36: The cliché of a well-disguised iron hand in velvet glove. **1968** LDurrell *Tunc* (NY) 58: That velvet prick in an iron mitt. **1968** EPHoyt *A. Woollcott* (NY) 187: His best mailed-fist-in-velvet-glove manner. **1969** CBush *Deadly* (NY) 36: He fits the cliché of the well-disguised iron hand in velvet glove. **1975** LBiggle *This Darkening* (NY) 137: His smile the velvet glove on the iron fist. TW 169(11).

H46 Let not one's left (right) **Hand** know *etc.*

1925 HHext *Monster* (NY) 24: You . . . don't tell your right hand what your left does. **1932** TSmith *Bishop's* (NY) 55: You don't believe in letting your left hand know what your right hand is doing. **1938** NBlake *Beast* (NY 1958) 183: He's the kind of man whose left hand is not allowed to know what his right hand is doing. **1941** EPhillpotts *Ghostwater* (NY) 81: He seldom let his left hand know what his right hand did. **1969** AGilbert *Missing* (NY) 21: Talk about your left hand not knowing what your right hand doesth. **1970** JAGraham *Something* (B) 135: Never let the right hand know what the left is doing. **1972** MDelving *Shadow* (NY) 49: The right hand not knowing what the left hand is doing. **1974** ROllard *Pepys* (NY) 283: The right hand rarely knew what the left was doing. **1981** AMorice *Men* (NY) 143: His right hand is out of communication with his left. EAP H41; Brunvand 65(3).

H47 Many **Hands** make light work

1928 WJerrold *Bulls* (L) 23: Many hands make light work. **1933** MPlum *Murder* (NY)

238: Many hands make light work. **1936** MBurton *Where Is* (L) 182: A matter of many hands making light work. **1944** PA Taylor *Dead Ernest* (NY) 107: Many hands make light work, and all that sort of thing. **1954** OAnderson *Thorn* (L) 19: Many hands make light work. **1957** CRice *Knocked* (NY) 188: Don't bite the many hands that make light work. **1961** MG Eberhart *Cup* (NY DBC) 127: Many hands make light work. **1962** AMStein *Home* (NY) 91: Many hands make light work and all that jazz. **1963** KVonnegut *Cat's* (NY) 224: "Many hands make much work light," old Chinese proverb. EAP H43; TW 169(7).

H48 One **Hand** for the ship *etc.*

1953 CBKelland *Sinister* (NY DBC) 36: The old sailor's injunction: One hand for the ship, one hand for yourself. **1963** J-YCousteau *Living Sea* (NY) 30: The old maxim, "One hand for the ship, one hand for yourself." EAP H45: Owners.

H49 One **Hand** washes the other

1935 RGraves *Claudius the God* (NY) 322: One hand washes the other. **1959** ESchiddel *Devil* (NY) 223: One hand washed another, as the saying goes. **1961** HActon *Last Bourbons* (L) 2: One hand washes the other. **1964** FPeters *Boyhood* (NY) 165: Love could be defined as "one hand washes the other." **1964** GVidal *Julian* (NY 1965) 351: One hand washes the other, as they say. **1971** JBlake *Joint* (NY) 208: One hand should wash the other. EAP H46.

H50 To be **Hand** in (and) glove (*varied*)

1900 CFPidgin *Quincy A. Sawyer* (B) 209: He is hand in glove with all the theatre managers. **1920** ACrabb *Samuel* (NY) 198: Stories that fitted as a hand and a glove. **1931** HBurnham *Murder* (NY) 251: I'd always been hand and glove with Lalla. **1931** LThayer *Last Shot* (NY) 3: Work together like a hand in a glove. **1936** JMWalsh *Crimes* (L) 34: You and Mentaz are hand in glove. **1938** ABoutell *Death* (NY) 189: If . . . Archie weren't hand and glove with the law. **1941** IAlexander *Revenge* (NY) 252: Phoebe and I have worked hand in glove. **1950** CDickson *Night* (NY) 47: He's hand-in-glove with the police. **1953** EBGarside *Man from* (NY) 92: This wench and I fitted like hand and glove. **1954** TDuBois *Seeing* (NY) 43: She was hand and glove with [him]. **1962** NMarsh *Hand in Glove* (B). **1966** RVanGulik *Murder* (NY) 114: That . . . captain must be hand in glove with them. **1967** AMarreco *Rebel* (L) 113: Emotion and action went hand in glove. **1974** AGarve *Case* (NY) 9: [They] complemented each other like hand and glove. EAP H51; Brunvand 65(1).

H51 To bite the **Hand** that feeds one (*varied*)

1928 ABCox *Amateur* (NY) 334: Why turn round and bite the hand that plotted with you, so to speak. **1930** CBarry *Avenging* (NY) 140: Soltan seems to have bitten the hand that fed him. **1933** LO'Flaherty *Martyr* (NY) 42: A cur bites the hand that feeds him. **1938** PMcGuire *Burial* (L) 220: I feel . . . like (if I may be permitted a vulgar expression) a mongrel which bites the hand that has fed it. **1939** EDean *Murder Is* (NY) 157: Feeling as though he had been bitten by the hand that was feeding him. **1956** RFenisong *Bite the Hand* (NY). **1957** *Punch* 2/20 271: Before you know where you are, their teeth are fixed in the hand they are feeding. **1959** *BHerald* 2/8 sec. IV 9: These pols are not going to turn around and bite the hand that elected them. **1961** FLockridge *Murder* (P) 19: Never bite the hand that might bite back. **1967** EWallach *Light* (NY) 348: He robbed the hand that fed him. **1970** JVizzard *See* (NY) 323: He did not want to bite the hand that freed him. **1974** SKrim *You* (NY) 53: And then biting, no, shitting all over the hands that fed him. EAP H55.

H52 To do something with one's left **Hand**
1970 SO'Toole *Confessions* (Minneapolis) 4: I did my schoolwork with my left hand. NED Left hand.

H53 To eat (feed) out of one's **Hand**
1922 DFox *Ethel* (NY) 191: Make him eat out of my hand. **1924** LSpringfield *Some Piquant* (L) 154: You'll have him feeding from the hand. **1928** JRhode *Tragedy* (NY) 133: He'd feed out of your hand. **1937** VWilliams *Mr. Treadgold* (L) 255: He eats out of her hand. **1940** MRRinehart *Great Mistake* (NY) 239: You'll have her eating out of your hand. **1950** RFoley *Hundredth* (NY) 86: The men . . . are eating out of your hand. **1956** AAkinson *Exit* (NY) 50: They'd eat out of your hand. **1963** HWaugh *Death* (NY) 26: You got her eating outa your hand like a frigging canary. **1969** DMDevine *Death* (L) 21: They were eating out of her hand. **1975** NFreeling *Bugles* (NY) 154: They'll eat out of your hand. **1977** PDickinson *Walking* (NY) 7: We have them eating out of our hat. NED Suppl. Eat 3d.

H54 To get (*etc.*) the upper **Hand**
1903 EChilders *Riddle* (NY 1940) 54: They got the upper hand. **1931** JJConnington *Boathouse* (B) 146: The upper hand. **1936** ECRLorac *Pall* (L) 31: They've got the upper hand. **1941** ISShriber *Murder Well Done* (NY) 71: It'll give Grandmother the upper hand. **1946** FLockridge *Death of a Tall Man* (P) 45: Skepticism fought for the upper hand. **1952** MInnes *One-man* (NY) 171: Fright will gain the upper hand. **1959** JABrussel *Just* (NY) 63: Curiosity gained the upper hand. **1960** EXFerrars *Fear* (NY) 116: One's own nature always gets the upper hand. **1962** MClifton *When They* (NY) 116: We've got the upper hand. **1975** MDelving *Bored* (NY) 58: My good sense got the upper hand. EAP H57; TW 169(14); Brunvand 65(7). Cf. next entry.

H55 To have (*etc.*) the whip **Hand**
1918 ERPunshon *Solitary* (NY) 196: He had the whip hand of me. **1924** JSFletcher *Safety* (NY) 199: Got the whip-hand. **1928** SMartin *Fifteen* (NY) 95: He held the whip handle. **1935** GBarnett *Murder* (L) 50: She's got the whip-hand. **1938** HAustin *Lilies* (NY) 276: He had the whip hand. **1940** ISShriber *Head over Heels* (NY) 164: She held the whip hand over you. **1956** AAkinson *Exit* (NY) 212: The villains held the whip-hand. **1959** BHalliday *Target* (NY) 176: He has the whip hand now. **1964** RBraddon *Year* (L 1967) 89: We must keep the whip hand over everyone. **1966** MG

Eberhart *Witness* (NY) 12: She did have the whip hand. **1970** BGrebanier *Uninhibited* (NY) 261: She held the whip hand over her. **1972** JBlish *Midsummer* (NY) 99: [He] did indeed have the whip hand. EAP H58: Hand; TW 169–70: Hand (15); Brunvand 65: Hand (8); *Oxford* 884: Whiphand. Cf. preceding entry.

H56 To keep one's **Hand** on one's ha'penny

1970 DClark *Deadly* (NY) 146: "You were trying to find out whether she'd been keeping her hand on her ha'penny or not." "Quite right. She took her hand off it when she was sixteen, I suspect. She's been taking it off at intervals ever since by the sound of things." *Oxford* 346–7.

H57 To lend a helping **Hand**

1953 DMDisney *Prescription* (NY) 20: I'm always ready to lend a helping hand. EAP H59.

H58 To live from **Hand** to mouth (*varied*)

1922 JSFletcher *Ravensdene* (NY) 151: Living from hand to mouth. **c1923** ACrowley *Confessions* ed JSymonds (L 1969) 639: Living from hand to mouth. **1933** AGilbert *Musical* (L) 99: Living, in a sense, from hand to mouth. **1937** RPEckert *Edward Thomas* (L) 53: Living a hand-to-mouth existence. **1941** JJConnington *Twenty-one* (B) 68: A hand-to-mouth business. **1949** NBlake *Head* (NY) 65: That hand-to-mouth kind of life. **1955** AWest *Heritage* (NY) 207: If you live from hand to mouth. **1957** JWyndham *Midwich* (NY) 15: The unregulated hand-to-mouth way of life. **1958** PDeVries *Mackerel* (B) 6: A kind of hand-to-mouth luxury. **1960** CDLewis *Buried* (L) 152: An emotionally hand-to-mouth existence. **1969** JGould *Poet* (NY) 84: They lived from hand to mouth. **1971** DDaiches *Third* (Sussex, Eng.) 12: A very hand-to-mouth way of preparing lectures. **1974** JFlaherty *Chez* (NY) 16: Lived . . . from hand-to-mouth. EAP H39; TW 170(18).

H59 To put one's **Hand** between the bark and the tree

1947 HCahill *Look* (NY) 13: Sometimes its pretty easy to put your hand between the bark and the tree. **1956** HCahill *Shadow* (NY) 270: Think you can get your hand between the bark and its tree anymore than Muggins could? *Oxford* 30: Bark.

H60 To put one's **Hand** to the plow *etc.*

1928 TCobb *Who Opened* (L) 276: He could not quite understand why Moina, having put her hand to the plough, should have thought . . . of looking back. **1930** MBurton *Hardway* (L) 67: He had put his hand to the plough. **1931** JHRYardley *Before the Mayflower* (NY) 333: Having once set his hand to the plough, he . . . refused to look back, or even aside. **1949** MBurton *Disappearing* (NY) 54: Having set his hand to the plough, would he consent to turn back? **1969** AGilbert *Mr. Crook* (NY DBC) 97: The one who having put his hand to the plow, never looked back. **1971** JBlake *Joint* (NY) 114: Don't put your hand on the plow if you're only going to take it off again. EAP H63.

H61 To throw in (up) one's **Hand**

1930 FDGrierson *Mysterious* (L) 241: He was not a man to throw in his hand. **1931** FBeeding *Three* (B) 226: I should not have expected him to throw up his hand. **1936** MBurton *Death* (L) 131: I chucked my hand in. **1946** CDickson *My Late* (NY) 246: He was just about ready to throw in his hand. **1956** BJFarmer *Death* (L) 128: Throwing his hand in. NED Suppl. Throw *v.*[1] 41g. Cf. *Oxford* 819: Throw up one's cards.

H62 To wait on **Hand** and foot (*varied*)

1923 JSFletcher *Charing Cross* (NY) 72: Waited on hand and foot. **1939** DDean *Emerald* (NY) 17: Servants to wait on you hand and foot. **1951** ESGardner *Fiery* (NY) 115: He was always dancing attendance on her hand and foot. **1953** AChristie *Funerals* (NY) 152: Waits on him hand and foot. **1970** SGBoswell *Book* (L) 68: They're waited on hand and foot. **1977** CWatson *Fourth* (B) 22: Waited on him hand and foot. NED Hand 56.

H63 To wash one's **Hands** of something

1916 EClodd *Memories* (L) 55: Washed his hands of the whole affair. **1923** EWallace

Clue of the New Pin (B) 168: I've washed my hands of the whole affair. **1932** DSharp *Code-letter* (B) 210: Mine host washed his hands of us. **1939** JDonavan *Coloured Wind* (L) 186: I washed my hands of the whole business. **1940** NRath *Death of a Lucky* (NY) 272: Sullivan has washed his hands of me. **1951** SSpender *World* (L) 135: I secretly washed my hands of social guilt. **1954** FCDavis *Another* (NY) 69: Force him to wash his hands of me. **1961** MKelly *Spoilt* (L) 183: I wash my hands of it. **1964** JWiles *March* (L) 132: I am washing my hands of the whole affair. **1972** DDevine *Three* (NY) 18: His father washed his hands of the black sheep of the family. **1974** MScherf *If You Want* (NY) 17: He . . . washed his hands of his employee. EAP H65; TW 170(22); Brunvand 65(9).

H64 With one **Hand** tied behind one's back

1959 HStone *Man Who* (NY) 101: Any time he wanted to he could do better himself with that proverbial one hand tied behind his back. **1962** DMDisney *Should Auld* (NY) 46: Something he could handle with one hand tied behind his back.

H65 To fly (go) off the **Handle**

1913 ECBentley *Trent's* (NY 1930) 84: He would fly off the handle. **1920** GDilnot *Suspected* (NY) 105: Don't fly off the handle. **1932** JDCarr *Poison* (NY) 181: Don't fly off the handle. **1937** CDickson *Ten Teacups* (L) 31: Never fly off the handle. **1942** JBell *Death . . . Medical Board* (NY 1964) 50: You fly off the handle. **1949** KMKnight *Bass* (NY) 55: Fly off the handle. **1951** TDubois *Foul* (NY) 140: They fly off the handle. **1957** LBeam *Maine* (NY) 202: Go clear off the handle. **1958** HCarmichael *Or Be* (NY) 180: Flying off the handle. **1961** WMasterson *Evil* (NY) 150: Flying off the handle. **1969** AGilbert *Missing* (NY) 10: Don't fly off the handle. TW 170(3,5).

H66 **Handsome** (*etc.*) is as handsome does (*varied*)

1900 CFPidgin *Quincy A. Sawyer* (B) 124: Handsome is as handsome does. **1911** JLondon *Letters* ed KHendricks (NY 1965) 338: Handsome is as handsome does. **1920**

LFBaum *Glinda* (C) 195: Handsome is as handsome does. **1922** JJoyce *Ulysses* (NY 1934) 72: Handsome is and handsome does. **1930** HBedford-Jones *Shadow* (NY) 173: Sensible is as sensible does. **1931** WWJacobs *Snug* (NY) 106: Handsome is as 'andsome does . . . It's an old saying but it's true. **1935** DMcCleary *Not for Heaven* (NY) 45: Big is as big does. **1936** AHuxley *Eyeless* (NY) 5: Ha dsome is as handsome doesn't, in your case. **1936** EQueen *Door* (Cleveland 1946) 6: Gentle is as gentle does. **1940** ECRLorac *Tryst* (L) 209: Handsome is as handsome does, as the sow said to the boar. **1941** HCBailey *Bishop's* (NY) 13: Dirty does as dirty is. **1941** CLittle *Black Paw* (NY) 24: Fancy is as fancy does. **1949** GHHall *End* (NY) 137: Common is as common does. **1951** IChase *New York 22* (NY) 148: "Handsome is as handsome does, we always say in our family." "And a very good saying, too." **1957** JCreasey *Model* (L 1961) 91: Handsome is as handsome does. **1960** JSymonds *Only Thing* (L) 26: But handsome is what handsome does. **1966** KAmis *Spectrum V* (L) 161: Beauty is as beauty does. **1974** SChance *Septimus* (Nashville) 60: Handsome is as handsome does. EAP H70. Cf. Pretty *below*.

H67 The **Handwriting** on the wall

1933 BRoss *Tragedy of Z* (NY) 175: We all saw the handwriting on the wall. **1936** NGayle *Murder* (L) 100: They fail to see the handwriting on the wall. **1945** GHCoxe *Jade Venus* (NY) 78: He could begin to see the handwriting on the wall. **1957** *NYTimes Magazine* 3/31 62: I saw the handwriting on the wall. **1965** SWeintraub *Reggie* (NY) 58: The handwriting had been on the wall for some time. **1970** JVizzard *See* (NY) 256: He had seen the handwriting on the wall. *Oxford* 923: Writing.

H68 Not care (give, worth) a **Hang**

1911 JCLincoln *Woman-Haters* (NY) 139: [Not] care a hang. **1923** JSFletcher *Exterior* (NY) 13: Don't care a hang. **1926** EDBiggers *Chinese* (NY) 132: I don't give a hang. **1932** PATaylor *Death* (I) 116: Didn't give one hang in hades. **1939** JRonald *This Way Out* (P) 210: I don't care hang. **1960**

DShannon *Case* (NY) 184: Not worth a hang. **1964** PMoyes *Falling* (NY 1966) 206: I don't care a hang. **1970** VCClinton-Baddeley *No Case* (NY) 66: No one cares a hang. DA Hang *n.* 2(3).

H69   Hang now . . . trial tomorrow

1973 BKnox *Storm* (NY) 88: Let's say I don't like the old approach of "Hang him now, we'll give him a fair trial tomorrow." EAP H71. Cf. First Fire *above*; Lydford Law *below*.

H70   Hanging and wiving go by destiny

1928 AWynne *Red* (P) 232: Hanging and wiving go by destiny. **1951** EMarshall *Viking* (NY) 49: King Alfred said that wiving and hanging go by destiny. EAP M106: Marriage; *Oxford* 350.

H71   Hanging is too good for (someone)

1920 AChristie *Mysterious Affair* (NY) 105: Hanging's too good for him. **1932** HCBailey *Mr. Fortune, Please* (NY) 234: Hanging is too good for that pair. **1937** MBeckett *Bullet* (L) 14: Hanging's too good for him. **1940** HReilly *Dead Can* (NY) 85: As the Irishman said, hangin's too good for her, they ought to kick her tail. **1946** ESHolding *Innocent* (NY) 130: Hanging's too good for a fellow like that. **1952** PMacDonald *Something* (NY) 220: Hanging's too good for him. **1960** GAshe *Man Who Laughed* (NY) 140: Hanging is too good for them. **1965** JPorter *Dover Two* (NY 1968) 73: Hanging's too good for the likes of him. EAP H72.

H72   Honest to (so help me) **Hannah**

1951 CArmstrong *Black-Eyed* (NY) 26: Honest to Hannah. **1957** BHitchens *End* (NY) 21: So help him Hannah. **1962** CDSimak *All the Traps* (NY) 179: So help me Hannah.

H73   As sure as Hannah Cook (*varied*)

1951 EGraham *My Window* (NY) 45: Sure as Hannah Cook. **1953** EBGarside *Man from* (NY) 188: He didn't give a Hannah Cook what anyone might say. 244: Not worth a Hannah Cook. Bartlett 1102a: Doesn't amount to Hannah Cook.

H74   Happy-go-lucky

1970 CDrummond *Stab* (NY) 63: They were a happy-go-lucky pair. EAP H78.

H75   As fast as a Hare

1926 LO'Flaherty *Tent* (L) 265: He was as fast as a hare. Cf. Whiting *NC* 420: Swift; Taylor *Prov. Comp.* 39: Rabbit.

H76   As mad as a March Hare (*varied*)

1900 CFPidgin *Quincy A. Sawyer* (B) 133: As mad as a March hare. **1924** TMundy *Om* (NY) 300: As mad as a March hare. **1930** WLewis *Apes* (NY 1932) 337: Mad as a March-hare. **1933** RCAshby *He Arrived* (NY) 255: Mad as a hare. **1934** GBurgers *Two O'Clock* (I) 144: Mad as a Martian hare. **1941** CFAdams *Decoy* (NY) 118: Crazy as a March hare. **1949** NMarsh *Wreath* (NY) 99: He's as mad as a March hare. **1958** PSJennison *Mimosa* (NY) 68: She was mad, mad as the April hare. Why do you suppose it was called an April hare? **1959** HEBates *Breath* (B) 110: Mad as those hares. **1966** JDCarr *Panic* (NY) 209: You're as mad as a March hare. **1969** AGilbert *Mr. Crook* (NY DBC) 159: She looked almost as sane as a March hare. **1976** MWarner *Medium* (NY) 24: As mad as the proverbial March hare. EAP H81.

H77   As timid (shy) **as a Hare**

1925 LPowys *Skin* (NY) 24: I was as timid as a brown hare. **1927** BAtkey *Smiler* (NY) 73: Shy as a hare. **1940** MBurton *Murder in* (L) 127: As timid as a hare. Cf. Whiting H111, H112. Cf. As timid as a Rabbit *below*.

H78   First catch your Hare (cat, rabbit, fish, bird, devil) (*varied*)

1922 DFox *Ethel* (NY) 123: Let's catch our cat first and skin him afterwards. **1922** JJoyce *Ulysses* (NY 1934) 172: Jugged hare. First catch your hare. **1924** RAFreeman *Blue* (NY) 50: They'll have to catch their hare before they can cook him. **1927** RA Freeman *Cat's Eye* (NY) 74: We had better catch our hare before we proceed to jug him. **1927** VLWhitechurch *Crime* (NY) 67: It's like Mrs. Beeton's cookery book—first catch your hare. **1929** RJCasey *Secret* (I) 214: But first, catch your rabbit. **1930**

WWoodrow *Moonhill* (NY) 158: You can't make a Welch rabbit, you know, without first catching your hare. **1931** HHolt *Necklace* (NY) 106: It's one thing to catch your hare, but skinning him is quite another matter. **1935** FBeeding *Death* (NY) 231: First get your fish, fry it afterwards. **1938** CFGregg *Brazen* (L) 150: There's another saying about first catching your hare. **1939** JPPhilips *Death Delivers* (NY) 206: You have to catch your bird . . . before you can eat it. **1951** FPratt *Double* (NY) 120: You know the old recipe for rabbit stew. First catch your rabbit. **1954** FCDavis *Another* (NY) 128: But first I had to catch my hare. **1959** HCarmichael *Marked* (NY) 154: There's an old saying, "First catch your hare." **1965** PAnderson *Star* (NY) 49: First catch your rabbit. **1967** JFDobie *Some Part* (B) 126: Don't kiss the devil until you catch him. **1973** ARoudybush *Gastronomic* (NY) 83: But, as the cookbook says, "first catch your hare." **1975** HDolson *Please* (P) 108: It's like those old recipes for jugged hare: "First catch a jugged hare and skin it." Brunvand 66(2); *Oxford* 262: First. Cf. Brunvand 20: Carp.

H79 To chase two **Hares** at the same time

1934 BThomson *Richardson Scores* (L) 168: We mustn't be running two hares at one and the same time. **1969** RGrayson *Voyage* (L) 39: Never chase two hares at the same time. EAP H82.

H80 To run like a **Hare**

1924 EWallace *Green* (B) 310: He ran like a hare. **1932** WMartyn *Murder* (NY) 252: The fellow ran like a hare. **1933** CBarry *Death* (NY) 61: He scooted like a hare. **1946** MBennett *Time to Change* (NY) 199: We both ran like March hares. **1960** PGWodehouse *Jeeves* (L) 37: I must run like a hare. Whiting H127. Cf. To run like a Rabbit *below*.

H81 To run with the **Hare** and hunt with the hounds (*varied*)

1920 GDilnot *Suspected* (NY) 56: He wants to run with the hare and hunt with the hounds. **1928** EBYoung *Murder* (P) 238: Running with the hare and hunting with the hounds. **1930** ABCox *Piccadilly* (NY) 326: He would try running with the hare instead of hunting with the hounds. **1936** DHume *Meet the Dragon* (L) 192: You can't hunt with the hounds and run with the fox. **1938** CFGregg *Brazen* (L) 243: Hannah . . . was trying the age-old game of endeavouring to run with the hare and hunt with the hounds, forgetting the biblical axiom that man cannot serve two masters. **1940** AMorton *Blue Mask* (P) 64: You could run with the hare as well as the hounds. **1946** ECrispin *Holy Disorders* (NY) 245: He would probably be a good deal less bold running with the hare instead of hunting with the hounds. **1950** MGEberhart *Hunt with the Hounds* (NY). **1954** RAldington *Pindorman* (L) 139: He wants to run with the writing hare and hunt with the critical hounds. **1958** *BHerald* 2/23 64: I am not running with the fox and at the same time baying with the hounds. **1961** TRobinson *When Scholars* (L) 203: I know it's hunting with the hounds when I'm running with the hares. **1965** JCleugh *Divine* (L) 91: Clement VII remained as determined as ever to go on hunting with the hare his own hounds were so persistently trying to bring down. **1968** JTMcIntosh *Take a Pair* (NY) 78: "He runs with the rabbit and the dogs." "The rabbit . . . Oh, you mean with the hare and the hounds." EAP H330: Hound.

H82 To start a **Hare**

1930 CBarry *Boat* (L) 163: I'm afraid I started that hare. **1930** RKeverne *Man in the Red Hat* (NY) 234: Jabez had started a new hare somehow. **1939** MBurton *Babbacombe* (L) 178: Don't let your imagination start any hares. Whiting H129.

H83 There is no **Harm** in trying (*very varied*)

1925 FSFitzgerald *Great Gatsby* (NY) 68: No harm in trying. **1934** CFGregg *Execution* (L) 100: No harm in hoping. **1937** WDickinson *Dead Man* (P) 83: Can't get shot for trying! **1939** JJConnington *Counsellor* (L) 158: There'd be no harm in trying. **1940** RDarby *Death Conducts* (NY) 63: Never shot a guy for tryin'. **1944** CWoolrich *Black Path* (NY) 55: There's no law against trying.

1949 AAFair *Bedrooms* (NY 1958) 144: There's no harm in trying. **1952** EPaul *Black* (NY) 112: But there's no harm trying, is there? **1956** MPHood *Scarlet* (NY) 69: It never hurts to try. **1959** RPowell *Pioneer* (NY) 94: They can't shoot you for trying. **1961** RSPrather *Dig That* (NY) 54: Can't hang a man for looking. **1964** CChaplin *Autobiography* (NY 1966) 74: There's no harm in trying. **1975** HLawrenson *Stranger* (NY) 65: They can't shoot me for trying. TW 172(2). Cf. There is Nothing *below*.

H84 To settle someone's **Hash**

1924 LTracy *Token* (NY) 152: I'll soon settle his hash. **1930** FWCrofts *Sir John* (NY) 82: This settles the hash about the major [*clears him*]. 268: Settle our hash [*clear us*]. **1941** HCBailey *Bishop's* (NY) 264: Cooking the hash of Grey. **1954** EFerrars *Lying* (L) 159: He'd settle his hash for him. **1959** EHuxley *Flame* (L) 177: That'll settle the beggar's hash. **1968** TMcGuane *Sporting* (NY) 133: If they settle [his] hash. **1969** RCook *Private* (NY) 62: I'll settle [his] hash. **1971** BWAldiss *Soldier* (L) 29: Settle your hash. **1975** ABrodsky *Madame* (NY) 148: To settle their hash. EAP H88; Brunvand 66(2).

H85 **Haste** makes waste

1936 VMcHugh *Caleb* (NY) 259: Haste makes waste. **1946** HRCampbell *Crime in Crystal* (NY) 136: Haste makes waste. **1956** *New Yorker* 9/1 33: Haste makes waste is an example of the deeply significant insights to be found in folk proverbs. **1957** *Time* 5/20 142: Haste Saves Waist. **1958** EMcBain *Lady* (NY 1964) 153: Muttering proverbs about haste making waste. **1961** JPhilips *Murder* (NY DBC) 89: Haste makes waste. **1968** EMirabelli *Way* (NY) 65: Haste makes waste. EAP H90.

H86 Make **Haste** slowly

1925 HBedford-Jones *Rodomont* (NY) 74: Make haste slowly. **1925** JICClarke *My Life* (NY) 30: Festina lente. **1928** BAtkey *Midnight* (NY) 24: Make haste a little more slowly. **1932** NTrott *Monkey* (NY) 61: *Festina lente.* Make haste slowly. **1937** CBClark *Purple* (NY) 257: It was well to "make haste slowly," as the proverb puts it. **1937** NGayle *Death* (NY) 197: You have to make haste slowly, as the saying is. **1952** DMDisney *Heavy* (NY) 148: You . . . will be making haste slowly. **1955** NMarsh *Scales* (B) 243: Your cry of *festina lente*. **1964** JAshford *Superintendent* (NY) 82: Let us remember to make haste slowly. **1966** GWBrace *Between Wind* (NY) 119: My sloop *Festina Lente* . . . Make Haste Slowly. **1970** LKronenberger *No Whippings* (B) 230: I decided to make haste, or preferably hay, slowly. **1972** HHarrison *Montezuma* (NY) 50: Not too fast, make haste slowly. EAP H91.

H87 Marry in **Haste** and repent at leisure (*varied*)

1904 SArmitage-Smith *John of Gaunt* (L) 273: Left to repent at leisure. **1919** JBCabell *Jurgen* (NY 1922) 273: I shall marry in haste and repeat [*sic*] at leisure. **1928** GDHCole *Man* (NY) 170: Mrs. Meston gets married . . . and repents without even a decent interval of leisure. **1937** RCWoodthorpe *Death in* (NY) 141: [Both] made a hasty marriage which they would repent at the proverbial tempo. **1954** HGardiner *Murder in Haste* (L). **1954** HGardiner *Murder* (L) 237: There's a lot of truth in that worn-out old saying about marrying in haste. **1959** FWakeman *Virginia* (L) 151: You know the old saying: "Better stay chaste than wed in haste." **1961** JBTownsend *John* (New Haven) 382: He grew angry in haste to repent at leisure. **1969** SMays *Reuben's* (L) 166: Marry in haste, repent you at leisure. Years spent to pay, for the minute's pleasure. **1969** RPearsall *Worm* (L) 185: Sinning in haste and repenting at leisure. **1971** PDennis *Paradise* (NY) 105: Marry in haste, repent at leisure. EAP H92.

H88 The more **Haste** the less (worse) speed (*varied*)

1926 FWCrofts *Cheyne* (NY) 69: The more haste frequently meant the less speed. **1929** CFGregg *Three Daggers* (NY) 243: It was a case of "more haste, less speed." **1934** FPitt *Naturalist* (L) 45: The old saying "more haste less speed." **1936** JMWalsh *Crimes* (L) 262: The old saw, the more haste the less speed. **1940** PWentworth *Rolling* (P) 261: More haste, worse speed, and all that sort of thing. **1946** FWCrofts *Death of a Train* (L) 233: The less haste the better. **1951** KBennett *Wink* (L) 165: Much haste and even more speed—the imperturable English proverb was unknown to the good Abbé. **1959** AGilbert *Death* (NY) 228: There's a lot of truth in the old proverbs . . . and one of them says "more haste less speed." **1961** GFowler *Skyline* (NY) 170: The truth of an old proverb . . . "The more haste, the less speed" [*a urinal joke*]. **1973** MInnes *Appleby's Answer* (NY) 84: Her more haste ended in less speed. EAP H94; TW 173(4).

H89 More **Haste** than speed
1940 KMKnight *Death Came* (NY) 212: More haste than speed. EAP H93.

H90 As thick as **Hasty** pudding
1909 JCLincoln *Keziah* (NY) 45: This fog is as thick as Injun-meal puddin'. **1917** JCLincoln *Extricating* (NY) 223: Thick as hasty-puddin'. TW 173. Cf. Oatmeal *below*.

H91 As black as one's **Hat** (*varied*)
1904 JCLincoln *Cap'n Eri* (NY) 82: He was black as your hat. **1928** NGordon *Professor's* (NY) 170: It's as black as your hat. **1935** VLoder *Death* (L) 247: Made the old judge look as black as the inside of a hat. **1940** HReilly *Murder in* (NY) 3: The alley was as black as your hat. **1953** AChristie *Pocket* (NY) 53: Black as your hat. **1955** CMWills *Death* (L) 35: The taps are as black as your hat—if you have a black hat. **1959** AGoodman *Golden* (NY) 113: It was black as the inside of your hat. **1968** LBlanch *Journey* (L) 124: Sables—black as your hat. **1974** THeald *Blue* (NY) 137: Black as your hat. EAP H96.

H92 A bad **Hat**
1922 VBridges *Greensea* (NY) 278: A bad hat. **1922** JJoyce *Ulysses* (NY 1934) 618: Faultfinding being a proverbially bad hat. **1932** GMitchell *Saltmarsh* (L) 40: Bad hat of the village. **1967** AChristie *Endless* (NY) 42: He's the bad hat of the family. TW 173(1).

H93 Here's your **Hat**, what's your hurry?
1932 JTFarrell *Young Lonigan* (NY 1935) 180: Here's your hat what's your hurry? **1965** RBissell *Still* (NY) 252: Here's your hat, what's your hurry. Berrey 58.5.

H94 If (something happens) I'll eat my **Hat** (boots)
1907 JLondon *Letters* ed KHendricks (NY 1965) 239: If . . . I'll eat my hat. **1910** JCLincoln *Depot Master* (NY) 196: If . . . I'll eat my Sunday hat. **1928** RAJWalling *That Dinner* (NY) 264: I'd eat my cap if we couldn't. **1930** AChristie *Murder* (NY) 118: Or I'll eat my boots. **1932** DLSayers *Have* (NY) 217: Or I'll eat my hat. **1932** HBurnham *Telltale* (NY) 167: If . . . I'll eat my hat. **1933** CWaye *Figure* (NY) 232: That's the very man, or I'll eat my boots. **1947** DBowers *Bells* (NY) 149: If . . . I'll eat— my boots. **1952** HFMPrescott *Man on* (NY) 43: If . . . I'll eat my hat. **1961** LPayne *Nose* (NY) 37: If . . . I'll eat your hat. **1967** CAird *Most Contagious* (NY) 57: If . . . I'll eat my hat. **1973** PMoyes *Curious* (NY) 24: If . . . I'll eat my hat. Partridge 378: Eat one's. Cf. Shirt *below*.

H95 To be knocked into a cocked **Hat**
1921 IOstrander *Crimson* (NY) 143: Knocked into a cocked hat. **1922** JJoyce *Ulysses* (NY 1934) 645: Knocking everything else into a cocked hat. **1932** JJFarjeon *Trunk-Call* (NY) 8: September's got August beaten into a cocked hat. **1938** MBrucker *Poison* (NY) 149: He had knocked her hopes . . . into a cocked hat. **1947** HCahill *Hat* (NY) 292: It knocked the profit into a cocked hat. **1957** *BHerald* 3/18 22: This delay . . . throws . . . the . . . system into a cocked hat. **1957** *NYTimes* 10/20 4E: The Brentano policy would have been knocked into a cocked hat. **1961** HFarrell *Death* (NY DBC) 128: Knocks our hopes . . . right into a cocked hat. **1969** SPalmer *Hildegarde* (NY) 122: It knocks it into a cocked hat. **1974** WCAnderson *Damp* (NY) 5: Knocked . . . into a cocked hat. **1976** JPorter *Package* (NY) 81: Knocked into a cocked hat. TW 173(7).

H96 To be sick in one's **Hat** *etc.*

1937 EGreenwood *Under the Fig* (NY) 7: He was a just man but there was no need for him to be sick in his own hat and then ram it on his head. Cf. The Bird that fouls *above.*

H97 To keep something under one's **Hat**

1924 WBMFerguson *Black* (NY) 300: Keep it under your hat. **1933** WCBrown *Murder* (P) 279: Keep this . . . under your hat. **1940** DHume *Invitation* (L) 218: Anything you can tell me I'll keep under my bonnet. **1948** CLLeonard *Fourth* (NY) 92: Keep it under your hat. **1955** BCarey *Fatal* (NY) 157: Keep this under your hat. **1956** RStout *Might* (NY) 74: Keeping our client under your hat. **1958** NMarsh *Singing* (B) 37: Keeping the whole thing under your cap. **1959** EHNisot *Sleepless* (NY) 130: We'll keep it under our hats. **1962** MCarleton *Dread* (NY) 36: Keep it under your hat. **1969** DClark *Nobody's* (NY) 149: Keep it under your hat. Wentworth 560: Under.

H98 To talk through one's **Hat**

1922 JJoyce *Ulysses* (NY 1934) 297: Talking through his bloody hat. **1924** VBridges *Red Lodge* (NY) 13: You're talking through your hat. **1931** DJohnson *Death of* (L) 281: I'm babbling—talking through my hat. **1933** GBegbie *Sudden* (L) 276: I'm not talking through my hat. **1936** RLehmann *Weather* (NY) 107: I'm talking through my cocked hat, as usual. **1944** CBrand *Green for Danger* (NY 1965) 47: He's just talking through his hat. **1949** NBlake *Head* (NY) 166: Talking through his hat. **1957** IAsimov *Earth* (NY) 187: You're talking through your hat. **1963** IFleming *On Her* (L) 200: Papa's talking through his hat. **1967** NFreeling *Strike* (NY) 34: Talking through his hat. Whiting *NC* 420(2).

H99 To throw one's **Hat** in the ring

1933 WChambers *Campanile* (NY) 156: You've thrown your hat in the ring. **1938** NMorland *Rope* (L) 45: His hat was in the ring. **1957** WGoldman *Temple* (NY) 227: My hat's in the ring. **1959** HPentecost *Lonely* (NY) 133: To throw his hat into the political ring. Brunvand 21: Castor; Berrey 225.2 etc. [*see Index*].

H100 Down the **Hatch**

1937 ESGardner *Murder up* (NY) 179: But here goes, down the hatch. **1960** TBDewey *Girl* (NY DBC) 150: Down the hatch. Colcord 95; Wentworth 159: Down.

H101 To keep under **Hatches**

1972 MGilbert *Body* (NY) 6: It was kept under hatches. EAP H98.

H102 As sharp as a **Hatchet**

1963 MGEberhart *Run* (NY) 82: A face as sharp as a hatchet. EAP H100.

H103 To bury the **Hatchet** (*varied*)

1919 SRohmer *Quest* (NY) 278: To bury the hatchet. **1936** KMKnight *Wheel* (NY) 235: They had buried the hatchet, as the saying goes. **1937** HAshbrook *Murder* (NY) 32: The hatchet had been buried. **1940** EDean *Murder Is* (NY) 30: All the hatchets seemed to be buried. **1944** MLong *Bury the Hatchet* (NY). **1953** WBlunt *Pietro's* (L) 242: The hatchet was buried. **1958** CHare *He Should* (L) 183: That's another hatchet buried. **1960** BWilliams *Borderline* (NY) 71: Bury the hatchet with Raquel. **1963** RCroft-Cooke *Bosie* (L) 347: He wanted to bury a number of rusty hatchets. **1972** HDPerry *Chair* (NY) 23: It turned out to be a bury-the-hatchet affair. **1974** RRosenbaum *Good* (NY) 183: With no hatchet to bury, no "Ax" to grind. **1975** SJPerelman *Vinegar* (NY) 55: Hatchets once buried and swords beaten into ploughshares. EAP H102; Brunvand 66.

H104 To take a **Hatchet** to break eggs

1956 *Punch* 5/16 578: There is an old proverb about taking hatchets to break eggs.

H105 **Hate** is akin to love

1956 ACLewis *Jenny* (NY) 62: Hate is akin to love, you know. *Oxford* 336: Greatest hate; Whiting H178: After hate comes love.

H106 As mad as a **Hatter;** Hatter-mad (*varied*)

1911 RAFreeman *Eye of Osiris* (NY 1929) 49: As mad as hatters. **1922** VBridges *Greensea* (NY) 211: As mad as a hatter. **1929** JBPriestley *Good* (NY) 259: Hatter-mad. **1933** JAston *First Lesson* (NY) 197: He's as mad as a hatter. **1933** JDCarr *The Mad Hatter Mystery* (L). **1934** PGWodehouse *Brinkley* (B) 261: As mad as some March hatters. **1938** RWhite *Run Masked* (NY) 7: Queer as hatters. **1948** WLewis *Letters* ed WKRose (L 1963) 439: As mad as a hatter. **1948** CBush *Curious* (NY) 165: Mad as a hatter [*angry*]. **1957** *New Yorker* 3/9 127: She gives every indication of being as mad as a hatter. **1963** HPentecost *Only* (NY DBC) 156: You're mad as a hatter. **1967** HBlyth *Old Q* (L) 174: He was as mad as a hatter. **1970** HCarvic *Miss Seeton Draws* (NY) 36: She's madder'n a hatter [*angry*]. **1976** GEklund *Grayspace* (NY) 53: I'm the maddest hatter in the room. TW 174.

H107 If one cannot **Have** what one likes, one must like what one has (*varied*)

1955 SNGhose *Flame* (L) 281: The English phrase, "When one has not what one wants one must want what one has." **1956** AGilbert *Riddle* (NY) 159: If you can't have what you like, you just like what you have.

H108 Them as **Has,** gets (to him that hath shall be given)

1933 CPenfield *After the Deacon* (NY) 66: Them as has, gets. **1937** GGoodchild *Operator* (L) 161: An English proverb . . . "To him that hath shall be given." **1939** AGilbert *Clock* (L) 100: There's no truer text than the saying that to him that has shall be given. **1953** OAtkinson *Golden* (I) 74: Them as has gits. **1958** *BTraveler* 11/12 5: Them as has, gits, the old saying goes. **1965** JMitchell *Joe Gould* (NY) 163: The old fundamental rule: "Them as has gits." **1970** DShannon *Unexpected* (NY) 71: Them as has gets. **1974** WDRoberts *Didn't Anybody* (NY) 113: Them as has, gets. Bradley 78; Matthew 25:29.

H109 To **Have** what it takes

1938 ESHolding *Obstinate* (NY) 215: He's got what it takes. **1955** NMarsh *Scales* (B) 290: You've got what it takes, as they say, and he's a widower. **1955** MInnes *Man from* (L) 218: He didn't really have what it takes. Berrey 128.2.

H110 To **Have** and to hold

1922 JSFletcher *Middle of Things* (NY) 147: The motto is *Have and Hold.* **1936** ESdePuy *Long Knife* (NY) 117: A woman to have but hard to hold. Lean II ii 913.

H111 What one never **Had,** one can never miss (lose) (*varied*)

1930 DLSayers *Documents* (NY) 16: What you've never had you don't miss, as the saying goes. **1936** JJFarjeon *Detective* (L) 119: You dinna miss whit you dinna ken. **1939** TBurke *Living* (L) 120: It has been said that what you've never had you never miss. **1955** WSloane *Stories* (L) 335: In this respect the old adage that a man does not miss what he has never had is far short of the truth. **1967** MWilkins *Last* (Englewood Cliffs, NJ) 48: You never miss what you don't have. **1969** RBlythe *Akenfield* (NY) 228: They say that what you've never had, you never miss. *Oxford* 485: Lose.

H112 As hungry as a **Hawk**

1928 GGardiner *At the House* (NY) 207: Hungry as a hawk. EAP H105.

H113 As keen as a **Hawk**

1933 EPhillpotts *Captain's* (NY) 36: Keen as a hawk. **1934** AFielding *Cautley* (L) 243: He . . . was as keen as a hawk. Whiting *NC* 420(1).

H114 As wild as a **Hawk**

1922 FPitt *Woodland* (L) 141: "As wild as a hawk" has passed into a proverb . . . it was the sparrow-hawk that was meant. **1938** PWentworth *Run!* (L) 317: They're as wild as hawks. **1940** JStagge *Turn* (NY) 48: This may sound wild as a hawk. **1951** EPaul *Murder on* (NY) 194: Lois was as wild as a hawk. **1957** *New Yorker* 7/6 19: When this part of town was as wild as a hawk. **1964** DMDisney *Hospitality* (NY) 104: They made me wild as a hawk. **1976** LEgan *Scenes* (NY) 121: She's wild as a hawk. TW 174(9).

H115 To know (tell) a **Hawk** from a handsaw

1931 GHolt *Green* (I) 223: In a southerly wind, Lord Stonecroft might know this Hawk from a handsaw. **1933** KTKnoblock *Take up* (NY) 154: Knew neither hawk nor handsaw nor camel nor compas. **1937** SPalmer *No Flowers* (L) 94: They don't know a hawk from a handsaw. **1950** SPalmer *Green* (NY) 92: I . . . can tell a hawk from a handsaw. **1956** RRobinson *Landscape* (L 1963) 118: He's the one who knows a hawk from a handsaw round this neck of the woods. **1965** RFoley *Suffer* (NY DBC) 114: He can still tell a hawk from a handsaw. **1968** MAllingham *Cargo* (NY) 150: I can tell a hawk from a handsaw. **1972** MInnes *Open* (NY) 34: One who knew a hawk from a handsaw. EAP H107; Brunvand 66(1).

H116 To watch like a **Hawk**

1927 RKing *Mystery* (NY) 38: He will be watching . . . like a hawk. **1931** TThayer *Greek* (NY) 16: Watch like the proverbial hawk. **1938** DBaker *Young Man* (B) 150: Jack watched the floor like a hawk. **1940** DBurnham *Last Act* (NY) 89: Her stepmother still watched over her like a hawk. **1948** PClark *Flight* (NY) 175: He watched every move Deshon made like a—like a caged hawk. **1953** SRansome *Shroud* (NY) 92: Watch her like a hawk. **1958** *NYTimes* 4/27 sec. VI 20: The carriers will be watching each other's meals like hawks, and thus is one instance where one may, with not only impunity but with a kind of literary joy, use that cliché. **1960** CWatson *Bump* (L 1963) 70: I have to watch them like a hawk. **1963** HPentecost *Tarnished* (NY DBC) 125: He must have watched Brock like a hawk. **1973** ELopez *Seven* (NY) 91: Watched me like a hawk. EAP H108; Brunvand 66(2).

H117 To come up through the **Hawsepipe**

1956 EGann *Twilight* (NY) 69: Everybody knew he come up through the hawsepipe the hard way. TW 175: Hawse-holes; Colcord 97.

H118 To hit the **Hay**

1955 MAllingham *Estate* (NY) 107: You must hit the hay. Wentworth 247; DA Hay d(2).

H119 To make **Hay** while the sun shines (*varied*)

1902 D'AStJohn *Madge Buford* (NY) 39: Let's make hay while the sun shines. **1919** JSClouston *Simon* (NY) 27: You have to make hay while the sun shines. **1920** RLHine *Cream* (L) 17: While it lasted he made whole stacks of hay. **1922** JJoyce *Ulysses* (NY 1934) 59: Make hay while the sun shines. **1926** AEHousman *Letters* ed HMaas (Cambridge, Mass. 1971) 233: Make hay while the sun shines. **1930** JGBrandon *Death* (L) 35: Gather hay while—oh—well, while the iron's hot. **1933** EECummings *Eimi* (NY) 83: Make hay while the sun shines. **1939** LBrock *Fourfingers* (L) 298: We should have to make hay while the sun was shining. **1951** JCollier *Fancies* (NY) 219: Why not make hey hey while the sun shines? **1957** *BHerald* 12/9 20: The congressional pols are making hay while the Administration's sun is behind a cloud. **1959** *BHerald* 10/3 2: Two groups of people were able to make hay while the sun didn't shine. **1964** IPetite *Elderberry* (NY) 150: Mountain beavers, who make hay while the moon shines. **1971** JJMarric *Gideon's Art* (NY) 104: Making hay while the sun shone. **1974** JLHess *Grand* (B) 26: A man who could make hay in a downpour. EAP H111; TW 175(3).

H120 As big as a **Haystack**

1931 CBush *Dead Man's* (L) 275: Things that stuck out as big as a haystack. TW 176; Brunvand 66.

H121 Not able to hit a **Haystack**

1957 MColes *Death* (NY) 84: You [*English*] say in your country that some men "could not hit a haystack." Partridge 381.

H122 Big **Head**, little wit *etc.* (*varied*)

1957 HPBeck *Folklore of Maine* (P) 65: Big head little wit, little head not a bit. **1960** VWilliams *Walk* (NY) 118: Small head, little wit. Big head not a bit. Whiting *NC* 421(6); Whiting H226; *Oxford* 530: Mickle head.

H123 Hard **Head**, soft heart (arse) (*varied*)

1930 MRRinehart *Door* (NY) 57: A hard head but a soft heart. **1960** VWilliams *Walk*

(NY) 29: A hard head carries a soft behind. **1967** IReed *Free-lance* (NY) 85: As my grandmother used to say, "A hard head makes a soft ass." Whiting *NC* 421(1): Soft mind.

H124   **Heads** I win, tails you lose

1922 JJoyce *Ulysses* (NY 1934) 171: I win tails you lose. **1926** AMarshall *Mote* (NY) 15: A sort of heads-I-win-tails-you-lose business. **1937** WSMasterman *Border* (NY) 78: Heads you win; tails I lose. **1944** LAG Strong *All Fall* (NY) 133: Heads you win, tails I lose. **1958** *New Yorker* 4/12 37: Heads, you win; tails, Harvard benefits. **1961** HPentecost *Deadly* (NY DBC) 31: Heads I win, tails you lose. **1964** LSDeCamp *Ancient* (NY) 134: A "heads I win, tails you lose" argument. **1970** PAlding *Murder* (NY) 20: It was a heads you win, tails I lose, situation. **1976** SWoods *My Life* (NY) 177: Heads you win, tails I lose. EAP H122.

H125   Not able to make **Head** or tail of something (*varied*)

1910 JCLincoln *Depot Master* (NY) 130: I couldn't make head or tail of [it]. **1923** HWNevinson *Changes* (NY) 47: I . . . could make both head and tail out of them. **1933** WCBrown *Murder* (P) 49: I can't make heads or tails out of it. **1936** PGWodehouse *Laughing* (NY) 2: Won't be able to make head or tail of it. **1940** JJConnington *Four Defences* (B) 210: You'll never make head or tail of stuff like that. **1949** RFinnegan *Bandaged* (L 1952) 9: Can't make head or tail of it. **1951** GHCoxe *Widow* (NY) 183: All of 'em bollixed up somehow so we don't know heads from tails. **1959** JPhilips *Killer* (NY) 204: I can't make head or tail out of it. **1964** LComber *Strange* (Rutland, Vt.) 62: Pao could not make head or tail of it. **1964** PGrosskurth *Symonds* (L) 49: Symonds could never make head or tail of the *Prolegomena*. **1975** EXFerrars *Alive* (NY) 138: I can't make head or tail of it. EAP H141; TW 176(10); Brunvand 67(2).

H126   Not to know if one is on his **Head** or his heels (*varied*)

1904 JCLincoln *Cap'n Eri* (NY) 130: I don't know . . . whether I'm on my head or my heels. **1928** GDHCole *Man* (NY) 213: Find out whether I am standing on my head or my heels. **1934** CMWills *Author* (L) 23: I didn't know whether I was on my head or my heels, as the saying is. **1940** MBurton *Murder in* (L) 10: I don't know whether I'm standing on my head or my heels. **1952** KMKnight *Death Goes* (NY) 93: She doesn't know whether she's on her head or her heels. **1957** JWyndham *Midwich* (NY) 61: Tom doesn't know whether he's on his head or his heels. **1961** JBlofeld *City* (L) 66: He didn't know if he was standing on his head or his feet. **1966** AAHomans *Education* (B) 77: I . . . did not know whether I was standing on my head or my heels. **1975** HCarmichael *Too Late* (NY) 11: I don't know whether I'm on my head or my heels. **1980** CHough *Bassington* (NY) 117: I hardly know if I'm on my head or my heels! EAP H127. Cf. Not to know which End *above.*

H127   To bang (*etc.*) one's **Head** against a (stone, brick) wall

1934 SPalmer *Murder* (L) 179: I've been beating my head against a stone wall. **1939** AWebb *Thank You* (L) 150: I'm getting tired of butting my head against a wall in this business. **1949** FKane *Green* (NY) 52: Stop banging your head against the wall. **1957** GAshe *Wait* (NY 1972) 133: You're just banging your head against a brick wall. **1958** *BangorDN* 9/28 8: We're beating our heads against a stone wall. **1966** TWells *Matter* (NY) 104: I was banging my head on a brick wall. **1970** HCarmichael *Death* (NY) 78: There was no use in butting his head against a brick wall. *Oxford* 688: Run.

H128   To be **Head** over ears in something

1923 JSFletcher *Exterior* (NY) 71: Your father is head over ears in that invention. **1929** CWells *Tapestry* (P) 213: Head and ears in debt. **1932** PMacDonald *Mystery* (NY) 12: He had fallen head over ears in love. **1933** GDHCole *Lesson* (L) 270: Head over ears in love. **1970** DJOlivy *Never* (NY) 37: Sheila was head over ears in calf love with him. EAP H120; TW 176-7(11).

H129　To be **Head** over heels in something (*varied*)

1900 CFPidgin *Quincy A. Sawyer* (B) 437: He's head over heels in love. **1917** JCLincoln *Extricating* (NY) 193: Head over heels in debt. **1923** EWallace *Clue of the New Pin* (B) 66: Head over heels in love. **1933** LRGribble *Yellow* (L) 76: The kid had been head over heels in love with her. **1933** RAJWalling *Follow* (L) 181: These two were heels over head in love. **1940** ISShriber *Head over Heels in Murder* (NY). **1952** AGarve *Hole* (NY 1959) 132: I've fallen for you head over heels. **1956** *New Yorker* 11/10 60: They're practicing falling head over heels in love. **1963** MRichler *Incomparable* (L) 89: Jock fell, as they say, head over heels in love. **1970** UO'Connor *Brendan* (L) 183: He fell head-over-heels for the play. **1972** JDCarr *Hungry* (NY) 198: Fallen head over heels in love with Jim. EAP H121; Brunvand 67(3).

H130　To be made a **Head** shorter

1914 PGWodehouse *Little Nugget* (NY 1929) 77: You needed making a head shorter. **1970** KLaumer *World* (NY) 54: I'd have been shorter by a head. EAP H142.

H131　To bite one's **Head** off

1954 HGardiner *Murder* (L) 194: There's no need to bite my head off. Berrey 284.3.

H132　To eat one's **Head** off

1932 PMacDonald *Rope* (L) 141: Eating his head off. **1932** BRoss *Tragedy of Y* (NY) 139: The police were eating their heads off. **1957** NMitford *Voltaire* (L) 52: He was eating his head off. EAP H133; Brunvand 67(4).

H133　To forget one's **Head** if it were not fastened on (*varied*)

1930 ACampbell *Murder* (NY) 143: You would forget your head, if it were not fastened to your shoulders. **1931** HGarland *Companions* (NY) 109: He would forget his head if it wasn't fastened on. **1934** MDavis *Murder* (NY) 64: You'd forget your head if it weren't fastened on. **1937** ATilton *Beginning* (NY) 54: He'd forget his head if it wasn't sewed on to the rest of him. **1950**

SSmith *Man with* (NY) 22: It was lucky her head was screwed on tight so she couldn't lose that. **1960** JBarry *Malignant* (NY) 95: She'd forget her head if it wasn't screwed on. **1963** The Gordons *Undercover* (NY DBC) 51: I'd lose my head if it weren't screwed on. Cf. To have one's **Head** screwed on *below*.

H134　To go and boil one's **Head**

1933 BReynolds *Very Private* (NY) 55: Go home and boil your head; 280. **1938** PGWodehouse *Code* (NY) 57: Tell him to go and boil his head. **1952** HWaugh *Last Seen* (NY) 133: Why don't you go soak your head? **1953** AChristie *Pocket* (NY) 176: I told Percy to go and boil his head. Partridge 75: Boil.

H135　To have a **Head** like a turnip

1961 CBush *Sapphire* (NY) 24: I've got a head like a turnip, as my old nurse used to say. I've forgotten the very thing I really came for. Cf. NED Turnip 4a: Turnip-headed.

H136　To have a **Head** too big for his hat

1934 BThomson *Richardson Scores* (L) 121: Take care your head doesn't get too big for your hat. **1940** RLGoldman *Snatch* (NY) 17: His head was always too big for his hat. **1954** MMcCarthy *Charmed* (NY) 293: Your head's too big for your hat. **1973** MSadler *Circle* (NY) 28: He's too big for his hat. Cf. Partridge 378: Hat, need a new, 381.

H137　To have an old **Head** on young shoulders (*varied*)

1910 EPhillpotts *Tales* (NY) 9: An old head on young shoulders; 190. **1929** KCStrahan *Footprints* (NY) 177: An old head on young shoulders. **1931** HSimpson *Prime* (NY) 227: One does not expect old heads on young shoulders. **1937** LAGStrong *Swift* (L) 93: You can't put old heads on young shoulders. **1941** CMRussell *Dreadful* (NY) 152: You have a wise old head on your young shoulders. **1954** OAnderson *Thorn* (L) 197: An old head on young shoulders. **1962** Bryher *Heart* (NY) 200: As the proverb says, "You can't put an old head on young shoulders." **1972** KCampbell *Thun-*

der (I) 51: You can't put an old head on young shoulders. **1973** MGilbert *Night* (NY) 220: An old head, one might say, on young shoulders. EAP H128.

H138 To have one's **Head** screwed on (*varied*)

1928 JJConnington *Mystery* (B) 34: His head's screwed on all right. **1928** GYoung *Treasure* (NY) 245: You've got your head screwed on backwards. **1931** WWJacobs *Snug* (NY) 20: You've got your 'ead on straight. 131: He's got his 'ead screwed on right. **1932** MTurnball *Return* (P) 77: [His] head was, in the language of the countryside, well screwed on. **1939** MBurton *Death Leaves* (L) 17: He's got his head screwed on the right way. **1940** JRhode *Murder at* (L) 139: Philip had his head screwed on straight. **1952** HTreece *Dark* (L) 200: If they hadn't had their heads screwed on the right way. **1957** GMalcolm-Smith *Trouble* (NY) 158: You screwed your head on good and tight this morning. **1959** GMitchell *Man Who* (L) 18: She's got her head screwed on tight. **1961** TRobinson *When Scholars* (L) 149: Here's someone with his head screwed on. **1966** ELinington *Date* (NY) 113: Ronnie had his head screwed on. **1970** JCreasey *Part* (NY) 130: [She] had her head screwed on. **1973** WJBurley *Death* (NY) 10: A sensible girl, got her head screwed on. *Oxford* 360; Partridge 738: Screwed.

H139 To have something on one's **Head** besides hair (lice) (*varied*)

1930 EDBiggers *Charlie* (NY 1943) 106: Nothing on my mind but my hair. **1941** ABCunningham *Strange Death* (NY) 143: There was something on his head besides the hair. **1969** HEBates *Vanished* (L) 77: My grandfather's old country adage that I had "something in my head besides lice."

H140 To keep one's **Head** above water

1919 CSLewis *Letters* ed WHLewis (NY 1966) 47: I am keeping my head above water. **1935** HWade *Heir* (L) 29: To keep . . . his own head above water. **1951** TDu-bois *Foul* (NY) 15: She would keep her own head above water. EAP H138; Brunvand 67(5).

H141 To make one's **Head** save his heels

1926 AFielding *Footsteps* (L) 38: I had to make my head save my heels. **1940** VRath *Death of a Lucky* (NY) 223: I've always said: "Let your head save your heels." **1964** CSSumner *Withdraw* (NY) 91: "Let your head save your heels," my father used to say to me. Whiting *NC* 421(10); Apperson 293(17).

H142 To put one's **Head** in a hornet's nest

1931 MAllingham *Gyrth* (NY) 44: I didn't want to put my head in a hornet's nest. **1932** MKennedy *Murderer* (L) 281: Put his head into a hornet's nest. Cf. Hornet *below*.

H143 To put one's **Head** (hand) in the lion's mouth (*varied*)

1925 FWCrofts *French's Greatest* (NY) 176: Putting her head into the lion's mouth. **1926** JArnold *Murder!* (L) 92: You'll put your head into the lion's jaws. **1926** HWade *Verdict* (L) 241: Putting one's head, in cold blood, into the lion's mouth. **1931** AC Edington *Monk's Hood* (NY) 3: He's sticking his head in the lion's mouth. **1932** DSharp *Code-letters* (B) 115: He'd never put his head in the lion's mouth. **1934** DFrome *They Called Him* (L) 180: His head was now inside the lion's den. **1954** SJepson *Black* (NY) 134: Having stuck my head in the lion's mouth and got it out again. **1958** SDean *Dishonor* (NY) 114: Putting her head in the tiger's mouth. **1959** EAllen *Man Who* (L 1967) 127: Poked his head deliberately into the Lion's cave. **1960** AGilbert *Out for* (NY 1965) 75: Shoving my head in the lion's den. **1969** LBruce *Death* (L) 138: Put my head in the lion's mouth. **1970** STerkel *Hard* (NY) 449: It's an old sayin': as long as you got your hand in the lion's mouth, you have to be easy till you get it out. **1970** RAtkin *Revolution* (NY) 215: He stuck his head into the lion's mouth. **1977** EXFerrars *Blood* (NY) 127: To put your head, so to speak, in the lion's mouth. EAP H62: Hand; TW 177(14).

H144 Two (three) **Heads** (*etc.*) are better than one (*varied*)

1911 FRS *Way of a Man With a Maid* (L) 100: Two heads are always said to be better than one. **1913** ECBentley *Trent's* (NY 1930) 182: Two heads will be better than one. **1916** MRJames *Letters* ed GMcBryde (L 1956) 63: They say two heads are better than one. **1919** JBCabell *Jurgen* (NY 1922) 172: The truism . . . that two heads are better than one. **1926** JSFletcher *Amaranth* (B) 130: Three heads are better than two. **1927** JSFletcher *Passenger* (NY) 136: Two opinions are better than one. **1927** LTracy *Mysterious* (NY) 157: Two 'eads is better'n one, if they're only sheep's 'eads. **1930** ER Burroughs *Fighting Man* (NY) 70: Two swords are better than one. **1930** WSMasterman *Yellow* (NY) 158: Four minds are better than two. **1931** AFielding *Upfold* (L) 146: Two are better than one. **1932** LFrost *Murder* (NY) 167: Three heads are better than two. **1934** JJFarjeon *Fancy Dress* (L) 175: Two minds are better than one. **1934** HHolt *Sinister* (NY) 167: They do say that two heads are better than one. **1935** BFlynn *Edge* (L) 73: Two heads are proverbially better than one. **1936** PCheyney *This Man* (L) 53: There's an old proverb that says that two watchdogs are better than one. **1936** BFlynn *Horn* (L) 74: Two heads are proverbially better than one—even fat heads. **1936** ECVivian *With Intent* (L) 204: The woman took her dog to market because two heads are better than one. **1937** DHume *Halfway* (L) 60: You know the old saying about two brains being better than one. **1937** JRhode *Proceed* (L) 228: Two heads are better than one, even if they're sheep's heads, as they say. **1941** KMKnight *Exit a Star* (NY) 237: Three heads are better than one. **1949** FBrown *Bloody* (NY) 195: Two heads are better than one, except on a boil. **1949** ESGardner *Dubious* (NY 1954) 103: "Two heads are better than one." "We're getting into the field of a different proverb now . . . At this point you can refer to the good old proverb that

too many cooks spoil the broth." **1950** SPalmer *Green* (NY) 33: Three heads are better than one. **1951** AChristie *They Came* (NY) 106: Two heads are better than one. **1954** HNearing *Sinister* (NY) 12: Two heads are better than one but three's a crowd. **1955** STroy *Half-way* (L) 142: It was a favorite saying . . . that two heads are better than one, even if they're only sheep's heads. **1956** *Time* 6/4 20: Three Heads Aren't Always Better Than One. **1957** *CSMonitor* 11/7 23: Two heads are better than one, of course. That's why it's a proverb. Because it's common sense in a capsule—. **1960** PGWodehouse *Jeeves* (L) 151: Four heads are better than three. **1962** LEgan *Against* (NY DBC) 97: They say two heads are better than one. **1962** MMcShane *Seance* (NY) 14: A case of many minds being better than one. **1963** EJHughes *Ordeal* (NY) 134: Many heads are always better than one. **1964** AMacKinnon *Report* (NY) 156: Two blood-streams being proverbially better than one. **1965** CKeith *Hiding-Place* (NY) 164: As the saying goes, two guns are better than one. **1966** LPDavies *Paper* (NY) 49: "Two heads are generally better than one," I said tritely. **1968** MSarton *Plant* (NY) 144: Two heads are better than one . . . especially when one is a sheep's head. **1970** PMoyes *Many* (NY) 62: Two heads are better than one. **1971** AGarve *Late* (NY) 26: Two heads, and all that . . . **1971** ADavidson *Peregrine* (NY) 50: Three heads are better than one, as Cerberus was once heard to howl. **1975** HDolson *Please* (P) 94: "Three heads are better than one." "That sounds like the old 'Two can live as cheaply as one.'" EAP H143; TW 177(22). Cf. Four Eyes *above*.

H145 A wise **Head** is better than a pretty face

1928 JAGade *Christian* (NY) 127: Time proved that "a wise head is better than a pretty face." Cf. Pretty *below*.

H146 To be knocked (struck) all of a **Heap**

1928 NGordon *Professor's* (NY) 226: It knocked me all of a heap. **1929** BFlynn *Billiard* (P) 97: I was struck all of a 'eap.

1936 GDHCole *Brothers* (L) 170: I'm knocked all of a heap. **1936** WSMasterman *Bloodhounds* (NY) 193: James was struck all of a heap, as the saying goes. **1949** MBurton *Disappearing* (NY) 202: He was struck all of a heap. **1952** EXFerrars *Alibi* (L 1967) 45: You look knocked all of a heap. **1974** JFleming *How To* (NY) 168: It knocked his man all of a heap. EAP H150.

H147 Cross my **Heart** and hope to die

1949 SJepson *Golden* (NY) 124: Cross my heart and hope to die, I won't. **1955** ES Gardner *Glamorous* (NY DBC) 90: I cross my heart and hope to die. **1964** JAshford *Superintendent* (NY) 212: Cross my heart, cut my throat, and hope to die. **1970** RCarson *Golden* (B) 151: Cross my heart and hope to die. **1972** JDMacDonald *Long* (P) 162: I swear to God, cross my heart and hope to die. Wentworth 131: Cross.

H148 Faint **Heart** never won fair lady (*varied*)

1925 JSFletcher *Secret* (B) 101: Nothing like the old proverb, you know—"faint heart." **1927** JMWalsh *Silver* (L) 42: Someone had said . . . something or other about "faint heart" and "fair lady." **1931** CJDaly *Third* (NY) 277: Faint heart never filled a spade flush. **1936** RDavis *Crowing Hen* (NY) 127: Faint heart never won fair Elinor. **1939** EMarsh *Number* (NY) 59: Faint praise never won fair lady. **1947** AAFair *Fools* (NY 1957) 175: Faint heart never won fair lady. **1951** JCollier *Fancies* (NY) 116: I can only remind you that faint heart never won fair lady. **1957** *TLS* 1/4 2: Faint heart and fair lady. **1960** EWolf *Rosenbach* (Cleveland) 533: The old saw about faint hearts and fair ladies. **1962** AGilbert *Uncertain* (NY DBC) 126: Faint heart never saved fair lady. **1971** EHCohen *Mademoiselle* (B) 111: Faint heart never won fair lady. **1977** VCanning *Doomsday* (NY) 182: Faint heart never won fair lady. Nothing venture, nothing win. EAP H157; Brunvand 67(1).

H149 It's a poor **Heart** that never rejoices

1913 HHMunro *When William* (L 1929) 13: It's a poor heart that never rejoices. **1932** JSFletcher *Four Degrees* (L) 69: Still, as they say, it's a poor heart that never rejoices. **1937** AGilbert *Murder* (L) 212: It's a poor heart that never rejoices. **1970** JBlackburn *Bury* (NY) 14: It's a sad heart that never rejoices. *Oxford* 638.

H150 Leal **Heart** never told a lie

1928 ACBrown *Dr. Glazebrook* (NY) 20: They say in Scotland that leal heart ne'er tel't a lee. Whiting H274: Good; *Oxford* 450: Leal.

H151 To have a **Heart** of gold (*varied*)

1912 ERBurroughs *Princess of Mars* (NY 1963) 159: A hideous creature with a heart of gold. **1930** CBush *Death* (NY) 73: [She had] a Continental upbringing but a heart of gold. **1936** HAdams *Old Jew* (L) 282: Not beautiful, perhaps, but with a heart of gold. **1937** CBush *Eight O'Clock* (NY) 225: A queer fellow . . . but a heart of gold, as they say. **1938** CBush *Tudor Queen* (L) 232: Hearts of gold plainly beat beneath her ample bodice and his cockney waistcoat. **1940** GDHCole *Wilson* (L) 184: It has been said . . . that the English people have a heart of gold. **1943** PATaylor *Going* (NY) 117: Her heart is pure gold an' a yard wide. **1952** MMillar *Vanish* (NY) 52: You got a heart of gold . . . cold and yellow. **1958** MUnderwood *Lawful* (NY) 51: She was the proverbially golden-hearted prostitute. **1964** NFreeling *Because* (NY 1965) 141: The tart with the heart of gold. **1965** JBrooks *Smith* (L) 249: A whore with a heart of gold. **1965** JMBrown *Worlds* (NY) 249: A prostitute with a heart which is a mine of gold. **1968** PDickinson *Skin* (L) 80: Not a whore with a heart of gold. **1972** PDJames *Unsuitable* (NY) 18: A large bosomy barmaid with a heart of gold. **1972** JDMacDonald *Long* (P) 174: There are no hookers with hearts of gold. **1973** GSheehy *Hustling* (NY) 19: The hooker with a Heart of Gold? That, I quickly discovered, is a male fallacy. **1974** CMartin *Whiskey* (NY) 103: The whore with a heart of gold is a stock character. EAP H162. Cf. Whorelady *below*.

H152 To have one's **Heart** go into his boots (*varied*)

1912 JCLincoln *Postmaster* (NY) 207: My heart went down into my boots. **1923** EWallace *Clue* (B) 157: My heart went down into my boots. **1929** BFlynn *Case* (P) 87: Clegg felt his courage sink into his boots. **1937** AGilbert *Murder* (L) 174: With his heart in his boots. **1940** JCLincoln *Out of the Fog* (NY) 123: My heart was somewhere down in my party shoes. **1955** DMDisney *Room* (NY) 101: Aggie's heart dropped into her best black shoes. **1957** THWhite *Master* (L) 223: Nicky's heart went into his boots. TW 178(11).

H153 To have one's **Heart** in his mouth

1925 AWynne *Sign* (P) 141: I have my heart in my mouth. **1938** BFlynn *Ebony* (L) 235: You've put our hearts in our mouths. **1971** MUnderwood *Trout* (NY) 146: My heart comes up into my mouth. EAP H165.

H154 To let one's **Heart** run away with his head (*varied*)

1932 CFGregg *Body* (L) 164: He had let his heart run away with his head. **1935** ECRLorac *Organ* (L) 212: Other people's hearts get the better of their heads. **1936** LWMeynell *On the Night* (NY) 48: The heart gives more people away than the hand. **1937** LRGribble *Who Killed* (L) 250: But women ever put their hearts before their heads. **1981** TEBClarke *Murder* (NY) 56: He's ruled by his heart more than his head. TW 179(15). Cf. EAP H166.

H155 To melt (*etc.*) a **Heart** of stone (*varied*)

1911 CPearl *Morrison of Peking* (Sydney 1967) 207: A letter that would have melted a heart of stone. **1931** WWJacobs *Snug* (NY) 71: A man must 'ave a 'art of stone if that didn't touch it. **1932** FBeeding *Take it* (B) 190: Whose tale of woe will melt the heart of a stone. **1951** JCollier *Fancies* (NY) 336: Her disappointment would have moved a heart of stone. **1963** NFitzgerald *Echo* (NY) 57: A smile that would have melted a heart of stone. **1967** GBrooks *If Strangers* (NY) 180: The proverbial heart of stone could not have withstood the pride

and satisfaction of the parish lady. **1971** JBlake *Joint* (NY) 89: I would have thought my pleading wails for a visit would melt a heart of stone. I guess you haven't got a heart of stone. **1975** BGelb *On the* (NY) 85: It took a heart of stone not to love him. **1975** AChristie *Curtain* (NY) 6: It would melt a heart of stone. EAP H169; Brunvand 67(2). Cf. Tears *below*.

H156 To take **Heart** of grace

1921 JSFletcher *Chestermarke* (NY) 157: [He] took heart of grace. **1922** JJoyce *Ulysses* (NY 1934) 110: The mourners took heart of grace. **1933** WADarlington *Mr. Cronk's* (L) 222: Cronk took heart of grace. **1941** NMarsh *Death and the* (B) 14: She seemed to take heart of grace. EAP H170; TW 179(19).

H157 To wear one's **Heart** on his sleeve

1913 JSFletcher *Secret* (L 1918) 103: It isn't Chandler's way to wear his heart on his sleeve. **1926** EWallace *Terrible* (NY) 118: I'm not the sort of bird who wears his heart on his sleeve. **1938** JRhode *Bloody* (L) 89: She's not the sort of girl who wears her heart on her sleeve. **1939** EPhillpotts *Monkshood* (L) 148: She does not wear her heart on her sleeve, as they say. **1947** HWade *New Graves* (L) 30: She did not carry her heart upon her sleeve. **1950** EQueen *Double* (B) 96: You've got to stop wearing your heart on your sleeve. **1954** HWade *Too Soon* (NY) 119: He wasn't one to wear his heart upon his sleeve, as the saying goes. **1955** JTrench *Dishonoured* (NY) 61: "I do rather wear my heart on my sleeve." "On your shoulder, I should say, in the form of a chip." **1959** LWhite *Meriweather* (NY) 18: She didn't carry her convictions on her sleeve, as the saying goes. **1965** RDSymons *Silton* (NY 1975) 67: A race . . . whose hearts are strangers to their sleeves. **1968** BKellner *C. VanVechten* (Norman, Okla.) 63: Carl's heart was still on his sleeve. **1970** AWRaitt *Prosper* (L) 19: She disdained to wear her heart on her sleeve. **1977** CAGoodrum *Dewey* (NY) 147: Don't wear your heart on your sleeve.

Whiting *NC* 422(1); *Oxford* (2nd ed) 698: Wears.

H158   In the seventh Heaven

1900 CFPidgin *Quincy A. Sawyer* (B) 242: In the seventh heaven of delight. **1930** FDBurdett *Odyssey* (L) 294: The seventh heaven of delight. **1934** LKirk *Whispering* (NY) 142: The seventh heaven of happiness. **1934** ACampbell *Desire* (NY) 113: In the seventh heaven of relief. **1935** JSFletcher *Carrismore* (L) 181: Smiler was in the seventh heaven of bliss. **1946** JDCarr *He Who Whispers* (NY) 18: His father is in the seventh heaven. **1951** JCollier *Fancies* (NY) 96: Ringwood was in the seventh heaven. **1958** PBranch *Murder's* (L 1963) 87: I was in Seventh Heaven. **1962** PDennis *Genius* (NY) 236: [He] was in seventh heaven. **1965** HWaugh *End* (NY) 102: Some new bride in Seventh Heaven. **1972** SBrooke *Queen* (NY) 52: In the seventh heaven of delight. *Oxford* 718.

H159   To move Heaven and earth

1912 JCLincoln *Postmaster* (NY) 47: He'd move heaven and earth to do it. **1922** JSFletcher *Rayner-Slade* (NY) 205: I'll move heaven and earth to get it. **1933** GDHCole *End* (L) 100: We'll move heaven and earth to find her father. **1940** JStagge *Turn* (NY) 88: Dawn would move heaven and earth to come home. **1944** RAJWalling *Corpse without* (NY) 96: To move heaven and earth to get a trace of him. **1951** RKing *Duenna* (NY) 190: The Tylers would move heaven and earth to prevent its disclosure. **1954** NBlake *Whisper* (L) 209: Edward was moving heaven and earth. **1960** NWilliams *Knaves* (NY) 49: Until he had moved heaven and earth. **1967** RFulford *Trial* (L) 38: They surely would have moved heaven and earth. **1975** TWells *Hark* (NY) 103: Rutgers is moving heaven and earth to get Alex out of jail. EAP H174; Brunvand 67–8(1).

H160   Too Heavy or too hot

1964 JKieran *Not Under* (B) xv: A salesman . . . offered to get me anything I wanted if it wasn't too hot to handle or too heavy to lift. The expression may have been old in the selling game but it was new to me. Whiting H316; *Oxford* 34: Bear. Cf. To take Anything *above*.

H161   Since Hector (Adam, Pluto) was a pup (*varied*)

1934 JTFarrell *Young Manhood* (NY 1935) 258: Haven't seen Dan since Hector was a pup. **1935** HWilliamson *Salar* (L) 284: I was working here with a gaff when Adam was a proper pup. **1938** PHaggard *Death Talks* (NY) 264: "The greatest publisher since Hector was a pup." "Who the hell is Hector?" **1941** ARLong *Four Feet* (NY) 13: I haven't been to a . . . party since Hector was a wee, sma' dog. **1959** AAnderson *Lover* (NY) 59: Since Pluto was a pup. Whiting *NC* 422: Hector; DARE i 9: Adam 2.

H162   As homely as a Hedge fence

1968 EBuckler *Ox Bells* (NY) 161: Homely as a hedge fence. Taylor *Prov. Comp.* 48. Cf. Mud fence *below*.

H163   To be down at the Heels

1950 SPalmer *Green* (NY) 106: A down-at-the-heels actress. **1974** JLHess *Grand* (B) 5: The city was down at the heels, down at the mouth. TW 180(5); Brunvand 68(1).

H164   To be set (rocked) back on one's Heels

1952 MVHeberden *Tragic* (NY) 126: It set her back on her heels. **1955** GBagby *Dirty* (NY) 135: It set her back on her heels. **1966** LPDavies *Who Is* (NY) 211: It must have rocked him back on his heels.

H165   To cool one's Heels

1929 JMWalsh *Mystery* (L) 140: He was left cooling his heels. **1936** ECVivian *With Intent* (L) 56: Leaving me to cool my heels. **1957** *Time* 12/16 4: To cool its heels. **1957** WFuller *Girl* (NY) 154: He's been cooling his heels in his own jail. **1961** CBush *Sapphire* (NY) 197: Let him cool his heels a bit longer. **1973** AWest *Mortal* (NY) 227: Cooling his heels in idleness. EAP H178; Brunvand 68(3).

H166 To have round **Heels** (*varied*)

1935 JEGrant *Green Shadow* (NY) 82: I have round heels as the current phrase so cunningly put it [*a girl speaks*]. **1939** CSaxby *Death Cuts* (NY) 147: She's got round heels. **1943** RChandler *Lady* (NY 1946) 35: Little round heels over there. **1956** SPalmer *Unhappy* (NY 1957) 91: I'm not one of your little round-heeled girls. **1958** DThorp *Only* (B) 76: Working girls don't come equipped with round heels. **1960** IWallace *Chapman* (NY 1961) 52: We are approaching the land of the round heels. **1964** SBecker *Covenant* (NY) 96: American officers . . . call Frenchwomen roundheels. **1965** GBagby *Mysteriouser* (NY) 113: No gal could ever get to be so exaggerately [*sic*] well rounded in the bosom without being somewhat round in the heel as well. **1965** JBrooks *Smith* (L) 84: "What does 'round-heeled' mean?" "Worn smooth in the cause . . . Think of the way you lay a woman, and the parts of her body that make contact with the bed. Buttocks, heels, shoulders—but it's the heels that do the work." **1967** DShannon *Rain* (NY) 120: Round heels aren't exclusively city. **1973** EMcBain *Let's Hear* (NY) 146: Her heels were round. Wentworth 434: Round-heels 2.

H167 To kick one's **Heels**

1928 WSMasterman *ZLO* (L) 158: In the meantime I must just kick my heels. **1938** BCobb *Fatal* (L) 79: Dad kicking his heels on the ship. **1959** JIMStewart *Man Who Wrote* (L) 15: Kicking my heels at Orly. EAP H179.

H168 To kick up one's **Heels**

1939 LRGribble *Arsenal* (L) 229: We saw the letters he had from women, and we know he kicked his heels up. **1956** D Wheatley *Ka* (L) 197: Kicking up her pretty heels with some lucky devil. **1964** HWaugh *Missing* (NY) 84: She could kick up her heels. EAP H180.

H169 To lay by the **Heels**

1915 JFerguson *Stealthy* (L 1935) 260: To lay by the heels the men who know. **1924** LTracy *Token* (NY) 181: Laying him by the heels. **1936** JMWalsh *Crimes* (L) 65: She knew enough to lay you by the heels. **1937** GDHCole *Missing* (L) 249: We've laid him by the heels. **1938** JRhode *Invisible* (L) 198: To lay her husband by the heels. **1955** HMHyde *United* (L) 23: His feat of laying . . . Bottomley by the heels. EAP H181.

H170 From **Hell**, Hull, and Halifax *etc.*

1966 JDCarr *Panic* (NY) 23: Isn't there an old prayer . . . which asks God to deliver us from "hell, Hull, and Halifax"? **1976** JRLAnderson *Death* (NY) 25: The . . . old saying, "From Hull, Hell and Halifax, good lord deliver us." EAP H190.

H171 From **Hell** (here) to breakfast (*varied*)

1930 JFDobie *Coronado* (Dallas) 104: I was going lickety-split hell-bent for breakfast. **1935** WSeabrook *Asylum* (NY) 45: Dragging me from hell to breakfast. **1938** MPage *Fast Company* (NY) 188: He could sue you from hell to breakfast. **1949** KMKnight *Bass* (NY) 223: Perjured himself from here to breakfast. **1951** DBOlsen *Cat* (NY) 161: I could hear the red mare going hell for breakfast. **1952** FPratt *Double* (NY) 199: Scattered across the country from hell to breakfast. **1956** RStout *Might* (NY) 114: Up to your neck in it hell for breakfast. **1959** RPowell *Pioneer* (NY) 59: They own it all from hell to breakfast. **1965** EQueen *Queens* (NY) 130: From hell to breakfast. TW 180(7).

H172 From **Hell** to Hackney (Halifax)

1934 JGBrandon *Murder* (L) 33: Trailing them from Hell to Hackney. **1945** MColes *Green Hazard* (NY) 47: I will curse them from Hell to Halifax. Cf. Whiting *Devil* 227(31a): From hell to Harvard; DA Hell d(6): Hell to Harlem.

H173 **Hell** and gone

1954 EQueen *Glass* (B) 7: I'm all scattered to hell and gone. **1958** FLockridge *Long* (P) 133: A post office, the hell and gone from anywhere. **1959** FSmith *Harry* (B) 54: This is somewhere hell and gone off New Guinea. **1960** FLockridge *Judge* (P) 70: The . . . apartment is what is called to hell and gone [*distance*]. **1964** FLockridge *Quest* (P) 155: It's sure to hell and gone. **1966** HHarrison *Make Room* (NY) 23: People are pouring in from all over hell and gone. Whiting *Devil* 227(35).

H174   Hell has no fury like a woman scorned (*very varied*)

1924 LSpringfield *Some Piquant* (L) 114: Hell hath no fury like a woman scorned. **1924** CWells *Furthest* (P) 216: "Hell has no fury like a woman scorned," as the poet puts it. **1929** BDuff *Central* (NY) 46: Get a woman to believing she's been ditched and the old saying "hell's fury" goes six ways. **1929** JJConnington *Case* (B) 128: The woman scorned, and hell let loose, eh? **1932** HFootner *Casual* (L) 187: Hell knoweth no fury like a woman starved. **1934** GWeston *His First* (NY) 16: You know the old saying: Hell hath no fury like a woman scorned. **1935** MJFreeman *Case* (NY) 145: Hell hath no fury like one woman scorned by another. **1935** ECRLorac *Death* (L) 255: I'm no believer in popular sayings as a rule, but the one about "Hell hath no fury" is true enough. **1936** TFuller *Harvard* (B) 3: Hell hath no fury like Cambridge in March or something. **1940** GHCoxe *Glass Triangle* (NY) 126: You've heard that one about hell having no fury like a woman scorned? **1940** PATaylor *Deadly* (NY) 142: Hell hath no fury like an armed woman. My mother told me that in my cradle. **1941** CCoffin *Mare's Nest* (NY) 80: There was an old proverb about a woman scorned. **1949** ESGardner *Dubious* (NY 1954) 17: You know the old saying about "Hell hath no fury like a woman scorned." **1950** SPalmer *Green* (NY) 7: Hell hath no fury like a woman who's been made a fool of. **1950** ECRLorac *And Then* (NY) 71: "Old proverbs have a way of working out." "Hell hath no fury . . . that old adage." **1953** ADean *Collector's* (NY DBC) 64: You know what the Bible said about a woman scorned . . . Hell ain't got no fury like. **1959** *NYTimes* 5/3 4E: Hell hath no fury like a Frenchman scorned. **1964** LLRue *World* (P) 44: The fury of a woman scorned cannot even be compared to the fury displayed by a mother in defence of her young. **1966** NMarsh *Killer* (B) 233: She really does bear out the Woman Scorned crack. **1969** DShannon

Crime (NY) 132: Hell having no fury like— a woman conned. **1970** RFoley *Calculated* (NY) 81: And there is always . . . the woman scorned. Oh please don't wince when I use clichés. **1970** NMonsarrat *Breaking* (L) 369: Hell hath no fury like an author thus fouled-up. **1970** RQuest *Cerberus* (NY) 172: Hell hath no fury like a homo scorned. **1972** EXFerrars *Foot* (NY) 208: Hell hath no fury like a woman whose cooking has been scorned. **1973** EJKahn *Fraud* (NY) 162: Hell hath no fury like a bilker bilked. **1975** NGuild *Lost* (NY) 67: Hell hath no fury like a woman scorned, so they said. **1981** MKWren *Seasons* (NY) 148: With the proverbial fury of a woman scorned, [she] stabbed Lee. Whiting *Devil* 220(1); Brunvand 68(3).

H175   In spite of (come) Hell and (or) high water (*varied*)

1926 CWTyler *Blue Jean* (NY) 207: In spite of Hades, Halifax, or high water. **1931** WBSeabrook *Jungle* (L) 61: In spite of hell and high water. **1933** REssex *Slade* (NY) 46: Come hell or high water. **1937** HAshbrook *Murder* (NY) 186: In spite of hell and high water. **1940** LFord *Old Lover's* (NY) 106: In spite of hell and high tide. **1954** EForbes *Rainbow* (B) 6: Come hell or high water. **1959** DLMathews *Fatal* (NY DBC) 76: Come hell or high water. **1963** MPHood *Sin* (NY) 192: Come devil or high water. **1973** AMorice *Death* (NY) 118: Come hell or high water. **1974** ELathen *Sweet* (NY) 10: Come hell, high water, or six inches of snow. Whiting *Devil* 223(10).

H176   Through Hell and high water

1926 MMTaylor *Heart* (L) 125: "Through hell and high water," to use a bromidic expression. **1934** GDilnot *Crook's* (L) 109: I'll stick to you through hell and high water. **1946** VSiller *One Alone* (NY) 83: Through hell or high water, she was his now. Whiting *Devil* 223–4(10).

H177   Till Hell freezes over

c1910 PGWodehouse *Leave it to Psmith* (L) 286: Pals till hell freezes! **1923** HGartland *Globe* (NY) 291: Until hell freezes over. **1928** RHFuller *Jubilee* (NY) 302: You'll wait till hell freezes over and thaws out again. **1928** CWood *Shadow* (NY) 228: Till hell freezes over, and even through the thaw. **1936** RKing *Constant God* (NY) 70: It can stay there till hell freezes over. **1941** DBHughes *Bamboo* (NY) 195: Could keep them till hell freezes over. **1959** *NYTimes* 1/ 18 61: I'll string along with Webb until hell freezes over. **1966** DMDisney *Magic* (NY) 148: Wait till hell freezes over. Whiting *Devil* 221(4).

H178 To be **Hell** on toast

1934 PATaylor *Cape Cod Tavern* (NY) 214: This selling books has been hell on toast. **1951** PATaylor *Diplomatic* (NY) 184: It's been simply hell on toast. Whiting *Devil* 226(28).

H179 To be **Hell** (*etc.*) on wheels (*varied*)

1928 CWood *Shadow* (NY) 120: They're hell on wheels. **1932** NKlein *No! No!* (NY) 80: Life was hell on wheels with Wolcott. **1933** DHoldridge *Pindorama* (NY) 69: How to be a son of a bitch on wheels. **1936** DHume *Meet the Dragon* (L) 215: They tell me he's hell on four wheels. **1938** JAllen *I Lost* (NY) 32: She's hell on wheels and hates your guts. **1939** HFootner *Murder That* (L) 209: You're a devil on wheels! **1940** WReed *No Sign* (NY) 161: My nieces were a pair of bitches on wheels. **1946** BHalliday *Blood* (NY 1960) 122: He thinks he's hell-on-wheels with the ladies. **1947** AAFair *Fools* (NY 1957) 52: A hellcat on wheels. **1948** CLLeonard *Fourth* (NY) 156: His wife's a bitch on wheels. **1954** RFMirvish *Texana* (NY) 56: He's no hell on wheels. **1963** MErskine *No. 9* (NY) 107: He's simply hell on wheels [*hard to deal with*]. **1965** RDrexler *I Am* (NY) 86: He thinks I'm sex on wheels. **1970** ELathen *Pick* (NY) 183: That woman must be plain on wheels. **1971** BBaxt *Affair* (NY) 111: You're hell on wheels [*hard to get along with*]. Whiting *Devil* 226–7(29).

H180 To come **Hell**-bent for election

1924 LThayer *Key* (NY) 147: Coming hell-bent-for-election. **1934** DGardiner *Drink* (NY) 28: Hell-bent-for-election. **1939** PA Taylor *Spring* (L) 66: He come around this curve hell-bent for election. **1944** MLong *Bury* (NY) 169: He had gone home hell-bent for election. **1950** MCarleton *Bride* (NY) 51: Run hell-for-election. **1965** JNichols *Sterile* (NY) 41: The hell-bent-for-election chaos. Whiting *Devil* 229(63); Berrey 53.16.

H181 To go **Hell**-bent for Kittery (Texas)

1935 AHobhouse *Hangover* (NY) 187: Going hell-bent for Kittery. **1935** SWilliams *Murder* (NY) 180: Going hell bent for Texas. Whiting *Devil* 225(18). Cf. Berrey 53.16.

H182 To go to **Hell** and back (*varied*)

1930 RGoldman *Murder* (L) 93: He would—to use a not very pretty popular phrase—go to hell and back for her. **1938** EHuxley *Murder* (NY) 100: She's the sort of girl who'd stick to a guy to hell and gone, and all the way back. **1957** COLocke *Hell Bent* (NY) 66: My sons will trail him from here to hell and back. Whiting *Devil* 227(34), 228(44).

H183 To go to **Hell** in a handbasket (*etc.*) (*varied*)

1926 JTully *Beggars* (NY) 255: Country's bound for hell in a handbasket. **1936** VMcHugh *Caleb* (NY) 326: Every last one of them boys figured he was going to heaven in a hand-basket. **1948** WLewis *Letters* ed WKRose (L 1963) 476: We are all going to Hell in a handbasket. **1951** RJHealey *New Tales* (NY) 228: The world was going to hell in a wheelbarrow. **1953** EQueen *Scarlet* (B) 129: He insists on going to hell on a shingle. **1956** *BHerald* 10/17 28: It would go to hell in a basket. **1956** CCockburn *In Time* (L) 75: His world was going to hell in a handcart. **1957** *Punch* 3/ 20 376: Going . . . to hell in a handcart. **1957** WRBurdett *Underdog* (NY) 130: Want to go to hell on a sled. **1957** DErskine *Pink* (NY) 19: The world was going to hell in a hack. **1959** *BHerald* 2/15 62: The bond market would go to hell in a hack. **1962** RMacdonald *Zebra* (NY) 171: The country would be headed for Hades in a handbasket. **1963** BWAldiss *Male* (L 1966) 103: The three of you can go to hell in a basket. **1964** RMacdonald *Chill* (NY) 167: Everything's gone to hell in a hand-car. **1966** EPangborn *Judgment* (NY) 126: Things went to hell in a bucket. **1967** RTraver *Jealous* (NY) 154: The Court . . . is generally plunging us to hell in a homemade handbasket. **1969** ACGraene *Personal* (NY) 309: My father would probably have gone to hell in a hack, as West Texas said. **1975** JDaniels *White* (NY) 121: Going to hell in a hack. Cf. Berrey 310.4: Go to hell on a poker.

H184   To have all **Hell** break loose

1931 HBurnham *Murder* (NY) 248: All hell had broke loose. **1940** GBagby *Corpse Wore* (NY) 217: All hell broke loose again. **1953** FKane *Poisons* (NY 1960) 117: All hell's going to break loose. **1959** KBulmer *Changeling* (NY) 119: All hell is scheduled to break loose. **1963** RCroft-Cooke *Bosie* (L) 159: All hell, as they say, broke loose. **1964** JWhite *Deadly* (NY) 43: All hell broke loose. **1976** JPorter *Package* (NY) 6: All hell broke loose. **1978** SWoods *Exit Murderer* (NY) 57: All hell broke loose. TW 180(8).

H185   To ride (*etc.*) **Hell** for leather

1906 CPearl *Morrison of Peking* (Sydney 1967) 189: Rode hell for leather. **c1923** ACrowley *Confessions* ed JSymonds (L 1969) 517: Going Hell for leather. **1933** CBush *Three Strange* (L) 156: They went hell-for-leather. **1935** FErskine *Naked* (L) 14: A man and a woman fighting hell for leather. **1959** *Time* 5/11 51: I get the orchestras to such a state of jitters they can't help playing hell-for-leather. **1962** PDennis *Genius* (NY) 304: Racing hell-bent for leather. **1969** ASJasper *Hoxton* (L) 68: Gave him hell for leather [*a scolding*]. **1971** ROulahan *Man Who* (NY) 19: A hell-for-leather liberal. **1976** EXFerrars *Cup* (NY) 177: Gone hell for leather home. Whiting *Devil* 229–30(64); Berrey 53.16.

H186   As fussy as a **Hen** (*varied*)

1930 MDalton *Body* (NY) 2: She fusses like a hen with one chick. **1934** JCLenehan *Carnival* (L) 39: He's as fussy as an old hen. **1950** IFletcher *Bennett's* (I) 303: Fussin' like an old hen. **1953** CHarnett *Nicholas* (NY) 158: All day long, as fussy as a hen. **1966**

DMDisney *At Some* (NY) 172: She'll fuss over you like a mother hen with one chick. **1969** DDoolittle ed *Only in Maine* (Barre, Mass.) 217: Charlie fussing over me like an anxious hen with one chick. TW 181(19).

H187   As jumpy (*etc.*) as a **Hen** (chicken) on a hot griddle (*varied*)

1927 FWCrofts *Ponson* (NY 1931) 86: He was all jumping like a hen on a hot griddle to be off. **1927** FWCrofts *Starvel* (NY) 334: French was like the proverbial hen on the hot griddle. **1928** RHFuller *Jubilee* (NY) 348: As uneasy as chickens on a hot stove. **1947** RDavies *Diary* (Toronto) 26: As jumpy as a hen on a hot griddle. Whiting *NC* 424(14); Taylor *Prov. Comp.* 48: Jump. Cf. Spider *below*.

H188   As mad (cross, sore) as a wet **Hen** (turkey) (*varied*)

1921 JCLincoln *Galusha* (NY) 322: He'll be crosser'n a hen out in a rainstorm. **1927** CAiken *Blue Voyage* (NY) 280: He was mad as a wet hen. **1935** CMRussell *Murder* (NY) 5: As cross as a wet hen. **1951** ADerleth *Far* (NY) 113: Madder'n a wet hen. **1956** *New Yorker* 10/27 25: My wife is mad as a wet hen. **1959** *BHerald* 9/24 13: The wife will be mad as a wet hen. **1960** LLevine *Great* (L) 264: Mad as wet turkeys. **1972** JPotts *Troublemaker* (NY) 47: Mad as a wet hen. **1975** HDolson *Please* (P) 166: Sore as a wet hen. EAP H202. As mad as a wet Cat *above*.

H189   As nervous as a **Hen** (*varied*)

1947 HCahill *Look* (NY) 134: He's been as nervous as two hens worrying about one lost chicken. **1963** DGardiner *Lion* (NY) 137: Nervous as a fussy old hen. **1967** AChester *Exquisite* (NY) 181: She was as nervous as a wet hen. Cf. EAP H201.

H190   As scarce (rare) as **Hen's** (turkey's) teeth (*varied*)

1920 BEStevenson *Gloved Hand* (NY) 29: As scarce as hen's teeth. **1931** LEppley *Murder* (NY) 204: Wells are scarcer than hen's teeth. **1933** EECummings *Eimi* (NY) 27: Taxis are scarcer than hen's teeth. **1941** MArmstrong *Blue Santo* (NY) 223: Alibis is scarcer'n hen's teeth. **1946** PATaylor *Punch*

(NY) 112: Getting information would be like pulling hen's teeth. **1951** MHead *Congo* (NY) 52: They being scarcer than hen's teeth. **1952** HReilly *Velvet* (NY) 103: Cabs were harder to find than hen's teeth. **1955** LCochran *Hallelujah* (NY) 82: As rare as a hen's tooth. **1958** *BangorDN* 8/2 23: "How do ye want yore steak?" "Rare as hen's teeth!" **1959** GMarx *Groucho* (NY) 248: They're as scarce as hen's teeth. (Why do people still insist on using this silly simile when even the rooster knows that the hen hasn't any teeth . . . and very little of anything else?) **1960** TWilliams *Three Players* (L) 105: As rare as hen's teeth. **1965** RVale *Beyond* (NY) 43: Food's been scarce as turkey's teeth. **1966** EVCunningham *Helen* (NY) 167: As rare as hen's teeth. **1968** MSarton *Plant* (NY) 145: As scarce as hen's teeth. **1974** CMartin *Whiskey* (NY) 120: Money was scarce as hen's teeth. TW 181(7).

H191 Crowing **Hens**, whistling girls *etc.*

1930 BABotkin ed *Folk-Say* (Norman, Okla.) 160: To tolerate crowing hens and whistling women. **1936** RDavis *Crowing Hen* (NY) iii [*title page*]: Whistling woman and crowing hen Are neither good for God nor men. **1954** EForbes *Rainbow* (B) 143: I suppose she came to a bad end—like crowing hens and whistling girls. **1957** LBeam *Maine* (NY) 92: Whistling girls and crowing hens, always come to some bad end. **1957** HPBeck *Folklore of Maine* (P) 65: Girls that whistle and hens that crow will make a living wherever they go. **1958** *BGlobe* 10/2 12: The old ditty is: Whistling girls and crowing hens always come to a bad end. But my father used to say: Girls that whistle and hens that crow can take care of themselves wherever they go. **1965** HBevington *Charley* (NY) 116: Whistling girls and crowing hens always come to some bad end. **1966** ARRandell *Sixty* (L) 93: "A whistling woman and a crowing hen are neither good for God nor men" is a very old saying firmly believed in by Fen folk. EAP H204, S21; *Oxford* 155: Crooning cow.

H192 To be the white **Hen's** chickens

1965 DCLunt *Woods* (NY) 17: In the York County [*Maine*] idiom of my grandfather Storer, they are the white hen's chickens [*good people*]. *Oxford* 752: Sons of. Cf. DARE i 304–5: Blue hen's chicken.

H193 To watch like a **Hen** with one chicken (*varied*)

1929 HFootner *Self-Made* (NY) 130: Watches over her like a hen with one chicken. **1934** CBush *Dead Shepherd* (L) 286: Palmer began hovering round . . . like a hen with a lone chick. **1955** JPotts *Death* (NY) 56: Like a mother hen . . . with one chick instead of the dozen she should have had. Taylor *Western Folklore* 17(1958) 16(2). Cf. EAP H201.

H194 To know **Hercules** by his foot

1930 ATrain *Adventures* (NY) 73: *Ex pede Herculem.* **1969** BLehane *Compleat* (L) 91: On the principle *ex pede Herculem.* **1972** QBell *Virginia* (NY) I 112: *Ex pede Herculem,* deducing Jacob from his room. EAP H209.

H195 Neither **Here** nor there

1909 JCLincoln *Keziah* (NY) 195: That's neither here nor there. **1924** EWallace *Green* (B) 204: Neither here nor there. **1926** MRJames *Letters to a Friend* ed GMcBryde (L 1956) 139: Neither here nor there. **1935** DHume *Murders* (L) 125: That's neither here nor there. **1939** DFrome *Mr. P. and the Old Angel* (L) 25: That's neither here nor there, as they say. **1943** HLMencken *Heathen Days* (NY) 149: What we saw . . . is neither here nor there. **1947** LFord *Woman* (NY) 98: Neither here nor there. **1951** KFarrell *Mistletoe* (L) 146: That is neither here nor there. **1956** PDeVries *Comfort* (B) 134: That's neither here nor there. **1965** HWaugh *End* (NY) 148: That's neither here nor there. **1969** ELathen *When* (NY) 179: That is neither here nor there. **1972** PWarner *Loose* (NY) 75: They are neither here nor there. **1975** JFraser *Wreath* (NY) 32: Friday night's neither here nor there. EAP H211.

H196 As cold as a **Herring** (*varied*)

1931 GFowler *Great* (NY) 91: He was knocked as cold as a Bismarck herring. **1931** LMcFarlane *Murder* (NY) 99: Knocked him cold as a herring. **1932**

MCJohnson *Damning* (NY) 166: I was as cold as a pickled herring. **1934** GFowler *Father Goose* (NY) 116: As cold as a herring. Cf. Wilstach 62: Fish. Cf. As cold as a Fish, Haddock *above.*

H197 As dead as a **Herring** (*varied*)

1926 SQuinn *Phantom* (Sauk City, Wisc. 1966) 38: He was dead as a herring. **1932** MCJohnson *Damning* (NY) 271: Dead as a herring. **1942** JShepherd *Demise* (NY 1962) 91: Heyworth is deader than a herring. **1950** CLittle *Black* (NY) 213: He's dead as a herring, although he still smells better. **1956** *BangorDN* 8/30 34: Your summer romance is as dead as a marinated herring. **1957** MPHood *In the Dark* (NY) 39: Dead as smoked herrings. **1962** ESherry *Girl* (NY DBC) 109: Dead as a herring. **1965** HHarrison *Bill* (NY) 176: Dead as a herring. EAP H214; Brunvand 69(1). Cf. As dead as a Fish, Haddock *above.*

H198 As thin as a (an August) **Herring**

1913 JCLincoln *Mr. Pratt's Patients* (NY) 27: She was thin as an August herring. NED Herring 2. Cf. Apperson 356: Lean; *Oxford* 450: Lean; Tilley H447 (quote 1666).

H199 Like **Herring** in a barrel (*varied*)

1917 GRSims *My Life* (L) 174: The proverbial herring in a barrel had by comparison comfortable accommodations. **1921** EMillay *Letters* ed ARMacdougall (NY 1952) 128: People packed in like herrings. EAP H216. Cf. Sardines *below.*

H200 He (she) who **Hesitates** is lost

1912 ERBurroughs *Gods of Mars* (NY 1963) 114: He who hesitates is lost . . . a true aphorism. **1928** BNewman *Round About Andorras* (L) 99: He hesitated and was lost. **1928** LTracy *Women* (NY) 32: The woman who hesitates is lost; the man who hesitates seldom or never does what he ought to do. **1930** WLewis *Apes* (NY 1932) 60: He who hesitates is lost. **1934** GEllinger *Return* (L) 81: Moya hesitated and was lost. **1950** RMacdonald *Drowning* (NY 1951) 3: He who hesitates is lost. **1959** DLMathews *Fatal* (NY DBC) 47: She was telling herself that he who hesitates is lost, and nothing ventured, nothing gained. **1973** JFleming *Alas*

(NY) 153: He who hesitates is lost, as his ould [*sic*] mother used to say. TW 409: Woman (6); Brunvand 69; *Oxford* 909: Woman.

H201 As tough (hard) as **Hickory** (*varied*)

1930 LMeynell *Mystery* (P) 174: He was as hard as hickory. **1939** TStevenson *Silver Arrow* (L) 196: As tough as hickory. **1968** JAiken *Crystal* (NY) 61: Tough as an old hickory root. TW 182(1). Cf. Brunvand 69.

H202 Not to see **Hide** nor hair of someone (*varied*)

1908 SHAdams *Flying Death* (NY) 95: Without finding hide or hair of the horse. **1921** IOstrander *Crimson* (NY) 42: Haven't seen hide or hair of you. **1932** HFootner *Dead Man's* (NY) 160: Ain't seen hide or hair of him. **1938** CCMunz *Land* (NY) 23: I ain't seen hide nor hair of him. **1940** PWentworth *Rolling* (P) 281: You won't see hair, hide or hoof of her, the she-devil. **1947** PWentworth *Wicked* (NY) 58: You wouldn't have seen hair, hide or hoof of me. **1948** BSBallinger *Body* (NY) 79: Haven't seen hide nor hair of any of 'em. **1954** JSanders *Freakshow* (B) 163: I ain't seen hide nor hair of him since. **1956** RFenisong *Bite* (NY) 144: She hadn't heard hide nor hair of them since. **1956** PWentworth *Fingerprint* (NY) 25: Never saw hair, hide or hoof of him. **1963** HWaugh *Death* (NY) 196: I ain't seen hide nor hair of any today. **1967** RPeterson *Another View* (NY) 29: I saw neither hide nor hair of a fox. **1974** DCavett *Cavett* (NY) 62: They never found hide nor hair of her. **1976** JPorter *Package* (NY) 17: She couldn't see hide or hair of any of us. EAP H219; Brunvand 69.

H203 To have one's **Hide** nailed to the barn door (*varied*)

1908 JCLincoln *Cy Whittaker* (NY) 360: He'll have your hide nailed on the barn door. **1950** SPalmer *Green* (NY) 9: I hate to see your hide nailed to the barn door. **1955** RDavies *Leaven* (L) 174: You seem to be the one who wants to hang [his] hide on the fence, as the boys used to say when we were young. **1972** JDCarr *Hungry* (NY) 20:

Your governor'll want to skin me and nail my hide to the door. **1975** JFoxx *Dead Run* (I) 28: They could tack my ass on the proverbial wall [*arrest and convict him*]. **1982** HPentecost *Past* (NY) 57: You can nail him to the barn door when you do. Cf. Mast *below.*

H204 To save one's **Hide**

1929 RJCasey *Secret* (I) 96: They are interested only in saving their hides. Whiting *NC* 424(2).

H205 Those that **Hide** can find (*varied*)

1922 JJoyce *Ulysses* (NY 1934) 542: Those that hides knows where to find. **1928** AR Martin *Cassiodore* (NY) 245: On the principle that hiders find. **1929** LBrock *Stoke Silver* (NY) 203: Who hides, finds. **1929** JJConnington *Grim* (B) 177: He who hides knows where to seek. **1933** MBurton *Fate* (L) 184: "They that hide can find." You know the old saying. **1939** CMWills *Calabar Bean* (L) 56: There's a saying . . . that those who hide know where to find. **1959** AGilbert *Death* (NY) 227: Them as hides knows where to find. EAP H220.

H206 **High**, wide and handsome

1930 The Aresbys *Murder* (NY) 259: He was out for a high, wide and handsome time. **1930** JGBrandon *Murder* (L) 190: Knock 'em high, wide, handsome and senseless. **1932** ORCohen *Star* (NY) 302: He was stepping high, wide and handsome. **1935** LThayer *Dead* (NY) 14: The old phrase "high, wide and handsome." **1938** PGWodehouse *Code* (NY) 82: Stepping high, wide and handsome. **1945** MWalsh *Nine Strings* (P) 118: Some wide and some high and all handsome. **1954** LFord *Invitation* (NY) 25: He'd been going high, wide and handsome. **1965** DoctorX *Intern* (NY) 323: I had missed high, wide and handsome. Wentworth 257.

H207 To be left **High** and dry

1937 RLGoldman *Judge Robinson* (L) 111: Left him high and dry. **1952** ECRLorac *Dog* (NY) 86: He'd left his wife high and dry, so to speak. **1956** JFStraker *Ginger* (L) 84: That . . . left him high and dry. **1957**

CCarnac *Late Miss* (NY) 109: I left them high and dry. Partridge 390.

H208 The **Higher** one comes the harder he falls (*varied*)

1952 TDuBois *Cavalier's* (NY) 118: The higher they come the harder they fall. **1955** KMKnight *Robineau* (NY) 48: The higher you go, the further you fall. Whiting *NC* 424–5.

H209 As plain as a **Highway**

1932 GDyer *Five* (B) 251: My procedure lay plain as a highway. Wilstach 293: The way.

H210 As ancient as the **Hills**

1934 MBurton *Murder* (NY) 67: It's as ancient as the hills. **1952** HPearson *Whistler* (NY) 25: As ancient as hills. **1962** RMacdonald *Zebra* (NY) 94: It's as ancient as the hills. TW 183(1).

H211 As old as the **Hills**

1908 JCLincoln *Cy Whittaker* (NY) 143: Old as the hills. **1920** ACrabb *Samuel* (NY) 199: As old as the hills. **1932** GKChesterton et al. *Floating* (NY) 53: Old as the hills. **1939** DHume *Heads* (L) 157: The trick was as old as the hills. **1950** HGreen *Nothing* (NY) 17: Old as the hills. **1958** RKing *Malice* (NY) 170: As old as the hills. **1959** *BangorDN* 8/24 9: This gag is older than the hills. **1960** HEBates *Aspidistra* (L) 115: It's as old as the hills. **1968** MAllingham *Cargo* (NY) 126: I am free, white and I feel as old as the hills. EAP H222.

H212 The far-off **Hills** are green (*varied*)

1937 LO'Flaherty *Famine* (NY) 391: It's an old story that the far-off hills are green. **1959** DCushman *Goodbye* (NY) 135: Always greener over the hill. **1968** GBagby *Another* (NY) 95: Another case of those far-off hills looking greener. Apperson 302(3); *Oxford* 373. Cf. The Grass is greener *above.*

H213 Not amount to a **Hill** of beans

1929 KCStrahan *Footprints* (NY) 223: Not that I think it will amount to a hill of beans. **1933** PGWodehouse *Heavy* (B) 306: [It] doesn't amount to a hill of beans. **1943** PATaylor *Going* (NY) 65: [It] doesn't amount to a hill of beans. **1954** AStone *Harvard* (B) 169: It didn't amount to a hill of beans. **1958** *BHerald* 6/24 35: Just never amounted to a hill of beans. **1976** CLarson *Muir's* (NY) 56: That didn't amount to a hill of beans. DA Hill 2b.

H214 Not care a **Hill** of beans

1957 WGoldman *Temple* (NY) 108: Didn't care a hill of beans for her. Cf. next entry.

H215 Not worth a **Hill** of beans

1930 SChalmers *Crime* (NY) 174: If he's worth a hill of beans. **1937** CBClason *Blind* (NY) 49: It wasn't worth a hill of beans. **1974** DCavett *Cavett* (NY) 135: Did they turn out to be worth a hill of beans to you, or even a handful? TW 183(6).

H216 Up **Hill** and down dale

1905 JBCabell *Line* (NY 1926) 125: René lied up-hill and down-dale. **1931** GDHCole *Dead Man's* (NY) 147: Cursed the taxi . . . up hill and down dale. **1934** MKennedy *Corpse* (L) 50: Cursed the van man up hill and sideways. **1951** JCollier *Fancies* (NY) 291: It's a bit of a wandering life for her—up hill and down dale, as the saying goes. **1959** EMButler *Paper* (L) 19: Abusing the regiment up hill and down dale. TW 183(5).

H217 Up to the **Hilt**

1937 JJConnington *Minor* (L) 144: It's confirmed up to the hilt. **1954** HWaugh *Rag* (NY) 177: I would back him to the hilt. NED Hilt 3.

H218 **Hindsight** is better than foresight (*varied*)

1931 GDyer *Three-Cornered* (B) 199: The much noted superiority of hindsight over foresight. **1931** DOgburn *Death* (B) 58: Hindsight is so clear. **1935** JHWallis *Politician* (NY) 115: Hindsight is better than foresight. **1936** KMKnight *Wheel* (NY) 270: Hindsight is always easier than foresight. **1941** HReilly *Three Women* (NY) 155: Hindsight was useless. **1958** *BHerald* 6/24 11: Hindsight is better than foresight. **1959** *NYTimes* 8/16 41: Hindsight is easier than foresight. **1960** HLivingston *Climacticon* (NY) 84: Hindsight is always easy. **1960**

DMDisney *Dark* (NY) 180: We have the advantage of hindsight. **1961** MMillar *How Like* (NY DBC) 230: Hindsight's not as good as foresight. **1970** AALewis *Carnival* (NY) 108: But hindsight is superior to foresight. **1970** RDAltick *Victorian* (NY) 234: Hindsight is always wiser than perception attempted in the midst of events. Whiting NC 425.

H219 As cold as the **Hinges** (of Newgate)

1937 DQBurleigh *Kristiana* (NY) 197: It's colder'n the hinges. **1968** EBuckler *Ox Bells* (NY) 164: Cold as the hinges of Newgate. DA Hinge b: Hinges of hell.

H220 As hot as the **Hinges** (of hell)

1930 JDosPassos *42nd* (NY) 127: Hotter'n the hinges of hell. **1940** MArmstrong *Man with* (NY) 53: Hotter than hinges, as the old saying is. **1942** CFAdams *What Price* (NY) 184: You're hotter than the hinges of hell [*wanted by police*]. **1943** RPSmith *Journey* (NY) 125: It was loaded with chile and hot as the hinges of hell. **1948** CLLeonard *Fourth* (NY) 23: It was hotter than the hinges of hell. **1953** JRMacdonald *Meet* (NY) 192: She's as hot as the hinges [*liable to arrest*]. **1959** BPalmer *Blind Man's* (NY) 11: Hot as the hinges. Whiting *Devil* 222(5); Taylor *Prov. Comp.* 50; Wilstach 204. Cf. TW 183: Black. Cf. Knobs *below*.

H221 A **Hint** is as good as a kick in the shins

1933 GHolt *Dark Lady* (L) 270: A hint's as good as a kick in the shins. TW 183(1).

H222 To have one on the **Hip**

1930 SFowler *King* (L) 259: We've got them on the hip now. **1934** AMeredith *Portrait* (NY) 21: She had him on the hip. **1938** NMarsh *Artists* (L 1941) 161: We have him on the hip. EAP H226; TW 183–4.

H223 **History** repeats itself (*varied*)

1913 EDBiggers *Seven Keys* (I) 370: You let history alone . . . or it'll repeat itself. **1919** HFAshurst *Diary* ed GFSparks (Tucson 1962) 101: History repeats itself. **1922** JJoyce *Ulysses* (NY 1934) 370: History repeats itself. 639: History repeating itself. **1932** GBucher *In the Line* (L) 308: History was repeating itself. **1936** PFleming *News* (NY) 103: It would not be my fault if history repeated itself. **1942** AMStein *Only the Guilty* (NY) 151: That history-repeats-itself stuff. **1944** WBThomas *Way of a Countryman* (L) 124: In this regard history is not repeating itself. **1951** CHare *English* (L) 228: History has repeated itself. **1955** AC Clark *Earthlight* (NY) 11: It has been truly said that history never repeats itself, but historical situations recur. **1957** *BangorDN* 1/23 10: We hope history repeats. 9/11 22: To say that "history repeats itself" sounds commonplace. **1957** *PMLA* 72 563: The well-known dictum that history repeats itself. **1957** NWYates *W.T.Porter* (Baton Rouge) 4: History never repeats itself exactly. **1959** *BangorDN* 8/18 2: The adage that history repeats itself. **1959** AGilbert *Death* (NY) 81: Any romantic claptrap about history not repeating itself. **1966** DRCowan *Pleasant* (NY) 45: History does not repeat itself, however much current events may simulate preceding ones. **1967** WTucker *Warlock* (NY) 184: History had not repeated itself. **1968** JRoffman *Daze* (NY) 76: History was said to repeat itself . . . the old cliché. **1974** SAGrau *Wind* (NY) 52: History is repeating itself. **1977** SKaminsky *Bullet* (NY) 150: History was repeating itself. TW 184; *Oxford* 374.

H224   To **Hit** one where he lives

1933 FDGrierson *Mystery* (L) 109: It hit the old boy where he lived. **1952** DMDisney *Heavy* (NY) 97: Something hits me where I live. **1957** DErskine *Pink* (NY) 135: We hit 'em where they live. **1957** JPotts *Man with* (NY 1964) 96: That one hit Monroe where he lived. **1961** JBlish *So Close* (NY) 15: It's hitting me right where I live. **1966** HPentecost *Hide* (NY) 7: They really hit you where you live. **1971** HPentecost *Deadly* (NY) 85: This story had hit him where he lived. Partridge 393.

H225   A **Hive** of bees in May is worth a load of hay

1957 HPBeck *Folklore of Maine* (P) 80: A hive of bees in May is worth a load of hay. Dunwoody 97: Swarm; *Oxford* 791: Swarm.

H226   As black (hot) as the **Hobs** of hell

1935 CStJSprigg *Corpse* (NY) 95: As hot as the hobs of hell. **1969** DClark *Nobody's* (NY) 108: The case against you could be made to look as black as the hobbs of hell. Cf. Hinges *above*, Knobs *below*.

H227   One's **Hobby-horse** (*varied*)

1929 RAldington *Death* (L) 151: George had mounted one of his hobby-horses. **1932** WSSykes *Harness* (NY) 103: Riding his hobby-horse. **1939** GDHCole *Greek* (L) 48: Preparing to mount a hobby-horse. **1941** MTYates *Midway* (NY) 133: Riding my favorite hobby-horse. **1943** NMarsh *Colour Scheme* (L 1960) 125: I'm riding my hobby horse to death. **1957** *New Yorker* 2/16 116: He is mounting an old hobby-horse. **1962** MAllingham *China* (NY) 47: I clamber up on this boring old hobby horse. **1965** JPorter *Dover Two* (NY 1968) 22: Climbed into the saddle of his hobby-horse. **1970** PMoyes *Many* (NY) 164: He was on his hobbyhorse, and enjoying the ride. **1974** WBridges *Gathering* (NY) 32: He rode his hobbyhorse off in all directions. EAP H231.

H228   **Hobson's choice** (*varied*)

1919 JSClouston *Man from the Clouds* (NY) 66: It was Hobson's choice. **1922** VBridges *Greensea* (NY) 14: A question of Hobson's choice. **1933** NBell *Lord* (B) 245: It's what you call Hobson's choice . . . like it or lump it. **1936** CFGregg *Henry* (L) 41: It was Hobson's choice. **1939** RHull *And Death* (L) 85: It was more or less a case of Hobson's choice. **1940** PATaylor *Deadly* (NY) 161: Ward was still torn between his Hobsonian choice of a . . . beachwagon . . . and a . . . sedan. **1946** CTGardner *Bones* (NY) 171: He faced a veritable Hobson's choice. **1951** GAxelrod *Hobson's Choice* (L). **1953** A Rhodes *Ball* (L) 255: Another of those Hobson choices with which Italy is always faced. **1958** EQueen *Finishing* (NY) 105: Luria was merely exercising the Hobson's choice of all policemen and going over the same old ground. **1964** RBlythe *Age* (B) 167: It was the heyday of Hobson's choice, of learning to actually live . . . without money. **1968** JTMcIntosh *Take a Pair* (NY)

180: "He sniffed and said he would wait because it was Hobson's choice." "He's wrong . . . Hobson's choice was take it or leave it. Charles just has to take it." **1969** PMcGerr *For Richer* (NY) 44: That calls for a husband apiece and your choices are very Hobson. **1975** ABrodsky *Madame* (NY) 57: Faced with this Hobson's choice, many opted for exile. **1976** JHerbers *No Thank You* (NY) 48: Cities are left with the Hobson's choice of firing the father in order to hire the son. **1980** RHFrancis *Daggerman* (NY) 167–8: It's Hobson's choice, Guv. If you can't go backwards, you have to go forwards. EAP H232.

H229 As dull as a **Hoe**

1935 *New Yorker* 9/21 19: Everything is as clean as a whistle and as dull as a hoe. EAP H234.

H230 As dirty as a **Hog**

1936 VRath *Murder* (NY) 212: I feel dirty as a hog. **1941** SHHolbrook *Murder out* (NY) 9: Dirty as a hog. EAP H236. Cf. As dirty as a Pig *below*.

H231 As fat as a **Hog**

1958 *CSMonitor* 10/23 22: Fat as a hog. TW 184(1). Cf. As fat as a Pig *below*.

H232 As happy as a **Hog** (*varied*)

1953 DCushman *Stay Away* (NY) 169: Happy as a hog in a brewery. **1971** DFJones *Denver* (NY) 25: [He] was as happy as a hog in an apple barrel. Cf. As happy as a Pig *below*.

H233 As independent (*etc.*) as a **Hog** (pig) on ice (*varied*)

1913 JCLincoln *Mr Pratt's Patients* (NY) 175: Independent as a hog on ice. **1937** RStout *Red Box* (L) 85: As independent as a hog on ice. **1939** RStout *Mountain Cat* (NY 1958) 199: She's as independent as a hog on ice. **1942** SHAdams *Tambay* (NY) 154: Klink tottered out, cool as a hog on ice. **1947** CBrand *Suddenly* (L) 51: He's as obstinate as a hog on ice. **1950** SPalmer *Green* (NY) 201: Mr. Big is as independent as a hog on ice. **1952** PGWodehouse *Pigs* (NY) 23: The calm insouciance of a pig on ice. **1956** *BHerald* 10/5 60: The Minnesota voter is independent and as hard to control as a hog on ice. **1956** SPalmer *Unhappy* (NY 1957) 159: All our people got jittery as a hog on ice. **1959** MPHood *Bell* (NY) 15: Obstinate as a hog on ice'n twice as independent. **1962** DTaylor *Blood* (NY) 198: A drunken Indian is as unpredictable as a pig on ice. **1969** JGould *Jonesport* (B) 169: "As independent as a hog on ice" is a standard Maine remark. **1972** FVWMason *Brimstone* (L) 271: Independent as pigs on ice. **1976** CLarson *Muir's* (NY) 144: He's as independent as a hog on a hot tin roof. Taylor *Prov. Comp.* 51, *Western Folklore* 17(1958) 16; DA Hog 10(1).

H234 Better my **Hog** dirty home than no hog at all

1981 AAndrews *Pig* (NY) 96: Better my hog dirty home than no hog at all. *Oxford* 54: Better.

H235 A **Hog** runs for his life *etc.*

1972 JGreenway *Down* (B) 179: I will give you from the Jamaicans one of life's most useful truths: *Hog run fo' him life—dog fo' him character.* Whiting *NC* 425(1).

H236 Root **Hog** or die

1934 FOursler *Joshua* (NY) 154: Root hog or die. **1943** HLMencken *Heathen Days* (NY) 215: Root, hog, or die. **1957** LBeam *Maine* (NY) 19: The saying, "Root, hog, or die." **1970** STerkel *Hard* (NY) 369: It was a ground hog case—root hog or die. TW 184(8); Brunvand 70(3).

H237 To eat (live) high on the **Hog**

1941 HLMencken *Newspaper Days, 1899–1906* (NY) 240: Eating very high on the hog. **1951** GBagby *Death* (NY) 67: Eating high on the hog. **1953** NKatkov *Fabulous* (NY) 44: Fanny had not been eating very high on the hog. **1956** RStout *Eat* (NY) 133: To live high on the hog. **1958** *NYTimes Book Review* 6/1 1: Are we living too high on the hog? **1959** JPhilips *Killer* (NY) 147: That's not living high off the hog. **1959** IWallach *Muscle* (B) 167: A swimming pool comes rather high on the hog. **1962** PDennis *Genius* (NY) 279: I've been living pretty high on the hog. **1967** NFreeling *Strike* (NY) 134: High on the hog [*living well*].

1968 KTopkins *Passing* (B) 32: [It] was still riding high on the hog. **1971** KLaumer *Deadfall* (NY) 190: Eating high on somebody else's hog. **1976** EFoote-Smith *Gentle* (NY) 75: Living high on the hog. **1981** JSScott *View* (NY) 5: With money enough to live off the high hog. Wentworth 256–7.

H238   To go the whole **Hog** (*varied*)

1921 EMillay *Letters* ed ARMacdougall (NY 1952) 127: Going the whole hog. **1922** JJoyce *Ulysses* (NY 1934) 364: I went the whole hog. **1933** DGBrowne *Dead* (L) 222: We may as well go the whole hog. **1940** MFitt *Death Starts* (L) 178: You are a whole-hogger! **1941** CMRussell *Dreadful* (NY) 230: Might as well . . . go the whole hog, vulgarly speaking. **1949** GHHall *End* (NY) 21: This man swallowed the idea whole-hog. **1958** CCockburn *Crossing* (L) 118: Got . . . drunk in the forthright, whole-hogging American fashion. **1960** JLodwick *Moon* (L) 143: Gone the whole hog. **1964** RBlythe *Age* (B) 218: [He] went the whole romantic hog. **1970** JAtkins *Sex* (L) 73: The third is whole hog, snatches at everything and catches nothing. **1970** GEEvans *Where* (L) 95: Go the whole hog. EAP H248; Brunvand 70(5); JAHirshberg "Going the Whole Hog" *Amer. Speech* 51(1979) 102–8. Cf. Brunvand 112: Pot.

H239   To know as little as a **Hog** knows about Sunday (*varied*)

1930 JFDobie *Coronado* (Dallas) 65: He knew as little about mining as a hog knows about Sunday. **1960** JBWest *Taste* (NY) 17: I know as much about it . . . as a hog knows about Easter Sunday. TW 184–5(7, 11, 12).

H240   To run **Hog**-wild

1945 BKendrick *Death Knell* (NY) 152: He'd run hog-wild. **1959** SDean *Merchant* (NY) 17: She ran hog-wild. **1972** CDSimak *Choice* (NY) 48: He would go hog wild. DA Hog 3b(10); Wentworth 261.

H241   To sleep like a **Hog** (*varied*)

1933 CWard *House Party* (L) 144: In a hog-like sleep. **1934** JSStrange *For the Hangman* (NY) 227: He sleeps like a hog. **1951** ES Holding *Too Many* (NY) 45: Slept . . . like

a hog. **1953** CLittle *Black* (NY) 108: Slept like hogs. EAP H250; TW 185(14). Cf. To sleep like a Pig *below*.

H242   Whole **Hog** or nothing

1930 CWalsh *Crime in India* (L) 98: It is either "whole hog" or nothing. **1932** TSmith *Bishop's* (NY) 30: It's whole hog or nothing. **1934** KCStrahan *Hobgoblin* (I) 279: Go whole hog or none. **1953** VPJohns *Murder* (NY 1962) 90: It was whole hog or none. **1959** *Republican Journal* 3/5 1: It's whole hog or nothing. Whiting *NC* 425(11).

H243   **Hogs Norton** where the pigs play the organs

1922 JJoyce *Ulysses* (NY 1934) 489: Hog's Norton where the pigs play the organs. *Oxford* 376; Tilley H505.

H244   Neither to **Hold** nor to bind

1928 WRoughead *Murderer's* (NY 1968) 352: He was neither to hold nor to bind [*to be restrained*]. **1961** MHHood *Drown* (NY) 92: Alec and his pals will be neither to hold nor to bind, as they say around here. **1970** DShannon *Unexpected* (NY) 100: Neither to hold nor bind, like they say [*of an uncontrolled girl*]. *Oxford* 377.

H245   Who can **Hold** what will away? (*varied*)

1964 JBLish *Doctor* (L) 58: That which will away is very hard to hold. **1971** ADavidson *Peregrine* (NY) 38: Who can hold . . . what will away? *Oxford* 377–8.

H246   As full of **Holes** as a colander (sieve, skimmer, swiss cheese)

1908 JCLincoln *Cy Whittaker* (NY) 256: As full of holes as a skimmer. **1928** SGluck *Last* (NY) 217: Your theory is as full of holes as a sieve. **1928** JRhode *Tragedy* (NY) 116: It was as full of holes as a colander. **1931** PATaylor *Cape Cod* (NY 1971) 114: His answers . . . were as full of holes as the proverbial Swiss cheese. **1932** DLSayers *Have* (NY) 337: The case . . . is as full of holes as a colander. **1946** CBush *Second Chance* (L) 179: It's got more holes than a ruddy colander. **1954** CCarnac *Policeman* (NY) 136: As a case it has as many holes in it as a colander. **1959** PMacDonald *List*

(NY) 209: Full of holes as one of those Swiss cheeses. **1966** PGWodehouse *Plum* (L) 193: As full of holes as a colander. **1967** LPDavies *Artificial* (NY) 63: Your p.m. is as full of holes as a sieve. **1972** AGarve *Case* (NY) 124: Your . . . theory is as full of holes as a sieve. EAP S200–2: Sieve.

H247 A **Hole**-and-corner (*etc.*) this or that

1920 JSFletcher *Dead Men's* (NY) 51: In hole-and-corner fashion. **1931** MKennedy *Death to the Rescue* (L) 89: A hole-in-the-corner existence; 288. **1932** VWilliams *Death* (B) 19: This hole-and-corner business. **1937** MAllingham *Late Pig* (L 1940) 58: Died in a hole-and-corner nursing home. **1941** HReilly *Three Women* (NY) 255: It was no hole-and-corner affair. **1951** ECrispin *Long* (L 1958) 82: Any such hole-and-corner business as anonymous letters. **1955** MInnes *Man from* (L) 178: Some small hole-and-corner immorality. **1966** HBlyth *Pocket* (L) 37: Bookmaking . . . was a . . . hole-in-the-corner affair. **1967** RJones *Three* (B) 14: Such a hole-and-corner manner. **1969** RPearsall *Worm* (L) 83: No scruffy hole-in-the-corner ménage. **1970** JAtkins *Sex* (L) 109: A promiscuity that has to hide its face and act in holes and corners. **1973** RRendell *Some* (NY) 174: To have a hole-in-corner, *sub rosa* affair. **1974** MG Eberhart *Danger* (NY) 183: No more hole-in-the-corner apartment for you. NED *s.v.*; Partridge 398.

H248 To crawl in a **Hole** and pull the hole after one (*varied*)

1937 ESGardner *Dangerous Dowager* (NY) 195: She crawled into a hole and pulled the hole in after her. **1951** ESGardner *Fiery* (NY) 109: I'm crawling into a hole and pulling the hole in after me. **1955** RStout *Before* (NY) 48: I've dug a hole and jumped in. **1958** ESGardner *Foot-loose* (NY) 6: Mildred only wanted to crawl in a hole and pull the hole in after her. **1964** RMacdonald *Chill* (NY) 120: You can't avoid it by crawling into a hole and pulling the hole in after you. **1970** CArmstrong *Protege* (NY DBC) 127: He dug himself a hole and pulled it in after him. Berrey 304.5, 305.4.

H249 To make a **Hole** in the Thames (*varied*)

1925 JSFletcher *Wolves* (NY) 171: I don't propose to go and make a hole in the Thames. **1930** RAJWalling *Squeaky Voice* (NY) 51: Why doesn't he make a hole in the water and have done with it? **1932** AGilbert *Body* (NY) 46: Shove 'imself under a train or make a hole in the river. **1935** FDGrierson *Death* (L) 222: I think he'd have made a hole in the Thames, or shot himself. *Oxford* 378: Water.

H250 To need as one needs a **Hole** in the head (*varied*)

1939 EQueen *Dragon's* (NY) 218: "Kerrie needs me!" "The way she needs a hole in the head." **1951** HQMasur *You Can't* (NY) 73: He needed more money like he needed the proverbial aperture in the skull. **1953** EPaul *Waylaid* (NY) 36: You need me like a hole in the head. **1958** BKendrick *Clear* (NY) 24: [He] needed money like a hole in his head. **1964** JCarnell *New Writings* (L) 34: I'd have missed you like a hole in the head. **1966** CArmstrong *Dream* (NY DBC) 77: She needed a nightcap like a hole-in-the-head. Wentworth 263.

H251 To pick **Holes** in something or other

1922 JJoyce *Ulysses* (NY 1934) 362: Picking holes in each other's appearance. EAP H252.

H252 To see a **Hole** through something or other (*varied*)

1934 BAWilliams *Hostile* (NY) 183: I can see a hole in a doughnut as far as the next. **1956** EDillon *Death* (L) 108: I can't help seeing a hole through a ladder. **1962** MG Eberhart *Enemy* (NY) 86: I can see through a hole in the wall as fast as anybody. TW 185(6), 212: Ladder.

H253 To beat one **Hollow**

1973 KAmis *Riverside* (NY) 24: It beats me hollow. EAP H253; Brunvand 70. Cf. DARE i 41: All hollow.

H254 Fed up (*etc.*) and far from **Home**

1962 IDavidson *Rose* (NY) 63: Fed up, frigged up, and far from home. **1967** AMontagu *Anatomy of Swearing* (NY) 313:

Fucked-up and far from home. Partridge 269: Fed-up.

H255   A **Home** (away) from home

1929 CBush *Perfect* (NY) 103: If you want a home from home. **1934** JVTurner *Murder* (L) 116: It was a sort of home from home for him. **1937** HCBailey *Clunk's* (L) 9: You make it a home from home. **1940** DHume *Invitation* (L) 23: A home from home. **1953** SBellow *Adventures* (NY) 477: His home away from home. **1954** THoward *Blood* (NY) 66: Your little home-away-from-home. **1959** STruss *Man to Match* (NY) 45: That isn't exactly a home from home. **1960** JMorris *Hired* (L) 90: This artificial little home from home. **1968** LDurrell *Tunc* (NY) 50: It is a home from home for us. **1970** MEChaber *Green* (NY) 75: My little home away from home. **1974** MG Eberhart *Danger* (NY) 10: It's his home away from home. NED Suppl. Home *sb*[1] 3.

H256   **Home** is where one hangs his hat (*varied*)

1930 JSFletcher *Green Rope* (L) 159: I'd nothing to do but go there and hang up my hat, as the saying is [*move into a new house*]. **1932** JStevens *Saginaw* (NY) 40: Any old place we hang our hats is home sweet home to us. **1937** LZugsmith *Home Is Where You Hang Your Childhood* (NY). **1938** ES Holding *Obstinate* (NY) 102: Home is where the hat is. **1954** SDeLima *Carnival* (NY) 118: Home is where you hang your hat. **1956** HCahill *Shadow* (NY) 12: Home is where you hang your skypiece. **1957** *New Yorker* 10/26 34: Home is where you check your hat. **1958** *Time* 11/3 96: Home is where one hangs the hangover. **1969** RReed *Conversations* (NY) 44: Home, they say, is where the hatrack is. **1973** GSheehy *Hustling* (NY) 112: Home is where your pimp is.

H257   **Home** is where the heart (hearth) is

1926 JCAddams *Secret* (NY) 116: Home's where the heart is. **1933** EECummings *Eimi* (NY) 85: Home is where the heart is. **1935** CBrooks *Three Yards* (L) 67: Where the heart is, there the home is also. **1944** HTalbot *Rim* (NY 1965) 123: Home is where the

hearth is. **1957** CRice *Knocked* (NY) 96: Home . . . was where the heart was. **1961** ESMadden *Craig's* (NY DBC) 6: Home is where the heart is. **1969** ACarter *Heroes* (L) 61: Home was where the heart was. **1971** ADavidson *Peregrine* (NY) 45: Home is where the hearth is. TW 186(1).

H258   **Home**, John (James), and don't spare the horses

1939 RHull *And Death* (L) 224: And now home, John, and don't spare the horses, as they say. **1946** MColes *Fifth Man* (NY) 215: Home, James, and don't spare the horses. **1955** NMarsh *Scales* (B) 240: Home, John, and don't spare the horses. **1967** RRendell *New Lease* (NY) 176: Home and don't spare the horses. Cf. Berrey 53.8, 245.12.

H259   One must leave **Home** to get the home news

1920 JSFletcher *Dead Men's* (NY) 182: You have to leave home to get the home news. **1937** JPMarquand *Late George* (B) 108: It seems one must leave home to learn the news of home. Whiting *NC* 426(3); *Oxford* 307: Go into the country.

H260   To be at **Home** when one's hat is on

1948 AWUpfield *Mountains* (NY) 39: He's at home when he's got his hat on. Tilley S580: Like a snail, he keeps his house (home) on his back (head). Cf. Snail travels *below*.

H261   To be **Home** and dry

1961 CWillock *Death* (L 1963) 148: In which case we're home and dry. **1972** DLees *Rainbow* (NY) 126: You would be home and dry. **1977** JThomson *Death* (NY) 160: We still might be home and dry. Partridge 400: Home and fried.

H262   To bring **Home** the bacon (*varied*)

1922 VSutphen *In Jeopardy* (NY) 147: It brought home the bacon. **1925** JGBrandon *Cork* (L) 13: To "bring home the bacon," to use the expressive American term. **1930** EWallace *Mr. Reeder* (NY) 261: Bringing home the bacon—if you'll excuse that vulgarity. **1937** MMPropper *One Murdered* (L) 113: Bring home the bacon. **1950** RLockridge *Foggy* (P) 76: This brought home the canned beans, if not the bacon. **1956** AGilbert *Riddle* (NY) 121: Brought home the bacon. **1957** *Republican Journal* 4/18 4: Whose husbands bring home the bacon. **1962** MStewart *Moon* (NY 1965) 180: Bringing home the bacon. **1968** RCroft-Cooke *Feasting* (NY) 196: All this did nothing, in vulgar terms, to bring home the bacon. **1970** DClark *Deadly* (NY) 10: It brings home the bacon. **1970** LKronenberger *No Whippings* (B) 236: They brought home—at Brandeis, a mere figure of speech—the bacon. NED Suppl. Bring 1d; Partridge 94; Wentworth 63: Bring home the groceries; Berrey 261.2, 373.4 etc. [*see Index*]. Cf. Dunmow flitch *above*.

H263   To one's long Home

1900 CFPidgin *Quincy A. Sawyer* (B) 369: Called to their long home. **1937** GGoodwin *White Farm* (L) 272: The old man goes to his long home. **1938** JJConnington *Truth* (L) 78: Gone to 'is long 'ome, as the Good Book says. **1954** JRRTolkien *Two* (L) 117: Gone at last to your long home. **1970** JLeasor *They Don't* (NY) 51: [She] had gone to her long home. **1973** DLeitch *God* (L) 164: [They] had gone to their long homes. EAP H258; TW 186(3).

H264   Who is she (he) when at Home?

1935 FWCrofts *Crime* (L) 160: Never heard of her. Who is she when she's at home? **1958** *New Yorker* 1/11 29: Who's she when she's at home? **1965** ASharp *Green Tree* (NY 1966) 74: And who is Mrs. Haskell when she's at home? **1973** JPorter *It's Murder* (NY) 48: Who's Inspector Dawkins when he's at home? Partridge *Suppl.* 1045: What is that?

H265   Homer (Jove) sometimes nods (*varied*)

1929 EDBiggers *Black* (I) 66: Famous God Jove, I hear, nodded on occasion. **1933** DGBrown *Dead* (L) 121: But Homer nodded. **1936** BFlynn *Horn* (L) 206: Our Homer has surely nodded. **1936** LWMeynell *On the Night* (NY) 21: You never know; Homer occasionally nodded. **1939** FBeeding *Ten Holy* (NY) 41: Homer may sleep as and when he likes. **1940** ECRLorac *Tryst*

(L) 141: Homer nodded, according to the adage of our youth. **1946** WPartington *T. J. Wise* (L) 265: Homer nowhere admits that he ever nodded. **1956** *Punch* 6/27 773: Even Homer fails to nod at times. **1957** PGreen *Sword* (L) 299: Once I caught him nodding: poor, faithful Homer. **1960** TCurley *It's a Wise* (NY) 41: There was a saying that even Homer nods. **1961** RA Heinlein *6XH* (NY) 137: Even Jove nods. **1969** RPearsall *Worm* (L) 377: Even Homer nods. **1976** JPorter *Package* (NY) 110: Even Homer was allowed the odd nod. EAP H261.

H266   Honesty (truth) is the best policy (*varied*)

1913 HTFinck *Food* (NY) 315: Honesty is by far the best policy. **1924** LO'Flaherty *Thy Neighbour's* (L) 280: Honesty was the best policy. **1928** JArnold *Surrey* (L) 59: Truth was the best policy. **1929** AAustin *Black* (NY) 73: Truth is always the best policy. **1934** FWCrofts *12:30* (L) 182: Honesty was his obvious policy. **1936** JRhode *Death Pays* (L) 116: "Honesty is the best policy" isn't a very moral proverb when you come to think of it. **1937** ECRLorac *These Names* (L) 244: Honesty is always the best policy—within reason. **1939** IJones *Hungry Corpse* (NY) 99: In a way, honesty is the best policy. **1954** HCecil *According* (L) 174: Honesty's the best policy. **1959** GMarx *Groucho* (NY) 95: Honesty is not always the best policy. **1961** GFowler *Skyline* (NY) 195: Honesty is the best fallacy. **1964** LLafore *Devil's* (NY) 188: Honesty would be the safest policy. **1967** RRendell *New Lease* (NY) 6: It's discretion, not honesty, that's the best policy. **1975** MVonnegut *Eden* (NY) 53: Honesty being the best policy. EAP H264; Brunvand 70. Cf. Silence is, Truth pays *below*.

H267   Honesty pays

1938 CHarris *Murder* (NY) 181: The conclusion that honesty pays. **1949** MGilbert *He Didn't* (NY DBC) 80: Honesty always paid. TW 186(2). Cf. Truth pays *below*.

H268   As smooth as Honey

1952 FO'Connor *Wise* (NY) 126: It goes as smooth as honey. Whiting H429.

H269 As sweet as **Honey** (*varied*)

1920 ACrabb *Samuel* (NY) 39: Sweet as honey. **1936** ECRLorac *Death* (L) 293: Them new Austins runs as sweet as honey. **1939** WMartyn *Noonday* (L) 150: She was sweet as honey. **1940** DWheelock *Murder at Montauk* (NY) 172: Sweet as honey. **1957** AAmos *Fatal* (NY) 97: Sweet as honey-pie. **1958** JLindsay *Life* (L) 93: Sweeter-than-honeycomb. EAP H265; Brunvand 70.

H270 Under **Honey** venom

1959 JPurdy *Malcolm* (NY) 134: Under all your honey runs a conduit of venom. Whiting H433.

H271 **Honi** *soit qui mal y pense* (*varied*)

1926 HWade *Verdict* (L) 92: *Honi soit qui mal y pense;* 179. **1933** CPenfield *After the Deacon* (NY) 64: *Honi soit qui mal y pense*—which I've heard translated "Mebbe so and mebbe not." **1937** TStevenson *Nudist* (L) 185: The classical formula of *Honi soit qui mal y pense.* **1947** PWentworth *Wicked* (NY) 210: *Honi soit qui mal y pense.* **1962** MInnes *Connoisseur's* (L) 69: *Honi soit qui mal y pense* . . . the old adage. **1965** MFrayn *Tin* (B) 180: He looked down at . . . the keyboard . . . *Honi soit key mal y pense.* **1967** JRichardson *Courtesans* (L) 52: The appropriate motto, *Honi soit qui mal y pense.* **1972** BLillie *Every* (NY) 26: After all, *honi soit qui Lily Pons. Oxford* 397: Ill be to him.

H272 There is (no) **Honor** among thieves (*almost always negative*)

1914 PGWodehouse *Little Nugget* (NY 1929) 176: Honour among thieves! **1920** GDilnot *Suspected* (NY) 109: The proverb . . . honour among thieves. **1926** EWallace *Terrible* (NY) 13: There is no honour among thieves, only amongst good thieves; 225. **1927** GDilnot *Lazy* (B) 81: There is possibly honour among thieves in a few exceptional cases. **1928** NGordon *Professor's* (NY) 30: There is an old proverb, "Honor among thieves." **1929** CGBowers *Tragic* (NY) 208: Disproving the theory that there is honor among thieves. **1930** EWallace *Fourth* (NY) 105: The falsity of the English adage that there is honour amongst thieves. **1931** EABlake *Jade* (NY)

235: Some reference to "honor among friends." **1932** VLoder *Death* (L) 119: There's a kind of loyalty among thieves. **1932** MRRinehart *Miss Pinkerton* (NY) 6: There is no honor among thieves. **1933** GDilnot *Thousandth* (L) 182: Honour among thieves—always a very thin thread—is apt to snap under such a strain. **1936** AACarey *Memoirs* (NY) 35: There is no honor among thieves. **1938** WJMakin *Queer Mr. Quell* (NY) 125: Dishonour among thieves, you know. **1939** NMorland *Knife* (L) 264: It proves the old principle of "No honor among rogues." **1940** EPaul *Mayhem* (NY) 258: So much for the proverbial honor among thieves. **1953** JFleming *Good* (L) 30: Honor among thieves is an outworn adage. **1957** *BHerald* 12/21 16: Another example of loyalty among thieves. **1958** SDean *Dishonor Among Thieves* (NY). **1961** BJames *Night* (NY DBC) 131: That honor-among-thieves legend. **1966** LLafore *Nine* (NY) 274: [He] was willing enough to show that there was no honor among thieves. **1970** PAlding *Murder Among Thieves* (NY). **1973** EJKahn *Fraud* (NY) 111: With picturesque contempt for the honor-among-thieves tradition. **1975** GHousehold *Red* (B) 188: Without even the illusion that there is honor among thieves. **1981** JBHilton *Playground* (NY) 25: There's a lot of talk about honor among thieves, but that must be when you get up among the higher echelons. EAP H272.

H273 A cloven **Hoof** (*varied*)

1909 JCLincoln *Keziah* (NY) 99: They say you can tell the Old Scratch by his footprints even if you can't smell the sulphur. **1932** PMcGuire *Black Rose* (NY) 54: I've seen a cloven hoof over a City desk before now. **1936** CBush *Monday Murders* (L) 79: There was no question of a cloven hoof. **1968** GSouter *Peculiar* (Sydney) 208: Now he . . . shows the cloven hoof. EAP F250; *Oxford* 129, 182.

H274 By **Hook** or crook

1904 WLewis *Letters* ed WKRose (L 1963) 15: By hook or crook. **1913** JSFletcher *Secret* (L 1918) 111: A man who must live by hook or by crook. **1923** ABlackwood *Epi-*

sodes (L) 31: By hook or by crook. **1933** RCAshby *He Arrived* (NY) 199: By hook or by crook. **1939** JJones *Murder al Fresco* (NY) 246: By hook or by crook, especially the crook. **1958** *TLS* 4/11 189: By hook or crook. **1959** *Time* 12/21 21: By hook or crook. **1972** LIsrael *Tallulah* (NY) 282: By hook or crook. **1975** ELathen *By Hook or by Crook* (NY). EAP H273; TW 187(1); Brunvand 71(1).

H275   **Hook**, line and sinker (*varied*)

1903 ADMcFaul *Ike Glidden* (B) 129: He caught the hook, line and whole bait. **1906** JCLincoln *Mr. Pratt* (NY) 112: Swallowed hook, line and sinker. **1923** ORCohen *Jim Hanvey* (NY) 131: Hook, line and sinker. **1930** WWoodrow *Moonhill* (NY) 74: Miss Arline will be there, hook, line and sinker. **1938** BFrancis *Death at* (L) 249: They swallowed my yarn—hook, line and sinker. **1940** GHCoxe *Lady Is Afraid* (NY) 87: One of those hook, line and sinker sort of things [*a hasty marriage*]. **1941** STowne *Death out of* (NY) 186: Robin swallowed it hook, line, sinker and fishing pole. **1950** ELinklater *Mr. Byculla* (L) 79: Nisbet swallowed his story hook, line and sinker. **1954** HGardiner *Murder* (L) 162: An elderly man who fell for her hook, line and sinker. **1957** *BHerald* 11/27 3A: The fact is that the Russians already are in there [*the Middle East*] hook, line and sinker. **1958** *BangorDN* 8/2 11: Your husband has swallowed some fish wives' tales hook, line and sinker. **1960** BKendrick *Aluminum* (NY DBC) 89: You swallowed it—hook, line and sinker, to coin a phrase. **1962** ESherry *Girl* (NY DBC) 89: She was going after Carlo hook, line and sinker. **1971** KLaumer *Deadfall* (NY) 188: She swallowed your story . . . hook, line and fisherman. **1975** MKWren *Multitude* (NY) 69: "And Maud fell for that?" "Clear down to the sinker." TW 187(2).

H276   On one's own **Hook**

1922 DFox *Ethel* (NY) 80: Going it alone on his own hook. **1924** IOstrander *Annihilations* (NY) 66: Go off on your own hook. **1935** MGEberhart *House* (L) 239: On his own hook. **1936** VMcHugh *Caleb* (NY) 56:

On my own hook. EAP H275; Brunvand 71(2).

H277   To get (be) off the **Hook**

1954 JPotts *Go* (NY) 77: It would get Hartley off the hook. **1959** LWibberly *Quest* (NY) 81: Get me off the hook. **1964** HWaugh *Missing* (NY) 49: That doesn't let the kid off the hook. **1968** DSkirrow *I Was* (NY) 71: I was off the hook. Not out of the doghouse altogether. **1972** DLees *Rainbow* (NY) 205: You are off the hook. Wentworth 267.

H278   To sling one's **Hook**

1922 JJoyce *Ulysses* (NY 1934) 420: Slung her hook, she did. **1949** CDickson *Graveyard* (NY) 162: Sling your hook, now [*get going*]! Partridge 402: Sling. Cf. TW 187(3).

H279   To be (*etc.*) through the **Hoops** (*varied*)

1922 JJoyce *Ulysses* (NY 1934) 145: I've been through the hoop myself [*out of money*]. **1933** GHolt *Six Minutes* (L) 251: The brute put both of them through the hoop [*abused them*]. **1937** BCobb *Fatal* (NY) 186: You'll have to take Baker through the hoop. **1939** CRawson *Footprints* (L) 29: [He] has her jumping through hoops. **1943** RChandler *Lady* (NY 1946) 228: She could make them jump through hoops. **1955** NMarsh *Scales* (B) 288: To put us through the hoops. **1964** CChaplin *Autobiography* (NY 1966) 501: An occasion of having to jump through the proverbial hoop for publicity. **1969** DClark *Nobody's* (NY) 72: Putting Torr through the hoop. Partridge 403.

H280   To go roll one's **Hoop**

1933 GFowler *Timber* (NY) 298: You can roll your little hoop. **1946** DBHughes *Ride the Pink* (NY 1958) 101: Telling him to go roll his hoop. **1955** ESGardner *Sun* (NY) 177: Now go roll your hoop. **1959** MMillar *Listening* (NY) 100: Tell him to go roll his hoop. **1961** AAFair *Bachelors* (NY DBC) 159: Why didn't he tell her to go roll her hoop? **1969** LHellman *Unfinished* (B) 72:

Why don't you go roll a hoop in the park? Berrey 253.8; Partridge 704: Roll.

H281   Not care a **Hoot** (*varied*)

1927 SBent *Ballyhoo* (NY) 174: The *Times* didn't care a hoot. **1927** TGann *Maya* (NY) 218: No one to care a hoot. **1928** AGMacleod *Marloe* (NY) 126: I don't care two hoots. **1936** AHuxley *Eyeless* (NY) 208: Didn't care two hoots. **1936** ECRLorac *Crime* (L) 19: I shan't care a blue hoot. **1939** CBarry *Nicholas* (L) 69: She don't care two yells in hell. **1949** EQueen *Cat* (B) 8: Who cares a hoot in Hell Gate what's caused it? **1952** KMKnight *Death Goes* (NY) 50: You never cared a hoot in hell about any of us. **1953** CDickson *Cavalier's* (NY) 236: You . . . didn't care two hoots and a whistle about it. **1957** CCarnac *Late Miss* (NY) 95: I don't care a blue hoot. **1970** HActon *Memoirs* (NY) 333: Not that Norman cared two hoots. **1971** HBevington *House* (NY) 67: Not care a hoot. DA Hoot, Hooter; Partridge 403; NED Suppl. Hoot *sb.*[2]

H282   Not give a **Hoot** (hootch) (*varied*)

1928 RGore-Browne *In Search* (NY) 26: I don't give a hoot. **1928** RHWatkins *Master* (NY) 146: Didn't give a hoot in hell. **1929** CBush *Perfect* (NY) 13: Not give two hoots. **1930** ALivingston *Trackless* (I) 204: He didn't give a hoot in Hades. **1932** RJCasey *News* (I) 29: I wouldn't give a hoot in a whirlwind. **1938** MTeagle *Murders* (NY) 154: I should give a holy hoot. **1946** VSiller *One Alone* (NY) 186: I don't give a hoot in hell. **1949** JEvans *Halo* (NY) 110: I don't give two hoots in a bathtub. **1950** MScherf *Curious* (NY) 23: Not giving a hoot in harrah who Passfield was. **1957** *BTraveler* 7/17 34: Others don't give a hoot. **1959** RLDuffus *Waterbury* (NY) 86: Very few . . . gave a hoot in hell (as we used to say). **1959** AAnderson *Lover* (NY) 92: I wouldn't give a hootch who's in it. **1960** COliver *Unearthly* (NY) 9: He didn't give two hoots in a rain barrel. **1964** JKieran *Not Under* (B) 239: He doesn't give a hoot about botany. **1965** MSpillane *Death* (NY) 15: I don't give a hoot in hell. **1970** GBagby *Killer* (NY) 29: It never gives a hoot in hell. **1970** RCarson

Golden (B) 196: Doesn't give a hoot. **1970** EQueen *Last* (NY) 111: I wouldn't give a hairy hoot in hell. DA Hoot; NED Suppl. Hoot *sb.*[2]

H283   Not matter a **Hoot** (*varied*)

1930 CBarry *Boat* (L) 100: It didn't matter a hoot. **1930** EWallace *White Face* (NY) 172: Something that maybe doesn't matter ten loud hoots. **1932** DHume *Bullets* (L) 36: It wouldn't matter two hoots. **1934** DFrome *They Called Him* (L) 146: It doesn't matter a twopenny hoot. **1953** JWyndham *Kraken* (L 1955) 87: It doesn't matter a hoot. **1954** JTey *Shilling* (NY) 149: As if it mattered a hoot. **1961** PMoyes *Down among* (NY) 21: It doesn't matter a hoot. **1972** JDCarr *Hungry* (NY) 250: It doesn't matter one twopenny hoot. **1972** ELathen *Murder* (NY) 61: It doesn't matter one hoot in hell. NED Suppl. Hoot *sb.*[2]

H284   Not worth a **Hoot** (*varied*)

1932 HLandon *Owl's* (L) 182: Your alibi isn't worth a hoot. **1936** JTMcIntyre *Steps* (NY) 399: Their lives weren't worth three hoots. **1940** MBoniface *Murder as* (NY) 7: Wouldn't be worth a hoot in hell. **1948** ESGardner *Lonely* (NY DBC) 21: Wouldn't be worth a hoot. **1956** *New Yorker* 9/1 32: Not worth a hoot. **1957** *Time* 2/25 88: Worth . . . not a hoot in hell. NED Suppl. Hoot *sb.*[2]

H285   Only a **Hop**, skip and a jump (away)

1956 NFitzgerald *Imagine* (L) 72: It's only a hop, skip and a jump from my place. **1964** ESGardner *Daring* (NY) 173: It's only a hop, skip and a jump. Amer. Herit. Dict. Hop[1] *n.*5.

H286   **Hope** deferred maketh the heart sick

1924 LSpringfield *Some Piquant* (L) 207: A hope so long deferred had made the heart of the Empire sick. **1938** ECRLorac *Slippery* (L) 36: Hope deferred maketh the heart sick. **1954** DCecil *Melbourne* (I) 151: Hope deferred maketh the heart lazy. EAP H279; Brunvand 71(1).

Hope

H287 Hope is cheap

1928 JGoodwin *When Dead* (NY) 316: Hope is cheap. **1933** HAdams *Strange Murder* (P) 27: Hope is cheap. Apperson 309(7): Hope is as cheap as despair.

H288 Hope lost, all lost

1934 AMeredith *Portrait* (NY) 109: You know—hope lost, all lost. Cf. Whiting H475: If it were not for Hope; *Oxford* 384.

H289 To live in **Hope** if one dies in despair

1951 DSDavis *Gentle* (NY 1959) 97: There was an expression my [*Irish*] mother used to use: we'll live in hope if we die in despair. **1961** MClingerman *Cupful* (NY) 18: Man lives in hope and dies in despair. **1967** JJDeiss *Captain* (NY) 182: The common people in Italy have a saying "Chi vive di speranza, muore disperato"—"Who lives in hope dies in despair." Of proverbs, who is more aware than a peasant . . .? EAP H284; Whiting *NC* 426.

H290 As mad (sore) as **Hops**

1924 CWells *Furthest* (P) 82: He was mad as hops. **1933** MPlum *Murder* (NY) 91: She'd be sore as hops. **1940** BHalliday *Private Practice* (NY 1965) 65: I was mad as hops at you. **1948** CDickson *Skeleton* (NY 1967) 55: Mad as hops. **1952** CDickson *Behind* (NY) 17: He was as mad as hops. **1959** SSterling *Body* (NY) 197: Mad as hops. **1965** DoctorX *Intern* (NY) 49: Mad as hops.

H291 Hops, Reformation *etc.*

1970 GEEvans *Where* (L) 245: The old jingle that used to be heard in Suffolk: "Hops, Reformation, bacca and beer, Came into England all in a year." *Oxford* 370: Heresy.

H292 He that bloweth not his own **Horn**, the same shall not be blown (*varied*)

1958 WDHassett *Off the Record* (New Brunswick, NJ) 180: Blessed is he that bloweth his own horn; otherwise it may not be blown. **1961** GFowler *Skyline* (NY) 24: He who tooteth not his own horn, the same shall not be tooted. **1967** MBerkeley *Winking* (B) 172: If you don't blow your own

horn who will? TW 189(12). Cf. To blow one's own Horn *below*.

H293 Horn of a bull *etc.*

1922 JJoyce *Ulysses* (NY 1934) 24: Horn of a bull, hoof of a horse, smile of a Saxon. Champion (Irish) 50(186): Beware of.

H294 Horns of cuckoldry

1911 CPearl *Morrison of Peking* (Sidney 1967) 208: The cuckold with the longest horns . . . in China. **1922** JJoyce *Ulysses* (NY 1934) 210: The hornmad Iago. 551: He hangs his hat smartly on a peg of Bloom's antlered head. **1929** JCPowys *Wolf* (NY) 2.519: You'll walk into the wood where they pick up horns. **1930** CTalbott *Droll* (NY) 19: [His] forehead stands greatly in danger Of horns from a stranger. **1930** WLewis *Apes* (NY 1932) 339: These two horns sprouting upon my forehead are *not* cuckoldic. **1931** GFowler *Great* (NY) 149: The horns of Cuckoldom. **1931** DFrome *Strange* (NY) 152: One sees the evidence of more than one pair of horns about this place. **1931** KTKnoblock *There's Been* (NY) 45: The horn-beast himself had been butchered with those who grew the horns on his forehead. **1931** TFPowys *Unclay* (L) 262: Wishing . . . that he might . . . crown the clergyman's forehead in an old and fashionable manner. **1931** TSmith *Stray* (NY) 106: Unaware of his horns. These husbands! **1931** TThayer *Greek* (NY) 316: Only one of Peros' horns would be on his head by my fixing. **1932** *Hot-cha* (L) 51: Fancy a boy like you putting horns on the head of his Father! **1932** GLane *Hotel* (L) 160: Why not a husband who suddenly found himself the wearer of horns? 230: He would have been wearing a large pair of horns on his brow. **1933** GFowler *Timber* (NY) 126: He was wearing horns as big as any bull moose. **1935** RBriffault *Europa* (NY) 263: More than the pair of horns. **1935** CGFinney *Circus* (NY) 150: On their brows they bear the ancient device of cuckoldry. **1937** RBriffault *Europa in Limbo* (NY) 118: Bride of Christ. Give horns to our Lord Jesus Christ. **1947** GMWilliams *Silk* (L) 62: I was like the gentleman in the Restoration play who sprouted horns. **1949** DKeene *Framed* (NY) 28: I thought you were going to drop over last night and grow some horns on Lyle. **1950** EPiper *Motive* (NY) 58: Why are you doing such an amateur cuckold job, Leo? Hold on to your horns. Your horns are slipping. **1951** CWillingham *Reach* (NY) 178: The one that's put those antlers on his head. **1953** EQueen *Scarlet* (B) 148: Let the other gent wear the horns. **1957** *Time* 12/16 98: French intellectuals are never happier than when planting the horns of a dilemma on another Frenchman's head. **1957** WHHarris *Golden* (NY) 191: That woman . . . had put the horns on him [*her lover*]. **1957** JLodwick *Equator* (L) 205: A man notoriously cuckolded by his wife . . . who pretends to be unaware that he wears horns. **1957** MShulman *Rally* (NY) 106: It was one thing to put horns on your wife. **1957** RStandish *Prince* (L) 154: Examining his brow in the mirror for signs of incipient horns. **1958** JBarth *End* (NY 1960) 82: A polishing of the horns we'd already placed on Joe's brow. **1958** PSJennison *Mimosa* (NY) 150: Webb is about to sprout horns. **1958** AMacKinnon *Summons* (NY) 75: The hazard here was no horned husband. **1960** JLodwick *Moon* (L) 326: A husband would wear the horns. **1963** ABurgess *Vision* (L) 141: To be cuckolded or certainly half-horned. **1963** ADuggan *Elephants* (L) 227: Publicly affix horns to his forehead. **1963** HMiller *Black* (NY) 196: The pair of horns which his wife Jedwiga had given him. **1964** ABoucher *Best Detective* (NY) 143: No dame's gonna make Sebastian Spinner wear neon horns. **1968** JUpdike *Couples* (NY 1969) 144: She's back from Maine with the horned monster. *Avec le coucou.* **1972** RLaxalt *In a Hundred* (Reno) 37: His wife put horns on his head. **1972** CTurney *Byron's* (NY) 11: He seems to have worn his horns with bland indifference. **1975** DEWestlake *Two* (NY) 161: I've applied the horns to other men's brows. EAP H289; TW 188(2).

H295 To argue the **Horns** off the devil

1937 RBriffault *Europa in Limbo* (NY) 312: You'd argue the horns off the devil that black is white and white black. Cf. Par-

tridge 17: Argue the leg off an iron pot. Cf. To talk the Horns, Leg *below*.

H296 To be **Horn** mad

1931 MNRawson *When Antiques* (NY) 208: Mrs. Pitcher did always make the neighbours "horn mad" with her complaining. EAP H292.

H297 To be on the **Horns** of a dilemma (*varied*)

1915 PGWodehouse *Something Fresh* (L 1935) 144: The phrase about the horns of a dilemma. **1922** JJoyce *Ulysses* (NY 1934) 393: He'll find himself on the horns of a dilemma. **1924** LTracy *Token* (NY) 189: Between the horns of a dilemma. **1931** GCollins *Phantom* (L) 145: Rather a horny old dilemma, what? **1937** RCWoodthorpe *Dead in* (NY) 186: Could a dilemma have three horns? **1942** WIrish *Phantom* (NY 1957) 66: He found himself between the horns of a dilemma. **1953** GRHEllis *Lesser* (L) 197: We are now on the horns of a moral dilemma. **1958** *BHerald* 11/20 24: I am on the horns of a dilemma. **1960** ASinclair *Project* (L) 149: He felt pierced through hip and thigh by the horns of the liberal dilemma. **1963** EJHughes *Ordeal* (NY) 138: There are two horns to this dilemma. **1968** RTruax *Doctors* (B) 198: They would not have to choose between the horns of a dilemma. **1969** LThomas *Between* (B) 176: Tossed upon the horns of a dilemma. **1975** SJPerelman *Vinegar* (NY) 41: I was on the horns of a dilemma. **1981** JBrett *Who'd Hire* (NY) 47: I was stuck . . . on the horns of Damocles, or whatever the phrase is. EAP H293.

H298 To blow (toot) one's own **Horn** (*varied*)

1911 JCLincoln *Women-Haters* (NY) 39: Far be it from me to toot my horn. **1932** CAndrews *Butterfly* (NY) 63: He didn't like to blow his own horn. **1932** MCJohnson *Damning* (NY) 302: Rollins here doesn't toot his own horn half loud enough. **1940** GPatten *Autobiography* ed HHinsdale (Norman, Okla. 1964) 186: A chance to blow my own horn. **1955** IAsimov *End* (NY) 82: These people blow their own horn. **1956** WBrinkley *Don't Go* (NY) 85: No one wants to blow his own horn. **1959** DCushman *Goodbye* (NY) 67: That grand old American custom of blowing my own horn. **1961** PDennis *Little* (NY) 135: I am simply blowing my own horn. **1962** HPentecost *Cannibal* (NY DBC) 51: It made me sick to hear him blow his own horn. **1971** DCWilson *Big-Little* (NY) 301: Professional folks . . . always like to toot their own horns. **1976** EMcBain *So Long* (NY) 39: I'm blowing my own horn. EAP H294; Brunvand 143: Tin Horn. Cf. Trumpet *below*.

H299 To draw (*etc.*) in one's **Horns** (*varied*)
1910 JCLincoln *Depot Master* (NY) 121: Haul in my horns. **1916** CSLewis *Letters* ed WHLewis (NY 1966) 29: Draw in your critical horns. **1928** DHLawrence *Lady* ("Allemagne") 120: They're having to draw their horns in. **1932** MPlum *Murder* (NY) 65: Didn't want to draw in his horns. **1935** LThayer *Sudden* (NY) 212: Pulled in his horns. **1939** RStout *Mountain Cat* (NY 1958) 123: I've seen you pull in your horns. **1941** CMRussell *Dreadful* (NY) 154: I'll make that Peck pull in his horns. **1954** TDuBois *Seeing* (NY) 62: You've got to pull in your horns. **1954** NBlake *Whisper* (L) 91: A . . . slight drawing-in, as it were, of sensitive horns. **1955** RChurch *Over the* (L) 22: He draws in his horns like a snail. **1968** DEAllen *British* (L) 208: They like drawing in their horns, tightening their belts. **1968** LTTanner *All the Things* (NY) 245: An unobstrusive pulling in of horns. EAP H295; TW 189(8).

H300 To talk the **Horns** off a billy-goat
1925 GBeasley *My First* (Paris) 306: Talk the horns off a billy-goat. **1934** HVines *This Green* (B) 95: Could talk the horns off a billy goat. Cf. Partridge 863: Talk the hind leg. Cf. To argue the Horns *above*; To talk the Leg *below*.

H301 As mad (angry) as a **Hornet** (*varied*)
c**1910** PGWodehouse *Leave it to Psmith* (L n.d.) 175: Madder than a hornet. **1920** GBMcCutcheon *Anderson Crow* (NY) 256: The poor dog was as mad as a hornet. **1932** EDBiggers *Keeper* (L) 110: Mad as a hornet. **1937** DQBurleigh *Kristiana* (NY) 22: Mad

as hornets. **1952** EPaul *Black* (NY) 151: Mad as a hornet. **1955** WSloane *Stories* (L) 313: At least twice as mad as the proverbial nest of hornets. **1962** LDRich *Natural* (NY) 13: People say "mad as a hornet," but actually hornets don't even get mad. **1964** ABoucher *Best Detective* (NY) 64: They're as angry as hornets. **1970** TKenrick *Only* (NY) 75: She was as mad as a hornet. **1974** CMartin *Whiskey* (NY) 260: Mad as a hornet. EAP H297; Brunvand 71(1). Cf. Taylor *Western Folklore* 17(1958) 16: Mean.

H302 To raise (*etc.*) a **Hornet's** nest (about one's ears)
1923 JSFletcher *Lost Mr L.* (NY) 162: She could raise a hornet's nest round the whole matter. **1929** HWade *Duke* (NY) 69: We don't want to bring a hornet's nest about our ears. **1931** JDCarr *Castle* (NY) 132: I shall have started a hornet's nest. **1934** EPOppenheim *Gallows* (B) 255: Stirring up a hornet's nest. **1950** EAMathew *Horse* (Belfast) 77: The election stirred up a veritable hornet's nest. **1956** AChristie *Dead Man's* (L) 194: We'd have a hornet's nest about our ears. **1961** MHHood *Drown* (NY) 150: You'll have a hornet's nest 'round your ears. **1964** ELathen *Accounting* (NY) 41: You're really going to stir up a hornet's nest. **1975** ELathen *By Hook* (NY) 66: [It] had stirred up a hornet's nest. EAP H298; Brunvand 71(3), 137: Swarm (3). Cf. To put one's Head *above*.

H303 As big as a **Horse**
1956 WMankowitz *Old* (B) 101: A heart as big as a horse. TW 190(6).

H304 As fit as a **Horse** (cart-horse)
1935 HHolt *Unknown* (L) 142: Murgatroyd was as fit as a horse. **1935** RAJWalling *Cat* (L) 265: I feel as fit as a cart-horse. **1939** LRGribble *Arsenal* (L) 54: He was as fit as a cart horse. **1961** BKnox *In at* (NY) 104: I'm as fit as a horse.

H305 As hungry as a **Horse**
1948 AHandley *Kiss* (P) 81: Hungry as a horse. **1960** JJMarric *Gideon's Fire* (NY) 208: I'm as hungry as a horse. Wilstach 207. Cf. To eat like a Horse *below*.

H306   As plain as a **Horse**

1965 HCarlisle *Ilyitch* (NY) 79: Plain as a horse [*a homely woman*]. Cf. TW 191(13): Ugly.

H307   As sick as a **Horse**

1900 CFPidgin *Quincy A. Sawyer* (B) 446: I'm allus sicker'n a horse. **1940** PATaylor *Criminal* (NY) 36: Sick as a horse. **1951** LFord *Murder Is* (NY) 85: He was sick as a horse. Taylor *Prov. Comp.* 72.

H308   As strong (powerful) as a **Horse** (stallion)

1923 JGollomb *Girl* (NY) 169: Strong as a horse. **1931** AChristie *Murder* (NY) 24: As strong as a horse. **1932** MTurnbull *Return* (P) 85: As strong as pack horses. **1933** NBrady *Fair Murder* (L) 93: Powerful as an 'orse. **1937** HCBailey *Clunk's* (L) 183: I am strong as a 'orse. **1953** ECRLorac *Speak* (NY) 103: She was as strong as a horse. **1958** TBrooke *Under* (NY) 247: Strong as a stallion. **1958** CHare *He Should* (L) 136: Jack was . . . as strong as a horse. **1964** WTrevor *Old Boys* (NY) 76: She seems strong as a horse. **1974** KAmis *Ending* (NY) 82: I'm as strong as a horse. TW 190(11).

H309   Enough to choke a **Horse** (goat, cow)

1920 ACrabb *Samuel* (NY) 291: A roll of bills big enough to choke a hoss. **1926** MRRinehart *Bat* (NY 1959) 27: They had reasons you could choke a goat with. **1937** QPatrick *Death* (NY) 51: There's that diamond ring. It's big enough to choke the proverbial goat. **1938** JSStrange *Silent* (NY) 265: Enough outstanding bills to choke a horse. **1956** *Arizona Highways* August 35: A roll of bills "big enough to choke a cow." **1961** JSStrange *Eye* (NY) 115: There's enough graft in it to choke a horse. **1963** ESGardner *Amorous* (NY DBC) 8: A roll of bills that would, I believe the expression they commonly use is, choke a horse. DARE i 645: Choke a horse. Cf. Partridge 150: To make a black man choke. Cf. Camel *above*.

H310   Enough to kill a **Horse**

1934 DFrome *Arsenic* (L) 45: Enough arsenic . . . to kill a horse. **1939** EDean *Murder Is* (NY) 197: I've enough work to do to kill a horse. **1940** ARLong *Corpse* (NY) 148: That's enough to kill a horse. **1961** MMillar *How Like* (NY DBC) 180: Enough arsenic to kill a horse.

H311   Enough to make a **Horse** laugh

1928 RPThompson *Giant Horse* (C) 142: You're enough to make a horse laugh. TW 191(22). Cf. Enough to make a Cat *above*.

H312   From the **Horse's** mouth (*varied*)

1925 JGBrandon *Bond* (L) 32: Straight from the horse's mouth. **1930** LCharteris *Last* (NY) 58: That's a tip from the stable. **1930** WLewis *Apes* (NY 1932) 429: That was from the horse's mouth. **1931** MAllingham *Gryth* (NY) 218: The whole story, hot from the horse's mouth. **1932** GKChesterton et al. *Floating* (NY) 110: Let us have it straight from the gee-gee's mouth. **1944** WLewis *Letters* ed WKRose (L 1963) 374: I speak from very near the horse's mouth. **1949** JReach *Late* (NY) 174: I'd get her a tip straight from the horse's mouth. **1952** JTey *Singing* (NY 1960) 62: As a source of information he was pure horse's mouth. **1956** MInnes *Old Hall* (L) 201: A tip straight from the horse's mouth. **1958** SEllin *Eighth* (NY 1959) 136: Every word of it right from under the horse's tail. **1959** PDeVries *Through* (NY) 9: Go straight to the horse's mouth and demand more money. **1961** PGWodehouse *Ice* (NY) 162: I had it straight from the horse's mouth. **1963** MCallaghan *That Summer* (NY 1964) 221: The political facts right out of the horse's mouth. **1969** RAirth *Snatch* (NY) 208: The tip straight from the horse's mouth. **1973** MInnes *Appleby's Answer* (NY) 21: Straight from the horse's mouth. **1973** JSymons *Plot* (NY) 173: That's official, from the horse's mouth. Or the horse's arse. Amer. Herit. Dict. Horse 10. Cf. NED Tip *sb.*[4] b.

H313   A **Horse** with white feet *etc*.

1957 HPBeck *Folklore of Maine* (P) 66: One white foot, buy him. Two white feet, try him. Three white feet, deny him. Four white feet and a slip in his nose, take him out and feed him to the crows. **1967** A

Christie *Endless* (NY) 149: That horse you're riding on has one white foot. Don't you know that it's bad luck to ride a horse with one white foot? **1967** MWilkins *Last* (Englewood, NJ) 96: "A horse with four white feet is only good for the crows," is an old Maine saying. *Oxford* 885: White foot.

H314 A lean **Horse** for a long race (*varied*)

1935 WMartyn *Nightmare* (L) 9: A spare horse for a long race. **1936** SLBradbury *Hiram* (Rutland, Vt.) 25: The old saying, "It takes a lean hoss for a long hard race." **1956** *BangorDN* 7/17: A lean horse for the race. **1957** *Republican Journal* 9/19 12: The old saw, "A lean horse to run a race." Whiting *NC* 427(2). Cf. Lean Wolf *below*.

H315 A one-**Horse** place (*etc.*)

1909 JCLincoln *Keziah* (NY) 6: This little one-horse place. **1910** JCLincoln *Depot Master* (NY) 88: A one-horse town. **1932** GMitchell *Saltmarsh* (L) 190: This somewhat one-horse village. **1934** MKennedy *Corpse* (L) 69: A one-horse river. **1940** JSStrange *Picture* (NY) 259: A little one-horse circus. **1954** EQueen *Bureau* (B) 91: This one-horse town. **1955** CMWills *Death* (L) 21: A one-horse town up north. **1971** PMoyes *Season* (NY) 39: This one-horse village. **1972** SAngus *Arson* (NY) 110: A one-horse town. TW 192(28).

H316 One may lead a **Horse** to water *etc.* (*varied*)

1924 HHMunro *Square* (L 1929) 191: Talk about bringing a horse to the water, we've brought water to the horse. **1927** GDHCole *Murder at Crome House* (NY) 79: It extended only so far as bringing the horse to water. There appeared to be innumerable reasons why he should not drink. **1929** HAdams *Caroline* (P) 66: Have you heard of the old proverb: "You can take a horse to the water but you can't make him drink"? . . . "Only foolish people find comfort in proverbs." **1929** ABCox *Poisoned* (NY) 109: You can take a filly to the altar, but you can't make her drunk. **1932** CBush *Unfortunate* (L) 15: Having dragged Dryden to the water, Travers was determined to make him drink.

1936 SLBradbury *Hiram* (Rutland, Vt.) 62: She not only led the horse to water but was able to make him drink against his will. **1937** PATaylor *Figure* (NY) 202: You can lead a horse to water, but even he won't drink the stuff. **1949** RLTaylor *W. C. Fields* (NY) 309: She could often lead Fields to the trough, and even make him drink. **1956** *NYPost* 11/2 12: There was some evidence today that Joe can occasionally lead a network to water and can even make it drink—a little, as long as it doesn't hurt. **1956** MGilbert *Be Shot* (L) 129: You can take your horses to the water. They will not always drink. **1957** *BangorDN* 3/28 24: You can lead a horse to water but you cannot make him drink. **1962** JSymonds *Bezill* (L) 173: One could drag a donkey to a well, but getting it to drink was another matter. **1965** JMBrown *Worlds* (NY) 150: Mrs. Parker's . . . "you may lead a whore to culture but you can't make her think." [*Using 'horticulture' in a word-game.*] **1966** JGaskell *Serpent* (NY 1968) 220: You can drag a goat to water, but can't make him drink. **1974** ELathen *Sweet* (NY) 132: You can lead a horse to water; you may be able to make him drink; you sure as hell can't expect the horse to thank you. EAP H312; TW 191(15).

H317 A short **Horse** is soon curried

1933 ISCobb *Murder* (I) 125: But a short horse was Clabby and soon curried. **1936** CGBowers *Jefferson in Power* (B) 164: It was a case of a short horse soon curried. **1941** ISCobb *Exit* (I) 214: A short horse . . . soon . . . curried. EAP H314; TW 190(4); Brunvand 72(2).

H318 That **Horse** will not jump (run)

1931 PBaron *Round* (NY) 126: That horse won't jump. **1933** REssex *Slade* (NY) 222: That horse won't run again. **1960** JSymons *Progress* (L) 179: I don't think that horse will run. Cf. *Oxford* 131: Cock won't fight. Cf. That Cat *above*.

H319 To back the wrong **Horse** (*varied*)

1929 ABCox *Layton* (NY) 286: I backed the wrong horse. **1929** HWilliamson *Beautiful* (NY) 248: You're backing the wrong 'oss.

1932 DFrome *Man* (NY) 255: Bull's backing the wrong horse. **1939** RAJWalling *Blistered Hand* (NY) 273: You're riding the wrong horse. **1944** BFischer *Hornet's* (NY) 169: You're backing the wrong horse. **1957** LHanson *Verlaine* (NY) 159: He had backed the wrong political horse. **1971** JMuir *Stranger* (NY) 150: You've been backing the wrong horse. **1976** MGilbert *Night* (NY) 52: They've backed the wrong horse. Berrey 168.4, 170.5, 216.3.

H320   To be a dark **Horse**

1916 MGibbon *Inglorious* (L 1968) 123: A bit of a dark horse. **1922** JJoyce *Ulysses* (NY 1934) 329: He's a bloody dark horse. **1928** AGMacleod *Marloe* (NY) 184: You're a dark horse [*keeping something back*]. **1940** JRhode *Death on* (NY) 260: He seems a pretty dark horse. **1953** JFleming *Good* (L) 22: I never thought you were a dark horse. **1955** DGarnett *Aspects* (L) 38: A bit of a dark horse. **1956** *BHerald* 8/12 5: Governor Clement appears to be among the dark horses of a grayish hue. **1960** FSWees *Country* (NY) 139: You're a dark horse as ever was. **1968** EHuxley *Love* (L) 67: Kate was reticent . . . she always was a dark horse. Wentworth 140.

H321   To be a gray (white) **Horse** of another color

1929 ORCohen *May Day* (NY) 154: That's a gray horse of another color. **1930** DFrome *In at the Death* (NY) 205: That's a white horse of a different color. **1930** KCStrahan *Death* (NY) 37: A gray horse of another color; 190. **1941** ISCobb *Exit* (I) 163: A gray horse of a mighty different color. **1961** ESGardner *Spurious* (NY) 185: But with the real Amelia coming, it's a gray horse of another color. TW 190(3).

H322   To be a **Horse** (cat, *etc.*) of another color (*varied*)

1922 JJoyce *Ulysses* (NY 1934) 618: It's a horse of quite another colour. **1925** JGBrandon *Bond* (L) 48: A horse of a totally different complexion. **1930** JGBrandon *Murder* (L) 94: A horse of a totally different colour. **1940** STowne *Death out* (NY) 141: But murder's a horse of another color. **1948** RMLovell *All Our* (NY) 23: My uncle was a horse of a different color. **1954** MMainwaring *Murder* (NY) 124: A horse of a different color. **1957** DErskine *Pink* (NY) 124: Dukemer in love was a horse of another color. **1958** *BangorDN* 7/18 23: An equine of a different hue. **1959** RCFrazer *Mark* (NY) 19: That's a cat of a different color. **1960** GAshe *Crime-haters* (NY) 11: But that's a cat with a different tail. **1962** LEgan *Borrowed* (NY DBC) 121: Ferguson was a horse of another color. **1964** IPetite *Elderberry* (NY) 146: To get a picture was a rodent of another color. **1967** EVCunningham *Samantha* (NY) 114: She was . . . a horse of another color. **1968** FHerbert *Santaroga* (NY) 197: That's a cat of quite different calico. **1971** EHCohen *Mademoiselle* (B) 55: A filly of a different color. **1972** WJBurley *Guilt* (NY) 165: That's a horse of another colour. **1981** JSScott *View* (NY) 135: His father was a duck of a different colour. EAP H306. Cf. A Bird of *above.*

H323   To be on (off) one's high **Horse**

1908 JCLincoln *Cy Whittaker* (NY) 360: Come off that high horse of yours. **1921** IOstrander *Crimson* (NY) 115: Down off your high horse. **1922** JJoyce *Ulysses* (NY 1934) 336: And he on his high horse about the Jews. **1933** VMacClure *Crying Pig* (L) 228: Take me off my high horse. **1938** RMBaker *Death* (NY) 220: You needn't get on your high horse. **1940** MBoniface *Murder as* (NY) 194: Climb off your high horse. **1944** MVenning *Jethro* (NY) 10: Climb down off that high horse. **1954** DMDisney *Last* (NY) 31: To climb down off her high horse. **1955** FCDavis *Night* (NY) 108: To make her get up on her precious high horse. **1959** DMDisney *Did She Fall* (NY) 137: It's time you climbed down off that high horse of yours. **1970** JCreasey *Part* (NY) 86: [He] stayed on his high horse. **1975** DRussell *Tamarisk* (NY) 174: The doctors . . . got on their high horse. EAP H320.

H324   To eat like a **Horse**

1910 JCLincoln *Depot Master* (NY) 41: Eatin' like a horse. **1937** JYork *Come Here* (NY)

76: He must eat like a horse. **1941** RStout *Alphabet* (NY) 268: I ate like a horse. **1951** MCHarriman *Vicious* (NY) 116: Woollcott . . . ate like a horse. **1957** TWicker *Devil* (NY) 40: He'll eat like a goldum horse. **1963** WHaggard *High* (NY DBC) 18: I eat like a horse. **1977** HDolson *Beauty* (P) 167: She ate like a horse. EAP H317; TW 192(32). Cf. As hungry as a Horse *above*.

H325   To flog a dead **Horse** (*varied*)

1924 RAFreeman *Blue* (NY) 152: You are flogging a dead horse. **1927** AGilbert *Tragedy* (NY) 269: A dead horse, I'm afraid [*no results*]. **1933** LRGribble *Yellow* (L) 31: Flogging a dead horse. **1933** VMarkham *Inspector* (L) 108: No use whacking dead dogs. **1935** NBlake *Question* (L) 192: The belabouring of that very dead donkey—police inefficiency. **1937** NBell *Crocus* (NY) 205: It's flogging a spent horse. **1941** RAldington *Life* (NY) 216: We were flogging a dead horse. **1948** CRBoxer *Fidalgos* (Oxford 1968) 89: At the risk of flogging a dead horse. **1957** *NYTimes Book Review* 3/24 8: Publishers don't believe in flogging a dead horse, but they concur in using the whip on a running horse. **1957** *PMLA* 72: 586: Perhaps I have erected a "live horse" to beat. **1958** *BHerald* 3/2 44: Official Washington is getting ready to try to flog a dead horse. **1958** RFraser *Jupiter* (L) 141: [He] appeared to be flogging a dead horse. **1959** *BHerald* 3/31 8: I'm not backing a dead horse. **1961** TWalsh *Eye* (NY DBC) 55: It's a dead horse . . . so stop beating it! **1962** EMcBain *Like* (NY) 51: Neither . . . were . . . anxious to whip a dead horse. **1963** EQueen *Player* (NY) 128: Maybe I'm clobbering a dead horse. **1964** AHunter *Gently* (NY) 111: The horse died years ago . . . We've been flogging him like mad and he hasn't twitched a muscle. **1970** HCarvic *Miss Seeton Draws* (NY) 147: An attempt to flog a dead horse. **1970** KLouchheim *By the Political* (NY) 139: We agreed this was beating a dead horse. **1975** EMcBain *Where* (NY) 46: I don't want him to continue flogging a dead horse, so to speak. **1977** CAlverson *Not Sleeping* (B) 185: What's the point of beating a dead horse? Berrey 796.7; Partridge 406; *Oxford* 269: Flog.

H326   To flog (*etc.*) a willing **Horse** (*varied*)

1924 VBridges *Red Lodge* (NY) 68: There is no sense in flogging a willing horse. **1929** TCobb *Crime* (L) 237: We mustn't overdrive a willing horse. **1930** Ex-PrivateX *War* (NY) 222: The willing horse being flogged and kicked to death. **1932** NBell *Disturbing* (NY) 246: I overworked a willing horse. **1939** CBClason *Dragon's* (NY) 254: I recall the proverb of the willing horse [*don't drive it to death*]. **1946** MColes *Fifth Man* (NY) 75: I have no wish to slaughter the willing horse. **1960** DHayles *Comedy* (L) 118: The willin' 'orse gets its back broke. **1968** MHolroyd *Strachey* (L) 2.294: She was simply driving willing horses too hard. Whiting H520; *Oxford* 768: Spur, 891: Willing; Partridge 288. Cf. EAP H319.

H327   To hold one's **Horses**

1920 GBMcCutcheon *Anderson Crow* (NY) 122: Hold your horses. **1924** HSKeeler *Voice* (NY) 293: Hold your horses. **1936** RStout *Rubber* (L) 156: Hold your horses. **1938** HHolt *Whispering* (L) 29: Now hold your horses. **1940** TChanslor *Our First* (NY) 248: He'll do well to hold his horses . . . or he'll find he has a mare's nest on his hands. **1952** JDCarr *Nine Wrong* (NY) 330: To make me hold my horses. **1958** HReilly *Ding* (NY DBC) 84: Not so fast Jack Harkaway—hold your horses. **1962** HWaugh *Born* (NY) 50: You just hold your horses. **1969** EStewart *Heads* (NY) 200: Hold your horses. TW 191–2(26).

H328   To lie as fast as a **Horse** can trot

1900 CFPidgin *Quincy A. Sawyer* (B) 360: Samanthy can lie faster'n a horse can trot. **1930** KCStrahan *Death* (NY) 200: You've been at it [*lying*], fast as a horse can trot. **1935** HFootner *Whip-poor-will* (NY) 243: That girl can lie faster than a horse can trot. EAP H318.

H329   To look a gift **Horse** in the mouth (*varied*)

1915 PGWodehouse *Something Fresh* (L 1935) 64: I must not look a gift horse in the mouth. **1919** KHoward *Peculiar* (NY) 225: I wouldn't look a gift-horse in the mouth. **1928** WGerhardi *Jazz* (L) 97: There is a Russian saying . . . "You don't look into the mouth of a gift horse." **1931** HKWebster *Who Is* (I) 105: Why look a gift horse in the mouth? **1934** GBurgers *Two O'Clock* (I) 147: Ride a gift horse to death. **1936** AGlanville *Death* (L) 98: There's no use looking a gift-horse in the mouth. **1937** CCrow *Four Hundred* (NY) 30: There is an old adage about not looking a gift horse in the mouth. **1948** ADerleth ed *Strange* (NY) 332: Get your head out of that gift-horse's mouth. **1949** DKeene *Framed* (NY) 55: Never look a gift horse in the mouth. Outside of it being unsanitary, it might bite you. **1951** ADerleth *Outer* (NY) 201: Inviting a gift horse to kick me in the face. **1956** *Punch* 6/27 774: One should look a gift horse in the mouth: especially if it needs fake teeth. **1957** *NYTimes Book Review* 1/13 4: A gift book . . . may be expected to enjoy the same dignified immunities as a gift horse. **1957** *BHerald* 5/10 55: Don't look a gift horse in the eye. **1957** MStirling *Fine* (L) 30: At no time . . . did she look a gift horse in the mouth, except to notice what an attractive mouth it had. **1959** *BHerald* 10/9 49: They not only do not look a gift horse in the mouth, but don't even pause to note whether it is a horse or a boa constrictor. **1959** MErskine *Graveyard* (NY) 79: So that in future you'll not only look a gift horse in the mouth, you'll count its teeth. **1963** MPHood *Sin* (NY) 26: Don't stick your nose in the gift horse's oral cavity. **1965** EQueen *Queens* (NY) 6: [He] was not one to look a gift horse under the crupper. **1965** JGaskell *Atlan* (NY 1968) 161: Rather looking gifthorses in their teeth. **1970** JAiken *Embroidered* (NY) 112: I wouldn't look a gift horse in the mouth. **1972** KBooton *Quite* (NY) 8: Who looks a gift dog in the mouth? **1972** JMcClure *Caterpillar* (NY) 7: Never look a gift horse in the saddle blanket. **1974** TWells *Have Mercy* (NY) 4: Don't count the teeth of gift horses. **1975** MKWren *Multitude* (NY) 70: So don't look a dark horse in the eye. TW 191(16); Brunvand 72(5).

H330 To swap **Horses** while crossing a stream (*varied*)

1929 RGraves *Good-bye* (L) 311: We have a proverb in England never to swap horses while crossing a stream. **1929** SWPierce *Layman* (NY) 58: It never pays to change horses in mid-stream. **1930** LThayer *They Tell* (NY) 133: No need to change drivers . . . when crossing a stream. **1931** LCArlington *Thorough* (L) 203: He would not "swap horses in the middle of the stream." **1936** ECRLorac *Death* (L) 129: It's no use changing horses in mid-stream. **1937** HSwiggett *Corpse* (B) 156: I say let's go ahead, never change horses, you know. **1941** CFAdams *Decoy* (NY) 72: Was Ruby getting ready to switch horses? **1945** HLawrence *Time to Die* (NY) 188: Mark . . . changed horses in mid-stream [*changed his mind*]. **1949** JEvans *Halo* (NY) 172: An election year and don't change horses while you're cleaning house. **1956** *TLS* 11/9 671: The Professor's view is that Shakespeare changed his horse amid stream. **1956** *JAFL* 69.358: Don't change horses in the middle of the stream. **1961** AAFair *Bachelors* (NY DBC) 160: Bernice had swapped horses in the middle of the stream. **1968** GSouter *Peculiar* (Sydney) 71: The argument that horses should not be changed in mid-stream. TW 191(18).

H331 To sweat like a **Horse**

1940 WCClark *Murder Goes* (B) 137: He was sweating like a horse. **1962** WHaggard *Unquiet* (NY DBC) 114: He was sweating like a horse. Berrey 245.12.

H332 To work for a dead **Horse** (*varied*)

1931 LCArlington *Through* (L) lv: One had to work up what we called the "dead horse." **1933** GYoung *Devil's* (NY) 101: I've got a dead horse to work off [*behind at poker*]. **1936** HChilds *El Jimmy* (P) 142: So he wouldn't have a "dead horse" to pay off when he got well. **1958** SBarr *Purely* (NY) 112: He would just say he never bought dead horses. **1959** *BHerald* 2/15 13: We'll be paying for a dead horse we no longer own. **1972** JGreenway *Down* (B) 311: With the dead-horse work of writing ahead of me [*an advanced payment*]. EAP H322.

H333 To work like a **Horse** (dray-horse)

1930 BFlynn *Creeping* (L) 221: I worked like a horse. **1931** JJConnington *Boathouse*

(B) 182: He worked like a horse. **1936** VLoder *Deaf-Mute* (L) 30: Working like a horse. **1950** MScherf *Curious* (NY) 66: Worked like a horse. **1964** BHecht *Letters* (NY) 1: They worked like cart horses. **1968** WASwanberg *Rector* (NY) 20: Work like a drayhorse. **1974** GPaley *Enormous* (NY) 122: Working like a horse. EAP H323. Cf. To work like a Mule *below.*

H334 Wild **Horses** couldn't do this or that (*varied*)

1900 CFPidgin *Quincy A. Sawyer* (B) 501: But horses shant drag it out of me. **1913** EDBiggers *Seven Keys* (I) 371: The proverbial wild horses couldn't do it [*pull a man away from a table*]. **1922** JJoyce *Ulysses* (NY 1934) 306: Wild horses shall not drag it from us. **1924** VBridges *Red Lodge* (NY) 163: Wild 'orses wouldn't keep 'im from work. **1932** FBeeding *Take It* (B) 225: Wild horses would not induce me to put my name to that contract. **1936** RGDean *Sutton* (NY) 44: Not that the time-worn wild horses could drag him away. **1940** NMorland *Gun* (L) 96: A man whom wild horses could not compel to speak. **1941** MBardon *Murder Does* (NY) 19: Wild elephants couldn't pull me out of this room. **1947** VSiller *Curtain* (NY) 50: Wild horses wouldn't make me sleep with a woman. **1956** *New Yorker* 11/17 220: But wild horses couldn't drag it out of us. **1959** SMarlowe *Blonde* (NY) 68: Wild horses couldn't have driven him away. **1965** MThomas *Such Men* (L) 25: Wild horses couldn't drag me away from that delicious meal. **1967** GBaxt *Swing* (NY) 46: Wild dogs couldn't keep her away. **1971** NMarsh *When* (B) 50: Kenneth, with a team of wild horses, wouldn't have bullied me into sightseeing at this ghastly hour. **1973** BBehan *My Life* (LA) 14: Wild horses wouldn't drag me back to the bottle. **1975** SJPerelman *Vinegar* (NY) 59: Wild horses tied tail to tail would never force me back there. EAP H316; TW 192(33). Cf. Brunvand 140: Team.

H335 **Horse-laugh**

1937 NMorland *Clue* (L) 160: Ha-ha—that's a horse-laugh, whatever such a

thing's supposed to be. **1938** HHolt *Whispering* (L) 97: Give him the horse-laugh. **1941** CFAdams *Decoy* (NY) 169: They gave me the horse laugh. **1951** JCollier *Fancies* (NY) 218: He was expected to laugh like a horse. **1955** DParry *Sea* (L) 101: Laughing like a horse. **1959** GMalcolm-Smith *If a Body* (NY) 177: Giving the homicide bureau the horse laugh. EAP H326.

H336 **Horse-sense**

1924 AChristie *Man* (NY) 112: Listen to horse sense. **1951** ELustgarten *Defenders* (NY) 39: Everyday horse-sense. **1952** AThorne *Young* (L) 51: It's just plain horse-sense. TW 192(27).

H337 To reckon without one's **Host**

1928 HRMayes *Alger* (NY) 75: He reckoned . . . without his hostess. **1931** CClausen *Jaws* (NY) 236: He reckoned without his host. **1931** APryde *Emerald* (NY) 163: He had reckoned without his host. **1936** RAJWalling *Dirty Face* (L) 298: He had reckoned without his hostess. **1952** HReilly *Velvet* (NY) 138: He reckoned without his host. EAP H327; TW 193.

H338 To be **Hot** and bothered

1933 VLoder *Death* (L) 86: You do seem to be hot and bothered about it. Berrey 173.5, 266.7, 284.8, 287.5, 288.5,8, 353.10,11; Spears 197.

H339 What gets **Hot** gets cold

1956 EMcBain *Mugger* (L 1963) 50: What gets hot gets cool. Whiting H552. Cf. EAP H328: Soon.

H340 To drop someone like a **Hot cake**

1931 LEppley *Murder* (NY) 163: Briel dropped my hand like a hot cake. **1937** CGGivens *All Cats* (I) 144: He dropped Rosemary like a hot cake. **1951** GHJohnston *Monsoon* (L) 252: The Indian will drop him like a hot cake. **1962** RMacdonald *Zebra-* (NY) 92: He dropped me like the proverbial hot cake. **1968** MRowell *Below* (L) 114: I got dropped like a hot cake. Wilstach 103: Potato. Cf. Partridge 120: Cakes, like hot. Cf. Brick, Chestnut, Coal *above,* Potato *below.*

H341   To sell (*etc.*) like **Hot cakes**

1914 CPearl *Morrison of Peking* (Sydney 1967) 302: Selling like hot cakes. **1922** JJoyce *Ulysses* (NY 1934) 125: It goes down like hot cake that stuff. **1927** JSFletcher *Bartenstein* (NY) 39: Newspapers sold like hot cakes on a cold day. **1931** APryde *Emerald* (NY) 60: It went off like hot cakes. **1933** GBegbie *Sudden* (L) 15: Sold even more rapidly than the proverbial hot cakes. **1936** LPaul *Horse* (NY) 68: They'll go like hotcakes. **1941** AChristie *Evil Under* (NY) 179: The press will be on it like hot cakes. **1949** PGWodehouse *Mating* (NY) 172: They sell like hot cakes. **1952** PGosse *Dr. Viper* (L) 130: Sold like hot cakes. **1957** *New Yorker* 7/13 22: We don't expect them to go like hot cakes. **1964** JPorter *Dover One* (NY 1966) 60: Sold like the proverbial hot cakes. **1967** RJones *Three* (B) 59: Memoirs sell like the proverbial hot cakes. **1975** BNByfield *Solemn* (NY) 111: It's selling like hotcakes. TW 53: Cake(7); Taylor *Prov. Comp.* 23; DA Hot cake 2; NED Suppl. Hot *a.* 12c.

H342   As sure as a **Hound dog** will suck eggs (*varied*)

1952 JKnox *Little* (P) 210: Sure as a hound dog'll suck hen eggs. **1954** LCochran *Row's End* (NY) 170: Every dog has to suck eggs sometime. Cf. Whiting *NC* 398(44): Like a suck-egg dog.

H343   As clean (white) as a **Hound's** (dog's, seal's) **tooth** (*varied*)

1925 EPhillpotts *Voice* (NY) 100: White as a dog's tooth. **1928** WMcFee *Pilgrims* (NY) 348: She's as clean as a hound's tooth. **1929** EQueen *Roman* (NY) 209: As clean as a hound's tooth. **1932** TSmith *Bishop's* (NY) 304: I'll pick 'em clean as a hound's tooth. **1939** BHalliday *Dividend* (NY 1959) 77: [His] record is as clean as a hound's tooth. **1940** AGaincs *While the Wind* (NY) 104: Garrick's desk had been swept clean as a hound's tooth. **1957** *BHerald* 3/28 6: As clean as a hound's tooth. **1958** *BangorDN* 7/11 10: Most Congressmen are first as clean as Ike's proverbial "hound's tooth." 9/6 10: As clean as the proverbial hound's

tooth. **1959** LColeman *Sam* (NY) 13: Cute as a hound's tooth. **1963** MRichler *Incomparable* (L) 51: I'm clean as a seal's tooth. **1972** HPentecost *Champagne* (NY) 41: Clean. Hound's tooth clean [*an automobile*]. **1974** GMcDonald *Fletch* (I) 174: He's as clean as a hound dog's tooth. **1980** HPentecost *Death* (NY) 10: Gone, clean as a hound's tooth, as my father used to say. EAP H329: White; Whiting *NC* 428(2).

H344   At the eleventh **Hour**

1967 HTravens *Madame* (NY) 149: At this last moment. The proverbial eleventh hour. **1970** DMDevine *Illegal* (NY) 175: At the eleventh hour. **1973** MInnes *Appleby's Answer* (NY) 157: At the eleventh hour. Brunvand 72.

H345   The darkest **Hour** is just before the dawn (*varied*)

1926 EPhillpotts *Jig-Saw* (NY) 163: Darkest before dawn, perhaps. **1927** GJNathan *Land* (NY) 208: It is always darkest just before dawn. **1928** AEWMason *Prisoner* (NY) 309: The darkest hour comes before the dawn. **1928** PGWodehouse *Meet* (NY) 134: It is always darkest before the dawn. **1929** FDGrierson *Murder* (L) 152: The old saying: the sky is darkest before the dawn. **1930** HWade *Dying* (L) 275: The darkest hour is before the dawn. **1935** FErskine *Naked* (L) 208: The old truism . . . "it was always darkest just before Dawn." **1936** FWCrofts *Loss* (NY) 172: Scientists and philosophers alike tell us that the darkest hour is that preceding the dawn. **1937** NForrest *Greek God* (L) 213: It's the classic dark before the dawn. **1939** EPaul *Mysterious* (NY 1962) 143: It was just before daylight, the hour when it is supposed to be darkest but actually is not. **1951** MCHarriman *Vicious* (NY) 42: The darkness before the dawn. **1951** RKing *Duenna* (NY) 59: I like clichés . . . they're comforting when you're in trouble. Like its always darkest just before the dawn, and the cloud with the silver lining. I like them because sometimes they turn out to be true. **1954** SDeLima *Carnival* (NY) 55: They say it's always darkest before day. **1956** WTenn

Human (NY) 99: "It's always darkest," he told himself with determined triteness, "before the dawn." **1960** LFletcher *Blindfold* (NY) 98: That old adage . . . It is always darkest before the dawn. Or an ill wind always blows some good. **1969** BCole *Funco* (NY) 209: It was the darkest hour of the night, just before dawn. **1970** JVizzard *See* (NY) 272: The deepest hour of darkness before the dawn. **1976** JRLAnderson *Death* (NY) 7: The truth of the proverb that it is always darkest just before dawn. EAP H331.

H346 An **Hour's** cold can suck out seven years' warmth

1959 *BHerald* 5/6 33: There's an auld Scotch proverb that says "An hour's cold can suck out seven years' warmth." *Oxford* 389.

H347 An **Hour's** sleep before midnight is worth two after

1930 ABCox *Vane* (L) 250: An hour's sleep before midnight's worth two after, I always say. Whiting *NC* 429(1); *Oxford* 389.

H348 A long **Hour** by Shrewsbury clock

1960 PGWodehouse *Jeeves* (L) 61: I've been hanging on to this damned receiver a long hour by Shrewsbury clock. Apperson 569: Shrewsbury.

H349 The morning **Hour** has gold in its mouth

1929 SLeacock *Iron Man* (L) 298: "The morning hour has gold in its mouth," adds the adage. Taylor *Proverb* 48–9, *Index* 82.

H350 As big as a **House**

1924 EWallace *Green* (B) 142: He is as big as a house. **1937** CDickson *Ten Teacups* (L) 123: A corporate alibi as big as a house. **1938** JTFarrell *No Star* (NY) 489: A head as big as a house. **1940** CLittle *Black Corridors* (NY) 89: She's getting as big as a house. **1946** JTShaw *Hard-Boiled* (NY) 27: A guy about as big as a house. **1952**

EQueen *King* (B) 26: An ex-wrestler, big as a house. **1953** RChandler *Long* (L) 133: She had a heart as big as a house. **1964** HBTaylor *Duplicate* (NY) 176: He's as big as a house. **1974** EMcBain *Bread* (NY) 58: Big as a house. Whiting *NC* 429(2).

H351 As plain (sure, tight) as **Houses**

1935 EGreenwood *Pins* (L) 232: It came to me suddenly, plain as houses. **1969** SAngus *Death* (L) 55: I had the thing tight as houses. **1973** GSereny *Case* (NY) 189: We could be sure as houses we'd get it.

H352 As safe as a **House**

1928 FWCrofts *Sea* (NY) 334: Both safe as a house. **1930** SChalmers *Affair* (NY) 174: She's as safe as a house. **1934** CWard *House Party* (NY) 295: You're as safe as a house. **1935** AWynne *Toll House* (P) 291: Safe as a house. Cf. Wilstach 333: A blockhouse.

H353 As safe as **Houses**

1931 MAllingham *Gryth* (NY) 12: You'll be as safe as houses. **1939** MInnes *Stop Press* (L) 428: "He would be as safe as houses." "Houses . . . are not particularly safe. The proverb is outmoded and deceptive." **1944** ECrispin *Gilded Fly* (NY 1970) 212: He'd still be as safe as houses. **1946** FWCrofts *Death of a Train* (L) 213: Safe as a house. **1957** FLockridge *Tangled* (P) 85: Planes are safe as houses nowadays. **1962** AChristie *Pale* (NY DBC) 176: Sitting pretty, safe as houses. **1972** JGores *Dead* (NY) 52: Safe as houses, silent as the fog, gentle as a kitten. Berrey 259.4; *Oxford* 691: Safe; Partridge 410.

H354 A **House** divided cannot stand (*varied*)

1930 CBarry *Avenging* (NY) 120: A house divided against itself cannot stand. **1963** DHayes *12th of Never* (NY DBC) 98: A house divided cannot stand. **1971** BEnglish *War* (L) 15: The city was a divided one, and very often, true to the proverb, it did not stand. EAP H334.

H355 One's **House** is his castle (*varied*)

1920 N&JOakley *Clevedon* (P) 150: An Englishman's house, et cetera, you know.

1922 JJoyce *Ulysses* (NY 1934) 341: True to the maxim that every little Irishman's house is his castle. **1928** AECoppard *Silver* (L) 216: An Englishman's castle's his birthright all the world over. **1932** JJFarjeon *Trunk-Call* (NY) 147: An Englishman's house was his castle. **1934** MPropper *Divorce* (NY) 142: A man's home is his castle. **1936** CFBregg *Tragedy* (L) 4: An Englishman's home was his castle. **1937** BHarvey *Growing Pains* (NY) 161: I come from a land where a man's home is his castle. **1938** NBlake *Beast* (NY 1958) 145: The Little Man's home is, traditionally, his castle. **1942** SLeacock *My Remarkable* (Toronto 1965) 35: An Englishman could look after himself; his home was his castle. **1948** HActon *Memoirs* (L) 9: The Englishman's home is his castle. **1954** ABoucher *Best from* (NY) 199: A man's home is his castle. **1957** *BHerald* 1/14 16: A Cape Codder's beach is his castle. **1957** *NYTimes Book Review* 5/12 31: If an Englishman's home is his castle, his club is his sanctuary. **1957** *Punch* 5/15 625: The Englishman's home is now probably a guest-house, and if he does have the misfortune to own a castle it is almost certain to be a guest-house. 8/28 227: The traditional privacy of an Englishman's home. **1958** *BHerald* 6/24 3: The Supreme Court, citing the adage that every man's home is his castle. **1958** WRoss *Immortal* (NY) 245: Is a man's grave his castle? **1960** PO'Connor *Lower* (L) 49: The Englishman's castle home. **1960** NWilliams *Knaves* (NY) 10: The maxim that an Englishman's house is his castle. **1961** WBromberg *Mold* (NY) 33: The Anglo-Saxon maxim that "a man's home is his castle." **1963** GMaxwell *Rocks* (NY) 103: An Englishman's home is his castle, but not a Scotsman's. **1968** RDuncan *How to Make* (L) 213: An Englishman's house is no longer his castle. **1970** KGiles *Death* (L) 50: An Englishman's Ford became his castle. **1971** JLord *Maharajahs* (NY) 166: At a . . . distance the trim . . . houses of the English squatted . . . each, as its occupant never doubted, a castle. **1973** TZinkin *Weeds* (L) 157: To the old saying about the Englishman's home must be added that his garden is his palace. **1974**

RSaltonstall *Maine* (B) 151: A man's home is his castle only when he does not turn it into a fortress to take advantage of his neighbors. EAP H339.

H356 To build a **House** on sand (*varied*)
1930 FDBurdett *Odyssey* (L) 74: The adage of the man who built his house on shifting sands. **1961** EWilliams *George* (NY) 417: Don't build castles on sand. **1965** LGralapp *Boom!* (NY) 21: Your house is built upon the sands . . . your bricks are made without straw. *Oxford* 698–9: Sand.

H357 To eat one out of **House** and home
1921 JCLincoln *Galusha* (NY) 404: He will eat me out of house and home. **1922** JJoyce *Ulysses* (NY 1934) 149: Eat you out of house and home. **1932** CAndrews *Butterfly* (NY) 164: Eating them out of house and home. **1935** GBullett *Jury* (L 1947) 280: Eat us out of house and home. **1944** MFitt *Clues* (NY) 177: Eat us all out of house and home. **1953** EBurns *Sex Life* (NY) 16: Ate themselves out of house and home. **1954** MProcter *Somewhere* (NY) 157: He'll drink us out of house and home. **1964** CRSumner *Withdraw* (NY) 29: Eat us out of house and home. **1972** SWoods *They Love* (NY) 51: Eating him out of house and home. EAP H343; TW 194(6).

H358 To fall (*etc.*) like a **House** of cards (*varied*)
1914 MAdams *In the Footsteps* (L) 201: It toppled them all down like a house of cards. **1925** FWCrofts *French's Greatest* (NY) 279: [He] soon demolished his house of cards. **1928** HAdams *Empty* (P) 243: I am building a house of cards; it keeps tumbling down. **1929** EDBiggers *Black* (I) 285: And house of cards would tumble about his ears. **1929** TLDavidson *Murder* (L) 123: The case against Rostov collapsed like a house of cards. **1930** MMPropper *Ticker-tape* (NY) 92: His structure of reasoning would collapse like a pack of cards. **1938** FDGrierson *Covenant* (L) 82: It's no good building up a house of cards, only to see it tumble down again. **1940** WCClark *Murder Goes* (B) 198: He saw his whole future crashing like a house of cards. **1940** CRaw-

son *Headless* (NY) 280: That would have brought the murderer's whole house of cards down about his ears. **1952** GBullett *Trouble* (L) 208: You will see it collapse like a house of cards. **1957** *Punch* 9/15 326: The whole pack of cards has collapsed. **1958** *NYTimes Book Review* 4/27 1: Yugoslavia, which fell apart like a house of cards. **1958** ELacy *Be Careful* (NY) 142: Then everything falls like a house of cards. **1963** GMaxwell *Rocks* (NY) 77: The whole card castle was falling to the ground. **1966** ELathen *Murder* (NY) 112: To bring the whole house of cards tumbling down. **1970** RMichaelis-Jena *Brothers Grimm* (L) 153: Hopes . . . collapsed like a house of cards. NED Card *sb.*² 1b.

H359 To get on (*etc.*) like a **House** afire (*varied*)

1906 JCLincoln *Mr. Pratt* (NY) 181: [Her] tongue going like a house afire. **1920** A Christie *Mysterious Affair* (NY) 15: Weeds grow like a house afire. **1922** JJoyce *Ulysses* (NY 1934) 154: Getting on like a house on fire. **1928** DHLawrence *Lady* ("Allemagne") 241: I read and I thought like a house on fire. **1934** BThomson *Inspector Richardson* (L) 208: I shall get on with her like a house on fire. **1941** MArmstrong *Blue Santo* (NY) 97: You two ought to get on like a house afire. **1952** MAllingham *Tiger* (NY) 107: They were getting on like a house on fire. **1952** WClapham *Night* (L) 49: He's going like a house on fire. **1959** MEChaber *So Dead* (NY) 34: Everything goes like the house on fire. **1962** ESGardner *Blonde* (NY DBC) 22: It would have gone over like a house afire. **1963** MMcCarthy *Group* (NY) 39: You come like a house afire. **1968** JHaythorne *None of Us* (NY) 91: We could have got on like a house on fire. **1970** JRoss *Deadest* (NY) 60: He and your husband get along like a house on fire. **1972** QBell *Virginia* (NY) II 103: He and Virginia got along like a house on fire. TW 194(5); Taylor *Prov. Comp.* 51.

H360 To put one's **House** in order

1930 ALivingston *Trackless* (I) 320: To put my house in order, as the old saying goes. NED Order *sb.* 27.

H361 A fine **How-de-do**

1957 *New Yorker* 9/14 46: A fine hoddeya do! TW 194.

H362 According to **Hoyle**

1920 ACrabb *Samuel* (NY) 200: Convicted according to Hoyle. **1931** HSKeeler *Matilda* (NY) 427: It isn't according to Hoyle. **1937** ATilton *Beginning* (NY) 88: It was not . . . according to Hoyle and Mrs. Post. **1940** CMWills *R. E. Pipe* (L) 14: This was not according to Hoyle. **1950** SPalmer *Green* (NY) 156: The case . . . wasn't going according to Hoyle. **1959** FLockridge *Murder* (P) 175: All according to Hoyle. **1960** RPrice *Upright Ape* (NY) 55: Operate clean, open and accordin' to Boyle [*sic*]. **1971** ELinington *Practice* (NY) 174: All according to Hoyle. *Enc. Brit.* (13th ed) XIII 841; *Amer. Herit. Dict.* Hoyle.

H363 As thick (plenty) as **Huckleberries**

1933 AMChase *Danger* (NY) 33: They're plenty as huckleberries. **1938** DCDisney *Strawstack* (NY) 229: Newspaper men are thick as huckleberries. **1959** MPHood *Bell* (NY) 9: Eggs were thicker'n huckleberries. **1963** MPHood *Sin* (NY) 21: Thicker'n huckleberries. TW 194(1).

H364 To be a **Huckleberry** above someone's persimmon (*varied*)

1924 CWells *Furthest* (P) 243: This case . . . is a huckleberry above your persimmon. **1960** VWilliams *Walk* (NY) 49: I wouldn't risk a huckleberry to a persimmon. TW 194–5(2).

H365 As big as old **Huffy**

1950 FFGould *Maine Man* (NY) 111: He was toddling around the yard as big as old Huffy. Cf. Whiting *Devil* 246(9): Old Harry; Berrey 406.3: Ill-tempered.

H366 **Hugger-mugger**

1905 JBCabell *Line* (NY 1926) 117: The poor dead lie together, hugger mugger. **1922** JJoyce *Ulysses* (NY 1934) 86: Hugger-mugger in corners. **1934** JJConnington *Ha-Ha* (L) 20: Life . . . is a hugger-mugger sort of affair. **1934** RForsyth *Pleasure Cruise* (NY) 60: You think there's some hugger-mugger behind the sudden death? **1936**

RAJWalling *Floating Foot* (NY) 205: He'd had enough of hugger-mugger. **1940** EDean *Murder Is* (NY) 273: There was a lot of huggermugger along the same lines [*nonsense*]. **1947** DBowers *Bells* (NY) 115: Living hugger-mugger as we do [*close together*]. **1953** ELinklater *Year* (L) 48: Back to hugger-mugger [*squalor*]. **1956** MInnes *Old Hall* (L) 182: Buried the poor girl in hugger-mugger. **1959** JHawkes *Providence* (L) 8: The general tasteless hugger-mugger of marble clocks, bronze versions of Hermes and the Dying Gaul, etc. **1961** MInnes *Old Hall* (L 1961) 178: Buried the poor girl in hugger-mugger. **1962** PZiegler *Duchess* (L) 266: Leave a taste of the hugger-mugger and unseemly. **1967** RBrett-Smith *Berlin* (NY) 39: All crammed together in a glorious hugger-mugger. **1971** EDahlberg *Confessions* (NY) 209: She was making ready, in hugger-mugger, to leave me. **1975** PDickinson *Lively* (NY) 21: Grey gravestones flanked it, hugger-mugger. EAP H352; Wentworth 276.

H367 To eat **Humble pie**

1924 ADHSmith *Porto* (NY) 48: Eat the humble-pie. **1928** ABCox *Amateur* (NY) 338: To eat as big a slice of humble pie as you can manage. **1932** CRyland *Notting* (L) 190: I must eat very humble pie. **1940** JStagge *Turn* (NY) 160: I loathed having to eat humble pie to her. **1946** RHuggins *Double Take* (NY 1959) 167: Humble pie gives me hives. **1953** MPHood *Silent* (NY) 130: Eating a slice of humble pie. **1955** AChristie *Hickory* (NY) 137: I'll eat humble pie. **1963** THWhite *America* (NY 1965) 76: I must begin to eat humble pie. **1966** NBlake *Deadly* (L) 158: Humble pie isn't one of my favorite dishes. **1970** NMonsarrat *Breaking* (L) 337: From humble pie to upper crust. **1973** VSPritchett *Balzac* (NY) 122: Balzac ate humble pie. **1980** JLehmann *Strange* (NY) 38: He [*Rupert Brooke*] ate humble pie with his tutor. EAP H354.

H368 To be over the **Hump**

1952 HReilly *Velvet* (NY) 112: She's over the hump. **1974** PHighsmith *Ripley's* (NY) 246: We're over the hump. Wentworth 276.

H369 With a **Hungarian** for a friend one does not need an enemy (*varied*)

1952 SBellow *Adventures* (NY) 5: If you have a Hungarian friend you don't need an enemy. **1958** ELacy *Be Careful* (NY) 95: As the saying goes, with pals like us he'll never need an enemy. **1959** AMStein *Never Need an Enemy* (NY). **1959** AMStein *Never* (NY) 167: We have an old saying here [*Yugoslavia*] . . . "Have a Hungarian for a friend and you'll never need an enemy." **1966** DHotchens *Man Who* (NY) 152: With a mother-in-law like her, he has no need of enemies. **1971** RMStern *You Don't Need an Enemy* (NY). **1979** COsborne *W. H. Auden* (NY) 199: With friends like this, Auden and Isherwood must have thought, who needs enemies?

H370 **Hunger** causes the wolf to sally from the wood

1905 JBCabell *Line* (NY 1926) 139: Hunger . . . causes the wolf to sally from the wood. Whiting H638; *Oxford* 392.

H371 **Hunger** is the best sauce (*varied*)

1934 VLincoln *February Hill* (NY) 43: Hunger's the best sauce. **1936** EMeynell *Sussex* (L) 19: Hunger is the best of all sauces. **1937** LO'Flaherty *Famine* (NY) 199: A hungry mouth doesn't pick and choose. **1954** RHaydn *Journal* (NY) 116: It is said that a hearty appetite needs no sauce. **1965** HHarrison *Bill* (NY) 106: Appetite was the sauce. **1970** MStewart *Crystal* (NY) 155: Hunger's the best sauce, they say. **1981** PDeVries *Sauce* (B) 201: Hunger is the best sauce, and starvation makes a banquet. EAP H357; TW 195(1). Cf. An empty Belly *above*.

H372 **Hunger** knows no laws

1937 DWhitelaw *Face* (L) 42: Hunger knows no laws. Cf. *Oxford* 392: Knows no friend. Cf. Necessity *below*.

H373 As hungry as a **Hunter**

1930 HFootner *Mystery* (NY) 23: He was hungry as a hunter. **1933** FDGrierson *Monkhurst* (L) 62: I'm as hungry as a hunter. **1944** LBrand *Green for Danger* (NY 1965) 39: So there 'e was, 'ungry as a 'unter. **1953** CHarnett *Nicholas* (NY) 32: He was hungry as a hunter. **1958** CLBlackstone *All Men* (NY) 28: I'm as hungry as a hunter. **1963** THWhite *America* (NY 1965) 30: Hungry as a hunter. TW 196.

H374   A **Hurrah's** nest

1941 LSdeCamp *Incomplete* (NY 1962) 148: His place is such a hurrah's nest. **1956** MPHood *Scarlet* (NY) 37: This place's a hurrah's nest. **1964** AMacKinnon *Report* (NY) 60: What a hurrah's nest! EAP H363.

H375   Not worth three **Hurrahs** in hell

1908 MDPost *Corrector of Destinies* (NY) 60: Not worth three hurrahs in hell. Cf. Whoops *below*.

H376   This **Hurts** me more than it does you

1931 HJForman *Rembrant* (NY) 224: It hurts me more than it does you. **1933** GDHCole *End* (L) 128: It hurts me more than it hurt you. **1940** RStout *Double for Death* (L) 192: This hurts me worse than it does you. **1955** BCarey *Fatal* (NY) 179: A "this hurts me more than it does you" manner. **1957** DJEnright *Heaven* (L) 133: This hurts me more than it does you. **1968** WTenn *Wooden* (NY) 210: This hurts me more than it does you.

H377   The **Husband** (wife) is always the last to know (*varied*)

1934 DFairfax *Masked Ball* (L) 15: It's generally the husband who's the last to know he's being deceived. **1936** RGDean *What Gentleman* (NY) 144: Is there not an adage to the effect that a husband is always the last to discover? **1949** ILeighton *Aspirin* (NY) 96: Like the proverbial injured husband, the President of the United States is always the last to hear news affecting the honor of his house. **1952** MRRinehart *Swimming* (NY) 203: Husbands are usually the last to know. **1957** WHHarris *Golden* (NY) 88: The old saying that the husband was always the last to know. **1959** AGilbert *Death* (NY) 28: They say the wife's always the last to hear. **1959** LWhite *Meriweather* (NY) 115: You know what they say . . . The wife is always the last one to know. **1966** SMarlowe *Search* (NY) 9: Husband's the last one to know, huh? **1968** ELathen *Stitch* (NY) 62: I know that the wife is always the last to know. **1969** DClark *Nobody's* (NY) 67: What about the common belief that the wife is always the last to know [*adultery*]? *Oxford* 159: Cuckold.

H378   Like **Husband** (wife), like wife (husband)

1938 NMorland *Case Without* (L) 11: Like husband, like wife. **1939** FGerard *Red Rope* (NY) 256: Like husband, like wife. **1957** GAshe *Wait* (NY 1972) 124: Like wife, like husband. Whiting H655: Such.

H379   To grin like a **Hyena**

1937 NMorland *Clue* (L) 69: Grinning like a hyena. TW 196(1).

H380   To laugh like a **Hyena**

1930 FRyerson *Seven* (L) 161: Laughin' like a hyena. **1932** GMitchell *Saltmarsh* (L) 60: Laughs like a hyena; 239. **1940** ECRLorac *Tryst* (L) 179: Laugh like a hyena. **1950** ECRLorac *And Then* (NY) 215: Still laughing "like a hyena." **1958** CCarnac *Affair* (NY) 43: The surgeons laughed like hyenas. **1968** KChristie *Child's* (L) 143: They are laughing like hyenas. TW 196(2).

I

I1 To dot the **I's** and cross the t's (*varied*)
c1923 ACrowley *Confessions* ed JSymonds (L 1969) 354: With every *t* crossed and every *i* dotted. **1930** ABCox *Piccadilly* (NY) 280: I'll dot his i's and cross his t's. **1935** CBarry *Shot* (NY) 185: I'll have to cross a few t's for you. **1939** MBurton *Babbecombe* (L) 195: I must dot the i's and cross the t's for you. **1945** PWentworth *She Came* (NY) 84: I don't need to dot the *i's* or cross the *t's*. **1950** MGEberhart *Never* (NY) 174: He would have had every i dotted and every t crossed. **1958** RKing *Malice* (NY) 48: "Following our instructions to a dotted *i*." . . . "Omit please, the crossed *t*. Clichés make me ill." **1960** NFitzgerald *Candles* (L) 160: To dot every "i" and cross every "t". **1964** SBecker *Covenant* (NY) 143: The Catholics never dotted their i's the way Calvin did. **1966** MSteen *Looking* (L) 112: I am obliged to cross t's and dot i's. **1968** PBarr *Deer Cry* (L) 195: Elevated language that did not dot the "i's". EAP I1.

I2 As calm as **Ice**
1929 DFrome *Murder* (L) 210: Calm as ice. Wilstach 42.

I3 As clear as **Ice**
1932 SHPage *Resurrection* (NY) 77: Clear as ice. TW 197(1).

I4 As cold (cool) as **Ice**; Ice-cold
1901 MLPeabody *To Be Young* (B 1967) 218: Feet as cold as ice. **1922** VThompson *Pointed* (NY) 37: Voice . . . cold as ice. **1925** LBrock *Deductions* (NY) 13: His face was as cool as a chunk of ice. **1928** JChancellor *Dark* (NY) 85: As cool as ice. **1928** SMartin *Fifteen* (NY) 200: The latter was as cool as ice. **1932** MBurton *Death* (L) 15: As cold as ice. **1933** GCollins *Dead Walk* (L) 71: Ice-cold anger. **1940** CBDawson *Lady Wept* (NY) 135: My whole body became as cold as ice. **1955** PWentworth *Gazebo* (L 1965) 46: His nose was as cold as ice. **1961** JSStrange *Eye* (NY) 124: They were cold as ice. **1962** ESGardner *The Case of the Ice-Cold Hands* (NY DBC). **1966** BKnox *Ghost* (NY) 45: He's . . . cold as ice. **1966** TWells *Matter* (NY) 24: She was as cool as a block of ice. **1974** BWAldiss *Eighty* (NY) 173: He went ice-cold. EAP I3, 3a; TW 197(2, 3); Brunvand 74(1).

I5 As hard as **Ice**
1922 VThompson *Pointed* (NY) 37: Voice . . . hard as ice. Taylor *Western Folklore* 17(1958) 16(1).

I6 As smooth as **Ice**
1930 TPerry *Owner* (NY) 194: Thornberry's voice was smooth as ice. **1932** RHMay *7 Murders* (NY) 204: Smooth as ice. **1952** FPratt *Blue* (NY 1969) 27: The doctor's voice was smooth as ice. EAP I5; Taylor *Western Folklore* 17(1958) 16(2).

I7 Not to cut (much, any) **Ice**
1915 JBuchan *Thirty-Nine* (NY) 17: He cuts no ice. **1924** CVanVechten *Tattooed* (NY) 143: It don't cut no ice. **1933** HAdams *Golf House* (P) 78: He will never cut much ice as the Americans say. **1935** BFlynn *Edge* (L) 81: That sort cuts little ice in an affair of this kind. **1952** EQueen *King* (B) 185: That

didn't cut any ice with me. **1958** RFraser *Jupiter* (L) 127: It won't cut any ice on earth. **1960** NBenchley *Sail* (NY) 157: That kinda talk don't cut no ice. **1966** LThayer *Dusty* (NY DBC) 129: They don't cut much ice either way. **1976** AChristie *Sleeping* (NY) 114: He didn't cut any ice with Helen. DA Ice 7(4); Wentworth 136–7.

I8   To break the Ice (*varied*)

1900 CFPidgin *Quincy A. Sawyer* (B) 222: To break the ice. **1913** ECBentley *Trent's* (NY 1930) 163: To have broken the ice. **1921** RLardner *Big House* (NY) 111: To break the ice. **1932** BFlynn *Murder* (P) 194: How was it you got him to break the ice? **1937** HWade *High Sheriff* (L) 233: A way of breaking the ice. **1946** PATaylor *Punch* (NY) 21: Help get the ice broken. **1949** RKing *Redoubled* (NY) 125: A delicate breaking of the ice. **1954** HCecil *According* (L) 60: I'm glad to have broken the ice. **1957** RFenisong *Schemers* (NY) 47: To have the ice broken. **1965** VRandolph *Hot Springs* (Hatboro, Penn.) 148: The girl tried to break the ice. **1966** LPDavies *Paper* (NY) 25: Once the ice was broken. EAP I6; Brunvand 74(2).

I9   To skate (*etc.*) **on thin Ice** (*varied*)

1914 JLondon *Letters* ed KHendricks (NY 1965) 414: How thin the ice is upon which I am skating. **1928** JJConnington *Tragedy* (B) 286: You skated over thin ice. **1930** FA Winder *Behind* (L) 178: Shaen was walking on thin ice. **1932** DLSayers *Have* (NY) 333: He was treading on thin ice. **1934** DHume *Too Dangerous* (L) 72: He had skated deliberately on the thin ice. **1936** AFielding *Mystery* (L) 173: She was on very thin ice. **1938** HHolt *Wanted* (L) 27: You're skating on horribly thin ice. **1940** ISShriber *Head over Heels* (NY) 250: Jerry was getting on pretty thin ice. **1951** MInnes *Paper* (NY) 34: The ice on which he was skating was paper-thin. **1957** *BHerald* 4/17 19A: Look at the thin ice on which these rabble-rousers are treading. **1958** GHCoxe *Impetuous* (NY) 59: We have been skating on thin ice. **1963** JNHarris *Weird* (NY DBC) 75: He skated on thin ice. **1966** MErskine *Family* (NY) 127: The kick he'd get out of skating on thin ice. **1972**

SNBehrman *People* (B) 107: I skated along on thin ice as well as I could. Whiting *NC* 429(5).

I10   As cold (cool) as an Iceberg

1932 VWilliams *Fog* (B) 291: Winstay was as cool as an iceberg. **1933** ESnell *And Then* (L) 103: Turn cold as an iceberg. **1954** HGardiner *Murder* (L) 246: As cold as an iceberg. Whiting *NC* 429; Brunvand 74(1).

I11   As cool as an Icicle

1939 WMartyn *Noonday* (L) 134: As cool as an icicle. TW 197(2).

I12   Idleness is the devil's workshop (*varied*)

1958 *BHerald* 1/27 20: The old proverb, "Idleness is the devil's workshop." **1962** EMcBain *Like* (NY) 79: He was fond of repeating an old Gypsy proverb that said something about idle hands being the devil's something-or-other. **1966** JStuart *My Land* (NY) 99: She told us that idleness was the devil's workshop. *Oxford* 395: Idle brain. Cf. Devil finds *above*.

I13   Idleness is the mother of vice (*varied*)

1961 WHLewis *Scandalous* (NY) 192: We recollect that idleness is the mother of all the vices. **1963** DHayes *12th of Never* (NY DBC) 58: Idleness leads to vice. **1971** TZinkin *Odious* (L) 22: Idleness is the mother of all evil. EAP I12; TW 198.

I14   Ifs, ands and (or) buts (*varied*)

1927 JSFletcher *Bartenstein* (NY) 170: "If ifs and buts were apples and nuts" . . . recalling an old rhyme familiar in childhood. **1930** CBush *Death* (NY) 192: Ifs and ans and pots and pans and all the rest of the jingle. **1941** ISShriber *Murder Well Done* (NY) 199: There were no ifs and buts about it. **1945** PWentworth *She Came* (NY) 181: If ifs and ans were pots and pans what would tinkers do? **1953** BCarey *Their Nearest* (NY) 90: Straight to the point, with no ifs, ands, or buts. **1959** DCushman *Goodbye* (NY) 173: There are no ifs and buts about it. It's down in black and white. **1963** ADean *Deadly* (NY) 11: So many ifs, ands, and buts. **1968** JPorter *Dover Goes* (NY) 84: I want no "ifs" and "buts" about it. **1970** STerkel *Hard* (NY)

342: There were no ifs, ands or buts about it. **1977** EPGreen *Rotten* (NY) 33: No ifs, ands, or buts. EAP I13.

I15 Ignorance is bliss

1928 GFairlie *Man Who Laughed* (NY) 100: How true the old saying was: "Ignorance is bliss!" **1970** ELathen *Pick* (NY) 135: Ignorance is bliss. TW 198; Brunvand 74. Cf. EAP I17.

I16 Ignorance of the law is no excuse (*varied*)

c1923 ACrowley *Confessions* ed JSymonds (L 1969) 307: Ignorance of the law excuses no man. **1928** JJConnington *Mystery* (B) 26: Ignorance of the law is no excuse. **1934** CKendrake *Clew* (NY) 229: Ignorance of the law excuses no one. **1939** CRawson *Footprints* (L) 274: Ignorance . . . is no excuse. **1957** *New Yorker* 3/2 35: Ignorance of the law is no excuse. **1957** *Cambridge Chronicle-Sun* 4/25 2: It is a fundamental law that ignorance of the law is no excuse. EAP I16.

I17 As big as Ike

1935 GGGivens *Rose Petal* (I) 148: His fingerprints were on the desk, big as Ike. **1940** CBDawson *Lady Wept* (NY) 223: He walked right in, as big as Ike.

I18 There's no Ill in a merry wind *etc.*

1929 KCStrahan *Footprints* (NY) 184: "There's nae ill in a merry wind," quo the wife when she whistled through the kink. Lean II ii 750.

I19 As rigid as an Image

1923 VWilliams *Orange* (B) 44: Rigid as any image. Cf. Wilstach 324: As if chiseled from stone. Cf. As rigid as a Statue *below*.

I20 As stiff as an Image (*varied*)

1903 MLPeabody *To Be Young* (B 1967) 267: He is as stiff as a wooden image. **1945** ACampbell *With Bated* (NY) 256: The two women stiff as images. Cf. Whiting I22: Stark; Wilstach 388: A marble statue, 559: Frozen statue. Cf. As stiff as a Statue *below*.

I21 To sit like an Image (*varied*)

1927 VWilliams *Eye* (B) 26: [He] sat like a graven image. **1929** ABCox *Layton* (NY) 96: To sit like a stone image. **1932** RAJWalling *Fatal* (NY) 129: Tolfree had sat like a graven image. **1933** GDHCole *End* (L) 67: Do you like sitting there like a graven image? **1945** PWentworth *She Came* (NY) 129: Lamb sat there like a image. **1961** ESherry *Call* (NY DBC) 100: If you sit . . . like a stone image. **1963** MErskine *No. 9* (NY) 76: Just sat like images. **1975** FMNivens *Publish* (NY) 134: She sat motionless as a carved image. Cf. TW 198(2): Slept. Cf. To sit like a Statue *below*.

I22 To stand like an Image (*varied*)

1909 JCLincoln *Keziah* (NY) 353: Stand still like a frozen image. **1912** ERBurroughs *Gods of Mars* (NY 1963) 35: Stood like a graven image. **1923** VWilliams *Orange* (B) 63: The men stood like graven images. **1931** PMacDonald *Crime* (NY) 62: Standing here like an image. **1933** REssex *Slade* (NY) 162: Jedbury stood like a graven image. **1965** RVanGulick *Willow* (NY) 146: Standing still as a graven image. Cf. Wilstach 384: Statues cut in stone. Cf. Indian, To stand like a Statue *below*.

I23 Imagination is a good stick but a bad crutch

1962 NFreeling *Death* (NY 1964) 146: Imagination steps into its place; a good stick but a bad crutch, as the English say. Cf. *Oxford* 468: Literature.

I24 Imitation is the sincerest form of flattery

1940 ECameron *Malice* (NY) 13: Imitation may be the sincerest form of flattery. **1955** PWentworth *Gazebo* (L 1965) 225: Imitation may be the sincerest form of flattery. **1963** THWhite *America* (NY 1965) 154: Imitation is the sincerest form of flattery. *Oxford* 402.

I25 First Impressions are untrustworthy (*varied*)

1929 GFairlie *Stone* (B) 156: First impressions are notoriously untrustworthy. **1970** DMDevine *Illegal* (NY) 60: First impressions were totally wrong. **1973** CJackson *Kicked* (NY) 23: First impressions, of course, are generally misleading. Cf. EAP I23. Cf. Appearances *above*.

I26 Given an **Inch** one takes an ell (*varied*)
1927 WDSteele *Man Who* (NY) 377: Give these old fellows an inch and they'll take a mile. **1928** RKing *Fatal* (NY) 6: An . . . aptitude for seizing an inch and making it an ell. 11: Billy caught the inch on the bound and at once proceeded to ell it. **1928** RMaury *Wars of the Godly* (NY) 52: George III was bitterly opposed to granting the catholics another inch, entertaining, as he did, the presentiment that they would take the proverbial mile. **1930** WLewis *Apes* (NY 1932) 394: Given an inch and will take an ell. **1931** CBush *Dead Man's* (L) 266: Give that sort of man an inch and he'll do you down for ten miles. **1933** WChambers *Campanile* (NY) 64: Give you an inch and you'll assume a mile. **1936** ECalmer *When Night* (NY) 64: Give you an inch and you want a mile. **1937** CGGivens *All Cats* (I) 287: Give a preacher an inch and he'll take a mile. **1937** GHeyer *They Found* (L) 26: People who given an inch grab an ell. **1937** PStong *Buckskin* (NY) 343: You give Sue an ell and she'll take a mile. **1946** KMKnight *Trouble* (NY) 141: Give that woman an inch and she'll take an ell. **1949** JSymons *Bland* (L) 201: It is axiomatic . . . that when once an inch has been allowed an ell will be taken. **1954** JHenry *Yield* (NY) 91: Give them an inch and they take yards. **1956** GMetalious *Peyton* (NY) 6: The theory that if a child were given the inch, he would rapidly take the proverbial mile. **1958** *NYTimes Book Review* 10/12 4: Give him a cliché and he takes a mile. **1958** CCockburn *Crossing* (L) 200: If you give a good newspaperman an inch he is capable of giving you half a column of hell. **1959** ASillitoe *Saturday* (NY) 202: He had given her an inch and she wanted a yard. **1962** AWUpfield *Will* (NY) 71: Gives him an inch, takes a yard. **1963** FArmitage *Five* (NY) 208: Give you a foot and you demand a mile. **1965** RNathan *Mallot* (NY) 158: Give them an inch and the next thing you know they're behind the oleander bushes. **1967** WASwanberg *Pulitzer* (NY) 160: Pulitzer . . . taking a mile when given a millimeter. **1968**

LDurrell *Tunc* (NY) 66: Gave me an inch and I took a mile. EAP H24; TW 198(2, 3).

I27 Not to see an **Inch** before one's nose (*varied*)
1922 JSFletcher *Rayner-Slade* (NY) 300: We men can't see an inch above our noses. **1928** EHamilton *Four* (L) 156: She . . . can't see an inch before her nose. **1931** AChristie *Murder* (NY) 162: He can't see a yard in front of his nose. **1934** LRGribble *Riddle* (L) 276: I can see a few inches before my nose. **1957** MProcter *Midnight* (NY) 55: They couldn't see an inch in front of their noses. EAP I26. Cf. Not to see . . . End *above*; To see . . . Nose *below*.

I28 To thrash (*etc.*) within an **Inch** of one's life
1922 JJoyce *Ulysses* (NY 1934) 460: Thrash the mongrel within an inch of his life. **1929** BThomson *Metal* (L) 209: He used to thrash him within an inch of his life. **1940** ACampbell *They Hunted* (NY) 120: Frightened within an inch of his young life. **1958** SDean *Dishonor* (NY) 68: It scared her within an inch of her life. TW 198(4); Brunvand 75(2).

I29 Honest **Indian** (Injun)
1940 CRawson *Headless* (NY) 8: Honest Injun, cross my heart. **1947** VWMason *Saigon* (NY) 133: "Honest Injun?" He chuckled at the homely phrase. **1961** HFarrell *Death* (NY DBC) 38: Even if I promise, honest Injun. DA Honest 3.

I30 An **Indian** giver
1936 VWBrooks *Flowering* (NY 1946) 521: The Indian-giver style. **1946** DWilson *Make With the Brain* (NY) 177: She is what Joe calls an Indian giver. **1952** FKane *Bare* (NY 1960) 142: You'll think I'm an Indian giver. **1954** JPotts *Go* (NY) 38: Indian giver. **1967** JPurdy *Eustace* (NY) 51: I'm not an Indian-giver. **1970** EQueen *Last* (NY) 18: I'm an Indian giver. EAP I36.

I31 The **Indian** sign
1931 ACEdington *Monk's Hood* (NY) 2: That guy must have the Indian sign on him. 94: Sometimes people get the Indian sign on

folks. **1934** FLGregory *Cipher* (NY) 218: He's got the Indian sign on you [*going to kill him*]. **1941** JKVedder *Last Doorbell* (NY) 222: His ex-wife had the Indian sign on him. **1956** CArmstrong *Dream* (NY 1958) 145: Ethel put the Indian sign on both of you. **1956** SPalmer *Unhappy* (NY 1957) 165: Your letters . . . put the Indian sign on the chief—or else he's giving you enough rope to hang yourself. **1965** HHowe *Gentle* (NY) 146: Mrs Gray must have had some kind of Indian sign on mother. **1970** CDBowen *Family* (B) 259: The Indian sign lay on my brother. DA Indian sign 3.

I32 The only good **Indian** (*etc.*) is a dead Indian (*etc.*) (*varied*)

1908 MRRinehart *Circular Staircase* (NY 1947) 175: They say the only good Indian is a dead Indian. **1912** ERBurroughs *Princess of Mars* (NY 1963) 72: The only good enemy is a dead enemy. **1926** TAWillard *City* (NY) 44: The Spaniards . . . made either good Christians or "good Indians" of all the inhabitants. **1929** RGraves *Good-bye* (L) 236: No good Fritzes but dead uns. **1930** BombardierX *So This Was War* (L) 11: The only good Germans were dead Germans. **1930** SEMorison *Builders* (B) 296: A good Indian is a dead Indian. **1930** SSassoon *Memoirs* (L) 16: There's only one good Boche, and that's a dead one. **1933** VLoder *Suspicion* (L) 173: The principle that the only good poacher was a dead poacher. **1934** JBCarr *Man with Bated Breath* (NY) 33: The saying in these parts that the only honest nigger is a dead nigger. **1935** CWells *Wooden* (P) 35: The only good Indian is a dead Indian. **1942** SLeacock *My Remarkable* (Toronto 1965) 46: As with the Indian, the only good teacher is a dead teacher. **1945** MColes *Green Hazard* (NY) 211: The only good German is a dead German. **1954** MBodenheim *My Life* (NY) 130: There is no good Indian but a dead Indian, we are told by the grandsons of men who have been scalped. **1957** *New Yorker* 1/19 38: I say the only good Indian is a dead Indian. **1957** PGallico *Thomasina* (NY) 43: Sayings like "The only good mouse is a dead mouse" [*said by a cat*]. **1959** *BHerald* 9/23 12: The only good Communist is a dead Communist. **1960** CDLewis *Buried* (L) 86: The only good German is a dead German. **1964** JWCampbell *Analog II* (NY) 54: The old saying, The only good Indian is a dead . . . drunk Indian. **1964** LSDeCamp *Ancient* (NY) 210: The only good Spaniard was a dead Spaniard. **1964** LLRue *World* (P) 82: The only good raccoon was a dead one. **1969** AGilbert *Missing* (NY) 124: What we used to say in the First War—the only good German's a dead German. **1970** MGEberhart *El Rancho* (NY DBC) 128: The only good Indian was a dead Indian. **1970** TKenrick *The Only Good Body's a Dead One* (NY). **1970** AHLewis *Carnival* (NY) 101: The only good snake was a dead snake. Brunvand 75(1); DA Good Indian 2. Cf. Only good Pig *below*.

I33 To stand like a wooden **Indian**

1930 CRawson *Headless* (NY) 125: He stood motionless as a wooden Indian. **1970** MG Eberhart *El Rancho* (NY DBC) 41: Don't stand there like a wooden Indian. Cf. DA Wooden 2(4). Cf. Image *above*.

I34 As blue as **Indigo**

1933 RAJWalling *Prove It* (NY) 153: Upper lip, as blue as Indigo. **1953** ERuggles *Prince* (NY) 333: It made him blue as indigo [*sad*]. **1960** AHLewis *Worlds* (NY) 152: I was as blue as indigo [*depressed*]. EAP I37; Brunvand 75.

I35 To sleep like an **Infant**

1919 KHoward *Peculiar* (NY) 50: Slept like an infant. TW 199(5). Cf. To sleep like a Babe *above*.

I36 First **Injure** and then hate

1932 JJConnington *Castleford* (B) 255: The old saying: "First injure, and then hate." Cf. EAP I44.

I37 As black as **Ink**; Ink-black

1908 MRRinehart *Circular Staircase* (NY 1947) 169: Ink-black prisons. **1920** MLevel *Tales of Mystery* (NY) 262: Black as ink. **1931** LCArlington *Through* (L) 63: The night . . . was black as ink. **1940** CLittle *Black Corridors* (NY) 191: These clouds are as black as ink. **1945** ACampbell *With Bated* (NY) 299: It was black as India ink. **1947** VWBrooks *Times of Melville* (NY) 420: Water as black as ink. **1959** SBeach *Shakespeare* (NY) 109: A black-as-ink cat. **1959** HWaugh *Sleep* (NY) 7: It was ink black. **1970** RZelazny *Isle* (NY) 153: The water was black as ink. **1976** MGilbert *Night* (NY) 224: Black as ink. EAP I46; TW 200(1); Brunvand 76.

I38   The **Ins** and outs

1930 RKeverne *Man in the Red Hat* (NY) 194: I know all the ins and outs. **1937** LRGribble *Who Killed* (L) 137: Something I didn't know the ins and outs of. **1939** HMiller *Capricorn* (NY 1961) 316: Learning the ins and outs of the job. **1951** ECRLorac *I Could* (NY) 28: All the ins and outs. EAP I47.

I39   As black (dark) as the **Inside** of this or that

1935 GDilnot *Murder* (L) 271: It's as dark as the inside of a dog's mouth. **1935** RHowes *Death* (NY) 141: Black as the inside of a chimney. **1941** CFAdams *Dewy* (NY) 26: The kitchen was darker than the inside of a black cat. **1950** ECBentley *Chill* (NY) 179: As dark as the inside of a cow, as you say. **1952** FVWMason *Himalayan* (NY 1953) 60: Black as the inside of a witch's cat. **1961** MHHood *Drown* (NY) 96: It'll be darker than the inside of Jonah's whale. TW 200(1).

I40   To be high in the **Instep**

1945 ATQuillerCouch *Memories* (Cambridge, Eng.) 33: She's too high in the insteps for the likes of me. **1954** EForbes *Rainbow* (B) 79: Nothing abashed her, I guess, for she was pretty high in the instep. EAP I48; TW 200.

I41   To add **Insult** to injury

1909 AEHousman *Letters* ed HMaas (Cambridge, Mass. 1971) 103: This adds insult to injury. **c1923** ACrowley *Confessions* ed JSymonds (L 1969) 424: Adding insult to injury. **1932** JSFletcher *Ninth Baronet* (NY) 227: Adding insult to injury, as the saying is. **1936** KCStrahan *Desert* (I) 78: Insult to injury. **1941** CLClifford *While the Bells* (NY) 144: That's adding insult to injury. **1951** JCFurnas *Voyage* (NY) 400: Added insult to

injury. **1957** *BHerald* 4/9 30: I just can't resist adding insult to injury. **1960** DShannon *Case* (NY) 95: Add insult to injury. **1963** HWaugh *Death* (NY) 133: But this was insult on injury. **1972** DShannon *Murder* (NY) 13: Talk about insult to injury. **1976** ACClark *Imperial* (NY) 61: Adding insult to economic injury. EAP I49.

I42   To get one's **Irish** up

1940 CSaxby *Death Joins* (NY) 31: Katiebelle . . . was getting her Irish up. **1953** BCarey *Their Nearest* (NY) 173: I'm beginning to get my Irish up. TW 200(3).

I43   The wild **Irish**

1922 JJoyce *Ulysses* (NY 1934) 24: Smiling at wild Irish. EAP I54.

I44   As cold as **Iron**

1956 SSmith *Shrew* (NY 1959) 149: His eyes were suddenly as cold as iron. Wilstach 61.

I45   As hard as **Iron**; Iron-hard (*varied*)

1929 LBrock *Stoke Silver* (NY) 296: The ground was as hard as iron. **1929** SMartin *Only Seven* (NY) 6: A . . . stick . . . hard as iron. **1940** JRhode *Death on* (NY) 228: She's as hard as a lump of iron. **1959** HCarmichael *Marked* (NY) 11: Frozen iron-hard. EAP I57; TW 200(2).

I46   As strong (tough) as **Iron**

1931 PMacDonald *Choice* (L) 64: Strong as iron. **1969** UKLeGuin *Left Hand* (NY) 210: He was tough as iron. **1974** LCarter *Valley* (NY) 18: Your heart was strong as iron. EAP I58; Brunvand 77(3).

I47   Strike while the **Iron** is hot (*varied*)

1918 BMalinowski *Diary* (NY 1967) 184: Strike while the iron is hot. **1924** CWells *Furthest* (P) 156: Being a hot iron striker. **1932** HWade *Hanging* (L) 123: Striking while the iron was hot; 249. **1938** JRhode *Bloody* (L) 226: The adage that one should strike while the iron was hot. **1945** GBellairs *Calamity* (NY) 126: The iron's hot . . . It's up to you to strike. **1954** KAmis *Lucky* (L) 48: To strike while the iron's hot, if you'll pardon the expression. **1956** *Republican Journal* 8/23 8: One who strikes while the iron is hot doesn't necessarily succeed in making warm friends. **1957** *Time* 12/30 61: Striking while Hagerty was still hot. **1958** JCoates *Widow's* (NY) 208: He'd better strike while the iron is hot. **1975** MButterworth *Man in* (NY) 122: Striking while the iron was hot. **1976** JFoxx *Freebooty* (I) 128: The adage of "striking while the iron is still hot." EAP I60; TW 201(5); Brunvand 77(7).

I48 To have **Irons** in the fire (*varied*)
1917 GRSims *My Life* (L) 289: Harris had a good many irons in the fire. **1921** JBCabell *Letters* ed PColum (NY 1962) 229: I have a variety of irons in the fire. **1930** HSKeeler *Fourth* (NY) 54: My business irons are lying in a cold fire. **1938** MSaltmarsh *Clouded* (NY) 296: It wouldn't hurt to have a second iron in the fire. **1941** HLMencken *Newspaper Days, 1899–1906* (NY) 308: He had many other irons in the fire. **1949** JDCarr *Conan Doyle* (NY) 41: Despite all these other irons clattering in and out of the fire. **1955** MO'Brine *Passport* (L) 214: [He] had some embarassing irons in certain fires. **1956** *New Yorker* 11/10 54: The Clementines had so many irons in the fire that the fire was in danger of going out. **1958** *New Yorker* 1/25 34: We have bigger irons in the fire now. **1958** *NYTimes Book Review* 4/6 8: As we say it in France, I have several chestnuts—you say irons—in the fire. **1958** HKoningsberger *Affair* (NY) 197: I have my own iron in the fire. **1962** MStewart *Moon* (NY 1965) 100: I like a lot of irons in the fire. **1967** EWallach *Light* (NY) 311: Two irons in the fire is what I always say [*a male lover and a lesbian lover*]. EAP H61.

I49 As bad as the **Itch**
1935 GHCoxe *Murder* (NY) 136: You guys are worse'n the itch. TW 201.

I50 To avoid like the **Itch**
1933 HAshbrook *Murder* (NY) 48: Avoid her like the itch. EAP H63: Shun.

I51 As white as **Ivory**; Ivory-white
1930 GFairlie *Suspect* (NY) 183: Her cheeks white as ivory. **1948** MColes *Among* (NY) 83: His face as white as ivory. **1950** SPalmer *Monkey* (NY) 21: Ivory-white baby. EAP I64; TW 201(2); Brunvand 77.

J

J1 Every man **Jack**

1904 JCLincoln *Cap'n Eri* (NY) 190: Every man Jack. **1924** JSFletcher *Safety* (NY) 124: Every man-Jack. **1935** CFGregg *Danger* (L) 137: Every man Jack of them. **1938** NMarsh *Death* (NY) 221: Every man Jack. **1957** *Punch* 2/20 276: Every man Jack in Britain. **1957** HEBates *Sugar* (L) 94: Every jack one of 'em. **1961** JDCarr *Witch* (L) 56: Every man jack of them. **1968** FLeiber *Swords* (NY) 141: Every man jack of them. **1971** ELinington *Practice* (NY) 122: Every man-jack of that crew. **1974** KAmis *Ending* (NY) 25: Every man jack. Apperson 190; Partridge 259.

J2 Fuck you, **Jack**, I'm all right (*varied*)

1967 AMontagu *Anatomy of Swearing* (NY) 313: Fuck you, Jack, I'm all right. **1968** KTopkins *Passing* (B) 32: The fuck-you-Buster war. **1975** HLawrenson *Stranger* (NY) 201: This "I'm all right, Jack" attitude. Partridge 305.

J3 **Jack** and Jill

1920 JSFletcher *Dead Men's* (NY) 297: Every Jack and Jill in the house. **1935** JSFletcher *Carrismore* (L) 224: Every Jack and Jill of 'em. EAP J2.

J4 **Jack**-in-office

c1923 ACrowley *Confessions* ed JSymonds (L 1969) 587: A swarm of useless jacks in office. **1932** JJConnington *Castleford* (B) 142: That jack-in-office Inspector. **1937** RPenny *Policeman's Holiday* (L) 126: An uppish country jack-in-office. **1944** ECrispin *Gilded Fly* (NY 1970) 155: Cheap minds and jacks-in-office. **1947** ECrispin *Dead* (NY DBC) 34: A jack-in-office. A nincompoop. **1961** JDCarr *Witch* (L) 208: Any Scotland Yard jack-in-office. **1967** AWaugh *My Brother* (L) 238: These jacks-in-office pestered him. **1970** PDickinson *Sinful* (NY) 186: An insolent damned jack-in-office. **1970** KLaumer *World* (NY) 101: That jumped-up jack-in-office. EAP J11.

J5 **Jack** is as good as his master (*varied*)

1931 LCArlington *Through* (L) 121: Jack was as good as his master. **1931** JJConnington *Boathouse* (B) 20: Jack is as good as his master. **1935** HAdams *Fate Laughs* (L) 42: Jack is as good as his master. **1960** AGilbert *One for* (NY 1965) 153: Jack is as good as his master and frequently a good deal better. **1967** FSwinnerton *Sanctuary* (NY) 211: The so-called democratic way of showing Jack to be as good as his master. **1972** MHardwick *Mrs. Dizzy* (NY) 36: Jack would be as good as his master. *Oxford* 408.

J6 A **Jack** of all trades (*varied*)

1920 AChristie *Mysterious Affair* (NY) 12: Jack of all trades. **c1923** ACrowley *Confessions* ed JSymonds (L 1969) 179: A widely travelled Jack-of-all-trades. **1939** RStout *Some Buried* (L) 249: A good stockman is a Jack of all trades. **1952** HTreece *Dark* (L) 80: The jack-of-all-trade legionaires. **1956** *BangorDN* 9/10 4: A literary Jack-of-all-trades. **1956** *Time* 9/17 98: Jack-of-all-literary-trades. **1956** MLSettle *O Beulah* (NY) 208: A jack of all trades better here . . . than

340

any master. **1957** *Time* 12/30 14: Jack of many professions. **1959** AGilbert *Prelude* (NY DBC) 48: These jack-of-all-trades women. **1968** JTMcIntosh *Take a Pair* (NY) 34: He's jack of many trades. **1968** GSouter *Peculiar* (Sydney) 204: He was a jack of all trades and had no difficulty in supporting his family. **1970** RFBanks *Maine* (Middletown, Conn.) 374: Freeman was a jack-of-all-trades. **1971** TCatledge *My Life* (NY) 29: I'd been jack-of-all-trades. **1972** BCatton *Waiting* (NY) 165: Gray was the most remarkable Jack-of-all-trades I ever met. **1974** BWAldiss *Eighty* (NY) 26: She was a jill-of-all-trades. EAP J4.

J7 A **Jack** of all trades and master of most (*varied*)

1930 SEMorison *Builders* (B) 164: Jack-of-all-trades and master of most. **1934** FWCrofts *Crime* (NY) 20: He was jack of all trades and master of all. **1941** VRath *Death Breaks* (NY) 43: Logan is a Jack-of-all-trades but master of a surprising number of them. **1959** *NYTimes Book Review* 2/1 7: Jack of all trades, and a master of them, too. **1971** WTeller *Cape Cod* (Englewood Cliffs, NJ) 45: Master of many trades and perhaps jack of none. **1973** JCEnk *Family* (Rockland, Me.) 239: A jack of all trades, who was adequate in most and very good in some. **1975** AHolmstead *Threshold* (NY) 46: One in every five . . . is a jack-of-all-trades who can do everything . . . and do it well.

J8 A **Jack** of all trades and master of none (*varied*)

1924 HCBailey *Mr. Fortune's Practice* (NY) 173: Jack of all trades and master of none. **1930** Ex-PrivateX *War* (NY) 216: A Jack of all trades and a master of none. **1932** PMacDonald *Rope* (NY) vii: He proved a refutation of the adage that a jack-of-all-trades can be master of none. **1933** JDCarr *Mad Hatter* (L) 147: A detective had to be a jack of all trades and a master of none. **1940** FWCrofts *Golden Ashes* (NY) 189: Jack of All Trades, with, I'm afraid, its contingent limitation. **1959** *BangorDN* 8/3 20: I've been sort of a jerk-of-all-jobs and master of none. **1959** CEMaine *Tide* (NY) 155: The jack of all trades, master of none. **1965** VPurcell

Memoirs (L) 240: We were jacks of all trades, and perhaps . . . masters of none. **1966** LBeers *Wild* (NY) 159: Vermonters are jacks-of-all-trades and masters of none. EAP J5; Brunvand 78(1).

J9 **Jack** shall have Jill (*varied*)

1905 JBCabell *Line* (NY 1926) 170: Jack has his Jill, and all ends merrily, like an old song. **1937** DLSayers *Busman's* (NY) 245: Jack shall have Jill, Naught shall go ill, The man shall have his mare again and all go well. **1941** PStong *Other Worlds* (NY) 390: Jill to have a Jack, Joan a Darby, Gretel a Hansel. **1965** MJones *Set* (L) 13: Jack shall have Jill, All shall go well. **1965** RDSymons *Silton* (NY 1975) 169: There is a Jack for every Jill. **1967** IBarea *Vienna* (NY) 171: Every Jack getting his Jill. EAP J7; TW 202(5).

J10 Before one can say **Jack Robinson** (*varied*)

1925 WAStowell *Singing Walls* (NY) 201: Before you could say "Jack Robinson." **1933** LThayer *Hell-Gate* (NY) 93: Before he could have said Jack Robinson. **1935** VWilliams *Clue* (B) 91: Quicker than you could say "Jack the Ripper." **1936** *New Yorker* 5/16 17: I would drown faster than you could say "Jack Robins." **1937** SPalmer *No Flowers* (L) 231: In less time than it takes to say the proverbial Jack Robinson. **1938** KMKnight *Acts* (NY) 74: Quicker'n ye could say Jack Robinson. **1940** EPaul *Mayhem* (NY) 53: While anyone who cared to said "Jack Robinson." **1943** FScully *Rogues* (Hollywood) 225: Before you could say James Harvey Robinson. **1954** EWalter *Untidy* (P) 22: Before you could say Jack Robinson. **1956** *New Yorker* 11/10 60: Before I could say "Jack Robinson," had I cared to say that, and had I known a Jack Robinson. **1957** *Punch* 2/27 299: Before anyone could say "Eric Robinson" I had switched off the TV. 4/3 447: Before you could say John Halifax. **1958** AAnderson *Lover* (NY) 66: Before you could say Sugar Ray Robinson. **1965** ANeame *Maud* (L) 104: Before you can say jack. **1969** RReed *Conversations* (NY) 217: Before you could say Paul Robeson. **1970** JVizzard *See* (NY) 347: Before the rest of them could say Mrs. Robinson. **1977** EP Green *Rotten* (NY) 148: Faster than you can say Jack Robinson. **1980** *BGlobe* 2/3 1: Last week in London, Christie's auction gallery sold a portrait of Jack Robinson quicker than one could say "Jack Robinson." Robinson, the British treasury minister before the American Revolution, was so hot-tempered, it was said, that swords would be drawn quicker than one could say "Jack Robinson," and his name went into the language. EAP J12; TW 202(3); Brunvand 78(2).

J11 Where the **Jackals** are, the lion cannot be far away

1938 MSaltmarsh *Clouded* (NY) 90: Where the jackals are, the lion won't be far away. See *Oxford* 467: Lion's provider.

J12 As stubborn as a **Jackass**

1932 GLane *Hotel* (L) 117: He was as stubborn as a jackass. Whiting *NC* 430(1). Cf. As stubborn as a Mule *below*.

J13 To act like a **Jack-in-the-box** (*varied*)

1912 JCLincoln *Postmaster* (NY) 144: Lucindy popped out like a jack-in-the-box. **1920** AChristie *Mysterious Affair* (NY) 197: In and out of the house like a jack-in-the-box. **1928** GDHCole *Man* (NY) 100: What a Jack-in-the-box the man was; 193. **1931** JDCarr *Lost* (L) 49: [It] shot up like a jack-in-the-box. **1934** AGMacleod *Case* (L) 176: Stott's jack-in-the-box-like appearance. **1940** EBQuinn *Death Is* (L) 165: [He] came out like a jack-in-the-box. **1951** HQMasur *You Can't* (NY) 128: I jerked upright like a jack-in-the-box. **1952** AGilbert *Mr. Crook* (NY DBC) 95: Popping out of the elevator like a Jill-in-the-box. **1957** JPotts *Man with* (NY 1964) 155: The ugly, jack-in-the-box question. **1961** GGFickling *Blood* (NY) 21: I bounced in front of him just like a jack-in-the-box. **1967** KLaumer *Planet* (NY) 22: Amos came out of his chair like a jack-in-the-box. **1973** KAmis *Riverside* (NY) 33: Popping up and down like a jack-in-the-box. *Oxford* 408.

J14 To fold up (*etc.*) like a **Jackknife** (knife) (*varied*)

1909 MRRinehart *Man in Lower Ten* (NY 1947) 220: I . . . folded up like a jackknife.

1931 HMSmith *Waverdale Fire* (L) 51: William shut up suddenly like a knife. **1939** LRGribble *Arsenal* (L) 22: He simply folded up like a jack-knife. **1947** GMWilliams *Silk* (L) 219: He went so far and then closed up like a knife.

J15 To hit the **Jackpot**

1941 ARLong *4 Feet* (NY) 149: We hit the jack-pot that time. **1949** EQueen *Cat* (B) 11: We hit the jackpot. **1957** LFord *Girl* (NY) 170: You hit the jackpot. **1958** SEllin *Eighth* (NY 1959) 83: Miller hit the jackpot. Wentworth 284.

J16 To see one in **Jail**

1940 RDarby *Death Conducts* (NY) 200: Well, see you in jail, as the lads say. **1955** FCDavis *Night* (NY) 107: See you in jail, to coin a phrase—and perhaps I'm not kidding either. Berrey 350.8: Church, funnies. Cf. See you in Church, Funny papers *above*.

J17 Plain (crazy) **Jane**

1922 JJoyce *Ulysses* (NY 1934) 121: Plain Jane, no damn nonsense. **1933** BReynolds *Very Private* (NY) 269: I look like crazy Jane. **1968** JRoffman *Grave* (NY) 47: I'm plain Jane.

J18 **January** warm, the Lord have mercy

1959 *NYTimes* 1/25 2E: An old proverb says, "January warm, the Lord have mercy!" Apperson 332(20); Dunwoody 93.

J19 As crazy (drunk, loony) as a **Jaybird**

1946 JStagge *Death's Old* (NY) 102: Crazy as a jaybird. **1956** WBrinkley *Don't Go* (NY) 212: We're all looney as a jaybird. **1961** DLoovis *Last* (NY) 46: Drunk as a jay bird.

J20 As happy as **Jaybirds**

1971 PTabor *Pauline's* (Louisville) 104: Those soldiers left her happy as jaybirds. Whiting *NC* 431(1).

J21 As naked as a **Jaybird**; Jaybird-naked

1934 KTKnoblock *Winter* (NY) 198: Naked as a jaybird. **1939** AMcRoyd *Double Shadow* (NY) 34: Nekkid as a jay bird, she was. **1941** BHalliday *Bodies* (NY 1959) 167: As naked as a jaybird in shedding time. **1945** MRRinehart *Yellow Room* (NY) 235: He was naked as a jaybird. **1951** LFord *Murder Is* (NY) 2:

You're nekkid as a jaybird. **1953** BMc-Million *Lot* (P) 155: Woman stripped jaybird naked. **1958** *New Yorker* 8/16 68: As naked, nearly, as a jaybird. **1960** JBWest *Taste* (NY) 78: Naked as a jaybird and as white as snow. **1968** JCFurnas *Lightfoot* (NY) 104: Naked as jaybirds. **1969** BCole *Funco* (NY) 21: Jay-bird naked. **1970** EQueen *Last* (NY) 46: As naked as a jaybird. **1973** HDolson *Dying* (P) 76: [There] you go naked-chested as a jay bird. Whiting *NC* 431(2, 3). Cf. Robin *below*.

J22 Jealousy implies love (*varied*)

1937 ECVivian *Tramp's* (L) 119: Jealousy implies love. **1967** PMcGerr *Murder* (NY) 178: Telling myself that jealousy is a form of love. Whiting J22; *Oxford* 491: Love is never.

J23 Jeddart justice

1928 JMBall *Sack-'Em-Up* (L) 105: "Jeddart justice" which is founded on the principle "to hang first and try afterwards." **1928** RTGould *Oddities* (NY) 269: Jeddart justice. **1958** *TLS* 1/31 55: All get "jeddart justice." *Oxford* 410. Cf. First Fire *above*; Jersey, Lydford *below*.

J24 To drive like Jehu

1934 HCBailey *Shadow* (NY) 120: Drive like Jehu. TW 203.

J25 To shake (shiver) like a Jelly

1922 JJoyce *Ulysses* (NY 1934) 731: He was shaking like a jelly all over. **1924** EWallace *Green* (B) 329: You're shivering like a jelly in an earthquake. **1929** CBarry *Clue* (NY) 89: He was shakin' like a jelly. **1931** GTrevor *Murder* (L) 57: The fellow was shivering like a jelly. **1936** HHolt *There Has Been* (L) 150: He may be shaking like a jelly. **1950** SPalmer *Monkey* (NY) 46: He shivered, like a dish of jelly. **1957** APowell *At Lady* (L) 230: Shaking like a jelly. **1964** DBagley *Golden* (NY) 39: He was shaking like a jelly. TW 203; Taylor *Prov. Comp.* 52.

J26 To tremble like a Jelly (*varied*)

1957 MPHood *In the Dark* (NY) 78: I was trembling like a bowl of apple jelly. **1959** GAshe *Pack* (NY) 84: She . . . began to tremble like a jelly. Wilstach 432: Like cold jelly.

J27 At (to) Jericho

1910 EPhillpotts *Tales* (NY) 168: She wished the farm at Jericho. **1929** GMitchell *Speedy* (NY) 258: You can go to Jericho wi' your old question. **1930** ECRLorac *Murder* (L) 51: I wish her at Jericho sometimes. **1935** FBeeding *Death* (L) 260: He would like to see us all at Jericho. **1936** ECRLorac *Crime* (L) 283: Enough TNT to blow us all to Jericho. **1958** CCarnac *Affair* (NY) 54: I could wish your . . . at Jericho. EAP J20.

J28 Jersey justice

1925 EMPoate *Pledged* (NY) 225: Jersey justice. DA Jersey 3(6) [*severe, but legal*].

J29 As black as Jet; Jet-black

1903 MLPeabody *To Be Young* (B 1967) 249: Jet-black major. **1922** JSFletcher *Ravensdene* (NY) 155: Black as jet. **1924** FWCrofts *Cask* (NY 1936) 96: Jet black hair. **1930** FBeeding *League* (B) 236: Birds . . . black as jet. **1933** CBush *April Fools* (L) 12: His hair was jet-black. **1937** PCoffin *Search* (NY) 145: His eyes were as black as jet. **1941** EDaly *Deadly* (NY 1947) 36: Eyes as bright and as black as jet. **1959** AWUpfield *Journey* (NY) 28: Her hair was jet black. **1972** JAnderson *Alpha* (NY) 68: Jet-black small cigar. EAP J26, 26a; TW 204(1, 2).

J30 As bright as Jet

1959 EMarshall *Pagan* (NY) 260: [Eyes] as bright as jet. Whiting J30.

J31 In a Jiff (*varied*)

1939 LBrock *Fourfingers* (L) 225: I'll be along in half a jiff. **1957** JCreasey *Model* (L 1961) 115: I'll be back in two jiffs. **1962** AMorton *If Anything* (L) 75: I won't be two jiffs. TW 204: Jiffy.

J32 The Jig is up

1921 EWallace *Daffodil* (B) 234: The jig is up. **1923** VWilliams *Orange* (B) 160: The jig's up. **1933** CWells *Clue* (NY) 308: The jig is up. **1936** PATaylor *Out of Order* (NY) 85: The jig was up. **1940** ABCunningham *Murder at* (NY) 192: The jig's up. **1941** I Alexander *Revenge* (NY) 85: The jig was up. **1951** HRigsby *Murder for* (NY 1952) 160: The jig was up. **1955** ESGardner *Glamorous* (NY DBC) 197: The jig is up. **1970** JVizzard

See (NY) 50: The jig was up. EAP J33; Brunvand 78.

J33   As patient as **Job** (*varied*)

1914 JLondon *Letters* ed KHendricks (NY 1965) 436: As patient as Job. **1934** CFGregg *Execution* (L) 254: Williams had the patience of Job. **1936** TDowning *Unconquered Sisters* (NY) 109: It's enough to try Job's own patience. **1953** CMRussell *Market* (NY) 41: Patient as Job. **1958** JYork *My Brother's* (NY DBC) 73: Patient as Job. **1970** JWechsberg *First* (NY) 257: He had needed the patience of Job. EAP J35; TW 205(5).

J34   As poor as **Job**

1960 KCicellis *Way* (L) 61: They're as poor as Job. EAP J36; TW 204(2).

J35   As poor as **Job's** cat

1928 RHFuller *Jubilee* (NY) 219: His family was poorer than Job's cat. EAP J37.

J36   As poor as **Job's** turkey

1906 JCLincoln *Mr. Pratt* (NY) 35: Poorer than Job's turkey. **1910** JCLincoln *Depot Master* (NY) 235: Poor as Job's pet turkey. **1921** MKSanders *D.Thompson* (B 1973) 76: Poor as Job's turkey. **1932** BABotkin ed *Land Is Ours* (Norman, Okla.) 267: As pore as Job's turkey. **1933** AMChase *Danger* (NY) 182: As poor as Job's turkey. **1942** RBurke *Here Lies* (NY) 79: Poor as Job's turkey. **1956** MLSettle *O Beulah* (NY) 212: Pore as Job's turkey. **1957** *BangorDN* 5/7 20: He's as poor as Job's turkey. EAP J38; Brunvand 78(1).

J37   A **Job's** comforter

1927 GDilnot *Lazy* (B) 90: A fine old Job's comforter you make. **1932** RThorndike *Devil* (NY) 172: The Job's comforter. **1936** GDHCole *Brothers* (L) 124: You really are a Job's comforter. **1952** RMacdonald *Ivory* (NY 1965) 16: He was a Job's comforter. **1970** JPorter *Dover Strikes* (NY) 158: A right Job's comforter. **1972** KCampbell *Thunder* (I) 152: That Job's comforter the landlord. EAP J40.

J38   Another **Job** is jobbed *etc.*

1967 RRendell *New Lease* (NY) 14: Another job jobbed . . . as the old woman said when

she jobbed the old man's eye out. *Oxford* 115: Char; Partridge 441: Jobbed.

J39   To give up as a bad **Job**

1931 GDHCole *Dead Man's* (L) 193: Dawes gave it up as a bad job. **1933** PMacDonald *Mystery* (NY 1958) 23: They've given it up as a bad job. **1945** MColes *Green Hazard* (NY) 22: The inspector was giving it up as a bad job. **1968** SPalmer *Rook* (NY) 127: To give it up as a bad job and go home. EAP J42.

J40   **John Blunt**

1931 EWallace *Ringer Returns* (NY) 186: I'm John Blunt [*a frank, candid man*]. Whiting J49.

J41   One's **John Hancock**

1917 JCLincoln *Extricating* (NY) 319: Put your John Hancock at the foot of this. **1935** FErskine *Naked* (L) 113: Come on, put your John Hancock on it! **1940** HSKeeler *Crimson Box* (L) 308: When he had his John Hancock half down. **1950** HReilly *Murder* (NY) 72: Until they put their John Hancock on the dotted line. **1958** HReilly *Ding* (NY DBC) 76: Joan . . . had left her John Hancock on the pearl brooch [*fingerprints*]. **1962** ESherry *Girl* (NY DBC) 45: A sample of your John Hancock. **1969** BJackson *Thief's* (NY) 132: All you do is write your John Henry. Wentworth 296.

J42   **Johnny-come-lately**

1940 CRawson *Headless* (NY) 45: Our bandmaster's a Johnny-come-lately. **1947** VW Mason *Saigon* (NY) 15: This Johnny-come-lately. **1951** DMDisney *Look* (NY) 211: Only in a Johnny-come-lately way. **1956** HCahill *Shadow* (NY) 106: No Johnny-come-lately. **1957** *NYTimes Book Review* 11/3 42: The angry young Jimmy-come-latelies. **1959** *NY Times* 12/13 2E: The Johnny-come-lately well fed liberal. **1961** JWebb *One for* (NY DBC) 103: You're a Johnny come lately. **1971** PTabor *Pauline's* (Louisville) 61: Johnny-come-lately characters. Wentworth 296.

J43   **Johnny-on-the-spot**

1924 MDPost *Walker* (NY) 266: Johnny-on-the-spot. **1928** WMcFee *Pilgrims* (NY) 436: Johnny on the job. **1936** CFGregg *Murder*

(NY) 202: He was Johnny-on-the-spot. **1937** DAllan *Brandon* (L) 160: Johnny on the spot, aren't you? **1940** WCClark *Murder Goes* (B) 14: I see the press is Johnny-on-the-spot. **1943** WMcCully *Doctors* (NY) 79: Miss Green would be Johnny on the spot. **1957** *Time* 8/19 70: Germans are Hans-on-the-spot. **1958** *Time* 5/12 19: A Johnny-on-the-spot expeditionary force. **1966** HWaugh *Pure* (NY) 43: You're Johnny-on-the-spot. **1976** RBDominic *Murder* (NY) 41: You were Johnny-on-the-spot. Wentworth 296. Cf. DARE i 594: Charlie-on-the-spot.

J44 A **Joke** is a joke
1917 JCLincoln *Extricating* (NY) 150: A joke's a joke. **1930** RGBrowne *By Way* (NY) 52: A joke's er joke. **1933** ABCox *Jumping* (L) 100: A joke's a joke, but this is too much. TW 205(1). Cf. Fun *above*.

J45 To keep up with the **Joneses**
1930 SEMorison *Builders* (B) 68: Keeping up with the Joneses. **1935** QPatrick *Grindle* (NY) 27: Roberta was just one of those Joneses nobody wanted to keep up with. **1951** AThorne *Man Who* (L) 42: An ecclesiastical keeping-up-with-the-Jones. **1954** EMarriner *Kennebec* (Waterville, Me.) 117: To keep up with the Joneses. **1959** RPowell *Pioneer* (NY) 162: You don't have any of that keeping-up-with-the-Joneses about gardening. **1962** KAmis *Spectrum(1)* (L) 125: The cult of "keeping up with the Joneses." **1966** JLymington *Froomb!* (NY) 141: There used to be a term. Keeping up with the Joneses. **1970** STerkel *Hard* (NY) 268: The notion of keeping up with the Joneses didn't exist. Wentworth 297. Cf. Whiting *NC* 432.

J46 A **Jot** or tittle
1935 GDHCole *Scandal* (L) 110: Not down to every jot or tittle. **1952** KMKnight *Death Goes* (NY) 83: To add one jot or tittle to a woman's sorrow. Brunvand 79; NED Jot *sb.*[1] (quote 1526), Tittle *sb.*[2]

J47 Not care (matter) a **Jot**
1929 GFairlie *Yellow* (B) 4: I didn't care a jot for that. **1929** TKindon *Murder* (NY) 68: It mattered not a jot. **1936** AGilbert *Courtier* (L) 133: He didn't care a jot. **1938** MBurton *Platinum* (L) 222: I don't care a jot. **1956**

FCauldwell *Firewalkers* (L) 138: You don't care a jot. **1966** TLang *Darling* (NY) 185: Warwick did not . . . care a jot. **1969** JDrummond *People* (NY) 166: I don't care a jot. **1970** HBlyth *Skittles* (L) 138: He cared not a jot. EAP J51.

J48 A **Judas** kiss (trick)
1919 LTracy *Bartlett* (NY) 243: Judas kisses. **1931** HWade *No Friendly* (L) 197: He was playing a Judas trick. **1933** DMarfield *Mystery* (NY) 284: A Judas kiss. **1938** LTanner *All the Things* (NY) 252: Given the Judas kiss. **1939** DCDisney *Golden Swan* (NY) 146: I gave my niece a Judas kiss. **1947** ECrispin *Dead* (NY DBC) 12: It's the kiss of Judas. **1960** ADean *Bullet* (NY) 188: A betrayal—a Judas kiss. **1962** PQuentin *Ordeal* (NY) 101: The kisses of Judas. EAP J55.

J49 To hang as high as **Judas**
1934 CDickson *White Priory* (NY) 233: Hang X higher than Judas. Cf. *Oxford* 414 [*a reference to Judas' hanging*]; NED Judas-tree. Cf. Haman *above*.

J50 As drunk as a **Judge**
1953 ANoyes *Two* (P) 20: Drunk as a judge. Cf. Whiting *NC* 432(3): Tight.

J51 As serious as a **Judge**
1929 TLDavidson *Murder* (L) 176: As serious as a judge. TW 205(1).

J52 As sober as a **Judge**
1910 EPhillpotts *Tales* (NY) 285: Sober as a judge. **1930** VStarrett *Blue Door* (NY) 4: I'm sober as a judge. **1935** TRoscoe *Murder* (NY) 118: Sober as the hypothetical judge. **1940** EBenjamin *Murder Without* (NY) 130: Soberer than any judge you ever saw. **1957** RAHeinlein *Door* (NY) 179: "Sober as a judge." . . . "That's no recommendation." **1958** *New Yorker* 8/2 20: We were as sober as a judge. **1970** UO'Connor *Brendan* (L) 231: As sober as a judge. EAP J57; Brunvand 79(2). Cf. Bishop *above*.

J53 As solemn as a **Judge**
1930 MBDix *Murder* (L) 166: Solemn as a judge. **1932** VLoder *Death* (L) 156: As solemn as a judge. **1969** AGilbert *Missing* (NY)

19: His voice was solemn as the proverbial judge. TW 206(3).

J54 Not by a **Jugful**

1913 JCLincoln *Mr. Pratt's Patients* (NY) 251: Not by a jugful. **1924** MDPost *Walker* (NY) 208: Not by a jugful. **1932** HLandon *Owl's* (L) 92: Not by a jugful. **1935** HHolt *Tiger* (L) 162: That isn't all . . . by a jugful. **1972** JDCarr *Hungry* (NY) 145: Not by a jugful. TW 206.

J55 To stew (fry) in one's own **Juice** (fat, gravy, grease, piss)

1920 GDilnot *Suspected* (NY) 196: To stew in your own juice. **1932** RCWoodthorpe *Public* (L) 27: Let him stew in his own juice. **1937** JYork *Come Here* (NY) 141: They can stew in their own juice. **1938** GDHCole *Mrs. Warrender's* (L) 57: Tell him to go and fry himself in his own fat. **1945** AChristie *Remembered* (NY) 18: Let him stew in his own juice. **1949** AMStein *Days* (NY) 87: Leave Pablo to stew in his own juice. **1950** VSReid *New Day* (L) 316: Leave him to stew in his own piss. **1952** EGCarey *Jumping* (NY) 163: And fry in his own juice. **1958** *BHerald* 4/24 15: Inclined to let these people stew in their own mess. **1958** MAMusmanno *Verdict* (NY) 339: Let him stew in his own juice. **1959** RVanGulik *Chinese* (NY) 44: Why not let the bastards stew in their own grease? **1961**

JAMichener *Report* (NY) 260: To stew in our own mental juices. **1961** LPayne *Nose* (NY) 35: He . . . should be allowed to stew in his own gravy for a while. **1964** SBecker *Covenant* (NY) 111: Let her stew in her own juice, or some equally original gem of folk wisdom. **1966** CRyan *Last Battle* (NY) 230: Fry in their own juice. **1973** JWhitehead *Solemn* (L) 133: Left Wise to stew in his own juice. **1975** HBHough *Mostly* (NY) 106: Let others stew in their own juice. *Oxford* 292: Fry (stew). Cf. EAP G166.

J56 As crazy as a **June bug**

1953 BMcMillion *Lot* (P) 89: She's crazy as a Junebug. **1960** LFletcher *Blindfold* (NY) 14: He's crazy as a June bug. Brunvand 79.

J57 Be **Just** before you are generous

1922 JJoyce *Ulysses* (NY 1934) 545: Be just before you are generous. EAP J58.

J58 **Justice** and mercy

1939 MHealy *Old Munster* (L) 151: Justice under his administration is tempered with mercy. **1955** *Partisan Review* 22.4 555: Fiedler wants mercy for the Rosenbergs and yet he fails, in the words of the common saying, to do them justice. EAP J59.

J59 **Justice** is blind

1961 RAKnowlton *Court* (L 1967) 175: Justice may be blind, but law isn't. EAP J61.

K

K1 To **Keep** oneself to oneself

1921 JSFletcher *Chestermarke* (NY) 14: [She] kept herself to herself. **1922** FPitt *Woodland* (L) 251: Keeps itself to itself. **1932** GHeyer *Footsteps* (L) 64: Keeps himself to himself, as the saying is. **1938** FDGrierson *Cabaret* (L) 179: Keeps herself to herself, as the saying is. **1950** JCannan *Murder* (L 1958) 491: They "keep themselves to themselves." **1957** GTrease *Snared* (L) 60: The national ideal, to keep oneself to oneself. **1962** LEgan *Borrowed* (NY DBC) 90: She—as the British say—keeps herself to herself. **1966** RMaugham *Somerset* (L) 65: He kept himself to himself, as the saying is. **1967** FSwinnerton *Sanctuary* (NY) 27: They kept themselves, as the saying is, to themselves. **1975** JBland *Death* (NY) 37: Each of them likes to keep himself to himself. EAP K2.

K2 To have had it up to one's **Keister**

1983 *BGlobe* 1/12 5: Ronald Reagan is . . . the first President to say of this time-honored process of unofficial communication between officialdom and journalists, "I've had it up to my keister with these leaks." Wentworth 301.

K3 As cold as **Kelsey**

1950 SPalmer *Green* (NY) 60: The dame . . . is right here on the floor . . . colder than Kelsey [*dead*].

K4 As dead (cold) as **Kelsey's** nuts

1961 NBogner *In Spells* (L) 15: Her first love is as dead as Kelsey's nuts—whoever Kelsey was. **1978** LBlock *Burglar* (NY) 67:

Now she's deader'n Kelsey's nuts. **1981** LBlock *Stab* (NY) 21: "It must be a pretty cold trail." "Colder'n Kelseys's legendary nuts." Cf. Wentworth 546: Tight as.

K5 **Kentish** men and Men of Kent

1928 RThorndike *Slype* (NY) 1: The famous river which divides the Kentish men from Men of Kent. **1928** CWells *Crime* (P) 127: The difference between a Kentish man and a Man of Kent. **1961** MErskine *Woman* (NY) 19: A cook who married a Kentish man or a man of Kent, I'm not sure which. *Oxford* 525.

K6 As black as a **Kettle**

1961 AWUpfield *White* (NY) 99: His new shirt, as black as a kettle. **1965** ANeame *Maud* (L) 72: His face was as black as a kettle. Taylor *Western Folklore* 17(1958) 16. Cf. As black as the Pot, Pot calls *below*.

K7 A different (another, fine, nice, pretty) **Kettle** of fish

1919 HRHaggard *She and Allan* (NY 1921) 78: Here's a pretty kettle of fish. **1924** LSpringfield *Some Piquant* (L) 46: Here was a pretty kettle of fish. **1924** LTracy *Token* (NY) 282: A nice kettle of fish. **1927** LTracy *Mysterious* (NY) 258: A nice kettle of fish. **1928** WMcFee *Pilgrims* (NY) 323: Fine kettle of fish she's cooked. **1930** NGordon *Silent* (NY) 205: We got landed with quite a different kettle of fish. **1931** LFalkner *M* (NY) 152: A fine kettle of stale fish. **1932** GCollins *Channel* (L) 198: Another kettle of fish. **1932** VLWhitechurch *Murder* (L) 182: A pretty kettle of fish you've provided for us. **1938** HHolt *Whispering* (L) 92: There's a nice kettle of fish to fry. **1938** KMKnight *Acts* (NY) 272: In a pretty kettle of fish. **1939** RPhilmore *Death in* (L) 48: She's quite a different kettle of fish. **1941** VRath *Death Breaks* (NY) 113: This is a pretty kettle of fish. **1950** TFuller *Keep Cool* (B) 16: This is a pretty kettle, you might say, of fish. **1951** ESGardner *Fiery* (NY) 197: They're both of them a pretty kettle of fish [*a bad lot*]. **1954** KAmis *Lucky* (L) 144: A very different kettle of fish. **1957** *BHerald* 5/19 19A: So here you have what your grandfather might have called a pretty kettle of fish. **1957** *New Yorker* 11/23 49: You and the Queen are different kettles of fish from me. **1957** VWMason *Gracious* (NY) 128: A very different and more complicated kettle of fish. **1960** FCrane *Death-wish* (NY DBC) 136: This was a fine kettle of fish. **1960** RWilson *30 Day* (NY) 93: A pretty stinking kettle of fish. **1964** DDeJong *Whirligig* (NY) 172: It would have been another kettle of fish. **1964** EPangborn *Davy* (NY) 207: An entirely different kettle of shoes of another color. **1965** AHeckstall-Smith *Consort* (NY) 61: A somewhat different kettle of fish that's likely to put the cat amongst the pigeons. **1970** HCarmichael *Death* (NY) 207: To prove it was a different kettle of fish. **1971** BWAldiss *Soldier* (L) 204: A different kettle of fish. EAP K5; TW 207(1).

K8 To be one's **Kettle** of fish

1950 AWUpfield *Widows* (NY) 97: It will be my kettle of fish, as they used to say when my grandfather was alive. **1976** JMcClure *Snake* (NY) 205: That's more my kettle of fish.

K9 A little **Key** will open a large door (*varied*)

1922 VThompson *Pointed* (NY) 317: A little key can open a very large door. **1934** SFowler(Wright) *Who Else* (L) 118: You can often unlock a large door with a small key. Cf. Spears 220: Key [*penis*].

K10 More **Kicks** than ha'pence (*varied*)

1914 MAdams *In the Footsteps* (L) 115: He had to accept the kicks which were in a hopeless majority over the halfpence. **1925** JGBrandon *Bond* (L) 184: Got all of the kicks and none of the ha'pence. **1928** VWilliams *Crouching* (B) 45: More kicks than pfennigs. **1930** MAllingham *Mystery* (NY) 310: More kicks than h'pence in our job. **1930** HFootner *Mystery* (NY) 209: We ordinary fellows have to take plenty of kicks among our ha'pence. **1938** SHorler *Gentleman* (NY) 66: I receive more kicks than ha'pence. **1940** MBurton *Murder in* (L) 96: Quite a lot of kicks and no halfpence. **1941** NMarsh *Death in Ecstasy* (NY) 241: A wish to have the ha'pence without the kicks. **1954** NBlake *Whisper* (L) 180: More hard knocks than halfpence in it. EAP K8.

K11 To be **Kicked** upstairs

1959 DMDouglass *Many* (L) 12: I was being kicked upstairs. **1965** CArmstrong *Turret* (NY) 42: Edie suspected that she'd been kicked upstairs. Berrey 67.4, 246.6.

K12 To seethe the **Kid** in its mother's milk

1931 MDalton *Night* (NY) 117: Would that not be—how do you say?—seething the kid in his mother's milk. **1932** JJConnington *Sweepstake* (B) 91: A bit like seething a kid in its mother's milk. **1932** AFielding *Death* (NY) 327: Seething a kid in its mother's milk to help hounds on the right trail. **1936** VLoder *Deaf-Mute* (L) 209: Seething the kid in the mother's milk. **1969** TBesterman *Voltaire* (NY) 373: We have too often seen the kid seethed in its mother's milk. Exodus 23:19.

K13 Of the same **Kidney**

1925 LBrock *Deductions* (NY) 138: Another individual of the same kidney. EAP K10.

K14 **Kilkenny** cats (*varied*)

1931 ELoban *Calloused* (NY) 65: Fighting like Kilkenny cats. **1931** APryde *Emerald* (NY) 36: As jealous of one another as Kilkenny cats. **1933** Anonymous *Modern Sinbad* (L) 166: To take cats to Kilkenny. **1936** RAJWalling *Floating Foot* (NY) 64: They were less cordial to each other than the Kilkenny cats. **1942** CFAdams *What Price* (NY) 251: They glared at each other like a couple of Kilkenny cats. **1950** ECRLorac *Accident* (NY DBC) 46: They were all quarrelling like Kilkenny cats. **1953** DMDickson

Prescription (NY) 31: We fought like Kilkenny cats. **1966** HTracy *Men* (L) 180: You're worse than the cats of Kilkenny. **1968** HEMaude *Of Islands* (Melbourne) 161: They wanted to kill each other off like Kilkenny cats. EAP K11. Cf. To fight like Cats *above*.

K15   To be in at the Kill

1934 WChambers *Murder* (NY) 195: And was in at the kill, as the saying goes. Amer. Herit. Dict. Kill *n.* 2.

K16   Kill or cure

1918 BMalinowski *Diary* (NY 1967) 282: Cure or kill. **1929** FBeeding *Pretty* (B) 275: It's kill or cure. **1933** JCMasterman *Oxford* (L) 235: I wanted to kill rather than to cure. **1940** NMarsh *Death of a Peer* (B) 290: Kill, as they say, or cure. **1950** EAMathew *Horse* (Belfast) 177: Kill or cure. **1956** RFenisong *Bite* (NY) 85: It would kill or cure. **1956** EXFerrars *Kill or Cure* (NY). EAP K12; Brunvand 30: Cure.

K17   To be dressed to Kill (*varied*)

1909 JCLincoln *Keziah* (NY) 11: He's dressed to kill. **1939** FGerard *Red Rope* (NY) 172: When she was got up to kill. **1941** ELFetta *Dressed to Kill* (NY). **1958** AWUpfield *Bachelors* (L) 94: There was one all dolled up to kill. **1970** CEWerkley *Mister* (NY) 137: She was all dressed up to kill. TW 208(1); Brunvand 80(1).

K18   Out of Kilter

1948 RFoley *No Tears* (NY DBC) 131: Everything has gone out of kilter with the world. **1962** EFRussell *Great* (NY) 119: Something is badly out of kilter. **1970** MGEberhard *El Rancho* (NY DBC) 66: Something out of kilter. **1972** MKaye *Lively* (NY) 5: Something had to be out of kilter. Amer. Herit. Dict. Kilter; NED Kelter 2.

K19   To kill with Kindness

1936 TAPlummer *Dumb* (NY) 184: He killed off the first with kindness—I don't think! **1940** AMcRoyd *Death in Costume* (NY) 135: If those people just don't kill me with kindness. **1948** ELipsky *Murder One* (NY) 116: He'll kill you with kindness. **1951** MCHarriman *Vicious* (NY) 61: We tried to kill it with kindness. **1957** DJEnright *Heaven* (L) 268: No need to kill ourselves with kindness. **1961** VWBrooks *From the Shadow* (NY) 133: I might be killed by so much kindness. **1966** ELinington *Date* (NY) 182: She's killing it with kindness. **1972** HTeichmann *Kaufman* (NY) 71: "I'll kill myself at eighty." . . . "How?" . . . "With kindness." **1974** AMorice *Killing with Kindness* (NY). EAP K17; Brunvand 80.

K20   As dead as King Tut

1954 JRMacdonald *Find* (NY) 60: This place is as dead as King Tut. Cf. Pharoah *below*.

K21   As happy as a King

1928 JRhode *Murders* (NY) 7: "As happy as a king" was to him no mere catch-word. **1932** AGask *Murder* (NY) 80: As happy as a king. **1937** RVercel *Lena* (NY) 74: As happy as a king. **1945** AChristie *Remembered* (NY) 65: We'll be as happy as kings. **1950** ECRLorac *Accident* (NY DBC) 6: We were as happy as kings. **1957** PGWodehouse *Butler* (NY) 44: We should all be as happy as kings. **1961** LWoolf *Growing* (L) 48: As happy as a king. **1964** TDubois *Shannon* (NY DBC) 137: He's happy as a king. EAP K18.

K22   A King can do no wrong

1928 AECoppard *Silver* (L) 216: A king can do no wrong. **1942** CHare *Tragedy at Law* (L 1953) 44: The King can do no wrong. *Oxford* 425.

K23   A King's chaff is better than other men's corn

1957 *TLS* 9/13 552: A king's chaff is proverbially better than other men's corn. *Oxford* 427.

K24   The King's (Queen's) English

1926 LBrock *Colonel Gore* (NY) 230: Spoke the King's English. **1937** NBerrow *One Thrilling* (L) 66: The King's English. **1961** CBlackstone *House* (L 1965) 112: Talk the Queen's English. **1961** FLockridge *Drill* (P) 140: Talks the King's English. **1966** JRoffman *Ashes* (NY) 54: Couldn't speak the Queen's English. **1973** AGilbert *Nice* (NY) 4: The Queen's English. Cf. EAP K28.

K25   The **King** is dead, long live the king

1935 DHume *Call in* (L) 114: She acted on the time-honoured phrase: "The king is dead, long live the king." **1960** NFitzgerald *Candles* (L) 113: The king is dead, long live the king! *Oxford* 426.

K26   The **King** of France with forty thousand men *etc.*

1975 ABrodsky *Madame* (NY) 54: Like the proverbial Duke of York, who marched his troops up the hill and then back down again. EAP K22.

K27   A **King's** ransom

1927 FLPackard *Two* (NY) 314: Worth a king's ransom. **1933** RAFreeman *Dr. Thorndyke Intervenes* (L) 76: It must have been worth a king's ransom. **1938** HFootner *Murder* (L) 223: None would have gone . . . for a king's ransom. **1940** JBentley *Mr. Marlow Stops* (B) 10: I wouldn't have him back for a king's ransom. **1964** GJenkins *River* (NY) 25: A king's ransom in diamonds. Whiting K47.

K28   To call the **King** one's cousin

1952 JTey *Singing* (NY 1960) 191: As they say in the far North, I wouldn't call the King my cousin. *Oxford* 99: Call the king.

K29   To live (eat) like a **King**

1930 GBMeans *Strange Death* (NY) 207: I live like a king. **1950** LKaufman *Jubel's* (NY) 283: He'll live like a king. **1957** *BHerald* 4/19 1: I lived like a king. **1963** UCurtiss *Wasp* (NY DBC) 34: They live like kings. **1964** WTrevor *Old Boys* (NY) 81: We eat like kings. **1970** RRendell *Best Man* (NY) 84: [He] had been living like a king. EAP K30.

K30   The two **Kings** of Brentford

1935 CFSchomberg *Between the Oxus* (L) 19: Two kings of Brentford create a situation intolerable to both. EAP K32.

K31   **King Charles's** head (*varied*)

1918 JBCabell *Letters* ed PColum (NY 1962) 84: A veritable King Charles's head. **1932** NBell *Disturbing* (NY) 38: Dear old King Charles Ellis his head! **1939** LBrock *Fourfingers* (L) 72: His King Charles' head was forgotten. **1949** RFoley *Girl* (NY) 140: Aldrich is my King Charles's head. **1956** AWilson *Anglo-Saxon* (L) 132: It was becoming a King Charles's head. **1957** VWheatley *H.Martineau* (Fair Lawn, NJ) 183: Slavery was her King Charles's head. **1959** *TLS* 7/17 424: Isis and Osiris are his King Charles's heads. **1965** RFoley *Suffer* (NY DBC) 69: There you have my sister's King Charles' head. **1970** RBernard *Deadly* (NY) 143: It was her King Charles's head. **1980** JGielgud *An Actor* (NY) 137: He [*Lord Alfred Douglas*] started on Wilde almost before I got through the door—Wilde was obviously his King Charles's head. *Oxford* 425.

K32   In the **Kingdom** of the blind *etc.* (*varied*)

1953 IAsimov *Second* (NY) 65: The seeing man in the kingdom of the blind. **1954** VWBrooks *Scenes* (NY) 82: He was the one-eyed man in the country of the blind. **1958** ECooper *Tomorrow's* (NY) 11: In the country of the blind, the one-eyed man is merely a psychotic. **1959** RMStern *Bright* (NY) 13: In the land of the blind . . . the one-eyed man is king. **1961** BWAldiss *Hothouse* (L) 92: In the country of the blind the one-eyed man is king. **1962** HMirrlees *Fly* (L) 102: Cotton was the one-eyed man who rules in the kingdom of the blind. **1966** DMarlowe *Dandy* (NY) 11: In the country of the blind, the one-eyed man is probably in a circus. **1974** JLHess *Grand* (B) 25: In this kingdom of the blind . . . the one-eyed man is king. EAP K33; TW 209.

K33   **Kingdom** come

1930 LTracy *Manning* (NY) 51: Send to kingdom come. **1930** AGilbert *Mystery* (NY) 273: We may wait for kingdom come. **1932** BABotkin ed *Land Is Ours* (Norman, Okla.) 267: Knock my plans all to kingdom come. **1946** KMKnight *Trouble* (NY) 217: Knocking Tad's alibi clean into kingdom come. **1968** JRoffman *Grave* (NY) 9: She could have gone on counting his sins till kingdome come. TW 209.

K34   To **Kiss** and make up (be friends)

1930 HAshbrook *Murder* (NY) 91: Kiss and make up. **1932** HCBailey *Case* (NY) 287:

Kiss and be friends. **1953** TWicker *Kingpin* (NY) 78: Why don't you kiss and make up. **1956** PWentworth *Fingerprints* (NY) 15: Kiss and be friends e'er night descends. **1958** CLBlackstone (NY) 166: We'll kiss and make up. **1965** DMDisney *Shadow* (NY) 144: Shall we kiss and make up? **1970** RDAltick *Victorian* (NY) 45: The couple kissed and made up. *Oxford* 429: Kiss and be friends.

K35 To **Kiss** and tell (*varied*)

1934 KWhipple *Killings* (NY) 175: A girl who kissed and told. **1936** DWheatley *They Found* (P) 252: The tradition that one might kiss a lot—but never tell! **1941** TFuller *Three Thirds* (B) 37: Old kiss-and-tell Jones. **1952** HCecil *No Bail* (NY) 63: Never kiss and tell or anything else. **1961** RLockridge *With One* (P) 102: Kissing and telling. **1966** EVCunningham *Helen* (NY) 86: The day of gentlemen who kiss and don't tell has gone away. **1970** SGraham *Garden* (NY) 149: [He] was a kiss and tell man. **1973** HPentecost *Beautiful* (NY) 73: I don't like to kiss and tell. EAP K35.

K36 Half-past **Kissing** time *etc.*

1922 JJoyce *Ulysses* (NY 1934) 354: It was half past kissing time, time to kiss again. **1946** ECrispin *Moving* (L 1970) 92: Half-past kissing time . . . time to kiss again. Partridge 457.

K37 **Kissing** goes by favor

1929 LThayer *Dead Men's* (NY) 3: Kissing goes by favour all along the line. EAP K36.

K38 The whole **Kit** and kaboodle (boodle)

1913 TDreiser *Traveler* (NY 1923) 376: The whole "kit and kaboodle." **1930** KCStrahan *Death* (NY) 135: The whole kit and kaboodle of us. **1931** EQueen *Dutch* (NY) 11: The whole kit and boodle of 'em. **1934** RJBlack *Killing* (NY) 24: She's the worst of the whole kit and boiling. **1941** TDuBois *McNeills Chase* (NY) 277: They all lied, the whole kit and boodle of them. **1943** PATaylor *Going* (NY) 17: She buys the whole kit and caboodle. **1945** HLawrence *Time to Die* (NY) 126: The whole kit and boodle. **1952** KMKnight *Valse* (NY) 88: The only thing in the whole kit and boodle

that I didn't go through with a fine-tooth comb. **1955** JO'Hara *Ten* (NY) 289: The whole kit and kaboodle. **1959** MPHood *Bell* (NY) 157: The kit 'n caboodle of you. **1961** BJames *Night* (NY DBC) 40: Here's the whole kit and caboodle. **1963** NBenchley *Catch* (NY) 102: The whole kit and kaboodle. **1972** BLillie *Every* (NY) 326: We took the whole kit and caboodle. TW 209; DARE i 501: Caboodle. Cf. Brunvand 80.

K39 As high (mad) as a **Kite** (lark) (*varied*)

1930 ATrain *Adventures* (NY) 490: Smash that law higher than a kite. **1935** LFord *Burn* (NY) 250: You'll hang higher than a kite. **1937** JDCarr *Burning* (NY) 279: Your alibi . . . is blown higher than a kite. **1937** LFord *Ill Met* (NY) 169: She was high as a kite [*drunk*]. **1939** MMGoldsmith *Detour* (L) 56: The bastard must be high as a kite on that weed. **1947** RDavies *Diary* (Toronto) 49: She was as high as a kite [*drunk*]. **1949** EQueen *Cat* (B) 136: I'm higher than the much-abused kite [*excited*]. **1956** HCahill *Shadow* (NY) 91: They'd run up the price. Higher'n a kite. **1957** BHerald 2/3 46: They carted me to the hospital higher than a kite [*insane*]. **1957** *New Yorker* 9/7 35: He would go higher than a kite [*angry*]. **1958** MCair *Burning* (NY) 75: He's higher than a kite [*drugs*]. **1959** WMiller *Cool* (B) 111: He's high as a kite on the junk. **1961** RAHeinlein *6XH* (NY) 129: The bastard had me higher'n a kite [*pregnant*]. **1964** JBPriestley *Sir Michael* (L) 95: Floating as high as a kite [*drunk*]. **1966** ACarter *Honeybuzzard* (NY) 117: High . . . higher than larks [*drugs or drink*]. **1967** MDolbier *Benjy* (NY) 258: Drunk as a lord and mad as a kite. **1968** MAllingham *Cargo* (NY) 20: As high as kites . . . full of pep pills or worse. **1970** ADean *Dower* (NY) 77: He was higher than a kite [*drugs*]. **1970** RFoley *Calculated* (NY) 155: I'd have been high as a kite [*drunk*]. TW 209(1); Brunvand 80. Cf. Rocket *below*.

K40 Go fly a **Kite**

1941 HAshbrook *Purple Onion* (NY) 176: She told me to go fly a kite. **1949** AAFair *Bedrooms* (NY 1958) 48: Go fly a kite. **1958** *Time* 4/28 4: Tell Reuther to go fly his socialistic kite. **1959** HCarmichael *Marked*

(NY) 131: Tell her boy friend to go fly a kite. **1974** RLockridge *Death* (NY) 26: It told the FBI to go fly a kite. Wentworth 194.

K41   Neither **Kith** nor kin

1933 JSFletcher *Who Killed* (L) 141: He hadn't neither kith nor kin, as the saying is. Brunvand 81; Tilley K117.

K42   As docile as a **Kitten**

1965 AAFair *Cut Thin* (NY DBC) 87: I'm docile as a kitten. TW 209(1).

K43   As friendly as a **Kitten**

1922 VBridges *Greensea* (NY) 103: As friendly as a kitten. **1953** CBKelland *Sinister* (NY DBC) 59: As friendly as a kitten. **1961** RLockridge *With One* (P) 185: Friendly as a kitten.

K44   As gentle (peaceful) as a **Kitten**

1936 JLatimer *Lady* (NY) 175: He's gentle as a kitten. **1961** MHHood *Drown* (NY) 134: Peaceful as a kitten. **1969** JBlackburn *Children* (NY) 52: Gentle as a kitten he is. TW 209(3); Brunvand 81(2).

K45   As happy as a **Kitten**

1968 RMStern *Merry* (NY) 74: Happy as a kitten. Cf. Wilstach 192: As a pussy.

K46   As helpless as a **Kitten**

1913 ERBurroughs *Warlord* (NY 1963) 54: As helpless as a kitten. **1937** AGilbert *Murder* (L) 250: More helpless than a kitten.

K47   As innocent as a **Kitten**

1938 PWentworth *Run!* (L) 45: She looked up at him as innocent as a kitten. **1964** EPangborn *Davy* (NY) 236: She looked innocent as a kitten. TW 209(5).

K48   As kind as a **Kitten**

1931 LSteffens *Autobiography* (NY) 1.86: She is kind as a kitten. TW 209(6).

K49   As playful as a **Kitten**

1972 SBrooke *Queen* (NY) 80: As playful as kittens. EAP K41.

K50   As pleased as a **Kitten**

1930 AAllen *Menace* (NY) 100: Pleased as a kitten. **1940** AGaines *While the Wind* (NY) 97: He seemed pleased as a kitten.

K51   As quiet as a **Kitten**

1957 RGibbings *Till I* (NY) 117: Quiet as a kitten. TW 209(8). Cf. As quiet as a Cat *above*.

K52   As soft as a **Kitten**

1935 JJConnington *In Whose* (L) 63: As soft as a kitten. Taylor *Prov. Comp.* 76: Soft.

K53   As spry (frisky) as a **Kitten**

1926 CWTyler *Blue Jean* (NY) 140: Spry as a kitten. **1967** MWilkins *Last* (Englewood, NJ) 125: The horses were frisky as kittens. TW 210(10). Cf. As spry as a Cat *above*.

K54   As weak as a **Kitten**

1913 EStVMillay *Letters* ed RMacdougall (NY 1952) 45: Weak as a kitten. **1932** LCharteris *White* (NY) 261: He did feel as weak as a kitten. **1934** MKing-Hall *Gay* (NY) 65: As weak as kittens. **1940** HBest *Twenty-fifth* (NY) 159: Weak as a kitten. **1952** KMKnight *Death Goes* (NY) 113: I'm as weak as a kitten. **1957** BWolfe *Limbo* (L) 157: Weak as a kitten. **1960** FSWees *Country* (NY) 91: As weak as a day-old kitten. **1967** RGarrett *Too Many* (NY) 188: I feel weak as a kitten. TW 210(12). Cf. As weak as a Cat *above*.

K55   **Kittens** will be cats

1932 HCBailey *Mr. Fortune, Please* (NY) 210: But kittens will be cats. TW 210(18).

K56   To have **Kittens** (*varied*)

1933 NBMavity *Fate* (NY) 2: Jimmy will have kittens if I don't. **1939** EDean *Murder Is* (NY) 209: Oscar is having a couple of kittens. **1949** GHHall *End* (NY) 17: She'll have kittens. **1952** KMKnight *Valse* (NY) 122: She was probably having kittens by now, with all that going on. **1957** CASmart *At Home* (NY) 21: Arnold was having kittens of his own [*nervous*]. **1962** ESGardner *Reluctant* (NY DBC) 90: Drake has been having kittens. **1962** NMarsh *Hand* (B) 122: Don't have kittens before they're hatched.

1969 RHarris *Wicked* (NY) 124: Janey came in having kittens. **1972** DDevine *Three* (NY) 101: She looked like she was going to have kittens. **1974** NWebster *Burial* (NY) 122: He's probably having kittens by now. Wentworth 307.

K57 On the **Knees** (in the lap) of the gods

1931 ABCox *Second* (NY) 180: That's on the knees of the gods. **1933** EPhillpotts *Captain's* (NY) 116: That's all on the knees of the gods, as they say. **1935** MGEberhart *House* (L) 201: It's on the lap of the gods. **1940** DHume *Invitation* (L) 129: Whatever happens afterwards lies in the proverbial lap of the powers that be. **1959** HCarmichael *Marked* (NY) 60: Your fate will be in the lap of the gods. **1966** JAiken *Beware* (NY) 98: Our beautiful campaign is hanging on the knees of the gods along with the sword of thingummy. *Oxford* 432.

K58 Since one was **Knee-high** to a this or that (*varied*)

1910 JCLincoln *Depot Master* (NY) 293: Ever since I was knee high to a kitchen chair. **1913** JCLincoln *Mr. Pratt's Patients* (NY) 2: Since I was knee-high to a horseshoe crab. **1924** TMundy *Om* (NY) 17: Before he was knee-high to a duck. **1927** CRogers *Colonel Bob* (NY) 29: Since she was knee-high to a grasshopper. **1930** JRussell *Cops* (NY) 169: When he was knee-high to a pup. **1938** HHolt *Wanted* (L) 121: Since she was knee-high to a grasshopper. **1947** GGallagher *I Found* (NY DBC) 40: You was no bigger than knee-high to a mosquito at the time. **1950** DAWollheim *Flight* (NY) 148: Since I was knee-high to a grasshopper. **1953** MPHood *Silent* (NY) 138: Since she was knee-high to a June bug. **1953** AUllman *Naked* (NY) 111: Since I was knee-high to spit. **1955** AHunter *Gently Does* (L) 92: When he was knee-high to a tin of paint. **1956** MPHood *Scarlet* (NY) 23: Since he was knee-high to a cricket. **1957** WHHarris *Golden* (NY) 173: Since I was knee-high to a duck. **1959** TRoscoe *Only* (NY) 46: When he was "knee-high to a nipper." **1961** MHHood *Drown* (NY) 182: Since I was knee-high to a bullfrog. **1972**

BLillie *Every* (NY) 11: I was a *petite* child, knee-high to a teacup. **1982** CMacLeod *Wrack* (NY) 165: When I was 'bout knee-high to a grasshopper. EAP K44; TW 210; Brunvand 81: Grasshopper; Wentworth 307.

K59 As easy as **Knife**

1931 RKeverne *Fleet* (NY) 236: Easy as knife. **1935** ECRLorac *Murder* (L) 125: Easy as knife.

K60 As keen as a **Knife**

1930 FRyerson *Seven* (L) 285: A wind as keen as a knife. **1937** NMorland *Clue* (L) 138: That girl's keener than a new knife. **1956** NMarsh *Death* (B) 194: As keen as a knife . . . A fanatic, in fact. TW 210.

K61 As sharp as a **Knife**

1913 JCLincoln *Mr. Pratt's Patients* (NY) 125: She was as sharp as a fish knife, that girl. **1931** RInce *When Joan* (L) 40: Her tongue was sharp as a knife. **1968** EWilliams *Beyond* (NY) 327: Says Myra, sharp as a knife. Whiting *NC* 433(1).

K62 Before one can say **Knife**

1903 EChilders *Riddle* (NY 1940) 76: Before you could say knife. **1922** MRJames *Letters* ed GMcBryde (L 1956) 119: Before you could say knife; 191 (1933). **1922** JJoyce *Ulysses* (NY 1934) 158: Toss off a glass of brandy neat while you'd say knife. **1933** RAFreeman *Dr. Thorndyke Intervenes* (L) 312: Before we can say "knife." **1938** NBerrow *Terror* (L) 92: Before you could say "knife." **1943** WLewis *Letters* ed WKRose (L 1963) 369: Before I could say knife. **1948** ECrispin *Buried* (L 1958) 14: Before you could say "knife." **1957** MSharp *Eye* (L) 12: Before you could say knife. **1959** CHassall *E.Marsh* (L) 536: Before you could say knife, let alone Jack Robinson. **1964** AHunter *Gently* (NY) 31: Before you could say "knife." **1970** JPorter *Dover Strikes* (NY) 62: Before you can say knife. **1973** AGilbert *Nice* (NY) 68: Before you can say knife. Partridge 459.

K63 To be on to something like (a) **Knife** (*varied*)

1930 AChristie *Murder* (NY) 88: [She] would have been on to it like a knife. **1935** FBeeding *Death* (NY) 90: The police were on to me like a knife. **1938** ECRLorac *Devil* (L) 46: I turned round like knife! **1951** PCheyney *Ladies* (NY DBC) 16: Olly would be on that like a knife.

K64 To go like a **Knife** through hot butter

1930 CBush *Dead Man* (NY) 9: Went through like a knife through hot butter. **1955** IFleming *Moonraker* (NY 1960) 147: We ran through France like a knife through butter. **1960** JWelcome *Stop* (NY) 71: [They] were going in like the proverbial hot knife through butter. Cf. *Oxford* 432. Cf. As easy as cutting Butter *above*.

K65 To have one's **Knife** into someone

1919 JSFletcher *Middle Temple* (NY) 226: Now's the time to have my knife into you. **1930** JSFletcher *South Foreland* (NY) 190: He's going to have his knife into somebody—to use a vulgar expression. **1936** LBrock *Stoat* (L) 140: They've got their knife into him. **1940** NMarsh *Death of a Peer* (B) 311: She's got her knife into Miss Tinkerton. **1941** GDHCole *Counterpoint* (NY) 32: He had his knife into Pelley. **1953** ECRLorac *Shepherd's* (NY) 111: She's got her knife into Jock. **1956** MProcter *Ripper* (NY) 193: If that young woman gets her knife into her . . . that's only a figure of speech. **1962** EGrierson *Massingham* (L) 213: You had your knife into the police. **1968** ELathen *Stitch* (NY) 126: She's had her knife into us. *Oxford* 432.

K66 To ride a **Knife** to the mill

1960 VWilliams *Walk* (NY) 92: A knife so dull my youngest boy could ride it to the mill and never scratch his britches. Whiting *NC* 444: Mill(1); *Oxford* 676: Ride to Rumford.

K67 To tend (*etc.*) to one's own **Knitting**

1935 PATaylor *Deathblow* (NY) 165: Stick to your knittin'. **1935** ESGardner *Counterfeit Eye* (NY) 141: You tend to your knitting and I'll tend to mine. **1937** LTWhite *Homicide* (NY) 54: I guessed I'd better tend my

own knitting. **1941** ESGardner *Empty Tin* (NY 1958) 126: Let's get back to our knitting. **1950** FO'Malley *Best* (NY) 5: Tend to your knitting. **1958** FDuncombe *Death* (NY) 67: Mind my own knitting. **1959** *BHerald* 8/27 19: The old saying of "tend to your own knitting." Berrey 245.15.

K68 As thin as a **Knitting needle**

1968 JAiken *Crystal* (NY) 141: He was thin as a knitting needle. Cf. Needle-thin *below*.

K69 As dry as the **Knobs** of hell

1937 MSandoz *Slogum* (B) 46: The Oxbow was dry as the knobs of hell. Cf. Hinges, Hobs *above*.

K70 Every **Knock** is a boost

1935 JHWallis *Politician* (NY) 217: Every knock was a boost. **1956** *BangorDN* 9/12 18: There is an old sports saying that "every knock is a boost." **1958** *BHerald* 3/23 sec. IV 16: Every knock is as good as a boost—another old saying has it. TW 207: Kick(1).

K71 As tough as a **Knot**

1946 VKelsey *Whisper Murder* (NY) 250: She was tough as a knot. EAP K51.

K72 Rather be a **Knot** in a log *etc.* (*varied*)

1957 *Time* 4/8 19: "I would rather be a lamppost on Seattle's Second Avenue" [*Dave Beck*] likes to say, "than own all of Miami Beach." **1969** APHannum *Look* (NY) 204: The heartfelt utterance of a returned mountain man who fervently declared, "I'd ruther be a knot on a log up hyur than the mayor of the city down yonder." Whiting *NC* 435: Laurel.

K73 To seek **Knots** in bulrushes

1958 LSdeCamp *Elephant* (NY) 43: You exhaust yourself seeking knots in bulrushes. *Oxford* 433.

K74 To look as if one had been pulled through a **Knot-hole** (*varied*)

1919 AMerritt *Moon Pool* (NY) 383: I feel as though I've been pulled through a knothole. **1934** HFootner *Murder* (NY) 11: You look as if you was drawed through a knothole. **1935** MGEberhart *House* (L) 166: I feel as if I'd been dragged through a knothole backward. **1936** CMRussell *Death* (NY)

299: You look like you'd been pulled through a rat hole. **1939** CSaxby *Death Cuts* (NY) 244: You look like you've been through six knot-holes. **1947** VWMason *Saigon* (NY) 287: He sure looked like he'd been drawn through a knothole feet-first. **1953** CMRussell *Market* (NY) 137: You look like you've been drawn through a knothole. **1957** VWMason *Gracious* (NY) 100: You look as if you'd been pulled through a knothole backwards. **1968** EBuckler *Ox Bells* (NY) 129: He looks as if he'd been pulled through a knothole and beat with a sutt bag. TW 211(3); Taylor *Prov. Comp.* 53. Cf. Bush *above*.

K75 **Know** me, come eat with me (*varied*)

1922 JJoyce *Ulysses* (NY 1934) 172: Know me, come eat with me. **1928** JSFletcher *Black House* (NY) 246: That good old English saying that you have got to live with people before you really know them. Whiting *NC* 442(33): To know a man. Cf. Winter *below*.

K76 **Know** thyself (*varied*)

1913 JCLincoln *Mr. Pratt's Patients* (NY) 94: Man, Know Thyself. **1957** GTrease *Snared* (L) 12: The Greek motto, *Know thyself*. **1965** JSUntermeyer *Private* (NY) 20: "Know thyself" is an ancient adage. **1966** NDevas *Two Flamboyant* (L) 231: "Know thyself" the wise men say. **1968** HCarvic *Picture* (NY) 161: They say self-knowledge is the first step to wisdom. **1969** JBrunner *Jagged* (NY) 96: *Gnothi seauton . . .* it means "know thyself." **1971** EDahlberg *Confessions* (NY) 3: Know thyself is a wise Socratic exhortation. EAP K54.

K77 Not **Knowing**, can't say

1937 NBersow *One Thrilling* (L) 145: Not knowing, can't say. **1950** ERPunshon *So Many* (NY) 130: Not knowing, can't say. TW 211: Knowing(1).

K78 One never **Knows** (you never know)

1924 VLWhitechurch *Templeton* (NY) 229: One never knows. **1933** CBarry *Murder* (L) 64: You never know. **1937** MBeckett *Bullet* (L) 21: But you never know. **1942** HCBailey *Nobody's* (NY) 26: You never know, you know. **1949** MAllingham *More*

Work (NY) 31: But you never know, do you? **1954** HWade *Too Soon* (NY) 63: One never knows. **1959** JBEthan *Black Gold* (NY DBC) 16: But, like the man says, you never know. **1963** FArmitage *Five* (NY) 100: But one never knows. **1968** RBissell *How Many* (B) 35: Well, you never know. Cf. You never know your Luck, One never can Tell *below*.

K79 One never **Knows** what he can do until he tries (*varied*)

1928 WMcFee *Pilgrims* (NY) 86: You don't know what you can do until you try. **1931** LEppley *Murder* (NY) 162: One never knows till he tries. **1938** CWitting *Michaelmas Goose* (L) 257: You never know what you can do till you try. **1959** PGraaf *Sapphire* (NY) 193: You never know till you try. **1971** RLockridge *Death* (P) 27: But we never know till we try, do we? **1974** SForbes *Some* (NY) 44: I figure you don't know if you don't try, you can't win all the time. **1981** JRoss *Dark* (NY) 60: One of Roger's maxims . . . was "you never know until you ask." *Oxford* 436.

K80 That's for me to **Know** and for you to find out

1943 EWTeale *Dune Boy* (NY 1957) 51: That's fer me t' know a' fer y' t' find out. **1956** EMcBain *Cop* (NY 1959) 75: That's for me to know and you to find out.

K81 To **Know** enough to go in when it rains (*varied*)

1921 JCLincoln *Galusha* (NY) 396: He knew enough to go in when it rained. **1928** RHFuller *Jubilee* (NY) 502: Democrats who had sense enough to get in out of the wet. **1929** LBrock *Stoke Silver* (NY) 107: When it rains . . . the wise child goes in out of it. **1930** EWallace *White Face* (NY) 88: You know enough to come in out of the rain. **1935** WIrwin *Julius* (NY) 122: She never did know enough to come in when it rains. **1935** RCWoodthorpe *Shadow* (NY) 246: The Americans have a proverb. "He's too big a fool to come in out of the rain." **1943** EWTeale *Dune Boy* (NY 1957) 124: People who didn't know enough to come in out of the rain. **1952** CDickson *Cavalier's* (NY) 9:

Just sense enough to come in out of the rain. **1958** *BHerald* 7/23 30: I do know enough to come in out of the rain. **1962** DMDisney *Find* (NY DBC) 85: An old fool that doesn't know enough to come in out of the rain. **1970** ADean *Dower* (NY) 106: They don't know when to come in outta the rain. **1973** JFleming *Alas* (NY) 135: Joshua knew when to come in out of the wet. **1975** HLawrenson *Stranger* (NY) 18: His mother treated him as if he didn't know enough to come in out of the rain. EAP K55; TW 211(2).

K82 What one doesn't **Know** won't hurt him (*varied*)

1908 JCLincoln *Cy Whittaker* (NY) 118: What they don't know won't hurt 'em. **1913** EDBiggers *Seven Keys* (I) 142: What you don't know won't hurt you. **1929** FLPackard *Big Shot* (NY) 282: Wot youse don't know won't hurt youse. **1931** WFaulkner *Sanctuary* (NY) 245: What they don't know caint hurt them. **1936** SWilliams *Aconite* (NY) 219: There's an American saying: "What you don't know won't hurt you any." **1937** GGoodwin *White Farm* (L) 260: What inna know inna wept over. **1940** RStout *Where There's* (NY) 215: What he don't know won't hurt him. **1941** CRice *Trial by Fury* (NY 1957) 122: What I don't know won't hurt you. **1951** JO'Hara *Farmer's* (NY) 133: The old saying, what I don't know won't hurt me. **1953** KMKnight *Akin* (NY) 38: According to the old saying, what she didn't know wouldn't worry her. **1958** *New Yorker* 8/30 31: What she don't know won't hurt her. **1961** RSPrather *Dig That* (NY) 137: Who was it said the things we don't know can't hurt us? **1964** DDeJong *Whirligig* (NY) 144: What Miss Sadie didn't know wouldn't bother her. **1964** HPentecost *Shape* (NY DBC) 46: As the old lady said, what you don't know can't hurt you. **1971** PTabor *Pauline's* (Louisville) 143:

There's a lot of common-sense in the old female adage: "What a man doesn't know won't hurt him." **1975** DEWestlake *Two* (NY) 10: What Ralph didn't know couldn't hurt me. Bradley 81.

K83 All **Knowledge** is useful

1960 JBall *Fall* (NY) 60: All knowledge is ultimately useful. Cf. *Oxford* 436: Knowledge is no burthen.

K84 **Knowledge** is power (*varied*)

1919 LMerrick *Chain* (L) 336: Knowledge is power. **1925** RAFreeman *Red Thumb* (L) 119: Knowledge, as the late Lord Bacon remarked with more truth than originality, is power. **1935** AChristie *Death* (L) 100: Knowledge is power. **1948** JErskine *My Life* (P) 221: Knowledge is power. **1950** AWUpfield *Widows* (NY) 192: Knowledge would bring power. **1956** *TLS* 7/13 425: Knowledge is power. **1962** ESGardner *Blonde* (NY DBC) 122: Knowledge is power. **1963** AA Fair *Fish* (NY DBC) 68: Knowledge is power. **1973** CAird *His Burial* (NY) 9: They said that knowledge was strength. **1976** SWoods *My Life* (NY) 191: They say knowledge gives a man power. EAP K56.

K85 To go (too) near the **Knuckle** (*varied*)

1930 WSMaugham *Cakes* (L 1948) 113: She goes pretty near the knuckle sometimes. **1931** HHolt *Necklace* (NY) 216: That was altogether too close to the knuckle. **1937** VLoder *Choose* (L) 132: It was too far off the knuckle to matter. **1954** JSymons *Narrowing* (NY) 15: Isn't some of this stuff going to be a bit near the knuckle? I mean, you mentioned Heath, who was the most vicious sort of sadist. **1958** PGWodehouse *Cocktail* (L) 44: It's a bit near the knuckle [*apt to hurt*]. **1961** RGorden *Doctor* (NY) 81: He started getting a bit near the knuckle for the ladies [*indelicate*]. **1962** AWaugh *Early* (L) 149: If an author was inclined to "go near the knuckle" [*off-color*]. Partridge 463. Cf. To be close to the Bone *above*.

L

L1 A **Labor** of love

1929 JJConnington *Grim* (B) 111: A labour of love. **1947** PMcGerr *Pick* (NY) 81: Hers was a labor of love. **1955** JCreasey *Murder* (NY DBC) 30: Here was a labor of love. **1960** MSpark *Bachelors* (L) 131: It's a labor of love. **1964** WBlunt *Cockerell* (L) 187: A labour of love. **1970** DShannon *Unexpected* (NY) 136: A labor of love. **1973** GSheehy *Hustling* (NY) 257: She thought of it as a labor of love. EAP L1.

L2 *Labor* omnia vincit

1970 OFriedrich *Decline* (NY) 361: *Labor omnia vincit. Oxford* 438: Labour overcomes. Cf. Love conquers all *below*.

L3 To have one's **Labor** (trouble) for his pains

1930 BReynolds *Stranglehold* (NY) 220: Let 'em have their trouble for their pains. **1941** HReilly *Three Women* (NY) 20: You'll have your trouble for your pains. **1956** MPHood *Scarlet* (NY) 53: You've had your labor for your pains. EAP L2.

L4 To have one's **Labor** in vain

1923 HWNevinson *Changes* (NY) 123: My labour had not been in vain. **1925** TRMarshall *Recollections* (I) 201: Your labor is in vain. **1933** MBurton *Fate* (L) 236: His labors were not in vain. **1956** *Punch* 7/11 33: Our labour will all have been in vain. **1970** JLeasor *They Don't* (NY) 8: Everything else is labour in vain. EAP L3.

L5 The **Laborer** is worthy of his hire

1920 AChristie *Mysterious Affair* (NY) 15: The labourer is worthy of his hire. **1924** TMundy *Om* (NY) 284: That Christian adage, that the laborer is worthy of his hire. **1934** FBeeding *One Sane* (B) 168: The labourer is worthy of his hire. **1937** GDilnot *Murder* (L) 203: The labourer is worthy of his hire. **1940** JJConnington *Four Defences* (B) 26: Thou shalt not muzzle the labourer who is worthy of his hire. The Bible says that, or something like it. **1950** OAnderson *In for* (NY) 145: The labourer is worthy of his hire. **1959** AGilbert *Prelude* (NY DBC) 9: The laborer is worthy of his hire. **1960** MSpark *Bachelors* (L) 29: No laborer who was worthy of his hire could be found. **1965** AHeckstall-Smith *Consort* (NY) 135: The laborer is not proving worthy of his hire. **1971** ELinington *Practice* (NY) 204: The laborer worthy of his hire. **1975** RStout *Family* (NY) 71: "But as somebody said, a man is worth his hire." "The laborer is worthy of his hire. The Bible. Luke." EAP L5; TW 212.

L6 **Ladies** first

1930 JJFarjeon *Following* (NY) 268: But ladies first, as the saying is. **1932** GLane *Hotel* (L) 231: You know the old saying, ladies first. **1932** THWhite *Darkness* (L) 273: Ladies first, if you'll excuse the proverb. **1945** EPhillpotts *They Were Seven* (NY) 203: Ladies come first.

L7 Go jump in the **Lake**

1936 CJKenny *This Is Murder* (L) 123: You can go jump in the lake. **1941** ESGardner

Turning Tide (NY) 77: Hazlitt can go jump in the lake. **1947** AAFair *Fools* (NY 1957) 26: Tell me to go jump in the lake. **1961** ESMadden *Craig's* (NY DBC) 63: He can go and jump in the lake for all I care. **1980** WODouglas *Court* (NY) 308: He [*Robert Kennedy*] told Rusk to go jump in the lake. Berrey 253.8.

L8   As docile as a Lamb

1904 JCLincoln *Cap'n Eri* (NY) 140: As docile as lambs. **1928** ESnell *Kontrol* (P) 117: The other was as docile as a lamb. EAP L7.

L9   As gentle as a Lamb

1906 JLondon *Letters* ed KHendricks (NY 1965) 219: As gentle as a lamb. **1922** VBridges *Greensea* (NY) 130: As gentle as a lamb. **1940** KSteel *Dead of Night* (B) 143: Gentle as a lamb. **1955** DMDisney *Room* (NY) 34: Gentle as a lamb. **1959** MMillar *Listening* (NY) 188: He's gentle as a lamb. EAP L8; TW 212(1).

L10   As happy as Lambs

1930 FIAnderson *Book* (NY) 146: We were as happy as lambs. Wilstach 193: Young lamb.

L11   As innocent as a Lamb

1924 TMundy *Om* (NY) 366: As innocent as lambs. **1930** TSmith *Topper* (NY) 262: Topper's as innocent as a lamb. **1933** CPenfield *After the Deacon* (NY) 161: Innocent as a new-born lamb. **1936** AGlanville *Death* (L) 75: Innocent as the proverbial lamb. **1945** CEVulliamy *Edwin* (L) 15: Innocent as a lamb unshorn. **1956** PMiller *Raven* (NY) 54: As innocent as lambs. **1964** HPentecost *Shape* (NY DBC) 133: He's as innocent as a lamb. **1971** RLockridge *Inspector's* (P) 179: Innocent as a lamb. TW 212–3(6); Brunvand 82(1).

L12   As meek as a Lamb

1928 CDane *Enter* (L) 16: Meek as lambs. **1940** ECameron *Malice* (NY) 186: He was meek as a lamb. **1950** DAWollheim *Flight* (NY) 41: Meek as a lamb. **1959** JBrunner *World* (NY) 133: Gone as meekly as lambs to the slaughter. **1961** CBeaton *Wandering* (L) 368: Meek as a lamb. **1966** ELinington

Date (NY) 31: Meek as little lambs. EAP L9; TW 213(7).

L13   As mild as a Lamb

1941 CWells *Murder . . . Casino* (P) 102: Talbot seemed as mild as a lamb. **1966** PGWodehouse *Plum* (L) 18: As mild as new-born lambs. EAP L10; TW 213(8).

L14   As peaceful as a Lamb

1919 LThayer *Mystery of the 13th Floor* (NY) 64: Peaceably as a lamb. **1928** PGWodehouse *Money* (NY) 227: As peaceful as a lamb. TW 213(9).

L15   As quiet as a Lamb

1905 JBCabell *Line* (NY 1926) 216: Quiet as a sucking lamb. **1920** GBMcCutcheon *Anderson Crow* (NY) 150: As quiet as a lamb. **1933** FDGrierson *Monkhurst* (L) 130: Quiet as a lamb. **1937** DLSayers *Busman's* (NY) 9: As quiet as a lamb. **1950** ECRLorac *Accident* (NY DBC) 75: He's as quiet as a lamb. **1959** PBoileau *Evil* (L) 106: Quiet as a lamb. **1968** JRoffman *Grave* (NY) 99: He stays as quiet as a lamb. EAP L13; Brunvand 82(3).

L16   As weak as a Lamb

1970 RPowell *Whom the Gods* (NY) 104: It makes me as weak as a new-born lamb. Wilstach 465: That can't stand etc. 466: The hour that it is yeaned.

L17   To go like a Lamb

1930 LCharteris *Enter* (NY) 128: He went like a lamb. Whiting L49 (quote c1390).

L18   To prefer Lamb to mutton

1972 WJBurley *Guilt* (NY) 91: Most men prefer lamb to mutton, if they can get it [*sex*]. Cf. Mutton *below.*

L19   To sleep like a Lamb

1913 JCLincoln *Mr. Pratt's Patients* (NY) 148: He was sleeping like a lamb. **1931** FBeeding *Death* (NY) 117: Sleeping like a lamb. **1933** CRobbins *Mystery* (NY) 109: Sleeping like a lamb; 202. **1940** TChanslor *Our First* (NY) 104: Sleeping like a lamb. **1951** MHead *Congo* (NY) 180: Sleeping like a lamb. **1961** DMDisney *Mrs. Meeker's* (NY) 47: Slept like lambs. TW 213(16).

L20   To take something like a **Lamb**

1967 RJones *Three* (B) 215: He took the remark from Mrs. Lewis like the proverbial lamb. EAP L15: Bear.

L21   To run like a **Lamplighter**

1944 CBrand *Green for Danger* (NY 1965) 70: She must have run like a lamp-lighter. Partridge 468. Cf. TW 213(1).

L22   As straight as a **Lance**

1954 ASeton *Katherine* (B) 568: You are still straight as a lance. Wilstach 392.

L23   From **Land's** End to John o' Groats *(varied)*

1919 JSFletcher *Middle Temple* (NY) 168: From Land's End to Berwick-upon-Tweed. **1923** JSFletcher *Lynne Court* (NY) 194: From Land's End to John o' Groats. **1928** JArnold *Surrey* (L) 107: From here to John o' Groats. **1930** EPOppenheim *Million* (B) 83: From John o' Groats to Land's End. **1935** GBarnett *Call-Box* (L) 147: She hasn't gone to Land's End or John o' Groat's. **1937** DWhitelaw *Face* (L) 94: From Land's End to John o' Groats. **1951** ECrispin *Long* (L 1958) 10: If you was to search from Land's End to John o' Groats. **1962** JCreasey *Death* (NY DBC) 47: Land's End to John o' Groats. **1964** RBlythe *Age* (NY) 90: Walked from Land's End to John o' Groats. **1965** AChristie *At Bertram's* (L) 103: He was at Land's End or John o' Groats. **1969** CBush *Deadly* (NY) 122: [He] might be anywhere by now. John o' Groats or Land's End. **1972** JRipley *Davis* (NY) 48: From Land's End to John o' Groats. **1980** MInnes *Going* (NY) 148: We can . . . be in at the kill, even if it's at Land's End or John o' Groats. EAP J45: John; *Oxford* 441.

L24   He that buys **Land** etc. *(varied)*

1933 RAFreeman *Dr. Thorndyke Intervenes* (L) 199: He that buys Land, buys Stones. He that buys meate buys bones. He that buys Eggs buys many Shelles. But he that buys good Beer buys Nothing Else. **1961** ESeeman *In the Arms* (NY) 38: When you buy meat, you buy plenty of bone. When you buy land, you buy plenty of stone. *Oxford* 96: Buys land.

L25   In the **Land** of the living

1927 JSFletcher *Lynne* (L) 188: In the land of the living. **1969** AGilbert *Missing* (NY) 130: In the land of the living. EAP L25.

L26   A **Land** flowing with milk and honey *(varied)*

1909 JCLincoln *Keziah* (NY) 326: An Eveless Eden flowing with milk and honey. **1927** FWCrofts *Starvel* (NY) 215: It was never a land flowing with milk and honey. **1930** The Aresbys *Murder* (NY) 95: A land of milk and honey. **1930** FRyerson *Seven* (L) 18: These here milk-and-honey preachers. **1937** HCBailey *Clunk's* (L) 26: A voice of milk and honey. **1945** CDickson *Curse* (NY) 115: He became all milk and honey. **1951** ACalder-Marshall *Magic* (L) 167: The land flowing with milk and honey. **1955** EJKahn *Merry* (NY) 63: A land flowing with milk, honey, gold, ravioli, and other lures. **1956** JDunbar *Golden* (B) 185: That land awash with milk and honey. **1957** *New Yorker* 1/19 26: The proverbial "Land of Milk and Honey." **1961** BAldiss *Primal* (NY) 20: His manner flowed with milk and honey. **1963** AHBroderick *Abbe* (L) 217: A Sahara flowing with milk and honey. **1964** PBecker *Rule* (L) 152: A land flowing with the proverbial milk and honey. **1965** VPurcell *Memoirs* (L) 40: Devonshire was a land flowing with milk and honey. **1969** CIrving *Fake* (NY) 91: The land of milk and honey, the United States. **1974** JFlaherty *Chez* (NY) 225: Westchester . . . was hardly the land of milk and honey. EAP L21. Cf. Brunvand 94: Milk(6).

L27   The **Land** of Nod

1930 SHorler *Curse* (NY) 61: In the land of Nod. **1936** BFlynn *Horn* (L) 218: In the land of Nod. **1940** EBenjamin *Murder Without* (NY) 235: I'm off to the land of Nod. **1965** HActon *Old Lamps* (L) 195: I'll leave him in the Land of Nod. **1968** EWilliams *Beyond* (NY) 268: Gran is in the Land o' Nod. **1974** EPHoyt *Horatio's* (Radnor, Penn.) 146: Carrie was in the Land of Nod. EAP L23; Brunvand 82(2).

L28   To see how the **Land** lays (lies)

1900 CFPidgin *Quincy A. Sawyer* (B) 298: To see how the land lays. **1903** EChilders

Riddle (NY 1940) 175: You see how the land lies. **1933** AGilbert *Musical* (L) 154: Learned . . . how the land lay. **1952** PQuentin *Black* (NY) 125: That's the way the land lies. **1961** RVanGulik *Chinese Lake* (L) 167: So that's how the land lies. **1975** AChristie *Curtain* (NY) 221: [He] knew exactly how the wind lay. EAP L26; Brunvand 82(3). Cf. Lay *below*.

L29 The **Landlord** never dies

1922 JJoyce *Ulysses* (NY 1934) 162: Landlord never dies they say. Cf. EAP K21: King; NED Landlord 1.

L30 A **Land-office** business

1940 CBDawson *Lady Wept* (NY) 228: I predict a land-office business. **1957** VWMason *Gracious* (NY) 53: We're doing a land-office business. **1960** CErwin *Orderly* (NY) 238: We were doing a land-office business. **1967** RTraver *Jealous* (B) 48: Doing a land-office business. DA Landoffice 2(1).

L31 A long **Lane** that has no turning

1910 EPhillpotts *Tales* (NY) 141: 'Twas a long lane that had no turning. **1928** SChalmers *House* (NY) 349: It's a long lane that has no turning. **1930** RKing *Murder* (NY) 261: You have reason when you say that a road does not lengthen without a turning at its end. **1934** EPhillpotts *Mr. Digweed* (L) 179: It's a long lane that has no turning. **1939** KSecrist *Murder Melody* (NY) 25: I'm that long lane you've heard about . . . an' I'm turnin' now. **1940** HReilly *Murder in* (NY) 188: It's a long lane that has no turning. **1954** WJohns *Fabulous* (B) 109: But there's no road that doesn't have a turning, as they say. **1959** *BHerald* 3/20 22: It's a long lane without a turning. **1965** ESGardner *Beautiful* (NY) 75: It's a long worm that has no turning. EAP L29. Cf. Worm *below*.

L32 To speak the same **Language**

1934 KWoods *Murder* (B) 40: They were very different as individuals, but, as the saying is, they spoke the same language. EAP L30.

L33 The deceptive **Lapwing**

1969 AGilbert *Mr. Crook* (NY DBC) 11: It isn't only the lady lapwing that can practice deception in the interests of its young. *Oxford* 442: Lapwing cries.

L34 As white as **Lard**; Lard-white

1931 RAFreeman *Dr. Thorndyke's* (NY) 273: Her face was as white as lard. **1952** NBlake *Dreadful* (L) 60: The lard-white face. **1966** HTravers *Madame* (NY) 103: A slice of calf as white as lard. **1968** JRoffman *Grave* (NY) 15: The lard-white skin.

L35 As blithe as a **Lark**

1921 ERBurroughs *Mucker* (NY) 288: Blythe as a lark. **1941** RAldington *Life* (NY) 177: He was as blithe as a lark on a May morning. EAP L31.

L36 As bright as a **Lark**

1928 EHamilton *Four* (L) 72: He appeared as bright and fresh as a lark. EAP L32.

L37 As cheerful as a **Lark**

1940 VRath *Death of a Lucky* (NY) 13: She's cheerful as a lark. EAP L33: Cheery.

L38 As chirpy (frisky) as a **Lark**

1932 LCharteris *White* (NY) 270: As chirpy as the proverbial lark. **1936** VMcHugh *Caleb* (NY) 202: Frisky as a lark. TW 214(4): Chipper.

L39 As fresh as a **Lark**

1930 AECoppard *Pink* (L) 176: Fresh as a lark. **1937** RAFreeman *Felo* (L) 46: As fresh as a lark. **1968** EWilliams *Beyond* (NY) 223: Fresh as larks. TW 214(4).

L40 As gay as a **Lark**

1929 JCPowys *Wolf* (NY) 2.501: He'll be gay as a lark. **1937** MDavis *Chess* (NY) 256: He was gay as a lark. **1938** EQueen *Four* (NY) 148: Gay as a lark. **1948** LFord *Devil's* (NY) 112: As gay as a lark. **1958** *New Yorker* 8/2 34: Gay as larks. EAP L34; Brunvand 82(1).

L41 As happy as a **Lark** (*varied*)

1925 JICClarke *My Life* (NY) 155: Happy as young larks. **1931** WWJacobs *Snug* (NY) 554: As happy as a skylark. **1936** *New Yorker* 7/25 62: She's as happy as a lark. **1947** HNicolson *Diaries III* ed NNicolson (NY 1968) 97: As happy and irresponsible as a lark. **1949** RStout *Trouble* (NY) 139: They could be as happy a larks. **1959** *BHerald* 2/22 3:

No birds and everyone is happy as a lark.
1960 ASinclair *Project* (L) 42: Happy as a
lark. **1970** WANolen *Making* (NY) 136: He
was happy as a lark. **1972** JCreasey *First*
(NY) 116: I ought to be as happy as a lark.
Oxford 527: Merry. Cf. As happy as a Bird
above.

L42 As merry as a **Lark**

1933 RAJWalling *Prove It* (NY) 159: She
came home merry as a lark. **1936** VMc-
Hugh *Caleb* (NY) 142: Merry as a lark. *Oxford* 527.

L43 To be up (rise) with the **Lark**

1917 JCLincoln *Extricating* (NY) 147: I rose
with the lark. **1930** AEWalter *Betrayal* (NY)
107: I get up with the lark. **1935** FDGrierson *Death* (L) 164: Wells rose, metaphorically speaking, with the lark. **1940** JLBonney *Death by* (NY) 90: Rising even earlier
than the lark. **1940** KSteel *Dead of Night* (B)
36: I was up with the lark. **1952** STruss
Death (NY) 146: Up with the lark. Work
like the devil. **1969** SAngus *Death* (L) 88:
[He] must have been up with the larks. EAP
L37: Rise; TW 214(10); Brunvand 82(2).
Cf. To be up with the Birds, To go . . .
Chickens *above*.

L44 Not to know as much as **Larrabee's** calf

1956 *BangorDN* 7/16 11: They don't know
as much as Larrabee's calf.

L45 As happy as **Larry**

1958 *New Yorker* 4/5 31: She was happy as
Larry. **1959** THWhite *Godstone* (NY) 192:
He was "as happy as Larry." **1966** NMarsh
Killer (B) 232: As happy as Larry. **1978**
NMarsh *Grave* (NY) 205: No brains and as
happy as Larry. **1982** GMitchell *Uncoffin'd*
(NY) 10: Mary was . . . as happy as Larry.
Partridge 470. Cf. Wentworth 313.

L46 **Last** but not least

1922 JJoyce *Ulysses* (NY 1934) 92: Last but
not least. **1937** SPalmer *No Flowers* (L) 26:
Last but not least. EAP L39; Brunvand
82(1).

L47 The **Last** of pea-time

1955 JBCabell *As I* (NY) 80: Feel sort of
like the last of pea-time and . . . tuckered
out. TW 278: Pea-time.

L48 **Last-in** first-out

1965 DAcheson *Morning* (B) 31: The rule
of last-in first-out pointed to me. Cf. *Oxford*
263: First up.

L49 To hang out the **Latch** string

1956 HCahill *Shadow* (NY) 178: Hung out
the latch string of prosperity. TW 215;
Brunvand 83.

L50 Better **Late** than never (*varied*)

1916 EClodd *Memories* (L) 125: Better late
than never. **1922** JJoyce *Ulysses* (NY 1934)
515: Better late than never. **1928** AHuxley
Point (L) 507: But to tell you the truth the
proverb needs changing. Better never than
early. **1932** GCollins *Channel* (L) 145: Better
late than never. **1948** MInnes *Night* (L
1966) 50: The adage better late than never.
1953 JRMacdonald *Meet* (NY) 58: Better
late than never. **1956** *New Yorker* 8/11 19:
Better never than late. **1963** RLPike *Mute*
(NY DBC) 46: What I always say is, better
late than never . . . I always say, a penny
saved is a penny earned, and for want of a
nail a kingdom was lost . . . One thing I
never say is, money is the root of all evil . . . ,
I'd love to sit here and talk proverbs all
morning, but time's awasting. **1969** DShannon *Crime* (NY) 9: Better late than never.
1976 GBagby *Two* (NY) 183: Better late
than never and all that. EAP L40; TW
215(1).

L51 Never too **Late** (old) to learn (*varied*)

1916 RFirbank *Inclinations* (Works 2, L
1929) 65: It's never too l-l-late to learn.
1932 PHerring *Murder* (L) 309: It's never
too old to learn. **1936** GMilburn *Catalogue*
(NY) 163: We never get too old to learn.
1938 JTFarrell *No Star* (NY) 317: It's never
too late to learn. **1957** JWyndham *Midwich*
(NY) 131: It's never too late to learn. **1965**
RLPike *Police* (NY) 99: It's never too late to
learn. **1974** DCory *Bit* (NY) 182: "You're
learning." . . . "They say it's never too late."
EAP L82; Brunvand 83(1).

L52 Never too **Late** to mend (change)

1910 EPhillpotts *Tales* (NY) 168: Never too late to mend. **1930** FBeeding *Four* (B) 10: It's never too late to change. **1931** CFGregg *I Have* (NY) 208: It's never too late to mend. EAP L41; Brunvand 83(2).

L53 As thin (lean) as a **Lath**

1924 VLWhitechurch *Templeton* (NY) 283: Thin as a lath. **1933** ERPunshon *Genius* (B) 288: He was as thin as a lath. **1939** CBClason *Dragon's* (NY) 45: Lean as a lath. **1941** IMontgomery *Death Won* (NY) 41: He was young, thin as a lath. **1958** *New Yorker* 1/4 19: Thin as laths. **1964** HBourne *In the Event* (NY) 148: Thin as a lath. **1968** MSteen *Pier* (L) 107: A woman as thin as a lath. **1970** AWRaitt *Prosper* (L) 31: He is as thin as a lath. **1978** JCash *Gold* (NY) 13: He's thin as a lath. EAP L42. Cf. Slat *below*.

L54 He that **Laughs** last laughs best (*varied*)

1908 JCLincoln *Cy Whittaker* (NY) 212: Them that laughs last laughs best. **1912** HHMunro *Unbearable* (NY 1928) 158: Fate would have the advantage of laughing last. **1925** WLewis *Letters* ed WKRose (L 1963) 148: An old saying, he laughs best who laughs last. **1926** JCAddams *Secret* (NY) 91: All depends who laughs last. **1928** SFWright *Deluge* (NY) 323: He laughs longest who laughs last. **1930** WLewis *Apes* (NY 1932) 578: He smiles best who smiles last. **1935** ESGardner *Counterfeit Eye* (NY) 120: The bird who laughs last is the one who laughs longest. **1939** GGoodchild *McLean Excels* (L) 256: The proverb—who laughs last laughs loudest. **1951** KBennett *Wink* (L) 199: Anxious lest the Devil should laugh last and longest. **1957** *Time* 2/18 38: The theory that he who laughs most laughs best. **1965** LAFiedler *Back* (NY) 7: He who laughs *first* laughs best. **1974** BWAldiss *Eighty* (NY) 29: "She who weeps least, weeps best." "We are proverbial. 'Least said, least mended.'" *Oxford* 445: Laughs (best).

L55 **Laugh** and grow fat

1929 WBSeabrook *Magic* (NY) 145: I laugh and grow fat. **1935** EGreenwood *Pins* (L) 160: Laugh and grow fat ain't a bad maxim. **1947** AGilbert *Death in* (L) 56: I believe in laughing. It may make you fat, but it does keep you young. EAP L44.

L56 **Laugh** and lie down

1922 JJoyce *Ulysses* (NY 1934) 194: The game of laugh and lie down. *Oxford* 444.

L57 **Laugh** before seven *etc.*

1966 NMonsarrat *Life(I)* (L) 9: Laugh before seven cry before eleven. Cf. *Oxford* 444: Laugh before breakfast. Cf. Rain before seven *below*.

L58 Those **Laugh** that win

1911 FRS *Way of a Man with a Maid* (L) 20: Those laugh that win. EAP L46; TW 215(3); Brunvand 83.

L59 To have the last **Laugh** (*varied*)

1932 LFrost *Murder* (NY) 209: Have the last laugh. **1935** DHume *Call in* (L) 247: The last laugh is with me. **1935** VWMason *Washington* (NY) 117: I've heard that the last laugh is the best. **1939** JPPhilips *Death Delivers* (NY) 32: If I can just have the last laugh once. **1941** CCoffin *Mare's Nest* (NY) 219: A last laugh is the best laugh. **1956** BCClough *More* (Portland, Me.) 127: It is the last laugh that lasts. **1957** *BHerald* 1/12 13: Wife has last laugh by getting divorce. **1958** CLBlackstone *All Men* (NY) 77: The last laugh was hers. **1963** RLFish *Isle* (NY DBC) 8: They would see who had the last laugh, which was always the most delectable. **1964** RLPike *Quarry* (NY) 50: It's the last laugh that counts. Amer. Herit. Dict. Laugh *n*. 2.

L60 To rest on one's **Laurels**

1931 MKennedy *Death in a Deck-Chair* (L) 96: Rest on your laurels. **1936** JRhode *Death at* (NY) 152: I shouldn't rest on your laurels yet. **1959** ASillitoe *Saturday* (NY) 76: She . . . rested on her laurels. **1969** ACarter *Heroes* (L) 173: Don't rest on your laurels. **1970** HCarmichael *Death Trap* (NY) 61: Rest on your laurels. **1974** ELathen *Sweet* (NY) 79: No time for a man to rest on his laurels. Cf. EAP L48; TW 215. Cf. Oars *below*.

L61 To lay out in **Lavender**

1937 PATaylor *Octagon* (NY) 139: An' that woman, she laid me out in lavender. Cf. EAP L49.

L62 The first **Law** of the sea *etc.*

1954 MMainwaring *Murder* (NY) 76: The first law of the sea . . . Never spit to windward.

L63 **Laws** are made to be broken

1928 WCWilliams *Voyage* (NY) 325: Laws are made to be broken. EAP P297: Promises. Cf. Rules *below.*

L64 **Laws** are silent amid arms

1923 HWNevinson *Changes* (NY) 292: Amid arms not only laws are silent, but so is reason. EAP L55.

L65 The **Law** does not care for little things

1930 CBush *Death* (NY) 201: *De minimis non curat lex.* **1951** RLHine *Relics* (NY) 174: The maxim "De minimis non curat lex." **1970** MInnes *Death* (L) 65: *De minimis non curat lex.* EAP L53.

L66 The **Law** (king, *etc.*) has long arms (*varied*)

1908 MRRinehart *Circular Staircase* (NY 1947) 175: The law has long arms. **1927** PBNoyes *Pallid* (NY) 37: Governments, proverbially, have long arms. **1952** MGreenberg *Five* (NY) 354: They say the arm of the law is long. **1956** BJFarmer *Death* (L) 206: Here Wigan approved of the rigour of the law, and the proverbial long arm. **1958** LSdeCamp *Elephant* (NY) 302: The king has a long reach. EAP K26: King.

L67 The **Law** is an ass (fool)

1928 JGoodwin *When Dead* (NY) 255: One of your English writers said the law was an ass. **1929** LBrock *Stoke Silver* (NY) 133: The Law had discovered once more that it was an ass. **1930** ATrain *Adventures* (NY) 571: You agree with Mr. Bumble that the law is an ass. **1930** EWoodward *House* (NY) 54: Everyone knew the law was a fool. **1936** JGBrandon *Pawnshop* (L) 48: The Law is such a damned ass. **1939** SRansome *Shroud* (NY) 34: Dickens made Bumble say the law is an ass. **1945** RLHines *Confession* (L) 39:

The law is an ass. **1954** HCecil *According* (L) 175: The law's an ass . . . but it can kick like one sometimes. **1959** ESGardner *Mythical* (NY) 276: You want to remember that the law isn't *always* an ass. **1961** LWoolf *Growing* (L) 240: The law, which everyone knew was an ass. **1969** JSteinbeck IV *In Touch* (NY) 70: The young are quick to see the law can be an ass. **1974** RLockridge *Death* (NY) 78: Everybody is an ass . . . as was once said about the law. *Oxford* 446.

L68 The **Laws** of the Medes and the Persians

1900 CFPidgin *Quincy A. Sawyer* (B) 210: As fixed as the laws of the Medes and Persians. **1912** JCLincoln *Postmaster* (NY) 121: Like the laws of the Medes and Possums. **1928** EHamilton *Four* (L) 64: One of the laws of the Medes and Persians that altereth not. **1930** JGBrandon *Death* (L) 112: The law of the Underworld . . . was as rigid as any of the ordinations of the Medes and Persians. **1938** RAJWalling *Grimy Glove* (NY) 220: Lanivet's word's the law of the Medes and Persians to him. **1942** HReilly *Name Your Poison* (NY) 50: A schedule whose rigidity would have made the Medes and Persians pale. **1947** GMWilliams *Silk* (L) 107: It's against all the laws of the Medes and Persians. **1952** JTey *Singing* (NY 1960) 67: The laws of the Medes and the Persians are not more unchangeable. **1959** AHocking *Victim* (NY) 42: One of those men whose self-made laws are as those of the Medes and the Persians. **1964** LWoolf *Beginning* (L) 83: It was contrary to the laws of the Medes and the Persians. **1971** WHMarnell *Once Upon* (NY) 159: The last was part of the law transmitted to The Store by the Medes and the Persians. **1975** DRussell *Tamarisk* (NY) 261: Not for all the laws of the Medes and the Persians. EAP L57.

L69 No **Law** west of (wherever)

1937 NMorland *Clue* (L) 182: Gives me the impression of "no law of God or man, west of fifty-three," or whatever the quotation is. **1959** *Time* 3/30 53: "There's no law west of Kansas City," the saying went, "and west of Fort Scott, no God." Cf. No Sunday *below.*

L70 One **Law** for the rich and another for the poor

1930 LTracy *Manning* (NY) 237: One law for the rich and another for the poor. **1937** VMacClure *Diva's* (L) 140: One law fer the rich an' another fer the pore. **1952** ES Holding *Widow's* (NY DBC) 99: There's one law for the rich, and one for the poor. **1960** JO'Hara *Ourselves* (NY) 64: One law for the rich and one for the poor. **1969** RPearsall *Worm* (L) 468: The adage that there was one law for the rich and one for the poor. TW 215 (2,3); *Oxford* 445–6.

L71 He who is his own **Lawyer** (doctor, physician) has a fool for a client (*varied*)

1931 GFowler *Great* (NY) 368: The first axiom of law is that an attorney defending himself has a fool for a client. **1933** CCNicole *Death* (L) 273: The old law adage about the lawyer who has a fool [*himself*] for a client. **1934** HAdams *Knife* (L) 47: No physician, it is said, can correctly diagnose his own case. **1946** ESedgwick *Happy* (B) 166: Physicians, as is notorious, cannot cure themselves . . . The lawyer who attends to his own business has a fool for a client. **1952** BKendrick *You Die* (NY) 191: There's an old saying in law—the man who tries to be his own lawyer has a fool for a client. **1956** *NYPost* 10/31 4: "A man who is his own advocate has a fool for a client," says one of the favorite aphorisms of the legal profession. **1956** RILee *Happy* (B) 170: There is an old saying that the doctor who treats himself has a fool for a doctor and a fool for a patient. **1957** *BHerald* 12/27 3: He who doctors himself has a fool for a physician. **1959** *NYTimes* 2/1 3: He who doctors himself has a fool for a physician. **1969** MDorman *King* (NY) 58: The theory that "a lawyer who represents himself in court has a damned fool for a client." **1972** A Roudybush *Sybaritic* (NY) 145: We lawyers have a saying that any man who acts as his own lawyer has a fool for a client. **1977** RHardin *Amateur* (I) 53: A lawyer representing himself has a fool for a client. EAP C310: Counsellor; TW 234: Man(7); Bradley 70: Doctor.

L72 When **Lawyers** stop lying in court

1933 NKlein *Destroying* (NY) 285: I'll talk to him when lawyers stop lying in court. Cf. EAP L63.

L73 The **Lay** (lie) of the land

1922 JJoyce *Ulysses* (NY 1934) 634: Sound the lie of the land first. **1933** HAshbrook *Murder* (NY) 113: So that's the lay of the land. **1933** JIronside *Marten* (L) 90: I want to get the lie of the land. **1955** AChristie *Hickory* (NY) 95: The lay of the land. **1959** ESGardner *Mythical* (NY) 254: You know the lay of the land. Amer. Herit. Dict. Lay *n*. Cf. To see how the Land *above*.

L74 **Lay-overs** to catch meddlers

1952 FO'Connor *Wise* (NY) 183: Lay-overs to catch meddlers. **1974** SAGrau *Wind* (NY) 149: Layovers to catch meddlers. CPWilson in FCBrown *Collection* I 557–8.

L75 As heavy (hard) as **Lead**

1906 JCLincoln *Mr. Pratt* (NY) 54: Heavier than lead. **1913** MPShiel *Dragon* (L) 38: Heavy as lead. **1933** ESnell *And Then* (L) 92: Heavy as lead. **1938** PWentworth *Run!* (L) 229: His heart . . . went as heavy as lead. **1941** VWMason *Rio Casino* (NY) 94: He is heavy as lead before cocktails. **1946** A Christie *Come, Tell Me* (L) 152: It [*a pillow*] is . . . as hard as lead. **1954** EXFerrars *Lying* (L) 148: His heart was heavy as lead. **1957** *New Yorker* 5/11 42: Her legs were as heavy as lead. **1961** WSanson *Blue Skies* (B) 16: Heavy as lead. **1970** CBrooke-Rose *Go When* (L) 115: I felt . . . heavy as lead. **1977** HDolson *Beauty* (P) 205: She felt suddenly as heavy as lead. EAP L68; TW 216(1).

L76 To get the **Lead** out of one's pants (*varied*)

1934 RWormser *Wax Face* (NY) 54: Get the lead out of his pants. **1936** RGDean *Sutton* (NY) 63: Shake the lead out of your tail! **1937** RGDean *Three Lights* (NY) 151: I've been hoping you'd shake the lead out of your tail. **1946** GHomes *Build* (NY) 129: Get the lead out of your can. **1951** DFontaine *Sugar* (NY) 142: How about someone telling Burkhardt to get the lead out of his pants? **1958** JBarry *Extreme* (NY) 189: Get the lead out of your pants. **1962** JBarry *Strange* (NY) 177: Can't you get the lead out of your pants? **1964** EPangborn *Davy* (NY) 61: Get the lead out of his butt. Wentworth 314.

L77 To put **Lead** in one's pencil (*varied*)

1929 HFergusson *In Those Days* (NY) 180: Here's to lead in his pencil and Jack in his jeans. **1966** NMonsarrat *Life(I)* (L) 338: This should put some lead in the pencil. **1966** WTrevor *Love* (L) 126: It'll put a bit of lead in your pencil [*a drink*]. Wentworth 314.

L78 One can be **Led** rather than driven

1928 FWCrofts *Sea* (NY) 21: You can lead better than you can drive. **1930** AChristie *Murder* (NY) 91: Can be led, not driven. **1939** DFrome *Mr. P. and The Old Angel* (L) 68: He couldn't be driven . . . he had to be led. **1950** OAnderson *In for* (NY) 153: As we say in Lincolnshire, I can be led but I won't be druv. **1953** AWUpfield *Murder Must* (NY) 153: You can lead 'em but never drive. EAP L71.

L79 **Leading strings**

1934 AWynne *Gold Coins* (P) 111: The man was in leading strings. **1944** HReilly *Opening Door* (NY) 14: She was out of Charlotte's leading strings. **1954** CCarnac *Policeman* (NY) 46: Kept the boy on leading strings. EAP L72.

L80 As frail as a **Leaf**

1959 FCrane *Buttercup* (NY DBC) 126: She seems frail as a leaf. Wilstach 158. Cf. Whiting *NC* 435(1): Fragile.

L81 As light as a **Leaf**

1940 DCCameron *Grave* (NY) 73: Her hand . . . light as a leaf and as tremulous. **1952** HFMPrescott *Man on* (NY) 299: Light as a leaf. **1962** AGilbert *Uncertain* (NY DBC) 116: A little woman, as light as a leaf. Whiting L138–40.

L82 As thick as **Leaves**

1929 PRussell *Red Tiger* (NY) 12: Poets and composers are as thick as leaves. TW 216(4).

L83 To shake like a **Leaf** (*varied*)

1920 AChristie *Mysterious Affair* (NY) 258: Your hand shook like a leaf. **1933** JLilienthal *Gambler's* (B) 269: He was shaking like a leaf. **1936** JSStrange *Bell* (NY) 4: You're shaking like a leaf. **1940** JRhode *Murder at* (L) 101: He was shaking all over like a leaf. **1943** VSiller *Echo* (NY) 225: He came out of his faint shaking like a leaf in the wind. **1950** MCarleton *Bride* (NY) 211: I shook like a leaf. **1951** ESGardner *Fiery* (NY) 172: I'm shaking like an autumn leaf. **1960** HSlesar *Enter* (NY 1967) 80: Shaking like a big fat leaf. **1962** MStewart *Moon-* (NY 1965) 215: Shaking like a leaf. **1966** LBeers *Wild* (NY) 25: I shook like a popple leaf. **1966** JStuart *My Land* (NY) 224: Armstrong . . . was shaking like a leaf in the wind. **1976** WMarshall *Hatchet* (NY) 186: [He] was shaking like a leaf. EAP L75; TW 216(6).

L84 To take a **Leaf** (page) from someone's book (*varied*)

1925 JSFletcher *False* (NY) 178: Let's take a leaf from the Frenchman's book. **1928** ABerkeley *Silk* (NY) 54: Taking a leaf out of the story-books. 149: We'll take a leaf out of the French notebooks. **1935** GBarnett *Call-Box* (L) 22: I'll take a leaf from your copy-book. **1939** HWPriwen *Inspector* (L) 171: You're taking a leaf out of your friend's book. **1946** ESedgwick *Happy* (B) 137: I took a leaf from his copybook. **1949** MGilbert *He Didn't* (NY DBC) 63: Taking a leaf out of the book of our friends. **1956** DMDisney *Unappointed* (NY) 150: He should have taken a leaf out of their book. **1967** JCrittenden *Balloons* (NY) 147: To take a page from Mr. Ormsby's book. **1968** HEL Mellersh *FitzRoy* (NY) 165: A leaf must be taken out of the Roman Catholic book. **1970** RDAltick *Victorian* (NY) 298: Dr. Pritchard took a leaf, so to speak, out of Dr. Palmer's prescription book. EAP L78.

L85 To tremble like a **Leaf**

1929 LO'Flaherty *House* (NY) 96: Trembling like a leaf. **1933** CStJSprigg *Crime* (L) 190: Look at your spoon, trembling like a leaf. **1956** MProcter *Pub* (NY) 92: Trembling like a leaf. **1977** JBHilton *Dead-Nettle*

(NY) 156: He was trembling like a leaf. EAP L76; TW 216(7); Brunvand 83: The Poplar's leaf.

L86   To turn over a new Leaf

1919 LMerrick *Chair* (L) 290: He has turned over a new leaf. **1922** JJoyce *Ulysses* (NY 1934) 453: He wanted to turn over a new leaf. **1929** TCobb *Crime* (L) 51: He really did try to turn over a new leaf. **1936** JJFarjeon *Detective* (L) 199: I am turning over a new leaf in my book of purity. **1940** CMWills *R.E.Pipe* (L) 36: To turn over a new leaf. **1950** MGEberhart *Never* (NY) 32: I've turned over a new leaf. **1955** AHocking *Poison* (NY) 116: I'd turn over a new leaf. **1960** RHolles *Captain* (L) 220: Look who's turned over a new leaf. **1965** DHitchens *Bank* (NY) 89: He was turning over a new leaf. **1970** JAGraham *Aldeburg* (B) 233: As evidence of the new leaf that had been turned over. **1977** LBlock *Burglars* (NY) 91: You're turning over a new leaf. EAP L79; Brunvand 83.

L87   Little Leaks sink the ship

1928 MPShiel *How the Old Woman* (L) 151: It's the little leaks sink the ship. EAP L80.

L88   A Leap in the dark

1903 EChilders *Riddle* (NY 1940) 271: It's a leap in the dark. **1924** CWells *Furthest* (P) 200: A leap in the dark. **1958** ECooper *Tomorrow's* (NY) 91: Mallory took a leap in the dark. EAP L81.

L89   A little Learning is a dangerous thing

1962 LWoolley *As I Seem* (L) 19: The proverbially dangerous little learning. **1968** JDHicks *My Life* (Lincoln, Neb.) 263: Despite the old adage, a little learning is probably better than none. *Oxford* (2nd ed) 374; TW 217(1).

L90   Least said soonest mended (*varied*)

1905 JBCabell *Line* (NY 1926) 25: The least said the soonest mended. **1920** JSFletcher *Dead Men's* (NY) 59: The old proverb . . . least said is soonest mended. **1925** EDBiggers *House* (NY) 147: The littlest said, sooner repairs are made. **1935** AFielding *Tragedy* (L) 115: "Least said soonest mend-

ed" was a wise old saw. **1937** GDHCole *Missing* (L) 235: I thought least said, soonest mended. **1950** SSmith *Man with* (NY) 21: Least said the better. **1954** CIsherwood *World* (L) 275: "Least said soonest mended" may be a truism. **1956** WMankowitz *Old* (B) 185: Least said soonest mended. **1969** GMFraser *Flashman* (NY) 224: Least said soonest mended. **1970** ACross *Poetic* (NY) 68: A case of least said soonest mended. **1974** GWheeler *Easy* (NY) 31: The less said the sooner mended, I always say. **1981** ACross *Death* (NY) 132: It did seem least said, soonest mended, as my dear mother used to say. EAP L86. Cf. Less *below.*

L91   As tough as Leather

1934 EJepson *Grinning* (L) 18: The Red Wop, as tough as leather. **1939** TScudder *J.W.Carlyle* (NY) 314: His will was tough as leather. **1957** *New Yorker* 7/13 32: Turkey as tough as leather. **1957** MPHood *In the Dark* (NY) 95: They'll be tough as leather. **1961** WEHuntsberry *Oscar* (NY DBC) 127: She's as tough as wet leather. **1964** WBlunt *Cockerell* (L) 4: You are as tough as leather. EAP L88; Taylor *Western Folklore* 17(1958) 16. Cf. Shoe leather *below.*

L92   To be on (fix on) like a Leech

1936 LAKnight *Night* (L) 127: I'm on to him like a leech. **1951** DBOlsen *Love Me* (NY) 169: She fixed on Burnell like a leech. TW 217(1).

L93   To cling like a Leech

1928 RHWatkins *Master* (NY) 74: The thug . . . clung like a leech. **1956** PWentworth *Fingerprint* (NY) 11: Fabian has clung like a leech. **1959** *New Yorker* 4/15 29: Clinging as a leech. Cf. Limpet *below.*

L94   To hang on like a Leech

1928 MThynne *Draycott* (NY) 50: Hang on like a leech. **1933** EPOppenheim *Murder* (NY) 19: They hung together like leeches. **1953** EReed *Maras* (NY) 54: They would hang on like leeches. **1958** *New Yorker* 9/27 40: They'll hang on like leeches. **1967**

JThompson *House* (NY) 49: She hangs on like a leech. EAP L91.

L95 To stick like a **Leech** (*varied*)

1922 JJoyce *Ulysses* (NY 1934) 180: No use sticking to him like a leech. **1924** JSFletcher *Time-Worn* (NY) 220: You and I stick together like leeches. **1930** JGBrandon *Murder* (L) 138: I'm gonna stick closer to you than ten leeches. **1937** PWentworth *Case Is Closed* (L) 238: She . . . stuck to it like a leech. **1941** PWentworth *Weekend* (P) 144: He stuck to me like a leech. **1951** MSpillane *Long* (NY) 97: I had stuck like a leech. **1955** MErskine *Old Mrs.* (NY) 77: The major stuck like the proverbial leech—and was just about as unpleasant. EAP L92. Cf. Limpet *below*.

L96 As green as a **Leek**

1938 GDHCole *Mrs. Warrender's* (L) 292: He was still as green as a leek. TW 217.

L97 A **Left-handed** (something or other)

1923 EWallace *Clue of the New Pin* (B) 80: A certain left-handed fame. **1938** JTFarrell *No Star* (NY) 536: The times is left-handed nowadays. **1940** CBDawson *Lady Wept* (NY) 164: That's a left-handed compliment. **1953** MPHood *Silent* (NY) 138: An apology . . . left-handed kind. **1959** HReilly *Not Me* (NY DBC) 39: Joan proceeded in her usual left-handed way [*uncomplimentary*]. EAP L96.

L98 **Leg** over leg as the dog went to Dover

1925 TRMarshall *Recollections* (I) 318: Leg over leg, the dog went to Dover. **1936** *New Yorker* 2/15 23: "Leg over leg, as the dog went to Dover," he [*Elihu Root*] used to drawl when the President [*T. Roosevelt*] started too rapidly on the road to utopia.

L99 Not have a **Leg** to stand on

1912 HFAshurst *Diary* ed GFSparks (Tucson 1962) 10: I had not a leg to stand on. **1924** VLWhitechurch *Templeton* (NY) 222: Not a leg to stand on. **1933** JVTurner *Amos* (L) 242: He had not got a leg to stand on. **1937** RCWoodthorpe *Death in* (NY) 18: He hasn't a leg to stand on. **1945** MBurton *Not a Leg to Stand on* (NY). **1948** JRhode *Death*

(NY) 33: She hasn't got a leg to stand on. **1954** JSanders *Freakshow* (B) 262: We ain't got a leg to stand on. **1959** ADean *Something* (NY) 174: He didn't really have a leg to stand on. **1962** WHaggard *Unquiet* (NY DBC) 168: She hadn't a leg to stand on. **1975** MDelving *Bored* (NY) 174: None of the others has a leg to stand on. TW 218(8).

L100 To be on one's last **Legs**

1922 JSFletcher *Ravensdene* (NY) 151: On his last legs. EAP L99.

L101 To get on one's hind **Legs**

1937 BThomson *Milliner's* (L) 62: Got on his hind legs. Partridge 477.

L102 To have a hollow **Leg**

1939 WChambers *You Can't* (NY) 5: Don't all tropical tramps have a hollow leg? **1953** EQueen *Scarlet* (B) 104: I have a hollow leg when I put my mind to it. **1955** CMKornbluth *Mindworm* (L) 107: Worple drank . . . like a man with a hollow leg. **1963** HPentecost *Only* (NY DBC) 36: That [*money for drink*] wouldn't take him too far with his hollow leg. **1965** RLFish *Diamond* (NY DBC) 61: This one had evidently been born with an empty leg [*a heavy drinker*]. **1969** RMacdonald *Goodbye* (NY) 47: She drinks like she's got a hollow leg. Amer. Herit. Dict. Hollow *adj.* 6.

L103 To pull one's **Leg** (to have one's leg pulled)

1919 JSClouston *Simon* (NY) 58: Pulling my leg; 59, 236. **1922** JJoyce *Ulysses* (NY 1934) 499: I won't have my leg pulled. **1933** BSKeirstead *Brownsville* (NY) 190: As the saying goes, to pull my leg. **1937** MKennedy *I'll Be Judge* (L) 216: She must have been pulling his leg. **1942** QMario *Murder Meets* (NY) 16: Someone's pulling your leg. **1953** RStout *Golden* (NY) 19: The woman might have been pulling his leg. **1958** NMarsh *Singing* (B) 99: I couldn't resist pulling your leg. **1966** JBall *Cool* (NY) 87: Linda had pulled his leg. **1975** JFraser *Wreath* (NY) 89: You could pull [his leg] so far. EAP L101.

L104 To stretch one's **Leg** according to his blanket

1969 RGrayson *Voyage* (L) 39: Stretch your legs according to the length of your blanket. *Oxford* 780: Stretch.

L105 To talk the **Leg** (arm, hind-leg) off something or other (*varied*)

1924 ROChipperfield *Bright Lights* (NY) 109: Talk the legs off an iron pot. **1928** JArnold *Surrey* (L) 297: You two would talk the leg off a piano. **1929** EWallace *Gunman's* (NY) 167: He can talk the hind leg off a donkey. **1929** DFrome *Murder* (L) 104: Talk your arm off. **1930** ABCox *Vane* (L) 52: He'd talk the hind-leg off a dead mule. **1930** TCobb *Crime* (L) 37: Ready to talk a horse's hind leg off. **1930** LTracy *Manning* (NY) 216: That little man can talk the hind leg off a dog. **1932** AGilbert *Body* (NY) 26: She'd talk the hind leg off a mule. **1936** DLSayers *Gaudy* (NY) 174: He'd talk the hind leg off a donkey. **1938** RMBaker *Death* (NY) 60: Father used to say she'd talk the legs off an iron pot. **1944** MVenning *Jethro* (NY) 82: I'll talk your arm off. **1949** BSBallinger *Body* (NY) 89: You're certainly talking my arm off. **1950** SPalmer *Monkey* (NY) 9: He talked our arm off. **1954** CCarnac *Policeman* (NY) 94: Talk the hind leg off any donkey. **1957** WRBurdett *Underdog* (NY) 10: He'll talk your arm off. **1960** PCurtis *Devil's* (NY) 48: I could talk the leg off an iron pot. **1963** RArnold *Orange* (L) 38: He could talk the hind-leg off a horse. **1969** AGilbert *Mr. Crook* (NY DBC) 131: You'd talk the hind leg off a goat. **1969** JLunt *Bokhara* (L) 82: Argue the hind leg off a donkey. **1972** EPeters *Seventh* (NY) 233: Andy can talk the leg off a table. **1973** ADean *Be Home* (NY) 65: They'll talk an arm off you. **1973** KAmis *Riverside* (NY) 10: Talking your hind leg off. **1975** MKWren *Multitude* (NY) 129: She could talk your left foot off. **1982** CMacLeod *Wrack* (NY) 27: She'd argue the left hind leg off'n a deaf mule. Whiting *NC* 436(2); Berrey 189.3; Partridge 17: Argue, 863: Talk; Apperson 619: Talk(8); *Oxford* 804: Talk. Cf. To talk one's Ear, To argue the Horns, To talk the Horns *above*.

L106 As sour as a **Lemon**

1901 HGarland *Companions on the Trail* (NY 1931) 76: He was sour as a lemon. Taylor *Prov. Comp.* 77.

L107 To get (pick) a **Lemon**

1931 HHolt *Midnight* (NY) 275: What has he handed me? A lemon. **1932** ORCohen *Star* (NY) 219: She had picked a lemon. NED Suppl. Lemon 1b (quote 1927); Partridge 477. Cf. Wentworth 317.

L108 To have the **Length** of someone's foot

1933 PWentworth *Seven Green* (L) 44: I'd taken the length of your foot in the first five minutes. **1941** EPhillpotts *Ghostwater* (NY) 121: She's got the length of his foot. **1952** GRaverat *Period* (L) 185: I am afraid he had the length of Uncle William's foot. EAP L104.

L109 The **Leopard** (tiger) cannot change his spots (*varied*)

1911 JCLincoln *Woman-Haters* (NY) 40: The leopard may or may not change his spots. **1916** RFirbank *Inclination* (Works 2, L 1929) 94: Can a leopard change its spots? **1927** LTracy *Mysterious* (NY) 149: The leopard has changed its spots. **1928** RKing *Fatal* (NY) 86: A friendly leopard, who had achieved the impossible and changed its spots. **1931** MAllingham *Police* (NY) 128: Can a leopard change his spots? **1931** TThayer *Greek* (NY) 284: It was a complete change of a leopard's spots. **1932** AWynne *White Arrow* (P) 268: Does the Ethiopian change his skin? **1933** DGBrowne *Dead* (L) 25: The Ethiopian cannot change his skin. **1936** VWBrooks *Flowering* (NY 1946) 148: Change his skin as he might, the young professor could not change his spots. **1945** ABarber *Noose* (NY) 182: The old tale of the leopard and the spots. **1957** *BHerald* 12/27 18: Even the Communist China tiger would change its spots. **1959** *BTraveler* 10/29 36: A leopard never changes its spots. **1960** HGold *Love* (NY) 30: A leopard coat can't change its spots. **1961** RJWhite *Smartest* (L) 118: We have it on the best authority that the leopard cannot change its spots. **1965** IRoss *Charmers* (NY) 248: I can no more change my habits than a leopard his spots. **1971** MUnderwood *Trout* (NY) 124: The leopard does not change his spots et cetera. **1972** JMDobson *Politics* (NY) 93: The Independents refused to believe he could change his spots. EAP E74: Ethiopian; TW 121–2: Ethiopian, 218: Leopard; *Oxford* 456: Leopard.

L110   The **Less** said the better
1928 HVO'Brien *Four-and-Twenty* (NY) 23: The less said about them the better. **1934** CCranston *Murder* (P) 258: The less said the better. **1960** HSDavies *Papers* (L) 7: The less said, the better. EAP L106. Cf. Least *above.*

L111   A **Liar** by the clock
1938 TDavis *Murder on* (NY) 139: He's a liar by the clock. **1947** HCahill *Look* (NY) 31: Both of them are liars by the clock. **1959** SDean *Merchant* (NY) 41: The lady is a liar by the clock. Cf. Shakespeare *1 Henry IV*, V.iv.143ff: Shrewsbury clock.

L112   A **Liar** needs a good memory (*varied*)
1922 JJoyce *Ulysses* (NY 1934) 268: Wonderful liar. But want a good memory. **1933** ECRLorac *Murder* (L) 256: I'm not a good liar . . . but I have a good memory. **1935** RAJWalling *Corpse* (NY) 107: The proverbial advice to liars that they should have good memories. **1946** CBush *Second Chance* (L) 113: Liars should have good memories. **1954** MKArgus *Rogue* (L) 16: Only people with good memories can afford to tell lies. **1959** ADean *Something* (NY) 118: A good liar had to have a phenomenal memory. **1959** MFitt *Mizmaze* (L) 155: And though she's a liar she has a poor memory, which is a bad combination. **1965** KLaumer *Galactic* (NY) 218: Diplomats and other liars require good memories. **1977** EXFerrars *Blood* (NY) 15: Don't tell any more lies than you've got to. They're a great strain on the memory. EAP L108.

L113   **Liberty** Hall
1913 JSFletcher *Secret* (L 1918) 165: The . . . yacht . . . was . . . a Liberty Hall. **1919** SLeacock *Frenzied* (Toronto 1971) 54: This is Liberty Hall. **1930** SHorler *Curse* (NY)

60: My shack is Liberty Hall. **1948** CBush *Curious* (NY) 90: This is Liberty Hall. **1958** PGWodehouse *Cocktail* (L) 58: This is Liberty Hall. **1961** PGWodehouse *Ice* (NY) 127: This is Liberty Hall. **1964** JBPriestley *Sir Michael* (L) 84: We're now in Liberty Hall. EAP L112.

L114   **Liberty** not license
1964 JBPriestley *Sir Michael* (L) 114: A certain amount of liberty . . . so long as it doesn't turn out to be license. EAP L110.

L115   A **Lick** and a promise
1909 JCLincoln *Keziah* (NY) 48: A lick and a promise. **1932** TThayer *Three Sheet* (NY) 35: We ain't had time to give it more than a lick an' a promise. **1936** EHFonseca *Death Below* (NY) 157: It's only a lick and a promise, but mostly promise. **1952** RFenisong *Deadlock* (NY) 39: I'd go up and give things a lick and a promise. **1957** EXFerrars *Count* (NY) 163: You know what these women are like—a lick and a promise. **1965** CArmstrong *Turret* (NY) 120: Give it a lick and a promise. **1967** VLincoln *Private* (NY) 91: Give the insides of the windows a lick and a promise. **1973** JBWest *Upstairs* (NY) 82: The cleaning staff went through the house with a "lick and a promise," as Mrs. Truman told me. **1977** RRendell *Judgment* (NY) 61: Giving it a lick and a promise. Whiting NC 436(1).

L116   If you can't **Lick** 'em, jine 'em (*varied*)
1947 HCahill *Look* (NY) 311: If you can't lick 'em, jine 'em. 471: If you can't beat 'em join 'em . . . An American proverb. **1949** JMMyers *Silverlock* (NY) 80: If you can't lick 'em, join 'em. **1956** FPohl *Alternating Currents* (NY) 154: If you can't lick 'em, join 'em, that's what the old man used to say. **1957** *BHerald* 4/24 17: I'm not a politician, but I understand one of their axioms is that if you can't defeat a man . . . the logical compromise is to join forces. **1957** CWilliams *Big Bite* (L) 124: If you can't whip 'em, join 'em. **1958** *NYTimes* 11/9 5E: The sound old theory that "if you can't lick 'em, you had better jine 'em." **1958** *BHerald* 11/25 18: The canny old saying, "If you can't

lick 'em, join 'em." **1958** *Time* 12/8 50: To a certain breed of Irishman, the one important motto to remember is: If you can't join 'em, lick 'em. **1961** DTrumbo *Additional* (NY 1970) 544: If you can't join 'em, beat 'em, which is an opposite of sorts. **1963** WTucker *Last* (NY) 101: If you can't join them, beat them. **1965** RDSymons *Silton* (NY 1975) 154: They say if you can't beat them, join them. **1971** VScannell *Tiger* (L) 61: If you can't lick 'em, don't join them. **1975** ABrodsky *Madame* (NY) 275: The time-honored thesis that when you can't fight 'em, join 'em.

L117   To put the (tin) **Lid** on something

1930 GCollins *Horror* (L) 145: That put the tin lid on all [*spoiled it*]. **1932** JMarsh *Murder* (L) 247: That puts the tin lid on everything. **1933** GDHCole *Lesson* (L) 119: That really does put the lid on it! **1956** RFoley *Last* (NY DBC) 51: That really puts the lid on it. **1970** ELathen *Pick* (NY) 9: This puts the lid on it. Partridge 480.

L118   One **Lie** begets another (*varied*)

1962 *BangorDN* 6/19 3: One lie draws ten after it. **1974** CMSmith *Reverend* (NY) 150: One lie often begot another. *Oxford* 460.

L119   As big as **Life**

1929 CJDutton *Streaked* (NY) 203: Walking up as big as life. **1934** KTKnoblock *Winter* (NY) 150: As big as life. **1953** TWicker *Kingpin* (NY) 2: There she was, big as life. **1959** RPHansen *There's Always* (NY DBC) 116: Welsh's name is on that paper as big as life. TW 219(2); Brunvand 84(1).

L120   As large as **Life**

1913 JCLincoln *Mr. Pratt's Patients* (NY) 303: As large as life. **1922** JJoyce *Ulysses* (NY 1934) 765: As large as life. **1923** JSFletcher *Lost Mr. L.* (NY) 199: She came up . . . large as life. **1933** AChristie *Tuesday* (NY) 47: Here is the mark as large as life. **1941** JBentley *Mr. Marlow Chooses* (B) 75: Fingerprints . . . large as life. **1953** GPhelps *Dry Stone* (L) 27: There he stood, as large as life. **1955** PMacDonald *Guest* (NY) 185: Large as life. EAP L118.

L121   As large (big) as **Life** and twice as natural (*etc.*)

1926 FBeeding *Little White* (L) 236: As large as life and twice as natural. **1932** MCJohnson *Damning* (NY) 229: Large as life and twice as natural. **1936** FBeeding *No Fury* (L) 36: Large as life and twice as natural. **1936** CFGregg *Murder* (NY) 51: As large as life and twice as ugly. **1938** SSeifert *Death Stops* (NY) 59: Big as life and twice as handsome. **1941** HBailey *Smiling Corpse* (NY) 105: Looking as big as life and twice as natural. **1949** MAllingham *More Work* (NY) 244: Large as life and twice as nosy. **1950** MRHodgkin *Student* (L) 166: Large as life and twice as natural. **1954** EWalter *Untidy* (P) 17: Big as life and twice as natural. **1957** *Punch* 1/30 181: Her purr large as life and twice as feline. **1958** WGraham *Wreck* (NY) 57: As large as life and twice as efficient. **1961** ZHenderson (NY) 180: Big as life and twice as natural. **1964** EPHoyt *Gentleman* (B) 109: Large as life and twice as meanlooking. **1970** JPorter *Dover Strikes* (NY) 149: You sat there large as life and twice as ugly. TW 219(4); Brunvand 84(2); Taylor *Prov. Comp.* 16.

L122   As natural as **Life** (and twice as handsome)

1913 JCLincoln *Mr. Pratt's Patients* (NY) 28: She was natural as life and . . . twice as handsome, as the saying is. 327: He said it as natural as life. TW 219(5).

L123   As sure as **Life** (and death)

1930 GCollins *Horror* (L) 163: Sure as life and death. **1934** ABliss *Murder* (P) 73: Sure as life somebody sneaked in. Whiting L236: Sicker.

L124   Into every **Life** some rain must fall

1935 HAshbrook *Most Immoral* (NY) 43: Into every life some rain must fall. **1940** RDarby *Death Conducts* (NY) 200: Into each life some rain is bound to fall. **1943** SShane *Lady . . . Millions* (NY) 25: Into every life some rain must fall. **1951** MHead *Congo* (NY) 50: Into every life some rain must fall. **1960** PGWodehouse *Jeeves* (L) 92: Still, into each life some rain must fall. **1968** PDeVries *Witch's* (B) 260: "Into each life some rain must fall," Pete said philosophically. **1972** RBernard *Illegal* (NY) 169: Into every life some rain must fall, as they say.

L125   It's a great (good) **Life** if one does not weaken

1928 VWilliams *Crouching* (B) 46: How do the smart Yankees put it? "It's a good life if you don't weaken." **1929** ACEdington *Studio* (NY) 18: It's a great life—if you don't weaken; 128. **1936** JDosPassos *Big Money* (NY) 61: New York's a great life if you don't weaken. **1968** EHuxley *Love* (L) 126: It's a great life if you don't weaken. Partridge 428: It's.

L126   **Life** is just a bowl of cherries (*varied*)

1933 GHolt *Dark Lady* (L) 45: Life is just a bowl of cherries. **1941** PStong *Other Worlds* (NY) 48: Life is Just a Bowl of Cherries. **1959** EMcBain *'Til Death* (L 1964) 38: Life is just a bowl of cherries. **1965** HWaugh *End* (NY) 37: He wouldn't think life was such a bowl of cherries. **1968** MRichler *Hunting* (Toronto) 58: Baseball was never a bowl of cherries for the Jewish player.

L127   **Life** is not a bed of roses (*varied*)

1928 RKing *Fatal* (NY) 30: Her life is not precisely a bed of roses. **1938** RAJWalling *Grimy Glove* (NY) 65: Life . . . is no bed of roses. **1941** LGBlochman *See You at* (NY) 277: Life isn't all a bed of orchids. **1947** HWade *New Graves* (L) 73: Doesn't sound a bed of roses. **1957** WHHarris *Golden* (NY) 47: Life with Ronald was still the proverbial bed of roses. **1960** BAskwith *Tangled* (L) 62: It's no bed of roses. **1968** KCLatrue *Bound* (NY) 75: Life . . . was not all a bed of roses. **1971** JJMarric *Gideon's Art* (NY) 191: You're on a bed of roses. EAP B96.

L128   **Life** is one damned thing after another (*varied*)

1929 VLWhitechurch *Robbery* (NY) 204: Life is just one damn thing after another. **1930** EStVMillay *Letters* ed ARMacdougall (NY 1952) 240: It's not true that life is one damn thing after another—it's one damn thing over and over. **1931** MKennedy *Death in a Deck-Chair* (L) 164: Life was just one thing after another. **1932** AMizner *Many* (NY) 20: Life was just one damned thing

after another. **1939** DDean *Emerald* (NY) 59: It's been one thing after another all week. **1953** ECRLorac *Shepherd's* (NY) 128: It's one damned thing after another. **1967** ESGardner *Queenly* (NY) 24: The life of a lawyer is just one damned thing after another. Cf. If it isn't one Thing *below*.

L129   **Life** is (too) short

1931 HCBailey *Fortune Speaking* (NY) 266: Life is short . . . but sweet. **1934** KLivingston *Dodd* (NY) 280: Life's too short. **1936** LWMeynell *On the Night* (NY) 95: Life's short anyway. **1941** CMRussell *Dreadful* (NY) 102: Life is short. **1963** JLeCarré *Spy Who* (NY 1965) 67: Life's too short. EAP L122; Brunvand 84(3).

L130   **Life** is sweet (*varied*)

1929 FBeeding *Pretty* (B) 158: Life is still rather sweet. **1931** JHRYardley *Before* (NY) 71: Life is very sweet. **1938** MECorne *Death* (NY) 157: Life is too sweet. **1952** APHerbert *Codd's* (L) 63: Life is sweet—however disgusting. **1956** ADuggan *Winter* (L) 81: Life is sweet. **1966** LPDavies *Who Is* (NY) 209: Life is always precious. TW 220(12); Brunvand 84(5); *Oxford* 462.

L131   One's **Life** is an open book (*varied*)

1926 EWallace *Colossus* (NY 1932) 229: Joseph's life was more or less an open book. **1934** EPOppenheim *Gallows* (B) 86: The life of an actress . . . is pretty much an open book. **1937** JBentley *Whitney* (L) 151: His life is a closed book to me. **1940** CSexby *Death Joins* (NY) 52: Life in San Carlos was an open book. **1959** JCreasy *Hit* (NY DBC) 49: "I should have thought she had a life as open as a book." "To coin a phrase." **1961** RFoley *It's Murder* (NY DBC) 59: Women are just an open book to you. **1963** TCaldwell *Late Clara* (NY) 179: She's as open as a book. **1967** GHousehold *Courtesy* (B) 30: My life is an open book. **1974** HCarmichael *Most* (NY) 74: My life is an open book. **1977** RRendell *Demon* (NY) 6: My life is an open book.

L132   A short **Life** and a merry one (*varied*)

1926 FBeeding *Little White* (L) 180: A short life and a merry one. **1933** KTKnoblock *Take up* (NY) 196: A quick life and a merry one. **1933** JWoodford *Five Fatal* (NY) 240: A short life and a sweet one. **1941** ESGardner *Haunted Husband* (NY) 63: A short life and a merry one. **1950** DMDisney *Fire* (NY) 47: A short life and a merry one. **1959** PGraaf *Sapphire* (NY) 145: A short life and a friendly one, I always say. **1959** GKersh *On an* (NY) 55: A short life and a merry one. EAP L124; Brunvand 84(4).

L133 Such is (that's) **Life**

1930 NGordon *Silent* (NY) 30: Such is life, you know. **1964** ABurgess *Eve* (L) 22: Well, that's life, as the saying goes. We must go when we're called. TW 220(14); Brunvand 85(8).

L134 There's **Life** in the old dog yet

1904 MLPeabody *To Be Young* (B 1967) 305: There's life in the old dog yet. **1930** ATrain *Adventures* (NY) 322: There is life in the old dog yet; 435, 694. **1937** JDonovan *Case* (L) 21: There's life in the old dog yet. **1947** NMarsh *Final* (B) 22: There is life in the old dog yet. **1966** MMcShane *Crimson* (NY) 52: Life in the old dog yet. **1973** DShannon *No Holiday* (NY) 153: Life in the old dog yet. Cf. *Oxford* 461: Horse.

L135 To be the **Life** and soul of the party (*varied*)

1919 SLeacock *Frenzied* (Toronto 1971) 56: The life and soul of the party. **1932** JRhode *Dead Men* (L) 97: The life and soul of the party. **1936** FDGrierson *Heart* (L) 84: The life and soul of any party. **1939** AWebb *Mr. Pendlebury Makes* (L) 56: The title of "life and soul of the party." **1950** MMurray *Neat* (NY DBC) 24: This was a party and Talmadge was determined to be the life and soul of it. **1954** RAldington *Pindorman* (L) 41: The life and soul of the party. **1958** RFenisong *Death of the Party* (NY). **1961** TRobinson *When Scholars* (L) 35: He'll be the life and soul of the party. **1968** DBagley *Vivero* (NY) 2: A life-and-soul-of-the-party type. **1970** MCollis *Journey* (L) 103: She was the life and soul of every occasion. **1972** EPeters *Seventh* (NY) 206: [He] had become what is commonly known as the life of the party. EAP L125.

L136 To bet one's sweet **Life**

1958 RMacdonald *Doomsters* (NY) 124: You bet your sweet life I am. **1968** MAllingham *Cargo* (NY) 107: You can bet your sweet life. DA Bet *v.* 11.

L137 To hang (hold) on for dear **Life**

1929 LRGribble *Gillespie* (L) 17: He . . . holds to it as though to dear life. **1936** PA Taylor *Crimson* (L) 252: Hung on for dear life. **1940** DWheelock *Murder at Montauk* (NY) 182: Aunt Tot hung on to his arm for dear life. **1941** ARLong *Four Feet* (NY) 225: The bell . . . was now ringing for dear life. **1966** JStuart *My Land* (NY) 67: Hanging onto the tree for dear life. **1967** SEMorison *Old Bruin* (B) 174: Holding on for dear life. **1969** AMoorehead *Darwin* (NY) 170: They hung on for dear life. **1971** DPryde *Nunaga* (NY) 128: Hanging on for dear life. Cf. TW 220(13).

L138 To live the **Life** of Riley (*varied*)

1928 GKnevels *Diamond* (NY) 10: I'm livin' the life of Reilly. **1940** HBest *Twenty-fifth* (NY) 132: Living the life of Riley. **1947** PBennett *Varmints* (NY) 281: This was the life of Reilly. **1948** NMailer *Naked* (NY) 271: Life of Riley. **1952** PHBonner *SPQR* (NY) 31: To live the life of Riley without doing a stroke of work. **1953** JMFox *Bright* (B) 67: He'd led the life of Riley, but [*then*] Riley had come home. **1956** *Punch* 5/23 624: We still speak of living the life of Riley. **1962** RMacdonald *Zebra* (NY) 50: He's living the life of Riley. **1970** NMonsarrat *Breaking* (L) 286: The life of Riley had begun. DA Life b(4); Amer. Herit. Dict. Life; SJRaff *Amer. Speech* 51 (1979) 94–101.

L139 To love more than one's **Life**

1932 FWCrofts *Sudden* (NY) 274: I loved Grinsmead more than my life. EAP L126.

L140 While there is **Life** there is hope (*varied*)

1919 LMerrick *Chain* (L) 240: While there is life there is hope. **1920** GBMcCutcheon *Anderson Crow* (NY) 55: While there's life there's hope. **1923** LThayer *Sinister* (NY) 149: While there's life there's hope. **1932** TThayer *Three Sheet* (NY) 311: While there's life, there's hope. **1935** GDHCole

Big Business (NY) 122: While there's life there's hope. **1941** ESHolding *Speak* (NY) 133: But while there is life, there is hope. **1945** EPhillpotts *They Were Seven* (NY) 136: What would life be without hope? **1956** *BHerald* 11/28 1: Where there is life, there is hope. **1957** *BangorDN* 7/29 26: "While there's life, there's hope," they say. **1959** *NYTimes* 5/17 5E: While man lives he will hope. **1960** HHarrison *Death World* (NY) 123: The old platitude: where there's life there's hope. **1965** HActon *Old Lamps* (L) 229: While there is drink there is hope. **1970** WANolen *Making* (NY) 214: I don't know the origin of the adage "Where there's life there's hope," but I can testify that whoever coined it sensed something deep within the soul of men. **1974** MInnes *Appleby's Other* (NY) 117: While there is death there is hope. **1975** PDickinson *Lively* (NY) 192: "Where there's hope there's life, like Mum used to say. D'you remember how she used to get that sort of thing inside out?" "She once told me that wild horses on bended knees couldn't get her into some store or other." EAP L128; TW 220(15); Brunvand 85(9).

L141   All in a **Lifetime**

1935 JTFarrell *Judgment* (NY) 234: It's all in a lifetime. **1938** RPhilmore *Short List* (L) 174: It's all in a lifetime. **1943** AAFair *Bats Fly* (NY) 89: Oh, well, it's all in a lifetime. **1956** *NYTimes Book Review* 8/26 29: It was all in a lifetime. **1957** PGWodehouse *Over* (L) 61: It was all in a lifetime and the first hundred years were the hardest. Brunvand 85.

L142   As quick as **Light**

1930 ANewell *Who Killed* (NY) 100: Quick as a light. **1969** JCreasey *Baron* (NY) 176: Quick as light. TW 220(2).

L143   As swift as **Light**

1925 JGBrandon *Bond* (L) 209: Swift as light. **1927** VBridges *Girl* (P) 105: Swift as light. Wilstach 412: Swifter than, 562.

L144   To go out like a **Light** (lamp) (varied)

1925 SQuinn *Phantom* (Sauk City, Wisc. 1966) 8: I went out like a light. **1932** GDyer *Five* (B) 72: I went out like a light. **1934**

HCorey *Crime* (NY) 137: He went out like a lamp. **1937** GBruce *Claim* (NY) 192: He was out like a light. **1940** CBDawson *Lady Wept* (NY) 218: Out like a light [*drunk*]. **1941** TChanslor *Our Second* (NY) 39: I'll go out like a light [*die*]. **1952** AGarve *Hole* (NY 1959) 72: He went out like a lamp [*fainted*]. **1953** CLittle *Black* (NY) 54: I slept very well . . . went out like a light. **1958** *New Yorker* 1/4 21: Out like a light [*drunk*]. **1959** MMillar *Listening* (NY) 18: I must have passed out like a light. **1961** FLockridge *Murder* (L) 150: Passed out like a light, as they say. **1965** AGilbert *Voice* (NY) 185: She was dead, out like a light. **1972** DLees *Rainbow* (NY) 48: He went out like a light [*drunk*]. **1973** ACharters *Kerouac* (San Francisco) 228: She was out like a light [*morphine*]. **1974** SForbes *Some* (NY) 162: Put myself out like light [*alcohol*]. **1976** JSScott *Bastard's* (NY) 27: You go out like a light [*sleep after sex*]. Taylor *Prov. Comp.* 53: Out; Wentworth 318.

L145   To hide one's **Light** (*etc.*) under a bushel (varied)

1906 JCLincoln *Mr. Pratt* (NY) 35: To hide his talents under a kitchen bushel. **1922** JJoyce *Ulysses* (NY 1934) 395: Females—who hide their flambeau under a bushel in an uncongenial cloister. **1924** LSpringfield *Some Piquant* (L) 279: Allow his light to be hidden under a bushel. **1933** WADarlington *Mr. Cronk's* (L) 310: You hid your light so long under a bushel. **1936** HAshbury *French* (NY) 128: Their quadroon sisters were far from being content to hide their shining lights under the proverbial bushel. **1939** GDHCole *Greek* (L) 204: He . . . did not believe in hiding his light under a bushel. **1940** CMWills *R.E.Pipe* (L) 173: We hide our light under a bushel. **1948** ME Chase *Jonathan* (NY) 27: Jonathan was never one to hide his candle under a bushel. **1952** AWUpfield *Venom* (NY) 95: Hiding his light under a bushel. **1957** *BangorDN* 3/12 10: Hiding our light under a bushel. **1957** *BHerald* 11/7 30: Moscow does not bury its light under a bushel. **1963** MMcCarthy *Group* (NY) 183: To hide her light under a bushel. **1968** CWatson *Charity* (NY) 173: You must stop hiding your light under a bushel. **1970** RPStearns *Science* (Urbana) 100: The Royal Society did not hide its light under a bushel. **1972** JMDobson *Politics* (NY) 89: Blaine hardly hid his light under a bushel. EAP B372: Bushel; TW 220(3); *Oxford* 371: Hide one's light.

L146 To see **Light** at the end of the tunnel

1962 *NYTimes* 12/13 4: We don't see the end of the tunnel, but I must say I don't think it is darker than it was a year ago, and in some ways lighter. [*Transcript of President John F. Kennedy's news conference of 12/ 12, in which he responded to a question about Vietnam.*] **1970** ELathen *Pick* (NY) 154: Beginning to see light at the end of the tunnel. **1972** MWilliams *Inside* (NY) 295: We had at last begun to see a light showing now at the end of the tunnel. **1974** ROllard *Pepys* (NY) 260: The King . . . could see light at the end of the tunnel. **1975** HDolson *Please* (P) 140: I'm beginning to see light at the end of the trap. **1976** IWallach *Five Thousand* (NY) 14: Remember that the light at the end of the tunnel is an interstellar orgasm.

L147 To stand in one's **Light**

1929 GDHCole *Poison* (NY) 345: Standing in her light. **1932** VLoder *Red Stain* (NY) 96: I didn't want to stand in his light. **1955** NLewis *Day* (L) 44: Far be it from me to stand in your light. EAP L132.

L148 As fast as **Lightning**

1931 RSAllen *Washington* (NY) 243: As fast as lightning. TW 221(1).

L149 As quick as **Lightning**; Lightning-quick (*varied*)

1900 CFPidgin *Quincy A. Sawyer* (B) 170: Quick as lightning; 277. **1904** JCLincoln *Cap'n Eri* (NY) 129: Quicker'n chain lightnin'. **1922** JJoyce *Ulysses* (NY 1934) 356: Quick as lightning. **1931** JTully *Blood* (NY) 25: Her mind was lightning quick. **1932** BRoss *Tragedy of X* (NY) 70: He's quick as lightning. **1959** ASillitoe *Saturday* (NY) 34: Quick as lightning. **1965** VRandolph *Hot Springs* (Hatboro, Penn.) 21: Quicker than greased lightning. EAP L135; TW 221(2); Brunvand 85(2).

L150 As swift as **Lightning**; Lightning-swift

1927 AHaynes *Crow's* (L) 309: Swift as lightning. **1931** SChalmers *Whispering* (NY) 219: It is as swift as a stroke of lightning. **1955** RStout *Before* (NY) 162: Something he knew to be lightning-swift. **1962** BWAldiss *Hothouse* (L) 233: As swift as the lightning. EAP L136; Brunvand 85(4).

L151 **Lightning** never strikes twice in the same place (*varied*)

1909 MRRinehart *Man in Lower Ten* (NY 1947) 228: Ghosts are like lightning; they never strike twice in the same night. **1914** PGWodehouse *Little Nugget* (NY 1929) 208: Sam, like lightning, did not strike twice in the same place. **1930** CFitzsimmons *Manville* (NY) 76: You don't believe that lightning strikes twice in the same place? **1937** CBClason *Blind* (NY) 205: I believe that lightning, contrary to tradition, does sometimes strike twice in the same spot. **1941** LThayer *Hallowe'en* (NY) 209: Aren't you in the habit of saying, "If lightning strikes twice in the same place, there's a reason." **1943** WMcCully *Doctors* (NY) 129: Remember the old saying about lightning . . . lightning had struck twice in the same place. **1954** WDexter *World* (NY 1966) 7: A saying that "Lightning never strikes in the same place twice." **1956** MGEberhart *Postmark* (NY) 168: Lightning may strike twice in the same place, but usually it doesn't. **1958** EMcBain *Lady* (NY 1964) 90: And to quote an old sawhorse, lightning never strikes twice in the same place. **1970** HCarvic *Miss Seeton Draws* (NY) 158: Lightning, as anyone knew, never struck in the same place. **1970** JWechsberg *First* (B) 132: Lightning never strikes twice, not in southern California, where thunderstorms are rare anyway. **1973** OSela *Portuguesa* (NY) 208: But luck, like lightning, doesn't often strike twice in the same place. TW 221(11). Cf. Bullets *above.*

L152 To act like greased (*etc.*) **Lightning** (*varied*)

1915 JBuchan *Thirty-Nine* (NY) 81: I went like blue lightning. **1919** KHoward *Peculiar* (NY) 89: She rattled it off like lightning.

1922 JJoyce *Ulysses* (NY 1934) 327: And off he pops like greased lightning. **1929** CBush *Perfect* (NY) 232: I'll come along with it like a streak of lightning. **1931** HReilly *Murder* (NY) 157: He beat it like a streak of greased lightning. **1933** GBegbie *Sudden* (L) 53: His quick brain began to work like lightning. **1937** RPenny *Policeman in* (L) 276: He acts like the proverbial lightning. **1955** MErskine *Old Mrs.* (NY) 180: He was off . . . like greased lightning, as the saying is. **1956** *BangorDN* 7/16 11: Going like streaked lightning down a peeled hickory. **1958** NMonkman *From Queensland* (NY) 39: The wasp moves like lightning. **1970** JCreasey *Part* (NY) 92: He moved like lightning. 155: It spreads like lightning. **1973** PMoyes *Curious* (NY) 85: A black form flashed like greased lightning. EAP L137; TW 221–2 (12–18).

L153   Like attracts like

1928 AEApple *Mr. Chang's* (NY) 165: Like attracts like. **1934** AFielding *Cautley* (L) 14: An instance of like attracting like. **1946** MBlankfort *Widow-Malern* (NY) 9: Like attracted like. **1947** HCahill *Look* (NY) 5: Like attracts like, as the fellow says. Cf. following entries.

L154   Like breeds (begets) like

1931 DFrome *Strange* (NY) 155: Like breeds like. **1969** APHannum *Look* (NY) 196: Like begets like in spite of the Devil. EAP L140: Produces; TW 222(2); Brunvand 86: Produces; *Oxford* 464: Breeds.

L155   Like calls to like

1910 EPhillpotts *Tales* (NY) 224: Like calls to like. **1940** CMWills *R.E.Pipe* (L) 152: Like calling to like. **1956** JWyndham *Tales* (NY) 92: There's this business of like calling to like. **1958** SJackson *Sundial* (NY) 200: Like calls to like. **1963** DMDisney *Here Lies* (NY) 63: Like called to like. **1964** EHuxley *Incident* (NY) 69: Like calls to like. **1970** FBarlow *Edward* (L) 284: It was like calling to like. **1971** MHarrison *Fanfare* (L) 141: Like was calling to like. TW 222(3): Loves. Cf. Turd *below*.

L156   Like cures (helps) like

1930 SChalmers *Crime* (NY) 27: On the principle of *similia similibus curantur*. **1942** SHAdams *Tambay* (NY) 218: You know the homeopathic principle, like cures like. **1958** TSterling *Silent* (L) 31: *Similia similibus curantur*. Like cures like. **1960** PO'Connor *Lower* (L) 18: Like helps like. TW 222(4); *Oxford* 464.

L157   Like knows like

1938 AEFielding *Black Cats* (NY) 114: Like has a way of knowing like. Whiting *NC* 437.

L158   Like should wed with like

1937 JSFletcher *Todmanhance* (L) 17: Like should wed with like. Whiting M175; *Oxford* 516: Marry your like.

L159   Like to like (*varied*)

1928 EJepson *Emerald* (NY) 55: Like to like. **1937** JEsteven *While Murder* (NY) 148: Like for like. **1953** JTMcIntosh *World* (NY 1956) 70: Like clings to like. **1967** Lord Kilbracken *Van Meergeren* (NY) 96: Like seeks out like. **1981** JSScott *View* (NY) 135: Like responds to like, and they were of a feather. EAP L141.

L160   Like it or lump it (*varied*)

1912 JCLincoln *Postmaster* (NY) 125: He'll have to like it or lump it. **1920** GBMcCutcheon *Anderson Crow* (NY) 281: If she didn't like [it] she could lump it. **1922** JJoyce *Ulysses* (NY 1934) 730: Now there you are like it or lump it. **1930** WLewis *Apes* (NY 1932) 180: You must like it or lump it. **1934** WMartyn *Death* (L) 53: You can like it or leave it. **1937** GHeyer *They Found* (L) 60: If you don't like it you'll have to lump it. **1940** ECBentley *Those Days* (L) 237: If the country did not like it, the country could lump it. **1952** MRRinehart *Swimming* (NY) 302: Take it or lump it. **1957** *Time* 7/22 46: Like it or lump it. **1961** JBingham *Night's* (L 1965) 54: If she didn't like it, she could lump it. **1964** JBPriestley *Sir Michael* (L) 144: If George doesn't like it, George can . . . lump it. **1970** VCHall *Outback* (Adelaide) 46: If you didn't like it you could lump it. **1974** SForbes *Some* (NY) 117: Like it or not, you'll have to lump it. EAP L142; TW 223(1); Brunvand 86.

L161 As fair as a **Lily**

1916 NDouglas *London Street Games* (L) 65: As fair as a lily. Whiting L276; Brunvand 86(1).

L162 As fresh as a **Lily**

1949 GFowler *Beau* (NY) 91: As fresh as a lily. Whiting L277.

L163 As pure as a **Lily**; Lily-pure

1934 JTFarrell *Young Manhood* (NY 1935) 182: My four sisters are as pure as a lily. **1941** NMarsh *Death in Ecstasy* (NY) 251: As pure as a lily. **1955** MO'Brine *Passport* (L) 14: Amadeo is as pure as the lily. **1959** AGoodman *Golden* (NY) 51: A girl should remain pure as a lily. **1961** HKlinger *Wanton* (NY) 139: Miss Norrell's lily-pure charms. Taylor *Prov. Comp.* 65.

L164 As white as a **Lily**; Lily-white

1920 ACrabb *Samuel* (NY) 12: He's lily-white. **1927** JTaine *Quayle's* (NY) 436: White as a lily. **1933** GBeaton *Jack* (L) 188: Lily-white hands. **1947** NBlake *Minute* (L) 26: My own lily-white hand. **1957** DJEnright *Heaven* (L) 106: Lily-white hands. **1970** STerkel *Hard* (NY) 438: My lily-white hands. **1974** CMSmith *Reverend* (NY) 212: I'll bet my lily-white arse he does. EAP L144, 144a; TW 223(2,3).

L165 To gild (paint) the **Lily** (*varied*)

1928 EDBiggers *Behind* (NY) 168: Gilding the lily. **1930** ATrain *Adventures* (NY) 2: The theory that a lily cannot be painted. **1932** RKeverne *William* (L) 92: To gild the lily. **1937** SFowler *Four Callers* (L) 260: To gild the lily is proverbial waste of time. **1940** MBurton *Murder in* (L) 248: The type that always seeks to gild the lily. **1947** LFord *Woman* (NY) 160: Gilding the lily. **1948** ES Gardner *Lonely* (NY DBC) 98: He's always gilding the lily and painting the rose. **1957** JLodwick *Equator* (L) 77: I made no attempt to gild my lily. **1959** EMcBain *King's* (NY) 30: Without any gilding of the lily. **1961** BAldiss *Primal* (NY) 120: It's positively gilding the lily. **1969** RRendell *Secret* (NY) 133: The lily that needs no gilding. Brunvand 86(3): Painting the lily; Oxford *DQ* (2nd ed) 447.39 [*Shakespeare*].

L166 To be out on a **Limb**

1931 ELoban *Calloused* (NY) 101: No wonder his attorney was out on a limb! **1937** RGDean *Three Lights* (NY) 242: He's out on a limb. **1944** HTalbot *Rim* (NY 1965) 7: Left you out on a limb. **1947** GGallagher *I Found* (NY DBC) 37: To go out on a limb for me. **1951** MHead *Congo* (NY) 176: I'm out on one hell of a shaky limb. Amer. Herit. Dict. Limb *n.* 5.

L167 As dry as a **Lime-kiln**

1936 CBarry *Poison* (L) 87: I'm as dry as a limekiln. TW 223.

L168 To attach oneself (cling) like a **Limpet**

1924 AChristie *Man* (NY) 80: Attached to her like a limpet. **1930** AChristie *Mysterious* (NY) 243: I can hardly attach myself to you like the proverbial limpet. **1931** EARobertson *Four Frightened* (NY) 41: The seat, to which everyone clung like a limpet. **1936** DWheatley *They Found* (P) 190: Clung to . . . life like a limpet. **1951** RKing *Duenna* (NY) 46: He had clung tenaciously to his swivel-chair like a true-blue limpet. **1955** CMcCormac *You'll Die* (NY) 154: Clinging to his waist like a limpet. **1965** NFreeling *Criminal* (L) 101: All journalists . . . cling like limpets to the coarse cliché. **1970** NMonsarrat *Breaking* (L) 149: I clung to office like any other minor limpet. **1975** HLawrenson *Stranger* (NY) 63: [He] clung to the bar like a limpet. Cf. Leech *above*.

L169 To stick like a **Limpet**

1922 JJoyce *Ulysses* (NY 1934) 373: Better not stick here all night like a limpet. **1927** RAFreeman *Magic* (NY) 281: Sticking to the bell-push like a limpet. **1935** JJConnington *In Whose* (L) 165: She stuck to that yarn of hers like a limpet to a rock. **1958** PGWodehouse *Cocktail* (L) 69: A . . . nurse who stuck to you like a limpet. **1959** NFitzgerald *This Won't* (L) 102: He's sticking like a limpet to His Nibs. **1960** LSdeCamp *Bronze* (NY) 30: My father . . . stuck to his subject like a limpet to a rock. **1962** PDJames *Cover* (NY 1976) 30: She sticks to him like a limpet. **1972** EPeters *Seventh* (NY) 141: I'm sticking to you like the proverbial limpet. **1976** JPorter *Package* (NY) 146: She would stick to the girls like the proverbial limpet. NED Limpet b (quote 1824). Cf. Leech *above*.

L170 As straight as a **Line**

1935 FDGrierson *Murder* (L) 50: He's straight as a line. **1938** FDGrierson *Covenant* (L) 12: He was as straight as a line [*honest*]. **1947** VWBrooks *Times of Melville* (NY) 292: Straight as a line. **1952** FPratt *Blue* (NY 1969) 30: [His] reasoning led straight as a line. EAP L147; TW 223(1).

L171 Hew to the **Line**, let the chips fall where they may

c1923 ACrowley *Confessions* ed JSymonds (L 1969) 890: Hew to the line, let the ships [*sic*] fall where they may. **1930** WLevinrew *Murder* (NY) 43: Let the ax fall where it may. **1930** CWells *Doorstep* (NY) 278: Let the chips fall where they may. **1937** SPalmer *Blue Banderilla* (NY) 206: Hew to the line, Oscar, let the chips fall where they may, even on the nigger in the woodpile. **1940** RLGoldman *Snatch* (NY) 218: You have hewed to the line and let the chips fall where they may. **1947** ELanham *Politics* (NY) 159: Let the chips fall where they may. **1949** ESGardner *Dubious* (NY 1954) 177: I hew to the line and the chips can fall where they want to. **1950** ESGardner *Musical* (NY) 197: We'll hew to the line . . . To hell with the chips. **1955** KMKnight *Robineau* (NY) 36: She hews to the line, let the quips fall where they may. **1958** *New Yorker* 7/12 23: And let the chaps fall where they may. **1959** *BHerald* 2/25 8: To use an expression of the street to "let the chips fall where they may." 3/8 14: Let the chips fall where they will. **1964** RMacdonald *Chill* (NY) 100: Let the truth be told, and the chips fall where they may. **1970** RMungo *Famous* (B) 159: Let the chips fall where they may. **1973** WMasterson *Undertaker* (NY) 16: The free-wheeling let-the-chips-fall-where-they-may little magazine. **1975** PMoyes *Black* (NY) 70: No matter where the chips may fall. Whiting *NC* 437(2); Bartlett 733a [*Roscoe Conkling*].

L172 To read between the **Lines**

1934 EPOppenheim *Gallows* (B) 278: One had to read between the lines. **1936** LRobinson *General* (NY) 24: Reading, as they say, between the lines it was too easy. **1953** AChristie *Funerals* (NY) 39: Cora . . . had read between the lines, and had crossed the t's and dotted the i's. **1966** HWaugh *Pure* (NY) 26: You can read between the lines. NED Line *sb.*^{2} 23a.

L173 To toe the **Line**

1922 JJoyce *Ulysses* (NY 1934) 309: Jack made him toe the line. **1937** LRGribble *Who Killed* (L) 43: She'll toe the line. **1953** JFleming *Good* (L) 212: If he didn't toe the line. **1956** EDillon *Death* (L) 40: He makes them all toe the line. NED Toe *v.* 2.

L174 To wash dirty **Linen** in public (*varied*)

1916 SRohmer *Tales* (NY 1922) 225: I have no dirty linen to wash. **1924** LThayer *Key* (NY) 182: Anybody's dirty linen. **1925** WAStowell *Singing Walls* (NY) 28: Washing our family linen in public. **1927** VWilliams *Eye* (B) 296: That'll save the washing of a heap of dirty linen. **1930** WLewis *Apes* (NY 1932) 421: There was no occasion to wash dirty linen in public. **1934** MDavis *Hospital* (NY) 80: Some linen is too foul to wash in public. **1935** CDickson *Red Widow* (NY) 217: I do not mean to conceal the dirty linen in the closet. **1939** CMRussell *Topaz Flower* (NY) 32: The family linen will be aired all right. **1941** GEGiles *Three Died* (NY) 67: They'll wash their own dirty linen. **1950** ECRLorac *And Then* (NY) 54: The washing of dirty linen in public. **1956** AM Wells *Night* (NY) 178: It looks as if all our dirty linen is going to be washed in public. **1958** AHeriot *Zenobia* (L) 210: To wash their dirty linen before a pagan public. **1959** SSterling *Body* (NY) 9: An old hand at washing dirty linen in public. **1960** A Sinclair *Project* (L) 152: One only washes clean linen in public. Dirty linen is kept between hard covers and censored. **1966** MFagyas *Widow* (NY) 40: Not by airing our dirty linen in public. **1970** WANolen *Making* (NY) 75: This was dirty-linen day. **1972** WJBurley *Guile* (NY) 52: Having the family's linen washed in public. EAP L151; Brunvand 87: Family; *Oxford* 868.

L175   As bold as a Lion
1939 DCCameron *Murder's Coming* (NY) 221: He acted bold as a lion. **1960** FCrane *Death-Wish* (NY DBC) 74: As bold as a lion. EAP L152; TW 223–4(1).

L176   As brave as a Lion
1903 EChilders *Riddle* (NY 1940) 65: He is brave as a lion. **1906** JLondon *Letters* ed KHendricks (NY 1965) 219: As brave as a lion. **1930** Ex-PrivateX *War* (NY) 200: Brave as a lion. **1938** WFaulkner *Unvanquished* (NY) 260: The colonel's brave as a lion. **1951** RStout *Curtains* (NY) 132: I'm as brave as a lion. **1958** SBarr *Purely* (NY) 145: As brave as a lion. **1967** FSwinnerton *Sanctuary* (NY) 161: As brave as a lion. EAP L153.

L177   As fierce as a Lion
1910 EPhillpotts *Tales* (NY) 195: Fierce as a lion. EAP L154; TW 224(4).

L178   As strong as a Lion
1920 EWallace *Three-Oaks* (L) 230: As strong as a lion. **1932** PMacDonald *Escape* (NY) 297: As strong as a lion. EAP L155; TW 224(7).

L179   The Lion and the lamb
1954 STruss *Other Side* (NY) 137: The lion . . . does not lie down with the lamb. **1962** STruss *Time* (NY) 97: The lion . . . does not lie down with the lamb. EAP L158.

L180   A Lion in the path (way)
1928 JRhode *Tragedy* (NY) 5: There's a lion in the path. **1949** MBurton *Disappearing* (NY) 29: There's only one lion in the path. **1952** AGilbert *Mr. Crook* (NY DBC) 158: [She] was a lion in the way. **1959** RVickers *Girl* (NY DBC) 71: There was still a lion in her path. EAP L160; TW 224(9).

L181   The Lion's share (portion)
1928 RHFuller *Jubilee* (NY) 119: The lion's share. **1930** ABCox *Piccadilly* (NY) 326: Get the lion's portion. **1935** HCBailey *Sullen* (NY) 300: Bure took the lion's share. **1951** HRigsby *Murder for* (NY 1952) 166: [He] got the lion's share. **1959** DAWollheim *Ma-*

cabre (NY) 185: [He] took the lion's share. **1964** RAHeinlein *Farnham's* (NY 1965) 81: She got the lion's share of liquor. **1972** QBell *Virginia* (NY) I 70: To have the lion's share of life. Brunvand 87(7); *Oxford* 467.

L182   Of Lions to make lambs (*varied*)
1934 CBush *100% Alibis* (L) 196: Wharton had a trick of finding lions and leaving lambs. **1934** PGWodehouse *Thank You* (B) 133: My visitor, who had gone up like a lion, came down like a lamb. **1940** GStockwell *Candy* (NY) 267: That was the lamblike Inspector Horme, roaring like a lion. EAP L162.

L183   To beard the Lion in his den
1900 CFPidgin *Quincy A. Sawyer* (B) 102: To beard the lion in his den. **1926** RAFreeman *Red Thumb* (L) 26: Beard the lion in their den. **1936** KCLenehan *Silecroft* (L) 210: I shall beard the lion in his den. **1955** JO'Hara *Ten* (NY) 266: I'm going to beard the lion in his den. **1959** SSterling *Body* (NY) 58: I'm going to beard the lion. **1972** AMenen *Cities* (L) 125: His sister . . . bearded the lion in his den of pleasure. **1975** NFreeling *Bugles* (NY) 130: To beard the lion in his den. EAP L163; Brunvand 87(5), 142: Tiger (1).

L184   To fight like a Lion
1930 EMarjoribanks *E.M.Hall* (L) 95: He had fought the case like a lion. **1956** AM Maughan *Harry* (NY) 391: He fought like a lion. EAP L164; TW 224(13).

L185   To walk (jump) into the Lion's den (mouth) (*varied*)
1915 JFerguson *Steal Thy* (L 1935) 289: They were walking . . . into the lion's den. **1921** JSFletcher *Orange-Yellow* (NY) 162: Walking . . . into the lion's den. **1932** DSharp *Code-Letter* (B) 159: He was walking rather too rashly into the lion's den. **1933** RAJWalling *Behind* (L) 143: What's made you jump into the lion's mouth? **1936** HWade *Bury Him* (L) 142: Shoved himself down the lion's mouth. **1939** DHume *Death Before* (L) 56: You dive into the lion's den. **1940** DHume *Five Aces* (L) 225: Walking into the lion's den single-handed. **1955** BBenson *Silver* (NY) 167: Back to the lion's

den again. **1967** EWallach *Light* (NY) 8: I had walked right into the lion's den. EAP L161: Mouth; *Oxford* 467: Mouth.

L186 From the **Lips** (teeth) outwards (*varied*)

1929 CReeve *Ginger* (NY) 3: He laughed—from the lips outward, as the saying goes. **1930** FBeeding *League* (B) 90: Granby might chuckle, but it was from the lips only. **1938** MSaltmarsh *Clouded* (NY) 46: Friends from the teeth outward. **1944** HReilly *Opening Door* (NY) 77: The smile didn't go any farther than his lips. EAP T191.

L187 To keep a stiff upper **Lip**

1912 JCLincoln *Postmaster* (NY) 41: Keep a stiff upper lip. **1928** SGluck *Last* (NY) 186: Keep a stiff upper lip. **1936** KMechem *Frame* (NY) 137: Keep a stiff upper lip. **1940** EDean *Murder Is* (NY) 92: Keep a stiff upper lip. **1941** TFuller *Three Thirds* (B) 83: To keep a stiff upper lip. **1950** SPalmer *Green* (NY) 23: Keeping a stiff upper lip. **1957** *Punch* 2/20 267: There is . . . surprise . . . that the Wodehouse upper lip should remain so stiff. EAP L169; Brunvand 87.

L188 To pay (give) **Lip-service**

1965 ESitwell *Taken Care* (NY) 38: To pay lip-service. **1972** MDelving *Shadow* (NY) 106: To give lip service. EAP L172.

L189 **Listeners** (*etc.*) never hear good of themselves (*varied*)

1900 CFPidgin *Quincy A. Sawyer* (B) 331: List'ners never hear any good of themselves. **1928** RGore-Browne *In Search* (NY) 267: Listeners never hear good. **1929** GMWhite *Square* (L) 151: [It] brought the proverb concerning eavesdroppers very forcibly home to my mind. **1934** DFairfax *Masked Ball* (L) 86: Listeners hear no good of themselves. **1939** RAJWalling *Blistered Hand* (NY) 13: The proverbial lot of the listener. **1941** CCoffin *Mare's Nest* (NY) 110: Eavesdroppers must expect to hear unpleasant things either about themselves or about others. **1952** DMDisney *Prescription* (NY) 168: Snoopers seldom learn anything pleasant. **1963** AWUpfield *Body* (NY) 182: The old saying, eavesdroppers seldom hear good of themselves. **1965** SForbes *Relative* (NY) 103: Eavesdropping . . . Did you hear anything good about yourself? **1967** RGarrett *Too Many* (NY) 119: There is an old adage to the effect that people who listen at keyholes often hear things that startle them. **1975** ARoudybush *Suddenly* (NY) 112: Don't you know that eavesdroppers never hear any good of themselves? EAP L174; TW 116: Eavesdropper, 225; Brunvand 41: Eavesdropper, 87: Listeners.

L190 Every **Little** (bit) helps (*varied*)

1923 JSFletcher *Charing Cross* (NY) 135: Every little helps. **1928** JJConnington *Mystery* (B) 152: "Everything helps," he said sententiously. **1931** HFootner *Easy* (L) 80: Every little helps, . . . as the old woman said when she beat up a dead fly in her currant cake. **1932** JSFletcher *Four Degrees* (L) 25: The smallest things help. **1932** DLSayers *Have* (NY) 399: Every little helps. **1940** JJConnington *Four Defences* (B) 81: Every little helps. **1940** MInnes *There Came* (L 1958) 49: Every little helps. **1950** STruss *Never* (NY) 49: Every little helps. **1956** AWUpfield *Man of* (NY) 144: Every little bit helps. **1957** *BHerald* 8/7 22: Every little 180,000 helps. **1960** DHayles *Comedy* (L) 160: Every little helps, as the old lady said when she piddled in the sea. **1961** BPym *No Fond* (L) 78: Every little helps, doesn't it? **1964** SRansome *Meet* (NY DBC) 49: Every little bit helps, to coin a cliché. **1965** WRBurkett *Sleeping* (NY) 98: Every little drop fills the bucket. **1972** SAngus *Arson* (NY) 10: Every little bit helps. **1977** JBHilton *Dead-Nettle* (NY) 39: Every little helps. EAP L177.

L191 A **Little** goes a long way

1925 JSFletcher *Secret* (B) 119: A very little of it goes a long way. **1932** RWhitfield *Virgin* (NY) 68: A little bit goes a long way. **1934** MKing-Hall *Gay* (NY) 161: A little of it goes a long way. **1962** PQuentin *Ordeal* (NY) 140: A little goes a long way. **1972** ELathen *Murder* (NY) 119: A little of [him] went a long way. TW 225(1).

L192 To say **Little** but think a lot (*varied*)

1930 CBush *Dead Man* (NY) 1: Norris . . . thought a lot but said little. **1930** BFlynn

Creeping (L) 185: If he said nothing there was no doubt that he thought a lot. **1930** JRhode *Venner* (L) 177: I shouldn't say much but I should think a bit. **1933** JVTurner *Who Spoke* (NY) 210: The less I say the more I think. **1937** JRhode *Death on the Board* (L) 151: He didn't say much but thought a lot. **1940** HAdams *Chief Witness* (L) 72: If like the sailor's parrot I have said little, I have thought a devil of a lot. **1952** EPempleton *Proper* (B) 91: "And otherwise I say nothing." "But you think all the more." EAP L183.

L193　He that **Lives** alone must ay be doing

1931 AWynne *Blue* (P) 194: Them as lives alone must aye be doing.

L194　He that **Lives** longest will see the most

1929 SMElam *Borrow* (L) 99: The longer one lives, the more one learns. **1929** BFlynn *Invisible* (L) 192: Those that live longest will see the most. **1932** JJConnington *Sweepstake* (B) 194: Them that lives longest'll see most. **1938** ECRLorac *Slippery* (L) 171: An adage that he who lives longest earns most. **1952** GKersh *Brazen* (L) 67: Those who live longest will see most. **1971** MErskine *Brood* (NY) 55: Those that live longest will see the most. TW 226(6); *Oxford* 474.

L195　**Live** and learn

1905 JBCabell *Line* (NY 1926) 102: We live and learn. **1909** JLondon *Letters* ed KHendricks (NY 1965) 282: We live and learn. **1919** LMerrick *Chain* (L) 259: One lives and learns. **1928** DHLawrence *Lady* ("Allemagne") 1: One must live and learn. **1932** PMcGuire *Black Rose* (NY) 237: He lived a little longer . . . and learned a little more. **1933** BRoss *Tragedy of Z* (NY) 160: We leave and learn. **1940** HRutland *Poison Fly* (NY) 80: Live and learn, you know. **1941** CCoffin *Mare's Nest* (NY) 162: Live and learn is what I say. **1952** FPratt *Double* (NY) 122: We live and learn. **1956** GMason *Golden* (NY) 235: I live and learn. **1957** JPMarquand *Life* (B) 41: Live and learn is always our motto. **1963** JKirkup *Tropic* (L) 194: We live and learn, they say. **1968** SWoods *Knives* (NY) 45: Who lives may learn. **1973** RCondon *And

Then (NY) 55: We lived and learned. **1975** ARoudybush *Suddenly* (NY) 155: Live and learn. EAP L187.

L196　**Live** and let live

1922 FPitt *Woodland* (L) 20: It lives and lets live. **1923** ABlackwood *Episodes* (L) 299: A live-and-let-live type of man. **1933** DG Browne *Cotfold* (L) 5: Live and let live . . . was *his* motto. **1934** WSharp *Murder* (NY) 61: A sort of live and let live and the devil take the hindermost. **1937** ECRLorac *Bats* (L) 119: They followed the adage of live and let live. **1941** EDaly *Murders in* (NY) 144: What I say is, live and let live. **1952** ESGardner *Grinning* (NY) 75: Live and let live is my motto. **1952** HHunter *Bengal* (NY) 65: I'm a live-and-let-liver. **1954** IFleming *Live and Let Die* (NY 1959). **1958** *BHerald* 11/1 22: Your motto was "live and let live." **1958** ECRLorac *People* (NY) 137: *Cosi, cosi*—meaning live and let live. **1959** PQuentin *Shadow* (NY) 17: Live and let live. That's an old Saskatchewan proverb. **1960** RMacdonald *Ferguson* (NY) 211: Live and let live is my motto. **1967** DShannon *Rain* (NY) 29: Live and let live, like they say. **1971** ELinington *Practice* (NY) 128: Live 'n let live, I always say. **1977** JRLAnderson *Death* (NY) 22: A policy of live and let live. EAP L188.

L197　One only **Lives** once (*varied*)

1928 WMcFee *Pilgrims* (NY) 439: You only live once. **1932** HFootner *Dead Man's* (NY) 72: A man only lives once. **1939** JPPhilips *Death Delivers* (NY) 90: You only got one life to live. **1940** HFootner *Murderer's* (NY) 148: We only live once. **1945** FLockridge *Pay off* (P) 84: You only live once. **1957** *New Yorker* 4/27 26: You only live once. **1959** JPhilips *Killer* (NY) 129: They say you only live once . . . which implies that you only die once. **1974** MDavis *Tell Them* (NY) 16: You have only one life to live. Cf. One Dies but once *above*.

L198　As quick as a **Lizard**

1958 *Time* 4/28 104: Quick as a lizard. Cf. Taylor *Prov. Comp.* 40: Fast.

L199 To sleep like a **Lizard**

1936 RAJWalling *Crimson Slippers* (L) 250: Slept like a lizard. NED Lizard 2 (quote 1600).

L200 As red as a boiled **Lobster**; Lobster-red

1938 PHaggard *Death Talks* (NY) 150: Smollett got as red as a boiled lobster. **1957** *Time* 4/29 20: Lobster-red with ire. **1959** IFleming *Goldfinger* (NY) 18: Red as a lobster. **1959** MPHood *Bell* (NY) 19: Red as a boiled lobster. **1967** RPeterson *Another View* (NY) 100: Their arms are lobster-red. EAP L194.

L201 **Lock**, stock, and barrel (*varied*)

1918 BMalinowski *Diary* (NY 1967) 241: Pack lock, stock and barrel. **1927** WLewis *Letters* ed WKRose (L 1963) 173: Come over . . . lock, stock and barrel. **1928** RThorndike *Slype* (NY) 42: Gone, lock, stock and barrel, off his rocker. **1938** AWebb *Mr. P.'s Hat* (L) 118: I'd bought up the furniture . . . lock, stock, and barrel, as the saying is. **1956** MInnes *Old Hall* (L) 132: The Jorys, lock, stock and barrel (to use a vulgar phrase). **1957** *Time* 12/23 49: To buy the rising paper, lock, stock and debt. **1957** VWMason *Gracious* (NY) 209: She's for Henry King lock, stock and barrel. **1959** *Time* 7/20 34: The only foreign city in the world run lock, stock, and barrel by the U.S. Navy. **1963** RCroft-Cooke *Bosie* (L) 302: He swallowed both [*stories*] lock, stock and barrel. **1964** LWoolf *Beginning* (L) 73: Symonds was a littérateur, lock, stock, and barrel. **1966** EConnell *I Had* (NY) 20: She wanted me lock, stock and her barrel of money. **1970** ACross *Poetic* (NY) 39: He's against it lock, stock, and barrel—or do I mean hook, line, and sinker? **1973** AMorice *Death* (NY) 33: Sell the dreadful place, lock, stock and stables. **1975** HDolson *Please* (P) 27: Mac's wife went for participation, lock, stock and mattress. TW 226; Brunvand 88; *Oxford* 775: Stock. Cf. EAP S439–41: Stock.

L202 As dead as a **Log**

1939 RStout *Some Buried* (L) 207: I was as dead as a log [*asleep*]. **1972** DEmrich *Folklore* (B) 50: He fell as dead as a log. EAP L195.

L203 As easy (simple) as rolling (falling) off a **Log** (*etc.*) (*varied*)

1920 GBMcCutcheon *Anderson Crow* (NY) 154: As easy as rolling off a log. **c1923** ACrowley *Confessions* ed JSymonds (L 1969) 385: As easy as falling off a log. **1925** FWCrofts *Pit-Prop* (NY) 123: As easy as tumbling off a log. **1930** JDosPassos *42nd* (NY) 320: It's easy as rolling off a log. **1930** ATrain *Adventures* (NY) 275: Simple as rolling off a log. **1933** GBegbie *Sudden* (L) 217: As easy and simple as falling off a log. **1933** JFerguson *Night* (L) 68: As easy as fallin' into a ditch. **1934** HHolt *Sinister* (NY) 191: Easy as falling off a roof. **1935** BFlynn *Edge* (L) 248: Easy as falling downstairs. **1940** KMKnight *Death Came* (NY) 138: Easy as rolling off a log. **1941** HCBailey *Orphan Ann* (NY) 32: As easy as falling downstairs. **1953** PGWodehouse *Ring* (L) 127: As simple as falling off a log. **1957** IFleming *From Russia* (NY 1958) 178: Simple as falling off a log. **1957** *BangorDN* 1/31 28: Easy as falling off a log. **1960** BCClark *Long* (NY) 24: Easy as fallin' off a saw log backwards. **1961** EWilliams *George* (NY) 339: It was as easy as falling off a log into four-leaved clover. **1964** JPorter *Dover One* (NY 1966) 98: Easy as falling off a tree. **1965** JPorter *Dover Two* (NY 1968) 136: As easy as falling off a chair. **1970** JAiken *Embroidered* (NY) 12: Easy as falling off a brick. **1975** ARoudybush *Suddenly* (NY) 45: As easy as falling off a log. TW 227(1); Brunvand 88(1–3).

L204 As still as a **Log**

1928 GGardiner *At the House* (NY) 217: Still as a log. **1929** CGLDuCann *Secret* (L) 139: Barney lay still as a log. EAP L197.

L205 To drop (go down) like a **Log**

1930 WAStowell *Marston* (NY) 80: Both men dropped in their tracks like logs. **1937** GBarnett *I Knew* (L) 346: Christopher went down like a log. **1937** RCWoodthorpe *Death in* (NY) 302: He went down like a log. **1962** ESherry *Girl* (NY DBC) 54: He dropped like a log. **1970** SGBoswell *Book* (L) 136: I dropped him like a log. **1972** WJBurley *Guilt* (NY) 163: The poor girl went down like a log.

L206 To fall like a **Log**

1920 EWallace *Three-Oaks* (L) 227: He fell like a log. **1925** JSFletcher *False* (NY) 293: He went down like a log. NED Log *sb.*[1] 1b (quote 1900).

L207 To lie like a **Log**

1905 JBCabell *Line* (NY 1926) 102: The Englishman lay like a log. **1910** EPhillpotts *Tales* (NY) 328: To lie like a log. **1931** RSabatini *Captain Blood Returns* (B) 230: He lay inert as a log. **1940** HCBailey *Mr. Fortune Here* (NY) 191: Tumble down and lie like a log. **1965** ASeyton *Avalon* (NY 1966) 207: She lay like a log in the box bed. EAP L198.

L208 To sleep like a **Log** (*varied*)

1905 HRHaggard *Ayesha* (NY) 108: Slept like a log. **1920** RLHine *Cream* (L) 300: He slept like a log. **1930** AAustin *Murder* (NY) 145: I slept like a log, as the old sayin' is. **1932** MKennedy *Murderer* (L) 163: He slept like the proverbial log. **1937** ATilton *Beginning* (NY) 161: Sleep like the proverbial log. **1941** AMStein *Up to No Good* (NY) 234: I was sleeping like a log. **1949** JReach *Late* (NY) 13: I slept like a log. Incidentally, has anyone ever seen a sleeping log? **1957** *BHerald* 4/1 27: I'm going to sleep like a log. **1957** *New Yorker* 5/11 33: Sleeping like a bloody log. **1963** AAFair *Fish* (NY DBC) 37: Slept like a log. **1973** TAWaters *Lost* (NY) 27: She was sleeping like a log, which I suppose [*meant*] that she was sleeping like a dead tree. **1974** JCreasey *As Merry* (NY) 151: People do sleep like logs. TW 227(7); Taylor *Western Folklore* 17(1958) 16; *Oxford* 477.

L209 At **Loggerheads**

1927 FEverton *Dalehouse* (NY) 124: At loggerheads. **1940** JLBonney *Death by* (NY) 58: The twins . . . are continually at loggerheads. **1968** TBarman *Diplomatic* (L) 87: Ministers were openly at loggerheads. EAP L199.

L210 To chop **Logic**

1928 RAFreeman *As a Thief* (L) 186: A lot of futile logic-chopping; 216. **1933** RAJWalling *Behind* (L) 125: In the mood for chopping logic. **1952** FPratt *Blue* (NY 1969) 77: I'll not chop logic against you. **1955** NMarsh *Scales* (B) 37: I can't chop logic with you. EAP L200.

L211 All **Lombard Street** to a china orange (*varied*)

1923 JSFletcher *Exterior* (NY) 141: I wouldn't mind laying a thousand pounds to a china orange. **1926** JSFletcher *Green Ink* (B) 195: I'll lay all Lombard Street to that coffee cup. **1927** JSFletcher *Bartenstein* (NY) 83: I'll lay all the world to a duck's egg. **1927** AGilbert *Tragedy* (NY) 246: It's all Lombard Street to a china orange. **1930** JSFletcher *Heaven-sent* (NY) 187: I'll lay every penny . . . to a China orange. **1934** CBush *Dead Shepherd* (L) 230: All Lombard Street to a pinch of dung. **1935** GDilnot *Murder* (L) 58: Bet all Wall Street to a doughnut. **1938** DHume *Good-bye* (L) 245: I'd bet all my money to a China orange. **1949** MGilbert *He Didn't* (NY DBC) 173: It's Lombard Street to a china orange they're all away. **1957** VWheatley *H.Martineau* (Fair Lawn, NJ) 205: It is all Lombard Street to a china orange. **1959** AGilbert *Death* (NY) 225: It's all Lombard Street to a china orange. *Oxford* 477; Apperson 377.

L212 The **Long** and short of it

1908 JCLincoln *Cy Whittaker* (NY) 390: The long and short of it is. **1922** JJoyce *Ulysses* (NY 1934) 367: Long and the short of it. **1923** JSFletcher *Charing Cross* (NY) 246: That's the long and short of it. **1933** CBarry *Murder* (L) 234: That's the long and the short of it. **1937** MBurton *Murder* (L) 23: The long and the short of it was. **1944** PATaylor *Dead Ernest* (NY) 191: The long and short of it is. **1950** CEVulliamy *Henry* (L) 83: The long and the short of it is. **1955** NMarsh *Scales* (B) 77: The long and the short of me is that I'm on my way. **1960** HLivingston *Climacticon* (NY) 166: The long and the short, beauty and the beast, May and December. **1965** MJones *Set* (L) 179: That's the long and the short of it. **1972** NMarsh *Tied* (B) 236: That's the long and the short of it. **1976** JFoxx *Freebooty* (I) 193: The long and short of it. EAP S179: Short; TW 227; Brunvand 88; *Oxford* 478.

L213   If **Looks** could kill *etc.*

1921 EWallace *Daffodil* (B) 31: If looks could have killed, Tarling would have died. **1922** VBridges *Greensea* (NY) 17: If looks could kill. **1931** WWJacobs *Snug* (NY) 253: If looks could ha' killed, as the saying is. **1935** CMRussell *Murder* (NY) 16: If looks could kill, as they say! **1943** MRRinehart *Episode* (NY) 168: If looks could have killed. **1962** ESGardner *Reluctant* (NY DBC) 34: If looks could kill. **1964** RDuncan *All Men* (L) 165: If looks could kill, both would have dropped dead. **1969** CMatthews *Dive* (LA) 21: If looks could kill, et cetera. **1973** TWells *Brenda's* (NY) 105: An if-looks-could-kill glare. Cf. Wilstach 240: A look that would split a pitcher.

L214   **Looks** (appearances, beauty, pretty) are not (is not) enough (*varied*)

1910 JCLincoln *Depot Master* (NY) 90: Looks ain't everything. **1929** EWallace *Dark Eyes* (NY) 10: Looks aren't everything. **1957** DMDisney *My Neighbour's* (NY) 30: Looks ain't everything. **1957** LHanson *Verlaine* (NY) 6: Appearances are not everything. **1959** HRigsby *Clash* (P) 32: They've got a saying around here—"Pretty's not enough." **1980** WStadiem *Class* (NY) 195: The family was a living refutation of the old adage that "beauty isn't everything." TW 228(3); *Oxford* 646: Prettiness.

L215   **Looks** break no bones

1930 DLSayers *Documents* (NY) 220: Looks breaks no bones, as the sayin' is. Cf. Sticks and stones *below.*

L216   **Look** before you leap (*varied*)

1928 WMcFee *Pilgrims* (NY) 168: You had better look before you jump. **1929** AFielding *Cluny* (NY) 39: His motto was "Leap before you look." **1931** CFGregg *Rutland* (NY) 201: If one looked too long one would never leap. **1934** JTFarrell *Young Manhood* (NY 1935) 160: Look twice before you leap. **1940** GBagby *Corpse Wore* (NY) 3: You should look ... before you leap. **1942** FLockridge *Hanged* (NY) 161: He looked before he leaped, and then he did not leap, but moved forward cautiously. **1957** *New Yorker* 8/10 72: Q. Then how am I to decide where to invest my money? A. *Look before you leap.* **1958** BAldiss *Starship* (NY 1960) 37: In quarters, a well-worn precept said "Leap before you look"; rashness was proverbially the path of wisdom. **1962** *BangorDN* 6/19 3: Think twice before you leap. **1967** GBaxt *Swing* (NY) 152: We leaped before we looked. **1971** BCraig *September* (NY) 35: I should look before I leap ... chuck in a stitch in time and you've cornered the bloody market in platitudes. **1971** NWebster *Flickering* (NY) 40: We've a proverb which goes "Look before you leap." **1979** GWest *Duke* (NY) 7: Bankers, lawyers, look-before-you-leapers. EAP L207; TW 228(1).

L217   As crazy (daft, dotty) as a **Loon**

1909 JCFletcher *Keziah* (NY) 281: Crazy as a loon. **1924** IOstrander *Annihilations* (NY) 236: Crazier than a loon. **1928** GKnevels *Diamond* (NY) 216: Giles is as daft as a loon. **1931** WFaulkner *Sanctuary* (NY) 57: You're crazy as a loon. **1935** VRSmale *I Knew* (NY) 264: Crazy as the proverbial loon. **1956** GMetalious *Peyton* (NY) 69: Crazy as a loon. **1957** *BangorDN* 1/21 58: He's crazy as a loon. **1961** HKlinger *Wanton* (NY) 155: She's as doty as a loon. EAP L212; Brunvand 89(1).

L218   As drunk as a **Loon**

1934 JTFarrell *Young Manhood* (NY 1935) 398: Drunk as a loon. **1954** SDeLima *Carnival* (NY) 126: You're as drunk as a loon. **1977** HDolson *Beauty* (P) 210: Drunk as a loon. TW 228(2); Brunvand 89(2).

L219   As mad as a **Loon**

1928 JChancellor *Dark* (NY) 30: As mad as loons. TW 228(3).

L220   To laugh like a **Loon**

1956 *NYTimes Magazine* 8/19 50: Laughing like loons. **1960** JBarry *Malignant* (NY) 52: Who ever made up the phrase "laugh like a loon"? Wilstach 227.

L221   To be knocked for a **Loop**

1927 JTully *Circus* (NY) 104: It sure knocked me for a loop. **1937** ESGardner

Dangerous Dowager (NY) 123: It knocked me for a loop. **1938** HWSandberg *Crazy* (NY) 134: Someone knocking you for a loop. **1941** KRoos *If the Shroud* (NY) 202: It'll knock him for a loop. **1954** JRMacdonald *Find* (NY) 109: It knocked Katie for a loop. **1957** CRice *Knocked for a Loop* (NY). **1973** ARoudybush *Gastronomic* (NY) 42: You'll knock them for a loop. Wentworth 308: Knock.

L222 As drunk (tipsy, tight) as a **Lord**

1925 HBedford-Jones *Rodomont* (NY) 100: He was drunk as a lord. **1932** FBeeding *Take It* (B) 76: As tight as a lord. **1932** NTrott *Monkey* (NY) 158: Tight as a lord. **1935** *New Yorker* 10/19 21: Drunk as a lord. **1936** GHeyer *Why Shout* (NY) 114: Drunk as a lord. **1938** CBrahms *Bullet* (NY) 230: Tight as a lord. **1954** ECRLorac *Shroud* (NY) 212: He's as drunk as a lord. **1956** *Arizona Highways* August 34: Drunker than a lord. **1962** EHuxley *Mottled* (L) 35: As drunk as lords. **1962** RO'Connor *Scandalous* (NY) 88: Tipsy as lords. **1967** MDolbier *Benjy* (NY) 259: Drunk as a lord. **1970** PAlding *Murder* (NY) 58: As drunk as the proverbial lord. **1975** RForrest *Child's* (I) 208: Drunk as a lord. EAP L213.

L223 As happy as a **Lord**

1932 EWallace *Frightened* (L) 99: He may be as happy as a lord. **1955** MAllingham *Estate* (NY) 233: Happy as a lord. EAP L215.

L224 As rich as a **Lord**

1974 GMcDonald *Fletch* (I) 36: They're all as rich as lords. EAP L217.

L225 To live like a **Lord**

1930 FAWinder *Behind* (L) 45: You will live like a lord. **1933** DGBrowne *Dead* (L) 92: The constable lives like a lord. **1943** AAbbott *Shudders* (NY) 49: They're living like lords. **1957** LHanson *Verlaine* (NY) 334: He lived like a lord. **1960** NFitzgerald *Candles* (L) 49: Living like a lord. Whiting *NC* 438(3); Brunvand 89.

L226 **Lord** love a duck

1922 JJoyce *Ulysses* (NY 1934) 176: Lord love a duck. **1927** LBamburg *Beads* (NY) 194: Lord love a duck! **1932** EWallace *Frightened* (L) 130: Lord love a duck! **1937** CRoberts *Victoria* (NY) 5: Gawd love a duck! **1957** RLongrigg *Switchboard* (L) 64: Lord love a duck. **1961** PGWodehouse *Ice* (NY) 25: Lord love a duck. **1965** NBenchley *Visitors* (NY) 68: Lord love a duck. Partridge 245: Duck, Lord love a.

L227 No great **Loss** without some small gain

1935 VWMason *Washington* (NY) 229: No great loss without some small gain. **1957** MPHood *In the Dark* (NY) 56: No loss without some small gain. TW 229(1).

L228 To cut one's **Losses**

1950 ECrispin *Sudden* (NY DBC) 89: She'll cut her losses and keep quiet. **1958** RMacdonald *Doomsters* (NY) 216: It's time to cut your losses. **1963** NFreeling *Question* (NY 1965) 96: He had cut his losses. NED Suppl. Loss *sb.*[1] 4.

L229 As salt as **Lot's** wife's arse

1922 JJoyce *Ulysses* (NY 1934) 624: The beef as salt as Lot's wife's arse. Partridge 496: Backbone.

L230 **Lots** of luck and all of it bad

1937 JYDane *Cabana* (NY) 186: We wish Chet lots of luck . . . and all of it bad. **1957** JWhitehill *Able* (B) 160: The people in town say that Papa George had a lot of luck and it was all bad. Cf. Partridge 498: Luck to (him).

L231 As crouse as a new-washed **Louse**

1935 LBarringer *Kay* (NY) 103: Cobby and crouse as a new-washed louse. *Oxford* 581: Nothing so crouse.

L232 As dead as a **Louse**

1938 SSeifert *Death Stops* (NY) 144: Dead as [a] louse. Whiting *NC* 438(1). Cf. Nit *below*.

L233 As hot as **Love** in hay time (a hay-mow)

1934 BAWilliams *Hostile* (NY) 204: It's hot as love in hay time. **1954** RKLeavitt *Chip* (P) 100: Such similes as "hotter'n love in a haymow." Taylor *Prov. Comp.* 50; *Western Folklore* 17(1958) 16.

L234 Be off with the old **Love** before one is on with the new (*varied*)

1924 JSFletcher *Safety* (NY) 306: There's a wise old saying . . . that it's well to be off with the old love before you are on with the new. **1928** AHuxley *Point* (L) 172: When it's a case of off with the old love and on with the new. **1931** HCBailey *Fortune Explains* (NY) 236: His lordship decided to be off with the old love. **1937** JFerguson *Death* (L) 259: There's a saying to the effect that it is wiser to be off with the old love before one is on with the new. **1940** JSStrange *Picture* (NY) 75: If he was off with the old love before he took on the new one. **1954** EForbes *Rainbow* (B) 80: He had an off-with-the-old, on-with-the-new temperament. **1958** HCarmichael *Into* (NY) 100: Off with the old and on with the new. **1966** DMDisney *Magic* (NY) 79: Off with the old love, on with the new. **1969** AGilbert *Mr. Crook* (NY DBC) 34: Always on with the new love before she's off with the old. TW 229(1).

L235 First **Love** is strongest

1910 JCLincoln *Depot Master* (NY) 305: First love's strongest, you know. *Oxford* 492: No Love. Cf. Girl *above*.

L236 For **Love** or money

1900 MLPeabody *To Be Young* (B 1967) 80: Wouldn't do another for love or money. **1931** JSFletcher *Malvery* (L) 163: Such as you couldn't buy for love or money. **1938** HWSandberg *Crazy* (NY) 130: They wouldn't come through for love or money. **1941** MGEberhart *With This Ring* (NY) 246: The saying is neither for love nor money. **1944** EDaly *Book of the Dead* (NY) 193: Couldn't get a cab for love or money. **1960** NFitzgerald *Candles* (L) 14: There isn't a bed to be had . . . for love nor money. **1967** RJones *Three* (B) 82: I can't drink the stuff for love or money. **1970** NMonsarrat *Breaking* (L) 73: We can't get those things for love or money. **1977** EXFerrars *Pretty* (NY) 68: For love or money. EAP L228; TW 229(2).

L237 **Love** at first sight (*varied*)

1906 JCLincoln *Mr. Pratt* (NY) 154: Fell in love with him at first sight. **1922** JJoyce *Ulysses* (NY 1934) 113: Hate at first sight. **1931** PBaron *Round* (NY) 127: A case of love at first slight. **1933** FDGrierson *Empty* (L) 122: Love at first sight. **1940** KRoos *Made up* (NY) 64: Murder isn't like love, it doesn't happen at first sight. **1948** EQueen *Ten* (B) 69: Love at first sight. **1950** GHCoxe *Frightened* (NY DBC) 95: This love-at-first-sight bromide. **1958** *New Yorker* 5/17 44: Very apt to fall in love at first sight. **1961** JPhilips *Murder* (NY DBC) 120: There is no such thing as love at first sight. **1962** SRansome *Night* (NY DBC) 8: That old bit about love at first sight wasn't strictly true. **1967** GBaxt *Swing* (NY) 114: It was love at second sight. **1972** JMcClure *Caterpillar* (NY) 110: Calf love at first sight. **1974** WDRoberts *Didn't Anybody* (NY) 20: *Love at first sight* was such a hackneyed phrase. EAP L232; TW 229–30(4); Brunvand 89(2).

L238 **Love** breeds love

1958 RFenisong *Death* (NY) 64: The cliché that "love breeds love." *Oxford* 489: Begets.

L239 **Love** (and a cough) cannot be hidden

1936 AFielding *Two Pearl* (L) 103: It is said that love cannot be hidden. **1936** DLSayers *Gaudy* (NY) 400: It is said that love and a cough cannot be hid. EAP L233.

L240 **Love** conquers all

1929 SQuinn *Phantom* (Sauk City, Wisc. 1966) 263: *Amor omnia vincit*—love conquers all. **1930** DOgburn *Ra-ta-plan!* (B) 48: Love conquers all; 58. **1952** EHahn *Love Conquers Nothing* (NY). **1952** EHahn *Love* (NY) 315: I would like to put on record somewhere the following revised proverb: ALL CONQUERS LOVE. **1957** LFord *Girl* (NY) 168: Love conquered all. **1960** EWolf *Rosenbach* (Cleveland) 351: *Amor* does not *vincit omnia*. **1963** FEvans *Pistols* (NY) 217: "Well love conquers where hate fails. *Amor vincit omnia*." "Hey, Father, that's a line from Chaucer!" "I know." "You ought to teach a course at Saint Felicitas sometime." **1969** RRendell *Secret* (NY) 45: Love was generally supposed to conquer all. **1970** JWechsberg *First* (B) 42: *Omnia vincit amor*. Whiting *Chaucer* 76. Cf. *Labor above*.

L241 Love in a cottage *etc.*

1924 CWells *Furthest* (P) 314: Love in a cottage. **1930** LPowys *Apples* (L) 269: It's not all love in the cottage, and not all love in the castle. *Oxford* 492.

L242 Love is blind (*varied*)

1905 JBCabell *Line* (NY 1926) 217: Love is blind. **1913** ERBurroughs *Warlord* (NY 1963) 36: They say love is blind. **1932** JCLenehan *Mansfield* (L) 182: Love is blind. **1933** HAdams *Woman* (L) 5: Love is said to be blind, or to make its victims blind. **1934** RJBlack *Killing* (NY) 92: Love is not only blind, but sometimes cock-eyed, too. **1935** *New Yorker* 11/2 28: Love is never blind. **1940** KMKnight *Death Came* (NY) 264: They say love makes folks blind: friendship does too, I calculate. **1940** EPaul *Mayhem* (NY) 34: Love is deaf as well as blind. **1951** JMFox *Aleutian* (B) 104: My mother told me love is blind. **1952** LKronenberger *Grand* (NY) 151: What remark could be stupider, Doctor, than that love is blind? These popular sayings are nonsense—I mean like "feed a cold" or "money is a curse." I give you my word of honor it's not. I've never regretted having money for a moment. **1954** MKArgus *Rogue* (L) 199: Love and faith are blind. **1956** BO'Donnell *Should Women* (L) 42: Love is . . . traditionally blind. **1958** RFenisong *Death* (NY) 102: The cliché that love is blind. **1961** HActon *Last Bourbons* (L) 91: Love is deaf as well as blind. **1962** JKnowles *Morning* (NY) 165: Neither love nor hate is blind. **1963** IGlackens *Yankee* (NY) 150: If love is blind, it is also deaf. **1970** DMDevine *Illegal* (NY) 134: I always heard that love is blind. **1970** RFenisong *Drop* (NY) 59: The cliché that love is blind. EAP L234; TW 230(6); Brunvand 12: Blind god, 89(3).

L243 Love is stronger than death

1929 RConnell *Murder* (NY) 198: There's an old saying in Yorkshire—a riddle, you might call it—What is stronger than death? The answer is: Love. **1930** NBMavity *Other Bullet* (NY) 272: They say that love is stronger than death. EAP L236; TW 230(9).

L244 Love's labor lost

1926 EWallace *Colossus* (NY 1932) 80: Love's labour lost. **1935** LBlow *Bournewick* (L) 18: Love's labour lost. **1937** JJConnington *Minor* (L) 129: Love's labour lost at the first try. **1970** BGrebanier *Uninhibited* (NY) 167: Love's labors lost. EAP L240.

L245 Love laughs at locksmiths (obstacles) (*varied*)

1910 JCLincoln *Depot Master* (NY) 370: Love laughin' at locksmiths. **1922** JJoyce *Ulysses* (NY 1934) 358: Love laughs at locksmiths. **1928** EOrczy *Skin* (NY) 330: Love laughs at locksmiths. **1930** GBMeans *Strange Death* (NY) 45: Love laughs at obstacles. **1932** TSmith *Bishop's* (NY) 4: Love has ever had the last laugh on the locksmith. **1935** VRSmall *I Knew* (NY) 76: It is an old saying that love laughs at all obstacles. **1937** WMartyn *Blue Ridge* (L) 263: He and love were alike in that they laughed at locksmiths. **1941** MTYates *Midway* (NY) 72: Locke laughs at lovesmiths. **1951** IChase *New York 22* (NY) 224: That's [*where*] the old saying, "Love laughs at locksmiths," comes from [*chastity belts*]. **1959** *BGlobe* 10/19 7: Love laughs at locksmiths, says an old adage. **1960** AGilbert *Out for* (NY 1965) 175: Love Laughs at Locks. **1964** CMackenzie *Life III* (L) 225: I was able to join with love and laugh at locksmiths. TW 230(7); Brunvand 89(5).

L246 Love makes liars

1934 MMitchell *Warning* (NY) 93: The maxim that love makes liars. EAP L248.

L247 Love makes the world go round (*varied*)

1928 AECoppard *Silver* (L) 255: [He] did not think it was love that makes the world go round. **1931** PWynnton *Ten* (P) 169: They say love makes the world go round. **1937** PGWodehouse *Crime Wave* (NY) 250: It's love that makes the world go round. **1949** JBonett *Dead Lion* (L 1953) 35: A saying . . . "It's love that makes the world go round." **1955** BBenson *Silver* (NY) 71: Love is supposed to make the world go 'round. **1958** HKoningsberger *Affair* (NY) 61: Love makes the world go round. **1964** HBTaylor

Duplicate (NY) 58: I like men and men like girls and this is what makes the world go around. **1965** KRoos *Necessary* (L) 40: [Love] doesn't make the world go round. *Oxford* 492. Cf. Money makes the world *below.*

L248 The **Love** of money is the root of all evil *(varied)*

1920 ACrabb *Samuel* (NY) 303: This money was the root of evil. **1925** BAtkey *Pyramid* (NY) 295: The root of all evil is mismanaged money . . . not just money because it is money. **1925** EBChancellor *Old Q* (L) 240: There is a foolish saying that money is the cause of all evil. **1929** AFielding *Mysterious* (NY) 286: Love of money, *love* of it, is the root of all evil, the old teachers were quite right. **1930** GDHCole *Corpse* (L) 102: The theory of money as the source of all evil. **1932** DLSayers *Have* (NY) 283: A contempt for money . . . is the root . . . of all evil. **1938** RMBaker *Death* (NY) 129: To prove the old adage that money is the root of all evil. **1939** JJConnington *Counsellor* (L) 40: Money's the root of all evil. St. Paul didn't say that, but never mind. **1939** DDean *Emerald* (NY) 81: If—as Solomon said—the love of money is the root of evil. **1946** GBellairs *Death in the Night* (NY) 32: Money's the root of all evil. **1948** EK Goldthwaite *Root of Evil* (NY DBC). **1952** DGBrowne *Scalpel* (NY) 291: Money is the root of most exhumations. **1953** HMyers *O King* (NY) 40: Money, the love of which is the root of all evil. **1957** *BHerald* 12/22 34: Money may be known as the "root of all evil." **1957** MPHood *In the Dark* (NY) 79: Old Timothy was wrong when he said money was the root of all evil. It's women. **1960** RHolles *Captain* (L) 132: Anybody who thinks money *isn't* the root of all evil must be nutters. **1961** DMDisney *Mrs. Meeker's* (NY) 185: The love of money is the root of all evil . . . Timothy, wasn't it? **1963** WMorris *Cause* (NY) 227: Havin' no money is the root of more evil than havin' too much. **1964** HMHyde *Norman* (L) 420: No truer statement in the whole Bible than "The root of all evil is the love of money." **1967** DShannon *Rain* (NY) 214: "Money . . . the root of all evil, like it says." "No, not

money . . . The love of money." **1968** NZierold *Three Sisters* (B) 163: The almighty dollar . . . was at the root not only of all evil but of everything. **1970** VCClinton-Baddeley *No Case* (NY) 18: Money is the root of all comfort. It was the love of money that St. Paul thought a bad thing. **1970** JWechsberg *First* (B) 127: Money is the root of all wealth. **1974** RRosenblum *Good* (NY) 98: "The old saying, 'Money is the root of all evil.'" . . . "You're wrong . . . the saying . . . is 'Love of money is the root.'" **1978** ACalder-Marshall *Two Duchesses* (NY) 58: Money was at the root of all her evils. **1980** WStadiem *Class* (NY) 64: Money, or lack thereof, was the root of all Virginian evil. EAP L239; TW 230(13); Brunvand 89(7).

L249 **Love** (nature) will find a way

1930 DOgburn *Ra-ta-plan!* (B) 58: Love will find a way. **1934** JJConnington *Ha-Ha* (L) 173: Nature ever finds a way. **1938** EQueen *Four* (NY) 23: Love will find a way. **1949** RStout *Trouble* (NY) 22: But love found a way. **1951** JCFurnas *Voyage* (NY) 255: Love will find a way. **1956** SWTaylor *I Have* (NY) 182: But love found its proverbial way. **1959** DMDouglass *Many* (L) 109: Love, it has been said, will find a way. **1964** AStratton *Great Red* (NY) 131: Love will find a way. **1977** VCanning *Doomsday* (NY) 98: As the old saying or proverb said, love would always find a way. *Oxford* 493.

L250 Never make **Love** before breakfast *(etc.)*

Uncle George and Aunty Mabel / fainted at the breakfast table. / Children, let this be a warning: / Never do it in the morning. [I cannot remember when I first heard this rhyme but it was not too long ago (now 1985)—perhaps a dozen years. *BJW*] **1932** CPSnow *Death* (NY) 28: One golden rule: Never make love before breakfast. **1937** JDCarr *To Wake* (L) 164: As the Frenchman said about love-making: "Never before the fish!"

L251 No **Love** lost between them

1900 CFPidgin *Quincy A. Sawyer* (B) 488: There never was any love lost between her and her sister. **1913** JSFletcher *Secret* (L

1918) 86: And no love lost between 'em. **1922** JJoyce *Ulysses* (NY 1934) 750: There was no love lost between us. **1924** WBMFerguson *Black* (NY) 13: No love lost between us. **1937** NBerrow *One Thrilling* (L) 210: There was . . . no love lost between those two. **1939** CFGregg *Danger* (L) 188: There *was* a marked lack of lost love between them. **1948** RFoley *No Tears* (NY DBC) 76: There wasn't much love lost between them. **1954** MAllingham *No Love Lost* (NY). **1954** WJohns *Fabulous* (B) 202: There is no love lost between the two nations. **1960** EWolf *Rosenbach* (Cleveland) 235: There was no love lost between these two giants. **1968** HWaugh *Con* (NY) 209: There's no love lost between [them]. **1971** DMDisney *Three's* (NY) 75: There's never been much love lost between you. **1974** JRichardson *Stendhal* (NY) 217: Little love was lost between them. EAP L244.

L252 One cannot live on **Love**

1959 PCurtis *No Question* (NY) 113: You can't live on love. **1969** SPalmer *Hildegarde* (NY) 137: In spite of the nauseating axiom to the contrary one cannot live on love. Whiting *NC* 439(7).

L253 When **Love** comes in at the door *etc.*

1929 NATemple-Ellis *Inconsistent* (NY) 162: When love comes in at the door, logic flies out at the window. Brunvand 89(6). Cf. EAP P265: When Poverty comes in at the door etc.

L254 Where **Love** is there the glance follows

1934 MKing-Hall *Gay* (NY) 121: There is a proverb, "Where love is, there the glance follows." Whiting L558.

L255 **Love** me little, love me long

1975 NFreeling *Bugles* (NY) 84: Love me only a little . . . but love me a long time. EAP L245.

L256 Plain and **Loved**, loved forever

1922 JJoyce *Ulysses* (NY 1934) 374: Plain and loved, loved forever, they say.

L257 To **Love** and leave (*varied*)

1933 HDuffy *Seven* (NY) 217: I must love you and leave you. **1937** NGayle *Death* (NY) 160: He loves 'em and leaves 'em. **1943** PCheyney *Dark Dust* (NY) 51: Love 'em and Leave 'em. **1953** EQueen *Scarlet* (B) 147: Love 'em and leave them the labor pains. **1957** GMalcolm-Smith *Trouble* (NY) 108: He seems to have been the sort of fellow who believed in loving 'em, leaving 'em, and telling 'em nothing. A good formula. **1959** *NYTimes Book Review* 9/13 3: The sailors' maxim, "Love 'em and leave 'em." **1964** LCohen *New York* (P) 124: Love 'em and leave 'em. **1965** AGilbert *Voice* (NY) 185: Love 'em and leave 'em—and never overstay your welcome, that was my motto. **1972** KCampbell *Thunder* (I) 109: I must love you and leave you. Partridge 497. Cf. Neck 'em *below.*

L258 As proud (vain) as **Lucifer**

1919 LThayer *Mystery of the 13th Floor* (NY) 122: He's as proud as Lucifer. **1931** LJVance *Lone Wolf's* (P) 19: Vain as Lucifer. **1932** JDCarr *Poison* (NY) 156: As proud as Lucifer. **1934** JGBrandon *One-Minute* (L) 219: As vain as Lucifer. **1936** DTeilhet *Crimson Hair* (NY) 49: Proud as Lucifer. **1941** CCoffin *Mare's Nest* (NY) 16: [We] were as proud as Lucifer. **1950** ELinklater *Mr. Byculla* (L) 26: As proud as Lucifer. **1958** JSStrange *Night* (NY) 50: Proud as Lucifer. **1962** HReilly *Day* (NY DBC) 32: Proud as Lucifer. **1963** MMcCarthy *Group* (NY) 237: Proud as Lucifer. EAP L250; TW 230–1(1); Brunvand 90(2).

L259 Better **Luck** next time

1925 BAtkey *Pyramid* (NY) 166: Better luck next time. **1930** WLewis *Apes* (NY 1932) 157: Better luck next time. **1939** FLGreen *On the Night* (L) 17: Better luck next time. **1947** ECrispin *Dead* (NY DBC) 153: Better luck next time. **1949** RStout *Trouble* (NY) 13: Better luck next time. **1954** THoward *Blood* (NY) 66: Better luck next time. **1963** HWaugh *Death* (NY) 145: Better luck next time. **1969** RStark *Blackbird* (NY) 42: Better luck next time. **1970** NMonsarrat *Breaking* (L) 135: Better luck next time. **1975** NGuild

Lost (NY) 117: Better luck next time. EAP L252; Brunvand 90(1).

L260 Luck in leisure
1937 JEsteven *While Murder* (NY) 203: There's luck in leisure. TW 231(4).

L261 Luck in odd numbers (*varied*)
1926 LO'Flaherty *Mr. Gilhooley* (L) 18: There's bad luck in odd numbers. **1930** JRhode *Peril* (NY) 64: There was luck in odd numbers, and the third might very well achieve its object. **1933** BRoss *Tragedy of Z* (NY) 142: It's the luck of odd numbers. **1963** NFitzgerald *Echo* (NY) 35: There's luck in odd numbers. *Oxford* 496.

L262 The **Luck** of the Irish
1923 LThayer *Sinister* (NY) 48: The luck of the Irish; 69, 153. **1935** LThayer *Dead* (NY) 172: We had the luck of the Irish. **1941** AAmos *Pray* (NY) 105: The proverbial luck of the Irish. **1950** SPalmer *Green* (NY) 70: If that isn't the luck of the Irish! **1952** EF Bleiber *Imagination* (NY) 352: The luck of the Irish. **1958** *BHerald* 4/27 sec. IV 5: You'd need the luck of all the Irish in the world to get it. **1969** JBoyd *Rakehells* (NY 1971) 26: "The luck of the Irish" is no chimera. Brunvand 76(2); Taylor *Western Folklore* 17(1958) 16: Irish (1).

L263 More by **Luck** than good (whatever) (*varied*)
1925 FWCrofts *French's Greatest* (NY) 108: More by luck than good guidance. **1929** VLoder *Between* (NY) 281: Luck more than skill guided the missile. **1930** WSMaugham *Cakes* (L 1948) 63: More by good luck than by good management. **1934** BThomson *Inspector Richardson* (L) 95: Rather by luck than good management. **1939** EPaul *Mysterious* (NY 1962) 80: It's better to have luck than skill. **1941** NMarsh *Death in Ecstasy* (NY) 107: More by good fortune than good management. **1941** VRath *Death Breaks* (NY) 288: That was more good luck than a good aim. **1947** RDavies *Diary* (Toronto) 7: More by good luck than good management. **1956** IFleming *Diamonds* (NY 1961) 156: More luck than good management. **1958** HReilly *Ding* (NY DBC) 71: More by good

luck than good guidance. **1958** HCarmichael *Or Be* (NY) 150: More by good luck than good judgement. **1961** ATCurtis *Poacher's* (L) 83: More by luck than skill. **1962** BWAldiss *Hothouse* (L) 61: Tony's plan ... succeeded through luck rather than judgment. **1962** GMaxwell *Ring* (NY) 74: It was more by accident than judgment. **1969** RCook *Private* (NY) 99: More by good luck than any management. **1976** JRLAnderson *Death* (NY) 84: More luck than judgment. **1976** LEgan *Scenes* (NY) 134: More luck than good management. EAP L255.

L264 To crowd (push, press, ride) one's **Luck**
1932 HFootner *Dead Man's* (NY) 111: Don't crowd your luck. **1939** GBagby *Bird* (NY) 214: He's bound to push his luck. **1939** WChambers *You Can't* (NY) 164: There's such a thing as crowding our luck. **1949** AAFair *Bedrooms* (NY 1958) 85: Don't crowd your luck too far. **1950** GHCoxe *Eye* (NY) 63: He ... did not want to crowd that luck too far. **1951** DMDisney *Straw* (NY) 201: He had pushed his luck as far as he should. **1964** GVidal *Julian* (NY 1965) 315: Press their luck too hard. **1967** RCowper *Phoenix* (NY) 147: We can't afford to ride our luck too hard. **1970** AAFair *All Grass* (NY DBC) 24: I didn't press my luck. **1971** LBiggle *World* (NY) 125: He did not believe in pressing his luck. **1976** EMcBain *So Long* (NY) 73: Don't press your luck.

L265 You never know your **Luck**
1923 JSFletcher *Markenmore* (NY) 173: You never know your luck. **1932** AGilbert *Body* (NY) 45: Some men don't know their luck. **1932** JWelzl *Thirty Years* (NY) 251: You never know your luck. **1953** ECRLorac *Speak* (NY) 60: You never know your luck. **1958** MUnderwood *Lawful* (NY) 33: I always say you never know your luck. **1960** NWoodin *Room* (L) 59: You never know your luck. **1961** FDurbridge *Case* (NY) 90: You never know your luck. **1976** JMcClure *Snake* (NY) 123: You never know your luck. Cf. One never Knows *above*; One never can Tell *below*.

L266 Once aboard the **Lugger** and the girl is mine

1928 HWade *Missing* (NY) 39: "Once aboard the lugger and the girl is mine." **1935** GWeston *Murder in Haste* (NY) 270: "'Once aboard the lugger,'" he quoted. Partridge 499.

L267 Shoot, **Luke**, or give up the gun

1967 JFDobie *Some Part* (B) 78: Shoot, Luke, or give up the gun. Cf. Shit or . . . Pot *below*.

L268 The **Lull** (calm) before the storm (*varied*)

1927 JMWalsh *Silver* (L) 67: The calm before the storm. **1928** ABCox *Amateur* (NY) 298: Merely a lull before the storm. **1928** JAFerguson *Man in the Dark* (NY) 101: The calm before the unsuspected storm. **1930** BombardierX *So This Was War* (L) 37: He says that this is only the lull before the storm. **1930** LCharteris *Last* (NY) 15: After the calm, the storm. **1931** RKing *Murder* (NY) 249: It is a commonplace to speak about the lull before a storm. **1932** RKing *Murder* (L) 210: The very well known lull before the storm. **1934** VLoder *Murder* (L) 44: The lull before the battle. **1934** GMSutton *Esquimo* (NY) 229: The dead calm portended a storm. **1945** GBellairs *Calamity* (NY) 129: Like the calm before the storm. **1947** ECrispin *Dead* (NY DBC) 23: Calm before the storm. **1959** JABrussel *Just* (NY) 118: The proverbial lull before the storm. **1961** ERChamberlin *Count* (NY) 203: It was the brief lull before the storm. **1962** AAFair *Try* (NY) 101: It was the quiet before the storm. **1967** TWells *Dead by* (NY) 11: The lull before the storm. EAP C14: Calm.

L269 To leave (be left) in the **Lurch**

1903 EChilders *Riddle* (NY 1940) 78: Left me in the lurch. **1920** EWallace *Three-Oak* (L) 13: Leave me in the lurch. **1937** CIsherwood *Lions* (Norfolk, Conn. 1947) 273: Left in the lurch. **1940** FWBronson *Nice People* (NY) 156: Left her brother in the lurch. **1948** FWCrofts *Silence* (NY) 22: Leave him in the lurch. **1953** SRansome *Shroud* (NY) 159: Leaving Brad in the lurch. **1957** JWyndham *Midwich* (NY) 107: Left in the lurch. **1960** JBell *Fall* (NY) 89: Leave you in the lurch. **1970** FBarlow *Edward* (L) 132: Left his wife and friends in the lurch. **1972** RBernard *Illegal* (NY) 23: Leaving his fiancée in the lurch. EAP L258.

L270 **Lydford** law

1953 RDuncan *Where* (L) 115: First hang and draw, then hear the cause in Lydford law. *Oxford* 459: Lidford. Cf. First Fire, Jeddart *above*.

L271 As easy as **Lying** (*varied*)

1905 JBCabell *Line* (NY 1926) 187: 'Tis as easy as lying. **1931** FBeeding *Death* (NY) 115: Easy as lying. **1933** HDuffy *Seven* (NY) 71: That's as easy as lying. **1952** CLittle *Black* (NY) 146: She fibs as easy as she breathes. TW 231. Cf. EAP L116.

L272 To watch like a **Lynx**

1925 FWCrofts *Pit-Prop* (NY) 136: He watched . . . with the sharpness of a lynx. **1926** JArnold *Murder!* (L) 122: He would watch me like a lynx. **1933** DGBrowne *Dead* (L) 89: She's watching us like a lynx. **1938** EPOppenheim *Curious* (B) 88: Watching her like a lynx. **1959** MFitt *Mizmaze* (L) 181: Watch him like a lynx. **1961** ANeame *Adventures* (NY) 31: I watched her like a lynx. **1966** NBlake *Deadly* (L) 90: I was watching Bertie like a lynx. **1970** VCHall *Outback* (Adelaide) 18: The diver . . . watched the Koepanger like a lynx. Cf. EAP L261; TW 231; Brunvand 90: Eyes of.

M

M1 As cold as a **Mackerel**

1945 HQMasur *Bury Me* (NY 1948) 41: She [is] colder'n a mackerel. **1948** DTrumbo *Additional* (NY 1970) 75: Knocked colder than a mackerel. **1955** PDennis *Auntie* (NY) 14: You'll be as cold as a mackerel by seven o'clock [*drunk*]. **1958** *BangorDN* 6/30 22: Out colder'n a couple of last week's mackerel. **1960** JBlish *Galactic* (L) 26: Cold as a mackerel. **1982** CMacLeod *Wrack* (NY) 26: Her feet was always colder'n a dead mackerel. Taylor *Prov. Comp.* 28: Cold. Cf. As cold as a Fish, Haddock, Herring *above*.

M2 As dead as a **Mackerel**

1930 EQueen *French* (NY) 6: Herrin was deader than a mackerel. **1931** ACEdington *Monk's Hood* (NY) 10: He's dead as a dried mackerel. **1932** PRoss *Tragedy of Y* (NY) 53: Deader than a last year's mackerel. **1933** EQueen *American* (NY) 95: He was deader'n an iced mackerel. **1940** WChambers *Dry* (NY) 30: Channing is deader'n a dessicated mackerel. **1949** ESGardner *Dubious* (NY 1954) 66: Dead as a mackerel. **1950** RPowell *Shark* (NY) 154: They would have to think up a nicer expression than dead as a mackerel. **1959** JHChase *Shock* (L) 86: As dead as a mackerel. **1965** ES Gardner *Beautiful* (NY) 150: Dead . . . as a mackerel. **1966** EVCunningham *Helen* (NY) 110: He was dead as a mackerel . . . That's a foolish saying. Like people, mackerel are alive before they are dead. **1973** JCEnk *Family* (Rockland, Me.) 109: She was as dead as a mackerel. TW 232. Cf. As dead as a Fish, Flounder, Haddock *above*.

M3 As mum as a **Mackerel**

1940 JJConnington *Four Defences* (B) 82: Be as mum as a mackerel. Cf. *Oxford* 552: Mute.

M4 **Mackerel** sky

1950 REGould *Yankee* (NY) 41: Mackerel sky, mackerel sky, never long wet, never long dry. **1953** BCClough *Grandma* (Portland, Me.) 51: Mackerel sky either wet or dry. **1957** HPBeck *Folklore of Maine* (P) 82: Mackerel skies and mare's-tails make tall ships carry low sails. *Oxford* 497; Apperson 389.

M5 The **Maggot** bites

1935 BFlynn *Case* (L) 202: You know what . . . Kemble's like when the maggot bites him. **1939** RAJWalling *Red-Headed Friend* (NY) 48: Nobody will ever know what maggot was biting him. **1969** RBlythe *Akenfield* (NY) 114: I have a tendency to do what I want to do, if the maggot bites. EAP M1; TW 232(3).

M6 To have **Maggots** in one's head (brain)

1931 GDHCole *Dead Man's* (L) 151: You've got maggots [*in your head*]. **1933** HMSmith *Crevenna Cove* (NY) 184: Had some maggot in his head. **1940** HFootner *Sinfully* (L) 90: She had started a maggot working in his brain. **1956** SPalmer *Unhappy* (NY 1957) 5: Rook was, as our English cousins say, a man with a maggot. He was always riding his hobby. **1958** TBrooke *Under* (NY) 234: He's got a brain full of maggots. He's more like a witch than a prophet. **1969** DClark

Nobody's (NY) 184: What maggot's got into your brain? **1972** SWoods *They Love* (NY) 52: What maggot have you got into your head? EAP M2; TW 232(2).

M7 To work like **Magic**

1938 PGWodehouse *Code* (NY) 157: It works like magic. **1952** RMacdonald *Ivory* (NY 1965) 179: It worked like magic. **1962** EX Ferrars *Wandering* (NY) 30: It worked like magic. Cf. Charm, Dream *above*.

M8 As curious as a **Magpie**

1919 HRHaggard *She and Allan* (NY 1921) 79: He was as curious as a magpie. **1959** ESherry *Defense* (NY) 77: As curious as a magpie. Wilstach 78.

M9 As merry as a **(Mag)pie**

1954 ASeton *Katherine* (B) 210: Jackie'll be merry as a pie. Whiting P174; *Oxford* 527.

M10 As talkative as a **Magpie**

1976 CIsherwood *Christopher* (NY) 102: Talkative as a magpie. Whiting *NC* 439(1).

M11 To chatter like **Magpies** (*varied*)

1900 CFPidgin *Quincy A. Sawyer* (B) 19: Chattering like magpies. **1926** JArnold *Murder!* (L) 205: We chattered away like a couple of magpies. **1936** TAPlummer *Dumb* (NY) 34: Chattering like magpies. **1939** JPPhilips *Death Delivers* (NY) 235: Benny was jabbering like a magpie. **1948** RFoley *No Tears* (NY DBC) 82: [She] chattered like a magpie. **1957** *Punch* 6/19 759: They chatter like a lot of magpies. **1958** ISdeCamp *Elephant* (NY) 31: Chattering like magpies. **1960** DHolman-Hunt *My Grandmothers* (L) 141: Women chattering like magpies. **1967** CDrummond *Death* (NY) 164: Old biddies chatter . . . like magpies. EAP M5; TW 232; Taylor *Western Folklore* 17(1958) 17.

M12 A **Mahon(e)** soldier

1968 EBuckler *Ox Bells* (NY) 166: "Lazy as a Mahone soldier." What was a Mahone soldier? No one could tell you. TW 232.

M13 A **Maid** that laughs is half taken

1975 DEWestlake *Two* (NY) 31: As John Ray pointed out way back in 1650, "A maid that laughs is half taken." *Oxford* 499.

M14 Old **Maids** (and bachelors) are experts on child care (*varied*)

1936 SLBradbury *Hiram* (Rutland, Vt.) 240: Old maids and baches know more about matrimony and raisin' kids than the critter that invented it. **1958** *BHerald* 3/9 40: He is in the unenviable position of a spinster who claims to be an expert on child care. EAP B8; TW 233(3).

M15 Old **Maids** lead apes in hell (*varied*)

1930 HAdams *Golden* (L) 69: There is a very old saying that it is the fate of old maids to lead apes in hell. There are plenty of references to it in Shakespeare and other Elizabethan writers. **1934** JFarnol *Winds* (B) 6: I'll die a maid to lead apes in hell. **1935** NChild *Diamond* (NY) 85: Mrs. Tendahl smiled painfully and shook her head with fascinated distaste and embarrassment, like an old maid seeing her first ape. **1953** MMainwaring *Murder* (NY) 25: When I start research into their lives, I may as well go lead apes in hell at once [*a young lady speaks of three dead old maids*]. **1968** PHJohnson *The Survival of the Fittest* (NY) 231: She was filled with the joy of being saved, at this late hour, from leading apes in hell. EAP M10.

M16 To splice the **Main-brace**

1940 HRutland *Poison Fly* (NY) 15: The girl had met naval officers at sherry parties, and secretly thought that splicing the mainbrace had more to do with that faraway look than the sea. **1960** *NYTimes* 2/21 2E: The Admiralty sent out to the Navy the traditional invitation to join the celebration—"Splice the mainbrace"—with a double ration of rum [*on birth of British prince Feb. 19*]. **1962** DAlexander *Tempering* (NY) 117: All hands be piped to splice the main brace [*have a drink*]. **1972** PRReynolds *Middle* (NY) 125: We spliced the main brace [*had a drink*]. EAP M11.

M17 As **Maine** goes so goes the nation

1956 *BHerald* 9/6 10: It is not necessarily true that "as Maine goes so goes the nation." **1957** *BangorDN* 8/28 18: The famed expression "As Maine goes so goes the nation." **1958** *BHerald* 7/11 18: The old slogan . . . "As Maine goes so goes the nation." **1958** *BangorDN* 9/8 8: "As Maine goes, so goes the nation" wasn't a saying that could be entirely counted upon. DA Go *v.* 6s. Cf. Brunvand 103: Old Keystone.

M18   From **Maine** to Florida (Georgia)
1948 LFord *Devil's* (NY) 94: Everybody from Maine to Florida. **1970** ELathen *Pick* (NY) 10: The countryside between Maine and Georgia. EAP G35: From Georgia to.

M19   As (whatever) as they **Make** them
1900 CFPidgin *Quincy A. Sawyer* (B) 375: As lucky as they make 'em. **1924** VLWhitechurch *Templeton* (NY) 136: As wily as they make 'em. **1933** EBailey *Death* (L) 12: Grimwood . . . is as mean as they make 'em. **1953** ECRLorac *Shepherd's* (NY) 178: He's as dumb as they make them. **1955** JBingham *Paton* (L 1964) 67: Honest as they make 'em. **1960** FSWees *Country* (NY) 111: You were as smart as they make them. Whiting *NC* 440(1). Cf. As pretty as they Come *above.*

M20   **Make** or break
1929 AFielding *Cluny* (NY) 35: It's make or break with me. **1930** MMPropper *Tickertape* (NY) 181: It more often breaks a person than makes him. **1937** ECRLorac *These Names* (L) 194: It's going to make or break me. **1955** MBennett *Long Way* (NY) 35: It will make or break each one of us. **1965** AGilbert *Voice* (NY) 189: It makes you or breaks you. EAP M12; Brunvand 91.

M21   **Make** or mar
1927 VBridges *Girl* (P) 82: It can make or mar his . . . career. **1950** ECRLorac *And Then* (NY) 152: We make or mar ourselves. **1952** AGarve *Hole* (NY 1959) 7: Made or marred. **1960** JJMarric *Gideon's Risk* (NY) 146: He could make or mar Gideon's future. EAP M13.

M22   All **Men** are liars
1937 JHunter *Three Die* (NY) 197: The good old adage that all men are liars. **1948** JSStrange *All Men Are Liars* (NY). **1956** MProcter *Pub* (NY) 147: All men are liars. Psalms 116.11. Cf. Tilley C822. Cf. Cretans *above.*

M23   All **Men** are mortal
1969 ECooper *Sea Horse* (NY) 106: All men are mortal. EAP M15.

M24   Better be an old **Man's** darling *etc.* (*varied*)
1929 JSFletcher *House* (L) 188: We have a phrase in our country—"An old man's darling." **1933** EJepson *Memoirs* (L) 69: Better to be an old man's darling than a young man's slave. **1940** JRhode *Death on* (NY) 223: It's not bad fun being an old man's darling. **1957** LBeam *Maine* (NY) 176: Never be an old man's darling. **1959** ADean *Something* (NY) 148: An old man's darling wasn't the role she saw herself playing. **1971** HGregory *House* (NY) 26: Better . . . to be an old man's darling than a young man's slave. *Oxford* 51.

M25   Beware a smiling **Man**
1956 SWTaylor *I Have* (NY) 210: The old proverb . . . Beware a smiling man. Whiting *NC* 440(12).

M26   A blind **Man** in a dark room *etc.*
1930 JJFarjeon *Mystery* (L) 108: According to tradition, a blind man once entered a dark room to look for a black cat that wasn't there. **1957** *TLS* 1/11 19: The proverbial blind man groping in a dark room for a black cat that is not there. Cf. To look for a black Cat *above.*

M27   Dead **Men** do not bite
1933 DGBrowne *The Dead Don't Bite* (L). **1939** EQueen *Dragon's* (NY) 250: Dead men don't bite. **1944** RAltrucchi *Sleuthing* (Cambridge, Mass.) 81: "Buried men bite not" seems to be one of the oldest bits of human prudence. *Oxford* 171: Dead men. Cf. Dead Dogs *above.*

M28   Dead **Men** tell no tales (*varied*)
1904 SArmitage-Smith *John of Gaunt* (L) 284: Dead men tell no tales. **1920** GDilnot *Suspected* (NY) 219: I had to make sure he would tell no tales [*kill him*]. **1922** VBridges *Greensea* (NY) 356: Dead men are notoriously reticent. **1924** LSpringfield *Some Piquant* (L) 261: Dead men, who notoriously cannot tell tales. **1928** JGoodwin *When Dead Men Tell Tales* (NY). **1929** FEverton

Hammer (NY) 95: Dead men tell no lies, but dying ones sometimes make mistakes. **1930** LThayer *They Tell No Tales* (NY). **1931** KTrask *Dead Men Do Tell* (NY). **1933** CWaye *Figure* (NY) 83: The proverb that dead men tell no tales is one of the few popular sayings based upon a correct appreciation of facts. **1935** TAPlummer *Creaking* (L) 158: Dead men can't talk. **1936** EPOppenheim *Advice* (B) 150: The most hackneyed of adages have their fallacy and dead men sometimes can spread consternation. **1937** WDickinson *Dead Man Talks Too Much* (P). **1939** HHolt *Smiling Doll* (L) 57: A man is silent in his grave. **1939** MStuart *Dead Men Sing No Songs* (L). **1940** HReilly *The Dead Men Can Tell* (NY). **1942** MColes *They Tell No Tales* (NY). **1945** BKendrick *Death Knell* (NY) 192: Dead men give no answers. **1957** *NYTimes* 3/24 6E: Dead men tell no tales. **1961** WBromberg *Mold* (NY) 151: A "dead-men-tell-no-tales" type of reaction. **1969** AGilbert *Missing* (NY) 174: This wasn't going to be a case of dead men—or dead women—telling no tales. **1972** JGreenway *Down* (B) 46: Dead men *do* tell tales. **1976** JJMarric *Gideon's Drive* (NY) 159: Dead men could not talk. EAP M23; TW 234(8).

M29 A drowning **Man** will clutch at a straw (*varied*)

1919 MScott *Behind Red Curtains* (NY) 70: With the desperation of a drowning man I clutched at the last straw of hope. **1921** ERBurroughs *Mucker* (NY) 299: As is a straw to a drowning man. **1925** AWynne *Sign* (P) 237: It is a poor enough straw with which to rescue any drowning man. **1927** RKing *Mystery* (NY) 16: But the straw floated unclutched down the stream. **1931** WVJacobs *Snug* (NY) 49: The proverbial grasp of a drowning man. **1931** HSKeeler *Matilda* (NY) 109: As a drowning man snatches at the proverbial straw. **1936** GCollins *Haven* (L) 224: Drowning men clutch at straws. **1940** CMWills *R.E.Pipe* (L) 207: With the air of a drowning man clutching at a straw. **1942** CFAdams *What Price* (NY) 72: [He] clung to this thought, rather like a drowning man to the proverbial straw. **1951** ESGardner *Angry* (NY

DBC) 127: The desperate attempt of a drowning man to clutch at a straw. **1953** NBlake *Dreadful* (L) 213: He clings to it as a drowning man to his proverbial straw. **1956** *BangorDN* 10/25 14: [It] is only a straw to a drowning man when he needs a log. **1956** DWheatley *Ka* (L) 287: I clutched at it as a drowning man would at a straw. **1961** ENowell *T.Wolfe* (NY) 332: Clutching . . . as a drowning man clutches at a straw. **1966** DSlavitt *Rochelle* (L) 22: Rochelle . . . was a straw for a drowning man on a heavily laden camel's back, in an ill wind. **1973** AMStein *Finger* (NY) 82: I was waiting for him to get by the drowning-and-clutching-at-straws stage. EAP M26; TW 233(1). Cf. To clutch at any Straw *below*.

M30 Every **Man's** dung is sweet in his own nose

1981 RDavies *Rebel* (NY) 109: You know the old country saying: "Every man's dung is sweet in his own nose."

M31 Every **Man** for himself (*varied*)

1923 JSFletcher *Exterior* (NY) 117: Every man for himself. **1923** DCScott *Witching* (Toronto) 193: Every man for himself. **1924** JJFarjeon *Master* (NY) 183: A case of *sauve qui peut*. **1925** JSFletcher *Wolves* (NY) 213: Every woman for herself. **1927** WDSteele *Man Who* (NY) 185: No creed but "save him who can"! **1955** CBrand *Tour* (NY) 112: It was every man for himself and what the French called *sauve qui peut*. **1959** *BHerald* 3/22 8A: It's every man for himself. **1965** JPhilips *Black* (NY DBC) 121: It's every man for himself when there's trouble. EAP E81; TW 122: Everyone.

M32 Every **Man** for himself and God for all (*varied*)

1954 HRAngeli *Pre-Raphaelite* (L) 136: "Each for himself and the devil take the hindmost" or, to put it more kindly—"Each for himself and God for all." **1965** FRussell *Secret* (NY) 80: Then it was "the good Lord for everyone and everyone for hisself." EAP E82; TW 235(15).

M33 Every **Man** for himself and the devil take the hindmost (*varied*)

1927 GDilnot *Lazy* (B) 263: It was each man for himself and the devil take the hindmost. **1927** WDSteele *Man Who* (NY) 384: And devil take the hindmost. **1928** ESnell *Kontrol* (P) 267: Each group for himself—and the devil take the hindmost. **1932** ACampbell *Murder* (NY) 212: Most people are for themselves and the devil take the hindmost. **1933** DHoldridge *Pindorama* (NY) 27: Devil-take-the-hindmost flight. **1936** LThayer *Dark of the Moon* (NY) 10: Every man for himself—and the devil take the hindmost. **1938** AEFielding *Black Cats* (NY) 149: Every man for himself, and the devil take the hindmost. **1941** PWilde *Design* (NY) 114: Free for all and the devil take the hindermost. **1954** OAnderson *Thorn* (L) 187: Every man for himself and to hell with everyone else. **1962** EF Russell *Great* (NY) 34: It's every man for himself and the devil take the hindmost. **1967** KLauner *Planet* (NY) 48: It'll be every man for himself, and the devil take the slow gun. Whiting M73; *Oxford* 229. Cf. Devil take *above*.

M34 Every **Man** has his price (*varied*)
1909 MRRinehart *Man in Lower Ten* (NY 1947) 282: The best of us have our price. **1922** JJoyce *Ulysses* (NY 1934) 107: Every man his price. **1924** HCBailey *Mr. Fortune's Patients* (NY) 24: All things can be bought for a price. **1925** HAdams *By Order* (L) 87: They say every man has his price. **1929** FDGrierson *Murder* (L) 107: Every woman has her price. **1930** ATrain *Adventures* (NY) 283: Every woman has her price. **1934** JRhode *Poison* (NY) 120: Talleyrand said that every man had his price. **1941** ES Gardner *Turning Tide* (NY) 97: Every man had his price. **1945** PATaylor *Proof* (NY) 95: Every man has his price. **1954** JTey *Shilling* (NY) 129: But every man has his price. **1957** IFleming *From Russia* (NY 1958) 48: There is a price for every man. **1962** DHonig *No Song* (L) 122: Every man has his price. **1964** HBourne *In the Event* (NY) 70: Every man has his price, so they say. **1970** JAtkins *Sex* (L) 136: Just as every man has his price so every woman can be seduced if you are persistent enough. **1973** TWells *Brenda's* (NY) 90: Every man has his price. Trite but true. EAP E84; Brunvand 91(5).

M35 Every **Man** is master of his own fortune
1926 JSFletcher *Massingham* (NY) 180: An ancient Latin proverb which tells us that every man is the master of his own fortune. *Oxford* 230.

M36 Every **Man** makes mistakes (*varied*)
1928 WSMasterman *2 LO* (L) 188: The best of men make mistakes. **1941** BHalliday *Bodies* (NY 1959) 162: Every man makes mistakes. **1957** GMalcolm-Smith *Trouble* (NY) 67: Isn't there a saying, "We all make mistakes," or something of the sort. **1963** KAmis *Spectrum III* (L) 39: Everybody makes mistakes. Cf. *Oxford* 502: Makes no. Cf. No Man is without faults *below*.

M37 Every **Man** to his taste (*varied*)
1919 LMerrick *Chair* (L) 122: Every man to his taste. **1922** JSFletcher *Ravensdene* (NY) 16: Every man to his taste. **1922** JJoyce *Ulysses* (NY 1934) 374: Everyone to his taste as Morris said when he kissed the cow. 445: *Chacun son goût*. **1927** CAiken *Blue Voyage* (NY) 352: Every man to his own trade, as the farmer said when he kissed the pig. **1928** HCMcNeile *Female* (NY) 36: *Chacun à son gout*. 178: Everyone to his taste. **1928** VStarrett *Seaports* (NY) 128: Every man to his taste, as the farmer said when he kissed the cow. **1930** PMacDonald *Rynox* (L) 83: Each man to his taste, as the French say. **1931** GFowler *Great* (NY) 134: Every man to his own pleasure. **1933** PMcGuire *Death* (NY) 53: Every man to his poison. **1933** SSVanDine *Dragon* (NY) 49: Every man to his own poison. **1934** SPalmer *Murder* (L) 134: But everyone to their own taste, as the old lady said when she kissed the cow. **1935** FBeeding *Norwich* (NY) 158: Every man to his kind. **1935** CJDaly *Murder* (NY) 151: Everyone to her own taste, as the old lady said when she kissed the pig. **1935** JEGrant *Green Shadow* (NY) 134: Well, every man to his own liking, as the sheep-herders say. **1936** PATaylor *Crimson* (L) 229: Ev'ryone to his own taste . . . as the feller said when he kissed his cow. **1950** ELinklater *Mr. Byculla* (L) 21: Well, everyone to his taste. **1956** *New Yorker* 9/22 45: Chacun à son gout is

very true. **1956** RLongrigg *High-pitched* (L) 155: *Chacun à son goût,* as the frogs say. **1956** EMcBain *Mugger* (L 1963) 27: For as the old maid remarked about kissing the cow, "It's all a matter of taste." **1959** LWibberly *Quest* (NY) 46: Well, everyone to his fancy. **1961** RKirk *Old House* (NY DBC) 9: Every man to his own humor. **1970** MBates *Jungle* (NY) 49: Each to his own distaste, as it were. **1975** JLangton *Dark* (NY) 49: Day goostibus . . . Each to his own poison. EAP E89; TW 235(18).

M38 Every **Man** to his trade (*varied*)

1917 JCLincoln *Extricating* (NY) 25: Every man to his job. **1928** GDHCole *Man* (NY) 302: Each to his trade. **1928** GGardiner *At the House* (NY) 93: Every man to his trade. **1934** BFlynn *Spiked* (P) 125: Every man to his own trade. **1936** BThomson *Dartmoor* (NY) 217: Every man to his job. **1946** AB Cunningham *One Man* (NY) 192: And every man to his tools. **1950** ECBentley *Chill* (NY) 213: Every man to his trade. **1959** MHarris *Wake* (NY) 226: Every man to his own trade. **1963** AWUpfield *Body* (NY) 123: Every man to his trade. EAP E87; TW 235(19).

M39 Fat **Men** are (this, that or the other) (*varied*)

1921 RLardner *Big House* (NY 1925) 151: An old saying that nobody loves a fat man. **1929** DAGPearson *Golden* (L) 11: What a fallacy it is about fat men having good tempers. **1932** HBurnham *Telltale* (NY) 237: He took the adage "Everybody loves a fat man" as seriously as a commandment. **1936** JTFarrell *World* (NY) 409: Tell me that all the world loves a fat man. **1941** JPhilips *Odds on* (NY) 8: Everybody loves fat men. **1951** LLariar *You Can't* (NY) 112: Nobody loves a fat man, remember? **1955** TBDewey *Mean* (NY) 27: He had the false geniality of the fat man which has so long been taken for granted. There aren't any happy fat men. **1957** WFuller *Girl* (NY) 43: Now I know why everybody loves a fat man. **1963** WTucker *Last* (NY) 45: He was a tremendously fat man who easily disproved the old saw that fat men were

happy men. **1965** HCarlisle *Ilyitch* (NY) 176: Fat men are supposed to be jolly. **1974** JOlsen *Man with* (NY) 145: Everybody loves a fat man. Whiting *NC* 441(18).

M40 Hasty **Man** never wants woe

1927 SSVanDine *Canary* (NY) 165: Hasty men never want woe. Whiting M97.

M41 A hungry **Man** is an angry man

1922 JJoyce *Ulysses* (NY 1934) 167: Hungry man is an angry man. *Oxford* 393. Cf. Brunvand 91(1).

M42 "I see," said the blind **Man**

1922 JJoyce *Ulysses* (NY 1934) 549: I see, says the blind man. **1933** RAJWalling *Prove It* (NY) 71: Nous verrons, dit l'aveugle! **1937** RAJWalling *Bury Him* (L) 181: But, like the French blindman, we should see. **1959** PDeVries *Through* (B) 262: I see said the blind man. Whiting H629; *Oxford* 456: Let me; Tilley G84.

M43 The last **Man** in the world (*varied*)

1922 JJoyce *Ulysses* (NY 1934) 755: I wouldn't marry him not if he was the last man in the world. **1931** WWJacobs *Snug* (NY) 487: She says she wouldn't have you if you were the only man in the world. **1968** MSteen *Pier* (L) 36: I wouldn't marry him if he were the last man on earth. Berrey 397.

M44 **Man** does not live by bread alone (*varied*)

1927 BAtkey *Man* (NY) 51: Man cannot live by bread alone. **1955** GBagby *Dirty* (NY) 83: Man does not live by bread alone. **1958** EQueen *Finishing* (NY) 155: Man does not live by bread alone. **1962** DGillon *Unsleep* (NY) 47: Hesketh said something about man not living by bread alone. **1968** PDickinson *Skin* (L) 151: Man cannot live by bed [*sic*] alone, still less two men. **1969** RNye *Tales* (L) 85: Man does not live by bread alone. Matthew 4:4.

M45 The **Man** in the moon

1924 WBMFerguson *Black* (NY) 305: No more idea than the man in the moon. **1926** EWallace *King* (NY) 143: I know no more about the murder than the man in the moon. **1932** JCLenehan *Mansfield* (L) 139: You might as well be axin' the man in the moon. **1932** PMacDonald *Rope* (L) 31: I don't know your Mr. Mallow from the man in the moon. **1934** JRhode *Robthorne* (L) 173: They're no more alike than my cat Topsey is to the man in the moon. **1936** DLSayers *Gaudy* (NY) 148: You might as well talk to the man in the moon. **1940** ECBentley *Those Days* (L) 256: I knew no more than the man in the moon. **1940** KSteel *Dead of Night* (B) 295: It's as plain as the man in the moon. **1950** JCannan *Murder* (L 1958) 73: You were no more looking for aspirin than the man in the moon is. **1950** EQueen *Double* (B) 200: Then who did, Kenny? The man in the moon? **1954** UCurtiss *Deadly* (NY 1955) 129: She had no more idea of who was wearing it than the man in the moon. **1958** *New Yorker* 8/30 17–19 [*an account of man-in-the-moon lore*]. **1961** RJWhite *Smartest* (L) 254: You know no more . . . than the man in the moon. **1965** PAudemars *Fair* (NY) 112: No more idea . . . than the man in the moon. **1970** DShannon *Unexpected* (NY) 100: Might as well have said it to the man in the moon. **1972** DWalker *Lord's* (B) 72: I might as well ask the man in the moon to build a fence. EAP M42; TW 236–7.

M46 **Man** is a fire, woman is tow *etc.*
1934 JFarnol *Winds* (B) 49: Man is a fire, woman's the tow, and the devil he comes and begins to blow. EAP M43; Oxford 259.

M47 A **Man** is as old (young) as he feels
1926 JSFletcher *Green Ink* (B) 240: A man's as old as he feels. **1931** FBeeding *Death* (NY) 39: A man is as large as he feels. **1932** CRyland *Notting* (L) 29: A man is as old as he feels. **1936** PGWodehouse *Young Men* (NY) 91: A man is as old as he feels. **1947** JDCarr *Sleeping* (NY) 21: I always say . . . that a person is as old as they feel. **1958** *BTraveler* 11/18 8: The old saying that "You're as young as you feel." **1965** HActon *Old Lamps* (L) 127: One is as old as one feels. **1966** TWells *Matter* (NY) 40: You're only as old as you think you are. **1968**

MRowell *Below* (L) 154: [Old men] tell you that they're as young as they feel. *Oxford* 505.

M48 A **Man** is as old as his arteries
1925 CMCampbell *Lazy Colors* (NY) 77: The truth of the old saying that a man is as old as his arteries. **1938** WNMacartney *Fifty Years* (NY) 221: A man is as old as his arteries, and a horse is as old as his teeth. **1950** SJepson *Hungry* (NY) 129: A man is as old as his arteries. **1952** JLeslie *Intimate* (NY) 15: A man is as young as he feels . . . a man is as old as his arteries. Bartlett 364b [*Thomas Sydenham*].

M49 A **Man** is known by the company he keeps (*varied*)
1911 HHMunro *Chronicles* (L 1927) 229: A man is known by the company he keeps. **1913** JSFletcher *Secret* (L 1918) 93: Another old saying—"A man is known by the company he keeps." **1918** EWEmerson *Early Years* (B) 301: A man is known by the company he keeps. **1924** JSFletcher *Mazaroff* (NY) 44: A man is known by the company he keeps. **1932** JTFarrell *Young Lonigan* (NY 1935) 162: The proverb, "Tell me your friends, and I'll tell you who you are." **1933** EECummings *Eimi* (NY) 146: A man is known by the company he keeps. **1937** MBurton *Murder* (L) 116: You mustn't judge a man by the company he keeps. **1937** WHMack *Mr. Birdsall* (NY) 193: Sometimes a man is known by the friends he hasn't. **1946** RLGreen *Andrew Lang* (Leicester, Eng.) 191: A man is known by his friends runs the old saying. **1959** *BangorDN* 9/10 34: They say a person is judged by the company he keeps. **1959** *BHerald* 10/25 28: A man is often known by the friends he knows. **1962** RO'Connor *Scandalous* (NY) 171: If a man can be judged by the enemies he makes as well as by the company he keeps. **1964** EPHoyt *Gentleman* (B) 110: If a writer is known by the company he keeps, he was a young man to watch. **1971** EHCohen *Mademoiselle* (B) 43: If a man, as the saying goes, is known by the company he keeps, it might be argued that a woman is known by the

men she is kept by. **1973** AGilbert *Nice* (NY) 57: You get known by the company you keep. EAP C271, M45; TW 233–4(4).

M50 **Man** is the measure of all things

1948 HBeston *Northern* (NY) 66: "Man the measure of all things." A good adage. *Oxford* 505.

M51 **Man** may work from sun to sun, but woman's work is never done (*more often the second part only*)

1928 AECoppard *Silver* (L) 35: They say a woman's work is never done, and that's gospel. **1936** VLoder *Deaf-Mute* (L) 45: I always say a woman's work is never done. **1939** HPentecost *Cancelled* (NY) 83: Man may work from sun to sun, but woman's work is never done. **1948** CSLewis *Letters* (NY 1966) 214: Like a woman, his work is never done. **1953** BCClough *Grandma* (Portland, Me.) 33: The expression "Woman's work is never done." **1956** RILee *Happy* (B) 200: There is an old saying that a woman's work is never done. **1969** ABarton *Penny* (L) 168: Man went forth to his work and to his labour until the evening, but woman's work was never done. **1969** JBoyd *Rakehells* (NY 1971) 117: Women work from sun to sun . . . but man's work is never done. **1973** CAird *His Burial* (NY) 162: Woman's work. It's never done. **1977** RRendell *Judgment* (NY) 53: Mrs. Samson used to say that a woman's work is never done. EAP W283; Brunvand 155: Woman (4); *Oxford* 909: Woman's.

M52 A **Man** of straw (*varied*)

1962 NMcLarty *Chain* (NY) 117: Don't build straw men to worry about. **1964** RBraddon *Year* (L 1967) 101: You are indeed men of straw. EAP M52.

M53 A **Man** or a mouse (*varied*)

1931 GFowler *Great* (NY) 53: Are you mice or are you men? **1934** VLoder *Murder* (L) 190: Less like a mouse and more like a man. **1938** PHaggard *Death Talks* (NY) 176: Are we taxpayers or are we mice? **1941** HBailey *Smiling Corpse* (NY) 81: Are you a man or a mouse? **1943** WMcCully *Doctors* (NY) 228: The doctors have to be mice, not men. **1946** PGuggenheim *Out of This Century* (NY) 250: Al Jolson's joke, "Are you man or mouse?" **1950** BCarey *Man who* (NY) 113: He thought of the worn . . . expression: Are you a man or a mouse? **1956** *Time* 6/4 118: This is the first time she acted like a woman—not a mouse—when I asked her to do something. **1956** BCClough *More* (Portland, Me.) 60: Getting a mouse instead of a man. **1957** *BHerald* 12/13 13: Will the rat get up and identify himself? Is he a man or a mouse? **1958** AMStein *Sitting* (NY) 88: A look that asked me if I was a man or a mouse. **1961** PGWodehouse *Ice* (NY) 62: Are you man or mouse? **1963** MRichler *Incomparable* (L) 174: Are we men or mice? **1967** JFDobie *Some Part* (B) 169: Be a man, or a mouse or a bob-tailed rat. **1976** MButterworth *Remains* (NY) 24: Are you a man or a mouse? EAP M55; *Oxford* 506.

M54 **Man** proposes, but God disposes (*varied*)

1930 FIAnderson *Book* (NY) 211: Man proposes and luck interposes. **1930** JGBrandon *Murder* (L) 242: Man proposes and . . . circumstance disposes. **1931** LCArlington *Through* (L) lvi: *L'homme propose mais Dieu dispose.* **1933** VWMason *Shanghai* (NY) 21: The old saying about "man proposes, God disposes." **1939** CMWills *Calabar Bears* (L) 238: There is an old proverb, "Man proposes, God disposes." **1942** ABMaurice *Riddle* (NY) 58: Man proposes, the sea disposes. **1944** RAJWalling *Corpse Without* (NY) 125: Man proposes and superman disposes. **1954** CBeaton *Glass* (NY) 299: Wittily Diór turns an epigram: "The couturier proposes, but the ladies dispose." **1956** *Punch* 11/14 595: Man proposes and woman just poses. **1957** *NYTimes* 5/19 3E: The President proposes and Congress disposes. **1958** PDeVries *Mackerel* (B) 100: Man proposes, woman accepts, as the fella said. **1959** *BHerald* 1/24 3: As the saying goes, a governor proposes, the legislature disposes. **1961** LNizer *My Life* (NY) 219: The saying that man proposes, but God disposes. **1963** JLudwig *Confusions* (Greenwich, Conn.) 88: Man proposes, wife disposes. **1969** BCole *Funco* (NY) 11: One proposes, not disposes. **1970** MZuckerman

Peaceable (NY) 38: The province proposed and the community disposed. EAP M56; TW 235(24); Brunvand 92(10).

M55 A merciful **Man** is merciful to his beast
1938 VLoder *Kill* (L) 38: The merciful man is merciful to his beast. EAP M65; Brunvand 91(3).

M56 No **Man** can serve two masters (*varied*)
1928 EWallace *Clever* (NY) 291: No man could serve two masters. **1934** HWade *Constable* (L) 188: No man can serve two masters. **1936** NGayle *Murder* (L) 101: "A man cannot serve two masters," he declared sententiously. **1939** MBurton *Babbacombe* (L) 219: It's a true saying that no man can serve two masters. **1940** DBillany *It Takes* (NY) 269: No woman can serve two masters. **1957** *BangorDN* 3/15 25: A man can't serve two masters. **1959** AWUpfield *Journey* (NY) 79: No man can serve two masters, but two masters may own a slave. **1960** NWoodin *Room* (L) 11: You cannot serve two bosses. **1966** SCRoberts *Adventures* (Cambridge, Eng.) 259: I believe it to be not impossible to serve two masters. **1968** JDHicks *My Life* (Lincoln, Neb.) 106: There is good authority for the dictum that no man can serve two masters. **1968** RLockridge *Plate* (P) 135: One cannot serve God and Mammon. **1971** EHCohen *Mademoiselle* (B) 35: It is a commonplace that it is difficult to serve two masters. It is even tougher to serve both a master and a mistress. **1975** JLangton *Dark* (NY) 206: I couldn't serve both God and Mammon at the same time. **1975** RO'Connor *Broun* (NY) 147: The adage that a man couldn't serve two masters. EAP M66.

M57 No **Man** is a hero to his valet (*varied*)
1914 HHMunro *Beasts* (NY 1928) 121: No one is a hero to one's own office-boy. **1927** WGerhardi *Pretty* (L) 154: There is even the proverb: "No man is a hero to his own valet." **1930** ATrain *Adventures* (NY) 389: No man is a hero to his children. He has far more chance with his valet. **1937** VWilliams *Mr. Treadgold* (L) 13: If a fellow's no hero to his valet . . . he's still less a hero to his tailor. **1946** WPartington *T.J.Wise* (L)

115: Few men are heroes to their valets. **1959** JBEthan *Black Gold* (NY DBC) 14: I guess no man's a hero to his secretary when she's his wife. **1962** HCarmichael *Of Unsound* (NY) 22: They say a man is never a hero to either his wife or his secretary. **1967** AChristie *Endless* (NY) 54: There is a saying by some great writer or other that no man is a hero to his valet. **1971** JMann *Charitable* (NY) 16: No man is a hero to his secretary. **1971** JHBPeel *Along* (L) 198: No man, they say, can long deceive his valet. **1974** EGertz *To Life* (NY) 61: No one is a hero to his valet. EAP M67.

M58 No **Man** is without faults (*varied*)
c1910 EWallace *Nine Bears* (L 1928) 33: We've all got our faults. **1943** PCheyney *Dark Dust* (NY) 140: No man is perfect. EAP M68. Cf. Every Man makes *above*; Nobody *below*.

M59 No **Man** should be judge in his own case
1943 HLMencken *Heathen Days* (NY) 118: One of the oldest of legal wheezes is to the effect that no man should sit as judge in his own case. EAP M69.

M60 Old **Men** for council, young men for war
1972 SBirmingham *Late John* (P) 165: The proverb "old men for council, young men for war." Cf. Whiting A70, C352, M252.

M61 One cannot keep a good **Man** down
c1923 ACrowley *Confessions* ed JSymonds (L 1969) 471: It is hard to keep a good man down. **1925** SJohnson *Professor* (NY) 244: There's an old saying, "You can't keep a good man down." **1928** WMcFee *Pilgrims* (NY) 337: It showed you couldn't keep a good man down. **1930** ABCox *Wychford* (NY) 163: You can't keep a good man down. **1942** HCBailey *Nobody's* (NY) 34: You can't keep a good man down. **1955** JPotts *Death* (NY) 182: Like the fellow says, you can't keep a good man down. **1960** SRaven *Brother* (NY) 140: You can't keep a good man down.

M62 One **Man's** loss is another man's gain (*varied*)

1927 JTully *Circus* (NY) 176: One man's loss is another man's gain. **1930** ATrain *Adventures* (NY) 738: One man's adversity is another man's opportunity. **1934** MBoyd *Murder* (B) 205: One man's loss is another man's gain, as they say. **1937** LAGStrong *Swift* (L) 190: His loss is our gain, as the saying is. **1939** FWCrofts *Fatal* (L 1959) 168: One man's gain meant another man's loss. **1950** ECRLorac *Accident* (NY DBC) 40: One man's death is proverbially another man's opportunity. **1960** DHayles *Comedy* (L) 53: One man's loss is another man's gain. *Oxford* 486: Loss.

M63 One **Man** may steal a horse *etc.* (*varied*)

1925 HWNevinson *More Changes* (L) 172: One man may steal a horse, when another may not look over the fence. **1930** AE Walter *Betrayal* (NY) 190: One may walk in the garden while another may not look over the fence. **1944** WLewis *Letters* ed WKRose (L 1963) 379: You may steal a horse, I may not look over a hedge. **1954** DCecil *Melbourne* (I) 293: One man can steal a horse, says the proverb, while another cannot look over the hedge. **1961** MLochhead *Elizabeth* (L) 82: Mr. Thackeray could ride off on a stolen horse, while Currer Bell might not look over the fence. *Oxford* 772: Steal a horse.

M64 One **Man's** meat is another man's poison (*very varied*)

1926 EPhillpotts *Jig-saw* (NY) 23: But one man's poison is another man's meat. **1928** RAFreeman *A Certain* (NY) 267: What is one man's meat is another man's poison. **1928** DHLawrence *Lady* ("Allemagne") 296: One man's meat is another man's poison. **1930** MBurton *Hardways* (L) 135: What's one man's meat is another man's poison. **1931** FBeeding *Death* (NY) 165: But one man's meat . . . as they say. **1933** SPalmer *Pepper Tree* (NY) 150: In spite of the proverb, what's one man's meat is not another man's poison. **1934** JJFarjeon *Mystery* (NY) 37: One man's blessing is another man's bane. **1938** MSaltmarsh *Clouded* (NY) 82: As the poet says, one woman's meat is another's indigestion. **1940** CFitzsimmons *One Man's Poison* (NY). **1942** FLockridge *Hanged* (NY) 52: One girl's poison, another girl's meat. **1944** RShattuck *Said* (NY) 176: One man's poison is another man's Ann Sheridan. **1951** GConklin *Possible* (NY) 213: One man's meat is another man's sawdust. **1955** WSloane *Stories* (L) 396: One man's meat may be another man's poison. **1956** *BHerald* 6/21 39: One man's truth is another man's cold broccoli. **1957** *New Yorker* 5/11 132: One man's war is another man's boredom. **1958** DGBrowne *Death* (L) 100: One man's tragedy is another man's joke. **1960** EBowen *Time* (NY) 14: One man's improvement is another man's poison. **1962** DTaylor *Blood-* (NY) viii: One man's meat may be another man's poison. **1965** JMBrown *Worlds* (NY) 177: One man's art is another man's hokum. **1967** PMcGerr *Murder* (NY) 103: "One man's floor is another man's ceiling." . . . "And one man's meat is another man's poison." . . . It takes genius to find new words for an old adage. **1967** DBloodworth *Chinese* (NY) 363: The tolerant principle that one man's heresy is, after all, another man's faith. **1970** JAtkins *Sex* (L) 34: One man's meat is another man's poison. **1972** HTeichmann *Kaufman* (NY) 118: One of Kaufman's greatest puns: "One man's Mede is another man's Persian." EAP M74.

M65 So many **Men**, so many opinions (*varied*)

1924 HHBashford *Augustus* (L 1966) 153: The old saying, so many men, so many opinions. **1925** EBChancellor *Hell Fire* (L) 252: *Quot homines tot sententiae.* **1928** EK Rand *Founders* (Cambridge, Mass.) viii: *Quot homines, tot sententiae.* **1929** GGranby *Secret* (NY) 160: *Tot homi—*I mean, *Tot canes, tot sententiae.* **1930** NDouglas *Three* (L) 189: *Quot homines, tot sententiae.* **1934** TMundy *Tros* (NY) 914: So many men, so many points of view. **1936** EQueen *Halfway* (NY) 110: *Quot homines, tot sententiæ* . . . So many men, so many opinions. **1956** *TLS* 9/21 546: It almost seems to be a case of *tot* *homines.* **1971** JHBPeel *Along* (L) 184: *Quot homines, tot sententiae.* EAP M78; TW 235(25).

M66   Threatened **Men** live long
1905 GDEldridge *Millbank Case* (NY) 237: Threatened men live long. **1933** JIronside *Marten* (L) 142: Threatened men are said to live long. **1963** AChristie *Mirror* (NY) 138: Threatened men live long, as they say. **1972** DShannon *Murder* (NY) 23: Threatened men live long, so they say. EAP F212: Folk; TW 236(35).

M67   To be a **Man** before one's mother
1938 JTFarrell *No Star* (NY) 176: You'll be a man before your mother. **1940** RAFreeman *Mr. Polton* (NY) 41: You'll be a man before your mother. **1948** LSdeCamp *Divide* (NY 1964) 103: You'll be a man before your mother. **1952** GKersh *Brazen* (L) 103: You'll be a man before your mother. **1956** HCahill *Shadow* (NY) 197: Ye'll be a plowman b'fore y'r mither. TW 236(39).

M68   To be a **Man** for one's money
1933 GYoung *Devil's* (NY) 277: You are a man for my money. **1939** AWebb *Thank You* (L) 130: Parsons is the man for my money. Partridge 507.

M69   To be low **Man** on the totem pole
1967 DHitchens *Postscript* (NY) 12: Low man on the totem pole. **1970** NMonsarrat *Breaking* (L) 318: I was low man on the scholastic totem-pole. **1975** ARoudybush *Suddenly* (NY) 132: He's hardly high man on the totem pole.

M70   To kick a **Man** when he is down (*varied*)
1924 LSpringfield *Some Piquant* (L) 83: Akin to kicking a man who was down. **1925** IOstrander *Neglected* (NY) 116: I don't believe in kicking a fellow when he's down. **1933** HFootner *Ring* (NY) 205: Don't kick a man when he's down. **1934** RWormser *Wax Face* (NY) 96: Never kick a man when he's down. **1939** HFootner *Murder That* (L) 214: When a man is down, they all rush to kick him. **1949** FCrane *Flying* (NY) 15: We never kick even a man when he is down.

1953 NLangley *Rift* (NY) 5: Never kick a man except when he is down. **1954** EQueen *Bureau* (B) 173: I don't mind kicking a man when he's down. **1958** JSymons *Pipe* (NY) 85: Don't-hit-a-man-when-he's-down Jerry. **1961** RGordon *Doctor* (NY) 24: The code of never kicking a man when he's down. **1966** MWorthington *Strange* (NY) 62: The time to kick a man was when he was down. **1970** MMcGrady *Stranger* (NY) 156: There can be no harm in kicking a man when he's up. **1971** MScherf *Beautiful* (NY) 101: You can't kick a dog when it's down, can you? EAP M80.

M71   To see a **Man** about a dog (*varied*)
1930 ABCox *Second* (NY) 224: I think he said something about having to see a man about a dog. **1930** CBush *Dead Man* (NY) 35: I'm going out of town for the weekend—seeing a bloke about a little dog. **1932** NKlein *No! No!* (NY) 107: I'm going out to buy a dog and then I'll take you home. **1937** WDickinson *Dead Man* (P) 245: He said he wanted to see four guys about a dog [*toilet*]. **1938** RWhite *Run Masked* (NY) 211: I've got to see a man about a dog [*cf. pp. 94–5 for other American euphemisms for going to the toilet*]. **1941** SHHolbrook *Murder out* (NY) 174: The sheriff . . . left the room for a moment to see a man about a couple of dogs. **1944** CWoolrich *Black Path* (NY) 164: There's an old saying in my language. To change it around a little, I'm going to see a dog—about a lady. **1957** CCarnac *Late Miss* (NY) 168: I'll go and see a man about a dog [*on an errand*]. **1958** RFenisong *Death* (NY) 155: I have to see a man about a dog license. **1960** DHolman-Hunt *My Grandmothers* (L) 172: I must go and see a man about a dog. **1967** OHesky *Time* (NY) 54: Going to see a man about a guinea pig [*toilet*]. **1973** JSymons *Plot* (NY) 92: I'm just going to see a man about a dog. Wentworth 456; Partridge 742: See a man [*but not to urinate*].

M72   To separate the **Men** from the boys
1956 AAFair *Beware* (NY DBC) 99: This is the kind of stuff that separates the men

from the boys. **1962** RGTugwell *Light* (NY) 340: Separate the men from the boys. **1964** FPohl *Seventh Galaxy* (NY) 168: A . . . test for separating the men from the boys. **1984** JGould *No Other* (NY) 119: Separates the men from the boys.

M73 To wait for dead **Men's** shoes (*varied*)

1928 JGoodwin *When Dead* (NY) 13: Waiting for dead men's shoes. **1928** ESnell *Blue* (P) 59: It had been a case of dead men's shoes. **1929** DHammett *Red Harvest* (NY) 254: Trying to get into the dead men's shoes. **1931** EQueen *Dutch* (NY) 116: He who waits for a dead man's shoes is in danger of going barefoot. **1935** JJConnington *In Whose* (L) 39: He waited for dead men's shoes. **1935** EGreenwood *Pins* (L) 43: It's no good thinking of dead men's shoes. **1944** MLong *Bury* (NY) 53: Archibald . . . is trying to step into a dead man's shoes. **1953** VPJohns *Murder* (NY 1962) 145: Eager to fill the dead man's shoes. **1957** PGWodehouse *Butler* (NY) 4: Waiting for dead men's shoes. **1969** DClark *Nobody's* (NY) 123: A chance of stepping into a very comfortable pair of dead man's shoes. EAP M81; TW 234(9).

M74 What **Man** has done man can do (*varied*)

1934 CFGregg *Execution* (L) 200: What man has done man can do! **1952** MColes *Alias* (NY) 38: What man has done man can do. **1960** FSWees *Country* (NY) 72: Where one can go, another can, too. Cf. *Oxford* 199: Done ill once.

M75 A wise **Man** may change his mind, a fool never

1934 HWade *Constable* (L) 73: A wise man may change his mind. **1954** AWBarkley *That Reminds* (NY) 42: A wise man may change his mind, a fool never does. TW 236(36).

M76 A young **Man** married is a young man marred

1945 ACampbell *With Bated* (NY) 202: The cynical quotation, *A young man married is a young man marred.* **1961** RKirk *Old House* (NY DBC) 14: A young man married is a

young man marred. *Oxford* 513: Marriage makes.

M77 Young **Men** may die, old men must

1970 DCraig *Young Men May Die* (NY). **1970** DCraig *Young* (NY) 6: Young men may die; old men must. *Proverb.* EAP M90; TW 236(37).

M78 Young **Men** (*etc.*) think old men are fools *etc.*

1930 AChristie *Murder* (NY) 312: She used to say, "The young people think the old people are fools—but the old people *know* the young people are fools." TW 236(41).

M79 **Manners** make the man (*varied*)

1918 EWEmerson *Early Years* (B) 484: The proverbial saying, "Manners make the man." **1929** JCameron *Seven* (L) 194: Manners makyth man. **1929** EBYoung *Dancing* (P) 196: If manners really made men. **1933** AJRees *Aldringham* (NY) 127: If manners alone made a man. **1938** AWebb *Mr P.'s Hat* (L) 191: Manners maketh man, eh? Cant! Humbug! **1946** NGidding *End over End* (NY) 21: Manners maketh man. Don't pee in the dining room. **1957** PGWodehouse *Over* (L) 36: Manners makyth Man is the motto of the American of today. **1958** *New Yorker* 5/3 34: Manners makyth man. **1959** *Time* 8/3 82: Unfortunately mannerisms do not make the man. EAP M93.

M80 **Many** are called but few are chosen

1971 DWeeks *Corvo* (NY) 42: Many are called, but few are chosen. EAP M95; TW 237.

M81 To be (right) off the **Map**

1928 HAdams *Empty* (P) 14: [It] was almost off the map. **1930** EWoodward *House* (NY) 93: He's vanished off the map. **1939** GBarnett *There's Money* (L) 131: A bit too much off the map for my liking. **1946** HCBailey *Life Sentence* (NY) 33: Rather off the map, Bridcombe. **1957** AWilson *A Bit off the Map* (L). **1959** MErskine *Graveyard* (NY) 18: A place right off the map. **1964** NFreeling *Because* (NY 1965) 160: Very primitive and off the map. NED Suppl. Map *sb.*[1] 1e. See Partridge 508–509.

M82 As cold as **Marble**; Marble-cold

1931 LRGribble *Grand* (L) 29: A face as cold . . . as marble. **1940** JBentley *Mr. Marlow Stops* (B) 87: Her hand was marble cold. **1971** EPeters *Knocker* (NY) 38: The hand . . . marble-cold. EAP M96; TW 237(1); Brunvand 92(1).

M83 As hard (firm, smooth) as **Marble**

1924 JSFletcher *Safety* (NY) 192: Hard as marble. **1939** AMcRoyd *Double Shadow* (NY) 55: His face was as hard and smooth as marble. **1959** HEBates *Breath* (B) 131: A skin as hard as marble. **1959** SMarlowe *Blonde* (NY) 29: Her buttocks looked as firm as marble. **1970** TKenrick *Only* (NY) 142: Cold, marble-hard flesh. **1975** JBland *Death* (NY) 139: His pale face as hard as marble. TW 237(2,5).

M84 As pale as **Marble**

1928 AWynne *Red* (P) 211: She was as pale as marble. **1934** PHunt *Two Knocks* (L) 35: Her cheeks pale as marble. TW 237(4); Brunvand 92(3).

M85 As still (immobile) as **Marble**; Marble-still

1928 AGilbert *Mrs. Davenport* (NY) 97: He was still as marble. **1929** STruss *Living* (NY) 161: A face immobile as marble. **1941** CBClason *Green Shiver* (NY) 7: He stood marble still. **1954** ASeton *Katherine* (B) 59: She stood up, marble-still. **1957** STruss *Truth* (NY) 91: She was as still as marble. TW 237(6); Brunvand 93(5).

M86 As white as **Marble**; Marble-white

1929 FDaingerfield *Linden* (NY) 33: Her face, white as marble; 235. **1939** HCBailey *Great Game* (L) 253: Face . . . white as marble. **1950** MGEberhart *Hunt* (NY) 228: Camilla was marble white. **1951** JCollier *Fancies* (NY) 36: White as marble and as cold. **1958** JSStrange *Night* (NY) 229: White as marble. **1966** HRFKeating *Death* (NY) 59: [He] was as white as pure marble. **1970** CBrookhouse *Running* (B) 39: Naked, white and strong as marble. **1970** JJMarric *Gideon's Sport* (NY) 36: Marble-white shoulders. EAP M98; TW 237(7); Brunvand 93(6).

M87 As hard as **Marbles**

1939 BHalliday *Dividend* (NY 1959) 65: Her eyes were . . . hard as two marbles. **1954** MAllingham *No Love* (NY) 123: His eyes had become as hard as marbles. Cf. Pebbles *below*.

M88 To lose one's **Marbles**

1957 *New Yorker* 10/19 33: Assumed we had lost our marbles [*were insane*]. **1957** SDean *Murder* (NY) 179: He's lost most of his marbles. **1960** HGold *Love* (NY) 88: A professor . . . who had dropped his marbles. **1966** DHitchens *Man who Cried* (NY) 120: You've lost your marbles. Amer. Herit. Dict. Marble 5.

M89 **March** comes in like a lion *etc.* (*varied*)

1925 GBeasley *My First* (Paris) 187: I had come in like a lamb and was going out like a lion. **1929** JBPriestley *Good* (NY) 469: March came in like a lion and seems to be going out like one. **1933** DGBrowne *Cotfold* (L) 2: March . . . came in like a ravaging lion, as the saying is. **1936** PQuentin *Puzzle* (NY) 170: Such typically March weather . . . In like a lion, you know. **1937** WBrewster *October* (Cambridge, Mass.) 94: The month came in "like a lamb" and is going out "like a lion." **1939** LRGribble *Arsenal* (L) 12: The lion and the lamb of March seem content with each other's company. **1952** MBancroft *Upside* (B) 150: March came in like a lion and went out like a lamb. **1956** *NYTimes* 12/30 7F: The Christmas season could be described as the proverbial month of March in reverse: In like a lamb, out like a lion. **1957** *BangorDN* 3/2 1: March came in like a lion Friday. **1965** RDSymons *Silton* (NY 1975) 156: March comes in like a lamb, but he will . . . roar before the month is out. **1968** MSarton *Plant* (NY) 163: March is apt to be more lionlike than lamblike around here [*Nelson, NH*]. **1970** RMungo *Famous* (B) 198: March comes in like a lion. **1974** CMSmith *Reverend* (NY) 224: March . . . was going out like a lamb. EAP M100.

M90 To go up **March** hill

1948 HBeston *Northern* (NY) 63: "Up March hill we go," to use an old phrase.

1949 JSStrange *Unquiet* (NY) 25: If I can just get up March hill I will be all right. EAP M100.2.

M91 To steal a **March**

1938 JCLanehan *Guilty* (L) 301: He's stolen a march on us. EAP M99.

M92 The gray **Mare** is the better horse (*varied*)

1910 EPhillpotts *Tales* (NY) 166: Prepared to let her be the gray mare. **1927** NSLincoln *Dancing* (NY) 76: She's the gray mare in the stable. **1929** EWHowe *Plain* (NY) 2: I often heard father say his mother was "the better horse" of his parents, as she ruled the family. **1931** CWells *Skeleton* (NY) 125: His . . . wife fell gracefully into the role of Gray Mare. **1933** RAFreeman *Dr. Thorndyke Intervenes* (L) 31: The gray mare was the better horse. **1950** EJohn *Ride* (NY) 304: I have heard that the gray mare is the better horse. **1960** BAskwith *Tangled* (L) 113: She's the grey mare. **1962** AGilbert *Uncertain* (NY DBC) 74: She had considered the gray mare to be the better horse. EAP M100.3; TW 238(1); Brunvand 93.

M93 A **Mare's** nest

1903 EChilders *Riddle* (NY 1940) 146: A mare's nest. **1924** AChristie *Man* (NY) 218: A mare's nest. **1932** CFGregg *Body* (L) 127: You've stirred up a mare's nest. **1935** HAdams *Body* (L) 189: No time to chase mare's nests. **1935** DOgburn *Will* (NY) 221: And as for mare's nests, I've never had the faintest notion what they were . . . I suppose they're in the category of hens' teeth, aren't they, and snakes' hips? **1937** DLSayers *Busman's* (NY) 215: He has found a mare's nest full of cockatrice's eggs. **1939** GBagby *Bird* (NY) 50: A mare's nest of hair and hairpins. **1941** CCoffin *Mare's Nest* (NY). **1944** EDaly *Book of the Dead* (NY) 147: "I don't want to get mixed up in a mare's nest." "Some day I must come up and give you a short frank talk on the use of the metaphor." **1945** PWentworth *She Came* (NY) 120: Come back with a mare's nest full of eggs. **1954** JBingham *Third* (NY) 236: The whole thing had been a mare's nest. **1958** HCarmichael *Into* (NY) 38: We are chasing a mare's nest. **1962** PDennis *Genius* (NY) 138: A mare's nest of extraneous bits of paper. **1963** AAFair *Fish* (NY DBC) 125: You steered me into a mare's nest. **1970** PAnderson *Tau* (NY) 80: The cabin was a mare's nest. Dresser drawers had burst open and scattered their contents. **1970** HCarvic *Miss Seeton Draws* (NY) 181: You're stirring up a mare's nest with hornets in it. **1981** ACross *Death* (NY) 38: No doubt the whole thing would turn out to be a mare's nest. (Now where had that phrase come from?) **1981** RRendell *Death* (NY) 106: He delivered one of his . . . confused metaphors. "It was a case of making a mare's nest out of a molehill." TW 238(2); *Oxford* 512.

M94 To shoe the wild **Mare**

1971 JBlake *Joint* (NY) 228: You can't be all that busy shoeing the wild mare. *Oxford* 725.

M95 Tell that to the **Marines**

1910 EPhillpotts *Tales* (NY) 205: Tell that tale to the marines. **1920** ACrabb *Samuel* (NY) 59: Tell that to the marines. **1932** CFitzsimmons *No Witness* (NY) 195: Tell that to the marines. **1933** ECRLorac *Case* (L) 263: Tell that yarn to the horse-marines. It won't wash. **1947** PMcGerr *Pick* (NY) 203: Tell that to the marines. **1954** GFowler *Minutes* (NY) 230: You can't tell that to the Marines. **1960** SRaven *Doctors* (L) 71: You can tell that to the Marines. **1965** HActon *Old Lamps* (L) 115: Tell that to the horse-marines. **1975** DRussell *Tamarisk* (NY) 111: Tell that to the marines. EAP M101. Cf. Muldoon, Sweeney *below*.

M96 To swear like a **Marine**

1941 MVHeberden *Lobster Pick* (L) 81: He was swearing like a marine. **1955** FCrane *Death* (NY) 104: King swore like the Marines. Cf. To swear like a Trooper *below*.

M97 To have one's **Market** made

1900 CFPidgin *Quincy A. Sawyer* (B) 180: That sort of look that girls have when their market's made. Cf. Tilley M672.

M98 **Marriage** and hanging go by destiny (*varied*)

1938 MSaltmarsh *Clouded* (NY) 218: Marriage and hanging go by destiny. **1970** ACross *Poetic* (NY) 91: "A wedding is destiny, and hanging likewise." "Did *Piers Plowman* say that?" ... "No. John Heywood." EAP M106.

M99 **Marriage** is a lottery

1924 HHMunro *Square* (L 1929) 166: [He] used to declare that marriage was a lottery. Like most popular sayings, simile breaks down on application. *Oxford* 513.

M100 **Marriage** is more than four bare legs in a bed

1937 DLSayers *Busman's* (NY) 187: "There's more to marriage, as they say, than four bare legs in a bed" ... "Or legs in silk stockings, neither." *Oxford* 513–4.

M101 **Marriages** are made in heaven (*varied*)

1911 JSHay *Amazing Emperor* (L) 178: Divorces, like marriages, were made in heaven. **1916** RFirbank *Inclinations* (Works 2, L 1929) 127: Marriages are made in heaven. **1919** JBCabell *Jurgen* (NY 1922) 273: A marriage ... hall-marked "Made in Heaven." **1926** EWallace *King* (NY) 133: Marriages really are made in heaven. **1939** JDonavan *Coloured Wind* (L) 248: Matches are made in Heaven, they say. **1942** QMario *Murder Meets* (NY) 30: A marriage made in Heaven. **1945** GDaniel *Cambridge* (L 1952) 210: He told me that happy marriages were made in heaven. **1951** JCollier *Fancies* (NY) 309: I believe marriages are made in Heaven. **1953** VPJohns *Murder* (NY 1962) 24: The marriage ... having been ordained in heaven. **1962** RMacdonald *Zebra* (NY) 10: The standard female illusion that all marriages are made in heaven. **1963** MAshley *Stuarts* (L) 35: Marriage was made at the attorney's table rather than in Heaven. **1965** RHardwick *Plotters* (NY) 33: Her marriage ... was not one of those made in heaven, assuming there was such a marriage. **1970** BWAldiss *Hand-reared* (L) 27: Marriages (I was told as a kid) are made in heaven. **1971** PRu-

benstein *Groupsex* (NY) 178: All marriages aren't made in heaven. **1980** HPentecost *Death* (NY) 113: Made in heaven, that marriage, they all said. EAP M117: Matches; *Oxford* 514.

M102 It is better to **Marry** than to burn (*varied*)

1919 JBCabell *Jurgen* (NY 1922) 273: The saying that it is better to marry than burn. **1933** EJepson *Memoirs* (L) 79: It was better to marry than burn. **1938** JJConnington *For Murder* (L) 94: Better to marry than burn. **1958** JByrom *Or Be* (L 1964) 149: I suppose it's better to marry than to burn. **1960** JO'Hara *Ourselves* (NY) 310: St. Paul said it's better to marry than to burn. **1962** PHNewby *Barbary* (L) 27: Not entirely true, this saying that it was better to marry than burn. **1973** JPorter *It's Murder* (NY) 58: It is better to marry than burn. EAP M108.

M103 To be nailed to the **Mast**

1930 LFalkner *Murder* (NY) 134: Got him nailed to the mast! **1933** EDTorgerson *Cold Finger* (L) 165: We had this bird Thurber nailed to the mast. Cf. Hide *above*.

M104 Better **Master** than man

1931 JSFletcher *Solution* (NY) 140: Better master than man!—that's what I say. Cf. Tilley M710: Better speak to the master than the man.

M105 Like **Master** (dog) like dog (master)

1926 AFielding *Footsteps* (L) 287: Like master, like dog. **1930** MAllingham *Mystery* (NY) 101: They say like dog, like master. **1945** FBunnamy *King Is Dead* (NY) 25: Like master, like dog. **1952** ETempleton *Proper* (B) 168: Like master, like dog. **1962** RLockridge *First* (P) 184: Like dog, like master. Cf. next entry.

M106 Like **Master**, like man

1928 NSLincoln *Secret* (NY) 159: Like master, like man. **1937** LRGribble *Case-book* (L) 99: Like master like man is a saying not always true. **1939** VHanson *Casual* (NY) 12: Like master, like man, they say. EAP M109; TW 239(4).

M107 As thin as a **Match(-stick)**; Match-stick-thin

1932 JJFarjeon *Trunk-Call* (NY) 19: The man was as thin as a match. **1938** EHuxley *Murder* (NY) 88: Her arm, thin as a match-stick. **1966** MErskine *Family* (NY) 94: His arms and legs were match-stick-thin. Cf. Whiting *NC* 443: Fat. Cf. As thin as a Stick *below*.

M108 As near as makes no **Matter**

1929 OGray *Bagshot* (NY) 164: As near as makes no matter. **1941** HCBailey *Bishop's* (NY) 203: As near as no matter. **1947** HWade *New Graves* (L) 186: I'm as sure as no matter. **1957** *Punch* 8/28 243: As damn near out of the red as made no matter. **1959** HReilly *Not Me* (NY DBC) 76: As near nothing as didn't matter. **1970** PMoyes *Many* (NY) 156: As near as makes no matter. Berrey 21.18, 40.4, 6; Partridge 513. Cf. As near as Nothing, Odds *below*.

M109 As meddlesome as **Mattie**

1939 JJones *Murder al Fresco* (NY) 92: You old meddlesome Mattie. *Oxford* 523.

M110 **May** and December (*varied*)

1920 JSFletcher *Exterior* (NY 1923) 12: May and December—she's twenty-five, and [he's] fifty years older. **1922** JJoyce *Ulysses* (NY 1934) 367: Marry in May and repent in December. **1928** EWallace *Sinister* (NY) 74: Kill that crazy May and December bug. **1932** WMartyn *Murder* (NY) 18: There's nothing in this May and December business. **1938** BFlynn *Five Red* (NY) 11: Sneering suggestions that coupled May with December. **1938** MTeagle *Murders* (NY) 210: I guess the saloon keeper thought I was the December husband checking up on my April wife. **1941** JShore *Rattle* (NY) 126: May and December—or June and October, if you like. **1949** JStagge *Three* (NY) 39: Are the textbooks against May and September [*marriages*]? **1952** EPaul *Black* (NY) 211: This June and December romance. **1953** STruss *Doctor* (NY) 63: A romance of May and December. **1957** PJFarmer *Green* (NY) 25: The December-May marriages. **1959** RMartin *Key* (NY DBC) 63: June and December. **1966** ALoos *Girl* (NY) 53: A May-December love story. **1967** RGarrett *Too Many* (NY) 63: A May-December marriage. **1971** HLemay *Inside* (NY) 113: The May-December wedding. **1974** JKaplan *Lincoln Steffens* (NY) 285: The May-and-December marriage. EAP D89, J16; TW 203: January (2); *Oxford* 518: May and December.

M111 **May bees** do not fly in September

1953 MPHood *Silent* (NY) 47: "Maybe . . ." "Maybes don't fly in September." EAP M123.

M112 As gay as a **May bug**

1956 BJChute *Greenwillow* (NY) 175: Gay as a May-bug. Cf. NED Chovy: "The popular name in the East of England of the June-bug," also May-bug. Cf. June bug *above*.

M113 As merry as **May-day**

1934 KCStrahan *Hobgoblin* (I) 169: Merry as May-day. Cf. Apperson 414: Merry month of May; Wilstach 259: As the month of May.

M114 As chipper (fresh) as a **May morning**

1931 MNRawson *When Antiques* (NY) 207: Looking fresh and sweet as a May morning. **1948** DCDisney *Explosion* (NY DBC) 63: A suspect as chipper as the May morning. Whiting M422: May. Cf. TW 240(1).

M115 The (real) **McCoy** (Mackay) (*varied*)

1934 BThomson *Richardson Scores* (L) 101: 'E was the real Mackay. **1935** JdeMeyer *Bailey's* (NY) 182: We're going to talk McCoy. **1937** GDyer *Long Death* (NY) 114: It's a McCoy snatch . . . a real kidnapping. **1938** HReed *Swing Music* (NY) 67: Talk about your clear McCoy! **1940** HReilly *Dead Can* (NY) 93: The real McCoy with feathers on it. **1942** NMarsh *Enter Murderer* (NY) 89: The cartridges . . . were the real Mackay. **1951** EQueen *Origin* (B) 65: If this were the McCoy. **1955** CMWills *Death* (L) 88: These chaps are the real McCoy. **1957** VWMason *Gracious* (NY) 82: This document is the McCoy. **1964** JPhilips *Laughter* (NY DBC) 129: It wasn't the real McCoy. Partridge 503; Wentworth 335, 423.

M116 Ka (scratch) **Me** and I'll ka (scratch) thee

1905 JBCabell *Line* (NY 1926) 101: Ka [*claw*] me and I ka thee. **1934** JSFletcher *Murder* (NY) "Ca me, and I'll ca thee," as our Scotch friends say. **1971** WHWalling *No One* (NY) 135: Scratch me and I'll scratch you. EAP S76; *Oxford* 416, 706.

M117 Love **Me**, love my dog (*varied*)

1908 SHAdams *Flying Death* (NY) 91: Case of "Love me, love my bugs." **1922** JJoyce *Ulysses* (NY 1934) 616–7: Love me, love my dirty shirt. **1930** MPShiel *Black Box* (NY) 32: Those who love me must love my sheep. **1933** GBeaton *Jack* (L) 166: This sort of love-me-love-my-dog life. **1935** *New Yorker* 10/19 24: Love me, love my dog. **1937** CRoberts *Victoria* (NY) 275: Love me, love my novelist. **1947** GKersh *Prelude* (NY) 94: Love Me, Love My Dog. **1957** DRMorris *Warm* (NY) 125: Love you, love your dog. **1962** HPentecost *Cannibal* (NY DBC) 88: Love me, love my dog. **1976** CIsherwood *Christopher* (NY) 46: Love me, love my dog. TW 240; *Oxford* 492.

M118 **Mealy-mouthed**

1921 JSFletcher *Chestermarke* (NY) 236: A . . . smooth-tongued mealy-mouthed chap. EAP M128.

M119 The golden **Mean**

1931 RScarlett *Cat's* (NY) 235: The old school-book moral of the golden mean. **1932** ARolls *Lobelia* (L) 135: To choose the golden mean. **1936** GDHCole *Brothers* (L) 112: The golden and conservative mean. **1940** PBuranell *News Reel* (NY) 34: You've heard about the old gag—the golden mean. EAP M130.

M120 There is a **Mean** (measure) in all things

1919 RFirbank *Valmouth* (Works 3, L 1929) 117: There's a mean in all things. **1958** MRenault *King* (NY 1960) 82: There is measure in everything. *Oxford* 520: Measure. Cf. Medium, Moderation *below*.

M121 The **Measure** of a bride is her broth

1933 AWynne *Cotswold* (P) 22: But I do say, the measure o' a bride is her broth. Yon's a good old Scotch proverb.

M122 To take the **Measure** of someone's foot

1929 GDHCole *Poison* (NY) 170: She'd pretty well taken the measure of Cayley's foot. Cf. *Oxford* 521.

M123 The blacker the **Meat** the sweeter the bone

1935 DLCohn *God Shakes* (NY) 297: Some niggers say de blacker de meat de sweeter de bone, but I does't bleeve dat. Cf. Spears 32: Black meat. Cf. The nearer the Bone *above*.

M124 To be one's **Meat** and drink

1913 JSFletcher *Secret* (L 1918) 140: It was all meat and drink to the clerk. **1926** JSFletcher *Dead Men's* (NY) 11: Peace and quiet is meat and drink to an ageing man. **1935** HCBailey *Sullen* (NY) 47: A pretty girl was meat and drink to him. **1938** WMartyn *Murder Walks* (L) 21: The incident was meat and drink to him. **1941** DKent *Jason* (NY) 27: Publicity . . . was meat and drink to him. **1959** HCarmichael *Marked* (NY) 130: Flattery was meat and drink to her. **1960** STruss *One Man's* (NY) 137: Dreadful happenings are meat and drink for the *Daily Snapshot*. EAP M138.

M125 As mad as a **Meat ax**

1943 NMarsh *Colour Scheme* (L 1960) 105: You're mad as a meat axe. **1955** NMarsh *Scales* (B) 281: As mad as a meat-ax [*insane*]. Cf. DA Meat ax 2.

M126 To be bad **Medicine**

1925 HBedford-Jones *Rodomont* (NY) 125: It's bad medicine for us all. **1931** KTrask *Murder* (NY) 122: These Spig women were bad medicine. **1943** PCheyney *Dark Dust* (NY) 133: Serilla was bad medicine. EAP M142.

M127 To take (swallow) one's **Medicine**

1911 CKSteele *Mansion* (NY) 228: Take his medicine. **1921** IOstrander *Crimson* (NY) 278: To take my medicine. **1927** ORCohen *Outer* (NY) 251: Dad will take his medicine like a man. **1931** KTrask *Murder* (NY) 136: I'll take my medicine. **1936** DHume *Meet the Dragon* (L) 11: I'll swallow my medicine. **1939** MPropper *Hide the Body* (NY) 190:

We'll have to swallow our medicine. **1952** RFenisong *Deadlock* (NY) 168: I had to take my medicine. **1955** BCarey *Fatal* (NY) 65: Take my medicine like a man. **1956** *BangorDN* 8/25 2: I'm guilty and I want to take my medicine. **1964** RAHeinlein *Farnham's* (NY) 65: Come back and take your medicine. EAP M143: Swallow; TW 241(2): Take.

M128 There is a **Medium** in all things
1922 JJoyce *Ulysses* (NY 1934) 452: There's a medium in all things. Play cricket. EAP M144. Cf. Mean *above*.

M129 To speak right out in **Meeting**
1924 CWells *Furthest* (P) 123: I'm going to speak right out in meeting. TW 241(2).

M130 To have a **Memory** like a sieve
1935 BThomson *Richardson Solves* (L) 102: A memory like a sieve. **1938** JJConnington *For Murder* (L) 37: I've got a memory like a sieve. **1960** PGWodehouse *Jeeves* (L) 195: A memory like a sieve. Taylor *Prov. Comp.* 72: A mind like a sieve. Cf. EAP S200–3.

M131 To have a **Memory** like a steel trap
1958 PGWodehouse *Cocktail* (L) 144: She has a memory like a steel trap. **1968** BHays *Hotbed* (NY) 142: He had a memory like a steel trap. **1970** RBernard *Deadly* (NY) 167: He has a mind like a steel trap. Cf. TW 352: Steel trap.

M132 To be **Merry** and wise
1960 LLevine *Great* (L) 57: Who made you so merry and wise? EAP M150; TW 241(1).

M133 **Method** in one's madness
1911 JSHay *Amazing Emperor* (L) 280: A certain method in his madness. **1922** JJoyce *Ulysses* (NY 1934) 158: Method in his madness. **1924** JJFarjeon *Master* (NY) 171: I had some method in my madness. **1933** DGBrowne *Cotfold* (L) 200: There's a method in my madness. **1941** GBenedict *Deadly Drops* (NY) 64: Method in Mayne's madness. **1950** SPalmer *Green* (NY) 224: I still don't see any method in your madness. **1954** JWKrutch *Voice* (NY) 45: There is method in the saguaro's seeming madness. **1961** ALee *Miss Hogg* (L) 102: There's

method in her madness. **1966** NMarsh *Killer* (B) 192: Method in her madness. **1976** SBrett *So Much* (NY) 150: Method in his madness. EAP M151; Brunvand 94.

M134 As old as **Methuselah** (*varied*)
1900 CFPidgin *Quincy A. Sawyer* (B) 339: I'm as old as Methooselah. **1908** JCLincoln *Cy Whittaker* (NY) 62: She's old enough to be Methusalom's grand marm. **1909** JCLincoln *Keziah* (NY) 101: I'm as old as Methusaleh. **1919** JSFletcher *Middle Temple* (NY) 226: As old as Methusalem. **1931** JDBeresford *Innocent* (NY) 5: A woman . . . at least as old as Methuselah. **1938** CKnight *Ginger Lei* (NY) 122: He'd live to be as old as Methuselah. **1956** *BangorDN* 7/24 11: Older than Methuselah. **1958** MColes *Come* (NY) 222: As dead as Methuselah. **1969** AGilbert *Missing* (NY) 38: Half as old as Methuselah. EAP M152; TW 242(2).

M135 **Meum** (mine) and tuum (thine)
1923 JSFletcher *Copper* (NY) 101: Their sense of mine and thine . . . is inadequate. **1929** RAJWalling *Murder* (NY) 210: His sense of Meum and Tuum was not very strong. **1930** JGBrandon *Death* (L) 46: He knows not the meaning of the words *meum* or *tuum*. **1935** ECRLorac *Organ* (L) 95: Without bothering over the right and wrong, the mine or thine. **1937** ECVivian *Tramp's* (L) 10: *Meum* and *tuum* had no place in his vocabulary. **1940** HReilly *Murder in* (NY) 41: She had never been taught the difference between *meum* and *tuum*. **1958** EStarkie *Baudelaire* (NY) 174: The difference between "mine and thine." **1962** HMirrlees *Fly* (L) 64: Jacobean scholars had very little sense of *meum and tuum*. **1966** HTracy *Men* (L) 176: A woman who cannot distinguish between *meum* and *tuum*, as it were. EAP M153.

M136 Many a **Mickle** (pickle) makes a muckle (*varied*)
1933 JCLenehan *Death* (L) 80: The aphorism that "many a mickle makes a muckle." **1946** WPartington *T.J.Wise* (L) 32: The old saw that many a pickle makes a mickle. **1958** RLDuffus *Williamstown* (NY) 85: It's the mickles [that] make the muckle. **1965**

JGrimmelshausen *Simplicius* trans. G Schulz-Behrend (I) 196: "Many a mickle makes a muckle" . . . when what he really meant was, "A lot of toothpicks make me a roaring fire." **1968** MConnelly *Voices* (NY) 91: "Many a mickle makes a muckle, but only God can make real maple syrup." EAP M154.

M137 As rich as **Midas**

1933 SRohmer *Tales* (NY) 85: I am as rich as Midas. **1977** EPGreen *Rotten* (NY) 48: Rich as Midas.

M138 To have the **Midas** touch

1940 RKing *Holiday* (NY) 26: He had the Midas touch, if you don't mind the cliché. NED Midas 1.

M139 To be knocked into the **Middle** of next week

1921 JCLincoln *Galusha* (NY) 250: Knocked into . . . the middle of next week. **1922** JJoyce *Ulysses* (NY 1934) 247: That fellow would knock you into the middle of next week. **1928** JArnold *Surrey* (L) 261: Knock whoever it was into the middle of next year. **1933** GHolt *Dark Lady* (L) 244: I'll knock you into the middle of next week. **1938** CFGregg *Brazen* (L) 45: A punch which would have knocked most men into the middle of next week. **1955** ESGardner *Glamorous* (NY DBC) 17: I've heard the expression "being knocked into the middle of next week." **1956** DWheatley *Ka* (L) 66: Blown into the middle of next week. **1962** AMStein *Home* (NY) 112: Knocked this character into the middle of next week. TW 242(2); NED Week *sb.* 6d.

M140 As black as **Midnight**

1915 JFerguson *Stealthy* (L 1935) 251: Black as midnight. **1955** GBrewer *Red Scarf* (NY) 29: It was as black as midnight. **1960** MCronin *Begin* (NY) 110: As black as midnight in Connemara. **1969** RHarris *Wicked* (NY) 211: My character's as black and desperate as midnight. EAP M155.

M141 As dark as **Midnight**

1965 JFWest *Time* (NY) 49: Gonna be darker'n midnight in a witch's womb before a feller can say scat. EAP M156; TW 242(2).

M142 As still as **Midnight**

1957 CDBowen *Lion* (B) 416: Still as midnight. EAP M158; TW 242(3); Taylor *Western Folklore* 17(1958) 17.

M143 **Might** makes right (*varied*)

1933 HHDunn *Crimson* (NY) 190: Might was still right. **1956** WMankowitz *Old* (B) 150: Right is might. **1957** *Time* 3/4 28: Might was still right. **1957** *BangorDN* 9/5 23: The theory that might makes right. **1961** RJWhite *Smartest* (L) 283: Thomas Carlyle . . . said that might is right. **1962** DMDisney *Should Auld* (NY) 98: The strong prevailed over the weak: Might made right. EAP M159: Overcomes; TW 242(1); Brunvand 94(1).

M144 With **Might** and main

1920 GBMcCutcheon *Anderson Crow* (NY) 146: With all his might and main. **1933** GRichards *Memoirs* (NY) 219: Cried out . . . with might and main. **1937** PATaylor *Figure* (NY) 182: Asey listened with all his might and main. **1947** GLGower *Mixed* (L) 140: Striving might and main. **1954** MMcCarthy *Charmed* (NY) 250: She had fought with might and main not to know. **1958** FMaclean *Person* (L) 181: Cannon . . . booming away with might and main. **1966** EFuller *Successful* (NY) 37: With all my might and main. **1971** ADavidson *Peregrine* (NY) 129: With might and main. **1974** AMorice *Killing* (NY) 127: With might and main. EAP M160; TW 242(2); Brunvand 94(3).

M145 A country **Mile**

1959 DMDisney *No Next* (NY) 34: Out in front by a country mile. **1960** IWallace *Chapman* (NY 1961) 81: You don't get within a country mile of her. **1971** KLaumer *Deadfall* (NY) 87: Not good enough, bub. Not by a country mile. **1981** ELathen *Going* (NY) 153: He was out by a country mile. Whiting *NC* 444; DARE i 802.

M146 To stick (stand) out a **Mile** (*varied*)

1926 MLewis *Island* (L) 156: The principal ones . . . should stick out a mile. **1932** WLHay *Who Cut* (L) 178: It is sticking out a mile. **1938** HHolt *Whispering* (L) 105: It stands out a mile. **1939** VWilliams *Fox*

Prowls (B) 211: The thing sticks out a foot. **1945** GDaniel *Cambridge* (L 1952) 133: It sticks out a mile. **1948** EDaly *Book* (NY) 54: Something stands out a mile. **1951** JCreasey *Puzzle* (L 1962) 115: The possible reason stood out a mile. **1954** CCarnac *Policeman* (NY) 166: It sticks out a mile. **1971** CAird *Late* (NY) 119: She's neurotic all right. Sticks out a mile. **1971** MUnderwood *Trout* (NY) 106: It stuck out a mile. Berrey 171.5. Cf. Yard *below*.

M147   To talk a **Mile** a minute

1959 DTracy *Big* (NY DBC) 23: Talking a mile a minute. **1972** JDMacDonald *Long* (P) 79: He talks to me a mile a minute.

M148   As meek as **Milk**

1938 NBlake *Beast* (NY 1958) 92: Meek as milk [*a boat under way*]. **1941** BDougall *I Don't Scare* (NY) 138: She was . . . meek as milk. **1970** MStewart *Crystal* (NY) 24: Meek as milk [*a woman*]. TW 243(1); Taylor *Western Folklore* 17(1958) 17.

M149   As mild as **Milk** (*varied*)

1919 JSClouston *Man from the Clouds* (NY) 136: Mild as milk. **1924** AChristie *Man* (NY) 86: He looks mild as milk. **1932** DFrome *Man* (NY) 212: Mild as milk [*a man*]. **1938** RAJWalling *Coroner* (L) 265: The auld mon was mild as a dish o' milk. **1939** IJones *Hungry Corpse* (NY) 246: I'm mild as goat's milk. **1941** AChristie *Evil Under* (NY) 132: Mild as milk. **1949** JSymons *Bland* (L) 143: The Inspector's voice was as mild as milk. **1966** NMonsarrat *Life (I)* (L) 216: The weather was mild as milk. **1971** HCarvig *Witch* (NY) 84: Looked as mild as milk [*a woman*]. TW 243(2).

M150   As pale as **Milk**

1942 HCBailey *Nobody's* (NY) 75: Pale as milk. **1959** AGilbert *Death* (NY) 44: A face as pale as milk. Wilstach 283.

M151   As smooth (bland) as **Milk**; Milk-smooth

1940 AGilbert *Dear Dead* (L) 140: Crook's voice was as smooth as milk. **1960** RMacdonald *Ferguson* (NY) 75: Her skin was as smooth as milk. **1969** RHarris *Wicked* (NY) 69: Such milk-smooth authority. **1975**

NGuild *Lost* (NY) 56: Her voice was bland as milk. Cf. As smooth as Cream *above*.

M152   As sweet as **Milk**

1953 MPHood *Silent* (NY) 67: Her voice is sweet as milk. EAP M161; TW 243(3).

M153   As white as **Milk**; Milk-white (*varied*)

1916 NDouglas *London Street Games* (L) 64: As white as milk. **1922** JJoyce *Ulysses* (NY 1934) 55: Milk white teeth. **1927** VWilliams *Eye* (B) 49: Milk-white teeth. **1928** DHLawrence *Lady* ("Allemagne") 251: He was white as milk. **1937** LCharteris *Thieves'* (NY) 14: Her face had gone as white as milk. **1940** AGaines *While the Wind* (NY) 28: None . . . turned white as skimmed milk. **1944** RAltrocchi *Sleuthing* (Cambridge, Mass.) 26: A milk-white virgin. **1951** ECrispin *Long* (L 1958) 37: A face as white as skimmed milk. **1952** HReilly *Velvet* (NY) 79: Philip went as white as milk. **1958** MKenton *Candy* (NY 1965) 75: The milk-white V the panties made. **1964** JBlish *Doctor* (L) 212: His face white as milk. **1970** MStewart *Crystal* (NY) 292: Breasts . . . milk-white. **1974** JCreasey *As Merry* (NY) 11: Milk-white skin. EAP M162, 162a; TW 243(4); Brunvand 94(1): Milk-white.

M154   **Milk**-and-water

1935 DHume *Murders* (L) 185: A milk-and-water lad. **1939** RStout *Mountain Cat* (NY 1958) 157: That was milk and water stuff. **1941** AWebb *Suicide Club* (L) 60: The halls [*music halls*] are milk and water now compared to what they used to be. **1949** MMuggeridge *Affairs* (L) 97: A rather milk-and-water liberalism. **1951** AChristie *They Came* (NY) 125: Milk as milk and water. **1960** LFielden *Natural* (L) 196: A milk-and-water Liberal. **1965** AChristie *At Bertram's* (L) 96: An unbelieveably milk-and-water Miss. **1972** MGilbert *Body* (NY) 133: They're milk and water beside that little patch of London. **1976** IAsimov *Murder* (NY) 145: His own milk-and-water style. EAP M164.

M155   The **Milk** in the coconut

1900 CFPidgin *Quincy A. Sawyer* (B) 303: That's the "milk in the cocoanut" [*the explanation*]. **1922** JJoyce *Ulysses* (NY 1934)

314: That explains the milk in the coconut. **1930** GBaxter *Ainceworth* (NY) 102: That really is the milk in the cocoanut; 275. **1934** CBush *100% Alibis* (L) 255: Then the milk is found in the coconut. **1950** MRHodgkin *Student* (L) 82: Now we get to the milk in the cocoanut. **1968** CMackenzie *Octave Seven* (NY) 259: I wondered what the milk in the coconut was. **1973** WJBurley *Death* (NY) 99: He began to wonder whether there was going to be any milk in the coconut. TW 243–4(6); Brunvand 94(4).

M156 Skimmed **Milk** masquerading as cream

1952 MO'Brine *Corpse* (L) 57: There's a saying about skimmed milk masquerading as cream. Cf. Mutton *below*.

M157 To cry over spilled **Milk** (*varied*)

1905 JBCabell *Line* (NY 1926) 210: A wise man does not meditate unthriftly upon spilt milk. **1912** HHMunro *Unbearable* (NY 1928) 171: There is nothing to be gained by crying over spilt milk. **1920** GDilnot *Suspected* (NY) 136: No good crying over spilt milk. **1926** Anonymous *Great American Ass* (NY) 94: No use crying over spilt cream. **1931** CBrooks *Ghost* (NY) 65: It's no use crying over spilt milk. **1932** BRoss *Tragedy of Y* (NY) 300: No use crying over spilt milk. **1939** JDonavan *Coloured Wind* (L) 122: It's no good crying over spilt milk. **1951** OSwenson *Northwest* (L) 143: I knew that spilled milk was never regained by crying over it. **1956** RMacdonald *Barbarous* (NY) 126: No use crying over spilled blood. **1957** *Punch* 2/6 225: There should be no crying over spilt opportunities. **1959** KWaterhouse *Billy* (L) 53: "It is better to cry over spilt milk than to try and put it back in the bottle," a saw that did not strike me for one as being particularly smart. **1961** GBagby *Evil* (NY) 108: A . . . no-use-crying-over-spilt-milk attitude. **1962** D Honig *No Song* (L) 253: We can't cry over what's spilled. **1969** LWoolf *Journey* (L) 210: Even the false proverbs tend to become true for old people, for instance, that it is no good crying over spilt milk. **1971** ELathen *Longer* (NY) 51: She was not weeping over spilt milk. **1971** HPentecost

Deadly (NY) 91: Oh well—spilled milk and all that. **1973** JPorter *It's Murder* (NY) 7: No good crying over spilt milk. EAP M166; Brunvand 94(2).

M158 The **Mills** of God grind slowly *etc.*

1927 AGilbert *Tragedy* (NY) 224: There's an adage about the mills of God. **1929** WKSmith *Bowery* (NY) 37: The inevitable workings of the mills of the gods that grind slowly but surely. **1947** AGilbert *Death in* (L) 133: The mills of God grind slowly, but they grind exceeding small. **1956** EDillon *Death* (L) 127: The mills of God grind slowly . . . but they grind exceeding small. **1957** *BangorDN* 1/24 22: The mills of God grind slowly, yet they grind exceeding small. **1974** NWebster *Burial* (NY) 38: They operate like them. When it comes to action they grind exceeding slow. *Oxford* 314: God's mill.

M159 The **Mill** will never grind with the water that is past

1937 HCBailey *Clunk's* (L) 62: The mill will never grind with the water that is past. *Oxford* 531.

M160 To have been through the **Mill**

1927 JMWalsh *Silver* (L) 13: You've been through the mill. **1933** AGilbert *Musical* (L) 189: I've been through the mill. **1935** BFlynn *Case* (L) 131: I've been through the mill. **1969** MDorman *King* (NY) 160: He had been through the mill. TW 244(1); Brunvand 95.

M161 As calm as a **Millpond** (pond)

1906 JCLincoln *Mr. Pratt* (NY) 130: As calm as a millpond. **1934** SPalmer *Silver Persian* (NY) 22: The sea's calm as a millpond. **1955** IFleming *Moonraker* (NY 1960) 167: Calm as a millpond. **1957** MPHood *In the Dark* (NY) 32: The sea was calm as a millpond. **1960** TWilliams *Three Players* (L) 197: Richard was . . . as calm as a duckpond. **1964** MColes *Knife* (NY DBC) 93: Calm as a mill-pond. **1972** JBonett *No Time* (NY) 19: The sea . . . as calm as a mill-pond. **1973** BBehan *My Life* (LA) 201: The sea had been as calm as a pond. EAP M170.

M162 As placid as a **Millpond**

1965 JGaskell *Atlan* (NY 1968) 30: The water . . . placid as a millpond. **1969** A Roudybush *Capital* (NY) 47: Thisbie's life was as placid as a pond. Wilstach 293: Millpond.

M163 As smooth as a **Millpond** (pond)

1909 JCLincoln *Keziah* (NY) 273: Smooth as a pond. **1928** ALivingston *Monk* (NY) 255: As smooth as a millpond. **1934** HFootner *Dangerous* (L) 40: The sea was as smooth as a pond. **1937** DduMaurier *The duMauriers* (NY) 168: The sea was as smooth as the proverbial millpond. **1957** CThomas *Leftover* (L) 109: The sea ought to be . . . as smooth as a mill pond: Has anyone ever seen a mill pond? **1970** PAlding *Guilt* (NY) 169: As smooth as a pond. EAP M171; TW 291: Pond(1).

M164 As still as a **Millpond** (pond)

1968 BRoueché *What's Left* (B) 5: The Canal lay as still as a pond. EAP M172; Brunvand 95.

M165 To be like a **Millpond**

1930 FDGrierson *Mysterious* (L) 21: The sea was like a millpond. **1934** DGBrowne *Plan XVI* (NY) 141: The sea was like the mill-pond we journalists have made familiar. 272: The sea that night being like the proverbial mill-pond. **1941** RAldington *Life* (NY) 274: The Channel passage . . . ought to be the proverbial mill-pond.

M166 As hard as the nether **Millstone**

1910 EPhillpotts *Tales* (NY) 76: Hard as the nether millstone. **1928** GGardiner *At the House* (NY) 288: As hard as the nether millstone. EAP M173.

M167 To be a **Millstone** around one's neck (*varied*)

1925 BAtkey *Pyramid* (NY) 202: A millstone has fallen from my neck. **1928** AGilbert *Mrs. Davenport* (NY) 30: A millstone round your neck. **1932** AGilbert *Body* (NY) 213: A grindstone round her neck. **1937** MBurton *Clue* (NY) 158: She would find Neurolith Ltd. a millstone round her neck. **1940** EHealy *Mr. Sandeman* (NY) 51: I'm a millstone around your neck. **1949** JReach *Late* (NY) 202: A millstone around his neck all the rest of his life. **1956** NFitzgerald *Imagine* (L) 129: The "Major" who hung like a golden millstone around his neck. **1959** BBenson *Seven* (NY) 103: Mrs. Hancock was a millstone around her daughter's neck. **1967** WStClair *Lord Elgin* (L) 180: The collection [was] becoming a millstone round his neck. **1972** JGreenway *Down* (B) 25: This millstone on my back. **1974** JP Hennessy *R.L.Stevenson* (NY) 237: A millstone round his neck. EAP M174; TW 244(2).

M168 Great **Minds** think alike (*varied*)

1921 P&MThorne *Sheridan* (NY) 26: Great minds [*no more*]. **1930** JGBrandon *McCarthy* (L) 183: Strange how great minds think alike. **1932** LCharteris *White* (NY) 205: Curious how great minds think alike. **1935** VWMason *Washington* (NY) 233: Great minds flow in the same channel. **1936** ABliss *Four Times* (P) 166: Peculiar how two minds will work along the same channel. **1940** JBentley *Mr. Marlow Stops* (B) 83: Great minds think alike. **1950** STruss *Never* (NY) 194: Great minds think alike. **1959** TWalsh *Dangerous* (B DBC) 98: Great minds and same channels. **1960** STruss *One Man's* (NY) 39: Great minds think alike. **1961** ESGardner *Spurious* (NY) 67: Great minds run in the same channel. **1976** RBDominic *Murder* (NY) 126: Great minds work alike. Whiting *NC* 444–5; *Oxford* 326–7: Good wits jump; Bradley 85: Run in the same channels.

M169 A sound **Mind** in a sound body (*varied*)

1930 FDBurdett *Odyssey* (L) 253: The old Latin adage: *Mens sana in corpore sano.* **1936** VMcHugh *Caleb* (NY) 168: You know the old sayin' 'bout a sound mind in a sound body. **1937** TStevenson *Nudist* (L) 40: A sound mind in a sound body, as the old tag has it. **1958** NFitzgerald *Suffer* (L) 166: An example of a healthy mind in a healthy body. **1962** EFRussell *Great* (NY) 60: A healthy mind in a healthy body. **1970** JWechsberg *First* (B) 134: *Mens sana in corpore sano.* **1973** HPentecost *Beautiful* (NY)

15: Sound body leads to a sound mind and sound thinking. EAP M179.

M170 Enough to make a **Minister** swear

1904 JCLincoln *Cap'n Eri* (NY) 57: Enough to make a minister swear. EAP M181. Cf. Saint *below*.

M171 **Ministers'** sons and deacons' daughters (*varied*)

1925 BBLindsay *Revolt* (NY) 95: The old saying about some ministers' sons and deacons' daughters. **1936** VWBrooks *Flowering* (NY 1946) 42: The "ministers' sons" who became proverbial were sons of the brimstone God of the inland regions. **1944** VWBrooks *Washington Irving* (NY 1946) 340: And, if he [*N.P.Willis*] was not the proverbial minister's son, he behaved for the rest of his life as if he had been. **1957** *NYTimes Book Review* 11/17 24: It has often been said of the children of ministers in this country that they go either to the dogs or glory. Whiting *NC* 462: Preacher's son.

M172 As horny (promiscuous, sleek, smooth) as a **Mink**

1959 DMarkson *Epitaph* (NY) 129: Promiscuous as a mink. **1962** ABoucher *Best from Fantasy* (B) 130: She was . . . as sleek as a mink. **1964** HKemelman *Friday* (NY 1965) 66: You're as horny as a mink. **1964** SRansome *Meet* (NY DBC) 11: A smooth job . . . as a mink. See Wentworth 339: Mink. Cf. Otter *below*.

M173 As hot as a (bull) **Mink**

1950 BBird *Death* (NY) 212: After a cryptic agreement that it was "hot as a bull mink." **1954** EMarriner *Kennebec* (Waterville, Me.) 298: This room's hot as a mink.

M174 To go for a **Minnow** (mackerel) and catch a whale (*varied*)

1933 EBBlack *Ravenelle* (NY) 221: Sent out for a minnow, he had caught a whale. **1934** HReilly *McKee* (NY) 1: Fishing for a minnow . . . he caught a whale. **1958** DGBrowne *Death* (L) 177: If ever a man went fishing for a mackerel and caught a whale.

M175 As big as a **Minute**

1930 CWells *Doorstep* (NY) 127: A village about as big as a minute. **1937** CGGivens *All Cats* (I) 253: This here puppy was about as big as a minute. **1941** ISCobb *Exit* (I) 361: About as big as a minute. **1952** JKnox *Little* (P) 32: About as big as a handful of minutes. **1954** MMcCarthy *Charmed* (NY) 38: He felt . . . about as big as a minute. **1961** ESeeman *In the Arms* (NY) 62: She warn't no bigger than a minute. **1964** AM Stein *Blood* (NY) 87: She was no bigger than a minute. **1970** RFenisong *Drop* (NY) 161: The boy's no bigger than a minute. **1971** PRubenstein *Groupsex* (NY) 62: She is as big as a minute. Taylor *Prov. Comp.* 16.

M176 Look out for the **Minutes** and the hours will look out for themselves

1954 EForbes *Rainbow* (B) 45: If you look out for the minutes the hours will look out for themselves. TW 245(1).

M177 In the **Mire**

1940 DHume *Five Aces* (L) 88: You wouldn't land me in the mire. EAP M188.

M178 As smooth as a **Mirror**

1940 AAFair *Gold Comes* (NY) 148: She's smooth as a mirror inside. **1953** ECrandall *White* (B) 3: A lawn . . . smooth as a mirror. EAP M189.

M179 **Misery** loves company (*varied*)

1921 JBCabell *Figures* (NY 1925) 173: Misery loves company. **1923** LThayer *Sinister* (NY) 157: Misery loves company. **1929** SGEndore *Casanova* (NY) 314: From Francesca came little consolation, unless it be the company of misery. **1935** CMRussell *Murder* (NY) 293: Misery loves company. **1937** GDilnot *Murder* (L) 188: Someone once said that misery loves company. **1948** EQueen *Ten* (B) 120: Misery likes to have company. **1954** JSanders *Freakshow* (B) 163: Misery loves company. **1958** *New Yorker* 4/5 77: The old saying . . . misery does love company. **1959** *BHerald* 3/13 43: The proverb that misery loves company. **1962** GMalcolm-Smith *Lady* (NY DBC) 127: Misery . . . can love some pretty odd company. **1968** ELathen *Stitch* (NY) 158: Misery loves company. **1970** OFriedrich *Decline* (NY) 111: Misery would love company. **1973** TAWaters *Lost* (NY) 77: The theory that anger loves company. EAP M192; TW 246(2); Brunvand 95.

M180 Misfortunes (troubles *etc.*) never come singly (*varied*)

1903 ADMcFaul *Ike Glidden* (B) 272: Sorrow comes in battalions never alone. **1925** RAFreeman *Red Thumb* (L) 107: Misfortunes are proverbially sociable. **1928** MChideckel *Strictly* (NY) 31: Troubles never come singly. **1929** AFielding *Cluny* (NY) 27: Misfortunes never come singly. **1930** ABCox *Vane* (L) 251: Troubles never come singly. **1930** HMSmith *Inspector Frost in the City* (NY) 117: Disappointments never come singly. **1932** MKennedy *Murderer* (L) 136: Misfortunes never come singly. **1935** JRhode *Hendon's* (L) 98: Troubles never come singly, as they say. **1937** LPendleton *Down East* (NY) 38: The old saying, "misfortunes never come singly." **1938** ECRLorac *John Brown's* (L) 120: They say accidents never come singly. **1940** GStockwell *Candy* (NY) 196: All the proverbs about trouble coming double are correct. **1949** MColes *Diamonds* (NY) 47: They say troubles never come singly. **1951** JCollier *Fancies* (NY) 93: They say, though, that blessings never come singly, any more than misfortunes. **1956** AChristie *Dead Man's* (L) 223: Troubles never come singly, as they say. **1958** WMiller *Way* (B) 10: Trouble always comes singly, he thought, with the sceptic's special pleasure in seeing another Old Saying undone. **1959** EHuxley *Flame* (L) 140: Troubles did not come singly to Sammy. **1960** HRobertson *Swan* (NY) 111: Troubles never come singly. **1964** EHuxley *Incident* (NY) 49: Troubles never come singly. **1968** NBowen *Hear* (NY) 4: Trouble will come. And it always comes in bunches, like bananas. **1971** RMurphy *Stream* (NY) 93: Misfortunes seldom come singly. **1973** JCashman *Gentleman* (NY) 141: They say troubles come by the sackload. EAP M194; TW 246(1). Cf. Brunvand 19: Calamity. Cf. All Things come in threes *below*.

M181 A **Miss** is as good as a mile (*varied*)

1924 WBMFerguson *Black* (NY) 211: A miss is as good as a mile. **1932** LAdamic *Laughing* (NY) 316: An inch is as good as a mile. **1932** JLMitchell *Three* (I) 178: Claim it missed by inches, but they were as good as so many miles. **1933** EECummings *Eimi* (NY) 157: A miss is as good as a mile. **1951** NMitford *Blessing* (NY) 242: A miss is as good as a mile might be taken as their motto by French pedestrians. **1952** BWolfe *Limbo* (L) 293: A myth is as good as a smile. **1957** *BangorDN* 9/10 2: A Miss was better than a mile tonight as Winifred Ann Zebley won her case in traffic court. **1958** SBedford *Best* (L 1961) 158: In these things a miss is as bad as a mile. **1959** *Time* 7/20 18: A miff was as good as a smile. **1959** SBedford *Trial* (NY) 170: In these things a miss is as bad as a mile. **1962** ADuggan *Lord* (L) 70: A miss was as good as a mile. **1969** SWilson *Away* (NY) 305: A miss is as good as a mile. EAP M195.

M182 **Miss** (Mrs., Mr.) Right

1922 JJoyce *Ulysses* (NY 1934) 362: Till Mr Right comes along. 640: Miss Right came on the scene. **1926** HAdams *Crooked* (L) 171: With Mrs. Right he'd be so rich [*the right kind of woman*]. **1937** GStockwell *Death* (NY) 103: Where Cora . . . could meet Mr. Right. **1957** DErskine *Pink* (NY) 41: Still looking for Mr. Right. **1958** WRoss *Immortal* (NY) 170: They're . . . victims of folklore who believe that there is only one Mister Right for every Miss Wrong. **1961** WCooper *Scenes* (NY) 232: Waiting for Miss Right to come along. **1965** RBissell *Still* (NY) 34: Mr. Right hasn't shown up yet. **1966** MMcShane *Night's* (NY) 78: She's waiting for Mr. Right. Partridge 698: Right, Mr; Wentworth 340: Mister Right 2.

M183 To be from **Missouri** (*varied*)

1921 P&MThorne *Sheridan* (NY) 12: I'm from Missouri. **1928** WAWolff *Trial* (NY) 312: Like the proverbial man from Missouri, I have to be shown. **1930** SChalmers *Crime* (NY) 75: I'm not from Missouri, but somebody'll have to show me. **1930** CWells *Doorstep* (NY) 184: I'm a hundred per cent

Missourian. I just had to get outside evidence. **1934** JTFarrell *Young Manhood* (NY 1935) 398: I'm from Missouri . . . show me. **1935** CBarry *Death Overseas* (L) 141: How many Englishmen know the expression, "I'm from Missouri," and what it means? **1939** NMorland *Knife* (L) 35: The desk sergeant . . . comes from Missouri . . . That's an Americanism for disbelief. **1948** GHJohnston *Death Takes* (L 1959) 111: I'm from Missouri, see, and I don't know nothin'. **1959** *NYTimes* 9/20 3E: If there are 50 states why does everybody keep saying he's from Missouri. **1959** JABrussel *Just* (NY) 101: This juror was "from Missouri and had to be shown." **1962** KAmis *Spectrum(1)* (L) 280: I'm from Missouri . . . I'll see for myself. **1964** EMcBain *Ax* (NY) 97: I'm from Missouri. **1970** WANolen *Making* (NY) 169: They're from Missouri when it comes to surgical procedures. DA Missouri 4d.

M184   Like **Mistress**, like maid (*varied*)
1936 GHeyer *Behold* (NY) 2: Like mistress, like maid. **1939** CSaxby *Death Cuts* (NY) 141: Like mistress, like maid. **1940** HReilly *Death Can* (NY) 275: Like mistress, like maid. **1955** SNGhose *Flame* (L) 46: Such mistress, such Nan; such master, such man. **1969** GBagby *Honest* (NY) 38: I told her I would be mistress in my own house. *Oxford* 536: Such; Tilley M1022.

M185   To give (get) the **Mitten** (*varied*)
1906 JCLincoln *Mr. Pratt* (NY) 328: She gave him the mitten. **1924** JSFletcher *Time-Worn* (NY) 189: Given 'em both the mitten, as they say. **1932** JSFletcher *Man in the Fur Coat* (L) 165: George . . . had given Samantha the mitten. **1935** CCranston *Murder* (P) 178: Hand you the mitten. **1938** PGWodehouse *Code* (NY) 11: She handed Gussie the temporary mitten. **1941** TDowning *Lazy Lawrence* (NY) 275: Giving him the mitten. **1941** CMRussell *Dreadful* (NY) 10: What you called "given the mitten" in your day. **1961** MHHood *Drown* (NY) 83: Margy gave him the mitten. **1968** EBuckler *Ox Bells* (NY) 174: You had got what was

known as the "mitten." TW 247(2); Brunvand 95.

M186   **Moderation** in all things
1932 TCobb *Death* (L) 79: There's moderation in all things. **1936** JTMcIntyre *Steps* (NY) 92: Moderation, which should be the check upon all things. **1950** ECRLorac *And Then* (NY) 202: Motto, moderation in all things. **1956** AWUpfield *Battling* (L 1960) 46: Moderation in all things. **1957** CLandon *Unseen* (NY) 103: Moderation in all things. *Oxford* 520: Measure (quote 1594). Cf. Mean, Medium *above*.

M187   As slow as **Molasses** (treacle) (*varied*)
1932 TThayer *Three Sheet* (NY) 122: Slow as molasses. **1936** JTFarrell *World* (NY) 468: They're slow as molasses in January. **1937** PStong *Buckskin* (NY) 36: She's slower than molasses in January. **1939** KSecrist *Murder Melody* (NY) 60: You're slower'n cold molasses. **1940** WCClark *Murder Goes* (B) 77: Those bastards are slower than molasses in January. **1945** RPowell *Lay That Pistol* (NY) 129: A deep voice, soft and slow as molasses. **1953** EBGarside *Man from* (NY) 174: The courts are slow as treacle. **1957** MPHood *In the Dark* (NY) 50: He was slower than molasses on a cold day. **1957** VWMason *Gracious* (NY) 88: Liquor flows around here like cold molasses. **1959** *BHerald* 4/25 25: But Sandy's awful smart, and Annie's no January molasses herself. **1959** DMDisney *Did She Fall* (NY) 99: "How's your Sherlocking going?" "About like molasses in January." **1976** MRReno *Final* (NY) 108: Slow as molasses. Whiting *NC* 445(1); Taylor *Prov. Comp.* 74; *Western Folklore* 17(1958) 17.

M188   As sweet as **Molasses**
1970 NMonsarrat *Breaking* (L) 533: As sweet as molasses. EAP M204.

M189   As thick as **Molasses** (treacle)
1933 HAshbrook *Murder* (NY) 48: They been as thick as molasses [*intimate*]. **1939** HMiller *Capricorn* (NY 1961) 97: The crowd thick as molasses. **1964** WHayward *It Never* (L) 98: The silence was thicker

than treacle. Whiting *NC* 445(2); Taylor *Prov. Comp.* 81: Thick.

M190   To break the **Mold** (*varied*)

1956 HCahill *Shadow* (NY) 176: My mother was a woman, like you said, but they don't make 'em like that now. They broke the mold. **1956** RFoley *Last* (NY DBC) 124: They broke the mold after they made Emily. **1957** *New Yorker* 2/16 133: Just before they made S. J. Perelman they broke the mold. NED Mould *sb.*³ 2c.

M191   As blind as a **Mole**

1933 RAJWalling *Behind* (L) 134: You're blind as a mole. **1939** LFord *Town* (NY) 203: I'd been blind as a mole. **1963** MMcCarthy *Group* (NY) 153: Blind as moles. **1968** JHarding *Sacha* (L) 24: As blind as a mole. **1976** CLarson *Muir's* (NY) 28: Blind as a mole. EAP M205.

M192   As gloomy as **Monday** morning

1952 PLoraine *Dublin* (L) 70: There was I, as gloomy as Monday morning. Whiting *NC* 445: Blue as. Cf. Taylor *Western Folklore* 17(1958) 17: Regular as.

M193   **Monday** for health *etc.*

1957 HPBeck *Folklore of Maine* (P) 60: Monday for health, Tuesday for wealth, Wednesday the best day of all, Thursday for crosses, Friday for losses, Saturday no luck at all. *Oxford* 537.

M194   Do not marry for **Money**, but marry where money is

1938 SKing *If I Die* (NY) 16: It's just as easy to fall in love with a girl with money as one without—a lot easier, I'd say. **1967** VSPritchett *Cab* (NY) 45: The saying, often heard in Yorkshire: "Dinna tha' marry money, go where money is." **1968** WHaggard *Cool Day* (NY) 31: He'd have heard the ancient saw. Never marry for money, but marry where money is. **1972** PDJames *Unsuitable* (NY) 124: My mother used to say, "Don't marry for money, but marry where money is." Cf. Whiting *NC* 446(4).

M195   Lend one's **Money**, lose one's friend

1930 TPerry *Owner* (NY) 28: There is an old Chinese proverb that says: "Lend your money; lose your friend." **1955** CMWills *Death* (L) 118: Never lend your money . . . Happen you'll lose the friend you lend it to—which don't matter over much—but you'll likely lose your money into the bargain. **1960** HSleasar *Enter* (NY 1967) 137: You know what they say about lending money, it's a sure way to lose friends. EAP M207; *Oxford* 455. Cf. Enemy *above*.

M196   **Money** burns a hole in one's pocket (*varied*)

1931 HBurnham *Murder* (NY) 126: A [jewel] that the holder finds burning a hole in his pocket. **1931** MElwin *Charles Reade* (L) 206: Smith's four thousand were burning a hole in his pocket. **1935** SVestal *Wine Room* (B) 176: Money burned his pockets. **1943** NMarsh *Colour Scheme* (L 1960) 210: A piece of portentous information burnt holes in the pockets of his reticence. **1952** AGilbert *Mr. Crook* (NY DBC) 42: Money burning a hole in his pocket. **1956** RA Heinlein *Double* (NY 1957) 55: Your pay burning holes in your pockets. **1959** WHaggard *Venetian* (NY DBC) 27: He had money in his pocket and it was burning a hole in it. **1960** NFitzgerald *Candles* (L) 129: Kate's letters were burning a hole in his pocket. **1963** WMorris *Cause* (NY) 23: Now that Violet's got a little money she feels it burning a hole in her pocket. **1974** NWebster *Burial* (NY) 34: Visitors with money burning a hole in their pocket. TW 247(2); *Oxford* 538.

M197   **Money** cannot buy happiness (*varied*)

1925 GHGerould *Midsummer* (NY) 156: There are some things money can't buy. **1930** JSFletcher *Heaven-sent* (NY) 227: Money . . . can't buy love. **1957** *New Yorker* 10/26 178: Money can't buy happiness. **1966** EVCunningham *Helen* (NY) 5: If you can't buy happiness, you can buy a lot of comfort. **1966** ESGardner *Worried* (NY) 14: Money doesn't mean happiness. **1970** RRendell *Best Man* (NY) 41: It's true what they say, money can't buy happiness. **1971** PMoyes *Season* (NY) 141: They say that money doesn't bring happiness. Cf. EAP H77; *Oxford* 141: Content is happiness. Cf. Money is not *below.*

M198 Money flies

1937 HIngstad *East of the Great Glacier* (NY) 106: Yes, it is said that money flies! Cf. *Oxford* 675: Riches have wings.

M199 Money for jam

1929 TKindon *Murder* (NY) 111: Money for jam. **1933** AAllen *Loose* (NY) 10: It'll be money for jam, as the vulgar say. **1940** LBruce *Ropes and Rings* (L) 270: It was money for jam. **1945** GBellairs *Calamity* (NY) 144: Ten pounds—money for jam. **1955** NFitzgerald *House* (L) 250: 'Tis as money for jam slandering her [*very easy*]. **1955** CMWills (L) 138: These daily maids are just money for jam. **1959** *TLS* 6/5 330: The first book was . . . money for jam. **1963** RArnold *Orange* (L) 12: Time was money for jam. **1968** PGallico *Manxmouse* (NY) 106: The rest was money for jam. **1973** PMoyes *Curious* (NY) 80: Money for jam. Partridge 528.

M200 Money for old rope

1949 MGilbert *He Didn't* (NY DBC) 53: It was money for old rope when you walked into the joint. **1961** JWelcome *Beware* (L) 57: Money for old rope. Partridge 528.

M201 Money has no smell

1911 JSHay *Amazing Emperor* (L) 141: "Money," as Vespasian said, "has no smell." **1934** FBeeding *One Sane* (B) 36: What is it the Romans used to say? *Non olet pecunia*—money does not smell. **1936** CBClason *Fifth* (NY) 128: The smell of money is good whatever its source, states the proverb. **1937** AEFielding *Mystery* (NY) 200: "Money has no smell," he quoted. **1952** MAllingham *Tiger* (NY) 116: They say all money stinks. **1965** JLindsay *Thunder* (L) 287: Money, we all know, doesn't smell. **1973** EJBurford *Queen* (L) 107: "*Pecuniam non olet*"—money has no smell—was an excellent motto. Apperson 422(16).

M202 Money is not everything

1930 JSFletcher *Heaven-sent* (NY) 227: Money isn't everything. **1931** VWilliams *Masks* (L) 42: Money isn't everything, you know. **1937** AGilbert *Murder* (L) 12: Money isn't everything. **1941** ISCobb *Exit* (I) 458: Money may not be everything, as some are prone to say. **1948** EKGoldthwaite *Root* (NY DBC) 143: I've learned that money isn't everything. **1950** FFGould *Maine Man* (NY) 202: But money isn't everything. **1955** GBrewer *Red Scarf* (NY) 45: Money isn't everything. **1963** ESGardner *Amorous* (NY DBC) 149: Money wasn't everything in life. **1967** JDetre *Happy* (NY) 158: Money isn't everything. **1970** MGEberhart *El Rancho* (NY DBC) 73: As they say, money isn't everything. **1981** AMorice *Men* (NY) 187: A stale old cliché . . . money isn't everything. **1981** JRoss *Dark* (NY) 108: Somebody said that money doesn't mean everything. Cf. Money cannot *below.*

M203 Money is power

1908 JBailey *Letters and Diaries* (L 1935) 111: Money is power. **1922** JJoyce *Ulysses* (NY 1934) 31: Money is power. **1928** JGoodwin *When Dead* (NY) 62: Money is power. **1941** FCrane *Turquoise* (P) 89: Money is certainly power. **1952** MVHeberden *Tragic* (NY) 55: Money is also power. **1956** ABurgess *Time* (L) 196: Money is power. **1971** SKrim *Shake* (L) 182: Money is power. **1973** GSheehy *Hustling* (NY) 14: Money is power. EAP M210.

M204 Money is the sinews of war

1938 CBarry *Case Dead* (L) 76: Count on me for the . . . sinews of war. EAP M213.

M205 Money makes man

1950 CEVulliamy *Henry* (L) 203: Money maketh man . . . Pecunia est vita hominis. Whiting M628; *Oxford* 539.

M206 Money makes (attracts) money (*varied*)

1930 RAFreeman *Mystery* (NY) 226: As money makes money so knowledge begets knowledge. **1932** HFootner *Dead Man's* (NY) 85: Money attracts money. **1936** JStagge *Murder Gone* (L) 58: Money attracts money, you know. **1937** PLindsay *Gentleman Harry* (L) 42: Gold makes gold, he learned. **1938** BGraeme *Mystery* (P) 258: Money makes money. **1940** JCreasey *Here*

Comes (NY 1967) 71: Money doesn't make money . . . in spite of fools who like to think that adage worth following. **1940** MCharlton *Death of* (L) 232: Money always comes to money. **1946** DBHughes *Ride the Pink* (NY 1958) 36: Money met money and bred money. **1947** VWMason *Saigon* (NY) 285: Takes money to make money. **1951** HQMasur *You Can't* (NY) 67: Money goes to money. **1954** DMDisney *Last* (NY) 163: No wonder they say money breeds money. **1957** BHitchens *End* (NY) 209: Money made money. **1967** HBlyth *Old Q* (L) 219: The adage that money makes money. **1970** HBlyth *Skittles* (L) 88: Money makes money. *Oxford* 538.

M207 Money makes the mare go (*varied*)
1919 LThayer *Mystery of the 13th Floor* (NY) 379: Money makes the mare go. **1934** AWynne *Death* (P) 63: What makes the mare go is not money but credit. **1936** *New Yorker* 5/16 77: M-G-M . . . forces us to revise an old adage: Mayer makes the money go. **1942** HReilly *Name Your Poison* (NY) 61: Money, the thing that makes the mare go. **1953** OAtkinson *Golden* (I) 248: Money makes the mare go. **1956** *New Yorker* 7/28 23: Money makes the nightmare go. **1957** *BangorDN* 3/20 16: The old saying, "Money makes the mare go," could very well be transposed to read, "Money makes the horses pull." EAP M214.

M208 Money makes the world (wheels) go round
1929 EHope *Alice* (NY) 287: Money makes the world go 'round. **1966** ESGardner *Worried* (NY) 27: It takes money to make the wheels go around. **1966** ELathen *Murder Makes the Wheels Go 'Round* (NY). **1971** JPHennessy *Trollope* (B) 263: The blunt recognition that it is money as well as hard work and, possibly, love that makes the world go round. Cf. Love makes *above.*

M209 Money talks (*varied*)
1915 PGWodehouse *Something Fresh* (L 1935) 75: Money talks. **1930** EBlunden *Leigh Hunt* (L) 313: Money talks, the want of it talks louder. **1938** LRGribble *Tragedy*

(L) 272: Her belief that money shouts louder than words. **1941** CEVulliamy *Short History* (L) 264: Money talks, the vulgar say. **1951** JCollier *Fancies* (NY) 359: They say money talks . . . I think I can hear it . . . It has an ugly voice. **1957** *BangorDN* 3/4 8: The old adage—"money talks!" 4/17 4: There is an old saying that "money talks." **1961** RKirk *Old House* (NY DBC) 40: Money speaks. **1966** GButler *Nameless* (NY) 164: Money talks . . . It may only whisper but people hear it and listen. **1969** JMPatterson *Doubly* (NY) 166: Money and power talk. **1974** MKenyon *Sorry* (NY) 30: Money talks. Apperson 423(38); Partridge 528.

M210 Money will do most things (*varied*)
1930 JGBrandon *Murder* (L) 112: Money will do most things. **1938** JSStrange *Silent* (NY) 191: Money can cure a sight of ills. **1938** HMcCloy *Dance* (NY) 169: Money can do almost anything. EAP M216; *Oxford* 538, 540.

M211 Money works miracles
1939 JCreasey *Toff Goes On* (L) 247: Money works miracles. **1940** EQueen *New Adventures* (NY) 133: It is proverbial that money works miracles. Cf. Money is power, Money makes the mare, Money makes the world, Money talks, Money will *above.*

M212 No **Money**, no doctor
1955 LCochran *Hallelujah* (NY) 107: His rule of "No money, no doctor." Cf. No Dollars *above.*

M213 To have **Money** to burn
1924 AOFriel *Mountains* (NY) 13: Money to burn in the bank. **1929** PRShore *Bolt* (NY) 45: She's got money to burn. **1940** AMuir *Sands* (L) 115: He has money to burn. **1959** HReilly *Not Me* (NY DBC) 68: He would have money to burn. **1970** NMonsarrat *Breaking* (L) 474: With money to burn. **1974** MMcCarthy *Mask* (NY) 169: There was money to burn. Berrey 239.1, 377.1, 559.7.

M214 To make **Money** hand over fist
1922 JJoyce *Ulysses* (NY 1934) 173: Making money hand over fist. **1926** CJDutton

Flying (NY) 46: Making money hand over fist. **1954** EWalter *Untidy* (P) 13: Makes money hand over fist. **1958** JSStrange *Night* (NY) 53: Making money hand over fist. **1963** NMarsh *Dead* (B 1964) 22: Making money hand over fist. Amer. Herit. Dict. Hand; Partridge 371: Hand over fist.

M215 To pay one's **Money** and take one's choice (*varied*)

c1910 EWallace *Nine Bears* (L 1928) 26: You paid your money and he took his choice. **1929** GSeldes *You Can't* (NY) 361: You pay your money and you take your choice. **1930** GDHCole *Berkshire* (NY) 153: It's a case of you pays your money and you takes your choice. **1939** IJones *Hungry Corpse* (NY) 74: You pays your money and you takes your choice. **1940** JDonavan *Plastic Man* (L) 243: You can pay your money and take your choice. **1955** DMDisney *Trick* (NY) 147: So you pay your money and take your choice. **1957** CCarnac *Late Miss* (NY) 167: So you can pay your money and take your choice. **1962** HWaugh *Late* (NY) 69: You pays your money and you takes your pick. **1966** LPDavies *Who Is* (NY) 95: You pays your money and you takes your choice. **1969** ECooper *Sea Horse* (NY) 86: You pays your penny and you takes your choice. **1975** JFoxx *Dead Run* (I) 131: You pays your dues and you takes your chances. TW 248(11); Brunvand 95(1); DA Money b; *Oxford* 615.

M216 To spend **Money** like a drunken sailor

1931 PGWodehouse *Big Money* (NY) 6: Going through her capital like a drunken sailor. **1935** RStout *League* (NY) 96: Spending money like a drunken sailor. **1938** JGEdwards *Odor* (NY) 85: He's been spending his money like a drunken sailor. **1940** PATaylor *Deadly* (NY) 29: Spend money like a drunken sailor. **1951** ADean *August* (NY) 51: Throwing money around like a drunken sailor. **1959** SBeach *Shakespeare* (NY) 197: He spends his money like a drunken sailor. **1966** MSteen *Looking* (L) 57: I spent it like a drunken sailor. **1969**

CIrving *Fake* (NY) 153: To spend money like the proverbial drunken sailor on shore leave. Cf. EAP S19.

M217 To spend (*etc.*) **Money** like water (*varied*)

1924 CVanVechten *Tattooed* (NY) 267: I saw money flowing like water. **1924** EWallace *Green* (B) 39: Spend money like water. **1925** EBChancellor *Old Q* (L) 187: Money passed through his hands like water. **1931** NFaulkner *Sanctuary* (NY) 171: Spent their money here like water. **1936** AMuir *Bronze* (L) 104: You spend money like water. **1946** ECrispin *Holy Disasters* (NY) 65: They can afford to waste lives like water. **1953** AChristie *Pocket* (NY) 160: Spending money like water. **1958** RHutton *Of Those* (L) 100: Money flowed like water. **1958** CCarnac *Affair* (NY) 71: Money is poured out like water. **1960** *TLS* 9/2 563: She had spent money like water. **1960** AWUpfield *Mystery* (L) 239: Money being spent like water. **1963** HPentecost *Only* (NY DBC) 30: Lucas spent money like water. **1972** RBraddon *Thirteenth* (NY) 166: Money that Mr. Robert was spending like water. EAP M217; TW 395: Water(17).

M218 To throw (*etc.*) good **Money** after bad (*varied*)

1927 JMWalsh *Silver* (L) 15: No further use in slinging good money after bad. **1929** KCStrahan *Footprints* (NY) 65: I don't believe in throwing good money after bad. **1930** FWCrofts *Sir John* (NY) 178: It . . . seemed like pouring good money after bad. **1936** RCarson *Revels* (NY) 231: There ain't sense in throwin' good money after bad. **1937** KCKempton *Monday* (NY) 212: Throwing good water after bad. **1940** ACampbell *They Hunted* (NY) 70: Throwing good money after bad. **1953** NBlake *Dreadful* (L) 123: I am not in the habit of throwing good money after bad. **1961** ER Chamberlin *Count* (NY) 98: The Serenissima never threw good money after bad. **1964** WMKunstler *Minister* (NY) 106: Good money after bad. **1971** RGMartin *Jennie* (NY) 283: A matter of giving good money to go the way of bad money. **1977**

CAGoodrum *Dewey* (NY) 9: To throw good money after bad. EAP M219.

M219   To whistle for one's **Money**

1932 CBush *Unfortunate* (L) 12: The expression "to whistle for one's money." **1932** JRhode *Mystery* (L) 18: You can whistle for your money. **1937** AGilbert *Murder* (L) 131: Then you can whistle for your money. EAP W135; TW 401: Whistle *vb*.

M220   As agile as a **Monkey**

1954 MErskine *Dead by* (NY) 173: Slater was as agile as a monkey. Whiting *NC* 446(1); Taylor *Prov. Comp.* 13.

M221   As artful as **Monkeys** (*varied*)

1927 GDilnot *Lazy* (B) 150: He's as artful as a wagon load of monkeys. **1931** EWallace *Black* (NY) 47: Them fellows are as hartful as monkeys. **1935** FBeeding *Death* (NY) 38: Artful as monkeys. **1937** PGWodehouse *Laughing* (NY) 69: He's as artful as a barrel-load of monkeys. Cf. As cunning *below*.

M222   As clever as a **Monkey** (*varied*)

1936 WSmith *Machine* (L) 172: As clever as a cartload of monkeys. **1938** FBeeding *Big Fish* (NY) 169: She is as clever as a monkey. **1939** CBarry *Nicholas* (L) 244: As clever as a cartload of monkeys. **1942** HCBailey *Nobody's* (NY) 44: Clever as a monkey. **1943** AAbbott *Shudders* (NY) 117: She was always clever as a bagfull of monkeys. **1957** AArmstrong *Strange* (NY) 12: He's clever as a hatfull of monkeys. **1968** EHuxley *Love* (L) 249: He's clever as a cartload of monkeys. **1968** JPorter *Dover Goes* (NY) 82: As clever as a box of monkeys. **1970** RQuest *Cerberus* (NY) 81: Clever as a monkey. **1975** AChristie *Curtain* (NY) 63: Clever as a barrel full of monkeys.

M223   As cunning (crafty, cute) as a **Monkey**

1925 JRhode *Paddington* (L) 129: He's as cunning as a bagful of monkeys. **1930** MBurton *Hardways* (L) 101: He was as cunning as a basket of monkeys. **1930** VLoder *Shop* (L) 79: Cunning as a monkey. **1933** CBush *Three Strange* (L) 214: He used to be crafty as a monkey. **1933** JVTurner *Amos* (L) 60: Naylor is as cunning as a bag of monkeys. **1934** LKirk *Whispering* (NY) 285: Cute as monkeys [*acute*]. **1940** JRhode *Murder at* (L) 150: Neddy is as cunning as a basket of monkeys. **1962** PDJames *Cover* (NY 1976) 24: And cunning as a wagonload of monkeys. **1969** HEBates *Vanished* (L) 60: Crafty as a monkey.

M224   As drunk as a **Monkey**

1925 FSFitzgerald *Great Gatsby* (NY) 92: As drunk as a monkey. **1938** MPage *Fast Company* (NY) 131: He was drunk as a monkey. **1960** JO'Hara *Imagine* (NY) 37: Drunk as a monkey. Cf. Wilstach 105: Ape.

M225   As mischievous as a **Monkey**

1943 GGCoulton *Fourscore* (Cambridge, Eng.) 51: Mischievous as a monkey. **1966** JDosPassos *Best* (NY) 83: Mischievous as a monkey. EAP M220.

M226   As pleased as a **Monkey** with four tails

1939 LBrock *Fourfingers* (L) 140: As pleased as two monkeys with four tails. Cf. Brunvand 96(1): With a red cap.

M227   As tricky as a **Monkey**

1934 RForsyth *Pleasure Cruise* (NY) 210: As tricky as a monkey. Whiting *NC* 446(3).

M228   The higher a **Monkey** goes the more he shows his behind (*varied*)

1950 VSReid *New Day* (L) 235: The higher monkey climbs, the more he exposes his underparts. **1977** VCanning *Doomsday* (NY) 24: The higher an ape climbs the more he shows his bare behind. EAP M223; *Oxford* 372: Higher.

M229   A **Monkey's** allowance

1964 JAiken *Silence* (NY) 182: She had you cast for the monkey's allowance whichever way things went. *Oxford* 541.

M230   **Monkey** see, monkey do (*varied*)

1934 RHare *Hand* (NY) 59: "Monkey see, monkey do," as the saying goes. **1945** PA Taylor *Proof* (NY) 125: Monkey see, monkey do. **1953** SBellow *Adventures* (NY) 9: Monkey hears, monkey says. **1956** *BangorDN* 11/26 20: Monkey see, monkey do. **1968** LBaldridge *Of Diamonds* (B) 238:

Monkey see, monkey do. HWJanson *Apes and Ape Lore in the Middle Ages and the Renaissance* (L 1952) 35, 58.

M231   Softly, softly, catchee **Monkey**

1939 HCBailey *Veron* (L) 172: Softly talkee, catchee monkey. **1940** RAFreeman *Mr. Polton* (NY) 33: Softly, softly, you catch the monkey. **1965** HHowe *Gentle* (NY) 11: Softly, softly catches the monkey. **1968** AChristie *By the Pricking* (NY) 139: Softly, softly, catchee monkey. Champion (Jamaican) 629: 371.

M232   The three Chinese **Monkeys** (*varied*)

1931 LMcFarlane *Murder* (NY) 100: See nothin', hear nothin', and say nothin', that's my motto. **1931** PATaylor *Cape Cod* (NY 1971) 236: Pretend you're one of them monkeys as can't see nor hear nor talk no evil. **1939** IOelrichs *Man Who* (NY) 103: Hear no evil, see no evil and speak no evil. **1941** GBenedict *Deadly Drops* (NY) 114: Mr. Cannon, who sees no evil, hears no evil, and especially talks no evil. **1941** MPRea *Compare* (NY) 130: I see nothing, hear nothing, say nothing. **1953** SRansome *Hear No Evil* (NY). **1954** MProcter *Somewhere* (NY) 16: Like the three wise monkeys they were. Hear nowt, see nowt, say nowt. **1955** MAllingham *Estate* (NY) 158: Old Henry hears nothing, sees nothing, says nothing. He's the proverbial cartload of monkeys. **1959** DMDisney *Did She Fall* (NY) 82: We're like the three monkeys: we hear no evil, see no evil, speak no evil. **1959** ESGardner *The Case of the Mythical Monkeys* (NY). **1964** AChristie *Caribbean* (NY) 173: See no evil, hear no evil, speak no evil. **1965** AChristie *At Bertram's* (L) 204: More Chinese monkeys . . . see no evil, hear no evil, speak no evil. **1970** JVizzard *See No Evil: Life Inside a Hollywood Censor* (NY). **1973** OSela *Portuguese* (NY) 162: Like one of the proverbial three monkeys he was seeing no evil, and even if he did, he was certainly not speaking about it. **1983** ACairns *Strained* (NY) 116: You put me in mind of the three wise monkeys, all of whose friends must have been quite above reproach as well. Like Caesar's wife. Cf. Tilley N275: Hear. Cf. Hear All *above*.

M233   To be a **Monkey's** uncle

1939 CBClason *Dragon's* (NY) 71: Well, I'll be a monkey's uncle. **1955** KMKnight *They're* (NY) 176: Well, I'll be a monkey's uncle.

M234   To be more fun than a barrel of **Monkeys**

1931 HFootner *Easy* (L) 215: The old lady was more fun than a barrel of monkeys. **1957** *BHerald* 2/15 10: As the monkey at the zoo would say, "It was more fun than a barrel of people." **1957** *NYTimes Book Review* 8/11 4: It would be difficult to say what the result is more fun than. The proverbial barrel of monkeys? A greased pig? **1957** *Time* 11/25 126: Monkeys, more fun than a barrel of. Whiting *NC* 446(2,4); Taylor *Prov. Comp.* 43: Funny.

M235   To have a **Monkey** on one's back (*varied*)

1951 AThorne *Man Who* (L) 42: The bawdy black monkey on your shoulder. **1957** CThompson *Halfway* (NY) 175: Ann was the monkey on my back. **1958** TEDikty *Six From* (NY) 106: When a man's a dope addict, they say he has a monkey on his back. **1959** BHecht *Sensualists* (NY) 131: A poor . . . actor with the monkey on his back [*dope*]. **1963** SForbes *Grieve* (NY) 15: That's one of the monkeys on my back. **1967** VSPritchett *Cab* (NY) 54: He's got a monkey on his back [*disgruntled*]. Partridge 529; Wentworth 343. Cf. *Oxford* 64: Black dog. Cf. To have a black Dog *above*.

M236   To make a **Monkey** of someone

1923 ORCohen *Jim Hanvey* (NY) 97: Make a monkey of me. **1933** WChambers *Campanile* (NY) 64: Made monkeys of the local detective bureau. **1937** PCoffin *Search* (NY) 235: He'll make a monkey out of this rustic bumpkin. **1955** MO'Brine *Passport* (L) 7: Making monkeys of themselves over tramps. **1959** JBrunner *World* (NY) 35: We've been made monkeys of. **1961** CJenkins *Message* (L) 195: Making a monkey out of him. **1961** RStout *Final* (NY) 64: He was making monkeys of us. **1976** JMcClure *Snake* (NY) 57: They're truly making monkeys of us. Whiting A148: Ape; Cole 56; Berrey 151.8.

M237   To put it where the **Monkey** (Jocko) put the nuts

1922 JJoyce *Ulysses* (NY 1934) 242: You can put that writ where Jacko put the nuts. **1948** WMiller *Fatal* (NY) 41: You can put that story where the monkey put the nuts. **1968** JRAckerley *My Father* (L) 43: Put it where the monkey put the nuts. Partridge 672: Put.

M238   To throw a **Monkey-wrench** (spanner) into the works (*varied*)

1929 ACEdington *Studio* (NY) 132: You've thrown the monkey wrench in the machinery; 150. **1929** WScott *Mask* (P) 24: It fell like a spanner into a machine. **1930** CBarry *Boat* (L) 107: I'll throw a monkey-wrench into your dirty little works. **1932** SJepson *Mystery* (NY) 57: Help drop a spanner in their evil machinery. **1936** JSStrange *Bell* (NY) 271: Threw a monkey wrench into the case against Lynch. **1938** HHolt *Whispering* (L) 66: Putting a spanner in the wheels of the law. **1940** HAshbrook *Murder Comes* (NY) 7: I'll stick all kinds of monkey wrenches into everybody's works. **1945** MWalsh *Nine Strings* (P) 212: I am trying to take a spanner out of the works. **1947** MCarleton *Swan* (NY) 69: Thrown a monkey wrench into the machinery. **1951** DMDisney *Straw* (NY) 185: She was out to throw a monkey wrench in the wedding plans. **1953** AChristie *Funerals* (NY) 117: Cora certainly threw a spanner into the works. **1958** *BHerald* 5/22 9: But every time he appears to be making some progress, Gov. Furcolo throws a monkey wrench at him. **1958** EStarkie *Baudelaire* (NY) 316: It would be a spanner in the works of the case for the prosecution. **1963** MAshley *Stuarts* (L) 79: Elizabeth tried to throw a spanner into the works. **1965** PDeVries *Let Me* (NY 1966) 49: Throwing a monkey wrench into the romantic works. **1969** RPearsall *Worm* (L) 32: Threw spanners into the government machine. **1974** HCarmichael *Most* (NY) 187: [It] seems to throw a spanner in the works. DA Monkey wrench 2; NED Suppl. Monkey 17a.

M239   In a **Month** of Sundays (*varied*)

1910 EPhillpotts *Tales* (NY) 43: A month o' Sundays. **1922** JJoyce *Ulysses* (NY 1934) 101: Haven't seen you for a month of Sundays. **1924** VBridges *Red* (NY) 137: A month o' Sundays. **1931** EWallace *Black* (NY) 138: If you spent a week of Sundays. **1932** BRoss *Tragedy of Y* (NY) 36: As quaint a collection . . . as you'll find in a world of Sundays. **1937** VGielgud *Death in Budapest* (L) 106: In a month of Sundays. **1939** VWilliams *Cat Prowls* (B) 17: We ain't seen you in a row o' Sundays. **1941** CRice *Right Murder* (NY) 183: It's like having a month of Sundays. **1946** KMKnight *Trouble* (NY) 9: Clem's dressed up like a month of Sundays. **1948** KBercovici *Savage* (NY) 105: I haven't had a man in a year of Sundays. **1951** JCreasey *Puzzle* (L 1962) 165: A face as long as a month of Sundays. **1958** MHastings *Cirk* (NY) 14: Once in a month of Sabbaths. **1959** ESchiddel *Devil* (NY) 273: In a month o' blue moons. **1960** RWatters *Murder* (Dublin) 217: A penance that'll keep him on his knees for a month of Sundays. **1966** DMDisney *At Some* (NY) 176: It'd be a long week of Sundays. **1971** CAird *Late* (NY) 151: Not in a month of Sundays. **1973** HDolson *Dying* (P) 53: The greatest roses you'll see in a month of Sundays. TW 248–9; Brunvand 96; *Oxford* 541.

M240   The **Moon** is made of green cheese (*varied*)

1928 BAtkey *Midnight* (NY) 138: That's only a moon—just a common or garden moon. Did you think it was a cheese on fire? **1929** JJFarjeon *Appointed* (NY) 188: "I don't think the moon is made of green cheese, but it may be" was one of his stock phrases. **1930** ABCox *Vane* (L) 247: Suppose the moon turned into a pink cheese. **1930** NBMavity *Case* (NY) 159: I'd have believed that the moon was made of green cheese if she said so. **1932** PATaylor *Death* (I) 238: None of us . . . can prove that the moon is or is not made of green cheese. **1937** CRCooper *Here's to Crime* (B) 257: The type of girl who will believe that the moon is not made of green cheese, but Camembert. **1941** AAmos *Pray* (NY) 181:

I'd believe the moon was made of Roquefort. **1941** RHLindsay *Fowl Murder* (B) 69: Yes, and I can say the moon is made of green cheese, but I can't eat it. **1947** TKyd *Blood* (P) 187: They'd claim the moon was made of green cheese if Mrs. Duvoisin did. **1956** MPHood *Scarlet* (NY) 23: The moon'll be made of green cheese before that happens. **1958** *Time* 12/1 17: A rocket-shot earth-mouse lands on the moon, made as it is of green cheese, and orders: "Take me to your Liederkranz." **1958** AMacKinnon *Summons* (NY) 166: He'll get you green cheese from the moon. **1961** OHesky *Purple* (L) 109: The tone of one who asks you whether you think the moon is made of green cheese. **1969** AGilbert *Mr. Crook* (NY DBC) 148: Maybe the moon's made of green cheese. **1976** CCalloway *Of Minnie* (NY) 248: Ned was a fantastic publicist. Man, he could sell blue cheese off the face of the moon. **1979** GWest *Duke* (NY) 209: Other people promise that the moon is made of cheese. EAP M231; TW 249(3).

M241 The **Moon** with a little red fence around it
1937 CBClason *Purple* (NY) 213: Offer a lawyer the moon, and he'll ask you to put a red fence around it. **1959** TRoscoe *Only* (NY) 83: He wants the Moon with a Little Red Fence around it. **1960** ASeager *Death* (NY) 26: I promised her the moon with a little red fence around it. Cf. The World with a fence *below.*

M242 Once in a blue **Moon** (*varied*)
1919 LMerrick *Chair* (L) 170: Once in a blue moon. **1920** ACrabb *Samuel* (NY) 176: Once in a blue moon. **1922** JJoyce *Ulysses* (NY 1934) 362: Once in a blue moon. **1930** ALivingston *Trackless* (I) 282: Once in a couple of green moons. **1934** CBush *100% Alibis* (L) 176: Not once in a blue moon, as the saying is. **1941** ABCunningham *Strange Death* (NY) 9: Only once in a blue moon. **1947** ELustgarten *One More* (NY 1959) 84: Once in a blue moon. **1954** EQueen *Glass* (B) 189: Once in a blue moon. **1958** *BangorDN* 7/18 15: Once in a blue moon. **1966** RLockridge *Murder* (NY) 50: Once in a blue moon. **1974** PHighsmith *Ripley's* (NY) 13: Once in a blue moon. **1976** JPorter *Package* (NY) 56: Once in a bloody blue moon. *Oxford* 595: Once.

M243 To bay the **Moon**
1937 GGoodwin *White Farm* (L) 269: They might as well have bayed the moon. **1962** FCrane *Amber* (NY) 21: I'll marry him and they can bay the moon. EAP M232. Cf. *Oxford* 541.

M244 To be over the **Moon**
1964 HBourne *In the Event* (NY) 153: Pip was over the moon [*happily excited*]. Cf. TW 249(4).

M245 To cry for the **Moon** (*varied*)
1905 JBCabell *Line* (NY 1926) 238: Lacking the moon he vainly cried for, the child learns to content himself with a penny whistle. **1924** ROChipperfield *Bright* (NY) 4: Too sensible to cry for the moon. **1932** GMitchell *Saltmarsh* (L) 282: He has given up sighing for the moon. **1951** JCollier *Fancies* (NY) 202: You might as well cry for the moon. **1955** RStout *Before* (NY) 144: What he wanted was the moon. **1962** FCrane *Amber* (NY) 167: Right away they want the moon. **1964** RRendell *From Doon* (L 1966) 118: Crying for the moon. *Oxford* 158: Cry.

M246 To shoot the **Moon**
1930 WSMaugham *Cakes* (L 1948) 89: The Driffields had shot the moon [*absconded*]. **1939** RPenny *She Had* (L) 119: Added something about shooting the moon—clearing out without paying his rent, in other words. **1940** NMarsh *Death of a Peer* (B) 13: I fancy we were shooting at the moon. **1946** RHuggins *Double Take* (NY 1959) 53: I was shooting the moon. **1949** JEvans *Halo* (NY) 59: Just shooting the moon. **1956** SDean *Marked* (NY) 53: Wouldn't that be shooting the moon and shooting blind? *Oxford* 726–7.

M247 **Moonlight** does not dry mittens
1956 *BangorDN* 7/18 3: Mr. Bradford also passes on another Maine saying to us: "Moonlight doesn't dry mittens." Dick says this is a special favorite of Carl Sandburg, the poet. What does it mean, Dick?

M248 A **Moonlight** flit

1935 CFGregg *Danger* (L) 229: Prince had not executed a moonlight flit. **1940** DBillany *It Takes* (NY) 190: He had . . . done what I believed is termed a moonlight flit. **1946** GBellairs *Death in the Night* (NY) 132: The man . . . did a moonlight flit, owing thirteen weeks' rent. **1954** JSymons *Narrowing* (NY) 192: Done a moonlight flit. **1960** JPudney *Home* (L) 66: The proprietor's "moonlight flit." **1968** MAllingham *Cargo* (NY) 135: Jonah did a moonlight flit on Saturday afternoon. **1970** JPorter *Dover Strikes* (NY) 173: Planning a moonlight flit. EAP M236.

M249 To be **Moonshine**

1929 JJConnington *Grim* (B) 166: The whole idea turned out to be moonshine. TW 249(2).

M250 The **More** it changes the more it is the same (*varied*)

1929 SQuinn *Phantom* (Sauk City, Wisc. 1966) 232: We have a proverb concerning history: Plus ça change plus c'est la même chose. **1931** LCArlington *Through* (L) 6: The oft quoted tag the more she changes the more she remains the same. **1955** STruss *False* (NY) 156: The more it changes the more it is the same thing. **1972** OFriedrich *Before* (NY) 9: To misquote the old saying, the more things remain the same, the more they change. **1975** HBlack *My Father* (NY) 183: The more things change the more they are the same. Bartlett 627a [*Alphonse Karr*].

M251 The **More** the merrier

1901 JLondon *Letters* ed KHendricks (NY 1965) 123: The more the merrier. **1913** EDBiggers *Seven Keys* (I) 98: The more the merrier. **1928** SFWright *Deluge* (NY) 223: *The fewer the better fare* was his motto. **1932** HBest *Mystery* (NY) 3: The more the merrier. **1935** HHolt *Unknown* (L) 203: The more the merrier. **1941** GWYates *If a Body* (NY) 232: The more the merrier. **1955** DParry *Sea* (L) 78: The more the sins, the merrier. **1956** *New Yorker* 11/17 111: A case of the more the merrier. **1957** *BangorDN* 9/7 23: The more the follier. **1958** *BangorDN* 7/10 22: The more the merrier. **1962** HEBates *Golden* (L) 142: The more the merrier. **1974** LBlack *Life* (NY) 150: The more the merrier. **1976** JMcClure *Snake* (NY) 151: The more the merrier, as they say. EAP M241; TW 250(1).

M252 There is **More** here than meets the eye (ear) (*varied*)

1915 JFerguson *Stealthy* (L 1935) 150: There's more in this affair than meets the eye. **1924** LTracy *Token* (NY) 81: More in this than meets the eye. **1926** JSFletcher *Great* (NY) 212: There was more in the news than perhaps met the ear. **1932** SHPage *Resurrection* (NY) 140: There's more to this than one sees on the surface. **1933** CBush *Three Strange* (L) 22: There was more in his chatter than met the ear. **1936** EPhillpotts *Close Call* (L) 30: There's much more in this than meets the eye. **1937** KMKnight *Seven* (NY) 210: There's more to this than meets the eye. **1938** KMKnight *Acts* (NY) 95: There's more to this than meets the eye, to coin a phrase. **1941** AMStein *Up to No Good* (NY) 79: There's more to this than meets the naked eye. **1945** RLockridge *Death in the Mind* (NY) 45: There was more to what Evans said than met the eye. **1947** PMcGerr *Pick* (NY) 51: There's more going on than meets the eye. **1952** KMKnight *Death Goes* (NY) 80: More to it than meets the naked eye. **1955** ACClark *Earthlight* (NY) 71: There may be more in that talk of his than meets the ear. **1955** BHitchens *F.O.B.* (NY) 52: There's more than meets the eye there. **1957** *Punch* 9/25 347: More in the affair than meets the eye. **1958** *NYTimes Book Review* 7/13 6: There was more here than first struck the eye. **1960** PCurtis *Devil's* (NY) 168: There was more in Wesley than meets the eye. **1964** NBenchley *Winter's* (NY) 63: There must be something more here than meets the eye. **1965** GBagby *Mysteriouser* (NY) 71: There's more than meets the eye in the business. **1967** RGarrett *Too Many* (NY) 11: There is more to this killing than meets the eye. **1973** KCampbell *Wheel* (I) 102: There was rather more than met the eye. **1977** CAGoodrum *Dewey* (NY) 57: There's more to this than meets the eye. EAP M240; TW 250(2).

M253 To bite off **More** than one can chew

1922 JJoyce *Ulysses* (NY 1934) 167: Bitten off more than he can chew. **1926** EPhillpotts *Jig-saw* (NY) 264: And discover you'd bit off more than you could chew. **1937** WMartyn *Old Manor* (L) 198: Bitten off more than you can chew. **1939** CWard *House Party* (L) 140: He might bite off more than he could chew. **1948** MInnes *Night* (L 1966) 34: [She] had bitten off more than she could chew. **1955** RPHansen *Walk* (NY DBC) 95: You bought yourself a bit bite.... It's more than you can chew. **1956** *Time* 10/1 52: He has never yet bit off a thing without knowing clearly in advance exactly how it should be chewed. **1956** *Speculum* 31 506: Here the author is obviously biting off more than he can chew. **1961** LPayne *Nose* (NY) 279: She'd bitten off more than she could chew. **1967** AWaugh *My Brother* (L) 329: I had bitten off more than I could chew. TW 30: Bite (2); Brunvand 11: Bite; Whiting *NC* 371: Bite(2).

M254 As dead as a **Morgue**

1932 BRoss *Tragedy of Y* (NY) 252: This place is deader than the Morgue. **1939** EDean *Murder is* (NY) 71: If Charles Street wasn't dead as a morgue. **1955** BBenson *Silver* (NY) 48: It's as dead as a morgue. Cf. As dead as the Tomb *below*.

M255 As quiet (silent) as a **Morgue**

1932 WFEberhardt *Dagger* (NY) 75: The office was as quiet as a morgue. **1946** AE Martin *Death in the Limelight* (NY) 63: Quiet as the morgue. **1959** PSomers *Shivering* (NY) 57: The place was as silent as a morgue. Cf. As quiet as the Grave *above*; Tomb *below*.

M256 As calm as **Morning**

1930 JSFletcher *Behind* (NY) 225: As calm as a summer morning. TW 250(3). Cf. Brunvand 96: Morn.

M257 As fresh as the **Morning**

1933 HAshbrook *Murder* (NY) 119: Fresh as the summer morning. **1968** JHaythorne *None of Us* (NY) 48: Caroline looked as fresh as the morning. TW 250(5).

M258 **Morning** brings counsel

1939 WMartyn *Noonday* (L) 146: Morning brings good counsel. **1945** CBrahms *Six Curtains* (L 1953) 109: The morning brings its own counsel. Cf. *Oxford* 566: Night.

M259 To get up early in the **Morning** (*varied*)

1928 RHFuller *Jubilee* (NY) 258: They would have to get up early in the morning if they intended to get the better of him. **1939** MHealy *Old Munster* (L) 165: One had to get up very early in the morning to be ahead of Maurice. **1959** AGilbert *Prelude* (NY DBC) 41: Have to get up pretty early in the morning to catch the old man napping. **1968** EBuckler *Ox Bells* (NY) 214: You have to get up early in the morning to get ahead of her. TW 250(9).

M260 As fresh as a **Morning glory**

1949 GFowler *Beau* (NY) 66: As fresh as a morning glory. **1960** BBarzman *Twinkle* (NY) 161: She was fresh as a morning glory. **1974** GMcDonald *Fletch* (I) 173: You sound as fresh as a morning glory. Cf. As fresh as a Daisy *above*.

M261 **Morton's** fork

1962 EGrierson *Massingham* (L) 42: That was a clever "Morton's Fork" kind of question. *Oxford* 545.

M262 As dead (mad) as **Moses**

1928 FBeeding *House* (NY) 148: Mad as Moses. **1946** CDickson *My Late* (NY) 113: The sentence would be quashed as dead as Moses.

M263 As meek as **Moses**

1910 EPhillpotts *Tales* (NY) 195: Meek as Moses. **1913** JCLincoln *Mr. Pratt's Patients* (NY) 251: As meek as Moses. **1921** JCLincoln *Galusha* (NY) 296: You was meek . . . as Moses's grandmother. **1936** JMetcalfe *Sally* (NY) 148: Meek as Moses. **1938** ME

Corne *Death* (NY) 109: These meek as Moses guys. **1951** LBrown *Cleopatra* (NY) 27: Meek as Moses. **1959** HLGold *World* (NY 1961) 172: Meek as Moses. **1965** JBall *In the Heat* (NY) 81: As meek as Moses. EAP M252. Cf. Brunvand 96: Patience.

M264   Where was **Moses** when the candle (light) went out?

1922 JJoyce *Ulysses* (NY 1934) 714: Where was Moses when the candle went out? **1934** RForsyth *Pleasure Cruise* (NY) 87: Where was Moses when the light went out? **1938** LBarret *Though Young* (NY) 138: I never did find out where Moses was when the light went out.

M265   To see the **Mote** in another's eye *etc.*

1922 JJoyce *Ulysses* (NY 1934) 320: Some people, says Bloom, can see the mote in others' eyes but can't see the beam in their own. **1929** ABCox *Poisoned* (NY) 259: Mrs. Bendix loses sight of the beam in her own eye on learning of the mote in her husband's. **1929** GEdinger *Pons* (L) 14: He set up a wood store with the beams he took out of his own eye. **1931** CBush *Dead Man's* (L) 96: He referred to the mote in the eye. **1939** RStout *Crime on* (L) 127: When you finish with my mote . . . I'll help you with your beam. **1956** *NYTimes* 12/16 8E: It was felt that Mr. Nehru could see the mote in the West's eye but ignored the beam in Russia's eye. **1957** *NYTimes* 2/24 8E: Beam in our eye. **1967** JAxelrad *Freneau* (Austin) 237: He saw the mote in Jefferson's eye, while the beam in his own remained invisible. **1967** RGarrett *Too Many* (NY) 21: It was still easier to see—and to remove—the speck in one's brother's eye than to see the beam in one's own. **1970** RDAltick *Victorian* (NY) 300: The beam was always in the other papers' eye. **1974** DCavett *Cavett* (NY) 229: The mote in one's eye can feel like a mountain. EAP M255; TW 18: Beam; Brunvand 96.

M266   The **Moth** and the candle (*varied*)

1913 EDBiggers *Seven Keys* (I) 2: Courtiers hovered as moths about a flame. **1926** MLewis *Island* (L) 46: The poor human moths who singed their wings as they flut-

tered round her. **1927** AWynne *Sinners* (P) 44: The moths love to burn their wings at a bright candle. **1928** JEsteven *Door* (NY) 169: Like the proverbial moth to the flame. **1929** RJCasey *Secret* (I) 298: "An old flame?" . . . "Call him a new moth." **1930** NBMavity *Case* (NY) 132: You're not the first moth to be singed in a flame. **1930** RAJWalling *Squeaky Voice* (NY) 148: Is it unwise for a moth to fly into a candle? It is. But you can't stop him. **1932** WMartyn *Trent* (NY) 87: I simply make a noise like a candle and moths flock toward me. **1933** AFielding *Tall House* (NY) 136: He flutters around any casino candle like the proverbial moth. **1936** TDowning *Murder* (L) 239: At the risk of being trite, the moth and the flame. **1941** KSecrist *Murder Makes* (NY) 47: I was drawn to them [*women*] like a moth to a candle. **1952** JDrummond *Naughty* (L) 149: Yet the moth must go to her flame. **1957** RChurch *Golden* (NY) 189: I went at it as a moth to a candle-flame. **1960** JLodwick *Moon* (L) 265: The candle sends no invitation to the moth. **1962** MGEberhart *Enemy* (NY) 81: Neville was drawn to her like a moth to a candle flame. **1966** ACarter *Honeybuzzard* (NY) 3: All the clichés fitted her: Candle-flame for moths. **1972** JGores *Dead* (NY) 152: He would always go for the wrong decision as a moth would always go for the candle. **1974** SChance *Septimus* (Nashville) 38: I am drawn as a moth to a candle. EAP F200: Fly; TW 251(1); Whiting B623: Butterfly; Brunvand 96; *Oxford* 271: Fly.

M267   Does your **Mother** know you're out? (*varied*)

1932 HCBailey *Red Castle* (NY) 73: Does your mother know you're out? **1935** EGreenwood *Deadly* (NY) 45: Does your grandmother know you're out, as they say. **1956** GMetalious *Peyton* (NY) 136: I wonder if his mother knows he's out. **1958** RLDuffus *Williamstown* (NY) 128: There was an extremely funny saying, as we thought, in those days [*1898*]. Does your mama, we would ask, know you're out? **1965** ESitwell *Taken Care* (NY) 90: They inquired . . . if our mothers knew we were out. **1966** CMBowra *Memories* (L) 103:

Does your mother know you are out? **1967** BRussell *Autobiography* (B) 231: Does your mother know you're out? TW 251(3).

M268   Every **Mother's** son

1909 JCLincoln *Keziah* (NY) 53: Every mother's son. **1940** EDean *Murder is* (NY) 285: Every mother's son. **1941** KSecrist *Murder Makes* (NY) 197: Every mother's son of you. **1956** *New Yorker* 10/20 30: Every mother's son of us. **1958** VCanning *Dragon* (NY) 241: Every mother's son of 'em. **1961** TWalsh *Eye* (NY DBC) 51: Every last mother's son of us. EAP M256; TW 251(2).

M269   Like **Mother**, like daughter (*etc.*)

1920 GBMcCutcheon *Anderson Crow* (NY) 232: Like mother, like daughter. **1934** GMitchell *Death* (L) 171: Like mother, like son. **1953** MPHood *Silent* (NY) 30: Like mother, like daughter's true words. **1955** MErskine *Old Mrs.* (NY) 126: Like mother, like daughter. **1956** NMarsh *Death* (B) 31: Like mother, like maid. **1956** HRoth *Crimson* (NY) 23: Like mother, like daughter—and like father, like son. **1962** PQuentin *Ordeal* (NY) 134: Like mother, like daughter. **1969** TBesterman *Voltaire* (NY) 22: Like mother, like son. **1973** ELopez *Seven* (NY) 231: Daughter like mother like daughter . . . And son like father like son. **1975** EXFerrars *Alive* (NY) 34: Like mother like child. EAP M258.

M270   **Mother** (papa) knows best

1931 CWells *Horror* (P) 35: Mother knows best. **1937** WDickinson *Dead Man* (P) 141: Mother knows best! **1953** BCClough *Grandma* (Portland, Me.) 87: The old fashioned phrase "Mother knows best." **1955** KMKnight *Robineau* (NY) 187: After all, Papa knows best. **1958** AChristie *Ordeal* (NY DBC) 79: Mother knows best. **1968** WTenn *Wooden* (NY) 239: The maxim . . . Mother Knows Best.

M271   One's **Mother** would not know him (*varied*)

1924 FWCrofts *Cask* (NY 1936) 281: Your own mother wouldn't know you. **1926** JArnold *Murder!* (L) 292: He's had [the jewels] all cut and reset, until their own mother wouldn't be able to swear to 'em. **1931** LCArlington *Through* (L) 131: Gave him such a hammering that his own mother would not have known him. **1933** FLPackard *Hidden* (L) 196: His own mother had she been alive, as the trite expression had it, would not have recognized him. **1948** LSdeCamp *Divide* (NY 1964) 68: Smashed it up so its own mother wouldn't know it. **1953** JFleming *Good* (L) 194: His own mother wouldn't know him. **1957** *Time* 12/30 2: I am sure his own mother wouldn't recognize him. **1962** JWain *Sprightly* (L) 70: I'll send you home so your mother won't know you. **1970** JJMarric *Gideon's Sport* (NY) 112: I'll fix you so your own mother won't bloody know you. **1979** GBaxt *Neon* (NY) 14: His mother wouldn't have known him, either, the way his face was bashed in. TW 251(4).

M272   Old **Mother Hawkins** is plucking geese

1960 ILee *Edge* (NY) 235: It's old Mother Hawkins a-plucking geese [*snowing*]. Cf. *Oxford* 887: Widecombe folks.

M273   **Mother tongue**

1929 POldfield *Alchemy* (L) 181: English was the mother-tongue. **1938** FDGrierson *Cabaret* (L) 101: He chose his mother tongue to swear in. **1957** MColes *Death* (NY) 30: His mother tongue had been French. **1958** AMStein *Sitting* (NY) 34: I shifted over to the mother tongue. **1970** AHalper *Good-bye* (C) 178: English was not his mother tongue. EAP M262; TW 251.

M274   **Mother-wit**

1930 ABrown *Green Lane* (L) 117: Mother-wit. EAP M264; TW 251; Brunvand 96.

M275   As big as a **Mountain**

1957 WGoldman *Temple* (NY) 42: Felix . . . big as a mountain. **1967** RRendell *New Lease* (NY) 181: A guilt complex as big as a mountain. EAP M266.

M276   If the **Mountain** will not come to Mahomet *etc.*

1910 JCLincoln *Depot Master* (NY) 11: The mountain must come to Mahomet. **1924** JJFarjeon *Master* (NY) 95: If the mountain won't come to Mohammed, Mohammed must go to the mountain. **1930** HFootner *Viper* (L) 93: The mountain is coming to Mahomet. **1931** HJForman *Rembrant* (NY) 129: Ah, Mohammed himself . . . or is it the mountain? **1931** VStarrett *Dead Man* (NY) 143: The appearance of the mountain bearing down on Mahomet. **1932** JJFarjeon *Z* (NY) 111: Mohamed went to the mountain because the mountain would not come to him. **1939** TScudder *J.W. Carlyle* (NY) 210: Various mountains were now coming to Mahomet. **1942** VCaspary *Laura* (NY 1957) 7: Mahomet had not rushed out to meet the mountain. **1951** AChristie *They Came* (NY) 184: If Mohammed won't come to the mountain, the mountain must come to Mohammed. **1957** DJEnright *Heaven* (L) 265: If Mahomet can't get away from the mountain, then the mountain must get away from Mahomet. **1962** PDennis *Genius* (NY) 11: The mountain came to Mohammed. **1969** RStout *Death* (NY) 48: The mountain comes to Mohammed. **1970** RCowper *Twilight* (NY) 145: The mountain will eventually come to Mahomet, and when it does Mahomet will have to be prepared to meet it halfway. **1974** CMSmith *Reverend* (NY) 34: If Mahomet won't go to the mountain, then the mountain will have to go to Mahomet. EAP M268.

M277 The **Mountain** was in labor and produced a mouse (*varied*)

1931 WMorton *Mystery* (NY) 198: The mountain laboured and brought forth—that. **1932** NBell *Disturbing* (NY) 80: Does it need so big a mountain as psycho-analysis to give birth to such a mole-hill of conjecture? **1936** CFGregg *Tragedy* (L) 151: A veritable mouse after a mountain of labour. **1940** CBush *Climbing Rat* (L) 62: The mountain, having been in that much labour, produced the following conventional mouse. **1947** NBlake *Minute* (L) 173: It was like watching a mouse bring forth a mountain. **1956** RStout *Might* (NY) 159: It struck me as a damned small mouse to come out of so big a mountain. **1957** BHerald 10/26 2: The Commonwealth labored with a mountain and came up with a mouse

in the person of Mattson. **1957** KFarrer *Gownsman's* (L) 75: You're longing to feel less mountainous and to see the Ridiculous Mouse. **1959** BHerald 4/26 6: He said the Senate had labored long and like the proverbial mountain it brought forth the proverbial mouse. **1959** EMButler *Paper* (L) 186: What mountainous knowledge, but often what mouse-like wisdom too! **1961** HFHutchinson *Hollow* (L) 35: A mountain of discontent had produced a mouse of reform. **1962** GMaxwell *Ring* (NY) 35: The mountain had travailed and brought forth a mouse. **1970** JVizzard *See* (NY) 144: The mountains are in labor, and out skurries a ridiculous mouse! EAP M269.

M278 To make a **Mountain** out of a molehill (*varied*)

1922 JSFletcher *Rayner-Slade* (NY) 223: Without . . . making mountains out of molehills. **1924** LSpringfield *Some Piquant* (L) 146: A mole-hill that he had assisted to make into a mountain. **1925** FWCrofts *Pit-Prop* (NY) 19: To be making a mountain out of nothing. **1932** WSMasterman *Flying* (NY) 154: We are making a mountain out of an ant-heap. **1935** GDHCole *Scandal* (L) 152: You're making mountains out of moonshine. **1936** AHuxley *Eyeless* (NY) 308: Making tragic mountains out of a simple amorous molehill. **1937** GFowler *Salute* (NY) 84: Don't make a mountain out of a mole-hill. **1938** PWTaylor *Murder in* (NY) 26: You're making a mountain out of a molehill. **1943** MVHeberden *Murder Goes* (NY) 18: You're making a mountain out of a molehill. **1949** NMarsh *Wreath* (NY) 125: Félicité makes emotional mountains out of sentimental mole-hills. **1951** DFontaine *Sugar* (NY) 248: We can't make a molehill out of a mountain. **1956** MPHood *Scarlet* (NY) 21: Guess I made the well-known mountain out of the molehill. **1957** NY Times Book Review 4/28 5: *Heaven and Hardpan Farm* achieves the wit and point, if not of a Magic Mountain, at least of a magic molehill. **1958** NYTimes Book Review 7/27 2: Mole Hill, West Virginia, has just changed its name to Mountain. **1959** JHawkes *Providence* (L) 155: Aren't you marvelling at the molehill and neglecting the mountain?

1959 BHecht *Sensualists* (NY) 186: She wouldn't be making mountains out of *mons Veneris*. **1962** MCarleton *Dread* (NY) 55: I made a mountain out of a molehill. **1962** JWoodford *Autobiography* (NY) 137: Never make a mountain out of an Antheil. **1965** RLFish *Diamond* (NY DBC) 105: We're really building up a fair mountain from a rather insignificant molehill. EAP M271.

M279   As dumb as a **Mouse**

1936 EPhillpotts *Close Call* (L) 156: Dumb as a mouse. Wilstach 106.

M280   As meek as a **Mouse**

1939 PWentworth *Blind Side* (P) 169: Looks as meek as a mouse. **1953** RBloomfield *Stranger* (NY) 168: The poor fool was meeker than any mouse. **1960** SDean *Murder* (NY DBC) 133: Meek as a mouse. **1963** NMarsh *Dead* (B 1964) 31: Meek as a mouse. Whiting *NC* 447(1).

M281   As mum as a **Mouse**

1932 AGilbert *Body* (NY) 44: As mum as a mouse. **1955** CBrand *Tour* (NY) 9: Mum as a mouse. Cf. As quiet, As still *below*.

M282   As nervous as a **Mouse**

1938 LAnson *Such Natural* (L) 145: I'm as nervous as a mouse. **1966** MErskine *Family* (NY) 91: She's as nervous as a mouse and he's deaf as a post. Wilstach 274.

M283   As quiet as a **Mouse** (*varied*)

1925 TFPowys *Mr Tasker* (L) 90: As quiet as mice. **1928** DHLawrence *Lady* ("Allemagne") 38: She had to be quiet as a mouse. **1935** MJFreeman *Case* (NY) 112: Quiet as the proverbial mouse. **1936** RGDean *What Gentleman* (NY) 86: Quiet as a mouse in a church pew. **1939** BHalliday *Dividend* (NY 1959) 86: I'll be as quiet as a mouse with rubbers on. **1941** VRath *Death Breaks* (NY) 230: Quiet, just like a mouse. **1953** EQueen *Scarlet* (B) 122: He's been quiet as a mouse. **1954** MProcter *Somewhere* (NY) 60: As quiet as a mouse. **1962** FLockridge *And Left* (P) 33: Quiet as a mouse. **1964** NFreeling *Because* (NY 1965) 132: Quiet as a mouse. **1973** BBehan *My Life* (LA) 199: They were quiet as fieldmice.

1976 MRReno *Final* (NY) 145: I'll be quiet as a mouse. EAP M275; Brunvand 97(1).

M284   As silent as a **Mouse**

1969 FSwinnerton *Reflections* (L) 88: I am as silent as a mouse. EAP M276. Cf. As mum *above*.

M285   As snug as a **Mouse**

1960 LLee *Edge* (NY) 23: I was snug as a mouse in a hayrick. TW 252(4).

M286   As still as a **Mouse**

1913 JSFletcher *Secret* (L 1918) 139: As still as a mouse. **1917** GRSims *My Life* (L) 13: Sit as still as a mouse. **1931** CBrooks *Ghost* (NY) 225: We sat still as two mice. **1932** HLandon *Owl's* (L) 113: As still as a dead mouse. EAP M277; Taylor *Western Folklore* 17(1958) 17.

M287   As timid as a **Mouse**

1958 PO'Connor *Memoirs* (L) 131: As timid as a mouse. **1968** GDurrell *Rosy* (NY) 210: She's as timid as a mouse. **1969** GMFraser *Flashman* (NY) 52: As timid as a mouse. Whiting *NC* 447(5).

M288   As weak (harmless) as a **Mouse**

1925 HHext *Monster* (NY) 295: As weak as a mouse. **1933** JGregory *Case* (NY) 125: Dora is as harmless as a mouse. Whiting M734.

M289   The **Mouse** and the lion

1944 RShattuck *Said* (NY) 171: Don't laugh—a mouse helped a lion once, didn't she? **1949** MGilbert *He Didn't* (NY DBC) 112: Talk about the mouse and the lion! *Oxford* 467: Lion.

M290   A **Mouse** in the house, outside a lion

1956 AWUpfield *Battling* (L 1960) 26: In the house he was a mouse. Outside he was a lion. EAP L14: Lamb; Whiting L38. Cf. TW 212: Lamb (2).

M291   The **Mouse** with one hole (*varied*)

1928 VWilliams *Crouching* (B) 288: "The mouse that only turns to one poor hole, can never be a mouse of any soul," he quoted gaily. **1945** RLHines *Confessions* (L) 115: Wretched the mouse that hath but one hole. *Oxford* 548.

M292 Not hurt a **Mouse**

1937 PCoffin *Search* (NY) 74: He doesn't look as though he'd hurt a mouse. Cf. Not hurt a Flea, Fly *above*.

M293 Big **Mouth**, small brain

1958 RChandler *Playback* (L) 126: Big mouth, small brain. Cf. *Oxford* 900: Wise head.

M294 Keep your **Mouth** shut and your eyes open

1930 DDeane *Mystery* (L) 157: Keep yer mouth shut and yer eyes open. *Oxford* 419: Keep.

M295 A shut **Mouth** catches no flies (*varied*)

1926 TAWillard *City* (NY) 254: A shut mouth catches no flies. **1970** UO'Connor *Brendan* (L) 22: A shut mouth will catch no flies. **1971** RLFish *Rub* (NY) 117: He was a great believer in the Norwegian proverb that a shut mouth catches no reindeer. **1972** RHGreenan *Queen* (NY) 97: In a closed mouth, flies do not enter. *En boca cerrada no entran moscas.* EAP M281.

M296 To be down in the **Mouth**

1936 RAJWalling *Dirty Face* (L) 271: The poor dear man's right down in the mouth. **1950** FFGould *Maine Man* (NY) 83: Father was pretty down in the mouth. **1959** PCurtis *No Question* (NY) 18: I began to feel very down in the mouth. **1969** MGilbert *Etruscan* (L) 60: He looks a little down in the mouth. EAP M285.

M297 To have a **Mouth** like a lime-kiln

1935 ECRLorac *Murder* (L) 164: The expression "a mouth like a lime-kiln." TW 223: Lime kiln.

M298 To have a **Mouth** like the bottom of a parrot's cage (*varied*)

1938 CBarry *Case Dead* (L) 176: My mouth feels like the bottom of a parrot's cage. **1957** FHoyle *Black* (L) 136: I've got a mouth like the bottom of a parrot's cage. **1959** EHuxley *Flame* (L) 94: His mouth felt like the inside of a parrot's cage.

M299 To have a poor **Mouth**

1951 DSDavis *Gentle* (NY 1959) 75: She had the poor mouth as his [*Irish*] mother

would have said [*pleaded poverty*]. **1961** DLoovis *Last* (NY) 114: Stanley had a poor mouth [*talked poverty*]. **1968** EBuckler *Ox Bells* (NY) 165: Make a poor mouth. EAP M290; Brunvand 97(1).

M300 To make one's **Mouth** water

1940 RDarby *Death Conducts* (NY) 134: It makes my mouth water to think of it. EAP M291.

M301 To open one's **Mouth** and put one's foot in it (*varied*)

1922 JJoyce *Ulysses* (NY 1934) 632: Open thy mouth and put thy foot in it. **1925** GBeasley *My First* (Paris) 306: Every time I opened my mouth I put my foot in it. **1931** MAHamilton *Murder* (L) 299: Shedlock never got up [*to speak*] without putting his foot in it. **1940** HAdams *Chief Witness* (L) 186: I do sometimes open my mouth and put my foot in it. **1953** GHolden *Killer* (NY) 112: One of those . . . people whose foot would be constantly popping into her mouth. **1956** JJMarric *Gideon's Week* (L) 40: I opened my mouth and you put your foot in it. **1956** MColes *Birdwatcher's* (NY) 168: I am a blundering fool with two left feet and I put them both in my mouth every time I open it. **1967** JWCampbell *Analog 5* (NY) 234: I'll try to keep my foot out of my mouth. **1970** VCHall *Outback* (Adelaide) 76: Every time you open your mouth you put your foot in it. **1977** CWatson *Fourth* (B) 19: [He] had no equal for placing the foot squarely in the mouth. *Oxford* 599: Open.

M302 **Much** in little

1934 HReilly *McKee* (NY) 261: Multum in parvo. So much in so little. EAP M295.

M303 **Much** of a muchness

1923 JSFletcher *Markenmore* (NY) 262: Pretty much of a muchness. **1935** ECRLorac *Death* (L) 179: They're all much of a muchness. **1937** ERPunshon *Mystery* (NY) 106: Much of a muchness. **1945** HCBailey *Wrong Man* (NY) 57: His sort were much of a muchness. **1959** ESchiddel *Devil* (NY) 247: It was . . . too much of a muchness, and she was nearing the end of her rope. **1961** OManning *Great* (NY) 34:

All Rumanians are much of a muchness. **1965** MFrayn *Tin* (B) 29: They were all much of a muchness. *Oxford* 549.

M304 **Much** wants more

1929 JSFletcher *Ransom* (NY) 202: An old adage to the effect that much wants more. *Oxford* 550.

M305 To have too **Much** of a good thing (*varied*)

1928 JArnold *Surrey* (L) 187: You can have too much of a good thing. **1936** JVTurner *Below the Clock* (L) 68: This is too much of a good thing. **1938** RTorrey *42 Days* (NY) 116: Too much is too much. **1940** GStockwell *Candy* (NY) 16: Can't get too much of a good thing. **1966** LLafore *Nine* (NY) 50: You can't have too much of a good thing. **1967** RPeterson *Another View* (NY) 87: Too much of anything is not a good thing. However much a vile cliché and a platitude, this is true. EAP M296.

M306 Too **Much** is enough

1944 CDickson *He Wouldn't* (NY) 16: Too much, they say, is enough. **1964** IPetite *Elderberry* (NY) 116: A phrase of Grandpa's: "Too much is enough." Cf. Whiting *NC* 447(2); Apperson 640–1.

M307 As common as **Muck**

1937 NBell *Crocus* (NY) 281: Millionaires are as common as muck. **1976** MButterworth *Remains* (NY) 29: They are all as common as muck. Cf. As common as Dirt *above*, Mud *below*.

M308 As mean as **Muck**

1937 ECRLorac *Bats* (L) 112: Mean as muck [*stingy*]. **1940** MCharlton *Death of* (L) 263: Mean as muck, he is. **1959** JJMarric *Gideon's Staff* (NY) 16: They're going to [be] . . . mean as muck. **1970** DClark *Deadly* (NY) 81: Mean as muck they were. And twice as nasty. Cf. Whiting M794: Vile.

M309 As sick as **Muck**

1939 FGerard *Red Rope* (NY) 93: Dame Susan was as sick as muck. Partridge *Suppl.* 1015.

M310 Where there is **Muck** there is money (*varied*)

1935 LMNesbitt *Desolate* (L) 46: Where there's muck there's money. **1957** *Punch* 5/22 651: Where there's muck, there's brass. **1971** CIsherwood *Kathleen* (NY) 260: "Where there's muck there's money" was their slogan. **1975** MDelving *Bored* (NY) 12: You know what they say in Gloucestershire—"Where there's muck, there's money." *Oxford* 550.

M311 As clear as **Mud**

1925 HHext *Monster* (NY) 232: All's clear as mud. **1928** JChancellor *Dark* (NY) 233: It's as clear as mud. **1936** RDavis *Crowing Hen* (NY) 251: It's all as clear as the proverbial mud. **1939** NMarsh *Overture* (NY) 226: It's as clear as mud in your eye. **1954** EXFerrars *Lying* (L) 153: Clear as mud. **1958** JLindsay *Life* (L) 81: Clear as mud. **1961** PMoyes *Down Among* (NY) 125: Clear as mud [*obvious*]. **1962** NMarsh (B) 95: Clear as mud. **1972** NMarsh *Tied* (B) 116: Everything had become as clear as mud. EAP M297; Brunvand 97(1). Cf. Ditchwater *above*; As plain as Mud, As clear as Pea soup, Treacle *below*.

M312 As common as **Mud**

1929 RHuch *Deruga* (NY) 176: Common as mud. **1937** DLSayers *Busman's* (NY) 306: It's as common as mud. **1951** EGraham *My Window* (NY) 185: Common as mud. Cf. As common as Dirt, Muck *above*.

M313 As mad as **Mud**

1930 RKeverne *Man in the Red Hat* (NY) 81: Joan will be mad as mud. Whiting *NC* 447(3).

M314 As plain as **Mud**

1930 SHorler *Curse* (NY) 150: As plain as mud. **1931** JTully *Blood* (NY) 242: Plain as mud. **1934** JJFarjeon *Sinister* (NY) 111: As plain as mud. **1936** JMetcalfe *Sally* (NY) 591: Plain as mud. Cf. As clear *above*.

M315 As rich as **Mud**

1908 JCLincoln *Cy Whittaker* (NY) 7: Rich as dock mud. **1924** AOFriel *Mountains* (NY) 13: Rich as mud. **1954** MHastings

Cork (NY) 246: She's as rich as mud. TW 254(3).

M316   As sick as **Mud**

1917 MGibbon *Inglorious* (L 1968) 276: Watson must be as sick as mud. **1933** GBegbie *Sudden* (L) 65: Mother would be as sick as mud. **1957** PGWodehouse *Butler* (NY) 107: He was as sick as mud. **1974** PGWodehouse *Cat-Nappers* (NY) 101: As sick as mud. Cf. Muck *above.*

M317   As thick as **Mud**

1928 CKingston *Guilty* (L) 65: Other folk with whom she's as thick as mud now. **1930** ALivingston *Murder* (I) 166: Thick as mud. **1932** EQueen *Egyptian* (NY) 42: You're thicker than mud. Whiting *NC* 447(4).

M318   Here's **Mud** in your eye

1927 FLPackard *Devil's* (NY) 126: Here's mud in your eye! **1937** DWhitelaw *Face* (L) 177: Here's mud in your eye. **1952** PMacDonald *Something* (NY) 114: Mud in your eye. **1962** KAmis *Spectrum(1)* (L) 259: Mud in your eye . . . Drink up. **1969** JMPatterson *Doubly* (NY) 128: All mud in your eye [*deception*]. **1980** BGlobe 5/5 33: Q. Do you know where the toast "Here's mud in your eye" came from? A. It's attributed to author VanWyck Mason who used it in his book, "The Bucharest Ballerina Murders" in 1940. Amer. Herit. Dict. Mud 3.

M319   **Mud** (*etc.*) sticks (*varied*)

1926 JJConnington *Death* (NY) 204–5: Some of his dirt may stick in some people's minds. **1929** WMartyn *Recluse* (NY) 68: If enough mud is thrown at a man . . . some of it will stick. **1929** PRShore *Bolt* (NY) 282: Mud that is once thrown sticks forever. **1933** CBarry *Wrong Murder* (NY) 44: You have heard the old proverb about mud thrown against a wall. Some of it sticks. **1937** JJConnington *Minor* (L) 117: Some mud always sticks. **1939** CSaxby *Death Cuts* (NY) 52: Slime sticks. **1950** ECRLorac *Accident* (NY DBC) 135: Throw enough mud and some of it sticks. **1953** ECRLorac *Shepherd's* (NY) 75: You're saying that mud sticks; it's an old adage. **1962** BCleeve *Death* (NY) 151: If he flings enough mud, some of it must stick. **1964** JAiken *Silence*

(NY) 176: Tar sticks. **1966** MErskine *Family* (NY) 133: Some mud must have stuck to her skirts. **1968** WHaggard *Cool Day* (NY) 95: He wanted the story, he wanted the dirt. Dirt could stick. **1973** JWhitehead *Solemn* (L) 148: When mud is thrown some of it is bound to stick. **1983** JMann *No Man's* (NY) 156: It's the proverbial situation. Mud sticks. No smoke without a fire. EAP D188; *Oxford* 189: Dirt.

M320   No **Mud** without a puddle

1945 CEVulliamy *Edwin* (L) 202: There's no mud without a puddle, as they say. Cf. Whiting *NC* 457: Piddle. Cf. Where there is Smoke *below.*

M321   As homely (ugly) as a **Mud fence** (*varied*)

1931 CWells *Horrors* (P) 180: The type of beauty commonly ascribed to a mud fence. **1932** HBurnham *Telltale* (NY) 92: Homely's a mud fence. **1936** CBClason *Fifth* (NY) 105: Daughter homelier than mud fence. **1941** ELFetta *Dressed* (NY) 110: He's ugly as a mud fence. **1944** MVenning *Jethro* (NY) 219: She's homely as a log fence. **1949** AAFair *Bedrooms* (NY 1958) 114: She's a girl—homely as a mud fence. **1956** MLSettle *O Beulah* (NY) 336: She's ugly as a mud fence. **1957** LBeam *Maine* (NY) 201: Ugly as a mud fence. **1959** *BangorDN* 7/4 9: I wish I were homely as a mud fence. **1965** JFWest *Time* (NY) 34: Ugly as a mud fence daubed with chinquapins. TW 254. Cf. Hedge fence *above*; Stump fence *below.*

M322   To go around the **Mulberry** bush (*varied*)

1930 JGBrandon *Murder* (L) 63: Then it'll be "Here we go round the mulberry bush" for all of us. **1931** JJFarjeon *House* (NY) 183: It won't help to go round and round the Mulberry Bush. **1931** MMagill *Death* (P) 74: Someone has been leading you round the mulberry bush. **1936** LRGribble *Malverne* (L) 209: What's the object of this dancing round the mulberry-bush [*evasion*]? **1937** CDickson *Ten Teacups* (L) 241: You've led him an awful dance around the gooseberry bush. **1939** EQueen *Dragon's* (NY) 172: Beat all around the mulberry bush to find out. **1940** BHalliday *Private Practice* (NY 1965) 149: I'm no good at riddles or beating around the mulberry bush. **1948** GHJohnston *Death Takes* (L 1959) 162: All the old kiss-in-the-ring and round-and-round-the-mulberry-bush stuff. **1954** ECRLorac *Shroud* (NY) 165: So here we go round the mulberry bush again. **1961** RFoley *It's Murder* (NY DBC) 115: Here we go round the mulberry bush. **1961** LPayne *Nose* (NY) 208: We'd been all round the mulberry bush. **1973** TWells *Brenda's* (NY) 122: We trotted around our verbal mulberry bush. NED Mulberry 4. Cf. To beat about the Bush *above.*

M323 Tell it to **Muldoon**

1959 DMDisney *Did She Fall* (NY) 48: You can tell that to Muldoon. Cf. Marines *above.*

M324 As balky as a **Mule**

1941 SMarshall *Some Like* (NY) 195: You're balkier than a Missouri mule. Whiting *NC* 448(2).

M325 As dead as a **Mule** (*varied*)

1928 JArnold *Surrey* (L) 118: As dead as a mule. **1934** ABCox *Mr Pidgeon's* (NY) 100: As dead as a dead mule—and that's the deadest thing I know.

M326 As headstrong (determined) as a **Mule**

1937 LFord *Ill Met* (NY) 91: Rosemary's as headstrong as a mule. **1940** PWentworth *Rolling* (P) 157: She could be as determined as a mule. TW 254(3).

M327 As obstinate (independent) as a **Mule** (donkey)

1929 CReeve *Ginger* (NY) 265: Obstinate as a mule. **1938** JRhode *Bloody* (L) 51: He was as obstinate as a mule. **1950** SJepson *Hungry* (NY) 34: Independent as a damned stuffed mule. **1954** KAmis *Lucky* (L) 238: Obstinate as a mule. **1956** ACLewis *Jenny* (NY) 20: Papa is obstinate as a donkey. **1971** PDJames *Shroud* (L) 211: As obstinate as an army mule. **1973** KAmis *Riverside* (NY) 117: Obstinate as a damn mule. EAP M299.

M328 As strong as a **Mule**

1935 HMcCoy *They Shout* (NY) 52: They're strong as mules. **1972** COverstreet *Boar* (NY) 1: He looked as strong as a mule. Whiting *NC* 448(6).

M329 As stubborn as a **Mule**; Mule-stubborn

1908 JCLincoln *Cy Whittaker* (NY) 178: Stubborn as a balky mule. **1922** JJoyce *Ulysses* (NY 1934) 425: Stubborn as a mule. **1927** BAtkey *Smiler* (NY) 8: As stubborn as a mule. **1937** MBurton *Clue* (NY) 158: She was as stubborn as a mule. **1940** JP Phillips *Murder in Marble* (NY) 15: He's as stubborn as all the Missouri mules in captivity. **1952** MRRinehart *Swimming* (NY) 27: As stubborn as a mule. **1958** CSibley *Malignant* (NY) 135: As stubborn as a team of Georgia mules. **1968** BKnox *Figurehead* (NY) 126: About as mule-stubborn as they come. **1970** WMasterson *Death* (NY) 30: Stubborn as a mule. **1971** ELathen *Longer* (NY) 216: She may be stubborn as a mule. EAP M300. Cf. Jackass *above.*

M330 As tough as a **Mule**

1947 RHichens *Yesterday* (L) 265: I was as tough as an old mule. Whiting *NC* 448(8).

M331 To kick like a **Mule**

1936 SFowler *Was Murder Done?* (L) 33: He'll kick like a mule. Whiting *NC* 448(12); Taylor *Prov. Comp.* 58.

M332 To work like a **Mule**

1962 WHaggard *Unquiet* (NY DBC) 108: Working like a mule. **1977** HDolson *Beauty* (P) 159: We work like mules. Cf. To work like a Horse *above.*

M333 In a **Multitude** of counselors there is safety

1932 JSFletcher *Four Degrees* (L) 30: Multitude of counsellors. **1935** CWells *Wooden* (P) 69: In a multitude of counselors there is safety, but too many cooks spoil the broth. EAP M301.

M334 **Mum**'s the word

1900 CFPidgin *Quincy A. Sawyer* (B) 157: Mum's the word. **1913** JSFletcher *Secret* (L 1918) 223: Mum's the word. **1922** JJoyce

Ulysses (NY 1934) 150: Mum's the word. **1932** STruss *Coroner* (NY) 113: Mum's the word. **1941** AMStein *Up to No Good* (NY) 51: Mum's the word. **1946** AEMartin *Death in the Limelight* (NY) 241: Mum's the word. **1965** HActon *Old Lamps* (L) 266: Mum's the word. **1966** GButler *Nameless* (NY) 27: "Mum's the word." She was fluent in out-of-date, half jocular slang. **1972** NMarsh *Tied* (B) 73: Mum's the word. **1974** SChance *Septimus* (Nashville) 55: Mum's the word. EAP M302; TW 254(1).

M335 Mumbudget

1949 NMarsh *Wreath* (NY) 274: You cry mum and I'll cry budget! *Oxford* 551.

M336 Murder breeds murder (*varied*)

1935 MGEberhart *House* (L) 139: Murder breeds murder. **1937** WDickinson *Dead Man* (P) 292: The trouble with one murder is that it breeds another. **1939** MPropper *Hide the Body* (NY) 144: Murder breeds murder. **1948** MInnes *Night* (L 1966) 173: Crime breeds crime. **1958** RKing *Malice* (NY) 98: The chilling cliché that "murder breeds." **1959** JPhilips *Killer* (NY) 119: Murder breeds murder. TW 254(2). Cf. One Murder *below*.

M337 Murder will out (*varied*)

1904 JCLincoln *Cap'n Eri* (NY) 274: There! The murder's out. **1920** ACrabb *Samuel* (NY) 191: Murder, contrary to the old saying, does not always out. **1922** JJoyce *Ulysses* (NY 1934) 99: Murder will out. **1926** LTracy *Gleave* (NY) 28: "Murder will out" says the old saw, which, like many another tag of proverbial philosophy, is profoundly inaccurate. **1936** EPearson *More Studies* (NY) 44: The ancient falsehood, "murder will out." **1940** HFootner *Murderer's* (NY) 9: The old gag . . . that murder will out. **1948** DCDisney *Explosion* (NY DBC) 132: Murder can't be hidden. Murder must out. **1952** AWUpfield *New Shoe* (L 1968) 50: Murder always will out some time or another. **1957** *BHerald* 5/12 IV 16: The adage of "murder will out" is a fallacy. **1959** *BHerald* 2/13 14: Murder will out—perhaps. **1959** TRoscoe *Only* (NY) 194: Only the most naive layman be-

lieves the myth that "murder will out." **1962** MAllingham *China* (NY) 279: My old copy-book was dead right. *Murder will out.* **1970** CDrummond *Stab* (NY) 94: Murder will out. **1974** JOlsen *Man With* (NY) 28: Mythology and Shakespeare hold that murder will out. EAP M305; TW 254(4); Brunvand 97. Cf. Truth will out *below*.

M338 One **Murder leads to another (*varied*)

1929 AGilbert *Death* (NY) 188: It's an axiom that one murder usually leads to a second. **1934** AWynne *Gold Coins* (P) 204: It's an old rule, as you know, that one murder deserves another. **1937** HAshbrook *Murder Makes Murder* (NY). **1947** GKersh *Prelude* (NY) 183: "Why don't you see, one murder makes many." . . . "I've heard that said about marriage." **1949** SJepson *Golden* (NY) 204: One murder leads to another. It is almost an axiom. **1960** AWUpfield *Mystery* (L) 233: One murder very often demands another. Cf. Murder breeds *above*.

M339 To get away with **Murder

1929 JBPriestley *Good* (NY) 536: You'd get away with murder. **1932** MMiller *I Cover* (NY) 50: He is getting by with murder. **1941** EDaly *Murders in* (NY) 12: They got away with murder. **1959** JHChase *Shock* (L) 188: Who says you can't get away with murder? **1960** HReilly *Follow* (NY DBC) 42: She got away with murder. **1968** JCaird *Murder* (NY) 97: George gets away with murder. **1976** JJMarric *Gideon's Drive* (NY) 92: Thieves can get away with murder. Wentworth 349.

M340 The **Murderer (criminal) returns *etc.* (*varied*)

1922 JJoyce *Ulysses* (NY 1934) 374: Must come back. Murderers do. **1923** JSFletcher *Markenmore* (NY) 320: The murderer's old trick . . . of hanging round the scene of his crime. **1926** BHecht *Count* (NY) 67: The murderer always returns to the scene of his crime. **1930** NBMavity *Case* (NY) 197: They say a murderer always comes back . . . maybe not. There's lots of old sayings that folks don't take much stock in any more. **1930** EDTorgerson *The Murderer Re-*

turns (NY). **1938** ZPopkin *Death Wears* (P) 100: The old line about a murderer revisiting the scene of his crime is that much hooey. **1940** GStockwell *Candy* (NY) 221: Let's put our faith in another of the good old proverbs and take it for granted that murderers do hover about the scene of their crimes. **1950** AWUpfield *Widows* (NY) 57: It had been the murderer who had returned to the scene of his crime. **1956** MProcter *Pub* (NY) 179: Once again it had happened, the traditional thing. The murderer had returned to the scene of his crime. **1958** AMStein *Sitting* (NY) 47: It could have been the criminal returning to the scene of the crime or it could have been a dog returning to his vomit. **1958** PUstinov *Add a* (B) 150: I know . . . that in detective stories criminals always return to the scene of their crime, but they usually allow a decent interval of time to elapse. **1961** GGFickling *Blood* (NY) 27: Don't tell me you believe the criminal always returns to the scene of his crime? **1963** NFitzgerald *Echo* (NY) 177: Perhaps the murderer is returning to the scene of his crime. **1973** TAWaters *Lost* (NY) 88: There was also his odd behavior in (to use the classic expression) returning to the scene of the crime—or at least the victim.

M341   As soft as **Mush**

1939 MMGoldsmith *Detour* (L) 30: I'd go soft as mush. **1939** HMiller *Capricorn* (NY 1961) 81: The asphalt was soft as mush. **1953** RChandler *Long* (L) 294: Soft as mush. **1959** MScherf *Never Turn* (NY) 59: Gordon was soft as mush with youngsters. Whiting *NC* 449(1); Taylor *Western Folklore* 17(1958) 17.

M342   To spring up like **Mushrooms**

1933 FDGrierson *Mystery* (L) 83: They spring up like mushrooms. **1956** *NYTimes Magazine* 7/8 15: They have sprung up again like mushrooms. EAP M307.

M343   To face the **Music**

1911 JCLincoln *Woman-Haters* (NY) 249: Face the music. **1913** EDBiggers *Seven Keys* (I) 293: I must face the music, as the vulgar expression goes. **1924** WBMFerguson *Black* (NY) 132: Face the music. **1933** EB Black *Ravenelle* (NY) 141: Face the music. **1939** CMWills *Death at* (L) 44: Afraid to face the music. **1941** MArmstrong *Blue Santo* (NY) 289: I'll have to face the music. **1956** BO'Donnell *Should Women* (L) 181: Left Mary to face the music. **1968** PGunn *My Dearest* (NY) 202: She remained to face the music. TW 255; *Oxford* 237.

M344   What **Must** be, must be

1913 HHMunro *When William* (L 1929) 13: What must be, must be. **1923** EMPoate *Behind* (NY) 204: But what must be, must be. **1937** JJFarjeon *Holiday* (L) 198: But what must be, must be. **1940** LMacNeice *Strings* (L 1965) 9: What must be must be. **1945** EPhillpotts *They Were Seven* (NY) 89: What must be must be. **1957** JMerrill *Seraglio* (NY) 113: If one must, one must. EAP M310; TW 255. Cf. What Will be will be *below*.

M345   As hot as **Mustard**

1929 PGWodehouse *Fish* (NY) 138: He was always as hot as mustard. **1938** PGWodehouse *Code* (NY) 261: Something hotter than mustard. **1954** EForbes *Rainbow* (B) 184: It had been hotter than mustard for weeks. **1968** RBusby *Main Line* (NY) 97: Hot as mustard they are [*crime squad*]. Tilley M1332.

M346   As keen (shrewd) as **Mustard**; Mustard-keen

1924 DMackail *Majestic* (NY) 302: As keen as mustard. **1932** TCobb *Who Closed* (L) 192: Jeremy was as keen as mustard on Freda. **1936** AFielding *Mystery* (L) 87: He . . . looked as keen as mustard. **1941** A Webb *Suicide Club* (L) 137: He was as keen as mustard. **1945** CDickson *Curse* (NY) 170: That fellow's as shrewd as mustard. **1958** *Time* 11/10 8: Keen as mustard. **1959** EHuxley *Flame* (L) 6: He was keen as mustard. **1965** MFrayn *Tin* (B) 62: Keen as mustard. **1968** JJMarric *Gideon's Ride* (NY) 180: [He] says he's mustard keen. Partridge 450: Keen.

M347   As sharp as **Mustard**

1929 EWallace *Ringer* (NY) 71: She's as sharp as mustard. Cf. Wilstach 342: As if he had lived on Tewksbury mustard.

M348 **Mustard** with mutton is the sign of a glutton

1966 NMonsarrat *Life(I)* (L) 9: Mustard with mutton was the sign of a glutton. Cf. Whiting M813.

M349 To stick like a **Mustard** plaster (*varied*)

1937 GBruce *Claim* (NY) 49: Stick to him like a mustard plaster. **1952** FVWMason *Himalayan* (NY 1953) 154: You are going to stick closer . . . than a mustard plaster. Cf. Berrey 419.1, 441.1.

M350 As dead as **Mutton** (*varied*)

1911 HHMunro *Chronicles* (L 1927) 234: He was as dead as mutton. **1926** JJConnington *Death* (NY) 29: As dead as mutton. **1931** QPatrick *Cottage* (P) 110: Dead as the proverbial mutton. **1935** CBarry *Death* (NY) 277: He was as dead as frozen mutton. **1939** JRWarren *Murder from* (NY) 37: Dead as mutton. **1940** MBurton *Murder in* (L) 14: As dead as frozen mutton. **1941** EXFerrars *Rehearsals* (NY) 161: Dead as cold mutton. **1948** CBush *Curious* (NY) 133: Dead as mutton. **1957** MProcter *Midnight* (NY) 232: As dead as mutton. **1961** CBush *Sapphire* (NY) 59: Deader than New Zealand mutton. **1964** LPayne *Deep* (L) 70: The receiver's as dead as mutton. **1970** AFreemantle *Three-Cornered* (NY) 255: Dead as mutton. **1974** JBrunner *Total* (NY) 182: Dead as mutton. TW 255(1); *Oxford* 170.

M351 **Mutton** dressed as lamb (*varied*)

1922 JJoyce *Ulysses* (NY 1934) 541: Mutton dressed as lamb. **1932** GLane *Hotel* (L) 173: I look like a hen—mutton dressed like lamb. **1933** JGrigsby *Island* (L) 80: And dat . . . is what ye maun call, "mutton dressed up as lamb." **1937** DLSayers *Busman's* (NY) 260: At 'er age! Mutton dressed as lamb. **1950** JCannan *Murder* (L 1958) 51: Looking like mutton dressed as lamb. **1955** CMWills *Death* (L) 26: Old ewe dressed as lamb. **1957** *Punch* 1/21 166: This reversing of the usual phrase about mutton dressed as lamb. **1959** GAshe *Pack* (NY) 95: There's a familiar saying, mutton dressed up as lamb. **1963** AChristie *Clocks* (NY) 126: There is a proverb or saying. Something about mutton dressed as lamb. **1964** JAshford *Superintendent* (NY) 138: There's over fifteen years between 'em, or I can't tell lamb from mutton. **1977** RRendell *Judgment* (NY) 15: [She] was mutton dressed as lamb. *Oxford* 589: Old ewe dressed lamb fashion. Cf. To prefer Lamb; Skimmed Milk *above.*

M352 To return to one's **Muttons** (*varied*)

1906 HGarland *Companions on the Trail* (NY 1931) 296: Return to your muttons. **1928** RBenchley *20,000 Leagues* (NY) 217: But to return to our mittens [*sic*]. **1928** RKing *Fatal* (NY) 15: And now to our muttons. **1930** ECRLorac *Murder* (L) 240: *Revenons à nos moutons.* **1936** AFielding *Two Pearl* (L) 108: To return to our mutton. **1958** RFraser *Jupiter* (L) 64: I thought best to return, as the French say, to my muttons. **1960** PO'Connor *Lower* (L) 54: We very quickly got down to our muttons. **1976** JPorter *Package* (NY) 142: Con returned to her muttons. **1977** PDJames *Death* (NY) 179: Ah well, to our muttons. TW 255(3).

N

N1 As dead as a **Nail**

1928 DHLawrence *Lady* ("Allemagne") 181: The . . . faculty was dead as nails. **1962** FLeiber *Shadows* (NY) 81: He's dead as a nail. TW 256(1). Cf. Doornail *above.*

N2 As hard as **Nails**; Nail-hard (*varied*)

1905 FMWhite *Crimson Blind* (NY) 368: He was hard as nails. **c1910** PGWodehouse *Leave it to Psmith* (L n.d.) 49: She is as hard as nails. **1922** JJoyce *Ulysses* (NY 1934) 56: Hard as nails at a bargain. **1929** BFlynn *Invisible* (L) 35: Hard as a bag of nails. **1936** EBQuinn *One Man's* (L) 253: Nail-hard. **1937** CBush *Hanging Rope* (L) 153: She's hard as nails. **1938** JGloag *Documents* (L) 151: Hard as a keg of nails [*a man*]. **1956** RRobinson *Landscape* (L 1963) 124: Hard as nails.**1957** B*Herald* 3/31 43: He could be hard as nails. **1970** JAtkins *Sex* (L) 144: Whether he be hard as nails. **1974** MInnes *Appleby's Other* (NY) 61: She was as hard as nails. *Oxford* 352.

N3 As naked as a **Nail**

1967 JPurdy *Eustace* (NY) 188: Stark naked as a nail. Whiting N1; Whiting *NC* 449(1); *Oxford* 554.

N4 As sharp as **Nails**

1939 AChristie *Murder Is* (L) 77: As sharp as nails [*bright*]. **1972** SAngus *Arson* (NY) 72: Miss Cope . . . was sharp as nails. **1974** DCory *Bit* (NY) 57: [Tracy was] sharp as a nail. Whiting N4.

N5 As tough as (old) **Nails**

1935 CGGivens *Rose Petal* (I) 28: Tough as nails. **1940** CFGregg *Fatal Error* (L) 226: As tough as nails. **1946** JDCarr *He Who Whispers* (NY) 249: The young lady is as tough as nails. **1962** FHoyle *A for Andromeda* (NY 1964) 17: Tough as old nails. **1968** EWilliams *Beyond* (NY) 242: Tough as nails. **1970** RByrne *Memories* (NY) 76: He was tough as nails. **1975** HCarmichael *Too Late* (NY) 160: She was a good soul. Tough as old nails on the outside. Whiting *NC* 449(2); Taylor *Prov. Comp.* 83.

N6 To chew **Nails** (*varied*)

1937 PATaylor *Octagon* (NY) 200: You look mad enough to chew nails. **1940** MSScott *Crime Hound* (NY) 103: You look as if you could bite a nail in two. **1957** MPHood *In the Dark* (NY) 58: Looking mad enough to chew nails. **1960** WMasterson *Hammer* (NY DBC) 134: Blossom's ready to chew nails and spit tacks. TW 256(9).

N7 To drive another **Nail** in one's coffin (*varied*)

1926 HAdams *Sloane* (NY) 18: That's the last nail in the coffin. **1927** AGilbert *Tragedy* (NY) 135: It is another nail in her coffin. **1936** JRhode *Death at* (NY) 119: [It] seemed to drive another nail into Philip's coffin. **1941** STowne *Death out of* (NY) 148: Driving the last nail in the man's coffin. **1949** LTreat *Trial* (NY DBC) 112: He had pounded in the first nail of Nicky's coffin. **1955** BCarey *Fatal* (NY) 113: It will be the final nail in your coffin. **1958** HRobertson

Crystal-Gazers (NY) 180: That's the last nail in Graham's coffin. **1965** CBeaton *Years* (L) 119: Birthdays . . . now another nail in my coffin. **1971** JFraser *Death* (NY) 138: Everyone of them [*cigarettes*] is a nail in your coffin. **1971** DGilman *Elusive* (NY) 133: Each dollar will be a nail in their coffin. **1977** KClark *Other* (NY) 157: One more nail in my coffin from the Tory point of view. EAP N7.

N8　To hit the **Nail** on the head (*varied*)

1912 JCLincoln *Postmaster* (NY) 100: You've hit the nailhead. **1916** NDouglas *London Street Games* (L) 119: Hit the nail on the head. **1925** AEHousman *Letters* ed HMaas (Cambridge, Mass. 1971) 25: Hit the nail on the head. **1931** WHLewis *Letters* (NY 1966) 143: Hits the nail on the head. **1936** DFrome *Mr. Pinkerton Has the Clue* (NY) 265: That's hitting the old nail square on the head. **1943** CEVulliamy *Polderoy* (L) 256: To hit the nail on the head. **1945** MBurton *Not a Leg* (NY) 45: He has an uncanny way of finding the head of a nail and hitting it hard. **1952** HReilly *Velvet* (NY) 87: Kit appeared to have hit the nail on the head. **1956** *BangorDN* 9/27 24: It hits one of the nails squarely on the head. **1956** PDeVries *Comfort* (B) 16: I like to hit the nail on the head with a saw. **1958** *Time* 4/28 6: You hit the nail on our theological heads. **1960** FWarburg *Occupation* (B) 167: Hit the nail on the head. **1969** HShapley *Ad Astra* (NY) 169: So I hit that nail on the head all right. **1972** RHGreenan *Queen* (NY) 103: You've hit the nail right on the head. EAP N9; TW 256(10); Brunvand 98(2).

N9　To pay (cash) on the **Nail** (*varied*)

1922 JJoyce *Ulysses* (NY 1934) 540: What will you pay on the nail? **1928** HVMorton *In Search* (NY) 179: The saying "to pay on the nail." **1931** JSFletcher *Murder* (NY) 85: There it was, down on the nail, as they say; 156. **1937** LRGribble *Who Killed* (L) 121: I was paid on the nail. **1941** FWCrofts *Circumstantial* (NY) 100: They paid that on the nail. **1955** CBrand *Tour* (NY) 202: Paying on the nail. **1959** ECRLorac *Last* (NY) 96: He'd pay for it on the nail. **1963** NFreeling

Question (NY 1965) 48: Paid on the nail. **1971** EPeters *Knocker* (NY) 49: They pay on the nail for everything. **1973** EJBurford *Queen* (L) 63: It was cash on the nail all the way. EAP N4; TW 57: Cash(2), 256(4).

N10　As busy as a **Nailer**

1928 HFootner *Velvet* (NY) 1: As busy as a nailer. **1974** WStegner *Uneasy* (NY) 87: As busy as a nailer. NED Nailer 1b.

N11　As sure as one's **Name** is (whatever)

1923 JSFletcher *Charing Cross* (NY) 300: As sure as my name's what it is. **1932** RThorndike *Devil* (NY) 311: As sure as my name's mud, he's dead. **1948** CBush *Curious* (NY) 152: As sure as my name's what it is. **1961** ANeame *Adventures* (NY) 131: As sure as my name is Maud. TW 257(1). Cf. Brunvand 98.

N12　A good **Name** is better than great riches

1961 HKlinger *Wanton* (NY) 27: "A good name is rather to be chosen than great riches." "Proverbs." EAP N10.

N13　If one has the **Name** he might as well have the game (*varied*)

1940 KMKnight *Death Came* (NY) 118: Wants the game without the name. **1941** CLClifford *While the Bells* (NY) 159: If he had the name he might as well have the game. **1951** AMStein *Shoot* (NY) 94: It would be a pity to have the name without having the game. **1956** ACLewis *Jenny* (NY) 71: You might as well have the name with the fame. **1959** SMarlowe *Blonde* (NY) 117: At least . . . I had the game as well as the name. **1963** MPHood *Sin* (NY) 132: Only a fool had the name without the game. **1966** DMDisney *At Some* (NY) 206: She might as well have the game as the name. **1971** ADavidson *Peregrine* (NY) 65: Some get the name, whereas others play the game. **1973** AMStein *Finger* (NY) 128: I wouldn't want the name without the game. **1981** JBrett *Who'd Hire* (NY) 112: If I've got the name, I might as well have the game. TW 257(4); *Oxford* (2nd ed) 442.

N14 No **Names**, no pack drill (*varied*)

1931 PMacDonald *Crime* (NY) 7: No names ... no pack drill. **1935** LRGribble *Mystery* (L) 281: No names, no packdrill. **1939** VWilliams *Fox Prowls* (B) 165: No names, no court martials. **1947** DBowers *Bells* (NY) 200: No names, no pack drill. **1954** JTey *Shilling* (NY) 33: No names, no pack drill. **1957** *Punch* 8/7 147: No names no pack-drill. **1961** ATCurtis *Poacher's* (L) 110: "No names, no pack drill, sir," I said, using the popular expression of the day. **1967** CDrummond *Death* (NY) 40: No names, no pack drill. **1970** JJMarric *Gideon's Sport* (NY) 14: No names, no packdrill. **1974** JFleming *How To* (NY) 133: No names, no pack-drill. Partridge 565: No names.

N15 To change the **Name** but not the letter *etc.*

1926 AFielding *Footsteps* (L) 275: Changed her name and not her letter. Unlucky. **1940** VRath *Death of a Lucky* (NY) 143: Change the name but not the letter; change for worse and not for better. **1957** HPBeck *Folklore of Maine* (P) 79: Change the name and not the letter is a change for worse and not for better. **1962** DMDisney *Find* (NY DBC) 8: An old saying popped into his mind: "Change your name but not the letter, change for worse and not for better." **1971** CAird *Late* (NY) 153: Change the name and not the letter ... change for worse and not for better. **1976** LEgan *Scenes* (NY) 44: Just like that thing says, change the name an' not the letter, change for worse—. TW 257(5).

N16 To have one's middle **Name** (whatever)

1931 CFGregg *I Have* (NY) 20: Careful is my middle name. **1932** GLane *Hotel* (L) 86: Depression is my middle name. **1939** MArmstrong *Murder in* (NY) 154: Hurry is my middle name, as the saying is. **1950** LAGStrong *Which I* (L) 118: Caution was not only his middle name; it was his first and third. **1952** MRRinehart *Swimming* (NY) 15: Trouble was her middle name. **1956** ESGardner *Demure* (NY) 46: Trouble is my middle name. **1981** JBrett *Who'd Hire*

(NY) 69: Subtle, in fact, might have been my middle name.

N17 To have one's **Name** mud

c1910 EWallace *Nine Bears* (L 1928) 21: My name's Mud in the city. **1936** NBlake *Thou Shell* (L) 189: My name will be mud. **1965** JBrooks *Smith* (L) 146: Smith's name ... became mud among the girls. **1966** PGWodehouse *Plum* (L) 90: His name will be mud. **1974** PGWodehouse *Cat-Nappers* (NY) 129: Her name would be mud. **1981** RDavies *Rebel* (NY) 211: Rabelais's name would have been mud. Partridge 539: Mud.

N18 See **Naples** and die (*varied*)

1922 JJoyce *Ulysses* (NY 1934) 711: The bay of Naples (to see which was to die). **1933** EJepson *Memoirs* (L) 156: I did not wish to see Naples and die. **1942** HCBailey *Nobody's* (NY) 3: See Naples and die. **1948** RFoley *No Tears* (NY DBC) 73: That saying "See Naples and die." **1955** CMWills *Death* (L) 74: See Naples and Die. **1958** *BHerald* 7/23 31: See Naples and live. **1960** KMKnight *Invitation* (NY DBC) 16: The old saying, "See Naples and die." **1970** HCarvic *Miss Seeton Draws* (NY) 35: See Naples ... and I'll stand your wreath myself. **1972** VTrefusis *From Dusk* (L) 85: "Peter wanted to see Capri and die!" "You mean Naples." "Same thing. Why so literal?" TW 257; *Oxford* 709.

N19 To be caught **Napping**

1926 MRRinehart *Bat* (NY 1959) 113: Not to be caught napping. **1937** NBlake *There's Trouble* (NY) 265: Gurney was not to be caught napping. **1957** NBlake *End* (L) 195: He had no intention of being caught napping. **1971** MErskine *Brood* (NY) 139: I'm a hard man to catch napping. EAP N14.

N20 Human **Nature** is human nature (*varied*)

1934 JJConnington *Ha-Ha* (L) 62: Human nature's human nature. **1936** ECRLorac *Death* (L) 156: Human nature's the same all the world over. **1939** AChristie *Sad Cypress* (NY 1958) 64: Human nature's human nature. **1952** ECRLorac *Dog* (NY)

140: Human nature is human nature. EAP N15.

N21 Let **Nature** take its course

1937 JDCarr *Four False* (NY) 290: In the words of the improving proverb, let nature take its course. **1937** KRoberts *Northwest* (NY) 357: Let Nature take its course. **1940** RDarby *Death Conducts* (NY) 98: Let nature take its course. **1950** FFGould *Maine Man* (NY) 84: I am letting nature take its course. **1959** PAnderson *Perish* (NY) 166: Nature could take its course. **1960** JSymons *Progress* (L) 207: Resigned to letting nature take its course. **1965** HActon *Old Lamps* (L) 188: Let nature take its course. TW 258(6). Cf. *Oxford* 556.

N22 **Nature** abhors a vacuum (*varied*)

1922 JJoyce *Ulysses* (NY 1934) 162: Nature abhors a vacuum. **1928** GDHCole *Man* (NY) 166: Nature abhors a vacuum. **1936** SFowler *Was Murder Done?* (L) 46: It is proverbial that nature abhors a vacuum. **1938** NMorland *Case Without* (L) 95: Did Nature overlook a vacuum for once when she made your head? **1946** ESedgwick *Happy* (B) 79: Experience like all nature abhors a vacuum. **1950** STruss *Never* (NY) 166: To Miss Purdue a state of suspended animation was as abhorrent as Nature's vacuum. **1956** *New Yorker* 11/10 55: Nature abhorred a vacuum. **1965** ESitwell *Taken Care* (NY) 33: Nature, far from abhorring a vacuum, positively adores it. **1968** WTenn *Wooden* (NY) 145: Nature abhors self-destruction even more than a vacuum. **1970** AKarmel *My Revolution* (NY) 279: Nature abhors a vacuum. **1974** BWAldiss *Eighty* (NY) 218: Nature abhors any vacuum. EAP N17.

N23 **Nature** cures the disease *etc.*

1968 JGould *Europe* (B) 22: Proving the old saying that nature cures the disease and the treatment amuses the patient.

N24 **Nature** has given us two ears *etc.*

1931 PBaron *Round* (NY) 252: "Nature has given us two ears, two eyes, and but one tongue, to the end that we shall see and hear more than we speak." *Oxford* 555.

N25 **Nature** is deeper than nurture (*varied*)

1939 EPhillpotts *Monkshood* (L) 18: Nature is deeper than nurture. **1946** MInnes *Unsuspected* (NY) 38: Nature had had its moment; nurture supervened. *Oxford* 556, 583.

N26 One can drive **Nature** out with a pitchfork *etc.*

1927 DYates *Blind* (NY) 173: A proverb—"You can drive Nature out with a pitchfork, but she'll always come back." **1933** EJepson *Memoirs* (L) 92: Finding Nature repulsive and trying to expel her with a fork. **1956** AMenen *Abode* (NY) 59: Having driven Nature out with a pitchfork, she was allowed to crawl back by a series of well-worn stratagems. EAP N18.

N27 One cannot change (human) **Nature**

1938 SHAdams *World* (B) 54: You can't change nature. **1951** KFarrell *Mistletoe* (L) 165: What I say is, you can't change human nature. TW 258(11).

N28 To eat like a **Navvy**

1937 DInce *In Those* (L) 40: It . . . made so slender a child eat like a navvy. See NED Navvy 1 = laborer engaged in digging etc. Cf. Trojan *below*.

N29 To swear (curse) like a **Navvy**

1915 JBuchan *Thirty-Nine* (NY) 69: [He] swore like a navvy. **1955** DParry *Sea* (L) 28: Cursing like a navvy. Cf. Stevedore, Trooper *below*.

N30 To work like a **Navvy**

1931 JWVandercook *Forty* (NY) 96: I worked like a navvy. **1935** AFielding *Tragedy* (L) 157: Every one worked like a navvy. **1941** NMarsh *Death at the* (B) 324: He worked like a navvy. **1949** MAllingham *More Work* (NY) 43: Works like a navvy. **1960** JBell *Fall* (NY) 136: Work like a navvy. Cf. Stevedore, Trojan, Trooper *below*.

N31 **Neat** but not gaudy

1927 BAtkey *Man* (NY) 76: Neat and not gaudy. **1937** CBClason *Blind* (NY) 84: Neat but not gaudy. Brunvand 98(1); *Oxford* 557.

N32 Necessity is the mother of invention (*varied*)

1929 TLDavidson *Murder* (L) 82: You call necessity the mother of invention. **1934** REast *Bell* (L) 206: Necessity . . . was the mother of invention. **1939** DCDisney *Golden Swan* (NY) 218: And, as wiser folk than I have observed, necessity is the mother of invention. **1950** DAWollheim *Flight* (NY) 40: Necessity is the mother of invention. **1953** BCClough *Grandma* (Portland, Me.) 52: Another saying, "Necessity is the mother of invention." **1956** *Punch* 7/18 81: Necessity becomes the mother of ingenuity. **1958** *New Yorker* 7/12 78: Necessity mothered the invention of a deputy President. **1960** *BangorDN* 2/15 11: If necessity is the mother of invention, the father is "Pat. Pending." **1966** AMStein *I Fear* (NY) 163: Necessity . . . is invention's mom. **1971** WHMarnell *Once Upon* (NY) 85: Necessity can have other children besides invention. **1978** AJLerner *Street* (NY) 189: In America invention is the mother of necessity. EAP N23.

N33 Necessity knows no law (*varied*)

1926 JTully *Beggars* (NY) 280: Of proverbs, rolling hackneyed down the ages, the truest of all is that "necessity knows no law." **1930** ATrain *Adventures* (NY) 132: The maxim is not that "Necessity is the first law of Nature," but that "Necessity knows no law." **1930** *American Mercury* March 302: Jim [Ferguson, of Texas] kept on talking about Necessity Grigg . . . "You know the old proverb 'Necessity knows no law.' Judge Grigg knows so little about law that you could properly say he don't know any" . . . The name has stuck ever since. **1931** EWallace *Black* (NY) 318: *Necessitas non habet legem.* **1939** REHoward *Almuric* (NY 1964) 19: Necessity recognizes few limitations. **1952** HReilly *Velvet* (NY) 161: Desperation knows no laws. **1958** LSdeCamp *Elephant* (NY) 257: A Greek saying that necessity knows no law but to conquer. **1959** STruss *Man to Match* (NY) 76: We are in a state of necessity . . . which, as a more exalted person once remarked, knows no law. **1964** MColes *Knife* (NY DBC) 76: Necessity knows no law. **1969** PAnderson *Beyond* (NY) 121: We have a saying that necessity knows no law. **1977** STWarner *Kingdoms* (NY) 107: Necessity knows no law. EAP N22; TW 258–9(3). Cf. Hunger *above.*

N34 Neck and crop

1917 JCLincoln *Extricating* (NY) 130: Pitch us all out, neck and crop. **1937** GDHCole *Missing* (L) 30: Turn you out neck and crop. **1939** FGerard *Red Rope* (NY) 223: Chucked out neck and crop. **1956** *Punch* 5/23 628: Mr Lennot-Boyd bowled out the Socialist middle stump, neck, crop, hook, line and sinker. **1957** LBeam *Maine* (NY) 202: He ought to be lambasted neck and crop. *Oxford* 558. Cf. Brunvand 99: Neck (and heels).

N35 Neck of the woods

1910 JCLincoln *Depot Master* (NY) 107: This neck of the woods. **1924** EMillay *Letters* ed ARMacdougall (NY 1952) 187: This neck of the woods. **1933** RJCasey *Hot Ice* (I) 86: In this neck of the woods. **1938** CBarry *Case Dead* (L) 52: In this neck of the woods. **1945** MRRinehart *Yellow Room* (NY) 79: In this neck of the wood. **1950** MCarleton *Bride* (NY) 149: In this neck of the woods. **1966** GBagby *Dirty* (NY) 48: In Fred's neck of the woods. **1968** DFGalouye *Scourge* (NY) 5: In his neck of the woods. **1974** MButterworth *Villa* (NY) 52: In this neck of the woods. TW 259(1).

N36 Neck or nothing

1910 EPhillpotts *Tales* (NY) 301: 'Twas neck or nothing. **1919** LTracy *Bartlett* (NY) 282: Neck or nothing. **1922** JJoyce *Ulysses* (NY 1934) 463: Neck or nothing. **1930** WLewis *Apes* (NY 1932) 501: A neck-or-nothing point. **1936** FBeeding *Nine Waxed* (NY) 136: Your neck-or-nothing men. **1941** VWMason *Rio Casino* (NY) 281: It was neck or nothing. EAP N28.

N37 One's **Neck** feels the weight of his buttocks

1938 MInnes *Lament* (L) 197: I only wish that his neck, in our good Scots phrase, could feel the weight of his buttocks. Whiting *Drama* 353.691; Whiting *Scots* I 154: Craig(1).

N38 To get it in the **Neck**

1926 JTully *Beggars* (NY) 200: The good guys always get it in the neck. **1938** ECRLorac *Devil* (L) 199: His appearance was, in the peculiar Cockney idiom, that of one who had "got it in the neck" [*had a beating*]. **1939** LFord *Mr Cromwell* (NY) 133: He got it in the neck first [*was killed*]. **1954** RFMirvish *Taxana* (NY) 74: The girl always gets it in the neck. **1957** HEBates *Summer* (B) 31: I'll get it in the neck if you do. Wentworth 352. Cf. To get it . . . Chicken *above*.

N39 To stick one's **Neck** out

1939 JNDarby *Murder in* (I) 237: Don't stick your neck out! **1941** MTYates *Midway* (NY) 131: I cursed myself for sticking my neck out. **1951** GBagby *Death* (NY) 35: No use sticking your neck out. **1959** CHenry *Hostage* (NY) 191: He stuck his neck out for us. **1960** FSWees *Country* (NY) 71: She's sticking her own neck out. **1963** PMHubbard *Flush* (L 1964) 32: Don't stick your neck out. Wentworth 520: Stick.

N40 **Neck** 'em and nick 'em

1934 HReilly *McKee* (NY) 105: You know the old saying, "Neck 'em and nick 'em." Cf. Partridge 559: Nick = to cheat; Wentworth 351: Neck v. 2. Cf. To Love *above*.

N41 To raise **Ned**

1930 CFitzsimmons *Manville* (NY) 16: "Raised Ned" when I told her. **1947** KMKnight *Blue* (NY) 54: Raise particular Ned. **1967** AWEckert *Wild* (B) 119: I'd raise Ned with [him]. TW 259; Brunvand 99(1).

N42 As bright as a new **Needle**; Needle-bright

1938 RAJWalling *Grimy Glove* (NY) 131: Alert and bright as a new needle. **1972** MWilliams *Inside* (NY) 110: A delightful character, needle-bright. Cf. As bright . . . Pin *below*.

N43 As clean (straight) as a **Needle**

1957 NBlake *End* (L) 46: Walked out of his blood-bath as clean as a needle. Cf. As . . . Pin *below*.

N44 As naked as a **Needle**

1955 MBorowsky *Queen's* (NY) 321: Naked as a needle. **1955** Henry Kuttner *No Boundaries* (NY) 121: Naked as needles. Whiting N64; Oxford 553.

N45 As sharp as a **Needle**; Needle-sharp

1922 JJoyce *Ulysses* (NY 1934) 365: Sharp as needles they are. **1925** HHext *Monster* (NY) 233: Sharp as a needle he was. **1937** RBriffault *Europa* (NY) 311: As sharp as a needle. **1939** JRonald *This Way Out* (P) 148: Eyes sharp as needles. **1939** NMarsh *Overture* (NY) 141: Her thoughts needle-sharp. **1940** JStagge *Turn* (NY) 178: The word came sharp as a needle. **1949** NMarsh *Wreath* (NY) 18: An eye as sharp as a needle. **1953** DGarnett *Golden* (L) 52: Wits as sharp as a needle. **1957** YBridges *How Charles* (L) 36: His mind was needle-sharp. **1959** HEBates *Breath* (B) 21: Sharp as a packet o' needles. **1964** JJMarric *Gideon's Lot* (NY) 42: He's sharp as a needle. **1972** RRendell *No More* (NY) 125: Elsie was sharp as a needle but bone ignorant. **1973** AGilbert *Nice* (NY) 229: Sharp as a darning needle. EAP N33; TW 259(1).

N46 **Needle**-thin

1934 EQueen *Adventures* (NY) 220: A tall, needle-thin man. **1972** AGarve *Case* (NY) 76: She was tall, needle-thin. Cf. Knitting needle *above*.

N47 **Needles** and pins, when a man marries *etc.*

1930 ATrain *Adventures* (NY) 373: Once a man's married his troubles not only begin but never end. **1937** DLSayers *Busman's* (NY) 94: When a man's married . . . his troubles begin. **1967** VSPritchett *Cab* (NY) 13: Needles and pins, needles and pins, when a man marries, his trouble begins. Oxford 559.

N48 No **Needle** is sharp at both ends

1945 RLHines *Confessions* (L) 97: "No needle," saith the proverb, "is sharp at both ends."

N49 To look for a **Needle** in a bottle of hay (*varied*)

1922 JSFletcher *Rayner-Slade* (NY) 59: Get to the bottle of hay and begin prospecting for the needle. **1924** JSFletcher *King* (NY) 71: The proverbial needle in the bottle of hay. 261: It is poor work to look for a needle in a pottle [*sic*] of hay. **1931** MA Hamilton *Murder* (L) 191: Talk about a needle in a bottle of hay. **1935** VGielgud *Death* (L) 190: There was a proverb about needles in bottles of hay. **1937** JJConnington *Minor* (L) 286: It sounds like hunting for a needle in a bottle of hay. **1938** JJConnington *Truth* (L) 83: "A needle in a bottle of hay, probably." "So long as it isn't a mare's nest." *Oxford* 559 [*bottle only*].

N50 To look for a **Needle** in a haystack (*etc.*) (*very varied*)

1908 HMSylvester *Olde Pemaquid* (B) 225: Looking for a needle in a haystack. **1914** PGWodehouse *Little Nugget* (NY 1929): Finding the needle in this human bundle of hay. **1915** RFirbank *Vainglory* (Works 1, L 1929) 213: It's like looking for a needle in a bundle of hay. **1923** LThayer *Sinister* (NY) 68: Like looking for a needle in a haystack. **1924** HCBailey *Mr. Fortune's Practice* (NY) 132: A needle in a bundle of hay. **1924** GRFox *Fangs* (NY) 89: Looking for a needle in a haystack is . . . simple as can be. If the needle is there, and the hay is removed straw by straw, the implement will surely be found. But we were not sure that the needle was in our haystack. **1925** GHGerould *Midsummer* (NY) 139: As well have looked for a needle in a haymow. **1928** DLSayers *Dawson* (NY) 137: Hunting for a single dog-collar in the States must be like the proverbial needle. **1928** LThomas *Raiders* (NY) 276: As scarce as the proverbial needle in the strawstack. **1930** JSFletcher *Heaven-sent* (NY) 41: Like looking for a needle in a bundle of hay. **1930** AGilbert *Night* (NY) 178: Like looking for the proverbial needle in a load of hay. **1931** JDBeresford *Innocent* (NY) 152: Like looking for a needle in all the hayfields of the world—a needle moreover that's been lost for two years. **1931** HWade *No Friendly* (L) 194: The proverbial needle would have been no less easy to find. **1935** JO'Neill *Land* (L) 217: Like looking for a needle in a bundle of straw. **1938** PWentworth *Run!* (L) 162: Looking for a needle in a bundle

of hay. **1939** LRGribble *Arsenal* (L) 252: Looking for a needle in a haystack. . . Not many years ago an American tried to find the answer to that stock problem. It took him some eighty-odd hours, working steadily. **1940** EBenjamin *Murder Without* (NY) 126: It's like looking for that needle in the camel's eye. **1941** GDHCole *Counterpoint* (NY) 229: Like looking for a needle in a load of hay. **1945** MInnes *Appleby's End* (NY) 157: The needles put into the haystack to serve as a red herring. **1947** HLawrence *Death of* (NY) 218: Where Bessy and Beulah were concerned, an axiom was an old saw that didn't cut. With his own eyes he had seen them find needles in haystacks and thread them with camels. **1948** JTey *Franchise* (NY 1955) 173: The proverbial needle just gives itself up by comparison. **1950** HClement *Needle* (NY) 127: After all, the smart way to hunt for a needle in a haystack is to use a magnet. **1951** FLockridge *Murder Comes* (P) 112: Pam feels that there's always a needle in every haystack. **1957** *New Yorker* 5/4 153: A needle-in-the-haystack hunt. **1957** *Punch* 7/24 93: The kind of people who cannot see a needle until someone has built a haystack round it. **1959** *BGlobe* 9/29 13: Cambridge Police had a needle in a haystack deal today, looking for a bearded beatnik in Harvard Square. **1959** JThurber *Years* (B) 93: It would be like looking for a broken needle in a hayfield. **1961** BAldiss *Primal* (NY) 134: The last straw in a haystack full of disciplinary needles. **1961** LDelRay *And Some* (NY) 81: There was about as much chance of one man finding her . . . as the proverbial needle. **1961** GHolden *Deadlier* (NY DBC) 20: Like looking for one particular needle in a needle factory. **1966** ECooper *All Fools* (NY) 36: You've got about as much chance . . . as of finding a needle in the proverbial but now obsolete haystack. **1968** MBorgenicht *Margin* (NY) 132: You know what kind of needle's-eye hunt it is. **1969** GBagby *Honest* (NY) 177: Needle in a haystack . . . or I should say one particular wisp of hay out of a haystack. **1974** LBlack *Life* (NY) 136: "The needle in the haystack—and we're not sure if it's a needle." "But we can be certain that the haystack exists, and conceals something." **1974** PNobile *Intellectual* (NY) 220: It's also possible to find a needle in a haystack. **1980** LBlock *Burglar . . . Spinoza* (NY) 113: The proverbial needle in the proverbial haystack would have been a piece of cake in comparison. **1980** THellerman *People* (NY) 182: [It] would have been like searching the white man's proverbial haystack for a dangerous needle. EAP N35; TW 259–60(2); Brunvand 99(2).

N51 To thread a moving **Needle**

1973 ELopez *Seven* (NY) 220: That old defence lawyer's proverb that "you can't thread a moving needle" [*of rape*]. Cf. Partridge 878: Thread the needle = to coït.

N52 **Needs** must

1919 JBCabell *Jurgen* (NY 1922) 16: Needs must, then. **1931** AWynne *Silver Scale* (P) 145: Needs does as needs must. **1944** ECrispin *Gilded Fly* (NY 1970) 23: It's a case of needs must. **1950** IFletcher *Bennett's* (I) 34: Needs must. *Oxford* 559–60.

N53 **Needs** must when the devil drives (*varied*)

1905 JBCabell *Line* (NY 1926) 37: Needs must when the devil drives. **1906** JCLincoln *Mr. Pratt* (NY) 316: Needs must if the old gentleman drives. **1923** JSFletcher *Copper* (NY) 137: Needs must where the devil drives. **1930** GBaxter *Ainceworth* (NY) 272: He said in his best French . . . "Needs must when Auld Nick drives," as the folks say where I come from [*Scotland*]. **1935** BFlynn *Edge* (L) 81: Needs must when the devil handles the reins. **1954** RHaydn *Journal* (NY) 115: Needs must, when the devil drives. **1958** CCarnac *Affair* (NY) 92: A case of needs must when the devil drives. **1960** LFielden *Natural* (L) 321: Needs must when the devil drives. **1967** FMBrodie *The Devil Drives: A Life of Sir Richard Burton* (NY). **1973** JPorter *It's Murder* (NY) 37: Needs must when the devil drives. EAP D142; TW 260.

N54 Two **Negatives** make an affirmative

1930 JCournos *Grandmother* (NY) 260: They say . . . that two negatives make a positive. **1931** MDalton *Night* (NY) 45: Two

negatives make an affirmative. I learnt that at school. **1972** RRendell *No More* (NY) 78: Two negatives make an affirmative. EAP N36.

N55 To feather one's **Nest** (*varied*)

1912 JCLincoln *Postmaster* (NY) 230: To feather their own nest. **1922** JJoyce *Ulysses* (NY 1934) 125: Feathered his nest well. **1923** ABlackwood *Episodes* (L) 299: They were feathering their nests. **1933** HHDunn *Crimson* (NY) 97: Collecting feathers for his own political nest. **1933** WHoltby *Mandoa* (NY) 58: Feather his nest. **1941** JBentley *Mr. Marlow Chooses* (B) 149: The feathering of a belated nest. **1957** *Punch* 1/23 169: A ruse to feather its own nest. **1957** *NYTimes Book Review* 3/3 35: Tallien had been feathering his nest. **1966** DMDisney *At Some* (NY) 61: You've both feathered your nests. **1971** MHarrison *Fanfare* (L) 3: Many a whore had wonderfully feathered her nest. **1980** JBell *Treachery* (NY) 35: Feather . . . for his own future nest. EAP N49.

N56 In vain is the **Net** spread in the sight of the bird (*varied*)

1925 BBLindsay *Revolt* (NY) 212: "Surely in vain the net is spread in the sight of any bird." **1930** HAdams *Golden* (L) 158: We are told that the snare is spread in vain in the sight of the bird, but is it true? **1935** CBush *Chinese Song* (NY) 200: In vain was the net spread in the sight of the bird. **1941** MColes *Drink* (NY) 78: In vain is the net spread in the sight of the bird. **1961** LSdeCamp *Dragon* (NY 1968) 168: In vain the net is spread in the sight of the bird. EAP N50.

N57 To be on **Nettles** (*varied*)

1938 MJohnston *Comets* (NY) 56: Tony waited like a man on nettles. **1951** MColes *Now* (NY) 211: [He] sits upon nettles until he has news of you. EAP N53; Brunvand 99.

N58 To grasp the **Nettle** boldly (*varied*)

1913 HFAshurst *Diary* ed GFSparks (Tucson 1962) 27: To grasp the nettle boldly. **1935** AChristie *Boomerang* (NY) 173: The bold thing—grasp the nettle. **1939** AGilbert *Clock* (L) 138: It's the old adage about grasping the nettle. **1940** GStockwell *Candy* (NY) 249: Grasp the nettle firmly. There was something in my copy book about it. **1943** HAdams *Victory* (L) 164: It is my nettle and I must grasp it. **1952** CRand *Hongkong* (NY) 171: The Reds had grasped the nettle firmly. **1955** IAsimov *End* (NY) 106: A proverb that went: "Grip the nettle firmly and it will become a stick with which to beat your enemy." **1957** JCreasey *Model* (L 1961) 11: I should grasp the nettle, take the bull by the horns, strike while the iron is hot. **1963** THWhite *America* (NY 1965) 163: I had to get out and pick a leaf [*of a nettle*] to see if the adage still held true. "Grasp the nettle and it will not sting." It did. **1969** AGilbert *Mr. Crook* (NY DBC) 10: Grasp the nettle boldly and then you'll rarely find it stings. *Oxford* 348: Handles.

N59 **Never** (forever) is a long time (*varied*)

1928 AGilbert *Mrs. Davenport* (NY) 215: Never's a long word. **1930** JFerguson *Murder* (NY) 136: Never's a long time. **1932** PHerring *Murder* (L) 193: Never is a long day. **1936** ESedgwick *Happy* (B) 289: Never is a long time. **1960** ABudrys *Unexpected* (NY) 8: Forever is a long time. **1966** BNaughton *Alfie* (L) 28: Never is a long time. **1971** JMacNab *Education* (NY) 26: Never is a long time. **1971** WHWalling *No One* (NY) 179: Never is rather a long time. *Oxford* 562. Cf. TW 144.

N60 To make no **Never-mind**

1937 JYDane *Cabana* (NY) 220: Make no never-mind if he did. **1940** JLBonney *Death by* (NY) 144: It don't make no never mind what your name is. **1941** GWYates *If a Body* (NY) 18: Don't make no never mind. **1962** FLockridge *And Left* (P) 83: To me . . . it makes no never mind. **1970** DShannon *Unexpected* (NY) 58: It wasn't no never-mind to me.

N61 Bad **News** travels fast (*varied*)

1904 SArmitage-Smith *John of Gaunt* (L) 250: Ill news flies fast. **1928** BAtkey *Midnight* (NY) 128: Bad news travels too fast. **1929** OGray *Bagshot* (NY) 304: The worse the news, the more quickly it must be told. **1933** JCMasterman *Oxford* (L) 89: Bad

news travels quickly. **1938** JJConnington *For Murder* (L) 176: Bad news travels like lightning. **1951** JMFox *Aleutian* (B) 193: Bad news travels too fast. **1953** MPei *Swords* (NY) 10: Bad news travels fast. **1960** NFitzgerald *Ghost* (L) 117: If I may coin a phrase, bad news travels fast. **1968** JCaird *Murder* (NY) 30: Ill news, as you may have heard, travels fast. **1970** HCarmichael *Death* (NY) 70: Bad news travels fast. **1973** CAird *His Burial* (NY) 95: Bad news—a far fleeter traveller—had already reached chez Osbourne. EAP N62; Brunvand 99.

N62 Good **News** travels fast

1954 JSymons *Narrowing* (NY) 69: "Good news travels fast" . . . this cliché. **1957** *Time* 7/8 18: Good news travels fast. **1960** HLivingston *Climacticon* (NY) 168: Good news travels fast. Cf. preceding entry.

N63 No **News** is good news (*varied*)

1924 IOstrander *Annihilations* (NY) 125: No news is good news. **1933** AEHousman *Letters* ed HMaas (Cambridge, Mass. 1971) 349: I hope no news is good news. **1940** CWorth *Trial* (NY) 33: To Aunt Ethel good news was no news. **1941** EStVMillay *Letters* ed ARMacdougall (NY 1952) 317: The old "no news is good news." **1947** HLawrence *Death of* (NY) 149: No news is good news, as the saying goes. **1954** CIsherwood *World* (L) 115: Any news is bad news. **1955** CArmstrong *Dream* (NY 1958) 139: No news is good news. **1963** CBlackstock *Mr. Christopoulos* (NY 1965) 142: The old cliché about no news being good news. **1964** CBrooke-Rose *Out* (L) 163: If no news is good news then news must be bad news. **1967** RHKuh *Foolish* (NY) 257: Thurman Arnold's flip slogan, "no nudes is good nudes." **1970** RFenisong *Drop* (NY) 95: How can even a fool believe that no news is good news? **1979** *BGlobe* 4/9 1: No Nukes is Good Nukes. [*A popular bumper motto 1979–1985.*] EAP N65.

N64 As drunk as a **Newt**

1957 HEBates *Sugar* (L) 112: Drunk as newts. **1959** HEBates *Breath* (B) 134: As drunk as a newt. **1962** HEBates *Golden* (L)

142: Drunk as newts. **1968** KRoberts *Pavane* (NY) 193: Robert . . . drunk as a newt.

N65   As pickled (plastered) as a **Newt**

1961 PMoyes *Down Among* (NY) 75: Pickled as a newt [*drunk*]. **1973** BKnox *Storm* (NY) 152: John was his usual, plastered as a newt [*drunk*].

N66   As pissed as a **Newt**

1966 NMonsarrat *Life(I)* (L) 285: I was pissed as a newt that night [*drunk*]. **1969** SMays *Fall Out* (L) 39: Kelly is as pissed as a newt [*drunk*]. **1972** JMcClure *Caterpillar* (NY) 115: Pissed as a newt and fed to the gills. **1976** MGilbert *Night* (NY) 208: Pissed as a newt [*drunk*]. Spears 302: Pissed = intoxicated.

N67   In the **Nick** of time

1913 ERBurroughs *Warlord* (NY 1963) 130: In the nick of time. **1924** RAFreeman *Blue* (NY) 28: In the nick of time. **1928** RKing *Fatal* (NY) 255: In the more than proverbial nick of time. **1937** CBush *Hanging Rope* (L) 102: Just in the nick of time. **1940** CWorth *Trail* (NY) 123: If we hadn't been on hand in the proverbial nick they might have come by it. **1954** NBlake *Whisper* (L) 103: In the nick, as they say, of time. **1956** PMiller *Raven* (NY) 183: In the nick of time. **1957** *Speculum* 32 536: In the nick of time. **1958** SDean *Dishonor* (NY) 187: But there he was, old Nick of Time, Johnny-on-the-spot. **1960** HWaugh *Road* (NY DBC) 133: What you did is known in the vernacular as "Arriving in the nick of time." **1966** SGCrawford *Gascoyne* (L) 26: Just in the nick of time. **1974** AChurchill *Splendid* (NY) 176: In the nick of time. **1976** JRLAnderson *Death* (NY) 177: In the nick of time. EAP N68.

N68   Do not take any wooden **Nickels** (*varied*)

1930 The Aresbys *Murder* (NY) 112: Don't take any wooden money. **1934** JTFarrell *Young Manhood* (NY 1935) 64: Don't take any wooden nickels. **1951** JMFox *Aleutian* (B) 200: As phony as a wooden nickel. **1954** EStreeter *Mr. Hobbs'* (NY) 39: Don't take any wooden money. **1957** *BHerald* 3/27 13: The old saying "Don't take any wooden

nickels." **1957** WRBurdett *Underdog* (NY) 119: Don't take any rubber quarters. **1959** *BangorDN* 9/10 12: An ancient American joke: "Don't take any wooden nickels." **1960** IWallace *Chapman* (NY 1961) 191: Don't take any wooden nickels. **1963** RA Heinlein *Glory* (NY) 261: Don't take any wooden nickels, as your tribesmen say. Berrey 21.3.

N69   Not care (give) a tin (plugged) **Nickel**

1909 JCLincoln *Keziah* (NY) 170: I really don't care a tin nickel for him. **1937** GDilnot *Murder* (L) 152: I don't care a plugged nickel. **1966** SGCrawford *Gascoyne* (L) 149: I don't give a plugged nickel. DA Plug *v.* 1b.

N70   Not worth a plugged **Nickel** (dime)

1930 CWells *Doorstep* (NY) 193: His life wasn't worth a plugged dime. **1934** EB Black *Crime* (NY) 74: Life isn't worth a plugged nickel. **1937** MDavis *Chess* (NY) 83: My reputation won't be worth a plugged nickel. **1941** HCBranson *I'll Eat You* (NY) 12: I wouldn't back him to the extent of a plugged nickel. **1949** RChandler *Little* (NY 1951) 208: I'm not worth a plugged nickel. **1958** RChandler *Playback* (L) 81: Your story . . . won't be worth a wooden nickel. **1964** LWhite *Ransomed* (NY DBC) 10: There wasn't one of them worth a plugged nickel. **1970** RZelazny *Isle* (NY) 142: I wouldn't have trusted him with a plugged nickel. Whiting *NC* 451: Worthless.

N71   As black as a **Nigger's** arse (heel)

1955 LCochran *Hallelujah* (NY) 132: Coffee as black as a Negro's heel and stout enough to talk back to the High Sheriff. **1969** SMays *Fall Out* (L) 94: Shades blacker than a nigger's arse. Taylor *Prov. Comp.* 18: Heel.

N72   A **Nigger** in the woodpile (*very varied*)

1908 JCLincoln *Cy Whittaker* (NY) 336: A nigger in the woodpile. **1912** JCLincoln *Postmaster* (NY) 192: Then he upset the woodpile and let out the darkey. **1924** CWells *Furthest* (P) 294: There's a very remarkable colored person in the woodpile. **1927** BAtkey *Smiler* (NY) 253: An Ethiopian was craftily concealed in the woodpile. **1929** KPreston *Pot Shots* (NY) 216: Like the Ethiopian in the wood pile. **1930** JJConnington *Two Tickets* (L) 279: Doesn't she spot the nigger in the fence? **1930** TFMadigan *Word Shadows* (NY) 71: There is bound to be a darky somewhere in such an autographic woodpile. **1936** ESGardner *Stu Hering* (NY) 55: There's a nigger in the woodpile somewhere. **1937** GBruce *Claim* (NY) 217: Like the proverbial woodpile, I'm looking for a nigger. **1940** GDHCole *Wilson* (L) 83: There was a bit of a nigger in the woodpile. **1940** JCLincoln *Out of the Fog* (NY) 346: There's a nigger in the cordwood. **1944** HTalbot *Rim* (NY 1965) 101: I smelled a nigger in the woodpile. **1945** MWalsh *Nine Strings* (P) 56: There was a murder in the woodpile. **1947** GLGower *Mixed* (L) 141: Showing, in Yankee parlance, who was "the nigger in the wood pile." **1950** SPalmer *Green* (NY) 4: There's a needle in the woodpile somewhere [*something wrong*]. **1954** AWUpfield *Death* (NY) 79: Seems to be a joker in the woodheap. **1957** *Time* 10/21 45: Was there a Welshman in the woodman? **1958** DGBrowne *Death* (L) 162: Just like him to see a nigger minstrel in every woodpile. **1961** LPayne *Nose* (L) 113: The nigger in the woodpile being the other chap [*triangle*]. **1964** LLafore *Devil's* (NY) 81: There are goats in the woodpile. **1967** CAird *Most Contagious* (NY) 142: There was a nigger in the family woodpile. **1968** MAllingham *Cargo* (NY) 51: Robin Goodfellow, the nigger in the original woodpile of Christianity in this country. **1970** TWells *Dinky* (NY) 123: You think there's a nigger in the woodpile? **1978** DNDurant *Bess* (NY) 188: Bamforth was the nigger in Bess's woodpile [*Bam. had betrayed the lady's secrets*]. TW 261(11); Brunvand 43: Ethiopian; *Oxford* 566.

N73 To sweat like a **Nigger** at election (*varied*)

1941 ISCobb *Exit* (I) 334: I'm sweating like a free nigger at election. **1953** BMcMillion *Lot* (P) 35: Sweat! . . . Like a nigger at election! **1953** JSanford *Land* (NY) 230: You sweat like a nigger at election. **1962** WMorris *North* (B) 59: I'm sweatin' like a nigger

at a free election. Whiting *NC* 450(10); Taylor *Prov. Comp.* 59.

N74 To work like a **Nigger** (*varied*)

1903 EChilders *Riddle* (NY 1940) 109: Works like a nigger. **1923** WLewis *Letters* ed WKRose (L 1963) 138: Working like a nigger. **1925** FBeeding *Seven* (B) 31: We work like negroes. **1930** AWaugh *Hot Countries* (NY) 202: Working like a nigger. **1931** JMWalsh *Company* (NY) 127: You've been working like a buck-nigger. **1937** NBell *Crocus* (NY) 283: He's been working about six times as hard as the proverbial nigger. **1953** ARhodes *Ball* (L) 152: In English you have the expression, to work like a nigger. **1955** Miss Read *Village* (L 1960) 135: She'd work like a nigger. EAP N43: Negro; TW 262(17); Brunvand 99(1). Cf. To work like a Black *above*, Slave *below*.

N75 As black as **Night**; Night-black

1922 JJoyce *Ulysses* (NY 1934) 740: As black as night. **1928** AWynne *Red* (P) 240: The man's face was as black as night. **1938** MBrucker *Poison* (NY) 199: Eyes . . . black as night. **1952** LBemelmans *How To* (L) 114: Wings as black as the night. **1959** SMarlowe *Blonde* (NY) 50: The night-black water. **1960** ADean *Bullet* (NY) 89: Black as night. **1964** IPetite *Elderberry* (NY) 28: Black as night and proud as Lucifer. EAP N70; Brunvand 100(1).

N76 As dark as **Night**

1925 HHext *Monster* (NY) 2: Richard was dark as night. EAP N71; TW 262(2); Brunvand 100(2).

N77 As sure (certain) as **Night** (day) follows day (night) (*varied*)

1925 JGBrandon *Cork* (L) 12: As sure as night follows day. **1935** BFlynn *Padded* (L) 23: As sure as night follows day. **1945** EPhillpotts *They Were Seven* (NY) 250: As certain as night follows day. **1954** JHenry *Yield* (NY) 87: As sure as day follows night. **1957** BHitchens *End* (NY) 203: As dependable as day following night. **1960** BCClark *Long* (NY) 201: Just as true as day would follow night. **1962** AMStein *Home* (NY) 31: It follows like the night the day. **1963** DGardiner *Lion* (NY) 68: Followed as the night the day. **1966** GWBrace *Between Wind* (NY) 115: As sure as night follows day. **1972** NMarsh *Tied* (B) 146: Doesn't follow as the night the day. Whiting *NC* 451(7); *Oxford* 228: Every day. Cf. Whiting D31.

N78 Night brings counsel (*varied*)

1928 LThayer *Darkest* (NY) 210: The saying that night brings counsel. **1928** SFWright *Island* (NY) 188: It is said that sleep brings counsel and courage. **1932** VLoder *Death* (L) 163: *La nuit porte conseil.* **1933** CBush *Three Strange* (L) 153: The night brings counsel. **1937** HCBailey *Black Land* (NY) 151: The night had brought counsel. **1967** NFreeling *Strike* (NY) 217: Night, they say, brings counsel. *Oxford* 566.

N79 One **Night** with Venus, three years with Mercury

1936 JMetcalfe *Sally* (NY) 553: One night with Venus, Sir; three years with Mercury.

N80 To turn **Night** into day

1925 HHext *Monster* (NY) 92: They turned night into day. **1932** JSFletcher *Four Degrees* (L) 71: They turn night into day, as the saying is. Berrey 313.2

N81 The **Nightingale** and the thorn

1966 COgburn *Winter* (NY) 93: Solitude is to the powers of perception what the thorn was to the nightingale which pressed its breast upon the point to provoke its most moving song. *Oxford* 566.

N82 As neat as **Ninepence** (sixpence)

1910 EPhillpotts *Tales* (NY) 173: All so neat as ninepence; 199. **1969** AGilbert *Mr. Crook* (NY DBC) 45: A . . . fellow . . . as neat as a new sixpence. Tilley N187.

N83 As nimble (quick) as **Ninepence**

1933 GRichards *Memoirs* (NY) 272: Nimble as ninepence. **1965** CMackenzie *My Life Octave Four* (L) 31: As quick as ninepence. EAP N77.

N84 As right (safe) as **Ninepence** (sixpence)

1919 KHoward *Peculiar* (NY) 178: I was as right as ninepence. **1922** VBridges *Greensea* (NY) 84: As right as ninepence. **1928** WGerhardi *Jazz* (L) 271: As right as six-pence. **1932** DHume *Bullets* (L) 13: As safe as ninepence. **1958** WGraham *Wreck* (NY) 204: They'll be right as ninepence. Partridge 562; Lean III ii 868.

N85 Ninepence to the shilling

1972 MHardwick *Mrs. Dizzy* (NY) 35: He was not quite nine-pence to the shilling. **1972** SWoods *They Love* (NY) 62: He's only about ninepence to the shilling [*dim-witted*]. *Oxford* 567.

N86 To go down like a **Ninepin** (*varied*)

1930 NGordon *Silent* (NY) 90: The stranger went down like a ninepin. **1932** CDawes *Lawless* (L) 249: You tumbled me over like a nine-pin. **1937** FWCrofts *Found* (NY) 288: He went down like a ninepin. **1950** CEVulliamy *Henry* (L) 73: They seem to go down like ninepins. **1951** JCollier *Fancies* (NY) 104: I should have been bowled over like a ninepin. **1956** DWheatley *Ka* (L) 50: Women had fallen for him like ninepins. **1965** AHeckstall-Smith *Consort* (NY) 38: The girls fall for him like ninepins. **1971** AGarve *Late* (NY) 155: The girls were going down like ninepins. EAP N79.

N87 To be dressed (up) to the **Nines** (*varied*)

1919 LTracy *Bartlett* (NY) 162: Dressed up to the nines. **1922** JJoyce *Ulysses* (NY 1934) 362: Dressed up to the nines. **1931** AChristie *Murder* (NY) 54: Dressed up to the nines. **1939** LBrock *Fourfingers* (L) 80: Always dressed up to the nines. **1941** CLClifford *While the Bells* (NY) 15: She was fixed up to the nines. **1951** AThorne *Man Who* (L) 212: All dressed up to the nines. **1957** RLongrigg *Switchboard* (L) 80: Dolled up to the nines. **1959** AHocking *Victim* (NY) 105: Tarted up to the nines. **1964** RCFaure *Summer* (NY) 142: Dressed to the nines. **1965** KLaumer *Galactic* (NY) 172: Armed to the nines [*synonomous with "armed to the teeth" (p. 174)*]. **1972** SNBehrman *People* (B) 293: Furred up and muffled to the nines. **1977** LBlock *Burglars* (NY) 104: Dressed to the nines. TW 262.

N88 To be **Nip** and tuck

1913 ERBurroughs *Thuvia* (NY 1963) 107: It would be nip and tuck. **1930** JCournos *Grandmother* (NY) 225: It was nip and tuck in a fair game. **1939** MGEberhart *Chiffon* (NY) 296: It was nip and tuck. **1948** HReilly *Staircase* (NY) 241: It was nip and tuck. **1952** KFCrossen *Future* (NY) 75: Nip and tuck. **1955** PDennis *Auntie* (NY) 149: It looks like nip and tuck. **1960** JBlish *Galactic* (L) 100: It will be nip and tuck. TW 262–3(2).

N89 As dead as a **Nit**

1910 EPhillpotts *Tales* (NY) 11: Dead as a nit. **1933** ISCobb *Murder* (I) 33: Dead's a nit. **1964** AHunter *Gently* (NY) 7: Dead as a nit. TW 263. Cf. Louse *above*.

N90 **Nits** make lice

1929 HFergusson *In Those Days* (NY) 97: "Nits make lice," they said. EAP N81; Brunvand 100; Tilley N191.

N91 Not to take **No** for an answer

1900 CFPidgin *Quincy A. Sawyer* (B) 96: I won't take no for an answer. **1922** VBridges *Greensea* (NY) 66: Won't take no for an answer. **1932** GHeyer *Footsteps* (L) 47: He wouldn't take No for an answer; 215. **1935** LNoel *Golden* (L) 70: They just won't take no for an answer. **1941** AWebb *Suicide Club* (L) 163: I can't take no for an answer. **1949** RKing *Redoubled* (NY) 119: I refused to take no for an answer. **1950** RMacdonald *Drowning* (NY 1951) 34: They'll never take no for an answer. **1956** *BangorDN* 11/28 20: That idiot won't take no for an answer. **1960** AHLewis *Worlds* (NY) 301: Wouldn't take no for an answer. **1963** BFarwell *Burton* (L) 73: He would not take no for an answer. **1970** BWAldiss *Hand-Reared* (L) 145: Your sexy Esmeralda is going to do it to you three times straight off, and I won't take no for an answer. **1976** MWarner *Medium* (NY) 123: One who wouldn't take no for an answer. EAP N82.

N92 **Nobody** is perfect (*varied*)

1929 EDBiggers *Black* (I) 286: Nobody is perfect. **1930** HFootner *Mystery* (NY) 180: Nobody is infallible. **1931** LHollingworth *Death* (L) 103: We ain't none of us perfect that I knows of. **1935** SVestal *Wine Room* (B) 45: Nobody is infallible. **1949** FLockridge *Spin* (P) 214: He had to be perfect. Well—nobody is. **1959** FCrane *Buttercup* (NY DBC) 113: Nobody is perfect. **1969** DClark *Nobody's Perfect* (NY). **1969** MDorman *King* (NY) 175: Nobody's perfect. **1969** NHale *Life* (B) 10: But, as I have always been told, nobody is perfect. **1970** WANolen *Making* (NY) 269: No one is infallible. **1973** EMcBain *Hail* (NY) 44: But nobody's perfect. Cf. No Man is without *above*.

N93 To be **Nobody's** business

1931 EWallace *Arranways* (NY) 190: The trouble she had made was nobody's business. **1932** LAdamic *Laughing* (NY) 41: You can hit like nobody's business. **1959** JHChase *Shock* (L) 118: What it did to Maddox was nobody's business. **1959** *BangorDN* 8/29 11: He smells like nobody's business. **1970** JRoss *Deadest* (NY) 85: Hating [him] like nobody's business. Whiting *NC* 452.

N94 To be **Nobody's** fool (*varied*)

1904 JCLincoln *Cap'n Eri* (NY) 133: Mrs. Snow ain't nobody's fool. **1924** CWells *Furthest* (P) 69: Fraser is nobody's fool. **1936** DFrome *Mr. Pinkerton has the Clue* (NY) 84: Dame Crosby wasn't nobody's fool, as they say. **1938** SCallaway *Conquistador* (NY) 123: Nobody's fool. Knows more than her prayers. **1941** GBagby *Red Is* (NY) 247: She's nobody's fool. **1956** DMDisney *Unappointed* (NY) 88: The father was nobody's fool. **1958** SBarr *Purely* (NY) 58: She was nobody's fool. **1961** ESherry *Call* (NY DBC) 87: Eliot was nobody's fool. **1970** GBagby *Killer* (NY) 166: He's nobody's fool. **1973** ADean *Be Home* (NY) 125: She was nobody's fool; she could put two and two together. TW 142: Fool(14).

N95 A **Nod** is as good as a wink to a blind horse (*varied*)

1906 JCLincoln *Mr. Pratt* (NY) 75: They say a nod's as good as a wink to a blind horse. **1920** AChristie *Mysterious Affair* (NY) 147: A wink is as good as a nod. **1921** APHerbert *House* (NY) 108: A nod's as good as a wink, they say. **1927** EPhillpotts

Jury (NY) 141: And a nod's as good as a wink to a blind horse. **1931** HMSmith *Waverdale Fire* (L) 36: I only want a wink, and I am not a blind horse. **1931** BGraeme *Murder* (P) 147: The English have a saying—a nod is as good as a smile to a dumb horse. **1936** JDosPassos *Big Money* (NY) 365: You know the one about a nod's as good as a wink to a blind mule. **1948** MColes *Among* (NY) 179: A wink's as good's a nod to a blind 'orse. **1951** CHare *English* (L) 27: A nod's as good as a wink. **1956** MInnes *Appleby* (L) 143: To a policeman, a wink . . . ought to be as good as a nod, any day. **1965** MFrayn *Tin* (B) 144: A nod's as good as a wink. **1965** AGilbert *Voice* (NY) 79: A nod's as good as a wink to a blind horse. **1969** JMasters *Casanova* (L) 55: To Casanova a nod was as good as a wink. **1971** BCraig *September* (NY) 8: He nodded and winked, but for all the effort, one was as good as the other. **1977** VCanning *Doomsday* (NY) 75: For them a nod was as good as a wink. EAP N84. Cf. Brunvand 154: Wink(2).

N96 Noli-me-tangere

1931 APryde *Emerald* (NY) 68: His little Louis was strictly noli-me-tangere. *Oxford* 575.

N97 As clear as Noonday (noontide)

1919 JSFletcher *Middle Temple* (NY) 245: Clear as noontide. **1922** JSFletcher *Middle of Things* (NY) 134: As clear as noonday. Cf. As clear as Day, Daylight *above*.

N98 As cool as the North Pole

1922 JSFletcher *Ravensdene* (NY) 177: As cool as the North Pole. Clark *Similes* 208: Cold.

N99 As plain (clear) as the Nose on one's face (varied)

1905 GDEldridge *Millbank Case* (NY) 196: As plain as the nose on your face. **1924** IOstrander *Annihilations* (NY) 45: As plain as the nose on your face. **1929** WScott *Mask* (P) 218: Plain as my nose. **1930** WLewis *Apes* (NY 1932) 371: It's as plain as the nose on your face. **1930** HCMcNeile *Tiny* (NY) 193: As clear as the nose on your face. **1938** AGilbert *Treason* (L) 115: As clear as the

nose on your face. **1938** RAJWalling *Grimy Glove* (NY) 273: Plain as my nose. **1939** HFootner *Murder That* (L) 223: This case is as plain as the nose before your face. **1940** PATaylor *Deadly* (NY) 46: It's clearer than the nose on your face. **1946** VSiller *One Alone* (NY) 189: It's as plain as the nose on your face. **1950** SPalmer *Monkey* (NY) 56: It's as plain as the nose on your face. **1957** *NYTimes* 3/24 2E: The law is as plain as the nose on your—my face. **1957** *Time* 4/22 67: Plain as nose above water. **1958** ESGardner *Foot-loose* (NY) 94: As obvious as the nose on your face. **1959** MProcter *Killer* (NY) 32: There's one thing that stands out like the nose on your face. **1960** JSymon *Progress* (L) 236: It's as plain as the nose on King Solomon's face. **1961** LPayne *The Nose on My Face* (NY). **1969** GBagby *Honest* (NY) 76: It's as plain as the nose on your face. **1975** JLangton *Dark* (NY) 95: It was plain as the nose on his face. EAP N91; Brunvand 100(1).

N100 As sure as you have a Nose on your face

1939 IOellrichs *Man Who* (NY) 5: As sure as you've got a nose on your face. Wilstach 561: I . . . my.

N101 He that has a great Nose etc.

1945 RLHine *Confessions* (L) 137: "He that hath a great nose," saith the proverb, "thinks everybody is speaking of it." *Oxford* 334: Great nose.

N102 To cut off one's Nose to spite one's face (varied)

1928 TCobb *Who Opened* (L) 127: He cut off his nose to spite his face. **1937** AEFielding *Mystery* (NY) 120: She was the type to cut off her nose *con brio* to spite her face. **1938** KMKnight *Acts* (NY) 28: Like cutting off all your noses to spite my face. **1946** GBellairs *Death in the Night* (NY) 72: Cutting off her nose to spite her face. **1950** ECrispin *Sudden* (NY DBC) 89: She's perfectly capable of cutting off her nose to spite her face. **1956** *Punch* 5/23 629: But Socialists are unlikely to cut off their noses to spite Mr. Shinwell's face. **1959** *BangorDN* 11/19 7: The restrictions . . . cut off the

Icelander's nose to spite his face. **1960** HLGold *Bodyguard* (NY) 27: I wonder whether cutting off my nose wouldn't, in the long run, be beneficial for my face. **1964** TDubois *Shannon* (NY DBC) 72: We cut off our own noses when we kicked out England. **1973** AGilbert *Nice* (NY) 149: You're cutting off your nose to spite your face. **1976** MGilbert *Night* (NY) 85: They are cutting off their noses to spite their scholastic faces. EAP N95.

N103 To hold (keep) one's **Nose** to the grindstone (*varied*)

1903 EChilders *Riddle* (NY 1940) 207: I was holding his nose to a very cruel grindstone. **1928** EO'Neill *Strange* (NY) 166: You'll have to get your nose on the grindstone. **1932** JHWallis *Capital* (NY) 251: He's holding their noses to the grindstone. **1937** PStong *Buckskin* (NY) 339: She keeps his nose to the grindstone. **1941** RAldington *Life* (NY) 320: The next three years were pretty much nose-to-the-grindstone. **1941** AAFair *Double* (NY) 65: His nose had worn a groove in the grindstone. **1955** PWentworth *Gazebo* (L 1965) 226: Her nose very firmly held to the grindstone. **1957** *BangorDN* 4/1 21: Keep your nose on the grindstone. **1967** JDetre *Happy* (NY) 25: I can lift my nose from the grindstone. **1970** CArmstrong *Protege* (NY DBC) 21: I'm doing business at the old grindstone. **1970** JAGraham *Aldeburg* (B) 11: "Keep your nose to the ground." "Grindstone." "Excuse me." . . . "Nose to the grindstone. Ear to the ground." **1976** RBDominic *Murder* (NY) 55: Keep your nose to the grindstone. EAP N96; TW 264(5).

N104 To keep one's **Nose** clean

1938 LRGribble *Tragedy* (L) 199: Takes me all my time to keep my nose clean. **1940** ECameron *Malice* (NY) 144: Long's we keep our noses clean. **1952** FKane *Bare* (NY 1960) 117: Keep your nose clean. **1958** MProcter *Three* (NY) 28: We'll keep our noses clean. **1963** ITRoss *Man Who Would* (NY DBC) 140: Just keep your nose clean. **1969** CBush *Deadly* (NY) 28: "His nose is clean?" "Clean as they come." **1971** KLaumer *Deadfall* (NY) 65: Keep the nose clean.

Berrey 105.4, 144.2 [*etc. see Index, s.v. Keep one's*]; Partridge 450: Keep your.

N105 To lead (be led) by the **Nose**

1921 P&MThorne *Sheridan* (NY) 278: Leading men . . . around by the nose. **1933** QPatrick *S.S. Murder* (NY) 125: She leads Mrs. Clapp by the nose. **1945** LGay *Unspeakables* (NY) 112: He led the Emperor by the nose. **1955** BCarey *Fatal* (NY) 81: Eloise led her elders around by the nose. **1956** PMiller *Raven* (NY) 101: Led him by the nose. **1961** RAHeinlein *6XH* (NY) 57: He led you around by the nose. **1964** NFreeling *Because* (NY 1965) 171: His cockiness led him by the nose. **1974** HCarmichael *Most* (NY) 93: I don't like being led by the nose. EAP N97.

N106 To look down one's **Nose** at someone

1940 GStockwell *Candy* (NY) 11: He looks down his nose at me. **1950** EQueen *Double* (B) 71: To look down their noses at me. **1956** FCauldwell *Firewalkers* (L) 59: They . . . look down their noses at her. **1970** FDorn *Forbidden* (NY) 78: To look down their noses at him. Partridge 493: Look.

N107 To pay through the **Nose** (*varied*)

1911 JLondon *Letters* ed KHendricks (NY 1965) 350: I have paid through the nose. **1922** JJoyce *Ulysses* (NY 1934) 624: Poor people that paid through the nose always. **1924** HCBailey *Mr. Fortune's Practice* (NY) 123: Pay through the nose for it. **1930** WLewis *Apes* (NY 1932) 242: He pays through the nose. **1936** HReilly *Mr. Smith's* (NY) 217: I hope you didn't pay through the nose. **1949** JSymons *Bland* (L) 23: Pay through the nose. **1954** GFowler *Minutes* (NY) 230: The government made him pay through the nose. **1957** JBrooks *Water* (L) 158: You're charging him through the nose. **1960** KO'Farrell *I Made* (NY) 78: Do they pay? Right through the nose. **1964** JJMarric *Gideon's Lot* (NY) 36: He would make old Adam pay through the nose. **1971** NMarsh *When* (B) 105: We've paid him through the neck. **1977** CAlverson *Not Sleeping* (B) 13: Fred . . . paid through the nose. Cf. To pay through the Teeth *below*.

N108 To poke one's **Nose** in

1923 JSFletcher *Copper* (NY) 65: Poking my nose into other people's affairs. TW 264(11): Stick.

N109 To put someone's **Nose** out of joint (*varied*)

1919 LMerrick *Chair* (L) 299: The nose of our brave Silvestre is out of joint. **1920** JSFletcher *Dead Men's* (NY) 152: I was to put his nose out [*take his place*]. **1920** AJRees *Hand in the Dark* (NY 1929) 139: She'd put her nose out of joint, as the saying is. **1922** JJoyce *Ulysses* (NY 1934) 343: As per usual somebody's nose was out of joint. **1932** HCBailey *Case* (NY) 11: That put the Evanly one's nose out of joint. **1941** DBHughes *Bamboo* (NY) 73: And perhaps her nose was out of joint. **1948** JTey *Franchise* (NY 1955) 68: Her nose had been put out of joint. **1953** OAtkinson *Golden* (I) 67: Somebody's nose will be out of joint. **1957** VWMason *Gracious* (NY) 53: Susan's pretty little nose is getting out of joint. **1958** PDWestbrook *Biography* (NY) 62: A first child . . . when a second child is born is described as . . . "having his nose broke." **1960** BKendrick *Aluminum* (NY DBC) 40: My nose has been out of joint [*made errors*]. **1962** HWaugh *Late* (NY) 70: Her nose would be out of joint. **1970** AEHotchner *Treasure* (NY) 47: It didn't put Arnold's nose out of joint [*frighten, make suspicious*]. **1977** HDolson *Beauty* (P) 62: Her nose is out of joint. EAP N99.

N110 To rub someone's **Nose** in it

1955 GBagby *Dirty* (NY) 175: You don't have to rub my nose in it. **1956** BWAldiss *Saliva* (L) 59: They won't believe anything till you rub their noses in it. **1970** AHerbert *A.P.H.* (L) 208: I wish to rub the nation's nose in it.

N111 To see no farther than one's **Nose** (*varied*)

1929 JHawk *It Was Locked* (NY) 150: The jury saw only as far as their noses. **1930** EMChannon *Chimney* (B) 220: The police don't always see farther than their noses. **1936** LBruce *Case* (L) 240: [He] sees no farther than his nose. **1941** CBClason *Green*

Shiver (NY) 194: Cops too stupid to look beyond their noses. **1949** RFoley *Girl* (NY) 105: [They] don't see beyond their noses. **1952** HTreece *Dark* (L) 23: You see no further than your nose. **1960** JJMarric *Gideon's Risk* (NY) 52: The only one who can see further than his nose. **1974** WBridges *Gathering* (NY) 107: [He] could not see beyond his nose. TW 264(7); *Oxford* 709: See. Cf. Not to see the End, Inch *above*.

N112 To thumb one's **Nose**

1962 ABurgess *Wanting* (L) 133: A new life was preparing to thumb its nose—in the gesture once known as "fat bacon." **1971** PTabor *Pauline's* (Louisville) 24: Thumbing my nose at the . . . ethics of my elders. **1973** JBrooks *Go-Go* (NY) 80: To thumb one's nose at the whole world. DA Thumb *v.* 2; NED Suppl. Thumb *v.* 5; Berrey 346.5.

N113 A wax **Nose**

1958 *Time* 9/1 4: The Bible, to the [Jehovah's] Witnesses, is a wax nose which may be twisted according to their interpretation. EAP N94.

N114 **Nosey Parker** (*varied*)

1915 PGWodehouse *Something Fresh* (L 1935) 132: Nosey Parker. **1924** WBMFerguson *Black* (NY) 276: Mr. Nosey Parker. **1931** LRGribble *Grand* (L) 16: You and your damned nosey-parkering. **1936** LBruce *Case* (L) 164: There have been Parkers less sane and more sinister than the proverbial Nosey. **1939** VWilliams *Fox Prowls* (B) 177: This Nosey Parker, as the English say. **1945** JSymons *Immaterial* (L 1954) 138: You're Mr. Nosey Parker. **1954** MHastings *Cork* (NY) 181: You're a Nosy Parker. **1963** LEgan *Run* (NY DBC) 11: Damn little nosy-parker. **1968** JBell *Death* (P) 67: The bloody young nosey parker. **1970** PDickinson *Sinful* (NY) 70: Too Nosey Parkerish an occupation. **1975** HCarvic *Odds on* (NY) 35: Nosey lot of Parkers. NED Suppl. Nosey 3b.

N115 As easy as **Nothing**

1931 HCBailey *Fortune Explains* (NY) 127: Get away with murder as easy as nothing. TW 265(1).

N116 As near as **Nothing**

1928 RAJWalling *That Dinner* (NY) 169: As near as nothing. **1935** CStJSprigg *Perfect* (NY) 111: As near as nothing. **1937** NBlake *There's Trouble* (L) 283: He as near as nothing got past the constable. **1960** JBell *Fall* (NY) 28: He as near as nothing went over. Cf. Matter *above*; Odds *below*.

N117 Believe **Nothing** that you hear *etc.* (*varied*)

1933 REssex *Slade* (NY) 141: It's a good plan to believe half you see and nothing you hear. **1941** Lord Berners *Romance of a Nose* (L) 64: Theodotos always used to say we should believe nothing of what we're told and only half of what we see. *Oxford* 43: Believe.

N118 Blessed are they that expect **Nothing** *etc.* (*varied*)

c1923 ACrowley *Confessions* ed JSymonds (L 1969) 249: Blessed are they that expect nothing; for they shall not be disappointed. **1938** ECRLorac *Slippery* (L) 36: Blessed is he that expects nothing. A sound adage. **1958** LBachmann *Lorelei* (NY) 100: I know enough not to expect anything from anyone. That way I'm never disappointed. **1959** ECooper *Seed* (NY) 43: He who expects little is rarely disappointed. **1967** JBrunner *Quicksand* (NY) 124: Blessed are they who expect the worst, for they shall get it! EAP N104. Cf. Brunvand 101(2).

N119 Do **Nothing** hastily but catching of fleas

1969 BLehane *Compleat* (L) 25: Do nothing hastily but catching of fleas. *Oxford* 580.

N120 Here goes **Nothing**

1932 MCJohnson *Damning* (NY) 6: Here goes nothing. **1941** JPhilips *Odds on* (NY) 196: Well, here goes nothing. **1952** FVWMason *Himalayan* (NY 1953) 76: Here goes nothing. **1959** AMStein *Never* (NY) 112: Here goes nothing. **1971** PDennis *Paradise* (NY) 319: Here goes nothin'. **1976** CLarson *Muir's* (NY) 119: Here goes nothing.

N121 **Nothing** for nothing (*varied*)

1927 GDilnot *Lazy* (B) 95: Nowt for nowt is my motto. **1937** ECRLorac *These Names* (L) 168: Nothing for nothing's a good motto. **1940** JJConnington *Four Defences* (B) 128: Nothing for nothing, and damned little for three pence. **1959** TWalsh *Dangerous* (B DBC) 118: Nothing for nothing . . . The old doorman's motto. **1973** JPorter *It's Murder* (NY) 109: You get nothing for nothing in this world. **1981** NFreeling *Arlette* (NY) 32: Nothing for nothing and not much for sixpence. *Oxford* 579.

N122 **Nothing** is impossible (*varied*)

1928 WSMasterman *2 LO* (L) 79: There is no such thing as impossible. **1936** LWMeynell *On the Night* (NY) 72: All things are possible. **1937** DAllan *Brandon* (L) 128: Nothing is impossible. **1940** CRawson *Headless* (NY) 4: Nothing is impossible. **1945** EPhillpotts *They Were Seven* (NY) 27: Nothing's impossible. **1961** SBlanc *Green* (NY DBC) 154: Nothing is impossible. **1961** MKelly *Spoilt* (L) 154: Everything is possible. **1965** WRBurkett *Sleeping* (NY) 220: Nothing is impossible. *Oxford* 580. Cf. Anything is possible *above*.

N123 **Nothing** is so bad but that it might be worse (*varied*)

1917 JCLincoln *Extricating* (NY) 33: Nothin's so bad but what it might be wuss. **1948** PCheyney *Dance* (NY DBC) 58: Nothing is never as bad as it looks. *Oxford* 580–1.

N124 **Nothing** is sure in this world (*varied*)

1928 JJConnington *Tragedy* (B) 240: Nothing's sure in this world. **1975** AMancini *Minnie* (NY) 73: Nothing's certain in this life. Cf. Whiting N154; *Oxford* 580.

N125 **Nothing** succeeds (fails) like success (*varied*)

1928 CJDaly *Man* (NY) 12: Nothing succeeds like success. **1936** KConibear *North Land* (L) 113: Among foxes, as elsewhere, nothing succeeds like success. **1943** AAbbott *Shudders* (NY) 82: A banal moral, nothing succeeds like success. **1947** AGilbert *Death in* (L) 68: Nothing succeeds like looking successful. **1950** ERPunshon *So Many* (NY) 13: Nothing fails like success, someone has said. **1957** *NYTimes* 10/13 3E: Nothing succeeds like success. **1960** DHayles *Comedy* (L) 217: Nothing fails like failure. **1962** ESGardner *Ice-cold* (NY DBC) 36: Nothing succeeds like success. **1963** EMcBain *Ten* (NY) 110: Nothing succeeds like success, that's how the saying goes. **1970** MMcGrady *Stranger* (NY) 118: Nothing succeeds like excess. **1970** SO'Toole *Confessions* (Minneapolis) 46: The guiding principle that nothing fails like success. TW 359: Success(1); Brunvand 136: Success; *Oxford* 581. Cf. Success *below*.

N126 **Nothing** venture, nothing have (*varied*)

1923 JSFletcher *Lost Mr. L* (NY) 260: Nothing venture, nothing have. **1928** DHLawrence *Lady* ("Allemagne") 221: Nothing venture, nothing win. **1932** TSmith *Topper Takes* (NY) 149: Nothing ventured nothing gained. **1936** LWMeynell *On the Night* (NY) 20: Risk nothing, win nothing. **1938** A Christie *Death on the Nile* (NY) 318: Nothing venture, nothing have. **1954** HClement *Mission* (NY) 123: Nothing venture, nothing gain. **1957** THWhite *Master* (L) 251: Nothing venture, nothing win. **1964** PKinsley *Three* (L) 100: If you never take a risk, you never win anything. **1966** DGilman *Unexpected* (NY) 11: Nothing ventured, nothing gained. **1966** HTracy *Men* (L) 141: Nothing venture, nothing win. **1970** RDAltick *Victorian* (NY) 165: Nothing ventured, nothing gained. **1970** OFriedrich *Decline* (NY) 291: Nothing venture, nothing lost. EAP N113; TW 265 (11,13); Brunvand 101(3).

N127 **Nothing** will come of nothing (*varied*)

1952 MInnes *One-Man* (NY) 44: Nothing will come of nothing. **1958** NMonkman *From Queensland* (NY) 92: *Ex nihilo nihil fit*—nothing can come out of nothing. **1961** ESeeman *In the Arms* (NY) 53: My mother always said, "What comes out a' nothin' will go back into it again." EAP N115; TW 265(5).

N128 Say **Nothing** and saw wood

1937 JMWalsh *White Mask* (L) 13: His motto . . . "Say nothing and saw wood."

N129 Thank you for **Nothing** (*varied*)

1928 HWade *Missing* (NY) 196: Thank you for—twice nothing. **1933** ECRLorac *Case* (L) 167: Thank you for nothing. **1937** HCBailey *Clunk's* (L) 308: A sort of thank you for nothing. **1940** JJFarjeon *Friday* (I) 103: Thank you for nothing. **1946** GBellairs *Death in the Night* (NY) 171: Thank you for nothing. **1952** JDCarr *Nine Wrong* (NY) 317: Thanks for nothing. **1956** GGreene *Quiet* (NY) 4: Thank him for nothing. **1963** EVCunningham *Alice* (L 1965) 89: Thanks for nothing. **1967** LPDavies *Artificial* (NY) 135: Thanks for nothing. **1974** HCarmichael *Most* (NY) 145: Thanks for nothing. **1977** DWilliams *Treasure* (NY) 127: Thank you for nothing. EAP N116.

N130 There is **Nothing** (nowt) as queer as folks (*varied*)

1936 LWMeynell *On the Night* (NY) 230: The old, old truth that queer though nature may be in parts, there's "nowt as queer as folk." **1970** DClark *Deadly* (NY) 82: There's nowt as queer as fowk. **1971** EMannin *Young* (L) 178: The North Country saying applies—"There's nowt so strange as folks." **1976** JPorter *Package* (NY) 127: There was nothing so queer as folks. **1979** JGash *Grail* (NY) 76: There's nowt as odd as folk. TW 141: Folks(1).

N131 There is **Nothing** like trying

1929 JBPriestley *Good* (NY) 406: There's nothing like trying. **1936** HBellamann *Gray Man* (NY) 153: There's nothing like trying. **1939** DHume *Make Way* (L) 79: There's nothing like trying. TW 265(7). Cf. Harm *above*.

N132 There is **Nothing** new under the sun

1906 HNewbolt *Old Country* (L) 92: There is nothing new under the moon. **1922** JJoyce *Ulysses* (NY 1934) 370: Nothing new under the sun. **1928** CKingston *Guilty* (L) 28: There's nothing new under the sun. **1930** WWoodrow *Moonhill* (NY) 179: There is nothing new under the sun. **1936** HWPonder *Cambodian* (L) 267: The truth of the aphorism that there is nothing new under the sun. **1954** CBEaton *Glass* (NY)

133: There is nothing new under the sun. **1959** JJMarric *Gideon's Staff* (NY) 118: There's nothing new under the sun. **1964** LCPowell *Little* (NY) 121: There is nothing new under the sun. EAP T57: Thing; *Oxford* 580: Nothing.

N133 To be like **Nothing** on earth (*varied*) **1926** JArnold *Murder!* (L) 207: I feel like nothing on earth. **1932** HCBailey *Case* (NY) 11: Looking like nothing on earth. **1936** RAJWalling *Crimson Slippers* (L) 77: The girl looked like nothing on earth. **1942** HReilly *Name Your Poison* (NY) 32: Feeling . . . like "nothing on earth." **1945** AT QuillerCouch *Memories* (Cambridge, Eng.) 80: [His] lectures were like nothing on earth, as the saying is. **1948** PCheyney *Dance* (NY DBC) 53: It tasted like nothing on earth. **1961** RFoley *It's Murder* (NY DBC) 148: You, looking like nothing on earth. **1966** WTrevor *Love* (L) 256: It tastes like nothing on earth. Partridge 572.

N134 To be **Nothing** to write home about **1928** GDHCole *Man* (NY) 181: He was . . . bleeding a bit, but nothing to write home about. **1936** LThayer *Dead End* (NY) 34: Nothing to write home about. **1949** NMarsh *Wreath* (NY) 146: Nothing to write home about. **1958** BNichols *Rich* (NY) 88: Nothing to write home about. **1969** RRendell *Secret* (NY) 3: It's not as if he was all that to write home about. **1972** GRDickson *Pritcher* (NY) 25: My life was nothing to write home about. Partridge 572.

N135 To know from **Nothing** **1952** FPratt *Double* (NY) 172: He just don't know from nothing. **1953** RChandler *Long* (L) 240: I got a woman who didn't know from nothing. **1962** HWaugh *Late* (NY) 14: The maid will know from nothing. **1964** DDeJong *Whirligig* (NY) 148: They don't know from nothing. Wentworth 358.

N136 To sit up and take **Notice** **1924** LSpringfield *Some Piquant* (L) 165: Even America sat up and took notice. **1933** EBBlack *Ravenelle* (NY) 132: Make you sit up and take notice. **1939** HWPriwen *Inspector* (L) 232: We'll make the world sit up and take notice. **1946** ABCunningham

Death Rides (NY) 93: People would sit up and take notice. **1949** JReach *Late* (NY) 82: Make the world sit up and take notice. **1957** BVanOrden *309 East* (NY) 25: Something will make you sit up and take notice. **1960** JJMarric *Gideon's Fire* (NY) 135: Someone is sitting up and taking notice. **1967** MHolroyd *Strachey* (L) 1.212: Caused the inhabitants of Sodom to sit up and take note. **1970** MEChaber *Green* (NY) 32: I was beginning to sit up and take notice. Partridge 772: Sit up.

N137 **Now** or never **1903** EChilders *Riddle* (NY 1940) 336: It's now or never. **1919** JBCabell *Letters* ed PColum (NY 1962) 122: Now or never. **1931** ACEdington *Monk's Hood* (NY) 181: Now or never. **1938** EHeath *Death Takes* (NY) 31: It was now or never. **1941** JJConnington *Twenty-one* (B) 290: It was now or never. **1949** GHHall *End* (NY) 211: It's now or never. **1951** MColes *Now or Never* (NY). **1958** HKoningsberger *Affair* (NY) 126: One of those now or never moments. **1970** MBates *Jungle* (NY) 48: It was now or never. **1975** DEWestlake *Two* (NY) 114: It's now or never. EAP N118; TW 266; Brunvand 101.

N138 To have one's **Number** **1930** EQueen *French* (NY) 104: Marchbanks had her number. **1937** RStout *Red Box* (L) 206: We've got your number. **1964** DDeJong *Whirligig* (NY) 85: I got his number, the big phony. Wentworth 359.

N139 To have one's **Number** come up **1928** JArnold *Surrey* (L) 98: This . . . is where my number is up. **1949** JLane *Murder Spoils* (NY) 106: Why am I still alive? When's my number coming up? **1968** HHarrison *Deathworld* (NY) 13: When your numbers came up it was certain death. **1969** JBrunner *Jagged* (NY) 160: If your number comes up then your number comes up. **1974** SAGrau *Wind* (NY) 171: When your number's up, it doesn't matter where you are. **1978** BKnox *Witchrock* (NY) 47: If your number comes up—. Partridge 574.

N140 To look after **Number** one (*varied*)

1910 JCLincoln *Depot Master* (NY) 6: Look out for number one. **1922** JJoyce *Ulysses* (NY 1934) 150: All for number one. **1924** LSpringfield *Some* (L) 271: Look after Number One. **1934** HFootner *Murder* (NY) 126: Takes damned good care of number one. **1946** JTShaw *Hard-Boiled* (NY) 30: Looked out for number one. **1952** AWUpfield *Venom* (NY) 82: She's out for Number One. **1957** THWhite *Master* (L) 150: [He] knew how to look after number one. **1961** NBlake *Worm* (L) 33: He was out for Number One every time. **1964** FLockridge *Quest* (P) 25: Comes a time, like they say, a man's got to think of number one. **1970** WMasterson *Death* (NY) 214: We all look out for number one. EAP N120.

N141 To lose the **Number** of one's mess (*varied*)

1933 GBegbie *Sudden* (L) 131: Jake's lost his number. **1933** GCollins *Dead Walk* (L) 208: Here's where that Johnny lost the number of his mess. EAP N121.

N142 As brown as a **Nut**; Nut-brown

1910 EPhillpotts *Tales* (NY) 293: Nut-brown. **1932** MPlum *Murder* (L) 68: The nut-brown type. **1937** GGoodwin *White Farm* (L) 218: His face was brown as a nut. **1943** AAbbot *Shudders* (NY) 198: A nut-brown gnome. **1952** MMurray *Doctor* (NY DBC) 4: His skin was as brown as a nut. **1957** *New Yorker* 2/16 116: His nut-brown whiskey. **1962** JLindsay *Fanfrolico* (L) 193: Brown as a nut, honest as the day. **1968** KRoberts *Pavane* (NY) 84: Brown as a nut. **1970** ELathen *Pick* (NY) 11: Nut-brown pate. **1972** SCloete *Victorian* (L) 85: Nut-brown men. **1981** JGodden *In Her* (NY) 55: He . . . was soon as brown as a nut. EAP N127; TW 266(1); Brunvand 101(1); Taylor *Western Folklore* 17(1958) 17(1).

N143 As sound (healthy) as a **Nut** (*varied*)

1925 JGBrandon *Cork* (L) 276: A clever idea . . . sound as nuts. **1929** FMPettee *Palgrave* (NY) 37: Appears sound as a hazelnut. **1930** KCStrahan *Death* (NY) 152: Place as sound as a nut. **1939** HMiller *Capricorn* (NY 1961) 156: Healthy as a nut. **1954**

EMarriner *Kennebec* (Waterville, Me.) 238: Sound as a nut. **1970** JVizzard *See* (NY) 155: Sound as a nut. **1973** HDolson *Dying* (P) 31: She might have been sound as a nut [*sane*]. EAP N124; Brunvand 101(2).

N144 As sweet as a **Nut** (*varied*)

1927 CRogers *Colonel Bob* (NY) 27: Sweet as nuts. **1932** CBush *Unfortunate* (L) 268: The place smelt as sweet as a nut. **1936** JVTurner *Below the Clock* (L) 202: It was all as sweet as a nut. **1940** CFGregg *Fatal Error* (L) 141: As sweet as a nut. **1951** ECrispin *Long* (L 1958) 10: Sweet as a nut, that wood is. **1966** MMcShane *Night's* (NY) 131: Running as sweet as a nut [*a machine*]. **1975** JFraser *Wreath* (NY) 47: Sweet as a nut [*of a situation*]. TW 266(7); Taylor *Western Folklore* 17(1958) 17(2); *Oxford* 793: Sweet.

N145 A hard (*etc.*) **Nut** to crack (*varied*)

1913 JSFletcher *Secret* (L 1918) 196: She's going to be a difficult nut to crack. **1927** HHBashford *Behind* (NY) 287: The house . . . was going to prove a hard nut to crack. **1928** AGilbert *Mrs. Davenport* (NY) 285: You'll find that a tough nut to crack. **1930** WLewis *Apes* (NY 1932) 169: This hard nut to crack. **1936** LRGribble *Riley* (L) 30: We got a mighty tough nut to crack. **1944** HReilly *Opening Door* (NY) 163: That's a pretty tough nut to crack. **1951** FCrane *Murder in* (NY) 113: It will be a tough nut to crack. **1960** COliver *Unearthly* (NY) 26: It would have been a tough nut to crack. **1968** LPDavies *Grave* (NY) 146: She'll be a hard nut to crack. **1970** RRendell *Best Man* (NY) 89: [He] was an easier nut to crack. EAP N126.

N146 In a **Nutshell**

1921 JSFletcher *Orange-Yellow* (NY) 109: To put it in a nutshell. **1922** JJoyce *Ulysses* (NY 1934) 33: Put the matter into a nutshell. **1931** HCBailey *Fortune Speaking* (NY) 177: You have it in a nutshell. **1936** EPOppenheim *Advice* (B) 41: Puts the case in a nutshell. **1940** RLGoldman *Snatch* (NY) 16: There it is in a nutshell. **1948** PCheyney *Dance* (NY DBC) 137: To put this whole thing in a nutshell. **1951** MGilbert *Death Has* (NY) 216: That's the matter in a nutshell. **1957** WMorris *Love* (NY) 45: The new show business in a nutshell. **1961** FLeiber *Silver* (NY) 120: Sexuality in a nutshell. **1964** JAiken *Silence* (NY) 27: You can put it in a nutshell. **1973** APrice *Colonel* (NY) 51: The whole thing in a nutshell. **1975** PMoyes *Black* (NY) 93: To put it in a nutshell. EAP N131.

O

O1 As sound as an **Oak**

1933 BPerowne *Return* (NY) 277: Marlowe was as sound as oak. Wilstach 375.

O2 As strong as an **Oak**

1927 RKing *Mystery* (NY) 105: He was . . . strong as an oak. Lean II ii 878: Oak.

O3 As sturdy (steady) as an **Oak**

1935 DMagarshack *Death* (NY) 340: As sturdy as an oak. **1937** DQBurleigh *Kristiana* (NY) 276: His voice was . . . steady as an oak. EAP O1.

O4 Big **Oaks** from little acorns grow (*varied*)

1920 BEStevenson *Gloved Hand* (NY) 337: Tall oaks from little acorns grow. **1932** HBurnham *Telltale* (NY) 199: What big oaks grow from tiny acorns! **1943** NDavis *Sally's* (NY) 87: Big oaks from little acorns. **1948** HAustin *Drink* (NY) 102: The adage . . . great oaks from little acorns grow. **1951** ESGardner *Fiery* (NY) 31: Big oaks grow from tiny acorns. **1956** RMacdonald *Barbarous* (NY) 149: Great oaks from little acorns grow. **1962** DTaylor *Blood* (NY) 36: Great oaks from little acorns grow. **1964** HMHyde *Norman* (L) 128: "Little acorns into great oaks grow." **1973** AGilbert *Nice* (NY) 87: Big oaks from little acorns grow. **1974** BWAldiss *Eighty* (NY) 35: Big blokes from little acorns grow. **1977** VCanning *Doomsday* (NY) 72: Great oaks from little acorns grow was his motto. TW 268(1); Brunvand 1: Acorn(2). Cf. *Oxford* 584. Cf. Events *above*.

O5 To put in one's **Oar** (*varied*)

1904 JCLincoln *Cap'n Eri* (NY) 72: I shan't put my oar in. **1924** CWells *Furthest* (P) 178: Get in my oar first. **1928** JJConnington *Mystery* (B) 110: You're not to go putting in your oar when it's not wanted; 152. **1932** JSFletcher *Four Degrees* (L) 37: Did Paley shove his oar in here? **1936** MBurton *Where Is* (L) 135: Mrs. Prentice put her oar in and upset the apple-cart. **1938** EHeath *Death Takes* (NY) 145: Caxton had to put in his ironical oar. **1940** JJConnington *Four Defences* (B) 92: If I shove my oar in. **1940** NMorland *Gun* (L) 204: Just let me get my oar in first. **1948** MColes *Among* (NY) 57: They keep on sticking their oar in. **1952** JMFox *Shroud* (B) 14: You stuck in your oar. **1958** HMasur *Murder* (NY 1959) 50: Lord stuck his oar in, trying to smooth Herbert's ruffled feathers. **1961** JSStrange *Eye* (NY) 191: Just stick in our oar. **1963** RLPike *Mute* (NY DBC) 37: Chalmers has a chance to get his oar in and muddy up the waters. **1970** DJOlivy *Never* (NY) 167: He put his oar in. **1973** WMasterson *Undertaker* (NY) 164: You keep puttin' your oar in where it don't belong and somebody's gonna shove it down your throat. **1977** JThomson *Death* (NY) 68: Shoving his oar in. EAP O4; TW 268(3); Brunvand 102.

O6 To rest on one's **Oars**

c1923 ACrowley *Confessions* ed JSymonds (L 1969) 403: To rest on my oars. **1935** FWCrofts *Crime* (L) 245: Inclined to rest on his oars. **1952** HReilly *Velvet* (NY) 118: She . . . had been inclined to rest on her oars. **1957** LHanson *Verlaine* (NY) 17: Ready to rest on his oars. **1968** MHolroyd *Strachey* (L) 2.687: Rest on his oars. EAP O3: Lie. Cf. Laurels *above*.

O7 To be off one's **Oats**

1930 HCMcNeile *Tiny* (NY) 58: Mary seems a bit off her oats. **1952** STruss *Death* (NY) 112: The master's been off his oats lately. Partridge 269: Feed.

O8 To feel one's **Oats**

1906 JCLincoln *Mr. Pratt* (NY) 12: Begun to feel her oats. **1929** GSeldes *You Can't* (NY) 148: Certainly the country is feeling its nationalistic oats. **1936** CFGregg *Henry* (L) 263: Ellis was feeling his oats. **1947** PMcGerr *Pick* (NY) 142: Your boss seems to be feeling his oats. **1953** DGarnett *Golden* (L) 130: To use a forgotten idiom, he was feeling his oats. **1959** DAngus *Ivy* (I) 19: Your father . . . is feeling his oats this morning. **1962** AAFair *Try* (NY) 36: I got feeling my oats [*sexually excited*]. **1967** GFWeston *Boston* (B) 216: The Quakers began to feel their oats. **1974** PGWodehouse *Cat-Nappers* (NY) 168: He was feeling his oats. TW 268(1).

O9 To know one's **Oats**

1933 RJCasey *Hot Ice* (I) 78: You boys know your oats. Berrey 257.8; Wentworth 310: Know.

O10 To sow one's wild **Oats** (*varied*)

1910 EPhillpotts *Tales* (NY) 147: Sown his wild oats. **1914** MAdams *In the Footsteps* (L) 86: Sowing his wild oats. **1922** JJoyce *Ulysses* (NY 1934) 589: Just a few wild oats. **1924** WBMFerguson *Black* (NY) 130: Sown a fine crop of wild oats. **1932** RKing *Murder* (L) 256: [He] sowed one little wild oat. **1933** FDell *Homecoming* (NY) 207: Sowing his intellectual wild oats. **1934** WSutherland *Death Rides* (L) 145: The so-called wild oats had failed to sprout. **1936** DLSayers *Gaudy* (NY) 270: Sown her wild oats in public. **1940** AMStein *Sun* (NY) 154: I'm the wild-oat boy, the wastrel. **1957** LHanson *Verlaine* (NY) 120: Coppée had sown his wild oats at high speed. **1958** EPargeter *Assize* (L) 135: They had sown wild oats lavishly in those days. **1966** HJBoyle *With a Pinch* (NY) 189: Sprinkled wild oats to grow on somebody else's lawn. **1966** LLafore *Nine* (NY) 44: His wild oats have been, as it were, frostbitten. **1967** AChristie *Endless* (NY) 115: To sow their wild oats. That's your English saying, isn't it? **1974** AChurchill *Splendid* (NY) 176: To sow wild oats before marriage. **1976** CIsherwood *Christopher* (NY) 29: Seldom have wild oats been sown so prudently. **1979** RDahl *My Uncle* (NY) 7: I was impatient to sow a few bushels of wild oats in foreign fields. **1981** AMStein *Body* (NY) 19: We sowed the proverbial wild oats. EAP O6; Brunvand 102.

O11 As thick as **Oatmeal**

1957 MScherf *Judicial* (NY) 13: The traffic was thick as oatmeal. Wilstach 421. Cf. Hasty pudding *above*.

O12 He who cannot **Obey** cannot give orders

1934 CFGregg *Inspector* (L) 27: One who cannot learn to obey cannot give orders. EAP O9.

O13 To spit (piss) in the **Ocean**

1957 AAmos *Fatal* (NY) 185: They might as well spit at the ocean. **1962** MClifton *When They* (NY) 192: It'll be like pissin' in the ocean compared to the money we can promote. **1977** WMiller *Fishbait* (Englewood Cliffs, NJ) 368: What difference does it make? He's just spitting in the ocean. Cf. Partridge 635: Pissed in the sea. Cf. *Oxford* 870: Water into the sea, cast. Cf. Drop *above*.

O14 As near as makes no **Odds**

1928 ABerkeley *Silk* (NY) 171: As near as makes no odds. **1933** HCMcNeile *Bulldog . . . Strikes* (NY) 209: As near as makes no odds. **1970** DMDevine *Illegal* (NY) 127: As near to it as makes no odds. **1972** AGarve *Case* (NY) 97: Near as makes no odds. TW 269(3). Cf. Matter, As near as Nothing *above*.

O15 No **Offense** meant, none taken (*varied*)

1928 EBYoung *Murder* (P) 158: No offense being meant, none is taken. **1930** KCStrahan *Death* (NY) 15: No insult taken if none intended. **1934** JJFarjeon *Windmill* (L) 25: Where there's no harm meant there's none done. **1956** BJChute *Greenwillow* (NY) 122: "No offence, I hope" . . . "None offered, none taken." **1956** WMankowitz *Old* (B) 175: No harm meant none taken.

O16   Offense is the best defense (*varied*)

1928 EALehman *Zeppelins* (NY) 271: Offensive is the best defensive. **1933** AF Tschiffely *Ride* (NY) 239: I took the offensive, which proved to be the best defence. **1937** DQBurleigh *Kristiana* (NY) 195: The best defence is a good offence. **1949** JReach *Late* (NY) 91: A good offence is the best defence. **1958** B*Herald* 2/6 20: The old military adage that offence is the best defence. **1958** *BangorDN* 7/28 10: A good offense is the best defense. **1959** RArmour *Drug* (NY) 133: The old military axiom that for every offense there is a defense. Cf. Attack *above*.

O17   As smooth as Oil

1927 HHBashford *Behind* (NY) 201: The surface of the water was as smooth as oil. **1937** BHKendrick *Whistling* (NY) 157: The doctor goes on smooth as oil. **1944** LAG Strong *All Fall* (NY) 165: Ellis's voice was smooth as oil. **1962** HPentecost *Cannibal* (NY DBC) 97: He said, smooth as oil. **1970** MStewart *Crystal* (NY) 198: Her voice was smooth as oil. EAP O14; TW 269(1).

O18   Oil and water will not mix (*varied*)

1910 JLondon *Letters* ed KHendricks (NY 1965) 297: We cannot mix oil and water. **1933** CBush *April Fools* (L) 105: Subterfuge and Taylor Samuels were oil and water. **1934** ACampbell *Desire* (NY) 18: Oil and water will not mix. **1935** HAdams *Body* (L) 202: Oil and vinegar never really mix. **1947** JDCarr *Sleeping* (NY) 128: They're oil and water. They won't mix. **1951** ACalder-Marshall *Magic* (L) 41: They were as unmixable as oil and water, as antipathetic as dog and cat. **1954** RKLeavitt *Chip* (P) 162: For oil and water don't mix. **1960** JO'Hara *Ourselves* (NY) 371: Oil and water . . . they don't mix. **1967** AMarreco *Rebel* (L) 180: Mixed about as well as oil and water. **1972** SBirmingham *Late John* (P) 210: As surely as oil and water won't mix and cream rises to the top. **1974** MDavis *Tell Them* (NY) 14: An oil-and-water combination of shyness and impudence. EAP O16.

O19   To burn the midnight Oil

1930 MBDix *Murder* (L) 28: Burned the midnight oil. **1937** GGoodchild *Having No* (L) 296: To burn the midnight oil. **1940** JLBonney *Death by* (NY) 40: Burning the midnight oil. **1944** LLariar *Man . . . Lumpy Nose* (NY) 128: He had burned the midnight oil. **1958** MAMusmanno *Verdict* (NY) 33: To burn the midnight oil. **1959** PGraaf *Sapphire* (NY) 18: I've been burning the midnight oil. **1967** LPDavies *Lampton* (NY) 62: Burned the midnight oil. **1968** BBlack *Associate* (NY) 27: Why burn the midnight oil? **1970** JVizzard *See* (NY) 100: We used to burn the midnight oil. **1976** SWoods *My Life* (NY) 13: To burn the midnight oil. EAP O18: Consume; *Oxford* 92: Burn.

O20   To pour Oil on the troubled flames (*varied*)

1938 HAdams *Damned* (L) 34: To pour oil on troubled flames. **1938** NBlake *Beast* (NY 1958) 64: Pouring oil, as they say, on the flames. **1959** MSarton *I Knew* (NY) 109: Pouring fire on the troubled oil, so to speak. **1962** ESGardner *Blonde* (NY DBC) 58: I tried to act the part of a peace maker . . . I poured oil on the troubled flames. EAP O19; TW 269(3).

O21   To pour Oil on troubled waters (*varied*)

1903 MLPeabody *To Be Young* (B 1967) 304: Pour oil on the troubled waters. **1921** RFirbank *Princess* (Works 3, L 1929) 145: I always pour oil on troubled waters. **1927** WBFoster *From Six* (NY) 84: The doctor . . . poured oil upon the angry sea. **1927** JMWalsh *Silver* (L) 29: She was oil on the waters that he travelled. **1929** JHawk *It Was Loaded* (NY) 30: In time to pour balm on troubled waters. **1932** PMacDonald *Mystery* (NY) 127: Distributing oil upon angry waves. **1936** WSmith *Machine* (L) 46: Tried . . . to pour oil on the troubled waters. **1938** TDubois *Death Wears* (B) 124: I had poured as much oil as I possessed, and was apparently pouring it upon flames rather than troubled waters. **1940** EDean *Murder Is* (NY) 19: She would have to be the oil on the troubled waters. **1940** ARLong *Corpse* (NY) 41: To calm the troubled waters with the oil of conversation. **1951** TDubois *Foul* (NY) 72: Oil on the troubled waters, as it were. **1952** LKronenberger *Grand* (NY) 89: You go nowhere without your little jar of oil to pour on troubled waters. **1956** DWheatley *Ka* (L) 260: Compton offered to pour oil on the troubled waters. **1961** CWillock *Death* (L 1963) 73: Crayne had a small barrel of oil ready to pour on the rapidly troubling waters. **1965** ADavidson *Rork!* (NY) 102: The old proverb about "pouring oil on troubled waters." **1969** AC Greene *Personal* (NY) 87: Trying to pour oil on the troubled waters. **1970** RCowper *Twilight* (NY) 34: [He] hastened to pour alcohol on the troubled water [*a drink to avert a row*]. **1974** JPHennessy *R.L.Stevenson* (NY) 25: To pour oil upon the most troubled of waters. **1981** JBrett *Who'd Hire* (NY) 21: It was a sound like oil on the proverbial waters. Soothing, that's what it was. EAP O20; Brunvand 102(2).

O22   To strike Oil

1925 FWCrofts *Groote* (NY) 273: On his fourth call he struck oil. **1933** GDHCole *End* (L) 72: Jay . . . struck oil. **1939** AWebb *Thank You* (L) 194: Did you strike oil? **1948** GHCoxe *Hollow* (NY) 223: You struck oil. **1959** SFarrar *Snake* (NY) 125: The moment I strike oil. **1967** HTravers *Madame* (NY) 44: He struck oil at his . . . first interrogation. Partridge 581.

O23   As black as Old Nick's hat

1960 LLevine *Great* (L) 173: It was black as Old Nick's hat. EAP O23; Brunvand 103: Old Nick.

O24   As mischievous as the Old Scratch

1903 ADMcFaul *Ike Glidden* (B) 1: Mischev'ous as the old Scratch. Taylor *Prov. Comp.* 64: Proud. Cf. TW 270; *Oxford* 592; Brunvand 103: Old Scratch [*devil*].

O25   As dark as Old Tilly's pocket

1957 MPHood *In the Dark* (NY) 17: His face darker'n Old Tilly's pocket.

O26   As proud as Old Tilly

1953 MPHood *Silent* (NY) 91: He was proud as old Tilly. Cf. Old Scratch *above.*

O27   The Olive branch (*varied*)

1917 GRSims *My Life* (L) 10: I was the olive branch. **1928** GDHCole *Man* (NY) 286: I come with an olive-branch. **1931** GFowler *Great* (NY) 293: Your olive branches are made of poison-ivy. **1934** CKendrake *Clew* (NY) 47: I'm trying to hand you an olive branch. **1940** ECameron *Malice* (NY) 36: Tim . . . extended the olive branch. **1947** RHichens *Yesterday* (L) 404: The symbol of the olive branch was as nothing compared with the symbol of Mr. Chamberlain's umbrella. **1958** AMacKinnon *Summons* (NY) 173: I'm a peace envoy with an olive branch in my mouth. **1960** JSymons *Progress* (L) 74: It was an olive branch extended reluctantly. **1965** DHitchens *Bank* (NY) 153: He came offering us the olive branch, as the saying goes. **1970** JCreasey *Part* (NY) 170: "Drink?" he invited, obviously as an olive branch. **1972** DDevine *Three* (NY) 160: It was . . . an olive branch. EAP O25; TW 270.

O28   One cannot make an Omelet without breaking eggs (*varied*)

1913 JSFletcher *Secret* (L 1918) 108: You cannot make an omelet without breaking eggs. **1924** HHMunro *Square* (L 1929) 108: One cannot have an omelette without breaking eggs. **1926** BNiles *Black Haiti* (NY) 58: You could not make an omelet without breaking the eggs. **1931** APryde *Emerald* (NY) 72: Rudolph in making his omelettes broke plenty of eggs. **1931** PWynnton *Ten* (P) 207: You can make omelettes without breaking eggs, I suppose. **1937** CBClason *Blind* (NY) 242: One cannot make an omelet without breaking the eggs, as the proverb puts it. **1942** CHare *Tragedy at Law* (L 1953) 140: One can't make an omelet without breaking eggs. **1948** ESherry *Sudden* (NY) 215: "The omelet is made," he said sententiously. "We cannot conjure the eggs back into their shells." **1951** KBennett *Wink* (L) 105: Omelets, proverbially, are not made without breaking eggs. **1957** *Time* 7/8 10: It's like taking an omelet and trying to put it back in the eggshells. **1957** WGHardy *City* (NY) 108: You can't cook an omelet without burning firewood. **1958** AChristie *Ordeal* (NY DBC) 157: You can't make an omelette without breaking eggs, as the French say. **1959** RMacDonald *Galton* (NY) 65: You can't make a Hamlet without breaking egos. **1961** RJWhite *Smartest* (L) 261: But as the Frenchman said, you can't make an omelette without breaking eggs. **1968** HHarrison *Deathworld* (NY) 172: Someone a long time ago said that you cannot make an omelet without breaking eggs. **1971** RLWolff *Strange* (B) 209: You can't make an omelette without breaking eggs. **1977** CAlverson *Not Sleeping* (B) 206: Who was it that said that you can't make an omelette without breaking eggs? **1980** EXFerrars *Witness* (NY) 78: I believe you [*English*] have a saying that it is impossible to make an omelet without breaking eggs. **1981** BSuyker *Death* (NY) 92: "You can't make an omelet ..." "... without breaking a cliché." *Oxford* 594.

O29   Once is enough

1925 FWCrofts *Groote* (NY) 100: Once was enough for me. **1930** GHolt *Trail* (L) 61: Once is enough for Santa Teresa. **1954** KMKnight *High* (NY) 45: Once is enough. **1964** DCecil *Max* (L) 457: Once is enough. **1968** RStout *Father* (NY) 132: Once is enough. **1970** RRendell *Best Man* (NY) 166: Once is enough. **1973** AMStein *Finger* (NY) 34: Once was enough. Whiting O33: Once ought to suffice.

O30   It takes One to know one (*varied*)

1955 BBenson *Silver* (NY) 72: It takes one to know one. **1959** ESchiddel *Devil* (NY) 282: It takes one to tell one. **1960** RPrice *Upright Ape* (NY) 25: It takes one to know one. **1967** TWells *Dead by* (NY) 46: Isn't there an expression ... takes one to know one? **1972** KBooton *Quite* (NY) 118: It takes one to know one. **1973** JPorter *It's Murder* (NY) 134: It takes one to spot one. **1974** GWheeler *Easy* (NY) 30: Takes one to catch one, I always say.

O31   One was afraid *etc.*

1906 JCLincoln *Mr. Pratt* (NY) 275: One was afraid to say so and t'other dassent. **1928** HAsbury *Gangs* (NY) 97: One was afraid and the other dasn't. TW 270(3).

O32   There is One (easy mark, mug, fool, sucker) born every minute

1913 JCLincoln *Mr. Pratt's Patients* (NY) 330: There's an easy mark born every minute. **1931** LCharteris *Wanted* (NY) 285: It is said that there is a mug born every minute. **1941** AWebb *Suicide Club* (L) 232: They say there's a fool born every minute. **1952** AGilbert *Mr. Crook* (NY DBC) 134: Scotland Yard will tell you there's a mug born every minute. **1952** JDrummond *Naughty* (L) 149: Yet one born every minute, they say. **1955** MO'Brine *Passport* (L) 33: There's a saying about one born every minute. **1956** *New Yorker* 5/26 89: There's a sucker born every minute. **1960** AGarve *Golden* (NY DBC) 130: You're not the only sucker in the world ... One born every minute. **1969** JMasters *Casanova* (L) 25: There's one born every minute. **1974** JCreasey *As Merry* (NY) 62: There's one born every minute. Wentworth 527: Sucker 1.

O33   To be One for the book

1936 HAustin *It Couldn't* (L) 120: Well, that's one for the book. **1942** FLockridge *Death ... Aisle* (P) 49: That's one for the book. **1955** AHunter *Gently Does* (L) 20: That's one for the book. **1959** LWibberly *Quest* (NY) 87: This is one for the book. Berrey 20.4.

O34   To have One for the road

1932 WLHay *Who Cut* (L) 128: What about one for the road, then bed? **1934** JVTurner *Murder* (L) 257: Have one for the road. **1945** MColes *Green Hazard* (NY) 32: We'll have one for the road. **1948** ECrispin *Buried* (L 1958) 43: How about one for the road. **1959** SMarlowe *Blonde* (NY) 69: Orin talked him into one for the road. **1963** GMaxwell *Rocks* (NY) 50: The host must always offer one for the road. **1971** PTabor *Pauline's* (Louisville) 105: You deserve one for the road before you leave [*sex*]. **1974**

WCAnderson *Damp* (NY) 41: We'll have one for the road. Wentworth 365.

O35   To have **One** over the eight (*varied*)

1925 JGBrandon *Cork* (L) 32: She'd had one over the eight, as the saying is. **1932** GCollins *Channel* (L) 113: You've had about nine over the eight. **1934** AChristie *Three Acts* (NY) 76: The young gentleman must have had one over the eight, as the saying goes. **1947** PMcGerr *Pick* (NY) 141: When he was one over the eight. **1955** PMac-Donald *Guest* (NY) 165: He's one over the eight. **1958** NMarsh *Singing* (B) 251: I'd had one or two drinks over the eight. **1971** AGarve *Late* (NY) 83: He'd had one over the eight. Berrey 106.7; Partridge 255.

O36   To do something like **One o'clock**

1958 RMaugham *Man with Two* (NY) 64: I've heard him cursing your father like one o'clock. **1970** VCClinton-Baddeley *No Case* (NY) 178: It's going to rain like one o'clock. Berrey 20.5.

O37   As bald-headed (naked) as an **Onion**

1936 CGGivens *Jig-time* (I) 15: As bald-headed as an onion. **1944** MBramhall *Murder Solves* (NY) 135: Naked as a peeled onion. TW 270(1).

O38   To know one's **Onions**

1928 WCWilliams *Voyage* (NY) 321: The best of them do know their onions. **1932** SHPage *Resurrection* (NY) 250: Clara knows her onions. **1934** JTFarrell *Young Manhood* (NY 1935) 31: She knew her onions. **1947** AGilbert *Death in* (L) 154: He knew his onions. **1953** ECRLorac *Speak* (NY) 59: If I know my onions. **1956** WMankowitz *Old* (B) 40: There's a fellow really knows his onions. **1961** MInnes *Silence* (NY) 61: As the vulgar say, they know their onions. **1966** WTrevor *Love* (L) 68: As the saying goes, I know my onions. **1974** JFleming *How To* (NY) 110: She knows her onions. Partridge *Suppl.* 1009: Know; Wentworth 310: Know.

O39   The **Onlooker** (looker-on) sees most of the game (*varied*)

1922 JJoyce *Ulysses* (NY 1934) 365: On-lookers see most of the game. **1925** HAd-ams *By Order* (L) 61: They say the looker-on sees most of the game. **1926** FWCrofts *Cheyne* (NY) 16: The outsider sees most of the game. **1928** EHamilton *Four* (L) 303: Onlookers are generally supposed to see most of the game. **1930** HAshton *Doctor* (NY) 281: Dummy [*at bridge*] sees most of the game. **1932** AFielding *Death* (NY) 154: On the principle that outsiders see more than insiders. **1935** GBullett *Jury* (L 1947) 23: Onlookers see most of the game. **1938** NForrest *Death Took* (NY) 103: The on-looker sees most of the game, they say. **1938** NForrest *Publisher* (NY) 244: The usual principle of the beholders seeing most of the game was making itself felt. **1947** NMarsh *Final* (B) 257: Please don't tell me the onlooker sees most of the game. In this instance, she sees as little as possible. **1956** AGilbert *Riddle* (NY) 195: You know the old saying about the looker-on seeing most of the game. **1957** MStirling *Fine* (L) 76: It is possible that onlookers . . . though they may see some of the game do not always succeed in making sense of what they think they've seen. **1959** NFitzgerald *This Won't* (L) 123: 'Tis an Irish proverb—the hurler on the ditch sees most of the game [*the game of hurling*]. **1962** EXFerrars *Wandering* (NY) 156: As the looker-on seeing most of the game. **1969** RCook *Private* (NY) 156: But as a professional on-looker I'm accustomed to seeing a good deal of a good many games. **1971** DClark *Sick* (NY) 25: Onlookers seeing most of the game. **1973** JMann *Troublecross* (NY) 159: The onlooker sees most of the game. EAP L209: Looker-on.

O40   **Open** and shet, sign of wet

1953 BCClough *Grandma* (Portland, Me.) 51: Open and shet, sign of wet. **1957** HPBeck *Folklore of Maine* (P) 82: Open and shet, sure sign of wet. Cf. Dunwoody 45: If clouds open and close, rain will continue; Cole 58: An open and-shut day.

O41   To be **Open** and shut

1925 JGBrandon *Cork* (L) 210: An open and shut case. **1928** WAWolff *Trial* (NY) 190: The case was open and shut. **1951** ESGardner *Angry* (NY DBC) 52: Looks like an open-and-shut case. **1952** EPaul *Black* (NY) 184: It's open and shut. **1960** WMasterson *Hammer* (NY DBC) 57: It's a long way from open and shut. **1961** RSPrather *Dig That* (NY) 97: It was an open and shut case. **1970** HCarvic *Miss Seeton Draws* (NY) 126: It's open and shut. **1974** PNobile *Intellectual* (NY) 197: It's an open and shut case. NED Suppl. Open and shut 22c; DA Open *a.* 4(1).

O42 To grin like an **(O)possum**

1957 *BangorDN* 1/12 21: Grinnin' like a possum. TW 271(4).

O43 To play **(O)possum**

1919 EWallace *Secret House* (NY) 219: Play 'possum. **1931** MJFreeman *Murder* (NY) 102: Playing possum. **1938** ECRLorac *Devil* (L) 165: Lying doggo, playing possum. **1947** DBowers *Beth* (NY) 20: She does play possum. **1953** JMFox *Code* (B) 160: You're playing possum. **1957** LDelRay *Robots* (NY) 106: Dead . . . or playing possum. **1963** JMarric *Gideon's Ride* (NY) 93: Gideon played the old game of possum. **1967** LPDavies *Psychogeist* (NY) 128: A patient's playing possum. **1970** TKenrick *Only* (NY) 241: Playing possum. EAP O34; Brunvand 103(1).

O44 **Opportunity** knocks but once *(varied)*

1920 AJRees *Hand in the Dark* (NY 1929) 72: Opportunity seldom knocks twice at any man's door. **1928** MPShiel *How the Old Woman* (L) 33: Opportunity never comes twice. **1930** JDosPassos *42nd* (NY) 200: Opportunity knocks but once at a young man's door. **1930** SBHustvedt *Ballad Books* (Cambridge, Mass.) 183: Opportunity was soon to knock at his door and to find him waiting with his hand on the latch. **1936** JTFarrell *World* (NY) 103: When Old Man Opportunity knocked on his door, he was out in the alley horsing around. **1936** LThayer *Dead End* (NY) 228: Opportunity that shouldn't be missed. Don't knock twice, as the saying is. **1940** HSKeeler *Crimson Box* (L) 235: One who . . . did not allow Opportunity to thunder at his door. **1941** PWentworth *Weekend* (P) 200: Opportunity never knocks twice at any man's door. **1958**

New Yorker 5/24 40: Grateful to opportunity for knocking twice. **1958** GMitcham *Man from* (NY) 38: Opportunity only knocked once. **1968** KCLatrue *Bound* (NY) 295: Opportunity knocked a second time. **1972** KCConstantine *Vicksburg* (NY) 148: Opportunity knocks several times . . . but chance never knocks. EAP F274: Fortune; Whiting *NC* 453(1); *Oxford* 282: Fortune.

O45 **Opportunity** makes the thief *(varied)*

1924 HCBailey *Mr. Fortune's Practice* (NY) 174: Opportunity makes the thief or what not. **1929** CWells *Tapestry* (P) 80: Opportunity creates the sinner. **1938** HCBailey *This Is Mr. Fortune* (L) 28: Opportunity makes the thief. **1962** BCleeve *Death* (NY) 80: Contrary to popular belief, opportunity does not make the criminal, but character and need. EAP O33.

O46 **Opposites** attract *(varied)*

1918 JWatson&AJRees *Mystery of the Downs* (NY) 244: It may have been the attraction of opposites. **1928** EBYoung *Murder* (P) 57: If the attraction of opposites counts for anything. **1929** RKing *Murder* (NY) 237: They say that opposites are attracted to one another. **1930** ABCox *Vane* (L) 7: It is often remarked that opposites make a happy marriage. **1938** RAJWalling *Grimy Glove* (NY) 22: There never was a clearer case of the attraction of opposites. **1945** MColes *Green Hazard* (NY) 194: Opposites attract. **1948** GHCoxe *Hollow* (NY) 68: It has been said that opposites attract each other. **1952** DBOlsen *Enrollment* (NY) 189: If unlikes attracted, as the saying went, they should be glued for eternity. **1960** FWarburg *Occupation* (B) 44: The attraction of opposites. **1968** KRoberts *Pavane* (NY) 28: It had been the attraction of opposites. **1970** HBlyth *Skittles* (L) 83: Opposites frequently attract each other. **1971** EHCohen *Mademoiselle* (B) 5: Did opposites attract? Not at all. **1974** JQuintero *If You* (B) 32: People always say that opposites attract.

O47 Obey **Orders** if you break owners

1976 JRLAnderson *Death* (NY) 73: I was brought up on the old sea maxim, obey orders if you break owners. 137: Obey orders if you break owners—that's an old Merchant Service saying. TW 271. Cf. EAP O37; Colcord 136.

O48 Orders are orders

1930 WLevinrew *Murder* (NY) 181: Orders is orders. **1930** NATemple-Ellis *Man Who Was There* (NY) 96: Orders are orders. Cf. Business, Duty *above*; Rules *below*.

O49 To act like an **Ostrich** (*varied*)

1924 CVanVechten *Tattooed* (NY) 240: With your silly ostrich head in the sand. **1929** TLDavidson *Murder* (L) 91: You had your head stuck in a cupboard—like an ostrich. **1932** FBeeding *Murder* (B) 194: It is foolish to put one's head in the sand. **1932** MThynne *Murder* (NY) 171: Stop behaving like the proverbial ostrich. **1935** EGreenwood *Deadly* (NY) 129: About her "Goings on" he preferred to maintain the proverbial ostrich attitude. **1939** DBOlsen *Death Cuts* (NY) 62: Go bury your head in the sand like an ostrich. **1947** DBowers *Bells* (NY) 184: Go on playing ostrich. **1949** JSStrange *Unquiet* (NY) 61: Where do you keep your head? In the sand? **1954** SJepson *Black* (NY) 77: You won't save yourself by sticking your head in the sand. **1964** AChristie *Caribbean* (NY) 3: Bury your head in the sand like a very delightful ostrich. **1966** MWorthington *Strange* (NY) 209: I lived with it, much like the proverbial ostrich, burying my face and pretending there was no sand storm at all. EAP O38.

O50 As sleek as an **Otter**

1959 MProcter *Killer* (NY) 13: As sleek as an otter. Cf. Mink *above*.

O51 An **Ounce** of fact is worth a pound of theory (*generalization*)

1931 MDalton *Night* (NY) 80: Now an ounce of fact . . . is worth a pound of theory. **1968** ABridge *Facts* (NY) 90: An ounce of fact is worth a pound of generalizations. Cf. TW 272(3): Experience.

O52 An **Ounce** of patience *etc.*

1930 ALivingston *Trackless* (I) 41: An ounce of patience is better than a pound

of tribulation. Cf. *Oxford* 601: Ounce of mirth.

O53 An **Ounce** of practice is worth (whatever) (*varied*)

1927 BAtkey *Man* (NY) 221: Half a pint of practice is worth a gallon of theory any day. **1930** VLoder *Essex* (L) 85: An ounce of practice is worth a pound of speculation. **1933** EO'Duffy *Bird Cage* (NY) 222: An ounce of practice is worth a ton of theory. *Oxford* 601.

O54 An **Ounce** of prevention is worth a pound of cure (*varied*)

1928 PThorne *Spiderweb* (P) 39: The old copy book maxim about the ounce of prevention. **1931** PATaylor *Cape Cod* (NY 1971) 82: An ounce o' prevention's worth a pound o' cure. **1933** RMarshall *Arctic* (NY) 270: An ounce of prevention is worth a pound of cure. **1938** MPage *Fast Company* (NY) 4: An ounce of prevention is better than a poke in the eye with a sharp stick. **1941** ESGardner *Turning Tide* (NY) 229: I felt that an ounce of precaution would be better than a pound of struggle. **1951** LBrown *Cleopatra* (NY) 155: An ounce of prevention was worth a pound of cure. **1958** *BHerald* 11/10 36: The old adage of an ounce of prevention being worth a pound of cure. **1959** *BGlobe* 5/22 22: An ounce of prevention is worth a pound of cure. **1971** TRosebury *Microbes* (NY) 212: An ounce of prevention, says grandma, is worth a pound of cure. EAP O42. Cf. Prevention *below*.

O55 As big as all **Outdoors** (*varied*)

1913 JCLincoln *Mr. Pratt's Patients* (NY) 234: A heart . . . big enough to take in all outdoors. **1938** EQueen *Devil* (NY) 174: Heart as big as all outdoors. **1949** RFoley *Girl* (NY) 99: A heart as big as all outdoors. **1952** GVidal *Judgment* (NY) 211: She has a heart as big as all outdoors. **1958** *BangorDN* 7/8 12: Shorty has a spirit as big as all out of doors. **1959** *NYTimes* 5/17 17XX: It looks larger than all outdoors. **1963** HPentecost *Tarnished* (NY DBC) 30: Her impulses were as generous as all outdoors. TW 272(1);

Taylor *Western Folklore* 17(1958) 13; DARE i 46: All outdoors 2.

O56   As hot as an **Oven**

1967 VSNaipaul *Flag* (L) 108: It's as hot as a bloomin' oven. EAP O46; TW 272(2); Taylor *Western Folklore* 17(1958) 17.

O57   As blind as an **Owl**

1931 WMorton *Mystery* (NY) 154: Blind as an owl. **1946** MBennett *Time to Change* (NY) 117: Blind as an owl. **1954** THoward *Blood* (NY) 74: Blind as an owl [*drunk*]. TW 272(2); *Oxford* 67.

O58   As boiled as an **Owl**

1954 MMcCarthy *Charmed* (NY) 70: Boiled as an owl. **1959** FCrane *Buttercup* (NY DBC) 97: Boiled as an owl. **1959** *Newsweek* 7/6 18: He was boiled as a hootowl. DARE i 324: Boiled owl. See DA Owl [*for boiled (drunk) owl phrases*].

O59   As crazy as an **Owl**

1937 WDickinson *Dead Man* (P) 293: He's crazy like an owl. **1937** SPalmer *No Flowers* (L) 35: Joel is crazy as a hoot-owl. **1953** RFMirvish *Eternal* (NY) 32: Crazier than a hoot owl. **1955** KMKnight *Robineau* (NY) 29: Crazy as a hoot owl. Taylor *Prov. Comp.* 30.

O60   As drunk as an **Owl**; Owl-drunk (*varied*)

1922 JJoyce *Ulysses* (NY 1934) 300: He brought him home as drunk as a boiled owl. **1927** HCNewton *Crime* (NY) 74: As drunk as an owl. **1930** JFDobie *Coronado* (Dallas) 28: Got as drunk as a covey of biled owls. **1933** JDCarr *Mad Hatter* (L) 186: He was as drunk as a hoot-owl. **1936** LPaul *Horse* (NY) 31: She was as drunk as a boiled owl. **1937** GDilnot *Murder* (L) 97: He was drunk as an owl. **1940** CDickson *And so to Murder* (NY) 68: They're all drunk as hoot-owls. **1951** ADerleth *Far* (NY) 268: Drunker than owls. **1953** RBloomfield *Stranger* (NY) 151: Drunk as a hoot owl. **1956** *Arizona Highways* June 12: The resultant bobbing and swaying is comical, indeed, and has probably given rise to the expression "drunk as a hoot owl." **1961** MHHood *Drown* (NY) 47: Drunker'n a

hoot owl. **1962** JLindsay *Fanfrolico* (L) 35: He was owl-drunk. Taylor *Western Folklore* 17(1958) 17: Boiled owl; DARE i 324: Boiled owl 2. Cf. As plastered, tight *below*.

O61   As grave (gloomy) as an **Owl**

1935 RAJWalling *Five Suspects* (L) 122: Looking grave as an owl. **1941** HAshbrook *Purple Onion* (NY) 14: You're both as gloomy as owls. **1964** GSimenon *Maigret's Dead* (NY DBC) 44: He was as grave as an owl. Brunvand 104(1).

O62   As plastered (pissed) as an **Owl**

1940 DTeilhet *Broken Face* (NY) 66: Plastered as a hoot owl. **1945** ABarber *Noose* (NY) 186: Get plastered as an owl. **1964** PKinsley *Three* (L) 135: I'm as pissed as an owl [*drunk*]. Cf. As drunk *above*.

O63   As serious (glum) as an **Owl**

1939 AWebb *Thank You* (L) 161: As serious as an owl. **1959** MNeville *Sweet* (L) 13: The boy had looked as glum as an owl. Wilstach 340.

O64   As sober as an **Owl**

1932 PHerring *Murder* (L) 56: Sober as an owl [*not drunk*]. **1936** RLehmann *Weather* (NY) 130: As sober as an owl. **1946** AB Cunningham *Death Rides* (NY) 120: Sober as an owl.

O65   As solemn as an **Owl**

1906 JCLincoln *Mr. Pratt* (NY) 39: Solemn as an owl. **1909** JCLincoln *Keziah* (NY) 107: As solemn as a stuffed owl. **1928** JRhode *Tragedy* (NY) 108: Solemn as an owl. **1930** WLewis *Apes* (NY 1932) 281: As solemn as an owl. **1954** MKArgus *Rogue* (L) 82: I'll be solemn as an owl. **1957** VWMason *Gracious* (NY) 49: You look solemn as a boiled owl. **1957** TWicker *Devil* (NY) 49: Solemn as a hoot owl. **1965** WRBurkett *Sleeping* (NY) 228: Solemn as an owl. **1975** MErskine *Harriet* (NY) 39: Geoffrey nodded, solemn as an owl. TW 272(5); Brunvand 104(2).

O66   As sore as a boiled **Owl**

1929 WKSmith *Bowery* (NY) 101: [He] is as sore as a half-boiled owl. **1932** GDyer *Five* (B) 24: Sore as a boiled owl. **1939** EDean

Murder Is (NY) 34: Sore as a boiled owl. **1940** RAHeinlein *Puppet* (NY 1965) 72: She was sore as a boiled owl. **1956** RFoley *Last* (NY DBC) 32: He's sore as a boiled owl.

O67   As stupid as an **Owl**

1934 JRhode *Shot* (L) 32: Stupid as an owl. **1934** AWynne *Gold Coins* (P) 55: Stupid as owls. **1966** NMarsh *Killer* (B) 258: I'm being stupid as an owl. EAP O48.

O68   As tight as an **Owl**

1913 JCLincoln *Mr. Pratt's Patients* (NY) 66: Drunk, tighter'n a b'iled owl. **1925** PG Wodehouse *Sam* (NY) 48: He was tight as an owl. **1933** AGilbert *Musical* (L) 121: He was as tight as an owl. **1938** WMartyn *Murder Walks* (L) 142: He was as tight as two owls. **1947** HWade *New Graves* (L) 111: Tight as an owl. **1970** UO'Connor *Brendan* (L) 20: As tight as an owl. **1978** JGould *Trifling* (B) 177: Tighter'n a constipated hootowl [*drunk*]. Cf. As drunk *above*.

O69   As tough as a boiled **Owl**

1900 CFPidgin *Quincy A. Sawyer* (B) 74: He is tougher'n a biled owl. **1953** KMKnight *Akin* (NY) 96: Tough as [a] boiled owl, that girl is. **1959** *BangorDN* 7/22 7: Tough as a boiled owl. DARE i 324: Boiled owl 3.

O70   As wise as an **Owl**

1936 PKelway *Hedge Folk* (L) 57: "As wise as an owl" is a well-known saying. **1954** HGardiner *Murder* (L) 120: As wise as an owl. **1960** JBWest *Taste* (NY) 35: He looked as wise as an owl. TW 272–3(8); Brunvand 104(3); Taylor *Prov. Comp.* 89.

O71   The **Owl** in the oak (*varied*)

1930 SMartin *Trial* (NY) 166: Let me remind you of the adage about the owl in the oak. **1952** AGilbert *Mr. Crook* (NY DBC) 55: There's a proverb . . . Something about an owl in an oak. **1952** CEVulliamy *Don* (L) 58: You look like an owl in a hollow tree. Cf. EAP O50.

O72   To bring **Owls** to Athens

1970 WBreem *Eagle* (NY) 60: You have brought owls to Athens. EAP O52.

O73   To stare like a (boiled) **Owl**

1935 NMarsh *Nursing* (B 1972) 79: Nash . . . stared like a boiled owl at the inspector. **1951** MColes *Now* (NY) 28: Just sat and stared like an owl. TW 273(10).

O74   As big as an **Ox**

1930 JFDobie *Coronado* (Dallas) 102: He had a heart "as big as an ox." EAP O53; Brunvand 104.

O75   As dumb as an **Ox**

1955 JBingham *Paton* (NY 1964) 67: Dumb as an ox. **1959** *BangorDN* 7/22 7: Dumb as an ox. Whiting *NC* 454(2).

O76   As healthy as an **Ox** (horse)

1933 WPrice *Death* (NY) 55: You're healthy as an ox. **1934** AHalper *Foundry* (NY) 404: As healthy as a horse. **1940** MBoniface *Murder as* (NY) 13: I'm healthier than an ox. **1956** GMetalious *Peyton* (NY) 45: She was as healthy as a horse. **1964** LLafore *Devil's* (NY) 126: He's as healthy as an ox. **1974** MDavis *Tell Them* (NY) 17: "She was as healthy as a—a gazelle." . . . "A gazelle? Isn't it a horse?"

O77   As strong as an **Ox** (*varied*)

1919 LThayer *Mystery of the 13th Floor* (NY) 184: As strong as an ox. **1931** MAllingham *Police* (NY) 235: The man was as strong as an ox. **1934** RHare *Hand* (NY) 51: He's as strong as an ox. **1941** ESGardner *Empty Tin* (NY 1958) 1: She was strong as an ox. **1954** CBeaton *Glass* (NY) 47: As strong not as the proverbial ox but . . . as a Rolls Royce engine. **1956** EMcBain *Mugger* (L 1963) 13: I'm as strong as an ox. **1960** JO'Hara *Imagine* (NY) 19: Joe's strong as an ox. **1965** PDeVries *Let Me* (NY 1966) 25: Strong as an ox and twice as bright. **1970** JAGraham *Aldeburg* (B) 65: Strong as an ox. **1974** KAmis *Ending* (NY) 159: Adela's as strong as an ox. TW 273(2).

O78   As stubborn as an (off-)**Ox**

1910 JCLincoln *Depot Master* (NY) 10: Stubborn as an off ox. **1954** EForbes *Rainbow* (B) 7: That painting feller is an off-ox if ever I saw one. **1970** RBernard *Deadly* (NY) 18: He's stubborn as an ox. **1975** ELathen *By Hook* (NY) 155: Paul was stubborn as an ox. DARE i 11: Adam's off-ox 2. Cf. TW 273(5). Cf. As slow as God's off-ox *above*.

O79 The black **Ox** has trod on one's toe (*varied*)

1929 TKenyon *Witches* (NY) 343: She was ready to settle down and let the Black Oxen do their will with her. **1930** WLewis *Apes* (NY 1932) 593: The black ox hath trodden on her toe. **1957** DJEnright *Heaven* (L) 109: "The black ox hath trodden on her toe." . . . Proverbial for "care has come upon her." **1964** ABurgess *Nothing* (L) 6: The black ox treadeth upon your foot. TW 273(10); *Oxford* 64–5.

O80 It depends on whose **Ox** is gored (*varied*)

1958 *BHerald* 8/24 6: Evidently it depends on whose ox is gored. **1958** *NYTimes Book Review* 10/19 18: Depended on whose ox was gored. **1960** *NYTimes* 3/13 9E: The enduring moral of Noah Webster's fable No. 8 ". . . It depends on whose ox is gored." **1960** *BHerald* 10/23 15: Own ox not gored. **1971** ELinington *Practice* (NY) 71: Whose ox is gored. **1972** JLHensley *Legislative* (NY) 111: It's just whose ox is being gored. TW 273(11).

O81 To be able to eat an **Ox** (horse) (*varied*)

1930 ABCox *Vane* (L) 206: I'm so hungry I could eat an ox. **1933** CJDaly *Murder* (NY) 104: I'm hungry enough to eat the proverbial ox. **1952** CLittle *Black* (NY) 54: I could eat a horse. **1955** AWest *Heritage* (NY) 144: He could eat a horse. **1965** ESGardner *Troubled* (NY) 62: I could have eaten a live horse. Cf. *Oxford* 393: Hungry.

O82 To muzzle the **Ox** *etc.*

1942 HCBailey *Nobody's* (NY) 65: Do not muzzle the ox that treadeth out the corn. **1957** RChurch *Golden* (NY) 171: Thou shalt not muzzle the ox that treads the corn. EAP O55.

O83 **Oxford** is the home of lost causes

1967 AMontagu *Anatomy* (NY) 285: Oxford . . . is proverbially the home of lost causes. *Oxford* 605.

O84 As close as an **Oyster** (*varied*)

1914 MAdams *In the Footsteps* (L) 236: Rural folk are as close as an oyster. **1927** GDHCole *Murder at Crome House* (NY) 151: As close as an oyster. **1928** RAFreeman *A Certain* (NY) 11: Close as a lock-jawed oyster. **1929** VLoder *Between* (NY) 248: As close-mouthed as an oyster. **1936** JGBrandon *Pawnshop* (L) 275: She was closer than any oyster. **1937** VMacClure *Diva's* (L) 245: Keep your mouth as close as a fresh oyster. **1939** FGerard *Red Rope* (NY) 94: He'll be closer than the proverbial oyster. **1940** CMWills *R.E.Pipe* (L) 59: He was as close as the proverbial oyster. **1959** GMitchell *Man Who* (L) 194: They can be as close as oysters. TW 273(1). Cf. As close as a Clam *above*.

O85 As dumb as an **Oyster** (clam)

1928 HFootner *Velvet* (NY) 16: She's dumb as an oyster. **1930** JGBrandon *Murder* (L) 104: They go as dumb as clams. **1932** VLWhitechurch *Murder* (L) 239: Blaythwait is as dumb as an oyster. **1946** HCBailey *Life Sentence* (NY) 114: She's dumb as an oyster. **1964** MGEberhart *Call* (NY DBC) 112: Sitting . . . dumb as oysters. TW 273(2).

O86 As glum as an **Oyster**

1963 MPHood *Sin* (NY) 182: Frank's glum as an oyster. Wilstach 181.

O87 As mum as an **Oyster** (clam)

1911 CKSteele *Mansion* (NY) 80: I'll be mum as an oyster. **1913** JCLincoln *Mr. Pratt's Patients* (NY) 228: She was mum as a clam. **1930** NBMavity *Case* (NY) 43: Mum as a clam; 287. **1931** SHorler *Evil* (NY) 152: I'll be as mum as an oyster. **1932** MSt Dennis *Death Kiss* (NY) 138: He kept mum as an oyster. **1935** KSproul *Mystery* (NY) 121: As mum as a clam. **1936** AACarey *Memoirs* (NY) 81: Mum as sleeping clams. **1954** HRAngeli *Pre-Raphaelite* (L) 250: As mum as an oyster. **1969** AGilbert *Mr. Crook* (NY DBC) 123: Mum as an oyster. Whiting *NC* 454(2).

O88   As secret(ive) (discreet) as an **Oyster** (clam)

1926 RAFreeman *Puzzle* (NY) 129: As secret as an oyster. **1930** HCMcNeile *Guardians* (NY) 70: He was as secretive as an oyster. **1931** VLWhitechurch *Murder* (NY) 223: As secretive as the proverbial oyster. **1967** VLincoln *Private* (NY) 60: Andrew was secretive as a clam. **1970** RQuest *Cerberus* (NY) 9: She's as discreet as an oyster.

O89   **Oysters** are only good in the R months (*varied*)

1922 JJoyce *Ulysses* (NY 1934) 172: June has no ar no oysters. **1934** AGilbert *Man in Button* (L) 245: Alibis are suspect just now; they're like oysters in R-less months. **1947** RHichens *Yesterday* (L) 24: A month with R in it had just come in. No oysters had been provided. **1950** Lord Dunsany *Strange* (L) 141: On a day of some month with an R in it, and plenty of oysters. **1970** RFoley *Calculated* (NY) 177: Oysters . . . I'm always so glad when the month has an R in it. **1972** RLPike *Gremlin* (NY) 99: Any month with an R in it is a good month for oysters. EAP O58.

O90   To close up like an **Oyster** (clam)

1924 FWCrofts *Cask* (NY 1936) 183: He had closed up like an oyster in its shell. **1930** CClausen *Gloyne* (NY) 238: She'd . . . close up like a clam. **1936** ESdePuy *Long Knife* (NY) 241: She closed up like a—well, I suppose you can say like a clam. **1956** MProcter *Ripper* (NY) 73: She might close up like an oyster. Berrey 205.2: Clam.

O91   To shut up like an **Oyster** (*varied*)

1920 GDilnot *Suspected* (NY) 17: Their mouths shut tight as oysters. **1926** HWade *Verdict* (L) 98: Shut up like an oyster. **1928** GFairlie *Man Who Laughed* (NY) 187: My direct question shut him up like an oyster. **1936** RAJWalling *Crimson Slippers* (L) 272: Thibaud shut up like an alarmed oyster. Cf. Wilstach 426: Locked tight as an oyster. Cf. To shut up like a Clam *above*.

P

P1 To mind one's **P's** and Q's (*varied*)

1921 JSFletcher *Orange-Yellow* (NY) 70: Mind your p's and q's. **1931** LCArlington *Thorough* (L) 195: We have to be on our P's and Q's. **1933** MKennedy et al. *Ask* (L) 145: It wasn't for me to say his P's and Q's for him. **1936** PATaylor *Crimson* (L) 123: Hilda minded her p's and q's. **1940** LMacNeice *Strings* (L) 99: I'm minding my pees and peeing my queues. **1948** AWUpfield *Author* (Sydney 1967) 81: He would have to mind his p's and q's. **1952** IGordon *Night* (NY) 139: Just see to it that he minds his p's and q's. **1959** LColeman *Sam* (NY) 213: That cat . . . had better watch his P's and Q's. **1960** LLevine *Great* (L) 379: Mind your peas and queues. **1964** BKaufman *Up the Down* (NY 1966) 83: I had to watch my peas and ques. **1973** CAird *His Burial* (NY) 131: Got to mind my p's and q's. **1974** HCarmichael *Most* (NY) 69: To watch your Ps and Qs. EAP P1.

P2 It is the **Pace** that kills

1927 LTracy *Mysterious* (NY) 93: The time-honored sporting adage has it: "It's not the miles we travel but the pace that kills." **1957** JMerrill *Seraglio* (NY) 43: This is the pace that kills. TW 274; *Oxford* 606.

P3 To be sold a **Packet**

1932 PHerring *Murder* (L) 94: Somebody sold you a packet. Partridge 598. Cf. Bill *above*.

P4 To get one's **Packet** (*varied*)

1937 GBarnett *I Knew* (L) 66: This is where she caught her packet [*was killed*]. **1940** JRhode *Death on* (NY) 19: A poor chap that got a packet [*was killed*]. **1952** MAllingham *Tiger* (NY) 104: The Major just got his packet [*killed*]. **1954** ECRLorac *Shroud* (NY) 33: He copped his packet as soon as he landed. Partridge 598: Cop, stop.

P5 As fast (plain) as **Paddy's** pig

1926 MRRinehart *Bat* (NY 1959) 24: Ran away . . . as fast as Paddy's pig. **1955** LWibbley *Mouse* (NY 1958) 136: It's as plain as Paddy's pig.

P6 As Irish as **Paddy's** pig (*varied*)

1955 DMDisney *Room* (NY) 102: She's as Irish as Paddy Murphy's pig. **1963** HPentecost *Only* (NY DBC) 6: As Irish as Paddy's pig. **1972** BLillie *Every* (NY) 15: MacBride, as Irish as Paddy's immortal porker. Whiting *NC* 454.

P7 As stiff as **Paddy's** father *etc.*

1958 *New Yorker* 4/5 32: I'm as stiff as Paddy's father when he was nine months dead. **1965** JMBrown *Worlds* (NY) 125: As shtiff [*stiff*] as Paddy's father and him nine days dead. Wilstach 559.

P8 From **Padstow Point** *etc.*

1948 IFletcher *Roanoke* (I) 18: From Padstow Point to Lundy Light is a sailor's grave, by day or night. Apperson 481.

P9 He is well **Paid** that is well satisifed

1919 JBCabell *Jurgen* (NY 1922) 84: He is well paid that is well satisfied. TW 277(2).

P10   A **Pain** in the arse (*varied*)

1941 GEGiles *Three Died* (NY) 4: It's a pain in the you-know-what. **1956** EMcBain *Pusher* (NY 1959) 351: This is a big pain in the ass. **1959** HLGold *World* (NY 1961) 171: James was only a pain in the rump. **1960** EMcBain *Give the Boys* (NY) 122: She's a very attractive girl. A pain in the ass, but very attractive. **1970** WANolen *Making* (NY) 25: He was . . . a real pain in the ass. **1972** RHGreenan *Queen* (NY) 32: She becomes more of a pain in the rump. **1972** ELathen *Murder* (NY) 178: Billy was a pain in the rear. **1975** PMoyes *Black* (NY) 136: He's nothing but a pain in the ass. Wentworth 372.

P11   A **Pain** in the neck (*varied*)

1925 JGBrandon *Cork* (L) 131: A pain in the neck. **1930** CBarry *Boat* (L) 44: You're a pain in the neck to me. **1937** QPatrick *Death* (NY) 160: Princess Walonska who, between you and me, is a pain in several places beside the neck. **1939** KSecrist *Murder Melody* (NY) 230: You're the well-known pain in my neck. **1947** KMKnight *Blue* (NY) 164: He told me it was a pain in the neck. **1948** WPMcGivern *But Death* (NY) 38: She was a pain in the neck. **1958** *New Yorker* 5/10 34: A wife who is a pain in the neck. **1959** *BangorDN* 8/7 11: Enough to give any girl a pain in the neck. **1967** JDCarr *Dark* (NY) 160: He may be a pain in the neck. **1968** RStout *Father* (NY) 112: It can be a pain not only in the neck but also in . . . the ass. **1975** PDickinson *Lively* (NY) 63: A pain in the neck. Wentworth 372.

P12   As clear as **Paint**

1928 HdeVStackpoole *Mystery* (NY) 17: It's clear as paint. **1932** PMcGuire *Three* (NY) 129: All the tracks since are clear as paint. Wilstach 56.

P13   As clever as **Paint**

1932 RThorndike *Devil* (NY) 268: He's clever as paint. **1938** GDHCole *Mrs. Warrender's* (L) 113: She was clever as paint at her job. **1967** VPowell *Substantial* (L) 18: As clever as paint. Wilstach 58.

P14   As fresh as **Paint** (*varied*)

1920 EWallace *Three-Oaks* (L) 172: Fresh as paint. **c1923** ACrowley *Confessions* ed JSymonds (L 1969) 435: As fresh as paint. **1935** ECRLorac *Affair* (L) 41: I'm as fresh as paint. **1940** ACampbell *They Hunted* (NY) 94: Fresh as paint, eyes a-sparkle. **1950** EC Bentley *Chill* (NY) 17: You look as fresh as paint. **1951** HRigsby *Murder for* (NY 1952) 47: The driver was fresh as new paint [*impudent*]. **1952** PHBonner *SPQR* (NY) 176: The caviar which is light grey and fresh as paint. **1959** EWeeks *In Friendly* (B) 3: Every impression was as fresh as red paint. *Oxford* 287.

P15   As handsome as **Paint**

1959 EMButler *Paper* (L) 109: He was handsome as paint. NED Suppl. Paint *sb.* 2e.

P16   As plain as **Paint**

1937 CDickson *Ten Teacups* (L) 167: You said to me, as plain as paint. **1962** CDSimal *All the Traps* (NY) 187: It was plain as paint.

P17   As pretty as **Paint**

1930 FRyerson *Seven* (L) 19: Pretty as paint, but a minx. **1937** VWilkins *And So—Victoria* (NY) 326: She's as pretty as paint. **1940** PWentworth *Rolling* (P) 77: We used to say "As pretty as paint." **1949** NMarsh *Wreath* (NY) 212: It's as pretty as paint. **1956** *BHerald* 12/15 9: Angela Greene pretty as paint. **1957** EMButler *Heine* (NY) 168: As pretty as paint. **1960** HReilly *Follow* (NY DBC) 98: Pretty as paint. **1971** EPeters *Knocker* (NY) 73: She's . . . still as pretty as new paint. TW 274(1).

P18   As smart as **Paint**

1929 HFootner *Doctor* (L) 143: Smart as paint. **1933** REssex *Slade* (NY) 52: He can be as smart as paint. **1945** MBurton *Not a Leg* (NY) 111: As smart as paint. **1958** C Oman *Garrick* (L) 219: She [*Mrs. Abington*] was as smart as paint and as hard as nails. NED Suppl. Paint *sb.* 2e.

P19   Not to touch with a **Pair** of tongs

1934 CBrackett *Entirely* (NY) 191: He wouldn't touch it with tongs. **1936** PGWodehouse *Laughing* (NY) 125: I wouldn't touch you with a pair of tongs. EAP P9. Cf. Pole *below*.

P20   To be a different **Pair** of shoes (trousers) (*varied*)

1919 LMerrick *Chair* (L) 83: With me it will be a different pair of shoes. **1922** JJoyce *Ulysses* (NY 1934) 493: That is another pair of trousers. **1929** GDHCole *Poison* (NY) 165: It's quite a different pair of shoes. **1930** JJConnington *Eye* (B) 215: Proof's another pair of shoes altogether. **1933** JBPriestley *I'll Tell* (NY) 151: That's another pair of shoes altogether, as the sayin' is. **1937** AChristie *Cards* (NY) 209: Shaitana was a very different pair of shoes. **1938** MSaltmarsh *Clouded* (NY) 266: Whether they find him . . . is a very different pair of trousers. **1952** AGilbert *Mr. Crook* (NY DBC) 40: Drugs are a different pair of shoes. Partridge 601. Cf. To be a Horse *above*.

P21   To show a clean **Pair** of heels

1925 FBeeding *Seven* (B) 103: Show a clean pair of heels. **1926** MLewis *Island* (L) 79: To show the gentleman a clean pair of heels. **1932** VLWhitechurch *Murder* (L) 230: Henlow had shown a clean pair of heels. **1933** JSFletcher *Mystery* (L) 111: He's made a clean pair of heels. **1940** JCreasey *Here Comes* (NY 1967) 40: [He] had shown Kohn a clean pair of heels. **1955** MInnes *Man from* (L) 114: Show those people a clean pair of heels. **1962** DMDisney *Should Auld* (NY) 185: To get out with a clean pair of heels. **1964** RConquest *World* (NY) 133: To show a . . . a clean pair of heels. **1975** SJPerelman *Vinegar* (NY) 186: I showed her a clean pair of heels. EAP P11; TW 274(1).

P22   As flat as the **Palm** of one's hand

1927 GDilnot *Lazy* (B) 248: It's as flat as the palm of your hand. Cf. Wilstach 144: As your hand. Cf. As flat as one's Hand *above*.

P23   As naked as the **Palm** of one's hand

1932 TSmith *Bishop's* (NY) 175: You're as naked as the palm of my hand. **1951** JCollier *Fancies* (NY) 141: As naked as your hand.

P24   To grease (oil) the **Palm** (*varied*)

1925 SQuinn *Phantom* (Sauk City, Wisc. 1966) 12: I grease the palm of a servant. **1935** JTFarrell *Judgment* (NY) 445: Get their palms greased by Moscow gold. **1939** GDHCole *Double* (NY) 93: Greasing the palm of office. **1940** RDarby *Death Conducts* (NY) 185: To oil all the many extended palms. **1947** FCrane *Murder on* (NY) 57: There are palms to be oiled. **1953** JMFox *Bright* (B) 208: They tell me greased palm loses grip. **1956** FWinwar *Wingless* (NY) 21: Get rid of this guide by oiling his palm. **1965** HWaugh *End* (NY) 136: Palms to be greased. **1970** RRendell *Best Man* (NY) 110: [He] greased your palm a bit. **1973** EJBurford *Queen* (L) 30: The golden ointment of palm grease. EAP P13. Cf. Brunvand 106.

P25   To have in the **Palm** of one's hand

1955 KAmis *That Uncertain* (L) 209: Vernon's got that committee in the palm of his hand. **1972** SNBehrman (B) 172: He had the audience in the palm of his hand.

P26   To know like the **Palm** of one's hand

1929 JJConnington *Case* (B) 7: I know this end of the town like the palm of my hand. **1932** PMcGuire *Three* (NY) 90: [He] knew the country about here like the palm of his hand. **1950** JCannan *Murder* (L 1958) 116: I know 'em like the palm of me 'and. **1955** EWSmith *One Eyed* (NY) 231: I know it like the palm of my hand. **1962** HReilly *Day* (NY DBC) 30: Mary knew the countryside like the palm of her hand.

P27   As flat as a **Pancake** (*varied*)

1924 LO'Flaherty *Thy Neighbour's* (L) 67: As flat as a pan-cake. **1933** ECRLorac *Murder* (L) 156: And that's flat, as the pancake said. **1936** GDyer *Catalyst* (NY) 60: She had left him flatter than the proverbial pancake. **1949** JSStrange *Unquiet* (NY) 166: It's flat as a pancake. **1951** NMitford *Blessing* (NY) 7: My life is as flat as a pancake. **1958** *BangorDN* 8/30 22: Stomach as flat as a pancake. **1963** MLynn *Mrs. Maitland* (NY) 27: The . . . tyre was as flat as the proverbial pancake. **1964** VSPritchett *Foreign* (L) 204: It was as flat as one of those pancakes of Persian bread. **1971** DFJones *Denver* (NY)

125: Her voice was flatter than a pancake. **1975** HBHough *Mostly* (NY) 78: Because . . . he had a flat nose he was called "Lord Pancake." EAP P15. Cf. Flapjack *above*.

P28 To sell like **Pancakes** on Shrove Tuesday

1952 RMarshall *Jane* (NY) 124: Selling like pancakes on Shrove Tuesday. Cf. NED Pancake 3: Pancake day, Shrove Tuesday.

P29 **Pandora's** box

1908 JBailey *Letters and Diaries* (L 1935) 110: Kept Pandora's box . . . half shut. **1930** JJFarjeon *Mystery* (L) 95: Pandora was natural when she opened the box of evil. **1939** MArmstrong *Murder in* (NY) 211: I had unlocked Pandora's box. **1940** RAHeinlein *Puppet* (NY 1965) 202: Pandora's box has a one-way lid. **1952** FCDavis *Tread* (NY) 92: To open that Pandora's box with its store of unknown evils. **1956** *TLS* 8/3 460: Pandora and her box are proverbial. **1957** JWyndham *Midwich* (NY) 155: Another little gimmick out of Pandora's infinite evolutionary box. **1965** ESitwell *Taken Care* (NY) 79: I have . . . seen two Pandora's boxes opened. **1966** NBlake *Morning* (NY) 179: The well-known box had the same effect on Pandora. **1967** JAxelrad *Freneau* (Austin) 361: The one treasure that remained in Pandora's box . . . hope. **1969** JJDeiss *Roman* (NY) 135: The "specter haunting Europe" indeed had been let out of Pandora's capitalist box. **1970** JFrazer *Deadly* (NY) 151: A pandora box filled with mystery and evil. **1970** KGiles *Death* (L) 35: A kind of walking Pandora's box. **1974** HCarmichael *Most* (NY) 93: It was like Pandora's Box in reverse. EAP P17.

P30 As quick as a **Panther**

1934 EBBlack *Crime* (NY) 310: Stevenson was quick as a panther. **1941** SHHolbrook *Murder out* (NY) 19: The . . . girl moved quickly as a panther. **1954** HWade *Too Soon* (NY) 200: Quick as a panther. Cf. TW 275(1).

P31 To scream like a **Panther**

1933 PATaylor *Mystery* (NY) 146: Her screams would have put the proverbial stricken panther to shame. TW 275(8); Brunvand 106.

P32 To be caught with one's **Pants** down (*varied*)

1922 JJoyce *Ulysses* (NY 1934) 99: Must be careful about women. Catch them once with their pants down. Never forgive you after. **1929** DHammett *Red Harvest* (NY) 143: I've got you with your pants down. **1934** ABinns *Lightship* (NY) 293: We would be caught with our pants down. **1938** EHuxley *Murder* (NY) 45: She had caught him with his pants down this time. **1941** GBagby *Here Comes* (NY) 214: We've got you with your pants down in more ways than one. **1948** BSBallinger *Body* (NY) 107: No one has caught him with his pants down yet. **1951** LLariar *You Can't* (NY) 111: She caught me with my mental pants down. **1959** *TLS* 7/10 407: Here [*in 1929*] were the "better elements" caught with their pants down, as Americans coarsely put it. **1960** BKendrick *Aluminum* (NY DBC) 128: Ted is caught with his breeches down. **1966** NBlake *Morning* (NY) 93: Joseph caught you with your pants down, so to speak. **1968** RDuncan *How to Make* (L) 337: Being caught with your trousers down. **1971** TPace *Fisherman's* (NY) 111: Really got old Porky with his pants down. **1974** JFlaherty *Chez* (NY) 25: He gets caught with his pants down. Berrey 178.3.

P33 To keep one's **Pants** on

1936 EQueen *Halfway* (NY) 39: Keep your pants on. **1938** WEHayes *Black* (NY) 236: Keep your pants on. **1949** RFinnegan *Bandaged* (L 1952) 129: Keep your pants on. **1953** EQueen *Scarlet* (B) 70: Keep your pants on. **1965** RSPrather *Dead Man's* (NY) 187: Keep your pants on. Cf. To keep one's Hair *above*; Shirt, Wig *below*.

P34 To scare the **Pants** off someone

1934 CDickson *White Priory* (NY) 242: It scared the pants off me. **1939** JPPhilips *Death Delivers* (NY) 79: The pants are scared right off him. **1941** RPKoehler *Sing a Song* (NY) 68: I hope John scares her pants off. **1951** AMStein *Shoot* (NY) 180: You walked in and scared the pants off her. **1956**

GHCoxe *Man on* (NY 1958) 62: Scaring the pants off me. **1972** BLillie *Every* (NY) 227: That scared the pants off me. **1974** MButterworth *Villa* (NY) 144: I scared the pants off old Susannah. Berrey 300.8.

P35   As pale (pallid) as **Paper**

1929 HFootner *Doctor* (L) 68: He was as pale as paper. **1930** VLoder *Essex* (L) 13: Her face as pallid as a sheet of paper. **1936** RAJWalling *Dirty Face* (L) 42: His face pale as paper. **1946** PQuentin *Puzzle for Fools* (NY) 98: Her face was as pale as paper. **1957** JDCarr *Fire* (NY) 57: As pale as paper. **1962** KAmis *Spectrum(1)* (L) 137: His face as pale as paper. **1974** JBrunner *Total* (NY) 155: Cheeks . . . paper-pale. EAP P18.

P36   As thin as (tissue) **Paper**; Paper-thin

1927 WDSteele *Man Who* (NY) 81: As thin as paper. **1931** JRhode *Tragedy* (NY) 189: The walls . . . are as thin as tissue paper. **1934** VGielgud *Death* (L) 50: That story . . . had been as thin as tissue paper. **1937** NBerrow *One Thrilling* (L) 118: Those phials are paper-thin. **1951** WCWilliams *Autobiography* (NY) 318: Thin as paper as she is. **1970** DStuart *Very* (NY) 211: Kennedy's margin of victory was paper thin. EAP P19; Whiting P23.

P37   As tight (close) as the **Paper** on the wall (*varied*)

1932 MRRinehart *Miss Pinkerton* (NY) 77: He was as tight as the paper on the wall. **1951** FCrane *Murder in* (NY) 122: She's tighter'n paper on a wall [*avaricious*]. **1961** PGWodehouse *Ice* (NY) 12: He and Sally had been closer than the paper on the wall. **1970** PMoyes *Many* (NY) 212: Stick to Dolly closer than the paper on the wall. **1974** MGEberhart *Danger* (NY) 75: You are as tight as the paper on the wall. Berrey 376.7.

P38   As white as **Paper**; Paper-white (*varied*)

1906 JCLincoln *Mr. Pratt* (NY) 300: He was white as paper. **1925** BAtkey *Pyramid* (NY) 200: A paper-white face. **1930** CBush *Dead Man* (NY) 55: His face seemed white as paper. **1933** GCollins *Dead Walk* (L) 57: A paper-white face. **1940** ISShriber *Head over Heels* (NY) 91: You're as white as paper. 158: A paper-white face. **1942** MGEberhart *Wolf* (NY) 13: Drue went as white as paper. **1950** ECrispin *Sudden* (NY DBC) 143: Her face muddy and paper-white. **1951** IChase *New York 22* (NY) 150: Her face white as paper. **1959** AGilbert *Death* (NY) 211: Cathie turned as white as paper. **1969** AGilbert *Mr. Crook* (NY DBC) 39: She was white as paper. **1972** EPeters *Seventh* (NY) 179: [The face] was white as paper. EAP P20; Whiting P24: Paper-white.

P39   To fit like the **Paper** on the wall

1931 PBaron *Round* (NY) 163: Fits like the paper on the wall. **1935** PMacDonald *Death* (NY) 287: It fits . . . like the paper on the wall. **1961** FSinclair *But the Patient* (NY) 166: Fits this place like the paper on the wall. Taylor *Prov. Comp.* 61.

P40   To go peddle one's **Papers**

1930 DFrome *In at the Death* (NY) 163: Told him to go peddle his papers—as we say in America. **1933** CCNicole *Death* (L) 177: Go sell your papers. **1942** FLockridge *Hanged* (NY) 187: Go peddle your papers. **1953** CBKelland *Sinister* (NY DBC) 61: Go peddle your papers. **1961** AAFair *Bachelors* (NY DBC) 26: Why doesn't Dowling go peddle his own papers? **1969** HPentecost *Girl Watcher* (NY) 146: She . . . told him to go peddle his papers. Wentworth 380.

P41   As busy as a one-armed **Paper hanger** (*varied*)

1929 KPreston *Pot Shots* (NY) 196: Busier than the proverbial one-armed paper hanger with the hives. **1933** AGMacLeon *Case* (NY) 285: As the saying goes, he'd have to be just about as busy as a one-armed paperhanger with the itch. **1937** KPKempton *Monday* (NY) 238: Busier than a one-armed paper hanger. **1956** *New Yorker* 8/4 25: I . . . useta be busier than a one-eyed paperhanger. **1961** PGWodehouse *Ice* (NY) 43: Busy as that famous one-armed paper hanger. **1964** JPhilips *Laughter* (NY DBC) 104: He was busier than the proverbial one-armed paperhanger. **1970** JLeasor *They Don't* (NY) 139: I worked like a one-armed paper hanger when the paste is nearly gone. **1977** JLHensley *Rivertown* (NY) 72: They keep him busier than a one-armed paper hanger. Whiting *NC* 454–5; Wilstach 40.

P42 As dry as **Parchment**; Parchment-dry
1971 MUnderwood *Trout* (NY) 33: Parchment-dry tone. EAP P21.

P43 As pale (white) as **Parchment**
1930 VMarkham *Black Door* (NY) 260: You're as pale as parchment. **1933** "Diplomat" *Death* (NY) 130: His face white as parchment. **1938** AWebb *Mr P's Hat* (L) 240: A face . . . as pale as parchment. Wilstach 282.

P44 As talkative as a **Parrot**
1936 JBude *Sussex* (L) 222: As talkative as a parrot. Whiting *NC* 455(1); Brunvand 106(1); *Oxford* 760: Speak.

P45 **Parthian** arrow (shot, shaft)
1900 CFPidgin *Quincy A. Sawyer* (B) 475: After shooting this Parthian arrow. **1926** AMarshall *Mote* (NY) 258: Parthian shot. **1933** DGBrowne *Cotfold* (L) 71: The Parthian shaft was discharged. **1933** CStJSprigg *Crime* (L) 153: Satisfied with this Parthian arrow, he went. **1952** JFleming *Man Who* (NY) 147: He was a great exponent of the Parthian shot. **1961** ANeame *Adventures* (NY) 76: I . . . let fly a Parthian shaft. **1961** JBTownsend *John* (New Haven) 26: To shoot the Parthian arrow. **1966** AChristie *13 Clues* (NY) 106: With that Parthian shot he departed. EAP P26; Brunvand 106.

P46 As plump as a **Partridge** (capon)
1920 GBMcCutcheon *Anderson Crow* (NY) 232: As plump as a partridge. **1934** AMeredith *Portrait* (NY) 45: You're getting as plump as a partridge. **1952** ETempleton *Proper* (B) 45: As plump as a partridge. **1957** JDCarr *Fire* (NY) 142: Plump as a partridge. **1959** PMoyes *Dead Men* (L) 27: A man plump as a capon. EAP P27.

P47 Hear the other **Party**
1967 AJToynbee *Acquaintances* (L) 276: *Audi alteram partem* is a binding precept. EAP P29.

P48 This, too, shall **Pass** (*varied*)
1951 HMcCloy *Through* (NY) 148: We know so well that saddest of old sayings: "This, too, will pass . . ." **1964** HMHyde *Norman* (L) 550: But all things change. **1966** DHitchens *Man Who Cried* (NY) 142: Try to be of good cheer . . . This too shall pass. **1966** CArmstrong *Dream* (NY DBC) 22: "This, too, shall pass," she told herself mockingly. **1967** SForbes *Encounter* (NY) 167: The Senator and I had a favorite saying . . . this, too, will pass. **1984** *BGlobe* 10/14 9: Q. Who was the king with the motto: "This, too, shall pass"? A. The phrase is attributed to King Solomon, according to researchers at the Boston Public Library. A sultan had asked Solomon to develop a phrase useful in both adversity and prosperity. Solomon chose: "And this, too, shall pass away." Whiting T99: All things must go (pass); Brunvand 141: This (Persian).

P49 Distant **Pastures** are greener (*varied*)
1936 CJKenny *This Is Murder* (L) 10: Other pastures look greener. **1954** EForbes *Rainbow* (B) 51: Old adage about greener pastures, I guess. **1960** KCrichton *Total* (NY) 36: Finding the distant pastures no greener. **1960** ESGardner *Shapely* (NY DBC) 50: A guy who sees green pastures on the other side of the fence. **1964** RMacdonald *Chill* (NY) 67: I suppose distant pastures look greenest. **1965** RDSymons *Silton* (NY 1975) 104: Distant pastures and lush and green. **1968** WGRogers *Ladies* (L) 129: Lawrence, to whom new pastures always looked green. **1971** EHCohen *Mademoiselle* (B) 208: Distant pastures are greener. **1974** WSnow *Codline* (Middletown, Conn.) 17: Believing . . . that distant fields are greener. 286: A case of another man's pasture greener than our own. Cf. Grass is greener *above*.

P50 A **Paternoster** while
1953 CHarnett *Nicholas* (NY) 87: I shall be no more than a Paternoster while. *Oxford* 612.

P51 **Patience** and shuffle the cards (*varied*)
1970 GMFraser *Royal* (L) 24: Courage—and shuffle the cards. **1977** JRLAnderson *Death* (NY) 85: Patience, as Cervantes ob-

served somewhere—Patience and shuffle the cards. EAP P34.

P52   Patience is a virtue

1923 CJDutton *Shadow* (NY) 227: They tell me that patience is a rare and great virtue. **1932** GKChesterton et al. *Floating* (NY) 227: Patience is a virtue. **1933** EPhillpotts *Captain's* (NY) 133: Patience is a virtue. **1941** ESHolding *Speak* (NY) 124: She was not sure that patience was a virtue. **1946** FLockridge *Murder Within* (P) 12: I can only advise patience . . . It is an excellent virtue. **1958** RKing *Malice* (NY) 107: They say that patience is a virtue. **1965** HSLatham *My Life* (NY) 22: Patience is a virtue. **1976** JFoxx *Freebooty* (I) 49: Patience was a virtue. EAP P35; TW 276–7(1).

P53   Patience moves mountains

1957 SAlexander *Michelangelo* (NY) 62: Patience moves mountains.

P54   With Patience and saliva *etc.*

1970 AEHotchner *Treasure* (NY) 129: A very old Spanish proverb that loses nothing in translation: "With patience and saliva, the elephant fucketh the ant." **1984** HResnicow *Gold Deadline* (NY) 86: The apothegm, "Con paciencia y saliva un elefante se cogio una hormiga." . . . "With patience and spit, an elephant screws an ant," and "screws" is an euphemism. Cf. TW 281: Perseverance; *Oxford* 613: Patience, time, and money.

P55   Paul(ine) Pry

1920 N&JOakley *Clevedon* (P) 179: You are a damned Paul Pry. **1930** CWells *Doorstep* (NY) 72: Miss Pauline Pry. *Oxford* 614.

P56   He that cannot Pay, let him pray

1954 RStout *Three* (NY) 101: He that cannot pay, let him pray. *Oxford* 614.

P57   To strike Pay dirt

1945 HQMasur *Bury Me* (NY 1948) 29: And struck pay dirt at our first stop. **1953** EQueen *Scarlet* (B) 54: I've hit pay dirt on this one. **1962** ESGardner *Reluctant* (NY DBC) 91: He's struck pay dirt. Wentworth 378.

P58   Forehand Payments *etc.*

1928 ACBrown *Dr. Glazebrook* (NY) 148: The old Scots adage that "fore-hand payments make hind-hand work." *Oxford* 614: Pay beforehand. Cf. EAP P39.

P59   As close(ly) as Peas in a pod

1924 DMackail *Majestic* (NY) 44: Resemble . . . as closely as peas in a pod. **1932** SJepson *Mystery* (NY) 157: Him an' Joe were as close as peas in a pod. Taylor *Prov. Comp.* 27: Close.

P60   As easy (simple) as shelling Peas

1919 HRHaggard *She and Allan* (NY 1921) 133: The thing was simple as shelling peas which, notwithstanding the proverb, in my experience is not simple at all. **1926** JSFletcher *Green Ink* (B) 101: Easy as shelling peas. **1931** DLSayers *Suspicious* (NY) 383: Simple as shelling peas. **1935** JRhode *Mystery* (L) 192: Easy as shelling peas. **1941** EPhillpotts *Ghostwater* (NY) 261: It's as simple as shelling peas. **1952** JDCarr *Nine Wrong* (NY) 27: Easy as shelling peas. **1976** JPorter *Package* (NY) 18: As easy as shelling peas. Partridge 754: Shelling.

P61   As like as two Peas (*very varied*)

1919 SRohmer *Quest* (NY) 279: They are like as two peas in a pod. **1924** ROChipperfield *Bright* (NY) 182: As alike as peas in a pod. **1924** LO'Flaherty *Thy Neighbour's* (L) 45: As like as two peas. **1928** TFPowys *House* (L) 182: A town as nearly like his own as one pea is to another. **1929** JSFletcher *Ransom* (NY) 58: As like it as a split pea is to the other half. **1929** FKing *Ghoul* (NY) 295: As like to him as the proverbial pea. **1930** EPearson *Instigation* (NY) 53: The traditional likeness of one pea to its brother. **1931** VWilliams *Masks* (L) 156: Looked as much alike as a row of peas in a pod. **1934** BFlynn *Spiked* (P) 218: They're as like as the proverbial two peas. **1937** GGoodwin *White Farm* (L) 268: As alike as split peas. **1941** TDuBois *McNeills Chase* (B) 6: If Professor Sayres and Professor Fuller were not as alike as two rather withered peas, they were certainly birds of a feather. **1949** SJepson *Golden* (NY) 107: I am like Ruperto—indeed, in nearly everything we are of the same peapod. **1950** JCannan *Murder* (L 1958) 11: All as alike as two peas. **1957** *Punch* 5/29 683: As like as two P's and Q's in a pod. **1968** JTStory *I Sit* (L) 70: You're like two peas in a pod. **1971** HPentecost *Deadly* (NY) 14: Alike as two peas in a pod, to coin a cliché. **1974** JBrunner *Total* (NY) 133: As alike as peas. EAP P41; Brunvand 107.

P62 As snug as a **Pea** in a pod

1938 PWentworth *Run!* (L) 238: Snug as . . . a pea in a pod. **1956** GMetalious *Peyton* (NY) 124: Snug as peas in a pod. Cf. As snug as a Bug, Cricket *above*.

P63 As thick as **Peas** (*varied*)

1928 FLPackard *Tiger* (NY) 151: Whitie and the magpie being as thick as peas. **1929** JMWalsh *Mystery* (L) 242: The clues . . . were as thick as peas in a pod. **1937** LRGribble *Case-Book* (L) 79: [They] were thick as peas. **1957** WGHardy *City* (NY) 43: As thick . . . as three peas in the same pod. **1957** MPHood *In the Dark* (NY) 52: Grew up together, always thicker'n two peas in a pod. **1965** AChristie *At Bertram's* (L) 147: Clergymen are as thick as peas in a pod in there. Whiting *NC* 455(2).

P64 Not give two **Peas**

1958 JByrom *Or Be* (L 1964) 134: I wouldn't give two peas. Whiting P98.

P65 To be like a **Pea** (flea) in a frying-pan (shovel)

1924 RAFreeman *Blue* (NY) 233: He is . . . hopping about like a pea in a frying-pan. **1938** HHolt *Wanted* (L) 97: You're like a pea in a hot frying-pan. **1944** RAJWalling *Corpse Without* (NY) 78: He's been like a flea on a hot plate. **1965** PGWodehouse *Galahad* (L) 30: He behaved like a pea on a hot shovel. EAP P45.

P66 To tear up the **Pea patch**

1957 JPotts *Man with* (NY 1964) 128: Disrupted my . . . schedule. Tore up the pea patch in general. **1961** JSStrange *Eye* (NY) 92: The girl had really torn up the pea patch [*taken up with a married man*]. **1972** JPotts *Troublemaker* (NY) 67: Your mother's

tearing up the pea patch looking for you. Wentworth 538: Tear.

P67 As clear as **Pea soup**

1928 JArnold *Surrey* (L) 237: Clear as peasoup [*here, quite clear*]. **1959** AWUpfield *Journey* (NY) 119: Clear . . . as pea soup. Cf. Ditchwater, As clear as Mud *above*.

P68 As thick as **Pea soup**

1934 APeters *Who Killed* (NY) 203: It's as thick as pea soup outside [*fog*]. **1936** JSStrange *Bell* (NY) 12: It [*fog*] was thick as pea soup. **1940** MArmstrong *Man with* (NY) 125: It's as thick as pea soup [*a plot*]. **1949** JSStrange *Unquiet* (NY) 127: It's thicker'n pea soup [*fog*]. Whiting *NC* 455; Taylor *Prov. Comp.* 81.

P69 In **Peace** prepare for war (*varied*)

1931 STruss *Hunterstone* (NY) 182: If you see peace, prepare for war, as the Roman gentleman said. **1934** HCBailey *Shadow* (NY) 175: *Si vis pacem, para bellum.* If you want peace, prepare for war. EAP P49; Brunvand 143: Time(2).

P70 As pretty as a **Peach**

1940 MArmstrong *Man with* (NY) 188: A charming girl. Pretty as a peach. **1949** FCrane *Flying* (NY) 9: Rosemary is said to be pretty as a peach. Whiting *NC* 455(1); Taylor *Prov. Comp.* 64.

P71 As proud as a **Peacock**; Peacock-proud

1904 JLondon *Letters* ed KHendricks (NY 1965) 156: Prouder than a peacock. **1953** FCDavis *Drag* (NY) 64: We're all as proud as peacocks. **1953** RDuncan *Where* (L) 119: The baker was as proud as a cock. **1959** SRansome *I'll Die* (NY) 156: Grateful and peacock-proud. **1966** DMDisney *At Some* (NY) 259: Proud as a peacock. **1968** JRoffman *Grave* (NY) 44: As proud as a peacock. **1971** DClark *Sick* (NY) 136: Proud as a peacock and twice as vain. **1971** VScannell *Tiger* (L) 78: Peacock-proud in their prickly new uniforms. EAP P54; TW 278(2).

P72 As vain as a **Peacock**

1921 CSLewis *Letters* ed WHLewis (NY 1966) 67: He's as vain as a peacock. **1931** MGEberhart *From This* (NY) 270: You're as vain as any peacock. **1933** GWeston *Murder* (NY) 256: As vain as a peacock. **1957** *TLS* 9/20 564: As vain as peacocks. **1958** CCockburn *Crossing* (L) 88: As vain as a peacock. **1961** HReilly *Certain* (NY DBC) 28: As vain as a peacock. **1979** CMacLeod *Luck* (NY) 107: My uncle Elmer, who was vain as a peacock, cheap as dirt, and homely as a mud fence. EAP P55; Brunvand 107; Taylor *Western Folklore* 17(1958) 17.

P73 For **Peanuts** (*varied*)

1942 FGruber *Buffalo Box* (NY) 90: I'll bet you're working for peanuts. **1957** BHitchens *End* (NY) 54: She didn't get that for peanuts. **1962** PDennis *Genius* (NY) 139: He'll do it for peanuts. **1968** MAllingham *Cargo* (NY) 97: Those two are not playing for peanuts. Wentworth 379.

P74 To hunt for **Pears** on an elm tree

1954 TDuBois *Seeing* (NY) 151: "You're hunting for pears on an elm tree" . . . It was the Spanish proverb. EAP P57.

P75 As white as **Pearls**; Pearl-white

1959 LGOfford *Walking* (NY DBC) 102: Margaret's face grew slowly pearl-white. **1962** EHuxley *Mottled* (L) 300: Teeth . . . white as pearls. Whiting P88; Brunvand 107(1); Clark *Similes* 225.

P76 To cast **Pearls** before swine (*varied*)

1925 RAFreeman *Red Thumb* (L) 101: The priceless pearl of her love was cast before . . . an unappreciative swine. **1925** PG Wodehouse *Sam* (NY) 96: The proverb about casting pearls before swine. **1928** DLSayers *Dawson* (NY) 63: Not to cast the jewels of my eloquence into the pig-bucket. **1935** MThomas *Inspector* (L) 24: As if every word were a pearl, and his hearers swine. **1941** RAldington *Life* (NY) 68: In comparison . . . the proverbial casting of pearls was a hopeful enterprise. **1945** RLHines *Confessions* (L) 219: A casting of artificial pearls before real swine. **1952** VPJohns *Murder* (NY 1962) 39: She might not have seemed just the swine not to cast pearls before. **1957** CPLee *Athenian* (NY) 194: I remembered the definition of education I once heard: "The casting of false pearls before real swine." **1958** *NYTimes Book Review* 4/27 5:

Mr. Miller is casting pearl onions before real swine. **1958** SBarr *Purely* (NY) 34: Imitation pearls before real swine, as the saying goes. **1965** JMaclaren-Ross *Memoirs* (L) 160: Pearl of wit too precious to cast before swine. **1968** JHaythorne *None of Us* (NY) 71: Mother regarded me as a pearl and my girl friends as swine. **1971** HGregory *House* (NY) 138: Throwing pearls before swine. **1974** DCavett *Cavett* (NY) 168: Woody had been casting pearls over the heads of swine. **1976** CTrowbridge *Crow* (NY) 101: Pick up your profession [*teaching*]: what some cynic has called "the casting of false pearls before real swine." **1981** AAndrews *Pig* (NY) 96: Pearls before swine. EAP P58; TW 278(2); Brunvand 107(3).

P77 As game as a **Pebble**

1932 BFlynn *Murder* (P) 202: As game as a pebble. **1934** HCorey *Crime* (NY) 221: She is as game as a pebble. Wilstach 167.

P78 As hard as **Pebbles**

1958 CLBlackstone *Dewey* (L 1965) 110: Her eyes were as hard as pebbles. Cf. Marbles *above*.

P79 To be the only **Pebble** on the beach (*varied*)

1924 CVanVechten *Tattooed* (NY) 143: She ain't the only pebble on the beach. **1931** MKennedy *Death to the Rescue* (L) 214: She doubtless thought she was the only pebble on the beach, to employ a vulgar phrase. **1932** BFlynn *Crime* (NY) 125: I am not the only pebble on the foreshore. **1932** RA Freeman *When Rogues* (L) 38: He was not the only pebble on the beach, as the vulgar saying has it; 59. **1939** FGerard *Red Rope* (NY) 210: You're not the only pebble on the beach. **1957** *BHerald* 9/25 39: They got to be showed they ain't the only puddles on the beach. **1958** *BangorDN* 7/25 11: Some fellows don't realize they aren't the only pebbles on the beach. **1959** TRoscoe *Only* (NY) 74: One girl isn't the only pebble on the beach at a beach resort. **1959** ASillitoe *Saturday* (NY) 198: There was always more than one pebble on the beach. **1969** AGilbert *Mr. Crook* (NY DBC) 118: He wasn't the only pebble on the beach. **1969** JAiken *Crys-*

tal (NY) 150: You're not the only apple on the tree. Whiting *NC* 456; Wentworth 380.

P80   To cry **Peccavi**

1931 VMeik *People* (L) 136: I cry *peccavi.* **1939** HFootner *Murder That* (L) 31: I must cry peccavi. EAP P61.

P81   A **Peck** of March dust *etc.*

1977 STWarner *Kingdoms* (NY) 67: A peck of March dust was worth a king's ransom. Whiting B611; *Oxford* 511: March dust.

P82   To be in a **Peck** of troubles

1910 EPhillpotts *Tales* (NY) 75: A proper peck of troubles. **1931** ACEdington *Monk's Hood* (NY) 306: In a peck of trouble. **1938** RAJWalling *Grimy Glove* (NY) 170: The padre had brought a peck of troubles on his head. **1941** GBagby *Here Comes* (NY) 61: The family's in a peck of trouble. **1957** RPHansen *Mark* (NY DBC) 32: You got yourself a peck of trouble. **1970** WANolen *Making* (NY) 251: Got us into a peck of troubles. **1974** MGEberhart *Danger* (NY) 38: The whole world is in a peck of trouble. EAP P62.

P83   To eat one's **Peck** of dirt *(varied)*

1916 RFirbank *Inclinations* (Works 2, L 1929) 58: You've got to eat a peck of dirt before you die. **1935** PATaylor *Deathblow* (NY) 87: Everyone should eat his peck of dirt. **1943** MVenning *Murder through* (NY) 213: There's a certain number of things that have to happen to everybody in his lifetime . . . you have to eat a peck of dirt and swallow a dozen flies. **1952** GKersh *Brazen* (L) 208: Every man must eat a bushel of dust before he dies. **1958** *BHerald* 10/15 24: You have to eat a peck of dirt in your life. EAP P64.

P84   To keep one's **Pecker** up

1920 EWallace *Three-Oaks* (L) 178: Just keep your pecker up. **1922** JJoyce *Ulysses* (NY 1934) 320: Keep your pecker up. **1932** JJFarjeon *Trunk-Call* (NY) 156: Keep your pecker up. **1935** BGrimshaw *Victorian* (NY) 147: Keep your pecker up. **1940** LBruce *Ropes and Rings* (L) 181: Keep your pecker up. **1946** CBush *Second Chance* (L) 244: Keep your pecker up. **1957** RLongrigg *Switchboard* (L) 126: Keep your pecker up. **1959** MPHood *Bell* (NY) 80: Man's got to keep his pecker up. **1966** JGaskell *Serpent* (NY 1968) 387: You need to keep your pecker up. **1969** PTheroux *Girls* (B) 13: Keep your pecker up. *Oxford* 419: Keep.

P85   A (round or square) **Peg** in a (square or round) hole *(very varied)*

1922 VSutphen *In Jeopardy* (NY) 10: Whittling my . . . peg to fit my allotted hole. **1927** BAtkey *Man* (NY) 227: The round peg in the circular hole. **1927** AHaynes *Crow's* (L) 5: A square peg in a round hole. **1929** WScott *Mask* (P) 146: Hesse is a bit of a square peg. **1929** JMWalsh *Mystery* (L) 57: He . . . found . . . that he was a round peg in a square hole or a square peg in a round hole, whichever you like. **1930** LBrock *Murder* (NY) 12: In this world the supply of pegs is very large. The number of holes, round and square, is comparatively limited. **1930** WLewis *Apes* (NY 1932) 533: A square peg in a square hole. **1931** JHRYardley *Before the Mayflower* (NY) 34: A round peg in a round hole was Captain John Smith. **1932** LAdamic *Laughing* (NY) 311: A square peg in a round hole, or *vice versa.* **1933** GHolt *Dark Lady* (L) 145: It was all as neat and fitting as a square peg in a round hole. **1934** CBush *Dead Shepherd* (L) 15: An attempt to fit round pegs into round holes. **1934** JRhode *Poison* (NY) 107: A square peg in a round hole. **1936** GWBrace *Islands* (NY) 91: A very square peg, she thought, and reflected that the hole she had had in mind was certainly round. **1936** BThomson *Who Killed* (NY) 43: The country has got on pretty well for the last few centuries with square men in round holes. **1937** MBurton *Murder* (L) 103: A square peg in a round hole. **1937** WLewis *Letters* ed WKRose (L 1963) 245: You are the perfect round peg in the round hole. **1939** FGerard *Red Rope* (NY) 50: Something of a square peg in a round hole. **1943** GGCoulton *Fourscore* (Cambridge, Eng.) 155: At last the square peg was finding a square hole. **1953** FLockridge *Curtain* (P) 13: The roundest of pegs in a perfectly rounded hole. **1955** RDavies *Leaven* (L) 211: There's much to be said for the square peg in the round hole, as the

Cubist told the Vorticist. **1956** MPHood *Scarlet* (NY) 130: A pleasant round peg in a very square hole. **1957** BWAldiss *Space* (L) 110: A round peg with a square hole somewhere inside him. **1957** *Punch* 2/6 229: Square pegs, displaced persons, round holes. **1957** *Punch* 2/27 309: Help to put the round and square pegs into their respective holes. 9/18 326: It is never the policy . . . to put a square peg into a round hole. **1957** *NYTimes* 9/29 37: Why put a square egg in a round roll? **1957** *BHerald* 11/24 3A: Square peg; round hole. **1957** RStandish *Prince* (L) 71: He was the traditional square peg in the round hole. **1957** IWallace *The Square Pegs* (NY). **1958** *Time* 10/6 94: A hip peg in a square world. **1958** PBranch *Murder's* (L 1963) 53: Many a square peg has eventually fitted into a round hole. **1959** DTaylor *Joy* (NY) 54: A square peg is withdrawing from a round hole. **1960** JPudney *Home* (L) 127: Square pegs in round holes. **1962** AWUpfield *Death* (NY) 179: A round peg in a square hole. **1964** CBrooke-Rose *Out* (L) 106: A square peg in a round hole. **1965** LBiggle *All the Colors* (NY) 100: If they were given to classifying things in terms of round holes, he was the square peg. **1967** RLockridge *Murder* (P) 51: A square bitch in a round hole. **1972** WJWatkins *Ecodeath* (NY) 9: A round peg in the square hole. **1973** RCondon *And Then* (NY) 217: The square-peg-round-hole men. *Oxford* 685: Round peg.

P86 To take (someone) down a **Peg** (or two)
1909 JCLincoln *Keziah* (NY) 84: He was took down a few pegs. **1919** CPearl *Morrison of Peking* (Sydney 1967) 378: Taken down a peg or two. **1932** ABCox *Murder* (L) 269: It was time to take him down a peg. **1939** AWebb *Mr. Pendlebury Makes* (L) 236: He needed taking down a peg or two. **1941** MTYates *Midway* (NY) 4: To take me down a peg. **1948** TKyd *Blood* (P) 9: To take him down a peg. **1955** DMDisney *Room* (NY) 126: It will take her down a peg or two. **1961** JSStrange *Eye* (NY) 68: Taking him down a peg. **1964** PKDick *Martian* (NY) 77: Ought to be taken down a peg or two. **1972** JDCarr *Hungry* (NY) 74: Don't try to take me down a peg. EAP P68; Brunvand 107.

P87 To pile **Pelion** on Ossa (*varied*)
1924 LSpringfield *Some Piquant* (L) 217: Piled Pelion upon Ossa. **1932** IGreig *Baxter's* (L) 244: It is piling Pelion upon Ossa. **1935** VWMason *Yellow Arrow* (L) 279: As though to pile the Pelion of sensation on the Ossa of the dramatic. **1940** CDickson *Plastic Man* (L) 248: That is piling Pelion on Ossa. **1950** ECRLorac *And Then* (NY) 202: There was Pelion piled on Ossa. **1955** WTenn *Of All* (NY) 82: Having achieved Ossa she cast about for Pelion. **1959** JThurber *Years* (B) 15: This day, however, the Ossa on the Pelion of his molehill miseries was the lost and found Jeannie. **1960** NFitzgerald *Ghost* (L) 204: This is piling a Pelion of absurdity on an Ossa of unlikelihood. **1961** LSdeCamp *Dragon* (NY 1968) 251: You might as well pile a Pelion of folly on an Ossa of impulse. **1971** CBeaton *My Bolivian* (L) 138: Pelion on Ossa, gilt on gingerbread. EAP P69.

P88 The **Pen** is mightier than the sword
1924 JSFletcher *Time-Worn* (NY) 203: The pen is mightier than the sword. **1937** WMartyn *Blue Ridge* (L) 316: That venerable proverb, "The pen is mightier than the sword." **1938** MSaltmarsh *Clouded* (NY) 113: Everyone says the pen is more pointed than the sword. **1946** HHowe *We Happy* (NY) 163: The pen was mightier than the sword. **1958** CCockburn *Crossing* (L) 104: I have . . . had . . . difficulty in believing that the pen really is mightier than the sword. **1958** RFraser *Jupiter* (L) 144: The pen is mightier than the sword. **1958** PUstinov *Add a* (B) 43: The pen is mightier than the sword. **1970** JWechsberg *First* (B) 125: The theory that the pen is mightier than the sword. **1973** EJKahn *Fraud* (NY) 244: How much less mighty is the pen than the sword. *Oxford* 618.

P89 As bright (pretty) as a (new) **Penny**
1936 VMcHugh *Caleb* (NY) 323: Bright's a new penny. **1952** JLeslie *Intimate* (NY) 177: Hair . . . as bright as a new penny. **1955** LWhite *Flight* (NY 1957) 13: Pretty as a new penny. **1958** HMasur *Murder* (NY 1959) 87: Bright as a penny. **1961** DLoovis *Last* (NY) 186: She was bright as a penny. **1966**

ACarter *Honeybuzzard* (NY) 22: The morning was as bright as a new penny. **1976** CLarson *Muir's* (NY) 88: Bright as a penny. Whiting *NC* 456(3). Cf. To shine *below*.

P90 A bad **Penny** always turns up (*varied*)
1914 PGWodehouse *Little Nugget* (NY 1929) 230: He turns up again like a bad ha' penny. **1922** JJoyce *Ulysses* (NY 1934) 154: Turn up like a bad penny. **1928** DHLawrence *Lady* ("Allemagne") 312: Michaelis turned up like a bad penny. **1929** DLSayers *Lord Peter* (NY) 152: Come back like a bad half penny. **1930** WLewis *Apes* (NY 1932) 73: Like a bad penny . . . the thing had turned up. **1930** JRhode *Peril* (NY) 191: He's sure to turn up again like the proverbial bad half penny. **1933** MBurton *Fate* (L) 41: He'll turn up again, like the proverbial bad halfpenny. **1947** MBurton *Will in the Way* (NY) 84: He turned up again like the proverbial bad penny. **1951** PCheyney *Ladies* (NY DBC) 157: I'm rather like a bad penny. I always turn up. **1952** RPowell *Shot* (NY) 89: Turning up like a bad nickel. I used to turn up like a bad penny, but inflation came along. **1957** MBryan *Murder* (NY) 33: He's like a bad penny, she thought. Only shows up when he's not wanted. **1964** ELathen *Accounting* (NY) 29: On the bad-penny principle that governs human affairs. **1964** RStewart *Professor* (NY) 240: "The black penny has returned." "Bad penny." **1967** RRendell *New Lease* (NY) 97: Back again . . . like the proverbial bad pennies. **1970** RLPike *Reardon* (NY) 62: Bob used to call me his Bad Penny, because he said he hoped I'll always show up. **1975** ELathen *By Hook* (NY) 100: Like the bad penny that keeps turning up. EAP P72; Brunvand 108(3).

P91 In for a **Penny**, in for a pound (*varied*)
1919 LThayer *Mystery of the 13th Floor* (NY) 218: In for a penny, in for a pound. **1932** PMacDonald *Escape* (NY) 224: In for a penny, in for a pound. **1938** ECRLorac *Slippery* (L) 139: In for a penny, in for a pound. **1948** FWCrofts *Silence* (NY) 31: The in-for-a-penny-in-for-a-pound argument. **1950** OAnderson *In for a Penny* (NY). **1956** SPalmer *Unhappy* (NY 1957) 147: In for a dime, in for a dollar. **1959** JWyndham *Outward* (NY) 48: In for a penny, in for a pound. **1967** JDCarr *Dark* (NY) 168: In for a penny, in for the whole bankroll. **1971** DGilman *Elusive* (NY) 93: In for a penny, in for a pound. **1972** JBonett *No Time* (NY) 123: Well, in for a penny if we couldn't have the pound, as you might say. **1973** OSela *Portuguese* (NY) 139: In for a dime, in for a dollar. EAP P73.

P92 Look out for the **Pennies** and the pounds will look out for themselves (*varied*)
1922 JJoyce *Ulysses* (NY 1934) 709: Having taken care of the pence, the pounds having taken care of themselves. **1930** WS Maugham *Cakes* (L 1948) 91: Look out for the pence . . . and the pounds'll look after themselves. **1936** *New Yorker* 4/18 18: If you take care of the pennies, the dollars will take care of themselves. **1944** RAJWalling *Corpse Without* (NY) 50: If you look after the pennies the pounds take care of themselves. **1957** LBeam *Maine* (NY) 165: Save the pennies and the dollars will take care of themselves. **1960** DHayles *Comedy* (L) 147: Look after the pennies and the pounds will look after themselves. **1960** CDLewis *Buried* (L) 132: A theory that, if you look after the pennies, you can do what you like with the pounds. **1962** EHuxley *Mottled* (L) 198: As my father used to say, take care of the seconds, and the hours will take care of themselves. **1965** MFrayn *Tin* (B) 5: Look after the small things and the big things will look after themselves. **1967** MBerkeley *Winking* (B) 25: Take care of the pennies and the dollars will take care of themselves. *Oxford* 798–9: Take.

P93 No **Penny**, no paternoster
1925 JICClarke *My Life* (NY) 74: The churchly motto, "No penny, no Paternoster." **1940** DTeilhet *Broken Face* (NY) 16: No penny, no paternoster. EAP P74.

P94 The **Penny** drops
1946 GBellairs *Death in the Night* (NY) 115: Colloquially, the penny hadn't dropped. **1952** PLoraine *Dublin* (L) 149: At last . . . the penny seemed to have dropped [*things*

got started]. **1961** CMacInnes *Mr. Love* (NY) 33: Suddenly the penny dropped [*he understood*]. **1964** SJay *Death* (NY) 170: The penny wouldn't drop. **1970** RCowper *Twilight* (NY) 40: The penny's dropped, has it? **1970** KGiles *Death* (L) 78: Your general inquiry dropped the penny.

P95   A **Penny** for one's thoughts (*varied*)
1911 FRS *Way of a Man with a Maid* (L) 188: A penny for your thoughts. **1922** JJoyce *Ulysses* (NY 1934) 354: A penny for your thoughts. **1924** JJFarjeon *Master* (NY) 203: I'm quite willing to hear your thoughts . . . and to pay a penny for them. **1932** RKing *Murder* (L) 246: I wouldn't give two cents . . . for your thoughts. **1932** JTFarrell *Young Lonigan* (NY 1935) 114: A penny for your thoughts. **1936** AHuxley *Eyeless* (NY) 137: A penny for your thought. **1941** BDougall *I Don't Scare* (NY) 166: It wouldn't have taken a penny to read his thoughts. **1950** EHemingway *Across* (NY) 185: Nobody would give you a penny for your thoughts, he thought. **1952** JWKrutch *Desert* (NY) 90: He was offered a penny for his thoughts. **1959** IWallach *Muscle* (B) 41: A penny for your thoughts. **1960** RWilson *Thirty Day* (NY) 106: A penny for your thoughts. **1968** KChristie *Child's* (L) 30: A penny for your thoughts. **1974** DGQuintano *Weekend* (NY) 39: Penny for 'em . . . to coin a phrase. **1976** MRReno *Final* (NY) 107: I wouldn't have needed to pay a penny for the thoughts of any of them. EAP P76; TW 279(2); Brunvand 107(1).

P96   A **Penny** saved is a penny earned (*varied*)
1929 DHammett *Red Harvest* (NY) 41: I became proverbial: "Money saved is money earned." **1933** PGWodehouse *Heavy* (B) 183: A penny saved is a penny earned. **1936** JTFarrell *World* (NY) 301: Penny saved was a penny earned. **1940** RAFreeman *Mr. Polton* (NY) 39: A penny saved is a penny earned. **1949** JEvans *Halo* (NY) 46: A penny saved was a penny earned. **1957** *NY Times* 9/22 3E: A penny saved is a penny earned. **1957** LDelRay *Robots* (NY) 52: A penny saved is a penny earned. **1958** *NY Times* 5/25 1F: Business acts on theme "A

penny saved . . ." **1958** *BangorDN* 9/15 19: You told me that a penny saved was a penny earned. **1963** AHLewis *Day* (NY) 41: A penny saved is a penny earned . . . a cliché. **1969** SMays *Reuben's* (L) 76: A penny saved is a penny gained. **1970** HCarmichael *Death* (NY) 171: My old mother used to say a penny saved was a penny earned. EAP P77; Brunvand 107(2). Cf. TW 279–80(3).

P97   **Penny**-wise and pound-foolish (*varied*)
1931 MElwin *Charles Reade* (L) 86: Penny-wise, pound-foolish. **1937** EJepson *Memories* (L) 125: Penny Royal, pound foolish. **1940** AAFair *Gold Comes* (NY) 92: She's penny-wise and pound-foolish. **1949** MG Eberhart *House* (NY DBC) 115: She was penny wise and pound foolish. **1950** MCarleton *Bride* (NY) 5: Penny-wise, pound-foolish. **1956** WMankowitz *Old* (B) 173: Penny wise pound foolish. **1959** *BHerald* 8/16 36: Penny-wise and dollar-foolish. **1960** *BTraveler* 5/10 1: Penny wise and pound foolish. **1965** GHolden *Don't Go* (NY) 103: A tendency toward penny wisdom and pound foolishness. **1970** KLouchheim *By the Political* (NY) 77: The Republicans are penny-wise and people-foolish. **1973** RCondon *And Then* (NY) 175: This boiler was not a matter of being penny-wise. It was strictly a matter of being pound foolish. EAP P79.

P98   To be without a **Penny** (*etc.*) to bless oneself with (*varied*)
1928 JJConnington *Tragedy* (B) 19: Without a farthing to bless ourselves with. **1929** PRShore *Bolt* (NY) 255: They hadn't a penny to bless themselves with. **1930** TCobb *Crime* (L) 55: A man without a penny to bless himself. **1932** MBurton *Death* (L) 137: I hadn't a bean to bless myself with. **1939** VHansom *Casual* (NY) 34: Not a dime to bless themselves with. **1945** JRhode *Shadow of a Crime* (NY) 138: Neither of us had a penny to bless ourselves with. **1948** JRhode *Death* (NY) 80: Hardly a bean to bless themselves with. **1956** AC Lewis *Jenny* (NY) 263: She had not a penny to bless herself with. **1956** MLSettle *O Beulah* (NY) 86: [He] ain't got a penny to bless himself with. **1962** JCreasey *Death* (NY DBC) 13: He'll never have a penny to bless him-

self with. **1965** AChristie *At Bertram's* (L) 12: She'd only got twopence or so a year to bless herself with. Whiting P115; *Oxford* 156: Cross. Cf. next entry.

P99 To be without two **Pennies** to rub together (*varied*)

1928 EHamilton *Four* (L) 274: [They] haven't two shillings in the world to rub together. **1936** TAPlummer *Dumb* (NY) 216: Marly hadn't two coins to jingle together. **1938** EHeath *Death Takes* (NY) 220: He lived ... without one penny to rub against another. **1950** RMacdonald *Drowning* (NY 1951) 40: The rest of them didn't have one nickel to clink against another. **1955** JBingham *Paton* (L 1964) 47: She hasn't got two ha'pence to rub together. **1955** BHitchens *F.O.B.* (NY) 168: Jane's never had two dimes to rub together. **1960** JBWest *Taste* (NY) 9: I hardly had a dime to rub against a quarter. **1968** DBagley *Vivero* (NY) 42: Those two haven't two cents to rub together. **1969** RBlythe *Akenfield* (NY) 81: He hadn't got two ha' pennies to rub together. **1971** PDennis *Paradise* (NY) 48: She ... probably didn't have two pesos to rub together. **1974** JCreasey *As Merry* (NY) 36: A young girl who hasn't two pennies to rub together. Cf. preceding entry.

P100 To cost a pretty **Penny** (*varied*)

1919 LMerrick *Chair* (L) 31: It must have cost a pretty penny. **1920** ACrabb *Samuel* (NY) 77: It's costing us a pretty penny. **1930** The Aresbys *Murder* (NY) 112: [Cost] a pretty penny. **1955** JEGill *House* (NY) 79: Cost the family a pretty penny. **1955** VWMason *Two* (NY) 88: Turning a pretty penny. **1961** FSinclair *But the Patient* (NY) 96: Put her back a pretty penny. **1966** MGEberhart *Witness* (NY) 118: It must have cost Boyd an ugly penny. **1967** WTucker *Warlock* (NY) 68: I'd give a pretty penny to find out! **1974** CMSmith *Reverend* (NY) 70: That must cost a pretty penny. Berrey 551.7.

P101 To shine like a new **Penny**

1935 BGraeme *Body* (L) 141: Black it was, and shining like a new penny. Whiting *NC* 456(8). Cf. As bright *above*.

P102 To take **Pennies** (money) from a blind man (*varied*)

1923 DFox *Doom* (NY) 241: Like taking pennies out of a blind beggar's cup. **1930** BFlynn *Creeping* (L) 112: It's like taking money from a blind man. **1937** GDilnot *Murder* (L) 202: Stick to something honest, like pinching pennies from a blind man's box or taking candy from a kid. **1941** EDaly *Murders in* (NY) 248: I've heard of taking pennies from a blind beggar. **1955** JPotts *Death* (NY) 86: He'd steal pennies out of a blind man's cup. **1957** MProcter *Midnight* (NY) 88: His had been a crime of proverbial meanness. He had stolen the pitiful takings of a blind beggar. **1965** AGilbert *Voice* (NY) 93: Threatening her was like taking pennies out of a blind man's hat. **1972** WJBurley *Guilt* (NY) 85: It was like taking money from a blind man. Berrey 145.6.

P103 To take **Pennies** from a dead man's eyes (*varied*)

1929 CRJones *King* (NY) 222: Hilda Hounten, typifying the proverbial sneak-thief, who would take the proverbial pennies from the proverbial eyes of the proverbial dead man, chose the lady's ring and pin. **1931** MNRawson *When Antiques* (NY) 249: So mean that "he'd steal the pennies off a dead man's eyes." **1936** JDosPassos *Big Money* (NY) 381: Jim would take the pennies off a dead man's eyes. **1939** MArmstrong *Murder in* (NY) 149: Adeline would steal the pennies off a dead nigger's eyes. **1958** RMacdonald *Doomsters* (NY) 132: You'd steal the pennies off a dead man's eyes and sell his body for soap. **1965** JPotts *Only Good* (NY) 90: You'd steal the pennies off a dead man's eyes. **1974** SChance *Septimus* (Nashville) 60: He would steal the halfpennies out of the baby's moneybox to put on his granny's eyelids. TW 280(8); Berrey 145.6.

P104 To turn an honest **Penny** (*varied*)

1922 JCFletcher *Herapath* (NY) 183: Turning an honest penny. **1933** DGBrowne *Dead* (L) 91: He turned a dishonest penny or two. **1939** AMcRoyd *Double Shadow* (NY) 86: I never even turned a crooked penny. **1942** MGEberhart *Wolf* (NY) 265: To turn an honest penny. **1953** HBPiper *Murder* (NY) 178: Anything to turn a dishonest dollar. **1956** CArmstrong *Dram* (NY 1958) 143: Or earn an honest penny. **1967** VThomson *V.Thomson* (L) 74: Without turning an honest penny. EAP P80.

P105 Not worth a **Penny-farthing**

1935 JCorbett *Man They Could Not Kill* (L) 131: His life is not worth a penny farthing. Cf. EAP P75.

P106 As red as a **Peony**

1934 EBove *Murder* (B) 221: The chief flushed as red as a peony. **1949** JDCarr *Below* (NY) 41: As red in the face as a peony. TW 280(1).

P107 More **People** know Tom Fool than Tom Fool knows (*varied*)

1931 EPhillpotts *Found* (L) 90: More people know Tom-fool than Tom-fool knows. **1936** LWMeynell *On the Night* (NY) 120: More people know Tom Fool than Tom Fool knows. **1950** LAGStrong *Which I* (L) 30: As my old aunt used to say, "More know Tom Fool than Tom Fool knows." **1953** ERuggles *Prince* (NY) 132: Everybody knows Tom Fool. **1964** DForbes-Robertson *My Aunt* (NY) 20: More fools know Tom Fool than Tom Fool knows. **1965** AGilbert *Voice* (NY) 26: It would be a case of more people knowing Tom Fool than Tom Fool knows. **1969** AGilbert *Mr. Crook* (NY DBC) 20: More people know Tom Fool than Tom Fool knows. *Oxford* 543: More know.

P108 **People** who live in glass houses should not throw stones (*varied*)

1914 PGWodehouse *Little Nugget* (NY 1929) 196: We are both in glass houses. Don't let us throw stones. **1928** HCrosby *Shadows* (Paris) 75: People in glass houses should not take baths in the day time. **1929** SGluck *Shadow* (NY) 248: You're a fine one to throw stones! [*one liar to another*]. **1934** JTFarrell *Young Manhood* (NY 1935) 362: People who live in glass houses, shouldn't fling bricks. **1934** JHHoulson *Blue Blazes* (L) 88: Remember the old proverb . . . "People who live in glass houses gather no moss." **1934** WLewis *Letters* ed WKRose (L 1963) 229: People who live in glass houses invar-iably throw stones. **1940** HBest *Twenty-fifth* (NY) 241: People who live in glass houses shouldn't throw stones. **1940** CLittle *Black Corridors* (NY) 146: You're living in a glass house to be throwing stones. **1951** PMcGerr *Death in* (NY) 135: The old practical policy of not starting stones flying when you're in a glass house. **1956** *BHerald* 6/11 23: The old sayin' about "People which live in glass houses should pull down the shades." **1957** JYork *Come Here* (NY) 155: If your own house has glass windows, you shouldn't throw stones. **1958** *BangorDN* 8/22 19: "Let the one who has not sinned cast the first stone." . . . No one is entirely without sin and therefore (according to that proverb) no one should cast stones. If you are through living in a glass house, go ahead and cast a few. **1959** *Time* 3/2 12: People in glass houses shouldn't throw stones. **1960** RWilson *Thirty Day* (NY) 98: As a dweller myself in a big glass house I was especially vulnerable to rocks. **1968** MHolroyd *L.Strachey* (L) 2.501: Throwing stones at others from within his own glass house. **1968** MMackay *Violent* (NY) 450: Louis was himself hardly one to throw stones out of the glass house of his Edinburgh youth. **1969** JDrummond *The People in the Glass House* (NY). **1970** JPorter *Dover Strikes* (NY) 195: People who live in glass houses shouldn't go around calling the pot black. EAP H333: House; Brunvand 72–3: House (3); *Oxford* 360: Head.

P109 Rich **People** have mean ways *etc.*

1967 JFDobie *Some Part* (B) 68: Rich people have mean ways and poor people have poor ways. Whiting *NC* 410: Folks.

P110 Young **People** will be young people

1931 JDCarr *Castle* (NY) 149: Young people will be young people. **1931** WWJacobs *Snug* (NY) 377: Young people will be young people. TW 280(4). Cf. Boys will, Girls *above*.

P111 As hot as cayenne **Pepper**

1937 ASoutar *One Page* (L) 234: And the article was as hot as cayenne pepper. EAP P86.

P112 To avoid like a **Pest** (pestilence)

1942 ABMaurice *Riddle* (NY) 25: They avoided it as a pestilence. EAP P90. Cf. Plague *below*.

P113 To be hoist with one's own **Petard** (*varied*)

1924 TMundy *Om* (NY) 80: That hoists him with his own petard. **1931** LTracy *Sandling* (NY) 286: The time-honoured position of the engineer hoist by his own petard. **1938** WChambers *Dog* (NY) 143: He's sunk on his own petard. **1950** IFletcher *Bennett's* (I) 183: Hoist on his own petard. **1956** MInnes *Appleby* (L) 189: The engineer—as Hamlet, once more, has it—was hoist with his own petard. **1959** *BHerald* 8/27 20: Has the Legislature hoist itself on its own economy petard. **1959** AGilbert *Death* (NY) 69: [She] was hoist on her own petard. **1963** JJMarric *Gideon's Ride* (NY) 193: How apt the trite sayings are . . . Hoist with his own petard. **1967** DBloodworth *Chinese* (NY) 39: Rarely has a man been hoist by such a fusillade of his own petards. **1967** FGruber *Pulp* (LA) 49: I was raised on my own petard and couldn't back down. **1969** JBoyd *Rakehells* (NY 1971) 151: Tamar was hoist on my petard [*sexual*]. **1972** JRathbone *Trip* (NY) 167: *Hoist him on his own petard* was the phrase that occurred to him, though he was rather vague as to what a petard was. **1977** RRendell *Judgment* (NY) 84: The hoisting of Eunice with her own petard. EAP P91.

P114 To rob **Peter** to pay Paul (*varied*)

1922 JJoyce *Ulysses* (NY 1934) 330: Robbing Peter to pay Paul. **1925** JGBrandon *Cork* (L) 105: Robbing Policeman Peter . . . to pay Policeman Paul. **1932** HLandon *Owl's* (L) 287: Borrowing from Peter to pay Paul. **1937** RBriffault *Europa* (NY) 426: He has robbed both Peter and Paul. **1939** JDCarr *Black Spectacles* (L) 200: You are robbing Peter to hang Paul. **1948** CRBoxer *Fidalgos* (Oxford 1968) 118: Robbing Peter to pay Paul. **1957** *BangorDN* 2/23 10: A case of robbing Taxpayer Peter to pay Taxpayer Paul. **1957** *BHerald* 12/7 4: But we must not steal from Humanities Peter to pay Science Paul. 5: We were trying to rob Peter to pay Paul. **1958** *BHerald* 9/25 3: Gibbons . . .

charged . . . that Gov. Furcolo "has been robbing Peter to pay pals." **1958** *New Yorker* 8/30 32: He is robbing Pater to paw Peale. **1959** BPalmer *Blind Man's* (NY) 51: I'm borrowing from Peter to pay Paul. Don't frown, darling. It's just a silly English thing—a saying, you know. **1960** *BHerald* 3/26 6: The robbing of the railroad Peter to pay the Paul of maritime transportation. **1960** *BangorDN* 4/22 14: Robbing Peter to pay Paul. **1973** JBWest *Upstairs* (NY) 123: Borrowing from Peter to pay Paul. **1976** EFoote-Smith *Gentle* (NY) 113: You've got to rob George to pay Paul. EAP P92; TW 281.

P115 **Petticoat** government

1904 JCLincoln *Cap'n Eri* (NY) 169: Petticoat government was wearing on him. **1922** JJoyce *Ulysses* (NY 1934) 515: Petticoat government. **1929** GMitchell *Speedy* (NY) 256: No petticoat government here. **1964** SSKlass *Everyone* (NY) 89: Living under petticoat government. EAP P93.

P116 To be in the wrong **Pew**

1931 TThayer *Greek* (NY) 266: They were in the wrong pew. **1934** HReilly *McKee* (NY) 142: You're in the wrong pew. **1938** VWMason *Cairo* (NY) 215: A case of right church, but wrong pew. **1941** KSecrist *Murder Makes* (NY) 129: You're in the right church, but the wrong pew. **1952** RFenisong *Deadlock* (NY) 83: Wandered into the wrong pew. **1957** *BangorDN* 5/7 20: You got in the wrong pew. TW 282(2).

P117 As dead as **Pharoah**

1953 RChandler *Long* (L) 102: The place seemed to be as dead as Pharoah. Wilstach 83. Cf. King Tut *above*.

P118 A **Philadelphia** lawyer (*varied*)

1903 ADMcFaul *Ike Glidden* (B) 256: It 'ud take a Phillydelphy lawyer to figger out. **1930** KCStrahan *Death* (NY) 240: Take a Philadelphia lawyer to make sense of it. **1932** JTFarrell *Young Lonigan* (NY 1935) 153: You shoulda been a Philadelphia lawyer with all them there words you use. **1938** PHaggard *Death Talks* (NY) 105: Made out by a Philadelphia lawyer, and it holds like iron. **1947** HCahill *Look* (NY) 1: Take a

Philadelphia lawyer to follow these wet roads. **1958** *BHerald* 6/6 23: If anyone can explain this he can take credit away from a Philadelphia lawyer. **1959** *NYTimes* 8/16 5: It could puzzle a Philadelphia lawyer. The corniness that caused New Englanders to say that "three Philadelphia lawyers were a match for the devil." **1960** *BHerald* 2/12 2: It would take 1000 Philadelphia lawyers to guarantee the purposes of this bill. **1960** AHLewis *Worlds* (NY) 10: The term "Philadelphia lawyer," used either in praise or opprobrium, has international significance. **1961** FBiddle *Casual* (NY) 399: A Philadelphia lawyer, in spite of the adage, could be curiously naive. **1962** RBissell *You Can* (NY) 231: An even dozen Philadelphia lawyers could make neither head, tail, or feathers of him. EAP P95.

P119 To appeal from **Philip** drunk to Philip sober (*varied*)

1922 JJoyce *Ulysses* (NY 1934) 509: Philip Drunk . . . Philip Sober. **1925** TRMarshall *Recollections* (I) 367: To appeal from Philip drunk to Philip sober. **1928** EBYoung *Murder* (P) 88: "I've only seen him sober." "And Philip drunk may be a different kind of bloke altogether." **1961** VCBrooks *From the Shadow* (NY) 60: Appeals from America drunk to America sober. EAP P96.

P120 **Physician** heal thyself (*varied*)

1933 MKennedy *Bull's Eye* (L) 50: Physician, 'eal thyself. **1950** SJepson *Hungry* (NY) 128: Physician, heal thyself. **1961** MErskine *Woman* (NY) 124: A clear case of "Physician, heal thyself." **1963** WMasterson *Man on* (NY DBC) 131: Heal Thyself, Doctor. **1963** EMCottman *Out-Island* (NY) 203: It was a case of "Physician, Heal Thyself." **1970** RRendell *Best Man* (NY) 38: Physician, heal thyself. EAP P102.

P121 In a **Pickle** (*varied*)

1919 JBCabell *Jurgen* (NY 1922) 36: Into an ugly pickle. **1921** ERBurroughs *Mucker* (NY) 59: Pretty pickle you've got yourself into. **1927** EHBall *Scarlet* (NY) 203: You have me in rather a pickle, as we vulgar Americans call it. **1937** LPendleton *Down East* (NY) 169: Grandfather was sure in a pickle. **1938** MBurton *Death* (L) 212: He'll find the house in the very dickens of a pickle. **1953** RBissell *7½ Cents* (B) 86: We'll be in a fine pickle of fish. **1954** RStout *Black* (NY) 64: We're in a pickle. **1960** RStout *Too Many* (NY) 175: You're in a pickle. **1962** HPentecost *Cannibal* (NY DBC) 109: We're all in a hell of a pickle. **1963** AHLewis *Day* (NY) 23: Her father's departure left Hetty in the proverbial pickle. EAP P104.

P122 To quarrel like two **Pickpockets**

1936 RAJWalling *Floating Foot* (NY) 39: You and I quarrelled like two pickpockets. Cf. EAP P105; *Oxford* 7: Agree.

P123 As beautiful as a **Picture**

1932 PHerring *Murder* (L) 280: His wife came out as beautiful as a picture. TW 282(1); Brunvand 108(1).

P124 As pretty as a **Picture**

1906 JCLincoln *Mr. Pratt* (NY) 316: As pretty as a picture. **1919** LMerrick *Chair* (L) 214: She was as pretty as a picture. **1924** IOstrandes *Annihilations* (NY) 47: Pretty as a picture. **1933** MAllingham *Sweet* (L 1950) 48: Pretty as a picture. **1957** *New Yorker* 10/5 49: Pretty as pictures. **1962** DTaylor *Blood* (NY) 99: She was as pretty as a picture with a million-dollar smile. **1966** JBell *Death* (NY) 57: Pretty as a picture. **1974** AMenen *Fonthill* (NY) 120: As pretty as a picture. TW 283(4); Brunvand 108(2). Cf. Postcard *below*.

P125 As good as the **Pictures**

1938 LBrock *Silver Sickle* (L) 116: Good as the pictures, isn't he? Cf. Play *below*.

P126 As cute as **Pie**

1957 *BangorDN* 3/14 30: Cute as pie. Taylor *Prov. Comp.* 31.

P127 As easy as **Pie** (*varied*)

1925 AJSmall *Death* (NY) 99: As easy as eating pie. **1925** GKnevels *Octagon* (NY) 49: As easy as pie to open. **1937** JBentley *Landor* (L) 277: It was as easy as pie. **1949** NBlake *Head* (NY) 135: As easy as pie. **1951** MSpillane *Long* (NY) 40: As easy as eating pie. **1955** PDennis *Auntie* (NY) 251: It was easy as pie. **1961** HKuttner *Bypass* (NY) 49:

It was easy as pie. **1968** RBissell *How Many* (B) 142: It's been easy as pie to stay on the wagon. **1976** JPorter *Package* (NY) 175: As easy as pie. Whiting *NC* 457(1); Taylor *Prov. Comp.* 38; *Western Folklore* 17(1958) 18: Pumpkin pie. Cf. As simple *below.*

P128 As good as **Pie**

1900 CFPidgin *Quincy A. Sawyer* (B) 180: She is just as good as pie to me. TW 283(1).

P129 As nice (pleasant) as **Pie**

1908 JCLincoln *Cy Whittaker* (NY) 388: She was nice as pie. **1922** JJoyce *Ulysses* (NY 1934) 309: Nice as pie. **1928** DMarquis *When the Turtles* (NY) 94: As pleasant and sociable as pie. **1940** HRutland *Poison Fly* (NY) 215: I've been as nice as pie. **1953** JRMacDonald *Meet* (NY) 184: She was as nice as pie. **1970** ACross *Poetic* (NY) 132: He's nice as pie underneath. Whiting *NC* 457(3); Taylor *Western Folklore* 17(1958) 17.

P130 As plain as **Pie**

1932 DLSayers *Have* (NY) 284: As plain as pie. **1953** NBlake *Dreadful* (L) 101: It was all plain as pie. **1957** COLocke *Hell Bent* (NY) 138: It is just as well to make it plain as pie.

P131 As polite (agreeable) as **Pie**

1937 KRoberts *Northwest* (NY) 334: Polite as pie. **1941** DVanDeusen *Garden Club* (I) 88: As polite as pie. **1947** VWMason *Saigon* (NY) 172: Agreeable as pie. **1965** HVan Dyke *Ladies* (NY) 14: Etta was as polite as pie.

P132 As simple as **Pie** (*varied*)

1929 AGray *Dead* (L) 58: The whole thing is as simple as pie. **1931** EQueen *Dutch* (NY) 183: Simple as eating pie. **1936** LPaul *Horse* (NY) 136: It had been as simple as mince pie. **1938** CRawson *Death from* (L) 221: It's as simple as pie. **1954** MMcCarthy *Charmed* (NY) 30: It's simple as pie. **1958** RKing *Malice* (NY) 135: Simple as pie. **1960** HSlesar *Enter* (NY 1967) 110: Simple as pie. **1964** AStratton *Great Red* (NY) 217: As simple as pi—or, rather two pis. Cf. As easy *above.*

P133 As sweet as **Pie**

1930 DOgburn *Ra-ta-plan!* (B) 283: Looking sweet as pie. **1937** RLGoldman *Judge Robinson* (L) 83: Wilks was sweet as pie. **1959** *BHerald* 3/8 24: He gave up, sweet as pie. **1964** DMDisney *Departure* (NY DBC) 117: Sweet-as-pie Mrs. Newton. **1964** R Stewart *Professor* (NY) 237: Sweet as pie. **1970** BWAldiss *Hand-reared* (L) 42: Mother was sweet as pie. Whiting *NC* 457(4); Taylor *Prov. Comp.* 80.

P134 **Pie** in the sky

1941 HAshbrook *Purple Onion* (NY) 247: We'll have pie in the sky. **1957** *Time* 12/9 100: Pie in the sky. **1958** *NYTimes* 4/20 57: A series of pie-in-the-sky projects. **1962** CKeith *Missing* (NY) 86: Yearning for pie in the sky. **1964** FArcher *Malabang* (NY DBC) 44: His pie-in-the-sky venture. **1972** HDPerry *Chair* (NY) 226: The money was pure "pie in the sky." **1977** PDickinson *Walking* (NY) 221: It's pie in the sky. Partridge 626.

P135 To be **Pie** to (for) someone

1929 HWade *Duke* (NY) 76: That was pie to Sir Horace. **1935** GDilnot *Inside* (L) 58: It looked like pie to me [*easy*]. Wentworth 387–8.

P136 As short as **Pie crust**

1906 JCLincoln *Mr. Pratt* (NY) 239: She snapped him up short as pie crust. **1910** JCLincoln *Depot Master* (NY) 89: You're shorter'n pie crust. EAP P111.

P137 As common as **Pig** (hog's) tracks

1937 WMartyn *Blue Ridge* (L) 261: Lots of the folks here is just dirt to him, common as hog's tracks. **1957** *New Yorker* 3/2 31: Common as pig trash [*of a woman*]. **1967** JFDobie *Some Part* (B) 227: Our major . . . was as common as pigtracks. Taylor *Prov. Comp.* 29.

P138 As dirty as a **Pig**

1931 DAldis *Murder in a Haystack* (NY) 20: I'm dirty as a pig. **1944** MVenning *Jethro* (NY) 200: Dirty as a pig. EAP P112; Brunvand 108(1). Cf. As dirty as a Hog *above.*

P139 As drunk as a **Pig** (hog)

1927 LBamburg *Beads* (NY) 204: He's drunk as a hog. **1927** GDHCole *Murder at Crome House* (NY) 165: Drunk as a pig. **1936** KSCole *I'm Afraid* (B) 14: Drunk as a pig. **1937** GDilnot *Murder* (L) 81: He's as drunk as a pig. **1953** RPostgate *Ledger* (L) 186: Drunk as a pig. **1960** EMcBain *Give the Boys* (NY) 94: Drunk as a pig. **1968** JMills *Prosecutor* (NY) 80: Drunk as a pig. EAP H237: Hog.

P140 As fat as a **Pig**

1934 VLoder *Murder* (L) 20: Fat as a pig. **1940** CLittle *Black Corridors* (NY) 238: You'll get fat as a pig. **1953** CLittle *Black Iris* (NY) 107: Men can get fat as pigs. **1956** CArmstrong *Dream* (NY 1958) 27: She'd be fat as a pig. **1973** ARoudybush *Gastronomic* (NY) 65: I'll be fat as a pig. Cf. As fat as a Hog *above*.

P141 As happy as a **Pig** (*varied*)

1941 RPSmith *So It Doesn't* (L 1947) 121: She had been happy as a little pink pig in the sunshine. **1956** *BHerald* 12/4 16: Happy as pigs in mud. **1957** *New Yorker* 5/4 101: They're as happy as pigs till I show up. **1966** BKnox *Ghost* (NY) 91: He's as happy as a pig in a mud bath. **1978** MHoward *Facts* (B) 67: I was a smug Miss Muffet, happy as a pig in shit. **1979** JGash *Grail* (NY) 32: I'm as happy as a pig in muck. TW 283(6). Cf. As happy as a Hog *above*.

P142 As obstinate (stubborn, headstrong) as a **Pig** (hog)

1928 HWade *Missing* (NY) 260: He's as obstinate as a pig. **1935** VLoder *Dead Doctor* (L) 164: As stubborn as a pig. **1937** LO'Flaherty *Famine* (NY) 29: He's as headstrong as a pig. **1940** MAllingham *Black Plumes* (L) 133: Obstinate as a pig. Wilstach 277.

P143 As proud as a **Pig** in hog waller

1961 MHHood *Drown* (NY) 16: Proud of himself as a pig in hog waller. Cf. Wilstach 548: As a white washed pig.

P144 As proud as a **Pig** (with two tails)

1935 PATaylor *Tinkling* (NY) 284: Pegley's proud as a pig. **1938** ECRLorac *John Brown's* (L) 10: He's as pleased as a pig with two tails. *Oxford* 651: Proud.

P145 As slick as a greased **Pig**

1941 GEGiles *Three Died* (NY) 109: "Worked, eh?" "Slick as a greased pig." Whiting *NC* 458(8).

P146 In a **Pig's** arse

1959 CBrown *Terror* (NY) 11: In a pig's hindquarter. **1960** JBWest *Taste* (NY) 23: In a pig's ass. **1972** KCConstantine *Vicksburg* (NY) 62: In a pig's ass it does. **1974** GMcDonald *Fletch* (I) 8: In a pig's ass. Spears 299: Pig's ass! Cf. Wentworth 389: Pig's eye.

P147 In a **Pig's** eye

1927 WDSteele *Man Who* (NY) 311: You'd make it in a pig's eye. **1932** ORCohen *Star* (NY) 270: In a pig's eye it does. **1937** ATilton *Beginning* (NY) 203: Fishing boat in a pig's eye! **1941** AMStein *Up to No Good* (NY) 267: In a pig's eye [*disbelief*]. **1962** HWaugh *Late* (NY) 34: In a pig's eye it doesn't. **1966** MMcShane *Night's* (NY) 110: In a pig's eye you are. TW 283–4(8).

P148 On the **Pig's** back

1922 JJoyce *Ulysses* (NY 1934) 177: On the pig's back. **1981** LCutter *Murder* (NY) 62: "There you are at last—home." "Dry and on a pig's back. Sorry to be late." Partridge 628.

P149 The only good **Pig** is one with its throat cut

1938 RAJWalling *Grimy Glove* (NY) 158: The only good pig was one with its throat cut. Cf. *Oxford* 376: Hog. Cf. Indian *above*.

P150 A **Pig** in a parlor

1964 FSwann *Brass* (NY) 67: As much out of place as a pig in a parlor. Cf. Skunk, Whore *below*.

P151 **Pigs** in clover

1933 KCStrachan *Meriwether* (NY) 29: Pigs in clover. **1956** WMankowitz *Old* (B) 19: With their pigs-in-clover ways [*nasty*]. **1967** CDrummond *Death* (NY) 174: The top brass live like pigs in clover. **1967** NWollaston *Jupiter* (L) 126: Happy as a pig in . . . the proverbial clover. EAP P125.

Pig

P152 Pigs may fly (*varied*)

1931 APryde *Emerald* (NY) 93: "When he is—!" "When the pigs begin to fly." **1934** HVines *This Green* (B) 130: His mother's old saying . . . "That beats a hog a flying." **1935** VGielgud *Death* (L) 182: "She might talk, sir." "Pigs might fly." **1940** WCClark *Murder Goes* (B) 82: And maybe pigs have wings. **1952** PGWodehouse *Pigs Have Wings* (NY). **1954** EWalter *Untidy* (P) 106: When pigs fly, that's when. **1960** AGilbert *Out for* (NY 1965) 83: And pigs might fly. **1960** HInnes *Doomed* (NY) 133: Suppose pigs had wings. **1970** PMoyes *Many* (NY) 118: If that woman died from natural causes, then pigs can fly and I'm a Dutchman. **1977** STWarner *Kingdoms* (NY) 110: Mortals . . . long, like pigs in the proverbs, for wings. *Oxford* 625.

P153 Pigs see the wind (*varied*)

1955 RGraves *Homer's* (NY) 179: The Sicans say, "The old white sow can tell which way the wind blows, and is never mistaken." **1966** ARRandell *Sixty* (L) 96: Pigs are supposed to "see wind." *Oxford* 625.

P154 Pigs smell their own smells first

1966 NMonsarrat *Life(I)* (L) 66: Pigs smell their own smells first. *Oxford* 284: Fox the finder.

P155 To bleed like a (stuck) **Pig** (hog)

1928 WSMasterman *2 LO* (L) 196: He's bleeding like a stuck pig. **1930** LBrock *Murder* (NY) 115: Bleeding . . . like the traditional stuck pig. **1931** RFFoster *Murder* (NY) 51: He's bleeding like a pig. **1937** WE Turpin *These Low* (NY) 322: Bleedin' like a hog. **1938** WEHayes *Black* (NY) 268: He's bleeding like a stuck hog. **1950** Lord Dunsany *Strange* (L) 86: The phrase "bleeding like a pig." **1950** ECRLorac *Accident* (NY DBC) 150: Bleeding like a stuck pig. **1959** RVanGulik *Chinese* (NY) 135: You were bleeding like a pig. **1962** NMcLarty *Chain* (NY) 110: That agent, bleeding like a stuck pig. **1965** HMiller *Quiet Days* (NY) 150: That bitch is bleeding like a stuck pig. **1976** LEgan *Scenes* (NY) 46: I'm bleeding like a stuck pig. **1979** CMacLeod *Luck* (NY) 51:

"Bleeding like a stuck pig" was no fanciful metaphor. EAP P120.

P156 To bring one's **Pigs** (hogs) to market (*varied*)

1927 CBStilson *Seven* (NY) 185: He had brought his unwholesome eggs to the wrong market. **1930** AChristie *Mysterious* (NY) 61: You can take your pigs to a better market. **1930** RAFreeman *Mr. Pottermack* (NY) 157: Mr. Pottermack had brought his pigs to the wrong market. **1936** CGBowers *Jefferson in Power* (B) 74: I carried my pigs to a good market. **1939** FBeeding *Ten Holy* (NY) 172: We have brought our pigs to market. **1953** OAtkinson *Golden* (I) 253: Pap has taken his hogs to a pretty poor market. **1956** ACLewis *Jenny* (NY) 200: Are you still driving that pig to market? **1968** EBuckler *Ox Bells* (NY) 15: Some said she drove her pigs to a poor market when she first married Jim. **1968** BHays *Hotbed* (NY) 73: You fetched your ducks to a poor market. TW 284(14); *Oxford* 376: Hogs.

P157 To buy a **Pig** in a poke (*varied*)

1905 JBCabell *Line* (NY 1926) 147: He, also, is buying—though the saying is somewhat rustic—a pig in a poke. **1908** MDPost *Corrector of Destinies* (NY) 157: Sells you a pig in a poke. **1924** JSFletcher *King* (NY) 94: To buy a pig in a poke. **1932** PHerring *Murder* (L) 245: You're not buying a pig in a poke . . . You've seen its ears. **1935** CSt JSprigg *Perfect* (NY) 127: A pig in a poke is the proverb you're looking for. **1938** RAJWalling *Grimy Glove* (NY) 92: A pig in a poke . . . I don't buy. **1940** JDCarr *Man Who* (NY) 12: I do not buy pigs in pokes. **1948** MInnes *Night* (L 1966) 15: She must have been a pig in a poke. **1955** PMacDonald *Guest* (NY) 158: I wouldn't let a friend buy what we call a pig in a poke. **1956** *BangorDN* 12/22 10: Portland's pig in a poke. **1957** *BHerald* 3/28 22: To sell a pig in a poke. **1961** RJWhite *Smartest* (L) 31: I had bought a pig in a poke. **1964** FArcher *Malabang* (NY DBC) 108: I'm supposed to buy a pig in a poke. **1971** PDennis *Paradise* (NY) 213: A vision of a pig in a poke growing into a huge white elephant. **1972** SBirmingham *Late John* (P) 224: It was a five-

489

figure pig in a poke. EAP P121; TW 284 (15); Brunvand 109(2).

P158   To drink like a **Pig**

1934 CDWoodyatt *Satan's* (NY) 140: Drink like a pig. **1948** NMailer *Naked* (NY) 206: Get drunk like pigs. **1950** MRHodgkin *Student* (L) 72: He drank like a pig. **1951** PCheyney *Ladies* (NY DBC) 49: He was drinking like a pig.

P159   To eat like a **Pig** (hog)

1922 JJoyce *Ulysses* (NY 1934) 151: Eat pig like pig. **1930** FRyerson *Seven* (L) 162: Eats like a hog. **1933** PStong *Strangers* (NY) 127: They eat like pigs. **1944** MLong *Bury* (NY) 108: Gordon ate like a hog. **1957** WHHarris *Golden* (NY) 199: Ate like the proverbial pig. **1958** ELacy *Be Careful* (NY) 113: Betty ate like a pig. Whiting *NC* 425: Hog (9).

P160   To gape like a stuck **Pig**

1933 GDilnot *Thousandth* (L) 90: Gaping like a stuck pig. Wilstach 168.

P161   To have the wrong (right) **Pig** by the ear

1926 SQuinn *Phantom* (Sauk City, Wisc. 1966) 36: You've got the wrong pig by the ear. **1928** ALivingston (NY) 255: Norvallis has the right pig by the ear. EAP P122. Cf. Sow *below*.

P162   To lead **Pigs** through shit

1971 PDennis *Paradise* (NY) 287: You're not fit to lead pigs through shit. Cf. Guts *above*.

P163   To live like a **Pig** *etc.*

1970 NMonsarrat *Breaking* (L) 419: That guy lives like a pig with its ass in butter. EAP P124.

P164   To scream like a stuck **Pig**

1961 HCromwell *Dirty* (LA) 239: She screamed like a stuck pig. TW 284(19). Cf. Brunvand 109(3): Cried.

P165   To sleep like a **Pig**

1923 EWallace *Clue of the New Pin* (B) 63: You were sleeping like a pig. **1933** EJepson *Memoirs* (L) 146: They slept like pigs. **1963** BHecht *Gaily* (NY) 70: He'll sleep like a pig. EAP P127. Cf. To sleep like a Hog *above*.

P166   To snore like a **Pig** (hog)

1932 GHeyer *Footsteps* (L) 175: Snoring like a pig. **1932** PMacDonald *Escape* (NY) 153: Snoring like a hog. **1933** MKennedy *Bull's Eye* (L) 255: Richard's still snoring like a hog. **1939** VWilliams *Fox Prowls* (B) 157: He's snoring like a pig. **1958** HCarmichael *Into* (NY) 119: You snore like a pig. **1962** EAmbler *Light* (L) 187: You snore like a pig. **1962** EFRussell *Great* (NY) 172: Snoring like a pig. **1970** CDrummond *Stab* (NY) 55: Snoring like a hog. **1973** ELopez *Seven* (NY) 25: Snoring away like a pig. Whiting H407: Rout . . . hog; Brunvand 109(4); *Oxford* 685: Routing . . . hog.

P167   To squeal (bleat) like a (stuck) **Pig**

1933 HMSmith *Crevenna Cove* (NY) 24: He squeals like a stuck pig. **1937** SFowler *Post-Mortem* (L) 188: I think he'll squeal like a stuck pig. **1941** JKVedder *Last Doorbell* (NY) 243: He was bleating like a stuck pig. **1944** CWoolrich *Black Path* (NY) 117: He'll squeal like a stuck pig. **1957** RStandish *Prince* (L) 52: Losses made him squeal like the proverbial stuck pig. **1966** ELathen *Murder* (NY) 73: He squealed like a pig. **1967** RVanGulik *Necklace* (NY) 86: Squealed like a pig. EAP P128.

P168   To stand like a stuck **Pig**

1930 EWallace *India* (NY) 7: Don't stand there mooning like a stuck pig. **1933** ESnell *And Then* (L) 139: Don't stand there like a stuck pig. **1936** GDHCole *Last Will* (NY) 158: Don't stand there like a stuck pig. **1940** HReilly *Murder in* (NY) 230: Don't stand there like a stuck pig. **1963** AChristie *Mirror* (NY) 174: Harry just stood there like a stuck pig.

P169   To stare like a stuck **Pig**

1928 SFWright *Deluge* (NY) 128: They "stare like a stuck pig." EAP P129.

P170   To sweat like a (stuck) **Pig** (hog)

1928 BAWilliams *Dreadful* (NY) 91: Sweating like a pig. **1941** CLClifford *While the Bells* (NY) 107: I sweat like a pig. **1949** MAllingham *More Work* (NY) 195: The old gentleman was sweating like a pig. **1952** W Clapham *Night* (L) 229: Casey was sweatin' like a pig. **1959** TWalsh *Dangerous* (B DBC)

153: What are you sweating for like a stuck pig? **1961** FPohl *Turn Left* (NY) 7: He was sweating like a hog. **1970** NMonsarrat *Breaking* (L) 500: Sweating like a pig. Taylor *Western Folklore* 17(1958) 17(4).

P171 To yell (holler) like a stuck **Pig**

1952 EPaul *Black* (NY) 166: You yelled like a stuck pig. **1954** MLSettle *Love* (L) 145: He'd holler like a stuck pig. **1969** HPentecost *Girl Watcher* (NY) 122: He began to yell like a stuck pig.

P172 As plump as a **Pigeon**

1922 JJoyce *Ulysses* (NY 1934) 434: Plump as a pampered pouter pigeon. **1956** MProcter *Ripper* (NY) 58: The young barman was as plump as a pigeon. **1957** SAlexander *Michelangelo* (NY) 454: She was . . . plump as a pigeon. TW 285(1).

P173 As straight as a homing **Pigeon** (*varied*)

1941 MHolbrook *Suitable* (NY) 2: Straight as a homing pigeon. **1946** JTShaw *Hard-Boiled* (NY) 411: Straight as a homing pigeon. **1947** GGallagher *I Found* (NY DBC) 93: The unerring instinct of a homing pigeon. **1957** CCarnac *Late Miss* (NY) 143: You came direct here like a homing pigeon. Cf. Whiting *NC* 443: Martin.

P174 To be one's **Pigeon**

1922 VBridges *Greensea* (NY) 67: That's his pigeon. **1933** ABCox *Jumping* (L) 257: This is your pigeon. **1940** MCharlton *Death of* (L) 141: It isn't your pigeon. **1956** RFenisong *Bite* (NY) 13: Blackmail wasn't your pigeon. **1970** HCarvic *Miss Seeton Draws* (NY) 99: It wasn't his pigeon. **1973** JMann *Troublecross* (NY) 156: It's not really my pigeon. NED Suppl. Pidgin c; Partridge 628(6).

P175 As plain (clear) as a **Pikestaff** (*varied*)

1905 JBCabell *Line* (NY 1926) 186: It was plainer than a pike-staff. **1919** SLeacock *Frenzied* (Toronto 1971) 37: As plain as a pikestaff. **1922** JJoyce *Ulysses* (NY 1934) 295: I'm after seeing him . . . as plain as pikestaff. **1924** FWCrofts *Cask* (NY 1936) 142: As plain as a pikestaff. **1930** LBrock *Murder* (NY) 179: As clear as a pikestaff.

1930 JBude *Loss* (L) 237: An imprint . . . as clear as a pikestaff. **1933** MBurton *Fate* (L) 22: All these things ought to be as plain as a pikestaff to you. A deal plainer, in fact, because you probably wouldn't recognize a pikestaff if you saw one. **1934** EPhillpotts *Mr. Digweed* (L) 205: As plain as the proverbial pikestaff. **1935** VGielgud *Death* (L) 99: It's as plain as our old friend the pikestaff and about as useful. **1939** AWebb *Mr. Pendlebury Makes* (L) 178: It's as plain as the—eh—proverbial pikestaff, which should, by the way, be packstaff. **1952** PLoraine *Dublin* (L) 116: It was as plain as a pikestaff. **1953** CCarnac *Policeman* (NY) 152: It looks as plain as a pikestaff. **1964** AHunter *Gently* (NY) 110: Plainer than a pikestaff. **1970** PMoyes *Many* (NY) 122: As plain as a pikestaff. EAP P134.

P176 As stiff as a **Pikestaff**

1929 JCPowys *Wolf* (NY) 1.382: Stiff as a pikestaff. TW 285(2).

P177 As straight as a **Pikestaff**

1944 HReilly *Opening Door* (NY) 105: As straight as a pikestaff. TW 285(3).

P178 **Pilgarlic**

1931 LPowys *Pagan's* (NY) 103: The venerable head of this old pilgarlic. EAP P135.

P179 To gild the **Pill** (*varied*)

1932 RCWoodthorpe *Public* (L) 69: Gild the pill. **1967** HCole *Christophe* (NY) 232: There was very little gilt on the pill. **1969** TBesterman *Voltaire* (NY) 34: The pill was sugar-coated and even gilded. EAP P139.

P180 To swallow a bitter **Pill**

1940 DWheelock *Murder at Montauk* (NY) 139: A bitter pill for Mrs. Jessup to swallow. EAP P140; Brunvand 109.

P181 As straight as a **Pillar**

1941 VWMason *Rio Casino* (NY) 106: Straight as a pillar. Cf. Whiting P204: Upright.

P182 From **Pillar** to post (*varied*)

1900 JLondon *Letters* ed KHendricks (NY 1965) 85: Knocked from pillar to post. **1923** HGartland *Globe* (NY) 259: To be kicked from pillar to post. **1930** SGlueck *500 Crim-*

inal Careers (NY) 56: Wandering from pillar to post. **1938** PATaylor *Banbury* (NY 1964) 245: Scamperin' around from pillar to post, an' from post to pillar. **1940** PWentworth *Rolling* (P) 41: They were running him round from pillar to post. **1941** FCharles *Vice Czar* (NY) 265: Or am I just another one of your women to be bandied about from pillar to post? **1956** *BangorDN* 5/25 9: Eisenhower needs in Congress Republicans upon whom he can count—not those who jump from pillar to post. **1956** *Time* 9/17 108: He was shuttled between expensive pillar and posh post. **1958** *NYTimes* 7/27 5E: Editorial writers battered the United States Government from pillar to post. **1960** MCohen *Rider Haggard* (L) 24: Rider's pillar-to-post education. **1963** VSheean *Dorothy* (B) 255: Red was constantly moving from pillar to post. **1974** GMeyer *Memphis* (NY) 227: A pillar-to-post existence. EAP P246: Post; TW 285(2); Brunvand 109, 112: Post.

P183 A **Pillar** of the church

1931 CBrooks *Ghost* (NY) 241: He was a pillar of the church. **1934** MHBradley *Unconfessed* (NY) 125: She's a pillar in the Presbyterian church. **1966** HWaugh *Pure* (NY) 89: Pillar of the church. EAP P143.

P184 As bright as a new **Pin**

1935 CBarry *Death* (NY) 88: As bright as a new pin. **1939** PWentworth *Blind Side* (P) 171: As bright and neat and clean as a new pin. **1959** AGilbert *Prelude* (NY DBC) 27: Everything was as bright as a new pin. EAP P146; Brunvand 109(3). Cf. As bright . . . Needle *above.*

P185 As clean as a **Pin** (button)

1924 LO'Flaherty *Thy Neighbour's* (L) 205: As clean as a new pin. **1932** FBeeding *Take It* (B) 86: All clean as a new pin. **1941** AB Cunningham *Strange Death* (NY) 66: She was as clean as a pin. **1948** CBush *Curious* (NY) 19: The house is as clean as a new pin. **1954** CCarnac *Policeman* (NY) 41: Clean and neat as the proverbial new pin. **1957** *BangorDN* 3/19 18: All feet clean as a pin. **1957** *Punch* 10/2 393: A room . . . clean as a new button. **1959** FCrane *Buttercup* (NY

DBC) 90: She's clean as a pin and the salt of the earth. **1970** PMoyes *Many* (NY) 116: The room . . . was clean and trim as a new pin. **1975** JFraser *Wreath* (NY) 25: It's as clean as a new pin [*a corpse*]. Whiting *NC* 458(1); Brunvand 109(2).

P186 As like as two **Pins** (row of pins)

1931 PGWodehouse *If I Were You* (NY) 105: Like me as two pins. **1935** JRhode *Corpse* (L) 177: They are as alike as two pins. **1945** HCBailey *Wrong Man* (NY) 145: In sex matters men and women were like a row of pins. **1957** JBrooks *Water* (L) 213: They're as alike as two pins. Whiting *NC* 458(2).

P187 As neat as a (new) **Pin**

1930 EBarker *Redman* (NY) 220: Neat as a new pin. **1941** RHLindsay *Fowl Murder* (B) 173: Throat cut from front to back—neat as a pin. **1957** *BHerald* 4/7 40: The place was as neat as a pin. **1959** AGilbert *Death* (NY) 42: Leaving the place as neat as the proverbial new pin. **1960** AGilbert *Out for* (NY 1965) 47: The place is so neat it 'ud make the proverbial pin look messy. **1970** RFenisong *Drop* (NY) 121: Neat as a pin. **1973** AGilbert *Nice* (NY) 54: Neat as the proverbial new pin. EAP P147; Brunvand 109(1).

P188 As sharp as a **Pin**

1957 *Punch* 9/23 368: With shoes as sharp as pins. **1959** SMartin *Third* (NY) 125: Sharp as a pin. Whiting *NC* 458(4); Taylor *Prov. Comp.* 71.

P189 As slick as a (new) **Pin**

1930 JSFletcher *Investigators* (NY) 126: You're as slick as a new pin. **1939** JPPhilips *Death Delivers* (NY) 278: Everything worked slick as a pin. **1952** AAFair *Top* (NY) 32: The cabin was slick as a pin. TW 286(4).

P190 As smart as **Pins**

1934 GSinclair *Cannibal* (NY) 177: Smart as pins. Whiting *NC* 458(5).

P191 As spruce as a new **Pin**

1928 LBrock *Slip-Carriage* (NY) 304: Spruce as a new pin. **1962** JJMarric *Gideon's March* (NY) 91: Was as spruce as a new pin.

P192   As straight as a **Pin**

1941 FCrane *Turquoise* (P) 54: Straight as a pin [*a man*]. TW 286(5). Cf. As clean as a Needle *above*.

P193   As tidy as a (new) **Pin**

1931 HWade *No Friendly* (L) 215: Tidy as a new pin. **1959** HLGold *World* (NY 1961) 87: Everything was as tidy as a pin.

P194   As trim as a **Pin**

1934 EQueen *Adventures* (NY) 331: The room was as trim as a pin. **1968** JAiken *Crystal* (NY) 211: Eleanor, trim as a pin.

P195   For two **Pins** one would (do this or that)

1925 JGBrandon *Bond* (L) 103: For two pins . . . I'd go down. **1932** GHolt *Drums* (L) 138: For two pins I'd knock you right down. **1945** GDaniel *Cambridge* (L 1952) 24: For two pins I'd throttle him. **1954** HCecil *According* (L) 179: For two pins he'd say he'd done it. **1959** HEBates *Breath* (B) 156: For two pins I'd have my blasted face lifted. **1967** LPDavies *Artificial* (NY) 14: For two pins . . . I'd do just that. **1970** JPorter *Dover Strikes* (NY) 104: For two pins he'd do it now. **1972** HCarmichael *Naked* (NY) 79: For two pins I'd tell you.

P196   Not a **Pin** to choose

1919 LMerrick *Chair* (L) 62: There is not a pin to choose between the pair of you. **1928** GGardiner *At the House* (NY) 188: Not a pin to choose between it and his master's. **1931** WWJacobs *Snug* (NY) 341: There didn't seem to be a pin to choose between 'em. **1956** HReilly *Canvas* (NY 1959) 99: There wasn't a pin to choose between them. Brunvand 109(4).

P197   Not care a **Pin** (two pins) (*varied*)

1917 MGibbon *Inglorious* (L 1968) 228: I don't care a pin. **1922** JJoyce *Ulysses* (NY 1934) 347: But not a pin cared Ciss. **1922** DLindsay *Haunted Woman* (L 1964) 15: I don't care two pins. **1931** LTracy *Sandling* (NY) 196: No one . . . cared a pin. **1933** EBailey *Death* (L) 101: I don't care a packet of pins. **1933** GBeaton *Jack* (L) 115: [Not] care two pins if I reap pains or pleasures. **1938** NShepherd *Death Walks* (L) 106: He

didn't care a bent pin for what [they] said. **1950** JCannan *Murder* (L 1958) 115: He didn't care a pin. **1953** EBigland *Marie* (L) 240: She cared not a pin. **1962** ADuggan *Lord* (L) 172: She didn't care a pin. **1964** HBTaylor *Duplicate* (NY) 98: That girl didn't care two pins. EAP P149.

P198   Not give a **Pin**

1926 LO'Flaherty *Mr. Gilhooley* (L) 156: He didn't give a pin for them. **1960** CBeaton *My Royal* (NY) 78: I didn't give a pin. **1963** MPHood *Sin* (NY) 109: I don't give a pin. EAP P152.

P199   Not matter two **Pins** (a pin)

1922 JSFletcher *Rayner-Slade* (NY) 290: Not matter two pins. **1930** ABrown *Green Lane* (L) 200: That don't matter a pin. EAP P148; Tilley P334 (quote 1604).

P200   Not worth a **Pin**

1928 VMarkham *Death* (NY) 334: His evidence . . . isn't worth a pin. EAP P155.

P201   See a **Pin** *etc.*

[As a child (c1912) I remember hearing: See a pin and pick it up, All the day you'll have good luck. See a pin and leave it lie, You'll be poor before you die. *BJW*] **1963** BKnox *Grey* (NY) 163: See a pin and pick it up, all the day we'll have ruddy good luck. **1965** JSUntermeyer *Private* (NY) 127: See a pin, pick it up—all the day you'll have good luck. **1966** AChristie *13 Clues* (NY) 4: They do say: "See a pin and pick it up, all the day you'll have good luck." **1969** SMays *Reuben's* (L) 164: See a pin and pick it up, And all the day you'll have good luck. See a pin and let it lie, Before the evening you will cry. *Oxford* 626.

P202   To be in a merry **Pin**

1934 NMarsh *Man Lay* (B 1972) 179: I see you are in a merry pin. EAP P156; *Oxford* 528: Merry.

P203   To be on **Pins** and needles (tacks) (*varied*)

1911 MLevel *Grip of Fear* (NY) 88: On pins and needles. **1922** JJoyce *Ulysses* (NY 1934) 737: On pins and needles about the shop girl in that place on Grafton Street. **c1923**

ACrowley *Confessions* ed JSymonds (L 1969) 799: On pins and needles. **1933** WChambers *Campanile* (NY) 218: I've been on pins and needles. **1934** LRGribble *Death* (L) 177: I've got pins and needles [*nervous*]. **1935** Edwin Greenwood *Pins and Needles* (L). **1938** HWSandberg *Crazy* (NY) 16: Here we've been sitting on tacks, while you knew all the time. **1940** HSKeeler *Crimson Box* (L) 31: I'll be sittin' on red-hot needles an' pins. **1945** PWentworth *She Came* (NY) 95: It gives me pins and needles all over to watch her. **1947** PWentworth *Wicked* (NY) 199: It gives me pins and needles to think of it. **1954** ESGardner *Restless* (NY) 164: The doctor who treated you is on pins and needles. **1955** EJKahn *Merry* (NY) 213: With the audience alternately on pins and needles and in stitches. **1961** JAMichener *Report* (NY) 123: I sat on needles waiting. **1969** HWaugh *Run* (NY) 62: I'm not cool. I'm on pins and needles. **1973** MGEberhart *Murder* (NY) 206: Seth must have been on pins and needles. EAP P160; Brunvand 109(6); *Oxford* 626.

P204 To hear a **Pin** drop (*varied*)

1919 LMerrick *Chair* (L) 222: One might have heard a pin drop. **1920** AChristie *Mysterious Affair* (NY) 138: You could have heard a pin drop. **1927** FWCrofts *Starvel* (NY) 269: While French was speaking the proverbial pin could have been heard, had any one tried the experiment of dropping it in the courthouse. **1931** MAHamilton *Murder* (L) 301: The silence now was such that the proverbial pin could have been heard dropping. **1932** MCJohnson *Damning* (NY) 41: One could almost have heard the proverbial drop of a pin. **1935** VGielgud *Death* (L) 28: There was a little pause, during which the proverbial pin would probably have dropped unobserved. **1936** WSMasterman *Rose* (NY) 264: In the hush that followed, the proverbial pin could have been heard to drop. **1940** JSStrange *Picture* (NY) 259: One could have heard the proverbial pin or a straw falling in the silent room. **1949** SJepson *Golden* (NY) 206: There was a moment's pin-dropping quiet. **1951** ADean *August* (NY) 33: You could have heard a pin drop. **1953** ANoyes *Two*

(P) 318: He was not going to drop the traditional pin [*to be heard*]. **1958** RHutton *Of Those* (L) 55: You could have heard the proverbial pin drop. **1959** AGilbert *Prelude* (NY DBC) 140: You could hear the proverbial pin drop. **1961** ESherry *Call* (NY DBC) 131: You could have heard the legendary pin. **1963** JGBallard *Passport* (NY) 33: "It's one of those *proverbial* sounds." . . . "A pin dropping." **1970** JJMarric *Gideon's Sport* (NY) 161: Absolute hush, pin-drop quiet. **1976** RBDominic *Murder* (NY) 105: You could have heard a pin drop. EAP P162; Brunvand 109(5).

P205 To shine like a new **Pin**

1937 GGoodchild *Call McLean* (L) 164: Shining like a new pin. **1939** JRonald *This Way Out* (P) 35: Shinin' like a noo pin. TW 286(12).

P206 As straight as a **Pine**

1954 AStone *Harvard* (B) 7: Straight as a pine. **1959** PDeVries *Through* (B) 31: Straight as a pine. **1963** MPHood *Sin* (NY) 138: An old woman, straight as a pine. EAP P165; Brunvand 110(1).

P207 As tough as a **Pine** knot

1950 FFGould *Maine Man* (NY) 52: They were tough as a pineknot. **1960** BCCleak *Long* (NY) 151: He was tough as a pine knot. Whiting *NC* 459.

P208 As pretty as a **Pink**

1909 JCLincoln *Keziah* (NY) 266: Girl . . . pretty as a pink. TW 286(1).

P209 Put that in your **Pipe** and smoke it

1922 JJoyce *Ulysses* (NY 1934) 356: They could put that in their pipe and smoke it. **1924** LO'Flaherty *Informer* (L) 148: Put that in your pipe and smoke it. **1936** JBude *Death* (L) 172: You can put that in your pipe and smoke it. **1938** PMacDonald *Warrant* (NY 1957) 288: And if you put that all in your pipe, how long before we get any smoke? **1953** RBissell *7½ Cents* (B) 129: Put that in your pipe and smoke it. **1959** *BHerald* 1/11 5A: Alcorn would do well to put a single political fact in his pipe and smoke it. **1959** MPHood *Bell* (NY) 147: Put that in your pipe 'n smoke it. **1964** BHecht *Letters*

(NY) 4: Put that in your pipe and smoke it. TW 256(1); *Oxford* 657: Put.

P210   To smoke the **Pipe** of peace

1917 GRSims *My Life* (L) 323: The pipe of peace was smoked. **1919** HRHaggard *She and Allan* (NY 1921) 127: Smoking the pipe of peace. **1939** FWCrofts *Fatal* (L 1959) 95: Offer to smoke the pipe of peace. EAP P169; Brunvand 110.

P211   To pay the **Piper** (*varied*)

1922 JJoyce *Ulysses* (NY 1934) 268: Paying the piper. **1926** BHecht *Count* (NY) 250: Not having danced, he refused to pay the fiddler. **1926** AFielding *Footsteps* (L) 14: He who pays the piper—you know. **1927** VBridges *Girl* (P) 141: You're the one who's paid the piper . . . its only fair that you should call the tune. **1929** EHope *Alice* (NY) 41: He who eats pie must pay the piper. **1931** WMillis *Martial* (NY) 90: Having called the tune, we . . . refused to pay the piper. **1934** CCDobie *Portrait* (NY) 214: Folks that dance must pay the piper. **1938** JDonovan *Beckoning Dead* (L) 89: If he paid the piper he should have some say at least in calling the tune. **1938** SFowler *Jordans* (L) 265: It is a matter of proverbial equity that he who pays the piper should call the tune. **1943** VSiller *Echo* (NY) 62: I've known . . . that I would have to pay the piper. **1948** HReilly *Staircase* (NY) 168: I danced the tune and refused to pay the piper. **1952** MVHeberden *Tragic* (NY) 120: The slogan "He who pays the piper calls the tune." **1955** RStout *Before* (NY) 65: Since I have to pay the piper I'm going to dance. **1957** JLodwick *Equator* (L) 47: She who blows the bellows calls the tune. **1958** *JAFL* 71.78: If I do not appear to keep pace with my neighbor, perhaps it is because I am paying a different piper. **1964** TDuBois *Shannon* (NY DBC) 32: He was still the piper who called the tune. **1968** ECooper *Five* (NY) 33: Whoever pays the pauper calls the tune. **1969** JPVDBalsdon *Life* (NY) 96: Who pays the fiddler calls the tune. **1972** PMHubbard *Whisper* (NY) 64: He didn't want to call the tune if it meant paying the piper. **1973** WMasterson *Undertaker* (NY) 87: [He's] been callin' the tune and payin'

the fiddler here for a mighty long time. **1980** WODouglas *Court* (NY) 344: We all know that "he who pays the piper calls the tune." EAP P174; Brunvand 110.

P212   **Piping** hot

1932 RCWoodthorpe *Public* (L) 78: News must always be piping hot. **1967** COSkinner *Madame* (B) 276: The food, piping hot. EAP P176.

P213   To swear like a **Pirate**

1930 CWells *Doorstep* (NY) 4: Swore like a pirate. **1931** HGarland *Companions* (NY) 212: Swore like a pirate. **1956** BCClough *More* (Portland, Me.) 104: Swore like a pirate. EAP P177.

P214   As poor as **Piss**; Piss-poor

1953 SBellow *Adventures* (NY) 323: He was piss-poor. **1961** HCromwell *Dirty* (LA) 17: It was a piss-poor answer. **1963** ABurgess *Vision* (L) 243: Poor as piss. **1977** CDSimak *Heritage* (NY) 169: I'm a piss-poor witch. **1979** RBarnard *Death* (NY) 129: He'd tried all the local beers, piss-poor imitations in his opinion. Spears 302: Piss-poor.

P215   To be full of **Piss** and vinegar (*varied*)

1951 AThorne *Man Who* (L) 49: Bill, yes, as full of piss as he always was. **1955** PDennis *Auntie* (NY) 180: Fulla piss and vinegar. **1956** SDean *Marked* (NY) 107: Other two [*dogs*] are full of fizz and vinegar. **1956** WMankowitz *Old* (B) 104: You're full of piss and wind. **1960** LFletcher *Blindfold* (NY) 120: Full of firewater and vinegar, ready to go back to work. **1962** AMStein *Home* (NY) 33: Full of spit and vinegar. **1964** CChaplin *Autobiography* (NY 1966) 233: They do look full of piss and high purpose. **1964** EPangborn *Davy* (NY) 245: Fifty-six, full of piss and vinegar and meanness. **1982** JLivingston *Piece* (NY) 116: I was full of piss and vinegar. **1982** BPronzini *Gun* (NY) 56: Full of . . . what folks used to call piss and vinegar. Wentworth 393. Cf. All Wind *below*.

P216   To have the **Piss** (shit) scared out of one (*varied*)

1934 HMiller *Tropic of Cancer* (NY 1962) 158: That scared the shit out of me. **1960**

BKellner *C.VanVechten* (Norman, Okla. 1968) 299: I have had the piss scared out of me. **1966** JDosPassos *Best* (NY) 99: We'd be scared pissless. **1972** JBall *Five* (B) 83: You scared the pee out of me. **1975** EMcBain *Where* (NY) 87: You scared the shit out of me. Cf. Spears 339: Fartless, shitless, spitless; Berrey 300.8: Tar, 300.11: Scared spitless.

P217 To pour **Piss** out of a boot *etc. (varied)*
1956 SWTaylor *I Have* (NY) 193: The old man didn't have the gumption and common sense to pour sand from a boot. **1957** JWhitehill *Able* (B) 62: He couldn't pour bilge out of a boot if the directions were on the heel. **1958** *BHerald* 3/19 43: Truman replied: "He probably felt that the little man from Missouri didn't know enough to pour beer out of a boot even if the instructions were written on the heel." **1964** FCormier *LBJ* (NY 1977) 93: I had heard him [*LBJ*] insist that men . . . were unable "To pour piss from a boot with the instructions written on the heel." **1971** TPace *Fisherman's* (NY) 51: Some council. They couldn't pour piss out of a boot. **1975** JDaniels *White* (NY) 27: [He] hasn't got sense enough to pour piss out of a boot. **1976** BMooney *LBJ* (NY) 275: [They] lacked sense enough to pour piss out of a boot. NADS 15.3 (1933) 7: Pour piss or water.

P218 As easy as **Pissing** against the wall
1969 RGrayson *Voyage* (L) 39: Always pee when you get the opportunity [*his father's advice*]. **1975** JHough *Guardian* (B) 142: Easy as pissing against the wall. Cf. Partridge 253: Pissing the bed.

P219 The more one **Pisses** the less he cries
1934 FOursler *Joshua* (NY) 5: Always remember, boys, the more you pee, the less you cry; 199, 272. **1983** HHBroun *Whose Little* (NY) 120: When I burst into tears . . . she would remark mildly, "the more you do of that, the less you'll do of something else." Partridge 635: Piss the less.

P220 Never get in a **Pissing** contest (match) with a skunk
1970 JVizzard *See* (NY) 240: Never engage in a pissing contest with a skunk. You're

bound to lose. **1975** HLawrenson *Stranger* (NY) 155: Never get in a peeing match with a skunk.

P221 As pie-eyed as a **Piss-ant**
1932 BAButkin ed *Land Is Ours* (Norman, Okla.) 150: Got pie-eyed as a piss-ant.

P222 As hot as a **Pistol**
1956 *New Yorker* 10/27 139: He can be . . . as hot as a pistol. **1957** JPMarquand *Life* (B) 44: He was hot as a pistol. **1960** DKarp *Enter* (NY) 105: He's as hot as a two-dollar pistol. **1963** IFleming *On Her* (L) 206: I'm hot as a pistol [*in danger*]. **1970** STerkel *Hard* (NY) 298: Their leadership was hot as a pistol. Taylor *Prov. Comp.* 50. Cf. Wentworth 272: Hot (11,12,13).

P223 As black as the **Pit** (of Tophet)
1928 JJConnington *Tragedy* (B) 65: The cave's as black as the pit. **1934** HFootner *Dangerous* (L) 58: It was black as the pit. **1935** VWilliams *Clue* (B) 154: As black as the pit of Tophet. **1936** AGlanville *Death* (L) 257: The study was as black as the Pit. **1942** ESHolding *Kill Joy* (NY) 36: The big room was black as the pit. Whiting *Devil* 247(11); Taylor *Western Folklore* 17(1958) 17: A pit.

P224 As dark as the **Pit**
1927 GDilnot *Lazy* (B) 180: It's as dark as the pit in here. **1959** EFenwick *Long Way* (NY DBC) 70: Dark as the pit in here. Whiting *Devil* 247(11).

P225 To fall into the **Pit** one digs for others
1930 AGilbert *Night* (NY) 281: He didn't study the psalms enough . . . and so he forgot that the pit he had digged for you might easily prove his own undoing. **1932** FWCrofts *Double* (NY) 297: Digging a pit and falling into it oneself. **1936** AFielding *Two Pearl* (L) 36: Ann had dug a pit, and was now about to fall into it herself. **1945** HCBailey *Wrong Man* (NY) 194: Whoso diggeth a pit himself shall fall therein. **1961** SRansome *Some Must* (NY 1963) 148: I dug this hole and fell into it. **1964** LCohen *New York* (P) 195: The republicans would fall into the pit they had just dug. **1968** PDickinson *Skin* (L) 146: What pits one digs for

one's own feet. **1973** DDelman *He Who Digs a Grave* (NY). EAP P182. Cf. Biter *above*; To make a Rod, Snare *below*.

P226   As black as **Pitch**; Pitch-black

1904 JCLincoln *Cap'n Eri* (NY) 191: Pitch-black night. **1910** EPhillpotts *Tales* (NY) 203: 'Twas black as pitch. **1924** TMundy *Om* (NY) 331: Black as pitch. **1932** WCBrown *Laughing* (P) 195: Pitch black shadow. **1936** NMorland *Clue* (L) 207: The road as black as pitch. **1954** SJepson *Black* (NY) 74: It was as black as pitch. **1956** RFoley *Last* (NY DBC) 57: It's as black as pitch. **1966** HTreece *Green* (L) 233: A darkness as black as pitch. **1970** TKenrick *Only* (NY) 181: Pitch-black inside. EAP P183; TW 287(1,2); Brunvand 110(1).

P227   As dark as **Pitch**; Pitch-dark

1910 EPhillpotts *Tales* (NY) 304: Dark as pitch. **1911** HHMunro *Chronicles* (L 1927) 6: It was nearly pitch-dark. **1923** JGollomb *Girl* (NY) 18: Dark as pitch. **1924** L O'Flaherty *Thy Neighbour's* (L) 177: Pitch dark. **1931** MBurton *Menace* (L) 166: It was pitch dark. **1937** MBurton *Murder* (L) 13: Dark as pitch. **1939** CSaxby *Death Cuts* (NY) 192: All dark as pitch. **1940** DBillany *It Takes* (NY) 158: It was dark as pitch in the garden. **1941** FCharles *Vice Czar* (NY) 149: Pitch-dark room. **1962** DTaylor *Blood* (NY) 171: It was dark as pitch. **1970** AAFair *All Grass* (NY DBC) 95: The night was as dark as pitch. **1970** EHahn *Times* (NY) 258: Pitch-dark room. EAP P184; TW 287(3,4); Brunvand 110(3), 111(4).

P228   He that touches **Pitch** will be defiled (*varied*)

c**1923** ACrowley *Confessions* ed JSymonds (L 1969) 639: If you touch pitch you will be defiled. **1925** EWallace *Face* (NY 1929) 76: You can't touch pitch—not that kind of pitch—without getting your hands black. **1929** RAldington *Death* (L) 118: By long dabbling in pitch [he] had become pitchy. **1930** AChristie *Murder* (NY) 248: Pitch soils. **1931** MAllingham *Police* (NY) 83: This affair is pitch. And in my experience, if you touch pitch you get your hands dirty. **1936** JMWalsh *Crimes* (L) 149: She had

touched pitch in many forms without being defiled. **1938** JJConnington *Truth* (L) 122: Can you touch pitch—or the proceeds of the sale of pitch—and keep your hands and your conscience clean. **1941** HRCampbell *Murder Set to Music* (NY) 42: I know you can't touch pitch without blacking your fingers. **1946** GHomes *Build* (NY) 188: You can't touch pitch forever and stay clean. **1947** AGilbert *Death in* (L) 119: Not that his firm ever touch this sort of thing. Pitch and all that, you know. **1948** FWCrofts *Silence* (NY) 44: "If we touch pitch," she began dolefully. **1957** AECoppard *It's Me* (L) 175: All three of them having touched the pitch were indelibly defiled. **1959** JIMStewart *Man Who Wrote* (L) 100: You can't touch pitch without being defiled. **1965** CBeaton *Years* (L) 72: However much pitch we wallowed in, it never stuck. **1970** DJOlivy *Never* (NY) 177: There was money to be had, legally, if she didn't mind touching a little pitch to get it. **1971** PNapier *Sword* (NY) 112: Tom . . . fearing to touch the pitch of rebellion and be defiled. **1977** KClark *Other* (NY) 25: He had not merely touched pitch; he had been up to his neck in it, and had not been defiled. EAP P185; TW 287–8(9).

P229   To queer one's **Pitch**

1919 LMerrick *Chair* (L) 46: You might queer your pitch. **1925** JRhode *Paddington* (L) 132: To queer our pitch. **1936** AMuir *Bronze* (L) 176: You may be queering our pitch. **1939** VBridges *Seven Stars* (L) 276: Threatened to queer his pitch. **1945** MAlan *Dark Prophecy* (NY) 187: I tried to queer your pitch. **1952** RVickers *Kynsard* (L 1965) 114: Queering your pitch. **1955** CMWills *Death* (L) 63: This "queering of his pitch"— as he phrased it. **1963** JBroderick *Don* (NY) 178: She had no reason to queer her pitch with him. **1969** PSCatling *Freddy* (NY) 117: I haven't queered your pitch. **1973** HCarvic *Miss Seeton Sings* (NY) 15: Mustn't queer the old girl's pitch. Partridge 636.

P230   Little **Pitchers** (pigs, jugs) have long ears (*varied*)

1927 OWarner *Secret* (NY) 134: Little pitchers have long ears. **1931** HBurnham *Murder* (NY) 228: The adage concerning "little pitchers." **1935** RGraves *Claudius the God* (NY) 51: Little pitchers have great ears. **1938** WNMacartney *Fifty Years* (NY) 216: Provided these big-eared little pitchers have not been prejudiced by what they have overheard. **1941** CCoffin *Mare's Nest* (NY) 123: I've disposed of our little pitcher [*a listener*]. **1941** VRath *Death Breaks* (NY) 182: Little pitchers do have long ears. **1945** FBonnamy *King Is Dead* (NY) 111: Little pitchers could have big mouths! **1949** AA Fair *Bedrooms* (NY 1958) 83: Little pitchers, over here, has big ears. **1952** HFMPrescott *Man on* (NY) 305: Little pitchers have long ears. **1956** MProcter *Ripper* (NY) 157: Little pigs have big ears. **1957** HEBates *Sugar* (L) 12: Little pigs have got big ears. **1960** PCurtis *Devil's* (NY) 91: A little jug with big ears. **1966** TWells *Matter* (NY) 158: Little pitchers have ears. **1970** RCowper *Twilight* (NY) 89: Certain pitchers have very long ears. **1970** MStewart *Crystal* (NY) 18: Young pigs have long ears. **1972** KCConstantine *Vicksburg* (NY) 73: Little pitchers have big ears. **1972** CWatson *Kissing* (NY) 130: Little pigs have big ears. **1972** CWatson *Kissing Covens* (NY) 131: [Her] mother would have prefaced such a catechism with the observation that "little pigs have big ears." *Oxford* 471: Little pitchers; NED Pig *sb.*[2]

P231 The **Pitcher** will go to the well once too often (*varied*)

1925 JGBrandon *Cork* (L) 23: [He] had carried the pitcher once too often to the well. **1925** EWallace *Face* (NY 1929) 32: There's a little old story about a pitcher and a well. **1926** JSFletcher *Massingham* (B) 257: You know the old proverb about the pitcher going to the well? **1930** WLewis *Apes* (NY 1932) 410: I should think he might get caught. The pitcher that goes often to the well. **1931** PBaron *Round* (NY) 10: You'll go to the well once too often. **1936** DHume *Bring 'Em Back* (NY) 157: You've taken your can to the water once too often. **1938** DHume *Good-bye* (L) 109: One day you'll . . . take your pitcher to the proverbial well once too often. **1940** MFitt *Death Starts* (L) 83: There's always a last time—the pitcher and the well, you know. **1948** NMailer *Naked* (NY) 557: She's gone to the well a little

too often and, well, frankly there's doctors involved. **1950** ERPunshon *So Many* (NY) 117: The old proverb, you know, the pitcher that goes to the well too often gets broken at last. **1959** *Time* 10/19 41: An old German proverb: "The pitcher goes to the well until it breaks." **1963** AChristie *Mirror* (NY) 185: The pitcher goes to the well once too often. **1971** RMStern *Murder* (NY) 155: He went to the well once too often—and fell in. **1973** DMDisney *Only Couples* (NY) 80: We can't take the pitcher to the well too often. **1974** PNobile *Intellectual* (NY) 198: They thought his bucket was going to the well a little too often. EAP P188; TW 288(1).

P232 Not to touch with a **Pitchfork**

1930 JGBrandon *Death* (L) 43: Something he wouldn't touch with a pitch-fork. **1935** GDilnot *Murder* (L) 139: I wouldn't touch that case with a pitchfork. Cf. Pair *above*; Pale *below*.

P233 To rain **Pitchforks** *etc.* (*varied*)

1913 TDreiser *Traveler* (NY 1923) 465: Raining pitchforks. **1930** JFDobie *Coronado* (Dallas) 149: It was raining pitchforks and bob-tailed heifers yesterday. **1937** GDyer *Long Death* (NY) 188: It was raining pitchforks and hammer-handles. **1940** CBDawson *Lady Wept* (NY) 210: It started raining pitchforks and nigger babies. **1955** DMDisney *Room* (NY) 74: It had been raining pitchforks. **1960** ASeager *Death* (NY) 4: It was raining pitchforks outside. **1978** JLangton *Memorial* (NY) 89: [Rain] was coming down like pitchforks. EAP P189; Brunvand 111. Cf. Stair-rods *below*.

P234 **Pity** is akin to love (*varied*)

1934 KTKnoblock *Winter* (NY) 209: It's an old saying that pity is like love. **1940** GStockwell *Candy* (NY) 92: It might just happen to be true that pity is akin to love. **1956** MProcter *Ripper* (NY) 216: Pity is akin to love, you know. *Oxford* 628. Cf. Brunvand 111.

P235 The jumping-off **Place**

1948 CLLeonard *Fourth* (NY) 95: It's the jumping-off place for nowhere. **1969** DDoolittle *Only in Maine* (Barre, Mass.) 99:

I felt that I had reached the proverbial jumping-off place. TW 288–9(3).

P236 A **Place** for everything *etc. (varied)*

1904 JCLincoln *Cap'n Eri* (NY) 160: Everything's got a place and is in it. **1919** LMerrick *Chair* (L) 128: "Everything in its place" is my motto. **1922** JJoyce *Ulysses* (NY 1934) 694: A place for everything and everything in its place. **1925** JRhode *Paddington* (L) 196: That proverbial Utopia, a place for everything and everything in its place. **1932** RThorndike *Devil* (NY) 63: I like a place for everything and everything in that place. **1935** JRhode *Hendon's* (L) 152: A place for everything, and everything in its place. **1956** *New Yorker* 10/6 42: "A place for everything," his father used to say, "and everything in its place." **1958** *NYTimes* 5/11 7E: A place for everyone—everyone in his place. **1959** AChristie *Ordeal* (NY) 30: A place for everything and everything in its place. **1960** HSDavies *Papers* (L) 16: Since there was a place for everyone, everyone must be put in his place. **1964** LPayne *Deep* (L) 41: My old mother used to say, "A place for everything and everything in its place." **1971** JFraser *Death* (NY) 53: A place for everything and everything in its place. **1974** OBleeck *Highbinders* (NY) 146: There was a place for everything and everything was in its place. TW 288(1); *Oxford* 628–9. Cf. There is a Time *below*.

P237 A **Place** in the sun

1937 WHMack *Mr. Birdsall* (NY) 238: A proper place in the sun. **1967** VLincoln *Private* (NY) 37: Lizzie longed for a place in the sun. *Oxford* 629.

P238 A **Place** set is a friend met *etc.*

1931 LEppley *Murder* (NY) 15: "I was brought up on the quotation or proverb about it. 'A place set is a friend met.'" . . . "You have it wrong . . . 'A place at table set in vain—there's one will not come back again.'"

P239 There is no **Place** like home

1900 CFPidgin *Quincy A. Sawyer* (B) 187: There is no place like home, they say. **1923** HWNevinson *Changes* (NY) 327: There's no place like home. **1941** RAldington *Life* (NY) 63: There's no place like home. **1952** FO'Connor *Wise* (NY) 11: There's no place like home. **1963** HCalvin *It's Different* (NY) 167: No place like home. **1965** HActon *Old Lamps* (L) 121: There's no place like home. **1975** HLawrenson *Stranger* (NY) 182: There's no place like home, be it ever so humble. TW 186: Home(2); *Oxford* 629. Cf. EAP H257.

P240 To be in two **Places** at once

1932 GKChesterton et al. *Floating* (NY) 56: You can't be in two places at once. **1934** MKennedy *Corpse* (L) 146: I can't be in two places at once. **1939** NMarsh *Overture* (NY) 100: You can't be in two places at once. **1961** HReilly *Certain* (NY DBC) 129: She couldn't be in two places at once. *Oxford* 851: Two.

P241 To go **Places** and see (do) things

1933 AWilliams *Death* (NY) 249: I like to go places and see things. **1934** GDean *Fifth Key* (NY) 225: I don't go places and do things, as the saying goes. Berrey 280.7.

P242 To avoid like the **Plague**

1928 ABCox *Amateur* (NY) 32: [He] avoids responsibility like the plague. **1928** HFootner *Velvet* (NY) 114: She was avoided like the plague. **1937** MDavis *Chess* (NY) 288: I avoid these people like the plague. **1940** EDean *Murder Is* (NY) 130: Eddie would avoid them like the plague. **1954** JPotts *Go* (NY) 77: He had also avoided her like the plague. **1955** LCochran *Hallelujah* (NY) 142: They avoided scandal . . . as they would the plague. **1961** MColes *Search* (NY DBC) 45: Avoid them like the plague. **1966** HBrown *Prose Styles* (Minneapolis) 115: To avoid it like the plague. Cole 44: Avoid. Cf. EAP P90: Pest. Cf. Pest *above*.

P243 To hate like the **Plague**

1933 JRhode *Dr. Priestley Lays* (NY) 65: He hates cars like the plague. **1958** *New Yorker* 8/2 30: He hated Teresa like the plague. **1975** FMNivens *Publish* (NY) 102: [He] hates Hope like the plague. Cf. Berrey 336.4: Poison, sin.

P244   To shun like the Plague

1940 GCKlingel *Anagua* (NY) 360: Other forms shun light like the plague. **1968** EBuckler *Ox Bells* (NY) 138: Shunned . . . the other like the plague. **1968** JPorter *Dover Goes* (NY) 40: Shun her as though she's got the proverbial plague. EAP P193.

P245   As Plain as plain

1926 LBrock *Colonel Gore* (NY) 139: As plain as plain. **1933** HWade *Policeman's* (L) 71: Plain as plain. **1934** AChristie *Calais Coach* (NY) 111: It was just as plain as plain could be. **1945** JSymons *Immaterial* (L 1954) 86: It was plain as plain. **1950** CDickson *Night* (NY) 158: As plain as plain. **1954** CHare *That Yew* (L) 29: I can see it all as plain as plain. **1965** MStewart *Airs* (NY 1966) 18: Lewis was in it, as plain as plain. **1968** AChristie *By the Pricking* (NY) 113: There it was plain as plain. **1971** HCarvig *Witch* (NY) 39: They saw it plain as plain. **1976** AChristie *Sleeping* (NY) 76: Abbott it says, plain as plain. Wilstach 293: As plainness. Cf. Clear *above*.

P246   As stiff (hard) as a Plank

1958 *NYTimes* 7/13 44: Stiff as a plank. **1958** HMasur *Murder* (NY 1959) 60: His palm was hard as a plank. **1962** NFreeling *Death* (NY 1964) 35: I was . . . stiff as an old plank [*cold*]. Whiting *NC* 459.

P247   To stick like a Plaster (*varied*)

1961 FLockridge *Ticking* (P) 59: Sticks around like a plaster to be a help. **1965** RSPrather *Dead Man's* (NY) 206: To stick to me like a plaster. Wilstach 388: Porous plaster. Cf. Berrey 332.5: Paper, wax, wet shirt.

P248   As flat as a Plate

1940 HCBailey *Mr. Fortune Here* (NY) 265: No cover, flat as a plate all round. Wilstach 145: Willow-pattern plate.

P249   To hand (be handed) on a silver Platter (plate) (*varied*)

1916 JLondon *Letters* ed KHendricks (NY 1965) 467: Presented to them . . . on a silver platter. **1922** JJoyce *Ulysses* (NY 1934) 135: Give it to them on a hot plate . . . the whole bloody history. **1931** HSKeeler *Matilda* (NY) 413: This picture . . . isn't handed to us on a silver platter. **1936** JBude *Death* (L) 56: Hands him a piping-hot clue on a plate. **1938** JStagge *Murder by* (NY) 189: You're handing me the solution on a golden platter. **1940** BHalliday *Private Practice* (NY 1965) 41: I handed you the case on a silver platter. **1945** AChristie *Remembered* (NY) 35: Everything handed to her on a golden platter. **1947** HCahill *Look* (NY) 12: Bring them the country on a silver platter. **1954** DAlexander *Terror* (NY) 82: Handed to us on a silver platter. **1955** JPotts *Death* (NY) 150: Success . . . handed to him on a silver platter. **1958** HMasur *Murder* (NY 1959) 83: "You'll turn him in?" "On a silver platter." **1959** *BTraveler* 8/21 20: It was handed to them on a silver platter. **1961** PGWodehouse *Ice* (NY) 74: The thing'll be handed to us on a plate. **1967** TWells *Dead by* (NY) 155: I wouldn't have a bitch like that on a silver platter. **1970** MEChaber *Green* (NY) 3: We can't hand it to them on a silver platter. **1975** EGundy *Naked* (NY) 130: "Don't you want him back?" "Not on a silver platter." Cole 52: Hand.

P250   As good as a Play

1909 JCLincoln *Keziah* (NY) 67: It's as good as a play. **1922** JJoyce *Ulysses* (NY 1934) 337: As good as any bloody play in the Queen's royal theatre. **1933** DGBrowne *Cotfold* (L) 192: It's as good as a play. **1934** BThomson *Richardson Scores* (L) 101: It was as good as a play. **1938** AGlanville *Body* (L) 25: It's as good as a play. **1941** PWentworth *Weekend* (P) 202: Good as a play. **1950** JBell *Summer* (L) 163: It's as good as a play. **1956** MLSettle *O Beulah* (NY) 330: 'Twas as good as a play. **1967** MErskine *Case with* (NY) 21: Good as a play. **1970** IOrigo *Images* (NY) 125: As good as a play. TW 289(2); *Oxford* 317: Good. Cf. Pictures *above*.

P251   Fair Play is a jewel

1930 FDBurdett *Odyssey* (L) 107: Fair play's a jewel. **1937** NBell *Crocus* (NY) 324: Fair play's a jewel. **1957** *Punch* 9/18 322: The adage . . . that fair play is a jewel. EAP P199.

P252   No **Play**, no pay

1935 VLoder *Death* (L) 13: No play no pay. TW 289(1): Play and pay. Cf. *Oxford* 628: Pitch and pay.

P253   A **Pleasure** shared is a pleasure doubled

1956 BWAldiss *Saliva* (L) 157: A pleasure shared is a pleasure doubled, as Mother used to say. Cf. Trouble shared *below.*

P254   What has been **Plowed** once is easier the second time

1956 HCahill *Shadow* (NY) 35: What's been plowed once is easier the second time. Cf. Spears 305: Plow = to coït. Cf. Slice *below.*

P255   The **Poacher** turns gamekeeper (*varied*)

1954 IFleming *Live* (NY 1959) 113: The poacher turned game-keeper. **1971** PNapier *Sword* (NY) 126: A stcrn poacher-turned-gamekeeper line. **1973** NMackenzie *Wells* (NY) 113: A case of gamekeeper turning poacher. **1975** JPearson *Edward* (NY) 86: The poacher was turning gamekeeper. **1979** MSecrest *Being* (NY) 233: The poacher must be made to turn gamekeeper. **1982** VWebb *Little* (NY) 74: On the AA principle: A reformed sinner is the best preacher. Whiting T76; *Oxford* 592: Old poacher.

P256   As dark (black) as a **Pocket** (*varied*)

1904 JCLincoln *Cap'n Eri* (NY) 343: It's darker'n a nigger's pocket. **1905** JBCabell *Line* (NY 1926) 136: The night was black as a pocket. **1911** JCLincoln *Woman-Haters* (NY) 182: Darker than a pocket. **1929** CWells *Tapestry* (P) 98: Dark as the black cat's pocket. **1935** SHPage *Tragic* (NY) 43: A hallway, as black as a pocket. **1935** CMRussell *Murder* (NY) 153: Black as a pocket. **1937** KMKnight *Seven* (NY) 205: Dark as a pocket in them woods. **1938** CHarris *Murder* (NY) 62: As dark as a blind man's pocket. **1941** AAmos *Pray* (NY) 145: It was as dark as a pocket. **1948** ESGardner *Lonely* (NY DBC) 140: Dark as the inside of a pocket. **1958** *New Yorker* 5/3 55: As black as a pocket. **1961** MHHood *Drown* (NY) 199: Darker'n a pocket. **1962** RGTugwell

Light (NY) 194: It had also been as dark as a pocket. **1972** JPotts *Troublemaker* (NY) 113: Dark as a pocket. TW 290.

P257   There are no **Pockets** in shrouds

1908 MRRinehart *Circular Staircase* (NY 1947) 108: There are no pockets in shrouds. **1950** ECRLorac *Accident* (NY DBC) 178: The old adage—"There's no pocket in a shroud." **1959** TRoscoe *Only* (NY) 132: There aren't any pockets in a shroud. **1962** YBridges *Poison* (L) 168: The clock which was as devoid of pockets as Edwin's shroud. *Oxford* 443: Last garment. Cf. Take *below.*

P258   To be ill (hit) in the **Pocket**

1933 LThayer *Hell-Gate* (NY) 46: She was ill—ahem—only in the pocket, if you'll excuse the expression. **1960** HQMasur *Send Another* (NY) 209: It hits them where they live—in the pocket. Cf. Whiting P449, S328.

P259   To have in one's **Pocket**

c1923 ACrowley *Confessions* ed JSymonds (L 1969) 495: I had the mourners, so to speak, in my pocket. **1934** MAllingham *Death of a Ghost* (NY 1958) 172: A competent painter very much in Max's pocket. **1939** GBarnett *There's Money* (L) 172: A future politician for Marne to have in his pocket. **1946** MInnes *Unsuspected* (NY) 277: Anybody . . . that we haven't got in our pocket. **1955** IFleming *Moonraker* (NY 1960) 150: London was in my pocket. **1957** RGraves *They Hanged* (NY) 219: He now had the coroner "in his breeches' pocket," as the cant saying is. **1967** WASwanberg *Pulitzer* (NY) 17: [He] seemed to have the President in his pocket. **1970** BRosmond *Benchley* (NY) 34: She had Edmund in her pocket. **1971** HCarvig *Witch* (NY) 16: She's got Treeves in her pocket. EAP P212.

P260   To live (sit) in one another's **Pockets** (*varied*)

1924 IICBailcy *Mr. Fortune's Practice* (NY) 27: They sat in each other's pockets. **1926** AFielding *Footsteps* (L) 152: I didn't want her to think I was going to sit in her pocket. **1931** ABCox *Top* (NY) 47: They did not live in each other's pockets. **1932** CDawes

Lawless (L) 50: You and he are not exactly in each other's pockets; 255. **1939** RHull *And Death* (L) 198: I didn't know then that you were living in his pocket. **1948** CDickson *Skeleton* (NY 1967) 206: They'd lived in each other's pockets. **1955** NMarsh *Scales* (B) 281: Rose and he sat in each other's pockets. **1961** GHolden *Deadlier* (NY DBC) 19: Some big place where people don't live in each other's pockets. **1965** DoctorX *Intern* (NY) 14: Living in each other's laps. 107: We sort of live in each other's hip pockets. **1970** VCClinton-Baddely *No Case* (NY) 13: They . . . had lived in each other's pockets. **1975** PDJames *Black* (NY) 102: She and Michael didn't exactly live in each other's pockets. NED Pocket 3d.

P261 As poor as **Podunk**

1963 MPHood *Sin* (NY) 54: We're poor as Podunk. See DA Podunk.

P262 A **Poet**, a painter, a Quaker *etc.*

1956 MLSettle *O Beulah* (NY) 171: Ye know what they do say—show me a poet, a painter, a Quaker, and I will show ye three liars. *Oxford* 607: Painters and poets.

P263 **Poets** are born, not made (*varied*)

1913 HTFinck *Food* (NY) 373: One is born a poet, saith the adage. **1930** IGoldberg *Tin Pan* (NY) 7: Poets, the wise saw tells us, are not made; they are born. *Oxford* 636. Cf. Brunvand 14: Born(2: Some spellers).

P264 To put too fine a **Point** on something

1968 AChristie *By the Pricking* (NY) 203: Not to put too fine a point on it, as the saying goes. TW 290(3).

P265 **Poison** is a woman's weapon (*varied*)

1920 AChristie *Mysterious Affair* (NY) 201: Poison was a woman's weapon. **1930** CSHammock *Why Murder* (NY) 58: Poison has always been a woman's weapon. **1931** ACEdington *Monk's Hood* (NY) 229: Women are slicker than men with poison. **1932** MRRinehart *Miss Pinkerton* (NY) 213: In a way poison is a woman's method. **1938** NBlake *Beast* (NY 1958) 141: Poison isn't a woman's weapon, as they glibly say; it's a coward's weapon. **1941** CCoffin *Mare's Nest* (NY) 80: Another folk belief that poison was a woman's weapon. **1952** MHBradley *Nice* (NY) 156: Women usually think of poison. **1952** MMurray *Doctor* (NY DBC) 97: You have conceived that poison is a woman's weapon. That, of course, is a fallacy. **1961** FSinclair *But the Patient* (NY) 172: Women are the traditional poisoners. **1962** SRansome *Night* (NY DBC) 142: As for poison, it's notoriously a woman's weapon. **1965** ADerleth *Casebook* (Sauk City, Wisc.) 128: Poison, after all, is primarily a woman's weapon. **1977** HDolson *Beauty* (P) 181: "Poisoned." "Which means a dame did it." **1977** RHardin *Amateur* (I) 139: I'm sure you're not saying that women murderers are all little old ladies who kill only with poison.

P266 To hate like **Poison**

1908 LDYoung *Climbing Doom* (B) 190: Hates like poison. **1920** AChristie *Mysterious Affair* (NY) 183: Hated him like poison. **1927** JTaine *Quayle's* (NY) 7: She will hate you like rat poison. **1932** TCobb *Who Closed* (L) 77: Hates like poison. **1936** FGérard *Concrete* (NY) 221: He hated the old man like poison. **1946** MColes *Fifth Man* (NY) 222: You hate him like rat poison. **1954** AStone *Harvard* (B) 80: [He] hated like poison to pay the taxes. **1956** NFitzgerald *Imagine* (L) 180: I hate him like poison. **1963** BHecht *Gaily* (NY) 35: She always hated me like poison. EAP P218; Taylor *Western Folklore* 17(1958) 18.

P267 To shun like **Poison**

1930 JWilliamson *American Hotel* (NY) 234: Shun it like poison. Tilley P459.

P268 As mean as **Poison water**

1956 BJChute *Greenwillow* (NY) 207: Mean as poison water. Whiting *NC* 460(2).

P269 To be better than a **Poke** in the eye *etc.*

1934 HHolt *Sinister* (NY) 193: It would be better than a poke in the eye with a burnt stick. **1960** GSAlbee *By the Sea* (NY) 127: Fifty cents is better than a poke in the eye with a forked stick. **1973** JCashman *Gentleman* (NY) 231: It was better than a poke in the eye with a blunt stick. **1974** WDRoberts *Didn't Anybody* (NY) 123: The lead [*infor-*

mation] was better than a poke in the eye with a sharp stick, as my grandmother used to say. Partridge 49: Better.

P270 As stiff as a **Poker**

1916 NDouglas *London Street Games* (L) 75: All as stiff as pocars. **1930** WLewis *Apes* (NY 1932) 35: As stiff as a poker; 322. **1938** SLeslie *Film* (L) 307: I was as stiff as many pokers in an Arctic frost. **1945** AChristie *Remembered* (NY) 127: As stiff as though she'd swallowed the poker. **1949** AMorton *Rope* (NY) 64: Stiff as a poker [*dead*]. **1954** TConnally *My Name* (NY) 195: Stiff as a poker. **1970** AAFair *All Grass* (NY DBC) 94: I was stiff as a poker. **1970** RFoley *Calculated* (NY) 62: She was as stiff as a poker. EAP P220.

P271 As straight as a **Poker**; Poker-straight

1926 AFielding *Footsteps* (L) 125: He's as straight as that poker and about as easy to bend. **1945** HLawrence *Time to Die* (NY) 65: It [*a woman's hair*] was as straight as a poker. **1950** BSpicer *Blues* (NY) 165: His back was poker-straight. TW 291(2).

P272 As cold as a **Polar bear**'s arse

1971 PDennis *Paradise* (NY) 223: It's cold as a polar bear's ass. Cf. Well digger *below.*

P273 As far apart as the **Poles** (*varied*)

1925 TRMarshall *Recollections* (I) 170: As far apart as the poles. **1933** REssex *Slade* (NY) 168: They are as the poles asunder. **1939** AChristie *Murder for* (NY) 17: You two are poles apart. **1944** HReilly *Opening Door* (NY) 7: They were as far apart as the poles. **1960** HRFKeating *Zen* (L 1963) 100: We were brought up poles apart. **1961** CBush *Sapphire* (NY) 86: His world and mine, to flog a cliché, were poles apart. **1971** JPope-Hennessy *A.Trollope* (B) 19: Art and morality are ever poles apart. EAP P221.

P274 As thin as a **Pole**

1934 DGardiner *Drink* (NY) 92: Thin as a pole. **1941** CLClifford *While the Bells* (NY) 25: [He was] thin as a pole. **1960** ADuggan *Cunning* (NY) 232: As thin as a pole. Clark *Similes* 224: Bean pole. Cf. Beanpole *above.*

P275 Not to touch with a ten-foot (barge) **Pole** (*varied*)

1912 JCLincoln *Postmaster* (NY) 95: I wouldn't touch it with a ten-foot pole. **1921** JCLincoln *Galusha* (NY) 279: He wouldn't touch [it] with a ten-foot pole. **1925** JGBrandon *Cork* (L) 136: Wouldn't touch him with a barge-pole. **1929** LBrock *Stoke Silver* (NY) 196: Hawkins wouldn't touch a firearm with a forty-foot pole. **1933** JGregory *Case* (NY) 252: I wouldn't touch it with a ten-foot pole. **1938** NMorland *Rope* (L) 142: I wouldn't 've touched it with a barge pole. **1940** JFBonnell *Death Over* (NY) 158: I wouldn't have touched Damator with a ten-foot pole. **1940** AGaines *While the Wind* (NY) 233: Garrick never would have touched her with a forty foot pole. **1940** CWorth *Trail* (NY) 69: I wouldn't stir it with a barge pole. **1952** MMurray *Doctor* (NY DBC) 94: Warn him not to touch the case with a barge pole. **1956** MScherf *Cautious* (NY) 19: I wouldn't touch a vitamin with a ten-foot pole. **1956** *Punch* 10/31 527: Glued to the rag you wouldn't touch with a barge-pole. **1957** CThompson *Halfway* (NY) 29: I wouldn't touch [her] with a ten-foot pole. **1959** *BHerald* 3/26 39: As American-born son would say—"Would not touch with ten-foot pole." **1961** PGWodehouse *Ice* (NY) 226: I wouldn't kiss her with a ten-foot pole. **1965** EQueen *Queens* (NY) 14: I wouldn't touch him with a skunk pole. **1968** JTStory *I Sit* (L) 8: He won't touch you with a bargepole. **1970** RBernard *Deadly* (NY) 44: We wouldn't touch him with a ten-foot yardstick. **1970** TWells *Dinky* (NY) 157: I wouldn't touch him with a ten-foot pole. **1976** JPorter *Package* (NY) 149: No reputable airline would touch the place with a barge pole. *Oxford* 833: Touch. Cf. Pair, Pitchfork *above.*

P276 To be up the **Pole**

1932 CDawes *Lawless* (L) 69: Bit of a mystery there . . . or I'm up the pole. **1932** DLSayers *Have* (NY) 295: Our friend Weldon is a bit up the pole financially. **1934** WGore *There's Death* (L) 224: That's up the pole [i.e. *out*]. **1958** NBlake *Penknife* (L) 36: You're certainly up the pole [*in trouble*]. **1958** NMarsh *Singing* (B) 141: The whole

Polecat

idea is completely up the pole [*nonsense*]. **1959** JFleming *Malice* (NY) 171: She'd drive any man up the pole. **1961** JDCarr *Witch* (L) 167: Do you want to drive me up the pole [*insane*]? Partridge 645 (2,5,6).

P277 To stink like a **Polecat**
1966 MFagyas *Widow* (NY) 4: You stink like a polecat. Whiting P291; *Oxford* 775.

P278 **Politeness** costs nothing (*varied*)
1931 HMSmith *Waverdale Fire* (L) 207: Politeness costs nothing, and wins everything. **1932** EWallace *Frightened* (L) 79: Politeness costs nothing. **1964** JCarnell *New Writings* (L) 14: Politeness costs nothing. EAP P225.

P279 **Politics** (*etc.*) makes strange bedfellows (*very varied*)
1927 NMartin *Mosaic* (NY) 266: Fear makes strange bedfellows. **1927** EPhillpotts *Jury* (NY) 106: Necessity makes strange bedfellows. **1928** JMBall *Sack-'Em-Up* (L) 127: Science, like politics, makes strange bedfellows. **1930** HLandon *Three Brass* (NY) 35: Poverty makes strange bedfellows. **1932** AMSullivan *Last Serjeant* (L) 136: Misfortune makes strange bedfellows. **1935** AGilbert *Man* (L) 219: Politics make strange bedfellows. **1935** JHWallis *Politician* (NY) 223: "Politics makes strange bedfellows" is an old saying. **1937** ABoucher *Case* (NY) 51: The very richness of Ashwin's tastes resembled poverty in its quality of making strange bedfellows. **1937** DWhitelaw *Face* (L) 65: Racing makes strange bedfellows. **1941** ISCobb *Exit* (I) 217: Politics makes estranged bedfellows. **1942** HRutland *Blue Murder* (NY) 212: War, which proverbially makes strange bedfellows. **1951** MHead *Congo* (NY) 49: What they say about politics and bedfellows is true enough. **1954** FCDavis *Another* (NY) 30: An old saying that politics makes strange bedfellows. **1954** JRMacDonald *Find* (NY) 157: Politics make stranger bedfellows than sex. **1956** *NYTimes* 11/11 30: The strangeness of political bedfellows. **1957** *BHerald* 2/4 16: Economics, like politics, makes strange bedfellows. **1957** RStandish *Prince* (L) 92: Expediency makes strange bedfellows. **1958** *NYTimes Book Review* 5/25 8: Like politics, the book

racket occasionally turns up some faintly surprising bedfellows. **1958** *Time* 5/26 108: Bedfellows make strange politics. **1959** *BHerald* 10/7 1: The old adage that politics makes strange bedfellows. **1959** NBlake *Widow's* (L) 18: Perversity makes strange bedfellows. **1960** SDean *Murder* (NY DBC) 98: Greed makes more strange fellows than politics. **1960** MInnes *New Sonia* (L) 150: Adversity makes strange bedfellows. **1963** JKirkup *Tropic* (L) 82: Necessity does indeed acquaint us with strange bedfellows. **1964** JKieran *Not Under* (B) 120: A war beats even politics for making strange bedfellows. **1967** JAxelrad *Freneau* (Austin) 286: Politics, reputed to make strange bedfellows, was to vindicate its reputation in the year 1797. **1969** HPentecost *Girl with* (NY) 156: Murder makes strange bedfellows. **1970** LKronenberger *No Whippings* (B) 31: Prohibition made strange barfellows, and bedfellows stranger still. **1972** AFriedman *Hermaphrodeity* (NY) 17: Politics makes strange bedfellows. **1973** BHowar *Laughing* (NY) 105: There will be strange bedfellows in politics as long as the double standard exists. EAP P226; *Oxford* 535: Misery.

P280 **Poor** but honest
1939 RHull *And Death* (L) 150: Born of poor but honest parents, as the saying is. **1949** EQueen *Cat* (B) 142: Poor but honest, he burned the midnight oil. **1953** CLittle *Black Iris* (NY) 68: Your people were poor but honest. *Oxford* 638. Cf. Brunvand 111(1): Poor but pious.

P281 **Poor** but (and, if) proud
1925 JSFletcher *False* (NY) 40: Proud, if poor. **1928** ABerkeley *Silk* (NY) 77: Poor but proud. **1929** CWells *Tapestry* (P) 169: She's poor and proud. **1937** NBlake *There's Trouble* (L) 250: Proud and poor. **1939** LFord *Town* (NY) 11: We're very proud, even if we are poor. **1940** AMorton *Blue Mask* (P) 145: They're the poor but proud type. **1946** GBellairs *Death in the Night* (NY) 116: Poor and proud. **1963** CArmstrong *Little Less* (NY) 12: Poor but proud. **1974** NWebster *Burial* (NY) 97: You could call us poor but proud. EAP P228; TW 291(2).

P282   As fat as a **Porpoise**

1913 JCLincoln *Mr. Pratt's Patients* (NY) 19: As fat as a porpoise. EAP P235.

P283   Any **Port** in a storm (*varied*)

1923 DCScott *Witching* (Toronto) 214: The adage "any port in a storm." **1926** RASimon *Weekend* (NY) 291: Any old port in a storm, you know. **1932** NTrott *Monkey* (NY) 45: The theory of any port in a storm. **1938** HHolt *Whispering* (L) 19: Any port in a snowstorm. **1950** ADerleth *Beyond* (NY) 269: Any port in a storm. **1956** *New Yorker* 9/29 121: Any portable [*typewriter*] in a storm. **1959** FBrown *Knock* (NY) 147: Any port in a storm. **1961** LThayer *And One* (NY DBC) 8: Any port in a storm. **1968** PMoyes *Death* (NY) 95: A case of any port in a storm. **1972** FFarmer *Will There* (NY) 276: You've been a port in a storm. **1972** HDPerry *Chair* (NY) 11: A good port in the occasional financial storm. EAP P238.

P284   As pretty as a **Posey**

1932 BABotkin ed *Land Is Ours* (Norman, Okla.) 258: Pretty as a posey. Taylor *Prov. Comp.* 64. See NED Posy 2: Bunch of flowers, nosegay.

P285   **Possession** is nine points of the law (*varied*)

1918 ERPunshon *Solitary* (NY) 34: Possession is nine-tenths of the law. **1928** RHFuller *Jubilee* (NY) 144: Possession isn't nine points of the law—it's all ten points. **1928** DLSayers *Dawson* (NY) 134: Possession is nine points of the law. **1935** AChristie *Boomerang* (NY) 213: Possession is nine points of the law. **1937** PATaylor *Figure* (NY) 101: There's a coarse, crass old adage that says possession is nine points of the law. **1941** GMitchell *Hangman's* (L) 130: Possession was going to be all ten points of the law. **1951** MInnes *Old Hall* (L 1961) 210: Possession nine-tenth of the law. **1953** LBaker *Snips* (NY) 97: Possession being nine points of the law. **1958** *BHerald* 11/20 7: Mrs Yanolis still had those mythical nine points of the law—possession. **1962** BLind *Vagabond* (NY) 43: Possession is nine points of the law. **1964** EFerrars *Legal* (L) 84: You'd find possession was nine points of

the law. **1973** FFelton *Peacock* (L) 18: Possession was, in this case, nine tenths of the law. EAP P240; TW 292; Brunvand 112.

P286   As deaf as a **Post** (*varied*)

1900 CFPidgin *Quincy A. Sawyer* (B) 71: He's deafer'n a stone post. **1926** RAFreeman *D'Arblay* (NY) 61: As deaf as a post. **1927** JSFletcher *Bartenstein* (NY) 71: He's as deaf as a post. **1930** WLewis *Apes* (NY 1932) 51: He's deaf as a post. **1931** HAshbrook *Murder* (NY) 54: Dead as a post. **1934** RJBlack *Killing* (NY) 68: I'm as deaf as a gate-post. **1938** JRice *Man Who* (NY) 80: Deaf as a post. **1939** ADemarest *Murder on* (NY) 194: Mrs. Evans, deaf as a lamp post. **1940** EDean *Murder Is* (NY) 10: She's deaf as a post. **1940** CBDawson *Lady Wept* (NY) 197: I was practically as deaf as seven posts. **1949** FLockridge *Spin* (P) 85: She's deaf as—I don't know. Are posts deaf, really? **1955** PWentworth *Gazebo* (L 1965) 125: As deaf as a post. **1957** CRice *My Kingdom* (NY) 185: He's as deaf as a whole fence full of posts. **1962** MGEberhart *Enemy* (NY) 42: Deaf as a post. **1971** JBlish *And All* (NY) 59: I'm deaf as a post. **1973** EMcBain *Let's Hear* (NY) 199: I was deaf as a post. EAP P242. Cf. Fence pole *above*.

P287   As dumb as a **Post**

1931 MGEberhart *From This* (NY) 207: Dumb as a post [*stupid*]. Whiting *NC* 461(2); Taylor *Western Folklore* 17(1958) 18.

P288   As stiff as a **Post**

1932 LFrost *Murder* (NY) 94: Miss Romany's stiffer'n a post. **1956** RRobinson *Landscape* (L 1963) 31: He was as stiff as a post. TW 292(2).

P289   As still as a **Post**

1929 WFaulkner *Sound* (NY) 258: As still as a post. **1967** HTravers *Madame Aubry Dines* (NY) 172: Standing as still as a post. EAP P244.

P290   As thin as a **Post**

1971 AGarve *Late* (NY) 131: Tall, and as thin as a post. TW 293(4).

P291   To be left at the **Post**

1912 JCLincoln *Postmaster* (NY) 242: He'll be left at the post. **1940** DWheelock *Murder at Montauk* (NY) 196: He'd be left at the post. **1958** RFenisong *Death* (NY) 59: I could have been left at the post. See NED Post *sb.*[1] 3c.

P292   As pretty as a **Postcard**

1958 RMacdonald *Doomsters* (NY) 42: Everything was as pretty as a postcard. **1960** PCurtis *Devil's* (NY) 22: As pretty as a postcard. Cf. Picture *above.*

P293   A **Postman's** holiday (*varied*)

1926 EDBiggers *Chinese* (NY) 10: He's like a postman who goes for a long walk on his day off. **1930** NBMavity *Case* (NY) 305: Like the postman's holiday. **1930** NBMavity *Other Bullet* (NY) 4: Postmen . . . are alleged to devote their vacations to long walks. **1934** TDowning *Cat Screams* (NY) 124: A postman's holiday for me. **1938** HReed *Swing Music* (NY) 127: My postman's holiday complex. **1950** BCarey *Man Who* (NY) 32: Talk about a "postman's holiday." **1957** *NYTimes Book Review* 6/17 7: A postman's holiday. Berrey 250.2. Cf. Busman *above;* Sailor *below.*

P294   As black as the **Pot**

1933 VLoder *Suspicion* (L) 124: As black as the pot. TW 293(1). Cf. Pot calls *below.*

P295   If one stirs the **Pot** he sees what comes to the surface

1968 SWoods *Knives* (NY) 74: He enjoys stirring the pot to see what comes to the surface. EAP P255.

P296   Not to have a **Pot** to piss in (*varied*)

1935 JMartin *Nathaniel West* (NY 1970) 268: Leave him alone, he hasn't got a pot to piss in. **1951** JO'Hara *Farmer's* (NY) 105: That little fellow there, he ain't got a pot to piss in. **1953** BMcMillion *Lot* (P) 236: That'll keep people from saying you ain't got a pot to piss in. **1958** RHiscock *Last* (NY) 6: Even if we don't have a pot to spit in, we eat good. **1960** DAlexander *Pennies* (P) 5: You didn't have a pot to spit in. **1960** CIrving *Fake* (NY) 185: I would be in a gutter some-where—an "old queen without a pot to piss in." **1971** TPace *Fisherman's* (NY) 48: Didn't have a pot to piss in, all his life. **1973** LHellman *Pentimento* (B) 240: You'll . . . die without a pot to piss in or a bone to chew. **1974** CCarpenter *Deadhead* (NY) 86: You know better than to think Dino has a pot to pee in! **1978** MHoward *Facts* (B) 110: My father said of us: "They don't have a pot to piss in." **1982** ECunningham *Kidnapped Angel* (NY) 102: [He] doesn't have a pot to pee in.

P297   The **Pot** calls the kettle black (*varied*)

1918 JBCabell *Letters* ed PColum (NY 1962) 77: The pot should not call the kettle black. **1920** WLewis *Letters* ed WKRose (L 1963) 117: Pot is calling the kettle black. **1922** JJoyce *Ulysses* (NY 1934) 752: The pan calling the kettle blackbottom. **c1923** ACrowley *Confessions* ed JSymonds (L 1969) 761: I still think the English pot as black as the German kettle. **1927** SBent *Ballyhoo* (NY) 281: Chicago with its machine-gun bandits . . . can hardly call the Denver kettle black. **1928** AYoung *On My Way* (NY) 242: It's a world of pots and kettles, a continual condemnation. Each calls the other black. **1930** Ex-PrivateX *War* (NY) 107: This propaganda on both sides is all a game of pots and kettles. **1931** SChase *Mexico* (NY) 299: The vulgar argument of kettle against pot. **1932** NOrde-Powlett *Cast* (B) 68: I haven't a right to criticize you; it's a case of the pot and the kettle. **1933** GHolt *Six Minutes* (L) 139: "You dirty crook," says the pot to the kettle. **1939** MElwin *Old Gods* (NY) 80: He was inviting a comparison of pot and kettle. **1940** MBoniface *Murder As* (NY) 222: The pot can't call the kettle black. **1952** EHahn *Love* (NY) 275: Talk about the pot calling the kettle black-arsed. **1956** *TLS* 5/11 280: Often involves the U pot in calling the non-U kettle black. **1956** *BangorDN* 9/11 8: If the kettle is black, so is the pot. **1957** *BHerald* 12/7 4: The Pot and the Kettle. **1958** *BHerald* 1/14 12: A case of the kettle calling the pot black. **1959** JThurber *Years* (B) 247: When it comes to money . . . I am not one to throw stones, but a pot is as black as a kettle. **1960** SRansome *Warning* (NY DBC)

35: Listen to the pot calling the kettle black. **1964** ABurgess *Eve* (L) 68: The aesthetic pot . . . calling the biological kettle black. **1968** JMerril *Daughters* (NY 1970) 87: The father-pot calling the mother-kettle neurotic. **1969** JSteinbeckIV *In Touch* (NY) 122: The pot generation calls the kettle generation black and the kettle boils over. **1970** MStocks *My Commonplace* (L) 119: Whose face was the dirtiest: the pot's or the kettle. **1975** EPeters *Crocodile* (NY) 64: I am the pot that calls the kettle black. **1981** AM Stein *Body* (NY) 21: That . . . is a case of the pot calling the kettle round [*two fat men involved*]. EAP P248. Cf. As black as a Kettle, Pot *above*.

P298 Shit or get off the **Pot** (*varied*)

1946 RFinnegan *Lying* (NY) 139: Either play or get off the piano. **1952** IGordon *Night* (NY) 157: Shit or get off the pot. **1959** MHarris *Wake* (NY) 32: He will either be in production or get off the pot. **1974** MDavis *Tell Them* (NY) 102: You mean, piss or get off the pot. **1974** EMcBain *Bread* (NY) 50: So shit or get off the pot, will you? **1977** CAlverson *Not Sleeping* (B) 90: You'd better . . . shit or get off the pot. Wentworth 468. Cf. Luke *above*.

P299 There is a **Pot** of gold at the end of the rainbow

1932 JJConnington *Sweepstake* (B) 40: To drive to the rainbow's end and dig up the crock of gold there. **1943** EWTeale *Dune Boy* (NY 1957) 52: A pot of gold at the end of the rainbow. **1951** RKing *Duenna* (NY) 52: The pot-of-gold stuff at the rainbow's end. **1956** IFleming *Diamonds* (NY 1961) 87: The proverbial pot of gold at the end of the rainbow. **1960** WMasterson *Hammer* (NY DBC) 133: The pot of gold at the end of the rainbow. **1966** DMDisney *Magic* (NY) 33: Pot of gold at the end of the rainbow. **1968** LBlanch *Journey* (L) 216: Sergei might have gone to America, seeking the proverbial pot of gold. **1970** WMasterson *Death* (NY) 126: Seeking a non-existent pot of gold at the end of the rainbow. **1974** ELathen *Sweet* (NY) 11: The legendary pot of gold at the end of some local rainbows. *Oxford* 221: End.

P300 To go to **Pot**

1922 JJoyce *Ulysses* (NY 1934) 162–3: Let them all go to pot. **1925** EMPoate *Pledged* (NY) 45: The younger generation is going to pot. **1937** DFrome *Black Envelope* (NY) 192: The place had gone to pot. **1939** JRWarren *Murder from* (NY) 39: Your deal . . . goes to pot. **1956** SPalmer *Unhappy* (NY 1957) 3: Criminology . . . has gone all to pot. **1960** JJMarric *Gideon's Fire* (NY) 61: The firm can go to pot. **1968** JPorter *Dover Goes to Pott* (NY). EAP P251.

P301 To piss in the same **Pot**

1950 GGrigson *Crest* (L) 158: Lancashire saying of intimacy . . . They piss in the same pot. *Oxford* 627: Quill.

P302 To put the big **Pot** in the little one (*varied*)

1930 JFDobie *Coronado* (Dallas) 252: The big pot was in the little one. **1941** ISCobb *Exit* (I) 394: Lorimer . . . had put the big pot in the little one. **1955** LCochran *Hallelujah* (NY) 131: Then the housewife would "put the big pot in the little pot and fry the skillet." Whiting *NC* 461(7). Cf. Quart *below*.

P303 A watched **Pot** never boils (*varied*)

1929 FEverton *Hammer* (NY) 133: A watched pot never boils, and [she] proved the old proverb a hundred times and again. **1933** SPalmer *Pepper Tree* (NY) 250: The watched pot was beginning to boil. **1935** VRath *Death* (NY) 165: If you let a pot simmer long enough, it fin'lly comes to a boil. **1936** LThayer *Dark of the Moon* (NY) 194: The pot has to simmer before it boils. **1956** AGilbert *Riddle* (NY) 48: Waiting for the watched pot . . . it's always a waste of time. **1958** *New Yorker* 7/12 78: If he was a watched pot, he would never boil. **1958** *New Yorker* 8/9 28: A Potted Watch Never Boils. **1960** ASinclair *Project* (L) 108: An unwatched can always boils. **1969** HFosburgh *Clearing* (NY) 2: It's like the pot that won't boil [*watched*]. **1970** RFenisong *Drop* (NY) 156: On the principle that a watched pot never boils. **1978** MRenault *Praise* (NY)

153: If he'd give over watching the pot, it might boil sooner. *Oxford* 869.

P304 As plain as a **Potato**

1959 MScherf *Never Turn* (NY) 162: She's not good looking—she's as plain as a potato.

P305 Small **Potatoes** (and few in a hill) (*varied*)

1908 JCLincoln *Cy Whittaker* (NY) 246: Small potatoes and few in a hill. **1929** LBrock *Murder* (NY) 5: My little lot is very small potatoes to bring you. **1934** RPTCoffin *Lost Paradise* (NY) 143: Small potatoes and few in a hill. **1942** CFAdams *What Price* (NY) 51: [It] seemed like rather small potatoes. **1955** SRansome *Frazer* (NY) 158: She . . . decided Smythe was small potatoes. **1957** CRice *My Kingdom* (NY) 238: Pretty small potatoes. **1960** JBarry *Malignant* (NY) 75: He's the smallest of small potatoes. **1963** MPHood *Sin* (NY) 141: Runty potatoes 'n few to the row. **1964** DMDisney *Hospitality* (NY) 47: Look like pretty small potatoes. **1971** PDennis *Paradise* (NY) 91: It was small potatoes. TW 293–4(13, 14).

P306 To drop (be dropped) like a hot **Potato** (*varied*)

1922 JJoyce *Ulysses* (NY 1934) 161: Drop him like a hot potato. **1926** MRRinehart *Bat* (NY 1959) 35: [He] dropped the revolver like a hot potato. **1933** HWade *Mist* (L) 3: Hilary had been dropped like a hot potato. **1939** WMartyn *Noonday* (L) 81: She'll drop him like a hot potato. **1946** ABCunningham *One Man* (NY) 51: I'm not going to be caught holding their hot potato. **1948** HStone *Corpse* (NY) 149: I dropped it like a hot potato. **1954** MProcter *Somewhere* (NY) 125: I dropped him like a hot potato. **1957** *Punch* 3/6 325: Anything new the Censor Cato would have dropped like a hot potato. **1958** *BHerald* 8/17 25: The controversion legislation . . . suddenly is bouncing around like the proverbial hot potato among opposing groups. **1966** HJBoyle *With a Pinch* (NY) 27: The suggestion was dropped like a hot potato. **1972** ELathen *Murder* (NY) 206: He dropped the idea like a hot potato. **1973** HDolson *Dying* (P) 126: Lucy . . . dropped that notion like a cold

potato. **1977** VCanning *Doomsday* (NY) 75: The police had been landed with a hot potato. TW 294(15); Brunvand 112(2). Cf. To drop . . . Brick, Chestnut, Coal, Hotcake *above*.

P307 To take a cold **Potato** to a chicken dinner

1937 EGowen *Old Hell* (NY) 42: Bringing the old woman here where you are at would be like toting a cold potato to a chicken dinner.

P308 **Pot-luck**

1927 RAFreeman *Puzzle* (NY) 194: Take pot-luck. **1930** EWallace *Red Aces* (NY) 9: You'll have to take pot luck. **1958** JCoates *Widow's* (NY) 11: He had come to take pot luck. **1961** LPayne *Nose* (NY) 78: I'll take pot-luck, as they say [*the chance of finding someone at home*]. **1968** JBell *Death* (P) 174: You'll have to take pot luck. **1976** MGilbert *Night* (NY) 32: Took pot luck [*of a chair to sit in*]. EAP P257.

P309 **Pot-valiant**

1941 LGBlochman *See You at* (NY) 81: She . . . was making herself pot-valiant to face the situation. EAP P258.

P310 All quiet along the **Potomac**

1930 LThayer *They Tell* (NY) 86: All's quiet along the Potomac. **1933** WCBrown *Murder* (P) 66: All quiet along the Potomac. **1936** RAJWalling *Floating Foot* (NY) 132: All quiet along the Potomac. **1961** LThayer *And One* (NY DBC) 110: All seems to be quiet along the Potomac tonight. Wentworth 4.

P311 As poor as **Poverty**

1908 JCLincoln *Cy Whittaker* (NY) 97: Poorer than poverty. **1921** JCLincoln *Galusha* (NY) 109: Poorer'n poverty. EAP P260; Brunvand 112.

P312 When **Poverty** comes in at the door *etc.* (*varied*)

1906 HNewbolt *Old Country* (L) 91: When logic comes in at the door, persuasion flies out of the window. **1911** HHMunro *Chronicles* (L 1927) 1: In spite of everything proverbs may say, poverty keeps together more homes than it breaks up. **1913** EDBiggers

Seven Keys (I) 106: When women come in the door, I fly out of the window, as the saying is. **1939** EPhillpotts *Monkshood* (L) 271: Future poverty shared with Julyan would have been withstood and love decline to fly out of the window. **1946** RPowell *Shoot If* (NY) 44: When forty-five caliber slugs come in the door, love flies out the windows. **1956** *Time* 10/22 43: When statehood flies in the window, the tax collector knocks at the door. **1970** JVizzard *See* (NY) 64: The Ten Commandments go right out the window, when love flies in. **1972** CTurney *Byron's* (NY) 217: Once suspicion enters the door, trust flies out the window. **1973** RStout *Please* (NY) 18: When sex comes in by the window, logic leaves by the door. **1977** PDJames *Death* (NY) 180: When murder comes in the window, privacy goes out the door. EAP P265.

P313 As dry as **Powder**

1938 RAJWalling *Grimy Gloves* (NY) 234: The dust ... is as dry as powder. **1954** JWKrutch *Voice* (NY) 135: The ground ... is dry as powder. EAP P266.

P314 Not worth **Powder** and shot

1928 JAFerguson *Man in the Dark* (NY) 147: The smaller fry were not worth his powder and shot. **1931** MAllingham *Police* (NY) 186: That's not worth powder and shot. EAP P267.

P315 Not worth the **Powder** to blow one to hell (*varied*)

1931 VWMason *Vesper* (NY) 9: He isn't worth the powder to blow him up. **1936** ABCaldwell *Turquoise* (NY) 107: Most of them aren't worth the powder to blow 'em to hell. **1940** HSKeeler *Crimson Box* (L) 196: He's not worth powder to blow him to hell. **1941** KMKnight *Exit a Star* (NY) 123: [Not] worth the powder to blow him to Jericho. **1948** DCDisney *Explosion* (NY DBC) 120: Not worth the powder to blow him to hell with. **1953** KMKnight *Akin* (NY) 152: He never was worth the powder to blow him to Jericho. **1957** TWicker *Devil* (NY) 14: Not worth the powder to blow him to hell. **1958** *BHerald* 10/6 16: A tiny island not worth the powder to blow it to kingdom

come. **1959** MScherf *Never Turn* (NY) 170: Collins' houses were never worth the powder to you know what. **1972** PKruger *Cold* (NY) 97: [Not] worth the powder to blow it up. **1982** CMacLeod *Wrack* (NY) 2: [He] ain't worth the powder to blow him to hell an' gone. EAP P268.

P316 To take a (run-out) **Powder**

1934 NChild *Diamond* (L) 143: To take a run-out powder. **1937** GBruce *Claim* (NY) 159: Taking a run-out powder. **1940** SMSchley *Who'd Shoot* (NY) 7: I took a run-out powder. **1950** RStout *In the Best* (NY) 167: Wolfe took a powder. **1959** BClifton *Murder* (NY) 18: Maybe he took a powder. **1961** GFowler *Skyline* (NY) 307: As the saying is, I take a powder. **1967** MDavis *Strange* (NY) 58: He took a run-out powder. **1971** VScannell *Tiger* (L) 90: He had taken a powder, got off his mark, vamoosed. Berrey 58.2, 215.4; Wentworth 405.

P317 More **Power** to one's elbow

1936 BThomson *Who Killed* (NY) 241: Well, more power to your elbow. **1939** RPhilmore *Death in* (L) 38: More power to his elbow. **1956** JFStraker *Ginger* (L) 15: More power to your elbow.

P318 **Practice** makes perfect

1900 CFPidgin *Quincy A. Sawyer* (B) 427: Practice makes perfect. **1921** JBCabell *Figures* (NY 1925) 88: Practice, that is the thing, they say, in all the arts. **1922** JJoyce *Ulysses* (NY 1934) 121: Practice makes perfect. **1931** WWJacobs *Snug* (NY) 454: Practice makes perfect. **1937** RPenny *Policeman's Holiday* (L) 6: Without even a practice to help make me perfect. **1940** DBurnham *Last Act* (NY) 179: Practice makes perfect. **1941** VWMason *Rio Casino* (NY) 253: Practice makes perfect. **1957** JPotts *Man with* (NY 1964) 69: Practice makes perfect, you know. **1958** RFraser *Jupiter* (L) 87: For practice indeed makes perfect. **1961** PDennis *Little* (NY) 150: Practice makes perfect. **1969** JCreasey *Baron* (NY) 36: A case of practice makes perfect. **1977** STWarner *Kingdoms* (NY) 84: Practice had made him nearly perfect. EAP P269.

P319 To **Practice** what one preaches (*varied*)

1903 ADMcFaul *Ike Glidden* (B) 136: He ought to be as willing to practise self-denial as to preach it. **1915** PGWodehouse *Something Fresh* (L 1935) 79: To practise what I preach. **1922** JJoyce *Ulysses* (NY 1934) 403: Let his practice consist better with the doctrines that now engross him. **1924** LSpringfield *Some Piquant* (L) 23: It failed to practise what it preached. **1930** WLewis *Apes* (NY 1932) 388: You practise what you preach. **1935** JTFarrell *Judgment* (NY) 341: Why don't you practice what you preach. **1941** ISCobb *Exit* (I) 317: Why should one practice what he preaches? **1947** GLGower *Mixed* (L) 154: I advised him to "preach what he practised, and not to practise what he preached." **1952** PGosse *Dr. Viper* (L) 217: Thicknesse practised what he preached. **1953** JSanford *Land* (NY) 135: Preach what you practice. **1956** PDeVries *Comfort* (B) 149: Yet, having preached platitudes I must now practise what I had preached. I must eat my own cooking. **1957** *BangorDN* 5/3 16: This is an example of how one government department practices the economy that President Eisenhower preaches. **1959** *BHerald* 6/25 31: It is not unfair to ask the President to practice what he preaches. **1965** JCleugh *Divine* (L) 209: Aretino practised what he preached. **1968** EHuxley *Love* (L) 100: You practice what I preach. **1968** ESprigge *Cocteau* (NY) 149: Cocteau did not preach what he practised. **1969** IBSinger *Day* (NY) 52: What others preached, he practiced. **1971** MRugoff *Prudery* (NY) 238: Others who did practice what they preached. **1973** WMasterson *Undertaker* (NY) 45: Practice what you preach. **1976** DWilliams *Unholy* (NY) 33: A priest who practices what he preaches. EAP P270; Brunvand 112, 113: Preaching(1).

P320 **Praise** to the face is open disgrace

1935 ERPunshon *Death* (L 1948) 32: As the old saw says "praise to the face is open disgrace." **1954** EWalter *Untidy* (P) 77: Praise to the face is open disgrace. **1964** EHemingway *Moveable* (NY) 150: Praise to the face was open disgrace. **1965** HHowe *Gentle* (NY) 193: Praise to the face is open disgrace. TW 295; *Oxford* (2nd ed) 515.

P321 As certain (sure) as **Preaching**

1936 SLBradbury *Hiram* (Rutland, Vt.) 141: As sartin as preachin'. **1949** KMKnight *Bass* (NY) 15: As sure as preaching. TW 295(1).

P322 As true as **Preaching**

1917 JCLincoln *Extricating* (NY) 225: True as preachin'. TW 295–6(5); Brunvand 113(2).

P323 **Pretty** is as pretty does

1929 AHayes *Crime* (L) 139: Pretty is as pretty does. **1935** TThayer *Cluck* (NY) 24: Pretty is as pretty does. **1936** ISCobb *Judge Priest* (I) 64: Purty is ez purty does, and not ez purty smells. **1940** TChanslor *Our First* (NY) 161: Pretty is as pretty does. **1959** FCrane *Buttercup* (NY DBC) 110: Pretty is as pretty does. **1961** HReilly *Certain* (NY DBC) 26: Pretty is as pretty does. **1963** SForbes *Grieve* (NY) 96: Pretty is as pretty does. **1976** IAsimov *Murder* (NY) 60: Pretty is as pretty does. TW 296(1); Brunvand 113(1). Cf. Handsome *above*.

P324 **Prevention** is better than cure (*varied*)

1927 RAFreeman *Magic* (NY) 138: Prevention is better than a post-mortem. **1930** RWallace *Seven Men* (NY) 64: Prevention is more important than attempting a cure—afterwards. **1931** WWJacobs *Snug* (NY) 509: Prevention is better than cure. **1954** EDillon *Sent* (L) 70: Prevention is better than cure. **1967** LPDavies *Lampton* (NY) 22: Prevention is better than cure. **1968** GWagner *Elegy* (L) 97: Prevention is better than cure. **1971** JJMarric *Gideon's Art* (NY) 43: Prevention's better than cure. EAP P275. Cf. Ounce *above*.

P325 To have to do with the **Price** of beans *etc.* (*varied*)

1931 PATaylor *Cape Cod* (NY 1971) 207: What's that got to do with the price of beans? **1934** AHalper *Foundry* (NY) 195: What's that got to do with the price of eggs? **1937** ATilton *Beginning* (NY) 203: What has that got to do with the price of beans? **1949** JSStrange *Unquiet* (NY) 111: What's that got to do with the price of fish? **1957** JMerrill *Seraglio* (NY) 188: What did that have to do with the price of beans? **1960** JBWest *Taste* (NY) 41: What's that got to do with the price of eggs in China? **1962** HWaugh *Born* (NY) 158: What's that got to do with the price of eggs? **1964** HPentecost *Shape* (NY DBC) 8: I don't see what it has to do with the price of eggs.

P326 All **Prick** and no pence

1922 JJoyce *Ulysses* (NY 1934) 424: Trinity medicals . . . All prick and no pence. Cf. Partridge 445: Judische compliment.

P327 A stiff **Prick** has no conscience (*varied*)

1933 LO'Flaherty *Martyr* (NY) 143: A thirsty throat is like another famous part of the human anatomy. It has no conscience. **1935** JTFarrell *Judgment* (NY) 94: You know, a John has got no conscience. **1939** HMiller *Capricorn* (NY 1961) 188: They say a stiff prick has no conscience, but a stiff prick that laughs too is phenomenal. **1947** HCahill *Look* (NY) 337: A hungry stomach has no conscience. **1966** RGrenier *Yes and Back* (L) 111: They said two things about a stiff pecker: (1) a stiff pecker has no conscience; and (2) a stiff pecker has no sense of humour. **1970** JAtkins *Sex* (L) 169: You know they say a stiff one knows no conscience. **1975** HLawrenson *Stranger* (NY) 25: The old adage "A stiff prick has no conscience." **1982** MDrown *Plowing* (NY) 115: A stiff prick has no conscience. Partridge 824: Standing; Taylor *Proverb* 171: Penis erectus non habet conscientiam.

P328 To kick against the **Pricks** (*varied*)

1928 ACBrown *Dr. Glazebrook* (NY) 79: Stop kicking against the pricks. **1932** RPertwee *Death* (B) 166: No use to kick against the pricks. **1937** HWade *High Sheriff* (L) 68: Kicking . . . against the pricks. **1941** CE Vulliamy *Short History* (L) 219: He kicked in vain at the tough and ubiquitous pricks of hypocrisy. **1948** CRBoxer *Fidalgos* (Oxford 1968) 162: Kicking against the pricks.

1956 *New Yorker* 11/10 55: There was no use kicking against the goad. **1959** JJMarric *Gideon's Staff* (NY) 23: You can't kick against the pricks. **1963** WHaggard *High* (NY DBC) 4: If there wasn't a prick to kick against Irene would seek one. **1981** JOsborne *Better* (NY) 163: From then on it was a beholden duty at all times for me to kick against the pricks. EAP P276; TW 296.

P329 **Pride** goes before a fall (*varied*)

1909 JCLincoln *Keziah* (NY) 202: Pride goes ahead of a tumble, I've heard tell. **1928** EKRand *Founders* (Cambridge, Mass.) 45: Pride goeth before a fall. **1928** RHWatkins *Master* (NY) 159: Pride goeth before a bump. **1933** JBCarr *Death* (NY) 255: Pride goeth before a fall. **1937** PWentworth *Case Is Closed* (L) 247: Pride had gone before a fall. **1938** BFlynn *Five Red* (NY) 86: Pride goes before destruction, remember. **1940** JJConnington *Four Defences* (B) 117: Pomposity goes before a fall. **1947** LFord *Woman* (NY) 157: It was merely pride that deserved its fall. **1949** GHHall *End* (NY) 192: Pride goeth before a fall. **1952** EPaul *Black* (NY) 172: It was wisely said that pride goeth before a fall. **1956** BCClough *More* (Portland, Me.) 96: As usual, pride went before a fall. **1965** JPorter *Dover Two* (NY 1968) 66: They say pride goes before a fall. **1966** NBlake *Deadly* (L) 49: Pride . . . comes before other and less painful kinds of falls. **1968** JRAckerley *My Father* (L) 114: Pride will have a fall. **1972** CTurney *Byron's* (NY) 165: Adversity had taught her . . . that pride does not always go before a fall, and that money is not necessarily the root of all evil. EAP P281; TW 296(1); Brunvand 113.

P330 To put one's **Pride** in his pocket (pocket one's pride) (*varied*)

1917 GRSims *My Life* (L) 226: Put his pride in his pocket. **1921** JSFletcher *Orange-Yellow* (NY) 19: He had put his pride in his pocket. **1932** WSMasterman *Flying* (NY) 246: I put my pride in my pocket. **1932** JVTurner *Death* (L) 253: You pocketed your pride. **1935** CBush *Chinese Song* (NY) 5: You've got to pocket a certain amount of pride. **1946** AEMartin *Death in the Limelight* (NY)

59: She'd pocket her pride. **1947** HLawrence *Death of* (NY) 48: Pocket your pride. **1962** MAllingham *China* (NY) 147: [She] put her pride in her pocket. **1968** EWilliams *Beyond* (NY) 332: The men took their pride out of their pocket. **1971** EHCohen *Mademoiselle* (B) 115: He pocketed his pride. **1972** JMangione *Dream* (B) 98: Pocketed their pride. EAP P282.

P331 To swallow one's **Pride**

1930 CFitzsimmons *Bainbridge* (NY) 181: I had to swallow my pride. **1956** GHCoxe *Suddenly* (NY) 47: I swallowed my pride. **1966** JAiken *Beware* (NY) 41: I finally swallowed my pride. **1970** WANolen *Making* (NY) 55: Swallowed my pride. EAP P283.

P332 As proud as a **Prince**

1955 CJay *Yellow* (NY) 89: As proud as a prince. Whiting P401.

P333 To live like a **Prince**

1924 EWallace *Green* (B) 27: Live like a prince. **1939** JNDarby *Murder in* (I) 282: Johnny could live like a prince. **1966** BHDeal *Fancy's* (NY) 70: All of them live like princes and princesses of the realm. EAP P290; Brunvand 113(2).

P334 As plain (clear) as **Print**

1921 ERBurroughs *Mucker* (NY) 153: As plain as print. **1930** WLewis *Apes* (NY 1932) 371: It's as plain as print. **1931** JJConnington *Boathouse* (B) 175: It's as plain as print to me. **1940** CDickson *And so to Murder* (NY) 270: It was plain as print. **1942** JDCarr *Emperor's* (NY) 289: As plain as print. **1958** CHare *He Should* (L) 45: As plain as print. **1962** NFreeling *Death* (NY 1964) 173: I could see, clear as print. **1975** EPeters *Crocodile* (NY) 147: It was as clear as print. EAP P291.

P335 **Procrastination** is the thief of time (*varied*)

1922 JJoyce *Ulysses* (NY 1934) 669: *Procrastination is the Thief of Time.* **1925** HWNevinson *More Changes* (L) 296: Procrastination the thief of other people's time. **1936** VMcHugh *Caleb* (NY) 290: I told 'em procrastination was the thief of time. **1939** DHume *Heads* (L) 194: They say that pro-

crastination is the thief of time. **1961** NBlake *Worm* (L) 173: Elimination . . . is the thief of time. **1965** JPotts *Only Good* (NY) 57: The message in High's fortune cookie said, "Procrastination is the thief of time." **1970** HActon *Memoirs* (NY) 290: They believed that punctuality was the thief of time. EAP P294.

P336 **Professors** are absent-minded (*varied*)

1928 EBYoung *Murder* (P) 23: We all know that professors are apt to be extremely absentminded—It's a byword. **1953** MMainwaring *Murder* (NY) 72: The proverbial absent-minded professor. Whiting *NC* 463.

P337 Small **Profits** and quick return

1956 MColes *Birdwatcher's* (NY) 121: What is that saying you have in England? Small profits and quick returns, is it? *Oxford* 744: Small.

P338 A forced **Promise** is no promise (*varied*)

1954 ADuggan *Leopards* (L) 26: A promise extorted by fear cannot bind. **1955** RGraves *Homer's* (NY) 166: A forced promise is no promise. **1970** DHarper *Hijacked* (NY DBC) 123: You don't have to stick to any promise forced under duress. Whiting O13.

P339 **Promises** are like pie crust *etc.* (*varied*)

1924 JSFletcher *Safety* (NY) 189: Promises are like pie-crust, as the old saying is . . . made to be broken. **1945** MBurton *Not a Leg* (NY) 145: Promises are like piecrusts, made to be broken. **1956** HCahill *Shadow* (NY) 69: Her promises brittle as pie crust. **1961** ATCurtis *Poacher's* (L) 170: Promises, some say, are made to be broken. **1964** HBourne *In the Event* (NY) 128: Pie-crust promises. **1981** GMitchell *Death-Cap* (NY) 147: Alibis, like promises and eggs, are made to be broken. EAP P297. Cf. Laws are made *above*; Rules *below*.

P340 **Promises** cost little

1953 WBlunt *Pietro's* (L) 171: Promises cost little. Cf. EAP W311: Good words cost nothing.

P341 A **Promise** is a debt (*varied*)

1931 HBurnham *Murder* (NY) 119: A promise is a debt. **1958** *BangorDN* 7/14 11: "A promise made—is a debt unpaid." Whiting B214; *Oxford* 649.

P342 **Promising** is one thing and doing is another (*varied*)

1924 HHMunro *Square* (L 1929) 119: Between the promise and the performance a cloud has arisen. **1935** ERPunshon *Death* (L 1948) 197: But promising's one thing and doing's another. EAP P298.

P343 The **Proof** of the pudding is in the eating (*varied*)

1904 JCLincoln *Cap'n Eri* (NY) 183: The proof of the pudding . . . is in the eating of it. **1922** JJoyce *Ulysses* (NY 1934) 150: Proof of the pudding. **1925** GBeasley *My First* (Paris) 211: As though that were sufficient proof of the pudding. **1931** VLoder *Death* (NY) 181: But the proof of the pudding's in the eating. **1937** RAFreeman *Felo* (L) 182: The proof of the pudding is in the eating, as the vulgar saying has it. **1945** PATaylor *Proof of the Pudding* (NY). **1949** HReilly *Murder* (NY) 32: The proof of the pudding was in the eating. **1951** CRCammell *Aleister* (L) 100: It is a trite saying that to prove the quality of the pudding one must eat it, but it is a true saying. **1955** *Partisan Review* 22 567: The final proof of Mama's pudding is given by Marjorie herself, who is shown eating it in Mamaroneck with a silver spoon. **1957** *New Yorker* 1/5 41: He is a proof-of-the-pudding man. **1966** NBlake *Morning* (NY) 19: The proof is in the pudding, as they say. **1971** CAird *Late* (NY) 77: The proof of the commercial pudding was always in the eating. **1972** JLDillard *Black* (NY) 252: The proof of the pudding . . . seems to be in the imitation. **1973** CAird *His Burial* (NY) 115: The proof of the police pudding isn't always in the eating. EAP P299.

P344 A **Prophet** is not without honor *etc.* (*varied*)

1903 EChilders *Riddle* (NY 1940) 4: I was not a prophet in my own country. **1923** JSFletcher *Copper* (NY) 91: Prophets . . . are said to have no honour in their own country. **1938** DBaker *Young Man* (B) 241: The prophet in his homeland is not supposed to be taken seriously. **1957** EMButler *Heine* (NY) 162: The proverbial fate of a prophet in his own times. **1959** *CSMonitor* 4/10 1: Kennan . . . was a prophet without honor in his own country or any other Western country. **1959** *BGlobe* 4/14 26: A new appreciation of that old proverb about the prophet. **1960** NWilliams *Knaves* (NY) 68: Astrologers, wizards and quacks are without honour in their own countries. **1961** MClingerman *Cupful* (NY) 75: A prophet is without honor under his own rooftree. **1963** MPutzel *Man in the Mirror* (Cambridge, Mass.) 104: Reedy had become a man not without honor in his home town. **1966** HMacDiarmid *Company* (L) 79: Prophets are proverbially without honour in their own country. **1973** JBrooks *Go-Go* (NY) 44: A prophet without honor not just in his own country but everywhere. **1980** LBarber *Heyday* (L) 196: [Asa Gray] was an American, and therefore a prophet without honour in his own country. EAP P301; TW 297.

P345 **Providence** (God, the Lord, the Almighty) looks after fools (babies, drunks *etc.*) (*varied*)

1906 JCLincoln *Mr Pratt* (NY) 98: They say the Almighty looks out for the lame and the lazy. **1911** HHMunro *Chronicles* (L 1927) 153: The protective Providence that looks after little children and amateur theatricals made good its traditional promise. **1919** LTracy *Bartlett* (NY) 141: There must be a special Providence that looks . . . after children and drunkards. **1924** WBMFerguson *Black* (NY) 29: The special Providence which is supposed to watch over the fool, sober or otherwise. **1925** TRMarshall *Recollections* (I) 128: The view that Providence looks after fools. **1928** RAFreeman *A Certain* (NY) 280: There is a Providence that watches over fools. **1930** MBDix *Murder* (L) 136: The Lord looks after fools [and] drunkards. **1930** IGoldberg *Tin Pan* (NY) 11: Doesn't Providence watch over babies and fools? **1930** MPShiel *Black Box* (NY) 112: The common saying that "God takes care of drunkards and babies." **1930** ATrain *Adventures* (NY) 129: The providence that sometimes watches over sailors, drunks and third parties. **1931** WMillis *Martial* (NY) 256: God takes care of drunken men, sailors, and the United States. **1933** CFitzsimmons *Red Rhapsody* (NY) 234: There is a divine providence what watches over fools and drunkards. **1938** WNMacartney *Fifty Years* (NY) 58: The kind Providence that looks after fools (and the delirious). **1940** AGilbert *Dear Dead* (NY) 151: The old proverb that Providence looks after fools and children. **1950** ECRLorac *Accident* (NY DBC) 126: The old adage that Providence helps those who help themselves. **1952** GBagby *Scared* (NY) 14: He'll be all right, you know—fools and drunkards. **1952** AWUpfield *New Shoe* (L 1968) 138: Drunks and babies are blessed with luck. **1955** STroy *Half-way* (L) 181: How you've found me, the God of fools and drunkards alone knoweth. **1965** RLFish *Diamond* (NY DBC) 67: There is a special Providence that watches over drunks and fools. **1966** EFuller *Successful* (NY) 235: Providence indeed watches over sailors, drunken men, and fools. **1970** RFenisong *Drop* (NY) 119: He'll be okay. You know what they say about drunks and fools. **1970** SGraham *Garden* (NY) 88: God takes care of children and drunks. **1972** DYoung *American* (NY) 384: God looks after fools, drunkards, and the United States. **1974** TWells *Have Mercy* (NY) 93: They say God watches out for fools and drunks. Whiting *NC* 415: God(11); *Oxford* 365: Heaven.

P346 As pious as a **Prune**

1954 EForbes *Rainbow* (B) 49: Jude sat there . . . looking pious as a prune. Cf. Taylor *Prov. Comp.* 64: So proper.

P347 To be full of **Prunes**

1940 RDarby *Death Conducts* (NY) 118: Mrs. Frank seemed as full of prunes as ever. **1941** AAFair *Spill* (NY) 45: I think Louie is full of prunes. Whiting *NC* 463(2).

P348 To have a **Pudding** in the oven

1965 JPorter *Dover Two* (NY 1968) 67: She'd got a pudding in the oven [*pregnant*]. Cf. Partridge 665.

P349 As full as a **Puggie**

1931 DLSayers *Suspicious* (NY) 337: Here's Campbell, fou' as a puggie. Partridge 666: Puggy-drunk.

P350 Between one and the ship's **Pump**

1909 JCLincoln *Keziah* (NY) 103: Between ourselves and the ship's pump. TW 298(3). Cf. Gate-post *above*.

P351 As straight as **Pump water**

1935 RAJWalling *Five Suspects* (L) 173: As straight and thin as two yards of pump water. **1968** MRowell *Below* (L) 100: My hair straight as pump water. Lean II ii 877: Yard of.

P352 To be some **Pumpkins**

1908 JCLincoln *Cy Whittaker* (NY) 387: We . . . are some punkins. **1925** SJohnson *Professor* (NY) 243: I do think I'm some "punkins." **1932** BRoss *Tragedy of X* (NY) 127: He's not small pumpkins. **1952** FKane *Bare* (NY 1960) 190: She thinks you're some pumpkins. **1973** JCashman *Gentleman* (NY) 25: They were some punkins. TW 298(6).

P353 As pleased as **Punch**

1901 MLPeabody *To Be Young* (B 1967) 206: As pleased as Punch. **1923** JSFletcher *Lynne Court* (NY) 89: Pleased as Punch. **1933** CBarry *Death* (NY) 257: You're as pleased as Punch. **1941** SMarshall *Some Like* (NY) 190: He was as pleased as Punch. **1950** MRHodgkin *Student* (L) 184: Your parents would be as pleased as punches. **1958** *New Yorker* 5/31 23: Mr. Rockefeller looked as pleased as Punch. **1960** AGilbert *Out for* (NY 1965) 27: As pleased as Punch. **1966** LPDavies *Paper* (NY) 130: As pleased as Punch. **1981** ELathen *Going* (NY) 142: Everett was pleased as punch. *Oxford* 651: Proud (pleased).

P354 As proud as **Punch**

1931 JDBeresford *Innocent* (NY) 47: As proud as Punch. **1931** DJohnson *Death of* (L) 5: She's as proud as Punch. **1934** FNHart *Crooked* (NY) 250: Proud as Punch. **1972** DPryde *Nunaga* (NY) 96: Proud as punch. **1973** DShannon *No Holiday* (NY) 102: Joe was proud as punch. *Oxford* 651.

P355   Not to pull one's **Punches**

1938 NJones *Hanging Lady* (NY) 172: I'm not going to pull any punches. **1949** MGilbert *He Didn't* (NY DBC) 91: He didn't pull any punches. **1957** ESGardner *Screaming* (NY) 145: I'm not going to pull any punches. **1960** CErwin *Orderly* (NY) 269: Pete never pulled any punches. **1970** DClark *Deadly* (NY) 12: You're not pulling your punches. Amer. Herit. Dict. Pull *v.* 10.

P356   As cute (tender) as a speckled **Pup**

1952 GMandel *Flee* (I) 77: I'm as tender as a speckled pup under a red cart. **1959** LColeman *Sam* (NY) 214: Cute as a speckled pup. Whiting *NC* 463(1).

P357   As friendly (gentle) as a **Pup** (*varied*)

1946 ABCunningham *Death Rides* (NY) 33: She had been friendly as a pup. **1948** DCDisney *Explosion* (NY DBC) 22: As friendly and forgiving as a spotted pup. **1956** MPHood *Scarlet* (NY) 4: Friendly as a speckled pup. **1962** ITRoss *Old* (NY DBC) 116: The boy was as gentle as a pup. Whiting *NC* 463: Puppy(1); Taylor *Prov. Comp.* 42: Puppy.

P358   As pretty as a spotted **Pup**

1940 LFord *Old Lover's* (NY) 191: Cecily's goin' to be as perty as a spotted pup. Whiting *NC* 463(1,2).

P359   As sick as a (poisoned) **Pup**

1937 HAustin *Murder* (L) 129: He gets sick as a poisoned pup. **1939** EAcheson *Murder to Hounds* (NY) 150: Felt sick as a pup. Cf. As sick as a Dog *above.*

P360   As sore (crabbed) as a **Pup** (*varied*)

1932 BRoss *Tragedy of Y* (NY) 277: He's sore as a pup. **1950** MCarleton *Bride* (NY) 41: He'll be sore as a pup. **1961** RFoley *It's Murder* (NY DBC) 118: Sore as a pup. **1963** MPHood *Sin* (NY) 38: Crabbed as a pup with a sore head. Whiting *NC* 463(3).

P361   To be sold a **Pup**

1925 AJSmall *Death* (NY) 202: He had sold Potsdam a . . . litter of pups. **1930** CBush *Death* (NY) 245: We've been sold a pup. **1930** HCMcNeile *Guardians* (NY) 129: You "haven't sold them a pup." **1937** DLSayers *Busman's* (NY) 350: You're handing me a nice pup. **1959** RVickers *Girl* (NY DBC) 29: The local police have sold you a pup. **1960** RWilson *30 Day* (NY) 147: They sold you a pup. **1966** JAiken *Beware* (NY) 28: I didn't sell you a pup, did I? Partridge 669.

P362   To swell (puff) up like a poisoned **Pup**

1940 HSKeeler *Cleopatra's* (L) 257: He swole up . . . like a p'izened pup. **1959** *BHerald* 5/12 39: I'm all puffed up like a pizened pup.

P363   To the **Pure** all things are (im)pure

1940 ARLong *Corpse* (NY) 34: To the pure all things are pure. **1949** JSymons *Bland* (L) 61: To the pure all things are impure. Brunvand 114(1).

P364   To make a silk **Purse** out of a sow's ear (*varied*)

1916 SRohmer *Tales* (NY 1922) 321: Trying to make a silk purse out of a sow's ear. **1919** HRHaggard *She and Allan* (NY 1921) 263: The difficulty of making silk purses out of sows' ears. **1922** JJoyce *Ulysses* (NY 1934) 542: This silken purse I made out of the sow's ear of the public. **c1923** ACrowley *Confessions* ed JSymonds (L 1969) 732: It is not only impossible to make a silk purse out of a sow's ear. It is an idealistic imbecility. **1933** NBMavity *Fate* (NY) 61: You can't make a silk purse out of a sow's ear. **1936** RCarson *Revels* (NY) 276: You're trying to make a silk purse out of a souse. **1936** FNebel *Fifty Roads* (B) 86: He had not the poet's aptitude for making a silk purse out of a sow's ear. **1940** CFAdams *Decoy* (NY) 121: You know the old gag about the silk purse and the sow's ear? Well, that's me—the sow's ear. **1950** LKaufman *Jubel's* (NY) 237: You can't act a sow's ear into a silk purse. **1951** DThompson *Phoenix* (L) 285: The men . . . did medieval work in medieval ways—making purses out of sow's ears. **1956** PDeVries *Comfort* (B) 40: But making a sow's ear out of a silk purse isn't any easier than the other way around. **1956** *NYTimes* 5/27 xi: The silk-purse-sow's-ear precept. **1956** *BangorDN* 8/31 7: "You can't make a silk purse out of a sow's ear." . . .

"A good scientist can." **1957** *NYTimes Book Review* 2/10 25: He made silk purses from sows' ears. **1957** *Time* 6/3 39: We don't believe that we can make a poet out of a sow's ear . . . not even in Iowa where we've got some damn fine sows' ears. **1957** *Punch* 8/21 221: Proving, I think, that not only can a sow's ear be turned into a silk purse but a silk purse can be lost forever in a pig's trotter. **1960** TPowell *Man-Killer* (NY) 83: You can't make a silk purse out of a sow's ear, but you can make a small one of pigskin. **1965** ASharp *Green Tree* (NY 1966) 66: They made the silk purse out of her sow's ear [*sexual intercourse*]. **1965** RHardwick *Plotters* (NY) 102: There's an old proverb . . . Something about sow's ears and silk purses. **1967** OHesky *Time* (NY) 88: We can change a sow's ear into tissue far finer than silk. **1968** WMuir *Belonging* (L) 67: Some pastries almost delicate enough to make silk purses were called "pigs' ears." **1970** LKronenberger *No Whippings* (B) 87: The backers' wives, who have been known to exhibit sows' ears and silk purses both. **1982** NDelbanco *Group* (NY) 59: The ironic adage . . . "you can't make a sow's ear of a silk purse." EAP P323.

P365 To hold the **Purse strings**

1929 MMPropper *Strange* (NY) 108: Mrs. Bend . . . holding the purse strings. **1951** RKing *Duenna* (NY) 47: Millay does hold the purse strings. **1958** JSStrange *Night* (NY) 59: Oh well, them as holds the purse strings rules the roost, as the saying goes. **1961** MErskine *Woman* (NY) 110: His father holds the purse strings. **1972** SWoods *They Love* (NY) 16: She held the purse strings. EAP P324.

P366 As mean as **Pursley**

1924 CWells *Furthest* (P) 225: "He was mean—meaner'n pussley." The New Englander can go no further. TW 299; DA Pusley b.

P367 When **Push** comes to shove (*varied*)

1967 JBrunner *Quicksand* (NY) 17: But if push comes to shove I shall tell him what I've told you. **1969** RStark *Dame* (NY) 67:

When push came to shove. **1971** DClark *Sick* (NY) 128: You mind your own barrow. If you can't push it, shove it. **1973** GSheehy *Hustling* (NY) 93: When push comes to shove. **1981** ELathen *Going* (NY) 195: When push comes to shove, when the day of reckoning approaches, when the curtain is about to fall.

P368 **Put** up or shut up

1924 CWells *Furthest* (P) 59: You've got to put up or shut up. **1929** CWells *Tapestry* (P) 233: You'll have to put up or shut up. **1931** HGarland *Companions* (NY) 154: Put up or shut up. **1932** HFootner *Dead Man's* (NY) 214: Pay up or shut up. **1940** EDean *Murder Is* (NY) 69: Put up or shut up. **1941** DCCameron *And So He* (NY) 218: Put up or shut up. **1954** MHyman *No Time* (NY) 132: Put up or shut up. **1958** *BHerald* 5/4 sec. I 12: It is time . . . to put up or shut up. **1962** VWMason *Trouble* (NY DBC) 33: To use the vernacular, either put up or shut up. **1970** GMFraser *Royal* (L) 37: Put up or shut up. **1972** MKramer *Mother* (NY) 52: Put up or shut up. Wentworth 414.

P369 As gray as **Putty**; Putty-gray

1937 LFord *Simple Way* (NY) 205: Face went putty-grey. **1939** DBOlsen *Death Cuts* (NY) 256: Her face had paled to a putty-gray. **1948** LFord *Devil's* (NY) 123: She was grey as putty.

P370 As soft as **Putty**

1939 HMiller *Capricorn* (NY 1961) 45: He went soft as putty. **1957** *BHerald* 3/31 43: He could be . . . soft as putty. **1965** HPearson *By Himself* (L) 202: As soft as putty. **1970** HCarvic *Miss Seeton Draws* (NY) 52: Soft as putty. TW 299.

P371 To be **Putty** in one's hands

1913 ERBurroughs *Warlord* (NY 1963) 125: They were as putty in my hands. **1931** HFootner *Easy* (L) 210: He was like putty in her hands. **1938** TDowning *Night* (L) 266: You're just like putty in his hands. **1956** PDeVries *Comfort* (B) 266: I'm weak, like putty in his hands. **1959** MFitt *Mizmaze* (L) 49: He was always putty in Althea's hands. **1962** CKeith *Missing* (NY) 48: He was putty in Sophia's hands. **1968** TMcGuane *Sporting* (NY) 206: I'm silly putty in your hands. **1972** LNiven *Ringworld* (L) 256: A thirty-year-old man would be putty in your hand. Cole 60. Cf. To be as Clay *above*; Wax *below*.

P372 A **Pyrrhic** victory

1917 GRSims *My Life* (L) 47: It was a pyrrhic victory. **1929** EBWhite *Letters* ed

DLGuth (NY 1976) 85: A pyrrhic victory. **1944** ECrispin *Gilded Fly* (NY 1970) 205: Its a Pyrrhic victory. **1955** SRansome *Frazer* (NY) 32: A Pyrrhic victory, that surprise acquittal. **1962** RSpeaight *W.Rothenstein* (L) 20: Whistler won a Pyrrhic victory. **1963** AHLewis *Day* (NY) 25: She won a Pyrrhic victory and handed the last laugh to Aunt Sylvia. **1971** JGreen *Mind* (NY) 26: Earth's victory had been a Pyrrhic one. EAP P326.

Q

Q1   To get a **Quart** in a pint pot (*varied*)
1934 CFGregg *Execution* (L) 97: You can't get a quart into a pint pot. **1940** NMorland *Gun* (L) 37: Managed to get a quart into a pint pot. **1958** *TLS* 7/18 409: But a quart cannot be got into a pint pot. **1960** JLodwick *Moon* (L) 20: It is impossible to place a gallon within a pint pot. **1978** PMcGinley *Bogmail* (NY 1981) 58: You can't put a quart into a pint pot. *Oxford* 659. Cf. To put the big Pot *above*.

Q2   A bad **Quarter** of an hour (*varied*)
1900 CFPidgin *Quincy A. Sawyer* (B) 146: Quincy, as the saying is, passed a "bad quarter of an hour." **1903** EChilders *Riddle* (NY 1940) 128: A *mauvais quart d'heure*. **1920** AChristie *Mysterious Affair* (NY) 271: She had a mauvais quart d'heure. **1931** MKennedy *Death to the Rescue* (L) 166: Andrews had given him a bad quarter of an hour. **1936** GDHCole *Brothers* (L) 313: He'd have had a *mauvais quart d'heure* there. **1937** CDickson *Ten Teacups* (L) 87: That woman's goin' to be in for a very uncomfortable quarter of an hour. **1960** RFraser *Trout's* (L) 73: Sparks will have a bad quarter of an hour. **1966** JDosPassos *Best* (NY) 223: Don Alfonso had passed a bad quarter of an hour. EAP Q5.

Q3   As certain as **Quarter Day**
1933 RAJWalling *Behind* (L) 293: It's as certain as Quarter Day. *Oxford* 580: Noth-

ing. Cf. As sure as Death *above*; Taxes *below*.

Q4   As dead as **Queen** Anne (*varied*)
1930 SFowler *King* (L) 98: As sure as Queen Anne's dead. **1932** PMcGuire *Three* (NY) 12: He's as dead as Queen Anne. **1933** DGBrowne *Dead* (L) 194: They're more dead than Queen Anne. **1958** *Time* 1/6 28: As dead as Queen Anne. **1958** WDHassett *Off the Record* (New Brunswick, NJ) 29: Mrs. Humphrey Ward was as dead as Queen Anne. **1966** JAiken *Beware* (NY) 68: Dead as Queen Anne. **1966** DMarlowe *Dandy* (NY) 245: He was as dead as Queen Anne. *Oxford* 170–1.

Q5   **Queen** Anne is dead
1914 HHMunro *Beasts* (NY 1928) 35: The saying "Queen Anne's dead." **1922** JJoyce *Ulysses* (NY 1934) 117–8: Queen Anne is dead. **1928** JRhode *Tragedy* (NY) 193: The news that Queen Anne is dead would be far too sensational for them to believe. **1933** VMarkham *Inspector* (L) 266: You've discovered Queen Anne's dead. **1936** ECVivian *With Intent* (L) 48: Queen Anne is dead. **1956** MInnes *Appleby* (L) 63: A man's voice announcing . . . that Queen Anne was dead. **1958** JDCarr *Dead Man's* (NY) 174: The earth is round and Queen Anne is dead. *Oxford* 659. Cf. EAP Q7.

Q6   To live like a **Queen**
1946 ABCunningham *One Man* (NY) 198: Mrs. Rider is living like a queen. Whiting *NC* 464(3).

Q7 To the **Queen's** taste

1932 LThayer *Glass Knife* (NY) 248: I'm sure you did it to the queen's taste. Cole 60.

Q8 In **Queer Street**

1923 JSFletcher *Exterior* (NY) 26: You're in Queer Street. **1936** CBush *Monday Murders* (L) 183: Find himself in Queer Street. **1937** HCBailey *Clunk's* (L) 59: Down Queer Street. **1941** JJConnington *Twenty-one* (B) 11: We'd be in Queer Street. **1945** GBellairs *Calamity* (NY) 65: Find himself in queer street on a murder charge. **1952** ECRLorac *Dog* (NY) 181: He'd be in queer street. **1956** DBatchelor *Taste* (L) 25: We're in Queer Street here. **1961** JDCarr *Witch* (L) 167: You'll find yourself in Queer Street. **1964** RBlythe *Age* (B) 19: Land ... in Queer Street. **1976** JPorter *Package* (NY) 43: In Queer Street. *Oxford* 659.

Q9 Ask a silly **Question**, get a silly answer (*varied*)

1916 RFirbank *Inclinations* (Works 2, L 1929) 138: Don't ask silly questions, if you don't want foolish answers. **1934** CRyland *Murder* (L) 92: If you ask me damned silly questions, I'm going to give you damned silly answers. **1941** SMarshall *Some Like* (NY) 5: If you ask foolish questions you'll get foolish answers. **1951** PATaylor *Diplomatic* (NY) 237: If I ask you silly questions ... I deserve silly answers. **1957** *BHerald* 1/15 27: Ask foolish questions, y're bound to get foolish answers. **1961** MNelson *When the Bed* (L) 189: Just a silly answer to a silly question. **1966** GKanin *Remembering* (NY) 46: Ask a stupid question and you'll get a stupid answer—so it goes in New Yorkese. **1967** SMorrow *Insiders* (NY) 139: Ask a crazy question, get a crazy answer. **1971** BWAldiss *Soldier* (L) 48: Ask a daft question ... get a daft bloody answer. **1971** MEChaber *Bonded* (NY) 61: Foolish questions deserve foolish answers. Cf. TW 300(2); *Oxford* 659.

Q10 Ask no **Questions** and be told no lies (*varied*)

1903 HLAdam *Trial of George Chapman* (L 1930) 94: If they ask me no questions I won't tell them no lies. **1922** JJoyce *Ulysses* (NY 1934) 260: Ask no questions and you'll hear no lies. **1931** CBush *Dead Man's* (L) 56: As his old nurse would say: "Ask no questions and you'll hear no lies." **1931** PWentworth *Danger* (P) 272: People asking damfool questions, get told lies. **1938** HAdams *Damned* (L) 183: If you ask no questions you hear no lies. A wonderful old maxim, that. **1938** JTFarrell *No Star* (NY) 335: Ask me no questions and I'll give you no answers. **1946** MColes *Fifth Man* (NY) 119: There is an English proverb which says that those who don't ask questions are not told lies. **1951** LSdeCamp *Rogue* (NY) 98: Ask me no questions and I'll tell you no lies. **1959** KWaterhouse *Billy* (L) 183: Ask no questions and you'll get no lies told. **1965** JMaclaren-Ross *Memoirs* (L) 323: Ask no questions, hear no lies. **1974** AMenen *Fonthill* (NY) 213: Ask no questions and you'll get told no lies. **1976** JSScott *Poor* (NY) 69: Ask no questions, hear no lies. EAP Q8.

Q11 The sixty-four dollar **Question** (*varied*)

1943 NDavis *Sally's* (NY) 160: That's the sixty-four dollar question. **1948** BSBallinger *Body* (NY) 82: That isn't the sixty-four-dollar question. **1956** ESGardner *Terrified* (NY) 25: That's the sixty-four dollar question. **1962** MStewart *Moon* (NY 1965) 124: The sixty-four-thousand-dollar question. **1969** KAmis *Green* (L) 79: Groping for the sixty-four-cent question. **1969** SViertel *Kindness* (NY) 302: The sixty-four dollar question (I have never found out why it was worth sixty-four). **1973** HPentecost *Beautiful* (NY) 48: The $64,000 question. **1973** TAWaters *Lost* (NY) 39: "The sixty-four dollar question" ... a phrase that dated him.

Q12 As nimble (volatile, slippery) as **Quicksilver**

1938 CBrahms *Bullet* (NY) 39: Nimble as quicksilver. **1944** HReilly *Opening Door* (NY) 77: She was as volatile as quicksilver. **1967** SMorrow *Insiders* (NY) 118: Slippery as quicksilver. Wilstach 274: Nimble.

Quid

Q13   A **Quid** pro quo

1919 JBCabell *Letters* ed PColum (NY 1962) 99: Ne quid pro quo. **1924** JSFletcher *Safety* (NY) 142: The *quid pro quo* or *quo pro quid.* **1935** RPenny *Lucky* (L) 138: A *quo* to catch a *quid.* **1936** ECBentley *Trent's Own* (NY) 95: To be sure of getting his quid before parting with his quo. **1940** RStout *Where There's* (NY) 176: I might for a quid pro quo. **1957** *NYTimes* 2/10 1E: One specific quid pro quo. **1962** AMStein *Home* (NY) 61: There is never a *quid* that doesn't have its pro *quo.* **1964** HBourne *In the Event* (NY) 102: *Quid pro quo* and fairs do. **1968** ESRussell *She Should* (NY) 45: For a small

quid . . . you got an awfully big *quo.* **1977** VCanning *Doomsday* (NY) 162: Time enough for the quid pro quos. EAP Q11.

Q14   On the **Q.T.**

1922 JJoyce *Ulysses* (NY 1934) 610: On the strict q.t. **1931** GDHCole *Dead Man's* (L) 115: On the q.t. **1939** MPropper *Hide the Body* (NY) 250: They met on the q.t. **1946** RFinnegan *Lying* (NY) 209: On the q.t. **1951** EQueen *Origin* (B) 66: On the q.t. **1960** WMasterson *Hammer* (NY DBC) 150: On the q.t. **1966** TWalshe *Resurrection* (NY) 47: On the q.t. **1972** HPentecost *Champagne* (NY) 31: On the Q.T. Partridge 674.

R

R1 **R** is the dog's letter

1945 MInnes *Appleby's End* (NY) 7: I am deep in the doggy letter ... What the grammarians were fond of calling *litera canina*. EAP R1.

R2 As jumpy (nervous) as a **Rabbit**

1937 JDCarr *Burning* (NY) 173: You're all as jumpy as rabbits. **1937** GStockwell *Death* (NY) 33: Amos was as jumpy as a rabbit. **1956** DEden *Death* (L) 140: The woman is as nervous as a rabbit. Cf. TW 301(5).

R3 As quick (spry) as a **Rabbit**

1939 JJFarjeon *Seven Dead* (I) 66: She went by me quick as a rabbit. **1941** RGDean *Murder in Mink* (NY) 72: Quick as a rabbit. **1949** RMLaurenson *Six Bullets* (NY) 113: Quick like a bunny rabbit. **1958** GGoodman *Killing* (NY) 73: Spry as a rabbit. Taylor *Prov. Comp.* 66. Cf. Bunny *above*.

R4 As scared (frightened) as a **Rabbit**

1929 AGray *Dead* (L) 51: As scared as a rabbit. **1944** MFitt *Clues* (NY) 50: Frightened as a rabbit. **1956** *New Yorker* 5/19 86: There's the proverbial scared rabbit. **1957** COLocke *Hell Bent* (NY) 177: I was scared as a rabbit. **1959** SRansome *I'll Die* (NY) 63: Scared as a rabbit. Taylor *Prov. Comp.* 71.

R5 As tame as a **Rabbit**

1939 HHolt *Smiling Doll* (L) 39: Crippen was as tame as a rabbit. Wilstach 563: Parlor rabbits.

R6 As timid as a **Rabbit**

1935 JDCarr *Death-Watch* (L) 50: Timid as a rabbit. Clark *Similes* 224. Cf. As timid as a Hare *above*.

R7 To jump like a **Rabbit**

1928 CBarry *Corpse* (NY) 177: I jumped like a rabbit. Whiting *NC* 464(1). Cf. TW 301(5). Cf. As jumpy as a Rabbit *above*.

R8 To pull a **Rabbit** out of a hat (*varied*)

1938 SFowler *Murder in* (L) 112: To bring his surprising explanation ... like a rabbit out of a hat. **1948** ESGardner *Lonely* (NY DBC) 26: You pulled this particular rabbit out of the hat. **1956** SDean *Marked* (NY) 120: You've pulled rabbits out of the hat before. **1959** CEMaine *Tide* (NY) 62: It might be possible to pull the rabbit out of the hat in time. **1962** HWaugh *Late* (NY) 143: You've been known to pull rabbits out of hats now and then. **1969** RPearsall *Worm* (L) 435: The professionals produced theories like rabbits from a hat.

R9 To run like a **Rabbit**

1926 EWallace *King* (NY) 172: You ran like rabbits. **1933** NBMavity *Fate* (NY) 11: Run like a rabbit. **1971** ELinington *Practice* (NY) 133: He ran like a rabbit. TW 310(7); Taylor *Western Folklore* 17(1958) 18(1). Cf. To run like a Hare *above*.

R10 **Raccoon** see Coon

R11 The **Race** is not to the swift *etc.*

1911 JSHay *Amazing Emperor* (L) 74: The battle was not to the strong. **1963** CBlack-

---

521

stock *Mr. Christopoulos* (NY 1965) 68: The race is not to the swift, nor the battle to the strong. **1968** GJones *History* (NY) 94: The race was to the swift and the battle to the strong. EAP R6; TW 301(1).

R12   To live at **Rack** and manger

1933 RBCGraham *Portrait* (L) 124: They roamed about, living at hack [*for rack*] and manger, on the inhabitants. EAP R7.

R13   As limp as a (wet) **Rag**

1922 JJoyce *Ulysses* (NY 1934) 327: As limp as a wet rag. **1923** DFox *Doom* (NY) 337: Limp as a rag. **1957** *BangorDN* 1/22 16: Limp as a rag. **1969** EPetaja *Nets* (NY) 46: Limp as a rag. TW 302(2): Limpsey; Whiting *NC* 464(2); Taylor *Western Folklore* 17(1958) 18. Cf. Dishrag *above*; Sack *below*.

R14   As weak as a **Rag**

1924 ADHSmith *Porto* (NY) 53: Weak as a rag. **1937** MWGlidden *Long Island* (NY) 171: I'm as weak as a rag. **1940** WChambers *Dry* (NY) 256: I rose . . . weak as a rag. Cole 67: Weak.

R15   To be like a red **Rag** to a bull (*varied*)

1916 SLeacock *Behind* (Toronto 1969) 62: A safety razor to a barber is like a red rag to a bull. **1922** JJoyce *Ulysses* (NY 1934) 576: Green rag to a bull. **1927** AWynne *Sinners* (P) 87: If ever a red rag had been waved in the face of a bull. **1932** JCLenehan *Mansfield* (L) 86: An effect similar to that which the proverbial red rag is said to have on a bull. **1935** JSFletcher *Eleventh* (NY) 127: The sight of that woman was as a red rag to a bull, as the saying is. **1939** JCreasey *Toff Goes on* (L) 132: Far worse than a red rag to a very angry bull. **1947** PWentworth *Wicked* (NY) 130: So many red rags to the official bull. **1958** WRoss *Immortal* (NY) 133: It was like waving a red flag to a bull. **1959** *NYTimes Book Review* 9/4 2: Critics to whom a writer's popularity with the ordinary reader is as the traditional red rag to a bull. **1967** MHolroyd *Strachey* (L) 1.203: Christianity was . . . like a red rag to a bull. **1974** ROllard *Pepys* (NY) 224: [They] were a red rag to Pepys. TW 302(8); *Oxford* 668: Red rag.

R16   To chew the **Rag**

1928 LTracy *Women* (NY) 82: We can't chew the rag here. **1954** DAlexander *Terror* (NY) 156: To chew the rag. **1963** ADean *Deadly* (NY) 35: No chewing the rag. Wentworth 97–8.

R17   To light a **Rag**

1961 ESeeman *In the Arms* (NY) 93: Pete lit a rag for the cabin. Whiting *NC* 464(4).

R18   To take the **Rag** off the bush

1957 VWMason *Gracious* (NY) 233: How that poison was injected "takes the rag off the bush," as we say at home. EAP R10.

R19   As limp as a **Rag doll**

1946 BHalliday *Blood* (NY) 132: Wilson was as limp and unconscious as a rag doll. **1968** DMDisney *Voice* (NY) 56: They were all as limp as rag dolls.

R20   **Rag-tag** and bobtail (*varied*)

1912 CPearl *Morrison of Peking* (Sydney 1967) 233: Such a rag-tag and bobtail. **1922** JJoyce *Ulysses* (NY 1934) 415: Giving the cry, and a tag and bobtail of all them after. **1924** WBMFerguson *Black* (NY) 13: Ragtag and bobtail. **1924** JSFletcher *Safety* (NY) 291: The rag-tag and bobtail. **1934** LKirk *Whispering* (NY) 252: All this rag, tag and bobtail. **1940** HRutland *Poison Fly* (NY) 166: All the rag tag and bobtail of information. **1941** ISCobb *Exit* (I) 493: Such itinerant raggle-taggle and bobtails. **1951** SMerwin *House* (NY) 93: His rag-tag-and-bobtail anarchists. **1954** HRAngeli *Pre-Raphaelite* (L) 43: The rag-tag, bob-tail and riff-raff. **1957** *NYTimes* 1/27 1x: A very funny ragtag and bobtail. **1964** JStoye *Siege* (L) 19: All the rag-tag and bobtail. **1967** EHahn *Romantic* (NY) 7: The ragtag and bobtail of the Latin Quarter. **1970** A Moorehead *Late* (L) 109: The ragtag and bobtail of the Paris system of law. TW 302(4); *Oxford* 797: Tag.

R21   As skinny (gaunt) as a **Rail**

1934 JTFarrell *Young Manhood* (NY 1935) 207: Skinnier than a rail. **1950** BCarey *Man Who* (NY) 37: Look at us, skinny as rails. **1958** PBranch *Murder's* (L 1963) 67: Gaunt as a rail. **1960** AHLewis *Worlds* (NY) 132: She was as skinny as a rail. **1971** DMDisney *Three's* (NY) 14: Skinny as a rail. **1975** MVonnegut *Eden* (NY) 140: He was skinny as a rail. Barbour 150.

R22 As stiff as a **Rail**

1935 VGielgud *Death* (L) 103: Whose back was as stiff as a rail. Clark *Similes* 22.

R23 As thin (slender) as a **Rail** (fence)

1928 HRMayes *Alger* (NY) 196: He was thin as a rail. **1941** SHHolbrook *Murder out* (NY) 9: Thin as a rail fence. **1948** KBercovici *Savage* (NY) 19: Thin as a rail. **1956** MSteen *Unquiet* (NY) 31: She was thin as a rail. **1961** LThayer *And One* (NY DBC) 28: Thin as the proverbial rail. **1969** AGilbert *Mr. Crook* (NY DBC) 3: Thin as the proverbial rails. **1970** CDBowen *Family* (B) 79: We remained thin as rails. **1973** AGilbert *Nice* (NY) 5: She was slender as a rail. TW 302(1).

R24 To be (go) off the **Rails**

1920 N&JOakley *Clevedon* (P) 30: You are a bit off the rails. **1928** JArnold *Surrey* (L) 68: He went off the rails. **1933** RAJWalling *Follow* (L) 294: I'm right off the rails. **1976** LEgan *Scenes* (NY) 67: He went off the rails. Partridge 684.

R25 As right (wrong) as **Rain** (*varied*)

1923 AGaul *Five Nights* (NY) 92: Wrong as rain. **1924** JSFletcher *Mazaroff* (NY) 14: Right as rain. **1933** WCBrown *Murder* (P) 283: Right as rain. **1936** RLehmann *Weather* (NY) 30: As right as rain. **1940** GDHCole *Wilson* (L) 99: I'm as right as rain. **1946** HRCampbell *Crime in Crystal* (NY) 127: You're right as rain. **1954** MHyman *No Time* (NY) 124: That's rightern rain on a tin roof. **1956** JBlish *They Shall* (L) 100: Right as rain. **1958** *BangorDN* 7/11 21: Yo're right as rain. **1959** JChristopher *Scent* (NY) 74: He was right as June rain after it. **1960** JBWest *Taste* (NY) 13: Right as spring rain. **1963** RArnold *Orange* (L) 150: As right as rain. **1977** EXFerrars *Blood* (NY) 32: I'd be as right as rain. *Oxford* 677.

R26 If the **Rain** is before the wind *etc.*

1933 MBurton *Fate* (L) 230: Do you know the old seaman's proverb? "If the rain's before the wind Halliards, sheets and braces mind." *Oxford* 662.

R27 A little **Rain** lays down a great wind

1935 CHaldane *Melusine* (L) 176: Before now a little rain hath laid down a great wind. Whiting R15; *Oxford* 662.

R28 It never **Rains** but it pours (*varied*)

1923 ABlackwood *Episodes* (L) 153: It never rains but it pours. **1933** BSKeirstead *Brownsville* (NY) 27: It never rains but it pours. **1940** JCLincoln *Out of the Fog* (NY) 162: The old saying . . . It never rains but it pours. **1946** MInnes *Unsuspected* (NY) 310: An auld proverb to the effect that it never rains but it pours. **1951** MCHarriman *Vicious* (NY) 244: It . . . never rains but it pours. **1957** JCheever *Wapshot* (NY) 92: It never rains but it pours. **1958** *BHerald* 11/5 33: It never rains but it hails. **1958** HKuttner *Murder* (NY) 124: It never rains but it pours, they say. **1963** WMankowitz *Cockatrice* (L) 125: It never rains but it pours pussy. **1964** MWiddemer *Golden* (NY) 66: The law of never raining but it pours. **1965** HActon *Old Lamps* (L) 282: It never rains but it shines. **1981** EVCunningham *Sliding* (NY) 5: It never rains but it pours. EAP R12; Brunvand 116(2).

R29 **Rain** before seven *etc.* (*varied*)

1936 SFowler *Hand in Print* (L) 140: "Rain before seven—." She knew the proverb. **1950** REGould *Yankee* (NY) 41: Rain before seven, clear before eleven. **1951** SSpender *World* (L) 22: Rain before seven, clear before eleven. **1953** BCClough *Grandma* (Portland, Me.) 51: Rain before seven, clear off before eleven. **1955** RChurch *Over the* (L) 172: Rain before seven, fine before eleven. **1971** WTeller *Cape Cod* (Englewood Cliffs, NJ) 89: Rain before seven, clear before eleven. Between one and two, we'll see what 'twill do. *Oxford* 662. Cf. Laugh before seven *above*.

R30 When it **Rains** in sunlight the Devil is beating his wife

1968 JUpdike *Couples* (NY 1969) 472: When it rains in sunlight, they say the Devil is beating his wife. *Oxford* 663: If it rains.

R31 To whistle down a **Rain barrel** (*varied*)

1954 AWBarkley *That Reminds* (NY) 34: [He] might as well have whistled down a rain barrel. **1957** *NYTimes* 12/8 7x: To protest is as useless as "shouting into a rain barrel." **1965** HPentecost *Sniper* (NY DBC) 133: This sniper isn't just whistling up a rainspout when he has a gun in his hands. Cf. Rat-hole, To whistle . . . Tree *below*.

R32 **Rainbow** at night, sailor's delight

1953 BCClough *Grandma* (Portland, Me.) 51: Rainbow at night, sailor's delight. *Oxford* 662–3.

R33 To have (give, take) a **Rain check**

1957 WFuller *Girl* (NY) 101: Maybe I can have a rain check. **1958** EMcBain *Lady* (NY 1964) 89: Give me a rain check. **1960** WMasterson *Hammer* (NY DBC) 50: I'll take a rain check. **1972** TWells *Die* (NY) 45: I'll take a rain check. Wentworth 418.

R34 As lean as a **Rake**

1934 HReilly *McKee* (NY) 262: Lean as a rake. *Oxford* 450.

R35 As thin as a **Rake**

1928 SHuddleston *Paris Salons* (NY) 234: Thin as a rake. **1933** ESnell *And Then* (L) 195: He was as thin as a rake. **1950** JCannan *Murder* (L 1958) 19: As thin as a rake. **1959** THWhite *Godstone* (NY) 193: As thin as a rake. **1963** MErskine *No. 9* (NY) 79: She was thin as a rake. **1964** RMacdonald *Chill* (NY) 261: He was as thin as a rake and as poor as Job's turkey. **1975** JvandeWetering *Outsider* (B) 127: Thin as a rake. Whiting *NC* 465(3).

R36 A reformed **Rake** makes the best husband (*varied*)

1924 HHMunro *Square* (L 1929) 241: Isn't there a proverb: "A relapsed husband makes the best rake"? **1925** EBChancellor *Hell Fire* (L) 43: The reformed rake . . . is proverbially not the worst sort of husband. EAP R14.

R37 As crooked as a **Ram's** horn

1922 JJoyce *Ulysses* (NY 1934) 366: Crooked as a ram's horn. **1928** RHFuller *Jubilee* (NY) 174: The legislature . . . was crooked as a ram's horn. **1939** TStevenson *Silver Arrow* (L) 189: As crooked as a ram's horn. **1953** KMKnight *Akin* (NY) 41: He's crooked as a ram's horn. Whiting R26; TW 303(1). Cf. *Oxford* 677: Right.

R38 As stiff (rigid) as a **Ramrod**; Ramrod-stiff

1920 GBMcCutcheon *Anderson Crow* (NY) 81: As stiff as a ramrod. **1930** CBush *Death* (NY) 100: Sitting rigid as a ramrod. **1932** PMcGuire *Three* (NY) 187: The sergeant was as stiff as a ramrod. **1933** BReynolds *Very Private* (NY) 96: Rigid as a ramrod. **1939** RAJWalling *Blistered Hand* (NY) 78: As stiff as a ramrod. **1941** CLClifford *While the Bells* (NY) 129: Stiff as a ramrod. **1955** PMacDonald *Guest* (NY) 56: As rigid as a ramrod. **1955** KMKnight *Robineau* (NY) 141: Her back ramrod-stiff. **1957** *Punch* 5/22 643: We all stood up, stiff as ramrods. **1959** CBrown *Terror* (NY) 110: His back ramrod-stiff. **1962** LDavidson *Rose* (NY) 239: His arms . . . stiff as ramrods. Whiting *NC* 465(1); Wilstach 389. Cf. As stiff as a Rod *below*.

R39 As straight as a **Ramrod**; Ramrod-straight

1912 JCLincoln *Postmaster* (NY) 134: As straight as a ramrod. **1919** LThayer *Mystery of the 13th Floor* (NY) 255: Straight as a ramrod. **1940** GHCoxe *Glass Triangle* (NY) 199: He stood ramrod-straight. **1948** CBush *Curious* (NY) 59: His back can suddenly be ramrod straight. **1956** *BHerald* 8/1 5: McKeon marched to the witness stand ramrod straight. **1957** *New Yorker* 5/25 28: Straight as a ramrod. **1958** *New Yorker* 1/1 46: They stood straight as ramrods. Whiting *NC* 465(2). Cf. As straight as a Rod *below*.

R40 As upright (erect) as a **Ramrod**

1929 AJSmall *Web* (NY) 173: Upright as a ramrod. **1930** JGBrandon *Death* (L) 15: As erect as a ramrod. **1953** ECRLorac *Speak* (NY) 96: She stood as erect as a ramrod. **1960** AChristie *Double* (NY DBC) 35: As upright as a ramrod. Wilstach 449.

R41 To sit (stand) like a **Ramrod**

1932 BRoss *Tragedy of X* (NY) 326: They . . . sat like ramrods. **1938** PATaylor *Annulet* (NY) 128: Basil sat like a ramrod. **1967** RBrett-Smith *Berlin* (NY) 9: Standing like a ramrod.

R42 Not bother (count, give, value at) a **Rap**

1921 ERBurroughs *Mucker* (NY) 102: Not give a rap. **1928** JJConnington *Mystery* (B) 234: It doesn't count for a rap. **1932** CDawes *Lawless* (L) 104: He don't value it a rap. **1940** ACampbell *They Hunted* (NY) 123: He doesn't bother a rap. *Oxford* 664: Not a rap. See NED Rap *sb.*² 1c.

R43 Not care a **Rap** (*varied*)

1903 EChilders *Riddle* (NY 1940) 95: I don't care a rap; 139. **1923** ABlackwood *Episodes* (L) 234: [Not] care a rap. **1933** GDHCole *Lesson* (L) 258: She never cared a rap. **1934** EQueen *Adventures* (NY) 79: Didn't care two raps in Hades. **1936** EBQuinn *One Man's* (L) 157: I don't care a continental rap. **1953** ANoyes *Two* (P) 73: I don't care a rap. **1958** HRobertson *Crystal-Gazers* (NY) 17: Rolle doesn't care a rap. **1962** DAlexander *Tempering* (NY) 10: She did not care a rap. **1962** RSpeaight *W.Rothenstein* (L) 263: Eric Gill did not care a rap of his fingers. **1968** FBaker *I Follow* (L) 109: Did not care a rap. **1972** RMaugham *Escape* (L) 192: He . . . doesn't care a rap. EAP R18.

R44 Not matter a **Rap**

1928 JJConnington *Mystery* (B) 172: I shouldn't say that it mattered a rap. **1928** ABCox *Amateur* (NY) 158: It wouldn't matter a rap. NED Rap *sb.*² 1c (quote 1875).

R45 Not worth a **Rap** (*varied*)

1919 JSClouston *Simon* (NY) 116: [Not] worth a rap. **1930** ABCox *Vane* (L) 67: And not a single one worth a twopenny rap. Cf. *Oxford* 664.

R46 As cute (cunning) as a **Rat** (*varied*)

1922 JJoyce *Ulysses* (NY 1934) 274: Hope he's not looking cute as a rat. 335: Cute as a shithouse rat. **1956** MScherf *Cautious* (NY) 101: As cute as a water closet rat. **1964** RBraddon *Year* (L 1967) 56: As cunning as a sewer rat.

R47 As poor as a **Rat**

1928 AEWMason *Prisoner* (NY) 299: We are poor as rats. **1939** CMWills *Calabar Bean* (L) 98: Poor as a rat, he is. **1940** JStagge *Turn* (NY) 12: We were poor as rats. **1952** GKersh *Brazen* (L) 66: Poor as a rat. **1962** AChristie *Pale* (NY DBC) 16: Poor as a rat. **1965** NFreeling *Criminal* (L) 154: We were as poor as rats. TW 304(4); *Oxford* 638: Poor. Cf. Church mouse *above*.

R48 As quick as a **Rat**

1932 EWallace *Frightened* (L) 289: That fellow's quicker than a rat. TW 304(5).

R49 As weak as a **Rat**

1928 EWallace *Sinister* (NY) 336: I was as weak as a rat from loss of blood. EAP R22.

R50 As wet as a drowned **Rat** (*varied*)

1921 JCLincoln *Galusha* (NY) 21: Wet as a drowned rat. **1936** PATaylor *Crimson* (L) 143: Lookin' like a drowned rat. **1939** NMarsh *Overture* (NY) 275: You're as wet as a water-rat. **1940** HReilly *Murder in* (NY) 228: She looked like a drowned rat. **1956** MPHood *Scarlet* (NY) 147: You resemble a drowned rat. **1961** PGWodehouse *Ice* (NY) 127: George, who was given to homely similes, thought she looked like a drowned rat. **1966** MGEberhart *Witness* (NY) 74: I'm wet as a drowned rat. EAP R23.

R51 A cornered **Rat** will fight (*varied*)

1926 AMerritt *Ship* (NY) 76: Even a cornered rat will fight. **1928** HAdams *Empty* (P) 231: A rat will fight when driven into a corner. **1929** RJCasey *Secret* (I) 317: There is an adage that a cornered rat will fight. **1933** ECVivian *Girl* (L) 278: A cornered rat always jumps. **1939** FGerard *Red Rope* (NY) 32: Fought with all the desperation of a cornered rat. **1941** HReilly *Three Women* (NY) 135: The trapped rat would fight. **1942** WABarber *Murder Enters* (NY) 275:

For even a trapped mouse will put up some sort of fight. **1948** ESherry *Sudden* (NY) 176: She's like a cornered rat trying to shove the blame on everybody within miles. **1950** RStout *In the Best* (NY) 74: I'll fight like a cornered rat. **1955** BBenson *Silver* (NY) 140: He was cornered like a rat, so he had to fight like a rat. Whiting *NC* 466(7). Cf. TW 303(1).

R52 **Rats** desert a sinking ship (*varied*)

1920 AJRees *Hand in the Dark* (NY 1929) 97: Like rats deserting a sinking ship. **1925** AJSmall *Death* (NY) 190: The rats smelt a sinking ship. **1927** AGilbert *Tragedy* (NY) 200: The proverbial case of the rats and the sinking ship. **1928** DHLawrence *Lady* ("Allemagne") 124: Like rats leave a sinking ship. **1932** JVTurner *Who Spoke* (L) 8: Scurrying from the boat with the blind rush of drowning rats. **1939** VWilliams *Fox Prowls* (B) 239: You know the saying about rats leaving the sinking ship. **1941** MHolbrook *Suitable* (NY) 201: Only rats desert a sinking ship. **1950** IFletcher *Bennett's* (I) 203: They crowd like rats leaving a sinking ship. **1957** PJFarmer *Green* (NY) 142: Give the rats a chance to desert the ship. **1959** JFleming *Malice* (NY) 29: Like rats deserting a sinking ship. **1961** JWebb *One for* (NY DBC) 96: Rats from a sinking ship and all that sort of jazz. **1965** LBiggle *All the Colors* (NY) 38: Wise men, as well as rats, desert sinking ships. **1968** JRAckerley *My Father* (L) 164: All his "men pals" . . . deserted him . . . like the proverbial rats on the sinking ship. **1972** LIsrael *Tallulah* (NY) 345: Tallulah castigated him for leaving a sinking ship. **1973** JBrooks *Go-Go* (NY) 345: To play the role of rats leaving a fleet of sinking ships. EAP R26.

R53 To be caught like a **Rat** in a trap (*varied*)

1903 MLPeabody *To Be Young* (B 1967) 257: Caught like rats in a trap. **1911** JSHay *Amazing Emperor* (L) 69: Caught like a rat in a trap. **1934** AGilbert *Man in Button* (L) 89: He must have been like the proverbial trapped rat. **1934** AMeredith *Portrait* (NY) 78: The whole household will descend, and

take me like the proverbial rat. **1936** WS Masterman *Bloodhounds* (NY) 262: Caught like a rat in a trap. **1950** ERPunshon *So Many* (NY) 223: Caught like rats in a trap. **1963** KAmis *Spectrum III* (L) 72: Caught like a rat in a trap. Whiting *NC* 466(3); Taylor *Prov. Comp.* 67. Cf. TW 304(7).

R54 To die like a **Rat** in a trap (*varied*)

1901 MLPeabody *To Be Young* (B 1967) 180: Drown like rats in traps. **1936** D Wheatley *They Found* (P) 187: I've got to die like a rat in a trap. **1939** CWard *House Party* (L) 219: Unless he wanted to die like a rat in a hole. Cf. Whiting *NC* 466(4): Like a rat, 466(8): Trapped like rats.

R55 To look as if **Rats** had slept in one's hair

1943 EWTeale *Dune Boy* (NY 1957) 194: My thatch of unruly hair . . . looked "like the rats had slept in it." Cf. Taylor *Prov. Comp.* 59: Look like a rat's nest.

R56 To smell a **Rat** (mouse) (*varied*)

1908 JCLincoln *Cy Whittaker* (NY) 341: It's one thing to smell a rat and another to nail its tail to the floor. 358: To smell a rat. **1913** JSFletcher *Secret* (L 1918) 213: Smell a rat. **1922** JJoyce *Ulysses* (NY 1934) 648: A remarkably sharp nose for smelling a rat of any sort. **1923** ORCohen *Jim Hanvey* (NY) 124: Smell a mice; even two or three mice. **1928** DHLawrence *Lady* ("Allemagne") 325: She smelled a rat. **1929** SQuinn *Phantom* (Sauk City, Wisc. 1966) 113: My nose scents the odor of the rodent. **1929** WBSeabrook *Magic* (NY) 292: He smelled a mouse. **1932** NJones *Hanging Lady* (NY) 264: So Arden knew I smelled a mouse. **1936** GHomes *Doctor* (NY) 261: Marjorie would have smelled a mouse. **1937** JJConnington *Minor* (L) 297: "Suppose he smells a rat?" . . . "What does a rat smell like?" **1940** RLGoldman *Snatch* (NY) 84: [He] seemed to smell a mouse. **1940** EPaul *Mayhem* (NY) 107: I smelled any number of rats. **1947** *New Yorker* 3/23 39: She smelled a rat. **1948** MColes *Among* (NY) 15: Somebody smelt a rat. **1950** SPalmer *Monkey* (NY) 41: I smell a mus giganticus . . . That's rat to you. **1956** *Punch* 7/4 1: Smelt any good rats lately? **1957** FHoyle *Black* (L) 174: Don't I detect a slight smell of rat in all this? **1960** SRaven *Brother* (NY) 83: Without smelling rats behind the arras. **1962** SRansome *Night* (NY DBC) 105: He smelled a pretty ripe rat. **1966** DMurphy *Tibetan* (NY) 116: I began to smell a large and unpleasant rat. **1967** ESGardner *Queenly* (NY) 144: To have smelled a mouse. **1971** JTMcIntosh *Coat* (NY) 71: They might smell a mouse. **1974** JKaplan *L.Steffens* (NY) 74: To smell rats, investigate, explore. EAP R29.

R57 Down a **Rat-hole** (*very varied*)

1925 GBeasley *My First* (Paris) 215: It was just like pouring water in a hole, my mother would say. **1934** SPalmer *Murder* (L) 152: Willis announced that he had found a rat-hole. "Do you know enough to pour sand in it?" called out Georgie. **1937** AGilbert *Murder* (L) 26: You were pouring your money into a sack without a bottom. **1937** GGoodchild *Murder Will* (L) 88: You're pouring good water down a bad hole. **1940** EBQuinn *Death Is* (L) 228: Willie's money was pouring like water into a basket. It had to stop. **1940** EPaul *Mayhem* (NY) 82: He's the only one among you with brains enough to pour sand in a rat hole. **1947** AAFair *Fools* (NY 1957) 87: It's just like pouring water down a rat hole. **1953** BCarey *Their Nearest* (NY) 47: Ever hear of pouring money down a rat-hole? **1956** SWTaylor *I Have* (NY) 102: [He] was without the sense to put sand in a rat hole? **1956** *NYTimes* 8/26 8E: That money is not poured down an absolute rat hole. **1957** *BHerald* 4/5 20: The expenditure of 50,000 for the study was "pouring corn down a rat hole." **1959** *BHerald* 2/12 3: Asking why more money should be thrown down a rathole. **1963** DGardiner *Lion* (NY) 136: Charley didn't have enough sense to pour sand down a rat-hole. Taylor *Prov. Comp.* 70: Sand. Cf. Drain, Rain barrel *above*.

R58 As close as a **Rat-trap** (trap)

1932 AGilbert *Body* (NY) 27: She'd be as close as a rat-trap. **1961** MColes *Search* (NY DBC) 148: A straight mouth as close as a

rat-trap. **1963** NMarsh *Dead* (B 1964) 84: I kept it close as a trap [*a secret*]. Cf. Steel trap *below*.

R59 As black as a **Raven** (raven's wing); Raven-black

1924 FWCrofts *Cask* (NY 1936) 192: Raven black hair. **1932** PMacDonald *Mystery* (NY) 6: Hair . . . black as a raven. **1934** DFrome *They Called Him* (L) 47: Darkness as black as a raven's wing. **1944** EDaly *Book of the Dead* (NY) 88: Hair . . . as black as a raven's wing. **1945** CEVulliamy *Edwin* (L) 77: Her hair was black as a raven's plume. **1949** SJepson *Golden* (NY) 131: Her hair was raven black. **1955** LBromfield *Passion* (C) 8: Raven's-wing black hair. **1956** EMcBain *Cop* (NY 1959) 41: His hair was raven black. **1957** *New Yorker* 3/23 35: Her hair was . . . black as a raven's wing. **1958** TBrooke *Under* (NY) 253: His hair is as black as the wing of a blackbird. **1958** BHalliday *Murder* (NY) 141: Hair . . . raven black. **1971** JBlake *Joint* (NY) 374: Eyes as black as the raven's wing. **1975** AChristie *Curtain* (NY) 211: [Hair] was as black as a raven. EAP R31; TW 304–5 (1,2); Brunvand 117. Cf. As black as a Crow *above*; Rook *below*.

R60 As glossy as a **Raven's** wing

1965 ASeton *Avalon* (NY 1966) 9: Hair, glossy as a raven's wing. TW 305(2).

R61 As hoarse as a **Raven**

1936 JCLenehan *Silecroft* (L) 78: He was as hoarse as a raven. **1969** FSwinnerton *Reflections* (L) 82: The phrase "as hoarse as a raven." Lean II ii 841.

R62 **Raw** head and bloody bones

1922 JJoyce *Ulysses* (NY 1934) 168: Rawhead and bloody bones; 566. **1928** VMarkham *Death* (NY) viii: Raw head and bloody bones. **1937** CGGivens *All Cats* (I) 311: Rawhead—and—Bloodybones is waiting just around the curve. **1941** ISCobb *Exit* (I) 59: Of Raw Head and Bloody Bones. **1951** JCFurnas *Voyage* (NY) 128: Her taste for raw head and bloody bones. **1964** ABurgess *Nothing* (L) 68: The law a raw head and bloody bones. EAP R32.

R63 As keen as a **Razor**

1926 JSFletcher *Great* (NY) 210: His interest . . . as keen as one of his own razors. **1941** TFuller *Reunion* (B) 186: Keen as a razor [*an ax*]. **1974** WSnow *Codline* (Middletown, Conn.) 268: A mind as keen as a razor. Whiting *NC* 466(1).

R64 As sharp as a **Razor**; Razor-sharp

1913 JCLincoln *Mr. Pratt's Patients* (NY) 269: He was as sharp as a razor. **1922** JJoyce *Ulysses* (NY 1934) 578: With teeth as sharp as razors. **1932** PMcGuire *Black Rose* (NY) 6: Her father's as sharp as a razor. **1940** HFootner *Sinfully* (L) 44: It's as sharp as a razor. **1958** LSdeCamp *Elephant* (NY) 216: He's sharp as a razor. **1961** MKelly *Spoilt* (L) 48: Clean, bright, and razor-sharp [*a museum*]. **1964** GSims *Terrible* (L 1967) 128: A razor-sharp mind. Like a steel trap. **1968** NBenchley *Welcome* (NY) 228: Keep your wits sharp as razors. **1970** JRoss *Deadest* (NY) 128: Her perceptions were razor-sharp. EAP R33; TW 305(4); Taylor *Western Folklore* 17(1958) 18: Razor sharp.

R65 There is **Reason** in all things

1929 RRodd *Secret* (NY) 81: There's reason in all things. **1930** LMeynell *Mystery* (P) 229: There's reason in all. **1934** ERPunshon *Crossword* (L) 19: There's reason in all things. **1936** RAJWalling *Floating Foot* (NY) 54: There's a reason for everything. TW 305(1); *Oxford* 666.

R66 **Red hair** a sign of lewdness (deceit) (*varied*)

1922 JJoyce *Ulysses* (NY 1934) 24: Red headed women buck like goats. **1929** FBeeding *Pretty* (B) 32: Always distrust a woman with red hair. **1929** PRShore *Bolt* (NY) 12: Relic of a forgotten fear, that made women cross their fingers when they saw a red-haired woman. **1930** JFarnol *Over the Hills* (B) 8: Ware o' the lad wi' the red poll, ay, and lassie too. **1941** FCharles *Vice Czar* (NY) 175: Redheads were hell on wheels. **1979** CNParkinson *Jeeves* (NY) 26: Then there are the girls with red hair—

don't trust them for a minute. EAP R42. Cf. Ginger *above*.

R67 To catch (be caught) **Red-handed** (*varied*)

1910 EPhillpotts *Tales* (NY) 314: Matthew caught her red-handed . . . with a poetry book. **1917** GRSims *My Life* (L) 268: Arrested red-handed [*murder with a knife*]. **1920** AChristie *Mysterious Affair* (NY) 146: Caught red-handed [*poison*]. **1925** BAtkey *Pyramid* (NY) 244: We will take him red-handed, no yellow-handed [*stealing gold*]. **1928** ABCox *Amateur* (NY) 74: Caught quite literally red-handed. **1930** EMarjoribanks *E.M.Hall* (L) 51: Caught redhanded with a bagful of silver. **1930** RScarlett *Beacon Hill* (NY) 276: Catch her literally red-handed [*cutting a throat*]. **1933** JAston *First Lesson* (NY) 257: Caught red-handed [*in bed*]. **1938** CBush *Tudor Queen* (L) 123: Caught him red-handed [*adultery*]. **1947** AGilbert *Death in* (L) 188: Catch the culprit red-handed, in possession of the letter. **1949** MGilbert *He Didn't* (NY DBC) 24: We got him red-handed, a few hours after the burglary. **1951** FCrane *Murder in* (NY) 82: They caught him red-handed growing marijuana. **1956** JJMarric *Gideon's Week* (L) 34: Caught red-handed in a fur salon. **1961** FBiddle *Casual* (NY) 296: Caught, red-handed, making away with an apple [*a dog*]. **1961** PMoyes *Down Among* (NY) 245: Caught Sir Simon red-handed [*digging*]. **1962** ESGardner *Ice-cold* (NY DBC) 93: You were caught red-handed [*handling dry ice*]. **1963** The Gordons *Undercover* (NY DBC) 38: I caught the cat redhanded [*with a duck in its mouth*]. **1963** HMiller *Black* (NY) 106: The pastor caught red-handed [*with a naked boy*]. **1966** WBlunt *Isfahan* (L) 105: Catching the man red-handed [*sexual intercourse*]. **1968** EQueen *House* (NY) 62: He caught you redhanded with the stolen horse. **1969** ACarter *Heroes* (L) 192: Caught red-handed stealing his peculiar honey. **1971** PMHubbard *Dancing* (NY) 73: I caught . . . a man red-handed doing good by stealth. **1973** TZinkin *Weeds* (L) 91: He was caught by his doctor, red handed [*breaking his diet*]. **1974** PGWodehouse *Cat-Nappers* (NY) 181: We caught him red-handed, or as red-handed as it is possible to be when stealing cats. **1978** NMarsh *Grave* (NY) 91: Someone who had been caught red-eared in the act of eavesdropping. TW 305.

R68 To draw a **Red herring** across the trail (*varied*)

1921 JSFletcher *Orange-Yellow* (NY) 275: To draw a red herring across the trail. **1922** JJoyce *Ulysses* (NY 1934) 643: To trail the conversation in the direction of that particular red herring. **1924** LO'Flaherty *Informer* (L) 84: A red herring of a story. **1926** JBlaikie *Egyptian Papyri* (L) 108: Seeing the vizier trail this manifest red herring over the scent. **1928** RBenchley *20,000 Leagues* (NY) 183: Trying to drag a fish, fowl, or good red herring across the trail. **1928** AJSmall *Master* (NY) 182: He's simply hitting us in the nose with a particularly smelly red herring. **1930** GMitchell *Mystery* (NY) 108: The skull was a red herring. **1930** DDeane *Mystery* (L) 319: Drawing red herrings and aniseed in front of the pack, so to speak. **1932** MThynne *Murder* (NY) 223: Davenport swallowed the red herring whole. **1937** RHull *Ghost* (NY) 243: I nicknamed him mentally the Red Herring. **1941** AAFair *Double* (NY) 273: They wanted to use me as an amatory red herring. **1941** SMarshall *Some Like* (NY) 274: He employed it [*a gun*] as a red herring by hiding it in my coat. **1949** NMarsh *Wreath* (NY) 289: His red herrings are more like whales. **1952** STruss *Death* (NY) 187: An open window as a red herring. **1955** MO'Brine *Passport* (L) 178: A red herring to send me on a wild goose chase. **1959** *BangorDN* 9/14 4: Southerners were dragging a very dead red herring across the enforcements of civil rights. **1960** HLivingston *Climacticon* (NY) 143: The Harvard red herring. **1963** JNHarris *Weird* (NY DBC) 43: "An irrelevant red herring." "Is a red herring ever relevant?" **1967** ESGardner *Queenly* (NY) 59: She . . . proved a beautiful red herring and sent the pack baying off on a false scent. **1968** RLockridge *A Plate of Red Herring* (P). **1972** WJBurley *Guilt* (NY) 115: You're as full of red herrings as a kipper factory. **1972** RLockridge *Write* (P) 191: Shepley was just

a red-bearded herring. **1973** CJackson *Kicked* (NY) 136: Gino's death had been a red herring. *Oxford* 668.

R69 As weak as a **Reed**
1959 EMarshall *Pagan* (NY) 101: I'm weak as a reed. EAP R44.

R70 To be a broken (*etc.*) **Reed** (*varied*)
1903 EChilders *Riddle* (NY 1940) 126: They were broken reeds. **1923** CSLewis *Letters* ed WHLewis (NY 1966) 90: Proved a broken reed. **1930** ABCox *Piccadilly* (NY) 318: A mistake to rely on a broken reed. **1939** MBurton *Babbacombe* (L) 11: I'm a bit of a broken reed. **1941** ABCunningham *Strange Death* (NY) 105: Sutton leaned on a broken reed. **1942** MGEberhart *Wolf* (NY) 92: Alexia . . . was . . . a broken reed [*crushed by the death of her husband*]. **1948** DCDisney *Explosion* (NY DBC) 96: Till is an awfully weak reed to lean on. **1951** HSaunders *Sleeping* (L) 117: He proved a broken reed. **1959** DMDouglass *Many* (L) 132: Books . . . are weak reeds on which to lean. **1960** NFitzgerald *Ghost* (L) 141: He'll be something of a broken reed. **1968** GBagby *Another* (NY) 156: He was leaning on a slender reed. **1970** RFoley *Calculated* (NY) 93: A slim reed to grasp. **1970** RQuest *Cerberus* (NY) 200: Anna had leaned on a broken reed. EAP R47. Cf. Staff *below*.

R71 To quiver (shake) like a **Reed**
1929 LO'Flaherty *House* (NY) 91: The doctor stood quivering like a reed. **1960** JBWest *Taste* (NY) 95: Shaking like a reed. Cf. Brunvand 117: Sway.

R72 To take a **Reef** in one's sail
1957 MBGarrett *Horse* (University, Ala.) 6: Took a new reef in his sail. EAP R48.

R73 Right (straight) off the **Reel**
1915 JFerguson *Stealthy* (L 1935) 115: Tell . . . the story straight off the reel. **1924** WBMFerguson *Black* (NY) 81: Right off the reel. Whiting *NC* 466.

R74 To hold the **Reins**
1940 MFitt *Death Starts* (L) 55: She holds the reins. EAP R50.

R75 Relax and enjoy it

1957 WGoldman *Temple* (NY) 23: So I began to relax and enjoy it. **1960** NBenchley *Sail* (NY) 43: We might as well relax and enjoy it. **1966** ELinington *Date* (NY) 7: And of course, same like advice to the young lady getting raped, relax and enjoy it. **1969** PSCatling *Freddy* (NY) 46: Then like the story says—relax and enjoy it.

R76 Republics are ungrateful (*varied*)

1949 RStout *Troubles* (NY) 77: The saying that democracies are always ungrateful. **1958** WDHassett *Off the Record* (New Brunswick, NJ) 217: If republics are ungrateful, democracies also are forgetful. **1962** VWBrooks *Fenollosa* (NY) 216: That republics are ungrateful had been known before the time of Wilkes. EAP R61.

R77 No **Rest** (peace) for the wicked (weary) (*varied*)

1931 BGraeme *Murder* (P) 132: There's no peace for the wicked. **1931** MMagill *Death* (P) 151: There's no rest for the wicked. **1933** EBailey *Death* (L) 47: There's no rest for the wicked. **1938** CBush *Tudor Queen* (L) 87: No rest for the wicked, they say, nor yet the ungodly. **1942** NMarsh *Enter Murderer* (NY) 165: No rest for the wicked. **1947** MBurton *Will in the Way* (NY) 99: No peace for the wicked. **1949** RMLaurenson *Six Bullets* (NY) 93: "The wicked know no rest," he said sententiously. **1961** HKlinger *Wanton* (NY) 61: No rest for the weary. **1966** EXFerrars *No Peace for the Wicked* (NY). **1967** RGarrett *Too Many* (NY) 211: There is no rest for the weary. **1969** LPDavies *Stranger* (NY) 167: No rest for the wicked. **1970** PAlding *Guilt* (NY) 160: There's no rest for the wicked. **1970** RRendell *Guilty* (NY) 15: There's no peace for the wicked. Isaiah 48.22: Peace; Brunvand 117: Wicked.

R78 Revenge is sweet (*varied*)

1928 HCMcNeile *Female* (NY) 264: Revenge is sweet. **1930** EMarjoribanks *E.M. Hall* (L) 347: Treacle is sweet, but revenge is sweeter. **1933** JVTurner *Amos* (L) 148: Revenge is sweet. **1938** JSStrange *Silent* (NY) 224: Revenge is sweet. **1940** GPatten *Autobiography* ed HHinsdale (Norman, Okla. 1964) 54: Revenge long deferred was doubly sweet. **1948** HAustin *Drink* (NY) 30: Revenge is sweet. **1957** EMButler *Heine* (NY) 267: Revenge was sweet to Heine. **1957** MProcter *Midnight* (NY) 162: Vengeance would be sweet indeed. **1959** EMcBain *King's* (NY) 222: Revenge isn't sweet. **1968** JRoffman *Grave* (NY) 78: Revenge was sweet. **1974** MDavis *Tell Them* (NY) 57: Revenge isn't sweet. **1975** HCarmichael *Too Late* (NY) 142: The old saying was still true: Sweet is revenge—especially to women. EAP R63; Brunvand 117.

R79 Rhyme or reason (*varied*)

1910 JLondon *Letters* ed KHendricks (NY 1965) 328: Little rhyme or reason. **1914** MAdams *In the Footsteps* (L) 133: Have neither rhyme nor reason. **1923** TFPowys *Black Bryony* (L) 129: Without rhyme or reason. **1931** APryde *Emerald* (NY) 18: Neither rhyme nor reason. **1933** AChristie *Lord Edgeware* (L) 128: Without rhyme or reason. **1934** GHeyer *Unfinished* (L) 43: Fugitive poems without rhyme or (said the uninitiated) reason. **1937** BHarvey *Growing Pains* (NY) 155: Verse . . . without rhyme or apparent reason. **1940** ECBentley *Those Days* (L) 130: The entire absence of rhyme or reason. **1942** WIrish *Phantom* (NY 1957) 87: Without rhyme or reason. **1955** *Partisan Review* 22.4 504: The problem, then, is a choice between rhyme and reason. **1955** ELacy *Best* (NY) 37: Shooting him without rhyme or reason. **1957** NMitford *Voltaire* (L) 81: A fairy tale without rhyme or reason. **1960** JLindsay *Roaring* (L) 132: Mrs B. . . . didn't know rhyme from reason. **1965** JDavey *Killing* (L) 30: What is its rhyme or reason? **1975** JHough *Guardian* (B) 163: There's no rhyme or reason in these things. **1978** JCash *Gold* (NY) 156: Greed knows no rhyme or reason. EAP R66; TW 306; Brunvand 118.

R80 As slick as a **Ribbon**

1930 LThayer *They Tell* (NY) 303: Slick as a ribbon. Whiting *NC* 467; Taylor *Prov. Comp.* 73.

R81 As straight as a **Ribbon**

1926 CJDutton *Flying* (NY) 139: The road was straight as a ribbon. Cf. As straight as a String *below*.

R82 Good **Riddance** to bad rubbish (*varied*)

1911 JCLincoln *Woman-Haters* (NY) 136: Good riddance to bad rubbish. **1924** CVanVechten *Tattooed* (NY) 285: Good riddance to bad rubbidge. **1928** VStarrett *Seaports* (NY) 36: Wish us godspeed and good riddance. **1932** JTFarrell *Young Lonigan* (NY 1935) 120: Good riddance to bad rubbish. **1938** JFarnol *Crooked* (NY) 23: Good luck and good riddance. **1939** RCSherriff *Hopkins* (NY) 294: Goodbye and good riddance. **1941** CMRussell *Dreadful* (NY) 110: Its good riddance to bad rubbish. **1952** EPaul *Black* (NY) 257: There's an old New England saying: "Good riddance to bad rubbish." **1953** SBellow *Adventures* (NY) 363: Good-by and good riddance. **1956** *BangorDN* 8/25 22: Good riddance to bad rubbish, I say. **1965** HActon *Old Lamps* (L) 158: A good riddance to bad rubbish. **1968** RBissell *How Many* (B) 29: Good riddance to bad rubbage. **1971** AChristie *Nemesis* (NY) 212: Bon voyage and good riddance. **1971** WHWalling *No One* (NY) 107: Good riddance, I'd say. EAP R76; Brunvand 118.

R83 To be taken for a **Ride**

1930 RScarlett *Beacon Hill* (NY) 34: I was being taken for a ride, as the saying goes. **1935** VGielgud *Death* (L) 249: Taking us for the proverbial ride. **1958** RPHansen *Deadly* (NY DBC) 152: They were taking Phipps for the well-known ride. **1959** STruss *Man to Match* (NY) 155: You've been taken for a ride. Wentworth 427.

R84 **Right** is right (*varied*)

1935 DHume *Murders* (L) 175: Right's right all the world over, I says. **1959** AGilbert *Death* (NY) 38: Still right's right. TW 307(2).

R85 To spend (lie) **Right** and left

1936 TAPlummer *Dumb* (NY) 13: He spent money right and left. **1960** GAshe *Man who Laughed* (NY) 120: She's lying right and left. Berrey 55.4, 255.5.

R86 To read the **Riot Act**

1930 RAJWalling *Squeaky Voice* (NY) 210: I read the Riot Act to her. TW 307.

R87 To sell (be sold) down (up) the **River**

1936 KSteel *Murder Goes* (I) 64: Kelly'd sold you down the river. **1938** EStVMillay *Letters* ed ARMacdougall (NY 1952) 304: I have sold myself down the river (or rather up the river, which is so much harder to swim). **1939** HPentecost *Cancelled* (NY) 262: He would have sold his own grandmother down the river for money. **1941** HAshbrook *Purple Onion* (NY) 246: Sell his own daughter . . . down the river. **1951** FCrane *Murder in* (NY) 124: But I won't be sold up the river. **1954** LFord *Invitation* (NY) 120: I'd sell my friends down the river. **1956** AGilbert *Riddle* (NY) 52: He's sold right up the river. **1958** *NYTimes Magazine* 5/11 14: The Weimar Republic had been sold down the river. **1958** SEllin *Eighth* (NY 1959) 271: I don't sell Ira down the river. **1963** JNHarris *Weird* (NY DBC) 22: She sent the boy up the river. **1967** EHahn *Romantic* (NY) 128: Selling himself down the river. **1973** AGilbert *Nice* (NY) 233: Selling him up the river. **1975** JDaniels *White* (NY) 80: Sold the New Deal down the river. **1977** PMoyes *Coconut* (NY) 167: [He] would have sold his grandmother down the river. TW 307(2).

R88 To set the **River** on fire (*varied*)

1930 SFDamon *T.H.Chivers* (NY) 84: Neither the Schuylkill nor any of the many rivers of Georgia showed the least sign of bursting into flame as yet. **1936** BThomson *Who Killed* (NY) 48: My writings have not yet set any river on fire. **1939** MArmstrong *Murder in* (NY) 22: Sam won't ever set the river afire. **1957** JCheever *Wapshot* (NY) 174: She's got this secret that will set the river on fire. **1975** RO'Connor *H.Broun* (NY) 89: [It] may or may not have set the Hudson on fire. EAP R93. Cf. To set the Thames, World *below*.

R89 All **Roads** lead to Rome (*varied*)

c1923 ACrowley *Confessions* ed JSymonds (L 1969) 232: All roads lead to Rome. **1924** JSFletcher *King* (NY) 271: The saying that all roads lead to Rome. **1929** TCobb *Crime* (L) 172: One has to follow every road . . . though only one can lead to Rome. **1934** FWCrofts *Crime* (NY) 195: There are many roads to Rome. **1946** ERolfe *Murder . . . Glass Room* (NY) 152: So all the roads really do lead to Rome. **1954** HGardiner *Murder* (L) 113: Every road leads to Rome. **1959** *NYTimes* 4/26 25: Even the Almighty has said that all roads lead to Rome. **1960** SRaven *Brother* (NY) 28: All roads lead to Rome, as they say. **1960** HRobertson *Swan* (NY) 166: All roads lead to London. **1971** ADavidson *Peregrine* (NY) 166: Every schoolboy . . . knows that all roads lead to Rome. **1975** ABrodsky *Madame* (NY) 27: Paris was in a sense the metaphorical Rome to [which] all roads lead. Whiting P52; *Oxford* 679–80.

R90 There is no royal **Road** to success

1938 FWCrofts *End* (L) 199: There was no royal road to success. **1968** FBaker *I Follow* (L) 31: There's no royal road to success. TW 308(4); *Oxford* 686.

R91 To be on the **Road** to Boston

1974 WSnow *Codline* (Middletown, Conn.) 261: She was already "on the road to Boston," as the Spruce Head people used to say [*pregnant*].

R92 To rule the **Roast**

1930 PFGaye *Good Sir John* (L) 84: Rule the roast. EAP R99; TW 308. Cf. Roost *below*.

R93 As naked as a **Robin**

1967 JPurdy *Eustace* (NY) 98: Amos . . . was naked as a robin. *Oxford* 553. Cf. Jaybird *above*.

R94 To go round **Robin Hood's** barn (*varied*)

1910 JCLincoln *Depot Master* (NY) 174: It's way round Robin Hood's barn. **1913** JCLincoln *Mr. Pratt's Patients* (NY) 283: After beating all around Robin Hood's barn by talking about the weather. **1930** MCKeator *Eyes* (NY) 194: Going the long-est way round a barn and getting lost on the journey. **1931** ACEdington *Monk's Hood* (NY) 179: You don't need to go round Robin Hood's barn to get him to talk. **1934** PATaylor *Sandbar* (NY) 103: Drove all over Robin Hood's barn. **1937** SPalmer *Blue Banderilla* (NY) 191: Which amounted to going twice around Robin Hood's barn. **1940** JSStrange *Picture* (NY) 15: It's all around Robin Hood's barn to the bridge. **1949** JDCarr *Below* (NY) 183: One of my eternal wanderings round Robin Hood's barn. **1953** KMKnight *Akin* (NY) 180: I wouldn't have gone all round Robin Hood's barn the way I did. **1956** *BHerald* 8/1 22: Getting into town via Robin Hood's barn. **1956** RAHeinlein *Double* (NY 1957) 19: Why do you think I went around Robinson's barn to get you out of there? **1961** JPhilips *Murder* (NY DBC) 101: Leave you to run around Robin Hood's barn. **1969** PAnderson *Satan's* (NY) 69: Let's not beat around the barn. **1971** ELinington *Practice* (NY) 26: He went all round Robin Hood's barn. **1973** HDolson *Dying* (P) 123: What are you leading up to with all this skulking around Robin Hood's barn? EAP R106.

R95 As firm as a **Rock**

1926 JSFletcher *Green Ink* (B) 195: He's firm as a rock. **1930** HHolt *Ace* (L) 13: Bannister remained firm as a rock. **1930** WLewis *Apes* (NY 1932) 127: It was firm as a rock. **1932** VWilliams *Death* (B) 237: The detective . . . firm as a rock. **1940** ACampbell *They Hunted* (NY) 23: Firm as a rock [*a man*]. **1956** ADuggan *Winter* (L) 56: The ponies . . . firm as rocks. **1959** CHassall *E.Marsh* (L) 427: Firm as a rock. **1961** DLMoore *Late Lord* (L) 194: He could be as firm as a rock. **1968** GHellman *Bankers* (NY) 153: [He] was firm as a rock. EAP R107; Brunvand 119.

R96 As hard as a **Rock**; Rock-hard

1929 HFergusson *In Those Days* (NY) 250: A poker face as hard as a rock. **1936** DTeilhet *Crimson Hair* (NY) 156: Cyrus is as hard as a rock. **1959** EHuxley *Flame* (L) 89: Men as hard as rocks. **1961** WMasterson *Evil* (NY) 132: Rock-hard arrogance. **1971** NBogner *Making* (NY) 150: He was . . .

hard as a rock [*penis*]. **1975** HPentecost *Time* (NY) 144: His rock-hard face. EAP R108. Cf. As hard as a Stone *below*.

R97 As rigid as a **Rock** (granite)

1931 ENWright *Strange* (Cleveland) 15: Jenks sat as rigid as rock. **1939** LFord *Town* (NY) 236: She was as rigid as granite. Wilstach 324. Cf. As rigid as a Stone *below*.

R98 As safe as a **Rock**

1927 AHaynes *Crow's* (L) 251: You are as safe as a rock. **1936** MBeckett *Escape* (L) 83: Simson . . . was safe as a rock, utterly trustworthy. Cf. Gibraltar *above*.

R99 As solid as a **Rock** (granite)

1931 CBush *Dead Man's* (L) 259: [They] stood . . . as solid as rocks. **1936** JGBrandon *Pawnshop* (L) 257: One thing stood solid as granite. **1937** DAllan *Brandon* (L) 39: And well off. Solid as a rock. **1940** AEVanVogt *Glass* (NY 1951) 99: Gray . . . solid as a rock [*a man*]. **1956** AAtkinson *Exit* (NY) 207: He was as solid as a rock. **1959** JWelcome *Run* (NY) 79: It was as solid as rock. **1970** M Stewart *Crystal* (NY) 481: [He] was as solid as a rock. **1974** HCarmichael *Most* (NY) 72: His friendship . . . was as solid as a rock. EAP R109.

R100 As sound as a **Rock**

1933 AGMacLeon *Case* (NY) 137: Sound as a rock. **1959** LColeman *Sam* (NY) 214: Sound as a rock [*a person*]. **1968** LDurrell *Tunc* (NY) 143: The firm is as sound as a rock. Wilstach 375.

R101 As steady as a **Rock**; Rock-steady

1926 MRRinehart *Bat* (NY 1959) 218: His right hand was as steady as a rock. **1947** CBrand *Suddenly* (L) 44: As steady as a rock. **1953** FKane *Poisons* (NY 1960) 113: The hand . . . was steady as a rock. **1954** HClement *Mission* (NY) 11: The deck [was] rock-steady. **1959** GCarr *Swing* (NY) 101: [His hands] were rock-steady. **1959** *CSMonitor* 4/11 12: The steady-as-a-rock rate. **1967** HStone *Funniest* (NY) 177: He was as steady as a rock. **1975** MHolroyd *Augustus* (NY) 57: Eyes . . . were rock-steady. Whiting *NC* 468(4). Cf. As steady as Stone *below*.

R102 As stiff as a **Rock**

1930 JSFletcher *Behind* (NY) 65: Hand . . . as stiff as a rock. Cf. Wilstach 389: A stone. Cf. As stiff as Stone *below*.

R103 As still as a **Rock**

1931 RAJWalling *Stroke* (L) 309: Parrish lay still as a rock. **1950** HReilly *Murder* (NY) 227: [He] was still as a rock. Cf. Wilstach 390: A stone. Cf. As still as Stone *below*.

R104 As strong as a **Rock**

1957 *NYTimes* 6/2 4E: His Government is as strong as a rock. TW 309(7).

R105 The **Rock** one split on

1935 HHolt *Tiger* (L) 113: That was the rock on which we often split. EAP R112.

R106 To be between a **Rock** (knot) and a hard spot (place)

1954 LCochran *Row's End* (NY) 40: I know you're between a knot and a hard place. **1959** *NYTimes* 4/19 76: It looks like we're caught between a rock and a hard spot [*from Kentucky*]. **1971** WHWalling *No One* (NY) 232: I'm caught between the proverbial rock and the hard spot. Berrey 173.5, 211.3, 256.13, 378.3, 933.4.

R107 To be on the **Rocks**

1934 DHume *Too Dangerous* (L) 162: I was on the rocks. **1936** SFowler *Was Murder Done?* (L) 167: The old man's too wily to let him run on the rocks. **1940** FWBronson *Nice People* (NY) 78: His firm is on the rocks. **1940** CMWills *R.E.Pipe* (L) 158: She's on the rocks [*broke*]. **1959** PCurtis *No Question* (NY) 74: You'll be on the rocks. **1962** IFleming *Spy* (NY) 155: The business might be on the rocks. Wentworth 367: On the.

R108 To have **Rocks** in one's head

1961 WEHuntsberry *Oscar* (NY DBC) 138: He thought I had rocks in my head. Wentworth 431.

R109 To sleep like a **Rock**

1930 WSMaugham *Cakes* (L 1948) 145: She sleeps like a rock. **1934** ABliss *Murder* (P) 169: Sleeping like a rock. **1940** DTeilhet *Broken Face* (NY) 269: You were sleeping like a rock. **1949** AMStein *Days* (NY) 92:

I'm going to sleep like a rock. **1954** SDe-Lima *Carnival* (NY) 153: I'll sleep like a rock. **1958** MAllingham *Tether's* (NY) 146: Sleeping like a rock. **1960** HWaugh *Road* (NY DBC) 36: Sleeping like a rock. **1965** LHWhitten *Progeny* (NY) 152: The boy sleeps like a rock. TW 309(5).

R110 To stand (sit) like a **Rock**

1931 RScarlett *Cat's* (NY) 45: Stood like a rock. **1939** WChambers *You Can't* (NY) 87: Frazier sat like a rock. TW 309(9).

R111 To go (be) off one's **Rocker**

1933 EBailey *Death* (L) 33: Go off her rocker. **1948** CDickson *Skeleton* (NY 1967) 182: Henry's gone off his rocker. **1953** CDickson *Cavalier's* (NY) 30: He's off his rocker at least. **1961** DLMathews *Very Welcome* (NY DBC) 94: He's off his rocker. **1963** RFoley *Backdoor* (NY DBC) 83: I think he's off his rocker. Wentworth 431.

R112 As high as a **Rocket**

1959 NMarsh *False* (B) 29: I'm in a tizzy . . . High as a rocket. Cf. Kite *above*.

R113 To go up (off) like a **Rocket**

1930 AMuir *Silent* (I) 223: He'll be off like a rocket. **1957** KFerrer *Gownsman's* (L) 102: Defay went up like a rocket. **1959** ESherry *Defense* (NY) 178: Your stock would go up like a rocket. TW 338: Sky-rocket; Brunvand 119.

R114 Up like a **Rocket** and down like the stick (*varied*)

1922 JJoyce *Ulysses* (NY 1934) 364: Up like a rocket, down like a stick. **1930** DLSayers *Strong* (NY) 90: Up like a rocket, down like the stick, you know. **1939** EMarsh *Number* (NY) 321: This book . . . went up like a rocket but . . . seemed to have come down like a stick. **1956** PWentworth *Fingerprint* (NY) 36: Up with the rocket and down with the stick. **1974** AMenen *Fonthill* (NY) 63: Up like a rocket and down like the stick. EAP R113.

R115 As stiff as a **Rod**

1953 CJay *Fugitive* (NY) 102: Kane lay stiff as a rod. **1962** ITRoss *Old* (NY DBC) 43: His backbone stiff as a rod. **1973** GSereny *Case* (NY) 204: Stiff as a rod. Cf. Ramrod *above*.

R116 As straight as a **Rod**

1973 GSereny *Case* (NY) 178: Mary sat straight as a rod. Cf. Ramrod *above*.

R117 Spare the **Rod** and spoil the child (*varied*)

1928 WJerrold *Bulls* (L) 205: Spare the rod and spoil the child. **1931** HMSmith *Waverdale Fire* (L) 92: His mother, mindful of Solomon, certainly did not spare the rod. **1938** JTFarrell *No Star* (NY) 253: Spare the rod and spoil the child. **1940** NBlake *Malice* (L) 85: Spare the rod and spoil the child. **1941** TChanslor *Our Second* (NY) 84: We spared the rod and spoiled a very engaging little girl. **1952** HFMPrescott *Man on* (NY) 324: Spare the rod, spoil the child. **1960** SDean *Murder* (NY DBC) 58: I spared the rod. I doubt if it will spoil the child. **1966** LPDavies *Paper* (NY) 74: A "spoil the rod, spare the child" doctrine. **1969** RPearsall *Worm* (L) 326: That most disgusting maxim, "Spare the rod and spoil the child." EAP R114.

R118 To have a **Rod** in pickle for someone

c1923 ACrowley *Confessions* ed JSymonds (L 1969) 881: The gods had a rod in pickle for her. **1935** VLoder *Dead Doctor* (L) 47: With a rod in pickle for Dr. Purton. **1938** MSaltmarsh *Clouded* (NY) 18: She's got rods in pickle for us. **1957** *New Yorker* 4/20 121: The Judge had another rod in pickle for him. **1958** DGBrowne *Death* (L) 146: You might find a rod in pickle for you. **1961** WHLewis *Scandalous* (NY) 127: The rod in pickle for the Parlement. **1963** RCroft-Cooke *Bosie* (L) 148: Wilde had a harsher rod in pickle for Ross. **1966** WDerry *Dr. Parr* (Oxford) 81: The Doctor had a rod in pickle for the Bishop. **1974** AMorice *Killing* (NY) 38: What is meant by putting a rod in pickle. EAP R115.

R119 To kiss the **Rod**

1931 HFootner *Easy* (L) 98: Able to force his victims to kiss the rod that chastened them. **1937** CIsherwood *Lions* (Norfolk, Conn. 1947) 19: Kissed the rod. **1956** AM Maughan *Harry* (NY) 15: Do not ask me to kiss the rod. **1964** BHecht *Letters* (NY) 35: Humility, such as induces sinners to kiss the rod. **1967** FSwinnerton *Sanctuary* (NY) 201: Kisses the rod. **1973** AWest *Mortal* (NY) 299: Solange kissed the rod. EAP R116.

R120 To make a **Rod** (stick) for one's own back (*varied*)

1927 LBamburg (NY) 46: He made a rod for his own back; 93. **1932** NBell *Disturbing* (NY) 69: I give you a stick for my back. **1939** HHolt *Smiling Doll* (L) 59: You might only be handing them a stick with which they might beat you. **1970** FBarlow *Edward* (L) 67: [They] made rods for their own backs. **1971** RFDelderfield *For My* (NY) 134: People who went out of their way to pickle rods for their own backs. EAP R117. Cf. Pit *above*.

R121 To rule with a **Rod** of iron

1932 VLWhitechurch *Murder* (L) 69: Rules locally with a rod of iron. **1937** ERPunshon *Mystery* (NY) 124: He rules her with a rod of iron, as the saying is. EAP R118.

R122 A **Roland** for one's Oliver (*varied*)

1919 HRHaggard *She and Allan* (NY 1921) 127: Give him a Roland for his Oliver. **1933** OMartyn *Body* (L) 121: A Roland for his Oliver. **1935** BFlynn *Case* (L) 90: A Childe Roland for a Bath Oliver. **1936** CBush *Monday Murders* (L) 131: I've a Roland for that Oliver. **1955** CMWills *Death* (L) 13: He might return a Roland for an Oliver. **1957** VWheatley *HMartineau* (Fair Lawn, NJ) 246: Gave him a Roland for his Oliver. **1958** EQueen *Finishing* (NY) 115: A Roland for his Oliver. **1968** MSteen *Pier* (L) 36: Returned a Roland for his Oliver. EAP R125.

R123 A **Roll** in the hay (*varied*)

1940 EQueen *New Adventures* (NY) 260: Ivy [*a mare*] keeps rolling in the hay. **1952** MEngel *Length* (NY) 82: It's a roll in the hay, which he's not averse to, but for him it's all the same in the dark, one roll or another. **1957** APowell *At Lady* (L) 179: As if marriage was one long roll in the hay. **1959** SRansome *I'll Die* (NY) 132: You'd been romping in the hay with Ruth. **1962** HWaugh *Late* (NY) 70: Donaldson and the

maid were rolling in the hay. **1963** MCallaghan *That Summer* (NY 1964) 145: Poor Emma Bovary's fugitive roll in the hay. **1965** HActon *Old Lamps* (L) 127: Have a rough and tumble in the hay. **1968** MAllingham *Cargo* (NY) 134: He's a one for his roll in the hay. **1973** JMann *Troublecross* (NY) 136: He had the odd roll in the hay with the pretty girls he met. Spears 331.

R124 **Rome** (the world) was not built in a day (*varied*)

1913 HHMunro *When William* (L 1929) 10: Rome wasn't built in a day. **1915** EBWhite *Letters* ed DLGuth (NY 1976) 13: Rome was not made in a day. **1923** JSFletcher *Lynne Court* (NY) 62: Rome was not built in a day. **1932** PATaylor *Death* (I) 177: Rome wasn't built in a day. **1934** CDKing *Obelists* (L) 37: World wasn't built in a day. **1938** VLoder *Wolf* (L) 17: Beards, like Rome, are not built in a day. **1939** HHolt *Smiling Doll* (L) 100: It took a hell of a long time to build Rome, so they tell me. **1940** DHume *Invitation* (L) 108: Soho wasn't built in a day. **1947** PMcGerr *Pick* (NY) 110: After all, Rome wasn't built in a day. **1952** GVidal *Judgment* (NY) 219: Rome was not built in a day. **1957** *Time* 3/11 80: Not only is Rome not rebuilt in a day. **1960** EBowen *Time* (NY) 122: Not built in a day, Rome did not fall in one. **1967** HStone *Funniest* (NY) 130: A beard like the one we were concerned with is like Rome. It isn't built in a day. **1970** RHeppenstall *French Crime* (L) 168: One of those who thought Rome could be built in a day. **1970** TAWaters *Probability* (NY) 20: After all, Rome wasn't torn down in a day, either. EAP R126; TW 310(1); Brunvand 156: World(3).

R125 To fiddle while **Rome** burns (*varied*)

1934 AGilbert *Man in Button* (L) 53: While he fiddles, Rome burns. **1945** PATaylor *Proof* (NY) 67: While you're fiddling around here Rome is doubtless burning. **1950** CDickson *Night* (NY) 73: What's the use fiddling while Rome burns? **1959** EHuxley *Flame* (L) 74: I am fiddling while Rome burns. **1962** JJMcPhaul *Deadlines* (NY) 188: They dread the accusation of fiddling while Rome burns. **1966** SWoods

Enter (NY) 160: You want to fiddle while Rome burns. **1970** HActon *Memoirs* (NY) 344: It was bad taste to fiddle while Rome was burning. **1971** LRhinehart *Dice* (NY) 296: He's a Nero fiddling while Rome burns. EAP R127.

R126   When in **Rome** do as the Romans do (*varied*)

1900 CFPidgin *Quincy A. Sawyer* (B) 340: When you are in Rome you must do as the Romans do. **1919** JBCabell *Jurgen* (NY 1922) 161: When in Rome—one must be romantic. **1925** EDBiggers *House* (NY) 8: When in Rome I make it a point not to do as the Bostonians do. **1926** HSKeeler *Spectacles* (NY 1929) 220: Being in Rome, he wore his toga resignedly. **1932** DSharp *Code-Letter* (B) 71: In Rome one should do as Rome does. **1947** DBowers *Bells* (NY) 145: When in Rome, behave as a Roman. **1948** KWilliamson *Atlantic* (L 1970) 285: The good old adage "When in Rome, do as Rome does." **1949** JBonett *Dead Lion* (L 1953) 97: When in Rome one studies the customs of the natives. **1953** DTrumbo *Additional* (NY 1970) 270: This is Rome, and we must all wear togas. **1956** *New Yorker* 8/25 51: The old saying about when in Rome. **1956** SPalmer *Unhappy* (NY 1957) 146: When in Rome wear a Roman nose and burn Roman candles. **1957** *New Yorker* 3/9 81: When in San Francisco do as natives do. **1958** SBarr *Purely* (NY) 35: When in Rome, show the Romans a trick or two. **1959** *BHerald* 9/21 31: When in Rome do the Romans as they'd do you. **1965** FPohl *Plague* (NY) 40: In Rome he would have to do Roman deeds. **1965** RVale *Beyond* (NY) 179: "What was that saying of the ancients about living as others do in Rome?" "When in Rome," Daly quoted. **1969** ELathen *When in Greece* (NY). **1971** NMarsh *When in Rome* (B). **1972** AMenen *Cities* (L) 141: Their refusal to do in Rome as the Romans did. EAP R128; Brunvand 119.

R127   The **Roof** falls in

1937 ERPunshon *Mystery* (NY) 244: He's getting out from under in case the roof falls in. **1939** DHume *Heads* (L) 197: Get out of this business before the roof falls in on you.

1955 MColes *Happy* (NY) 161: And then the roof fell in. **1960** JSymonds *Only Thing* (L) 156: The roof's going to fall in. **1970** AHalper *Good-bye* (C) 260: The roof had fallen in on him. TW 310(1).

R128   To hit the **Roof**

1973 AWest *Mortal* (NY) 284: George hit the roof. Partridge 393; Wentworth 432–3.

R129   As black as a **Rook**

1961 HEBates *Now Sleeps* (L) 75: Hair black as a rook. Wilstach 20: Young rook. Cf. As black as a Crow, Raven *above*.

R130   Not **Room** to swing a cat

1927 HAdams *Queen's* (P) 11: You couldn't swing a cat in 'em [rooms]. **1929** HMSmith *Jigsaw* (NY) 41: You said you couldn't swing a cat in that scullery. **1931** MMagill *Death* (P) 56: There's not enough room to swing a cat. **1932** JWelzl *Thirty Years* (NY) 216: It was hardly big enough to swing a cat in. **1933** WSharp *Murder* (NY) 196: You couldn't swing a cat below decks. **1951** DBOlsen *Love Me* (NY) 112: Aunt Elizabeth's old saying: "Not enough room to swing a cat." **1957** JCheever *Wapshot* (NY) 90: A room where you couldn't swing a cat around in. **1959** MProcter *Killer* (NY) 92: There was just enough space for a small man to swing a cat. **1964** DBagley *Golden* (NY) 12: A . . . flat . . . with hardly enough room to swing a cat. **1971** EPeters *Knocker* (NY) 60: There wasn't room to swing a cat, let alone a camera. **1972** DLees *Rainbow* (NY) 148: There'll be no one here for a while but by midnight you won't be able to swing a cat. **1977** CAlverson *Not Sleeping* (B) 58: You could have swung a cat in the room, but not a big one. EAP C79; TW 59–60(35).

R131   There is always **Room** at the top

1928 RGore-Browne *In Search* (NY) 148: There's always room at the top, as the man said who looked for the gas leak with a candle. **1937** BFlynn *Orange* (L) 255: You English have a saying that "there's always room at the top." **1958** SJackson *Sundial*

(NY) 187: There's always room at the top. **1960** NWoodin *Room at the Bottom* (L). Whiting *NC* 468.

R132 To prefer one's **Room** to his company (*varied*)

1922 JSFletcher *Ravensdene* (NY) 220: I should much prefer his room to his company. **1922** JJoyce *Ulysses* (NY 1934) 617: He desired the female's room more than her company. **1933** PWentworth *Seven Green* (L) 62: I can do with your room instead of your company. **1936** KMKnight *Clue* (NY) 222: I calc'late our room's worth more'n our company. **1943** HLMencken *Heathen Days* (NY) 10: Their room was preferred to their company. **1950** DMathew *Mango* (L) 18: They wanted his room rather than his company. **1960** RFraser *Trout's* (L) 48: One whose room is often preferred to his company. **1966** DMDisney *Magic* (NY) 52: You'd rather have my room than my company. EAP R130; Brunvand 119.

R133 To rule the **Roost** (*varied*)

1908 JCLincoln *Cy Whittaker* (NY) 207: I'm on top of the roost here. **1917** GRSims *My Life* (L) 104: Ruled the roost. **1922** JJoyce *Ulysses* (NY 1934) 633–4: Ruled the roost. **1928** DHLawrence *Lady* ("Allemagne") 5: To rule her own roost. **1936** LJHalle *Transcaribbean* (NY) 47: Ruled the roost. **1937** PBalfour *Lords* (L) 134: Rule the roost. **1941** CBClason *Green Sliver* (NY) 188: Grandma seemed to rule the roost. **1953** CSWebb *Wanderer* (L) 227: Superstition ruled the roost. **1956** *BHerald* 12/16 1A: Woman, no pampered chick, now rules roost. **1966** LPDavies *Paper* (NY) 147: He is the one who rules the roost. **1969** RCook *Private* (NY) 136: There you were, cock o' the roost. **1975** JPearson *Edward* (NY) 41: He ruled the roost. EAP R131. Cf. Roast *above*.

R134 Give one enough **Rope** and he will hang himself (*varied*)

1920 N&JOakley *Clevedon* (P) 51: We are giving you a little more rope. **1924** AChristie *Man* (NY) 222: There is such a thing as giving a man enough rope, and letting him hang himself. **1929** MGEberhart *Patient* (NY) 220: As a rule, given enough rope a man can hang himself. **1931** DFrome *Strange* (NY) 107: If he gave her enough rope she'd hang herself, as the saying goes. **1936** ISCobb *Judge Priest* (I) 297: The ancient homely saying—"Give a calf enough rope and he'll hang himself." **1936** LGilman *Shanghai* (NY) 10: Give a man enough rope and he'll lead a horse to water. **1937** RPenny *Policeman in* (L) 70: I think we'll give everybody plenty of rope, and hope the rest of the proverb will come true. **1938** MJFreeman *Scarf* (NY) 77: There's an old saying about giving a calf enough rope. **1940** JBentley *Mr. Marlow Stops* (B) 108: I'm going to give you a bit more rope on the assumption you'll hang yourself. **1941** ESGardner *Empty Tin* (NY 1958) 86: Tragg's going to give the boy a little rope and see if he'll get himself tangled up. **1954** GScott *Sound* (NY) 164: You give these little guys enough rope and they'll hang you. **1958** *BHerald* 1/15 9: Feeding Castro enough rope to hang himself. **1959** GHCoxe *Focus* (NY) 151: It looked smarter to give him plenty of rope and see where he led us. **1965** AGilbert *Voice* (NY) 172: If you want a man to hang himself you have to give him plenty of rope. **1968** WASwanberg *Rector* (NY) 44: One had only to give him a little rope and he would hang himself. **1970** DMDevine *Illegal* (NY) 217: Why did you give her so much rope? **1973** JBrooks *Go-Go* (NY) 135: Here's your rope . . . go ahead and hang yourself with it. **1973** EMcBain *Hail* (NY) 99: They had given him enough rope and he had hanged himself. EAP R135; Brunvand 120(2).

R135 **Ropes** of sand

1927 VWilliams *Eye* (B) 63: The fetters [of] matrimony . . . were as ropes of sand. **1931** LRGribble *Grand* (L) 129: It's no use trying to tie knots in ropes of sand. **1938** JCCaughey *McGillivray* (Norman, Okla.) 54: Ropes of Sand. **1965** HCarlisle *Ilyitch* (NY) 190: Busy making sand ropes and climbing up them. **1977** STWarner *Kingdoms* (NY) 154: He makes ropes of sand. EAP R137; Brunvand 120(1).

R136   To go (and) piss up a **Rope**

1972 KCConstantine *Vicksburg* (NY) 166: Aw, go piss up a rope.

R137   To know the **Ropes**

1905 FMWhite *Crimson Blind* (NY) 249: I knew the ropes. **1913** JSFletcher *Secret* (L 1918) 172: You know the ropes. **1923** ABlackwood *Episodes* (L) 277: He knew the ropes. **1933** DGBrowne *Cotfold* (L) 77: He knew the ropes. **1954** RJHealy *Tales* (NY) 197: You know the ropes, as we sailors say. **1957** *Punch* 2/13 244: Anyone who knows the ropes. **1969** AMoorehead *Darwin* (NY) 105: He knew the ropes. **1970** SGBoswell *Book* (L) 135: He knew the ropes. EAP R136; Brunvand 120(3).

R138   To learn the **Ropes**

1914 PGWodehouse *Little Nugget* (NY 1929) 61: To learn the ropes. **1936** HWade *Bury Him* (L) 17: To learn the ropes. **1958** *NYTimes* 5/11 53: He is learning the ropes. TW 311(4).

R139   To mention a **Rope** in the house of a man who has been hanged (*varied*)

1958 JSStrange *Night* (NY) 85: Never mention rope in the house of a man who has been hanged. **1974** EXFerrars *Hanged Man's House* (NY). **1974** EXFerrars *Hanged* (NY) 144: "Do you know the proverb, 'Don't talk of halters in a hanged man's house?'" "No, I don't think I've heard it before." **1974** JLHess *Grand* (B) 149: It was like mentioning rope in the house of a hanged man. TW 311(8); *Oxford* 684.

R140   To show one the **Ropes**

1940 GHCoxe *Glass Triangle* (NY) 140: I tried to show her the ropes. **1943** GHCoxe *Murder for Two* (NY) 8: Casey'll show you the ropes. **1970** DMacKenzie *Kyle* (B) 69: Show him the ropes. **1974** MButterworth *Villa* (NY) 34: I showed you the ropes. TW 311(7).

R141   As clean as a **Rose**

1949 RStout *Second* (NY) 29: She's still as clean as a rose. Wilstach 55: After rain. Cf. Lean II ii 814: Pink.

R142   As fresh as a **Rose** (*varied*)

1931 FDGrierson *Mystery* (L) 10: You look as fresh as a rose. **1938** EHeath *Death Takes* (NY) 79: He looked as fresh as a rose in the morning dew. **1940** MArmstrong *Man with* (NY) 66: Fresh as the first rose of summer. **1958** RChandler *Playback* (L) 105: She looked as fresh as a morning rose. **1960** LLevine *Great* (L) 355: Fresh as a rose. **1969** EAnderson *Miss* (B) 40: As fresh as a rose in the morning. EAP R142; TW 312(3).

R143   As red as a **Rose** (*varied*)

1900 EStVMillay *Letters* ed ARMacdougall (NY 1952) 13: She blused [*sic*] red as a June rose. **1913** MPShiel *Dragon* (L) 38: Red as a rose. **1922** JJoyce *Ulysses* (NY 1934) 643: *Red as a Rose is She*. **1935** DBennett *Murder* (NY) 141: Red as a rose. **1937** PWentworth *Case Is Closed* (L) 7: Red as a rose. **1950** IFletcher *Bennett's* (I) 127: Cheeks grew as red as roses. **1961** PGWodehouse *Ice* (NY) 119: Redder than the rose. **1968** PDickinson *Skin* (L) 151: Red as a rose. EAP R143; TW 312(5).

R144   No **Rose** without a thorn (*varied*)

1916 SLeacock *Behind* (Toronto 1969) 74: Every rose has its thorn. **1922** JJoyce *Ulysses* (NY 1934) 77: No roses without thorns. **1935** HAshbrook *Most Immoral* (NY) 43: Every rose has its thorn. **1943** SShane *Lady . . . Million* (NY) 25: Every rose has its thorn. **1955** STroy *Half-way* (L) 77: But there are no roses without thorns. **1959** AHocking *Victim* (NY) 57: There was a sharpish thorn hidden among the roses. **1961** WHLewis *Scandalous* (NY) 174: There is no rose without its thorn. **1965** HActon *Old Lamps* (L) 218: No rose without a thorn. EAP R145; Brunvand 120(2).

R145   To pluck a **Rose**

1957 GTrease *Snared* (L) 161: I have been to pluck a rose [*urinate*]. EAP R148.

R146   Sub **Rosa**

1913 JLondon *Letters* ed KHendricks (NY 1965) 370: Sub rosa. **1931** JSFletcher *Murder* (NY) 156: And all *sub rosa*, as the saying is. **1937** ECRLorac *These Names* (L) 91: Bartram must have grinned a bit *sub rosa*. **1943** AAbbott *Shudders* (NY) 44: By sub rosa means. **1954** MBodenheim *My Life* (NY) 231: Made love *sub rosa*. **1960** RMacdonald *Ferguson* (NY) 45: Gather ye subrosas while ye may. **1974** GNRay *Wells* (New Haven) xxi: Her sub rosa life. EAP R149; Brunvand 120(3).

R147 Under the **Rose**
1913 ECBentley *Trent's* (NY 1930) 44: Under the rose. c**1923** ACrowley *Confessions* ed JSymonds (L 1969) 859: It circulates under the rose. **1932** NBell *Disturbing* (NY) 189: Strictly under the rose. **1936** RKing *Constant God* (NY) 179: Born, as it were, under the rose. **1963** RAHeinlein *Glory* (NY) 263: Under the rose. **1969** PAnderson *Beyond* (NY) 194: Under the rose. **1972** JBall *Five* (B) 133: "Under the rose." "*Sub rosa* it is." EAP R150.

R148 **Rough** and ready
1927 FWCrofts *Starvel* (NY) 291: Rough and ready. **1937** MBurton *Murder* (L) 180: We're rough and ready. **1941** GBagby *Red Is* (NY) The rough-and-ready level. **1944** MFitt *Clues* (NY) 86: Rough and ready. **1960** RLDuffus *Tower* (NY) 110: Rough and ready. **1965** MAllingham *Mind* (NY) 142: Rough and ready. **1966** JRothenstein *Brave Day* (L) 174: The distinction I have drawn is rough and ready. **1971** JPope-Hennessy *Trollope* (B) 84: Rough and ready methods. EAP R152.

R149 To take the **Rough** with the smooth
1928 DHLawrence *Lady* ("Allemagne") 206: Tha mun ta'e th' rough wi' th' smooth. **1936** RHull *Keep It Quiet* (NY) 157: He would have to take the rough with the smooth. **1938** NBlake *Beast* (NY 1958) 212: We aim to take the rough with the smooth. **1940** PWentworth *Rolling* (P) 226: One just has to take the rough with the smooth. **1949** JStagge *Three* (NY) 126: One learns to take the rough with the smooth. **1952** PQuentin *Black* (NY) 127: We take the rough with the smooth. **1956** RParker *Harm* (NY) 7: You have to take the rough with the smooth. **1962** EAmbler *Light* (L) 6: To take the rough with the smooth. **1963** AHBrodrick *Abbé Breuil* (L) 177: Take the

rough with the smooth. EAP R153. Cf. To take the Bitter, Fat, Good *above*.

R150 To have a hard (long, tough *etc.*) **Row** to hoe (*varied*)
1928 AEApple *Mr. Chang's* (NY) 66: He had the common sense acquired by having had a rough row to hoe. **1928** LMatters *Jack the Ripper* (L) 76: [He] had a hard row to hoe. **1929** VLoder *Between* (NY) 296: I still had a long row to hoe. **1930** JDosPassos *42nd* (NY) 340: A stiff row to hoe. **1936** RAJWalling *Crimson Slipper* (L) 153: A hard row to hoe. **1941** ABCunningham *Strange Death* (NY) 202: You've got a hard row to hoe. **1953** GHolden *Killer* (NY) 136: You've got a hard row to hoe. **1954** CBeaton *Glass* (NY) 294: He realized there was a long row to be hoed. **1957** *Time* 4/22 67: Britain had an heroic row to hoe. **1958** *NYTimes Book Review* 4/27 34: An even more cruelly difficult row to hoe. **1960** BCClark *A Long Row to Hoe* (NY). **1960** EMcBain *Give the Boys* (NY) 85: A hell of a tough row to hoe. **1965** RSPrather *Dead Man's* (NY) 153: I had a long row to hoe. **1970** NMonsarrat *Breaking* (L) 217: A hard row to hoe. **1970** WANolen *Making* (NY) 199: Steve had a tough row to hoe. TW 312–3(1); *Oxford* 686. Cf. Brunvand 120(3).

R151 To have one's **Row** to hoe (*varied*)
1929 VLoder *Between* (NY) 197: I have a nice little row to hoe with this new evidence. **1954** EQueen *Glass* (B) 26: Drake's got his row to hoe. **1955** GBrewer *Red Scarf* (NY) 10: You must learn to hoe your own row. **1957** MBGarrett *Horse* (University, Ala.) 155: Each pupil hoed his own row, so to speak. Whiting *NC* 469; Brunvand 120(3); DA Row n.3.

R152 Not add up to (*etc.*) a **Row of beans**
1919 LTracy *Bartlett* (NY) 89: Won't amount to a row of beans. **1930** NGordon *Silent* (NY) 85: They don't care a row of beans. **1930** LTracy *Manning* (NY) 78: Don't amount to a row of beans. 206: That won't matter a row of beans. **1970** PMoyes *Many* (NY) 75: It doesn't matter a row of beans. **1970** PAlding *Guilt* (NY) 100: It didn't add up to a row of beans. **1970**

AMoorehead *Late* (L) 116: A Spanish colonel wasn't worth a row of beans. **1971** NMarsh *When* (NY) 210: It won't amount to a row of beans. **1972** MGilbert *Body* (NY) 152: It doesn't amount to a row of beans. DA Row *n.*5. Cf. Whiting B92: Bean.

R153   Not amount to (care, give, matter) a **Row of pins**

1917 CPearl *Morrison of Peking* (Sidney 1967) 344: Not amount to a row of pins. **1929** HHolt *Mayfair* (L) 172: It didn't matter a row of pins. **1932** RKeverne *William* (L) 139: She didn't seem to care a row of pins. **1935** PATaylor *Tinkling* (NY) 92: My obituary won't amount to a row of pins. **1940** HReilly *Dead Can* (NY) 185: Wouldn't have amounted to a row of pins. **1948** JErskine *My Life* (P) 147: Germany would never again amount to a row of pins. **1950** RFoley *Hundredth* (NY) 230: He didn't care a row of pins. **1957** *Punch* 2/13 240: The whole speech didn't really amount to more than a row of pins. **1964** BWAldiss *Dark* (L) 82: I don't give a row of pins. **1970** JPorter *Dover Strikes* (NY) 165: It doesn't matter a row of pins. Berrey 21.3. Cf. Whiting P210: Pin.

R154   There's the **Rub** (*varied*)

1922 JJoyce *Ulysses* (NY 1934) 611: That was the rub. **1931** LRGribble *Grand* (L) 211: There's the rub. **1935** BFlynn *Edge* (L) 62: Ay—there's the rub. **1949** ESGardner *Dubious* (NY 1954) 16: There's the rub. **1963** NFitzgerald *Echo* (NY) 253: That was the rub. **1965** JPhilips *Black* (NY DBC) 78: There's the rub, as the fellow said. **1970** ELathen *Pick* (NY) 8: There lies the rub. **1971** RMStern *You Don't* (NY) 9: That was where the rub came in. **1974** JFleming *How To* (NY) 75: And here was the rub. EAP R154.

R155   To cross the **Rubicon** (*varied*)

1928 HKWebster *Quartz* (NY) 11: Crossing the Rubicon. **1929** CWells *Tapestry* (P) 13: The Rubicon . . . crossed. **1937** GGVan Deusen *Henry Clay* (B) 184: Though he had crossed the Rubicon, he had not burned his bridges behind him. **1940** GCKlingel *Anagua* (NY) 235: It is the crossing of this Rubicon. **1943** EDaly *Nothing Can Rescue* (NY 1963) 13: That wedding was her Rubicon. **1954** MBodenheim *My Life* (NY) 198: Eager to cross the Rubicon of erotic experience. **1955** NFitzgerald *House* (L) 177: The culinary rubicon had been crossed. **1962** MMcShane *Seance* (NY) 119: Alfie crossed the Rubicon [*died*]. **1967** LGribble *They Had* (NY) 176: To cross his own murder Rubicon. **1968** WMuir *Belonging* (L) 32: London was a Rubicon Edwin had to cross. **1971** LRhinehart *Dice* (NY) 41: I stood . . . on my own personal Rubicon. **1974** RHelms *Tolkien's* (B) 91: Crossing the Rubicon. EAP R158; Brunvand 120.

R156   As red as **Rubies**; Ruby-red

1929 GFairlie *Yellow* (B) 26: Lips as red as rubies. **1931** LRGribble *Grand* (L) 115: The ruby-red mouth. EAP R160; TW 313.

R157   I'm not **Rude**, I'm rich

1940 AGilbert *Dear Dead* (L) 168: The old north country saying, "I'm not rude, I'm rich." **1960** AGilbert *Out for* (NY 1965) 97: It's like that Yorkshire saying—I'm not rude, I'm rich.

R158   To pull the **Rug** out from under one

1952 JMFox *Shroud* (B) 62: Pull the rug out from under me. **1956** *BangorDN* 6/9 12: Mr. Eisenhower almost pulled the rug from under his whole foreign-aid program. **1957** JBlish *Frozen* (NY) 18: He's not going to pull the rug out from under us twice. **1965** ESGardner *Beautiful* (NY) 52: I didn't like to jerk the rug out from under you. **1970** JRoss *Deadest* (NY) 159: You pulled the rug out from under his feet. **1975** ABrodsky *Madame* (NY) 210: Gould had the rug pulled out from under him.

R159   To sweep (something) under the **Rug** (carpet) (*varied*)

1955 *New Yorker* 8/6 50: They adopted the familiar Western approach of sweeping things under the rug. **1960** WMasterson *Hammer* (NY DBC) 31: We're trying to sweep things under the rug. **1963** MPHood *Sin* (NY) 14: Pushed under the rug. **1967** DBloodworth *Chinese* (NY) 296: The Chinese are only too often ready to sweep the dust of reality under the carpet of appearance. **1969** PHighsmith *Tremor* (NY) 201: You can sweep it under the carpet. **1973** JPorter *It's Murder* (NY) 56: Sweeping things under the carpet. Cole 64: Sweep the dirt under the beds.

R160   It's a poor **Rule** that does not work both ways

1904 LFBaum *Marvelous Land of Oz* (NY) 129: They say it is a poor rule that don't work both ways. **1929** EHope *Alice* (NY) 265: It's a poor rule that doesn't work both ways. **1938** WNMacartney *Fifty Years* (NY) 93: It was a poor rule that did not work both ways. EAP R161.

R161   **Rules** are made to be broken

1953 ACClarke *Expedition* (NY) 54: Rules are made to be broken. **1954** MColes *Brief* (NY) 114: Rules are made to be broken sometimes. **1960** PJFarmer *Strange* (NY) 69: Rules aren't made to be broken. No captain would subscribe to that proverb. **1961** JBingham *Night's* (L 1965) 126: "Rules are made to be kept." And broken— as the saying is. **1970** PPullar *Consuming* (L) 80: Rules, they say, are made to be broken and the Forest Laws were no exception. Cf. Exceptions, Laws are made, Promise is *above*.

R162   **Rules** is rules

1953 JSanford *Land* (NY) 28: But like it says in the saying: Rules is rules. Cf. Business, Duty, Orders *above*.

R163   **Rule** of thumb

1925 JGBrandon *Cork* (L) 13: The Rule of Thumb methods. **1932** PMacDonald *Rope* (L) 254: A case . . . of the rule-of-thumb sort. **1940** GDHCole *Murder at* (NY) 5: His old, rule-of-thumb methods. **1956** WBrinkley *Don't Go* (NY) 132: I have a rule of thumb . . . "What they don't know won't hurt me." **1958** VCanning *Dragon* (NY) 18: Work to a rule of thumb. **1959** SBedford *Trial* (NY) 161: We have a working rule of thumb. **1961** JBingham *Night's* (L 1965) 94: His gay charm and rule-of-thumb medical knowledge. **1967** RBrett-Smith *Berlin* (NY) 8: Rule of thumb and common sense. **1971** ELathen *Longer* (NY) 180: Thatcher was skeptical of most rules of thumb. **1972**

SCloete *Victorian* (L) 54: By rule of thumb. EAP R162.

R164   As straight as a **Ruler**

1931 HHolt *Necklace* (NY) 265: It was straight as a ruler. **1944** RAJWalling *Corpse Without* (NY) 63: A road . . . straight as a ruler. **1967** RBrett-Smith *Berlin* (NY) 35: Autobahn . . . straight as a ruler. **1974** JMurphy *El Greco* (NY) 135: A ruler-straight, one-lane road. **1982** JLivingston *Piece* (NY) 157: She was straight as a ruler [*honest*]. TW 314.

R165   A good **Run** is better than a bad stand

1943 MVHeberden *Murder Goes* (NY) 119: 'Tis better to make a good run than a bad stand. **1968** FHerbert *Santaroga* (NY) 233: A good run is better than a bad stand. Whiting *NC* 469.

R166   To be a different (last) **Run** of shad

1950 FFGould *Maine Man* (NY) 68: One of them . . . was of "a different run of shad." **1953** OAtkinson *Golden* (I) 182: Looks like the last run of shad. Cf. Whiting *NC* 455: Last of pea-time.

R167   To get (give) a **Run** for one's money (*varied*)

1906 JLondon *Letters* ed KHendricks (NY 1965) 205: I would give him a run for his money. **1922** JJoyce *Ulysses* (NY 1934) 160: He got a run for his money. **1927** CSLewis *Letters* ed WHLewis (NY 1966) 113: He has . . . had a . . . run for his money. **1936** PA Taylor *Out of Order* (NY) 219: I'll give you a run for your money. **1937** GBarnett *I Knew* (L) 277: He's had a good run for his money. **1941** PWilde *Design* (NY) 42: I'm going to give the crowd their money's worth. **1952** CEVulliamy *Don* (L) 191: We shall have a good run for our money. **1956** AWilson *Anglo-Saxon* (L) 25: We'll give you a bit of a run for your money. **1957** CWilliams *Big Bite* (L) 126: Give her just as good a run for her money in the hay. **1960** TWilliams *Three Players* (L) 105: You had a good run for your money. **1963** BHecht *Gaily* (NY) 102: You gave me a good run for my money. **1970** STerkel *Hard* (NY) 123: They could give a congressman a pretty good run for his money. NED Run *sb.*[1] 1d; Partridge 716.

R168   He who **Runs** may read

1926 RAFreeman *Puzzle* (NY) 176: He who runs may read those characteristics. EAP R166; Brunvand 121.

R169   **Run-of-the-mill** (-mine)

1941 JShore *Rattle* (NY) 132: They all look run-of-the-mill to me. **1949** RMLaurenson *Six Bullets* (NY) 175: Run of the mill legal work. **1950** BSpicer *Blues* (NY) 90: She was run-of-the-mine, but might do for fill-ins. **1952** DBOlsen *Enrollment* (NY) 103: The run-of-the-mill faculty wives. **1960** JMc Govern *Berlin* (NY DBC) 38: A run-of-the-mill floozie. **1967** RBendiner *Just* (NY) 146: The run-of-the-mill Republicans. **1970** RRendell *Guilty* (NY) 191: A natural run-of-the-mill infidelity. Amer. Herit. Dict. Run-of-the-mill; Wentworth 438.

R170   As straight as a **Rush**

1923 DCScott *Witching* (Toronto) 40: As straight as a rush. EAP R167.

R171   Not worth a **Rush**

1931 LPowys in MElwin *Life* (L 1946) 205: Not worth a rush or a cherry stone. **1934** JRhode *Shot* (L) 204: The evidence . . . was not worth a rush. EAP R174.

R172   Scratch a **Russian** and find a Tartar (*varied*)

1927 CMackenzie *Vestal* (NY) 303: Scratch a Russian and you find a Tartar. **1929** JHawk *It Was Locked* (NY) 33: Scratch a poet and you find a Tartar. **1947** AGilbery *Death in* (L) 81: Scratch a bachelor and you'll find a rake. **1955** DGarnett *Flowers* (L) 172: Scratch a Russian and you find a Tartar. **1967** DBloodworth *Chinese* (NY) 390: You had only to scratch a Russian Communist to find a Tatar. EAP R176.

S

S1 A Sabbath day's journey
1938 MBurton *Death* (L) 29: It's a Sabbath's day journey from the Club House. NED Sabbath-day 1b.

S2 As limp as a Sack
1935 CStJSprigg *Death* (NY) 164: As limp as a sack. Clark 215: Of potatoes. Cf. As limp as a Dishrag, Rag *above*.

S3 To fall like a Sack
1973 BKnox *Storm* (NY) 154: He fell like an emptied sack. EAP S4.

S4 To get the Sack
1924 GThorne *Ravenscroft* (NY) 7: You got the sack. TW 315(1); Brunvand 122; *Oxford* 26: Bag.

S5 To hold (be left holding) the Sack
1934 CFGregg *Execution* (L) 189: Left holding the sack. **1941** ESGardner *Empty Tin* (NY 1958) 119: I let Paul . . . hold the sack. **1946** GHomes *Build* (NY) 44: He had been left holding the sack. **1958** GHCoxe *Impetuous* (NY) 123: Leave Eastman holding the sack. *Oxford* 27: Bag. Cf. To leave . . . Baby, To be left . . . Bag *above*.

S6 Like a Saddle on a sow
1977 RThomas *Yellow-Dog* (NY) 186: That sits with the city like a saddle on a sow. *Oxford* 757: Sow to bear.

S7 To put the Saddle on the wrong horse
1981 JRoss *Dark* (NY) 147: Hoping that Rogers wasn't putting the saddle on the wrong horse. EAP S6.

S8 Better be Safe (sensible) than sorry
1929 EWHowe *Plain* (NY) 219: Better be safe than sorry. **1932** MPlum *Murder* (NY) 7: Better be safe than sorry. **1934** ERPunshon *Information* (B) 8: Better safe than sorry is a good motto. **1940** CFGregg *Fatal Error* (L) 17: Better be safe than sorry. **1952** HCecil *No Bail* (NY) 73: Better be sensible than sorry. **1957** PGallico *Thomasina* (NY) 93: Better safe than sorry. **1964** JAiken *Silence* (NY) 152: Your English precept, "Better safe than sorry." **1968** GBagby *Another* (NY) 112: Better be safe than sorry. *Oxford* 51: Better be sure.

S9 Safe and sound
1910 JCLincoln *Depot Master* (NY) 160: Safe and sound. **1916** AEHousman *Letters* ed HMaas (Cambridge, Mass. 1971) 147: Safe and sound. **1931** LEppley *Murder* (NY) 3: Safe and sound. **1940** AMChase *No Outlet* (NY) 220: Safe and sound. **1950** JCannan *Murder* (L 1958) 132: Safe and sound. **1959** KMKnight *Beauty* (NY) 104: Safe and sound. **1962** RLockridge *First* (P) 21: Safe and sound. **1965** MMcShane *Girl* (NY) 162: I'm looking safe and sound. EAP S9; TW 315(1).

S10 Safety first
1924 EWallace *Green* (B) 312: Safety first. **1937** ESGardner *Dangerous Dowager* (NY) 103: After all, you know, safety first. **1938** CFGregg *Brazen* (L) 46: Safety first is a fairly good motto, being but the modern equivalent of the discretion-valour theory. *Oxford* 691.

S11 There is **Safety** (strength, comfort) in numbers (*varied*)

1928 JChancellor *Dark* (NY) 7: Safety in numbers, you know. **1930** TFMadigan *Word Shadows* (NY) xiii: There is strength in numbers. **1934** GEllinger *Return* (L) 136: There is safety in a crowd and danger in this solitude. **1934** RAJWalling *Legacy* (NY) 186: Strength in numbers. **1936** JMetcalfe *Sally* (NY) 436: Up to a point there was "safety in numbers." **1943** HAdams *Victory* (L) 96: They say there is safety in numbers. **1943** EDaly *Nothing Can Rescue* (NY 1963) 110: There is no safety in numbers. **1953** GHolden *Killer* (NY) 111: The safety of unexpected and overwhelming numbers. **1956** RStout *Eat* (NY) 106: There's comfort in numbers. **1957** *BangorDN* 5/18 14: The old, true saying "there is safety in numbers." **1968** DBagley *Vivero* (NY) 216: There was comfort in numbers. **1969** AGilbert *Missing* (NY) 119: There's safety in numbers, declares the old saw. **1970** DMDevine *Illegal* (NY) 165: Safety in numbers. **1977** EP Green *Rotten* (NY) 87: There's safety in numbers. *Oxford* 691.

S12 As yellow as **Saffron**

1936 HFootner *Kidnapping* (L) 213: His face turned as yellow as saffron. **1954** ASeton *Katherine* (B) 174: Fog looks yellow as saffron. EAP S11; Brunvand 122: Saffron bag.

S13 As dry as the **Sahara**

1934 GWLee *Beale* (NY) 103: Make Beale Street as dry as the Sahara [*no liquor*]. **1939** HWPriwen *Inspector* (L) 316: I'm as dry as the Sahara. **1954** EMarriner *Kennebec* (Waterville, Me.) 300: Maine's prohibitory law made Maine as dry as the Sahara. **1959** ESAarons *Assignment* (Greenwich, Conn.) 94: I'm as dry as the Sahara. TW 315(1).

S14 Easier **Said** than done

1928 JArnold *Surrey* (L) 228: Easier said than done. **1936** ECRLorac *Pall* (L) 125: Easier said than done. **1948** FWCrofts *Silence* (NY) 206: Easier said than done. **1959** SMorrow *Murder* (NY) 17: That's easier said than done. **1967** RVanGulik *Necklace* (NY) 64: It was easier said than done. **1974** GMcDonald *Fletch* (I) 16: Easier done than said. EAP S59; TW 319(2); Brunvand 124.

S15 To have one's **Sail** too big for his boat

1946 ECrispin *Holy Disorders* (NY) 148: His sail was too big for his boat. *Oxford* 692: Sail too big.

S16 To be (all) plain **Sailing**

1920 JSFletcher *Dead Men's* (NY) 54: We had plain sailing. **1932** FWCrofts *Sudden* (NY) 201: They're all plain sailing. **1937** JRhode *Proceed* (L) 77: All was plain sailing. **1941** GDHCole *Counterpoint* (NY) 132: It all seems pretty plain sailing. **1953** JRhode *Mysterious* (NY DBC) 28: That was all plain sailing. **1955** DMDisney *Trick* (NY) 110: It was all plain sailing. EAP S16.

S17 A **Sailor** has a wife in every port (*varied*)

1922 JJoyce *Ulysses* (NY 1934) 372: Wife in every port they say. **1935** GHDoran *Chronicles* (NY) 275: Like sailors with sweethearts in every port. **1938** CWells *Missing* (P) 127: Like the traditional sailor, Stone had a friend in every port. **1939** GDHCole *Greek* (L) 46: The wife-in-every-port category of mankind. **1942** SLeacock *My Remarkable* (Toronto 1965) 34: The Jolly Jack Tar is supposed to have "a wife in every port." **1950** HReilly *Murder* (NY) 32: Someone else's wife in every port. **1956** MInnes *Old Hall* (L) 126: A sailor, they say, may have a wife in every port. **1963** ADuggan *Elephants* (L) 253: Sailors might have a wife in every port. **1963** MMcCarthy *Group* (NY) 55: Like a sailor with a wife in every port. EAP S18.

S18 A **Sailor** on leave hires a boat

1930 RKing *Somewhere* (NY) 24: You know as well as I do that a sailor on leave hires a boat and goes rowing. Cf. Busman, Postman *above*.

S19 To swear like a **Sailor**

1935 CGGivens *Rose Petal* (I) 28: Swears like a sailor. **1950** MLong *Louisville* (NY) 241: Swearin' like a sailor. **1976** EMcBain *So Long* (NY) 24: Swearing like a sailor. TW 316(8).

S20 As patient as a **Saint**

1964 HBTaylor *Duplicate* (NY) 129: You've been as sweet and patient as a saint. Wilstach 288: Any Christian saint of old; Clark 217.

S21 Enough to try a **Saint** (*very varied*)

1904 JCLincoln *Cap'n Eri* (NY) 44: Enough to try a saint. **1930** JSFletcher *Investigators* (NY) 115: Enough to make a saint swear. **1930** VWMason *Seeds* (NY) 6: It's enough to drive a man to drink. **1931** DOgburn *Death* (B) 101: Enough to provoke the proverbial saint. **1934** GOrwell *Burmese* (NY) 40: Try the temper of a saint. **1934** WSharp *Murder* (NY) 202: Things that would try the patience of fifty saints. **1941** HReilly *Three Women* (NY) 112: That girl would try the patience of a saint. **1941** LThayer *Hallowe'en* (NY) 56: It was enough to infuriate a saint. **1948** FWCrofts *Silence* (NY) 88: You're enough to make a saint swear. **1958** JSStrange *Night* (NY) 87: You'd try the patience of a saint. **1959** RMacdonald *Galton* (NY) 95: That brother of his would drive a saint to drink. **1961** ZHenderson *Pilgrimage* (NY) 192: She'd drive the devil to drink. **1962** HEBates *Golden* (L) 43: Enough to make a saint swear. **1966** BKnox *Ghost* (NY) 157: My old mother would say this was enough to make a saint spin in his grave. **1976** JPorter *Package* (NY) 67: Con had the patience of a bloody saint, but enough was enough. EAP S22; *Oxford* 696. Cf. Minister *above.*

S22 To be a plaster (tin) **Saint**

1933 VMacClure *Crying Pig* (L) 43: I'm not setting up as a tin saint. **1940** AMuir *Sands* (L) 19: You thought me a plaster saint. **1941** EXFerrars *Murder of a Suicide* (NY) 157: I don't mean . . . you ought to behave like a plaster saint. **1960** FLockridge *Judge* (P) 114: John was no plaster saint. Berrey 421.4, 437.10: Plaster.

S23 Young **Saint**, old devil

1936 VMcHugh *Caleb* (NY) 184: Young saint, old devil. EAP S23.

S24 To ride **Saint George**

1932 Anonymous *Hot-cha* (L) 92: There's nothing like riding St. George. Partridge 697: Riding.

S25 **Saint Valentine's** day (*varied*)

1939 MBurton *Death Leaves* (L) 149: Arnold remembered the saying that one should be able to see a grey goose at a furlong at six in the evening on St. Valentine's day. **1970** SGBoswell *Book* (L) 156: Fourteenth of February is coupling day for the birds and it was my father's day and it's my day. EAP S29.

S26 As cold as **Salt**

1951 DSDavis *Gentle* (NY 1959) 124: A face as cold as salt. Wilstach 62.

S27 As white as **Salt**

1932 DFrome *Man* (NY) 18: [He] turned as white as salt. Wilstach 470.

S28 Help one to **Salt**, help him to sorrow

1969 SMays *Reuben's* (L) 163: Help you to salt, help you to sorrow. Whiting *NC* 470(2).

S29 To be the **Salt** of the earth

1900 CFPidgin *Quincy A. Sawyer* (B) 580: He considered her to be the "salt of the earth." **1922** JJoyce *Ulysses* (NY 1934) 449: The salt of the earth. **1923** EWallace *Clue* (B) 260: The salt of the earth. **1933** GBegbie *Sudden* (L) 93: The Salt of the Earth. **1940** CWorth *Trail* (NY) 51: Worthy people, salt of the earth. **1947** FCrane *Murder on* (NY) 174: He's the salt of the earth. **1953** SBellow *Adventures* (NY) 432: Salt of the earth. **1957** *NYTimes Book Review* 11/17 3: "The salt of the earth" . . . an awesome cliché. **1961** EWilliams *George* (NY) 294: You are the salt of the earth, but it is salt for me which will never have any savor. **1968** MGibbon *Inglorious* (L) 282: The salt of the social earth. **1975** PMoyes *Black* (NY) 69: The salt of the earth. **1975** MVonnegut *Eden* (NY) 116: Salt-of-the-earth common sense. EAP S31; TW 316(2).

S30 To be (not) worth one's **Salt**

1906 JCLincoln *Mr. Pratt* (NY) 194: She was worth her salt. **1910** JCLincoln *Depot Master* (NY) 309: [Not] worth his salt. **1919** JBCabell *Jurgen* (NY 1922) 276: Made him worth his salt. **1920** GBMcCutcheon *Anderson Crow* (NY) 323: Worth your salt. **1922** JJoyce *Ulysses* (NY 1934) 176: You're worth your salt. **1932** JSFletcher *Man in the Fur Coat* (L)

103: No man's worth his salt who doesn't work. **1937** CBClason *Purple* (NY) 102: You wouldn't be worth your salt. **1941** MPRea *Compare* (NY) 27: I'm not worth my salt today. **1956** *NYHerald Tribune Book Review* 7/22 3: Any poet worth his salt would subscribe to this. **1959** *BHerald* 8/1 6: Any serviceman worth his salt. **1970** MJArlen *Exiles* (NY) 68: No novelist worth his salt. **1971** MHarrison *Fanfare* (L) 64: No French whore worth her salt. EAP S32; Brunvand 122.

S31 To earn one's **Salt**

1936 CGGivens *Jig-Time* (I) 186: I don't suppose they earned their salt. **1941** EL Fetta *Dressed* (NY) 221: To earn her salt. **1960** CErwin *Orderly* (NY) 207: She's not earning her salt. **1968** JGrant *Ross* (NY) 110: At least earning his salt. EAP S33.

S32 To eat someone's **Salt**

1928 AGilbert *Mrs. Davenport* (NY) 191: A man should eat another man's salt. **1934** CFGregg *Execution* (L) 144: I have eaten his salt. **1934** JSStrange *Chinese Jar* (L) 166: A man who would be loyal to his salt. **1936** VLoder *Deaf-Mute* (L) 206: Can't eat their salt any more, and think of putting salt on his tail afterwards. **1936** GHeyer *Behold* (NY) 214: I have eaten your salt . . . so I can't say what I should like to. **1940** AMuir *Sands* (L) 142: I don't feel too good about helping to pull him in while he's eating my salt. NED Salt *sb.*[1] 2b. Cf. *Oxford* 40: Before.

S33 To put **Salt** on a bird's tail (*varied*)

1927 BAtkey *Man* (NY) 33: Money's like a bird. If you're going to drop a pinch of salt on its rudder, you want to be lively about it. **1929** LBrock *Stoke Silver* (NY) 20: You must be very agile in putting salt on this bird's tail. **1929** AGilbert *Death* (NY) 80: We got near enough to put salt on his tail [*a thief*]. **1931** ENWright *Strange* (Cleveland) 24: Now that we have put salt on our bird's tail. **1932** RAFreeman *When Rogues* (L) 229: He'll want a bit of salt sprinkled on his tail before he'll get caught. **1939** EMarsh *Number* (NY) 364: My . . . failure to put salt on the tail of Opportunity. **1940** RAHeinlein *Puppet* (NY 1965) 177: The old saw about

how to catch a bird: it's no trouble if you can sneak up close enough to put salt on its tail. **1950** ECBentley *Chill* (NY) 77: The enemy have been trying to put salt on your tail again. **1961** GGFickling *Blood* (NY) 69: [She] could wind up with salt on her tail. **1963** CMackenzie *Octave One* (L) 145: My old nurse had told me that one could always catch birds by putting salt on their tails. EAP S36; TW 316–7(9).

S34 To rub **Salt** in the wound

1940 JSStrange *Picture* (NY) 18: This was rubbing salt in the wound. **1961** EPeters *Death* (NY) 67: Rubbing salt into the wounds. **1964** JPhilips *Laughter* (NY DBC) 8: Rubbing salt in old wounds. Taylor *Prov. Comp.* 70.

S35 To sit below the **Salt**

1928 AGilbert *Mrs. Davenport* (NY) 137: To sit below the salt. **1964** DForbes-Robertson *My Aunt* (NY) 172: I may sit below the salt. TW 316(1); *Oxford* 697.

S36 Back to the **Salt mines**

1955 WSloane *Stories* (L) 281: Well, back to the salt mines. **1958** PBranch *Murder's* (L 1963) 213: Back to the salt mines. **1960** IWallace *Chapman* (NY 1961) 286: Back to the salt mines. **1965** SRansome *Alias* (NY DBC) 28: Get back to the old salt mine. **1968** DFGalouye *Scourge* (NY) 127: It's back to the mines for me. **1975** MErskine *Harriet* (NY) 155: It's back to the salt mines for me. Wentworth 441.

S37 To go up **Salt River**

1952 DWecter *Sam Clemens* (B) 47: The Missouri phrases to "go up Salt River," or be "rowed up Salt River" signified defeat and banishment into the ultimate back water. EAP S37; TW 317; Brunvand 122–3.

S38 As safe as **Sam's** hog

1949 HLDavis *Beulah* (NY) 46: That river's as safe as Sam's hog this time of year. Cf. Apperson 549: Sam Babb's pig.

S39 **Sam Hill**

1926 CWTyler *Blue Jean* (NY) 239: What in the name of Sam Hill is the matter? **1930** ANewell *Who Killed* (NY) 187: What in Sam

Hill do you want? Brunvand 123; DA Sam 2. Cf. EAP S39.

S40 San Quentin quail

1954 JRMacdonald *Find* (NY) 60: She was Quentin quail, a fugitive from the sixth grade. **1963** SForbes *Grieve* (NY) 127: San Quentin quail. Wentworth 442.

S41 As dry as Sand

1946 JDCarr *He Who Whispers* (NY) 45: My throat is as dry as sand. Wilstach 105. Cf. TW 317(1).

S42 As (many as) the Sands on the seashore

1928 HAdams *Empty* (P) 16: My love affairs were as the sands on the seashore. EAP S43.

S43 To plow the Sands (waves)

1925 JSFletcher *False* (NY) 210: Ploughing the sands. **1935** BFlynn *Case* (L) 107: Buckinger hated to plough [the] sands. **1937** JFerguson *Death* (L) 14: Leaving no stone unturned, and ploughing the sands. **1959** WHMurray *Appointment* (NY) 34: We were ploughing waves to grow corn. *Oxford* 635.

S44 To treat someone like Sand in one's shoes

1950 RPowell *Shark* (NY) 196: And now you treat him like sand in your shoes. Cf. Partridge 940: Water. Cf. To treat someone like Dirt *above*.

S45 As happy (lively) as a Sandboy

1914 MAdams *In the Footsteps* (L) 18: As happy as a sandboy. **1932** WLHay *Who Cut* (L) 58: Happy as a sand-boy. **1933** JCLenehan *Death* (L) 28: Happy as a sandboy. **1934** WGore *There's Death* (L) 263: He was as lively as a sandboy. **1952** AWilson *Hemlock* (L) 122: She's as happy as a sandgirl. **1959** GAshe *Pack* (NY) 143: Happy as the proverbial sandboy. **1964** RBlythe *Age* (B) 34: He looked as happy as a sandboy. **1969** JMPatterson *Doubly* (NY) 36: As happy as two sandboys at low tide. NED Sand-boy 1; Partridge 726; Taylor *Western Folklore* 17(1958) 18 [*full discussion*].

S46 To work like a Sand hog

1959 *Time* 3/9 38: He also works like a sand hog. See DA Sand 2b(5) (quote 1904).

S47 As blue as Sapphires

1957 THWhite *Master* (L) 46: Eyes, as blue as sapphires. Taylor *Prov. Comp.* 70: Eyes like sapphires.

S48 To be packed like Sardines (*varied*)

1909 MRRinehart *Man in Lower Ten* (NY 1947) 333: Fastened up like sardines in a can. **1928** SHuddleston *Paris Salons* (NY) 102: We were squeezed together like the proverbial sardines. **1932** ORCohen *Star* (NY) 2: The crowd had hoped to pack itself like sardines. **1935** JSFletcher *Eleventh* (NY) 6: They're packed like sardines in a box. **1939** EMarsh *Number* (NY) 160: Crocodiles . . . as thick as sardines in a tin. **1939** HMiller *Capricorn* (NY 1961) 222: We're wedged in like sardines. **1940** GCKlingel *Anagua* (NY) 287: The tang [*a kind of fish*] were packed like the proverbial sardines. **1948** NMailer *Naked* (NY) 52: They had us packed in like sardines. **1951** WCWilliams *Autobiography* (NY) 212: We were packed like sardines into the small place. **1957** GDurrell *My Family* (NY) 72: Crammed together like sardines. **1965** HMiller *Quiet Days* (NY) 81: We were soon packed like sardines. **1966** SCRoberts *Adventures* (Cambridge, Eng.) 40: Into which we were jammed like sardines. **1976** JPorter *Package* (NY) 17: Packed like sardines in a tin. TW 318. Cf. Herring *above*.

S49 Satan rebukes sin

1936 HWade *Bury Him* (L) 321: It was not far from a case of Satan rebuking sin. **1936** RCWoodthorpe *Silence* (L) 111: Slade smiled at Satan rebuking sin. EAP S48.

S50 As smooth as Satin; Satin-smooth

1936 KCStrahan *Desert* (I) 85: He'd finished his plate off smooth as satin. **1939** WChambers *You Can't* (NY) 105: The satin-smooth surface of the water. **1954** HGardiner *Murder* (L) 29: Simon's voice was smooth as satin. **1964** DCecil *Max* (L) 10: Hair smooth as satin. EAP S49.

S51 Saturday's flitting and a short sitting

1957 HPBeck *Folklore of Maine* (P) 79: Saturday's flitting meant a short sitting. *Oxford* 699.

S52 A **Saturday** moon and a Saturday change *etc.*

1968 KMartin *Editor* (L) 119: You know the old saying: "A Saturday moon and a Saturday change, Never comes out but that it rains." Dunwoody 63.

S53 **Saturday** night dreamt *etc.*

1957 LBeam *Maine* (NY) 195: Saturday night dreamt, Sunday morning told, Sure to come to pass, Before the week's old. Hand in FCBrown *Collection* 6.409–10: 3139, 3140, 3142, 3143: Friday.

S54 **Sauce** for the goose is sauce for the gander (*varied*)

1922 JJoyce *Ulysses* (NY 1934) 275: Women. Sauce for the gander. 530: Sauce for the goose, my gander. **1925** HBedford-Jones *Rodomont* (NY) 117: Sauce for the gander is sauce for the goose. **1930** WLewis *Apes* (NY 1932) 308: What is sauce for the goose is sauce for the gander. **1931** HReilly *Painted Head* (NY) 145: But then, you know, what's sauce for the gander—. **1932** MKennedy *Murderer* (L) 103: What was sauce for her was by no means sauce for the colonel. **1933** TThayer *American* (NY) 17: It seemed a little thing to invert an adage and upon learning what sauce for the gander was—sauced herself, the little goose. **1939** CSaxby *Death Cuts* (NY) 171: But a gander at that needs a lot of sauce. **1951** ELustgarten *Defenders* (NY) 72: The traditional tag concerning sauce for the goose. **1958** *BangorDN* 7/26 11: An old saw: "What's sauce for the goose is sauce for the gander." **1959** *BHerald* 4/11 4: An old New England adage "What's good for the goose is good for the gander." **1959** RMartin *Key* (NY DBC) 61: It was sauce for the goose stuff. **1960** BWilliams *Border-line* (NY DBC) 63: He was playing around with Carlota . . . a goose and the gander sort of thing. **1970** RRendell *Best Man* (NY) 100: What was sauce for the gander was sauce for the goose. **1970** JVizzard *See* (NY) 350: What is sauce for the censors is sauce for the ganderers. **1971** HVanDyke *Dead* (NY) 154: What's good for the gander is good for the goose. **1972** ELathen *Murder* (NY) 215: Sauce for the gander did not sit well with her. **1974** HCarmichael *Most* (NY)

23: An old saying that what's sauce for the goose is sauce for the gander. **1981** PDe Vries *Sauce for the Goose* (B). EAP S53; Brunvand 123. Cf. Brunvand 51: Fish(1).

S55 As big as **Saucers**

1926 MRRinehart *Bat* (NY 1959) 97: Her eyes as big as saucers. **1940** CBDawson *Lady Wept* (NY) 145: Eyes as big as saucers. **1940** CLittle *Black Corridors* (NY) 266: Her eyes as big as saucers. **1953** MPHood *Silent* (NY) 65: His eyes big as saucers. **1954** HWaugh *Rag* (NY) 145: Her eyes were as big as saucers. **1960** DHolman-Hunt *My Grandmothers* (L) 201: Your eyes are as big as saucers. EAP S54; Brunvand 123. Cf. As big as a Dollar *above*.

S56 As large as **Saucers**

1932 PMcGuire *Three* (NY) 312: His eyes as large as saucers. **1938** AWUpfield *Bone* (L 1966) 202: His eyes became as large as saucers. Taylor *Western Folklore* 17(1958) 18.

S57 As round as **Saucers**; Saucer-round

1931 GCollins *Phantom* (L) 269: Whose eyes were round as saucers. **1941** GBagby *Red Is* (NY) 115: Delia's eyes were saucer-round. **1947** NMarsh *Final* (B) 42: Her eyes were as round as saucers. Cf. Taylor *Prov. Comp.* 70: Eyes like saucers.

S58 As wide as **Saucers**

1969 HPentecost *Girl with* (NY) 107: [His] eyes were wide as saucers. **1972** NMarsh *Tied* (B) 256: The Colonel opened his eyes as wide as saucers.

S59 Is **Saul** also among the prophets? (*varied*)

1928 RGore-Browne *In Search* (NY) 109: Is Saul also among the cynics? **1936** NBlake *Thou Shell of* (L) 118: So Saul also is among the sleuths. **1940** AGilbert *Dear Dead* (L) 110: Saul among the prophets. **1961** JDCarr *Witch* (L) 230: Is Saul also among the prophets? **1962** HMirrlees *Fly* (L) 295: Saul among the prophets. **1970** CDBowen *Family* (B) 114: Saul among the prophets! EAP S55.

S60 Let's not and **Say** we did

1940 EQueen *New Adventures* (NY) 147: Let's not and say we did. **1953** SBellow *Adventures* (NY) 149: Let's not and say we did. **1968** JUpdike *Couples* (NY 1969) 120: Let's not and say we did. Berrey 227.2.

S61 No sooner **Said** than done

1933 MAllingham *Sweet* (L 1950) 18: The thing is no sooner said than done. **1950** DAWollheim *Flight* (NY) 215: No sooner said than done. **1962** EGrierson *Massingham* (L) 19: No sooner said than done. EAP S60.

S62 Though I **Say** it that should not (*varied*)

1911 JCLincoln *Woman-Haters* (NY) 20: If you'll excuse my sayin' so that shouldn't. **1919** JSFletcher *Middle Temple* (NY) 168: Though I say it as shouldn't, as the saying is. **1931** ABCox *Second* (NY) 246: Though I say it as shouldn't. **1935** LThayer *Dead* (NY) 109: If I say it as hadn't ought to. **1942** ABMaurice *Riddle* (NY) 137: Though I say it that shouldn't. **1955** BCarey *Fatal* (NY) 18: If I do say so as shouldn't. **1967** NWollaston *Jupiter* (L) 117: It was my own idea, though I say it as shouldn't. **1968** RVanGulik *Poets* (NY) 6: A nice programme, though I say it myself. EAP S62.

S63 What is **Said** is not easily unsaid

1933 NBrady *Fair Murder* (L) 188: What's said isn't easy unsaid. TW 319(5). Cf. What is Done *above*.

S64 As quick as **Scat**

1900 CFPidgin *Quincy A. Sawyer* (B) 342: Quicker'n scat. **1927** WBFoster *From Six* (NY) 152: He got out quick's scat. **1933** ISCobb *Murder* (I) 228: Quicker'n scat. **1972** JGores *Dead* (NY) 77: Quick as scat. TW 319.

S65 Before one can say **Scat**

1933 WMarch *Company K* (NY) 45: Before you could say scat. **1941** HLMencken *Newspaper Days, 1899–1906* (NY) 232: Before I could say "scat." **1957** MPHood *In the Dark* (NY) 145: Before you could say scat. Whiting *NC* 471.

S66 Not to care whether **School** keeps or not (*varied*)

1913 JCLincoln *Mr. Pratt's Patients* (NY) 6: Before I cared whether school kept or not. **1920** ACrabb *Samuel* (NY) 72: Didn't care whether school kept or not. **1936** CMRussell *Death* (NY) 133: Lookin' like he didn't care whether school kept or not. **1938** MTeagle *Murders* (NY) 165: Tight enough not to care whether school kept or not. **1951** DWMeredith *Christmas* (NY) 196: She . . . didn't care if school kept, just wanted to drink and drink. **1952** EPaul *Black* (NY) 258: School could keep or not, into every life some rain must fall, so what? **1956** RAHeinlein *Double* (NY 1957) 105: They don't give a damn whether school keeps or not. **1965** DoctorX *Intern* (NY) 53: I didn't give a damn whether school kept or not. TW 320.

S67 A **Scotch** mist

1945 BKendrick *Death Knell* (NY) 175: The drizzle had turned to a fine Scotch mist. **1952** JDCarr *Nine Wrong* (NY) 261: What is called a Scotch mist, which merely soaks you through without the striking of one honest raindrop. **1958** AMacKinnon *Summons* (NY) 18: No "Scotch mist" . . . but rain of savage intensity. EAP S70.

S68 A **Scotch** warming pan

1952 CDickson *Behind* (NY) 17: He thought my "secretary" meant my Scotch warming pan. Partridge 734.

S69 Not care a **Scrap**

1937 JBentley *Whitney* (L) 255: I didn't care a scrap. **1967** JDCarr *Dark* (NY) 182: You don't really care a scrap. Cf. NED Scrap *sb.*[1] 2.

S70 Not matter (mind) a **Scrap**

1929 GMitchell *Speedy* (NY) 111: It really doesn't matter a scrap. **1932** FIles *Before* (NY 1958) 139: I wouldn't have minded a scrap. **1945** MAlan *Dark Prophecy* (NY) 77: It doesn't matter a scrap.

S71 To be up to **Scratch** (*varied*)

1922 JJoyce *Ulysses* (NY 1934) 635: The husband not being up to the scratch. **1928** JArnold *Surrey* (L) 311: Monty's come up to the scratch at last. **1928** MThynne *Draycott* (NY) 300: Come up to the scratch. **1934** GMitchell *Death* (L) 57: He always comes up to scratch. **1935** MMPropper *Family Burial* (L) 236: She wasn't up to scratch. **1939** FLGreen *On the Night* (L) 74: I have to be up to scratch [*in good physical condition*]. **1958** MHastings *Cork* (NY) 60: The old phrase . . . "up to scratch." EAP S75.

S72 To start from **Scratch** (*varied*)

1937 JDCarr *Four False* (NY) 174: We can begin at scratch. **1939** CRawson *Footprints* (L) 94: We'll start from scratch. **1948** TKyd *Blood* (P) 177: I'm starting from scratch. **1956** WTenn *Of All* (L) 62: You have to start right from scratch. **1959** AGilbert *Death* (NY) 171: It's always best to start from scratch. **1971** JCreasey *Murder* (NY) 38: We both start from scratch. Amer. Herit. Dict. Scratch *n.* 8; Cole 63.

S73 To have a **Screw** (hinge) loose

1929 ORCohen *May Day* (NY) 66: Max is entitled to have a screw loose. **1930** WLewis *Apes* (NY 1932) 215: He . . . has a screw loose. **1937** JDCarr *To Wake* (L) 165: Someone . . . who's got a hinge loose. **1937** PWentworth *Case Is Closed* (L) 27: He'd got a screw loose. **1945** ACampbell *With Bated* (NY) 120: Aggie had a screw loose. **1950** RStout *In the Best* (NY) 85: He's got a screw loose. **1958** AChristie *Ordeal* (NY DBC) 90: Having a screw loose. **1975** RStout *Family* (NY) 101: He really had a screw loose. TW 320(1); *Oxford* 706.

S74 To put the **Screws** on someone

1940 JPPhilips *Murder in Marble* (NY) 13: Putting the screws on Palmer. **1958** *NYTimes* 5/11 20: They put the screws on the people again. TW 320(2).

S75 To drag in by the **Scruff** of the neck

1933 CBush *April Fools* (L) 108: Introduced it? . . . He dragged it in by the scruff of the neck. Cf. Cole 49: By the ears. Cf. To lug in by the Ears *above*.

S76 Between **Scylla** and Charybdis (*varied*)

1930 ABCox *Piccadilly* (NY) 267: Those were the Scylla and Charybdis of the new problem. **1931** JHRYardley *Before the May-flower* (NY) 171: The barque of Colonial policy drifted perilously 'twixt Scylla and Charybdis. **1937** ECVivian *Tramp's* (L) 16: Scylla and Charybdis, devil and deep sea. **1941** MHolbrook *Suitable* (NY) 92: I saw Scylla looming on one side of me and Charybdis on the other. **1946** ECrispin *Moving* (L 1970) 83: Scylla and Charbydis [*sic*] are still after us. **1951** ADean *August* (NY) 160: It's like being between Scylla and Charybdis. **1955** WTenn *Of All* (NY) 3: The group that plays Scylla to the litterateur's Charybdis. **1957** CESellers *Polk* (Princeton) 279: To navigate the hazardous course between Scylla and Charybdis. **1962** HMirrlees *Fly* (L) 153: The true *via media* between the Scylla of progress and the Charybdis of regression. **1967** AMontagu *Anatomy* (NY) 279: To steer the swearer clear of the Scylla of profanity and the Charybdis of vulgarity. **1969** LWoolf *Journey* (L) 126: The Scylla of the takeover or the Charybdis of bankruptcy. **1970** JVizzard *See* (NY) 349: The Scylla and Charybdis of democracy. **1971** RMStern *Murder* (NY) 134: Who ever invented the myth of Scylla and Charybdis must have been in politics. EAP S78; TW 320–1.

S77 As deep as the **Sea**

1929 EJMillward *Copper* (NY) 192: Deep as the sea, is Sawny. **1935** RTrevor *Death* (L) 45: As deep as the sea [*a girl*]. **1956** BJFarmer *Death* (L) 170: Deep as the sea. TW 321(3).

S78 As wide as the **Sea**

1926 CJDutton *Flying* (NY) 48: A heart as wide as the sea. EAP S81.

S79 The **Sea** refuses no river

1969 RNye *Tales* (L) 124: The sea refuses no river. *Oxford* 707.

S80 To be at **Sea** (*varied*)

1919 MScott *Behind Red Curtains* (NY) 235: Gray is hopelessly at sea. **1922** JJoyce *Ulysses* (NY 1934) 335: Letting on to be all at sea. 607: Bloom was all at sea. **1930** EQueen *French* (NY) 189: I know you're at sea. **1938** LRGribble *Tragedy* (L) 253: Feeling very much at sea. **1953** EReed *Maras* (NY) 75: He's quite at sea over it. **1969** AGilbert *Miss-*

ing (NY) 47: He's all at sea. TW 321(7); Brunvand 124(2).

S81 Seagull, seagull, sit on the sand *etc.*

1980 EDodge *Morning* (Chester, Conn.) 195: [It] brings to mind an old [*Maine*] sailor's proverb: "Seagull, seagull, sit on the sand, it's always fair weather when you're on the land." Cf. Dunwoody 40.

S82 A Sea-lawyer

1930 CRawson *Headless* (NY) 215: A sea lawyer, eh? **1932** MKennedy *Murderer* (L) 80: A bit of a sea-lawyer. **1947** NBlake *Minute* (L) 97: He's a sea-lawyer. **1949** MBurton *Disappearing* (NY) 189: The skipper was . . . something of a sea-lawyer. **1959** RVickers *Girl* (NY DBC) 86: A pair o' sea lawyers. **1968** SCHutchison *History* (NY) 153: The whole amounted to no more than the rantings of a sea-lawyer. TW 321.

S83 As fat as a Seal

1940 JJConnington *Four Defences* (B) 142: As fat as a seal. EAP S88; TW 321(1).

S84 To come apart at the Seams (*varied*)

1936 SFowler *Hand in Print* (L) 29: Do I look a bit worn at the seams? **1950** SPalmer *Green* (NY) 53: He seemed to be coming a little apart at the seams. **1958** PGWodehouse *Cocktail* (L) 119: You appear to be coming apart at the seams somewhat. **1961** JPhilips *Murder* (NY DBC) 57: She comes apart at the seams. Wentworth 116: Come.

S85 There are Seasons in all things

1968 MKJoseph *Hole* (NY) 174: All things have their seasons. EAP S91.

S86 To be on the anxious Seat

1919 LThayer *Mystery of the 13th Floor* (NY) 134: I kept him on the anxious seat. **1930** WWoodrow *Moonhill* (NY) 169: Squirming on the anxious seat. **1941** ESGardner *Turning Tide* (NY) 107: Keep us in the anxious seat. DARE i 72: Anxious bench.

S87 A Secret shared is no secret (*varied*)

1926 AMerritt *Ship* (NY) 94: A secret shared by two runs risk of being known. **1929** APryde *Secret* (NY) 75: The broad and safe principle that a secret shared is no secret. **1934** CRushton *Another Crime* (L) 217:

As someone once said, a secret's no secret if you share it. Cf. Wilstach 338. Cf. Two can keep *below*.

S88 Once Seen is better than a hundred times heard

1947 HCahill *Look* (NY) 78: Once seen is better than a hundred times heard. Cf. TW 322(2, 3). Cf. Seeing *below*.

S89 Once Seen never forgotten

1936 DHume *Meet the Dragon* (L) 231: Once seen never forgotten. **1937** RPenny *Policeman's Holiday* (L) 187: Not easily to be forgotten, once seen. **1964** JPorter *Dover One* (NY 1966) 8: Once seen never forgotten. **1966** LPDavies *Paper* (NY) 102: Once seen never forgot.

S90 To see or to be Seen

1940 RKing *Holiday* (NY) 197: She had neither time to see nor to be seen. EAP S96.

S91 We shall See what we shall see

1929 WScott *Mask* (P) 163: We'll see what we'll see. **1931** PWynnton *Ten* (P) 196: We shall see what we shall see. TW 321(2); *Oxford* 710.

S92 Seeing is believing (*varied*)

1924 AChristie *Man* (NY) 246: Seeing is believing. **1924** AOFriel *Mountains* (NY) 156: They were seeing, and so, in part, believing. **1933** RAJWalling *Behind* (L) 6: Seeing is believing, says the most fallacious of all proverbs. It should be reversed. Believing is seeing. **1935** JSFletcher *Carrismore* (L) 190: Seeing is believing, so they say. **1938** ECRLorac *Slippery* (L) 231: Seeing's believing, as the old saw has it. **1939** CSaxby *Death Cuts* (NY) 154: Smelling's believing. **1944** FLockridge *Killing* (P) 63: Seeing's believing. **1948** MColes *Among* (NY) 22: Seein's believin', ain't it? **1951** RJHealey *New Tales* (NY) 185: Seeing is believing but feeling is knowing. **1956** *New Yorker* 9/22 45: Seeing is deceiving. It's eating that's believing. **1957** BVanorden *309 East* (NY) 20: [His] favorite adage was "seeing is believing." **1961** HReilly *Certain* (NY DBC) 107: People say seeing is believing. **1966** LNizer *Jury* (NY) 349: The old saying, seeing is believing. **1967** DBloodworth *Chinese* (NY)

165: The . . . Chinese know that believing is seeing. TW 321–2(1); *Oxford* 710. Cf. To Believe, Once Seen *above*.

S93 He that **Seeks**, finds

1966 ESConnell *Diary* (NY) 6: He that seeketh, findeth. EAP S98.

S94 **Self-praise** is no recommendation (*varied*)

1922 JSFletcher *Ravensdene* (NY) 149: Self-praise, they say, is no recommendation, though to be sure I'm no believer in the old proverb. **1940** ECBentley *Those Days* (L) 144: It has been wisely said, Self Prays is no Recommendation. **1943** FScully *Rogues* (Hollywood) 210: They say self praise stinks. **1966** NMarsh *Killer* (B) 55: Self praise, no recommendation's what they say. EAP P272.

S95 **Self-preservation** is the first law of nature (*varied*)

1929 EWallace *Ringer* (NY) 238: The first law of nature urged him to safety. **1930** TCobb *Crime* (L) 181: Self-preservation is supposed to be the first law of nature. **1938** EHeath *Death Takes* (NY) 240: Self-preservation is a primary law of nature. **1941** EL Fetta *Dressed* (NY) 265: The first law of man is self-preservation and all that. **1941** KMKnight *Exit a Star* (NY) 181: Self-preservation is the first instinct of sane man. **1947** LFord *Woman* (NY) 239: Self-preservation is the first law of nature. **1955** SNGhose *Flame* (L) 67: Self-preservation, they say, is a man's first duty. **1962** HCarmichael *Of Unsound* (NY) 35: Self-preservation is a natural instinct. **1962** CDSimak *All the Traps* (NY) 31: There is just one law for you—self-preservation. **1970** MGrant *Ancient* (NY) 251: Self-preservation is a natural instinct. **1972** JMcClure *Caterpillar* (NY) 213: Since when has guilt been stronger than self-preservation? **1975** PDJames *Black* (NY) 225: Self-preservation is the first law of nature. EAP S99.

S96 To be **Sent** for and didn't come

1968 EBuckler *Ox Bells* (NY) 162: Somethin' that was sent for and couldn't come. TW 322.

S97 (Not) To have the **Sense** that God gave geese (little fishes)

1941 ESHolding *Speak* (NY) 243: If I have the sense that God gave geese. **1959** KMKnight *Beauty* (NY) 169: He ain't got the common sense God gave to little fishes. Taylor *Prov. Comp.* 71: Goose.

S98 Where there is no **Sense** there is no feeling

1939 EMarsh *Number* (NY) 266: A proverb he had learned from his nurse: "Where there's no sense, there's no feeling." **1949** EQueen *Cat* (B) 195: Where there's no sense there's no feeling. **1967** RFenisong *Villainous* (NY) 123: Where there's no sense there's no feeling. Cf. EAP S101; Tilley S281 [*for form*]: Where no shame is there is no fear.

S99 As fleet as a **Shadow**

1969 EStewart *Heads* (NY) 54: A figure . . . moving . . . fleet as a shadow. EAP S109: Fleeting; Wilstach 146.

S100 As silent as a **Shadow**

1923 JSFletcher *Lost Mr. Linthwaite* (NY) 213: Silent as a shadow. **1954** KMKnight *High* (NY) 164: As silent as a shadow, she slipped around the corner. **1964** SGelder *Timely* (L) 47: Silent as a shadow. Wilstach 353(2); Clark 220.

S101 Follow a **Shadow** etc.

1966 EXFerrars *No Peace* (NY) 119: Follow a shadow, it still flies you. Seem to fly it, it will pursue. *Oxford* 272: Love, etc.

S102 To be afraid of one's own **Shadow** (*varied*)

1927 SHorler *Black* (L 1935) 125: The man would be afraid of his own shadow. **1932** PMcGuire *Three* (NY) 99: Nearly fright'n'd of his own shadder. **1940** TChanslor *Our First* (NY) 301: He was scared of his shadow. **1940** CBDawson *Lady Wept* (NY) 116: Probably running from her own shadow. **1949** MBurton *Disappearing* (NY) 70: Afraid of their own shadows in the moonlight. **1950** RFoley *Hundredth* (NY) 219: I'm getting afraid of my shadow. **1959** SFarrar *Snake* (NY) 136: A man who's scared of his own shadow. **1962** DMDisney *Should Auld* (NY)

99: Running from his own shadow. **1963** TCaldwell *Late Clara* (NY) 3: You think I'm jumping at shadows. **1966** MGEberhart *Witness* (NY) 18: Perhaps he was not afraid of his own shadow, but he was afraid of everything else. **1977** PMoyes *Coconut* (NY) 41: Fraid of their own shadows. EAP S110.

S103   To catch at the **Shadow** *etc.* (*varied*)

1919 LMerrick *Chair* (L) 186: She had thrown away the substance for the shadow. **1932** CDawes *Lawless* (L) 166: Pursuing the shadow and ignoring the substance. **1935** FBeeding *Death* (NY) 72: Like the dog in the fable, you preferred to drop the bone to snap at the shadow. **1938** DBowers *Postscript* (L) 88: You may be mistaking shadow for substance. **1950** MCarleton *Bride* (NY) 4: Snatch at the shadow, lose the substance . . . He was a great one for adages. There again you save time. Much of your thinking has been done for you. **1972** PDJames *Unsuitable* (NY) 143: He exchanged the substance for the shadow and now he has neither. **1975** DRussell *Tamarisk* (NY) 256: A sacrifice of real living for the shadow of legality. EAP S111.

S104   To fight **Shadows**

1969 RLockridge *Risky* (P) 42: You can't fight shadows. EAP S114.

S105   To follow like a **Shadow**

1933 VMacClure *Crying Pig* (L) 119: He used to follow her about like a shadow. **1939** TScudder *J.W.Carlyle* (NY) 330: He followed her like a shadow. **1960** STruss *One Man's* (NY) 145: That dog followed me about like a shadow. EAP S112; TW 323(4).

S106   To stick to one like a **Shadow**

1937 AFielding *Scarecrow* (L) 260: And stick to him like his shadow. **1940** PMcGuire *Spanish* (L) 260: You're to stick to me like my shadow. **1953** JTMcIntosh *World* (NY 1956) 110: I'll stick to you like a shadow. TW 323(4).

S107   To wear oneself to a **Shadow**

1923 EWallace *Blue Hand* (B) 47: Worn himself to a shadow. **1953** AChristie *Funerals* (NY) 62: Maude . . . has to work herself to a shadow. TW 323(6).

S108   As wet as a **Shag**

1963 NMarsh *Dead* (B 1964) 100: You're wet as a shag [*a bird*]. NED Shag *sb.*^{2} (*phrases* 1835, 1841).

S109   In two **Shakes** (*very varied*)

1906 JCLincoln *Mr. Pratt* (NY) 59: In less than three shakes of a herring's hind leg. **1910** JCLincoln *Depot Master* (NY) 152: In about two shakes of a heifer's tail. **1912** JCLincoln *Postmaster* (NY) 80: In two shakes of a heifer's tail. **1916** MGibbon *Inglorious* (L 1968) 165: In two shakes of a jiffy. **1921** ERBurroughs *Mucker* (NY) 150: In about two shakes. **1922** JJoyce *Ulysses* (NY 1934) 448: Do it in shake [*sic*] of a lamb's tail. **1926** EWallace *King* (NY) 256: In two shakes of a dog's tail. **1928** RKing *Fatal* (NY) 249: We have about two shakes of a short lamb's tail left. **1928** LThayer *Darkest* (NY) 186: In two shakes of a lamb's tail. **1928** RAJWalling *That Dinner* (NY) 136: In a brace of shakes. **1930** JGBrandon *Murder* (L) 241: Before, as you English say, "the shake of a lamb's tail." **1930** WLewis *Apes* (NY 1932) 228: In two shakes of a donkey's tail; 438. **1931** AArmstrong *Trail* (P) 27: In two shakes of a—of a—. **1932** PMacDonald *Rope* (L) 286: In two shakes of a cat's tail. **1933** VWMason *Shanghai* (NY) 12: Be back in two shakes. **1934** ERPunshon *Information* (B) 234: In two shakes of a donkey's tail. **1934** PATaylor *Sandbar* (NY) 270: In just about two shakes of the proverbial lamb's tail. **1934** PGWodehouse *Brinkley* (B) 208: In two shakes of a duck's tail. **1936** VMcHugh *Caleb* (NY) 187: In three shakes of a lamb's tail. **1937** GBruce *Claim* (NY) 86: In two shakes of the old lamb's tail. **1937** LPendleton *Down East* (NY) 54: In half the shake of a lamb's tail. **1940** HFootner *Murderer's* (NY) 166: I'd be there in three shakes. **1940** STowne *Death Out* (NY) 203: Before you can shake a lamb's tail. **1941** EPhillpotts *Ghostwater* (NY) 278: In two shakes of a duck's tail. **1941** GWYates *If a Body* (NY) 184: She got ready . . . in the proverbial number of shakes. **1945** HLawrence *Time to Die* (NY) 15: In two shakes of a lamb's tail. **1949** NBlake *Hear* (NY) 28: Put it to rights in two shakes of a cat's arse. **1951** HSaunders *Sleeping* (L) 234: I could get it for you in two flicks of a duck's tail. **1955** JO'Hara *Ten* (NY) 194: Two shakes of a ram's tail. **1956** *BangorDN* 8/11 25: I'll have it fixed in two shakes of a sheep's tail. **1957** RFenisong *Schemers* (NY) 176: They'll be along in two shakes. **1959** HEBates *Breath* (B) 29: Over there in two ticks of a donkey's tail. **1961** ZHenderson *Pilgrimage* (NY) 129: Supper'll be ready in two jerks of a dead lamb's tail. **1962** VWMason *Trouble* (NY DBC) 21: Three shakes of a lamb's tail. **1965** AAFair *Cut Thin* (NY DBC) 31: I'll be [there] in the shake of a cat's whisker. **1969** CBush *Deadly* (NY) 25: In a couple of shakes. **1974** KAmis *Ending* (NY) 46: In two shakes of a lamb's tail. **1977** HDolson *Beauty* (P) 52: In two shakes of a ram's tail. TW 323(1–4); Wentworth 559: Two. Cf. In two Ticks *below*.

S110   To be no great Shakes

1930 VLoder *Shop* (L) 52: Not that he was any great shakes himself. **1938** SCallaway *Conquistador* (NY) 141: He was no great shakes. **1959** PCurtis *No Question* (NY) 13: I was no great shakes as a teacher. **1971** DFJones *Denver* (NY) 160: It was no great shakes of a dinner. TW 323–4(5); Brunvand 124.

S111   The Shank of the evening

1933 RJCasey *Hot Ice* (I) 111: The shank of the evening. **1938** JSStrange *Silent* (NY) 56: Only [the] shank o' the evening. **1940** TChanslor *Our First* (NY) 297: It's the shank of the evening. **1946** VKelsey *Whisper Murder* (NY) 208: It's just the shank of the evening. **1952** PGWodehouse *Angel* (NY) 55: The shank of the evening. **1964** HKemelman *Friday* (NY 1965) 137: The night's young . . . Shank of the evening. **1973** HPentecost *Beautiful* (NY) 73: It was just the shank of the evening. Berrey 3.10.

S112   Shank's mare (pony)

1924 AOFriel *Mountains* (NY) 80: Shanks' mare. **1930** LBrock *Murder* (NY) 22: I'm relying on Shank's mare. **1930** WS Maugham *Cakes* (L 1948) 52: Shank's pony was good enough for them. **1934** BThomson *Richardson Scores* (L) 195: Shank's pony. **1947** HCahill *Look* (NY) 133: By shank's mare. **1952** FVWMason *Himalayan* (NY

1953) 51: We'll all travel shank's mare. **1957** *BHerald* 4/6 1: Shank's mare trip to Boston. **1961** MHHood *Drown* (NY) 55: Shank's mare's good enough for me. **1969** HEBates *Vanished* (L) 30: We travelled by Shank's Pony. EAP S115.

S113   As dumb (silly) as a Sheep

1954 ECRLorac *Shroud* (NY) 99: As dumb as sheep. **1956** NMarsh *Death* (B) 151: Silly as a sheep. Cf. Taylor *Prov. Comp.* 79: Stupid.

S114   As meek as a Sheep

1930 GMitchell *Mystery* (NY) 268: He's as meek as a sheep. Whiting S204.

S115   As well be hanged for a Sheep as a lamb (goat) (varied)

1912 JCLincoln *Postmaster* (NY) 220: We might as well be hung for old sheep as lamb. **1921** ASTuberville *Mediaeval Heresy* (L) 44: "As well be hanged for a sheep as a lamb" is a proverb of very general validity. **1928** DHLawrence *Lady* ("Allemagne") 150: We might as well be hung for a sheep as for a lamb. **1929** ABCox *Poisoned* (NY) 54: Having committed himself to this lamb, Moresby seemed disposed to look about for a sheep. **1932** AWynne *Green Knife* (P) 227: As well be hanged for a man as a sheep. **1936** JMWalsh *Crimes* (L) 57: She might as well be hung for a sheep as a lamb. **1938** MSaltmarsh *Clouded* (NY) 62: I might as well be hanged for a sheep as a goat. **1941** BHalliday *Bodies* (NY 1959) 161: You might as well swing for a skunk as a weasel. **1942** FLockridge *Hanged for a Sheep* (NY). **1950** HGreen *Nothing* (NY) 92: Might as well be hung for a lamb or whatever the silly phrase is. **1953** MPHood *Silent* (NY) 113: Might as well be killed for a sheep as a lamb. **1955** JO'Hara *Ten* (NY) 228: I might as well be hung for a sheep as a goat. **1958** AMacKinnon *Summons* (NY) 117: There's an old English belief that you might as well be hung for a sheep as a lamb. **1961** WCooper *Scenes* (NY) 98: I might as well be hung for a sheep as a lamb. **1962** ESGardner *Ice-cold* (NY DBC) 113: He might as well be hanged for a sheep as a goat, as the saying goes. **1963** HWaugh *Death* (NY) 109: We might's well get hung for a wolf as a sheep. **1965** BGrebanier *Great Shakespeare* (NY) 233: William Henry would as soon have been hanged for robbing a bank as for stealing a loaf. **1965** DKnight *Dark Side* (NY) 216: But in for a lamb, in for a sheep. **1968** JTMc Intosh *Take a Pair* (NY) 131: He had decided to be hanged as a sheep rather than as a lamb. **1970** WBlunt *Dream* (L) 84: He might as well be hanged for a sheep as for a lamb. **1972** RRendell *Murder* (NY) 167: Why not break one more and be hanged for a sheep? **1973** TWells *Brenda's* (NY) 107: Might as well be hung for a sheep as a goat. EAP S120.

S116　A (the) black **Sheep** (of the flock, family) (*varied*)

1909 JCLincoln *Keziah* (NY) 48: A black sheep. **1911** HHMunro *Chronicles* (L 1927) 96: The black sheep of a rather greyish family. **1915** RFirbank *Vainglory* (Works 1, L 1929) 79: The proverbial kind heart of a black sheep. **1922** JJoyce *Ulysses* (NY 1934) 453: Branded as a black sheep. **1922** EPower *Medieval English Nunneries* (Cambridge, Eng.) 395: Herself the blackest sheep in all the flock. **1925** JSFletcher *False* (NY) 234: There are black sheep in every flock, as the saying goes. **1929** EBarker *C.I.D.* (NY) 153: There's a—well, say a gray sheep in almost every family. **1930** MScott *Sportsman* (NY) 96: There are black sheep sometimes in the best of families. **1931** MAllingham *Police* (NY) 52: Every family has its black sheep. **1933** DLSayers *Murder* (NY) 31: The black sheep of the family. **1941** JShore *Rattle* (NY) 98: I'm the black sheep of the family. **1953** GPhelps *Dry Stone* (L) 56: He was something of a black sheep in the family. **1957** JBlackburn *Scent* (L) 143: There is said to be a black sheep in every family. **1964** ESGardner *Horrified* (NY DBC) 164: I'm the black sheep of the family. **1971** PRubenstein *Groupsex* (NY) 112: He was the black sheep again. EAP S123; Brunvand 125(1). Cf. There is . . . rotten Apple *above*.

S117　To count **Sheep** (*varied*)

1930 EWallace *Silver Key* (NY) 305: She lay for half an hour, counting sheep. **1932** PMcGuire *Black Rose* (NY) 19: You'd just stand there counting sheep over a stile until you were put to sleep. **1937** FDeLaguna *Arrow* (NY) 238: He saw not the proverbial sheep, jumping one by one a shadowy fence. **1940** WCClark *Murder Goes* (B) 141: At night he counts theories instead of sheep. **1941** EPOppenheim *Man Who* (B) 119: Martin closed his eyes . . . and counted the sheep passing through the farmer's gate. **1964** AChristie *Caribbean* (NY) 190: Nobody tells young women who can't sleep to count sheep. TW 325(15).

S118　To follow like **Sheep**

1930 JRhode *Peril* (NY) 8: The . . . world would follow them like sheep. EAP S132.

S119　To make (cast, throw) **Sheep's** (calf's) eyes

1922 JJoyce *Ulysses* (NY 1934) 758: He was throwing his sheeps eyes at those two. **1928** GDHCole *Man* (NY) 70: That girl made sheep's eyes at you. **1930** WLewis *Apes* (NY 1932) 225: It's no use your making sheep's eyes at *me!* **1936** SPalmer *Briar Pipe* (L) 170: Making calf's eyes at Violet. **1944** ECrispin *Gilded Fly* (NY 1970) 28: Making sheep's eyes at you. **1949** RKing *Redoubled* (NY) 35: Kicking any opening barrage toward sheep's eyes into a cocked hat. **1971** PNapier *Sword* (NY) 281: They were casting sheep's eyes at the empty plains of Canada. **1973** CAird *His Burial* (NY) 78: Making sheep's eyes at Miss Fenella. EAP S128; TW 325(12); Brunvand 125(5).

S120　To separate the **Sheep** from the goats (*varied*)

1929 EWallace *Girl* (NY) 192: Sorting the sheep from the goats. **1930** MBDix *Murder* (L) 222: We have to separate the goats from the sheep. **1938** KMKnight *Acts* (NY) 138: Divide the sheep from the goats. **1939** HReilly *All Concerned* (NY) 257: The separation of the sheep from the goats, the chaff from the wheat. **1950** MLong *Louisville* (NY) 155: Separate the sheep and the goats. **1958** DMDisney *Black* (NY) 120: You know, sheep from goats, wheat from chaff. **1962** NMcLarty *Chain* (NY) 126: To separate the goats from the sheep. **1965** DoctorX *Intern* (NY) 173: You get the sheep with the goats.

1972 JMcClure *Caterpillar* (NY) 27: Sorted the sheep from the goats. EAP S134; Brunvand 125(4). Cf. Wheat *below.*

S121 As pale as a **Sheet**

1919 MScott *Behind Red Curtains* (NY) 71: As pale as a sheet. **1932** NTrott *Monkey* (NY) 93: As pale as a sheet. **1948** MInnes *Night* (L 1966) 153: You're as pale as a sheet. **1960** TFurlong *Time* (NY) 55: He was as pale as a sheet. **1973** ACharters *Kerouac* (San Francisco) 194: He was pale as a sheet. TW 325(1); Taylor *Western Folklore* 17(1958) 18–9.

S122 As white as a **Sheet**; Sheet-white

1908 JCLincoln *Cy Whittaker* (NY) 113: White as a sheet. **1921** JCLincoln *Galusha* (NY) 339: White as the proverbial sheet, which means much whiter than some sheets. **1922** JJoyce *Ulysses* (NY 1934) 751: As white as a sheet. **1929** RConnell *Murder* (NY) 65: Her sheet-white face. **1931** FWCrofts *Mystery* (NY) 96: As white as a sheet. **1934** RKing *Lesser Antilles* (NY) 209: Leaving her sheet white. **1938** NMarsh *Artists* (NY 1941) 237: The face was sheet-white. **1939** JJones *Murder al Fresco* (NY) 5: As white as the proverbial sheet. **1942** MVHeberden *Murder Makes* (NY) 183: A sheet-white face. **1947** VSiller *Curtain* (NY) 131: Face turned sheet white. **1953** CJay *Fugitive* (NY) 28: White as a sheet, you are. **1956** *BangorDN* 5/23 31: You're white as a sheet. **1961** ALee *Miss Hogg* (NY) 72: Barbara went white as the proverbial sheet. **1965** DHitchens *Bank* (NY) 134: "You're pale as a sheet." "As white as a sheet. Pale as a ghost." "Or whatever. You're kind of green, even." **1969** RAirth *Snatch* (NY) 204: She went white as a sheet. **1969** AGilbert *Mr. Crook* (NY DBC) 43: The policeman was sheet-white. 119: Polly was as white as the proverbial sheet. **1970** STerkel *Hard* (NY) 326: Coughlin came back as white as any sheet. **1976** CLarson *Muir's* (NY) 13: White as a sheet. **1977** LKelly *Lermontov* (NY) 101: White as a sheet, thin as a nail. EAP S136; TW 325(2, 3); Brunvand 125(1).

S123 Three **Sheets** in the wind (*varied*)

1909 JCLincoln *Keziah* (NY) 357: He was three sheets in the wind. **1932** TSmith *Night Life* (NY) 59: Three sheets in the wind. **1934** SPalmer *Silver Persian* (NY) 229: [He] seems a few sheets in the wind. **1939** EDean *Murder Is* (NY) 139: When he was three-sheets in the wind. That means drunk. **1956** EMcBain *Cop* (NY 1959) 23: He just had a couple of sheets in the wind. **1958** PDeVries *Mackerel* (B) 82: He was three sheets in the wind. **1960** EMcBain *Heckler* (NY) 79: You had a couple of sheets in the wind. **1966** JDCarr *Panic* (NY) 41: You were three sheets in the wind. **1969** SMays *Reuben's* (L) 108: Good ten sheets in the wind. **1970** UO'Connor *Brendan* (L) 268: When he wasn't four sheets in the wind. **1972** DEmrich *Folklore* (B) 53: He was just three sheets in the wind. **1978** JCash *Gold* (NY) 94: Tinker Dill, three sheets sloshed in the White Hart. EAP S138; Brunvand 125(2).

S124 **Sheet anchor**

1913 JCLincoln *Mr. Pratt's Patients* (NY) 313: This was his sheet anchor. **1924** HHBashford *Augustus* (L 1966) 256: It was the sheet-anchor by which I clung to life. **1931** AWynne *Blue* (P) 319: Hogg's evidence was my sheet-anchor. **1937** MKennedy *I'll Be Judge* (L) 129: History had been her sheet-anchor. **1963** EMCottman *Out-Island* (NY) 108: The sounding rod . . . became my sheet anchor. **1968** MGibbon *Inglorious* (L) 254: Vane continued to be my sheet anchor. **1974** JWain *SJohnson* (NY) 168: He found it an indispensable sheet anchor. NED Sheet-anchor b.

S125 To be on the **Shelf**

1922 JJoyce *Ulysses* (NY 1934) 751: He thinks Im finished out and laid on the shelf. TW 326.

S126 Not twenty **Shillings** to the pound

1929 JBPriestley *Good* (NY) 412: No harm in him, y'r know; just hasn't got twenty shillings t' pound [*not very bright*]. Cf. *Oxford* 567: Nine-pence; TW 326(4).

S127 To be cut off with a **Shilling** (*varied*)

1928 DLSayers *Unpleasantness* (NY) 128: He might have cut me off with a shilling. **1929** TShannon *Catspaw* (NY) 237: He'd cut me off without even the proverbial shilling. **1930** JCournos *Grandmother* (NY) 168: She saw fit to leave them the proverbial shilling. **1930** GMitchell *Mystery* (NY) 21: Got himself cut off with the proverbial bob. **1935** NGayle *Sentry-Box* (NY) 92: Was Mr. Coulton cut off with the traditional shilling? **1936** HAdams *Old Jew* (L) 38: He cut you off with the proverbial shilling? **1936** RGDean *Sutton* (NY) 117: There would be nothing for her but the proverbial dollar. **1945** RLHines *Confessions* (L) 50: Cut . . . the children off with the proverbial shilling. **1947** NMarsh *Final* (B) 98: Planning how to lay out the proverbial shilling to advantage [*disinherited*]. **1952** RMarshall *Jane* (NY) 6: Cutting off his brother with the proverbial shilling. **1954** LFord *Invitation* (NY) 137: Jennifer has promised not to cut her off with that shilling the English talk about. **1961** JPhilips *Murder* (NY DBC) 28: Cut Loring off with the proverbial penny. **1964** JHillas *Today* (NY) 236: Neither the proverbial shilling nor a single article from my old home. **1969** VdeSolaPinto *City* (L) 8: His father did not exactly cut him off with the proverbial shilling. **1974** MInnes *Appleby's Other* (NY) 97: Leaving an only son the proverbial farthing. TW 326(2); *Oxford* 163: Cut.

S128 Don't give up the **Ship**

1908 JCLincoln *Cy Whittaker* (NY) 265: Don't give up the ship. **1934** JTFarrell *Young Manhood* (NY 1935) 402: As Napoleon said, don't give up the ship. **1940** JPPhilips *Murder in Marble* (NY) 197: Don't give up the ship, mate. **1964** RCFaure *Summer* (NY) 15: Don't give up the ship. **1965** JPotts *Only Good* (NY) 66: I'm not giving up the ship. **1974** GCEdmonston *T.H.E.M.* (NY) 167: Don't give up the ship. EAP S147.

S129 To spoil (lose) the **Ship** for a ha'porth of tar (*varied*)

1912 HHMunro *Unbearable* (NY 1928) 164: The good ship had been lost for the sake of the traditional ha'p'orth of tar. **1928** WMcFee *Pilgrims* (NY) 59: Don't lose the ship for a pennorth o' tar. **1930** FDGrierson *Blue Bucket* (NY) 18: It seemed a pity to spoil the ship, so to speak, for a ha'porth of tar. **1939** VWilliams *Fox Prowls* (B) 220: I'll not

have the ship spoiled for a ha'porth of tar. **1953** DGarnett *Golden* (L) 158: Don't let the ship sink for a ha'porth of tar. **1957** *Punch* 7/10 47: I replied it was a pity to spoil the ship for a ha'porth of tar. **1961** CBush *Sapphire* (NY) 71: No use spoiling the ship for a ha'porth of tar. **1965** PGWodehouse *Galahad* (L) 120: The old saying about spoiling ships for ha'porths of tar. **1975** NFreeling *Bugles* (NY) 95: They spoil the ship for a penny's worth of tar. **1978** JCash *Gold* (NY) 3: You don't spoil the ship for a ha'porth of tar. *Oxford* 723.

S130 When one's **Ship** comes in (home) (*varied*)

1923 HGartland *Globe* (NY) 286: When my ship comes in. **1928** JGoodwin *When Dead* (NY) 287: It is proverbially a pleasant sight to see one's ship come home. **1932** JJConnington *Sweepstake* (B) 77: Her ship seems to have come home. **1939** WChambers *You Can't* (NY) 24: When my ship comes in, if ever. **1940** GHCoxe *Lady Is Afraid* (NY) 258: Now his ship had come in. **1947** KMKnight *Blue* (NY) 128: Don't tell me you've got a ship coming in. **1951** ACalder-Marshall *Magic* (L) 33: When my ship comes in. **1957** *New Yorker* 4/6 38: If my ship comes in, I'll tell you what I'll do. **1960** NWilliams *Knaves* (NY) 44: His ship was coming home, he told him. **1966** MMcShane *Crimson* (NY) 32: The future, when her funeral barge came in. **1967** AChester *Exquisite* (NY) 178: One day Dickie's ship came in in more ways than one. **1967** JMSeton *By a Thousand* (NY) 4: The now half-forgotten, wholly enfeebled phrase "Wait till my ship comes in." TW 327(3); Brunvand 126; *Oxford* 723.

S131 To be **Shipshape**

1938 JJConnington *For Murder* (L) 224: All shipshape and in apple-pie order. EAP S156.

S132 To be **Shipshape** and Bristol fashion

1927 SHorler *Black* (L 1935) 312: Rounded up nice and shipshape and Bristol fashion [*arrested*]. **1928** RThorndike *Slype* (NY) 98: All of 'em working O.K., A-1, shipshape and Bristol fashion. **1932** VWilliams *Mystery* (B) 71: All shipshape and Bristol fashion.

1939 EAmbler *Coffin* (NY 1957) 36: Quite above board and Bristol fashion. **1942** SE Morison *Admiral* (B) 350: She was all "ship-shape and Bristol fashion." **1952** ECRLorac *Dog* (NY) 185: That's all shipshape and Bristol fashion. **1956** EGann *Twilight* (NY) 18: A shipshape and Bristol-fashion mate. **1965** JAshford *Superintendent's* (NY) 3: It'll all be shipshape and Bristol fashion. **1967** SE Morison *Old Bruin* (B) 86: All was "Ship-shape and Bristol fashion." **1970** NMonsarrat *Breaking* (L) 308: Ship-shape and Bristol fashion. **1973** JMann *Troublecross* (NY) 43: All shipshape and Bristol fashion. EAP S157.

S133   As white as a **Shirt**

1917 JCLincoln *Extricating* (NY) 164: You're as white as my shirt. Cf. EAP S159: Pale.

S134   I'll eat my **Shirt**

1931 GPahlow *Murder* (NY) 39: If he hasn't . . . I'll eat my shirt. **1933** KCStrahan *Meriwether* (NY) 111: If . . . I'll eat my shirt. **1933** "Diplomat" *Death* (NY) 168: Or I'll eat my shirt. Cf. Berrey 203.3. Cf. If . . . Hat *above*.

S135   Keep your **Shirt** on

1925 JGBrandon *Bond* (L) 7: Keep your shirt on. **1930** PMacDonald *Rynox* (L) 45: Keep your shirt in! **1948** CDickson *Skeleton* (NY 1967) 49: Keep your shirt on. **1950** RLockridge *Foggy* (P) 99: Keep your shirt on. **1961** The Gordons *Operation* (NY) 15: Keep your shirt on. **1967** ARose *Memoirs* (NY) 43: Keep your shirt on. Whiting *NC* 473(1); Wentworth 467; Cole 54. Cf. To keep one's Hair, Pants *above*; Wig *below*.

S136   From **Shirtsleeves** to shirtsleeves in three generations (*varied*)

1928 DLSayers *Dawson* (NY) 151: They do say, don't they, that from shirtsleeves to shirtsleeves is three generations? **1938** JCCaughey *McGillivray* (Norman, Okla.) 10: The hackneyed adage, shirtsleeves to shirtsleeves in three generations. **1952** CAmory *Last* (NY) 386: Shirtsleeves to shirtsleeves in three generations. **1964** RO'Connor *Jack* (B) 28: Shirtsleeves to shirtsleeves in three or four years. Bradley 91. Cf. Clogs *above*.

S137   As low as **Shit**

1966 HRDaniels *House* (NY) 74: I think you're lower than shit. Cf. Whale shit *below*.

S138   Not give a **Shit**

1922 JJoyce *Ulysses* (NY 1934) 587: I don't give a shit for him. **1957** WGoldman *Temple* (NY) 81: And I don't give a shit. **1960** MJones *Forest* (NY) 141: He don't give a shit. **1969** SFisher *Saxon's* (LA) 152: I don't give a shit. **1970** JVizzard *See* (NY) 85: Who gives a shit? **1974** OBleeck *Highbinders* (NY) 193: You wouldn't give much of a shit. **1975** MVonnegut *Eden* (NY) 44: Not many people gave a shit. **1979** LBlock *Burglar* (NY) 77: I don't particularly give a shit. **1982** JLivingston *Piece* (NY) 107: [None] of them give a shit if you're poisoning wells.

S139   Not worth (a) **Shit**

1965 HRoskolenko *When I Was Last* (NY) 190: [He] can't write worth a shit. **1969** RStark *Dame* (NY) 116: They's no stations worth shit. **1971** NBogner *Making* (NY) 256: I ain't worth a shit. **1975** EMcBain *Where* (NY) 156: [It] ain't worth a shit. **1979** GWest *Duke* (NY) 122: Your watch isn't worth shit.

S140   The **Shit** hits the fan (*varied*)

1954 DTrumbo *Additional* (NY 1970) 288: The shit was in the fan for fair. **1965** DoctorX *Intern* (NY) 330: I told [him] about this and the shit hit the fan. **1966** EConnell *I Had* (NY) 37: I have a feeling the well-known you-know-what has hit the fan. **1966** RGrenier *Yes and Back* (L) 145: Where were you when the shit hit the fan? **1967** IReed *Free-lance* (NY) 13: When the shit hits the fan, your life ain't gone to be worth two cents. **1970** DHarper *Hijacked* (NY DBC) 42: The fit has hit the Shan [*the news is out*]. **1970** NMonsarrat *Breaking* (L) 4: A short day before the fried egg hit the fan. **1970** WANolen *Making* (NY) 284: Things have hit the fan. **1974** GCEdmonston *T.H.E.M.* (NY) 125: "Flatulent feces!" . . . Art decided that something very like the alien's exclamation was about to hit the fan. **1975** MVonnegut *Eden* (NY) 46: The shit is on the fan or very close. **1977** LBlock *Burglars* (NY) 131: If the shit hits the fan he'll be right there in front of it. **1981** NFreeling *Arlette* (NY) 90: He'd throw a bit of bullshit up against the fan to keep you from getting uppity. **1983** JHyams *Murder at the Academy* (NY) 57: The shit's going to hit the fan.

S141 **Shit,** piss and corruption
1967 AMontagu *Anatomy of Swearing* (NY) 317: *Shit, piss and corruption!* is an early twentieth-century expression.

S142 To be **Shit** down one's pant leg
1959 ESchiddel *Devil* (NY) 248: It'll be shit down your pantleg if you don't, mister.

S143 To be **Shit** out of luck
1939 HMiller *Capricorn* (NY 1961) 57: You are shit out of luck. **1972** JBall *Five* (B) 166: You're shit outta luck. **1973** JDMacDonald *Turquoise* (P) 164: I was shit out of luck. Wentworth 468.

S144 To **Shit** where one sits
1953 SBellow *Adventures* (NY) 21: Don't shit where you eat. **1973** LHellman *Pentimento* (B) 85: She made the shit and now she sit in it and poke around. Cf. Bird that fouls, To be sick in one's Hat *above.*

S145 As crazy (lean) as a **Shitepoke**
1937 MSandoz *Slogum* (B) 200: Crazy as a shitepoke. **1941** ISCobb *Exit* (I) 361: As lean as a shitepoke. DA Shitepoke b.

S146 To be built like a brick **Shithouse** (*varied*)
1956 GMetalious *Peyton* (NY) 132: [She] was built like a brick shithouse. **1963** DHamilton *Ambushers* (NY) 87: I'm not built like a . . . brick outhouse. **1967** GBaxt *Swing* (NY) 93: Suave, sophisticated, [he was] still built like a brick crap house. **1968** KTopkins *Passing* (B) 11: Built like a brick shithouse, but a real lady. **1970** AALewis *Carnival* (NY) 187: Built like a brick donniker [*toilet*]. **1971** BWAldiss *Soldier* (L) 52: [She is] built like a brick shithouse. **1980** JMcClure *Blood* (NY) 56: This massive bloke, built like a brick shithouse. **1984** PTrumbull *Big Money* (NY) 170: They're both built like a brick shithouse.

S147 As black as one's **Shoe**
1959 FSmith *Harry* (B) 55: As black as your shoe. EAP S163.

S148 As close (snug) as **Shoe** to foot (*varied*)
1935 HFootner *Whip-poor-will* (NY) 32: As close to him as the shoe to his foot. **1940** KMKnight *Death Came* (NY) 79: You and I are going to get along together like a foot and an old shoe. **1967** RCowper *Phoenix* (NY) 62: As snug as an old shoe. Wilstach 504.

S149 As comfortable as an old **Shoe**
1948 FCrane *Black* (NY) 157: He . . . turned as comfortable as an old shoe. **1954** EForbes *Rainbow* (B) 240: Mrs. Squires was pleasant and comfortable as an old shoe. **1963** MCarleton *Dread* (NY) 120: As comfortable as an old shoe. **1977** PGWinslow *Witch* (NY) 69: As comfortable to him as an old shoe. Whiting *NC* 473(1).

S150 As common (ordinary) as an old **Shoe**
1934 SHAdams *Gorgeous* (B) 207: I'm common as an old shoe. **1948** DCDisney *Explosion* (NY DBC) 29: As common as an old shoe. **1948** NMailer *Naked* (NY) 558: I'm as ordinary as an old shoe. **1950** BCarey *Man Who* (NY) 14: Just as common as an old shoe [*a friendly man*]. Taylor *Prov. Comp.* 29.

S151 As dry as an old **Shoe**
1928 HKWebster *Clock* (NY) 289: My mouth's as dry as an old shoe. **1934** LO'Flaherty *Shame* (L) 252: She's dry like an old shoe.

S152 As easy (regular) as an old **Shoe**
1904 MLPeabody *To Be Young* (B 1967) 327: He really is as easy as an old shoe. **1910** HGarland *Companions on the Trail* (NY 1931) 445: He was as easy as an old shoe. **1941** ABCunningham *Strange Death* (NY) 167: The . . . house . . . looked easy as an old shoe. **1948** NMailer *Naked* (NY) 329: I'm as regular as an old shoe. TW 328(1).

S153 As plain as an old **Shoe**
1935 JHWallis *Politician* (NY) 192: As plain as an old shoe. **1940** MRRinehart *Great Mistake* (NY) 4: She was as plain as any old shoe. **1951** GPettuloo *Always* (NY) 179: He's

as plain as an old shoe. **1953** AJLiebling *Honest* (NY) 46: Plain as an old shoe. **1967** VLincoln *Private* (NY) 36: Emma . . . was plain as an old shoe. **1971** DMDisney *Three's* (NY) 63: She'll look . . . plain as an old shoe. TW 328(2). Cf. Sock *below*.

S154 As tight as a new **Shoe**

1949 AAFair *Bedrooms* (NY 1958) 49: She's tight as a new shoe. Taylor *Western Folklore* 17(1958) 19(2).

S155 If the **Shoe** fits, wear it (*varied*)

1930 DOgburn *Ra-ta-plan!* (B) 148: I have no desire that you shall wear any shoe that doesn't fit. **1933** KTKnoblock *Take Up* (NY) 68: If the shoe didn't fit, why did they wear it? **1934** JGregory *Emerald* (NY) 260: There's an old saying, you know, if the shoe fits, wear it. **1940** CRawson *Headless* (NY) 84: I didn't make any accusation. But you seem to be trying the shoe on. **1941** JShore *Rattle* (NY) 9: If the shoe fits anyone here, he can wear it. **1951** DHitchens *Stairway* (NY) 85: Try the shoe on. You'll find it fits. **1956** *BangorDN* 10/22 11: If the shoe fits one, let it fit all. **1957** *BangorDN* 8/28 24: There's a saying, . . . "If the shoe fits, wear it." **1958** *BHerald* 9/27 7: If the shoe fits, put it on. **1960** *BHerald* 5/4 17: If anyone thinks the shoe fits let him put it on. **1960** HQMasur *Send Another* (NY) 115: "Are you accusing me?" "Does the shoe fit?" EAP S164. Cf. Cap *above*.

S156 Not fit to tie someone's **Shoes** (shoe-laces, *etc.*) (*varied*)

1909 JCLincoln *Keziah* (NY) 86: People who aren't fit to tie his shoes. **1909** MRRinehart *Man in Lower Ten* (NY 1947) 327: Women not fit to touch my shoes. **1912** ERBur-roughs *Princess of Mars* (NY 1963) 77: Not fit to polish her shoes. **1924** WBMFerguson *Black* (NY) 109: Not fit to tie her shoes. **1929** RRodd *Secret* (NY) 99: Not fit to lick your boots. **1932** RPertwee *Death* (B) 208: Killed by someone whose boots he wasn't fit to black. **1933** AFielding *Tall House* (NY) 34: I'm not worthy to tie Alfreda's shoe-strings. **1939** AGilbert *Clock* (L) 50: She wasn't fit to black his boots. **1950** STruss *Never* (NY) 13: I wish you were fit to tie his bootlaces. **1962**

ESherry *Girl* (NY DBC) 118: We . . . weren't fit to tie his shoelaces. **1966** HMacDiarmid *Company* (L) 163: Men not fit to tie his shoe-laces. EAP S165, 170; *Oxford* 922: Worthy.

S157 To be in someone's **Shoes**

1913 JCLincoln *Mr. Pratt's Patients* (NY) 30: I wouldn't be in his shoes. **1923** JSFletcher *Exterior* (NY) 10: If you'd been in my shoes. **1931** PBaron *Round* (NY) 280: I shouldn't care to be in your shoes. **1939** CMWills *Death at* (L) 56: I shouldn't care to be in your shoes. **1956** *New Yorker* 11/10 60: I wouldn't have been in that man's shoes for a million dollars. **1970** MMcGrady *Stranger* (NY) 155: Put yourself in his shoes. EAP S168.

S158 To step into someone's **Shoes**

1938 LAnson *Such Natural* (L) 44: He'll step straight into Roger's shoes. **1939** MBurton *Death Leaves* (L) 93: Geoffrey murdered his nephew just for the sake of stepping into his shoes. NED Shoe *sb.* 2k.

S159 To throw (*etc.*) away like an old **Shoe**

1929 GDHCole *Poison* (NY) 249: Chucked away like an old shoe. **1930** HHolt *Ace* (L) 126: It cannot be thrown aside as easily as an old shoe. **1945** ACampbell *With Bated* (NY) 75: Aggie is to be cast aside like an old shoe. **1951** DMDisney *Straw* (NY) 80: He threw her over like an old shoe. **1954** HGardiner *Murder* (L) 181: I'd be tossed aside as carelessly as an old shoe. **1962** MGEberhart *Enemy* (NY) 92: You can't throw it away like an old shoe. *Oxford* 725.

S160 To wait for the other **Shoe** to fall

1975 BGelb *On the* (NY) 169: I'm waiting for the other shoe to fall [*another murder*]. **1976** CLarson *Muir's* (NY) 82: Let the other shoe drop, for God's sake.

S161 Where the **Shoe** pinches (*varied*)

1911 JCLincoln *Woman-Haters* (NY) 7: That's where the shoe pinches. **1924** LThayer *Key* (NY) 224: That's where the shoe pinches. **1928** BWoon *When It's Cocktail* (NY) 265: Here the shoe began to pinch. **1932** JJConnington *Sweepstake* (B) 178: That's where the shoe pinches. **1935** RCWoodthorpe *Shadow* (NY) 184: Only the wearer knows where the shoe pinches. **1936** EBClason *Death Angel* (NY) 156: That's where the shoe binds—and binds plenty. **1937** EForbes *Paradise* (NY) 193: Where the shoe is tightest, there the corn will come. **1945** HGreen *Loving* (L) 217: That's where the shoe pinches. **1956** *New Yorker* 11/10 60: The shoe pinched a little at first. **1961** DMDisney *Mrs. Meeker's* (NY) 64: That was where the shoe pinched. **1966** HPentecost *Hide* (NY) 190: The shoe is beginning to pinch our friend Bartram. **1973** HDolson *Dying* (P) 92: But if the shoe pinches . . . EAP S169; TW 328–9(6); Brunvand 126(1).

S162   As black as **Shoe buttons**

1930 WAStowell *Marston* (NY) 184: Eyes black as shoe buttons. **1933** VWMason *Shanghai* (NY) 162: Eyes as round and black as shoe buttons.

S163   As dead (tough) as **Shoe leather**

1947 JIams *Body* (NY) 55: He was . . . tough as shoe leather. **1964** EPangborn *Davy* (NY) 86: Dead as shoe-leather. Whiting *NC* 473: Tough. Cf. Taylor *Western Folklore* 17(1958) 19: Shoe(3). Cf. Leather *above*.

S164   As ever wore **Shoe leather** (*varied*)

1928 RAJWalling *That Dinner* (NY) 47: One of the finest men that go on boot-leather. **1935** BFlynn *Padded* (L) 191: The biggest rogues that ever wore shoe-leather. **1939** AMuir *Death Comes* (L) 35: A finer man never wore shoe-leather. **1958** MColes *Come* (NY) 93: As truthful a man as ever stepped in shoe-leather. **1968** KDetzer *Myself* (NY) 156: The worst boy that every walked on shoe leather. EAP S171.

S165   The **Shoemaker's** children (wife) are ill-shod (*varied*)

1940 HAdams *Chief Witness* (L) 51: What do they say about the cobbler's wife being ill-shod? **1965** SRansome *Alias* (NY DBC) 55: Like the shoemaker whose children go un-shod. Whiting S270; Apperson 566; *Oxford* 543: More bare.

S166   On a **Shoestring**

1925 JICClarke *My Life* (NY) 131: Founded [it] on a shoe string. **1930** HCrooker *Hollywood* (NY) 22: Pictures made on a shoe-string. **1931** HGarland *Companions* (NY) 187: His coming to New York on half a shoestring. **1936** FNebel *Fifty Roads* (B) 156: I'm heading for Canada on a shoestring. **1940** LFord *Old Lover's* (NY) 140: [They] are on a shoestring. **1956** BTraveler 10/30 33: Kennedy has been running his campaign on a political shoestring. **1957** *NY Times Book Review* 12/15 6: He started his monthly . . . on something less than a shoestring. **1957** HEBates *Summer* (B) 108: I might as well be a widow on a shoestring. **1965** JSUntermeyer *Private* (NY) 78: It had been done on the proverbial shoestring. **1968** MAllingham *Cargo* (NY) 230: The place is run on the well-known shoe string. **1968** SPalmer *Rook* (NY) 81: It was a shoestring, or at least one-man, operation. **1975** PDJames *Black* (NY) 57: We run on a shoe-string. Brunvand 126; NED Suppl. Shoe-string 2.

S167   As sure as **Shooting**

1920 ACrabb *Samuel* (NY) 84: Sure as shooting; 139, 300. **1925** BBLindsay *Revolt* (NY) 123: Sure as shooting. **1935** CDKing *Obelists* (NY) 251: As sure as shooting. **1937** PCoffin *Search* (NY) 78: Sure as shootin'. **1948** WMiller *Fatal* (NY) 97: Sure as shooting. **1949** FCrane *Flying* (NY) 199: Sure as shooting. **1959** *NYTimes* 12/20 9: He would be elected "as sure as shooting." **1967** TWells *Dead by* (NY) 29: Sure as shooting. Brunvand 126; Taylor *Prov. Comp.* 80.

S168   **Short** and sweet

1925 JSFletcher *Annexation* (NY) 24: What I say . . . is short and sweet. **1932** CRyland *Notting* (L) 111: Short and sweet. **1936** DTeilhet *Feather Cloak* (NY) 112: Short and sweet. **1940** AMuir *Sands* (L) 235: Short and sweet. **1948** CDickson *Skeleton* (NY 1967) 156: It'll be short, but it won't be sweet. **1950** CDickson *Night* (NY) 77: I'll tell 'em short and sweet. **1956** *BangorDN* 9/25 20: That was short and sweet. **1962** EMcBain *Like* (NY) 61: Make this short and sweet. **1969** JCheever *Bullet* (NY) 138: Make it short and sweet. **1973** MSadler *Circle* (NY) 130: Short and sweet. **1975** RStout *Family* (NY) 13: You're short and sweet. EAP S180; Brunvand 126(1).

S169 **Short** and sweet, like a donkey's gallop

1937 LAGStrong *Swift* (L) 237: Short and sweet, like a donkey's gallop. *Oxford* 727; Wilstach 555: Like an old woman's dance.

S170 As quick as a **Shot**

1929 AFredericks *Mark* (NY) 39: Quick as a shot. **1933** RCurle *Corruption* (I) 246: The climax will come as quick as a shot. Whiting *NC* 473(1).

S171 Like a **Shot** (out of hell, from a gun)

1913 JCLincoln *Mr. Pratt's Patients* (NY) 331: She was out of that kitchen like a shot. **1919** KHoward *Peculiar* (NY) 220: I'd do it like a shot. **1922** JJoyce *Ulysses* (NY 1934) 58: Value would go up like a shot. **1932** CFitzsimmons *No Witness* (NY) 299: I was driving . . . like a shot out of hell. **1934** RKeverne *He Laughed* (L) 94: He was after it like a shot from a gun. **1940** WReed *No Sign* (NY) 199: [He] headed for Bates Manor like a shot out of hell. **1950** MMurray *Neat* (NY DBC) 95: His own pony was away like a shot out of a gun. **1956** *Time* 9/17 76: Weldy beat it like a shot out of hell. **1970** VCHall *Outback* (Adelaide) 94: The wanted man would be off like a shot. **1971** JCreasey *Murder* (NY) 29: He'd come like a shot. **1982** SFrimmer *Dead* (NY) 101: And then he was off like the proverbial shot. TW 330(3); Taylor *Western Folklore* 17(1958) 19.

S172 Like **Shot** off a shovel

1922 JJoyce *Ulysses* (NY 1934) 339: Like shot off a shovel. **1951** EPaul *Murder on* (NY) 87: Started like shot off a shovel [*very fast*]. **1956** *Punch* 10/10 426: Mr. Chulkai then disappeared like shot off a shovel. **1961** EPeters *Death* (NY) 126: He goes like a shot off a shovel. EAP S181.

S173 A long **Shot** (*varied*)

1929 JJConnington *Case* (B) 123: It was just a long shot. **1939** GDHCole *Greek* (L) 230: Wilson noticed . . . that a long shot had come off. **1941** JShore *Rattle* (NY) 229: It was a long shot, but it went home. **1946** MInnes *What Happened* (NY) 143: I risked my long shot. **1962** AGarve *Prisoner's* (NY DBC) 88: It's the longest of long shots. EAP S182.

S174 Not by a long **Shot**

1919 JBCabell *Jurgen* (NY 1922) 322: Not . . . by a long shot. **1922** JJoyce *Ulysses* (NY 1934) 430: Not by a long shot. **1924** RO Chipperfield *Bright* (NY) 174: Not by a long shot. **1930** WLewis *Apes* (NY 1932) 17: Not by a long shot. **1949** RMLaurenson *Six Bullets* (NY) 54: Not by a long shot. **1970** RLockridge *Twice* (P) 171: Not by a hell of a long shot. **1976** RBDominic *Murder* (NY) 66: Not by a long shot. TW 330(2); Brunvand 126. Cf. Sight *below*.

S175 A **Shot** in the dark (*varied*)

1924 VLWhitechurch *Templeton* (NY) 202: A shot in the dark. **1930** LRGribble *Case* (NY) 188: A shot in the dark. But . . . it grazed the bull's eye. **1938** JCLanehan *Guilty* (L) 303: A shot in the dark. **1947** JIams *Body* (NY) 128: It's a shot in the dark. **1952** RPowell *A Shot in the Dark* (NY). **1957** SDean *Murder* (NY) 80: Shot in the dark. **1960** HWaugh *Road* (NY DBC) 80: Fellows tried a shot in the dark. **1962** HCarmichael *Of Unsound* (NY) 88: It was a blind shot in the dark. **1969** PZiegler *Black* (L) 62: A shot in the dark, or at least the twilight. **1970** TCoe *Wax* (NY) 51: A beautiful shot in the dark. **1977** JThomson *Death* (NY) 114: It was a shot in the dark. Berrey 179.2; Cole 62. Cf. Stab *below*.

S176 To call the **Shots** as one sees them

1938 CKnight *Ginger Lei* (NY) 166: I only call the shots as I see them. **1958** RMacdonald *Doomsters* (NY) 239: You really called the shots last night. **1962** GHCoxe *Man Who Died* (NY) 85: He called his shots as he saw them.

S177 To have a **Shot** in the locker (*varied*)

1913 JCLincoln *Mr. Pratt's Patients* (NY) 46: [He] had a shot left in the locker. **1914** PGWodehouse *Little Nugget* (NY 1929) 207: I still have a shot or two in my locker. **1931** LCArlington *Through* (L) 156: The final shot—generally the last left in the locker. **1933** HWade *Mist* (L) 69: It was the last shot in his locker. **1938** NMorland *Case Without* (L) 52: We have got a few shots in our locker. **1940** JCLincoln *Out of the Fog* (NY) 302: She . . . intended to keep a spare shot in the locker. **1941** GMitchell *Hangman's* (L) 273: He is at once the first and last shot in our locker. **1956** FDOmmanney *Isle* (P) 22: Zanzibar has another shot in the locker. **1958** RMacdonald *Doomsters* (NY) 216: There's plenty of shots in the old locker [*sexually potent*]. **1974** ROllard *Pepys* (NY) 188: Bleeding, the first and last shot in the medical locker of the seventeenth century. **1976** JPorter *Package* (NY) 61: She had more shots in her locker. EAP S184.

S178 Straight from the **Shoulder** (*varied*)
1931 ACEdington *Monk's Hood* (NY) 213: We have to speak straight from the shoulder. **1935** GBullett *Jury* (L 1947) 341: I told them so, straight from the shoulder. **1936** SGibbons *Miss Linsey* (NY) 185: That's straight from the shoulder, as they say. **1958** JYork *My Brother's* (NY DBC) 57: She would like it straight from the shoulder and wouldn't want him to beat about the bush. Wentworth 524: Straight.

S179 To give (turn) the cold **Shoulder**
1925 JSFletcher *Secret* (B) 57: I gave [him] the cold shoulder. **1939** WChambers *You Can't* (NY) 139: The movies . . . gave him the cold shoulder. **1951** ECrispin *Long* (L 1958) 30: She gives them the cold shoulder. **1956** JFStraker *Ginger* (L) 10: You've given him the cold shoulder. **1961** JRChild *Casanova* (L) 198: Turned the cold shoulder to him. **1965** IRoss *Charmers* (NY) 187: Chicago gave her the cold shoulder. **1972** RRendell *Murder* (NY) 63: Gave him the cold shoulder. TW 331(4); Brunvand 126; *Oxford* 133: Cold.

S180 To put one's **Shoulder** to the wheel (*varied*)
1925 FBeeding *Seven* (B) 10: Let every man put his shoulder to the wheel. **1935** JJConnington *In Whose* (L) 223: He had already put his shoulder to the wheel. **1955** PAnderson *Snake* (L) 178: Unless he put his shoulder to the wheel. **1957** *BangorDN* 4/1 21: Keep your shoulders to the wheel. **1964** BKaufman *Up the Down* (NY 1966) 69: Shoulder to wheel and nose to grindstone. **1964** ELathen *Accounting* (NY) 86: Put our shoulder to the wheel and march down the field. **1965** JPotts *Only Good* (NY) 66: I've barely laid my shoulder to the plow. **1969** JBurke *Firefly* (L) 88: Put your shoulder to the wheel, nose to the grindstone. **1971** TRosebury *Microbes* (NY) 305: We need to put our shoulders to the wheel and push. EAP S188.

S181 To get the **Show** on the road
1957 DRMorris *Warm* (NY) 134: Let's get the show on the road. **1959** SSterling *Body* (NY) 162: Let's get the show on the road. **1965** GHolden *Don't Go* (NY) 173: I hope you're ready to get your little show on the road. **1967** RTraver *Jealous* (B) 165: What is the current idiom?—kept the show on the road. **1973** BPronzini *Undercurrent* (NY) 14: Let's get the show on the road.

S182 To give the **Show** away
1958 HAlpert *Summer* (NY) 147: Sally would give the show away. Partridge 765.

S183 To get a short **Shrift** and a long day
1922 JJoyce *Ulysses* (NY 1934) 234: You'll all get a short shrift and a long day from me. Cf. NED Shrift *sb.* 9.

S184 As white as a **Shroud**
1928 VWilliams *Crouching* (B) 47: As white as a shroud. TW 331.

S185 Not know from a **Side** of sole leather
1956 *BangorDN* 7/24 11: I wouldn't know him from a side of sole leather. TW 332(3). Cf. Brunvand 127(1).

S186 On the right (fair, sunny) **Side** of fifty (*varied*)
1924 JSFletcher *Safety* (NY) 73: On the right side of fifty. **1926** HWade *Verdict* (L) 45: Barely on the right side of forty. **1928** WRoughead *Murderer's* (NY 1968) 4: Both were on the sunny side of thirty. **1936** HWade *Bury Him* (L) 23: On the right side of forty. **1943** WMcCully *Doctors* (NY) 45: On the sunny side of forty. **1956** ESGardner *Demure* (NY) 216: On the sunny side of thirty. **1965** HWaugh *End* (NY) 62: She was still on the fair side of thirty. TW 332(7). Cf. On the wrong Side *below*.

Side

S187   On the safe Side

1933 GCollins *Dead Walk* (L) 148: Nothin' like bein' on the safe side. *Oxford* 691: Safe.

S188   On the Side of the angels

1929 RBlaker *Jefferson* (NY) 4: On the side of the angels. **1951** DMDisney *Look* (NY) 71: Whose side was she on? The side of the angels, apparently. **1958** *NYTimes Book Review* 5/25 6: On the side of the angels. *Oxford* 13.

S189   On the wrong Side of fifty (*varied*)

1900 CFPidgin *Quincy A. Sawyer* (B) 13: On the shady side of fifty. **1925** FWCrofts *French's Greatest* (NY) 11: On the wrong side of sixty. **1940** MCharlton *Death of* (L) 28: The Colonel was on the wrong side of sixty. **1954** CHare *That Yew* (L) 24: Seems on the wrong side of fifty. **1972** KPedler *Mutant* (NY) 141: Most of the faces were on the wrong side of fifty. **1974** HCarmichael *Most* (NY) 124: She was the wrong side of fifty. EAP S193. Cf. On the right Side *above*.

S190   On the wrong Side of the blanket (*varied*)

1929 BFlynn *Case* (P) 229: Born the wrong side of the blanket. **1932** DLSayers *Have* (NY) 420: She thinks the wrong side of the blanket better than being left out in the cold. **1937** EGreenwood *Under the Fig* (NY) 32: Sinister bars and the wrong sides of blankets. **1939** AChristie *Murder for* (NY) 66: Even if you were born the right side of the blanket. **1946** MInnes *What Happened* (NY) 48: Born on the wrong side of the blanket. **1947** CBrand *Suddenly* (L) 30: Those entrancing glimpses of the wrong side of the blanket. **1955** RChurch *Over the* (L) 39: Children born on the wrong side of the blanket. **1957** JWyndham *Midwich* (NY) 151: Lot of wrong side of the blanket stuff in these parts. **1960** HInnes *Doomed* (NY) 15: The wrong side of the bloody blanket [*bastard*]. **1966** EFuller *Successful* (NY) 203: A litter of wrong-side-of-the-blanket puppies. TW 332(9); DARE i 276: Blanket; *Oxford* 924: Wrong.

S191   On the wrong Side of the tracks

1954 LFord *Invitation* (NY) 48: This date of yours must be horribly wrong side of the

tracks. **1961** JPhilips *Murder* (NY DBC) 7: You were born on the wrong side of the tracks. **1967** AChristie *Endless* (NY) 77: Your American phrase—I come from the wrong side of the tracks. **1970** AAFair *All Grass* (NY DBC) 86: People on the—well, on the other side of the tracks. **1970** JWechsberg *First* (B) 117: I'd never heard the expression "the wrong side of the tracks." DA Track *n.* 2c(8).

S192   There are two Sides to everything (*varied*)

1908 JCLincoln *Cy Whittaker* (NY) 258: There's always two sides to everything. **1916** SRohmer *Tales* (NY 1922) 199: There are always two sides to a case. **1924** CVanVechten *Tattooed* (NY) 179: There are two sides to every question. **1926** AFielding *Footsteps* (L) 144: There are two sides to every circle. **1931** SLeacock *Sunshine* (Toronto 1960) 49: There were two sides to everything. **1932** CBush *Unfortunate* (L) 12: Every question has two sides. **1940** MBurton *Mr. Westerby* (NY) 167: There are always two sides to a question. **1941** DVanDeusen *Garden Club* (I) 52: There were always two sides to a quarrel. **1949** RStout *Trouble* (NY) 95: But there's two sides to a bargain. **1956** *BHerald* 7/29 8: There are two sides to every argument. **1960** ADuggan *Cunning* (NY) 105: There are two sides to every quarrel. **1962** HWaugh *Late* (NY) 45: That's the other side of the coin. **1970** ACross *Poetic* (NY) 140: There are two sides to every question. **1970** WANolen *Making* (NY) 65: There were two sides to this particular coin. EAP S194, 195.

S193   To give the rough Side (edge) of one's tongue

1929 BFlynn *Case* (P) 143: She puts the rough edge of her tongue round Mr. Morgan. **1930** GMitchell *Mystery* (NY) 197: A boy that's had the rough side of me tongue. **1938** CAlington *Crime* (L) 74: The old brute's given him the rough side of his tongue. **1945** PWentworth *She Came* (NY) 37: I gave her the rough side of my tongue. **1953** ECRLorac *Shepherd's* (NY) 134: You'll get the rough side of my tongue. **1969** VdeSolaPinto *City* (L) 8: Jane would give him the rough edge of her tongue. **1969** FSwinnerton *Reflections* (L) 137: To give me the rough side of his tongue. *Oxford* 459: Lick.

S194 To hit the **Side** of a barn (a barn [door]) (*varied*)

1934 HReilly *McKee* (NY) 120: He wouldn't have been able to hit the side of a barn at ten paces. **1936** CFGregg *Henry* (L) 14: You couldn't hit a barn door. **1938** JTFarrell *No Star* (NY) 10: Your brother can't hit the blind side of a barn. **1940** DBurnham *Last Act* (NY) 197: I doubted whether Joan could hit a barn with a .45. **1952** MVHeberden *Tragic* (NY) 189: Carter couldn't hit a barn door at two feet. **1956** MColes *Birdwatcher's* (NY) 93: Now he is so blind he could not hit a barn unless, as they say, he was inside it with the door shut. **1961** FLockridge *Murder* (P) 99: I doubt if she could hit the side of a barn with a shotgun. **1965** RLPike *Police* (NY) 170: You couldn't hit the broadside of a barn. **1972** NWebster *Killing* (NY) 61: Probably . . . it [*a gun*] would be so inaccurate it wouldn't hit a barn door at the proverbial twenty paces. TW 17(3): Barn door; Cole 53: Hit . . . broad side.

S195 To know on which **Side** one's bread is buttered (*varied*)

1919 JSClouston *Simon* (NY) 133: He knows . . . which side his bread is buttered. **1922** JJoyce *Ulysses* (NY 1934) 313: He knows which side his bread is buttered. **1924** JJFarjeon *Master* (NY) 143: Knows which side his bread's buttered. **1930** RKeverne *Man in the Red Hat* (NY) 114: Price is no fool so far as his bread and butter is concerned. **1935** FDGrierson *Murder* (L) 233: I know which side my bread's buttered. **1947** HCahill *Look* (NY) 380: You'd think they'd know which side their bread was buttered on. **1950** GHCoxe *Eye* (NY) 16: He . . . knew which side his bread was buttered on. **1950** DMathew *Mango* (L) 207: He had always had a distaste for slang, the phrase about knowing which side a man's bread was buttered. **1957** JBlish *Frozen* (NY) 25: Which side do you think your bed [*sic*] is buttered on? **1961** AAFair *Bachelors* (NY DBC) 108: I know which side of the bread

has the butter. **1964** CWillock *Animal* (NY) 118: They saw which side their bread was buttered. **1969** JTrahey *Pecked* (Englewood Cliffs, NJ) 137: Sylvia . . . knew which side her girdle was buttered on. **1975** HLawrenson *Stranger* (NY) 9: He saw on what side his bread would best be buttered. **1976** MButterworth *Remains* (NY) 28: In the phrase of the vulgar, they know which side of their bloody bread is buttered. EAP S198; TW 332(11); Brunvand 127(2) [*varied*].

S196 To laugh on the other **Side** of one's face (*varied*)

1909 MRRinehart *Man in Lower Ten* (NY 1947) 245: I only hope you won't laugh on the wrong side of your face. **1925** BAtkey *Pyramid* (NY) 74: They will be laughing . . . on the wrong side of their mouths. **1927** SHorler *Black* (L 1935) 93: I want to see this fellow . . . smiling on the other side of his face. **1928** FDaingerfield *House* (NY) 112: He would laugh out of the other side of that mouth of his. **1928** HCMcNeile *Female* (NY) 230: You'll smile the other side of your face before long. **1930** JGBrandon *McCarthy* (L) 221: That'll make you grin . . . and on the wrong side of your mouth. **1936** RHull *Murder* (NY) 95: You'll laugh the other side of your face. **1941** TDuBois *McNeills Chase* (NY) 274: You'll be laughing out of the wrong side of your mouth. **1952** FCDavis *T.Read* (NY) 112: You'll be sneering on the other side of your pretty face. **1956** MProcter *Pub* (NY) 78: I'll make you laugh at the other side of your face. **1960** GAshe *Crime-Haters* (NY) 74: Make them laugh with the other sides of their faces. **1962** DAlexander *Tempering* (NY) 31: The laugh will be on the other side of your face. **1967** AChristie *Endless* (NY) 7: You'll laugh on the wrong side of your mouth. **1974** AMenen *Fonthill* (NY) 122: News that'll make you laugh on the other side of your face. EAP S196.

S197 To work (play) both **Sides** of the street

1944 HReilly *Opening Door* (NY) 116: She was working the same side of the street.

1957 *Time* 4/29 27: The men in the Kremlin were working both sides of the street. **1958** NMacNeil *Death* (Greenwich, Conn.) 16: You can't play both sides of the street in this racket. **1965** JPhilips *Black* (NY DBC) 54: She may decide to play both sides of the street.

S198   Up one **Side** and down the other

1934 BHughes *Murder* (NY) 48: She cursed Quinn up one side and down the other. **1937** ESGardner *D.A. Calls* (NY) 244: *The Blade* will be damning you up one side and down the other. **1970** STerkel *Hard* (NY) 47: They cursed him up one side and down the other.

S199   As leaky as a **Sieve**

1966 JAiken *Beware* (NY) 111: As leaky as an old sieve. EAP S200; Taylor *Western Folklore* 17(1958) 19. Cf. Colander *above*.

S200   To leak like a **Sieve**

1921 JCLincoln *Galusha* (NY) 149: We was leakin' like a sieve. **1940** CSaxby *Death Joins* (NY) 88: That . . . story leaks like a sieve. **1959** *BHerald* 4/11 5: It seems to have leaked like a sieve. **1961** PMoyes *Down Among* (NY) 52: Leaks like a bloody sieve. **1963** KAmis *Spectrum III* (L) 137: It leaks like a sieve. **1975** JDaniels *White* (NY) 262: The British censorship was leaking like a sieve. TW 333(1); *Oxford* 732.

S201   Not by a long **Sight**

1930 NBMavity *Other Bullet* (NY) 201: Not by a long sight. TW 333(2). Cf. Not by a long Shot *above*.

S202   Out of **Sight**, out of mind (*varied*)

1910 EPhillpotts *Tales* (NY) 79: Out of sight, out of mind. **1922** JJoyce *Ulysses* (NY 1934) 110: Out of sight, out of mind. **1922** FPitt *Woodland* (L) 82: Out of sight, out of mind. **1930** WLewis *Apes* (NY 1932) 72: Out of sight, out of mind. **1935** *New Yorker* 9/21 22: Just like the old saying, "Outta sight, outta mind." **1938** JGloag *Documents* (L) 144: To keep dames out of mind, if not out of sight. **1938** JRRTolkien *Hobbit* (B) 80: Out of sight and out of mind. **1945** JMarx *Groucho Letters* (NY 1967) 51: I was an out-of-sight, out-of-mind dog. **1949** GFowler *Beau* (NY) 38: His out-of-sight, out-of-mind tactics. **1953** EPaul *Waylaid* (NY) 265: Out of sight, out of mind, is a proverb common to all races. **1955** Miss Read *Village* (L 1960) 113: Out of sight was out of mind, wasn't it? And least said, soonest mended! Sensible sayings, both of 'em. **1957** *New Yorker* 11/16 103: Out of sight, but not quite out of mind. **1959** *BangorDN* 8/14 15: The saying "Out of sight—out of mind." **1964** AStratton *Great Red* (NY) 73: Out of the world's sight, out of the world's mind. **1966** ACarter *Honeybuzzard* (NY) 99: Out of sight, out of mind, was Emily's unconscious motto. **1966** DMarlowe *Dandy* (NY) 234: Aus dem Augen, aus dem Sinn, out of sight out of mind. **1968** LdeKLawrence *Lovely* (NY) 161: Out of sight, out of memory. **1975** NFreeling *Bugles* (NY) 77: Out of sight, out of mind. EAP S204; TW 333(1); Brunvand 127.

S203   A **Sight** for sore eyes (*varied*)

1900 CFPidgin *Quincy A. Sawyer* (B) 382: The sight of you is good for sore eyes. **1912** JCLincoln *Postmaster* (NY) 315: If this isn't good for sore eyes! **1930** MKennedy *Death* (L) 179: It wasn't exactly a treat for sore eyes. **1931** RAJWalling *Stroke* (NY) 189: He always was good for sore eyes. **1932** JCLenehan *Mansfield* (L) 32: A sight fit to cure sore eyes. **1935** CBarry *Death* (NY) 47: It's yerself 'at's a cure for sore eyes. **1940** D Burnham *Last Act* (NY) 108: A sight for sore eyes. **1949** MGilbert *He Didn't* (NY DBC) 17: You're a sight for sore eyes. **1954** MLSettle *Love* (L) 31: You're a sight for sore eyes. **1958** JYork *My Brother's* (NY DBC) 93: What a sight for sore eyes! **1966** RCrosby *I Was* (B) 141: You surely are a sight for sore eyes. **1970** RPowell *Whom the Gods* (NY) 111: The old saying, a sight for sore eyes, has wisdom in it. **1972** JBonett *No Time* (NY) 15: You're a sight for sore eyes. **1982** CMacLeod *Wrack* (NY) 94: You're a sight for sore eyes. EAP S205. Cf. Brunvand 44: Eye(4).

S204   To set one's **Sights** too high

1948 HReilly *Staircase* (NY) 37: She had set her sights too high. **1968** RCroft-Cooke

Feasting (NY) 65: He set his sights too high. Whiting *NC* 475.

S205 All **Signs** fail in dry weather

1943 EWTeale *Dune Boy* (NY 1957) 86: All signs fail in dry weather. EAP S208; Brunvand 127.

S206 **Silence** gives consent (*varied*)

1900 CFPidgin *Quincy A. Sawyer* (B) 340: Silence means consent. **1904** AEHousman *Letters* ed HMaas (Cambridge, Mass. 1971) 76: I will take silence to mean consent. **1919** JBCabell *Jurgen* (NY 1922) 72: Silence is a proverbial form of assent. **1922** JJoyce *Ulysses* (NY 1934) 490: Silence gives consent. **1928** PMacDonald *White* (NY) 198: Silence is avowal. **1928** HVO'Brien *Four-and-Twenty* (NY) 134: I take your silence for assent. **1929** CGBowers *Tragic* (NY) 172: Silence had not given consent. **1930** HAdams *Crime* (P) 180: Taking his silence for assent. **1930** ABCox *Second* (NY) 46: Her silence expressing her agreement. **1931** EABlake *Jade* (NY) 24: He seemed to take her silence for agreement. **1931** GTrevor *Murder* (L) 274: The other took his silence for acceptance. **1936** RAJWalling *Floating Foot* (NY) 4: The Professor's unusual silence gave consent. **1940** AEVanVogt *Glass* (NY 1951) 99: Their silence was consent. **1942** CHare *Tragedy at Law* (L 1953) 78: Silence being traditionally taken to mean consent. **1950** SPalmer *Monkey* (NY) 119: Taking silence for consent. **1954** STruss *Other Side* (NY) 165: Taking silence for at least tacit acquiescence. **1959** *NYTimes* 12/13 57: Silence means tacit assent. **1960** CBrossard *Double* (NY) 98: His silence of course meant agreement. **1962** MInnes *Connoisseur's* (L) 160: But I was silent. Or did I give an actual assent? **1969** PKDick *Galactic* (NY) 96: He said nothing. Mali took it for assent. **1970** HCarvic *Miss Seeton Draws* (NY) 141: There was a silence of consent. **1971** JMacNab *Education* (NY) 60: Silence implies assent. EAP S209; TW 333.

S207 **Silence** is the best policy

1931 LEppley *Murder* (NY) 89: Silence is sometimes the best policy. Cf. Honesty *above*. Cf. next entry.

S208 **Silence** is wisdom when speaking is folly

1965 HActon *Old Lamps* (L) 112: The proverb: silence is wisdom, when speaking is folly. EAP S210.

S209 As fine as **Silk**

1931 PATaylor *Cape Cod* (NY 1971) 299: Bill . . . was fine's silk. **1934** WMartyn *Death* (L) 260: "How-do-you do?" "Fine as silk." **1936** RHowes *Callace* (NY) 91: Fine as silk. **1956** BJChute *Greenwillow* (NY) 210: The words . . . fine as silk. **1962** ESherry *Girl* (NY DBC) 103: Fine as silk. EAP S212; TW 334(2); Brunvand 128(1).

S210 As sleek as **Silk**

1940 PMcGuire *Spanish* (L) 74: His hair was sleek as silk. Wilstach 358.

S211 As smooth as **Silk**; Silk-smooth

1930 JBude *Loss* (L) 226: It was working smooth as silk. **1930** LRGribble *Case* (NY) 107: Silk-smooth tones. **1932** MStDennis *Death Kiss* (NY) 135: An engine running smooth as silk. **1943** AAFair *Bats Fly* (NY) 38: Speeches that sound as smooth as silk. **1955** MGilbert *Country-House* (NY) 171: They're smooth as silk [*affable*]. **1957** *Time* 7/29 16: Everything went smooth as silk. **1965** MAllingham *Mind* (NY) 125: Keeping the interview as smooth as silk. **1968** RBissell *How Many* (B) 244: The royal coach . . . glides . . . smooth as precious silk out of the station. **1971** AGarve *Late* (NY) 63: The sea is as smooth as silk. **1973** ARoudybush *Gastronomic* (NY) 165: It's smooth as silk [*brandy*]. TW 334(3).

S212 As soft as **Silk**

1905 HRHaggard *Ayesha* (NY) 104: Hair . . . soft as silk. **1928** AECoppard *Silver* (L) 110: The soil's as soft as silk. **1939** DFrome *Mr. Pinkerton and the Old Angel* (L) 177: Voice . . . soft as silk. **1942** MGEberhart *Wolf* (NY) 48: A soft-as-silk voice. **1950** HReilly *Murder* (NY) 20: Hair as soft as silk. **1968** JMyrdal *Confessions* (NY) 33: Your blonde pubic hair as soft as silk. EAP S213; Brunvand 128(2).

S213 Silver-white

1936 HAdams *Chief* (L) 27: His silver-white hair. **1941** FCharles *Vice Czar* (NY) 149: Silver-white hair. EAP S216.

S214 Simon-pure

1912 JCLincoln *Postmaster* (NY) 165: Simon-pure. **1920** JSFletcher *Dead Men's* (NY) 217: The absolute Simon-pure. **1935** R Howes *Death* (NY) 184: A simon-pure lunatic. **1936** DTeilhet *Crimson Hair* (NY) 100: A simon-pure lie of the first water. **1946** HHowe *We Happy* (NY) 9: He's a simon-pure parlor snake. **1958** DGBrowne *Death* (L) 31: The real Simon Pure. **1958** HReilly *Ding* (NY DBC) 43: A simon pure first rate rat. **1962** PDennis *Genius* (NY) 118: The stories . . . are simon pure [*decent*]. **1965** HHowe *Gentle* (NY) 128: Simon-pure Yankee. EAP S217.

S215 As black as Sin

1913 ERBurroughs *Warlord* (NY 1963) 142: The way was black as sin. **1931** CFGregg *Rutland* (NY) 274: Black as sin. **1938** MBrucker *Poison* (NY) 112: A heart as black as sin. **1954** AStratton *Great Red* (NY) 49: Black as sin. **1960** EMcBain *Give the Boys* (NY) 62: Her hair was black as sin. **1961** EMcBain *Lady* (NY) 11: Hair, as black as sin. **1975** HCarvic *Odds on* (NY) 70: It was black as sin. Whiting *NC* 475(1); Taylor *Western Folklore* 17(1958) 19(1).

S216 As clever as Sin

1924 HCBailey *Mr. Fortune's Practice* (NY) 73: As clever as sin. **1935** DYates *She Fell* (NY) 156: They say "clever as sin," don't they? Taylor *Prov. Comp.* 27.

S217 As crooked as Sin

1929 JCameron *Seven* (L) 194: Crooked as sin. Whiting *NC* 475(2).

S218 As guilty as Sin

1925 FWCrofts *Groote* (NY) 120: He's as guilty as sin. **1968** JRoffman *Grave* (NY) 129: Looking as guilty as sin itself. Whiting *NC* 475(3).

S219 As homely as Sin

1900 CFPidgin *Quincy A. Sawyer* (B) 206: Homelier than sin. Taylor *Prov. Comp.* 49.

S220 As mean as Sin

1968 RDuncan *How to Make* (L) 169: As mean as sin. **1968** JHaythorne *None of Us* (NY) 12: He was as mean as sin [*frugal*]. Taylor *Prov. Comp.* 57.

S221 As naked (stubborn) as Sin

1938 HWSandberg *Crazy* (NY) 111: Naked as sin. **1970** ELathen *Pick* (NY) 96: He was stubborn as sin.

S222 As ugly as Sin (varied)

1917 JCLincoln *Extricating* (NY) 300: Ugly as sin [*disagreeable*]. **1928** CBarry *Corpse* (NY) 234: She is as ugly as the seven deadly sins. **1931** FLPackard *Gold Skull* (NY) 127: Ugly as sin. **1952** HCecil *Ways* (L) 91: She was ugly as sin. **1957** *New Yorker* 2/9 23: The new lights are as ugly as sin. **1960** JJMarric *Gideon's Fire* (NY) 107: She was as ugly as proverbial sin. **1965** HVanDyke *Ladies* (NY) 99: You're ugly as homemade sin. **1974** HCrews *Gypsy's* (NY) 170: As ugly as sin and sure as death. EAP S218; TW 335(8); Brunvand 128(1).

S223 It is a Sin to steal a penny or a pin

1956 DMDisney *Unappointed* (NY) 181: 'Tis a sin to steal a penny or a pin. Apperson 572(2): Pin.

S224 Old Sins have long shadows

1925 DVane *Scar* (NY) 23: Old sins have long shadows. **1933** HWade *Mist* (L) 239: Old sins have long shadows. **1939** AChristie *Sad Cypress* (NY 1958) 113: Old sins have long shadows, as they say. **1947** AGilbert *Death in* (L) 131: Old sins have long shadows. **1953** AChristie *Pocket* (NY) 55: And old sins have long shadows, as the saying goes. **1959** AGilbert *Death* (NY) 124: Old sins have long shadows, proclaimed the proverb. **1961** AGilbert *After* (NY DBC) 62: That saying "Old sins have long shadows." **1967** MErskine *Case with* (NY) 71: Old happenings cast long shadows. Cf. *Oxford* 592.

S225 Old Sins never die

1933 RJCasey *Hot Ice* (I) 126: Old Sins Never Die. Cf. preceding entry.

S226 One's **Sins** will find one out (*varied*)
1931 RAFreeman *Pontifex* (NY) 187: A good old proverb assures us that we may be sure our sins will find us out. **1932** BRoss *Tragedy of X* (NY) 298: Our sins come home to us. **1936** JCLenehan *Deadly* (L) 281: A case of "your sins will find you out." **1967** JBlish *Torrent* (NY) 217: Another of [his] proverbs: Be sure your sins will find you out. **1969** FSwinnerton *Reflections* (L) 21: The old saying, "Be sure your sin will find you out." Bradley 92: Be sure.

S227 To hate like **Sin**
1910 EPhillpotts *Tales* (NY) 81: Hated . . . worse than sin. TW 335(10).

S228 To **Sing** small
1906 JCLincoln *Mr. Pratt* (NY) 76: I was ready to sing small. **1909** JCLincoln *Keziah* (NY) 333: Have to sing small. **1932** CFGregg *Body* (L) 114: Big noises hate to sing small. EAP S222; TW 339: Small.

S229 **Sink** or swim
1904 LFBaum *Marvelous Land of Oz* (NY) 61: Let him sink or swim. **1921** JSFletcher *Orange-Yellow* (NY) 28: Swim or sink with it. **1933** HHolt *Scarlet* (L) 118: Left to sink or swim. **1937** FBeeding *Hell* (L) 284: It's sink or swim together. **1946** RFinnegan *Lying* (NY) 151: The sink-or-swim, do-or-die individualism. **1951** ADerleth *Outer* (NY) 162: We sink or swim. **1956** AWUpfield *Man of* (NY) 82: To employ a nautical cliché, "We sink or swim together." **1957** *BHerald* 3/10 3A: We have to sink or swim on our own. **1959** JPurdy *Malcolm* (NY) 39: Sink or swim, as the old saw has it. **1968** RTruax *Doctors* (NY) 306: The "sink or swim" method. **1974** JWain *SJohnson* (NY) 75: Swim, or sink. EAP S224; TW 335(1).

S230 All **Sir Garnet**
1917 GRSims *My Life* (L) 25: All Sir Garnet. **1933** NBell *Lord* (B) 5: All Sir Garnet [*first rate*]. **1936** LAKnight *Night* (L) 158: Seems all Sir Garnet [*okay*]. **1956** AWUpfield *Battling* (L 1960) 144: Everything all Sir Garno [*sic*]. **1961** RJWhite *Smartest* (L) 104: It's all Sir Garnet. Partridge 771.

S231 As sure as I'm **Sitting** here
1908 MRRinehart *Circular Staircase* (NY 1947) 128: Sure as I'm sitting here. **1924** EWallace *Green* (B) 279: As sure as I'm sitting here. **1936** JRhode *In Face* (L) 42: As surely as I'm sitting here. **1937** ECVivian *38 Automatic* (L) 152: As sure as I'm sitting here. **1947** HLawrence *Death of* (NY) 161: As sure as I'm sitting here. **1952** RFenisong *Deadlock* (NY) 80: As sure as I'm sitting here. **1970** STerkel *Hard* (NY) 220: As sure as I'm sitting here. TW 335(1).

S232 As true as I'm **Sitting** here
1948 JRhode *Death* (NY) 167: That's as true as I'm sitting here. **1954** EForbes *Rainbow* (B) 27: True as I'm sitting here. **1965** JLindsay *Thunder* (L) 424: True as I'm sitting here on my own bottom. TW 335(2).

S233 It is as cheap **Sitting** as standing (*varied*)
1921 JCLincoln *Galusha* (NY) 301: Jest as cheap settin' as standin' and consider'ble lighter on shoe leather, as the feller said. **1922** JJoyce *Ulysses* (NY 1934) 395: 'Tis as cheap sitting as standing. **1928** JJConnington *Mystery* (B) 270: It's as cheap sitting as standing. **1956** BJFarmer *Death* (L) 57: Never stand when you can sit. TW 335(4); *Oxford* 116: Cheap.

S234 To be **Sitting** pretty
1936 PGWodehouse *Laughing* (NY) 280: You'll be sitting pretty. **1939** GBarnett *There's Money* (L) 268: You're not sitting very prettily. **1943** RChandler *Lady* (NY 1946) 35: I am sitting pretty. **1955** MErskine *Old Mrs.* (NY) 142: Kenneth was sitting pretty. **1971** PDickinson *Sleep* (NY) 136: The kids here are sitting pretty. Wentworth 479.

S235 At **Sixes** and sevens
1919 CPearl *Morrison of Peking* (Sydney 1967) 380: At sixes and sevens. **1930** WLewis *Apes* (NY 1932) 413: All was at sixes and sevens in his head. **1934** JRhode *Venner* (NY) 225: You all seem to be at sixes and sevens [*of different opinions*]. **1937** AEFielding *Mystery* (NY) 75: The morning room looked like sixes and sevens. **1941** JKVedder *Last Doorbell* (NY) 30: I'm all at sevens

and eights. **1945** HGreen *Loving* (L) 209: Setting everyone about the place at sixes and sevens as he did. **1952** JSherwood *Ambush* (NY) 56: Everything here's at sixes and sevens. **1959** *BHerald* 11/23 10: A Europe "at sixes and sevens," to borrow a British phrase. **1962** VWBrooks *Fenollosa* (NY) 4: Everything was at sixes and sevens. **1966** LPDavies *Who Is* (NY) 117: His mind is at sixes and sevens [*slightly deranged*]. **1970** RRendell *Guilty* (NY) 123: We're all at sixes and sevens. **1974** JPHennessy *Stevenson* (NY) 248: He and Belle were frequently at sixes and sevens. EAP S227; TW 336(4); Brunvand 128.

S236 **Six** of one and half a dozen of the other (*varied*)

1919 LTracy *Bartlett* (NY) 84: We're six of one and half a dozen of the other. **1931** SChalmers *Whispering* (NY) 227: It's six and half-a-dozen for choice. **1931** AWynne *Silver Scale* (P) 31: Six of one and half a dozen of the other. **1941** RStout *Alphabet* (NY) 266: It is six of one and about three dozen of the other. **1945** JSymons *Immaterial* (L 1954) 85: It was six of one and a half dozen of the other. **1952** RGHam *Gifted* (NY) 42: It's six of one and a half dozen of the other. **1957** *New Yorker* 3/9 80: A case of six of one and six of the other. **1957** CRice *Knocked* (NY) 12: It was six of a half-dozen, he told himself, wondering if that was exactly what he meant. **1960** DKarp *Enter* (NY) 164: It's six of one and three for a nickel of the other. **1960** VWilliams *Walk* (NY) 41: He said the woman was six of a witch and the man was half-dozen of a devil. **1968** JMerrill *Daughters* (NY 1970) 45: I guess it's six of one and you-know-what of the other. EAP S228.

S237 As bright as **Sixpence**

1955 NMarsh *Scales* (B) 63: He's not exactly as bright as sixpence. **1965** AGilbert *Voice* (NY) 84: Bright [*in mind*] as a new sixpence even now.

S238 A quick **Sixpence** is better than a slow shilling

1953 OAtkinson *Golden* (I) 120: A quick sixpence is better than a slow shilling. Whit-

ing *NC* 476(1): Nimble; *Oxford* 567: Nimble ninepence.

S239 To lose a **Sixpence** and find a farthing

1940 HRutland *Poison Fly* (NY) 61: What's happened? Lost sixpence and found a farthing!

S240 To seek **Sixpences**

1920 JSFletcher *Dead Men's* (NY) 65: A . . . man . . . walking very fast with his eyes on the ground, as if, as the youngsters say, he was seeking sixpences. Cf. Whiting H126.

S241 To go it (*etc.*) like **Sixty**

1928 RHFuller *Jubilee* (NY) 403: Going it like sixty. **1939** IOellrichs *Man Who* (NY) 192: She was going like sixty. **1952** RMarshall *Jane* (NY) 29: Working like sixty. **1959** ESGardner *Deadly* (NY) 159: This car comes driving up there . . . coming like sixty. **1965** CArmstrong *Turret* (NY) 226: Her arm . . . hurt like sixty. TW 336(2); Brunvand 128.

S242 To cut down to **Size**

1952 KMKnight *Valse* (NY) 113: I'm going to cut him down to size. **1953** JDolph *Dead Angel* (NY) 50: I'll trim him down to size for you. **1960** MCronin *Begin* (NY) 110: Let's cut him down to size. **1972** ARoudybush *Sybaritic* (NY) 50: We'll have to cut you down to size.

S243 The **Skeleton** (*etc.*) at the feast (*varied*)

c1923 ACrowley *Confessions* ed JSymonds (L 1969) 906: They began to see me as a skeleton at the banquet. **1929** RAldington *Death* (L) 349: Like a death's-head at a feast. **1931** CWells *The Skeleton at the Feast* (NY). **1933** LGrex *Lonely Inn* (L) 211: He was a death's head at the feast. **1939** GDHCole *Double* (NY) 56: Roger calls her the death's head at the feast. **1946** CDickson *My Late* (NY) 39: I don't want to seem a death's head at the feast. **1954** AWUpfield *Sinister* (NY) 18: Looking like the skeleton at the feast. **1957** STruss *Truth* (NY) 148: Why must I be my own spectre at the feast? **1960** AWUpfield *Valley* (NY DBC) 142: The Skeleton at the Feast. **1961** FLeiber *Silver* (NY) 186: Don't let him feel like a spectre at the feast. **1969** JCaird *Loch* (NY) 111: Something of a death's head at the feast. **1969** UKLeGuin *Left Hand* (NY) 87: The spectre at the feast. **1969** RWeiss *Renaissance* (Oxford) 31: The proverbial skeleton at the Roman feast. TW 336(2); *Oxford* 739.

S244 The **Skeleton** in the closet (cupboard) (*varied*)

1900 CFPidgin *Quincy A. Sawyer* (B) 293: A skeleton in a closet. **1922** JJoyce *Ulysses* (NY 1934) 367: Skeleton in the cupboard. **1924** CVanVechten *Tattooed* (NY) 119: Skeletons dangled from the hooks in all their closets. **1930** JHawk *House* (NY) 34: These families always believe in keeping the skeleton locked tight in the proverbial cupboard. **1930** WLewis *Apes* (NY 1932) 501: If one has *that* skeleton always in one's family cupboard. **1933** DLSayers *Murder* (NY) 64: The skeleton in the water-closet. **1939** LBrock *Riddle* (L) 156: Dragged out of its dusty cupboard . . . a long-concealed skeleton. **1940** JJFarjeon *Friday* (I) 96: He has a skeleton in his cupboard . . . Not the conventional skeleton [*a woman*]. **1949** NBlake *Head* (NY) 24: Any skeletons in closets or black sheep. **1953** HBPiper *Murder* (NY) 162: There's nothing like a good murder to shake the skeletons out of the closets. **1956** *TLS* 11/2 649: There were more skeletons than one in the Rydal Mount cupboards. **1957** GLWatson *A.E.Housman* (L) 30: The skeleton still faintly rattled in the closet. **1957** NWYates *W.T.Porter* (Baton Rouge) 26: Slavery was usually kept in the editorial closet—the national skeleton. **1962** PMac Donald *Death* (NY) 98: I suppose we all have dirty linen in our closets, wrapped around the skeletons. **1967** CAird *Most Contagious* (NY) 143: The family skeleton in the family woodpile. **1967** VPowell *Substantial* (L) 81: Without any amorous skeleton in the cupboard of his private life. **1969** PDickinson *Old English* (NY) 172: You found the very gruesome skeleton in the . . . cupboard. **1970** WGSewell *People* (L) 50: A Western skeleton in their Chinese cupboard. **1976** RBDominic *Murder* (NY) 38: Hiding skeletons in the closet. **1976** EMcBain *So Long* (NY) 58: You open the closet door and find the skeletons hanging there. TW 336(3); Brunvand 128; *Oxford* 739.

S245 To be frightened out of one's **Skin** (boots)

1930 EWallace *White Face* (NY) 143: Frightened me out of my skin. **1932** TCobb *Death* (L) 233: I was frightened out of my skin. **1935** BThomson *Richardson Solves* (L) 41: He frightened him out of his boots. **1950** ERPunshon *So Many* (NY) 179: She seemed pretty well frightened out of her skin. Cf. To jump *below*.

S246 To be no **Skin** off one's nose (back[side], teeth, *etc.*)

1929 WFaulkner *Sound* (NY) 307: It was no skin off my back. **1932** MTurnbull *Return* (P) 90: 'Tain't no skin off my nose. **1933** WMarch *Company K* (NY) 141: It's no skin off my back-side. **1934** NChild *Diamond* (L) 11: It's no skin off your back. **1935** WChambers *13 Steps* (NY) 143: It's no skin off my knuckles. **1935** HLDavis *Honey* (NY) 53: It was no bark off his tail. **1936** JTFarrell *World* (NY) 243: It's no skin off your backside. **1936** TPainter *Motives* (NY) 12: No skin off my chin. **1940** GBagby *Corpse Wore* (NY) 207: The Queen's job is no skin off my nose. **1940** RDarby *Death Conducts* (NY) 255: It ain't no skin offa our elbows. **1941** GEGiles *Three Died* (NY) 181: No skin off my lovely butt. **1952** PHBonner *SPQR* (NY) 4: It's no skin off our behinds. **1952** HWaugh *Last Seen* (NY) 87: It's no skin off my teeth whether she's alive in Michigan City or dead in Boston. **1954** HStone *Man Who* (NY 1957) 15: Fatso was no skin off his nose. **1957** *BHerald* 6/6 16: And it isn't a single bit of skin off their noses. **1959** DTracy *Big* (NY DBC) 120: It won't be no skin off our tails. **1961** RAKnoelton *Court* (L 1967) 187: It's no skin off our butt. **1962** AMStein *Home* (NY) 20: It's no skin off your saddle. **1967** LJBraun *Cat* (NY) 52: It's no skin off my back. **1968** WTenn *Square* (NY) 174: It's no skin off my nose. **1970** SO'Toole *Confessions* (Minneapolis) 69: It was no skin off my back. **1970** RLPike *Reardon* (NY) 130: It wasn't any skin off his butt. **1973** CJackson *Kicked* (NY) 44: It's no skin off your nose. **1974** CCarpenter *Deadhead* (NY) 76: C'est la vie, you know. No skin off my proverbial. **1974** RRosenblum *Good* (NY) 24: It's no skin off my teeth. **1977**

HDolson *Beauty* (P) 133: No skin off my ass. Partridge 775: Nose; Berrey 21.3: Ear, elbow, nose, 275.1.

S247 To escape (*etc.*) by the **Skin** of one's teeth (*varied*)

1900 CFPidgin *Quincy A. Sawyer* (B) 159: He just got in by the skin of his teeth. **1913** JSFletcher *Secret* (L 1918) 198: He had escaped by the mere skin of his teeth. **1914** JLondon *Letters* ed KHendricks (NY 1965) 412: By the skin of my teeth. **1928** AEApple *Mr. Chang's* (NY) 163: Escaped by the bare skin of his teeth. **1932** RJCasey *News* (I) 118: She got there by the skin of her teeth. **1937** PWentworth *Case Is Closed* (L) 223: He just got a train by the skin of his teeth. **1941** AAFair *Spill* (NY) 8: He'd made it by the skin of his eyeteeth. **1943** PATaylor *Going* (NY) 169: She just misses lisping by the skin of her teeth. **1946** FWCrofts *Death of a Train* (L) 11: We were carrying on by the skin of our teeth. **1951** JSStrange *Reasonable* (NY) 175: For six years I lived by the skin of my teeth. **1956** EBigland *Lord Byron* (L) 103: By the skin of his teeth, Byron managed to evade a meeting. **1957** *Time* 9/30 18: I got there by the skin of my teeth. **1958** WDHassett *Off the Record* (New Brunswick, NJ) 319: Jesse had been hanging onto both jobs by the skin of his teeth. **1960** EWolf *Rosenbach* (Cleveland) 133: A touch of by-the-skin-of-your-teeth excitement. **1967** RTraver *Jealous* (B) 93: To coin a phrase, the nudists escaped by the skin of their teeth. EAP S236.

S248 To get out with a whole **Skin**

1928 RHFuller *Jubilee* (NY) 505: Get out with a whole skin. EAP S235.

S249 To get under one's **Skin**

1937 GBarnett *I Knew* (L) 164: He got under one's skin. Wentworth 482.

S250 To jump out of one's **Skin** (shoes)

1919 JSFletcher *Middle Temple* (NY) 225: I can't a-bear to be jumped out of my skin. **1922** JJoyce *Ulysses* (NY 1934) 744: I near jumped out of my skin. **1932** JJFarjeon *Z* (NY) 283: He nearly jumped out of his skin at the sound. **1937** LPowys in MElwin *Life* (L 1946) 250: I could jump out of my skin.

1939 IOellrichs *Man Who* (NY) 35: Don't go jumping out of your shoes. **1940** JRhode *Death on* (NY) 102: He nearly jumped out of his skin. **1951** JCollier *Fancies* (NY) 246: It made Charlie nearly jump out of his skin. **1952** EPaul *Black* (NY) 34: I jumped out of my shoes. **1957** The Gordons *Big* (NY) 55: I almost jumped out of my skin. **1960** MColes *Concrete* (NY) 108: You've made me jump out of my seven skins. **1967** LWoolf *Downhill* (L) 52: She "jumped out of her skin." **1970** RNeely *Walter* (NY) 131: The phone almost made me leap out of my skin. EAP S237. Cf. TW 337(5): Fly. Cf. To be frightened *above*.

S251 To save one's own **Skin**

1923 DFox *Doom* (NY) 207: Save your own skin. **1929** JJConnington *Case* (B) 262: One's own skin comes first. **1941** MHolbrook *Suitable* (NY) 194: I'd look after my own skin. **1959** JGill *Dead* (NY) 173: I want to save my skin. **1981** JSScott *View* (NY) 112: Save his own skin. TW 237(7).

S252 To keep one's **Skirts** clear (*varied*)

1922 VSutphen *In Jeopardy* (NY) 94: His personal skirts must be clear. **1927** WBFoster *From Six* (NY) 77: None of our skirts are clear in that matter; 84. **1927** GELocke *Golden* (NY) 55: His coat-tails are clear in the matter. **1931** JDCarr *Lost* (L) 112: He merely seems to have been clearing his own skirts. **1934** CFGregg *Execution* (L) 60: I want to keep my skirts clear. **1937** DQBurleigh *Kristiana* (NY) 245: Joe's skirts seem to be clear. **1941** ISShriber *Murder Well Done* (NY) 223: Your skirts aren't so clean yourself. **1963** JMUllman *Neon* (NY) 192: Keep their skirts clean. **1968** LSdeCamp *Great Monkey* (NY) 432: My skirts are clear. TW 337; Brunvand 128.

S253 As drunk as a **Skunk**

1940 BHalliday *Uncomplaining* (NY) 143: I'm drunk as a skunk. **1948** AHandley *Kiss* (P) 164: Drunk as a skunk. **1954** SDeLima *Carnival* (NY) 32: He was drunk as a skunk. **1958** *BangorDN* 8/6 11: My husband got drunk as a skunk. **1968** TMcGuane *Sporting* (NY) 118: Drunk as a skunk. **1975** FMNivens *Publish* (NY) 72: He was drunk as a skunk. **1978** CMacLeod *Rest You* (NY) 42: Jemima was drunk as a skunk, to coin a simile. Taylor *Western Folklore* 17(1958) 19(1).

S254   As popular as a **Skunk** (at a picnic)

1937 JGEdwards *Murder* (NY) 52: As popular as a skunk at a picnic. **1958** *Time* 7/7 68: As popular as a skunk. Cf. Cole 67: Welcome . . . garden party.

S255   Enough blue **Sky** to make a pair of breeches (*varied*)

1936 RWyndham *Gentle Savage* (L) 31: A patch of blue in the sky "large enough to cut a pair of breeches," or at least a pair of hiker's shorts. **1956** EGann *Twilight* (NY) 234: [Blue sky] about as big as a Dutchman's pants. Partridge 251: Dutchman's breeches; Taylor *Western Folklore* 17(1958) 15: Dutchman's trousers.

S256   Red **Sky** at night, sailors' delight *etc.* (*varied*)

1933 CPenfield *After the Deacon* (NY) 184: Red sky at night, sailors' delight. **1940** EPaul *Mayhem* (NY) 255: The old proverb: "Evening red and morning gray, Sure sign of a fair day." **1946** CDickson *My Late* (NY) 184: Red sky at morning, Sailors take warning. **1957** THWhite *Master* (L) 180: Red sky at night, shepherds' delight. **1961** CBlackstone *House* (L 1965) 154: Red sky at night is the shepherd's delight. Isn't that what the country people say? **1963** MPHood *Sin* (NY) 85: Red in the morning, Sailor take warning. **1964** AMacKinnon *Report* (NY) 27: "Red sky at morning, angler's warning," quoted Dr. John. **1969** SMays *Reuben's* (L) 166: Red sky at night, shepherd's delight; Red sky at morning, that be a warnin'. **1971** WTeller *Cape Cod* (Englewood Cliffs, NJ) 41: Red sky, in the morning, sailor take warning—that is what they say in New England. **1978** HPentecost *Deadly Trap* (NY) 42: Red sky at night, sailor's delight. **1981** JSScott *View* (NY) 25: We have a saying . . . "Red sky at night, shepherd's delight." **1983** HHBroun *Whose Little* (NY) 207: An old rhyme . . . "Red sky at night, sailor's delight, red sky at morning, sailor take warning." TW 122: Evening; *Oxford* 741.

S257   The **Sky** is the limit

1930 JFDobie *Coronado* (Dallas) 252: With the sky for the limit. **1937** ESGardner *Dangerous Dowager* (NY) 9: Aside from that, the sky's the limit. **1942** WIrish *Phantom* (NY 1957) 10: The sky's the limit. **1942** PGWodehouse *Money* (NY) 124: The sky might be the limit. **1950** FO'Malley *Best* (NY) 76: The sky was the limit. **1953** AA Fair *Some Women* (NY DBC) 152: The sky's the limit now. **1965** JNichols *Sterile* (NY) 62: The sky was the limit. **1968** TMcGuane *Sporting* (NY) 90: The sky was the limit. Partridge 484: Limit.

S258   When the **Sky** falls we shall all have larks (*varied*)

1922 JJoyce *Ulysses* (NY 1934) 290: And he waiting for what the sky would drop in the way of drink. **1931** PATaylor *Cape Cod* (NY 1971) 318: We can go on an' hope the sky falls an' lets down a shower o' skylarks an' rainbows. **1938** MInnes *Lament* (L) 41: The laverocks might be in fear of the skies falling, folks said, if those at the mickle house were taking to spend their silver like that. EAP S243.

S259   To blow (be blown) **Sky-high**

1930 HAdams *Crime* (P) 223: The case was blown sky high. **1930** IGreig *King's* (L) 147: It . . . blew the police theory sky-high. EAP S245; Brunvand 129.

S260   As lean as a **Slat**

1957 *New Yorker* 4/27 39: He . . . is as lean as a slat. Cf. Lath *above*.

S261   As thin as a **Slat**

1960 DKarp *Enter* (NY) 139: The lady, thin as a slat. **1969** SPalmer *Hildegarde* (NY) 59: Thin as a slat. Cf. Lath *above*.

S262   To have a **Slate** loose

1950 CDickson *Night* (NY) 20: She's got a slate loose. Partridge 780. Cf. Tile *below*.

S263   To wipe the **Slate** clean

1936 ECRLorac *Crime* (L) 9: The slate's wiped clean. **1958** SDean *Dishonor* (NY) 15: I was wiping the slate clean. Cole 68. Cf. Wentworth 582: Wipe off the slate.

S264 To work (toil) like a **Slave**

1925 EMillay *Letters* ed ARMacdougall (NY 1952) 194: Working like . . . slaves. **1935** FBeeding *Norwich* (NY) 4: I've worked like a slave. **1945** BKendrick *Death Knell* (NY) 48: He'd worked like a slave. **1955** MWheeler *Still* (L) 164: Worked like slaves. **1963** IFleming *On Her* (L) 147: Working like a slave. **1969** PSCatling *Freddy* (NY) 155: I've been working like a slave. **1971** DFJones *Denver* (NY) 174: We toiled like slaves. **1971** DPryde *Nunaga* (NY) 158: Working like a slave. EAP S247; Taylor *Western Folklore* 17(1958) 19(1). Cf. To work like a Black, Galley slave, Nigger *above*.

S265 The first **Sleep** is the soundest

1934 HFootner *Murder* (NY) 200: He may go according to the old saying that the first sleep is the soundest. Cf. Bradley 92; *Oxford* 389: Hour's sleep.

S266 Plenty of **Sleep** in the grave

1954 IFleming *Live* (NY 1959) 59: We'll get plenty of sleep in the grave. EAP S248.

S267 To have something (card, ace, *etc.*) up one's **Sleeve**

1908 JCLincoln *Cy Whittaker* (NY) 198: Somethin' up your sleeve. **1915** JBuchan *Thirty-Nine* (NY) 19: They've got the ace up their sleeve. **1922** JJoyce *Ulysses* (NY 1934) 176: He has some bloody horse up his sleeve. **1924** VLWhitechurch *Templeton* (NY) 214: A card up my sleeve. **1930** JSFletcher *Yorkshire* (NY) 271: He has a trump card up his sleeve. **1932** CBush *Unfortunate* (L) 160: The vicar had been a card up Parker's sleeve. **1933** ABCox *Jumping* (L) 279: They have . . . something up their sleeves. **1933** WCBrown *Murder* (P) 109: It's an ace up our sleeve. **1937** AChristie *Cards* (NY) 59: Our own deductions . . . we . . . keep up our sleeves. **1940** FWBronson *Nice People* (NY) 143: He had something up his sleeve. **1941** FWCrofts *Circumstantial* (NY) 274: He's generally got a trump up his sleeve. **1946** CBush *Second Chance* (L) 174: To have Nevall up her sleeve as a possible . . . second string. **1950** SPalmer *Monkey* (NY) 61: I have an extra ace up my sleeve. **1951** MHead *Congo* (NY) 9: I've got some-

thing up my sleeve. **1953** FKane *Poisons* (NY 1960) 71: I still have one card up my sleeve. **1956** *TLS* 6/8 349: There had always been another ace up the papal sleeve. **1956** *Arizona Highways* Sept. 37: What have you got up your sleeve now? **1958** CCarnac *Affair* (NY) 161: Latimer had another card up his sleeve. **1962** ABurgess *Clockwork* (NY 1965) 147: Nothing up our sleeves. **1968** GAshe *Death* (NY) 120: She may have something else up her sleeves. **1969** JTAppleby *Troubled* (L) 177: The king . . . had an ace up his sleeve. **1970** AChristie *Passenger* (NY) 34: Something funny up their sleeves. **1975** MKWren *Multitude* (NY) 162: Have an ace up his sleeve. Brunvand 1: Ace(2); Wentworth 2: Ace.

S268 To laugh in (up) one's **Sleeve**

1913 EDBiggers *Seven Keys* (I) 103: Laughing in their sleeves. **1931** WWJacob *Snug* (NY) 144: Laughing in your sleeves at me. **1936** CBush *Monday Murders* (L) 135: Laughing up his sleeve. **1938** JRRTolkien *Hobbit* (B) 231: Laughing in their sleeves at him. **1940** MBoniface *Murder as* (NY) 139: His silent way of laughing in his sleeve. **1951** EQueen *Origin* (B) 211: Laughing up his sleeve. **1957** BVanOrden *309 East* (NY) 123: He must have laughed up his sleeve. **1962** LEgan *Borrowed* (NY DBC) 167: Laughing up his sleeve. **1968** SMorrow *Dancing* (NY) 19: Laughing up his sleeve. **1975** EPeters *Crocodile* (NY) 4: Laughed up my sleeve. EAP S249; TW 338–9.

S269 A **Slice** from a cut cake is never missed (*varied*)

1937 CFGregg *Wrong House* (L) 170: It's like a slice from a cut cake or more so—it's never missed. **1960** GSAlbee *By the Sea* (NY) 96: What's another slice out of a cut pie? **1966** BNaughton *Alfie* (L) 92: They say a slice off a cut loaf is never missed. Whiting *NC* 477; Partridge 781; *Oxford* 724: Shive. Cf. Plowed *above*.

S270 To give a **Slice** of tongue pie

1952 GBullett *Trouble* (L) 236: My wife gave me a slice of tongue pie. Partridge 897.

S271 There's many a **Slip** between the cup and the lip (*varied*)

1922 JJoyce *Ulysses* (NY 1934) 634: The little misadventure . . . between the cup and the lip. **1923** JSFletcher *Charing Cross* (NY) 299: There's many a slip. 336: There's many a slip 'twix cup and lip—as the old saying goes. **1931** VLoder *Death* (NY) 278: There is many a slip between an arrest and a conviction. **1935** LAKnight *Super-Cinema* (L) 304: There is many a slip between cup and lip. **1935** RAJWalling *Corpse* (NY) 282: That proverbial slip between the cup and the lip. **1956** AMenen *Abode* (NY) 152: There's many a slip between the cup and the lip. **1961** LNizer *My Life* (NY) 492: They would permit no more slips between the cup and the lip. **1964** EXFerrars *Legal* (L) 134: The slip between the cup and the lip. **1965** HHowe *Gentle* (NY) 74: A slip 'twixt the cup and the lip of her full-bearded mate. **1976** EXFerrars *The Cup and the Lip* (NY). EAP S250; Brunvand 129.

S272 As black as **Sloes**; Sloe-black

1923 JSFletcher *Charing Cross* (NY) 125: Eyes black as sloes. **1927** CBStilson *Seven* (NY) 106: Sloe-black eyes. **1938** MSaltmarsh *Clouded* (NY) 78: Sloe-black eyes. **1941** CBClason *Green Shiver* (NY) 75: Sloe-black eyes. **1943** GGCoulton *Fourscore* (Cambridge, Eng.) 40: Eyes as black as sloes. **1952** AGilbert *Mr. Crook* (NY DBC) 46: His eyes were as black as sloes and as hard as chips of glass. EAP S252.

S273 **Slow** and steady wins the race (*varied*)

1921 JSFletcher *Chestermarke* (NY) 94: Slow and steady's the game here. **1930** TCobb *Sark* (L) 67: Slow and steady wins the race. **1936** RGDean *What Gentleman* (NY) 91: Slow and steady wins the race. **1952** GKersh *Brazen* (L) 116: Steady wins the game, as the English say. **1966** MMcShane *Crimson* (NY) 78: Slow but steady. *Oxford* 744.

S274 **Slow** but (and) sure (*varied*)

1913 JCLincoln *Mr. Pratt's Patients* (NY) 219: Slow but sure. **1922** JJoyce *Ulysses* (NY 1934) 413: Slow but sure. **1923** CWells *Affair at Flower Acres* (NY) 78: Slow and sure—that's my motto. **1932** JSFletcher *Four De-*

grees (L) 96: Slow and sure—no undue haste. **1932** BFlynn *Crime* (NY) 228: Mitchell came on slowly but surely. **1932** FDGrierson *Murder* (L) 245: It is slow but sure, as the proverb says. **1938** CWells *Missing* (P) 254: Slow but sure had to be the slogan. **1941** HCBailey *Bishop's* (NY) 220: Slow but unsure hitherto. **1951** EQueen *Origin* (B) 58: Slow and sure. **1958** KDGuinness *Fisherman's* (L) 24: Slowly, but not surely. **1968** IPetite *Life* (NY) 122: Slow but sure. **1971** ELathen *Longer* (NY) 204: Slow but sure. **1976** JPorter *Package* (NY) 167: Slow but sure is our motto. EAP S255.

S275 Plow deep while **Sluggards** sleep

1961 LNizer *My Life* (NY) 134: I like to "plough deep while sluggards sleep." EAP S256.

S276 As dead as a **Smelt**

1929 RPeckham *Murder* (NY) 285: This here gal is deader'n a smelt. TW 339.

S277 As smooth as a **Smelt**

1937 KPKempton *Monday* (NY) 306: You're—smooth as a smelt [*to a naked woman*]. Taylor *Western Folklore* 17(1958) 19(2); Cole 63. Cf. Trout *below*.

S278 To consume (burn) one's own **Smoke**

1925 GHGerould *Midsummer* (NY) 157: He kept his grief to himself; he burned his own smoke. **1930** TCobb *Sark* (L) 183: I can't consume my own smoke. **1936** FGérard *Concrete* (NY) 6: He kept his own counsel and consumed his own smoke. **1961** AGilbert *After* (NY DBC) 38: You do consume your own smoke. **1965** HHowe *Gentle* (NY) 230: We ought to consume our own smoke. *Oxford* 141: Consume.

S279 To go like **Smoke**

1931 PMacDonald *Murder* (L) 201: Drive like smoke. **1953** ECRLorac *Shepherd's* (NY) 155: The dog . . . was away like smoke, almost too fast. **1964** NFreeling *Because* (NY 1965) 155: He had to jump out and run like smoke. TW 340(2).

S280 To go up in **Smoke**

1931 WMorton *Mystery* (NY) 76: He seems to have gone up in smoke. **1956** PWentworth *Fingerprint* (NY) 236: Mirrie's chances had gone up in smoke. Cole 52.

S281 To vanish like **Smoke**

1925 BAtkey *Pyramid* (NY) 254: It all vanishes . . . like smoke. **1926** RAFreeman *Puzzle* (NY) 8: The staff . . . vanished into smoke. **1954** MBodenheim *My Life* (NY) 119: She vanished like smoke. **1959** HReilly *Not Me* (NY DBC) 4: The . . . cash . . . had vanished like smoke. EAP S262; TW 340(3).

S282 Where there is **Smoke** there is fire (*varied*)

1900 CFPidgin *Quincy A. Sawyer* (B) 192: Where there is so much smoke there must be some fire. **1921** ASTuberville *Medieval Heresy* (L) 186: On the principle that there is no smoke without fire. **1926** RASimon *Weekend* (NY) 103: Where there's so much smoke, there must be a woman. **1931** VWilliams *Masks* (L) 57: There was smoke, but no fire. **1932** SJepson *Mystery* (NY) 157: There's mostly fire where there's smoke, I've found. **1933** HWade *Hanging* (NY) 68: There's that old proverb about no smoke without fire. **1934** VWilliams *Masks Off* (B) 47: There was smoke, but no fire. **1936** JStagge *Murder* (L) 56: But where there's smoke and a pretty girl—there's usually fire. **1937** MBenney *Angels* (NY) 204: No smoke without fire—what gehennas of self-doubt that proverb must have been responsible for since it was first uttered! **1940** JJConnington *Four Defences* (B) 136: There's no smoke without fire, you know. **1940** JRhode *Murder at* (L) 7: A case of there being no smoke without fire. **1950** SPalmer *Green* (NY) 68: Where there's so much smoke mightn't there be some fire? **1957** *BangorDN* 2/8 22: There are rumors, and where there's so much smoke—. **1957** *Punch* 9/4 259: Where there's so much fire, there must be some smoke. **1959** *BangorDN* 8/12 11: The old saying of, "Where there's smoke there's fire." **1962** HPentecost *Cannibal* (NY DBC) 47: Sage remarks about "smoke and fire." **1964** EMcBain *Ax* (NY) 106: Hawes was not a firm believer in old adages, but there was an old adage that ran to the tune of "Where there's Smoke there's Fire." **1966** ELathen *Murder* (NY) 53: A great deal of smoke and very little fire. **1967** MGEberhart *Woman* (NY) 9: That damnable old thing people will always say—no smoke without fire. **1970** HActon *Memoirs* (NY) xiv: The adage that there is no smoke without fire. **1971** HVanDyke *Dead* (NY) 130: Where there's no smoke there's no fire—or is it the other way around? **1974** BFothergill *Mitred* (L) 91: Hyperbole . . . of a sort . . . calculated to produce smoke where in fact there was no fire. **1975** EMcBain *Where There's Smoke* (NY). **1975** HPentecost *Time* (NY) 51: There is a little smoke to justify the suspicion of a hidden fire. EAP S263; Brunvand 129.

S283 As slow as a **Snail**

1940 ECRLorac *Tryst* (L) 51: They've got the proverbial snail beat for slowness. Brunvand 130(1); Taylor *Prov. Comp.* 74.

S284 At a **Snail's** pace

1921 EWallace *Daffodil* (B) 204: Walked at a snail's pace. **1933** WCBrown *Murder* (P) 47: At a snail's pace. **1936** WMartyn *House* (L) 161: At a snail's pace. **1941** BHalliday *Bodies* (NY 1959) 164: Slowed to a snail's pace. **1943** PATaylor *Going* (NY) 90: Proceeded at a tired snail's pace. **1951** DMDisney *Straw* (NY) 16: At a snail's pace. **1959** EMButler *Paper* (L) 45: Went at a snail's pace. **1964** IMorris *World* (L) 87: At a snail's pace. **1968** SEdwards *Barbary* (Englewood Cliffs, NJ) 53: Slowed to the proverbial snail's pace. **1970** MStocks *My Commonplace* (L) 205: [It] seems a snail's progress. **1972** JRoffman *Bad* (NY) 35: Moving at a snail's pace. EAP S267; TW 340–1(2); Brunvand 130(2).

S285 A **Snail** travels with his house on his back

1973 AGilbert *Nice* (NY) 9: I do not travel like a snail with my house on my back. EAP S268. Cf. To be at Home *above*.

S286 To creep (move) like a **Snail**

1903 EChilders *Riddle* (NY 1940) 293: The train crept like a snail. **1941** FCrane *Turquoise* (P) 97: We moved like snails. EAP S269.

S287 As cold as a **Snake**

1946 PGuggenheim *Out of This Century* (NY) 309: He was as cold as a snake. **1952** TClaymore *Reunion* (NY 1955) 174: He was as cold as a snake. TW 341(2).

S288 As crafty as a **Snake**

1915 LPowys in MElwin *Llewelyn Powys* (L 1946) 127: As crafty as a snake. Wilstach 73.

S289 As crooked as a **Snake**('s tail)

1927 ORCohen *Outer* (NY) 196: He's crooked as a snake. **1937** DQBurleigh *Kristiana* (NY) 271: He's as crooked as a snake's tail. Whiting *NC* 477(2).

S290 As cunning as a **Snake** (serpent)

1936 BFlynn *Horn* (L) 269: He was as cunning as a snake. **1950** ESGardner *Musical* (NY) 268: She's cunning as a serpent. **1972** PMHubbard *Whisper* (NY) 147: She was as cunning as a snake. DA Snake *n.* 7(12) (quote 1855).

S291 As holy as a **Snake**

1945 GBellairs *Calamity* (NY) 88: A pious . . . humbug . . . As holy as a snake.

S292 As low as a **Snake's** (skunk's, worm's) belly (*varied*)

1927 JTully *Circus* (NY) 255: That man ain't human. He's lower'n a skunk's belly. **1934** LFord *Strangled* (NY) 120: Lower than a snake's belly. **1939** DFrome *Mr. Pinkerton . . . Old Angel* (L) 51: Pinkerton's heart, already lower than the proverbial underside of a snake. **1940** ISShriber *Head over Heels* (NY) 273: He's lower than a snake's— hmm—than a snake. **1941** CFAdams *Dewy* (NY) 123: Insurance dicks were considered even lower in the scale of things than the proverbial snake's abdomen. **1944** MVenning *Jethro* (NY) 225: I felt low as a snake's navel. **1952** JTey *Singing* (NY 1960) 164: He was lower than a worm's belly [*depressed*]. **1953** BBloch *Mrs. Hulett* (NY) 179: I am as low as a snake's belly. **1962** AAFair *Try* (NY) 25: A man who's lower than a snake's belly [*despondent*]. Whiting *NC* 477(6); Taylor *Western Folklore* 17(1958) 19(1), 20: Worm.

S293 As mad as a **Snake**

1962 JLeCarré *Murder* (NY 1964) 93: Sarah gets as mad as a snake. **1964** RBraddon *Year* (L 1967) 103: He's as mad as a cut snake . . . not to mention as a meat axe, a wheel, and a two bob watch. **1975** HBlack *My Father* (NY) 173: Mad as a snake. Cf. Wilstach 249: An adder.

S294 As mean as a **Snake**

1960 TPowell *Man-Killer* (NY) 106: He's feeling as mean as a snake. Whiting *NC* 477(7).

S295 As poor as a **Snake**

1933 JLilienthal *Gambler's* (B) 226: Poor as a snake. EAP S271.

S296 As quick (fast) as a **Snake**

1940 DBurnham *Last Act* (NY) 242: Moving quick as a snake. **1946** ERolfe *Murder . . . Glass Room* (NY 1948) 86: He was as fast as a snake. **1961** LSdeCamp *Dragon* (NY 1968) 279: She's quick as a snake. **1970** MStewart *Crystal* (NY) 512: Quick as a snake.

S297 As slimy as a **Snake**

1965 JJMarric *Gideon's Badge* (NY) 15: He's as slimy as a snake. Taylor *Prov. Comp.* 74: Slimmy [*sic*]; Clark 221.

S298 As slippery as a **Snake**('s belly)

1947 HCahill *Look* (NY) 309: Slippery as a snake's belly. **1971** JTMcIntosh *Coat* (NY) 153: You are as slippery as a snake. Cf. Wilstach 359: Serpent.

S299 As subtle as a **Snake**

1922 JSFletcher *Ravensdene* (NY) 243: As subtle as snakes. Wilstach 398.

S300 A **Snake** in the grass (*varied*)

1915 PGWodehouse *Something Fresh* (L 1935) 172: A snake in the grass. **1923** CWells *Affair at Flower Acres* (NY) 122: [He's] an old snake in the grass. **1928** GKnevels *Diamond* (NY) 103: Like serpents in the grass. **1928** DHLawrence *Lady* ("Allemagne") 240: The serpent in the grass was sex. **1931** ACEdington *Monk's Hood* (NY) 50: The viper hidden in the grass. **1933** TSmith *Turnabout* (NY) 271: You, like a snake in the grass, have fouled your own nest. **1947** FCrane *Murder on* (NY) 191: He glides in and out of the picture like a snake in the grass. **1954** RKLeavitt *Chip* (P) 126: The serpent under the innocent flowers. **1957** *Punch* 7/10 43: Snakes are to be looked for in grass. **1959** *BHerald* 4/21 35: Snakes in the grass—a big fat Anguis in the herba. **1964** JKieran *Not Under* (B) 74: I was a sneak in the grass. **1965** HActon *Old Lamps* (L) 48: A snake in the grass. **1972** COverstreet *Boar* (NY) 24: That two-faced bitch was worse than a snake in the grass. **1973** HDolson *Dying* (P) 55: He's the snake in the ointment. **1976** SBrett *So Much* (NY) 65: I may look like the innocent flower, but be the serpent under it. EAP S275; TW 341(1); Brunvand 130(1).

S301 To kill one's own **Snakes**

1955 KMKnight *They're* (NY) 77: I'll kill my own snakes. **1960** JBWest *Taste* (NY) 103: I kill my own snakes. Cf. To skin *below*.

S302 To scotch one's own **Snakes**

1931 ACEdington *Monk's Hood* (NY) 177: You scotch your own snakes! Cf. Shakespeare *Macbeth* III ii 13.

S303 To skin one's own **Snakes** (cats, skunks)

1933 ISCobb *Murder* (I) 151: Let 'em skin their own cats. **1934** HCorey *Crime* (NY) 62: I'm through. He can skin his own snakes. **1949** SSterling *Dead Sure* (NY) 130: You skin your own snakes. I'll take care of mine. **1969** LEGoss *Knight* (NY) 130: They skinned their own skunks. EAP S242: Skunks; TW 338: Skunk (4). Cf. To kill *above*.

S304 Wake **Snakes**

1941 ISCobb *Exit* (I) 202: Wake Snakes. TW 341(12).

S305 Before one can say **Snap**

1928 JJConnington *Mystery* (B) 171: Before you could say: "Snap!" **1961** JCreasey *Killing* (NY DBC) 139: Charley . . . is dead before we can say snap.

S306 Not care a **Snap** (of one's fingers)

1919 JBCabell *Jurgen* (NY 1922) 52: [Not] care a snap of my finger. **1929** TFPowys *Fables* (NY) 266: I care not a snap about

him. **1932** HLandon *Owl's* (L) 122: I don't care a snap of my fingers. **1936** RLGoldman *Judge* (NY) 89: You don't really care a snap. **1943** PATaylor *Going* (NY) 28: He didn't seem to care a snap. **1951** ECRLorac *I Could* (NY) 136: I don't care a snap. **1958** ECRLorac *People* (NY) 112: I didn't care a snap. **1974** SForbes *Some* (NY) 137: You don't care a snap. EAP S277.

S307 Not give a **Snap** of one's finger(s) (*varied*)

1912 ERBurroughs *Princess of Mars* (NY 1963) 114: I did not give the snap of my finger. **1922** JJoyce *Ulysses* (NY 1934) 767: I wouldn't give a snap of my two fingers for all their learning. **1932** TSmith *Topper Takes* (NY) 252: He did not give one snap of his fingers. **1959** EMarshall *Pagan* (NY) 49: He . . . did not give a snap of his finger. EAP S278.

S308 Not worth a **Snap** of one's finger(s)

1924 EWallace *Green* (B) 352: [Not] worth a snap of the fingers. **1933** HCMcNeill *Bulldog . . . Strikes* (NY) 205: Not worth the snap of a finger. **1964** ESGardner *Horrified* (NY DBC) 166: My life won't be worth a snap of my finger. Cf. Cole 63: To snap one's fingers at something.

S309 To be caught in one's own **Snare** (*varied*)

1931 HReilly *Murder* (NY) 155: The old fox caught in his own snare. **1935** MPropper *Election* (NY) 205: I was caught in my own snare. EAP S281. Cf. Pit, To make a Rod *above*.

S310 Not give a **Sneeze** in a cyclone

1954 EWalter *Untidy* (P) 168: I don't give a sneeze in a cyclone for your hunting. Cf. Not give a Fart *above*.

S311 Not worth a **Sneeze** (in a cyclone) (*varied*)

1935 HAustin *It Couldn't* (NY) 276: They're not worth a sneeze in a cyclone. **1945** HQMasur *Bury Me* (NY 1948) 210: Quimby's claim . . . isn't worth a sneeze in hell. Cf. Not worth a Fart *above*.

S312 Not to be **Sneezed** (sniffed) at

1919 LMerrick *Chair* (L) 94: Touquet was not a person to be sneezed at. **1922** JJoyce *Ulysses* (NY 1934) 648: The pecuniary emolument by no means to be sneezed at. **1928** AECoppard *Silver* (L) 15: It is not . . . to be sneezed at. **1930** EWallace *Silver Key* (NY) 79: Two thousand pounds . . . is not to be sniffed at. **1953** PIWellman *Female* (NY) 143: That's not to be sneezed at. **1957** WMorris *Love* (NY) 83: I suppose that's not to be sneezed at. **1966** ELathen *Murder* (NY) 101: An invitation . . . was not to be sneezed at. **1973** WMasterson *Undertaker* (NY) 94: That girl of hers ain't nothin' to sneeze at. EAP S282; Brunvand 130.

S313 To cock a **Snook**

1942 NMarsh *Enter Murderer* (NY) 219: Nigel cocked a snook at his friends. **1952** PLoraine *Dublin* (L) 80: If you choose to cock snooks at authority. **1956** EDillon *Death* (L) 81: Bradley had cocked a snook at Daly's mental powers. **1963** AMoorehead *Cooper's* (NY 1965) 11: To cock a snook at the respectable. **1967** AChristie *Endless* (NY) 70: The people laugh and cock a snook at them. **1970** AWRaitt *Prosper* (L) 21: It cocks a snook at a section of society. Partridge 165: Cock.

S314 As clean as **Snow**

1947 RBradbury *Dark Carnival* (Sauk City, Wisc.) 142: Clean as snow, white as linen. **1975** MKWren *Multitude* (NY) 148: A local woman, clean as new snow.

S315 As cold as **Snow**

1956 RMacdonald *Barbarous* (NY) 52: She was as cold as snow. Whiting S432.

S316 As innocent as (the driven) **Snow**

1933 BSKeirstead *Brownsville* (NY) 181: As innocent as snow. **1937** KMKnight *Seven* (NY) 83: You're as innocent as the driven snow. **1941** PWentworth *Weekend* (P) 71: As innocent as the driven snow. **1965** JPotts *Only Good* (NY) 55: That boy's as innocent as the driven snow. **1968** ASilitoe *Guzman* (L) 105: I'm as innocent as driven snow.

S317 As light as **Snow**

1956 RMacdonald *Barbarous* (NY) 92: He was light as snow. TW 342(3).

S318 As pale as **Snow**

1932 HFootner *Dead Man's* (NY) 259: She went as pale as snow. Wilstach 284: Young snow.

S319 As pure as (the) driven **Snow**; Snow-pure (*varied*)

1930 JDosPassos *42nd* (NY) 364: Their relations were pure as driven snow; 371. **1939** JJones *Murder al Fresco* (NY) 106: She's pure as the driven snow. **1939** RPenny *She Had* (L) 136: She may have been pure as the proverbial snow once, but she had drifted a good deal before I ever knew she existed. **1940** JSStrange *Picture* (NY) 139: They're innocent and pure as new-fallen snow. **1948** ESGardner *Lonely* (NY DBC) 137: [They] are pure as the driven snow. **1954** HGardiner *Murder* (L) 85: She was pure as driven snow. **1954** RKLeavitt *Chip* (P) 75: Snow-pure. **1958** JYork *My Brother's* (NY DBC) 8: She's got to be pure as driven snow. **1969** RMacdonald *Goodbye* (NY) 222: As pure as the driven snow. **1971** RLFish *Rub* (NY) 152: As pure as the driven snow. **1973** ELopez *Storm* (NY) 217: He was . . . as pure as the South Dakota snow. **1974** CMartin *Whiskey* (NY) 89: Pure as new snow. EAP S287; Taylor *Western Folklore* 17(1958) 19.

S320 As white as (the) driven **Snow**; Snow-white (*varied*)

1904 JCLincoln *Cap'n Eri* (NY) 141: Cloth snow-white. 183: Shells as white as snow. **1919** KHoward *Peculiar* (NY) 138: Snow-white caps. **1926** JJConnington *Death* (NY) 284: Character white as the driven snow. **1931** WWJacobs *Snug* (NY) 153: Bill's art is as white as snow. **1931** RInce *When Joan* (L) 184: A beard as white as the snows of Parnassus. **1933** FBeeding *Two Undertakers* (L) 101: Snow-white hair. **1934** EJepson *Grinning* (L) 124: A tress as white as the driven snow. **1950** FO'Malley *Best* (NY) 244: Her heart is white as snow. **1953** EWTeale *Circle* (NY) 16: One of the oldest similes in the world: "As white as the snow." **1955** RDavies *Leaven* (L) 242: You will be as white as driven snow. **1959** *New Yorker* 4/19 47: Snow-white hair. **1962** ADuggan *Lord* (L) 33: A skin as white as snow. **1970** MEChaber *Green* (NY) 81: Snow-white hair. **1974** BWAldiss *Eighty* (NY) 12: My soul was snow-white with fear. **1979** *BHerald* 3/19 3: He must be as white as the driven snow, as we say in Vermont. EAP S289, 293, 293a; TW 342 (6–10); Brunvand 130.

S321 Spring **Snow** is poor man's fertilizer

1968 MSarton *Plant* (NY) 99: I was to learn that [spring] snow is kind—"poor man's fertilizer," they call it. EAP S295; TW 342(1).

S322 To melt like **Snow**

1925 BAtkey *Pyramid* (NY) 95: Our capital melted like snow in the sun. **1932** VWilliams *Fog* (B) 193: The meeting melted like snow in the sun. EAP S296; TW 342–3(11).

S323 To vanish like **Snow** (*varied*)

1925 JSFletcher *Secret* (B) 42: Vanished as completely as last year's snows. **1943** AAMacGregor *Auld Reekie* (L) 120: Vanished overnight, "like snaw aff a dyke," as the Lowland folks say. **1962** DBickerton *Murders* (L) 68: The quarter-million vanished like snow in August. Whiting S447.

S324 Where are the **Snows** of yesteryear? (*varied*)

1935 FBeeding *Norwich* (NY) 45: Where were the snows of yester-year? **1936** VRath *Murder* (NY) 116: Where are the roses of yesteryear? **1958** SEllin *Eighth* (NY 1959) 208: Full of talk about the snows of yesteryear. **1964** CMacKenzie *Life III* (L) 58: Her tyranny was now with the snows of yesteryear. **1968** LBlanch *Journey* (L) 353: But the snows of yesteryear—where are they? Whiting S438.

S325 A **Snowball** (snowflake) in hell (*very varied*)

1920 GBMcCutcheon *Anderson Crow* (NY) 37: A crook ain't got any more chance than a snowball in—you know; 244. **1922** JJoyce *Ulysses* (NY 1934) 129: We haven't got the chance of a snowball in hell. **c1923** ACrowley *Confessions* ed JSymonds (L 1969) 479: I might as well have looked for a snowball in hell; 765. **1930** EMChannon *Chimney* (B)

213: The three hundred melted like a snowflake in hell. **1930** JCournos *Grandmother* (NY) 95: No more chance . . . than a snowball has . . . of surviving in hell. 230: It was a case of the proverbial snowball in hell. **1933** NBell *Lord* (B) 168: As much chance of splicin' Mrs. B. as a celluloid monkey's got of finding snowballs in Hell. **1933** HFootner *Ring* (NY) 140: My life won't be worth a snowflake in hell. **1934** BHughes *Murder* (NY) 116: My paper . . . would stand as much chance as a snowball in hell. **1940** LFord *Road* (NY) 6: I knew he hadn't the chance of the proverbial snowball. **1945** FAllan *First Come* (NY) 112: You'll be the proverbial snowball in hell. **1947** LFord *Woman* (NY) 131: I . . . didn't have the chance of the proverbial snowball on the steps of Capitol Hill. **1953** ESGardner *Hesitant* (NY) 117: The same chance as the proverbial snowball in hell. **1955** ELacy *Best* (NY) 119: Your opinion isn't worth a snowball in hell around here. **1957** CEMaine *High* (NY) 95: We don't stand a snowflake's chance in hell of surviving. **1958** *BHerald* 2/12 8: There is about as much chance for a fair investigation as a snowball has in—you know what I mean. **1959** *BHerald* 4/13 6: He had about as much chance of getting a fair trial "as a snowball in that place made famous by Dante." **1962** AAFair *Try* (NY) 151: Your license doesn't stand as much chance as a snowball. **1966** LPDavies *Who Is* (NY) 183: We won't stand a snowball's chance in hell. **1967** RJackson *Occupied* (L) 189: I haven't the chance of the proverbial snowball in Hades of getting out of the mess. **1971** PTabor *Pauline's* (Louisville) 142: A marriage that's got about as much chance of lasting as a snowball in hell. **1973** ADean *Be Home* (NY) 163: The trooper doesn't have the proverbial chance of a snowball in hell. Cf. EAP S298.

S326 To grow like a rolling **Snowball** (*varied*)

1924 RAFreeman *Blue* (NY) 124: Evidence began to grow like a rolling snowball. **1935** LRGribble *Mystery* (L) 125: Like the proverbial snowball, it'll grow and grow. **1966** RHardwick *Season* (NY) 94: The lie . . . was growing out of all proportion, like a snowball rolling down a hillside. **1973** HPentecost *Beautiful* (NY) 140: It's like a snowball, growing bigger and bigger. EAP S297.

S327 Not care a **Snuff**

1937 TStevenson *Nudist* (L) 94: I don't care a snuff. **1940** AMuir *Sands* (L) 247: He didn't care a snuff for law and order. TW 343(3).

S328 To be up to **Snuff**

1906 JLondon *Letters* ed KHendricks (NY 1965) 204: Right up to snuff. **1922** VThompson *Pointed* (NY) 121: The . . . valet . . . was up to snuff. **1938** LBarret *Though Young* (NY) 112: Vastly energetic . . . always up to snuff. **1959** PDeVries *Through* (B) 45: She came up to snuff. **1959** BHitchens *Man Who* (NY) 104: Not quite up to snuff. **1977** EPGreen *Rotten* (NY) 47: He wasn't up to snuff. TW 343(1); Brunvand 130; *Oxford* 749.

S329 As slick as **Soap**

1940 JSStrange *Picture* (NY) 259: That's slick as soap. **1969** RMacdonald *Goodbye* (NY) 120: I'm as clean as soap [*of crime*]. Whiting *NC* 478(1).

S330 As soft as **Soap**

1934 MMitchell *Warning* (NY) 23: I'm soft as soap. TW 343(1).

S331 Soft **Soap**

1929 DBHobart *Hunchback* (Racine) 194: How come all this soft soap? **1939** RPhilmore *Death in* (L) 225: I put a lot of soft soap on. **1951** ADerleth *Far* (NY) 118: A little soft soap will do the trick. **1959** A Christie *Ordeal* (NY) 120: Soft soap meaning nothing. EAP S304.

S332 To say (be) no **Soap**

1935 WChambers *Thirteen Steps* (NY) 204: He's just stubborn enough to say no soap. **1939** MMGoldsmith *Detour* (L) 32: It was no soap. Wentworth 358: No soap.

S333 As plain as an old **Sock**

1968 EBuckler *Ox Bells* (NY) 274: The whole Royal bunch were "as plain as an old sock." Clark 217: Plain as an old shoe. Cf. As plain . . . Shoe *above*.

S334 To pull up one's **Socks**

1932 DLSayers *Have* (NY) 144: He pulled up his socks and set to work. **1933** PGWodehouse *Mulliner* (NY) 113: Pull up the old socks and take a stab at the programme. **1954** AWUpfield *Sinister* (NY) 106: We'll have to pull up our socks. **1959** GBagby *Real* (NY) 184: I'd tell her she had to pull up her socks. **1965** PGWodehouse *Galahad* (L) 85: I'll spit on my hands and pull up my socks and leave no stone unturned or my name will be mud. Partridge 798.

S335 To put a **Sock** in it

1960 JSymons *Progress* (L) 120: Put a sock in it [*keep still*]. Partridge 798.

S336 Not give a **Sod**

1963 ABurgess *Vision* (L) 79: I don't give a sod who knows it. **1968** ASilitoe *Guzman* (L) 99: I didn't give a sod for any job.

S337 Old **Soldiers** never die *etc.* (*varied*)

1952 AWilson *Hemlock* (L) 160: Old soldiers never die. **1956** WMankowitz *Old Soldiers Never Die* (B). **1957** *New Yorker* 9/14 161: Clearly, old soldiers never die; they simply keep on arguing. **1957** *NYTimes* 11/3 E11: Old soldiers never die, they just fade away. **1957** *BHerald* 11/9 6: According to the saying old generals fade away. **1962** ITRoss *Old Students Never Die* (NY DBC). **1962** ITRoss *Old* (NY DBC) 3: "Old students never die," a cynical colleague once said, "they just stay away." Bartlett 1103a; *Oxford DQ* (2nd ed) 9.2.

S338 To come the old **Soldier** with someone

1934 JVTurner *Murder* (L) 127: Don't try to come the old soldier with me. **1973** JPorter *It's Murder* (NY) 120: Don't start coming the old soldier with me. *Oxford* 592.

S339 What the **Soldier** said is not evidence

1924 LSpringfield *Some Piquant* (L) 175: It is no more evidence than "what the soldier said." **1928** JJConnington *Tragedy* (B) 273: It can only be something like "what the soldier said." **1932** VLoder *Red Stain* (NY) 116: What the soldier said is not evidence. **1933** ECVivian *Girl* (L) 128: It's like what the soldier told the girl—not evidence. **1936**

RCWoodthorpe *Silence* (L) 241: What a certain soldier said, you know, wasn't evidence. **1952** AGilbert *Mr. Crook* (NY DBC) 81: What the soldier said isn't evidence. **1971** PMoyes *Season* (NY) 115: What the soldier said isn't evidence. Cf. *Pickwick Papers* ch. 34.

S340 As rich as **Solomon**

1943 EDaly *Nothing Can Rescue* (NY 1963) 13: As rich as Solomon. Taylor *Western Folklore* 17(1958) 19.

S341 As wise as **Solomon**

1917 JCLincoln *Extricating* (NY) 35: He looks wise as a cross between King Solomon and a cage full of owls. **1938** HAdams *Bluff* (L) 54: You were as wise as Solomon. EAP S314; TW 344(1).

S342 **Something** is better than nothing

1929 JSFletcher *Box* (NY) 218: Something's better than nothing. TW 345(2); *Oxford* 751: Somewhat.

S343 To have **Something** for nothing (*varied*)

1908 WHHudson *Land's End* (L) 111: But you can't have something for nothing. **1929** EWallace *Murder Book* (NY) 82: Something for nothing! **1945** GBellairs *Calamity* (NY) 24: You can't expect something for nothing. **1952** FPratt *Double* (NY) 9: You don't get something for nothing. **1959** *NYTimes Book Review* 5/17 1: The old political maxim that you can't beat something with nothing. **1964** AChristie *Caribbean* (NY) 24: You can't have anything for nothing. **1979** ELathen *When* (NY) 207: To get something you have to give something. TW 344–45(1).

S344 To have **Something** up one's sleeve beside his arm (*varied*)

1926 LThayer *Poison* (NY) 108: Something up your sleeve besides your arm. **1941** STowne *Death out of* (NY) 51: What has Pat got up her sleeve beside her arm? **1956** AGilbert *Riddle* (NY) 200: The chap had something up his sleeve besides his arm. **1959** AGilbert *Prelude* (NY DBC) 123: Got more up his sleeve than just his arm. **1962** AGilbert *Uncertain* (NY DBC) 24: You got anything up your sleeve except your arm? **1971** JTMcIntosh *Coat* (NY) 16: This creep

has something up his sleeve as well as his elbow.

S345 To look like **Something** the cat brought in (*varied*)

1915 PGWodehouse *Something Fresh* (L 1935) 124: Looking at me as if I were something the cat had brought in. **1929** NBMavity *Tule* (NY) 161: Look what the cat brought in. **1933** FDell *Homecoming* (NY) 295: As if he were something the cat had brought in. **1935** VWMason *Washington* (NY) 284: You look like what the cat brought home an' wouldn't eat. **1936** GMilburn *Catalogue* (NY) 32: Lookie what the cat's drug up and the kittens wouldn't eat. **1939** HCBailey *Great Game* (L) 228: She stared a bit too much. You know, what is this the cat brought in? **1941** RDarby *If This Be* (NY) 60: You look like something no self-respecting cat would dream of bringing in. **1947** NMarsh *Final* (B) 204: They all go out as if I was something the cat brought in. **1954** *Punch* 6/6 678: A socialist in the Carleton Club ought to feel like something the cat brought in. **1955** JO'Hara *Ten* (NY) 90: I'd look like something the cat dragged in. **1956** *New Yorker* 10/20 35: He . . . looked like something the cat dragged in. **1961** NBlake *Worm* (L) 90: He treated me like something the cat brought in. **1965** RHardwick *Plotters* (NY) 76: I feel like something the cat wouldn't bother to drag in. **1966** PGWodehouse *Plum* (L) 201: [He looks] like something the cat brought in, and not a very fastidious cat. **1979** CNParkinson *Jeeves* (NY) 92: Mr. Todd looked like something the cat had brought in—a cat, moreover, with an outstanding lack of discrimination. Partridge 483: Like something.

S346 A seventh **Son** of a seventh son (*varied*)

1913 EDBiggers *Seven Keys* (I) 211: Your seventh son of a son friend here has read my palm OK. **1940** EDean *Murder Is* (NY) 177: I'm the seventh son of a seventh son. **1958** *BHerald* 11/9 3A: It takes no seventh son of a seventh son to divine that. **1975** MButterworth *Man in* (NY) 151: I'm the seventh child of a seventh child. EAP S321.

S347 A **Son** of a sea cook

1950 FFGould *Maine Man* (NY) 72: Ye . . . half-witted son of a shore stayin' sea cook. **1964** FArcher *Malabang* (NY DBC) 109: You white-eyed son of a sea cook. TW 345(1); Colcord 172.

S348 To buy (sell) for a **Song** (*varied*)

1900 CFPidgin *Quincy A. Sawyer* (B) 441: You can buy such treasures for a mere song. **1924** LSpringfield *Some* (L) 160: Bought up for an old song. **1927** FLPackard *Devil's* (NY) 65: Picked her up for the proverbial song. **1932** AGilbert *Body* (NY) 251: Sold for the proverbial song. **1938** EPOppenheim *Curious* (B) 46: He would probably get it for an old song. **1945** GBellairs *Calamity* (NY) 7: He will buy it for a mere song. **1951** HQMasur *You Can't* (NY) 91: Nick picked it up for a song. **1957** RStandish *Prince* (L) 94: Houses to be picked up for the proverbial song. **1959** GDessart *Cry* (NY) 28: Bought for the proverbial song. **1962** VWBrooks *Fenollosa* (NY) 34: Bought for a song. **1968** KRoberts *Pavane* (NY) 196: She's sold herself for a pretty song. **1975** JHough *Guardian* (B) 176: Bought it for a song. EAP S327.

S349 To make a **Song** and dance about something (*varied*)

1927 VWilliams *Eye* (B) 230: It's not anything to make a song and dance about. **1931** MBurton *Menace* (NY) 155: That was nothing to make a song about. **1932** FWCrofts *Sudden* (NY) 167: It isn't much to make a song about. **1937** GDilnot *Murder* (L) 64: We don't want a song and dance about it in the newspapers. **1940** ECRLorac *Tryst* (L) 171: Stud always made a song and dance about locking up. **1941** EXFerrars *Rehearsals* (NY) 51: There's no point in my making a song and dance about it. **1951** CWillingham *Reach* (NY) 196: You keep giving me a song and dance. **1957** AWUpfield *Bushman* (NY) 44: He did make a song and dance about it. **1970** AAFair *All Grass* (NY DBC) 146: Put up the old song and dance. EAP S326.

S350 The **Sooner** the better

1915 JFerguson *Stealthy* (L 1935) 98: The sooner the better. **1924** CVanVechten *Tat-*tooed (NY) 261: The sooner the better. **1933** ABCox *Jumping* (L) 249: The sooner the better. **1939** HReilly *All Concerned* (NY) 73: The sooner it was over the better. **1950** FO'Malley *Best* (NY) 41: The sooner the better. **1956** DMDisney *Unappointed* (NY) 26: The sooner the better. **1964** FArcher *Malabang* (NY DBC) 129: The quicker, the better. **1966** JBell *Death* (NY) 98: The sooner the better. **1973** JPorter *It's Murder* (NY) 173: The sooner the better. EAP S328; Brunvand 131.

S351 As black as **Soot**; Soot-black

1925 HWilliamson *Son* (NY) 135: He was black as soot. **1932** JMO'Connor *Anonymous* (NY) 12: Soot-black hair. **1933** EPhillpotts *Captain's* (NY) 58: A face so black as soot. **1938** JLatimer *Dead Don't* (L) 57: As black, as dull, as coarse as soot [*hair*]. **1946** LCores *Let's Kill George* (NY) 8: A soot-black poodle. **1957** RGraves *They Hanged* (NY) 172: Black as soot. **1963** JYCousteau *Living Sea* (NY) 17: Black as soot. **1964** EHuxley *Incident* (NY) 206: His face black as soot. EAP S330; TW 345.

S352 A **Sop** to Cerberus (*varied*)

1931 PMacDonald *Murder* (L) 174: It's just a sop, as you might say, to Cerebus [*sic*]. **1932** JMarsh *Murder* (L) 159: "We could throw a sop to—to—." "To Cerberus." **1939** NBlake *Smiles* (L) 74: A sop to Cerberus. **1946** WPartington *T.J.Wise* (L) 82: Thrown as sops to Cerberus. **1948** HActon *Memoirs* (L) 340: The sop to Cerberus. **1958** JByrom *Or Be* (L 1964) 149: Flung as a sop to the Cerberus at the door. **1960** EWolf *Rosenbach* (Cleveland) 518: A sop to Cerberus. **1967** IBarea *Vienna* (NY) 98: A sop to Cerberus. EAP S332.

S353 It takes all **Sorts** (kinds) to make a world (*varied*)

1910 EPhillpotts *Tales* (NY) 294: It takes all sorts to make a world. **1924** HHMunro *Square* (L 1929) 120: It takes all sorts to make a sex. **1926** AMarshall *Mote* (NY) 32: It takes many men to make a world. **1930** LPowys *Apples* (L) 57: It takes, as they say, many minds to make a world. **1930** JSFletcher *Matheson* (L) 110: There's all sorts in life. **1932** EWallace *Frightened* (L) 26: It takes all sorts of people to make a world. **1937** CIsherwood *Lions* (Norfolk, Conn. 1947) 163: They say it takes all sorts to make a world. **1940** LFord *Old Lover's* (NY) 79: It takes all kinds to make a world. **1947** MCarleton *Swan* (NY) 63: It takes all sorts to make a world. **1947** FLockridge *Untidy* (NY) 24: Somebody said it takes all kinds to make a world. **1949** FLockridge *Spin* (P) 130: It takes all kinds to make a small world after all. **1951** RStout *Curtains* (NY) 38: It takes all kinds to make a Harvard Club. **1955** BBenson *Silver* (NY) 23: It takes all kinds to make a world. **1957** *Punch* 7/3 8: Still, it takes all sorts to make a world, I always say. **1958** VCanning *Dragon* (NY) 17: It takes all sorts to make a world. **1962** JSymonds *Bezill* (L) 51: It takes all sorts to make a world. **1963** KVonnegut *Cat's* (NY) 61: Well, I guess it takes all kinds . . . **1964** DMDisney *Hospitality* (NY) 182: It takes all kinds, they say. **1969** ASJasper *Hoxton* (L) 78: It took all sorts to create the poverty-stricken world we lived in. **1971** JThomson *Not One* (NY) 37: They say it takes all sorts to make the world. **1973** WJBurley *Death* (NY) 42: But it takes all sorts. Brunvand 131; *Oxford* 11: All sorts.

S354 To call one's **Soul** his own

1913 JCLincoln *Mr. Pratt's Patients* (NY) 251: Scared to say his soul was his own. **1929** FDaingerfield *Linden* (NY) 138: Foster didn't call his soul his own. **1933** VWilliams *Clock* (L) 265: He won't let me call my soul my own. **1940** EDean *Murder Is* (NY) 269: Not able to call my soul my own. **1949** MG Eberhart *House* (NY DBC) 15: I couldn't call my soul my own. **1966** PGWodehouse *Plum* (L) 216: She wouldn't let me call my soul my own. **1974** EXFerrars *Hanged* (NY) 104: Doesn't want the girl to call her soul her own. EAP S339.

S355 To wander about like a lost **Soul**

1924 CWells *Furthest* (P) 153: Wandering about like a lost soul. **1930** CBush *Dead Man* (NY) 5: [A] new member wandering round like the proverbial lost soul. Taylor *Prov. Comp.* 76–7; Cole 67.

S356 From **Soup** to nuts

1935 FGEberhard *Microbe* (NY) 244: Everything from soup to nuts. **1941** AAFair *Double* (NY) 186: I went through the joint from soup to nuts. **1953** BBloch *Mrs. Hulett* (NY) 17: Phi Beta from soup to nuts. **1955** PGWodehouse *French* (L) 52: I know them from soup to nuts. Berrey 94.19.

S357 To be in the **Soup**

c1910 PGWodehouse *Leave it to Psmith* (L n.d.) 33: In the soup. **1924** VBridges *Red* (NY) 14: In the soup. **1930** WLewis *Apes* (NY 1932) 137: Julius was left in the soup. **1939** MDalman *Missing* (L) 19: I'd be in the soup. **1941** HCBranson *I'll Eat You* (NY) 141: You're in the soup up to the neck. **1954** EDillon *Sent* (L) 93: He was sure he had me in the soup. **1961** CJenkins *Message* (L) 148: We're in the soup. **1963** RLFish *Isle* (NY DBC) 96: We may all end up in the soup. **1976** HPentecost *Fourteenth* (NY) 150: We're in the soup. Partridge 803; Wentworth 504.

S358 To spill the **Soup**

1960 RStout *Too Many* (NY) 162: One little slip would spill the soup. Berrey 198.4. Cf. To spill the Beans *above*.

S359 To take the **Sour** with the sweet

1956 *BHerald* 11/21 16: They must take the sour with the sweet. EAP S344; Whiting S945; *Oxford* 794: Sweet.

S360 As drunk as a **Sow** (*varied*)

1933 Anonymous *Modern Sinbad* (L) 51: Drunk as a sow. **1937** JRhode *Hop Fields* (L) 161: As drunk as the farmer's sow. **1956** MLSettle *O Beulah* (NY) 207: Uncle Taylor, drunk as a sow. EAP S346. Cf. David *above*.

S361 A still **Sow** drinks all the swill

1962 *BangorDN* 6/25 22: A still sow drinks all the swill. Brunvand 131; *Oxford* 774.

S362 To grease the fat **Sow**

1937 RWWinston *It's a Far Cry* (NY) 230: The principle, no doubt, of greasing the fat sow. *Oxford* 332.

S363 To have the wrong (right) **Sow** by the ear

1922 JJoyce *Ulysses* (NY 1934) 192: Has the wrong sow by the ear. **1923** JSFletcher *Lost Mr. Linthwaite* (NY) 172: You'd got the wrong sow by the ear. **1931** DLSayers *Suspicious* (NY) 330: He had the right sow by the ears. **1939** JJConnington *Counsellor* (L) 247: We've got the wrong sow by the ear. **1967** HBorland *Hill Country* (P) 188: My grandmother had a saying . . . "He's got the wrong sow by the ear." EAP S351; TW 346(2).

S364 As one **Sows** so shall he reap (*varied*)

1923 ECVivian *City of Wonder* (NY) 235: I have sown—I reap; 247. **1924** TMundy *Om* (NY) 61: As we sow, we reap. **1932** RThorndike *Devil* (NY) 215: Life generally makes us reap what we had sown. **1935** LThayer *Dead* (NY) 6: To reap what others sowed. **1951** HSaunders *Sleeping* (L) 104: As a man sows so shall he reap. **1958** HCarmichael *Or Be* (NY) 44: He's only reaping what he has been sowing for many years. **1964** CChaplin *Autobiography* (NY 1966) 62: The old proverb: "Whatsoever a man soweth, that shall he also reap." **1968** HHarrison *Deathworld* (NY) 41: As ye sow, so shall ye reap. EAP S352; Brunvand 117: Reap.

S365 To call a **Spade** a spade (*varied*)

1905 JBCabell *Line* (NY 1926) 216: Innocence that cannot endure the spoken name of a spade. **1909** MRRinehart *Man in Lower Ten* (NY 1947) 284: Call a spade a spade, although it may be a shovel. **1925** EBChancellor *"Old Q"* (L) 139: In these days . . . we have become accustomed when talking of spades to use no circumlocution or periphrasis whatever. **1926** PGWodehouse *Small Bachelor* (NY) 10: He called a Ford a Ford. **1927** WDSteele *Man Who* (NY) 301: Never wanted the word for a spade. **1933** GHolt *Six Minutes* (L) 11: [They] were . . . not civilized enough to call a spade anything but a spade. **1936** HAsbury *French* (NY) 371: A spade was never a spade in Kate Townsend's bagnio. **1937** PATaylor *Figure* (NY) 65: Outspoken sort. An old spade caller. **1940** NMorland *Gun* (L) 179: Maraday . . . was unused to hearing her own sex

call a spade by its proper name. **1940** CE Vulliamy *Calico Pie* (L) 64: A . . . style in which a spade was often a bloody shovel. **1952** RLGreen *Mason* (L) 207: A spade, not a spade, and not even a bloody shovel, but a horticultural implement of unimproved design. **1955** JCreasey *Murder* (NY DBC) 113: A Puritanical reluctance to call a spade a spade. **1956** *BHerald* 1/23 14: He trots out a filthy expression, presumably in the interests of calling a spade a spade. **1956** *NY Times Book Review* 7/15 8: He is still not one to call a spade a garden implement. **1956** *Harvard Summer News* 7/19 2: And when Dekker doesn't call a spade a spade, he calls it a steam-shovel. **1956** AWUpfield *Battling* (L 1960) 74: Sooner call a spade a bloody shovel than a trowel. **1956** AMenen *Abode* (NY) 144: Loving couples, sir, to call a spade a spade, littered that island. **1957** *Time* 8/26 61: Millions of readers like to have a spade of dirt called a spade of dirt. **1958** *Time* 5/26 20: With spade-calling confidence. **1958** *NYTimes Book Review* 7/27 6: He went about calling a spade what it jolly well was. **1958** *BHerald* 8/7 30: Why call a spade a spade if a more descriptive moniker is handy? **1958** LSdeCamp *Elephant* (NY) 38: I am a plain blunt man who calls a fig a fig and a spade a spade. **1960** *Time* 2/22 37: In the . . . warfare of Australian politics, spades are called bloody shovels. **1960** NWoodin *Room* (L) 128: Calling a spade a spade and a nightingale a nightingale. **1963** KVonnegut *Cat's* (NY) 159: Call a spade a spade and let the chips fall where they may. **1965** CPSmith *Where the Light* (NY) 371: The velvet of Victorian genteelness which required that no spade could be known as a spade. **1966** NDevas *Two Flamboyant* (L) 81: Some people are afraid of a spade being called a spade, or don't want to know there is such a thing as a spade. **1967** COSkinner *Madame* (B) 74: A coarse person . . . fond of calling a spade a dirty spade, but blessed with a heart of gold. **1969** AGilbert *Missing* (NY) 51: Her Saxon proclivity for calling a spade a spade. **1969** PHighsmith *Tremor* (NY) 83: She wasn't the kind of girl to call a spade a—a what? Anyway, she called a lay a roll in the hay. **1970** HActon *Memoirs* (NY) 67: [He] called a spade a bloody shovel. **1974** WSnow

Codline (Middletown, Conn.) 126: He not only called a spade a spade but told what was on the spade. **1978** CMacLeod *Rest You* (NY) 41: Bob made a thing of calling a spade by a more vulgar name. EAP S354; Brunvand 131.

S366 To pay off (*etc.*) in **Spades**

1951 LLariar *You Can't* (NY) 111: She paid off in spades. **1953** VPJohns *Murder* (NY 1962) 106: She had been insulted in spades. **1958** HPentecost *Obituary* (NY 1960) 69: My mother lit into me in spades. **1961** JWelcome *Beware* (L) 165: You can say that in spades. **1975** HPentecost *Time* (NY) 124: I'll give it back to him in spades. Double spades. Wentworth 505.

S367 **Spae** well and hae well

1931 HReilly *Murder* (NY) 74: You know the old saw, "Spae well and you'll hae well." NED Spae *v.* [*to foretell, to prophesy*].

S368 To walk **Spanish**

1900 CFPidgin *Quincy A. Sawyer* (B) 22: Learn . . . how to walk Spanish. **1906** JCLincoln *Mr. Pratt* (NY) 257: He moved then, "walking Spanish." TW 346.

S369 A small **Spark** can blow up an arsenal

1930 LTracy *Manning* (NY) 167: A mighty small spark can blow up an arsenal. EAP S361.

S370 To be as **Spark** and tinder

1919 JBCabell *Jurgen* (NY 1922) 87: You two would be as spark and tinder. TW 134: Fire(10); Whiting F182.

S371 As amorous as a **Sparrow**

1964 EDahlberg *Alms* (Minneapolis) 52: She was as amorous as a sparrow. Whiting S570: Hot and lecherous; Tilley S715 (quote c1640); *Oxford* 497: Lustful.

S372 As chipper as a **Sparrow**

1953 MLeinster *Great Stories* (L) 28: Chipper as a sparrow. **1966** LBeers *Wild* (NY) 22: He was chipper as a sparrow. Taylor *Prov. Comp.* 25. Cf. *Oxford* 621: Pert.

S373 To be up by **Sparrow-fart**

1968 MSarton *Plant* (NY) 154: I must be up by sparrow-fart [*an elderly New Hampshire woman speaking*]. Partridge 805: Day-break. Cf. Butterfly's fart *above*.

S374 To **Speak** as one finds

1933 CBush *Three Strange* (L) 191: Speak as you find . . . That's my motto. **1933** GMitchell *Saltmarsh* (P) 48: I speak of her as I found her. **1957** *Punch* 3/6 322: But, speaking as you find, as the saying goes. **1972** WJBurley *Guile* (NY) 42: George was wild, but, speak as you find, he was all right with me. *Oxford* 760.

S375 As straight as a **Spear**

1932 BRoss *Tragedy of Y* (NY) 199: The old actor . . . was standing straight as a spear. **1958** MRenault *King* (NY 1960) 231: She was straight as a spear. **1971** JBlish *And All* (NY) 177: Her old back as straight as a spear. TW 346(1).

S376 **Speech** is silver, silence is golden (*varied*)

1923 HWNevinson *Changes* (NY) 326: Silence is golden. **1930** AFielding *Murder* (NY) 201: Silence is not always golden nor speech silver. **1932** LCharteris *White* (NY) 179: There are times when silence is not only golden, but the best policy. **1938** BFlynn *Five Red* (NY) 95: Silence could be golden—and it could be guilt. **1952** C Amory *Last* (NY) 109: Baker had for his life-time motto, "Silence is golden." **1954** RKLeavitt *Chip* (P) 86: Silence, as the feller said, is golden. **1956** LBeam *Maine* (NY) 126: Speech is silver but silence is golden. **1961** BAldiss *Primal* (NY) 42: Speech is silver: silence is golden: print is dynamite. **1969** ABarton *Penny* (L) 92: Speech is silver; silence is golden. **1970** MCollis *Journey* (L) 199: Silence must indeed be golden. **1970** JWechsberg *First* (B) 341: A German proverb says, "Talk is silver, silence is golden." **1972** AFriedman *Hermaphrodeity* (NY) 15: Silence is the golden rule, remember. TW 346; Brunvand 127: Silence [*no speech*]; *Oxford* 763.

S377 As dumb as the **Sphinx**

1931 ALivingston *In Cold* (I) 123: I can be as dumb as the Sphinx. TW 346.

S378 As inscrutable as a (the) **Sphinx**

1930 CWells *Doorstep* (NY) 201: He could be as inscrutable as a sphinx. **1958** *BHerald* 5/6 6: Inscrutable as the sphinx. Wilstach 216.

S379 As silent (mum, mute) as a (the) **Sphinx**

1925 GBeasley *My First* (Paris) 92: I was as silent as a sphinx. **1936** RGDean *Sutton* (NY) 270: Mum as a Sphinx. **1940** CBDawson *Lady Wept* (NY) 118: You've been as silent as the sphinx. **1941** ISCobb *Exit* (I) 192: As mute as the Sphinx. **1962** HWaugh *Late* (NY) 142: You're as silent as the sphinx. Cole 62; Wilstach 353.

S380 **Spick** and span (*varied*)

1901 AEHousman *Letters* ed HMaas (Cambridge, Mass. 1971) 59: Looking painfully spick and span. **1913** JSFletcher *Secret* (L 1918) 46: The spick-and-span sailors. **1915** JBuchan *Thirty-nine* (NY) 72: Very spick and span. **1923** JSFletcher *Charing Cross* (NY) 40: The general spic-and-spanness of the man. **1933** WCBrown *Murder* (P) 58: Everything spick and span. **1939** EMarsh *Number* (NY) 200: All up-to-date spickness and spanness. **1956** SDean *Marked* (NY) 63: Cliché-clean, spick and span, neat and tidy, eat off the floor. **1958** MProcter *Man in* (NY) 167: All the others are spick and span. **1963** LJMilne *Valley* (NY) 132: Most insects keep themselves spic and span. **1966** LNizer *Jury* (NY) 74: The prison was spic and span. **1970** PMoyes *Many* (NY) 35: The kitchen . . . was spick and span. EAP S366.

S381 As mean as a blue **Spider**

1934 SHAdams *Gorgeous* (B) 93: Mean as a blue spider. Cf. *Oxford* 423: Killed.

S382 As nervous as a **Spider** on a hot plate

1930 WAStowell *Marston* (NY) 221: She was nervous too, like a spider on a hot plate. Taylor *Western Folklore* 17(1958) 19: To run like a spider on a hot stove. Cf. As jumpy as a Hen *above*.

S383 If you want to live and thrive let the **Spider** run alive

1957 HPBeck *Folklore of Maine* (P) 79: If you want to live and thrive let the spider run alive. *Oxford* 819: Thrive.

S384 To put a **Spider** in someone's biscuit

1965 MEchard *I Met* (NY) 39: Someday . . . somebody's goin' to put a spider in his biscuit. Whiting *NC* 480.

S385 What one saves at the **Spigot** he loses at the bung

1966 LBeer *Wild* (NY) 181: If you save at the spigot you lose at the bung. EAP S368.

S386 The living (*etc.*) **Spit** (*etc.*) of someone or something (*varied*)

1919 AMerritt *Moon Pool* (NY) 195: The living spit of him. **1927** NMartin *Mosaic* (NY) 199: The spitting image of this young millionaire. **1927** SWilliams *Drury* (NY) 101: It was Hal, or his spit and image. **1930** DLSayers *Strong* (NY) 131: One other case that was the dead spit of this one. **1932** MThynne *Murder* (NY) 91: It's the living spit of him. **1933** AMerritt *Burn Witch* (NY) 124: It was the lick-an'-spit of Peters. **1936** JBude *Sussex* (L) 10: The spit and image of the great-grandfather. **1936** MBurton *Where Is* (L) 32: The very spit and likeness of it. **1939** MHealy *Old Munster* (L) 161: The "dead spit," as the phrase goes, of Mr Justice Gibson. **1943** SShane *Lady . . . Million* (NY) 19: Roberta was the dead spit of her mother. **1944** RAltrocchi *Sleuthing* (Cambridge, Mass.) 177: The spitten image . . . of the deceased. **1950** IFletcher *Bennett's* (I) 63: He was the spit of his father. **1952** AGilbert *Mr. Crook* (NY DBC) 85: The spitting image of one her sister had just bought. **1952** RGHam *Gifted* (NY) 24: A little girl her spit and image. **1957** *BangorDN* 4/2 20: I'm the spittin' image of him. **1957** JCheever *Wapshot* (NY) 30: The spit and image of Mr. Forbes' pants. **1960** TBDewey *Girl* (NY DBC) 81: She was the spitting image of her sister. **1960** NFitzgerald *Candles* (L) 49: You'd be his splitten [*sic*] image. **1960** MInnes *New Sonia* (L) 156: You're the split [*sic*] image of her. **1963** PMHubbard *Flush* (L 1964) 100: The dead spit of each other. **1964** RDuncan *All Men* (L) 13: I was the living spit of my father. **1967** JWCampbell *Analog* 5 (NY) 20: Spittin' image, as the Americans say. **1967** VThomson *V.Thomson* (L) 128: Spitting image of Abraham Lincoln. **1972** JBonett *No Time* (NY) 67: Just like him, the spitting image. **1974** GPaley *Enormous* (NY) 16: His house was the spit of mine. TW 198: Image (3); *Oxford* 464: Like one, 766.

S387 As easy as **Spitting**

1929 AGray *Dead* (L) 12: As easy as spitting. **1938** MKRawlings *Yearling* (NY) 61: Easy as spittin'. Wilstach 516.

S388 **Spit-and-polish**

1946 VKelsey *Whisper Murder* (NY) 73: His spit-and-polish manners. **1952** AWUpfield *Venom* (NY) 12: They're all spit and polish and no guts [*automobiles*]. Partridge 811.

S389 To put a **Spoke** in one's wheel (*varied in form and sense*)

1900 CFPidgin *Quincy A. Sawyer* (B) 238: To put another spoke in Mr. Strout's wheel. **1911** CKSteele *Mansion* (NY) 294: I can put a spoke in his wheel. **1925** JGBrandon *Bond* (L) 257: That's put a spoke in your wheel. **1928** ABCox *Amateur* (NY) 269: She would . . . try to put her spoke into his wheel [*apparently, to assist*]. **1928** GFairlie *Man Who Laughed* (NY) 19: It's my job to break a spoke or two in this unpleasant Johnny's wheel. **1930** DOgburn *Ra-ta-plan!* (B) 65: Mr. Court might have felt he had more spokes to his wheel. **1936** AFielding *Missing Diary* (NY) 148: Put a spoke in his wheel. **1936** AGlanville *Death* (L) 28: I put my spoke into the wheel [*took part, aided*]. **1940** NBlake *Malice* (L) 96: That put a spoke in him. **1940** LBruce *Ropes and Rings* (L) 25: My brother . . . rashly put in his spoke [*tried to help*]. **1953** MMainwaring *Murder* (NY) 25: Mersey had put a spoke in our wheel. **1958** VCanning *Dragon* (NY) 233: George could put a spoke in his wheel. **1966** JGaskell *Serpent* (NY 1968) 338: Do anything to throw a spoke in my wheel. **1968** DBagley *Vivero* (NY) 35: If you put a spoke in their wheel. **1972** HPentecost *Champagne* (NY) 38: No one tried to put a spoke in the wheel. EAP S373.

S390 To drink like a **Sponge**

1931 MAllingham *Police* (NY) 109: Drank like a sponge. **1951** CLittle *Blackout* (NY) 73: Seems to be drinkin' like a sponge. **1962** MAllingham *China* (NY) 40: He drinks like a sponge. **1977** HDolson *Beauty* (P) 98: Wynn drinks like a sponge. Cf. NED Sponge *sb.*[1] 8.

S391 To throw in the **Sponge**

1949 RLTaylor *W.C.Fields* (NY) 155: Ziggie threw in the sponge. **1954** MMcCarthy *Charmed* (NY) 188: She throws in the sponge. **1957** CESellers *Polk* (Princeton) 160: Polk threw in the sponge. **1959** HWaugh *Sleep* (NY) 159: To throw in the sponge. **1962** NArvin *Longfellow* (B) 289: They had refused to throw in the sponge. Wentworth 543. Cf. Towel *below*.

S392 To throw up the **Sponge**

1910 EPhillpotts *Tales* (NY) 220: Throw up the sponge. **c1923** ACrowley *Confessions* ed JSymonds (L 1969) 535: The doctor threw up the sponge. **1936** ECRLorac *Pall* (L) 149: Threw up the sponge. **1937** JRhode *Death on the Board* (L) 33: He'd have to chuck up the sponge. **1940** ACampbell *They Hunted* (NY) 207: Thrown up the sponge. **1954** CBeaton *Glass* (NY) 298: Refusing to throw up the sponge. **1970** LGrafftey-Smith *Bright* (L) 188: Causing the French to throw up the sponge. TW 347(2).

S393 To be born with a silver **Spoon** in one's mouth (*varied*)

1922 JJoyce *Ulysses* (NY 1934) 167: Born with a silver knife in his mouth. That's witty, I think. Or no. Silver means born rich. Born with a knife. But then the allusion is lost. **1925** JSFletcher *Annexation* (NY) 262: You were born with a silver—or, rather a gold spoon in your mouth. **1930** APHerbert *Water* (NY) 88: Born with a silver spoon in his mouth. **1935** JTFarrell *Judgment* (NY) 422: Neither of us were born with silver spoons in our mouths. **1943** WLewis *Letters* ed WKRose (L 1963) 366: A silver spoon he found at birth stuck in his mouth by a good fairy. **1945** HLawrence *Time to Die* (NY) 95: Not born with a spoon in her mouth. **1953** BCClough *Grandma* (Portland, Me.) 49: Melissa was born with a silver spoon in her mouth. **1954** VWBrooks *Scenes* (NY) 101: Born "with a gold spoon in his mouth." **1957** *Time* 12/30 66: A great many were born with silver spoons in their mouths and golden bees in their bonnets. **1960** TWBurgess *Now I* (B) 9: It was my very good fortune to be born minus the proverbial silver spoon. **1962** CKeith *Missing* (NY) 160: He wasn't born with a silver spoon in his mouth. **1965** SWeintraub *Reggie* (NY) 20: Reggie was born with someone's silver spoon in his mouth. **1971** WHMarnell *Once Upon* (NY) 177: Boys who are born, not with a silver spoon in their mouths, but with a chisel in their hands [*cheaters*]. **1971** JJMarric *Gideon's Art* (NY) 96: Born with a diamond-encrusted spoon in your pretty mouth. **1976** GBagby *Two* (NY) 9: It's the sound one makes . . . when one has learned to talk around the silver spoon in one's mouth. EAP S375; Brunvand 132(1).

S394 The darkest **Spot** is just under the candle (*varied*)

1928 LThayer *Darkest Spot* (NY) 54: The darkest spot is immediately under the candle. 123: The same old proverb—the darkest place is just under the candle. **1933** RJCasey *Hot Ice* (I) 222: The darkest spot is right under the light.

S395 To be up the **Spout**

1926 LdeGSieveking *Bats* (L) 12: Arabella's up the spout. **1934** RPhilmore *Journey* (NY) 229: The corporation is likely to go up the spout. **1940** JDCarr *Man Who* (NY) 291: Your case . . . is up the spout. **1947** NMarsh *Final* (B) 204: Cedric's pretty well up the spout. **1956** DBatchelor *Taste* (L) 70: Enough to drive you up the spout [*a bad time*]. EAP S380; Brunvand 132.

S396 A **Sprat** to catch a mackerel (whale, herring) (*varied*)

1928 RThorndike *Slype* (NY) 302: You never risk a sprat to catch a mackerel, whereas I was risking a tiddler to catch a whale. **1930** JRhode *Peril* (NY) 249: This Gilray business is only a sprat to catch a mackerel. **1936** DVDuff *Horned* (L) 103: The old proverb about a sprat to catch a mackerel. **1936** RHull *Murder* (NY) 17: We must occasionally throw a sprat to catch a whale. **1938** ECRLorac *John Brown's* (L) 177: Offering me as the sprat to catch the

shark. **1939** TBurke *Living* (L) 238: Ask for a sprat and win a whale. **1941** JJConnington *Twenty-one* (B) 158: It's a sprat thrown out to catch a herring. **1953** IFleming *Casino* (L) 132: Vesper had been only a sprat to catch a mackerel. **1957** RArnold *Spring* (NY) 44: A sprat to catch a whale. **1961** EPeters *Death* (NY) 54: A sprat to catch a mackerel. **1968** JCFurnas *Lightfoot* (NY) 34: Morgan's pay checks were sprats to catch whales. **1970** DMDevine *Illegal* (NY) 203: The sprat to catch the mackerel. **1973** KCampbell *Wheel* (I) 140: An old Norfolk saying—set a sprat to catch a mackerel. **1973** JWhitehead *Solemn* (L) 152: This book was a mere sprat to catch herring. EAP S382.

S397 A **Springe** to catch a woodcock

1934 AGMacleod *Case of* (L) 257: A Springe to Catch a Woodcocke. **1945** FLockridge *Payoff* (P) 98: A springe—a trap to catch woodcocks. EAP S385; Brunvand 132.

S398 On the **Spur** of the moment (*varied*)

1900 CFPidgin *Quincy A. Sawyer* (B) 380: On the spur of the moment. **1922** DLindsay *Haunted Woman* (L 1964) 32: On the spur of the moment. **1932** ABCox *Murder* (L) 302: On the spur of the moment. **1936** LThayer *Dark of the Moon* (NY) 251: On the spur of the minute. **1942** FLockridge *Death . . . Aisle* (P) 158: It was the best the spurred moment provided. **1948** MInnes *Night* (L 1966) 202: On the spur of the moment. **1959** JBrunner *World* (NY) 71: A spur-of-the-moment arrangement. **1962** LEgan *Against* (NY DBC) 24: Spur-of-the-moment, crude lust. **1963** AChristie *Mirror* (NY) 243: On the spur of the moment. **1971** JMuir *Stranger* (NY) 10: At the spur of the moment. **1977** CAGoodrum *Dewey* (NY) 95: Not bad for the spur of the moment. EAP S388.

S399 To win (earn) one's **Spurs**

1912 ERBurroughs *Princess of Mars* (NY 1963) 56: Won my spurs. **1917** GRSims *My Life* (L) 287: Winning my spurs. **1933** FDGrierson *Empty* (L) 49: To win his spurs. **1936** VWBrooks *Flowering* (NY 1946) 40: Win his spurs. **1940** ECBentley *Those Days* (L) 76: He won his spurs as an orator. **1953**

IFleming *Casino* (L) 29: A young sapper who had earned his spurs. **1957** EMButler *Heine* (NY) 17: Win his commercial spurs. **1963** JNHarris *Weird* (NY DBC) 176: You've won your spurs. **1965** IRoss *Charmers* (NY) 46: Ned had won his spurs. TW 349(3); *Oxford* 892: Win.

S400   As chipper as a **Squirrel**

1959 *BHerald* 5/10 sec. III 3: He's as chipper as a squirrel. TW 349(1).

S401   Like a **Squirrel** in a cage

1928 HCrosby *Shadows* (Paris) 23: Like the proverbial squirrel in his cage. **1928** SGluck *Last* (NY) 120: The proverbial squirrel in a cage.

S402   A **Stab** in the dark

1946 ERolfe *Murder . . . Glass Room* (NY 1945) 45: I took a long chance, a stab in the dark. **1963** AAFair *Fish* (NY DBC) 105: A blind stab in the dark. **1963** JMUllman *Neon* (NY) 39: It was an accurate stab in the dark. Taylor *Prov. Comp.* 77; Cole 63. Cf. A Shot in the dark *above*.

S403   To blow one's **Stack**

1959 ESAarons *Assignment* (Greenwich, Conn.) 36: I'm afraid I blew my stack. **1959** GBagby *Real* (NY) 163: You can blow your stack from here to Christmas. **1975** HPentecost *Time* (NY) 127: [He] had blown his stack. Wentworth 46–7: Blow.

S404   To swear on a **Stack** of Bibles (*varied*)

1930 ALivingston *Murder* (I) 298: I'll swear it on a stack of Bibles. **1932** PMacDonald *Mystery* (NY) 78: I'd swear on a stack of Bibles as high as this room. **1946** CBush *Second Chance* (L) 209: I'd swear, not on a stack of Bibles but on the whole premises of the British and Foreign Bible Society. **1947** FCDavis *Thursday's* (NY) 189: You're still swearing to this on a stack of Bibles. **1954** FCDavis *Another* (NY) 108: I'll swear on a stack of Bibles that you're a pair of barefaced liars. **1959** KMKnight *Beauty* (NY) 170: I'll swear to it on a stack of Bibles. **1961** SSterling *Too Hot* (NY) 60: That, I swear on a stack of Bibles, I did not do. **1970** DShannon *Unexpected* (NY) 90: I swear on a stack of Bibles. **1975** EMcBain *Where*

(NY) 125: They swore on a stack of Bibles. TW 26: Bible.

S405   To be a broken **Staff**

1961 ERChamberlin *Count* (NY) 150: Louis proved a broken staff. Cf. EAP S897. Cf. Reed *above*.

S406   To pour (rain) **Stair rods**

1952 JTey *Singing* (NY 1960) 53: It's pouring stair-rods. **1966** WTrevor *Love* (L) 275: It being raining stair-rods. Cf. NED Stair *sb.* 5b (quote 1858). Cf. Pitchforks *above*.

S407   As stiff as a **Stake**

1950 FFGould *Maine Man* (NY) 37: Frozen stiff as a stake. EAP S400.

S408   To pull up **Stakes**

1938 HReed *Swing Music* (NY) 264: "You'll be pulling up stakes." "Or pushing up daisies." **1957** COLocke *Hell Bent* (NY) 12: The father . . . pulled up stakes. **1966** DMDisney *Magic* (NY) 54: You'd have to pull up stakes. **1970** SGBoswell *Book* (L) 54: You . . . picked up your stakes. **1975** MDelving *Bored* (NY) 110: They have to pull up stakes. EAP S402.

S409   To be a **Stalking** horse

1977 CAGoodrum *Dewey* (NY) 12: He'd used her as a stalking horse. EAP S403.

S410   As plain as I am **Standing** here

1929 BThomson *Metal* (L) 158: As plain as I'm standing here. Cf. next entries.

S411   As sure (certain) as I am **Standing** here (*varied*)

1920 AChristie *Mysterious Affair* (NY) 147: As sure as I stand here. **1921** EWallace *Daffodil* (B) 116: As certain as that I am standing here. **1924** JSFletcher *Safety* (NY) 154: As certain as I am that I'm standing here. **1933** AMChase *Danger* (NY) 203: I tell you as surely as I am standing here, I know he did not do it. **1942** MBurton *Death at Ash* (NY) 31: As sure as that I'm standing here. **1953** STruss *Doctor* (NY) 181: As sure as I stand here. **1958** STruss *In Secret* (NY) 114: As sure as I'm standing here. **1960** HQMasur *Send Another* (NY) 112: As sure as you're standing on God's green footstool. **1970** JCreasey *Part* (NY) 33: As sure as I'm standing here. **1972** KCConstantine *Vicksburg* (NY) 28: I know as sure as I'm standing here. TW 350(1). Cf. Sitting *above*.

S412   As true as I am **Standing** here (*varied*)
1930 MBurton *Hardway* (L) 18: It's as true as I stand here. **1955** DParry *Sea* (L) 80: As true as I'm here. **1956** SSmith *Shrew* (NY 1959) 113: True as I'm standing here. **1966** AGMartin *True Maine* (Freeport, Me.) 149: It's as true as I'm standing here. Whiting S667. Cf. Sitting *above*.

S413   As bright as **Stars**
1962 FLeiber *Shadows* (NY) 45: Max's eyes looked bright as stars. **1963** DMDisney *Here Lies* (NY) 156: Her eyes were bright as stars. EAP S408; TW 350(1).

S414   To be born under a lucky **Star**
1922 VBridges *Greensea* (NY) 114: Born under a lucky star. TW 350(6).

S415   A good **Start** often means a bad finish
1905 HRHaggard *Ayesha* (NY) 61: A good start often means a bad finish. Whiting *NC* 369: Beginning (2).

S416   As hard as a **Statue**
1963 KVonnegut *Cat's* (NY) 193: He was dead—as hard as a statue. **1966** ESConnell *Diary* (NY) 161: Face got hard as a statue.

S417   As immobile as a **Statue**
1932 WCBrown *Laughing* (P) 48: As dumb and immobile as a statue. **1938** EHeath *Death Takes* (NY) 20: He was as immobile as a statue. **1969** JBrunner *Jagged* (NY) 268: He was immobile as a statue.

S418   As motionless as a **Statue**
1929 JCameron *Seven* (L) 165: [They] stood motionless as statues. **1931** HGarland *Companions* (NY) 44: Motionless as a bronze statue. **1942** JShepherd *Demise* (NY 1962) 66: She sat motionless as a statue. **1971** WHWalling *No One* (NY) 237: Tanis . . . stood motionless as a basalt statue. TW 351(2).

S419   As rigid as a **Statue**
1908 SHAdams *Flying Death* (NY) 12: Colton stood rigid as a statue. **1926** RAFreeman *Puzzle* (NY) 210: Rigid as a marble statue and nearly as void of colour. **1930** JGBrandon *Murder* (L) 197: Stood as rigid as a statue. **1930** CWells *Doorstep* (NY) 314: Rigid as a statue. **1932** JCLenehan *Mansfield* (L) 43: Rigid as a statue. **1955** JEGill *House* (NY) 82: Her body rigid as a statue. **1966** HPentecost *Hide* (NY) 29: [She] sat rigid as a statue. **1977** PDJames *Death* (NY) 70: Rigid as a statue. Cf. Image *above*.

S420   As stiff as a (marble) **Statue**
1945 MInnes *Appleby's End* (NY) 101: As stiff as a statue, as they say. **1958** HTreece *Red Queen* (L) 125: Stiff as a marble statue. **1971** PJFarmer *To Your* (NY) 204: He toppled over, stiff as a statue. Wilstach 388. Cf. Image *above*.

S421   As still as a **Statue**; Statue-still
1928 ABCox *Amateur* (NY) 67: As still as statues. **1932** VWilliams *Death* (B) 256: Still as a statue. **1937** WBrewster *October* (Cambridge, Mass.) 138: As still as a statue. **1938** VWMason *Cairo* (NY) 86: She remained statue still. **1949** MColes *Diamonds* (NY) 204: [They] sat as still as statues and as silent. **1956** RMacdonald *Barbarous* (NY) 240: She was sitting . . . as still as a statue. **1961** RVanGulik *Chinese Lake* (L) 35: Still as a stone statue. **1961** UCurtiss *Hours* (NY) 178: She stood statue-still. **1964** JBlish *Doctor* (L) 210: They stood as still as statues. **1970** RRendell (NY) 135: Statue-still. **1971** DFJones *Denver* (NY) 152: Bette . . . was as still as a statue. **1971** JLymington *Nowhere* (NY) 64: The dog stood still as a statue. **1973** MGEberhart *Murder* (NY) 39: Lorraine sat statue-still. Brunvand 133(3); Whiting *NC* 481.

S422   As straight as a **Statue**
1941 GMitchell *Hangman's* (L) 282: Sat up straight as a statue. Clark 223.

S423   To sit like a **Statue**
1924 VLWhitechurch *Templeton* (NY) 303: [They] sat like two statues. **1926** CJDutton *Flying* (NY) 109: The cat sat there like a statue. **1945** GBellairs *Calamity* (NY) 170: [She] sat like a statue. **1954** MMaring *Murder* (NY) 153: [She] sat like a statue. TW 351(6). Cf. Image *above*.

S424 To stand like a **Statue**

1921 JSFletcher *Chestermarke* (NY) 172: He . . . stood like a statue. **1931** ABCox *Second* (NY) 85: Armorel was standing like a statue. **1959** MNeville *Sweet* (L) 206: She's standing like a statue. **1970** EHahn *Times* (NY) 38: Stood . . . like a statue. **1976** LEgan *Scenes* (NY) 170: She stood like a statue. EAP S418; Brunvand 133(4). Cf. Image *above*.

S425 To let (blow) off **Steam**

1922 JJoyce *Ulysses* (NY 1934) 80: Let off steam. **1940** FGruber *Talking Clock* (NY) 253: Just blowing off steam to Mickey. **1958** EPargeter *Assize* (L) 156: You were just letting off steam. TW 351(3); Wentworth 518.

S426 Under one's own **Steam**

1936 MGEberhart *Fair Warning* (NY) 202: Going out under his own steam. **1952** HWaugh *Last Seen* (NY) 34: She left . . . under her own steam. Cf. NED Steam *sb.* 7d.

S427 As blue as **Steel**; Steel-blue

1930 VStarrett *Blue Door* (NY) 298: Steel-blue eyes. TW 352(1); Brunvand 133(2): Steel-blue.

S428 As cold as **Steel**

1913 EDBiggers *Seven Keys* (I) 157: Eye . . . cold as steel. **1931** DFrome *Strange* (NY) 141: They [*eyes*] would turn cold as steel. **1933** NBMavity *Fate* (NY) 63: She was cold—cold as steel. **1939** NBlake *Smiler* (L) 269: Her voice, cold as steel. Whiting *NC* 481(1).

S429 As gray as **Steel**; Steel-gray

1925 AJSmall *Death* (NY) 11: Steel-grey eyes. **1956** MGEberhart *Postmark* (NY) 207: Eyes as cold and gray as steel. TW 352(4).

S430 As hard as **Steel**; Steel-hard

1913 JCLincoln *Mr. Pratt's Patients* (NY) 317: As hard as steel. **1931** JSFletcher *Murder* (NY) 241: The tones as . . . hard as steel. **1931** HKWebster *Who Is* (I) 90: A look . . . as hard as steel. **1957** CEMaine *High* (NY) 163: Hard as tempered steel. **1967** MDolbier *Benjy* (NY) 114: Steel-sharp eyes. Whiting S699.

S431 As strong as **Steel**

1923 DCScott *Witching* (Toronto) 40: He was as strong as steel. **1949** FCrane *Flying* (NY) 152: Fingers . . . strong as steel. **1959** GKersh *On an* (NY) 121: He was . . . strong as steel. Whiting S705.

S432 As tough as **Steel**

1913 JCLincoln *Mr. Pratt's Patients* (NY) 316: As tough as steel. **1924** JSFletcher *Safety* (NY) 192: Tough as steel. **1934** RKeverne *He Laughed* (L) 255: The man was tough as steel. Whiting *NC* 481(4).

S433 As true (straight) as **Steel**; Steel-true

1906 CPearl *Morrison of Peking* (Sydney 1967) 167: True as steel. **1918** CPearl *Morrison of Peking* (Sydney 1967) 359: True as steel. **1929** RAldington *Death* (L) 228: Steel-true. **1931** PGWodehouse *If I Were You* (NY) 152: Meech was true as steel. **1934** RJBlack *Killing* (NY) 59: "She's as true as—" Charlie hesitated, not wishing to employ the hackneyed simile "steel." **1934** PLindsay *London Bridge* (B) 232: You are as true as steel. **1940** WReed *No Sign* (NY) 18: His nose was as straight as steel. **1956** NMarsh *Death* (B) 200: True's steel. **1957** *TLS* 7/12 425: True as steel. **1964** TDubois *Shannon* (NY DBC) 102: True as steel [*truthful*]. **1967** MBerkeley *Winking* (B) 3: True as steel. EAP S420; TW 352(7); Brunvand 133(3).

S434 As smart (bright, clever) as a **Steel trap**

1912 JCLincoln *Postmaster* (NY) 193: He's smart as a steel trap; 227. **1928** RHFuller *Jubilee* (NY) 132: Smarter'n a steel trap. **1930** HSKeeler *Fourth* (NY) 132: A girl who was as bright as a steel trap. **1933** AMChase *Danger* (NY) 172: She's sharp, smart as a steel trap. **1936** AMChase *Twenty Minutes* (NY) 104: You were smart as a steel trap. **1948** ESherry *Sudden* (NY) 72: He's smart as a steel trap. **1952** PGWodehouse *Angel* (NY) 146: A little girl . . . smart as a steel trap. **1962** COSkinner *Elegant* (NY) 219: These great dolls were clever as steel traps. TW 352(5); Brunvand 133.

S435 To close (shut) like a **Steel trap**

1929 BThomson *Metal* (L) 119: His mouth shut like a steel trap. **1932** DFrome *By-Pass*

(L) 37: A mouth closed as tightly as a steel trap. Cf. Rat-trap *above*; Trap *below*.

S436   To kick (fight) like a (bay) **Steer**

1920 GBMcCutcheon *Anderson Crow* (NY) 130: She may kick like a bay steer. **1930** LTracy *Manning* (NY) 73: He kicked like a steer. **1938** HHolt *Wanted* (L) 154: The Home Office has been kicking like a steer. **1941** IAlexander *Revenge* (NY) 7: She kicked like a steer [*objected*]. **1952** JWPritchard *Every* (NY) 136: He kicked like a steer. **1956** CArmstrong *Dream* (NY 1958) 54: One should . . . kick like a steer. **1964** AMacKinnon *Report* (NY) 8: I've fought like a steer. Taylor *Prov. Comp.* 77.

S437   From **Stem** to stern

1917 JCLincoln *Extricating* (NY) 170: The whole of it from stem to stern. EAP S422; Brunvand 134.

S438   It is the first **Step** that counts (*varied*)

1926 APNewton *Travel* (L) 205: The French proverb—"The first step is the most difficult"—proved true once more. **1932** NBell *Disturbing* (NY) 209: It is the first step that counts. **1932** WBMFerguson *Murder* (NY) 235: The alluring first step on the proverbial road to ruin. **1937** EGreenwood *Under the Fig* (NY) 264: It is the first step that counts, we are told. **1960** FWarburg *Occupation* (B) 146: It's the First Step that Counts. **1968** ELustgarten *Business* (NY) 132: *C'est le premier pas qui compte*—so a French proverb instructs us. EAP S423; Brunvand 134.

S439   One **Step** at a time

1928 GDHCole *Man* (NY) 261: One step at a time. **1933** RAJWalling *Follow* (L) 41: A step at a time. **1941** CCoffin *Mare's Nest* (NY) 184: We take one step at a time. Cf. One Fence *above*.

S440   To watch one's **Step**

1929 RJCasey *Secret* (I) 72: Watch your step; 238. **1938** RPhilmore *Short List* (L) 55: You'd better watch your step. **1959** EHNisot *Sleepless* (NY) 84: He would have to watch his step. **1960** HInnes *Doomed* (NY) 165: Watch your step. **1965** HWaugh *Girl*

(NY) 66: A man had to watch his step. Berrey 154.4.

S441   To **Step** high

1920 GBMcCutcheon *Anderson Crow* (NY) 299: She stepped high, as the saying is. TW 353: Stepped.

S442   To be even **Stephen**

1925 PGWodehouse *Sam* (NY) 140: To split Even Stephen. **1935** CFGregg *Danger* (L) 100: It's even stephen they bring you back. **1941** ISCobb *Exit* (I) 231: The score stood even-Steven. **1953** EBurns *Sex Life* (NY) 225: An even-Stephen fight. **1958** *New Yorker* 10/4 132: The occupation worked out even-Stephen. **1958** MProcter *Three* (NY) 154: Even Steven it'll be. **1967** VLincoln *Private* (NY) 96: You're all even Stephen. TW 353.

S443   To be a **Stepmother** (*varied*)

1922 JJoyce *Ulysses* (NY 1934) 640: Rooked by some landlady worse than any stepmother. **1937** SFowler *Post-Mortem* (L) 226: Stepmothers . . . are traditionally unloved. **1962** RMacdonald *Zebra* (NY) 4: I have tried to be something better than the proverbial stepmother. **1970** MGEberhart *El Rancho* (NY DBC) 67: Nobody likes a stepmother. EAP S426.

S444   To go **Stern** over Crockett

1957 LBeam *Maine* (NY) 196: He didn't just fall down, he went stern over Crockett. Cf. Arse over *above*.

S445   **Steve Brodie** took a chance

1931 MJFreeman *Murder* (NY) 96: Steve Brodie took a chance. **1934** WSutherland *Death Rides* (L) 86: Steve Brodie took a chance! Cf. Wentworth 64: Brodie.

S446   To curse (work) like a **Stevedore**

1959 DLMathews (NY DBC) 93: He was cussing like a stevedore. **1962** PDennis *Genius* (NY) 17: I worked like a stevedore. Cf. To swear like a Navvy, To work like a Navvy *above*.

S447   **Stewed**, screwed, and tattooed

1955 JLatimer *Sinners* (NY) 27: Stewed, screwed and tatooed, as the saying goes.

S448 Any **Stick** will do to beat a dog (*varied*)
c1923 ACrowley *Confessions* ed JSymonds (L 1969) 338: Any stick is good enough to beat a dog with. **1934** FPratt *Heroic* (NY) 14: Clever at finding sticks to beat the Federalist dogs with. **1937** RCWoodthorpe *Death in* (NY) 290: Any stick good enough to do a rival down. **1958** *Time* 5/26 112: He would use any stick to beat a dog. **1958** VCanning *Dragon* (NY) 48: Any stick to beat a donkey. **1959** AGilbert *Death* (NY) 145: Any stick does to beat a dog. **1967** RJones *Three* (B) 254: People will use any stick to beat an enemy. **1968** JCleugh *History* (NY 1970) 99: Any stick would do to beat the Catholics. EAP S430; *Oxford* 769: Staff.

S449 As cross (jealous) as two **Sticks**
1922 JJoyce *Ulysses* (NY 1934) 347: Edy got as cross as two sticks. **1928** GDHCole *Man* (NY) 24: He's always as cross as two sticks. **1936** SGibbons *Miss Linsey* (NY) 66: Jealous as two sticks. **1936** SWilliams *Aconite* (NY) 104: You're as cross . . . as the two famous sticks. **1949** SJepson *Golden* (NY) 54: He's as cross as two sticks. **1954** UCurtiss *Deadly* (NY 1955) 21: As cross as two sticks. **1962** NMarsh *Hand* (B) 28: [He] would be as cross as two sticks. *Oxford* 155: Cross.

S450 As dry as a **Stick** (broomstick)
1935 RBriffault *Europa* (NY) 189: Dry as a broomstick. **1966** NMitford *Sun King* (L) 191: She had become . . . as dry as a stick. **1974** THeald *Blue* (NY) 162: Dry as a stick. TW 353(1).

S451 As stiff as a **Stick**
1959 BWAldiss *Vanguard* (NY) 87: As stiff as a stick. Whiting S724.

S452 As straight as a (any) **Stick**
1951 WCWilliams *Autobiography* (NY) 220: Nancy . . . straight as any stick [*erect*]. **1956** GMetalious *Peyton* (NY) 255: Sitting straight as a stick. Whiting *NC* 481(6); Taylor *Prov. Comp.* 78.

S453 As thin (skinny) as a **Stick**; Stick-thin
1939 AMuir *Death Comes* (L) 85: They [*legs*] were thin as sticks. **1954** ASeton *Katherine* (B) 102: She was small and thin as a stick. **1958** *New Yorker* 5/10 41: Skinny as a stick.

1960 LHolton *Pact* (NY DBC) 102: Her legs were thin as two sticks. **1961** CWillock *Death* (L 1963) 7: Tall and stick-thin. **1974** O Bleeck *Highbinders* (NY) 139: He was stick thin. Cf. Match *above*.

S454 More (this or that) than one can shake a **Stick** at
1904 JCLincoln *Cap'n Eri* (NY) 56: There's more Snows . . . than you can shake a stick at. **1927** JTully *Circus* (NY) 213: There was more hell . . . than you could shake a stick at. **1939** PATaylor *Spring* (L) 37: More indignant relatives than you could shake a stick at. **1941** TChanslor *Our Second* (NY) 163: More motives than we can shake a stick at. **1950** HReilly *Murder* (NY) 61: More scrapes than you can shake a stick at. **1960** PGWodehouse *Jeeves* (L) 82: More mystery stories than you could shake a stick at. **1969** RLockridge *Risky* (P) 150: More bathrooms than you can shake a stick at. EAP S429; TW 353(2).

S455 **Sticks** and stones may break my bones *etc.* (*varied*)
1936 SGGibbons *Miss Linsey* (NY) 110: Sticks and stones may break my bones, but hard words cannot hurt me. **1940** TChanslor *Our First* (NY) 222: Sticks and stones will break our bones, but words will never hurt us. **1943** EWTeale *Dune Boy* (NY 1957) 183: The old adage, Sticks and stones they break my bones, but words they never hurt me. **1949** RLTaylor *W.C.Fields* (NY) 47: Sticks and stones may break my bones, but names will never hurt me. **1952** FKane *Bare* (NY 1960) 191: Sticks and stones will break my bones but lies will never hurt me. **1957** *BHerald* 7/7 14: Sticks and stones can break your bones in the Soviet Union, and names can hurt a lot, too. **1957** *BangorDN* 8/28 10: The old adage of "Sticks and stones may break my bones but names will never hurt me." **1957** BGill *Day* (NY) 159: "You cheap dead-beat son of a bitch." "Sticks and stones." **1968** EMirabelli *Way* (NY) 85: Sticks and stones may break my bones but names will never hurt me. **1969** KHunt [JCreasey] *Too Good* (NY 1970) 130: Sticks and stones can break my bones but words can never hurt me. **1973** CJackson *Kicked*

(NY) 111: Sticks and stones . . . sticks and stones. **1975** EPeters *Crocodile* (NY) 118: Sticks and stones may break my bones, you know. *Oxford* 773. Cf. Looks *above*; Talking, Hard Words *below.*

S456   To be in a cleft (forked) **Stick**

1920 GDilnot *Suspected* (NY) 121: He had her in a cleft stick. **1933** NBell *Lord* (B) 246: He's got us in a cleft stick. **1938** NBerrow *Terror* (L) 222: I'm in a cleft stick. **1941** JRLangham *Pocket* (NY) 295: Robinson had him in a cleft stick. **1949** RFoley *Girl* (NY) 206: I was in a cleft stick. **1958** SBedford *Best* (L 1961) 65: That leaves her in a cleft stick. **1959** SBedford *Trial* (NY) 62: That leaves her in a cleft stick. **1963** RCroft-Cooke *Bosie* (L) 242: Bosie was in a cleft stick. **1967** VLincoln *Private* (NY) 151: The police were in a forked stick. **1972** MGilbert *Body* (NY) 69: We . . . are in a bit of a cleft stick. **1976** JJMarric *Gideon's Drive* (NY) 137: I'm in a cleft stick. Partridge 158: Cleft.

S457   To cut **Stick**

1908 JCLincoln *Cy Whittaker* (NY) 390: He'd gone, skipped, cut stick. **1926** JJConnington *Death* (NY) 204: Jimmy cut his stick. **1933** JSFletcher *Murder* (L) 84: He'd ha' cut his stick at once. **1940** CMWills *R.E.Pipe* (L) 168: Thinkin' of cutting my stick. **1957** RGraves *They Hanged* (NY) 99: Why don't you cut your stick and come to me? TW 353–4(7); Brunvand 134; DARE i 898: Cut stick.

S458   A **Stick-in-the-mud** (*varied*)

1922 JJoyce *Ulysses* (NY 1934) 433: You are a poor old stick in the mud. **1926** JJConnington *Death* (NY) 253: That stick-in-the-mud. **1934** WGore *There's Death* (L) 49: We've got stuck in the mud. **1940** LBrock *Stoat* (L) 21: A regular old stick-in-the-mud. **1948** NMailer *Naked* (NY) 203: He's kind of a stick-in-the-mud. **1952** KMKnight *Valse* (NY) 177: He was an old stick-in-the-mud. **1952** CMackenzie *Rival* (L) 11: These stink-in-the-muds [*sic*]. **1960** BAskwith *Tangled* (L) 38: She's a bit of a stick-in-the-mud. **1962** AMorton *If Anything* (L) 17: Old stick-in-the-mud. **1971** RFDelderfield *For My*

(NY) 116: A bit of a stick-in-the-mud. **1974** JOlsen *Man with* (NY) 66: He wasn't a stick-in-the-mud. TW 354.

S459   To hate (run, work) like **Stink**

1951 ECRLorac *I Could* (NY) 41: They hate me like stink. **1955** MAllingham *Estate* (NY) 56: You have to run like stink. **1972** DDevine *Three* (NY) 4: She just worked like stink. Partridge 832: Like stink.

S460   A **Stitch** in time saves nine (*varied*)

1919 KHoward *Peculiar* (NY) 239: A shock in time saves nine. **1932** LThayer *Glass Knife* (NY) 183: A stitch in time—. **1938** NBlake *Beast* (NY 1958) 108: How many stitches in time saves ten? **1947** PWentworth *Wicked* (NY) 13: The proverbial stitch in time. **1949** FCrane *Flying* (NY) 168: A stitch in time, making hay while the sun shines, that kind of stuff. **1949** SSterling *Dead Sure* (NY) 170: Let him take the stitch in time. **1950** OAnderson *In for* (NY) 30: An Itch in Time. **1955** MColes *Happy* (NY) 137: What says your English proverb? A stitch in time saves the camel's back? **1956** PDeVries *Comfort* (B) 45: A stitch in time sometimes saves nine. **1961** SSterling *Too Hot* (NY) 19: Get on with your stitch in time. **1962** DTaylor *Blood-* (NY) 228: Soonest done, soonest mended. A stitch in time saves nine. **1968** ELathen *A Stitch in Time* (NY). **1970** DClark *Deadly* (NY) 159: The old saying "a stitch in time saves nine." EAP S434.

S461   **Stock**-still

1926 LO'Flaherty *Tent* (L) 74: She listened stock-still. **1930** WLewis *Apes* (NY 1932) 211: He lay stock-still. **1970** CDrummond *Stab* (NY) 36: [He] stood stock still. EAP S442.

S462   To stand like a **Stock**

1956 MPHood *Scarlet* (NY) 110: Jetty stood like a stock. Cf. Whiting S745, 748.

S463   One's **Stomach** is a liar or it is lunch time

1951 MColes *Now* (NY) 72: It's just about lunch time or my stomach's a liar. *Oxford* 45: Belly is the truest clock.

S464 The **Stomach** (belly) thinks the throat is cut

1926 JTully *Beggars* (NY) 107: I woke up so hungry my belly thought my throat was cut. **1931** ACEdington *Monk's Hood* (NY) 85: My stomach thinks my throat's been cut. **1938** WFaulkner *Unvanquished* (NY) 70: My stomach think my throat cut. **1956** EDillon *Death* (L) 76: Me stomach thinks me throat is cut. **1960** JBWest *Taste* (NY) 101: My stomach felt like it thought my throat was cut. **1961** MHHood *Drown* (NY) 53: Your belly thinks your throat's cut. **1980** PDe Vries *Consenting* (B) 162: His stomach thought his throat was cut. *Oxford* 45: Belly.

S465 As bald as a **Stone**; Stone-bald

1928 HFAshurst *Diary* ed GFSparks (Tucson 1962) 263: He is . . . stone-bald. **1953** ELinklater *Year* (L) 29: Bald as a stone—bald as I am. Cf. Whiting S756: Bare.

S466 As bleak as **Stone**

1957 PKDick *Eye* (NY) 119: Saw Sylvester's face turn as bleak as stone. **1957** BHitchens *End* (NY) 219: [His] gaze was as bleak as stone.

S467 As blind as **Stone**; Stone-blind

1923 LThayer *Sinister* (NY) 170: He was stone blind. **1949** WIrish *Phantom* (NY 1957) 233: Drank himself stone-blind. EAP S451a; TW 355(2); Brunvand 134(2): Stone-blind; Whiting S757.

S468 As cold as (a) **Stone**; Stone-cold

1903 EChilders *Riddle* (NY 1940) 81: As cold as stone. **1908** MDPost *Corrector of Destinies* (NY) 110: As cold as a stone. **1922** JJoyce *Ulysses* (NY 1934) 538: We are stone cold. **1928** RAFreeman *As a Thief* (L) 20: Cold as stone. **1933** AAdams *Golf House* (P) 112: Leave you stone cold. **1956** AGilbert *Riddle* (NY) 95: As cold as a stone. **1959** MPHood *Bell* (NY) 161: Cold as a stone. **1964** JWiles *March* (L) 94: His face, cold as stone. **1967** JDHoran *Pinkertons* (NY) 262: [The faces] were cold as stone. **1969** GHCoxe *Easy* (NY) 110: He leaves me stone-cold dead. **1976** HPentecost *Fourteenth* (NY) 127: He played it stone-cold. EAP S452; TW 355(3); Brunvand 134(3).

S469 As dead as a **Stone**; Stone-dead

1911 CKSteele *Mansion* (NY) 39: Stone dead. **1924** LO'Flaherty *Spring* (L) 193: Stone dead. **1933** GDHCole *Lesson* (L) 265: Stone dead. **1933** EQueen *Siamese* (NY) 226: Dead as a stone. **1937** ECRLorac *Bats* (L) 180: Dead as a stone. **1956** MStewart *Wildfire* (NY) 144: Deid [*dead*] as a stone. **1963** NMarsh *Dead* (B 1964) 60: You'll be dead as a stone. **1970** HCarmichael *Death* (NY) 111: Stone-cold dead. **1970** KGiles *Death* (L) 82: He was stone dead. EAP S453, 453a; TW 355(5,6); Brunvand 134(4): Stone dead.

S470 As deaf as a **Stone**; Stone-deaf

1923 AGaul *Five Nights* (NY) 56: Stone deaf. **1930** WLewis *Apes* (NY 1932) 237: Stone-deaf. **1949** RFinnegan *Bandaged* (L 1952) 140: She's deaf as a stone. **1962** BRoss *Scrolls* (NY) 210: As deaf as a stone. **1964** BWAldiss *Greybeard* (L) 23: Meller was as thin as a staff and as deaf as a stone. Whiting S760.

S471 As drunk as a **Stone**

1959 FSmith *Harry* (B) 56: The chief is as drunk as a stone.

S472 As fixed (immobile) as **Stone**

1931 FBeeding *Death* (NY) 265: The faces of his audience were fixed as stone. **1932** STruss *Coroner* (NY) 261: She stood there, immobile as stone. Wilstach 142.

S473 As hard as (a) **Stone**

1930 CBarry *Avenging* (NY) 137: He is hard like a stone. **1930** JGBrandon *Death* (L) 109: His face . . . as hard as stone. **1951** JSStrange *Reasonable* (NY) 177: Her voice was hard as stone. **1956** EXFerrars *We Haven't* (NY) 156: My heart was as hard as stone. EAP S454; TW 356(9); Brunvand 135(6); Taylor *Western Folklore* 17(1958) 19. Cf. As hard as a Rock *above*.

S474 As heavy as a **Stone**

1955 CJay *Yellow* (NY) 106: As heavy as a stone. **1959** ELWithers *Salazar* (NY) 102: Feeling heavy as a stone. Whiting S764.

S475 As motionless as a **Stone** (granite)

1929 CGLDuCann *Secret* (L) 220: She was motionless as a stone. **1935** CRawson *Footprints* (L) 238: Stood motionless as granite. **1954** FCDavis *Another* (NY) 49: He . . . stayed as motionless as a stone. Wilstach 266: Above a grave.

S476 As naked as a **Stone**

1962 ABoucher *Best from Fantasy* (B) 67: He was naked as a stone, or an eel, or a pot, or a new-born babe. Whiting S766.

S477 As quiet as (a) **Stone**; Stone-quiet

1929 FBeeding *Pretty* (B) 147: She sat quiet as a stone. **1929** JCPowys *Wolf* (NY) 2.728: I sits quiet as stone. **1932** JGunther *Bright* (I) 229: The legation was stone quiet. **1970** RBernard *Deadly* (NY) 157: [He] was as quiet as stone. Wilstach 309.

S478 As rigid as **Stone**; Stone-rigid

1924 RAFreeman *Blue* (NY) 43: Face . . . rigid as stone. **1930** Private 19022 *Her Privates* (L) 384: He kept his face as rigid as stone. **1955** EWSmith *One Eyed* (NY) 119: Jeff, rigid as stone. **1960** CErwin *Orderly* (NY) 29: I just sat there stone-rigid. Wilstach 324. Cf. As rigid as a Rock *above*.

S479 As silent (mum) as **Stone**; Stone-silent

1931 DOgburn *Death* (B) 199: [She] always kept as mum as a stone. **1961** SClayton *Crystal* (L) 85: Visitors silent as stone. **1965** LHWhitten *Progeny* (NY) 155: She stood stone silent. Wilstach 353.

S480 As steady as **Stone**

1923 JGollomb *Girl* (NY) 16: As steady as stone. **1936** JWVandercook *Murder in Fiji* (NY) 245: He was steady as stone. Cf. Whiting S770: Steadfast. Cf. As steady as a Rock *above*.

S481 As stiff as **Stone**

1966 JGaskell *All Neat* (L) 88: She was stiff as a stone. **1971** EPeters *Knocker* (NY) 124: Erect and stiff as stone. Whiting S771; Wilstach 389. Cf. As stiff as a Rock *above*.

S482 As still as (a) **Stone**; Stone-still

1919 LMerrick *Chair* (L) 175: Stone-still. **1928** PMacDonald *White* (NY) 194: [He] was still as stone. **1932** LThayer *Glass Knife* (NY)

137: Still as stone. **1933** JGregory *Case* (NY) 10: Stone-still. **1937** NBerrow *One Thrilling* (L) 193: He sat, still as a stone. **1940** EBQuinn *Death Is* (L) 81: Still as stone. **1955** CJay *Yellow* (NY) 4: Still as a stone. **1957** *New Yorker* 12/7 80: The spectators were still as stones. **1963** CArmstrong *Little Less* (NY) 53: Ladd sat still as a stone. **1973** JCaird *Murder* (NY) 109: She lay still as stone. TW 356(11); Wilstach 390. Cf. As still as a Rock *above*.

S483 A rolling **Stone**

1923 ABlackwood *Episodes* (L) 258: The rolling stone went rolling. **1930** JWilliamson *American Hotel* (NY) 9: Americans had nearly all become great rolling stones. **1933** HWade *Hanging* (NY) 5: A rolling stone, if ever there was one. But he rolled to some purpose. **1940** PWentworth *Rolling Stone* (P). **1952** DGBrowne *Scalpel* (NY) 321: The shiftless rolling stone who had been almost everything by turns, but nothing long. **1957** *Punch* 9/4 259: A rolling stone, she is prone to muse/Is worth two in the bush. **1959** JChristopher *Scent* (NY) 28: He's a stone that genuinely loves rolling. **1964** SRansome *Meet* (NY DBC) 5: Like the proverbial stone, old boy, I keep rolling. **1966** NMitford *Sun King* (L) 120: A scamp, a rolling stone. NED Rolling stone 2.

S484 A rolling **Stone** gathers no moss (*very varied*)

1911 JCLincoln *Woman-Haters* (NY) 32: I'm a rolling stone—at any rate I haven't gathered any moss, any financial moss. **1921** JSFletcher *Orange-Yellow* (NY) 154: I've been a bit of a rolling stone . . . and I've falsified the old saying, for I've contrived to gather a good bit of moss in my rollings. **1927** GKChesterton *Secret* (NY) 4: The rolling stone from the West was glad to rest for a moment on this rock in the South, that had gathered so much moss. **1930** ABCox *Wychford* (NY) 200: A rolling stone gathers no moss. **1931** HAdams *Paulton* (P) 171: They say a rolling stone gathers no moss, but it isn't always true. It may roll until it strikes something good. **1932** SHPage *Resurrection* (NY) 29: A rolling stone gathers no moss, but it does get a polish. **1934**

FDGrierson *Murder* (L) 242: A rolling stone who . . . has gathered very little honest moss in his career. **1934** AHelper *Foundry* (NY) 134: A rolling stone . . . never gets to be a mossback. **1936** HAdams *Death* (L) 38: "Been a bit of a rolling stone." . . . "But you've gathered some moss." **1940** PWentworth *Rolling* (P) 8: That's the sort of moss a rolling stone like me doesn't gather. **1941** TDuBois *McNeills Chase* (NY) 143: He thought I was a rolling stone. Moss gathers no rolling stones. She was the moss. But the result was that the stone rolled more furiously than ever. **1943** FScully *Rogues* (Hollywood) 87: A rolling stone that gathered no boss [*sic*]. **1951** JCFurnas *Voyage* (NY) 305: The rolling stone at last . . . determined to gather moss. **1951** SJepson *Man Dead* (NY) 74: Andrew gathered no moss and was proud of it. **1953** JWKrutch *Best* (NY) 123: Moss grows rather quickly, and what a rolling stone really can't gather is lichens. **1955** JRRTolkien *Return* (L) 275: He is a moss-gatherer, and I have been a stone doomed to rolling. **1956** AWilson *Anglo-Saxon* (L) 83: Perhaps if a stone rolls slowly enough, it *will* gather moss. **1958** *New Yorker* 5/10 116: A stone for every kidney/ Can't gather moss today! **1967** VPowell *Substantial* (L) 160: To regulate her life, to cease rolling, and to gather some moss. **1967** JAxelrad *Freneau* (Austin) 185: Peter . . . was no rolling stone, and he knew how to gather the moss. **1968** MConnelly *Voices* (NY) 96: A rolling stone gathers no boss [*sic*]. **1972** DDevine *Three* (NY) 57: He had travelled light and gathered little moss. **1975** EMcBain *Where* (NY) 162: Whereas a rolling stone may gather no moss, a stitch in time most certainly saves nine. **1981** CMacLeod *Palace* (NY) 33: He's the original rolling stone, though I expect he's fairly mossy as far as money goes. EAP S456; TW 355(1); Brunvand 134(1).

S485 To be within a **Stone's** throw

1969 CHGardiner *Prescott* (Austin) 16: Within the proverbial stone's throw of the Prescott residence. Cole 64.

S486 To drop like a **Stone**

1914 PJBrebner *Christopher* (NY) 82: He dropped like a stone. **c1923** ACrowley

Confessions ed JSymonds (L 1969) 269: The deer dropped like a stone. **1925** JGBrandon *Cork* (L) 150: Dropped me like a stone. **1952** DBOlsen *Enrollment* (NY) 180: She dropped like a stone. **1970** RQuest *Cerberus* (NY) 186: He dropped like a stone. Wilstach 104.

S487 To fall like a **Stone**

1925 AWynne *Sign* (P) 293: The old man fell like a stone. Whiting S781.

S488 To go down like a **Stone**

1929 SMartin *Only Seven* (NY) 55: Black went down like a stone. Whiting S787 (quote 1395).

S489 To leave no **Stone** unturned (*varied*)

1909 MRRinehart *Man in Lower Ten* (NY 1947) 268: Not leave one stone unturned. **1922** JJoyce *Ulysses* (NY 1934) 316: Left no stone unturned. **1924** RAFreeman *Blue* (NY) 106: Leaving no stone unturned. **1933** EBBlack *Ravenelle* (NY) 41: You've certainly left no stone unturned. **1940** CRice *Corpse Steps* (NY) 245: "We're leaving no turn unstoned." "That's wrong . . . It's that we're leaving no worm unturned." **1941** MHolbrook *Suitable* (NY) 210: We leave no stone unturned, as the books say. **1946** MBennett *Time to Change* (NY) 153: Leave no scone [*sic*] unturned and all that sort of thing. **1947** AGilbert *Death in* (L) 110: To use a colloquialism, they left no stone unturned. **1950** RVickers *Murdering* (L 1955) 45: We like to leave no stone unturned. **1958** *BangorDN* 9/8 12: Dillaway has let no stone remain unturned. **1959** MInnes *Hare* (NY 1964) 48: "It's another of those tiresome stones." "Not to be left unturned." **1961** RLockridge *With One* (P) 94: Leave no stone unturned, as they say. **1961** AGilbert *After* (NY DBC) 33: Not believing in leaving stones unturned or wheels unshouldered. **1965** BGrebanier *Great Shakespeare* (NY) 37: His determination to leave no pebble unturned. **1971** JFraser *Death* (NY) 123: Some stones are better left without turning. **1981** JRoss *Dark* (NY) 25: He had not failed to look under every stone. EAP S457. Cf. Avenue *above*.

S490 To mark with a white **Stone**

1925 JSFletcher *Annexation* (NY) 75: Days as were marked with a white stone because of his reception of a tuck basket. **1933** VWilliams *Clock* (L) 234: Let us mark the day with a white stone. EAP S458.

S491 To sink like a **Stone**

1920 EWallace *Three-Oaks* (L) 219: Molly's heart sank like a stone. **1930** GCollins *Horror* (L) 266: Sank like a stone. **1936** FWCrofts *Loss* (NY) 13: The ship would sink like a stone. **1946** ESHolding *Innocent* (NY) 81: Paul sank like a stone. **1957** JBrooks *Water* (L) 236: He had sunk like a stone. **1960** COliver *Unearthly* (NY) 95: He would sink like a stone. **1968** CCowley *Fabled* (NY) 91: Sank like a stone. **1970** CDBowen *Family* (B) 89: She sank like a stone. EAP S459.

S492 To sit like a **Stone**

1928 AGilbert *Mrs. Davenport* (NY) 162: [He] sat like a stone. **1934** EQueen *Adventures* (NY) 152: The banker sat like stone. **1956** RLongrigg *High-pitched* (L) 224: I sat like a stone. **1974** MGEberhart *Danger* (NY) 19: Sitting like a stone. Whiting S787 (quote 1350).

S493 To sleep like a **Stone**

1935 DMagarshack *Death* (NY) 68: Slept like a stone. **1941** MTYates *Midway* (NY) 256: He slept like a stone.

S494 To stand like a **Stone**

1930 MPShiel *Purple Cloud* (NY) 19: I stood like stone. **1941** NMarsh *Death and the* (B) 78: Mandrake stood like a stone. **1958** DGBrowne *Death* (L) 178: She stood there like a stone. Whiting S786.

S495 **Stone-dead** has no fellow

1911 JSHay *Amazing Emperor* (L) 59: Stone-dead hath no fellow. **1939** HCBailey *Veron* (L) 137: There is an old saying . . . "Stone dead has no fellow." 139: I remember now it was Oliver Cromwell who said [it]. **1963** HMacInnes *Venetian* (NY) 59: Stone dead hath no fellow. *Oxford* 776.

S496 To fall between two **Stools** (*varied*)

1916 RFirbank *Inclinations* (Works 2, L 1929) 131: I fear she has fallen between two stools. **1927** GDilnot *Lazy* (B) 215: I don't want you to fall between two stools. **1928** SChalmers *House* (NY) 369: Watch you don't fall between two stools while reaching for too much. **1935** AGilbert *Man* (L) 45: She'd fallen between two stools. **1939** MElwin *Old Gods* (NY) 247: He was falling between the stools of scholarship and . . . story-telling. **1953** GRHEllis *Lesser* (L) 18: As it was he fell, psychologically speaking, between two stools. **1956** *NYTimes* 11/25 1E: An old proverb says a man can sit on only one stool at a time. **1957** *Punch* 6/19 759: Never fall between stools, darling. I usually say don't fall between stool pigeons. I'm the Mrs Malaprop of the world. **1957** CASmart *At Home* (NY) 75: The results fell between two or three stools. **1961** RKirk *Old House* (NY DBC) 155: Fallen between two stools. **1962** EHuxley *Mottled* (L) 82: Robin was caught between two stools. **1964** DForbes-Robertson *My Aunt* (NY) 157: He was accused of falling between two stools. **1971** MdeRichewiltz *Discretions* (B) 207: Take care not to slide between two chairs. **1973** JMann *Troublecross* (NY) 116: Bill apparently was caught between two stools, fires, duties or whatever. EAP S462; TW 356.

S497 To tend the **Store**

1966 SMarlowe *Search* (NY) 178: I came all the way to mind the store. **1972** ELathen *Murder* (NY) 105: Someone else minded the store. **1973** WMasterson *Undertaker* (NY) 53: When he wasn't mindin' the store I usually was.

S498 One **Story** is good until you hear the next

1922 JJoyce *Ulysses* (NY 1934) 124: One story good till you hear the next. EAP S467.

S499 That's my **Story** and I'll stick to it (*varied*)

1926 EDBiggers *Chinese* (NY) 221: That's my story, and I'll stick to it. **1930** TFMadigan *Word Shadows* (NY) 231: That was his story and, as the modern saying goes, he stuck to it. **1937** ITSanderson *Animal* (NY) 15: This is my story and I'm sticking to it. **1940** CRice *Corpse Stops* (NY) 196: He's our story and we're stuck with him. **1953** MMKaye *Death Walked* (L) 21: If that's your story, you stick to it. **1956** JWyndham *Tales* (NY) 48: That's your story, and you've got to stick to it. **1968** PMoyes *Death* (NY) 15: This was his story, and he was sticking to it. **1971** NBogner *Making* (NY) 45: That was Mel's story and he was sticking to it. Berrey 208.6.

S500 To cut (make) a long **Story** short

1922 JJoyce *Ulysses* (NY 1934) 642: To cut a long story short. **1926** FWCrofts *Cheyne* (NY) 212: To make a long story short. **1939** CBarry *Nicholas* (L) 240: To make a long story short. **1955** PDennis *Auntie* (NY) 50: To make a long story short. **1962** CWatson *Hopjoy* (NY) 72: To cut a long story short. **1972** JMcClure *Caterpillar* (NY) 198: To cut a long story short. **1975** HBlack *My Father* (NY) 196: To make a long story short. EAP S468.

S501 As warm as a **Stove**

1961 NBlake *Worm* (L) 120: Millie was warm as a stove. Whiting *NC* 482.

S502 The last (final) **Straw**

1908 JCLincoln *Cy Whittaker* (NY) 364: The final straw. **1922** JJoyce *Ulysses* (NY 1934) 540: The last straw. **1927** CSLewis *Letters* ed WHLewis (NY 1966) 116: The last straw. **1937** WETurpin *These Low* (NY) 109: This was the proverbial last straw. **1953** KMKnight *Akin* (NY) 121: Sophie's final betrayal could have been the proverbial last straw. **1954** DMDisney *The Last Straw* (NY). **1956** NFitzgerald *Imagine* (L) 142: The last straw should be one straw and not a damned barnful. **1970** JAiken *Embroidered* (NY) 174: The last straw. Whiting *NC* 482 (2); Brunvand 135(4); *Oxford* 443: Last.

S503 The last **Straw** that broke the camel's back (*varied*)

1911 JCLincoln *Woman-Haters* (NY) 130: The final straw that choked the camel. **1924** HSKeeler *Voice* (NY) 173: The straw that broke Iva's back. **1928** ACBrown *Dr. Glazebrook* (NY) 248: The last straw that would

break the camel's back. **1930** JFDobie *Coronado* (Dallas) 199: That was the straw that broke the camel's back. **1934** NBrady *Ebenezer* (L) 286: He found that cut the last straw on the camel's back. **1936** HAustin *Murder of a Matriarch* (NY) 91: Putting the final straw on a camel's back. **1938** BFlynn *Ebony* (L) 224: That would have placed the proverbial straw on the camel's back. **1939** DMDisney *Golden Swan* (NY) 44: The final straw that broke my back. **1940** RStout *Double for Death* (L) 118: It was the bleat of a camel whose back is bending under the last straw. **1947** FLockridge *Untidy* (NY) 37: "And anything might have—have been the last straw." . . . "Quotations! Old sayings! Camels with broken backs!" **1952** KM Knight *Death Goes* (NY) 39: The straw . . . that broke the camel's back. **1954** JSymons *Narrowing* (NY) 181: The last straw added to the pile that broke the camel's back. **1957** *BHerald* 7/1 10: The straw that broke the camel's back. **1960** FWarburg *Occupation* (B) 219: The last straw on the publishing camel's back. **1961** JPhilips *Murder* (NY DBC) 140: One of the straws that broke the camel's back. **1964** RCFaure *Summer* (NY) 156: The straw that broke the camel's back. **1971** MUnderwood *Trout* (NY) 185: The straw which breaks the camel's back. **1974** DCavett *Cavett* (NY) 48: The last, back-breaking straw. **1975** FMNivens *Publish* (NY) 120: That was the straw that put my back to the wall. **1982** SAllen *Talk* (NY) 227: So the Margulis murder was kind of a straw that broke the cliché's back. Whiting *NC* 482 (2); Brunvand 20: Camel(3); *Oxford* 443: Last.

S504 Not care two **Straws** (a straw) (*varied*)

1909 JCLincoln *Keziah* (NY) 228: Only one boy I cared two straws about. **1919** JBCabell *Jurgen* (NY 1922) 181: Not care a straw. **1922** JJoyce *Ulysses* (NY 1934) 724: Not that I care two straws who he does it with. **1923** ABlackwood *Episodes* (L) 222: Not care two straws. 246: A straw. **1924** LO'Flaherty *Spring* (L) 28: Not care a straw. **1928** DHLawrence *Lady* ("Allemagne") 84: She didn't care a straw. **1939** LBrock *Fourfingers* (L) 125: I don't care a Jack straw. **1955** JBingham *Paton* (L 1964) 151: Not that I care two blinking straws. **1959** ECooper

Seed (NY) 74: I don't care one straw—one single bloody straw. **1970** RFoley *Calculated* (NY) 144: He never cared two straws for you. EAP S473; TW 357(1); Brunvand 135(1).

S505   Not give a **Straw**

1956 CJay *Brink* (L 1962) 149: He just didn't give a straw. EAP S474; TW 357(2).

S506   Not matter two **Straws** (a straw)

c1923 ACrowley *Confessions* ed JSymonds (L 1969) 401: [Not] matter a straw. **1930** FWCrofts *Sir John* (NY) 146: Not that parental opposition . . . would have mattered two straws. **1933** PMacDonald *Menace* (NY) 157: It don't matter two straws in merry Hades. Whiting *Drama* 365(876).

S507   Not value a **Straw**

1931 RAFreeman *Mr. Pottermack's* (L) 147: Valued him not a straw. EAP S476.

S508   Not worth a **Straw**

1964 DHughes *Major* (L) 91: Nothing . . . was worth a straw. EAP S477; TW 357(4).

S509   A **Straw** (straws) in the wind

1939 AMorton *Alias Blue* (P) 73: [He] was a straw in the wind. **1956** *BangorDN* 11/3 10: It may be a straw in the wind of things to come. **1957** *TLS* 3/8 146: A straw in the same wind. **1959** *BHerald* 12/6 58: These divergent views are only straws in the wind. **1965** IRoss *Charmers* (NY) 276: Another straw in the wind. **1967** AMarreco *Rebel* (L) 232: The by-election was more than a straw in the wind. **1972** SBrooke *Queen* (NY) 138: These early rumours . . . were mere straws in the wind. **1975** HDolson *Please* (P) 98: Lucy . . . was ready to seize on straws in the wind and twist them to any desired shape. Amer. Herit. Dict. Straw *n.*3. Cf. next entry.

S510   **Straws** show which way the wind blows (*varied*)

1917 JCLincoln *Extricating* (NY) 124: A straw showing which way the wind blew. **1924** CWells *Furthest* (P) 293: Straws show which way the wind blows. **1926** LThayer *Poison* (NY) 115: It is not in my poor experience that straws blow against the wind. **1937** MBurton *Murder* (L) 139: The old ad-

age concerning straws and the wind. **1938** ECRLorac *Slippery* (L) 5: They say a straw shows which way the wind blows. **1941** MGEberhart *With This Ring* (NY) 217: Straws . . . showing which way the wind was blowing. **1953** ERuggles *Prince* (NY) 113: These were only straws, yet they showed how the wind blew. **1956** BJFarmer *Death* (L) 171: It's a straw to indicate the way of the wind. **1959** *NYTimes Book Review* 8/30 6: Straws to show which way the wind is blowing. **1960** HRobertson *Swan* (NY) 63: Nothing but straws in the wind . . . and they were all bent in the same direction. **1971** J Creasey *Murder* (NY) 30: Straws perhaps, but they add to my hunch. **1971** PDickinson *Sleep* (NY) 207: "You're clutching at straws." The straws are in the wind. You can also see the wind by the straws in it. Old Mongolian proverb. EAP S480. Cf. preceding entry.

S511   To clutch (*etc.*) at any **Straw**

1911 JSHay *Amazing Emperor* (L) 183: Ready to catch at any straw. **1924** GRFox *Fangs* (NY) 257: Grasping at every straw. **1927** FLPackard *Two* (NY) 292: Like catching at the proverbial straw. **1927** CWells *Where's Emily* (NY) 51: Grabbed at her as the possible last straw. **1933** FLPackard *Hidden* (L) 120: I may only be grasping at the proverbial straw. **1935** MBeckett *Tea Time* (L) 272: We seem to hang on straws in this case . . . And so far all the straws have broken. **1938** HHolt *Wanted* (L) 76: A pretty good straw at which to clutch. **1941** AAFair *Spill* (NY) 194: She was clinging to a straw of hope. **1947** ELustgarten *One More* (NY 1959) 178: People clutch at any straw for comfort. **1951** FLockridge *Murder Comes* (P) 31: That's grabbing a straw. **1959** HWaugh *Sleep* (NY) 91: It was grabbing for straws. **1961** GHCoxe *Last* (NY) 104: He kept grabbing at straws. **1962** HWaugh *That Night* (L) 143: He had been grasping for straws. **1965** WRBurkett *Sleeping* (NY) 13: Hanging onto [it] as if it were the proverbial straw. **1968** LPDavies *Grave* (NY) 30: I'm reduced to clutching at straws. **1973** PMoyes *Curious* (NY) 38: Clutching at straws. **1974** GMeyer *Memphis* (NY) 52: He was beginning to clutch at straws. **1977** LBlock *Burglars* (NY)

61: I am thirsty enough to grab at a straw. EAP S483; Brunvand 135(3). Cf. A drowning Man *above*.

S512 To move (be off) like a **Streak**

1929 CBush *Perfect* (NY) 42: Eaton moved like a streak. **1954** MAllingham *No Love* (NY) 205: She'd be off like a streak. TW 358(2).

S513 To talk a blue **Streak**

1906 JCLincoln *Mr. Pratt* (NY) 40: Talking a blue streak. **1928** RHFuller *Jubilee* (NY) 37: He talked a blue streak; 428. **1941** ES Gardner *Haunted Husband* (NY) 188: She talks a blue streak. **1953** ECrandall *White* (B) 107: She'll talk a blue streak. **1960** FLockridge *Judge* (P) 68: He's talking a blue streak. **1966** MWorthington *Strange* (NY) 140: Talking a blue streak. **1972** LIsrael *Tallulah* (NY) 83: Tallulah talked a blue streak. Whiting *NC* 482: Runs; Brunvand 135: Cuss; Berrey 189.3.

S514 To be up (down) one's **Street**

1933 JWVandercook *Murder* (NY) 186: The job was decidedly "up my street." **1936** PAJWalling *Crimson Slippers* (L) 75: It was not down his street. **1938** PGWodehouse *Code* (NY) 90: It ought to be right up Harold's street. **1954** MLSettle *Love* (L) 175: All this kind of going-on is just not up my street. **1957** CCarnac *Late Miss* (NY) 80: It's more up your street than ours. **1961** AGilbert *After* (NY DBC) 112: This is right up his street. **1971** MUnderwood *Trout* (NY) 112: Murder sounds right up his street. **1975** MErskine *Harriet* (NY) 102: Right up our street. Partridge 838–9.

S515 Not to know one's own **Strength**

1930 PMacDonald *Rynox* (L) 181: James doesn't know his own strength. **1936** KMKnight *Clue* (NY) 127: Didn't know his strength. **1938** MSaltmarsh *Clouded* (NY) 87: You don't realize your own strength, as the flea said to the elephant. **1946** LCores *Let's Kill George* (NY) 24: You don't know your own strength. **1947** GGallagher *I Found* (NY DBC) 72: I don't know my own strength. **1955** RFenisong *Widows* (NY) 143: You don't know your own strength. **1956** *BangorDN* 12/19 26: You don't know your

own strength. **1964** JJMarric *Gideon's Vote* (NY) 143: You don't know your own strength. **1976** JMcClure *Snake* (NY) 129: You don't know your own strength. Cf. NED Strength *sb.* 1d (quote 1636).

S516 To take in one's **Stride**

1935 BFlynn *Case* (L) 166: You've taken this in your stride. **1938** ESGardner *Shoplifter's Shoe* (NY) 22: Sarah takes it right in her stride. **1947** NMarsh *Final* (B) 250: She's taking it in her stride. **1949** SJepson *Golden* (NY) 196: She was . . . taking it in her stride. **1952** AThorne *Young* (L) 128: One should take these things . . . in one's stride. **1961** BPym *No Fond* (L) 250: Mother took it in her stride. Cole 65: Take something.

S517 To have two **Strikes** on (against) one

1955 AWest *Heritage* (NY) 122: You'd have had two strikes on you before you were even out of school. **1959** SDean *Price* (NY) 114: You have two strikes on you at home. **1960** TPowell *Man-Killer* (NY) 15: Vicky was born with two strikes against her. DA Strike *n.* 1b.

S518 As limp as a wet **String**

1940 JStagge *Turn* (NY) 19: I felt limp as a piece of wet string. **1956** *BangorDN* 6/30 2: I feel limp as a wet string. Cf. TW 358(1): Limber.

S519 As straight as a **String**

1920 ACrabb *Samuel* (NY) 39: She was . . . straight as a string. **1930** ALivingston *Murder* (I) 193: As straight as a string. **1936** HFootner *Kidnapping* (L) 136: She was straight as a string [*moral*]. **1937** WMartyn *Old Manor* (L) 52: Ware is as straight as a string. **1940** PATaylor *Criminal* (NY) 29: Straight as a string. **1965** HWaugh *Girl* (NY) 190: It's straight as string. **1969** RLockridge *Die* (P) 107: Straight as a string . . . has always seemed an odd simile to Shapiro, who knows how strings can tangle. TW 358(2); Brunvand 136(1). Cf. Ribbon *above*.

S520 To harp on one **String** (*varied*)

1905 FMWhite *Crimson Blind* (NY) 150: So you are harping on that string again. **1925** EBChancellor *Hell Fire* (L) 232: To harp over much on one string. **1932** ERPunshon *Cottage* (B) 67: Harp on one string. **1933** KCStrahan *Meriwether* (NY) 195: Paul had but one string to his harp. **1934** LRGribble *Riddle* (L) 143: How you do harp on one note! **1936** GdePekár *Wanderer* (L) 68: Forever harping on the same string. **1940** MBurton *Murder in* (L) 108: Still harping on the same string. **1940** HRutland *Poison Fly* (NY) 63: Do stop harping on that string. **1948** ESherry *Sudden* (NY) 60: Still harping on that string. **1957** GWJohnson *Lunatic* (P) 129: The tactical error of harping on one string. EAP S494.

S521 To have two (*etc.*) **Strings** to one's bow (*varied*)

1900 CFPidgin *Quincy A. Sawyer* (B) 76: That city chap had two strings to his bow. **1915** RFirbank *Vainglory* (Works 1, L 1929) 226: Second string to my bow. **1919** LTracy *Bartlett* (NY) 277: Find another string to your bow. **1922** JJoyce *Ulysses* (NY 1934) 73: Two strings to her bow. **1925** FWCrofts *Groote* (NY) 238: He was loath to give up one of the only two strings he had to his bow. **1928** EHBierstadt *Curious Trials* (NY) 262: The defense had two arrows to its bow. **1932** FBeeding *Murder* (B) 274: He was a second string to her bow. **1932** CRyland *Notting* (L) 289: It gave him two strings to his bow. **1935** JSFletcher *Eleventh* (NY) 162: The lady appears to have three strings to her bow. **1938** BFlynn *Five Red* (NY) 27: It's always well to have two strings to your bow. **1940** HFootner *Sinfully* (L) 153: He took along the dagger as a second string. **1940** RKing *Holiday* (NY) 114: As somebody always says, two bowstrings are better than one. **1943** MVHeberden *Murder Goes* (NY) 27: She had a third string to her bow. **1945** HCBailey *Wrong Man* (NY) 118: The ancient jingle: "Two strings to my bow, Two beaux to my string." **1945** MWalsh *Nine Strings to Your Bow* (P). **1953** DMDisney *Do Unto* (NY) 110: She's got a second string to her bow. **1957** *BHerald* 10/10 9: Now the reason for spending more money is because of the number of strings you put on your bow. **1957** AWilson *Bit* (L) 40: It's just as well to have a second string. **1958** MInnes *Long* (NY) 55: Perhaps she has Shakespeare

as a second string. **1962** HPentecost *Cannibal* (NY DBC) 43: I would have more than one string to my bow. **1966** WDerry *Dr. Parr* (Oxford) 87: Add a second string to his bow. **1967** WGolding *Pyramid* (NY) 46: What other strings did Evie have to her trim bow? **1970** CEClark *Eastern* (NY) 19: Gorges . . . still had one string to his bow. **1970** KLaumer *World* (NY) 160: I have more than one string to my bow—or should I say more than one beau to my string? **1973** HDolson *Dying* (P) 30: Grace had other strings to her bow. **1974** EPHoyt *Horatio's* (Radnor, Penn.) 36: Alger . . . had only one string to his bow. **1975** JLangton *Dark* (NY) 80: [They] seemed to have a couple of strings to their bow. EAP S495; TW 358(3); Brunvand 136(6). Cf. Arrow *above*.

S522 To pull **Strings**

1929 SMElam *Borrow* (L) 92: He would have to pull a few strings. **1932** FIles *Before* (NY 1958) 163: Johnnie had pulled every string he knew. **1933** LRGribble *Secret* (L) 281: People who can pull strings. Brunvand 136(4); NED String *sb.* 1i.

S523 Little **Strokes** fell big oaks

1957 *Time* 12/16 54: Little strokes fell big oaks. EAP S496.

S524 To be in a brown (blue) **Study**

1919 JSFletcher *Middle Temple* (NY) 18: In a . . . brown study. **1922** JJoyce *Ulysses* (NY 1934) 348: In a brown study. **1923** TFPowys *Left Leg* (L) 174: In a brown study, as 'tis called. **1930** SGluck *Blind Fury* (NY) 162: She undressed in a brown study. **1930** WWoodrow *Moonhill* (NY) 169: One of those horrid, faraway silences, which are spoken of in books as brown studies. **1936** EBQuinn *One Man's* (L) 57: Something brought me out of my blue study. **1937** ECRLorac *Bats* (L) 135: He went off into a blue study. **1941** ELFetta *Dressed* (NY) 128: Curtis' face was a brown study. **1950** D Mathew *Mango* (L) 161: He was in what used to be called a brown study. **1963** NBenchley *Catch* (NY) 196: I was in what's sometimes called a brown study. **1969** R Stark *Blackbird* (NY) 93: [He] roused himself from a brown study. **1970** ELathen *Pick* (NY)

153: Waking from a brown study. **1974** JBrunner *Total* (NY) 37: In a brown study of depression. EAP S498; Brunvand 136.

S525 The **Stuff** to give the troops

1930 LTracy *Manning* (NY) 165: That's the stuff to give the troops. **1932** WLHay *Who Cut* (L) 235: This was the stuff to administer to the troops. **1941** NMarsh *Death and the* (B) 4: That's the stuff to give the troops. **1948** WMiller *Fatal* (NY) 15: That's the stuff to give the troops. **1956** AWilson *Anglo-Saxon* (L) 392: That's the stuff to give the troops. **1957** *Punch* 1/2 64: That's the stuff to give the troops. **1971** MErskine *Brood* (NY) 24: That's the stuff to give the troops, she told herself, echoing an absurdly old-fashioned saying of her father's. **1977** PDJames *Death* (NY) 65: That's the stuff to give the troops. Partridge 842.

S526 To be a **Stumbling** block

1928 EHamilton *Four* (L) 157: The only stumbling block. **1936** MBurton *Murder* (L) 44: His existence had been a stumbling block to certain persons. **1938** JGBrandon *Cork Street* (L) 186: The stumbling-block in our way. **1948** MEChase *Jonathan* (NY) 142: A spiritual stumbling-block in his more mature years. **1955** LWhite *To Find* (NY) 120: The biggest stumbling block. **1961** CKeith *Missing* (NY) 162: An unimportant stumbling-block. **1968** LdeKLawrence *Lovely* (NY) 53: The inept idea . . . was a greatly confusing stumbling block. **1971** JHBPeel *Along* (L) 40: Gibbon's basic stumbling block. **1973** SWoods *Yet She* (NY) 35: The last item is the stumbling block. EAP S499.

S527 To be up a **Stump**

1928 EBarker *Cobra* (NY) 63: You are up a stump. **1939** RStout *Crime on* (L) 113: They are up a stump. **1953** SBellow *Adventures* (NY) 208: I'm up the stump. **1969** RStout *Death* (NY) 7: You're up a stump. **1973** RStout *Please* (NY) 146: You're up a stump. TW 359(7).

S528 To stir one's **Stumps**

1931 GDHCole *Dead Man's* (L) 20: Stir his stumps. **1937** DQBurleigh *Kristiana* (NY) 45: I'd better be stirring my stumps. **1940** MArmstrong *Man with* (NY) 54: Stir their stumps. **1943** PCheyney *Dark Dust* (NY) 140: It is time you . . . stirred your lazy stumps. **1950** GHCoxe *Frightened* (NY DBC) 44: He can just as well stir his stumps. **1956** MPHood *Scarlet* (NY) 158: You'd better stir your stumps. **1961** MGEberhart *Cup* (NY DBC) 106: We all better be stirring our stumps. **1963** AChristie *Clocks* (NY) 179: You can stir your stumps. **1970** KLaumer *World* (NY) 120: You'd better stir your stumps. EAP S501.

S529 As homely as a **Stump fence**

1956 *BangorDN* 7/20 5: Homelier than a stump fence built by moonlight. **1962** *BangorDN* 6/25 22: Homely as a stump fence. TW 359. Cf. Hedge fence, Mud fence *above*.

S530 As well be dead as out of **Style**

1967 JFDobie *Some Part* (B) 126: Just as well be dead as out of style. *Oxford* 603: Out of the world.

S531 If at first you don't **Succeed** *etc.* (*varied*)

1919 SLeacock *Frenzied* (Toronto 1971) 132: An old motto which runs, "If at first you don't succeed, try, try again." This is nonsense. **1919** LTracy *Bartlett* (NY) 143: If at first you don't succeed, try, try, try again. **1922** JJoyce *Ulysses* (NY 1934) 350: If you fail try again. **1928** WRoughead *Malice* (L) viii: I was thereby encouraged, reversing the order of the proverb, to try and try again. **1933** JJFarjeon *House* (NY) 103: Remember the old proverb . . . If at first you don't succeed, try, try again. **1940** HCBailey *Mr. Fortune Here* (NY) 118: If at first you don't succeed, try, try, try again. **1952** DGBrowne *Scalpel* (NY) 276: If at first you don't succeed, try, try again. **1956** *New Yorker* 8/11 19: If at first you don't succeed, fail, fail again. **1959** FLockridge *Murder Is* (P) 104: If at first you don't succeed, blame, blame again. **1961** RAHeinlein *6XH* (NY) 127: If at Last You Do Succeed, Never Try Again. **1968** JDHicks *My Life* (Lincoln, Nebr.) 32: The abominable maxim: "If at first you don't succeed, try, try again." Whiting *NC* 483. Cf. *Oxford* 238: Failure.

S532 **Success** begets (breeds) success

1927 NMartin *Mosaic* (NY) 110: Success begets success. **1957** *BHerald* 6/24 7: Success breeds success. **1967** JRichardson *Courtesans* (L) 51: It has always been evident that success creates success. **1969** RPearsall *Worm* (L) 251: Success breeds success. Cf. Nothing succeeds *above*.

S533 Never give a **Sucker** an even break

1931 TThayer *Greek* (NY) 263: Never give a sucker an even break. **1941** ESGardner *Turning Tide* (NY) 163: Never give a sucker a break. **1956** RAHeinlein *Double* (NY 1957) 87: Never give a sucker an even break. **1964** LCohen *New York* (P) 125: Never give a sucker an even break. Wentworth 527: Sucker *n*.1.

S534 Silly **Suffolk**

1931 CBush *Dead Man's* (L) 125: All the way to Suffolk—silly Suffolk, don't they call it? *Oxford* 734.

S535 As sweet as **Sugar**

1933 BReynolds *Very Private* (NY) 23: You're as sweet as sugar. **1939** MArmstrong *Murder in* (NY) 136: He'd be as sweet as sugar. **1950** FO'Malley *Best* (NY) 26: Sweet as sugar to me. **1957** HEBates *Sugar* (L) 6: She was as sweet as a sugar-ball. EAP S504; TW 359–60(1).

S536 As white as **Sugar**

1972 RHGreenan *Queen* (NY) 198: He was as white as sugar—or snow. Clark 225.

S537 To be neither **Sugar** nor salt (*varied*)

1930 ECVivian *Double* (L) 156: I'm no sugar . . . I don't melt for a drop o' rain. **1938** RTorrey *42 Days* (NY) 239: He ain't made of sugar or salt. Don't make a baby of him. **1957** LDelRay *Robots* (NY) 58: All she said was something about not being sugar, so she wouldn't melt. EAP S505.

S538 On a **Summer's** day

1931 CBush *Dead Man's* (L) 42: As modest a soul as you'd meet on a summer's day. EAP S508; TW 360. Cf. In a Day's march *above*.

S539 As bright as the **Sun**

1966 NMarsh *Killer* (B) 51: Bright as the sun. EAP S509; TW 360(1).

S540 As clear as the **Sun**

1943 CEVulliamy *Polderoy* (L) 275: A fact as clear as the noonday sun. EAP S511; TW 260(2). Cf. Sunlight *below*.

S541 As open as the **Sun**

1934 AFielding *Cautley* (L) 10: As open as the sun. **1934** HReilly *McKee* (NY) 139: Judith . . . was as open as the sun. Cf. As open as the Day, Daylight *above*.

S542 As plain as the **Sun**

1938 CDickson *Judas* (L) 181: It seems as plain as the sun. **1952** FCDavis *Tread* (NY) 126: As plain as the noonday sun. EAP S513. Cf. As plain as Day, Daylight *above*; Sunlight *below*.

S543 As regular as the **Sun**

1957 TWicker *Devil* (NY) 47: Regular as the sun comes up. TW 360(5).

S544 As sure as the **Sun** shines

1903 ADMcFaul *Ike Glidden* (B) 196: Just as sure as the sun shines. **1972** RRendell *No More* (NY) 134: As sure as the sun rises. EAP S516. Cf. Brunvand 137: Sunrise.

S545 The **Sun** always comes out on Saturday

1968 KMartin *Editor* (L) 119: You know the saying that the sun always comes out on Saturday. Dunwoody 101.

S546 The **Sun** is over (below) the yard-arm (*varied*)

1933 GBegbie *Sudden* (L) 38: Taking to tippling before the sun sank below the yard arm. **1936** RAJWalling *Floating Foot* (NY) 28: The sun was just over the yard-arm . . . and we observed the traditional ceremony. **1941** VWMason *Rio Casino* (NY) 53: Sun's over the yard arm. **1952** APHerbert *Codd's* (L) 74: When the sun, as the merry sailors say, is "over the yard-arm." **1955** *New Yorker* 8/20 23: The sun is over the yardarm, as they say . . . I shall now order raki. **1955** NMarsh *Scales* (B) 49: At about five o'clock, when the sun was over the yard-arm, he had a brandy and soda. **1957** *NYTimes Book*

Review 12/1 6: One or two drinks when the sun was over the yardarm. **1962** AWaugh *Early* (L) 229: The sun was "below the yard-arm." **1964** JAshford *Superintendent* (NY) 96: The sun may not be below the yardarm. **1968** JHaythorne *None of Us* (NY) 30: He did not look the type to wait until the sun was below the yard-arm. **1970** JAiken *Embroidered* (NY) 171: The sun ain't quite over the clothes-line yet, but this calls for a [drink]. **1971** RLockridge *Inspector's* (P) 42: Over the yardarm . . . whatever a yardarm may be. **1972** JBall *Five* (B) 112: "I know it's early, but the sun has been over the yardarm for some time. Name it." "Is a Coke OK?" **1976** GBagby *Two* (NY) 87: The moon is over the yardarm [*have a drink*]. **1981** AMorice *Men* (NY) 131: The doorbell rang at twenty minutes to six . . . I reminded myself that many Americans think nothing of starting on their martinis while the sun is still flying high above the yard arm, indeed are almost compelled to do so, if they are to be ready for dinner at half past six. TW 360–1(9).

S547 To think the **Sun** rises and sets in someone

1924 CWells *Furthest* (P) 212: She thinks the sun rises and sets in that man of hers. **1939** GBagby *Bird* (NY) 103: He thought the sun rose and set in that boy. **1941** TDowning *Lazy Lawrence* (NY) 112: [He] thinks the sun rises and sets in Wells. **1955** KMKnight *Robineau* (NY) 102: Tracy thought the sun rose and set in him. **1959** FCrane *Buttercup* (NY DBC) 16: She was sure that the sun rose and set in her little brother. **1960** DMDisney *Dark* (NY) 37: She thought the sun rose and set on him. **1966** HWaugh *Pure* (NY) 59: He doesn't seem to think the sun rises and sets on you.

S548 As sure as **Sunday**

1963 MPHood *Sin* (NY) 179: You go to hell sure's Sunday. Wilstach 561.

S549 No **Sunday** (Sabbath) east of soundings (*varied*)

1956 HCahill *Shadow* (NY) 130: It's like they said, them days. "No Sunday west of sundown and we're a month west of sundown."

1965 DCLunt *Woods* (NY) 20: Take off thet co't, young man, an' set to yer vittles. They's no Sundays east o' Bug Light [*a Maine story*]. **1967** SEMorison *Old Bruin* (B) 297: The old naval slogan, "no sabbath off soundings." **1970** GEEvans *Where* (L) 257: "Going up to Burton by train they used to say: 'There ain't no Sundays once you've passed Leicester Corner.' You were going into a seven-day week and you couldn't tell a Sunday from a weekday." EAP S1, S529.

S550 **Sunday-go-to-meeting** bonnet (*etc.*)

1900 CFPidgin *Quincy A. Sawyer* (B) 469: A new Sunday-go-to-meeting bonnet. **1905** GDEldridge *Millbank Case* (NY) 55: Got up in go-to-meetin' style. **1912** JCLincoln *Postmaster* (NY) 253: His Sunday-go-to-meetin' duds. **1946** GBellairs *Death in the Night* (NY) 68: His Sunday-go-to-meeting attire. **1952** AWUpfield *Venom* (NY) 83: The constable's Sunday-go-to-meeting uniform. **1957** D Rutherford *Long* (L) 71: Those Sunday-go-to-meeting suits. **1966** NMonsarrat *Life (I)* (L) 172: Sunday-go-to-meeting clothes. **1971** ADavidson *Peregrine* (NY) 116: These extra Sunday-go-to-market duds. TW 361.

S551 As clear as **Sunlight**

1935 ERPunshon *Death* (L 1948) 166: The darkest cipher . . . is clear as sunlight. **1938** LDSmith *Death Is* (P) 156: There's the picture clear as sunlight. Wilstach 57, 58. Cf. As clear as the Sun *above*.

S552 As honest as **Sunlight**

1946 VKelsey *Whisper Murder* (NY) 22: Honest as sunlight. Cf. Wilstach 202: The sun.

S553 As certain (sure) as **Sunrise**

1935 RAJWalling *Five Suspects* (L) 147: Certain as sunrise. **1976** MRReno *Final* (NY) 22: Sure as sunrise. Brunvand 137(2): Sure. Cf. TW 360(8). Cf. As sure as the Sun shines *above*.

S554 As clear as **Sunshine**

1933 FHShaw *Atlantic* (NY) 250: As clear as sunshine. **1956** JBarlow *Protagonists* (L) 75: You'll have a picture as clear as sunshine. TW 361(1). Cf. Sunlight *above*.

S555   As honest as **Sunshine**

1936 RStout *Rubber* (L) 73: Durkin was as honest as sunshine. Cf. Wilstach 202: The sun.

S556   To sing for one's **Supper**

1937 CKnight *Heavenly Voice* (NY) 79: You can at least sing for your supper now and then. **1953** JDolph *Dead Angel* (NY) 32: Singing for his supper. **1968** MAllingham *Cargo* (NY) 190: Now sing for your supper. **1970** CArmstrong *Protégé* (NY DBC) 12: It's like singing for his supper in reverse. *Oxford* 574: No song, no supper.

S557   As **Sure** as sure

1930 GMitchell *Mystery* (NY) 95: Sure as sure. **1939** JJConnington *Counsellor* (L) 83: I'm as sure as sure. **1946** MInnes *Unsuspected* (NY) 134: Sure as sure. Wilstach 402: As the most certain sure.

S558   Better to be **Sure** (careful) than sorry

1927 GABirmingham *Gold* (NY) 150: Better sure than sorry. **1930** FWCrofts *Sir John* (NY) 304: It is better to be sure than sorry. **1933** FWCrofts *Hog's Back* (L) 140: Better to be sure than sorry. **1947** GMWilliams *Silk* (L) 131: It's better to be sure than sorry. **1958** ECooper *Tomorrow's* (NY) 121: Better be careful than sorry. *Oxford* 51.

S559   **Suspicion** breeds suspicion

1948 FCrane *Black* (NY) 63: They say that suspicion breeds suspicion.

S560   One **Swallow** does not make a summer (*varied*)

1931 FBeeding *Death* (NY) 67: One swallow does not make a summer. **1934** TMundy *Tros* (NY) 520: And yet one swallow makes no summer. **1939** DDean *Emerald* (NY) 206: One swallow doesn't make a Spring. **1940** HSKeeler *Cleopatra's* (L) 173: Just as one swallow makes a summer. **1949** MAllingham *More Work* (NY) 19: No, two swallows don't make a summons . . . According to the adage one needs three for that. **1951** EMarshall *Viking* (NY) 264: One swallow does not make a summer but surely he heralds her soon blooming. **1954** RAldington *Pindorman* (L) 132: One swallow doesn't make a spring. **1956** *New Yorker* 8/11 43:

How many swallows make a summer? **1958** *BHerald* 4/16 29: One swallow doesn't make a summer, nor even a square meal. **1959** *NYTimes* 12/13 5X: One swallow does not make a spring. **1960** JLodwick *Moon* (L) 71: One swallow doesn't make a summer. **1963** MCallaghan *That Summer* (NY 1964) 22: Three swallows never make a summer. **1968** WMuir *Belonging* (L) 135: One Norman Douglas does not make a literary summer. **1970** HActon *Memoirs* (NY) 66: One swallow makes not a spring, nor even two swallows. **1971** EHCohen *Mademoiselle* (B) 92: After all, one swallow does not make a dinner. **1977** PMoyes *Coconut* (NY) 182: He's the first swallow of summer, as it were. **1980** WODouglas *Court* (NY) 215: It takes more than two swallows to make a summer. EAP S534; TW 362(5).

S561   As white as a **Swan**; Swan-white

1916 NDouglas *London Street Games* (L) 65: As white as a swan. **1946** ECrispin *Holy Disorders* (NY) 66: Swan-white hair. **1960** HInnes *Doomed* (NY) 99: White as a swan. EAP S536.

S562   A black **Swan**

1929 JBPriestley *Good* (NY) 11: Black Swan Inn. **1930** HLofting *Twilight* (NY) 6: He'll turn into a black swan. **1931** WMartyn *Scarlett* (L) 54: Trent was that *rara avis*. EAP S537; TW 362(1). Cf. Blackbird *above*.

S563   A **Swan** sings before he dies (*varied*)

1934 RCWoodthorpe *Death Wears* (NY) 97: The melodious charm of a dying swan. **1947** MCarleton *The Swan Sang Once* (NY). **1957** *Punch* 7/10 42: He sings before he dies. EAP S538; TW 362(2).

S564   A **Swan** song (*varied*)

1911 HHMunro *Chronicles* (L 1927) 190: Its swan song. **1917** GRSims *My Life* (L) 333: Sing his swan-song. **1922** JJoyce *Ulysses* (NY 1934) 200: Explain the swan-song too wherein he has commended her to posterity. **1929** SMElam *Borrow* (NY) 123: He had yet to sing his swan-song. **1930** GCollins *Horror* (L) 90: Singing his swan song on the same note. **1937** HCKittredge *Mooncursers* (B) 174: Without the accompanying swan song of ambergris. **1950** OAnderson *In for*

(NY) 139: That agonized swan-song of a broken heart. **1954** DCecil *Melbourne* (I) 422: His political swan-song. **1960** HRobertson *Swan Song* (NY). **1967** RJones *Three* (B) 52: Singing the swan-song for a way of life. **1969** DDoolittle *Only in Maine* (Barre, Mass.) 95: The swan song of the Stanley Steamer. **1969** HFosburgh *Clearing* (NY) 77: The hardwood forests are a swan song of sun and shadow. Amer. Herit. Dict. Swan song; NED Swan *sb.* 4b.

S565 To cut a **Swath**

1941 PWilde *Design* (NY) 170: She cut a wide swath. TW 362.

S566 By the **Sweat** of one's brow *etc.*

1900 CFPidgin *Quincy A. Sawyer* (B) 174: Man is obliged to earn his living by the sweat of his brow. **1931** JHRYardley *Before the Mayflower* (NY) 222: To toil for others by the sweat of one's brow. **1936** HAdams *Chief* (L) 134: I've gotten a bit by the sweat o' my brow. **1954** RJHealy *Tales* (NY) 222: Earns her bread and board by the sweat of her brow. **1959** DCushman *Goodbye* (NY) 137: Money earned by the sweat of my brow. **1960** MClifton *Eight* (NY) 44: Forced to live by the sweat of his brow. **1961** LNizer *My Life* (NY) 385: They earn their bread by the sweat of their browbeating. EAP S540; Brunvand 15: Bread(1).

S567 Tell it to **Sweeney**

1914 PGWodehouse *Little Nugget* (NY 1929) 117: Tell it to Sweeney! **1924** WBMFerguson *Black* (NY) 39: Tell all that to Sweeney. **1944** *New Yorker* 1/8 18: Tell it to Sweeney. **1954** KMKnight *High* (NY) 106: Oh nuts! Tell it to Sweeney. Wentworth 539: Tell. Cf. Marines *above*.

S568 As black as a **Sweep's** arse

1969 SMays *Reuben's* (L) 201: Black as a sweep's arse.

S569 **Sweets** to the sweet

1931 PWentworth *Danger* (P) 227: Sweets to the sweet. **1933** DLSayers *Hangman's* (NY) 152: Sweets to the sweets. **1946** ERolfe *Murder . . . Glass Room* (NY) 178: Sweets for the sweet is my principle. TW 362(2).

S570 To be in the same **Swim**

1922 JJoyce *Ulysses* (NY 1934) 80: All in the same swim. TW 362–3. Cf. Brunvand 138: Out of the swim.

S571 To lose on the **Swings** and gain on the roundabouts (*varied*)

1924 LSpringfield *Some Piquant People* (L) 243: That which he lost on the literary swings he regained on the city roundabout. **1928** RAJWalling *That Dinner* (NY) 35: The Corporation was managed on the principle of the swings and the roundabouts. **1932** JJConnington *Sweepstake* (B) 85: What one gained on the swings, one . . . lost on the roundabouts. **1936** DHume *Meet the Dragon* (L) 130: We'd lose more on the swings than we'd gain on the roundabouts. **1939** JJConnington *Counsellor* (L) 130: If you don't like the swings, try the roundabouts. **1956** *Punch* 8/8 165: When they lose on the roundabouts and more than make up on the swings. **1960** RDahl *Kiss* (NY) 115: What you lose on the swings you get back on the roundabouts. **1963** EFerber *Kind* (NY) 69: As the English saying goes, what you lose on the swings you gain on the turnabout. **1971** JBlake *Joint* (NY) 358: You lose it on the swings, you gotta make it up on the roundabouts. **1976** ACross *Question* (NY) 90: We rather expect to make a trifle more on the swings than we lose on the roundabouts. *Oxford* 796.

S572 As sharp as a **Sword**

1962 Bryher *Heart* (NY) 250: Her tongue was as sharp as any sword. Whiting S974; Whiting *NC* 484; Brunvand 138: Two-edged.

S573 At **Swords'** points (sword's point)

1900 CFPidgin *Quincy A. Sawyer* (B) 370: At swords' points. **1931** PATaylor *Cape Cod* (NY 1971) 14: They've been at swords' points. **1950** DMDisney *Fire* (NY) 103: They're at swords' points. **1956** BCClough *More* (Portland, Me.) 131: They started out at sword's point. EAP S545.

S574 He who lives by the **Sword** shall perish by the sword (*varied*)

1928 SFWright *Deluge* (NY) 352: He who liveth by the sword—. **1934** AMerritt *Creep*

(NY) 48: Those who live by the sword must die by the sword. **1943** MVHeberden *Murder Goes* (NY) 178: They that take the sword shall perish by the sword. **1954** AWUpfield *Sinister* (NY) 57: He that raiseth the sword shall die by the sword. **1955** DMDisney *Room* (NY) 184: Zimmerman, who had lived by the sword, had perished by the sword. **1959** NFitzgerald *Midsummer* (NY) 71: Who takes the sword, shall perish by the sword. **1963** RAusting *I Went to the Woods* (NY) 24: He who lives by the tree dies by the tree. **1964** LWoolf *Beginning* (L) 215: If you draw the sword you will perish by the sword. **1974** MDavis *Tell Them* (NY) 101: Once you told me people who use the sword are killed by the sword or something like that. EAP S546; TW 363(4).

S575 The **Sword** of Damocles (*varied*)

1919 HFAshurst *Diary* ed GFSparks (Tuscon 1962) 96: A sword of Damocles suspended over them. **1923** HGartland *Globe* (NY) 246: Holding the sword of Damocles over his head. **1926** LBrock *Colonel Gore* (NY) 326: The sword that had hung over their heads for two years had fallen. **1931** PATaylor *Cape Cod* (NY 1971) 270: It 'pears to me that the sword hangin' over your head is danglin' from an awful thin thread. **1933** AJRees *Aldringham* (NY) 30: The sword of Damocles about one's head. **1938** BFlynn *Five Red* (NY) 170: He must have lived under my sword of Damocles. **1941** BHalliday *Bodies* (NY 1959) 94: Hanging over his head, like a sword held by a hair. **1947** FCDavis *Thursday's* (NY) 148: Sibella has made herself the goddamndest sword of Damocles that anybody ever sweated under. **1954** *BHerald* 8/10 2: Control by Nasser over the canal amounts to a Sword of Damocles over Europe, a stranglehold over European economic life. **1957** SDean *Murder* (NY) 19: A bit of a sword of Damocles hanging over my head. **1965** SRansome *Alias* (NY DBC) 63: The sword would still hang overhead by a hair. **1967** JBlish *Torrent* (NY) 235: The sword of Damocles was hanging low; the thread was fraying. **1969** SViertel *Kindness* (NY) 313: The sword hung twice over my head. **1970** WMasterson *Death* (NY) 28: How can you ... be happy with a sword hanging over your head all the time? **1972** QBell *Virginia* (NY) I 44: A Dionysian sword above one's head. **1978** MKWren *Nothing's* (NY) 98: The Damoclean sword still hovered. EAP S550; TW 363(5).

S576 The **Sword** outwears the scabbard

1945 RLHines *Confessions* (L) 196: It is the sword that wears out the scabbard. *Oxford* 65: Blade.

S577 As sweet as **Syrup**

1906 JCLincoln *Mr. Pratt* (NY) 193: He was ... sweet as syrup. EAP S553.

T

T1 To a **T** (tee)

1900 CFPidgin *Quincy A. Sawyer* (B) 333: Suit him to a T. **1922** JJoyce *Ulysses* (NY 1934) 58: Dedalus takes him off to a tee. **1924** LTracy *Token* (NY) 274: Described . . . to a T. **1935** BFlynn *Padded* (L) 286: They fitted our man to the proverbial T. **1939** JJones *Murder al Fresco* (NY) 4: Little Thos suited me to T. **1941** JPhilips *Odds on* (NY) 66: She described Saxon to a T. **1947** PMcGerr *Pick* (NY) 31: It would suit me to a T. **1956** PWentworth *Fingerprint* (NY) 169: My sentiments to a T. **1959** *Speculum* 34.26: The method . . . fits John of Seville almost to a T. **1960** COLocke *Taste* (NY) 60: "Sure you know where you are?" "To a tee." **1968** EBuckler *Ox Bells* (NY) 56: [He] could take off anything to a T. **1970** TCoe *Wax* (NY) 150: Dorsey's room matched . . . Dorsey's character to a T. **1975** HBlack *My Father* (NY) 113: It was Daddy to a T. EAP T1; Brunvand 139. Cf. To a Tick *below.*

T2 As flat as a **Table**(top)

1954 EForbes *Rainbow* (B) 110: [The land] was flat as a table top, rich as pork gravy. **1964** VSPritchett *Foreign* (L) 63: It was flat as a table. TW 364(1).

T3 To turn the **Tables** (*varied*)

1912 JCLincoln *Postmaster* (NY) 180: Turn the tables. **1922** JJoyce *Ulysses* (NY 1934) 529: The tables are turned. **1924** HHBashford *Augustus* (L 1966) 89: The tables are turned. **1933** EBailey *Death* (L) 87: The turning of the tables. **1939** IJones *Hungry Corpse* (NY) 192: But to coin a phrase, the tables may soon be turned. **1940** JStagge *Turn of the Table* (NY). **1955** VWMason *Two* (NY) 266: I'm going to turn the tables. **1958** JDCarr *Dead Man's* (NY) 192: Are you turning the tables again? **1965** ADerleth *Casebook* (Sauk City, Wisc.) 33: But the tables turned. **1968** BHays *Hotbed* (NY) 10: I turned the tables on a friend. **1974** JQuintero *If You* (B) 114: The tables do turn with a vengeance. EAP T3.

T4 As hard as **Tacks**

1971 MScherf *Beautiful* (NY) 61: Her eyes were as hard as tacks. Taylor *Prov. Comp.* 46: Hard.

T5 As sharp as a **Tack**

1929 EWHowe *Plain* (NY) 21: Said to be "as sharp as tacks." **1951** JMFox *Aleutian* (B) 58: His quarters were sharp as a tack. **1952** PMacDonald *Something* (NY) 53: Sharp as a tack [*clever*]. **1959** ESGardner *Deadly* (NY) 41: They're sharp as a tack [*binoculars*]. **1961** MMillar *How Like* (NY DBC) 39: They're both sharp as tacks. **1970** CEWerkley *Mister* (NY) 217: Mr. Carnegie, sharp as a tack. Taylor *Prov. Comp.* 72: Sharp.

T6 As smart as a **Tack**

1956 MLSettle *O Beulah* (NY) 285: Peregrine is as smart as a tack. **1967** MGEberhart *Woman* (NY) 66: She was smart as tacks. **1968** DDempsey *Triumphs* (NY) 72: She was a smart talker, smart as a tack. Cf. Clark 221: Pin.

T7 Go sit on a **Tack**

1936 EQueen *Halfway* (NY) 240: Go sit on a tack. **1953** RStout *Golden* (NY) 37: She told Wolfe to go sit on a tack. Berrey 253.8.

T8 Let the **Tail** go with the hide

1959 DCushman *Goodbye* (NY) 167: Let the tail go with the hide. **1961** RAHeinlein *6XH* (NY) 139: Let the tail go with the hide. **1965** DKnight *Dark Side* (NY) 14: Let the tail go with the hide. *Oxford* 797: Tail follow the skin, Let the.

T9 The **Tail** wags the dog *(varied)*

1936 CFGregg *Murder* (NY) 48: The tail was beginning to wag the dog. **1939** HCBailey *Great Game* (L) 27: It's the tail wagging the dog. **1940** AAFair *Turn on* (NY) 118: It's a case of the tail wagging the dog. **1957** *Time* 11/18 76: It's a case of the dog wagging the world. **1957** BWAldiss *Space* (L) 195: A case of the tail wagging the dog. **1959** *Time* 5/4 54: The wags were tailing the top dog. **1959** *NYTimes Book Review* 11/29 62: The whole book trade knows how the paperback tail wagged this hardcover dog. **1961** GFowler *Skyline* (NY) 241: The tail wagging the dog, so to speak. **1966** EPangborn *Judgment* (NY) 193: The religious tail happened to wag the psychological dog. **1967** DBloodworth *Chinese* (NY) 183: The tael [*Chinese coin*] wags the dog. **1970** JVizzard *See* (NY) 258: He is the tail that wags the dog. **1977** DWilliams *Treasure* (NY) 61: The tail that wagged the dog. Oxford *DQ* (2nd ed) 295.15: The tail must wag the dog [*RKipling*].

T10 To have one's **Tail** between his legs *(varied)*

1925 EPhillpotts *Voice* (NY) 39: She had nothing to do but slink away with her tail between her legs. **1931** AFielding *Upfold* (L) 100: Talk of a dog with its tail between its legs. **1936** RCWoodthorpe *Silence* (L) 206: He's got his tail between his legs. **1939** EPhillpotts *Monkshood* (L) 137: Democracy puts its tail between its legs. **1945** MWalsh *Nine Strings* (P) 37: With my tail between my legs. **1952** CJay *Beat* (NY) 81: He slunk from the room, very like a dog with its tail between its legs. **1957** NBlake *End* (L) 127:

They ran away with their tails between their legs. **1965** RHardwick *Plotters* (NY) 32: Come running home with your tail between your legs. **1970** BWAldiss *Hand-reared* (L) 173: I had no intention of going home with my tail between my legs. **1971** PMoyes *Season* (NY) 197: To creep back to his wife with his tail between his legs. **1974** GWheeler *Easy* (NY) 124: He was running, with his tail between his legs. TW 365(4).

T11 To keep one's **Tail** up

1931 HHolt *Necklace* (NY) 33: We've got to keep our tails up. **1936** GCollins *Haven* (L) 186: Keep your tail up. **1938** GDHCole *Mrs. Warrender's* (L) 219: Keep your tail up till we meet again. Cf. TW 364–5(1).

T12 To turn **Tail**

1928 TCobb *Who Opened* (L) 67: He wouldn't have turned tail. EAP T9.

T13 Nine **Tailors** make a man *(varied)*

1919 JBCabell *Jurgen* (NY 1922) 239–40: How many tailors make a man [*nine implied*]. **1934** DLSayers *Nine Tailors* (NY) 65: Nine Taylors make a Manne; 99. **1937** RCWoodthorpe *Death in* (NY) 159: A ninth of a tailor, without muscle or thews. EAP T10.

T14 One cannot **Take** it with him

1929 EWallace *Murder Book* (NY) 35: Being an old man . . . he couldn't take his money with him. **1935** JLatimer *Headed* (NY 1957) 101: He can't take the dough with him, can he? **1943** DGoldring *South Lodge* (L) xv: We brought nothing with us into the world, so we can take nothing out of it. **1945** RLHines *Confessions* (L) 111: Bert Ballantine was right: "You can't take it with you when you die." **1952** AChristie *Mrs. McGinty* (NY) 56: You can't take it with you. **1953** VPJohns *Murder* (NY 1962) 53: Whatever his wallet contained he had presumably, and despite the adage, taken with him on his fiery journey [*burned to death*]. **1959** *BHerald* 10/21 31: I don't wonder we can't take it [*money*] with us—it goes before we do. **1960** SWilson *Away* (NY) 82: "You can't take it with you." "Damn it, I'm not dying." **1961** PGWodehouse *Ice in* (NY) 76: "Money isn't everything." "You can't take it with you." **1968** JRoffman *Daze* (NY) 177: You can't take your money with you to spend in a grave. **1973** EJKahn *Fraud* (NY) 223: When they went to Heaven they couldn't take their money with them. TW 365(1). Cf. There are no Pockets *above*.

T15   To Take it or leave it (*varied*)
1923 EWallace *Clue of the Blue Pin* (B) 97: Take it or leave it. **1937** NBlake *There's Trouble* (L) 181: He's got to take it or leave it. **1939** DCCameron *Murder's Coming* (NY) 223: You're one of them who can take it or leave it alone. **1940** ABCunningham *Murder at* (NY) 16: Take it or leave it. **1948** RMLovett *All Our* (NY) 114: Take it or leave it. **1951** DHitchens *Stairway* (NY) 71: I can take men or leave them alone. **1952** KFuller *Silken* (L) 120: As my dear father used to say: Take it or leave it. **1961** LPayne *Nose* (NY) 168: That's the truth. Take it or leave it. **1968** JFraser *Evergreen* (NY) 171: I can take 'em or leave 'em alone. **1969** GBagby *Honest* (NY) 101: It was a can-take-it-or-leave-it deal. *Oxford* 799.

T16   Judge not a Tale before its end
1939 JJConnington *Counsellor* (L) 103: Never judge a tale till you've heard the end of it. Cf. Whiting E78.

T17   One Tale is good until another has been heard
1937 SFowler *Four Callers* (L) 260: Is it not also proverbial that one tale has a good sound until the other side has been heard? *Oxford* 597–8. Cf. One Story *above*.

T18   To tell Tales out of school (*varied*)
1919 LTracy *Bartlett* (NY) 167: Told tales out of school. **1924** AChristie *Man* (NY) 143: I mustn't tell tales out of school. **1924** TFPowys *Mark Only* (L) 50: 'Tis tales out of school thee be telling. **1925** JGBrandon *Cork* (L) 235: If it ain't arskin' questions aht o' school. **1935** FYeager *Jungle* (NY) 247: He was always telling tales out of school. **1938** NMarsh *Death* (NY) 239: Aren't you talking out of school? **1952** RMacdonald *Ivory* (NY 1965) 88: I told tales out of school. **1954** DAlexander *Terror* (NY) 224: I'll tell you something out of school. **1961** GHCoxe *Error* (NY) 108: My wife's been talking out of school. **1966** JDosPassos *Best* (NY) 138: Told tall tales out of school. **1974** GMcDonald *Fletch* (I) 78: I guess I talked out of school. EAP T13; TW 365.

T19   A twice-told Tale
1934 JCameron *Body* (L) 79: Her twice-told tale. **1956** BJChute *Greenwillow* (NY) 42: The liking for a twice-told tale. EAP T16.

T20   To bury one's Talents in a napkin
1942 HCBailey *Nobody's* (NY) 228: He has talents, he buries them in a napkin. EAP T17.

T21   All Talk and no do (*varied*)
1934 ERPunshon *Death* (L) 168: All talk and no do. **1939** WMartyn *Noonday* (L) 111: All talk and no do. **1950** LKaufman *Jubel's* (NY) 90: It's always the ones who talk loudest who can do the least. **1967** FWeldon *And the Wife* (NY) 6: They do say that the men who talk most, do least [*sex*]. **1971** BWAldiss *Soldier* (L) 96: The old saying "Them as talks most does least." **1973** KAmis *Riverside* (NY) 139: A case of all talk and no do. Brunvand 139; DARE i 666: Cider; *Oxford* 804: Talkers. Cf. EAP T18. Cf. Words and deeds *below*.

T22   Talk is cheap (*varied*)
1917 JCLincoln *Extricating* (NY) 159: Talk's cheap. **1931** GFowler *Great* (NY) 286: The adage "Talk is cheap." **1933** LRGribble *Yellow* (L) 110: Threats are cheap. **1936** AFielding *Mystery* (L) 192: Talk was easy. **1939** CBarry *Nicholas* (L) 177: Words are cheap. **1948** NMailer *Naked* (NY) 227: Talk is pretty cheap. **1956** *BHerald* 8/2 10: Talk is cheap. **1956** HCahill *Shadow* (NY) 107: Talk's cheap but it don't pay off mortgages. **1957** *BHerald* 7/11 24: Nothing is cheap these days, including talk. **1970** DJOlivy *Never* (NY) 170: Talk's cheap, doesn't cost nothing at all. TW 365(3).

T23   To be a better Talker than doer
1961 WEHuntsberry *Oscar* (NY DBC) 66: He was simply a better talker than doer. EAP T20.

T24 Talking never killed anybody

1936 KMKnight *Wheel* (NY) 49: Talking never killed anybody. TW 365(2). Cf. Sticks and stones *above*; Hard Words *below*.

T25 As pale as Tallow

1958 JBlackburn *Scent* (L) 41: Their own faces as pale as tallow. Clark 217.

T26 On the Tapis

1927 JMWalsh *Silver* (L) 269: What's on the tapis tonight? **1954** MErskine *Dead by* (NY) 104: No one on the tappy, as the saying is [*under consideration*]. EAP T22. Cf. Carpet *above*.

T27 As black as Tar; Tar-black

1940 WReed *No Sign* (NY) 10: Her tar-black eyes. **1957** GDurrell *My Family* (NY) 26: Figs black as tar. **1959** TRoscoe *Only* (NY) 45: As black as tar. **1965** AGilbert *Voice* (NY) 102: Ted was looking as black as the famous tar barrel. EAP T23; TW 366(1,2). Cf. Coffee *above*.

T28 To beat (wallop) the Tar out of someone

1933 VWilliams *Clock* (L) 156: I can beat the tar out of him. **1949** GHHall *End* (NY) 182: He wanted, in his phrase, to wallop the tar out of the child. **1959** *BangorDN* 9/8 2: He would beat the tar out of one of this crew. Partridge 866; Wentworth 537(2).

T29 To catch a Tartar

1913 MPShiel *Dragon* (L) 47: "Catching a Tartar," as they say. **1926** APNewton *Travel* (L) 154: The phrase "To catch a Tartar" has become proverbial. **1938** CAlington *Crime* (L) 189: They'd caught a Tartar. **1945** MInnes *Appleby's End* (NY) 68: The expression to *catch a Tartar*. **1961** SDean *Credit* (NY) 21: She . . . caught a Tartar. **1974** JKaplan *LSteffens* (NY) 224: [He] had caught himself a tartar. EAP T26; Brunvand 139.

T30 Tastes differ (vary)

1908 LFBaum *Dorothy and the Wizard of Oz* (I) 169: Tastes differ. **1923** JSFletcher *Markenmore* (NY) 148: Tastes differ. **1931** HJForman *Rembrant* (NY) 267: Tastes dif-

fer. **1940** JJConnington *Four Defences* (B) 171: Tastes differ. **1941** CLittle *Black Paw* (NY) 144: Tastes differ. **1958** AMacKinnon *Summons* (NY) 118: Still, I suppose, tastes differ. **1966** PAnderson *Trouble* (NY) 157: Tastes vary. **1974** MInnes *Appleby's Other* (NY) 86: Tastes of course differ. EAP T28. Cf. Accounting *above*.

T31 To get a Taste (dose) of one's own medicine (*varied*)

1929 FAPottle *Stretchers* (NY) 256: To give the Huns a taste of their own medicine. **1932** TPerry *Never* (NY) 117: Gave Ben some of his own medicine. **1932** CFitzsimmons *No Witness* (NY) 174: She'll get a taste of her own medicine. **1939** HMiller *Capricorn* (NY 1961) 272: They got a dose of their own medicine. **1954** NBlake *Whisper* (L) 140: Give him some of his own medicine. **1956** *NYTimes* 8/14 14: A prescription that calls for the Republicans to get a little medicine of their own. **1957** *New Yorker* 4/27 31: A dose of our own medicine. **1968** JPorter *Dover Goes* (NY) 19: Give 'em a taste of their own medicine. **1968** LBaldridge *Of Diamonds* (B) 41: I gave him back some of his own medicine. **1973** HDolson *Dying* (P) 225: He was getting a dose of his own medicine. Cole 65: Take. Cf. TW 241: Medicine(2); Berrey 322.7.

T32 As sure (regularly) as Taxes

1909 JCLincoln *Keziah* (NY) 383: Sure's taxes. **1928** VMarkham *Death* (NY) 212: As sure as taxes. **1934** DGardiner *Drink* (NY) 35: As regularly as taxes. **1952** RPSmith *Time* (NY) 133: Sure as taxes. **1958** RA Heinlein *Methuselah's* (NY) 60: Sure as taxes. Brunvand 139(2). Cf. *Oxford* 580: Nothing. Cf. As sure as Death, Quarter Day *above*.

T33 (Not) for all the Tea in China (*varied*)

1940 LFord *Old Lover's* (NY) 2: I wouldn't have that . . . man for all the tea in China. **1948** PCheyney *Dance* (NY DBC) 113: It's all the tea in China to a bad egg that she killed Ricaud. **1950** SPalmer *Green* (NY) 36: Not for all the tea in China. **1952** AWUpfield *New Shoe* (L 1968) 128: Wouldn't live there for all the tea in China. **1957** EXFerrars *Count* (NY) 81: Couldn't do it myself at the moment for all the tea in China. **1961** HEBates *Now Sleeps* (L) 92: I bet all the tea in China that's how it got there. **1961** LPayne *Nose* (NY) 225: He wouldn't have turned back for all the tea in China. **1968** CWatson *Charity* (NY) 68: Not . . . for all the tea in China. **1974** JFleming *How To* (NY) 158: She's got all the tea in China. **1977** CRLarson *Academia* (NY) 103: You couldn't get me to take that course for all the tea in China. Partridge 148: China.

T34 As hard (tough) as **Teak**

1934 DHume *Too Dangerous* (L) 36: The kids are hard as teak. **1947** HWade *New Graves* (L) 127: Hard as teak, body and mind. **1961** EPeters *Death* (NY) 39: Tough as teak.

T35 To be the whole **Team** *etc.*

1906 JCLincoln *Mr. Pratt* (NY) 315: Jordan was a whole team and the dog under the wagon. **1958** JSStrange *Night* (NY) 125: You're not the whole team and the dog under the wagon too. TW 367(2).

T36 To eat (swear) like a **Teamster**

1929 SQuinn *Phantom* (Sauk City, Wisc. 1966) 220: He ate like a teamster. **1935** JTFarrell *Judgment* (NY) 431: Swearing like teamsters. Cf. Navvy, Stevedore *above*; Trooper *below*.

T37 To wring **Tears** from a stone

1948 HActon *Memoirs* (L) 329: It was enough to wring tears from a stone. **1951** DMDisney *Straw* (NY) 63: The young woman whose tragic circumstances would wring tears from a stone. **1966** DMurphy *Tibetan* (NY) 181: They . . . would wring a tear from a stone. Cf. *Oxford* 869–70: Water. Cf. To melt a Heart of stone *above*.

T38 One never can **Tell**

1913 EDBiggers *Seven Keys* (I) 39: You never can tell. **1923** JSFletcher *Copper* (NY) 32: You never can tell. **1933** EBBlack *Ravenelle* (NY) 163: Still you never can tell. **1938** SKing *If I Die* (NY) 59: Well, you never can tell, as the saying goes. **1945** AChristie *Remembered* (NY) 117: You never can tell. **1959** GHCoxe *Focus* (NY) 153: You

never can tell. **1961** LPayne *Nose* (NY) 244: He said . . . with Shavian philosophy, "You never can tell." **1968** PMoyes *Death* (NY) 37: It just shows you never can tell, doesn't it? **1973** THeald *Unbecoming* (NY) 151: There's no telling, is there? **1980** MFredman *You Can* (NY) 50: But as they say, you never can tell. TW 367; Brunvand 140(1). Cf. One never Knows, You never know your Luck *above*.

T39 One never can **Tell** till he tries

1926 MRRinehart *Bat* (NY 1959) 31: You never can tell what you can do till you try. **1955** VWMason *Two* (NY) 22: One never can tell till he tries. **1968** CDSimak *Goblin* (NY) 133: But you can't tell until you try. **1970** RCowper *Twilight* (NY) 104: You can never tell till you try.

T40 A **Tempest** (storm) in a tea-cup (teapot) (*varied*)

1911 JSHay *Amazing Emperor* (L) 57: A veritable storm in a tea-cup. **1913** MRRinehart *Jeannie Brice* (NY 1947) 378: A tempest in a teacup. **c1923** ACrowley *Confessions* ed JSymonds (L 1969) 196: A typhoon began to rage in the teacup. 896: A tempest in a teapot. **1929** CSLewis *Letters* ed WHLewis (NY 1966) 59: Making a storm in a teacup. **1930** SEMorison *Builders* (B) 102: One of those tempests in the colonial teapot. **1931** QPatrick *Cottage* (P) 14: These storms in a coffee cup. **1946** ESHolding *Innocent* (NY) 59: It's a tempest in a teacup. **1953** EQueen *Scarlet* (B) 108: It's a tempest in a cocktail shaker. **1954** HRAngeli *Pre-Raphaelite* (L) 161: A storm in a tea-pot. **1956** *Time* 10/22 20: Merely a tempest in a teapot. **1957** IWallace *Square* (NY) 189: There was a tempest amid the teacups. **1958** *BangorDN* 7/18 14: The tempest in the chowder pot. **1962** EGrierson *Massingham* (L) 28: One whose nature it was to fuss in a teapot. **1965** HHowe *Gentle* (NY) 240: This tempest in the Harvard teapot. **1967** IBarea *Vienna* (NY) 359: Small storms in small tea-cups. **1971** RGMartin *Jennie* (NY) 207: A teapot-tempest. **1977** PMoyes *Coconut* (NY) 39: A storm in a teacup. TW 367(2); Brunvand 140; *Oxford* 778: Storm.

T41 When angry count **Ten** (*varied*)

1930 CBarry *Boat* (L) 74: The next time you feel inclined to be nasty, count ten. **1933** TAPlummer *Alias* (L) 46: Some folks counted ten before speaking, when in anger. **1940** JBentley *Mr. Marlow Stops* (B) 209: I gritted my teeth, swallowed, counted ten. **1941** CRice *Trial by Fury* (NY 1957) 195: Malone counted ten and decided he could trust himself to speak. **1946** VKelsey *Whisper Murder* (NY) 35: The equivalent for him, of counting ten. **1953** DMDisney *Prescription* (NY) 156: Next time I'll count to ten before I lose my temper. **1957** *New Yorker* 7/13 25: Before Mrs. Engel answered this, she somehow managed to give the impression that she had counted up to ten. **1961** LPayne *Nose* (NY) 194: I . . . counted to ten, slowly . . . and the anger drained away. **1965** DMDisney *Shadow* (NY) 63: Before Maggie replied she counted to ten, as she frequently did when talking with her mother-in-law. **1967** SMarrow *Insiders* (NY) 128: Hoyt was angry suddenly. Count ten, he thought. **1972** KCConstantine *Vicksburg* (NY) 69: He appeared to be counting ten silently. **1974** THeald *Blue* (NY) 72: Bognor shut his eyes and counted ten. EAP T32.

T42 To fall like **Ten pins**

1972 TCBhaduri *Chambal* (Delhi) 2: The dynasty fell like ten pins. TW 368: Drop.

T43 To be on **Tenterhooks**

1921 IOstrander *Crimson* (NY) 268: On tenterhooks. **1922** JJoyce *Ulysses* (NY 1934) 617: Being on tenterhooks. **1930** WLewis *Apes* (NY 1932) 210: I was on tenterhooks. **1935** WSMasterman *Perjured* (NY) 41: I followed him, as the saying is, on tenterhooks. **1953** CHarnett *Nicholas* (NY) 131: You are on tenterhooks. **1958** HMasur *Murder* (NY 1959) 130: She was on tenterhooks. **1960** PCurtis *Devil's* (NY) 10: I should be on tenter-hooks. **1969** JBurke *Firefly* (L) 50: [He] kept him on tenterhooks. **1972** SNBehrman *People* (B) 224: "He was on tenterhooks . . ." "What are tenterhooks, anyway?" Sherwood explained: "Tenterhooks are the up-hol-ster-ry of the anxious seat." **1973** TZinkin *Weeds* (L) 81: We were on tenterhooks. EAP T36.

T44 As thick as **Tewkesbury** mustard

1935 BFlynn *Case* (L) 15: About as thick as Tewkesbury mustard [*unclear*]. *Oxford* 809.

T45 To set the **Thames** on fire (*varied*)

1922 JSFletcher *Middle of Things* (NY) 129: No ambition to set the Thames on fire. **1930** AChristie *Mysterious* (NY) 166: [He] will never set the Thames on fire. **1931** WLewis *Letters* ed WKRose (L 1963) 202: I have often wondered what people meant by setting the *Thames* on fire—or is that shire snobbery? Give me a foreign river. **1938** VLoder *Kill* (L) 23: The Thames is not readily set on fire by the debut of an amateur. **1942** AAMacGregor *Vanished* (L) 2: He was . . . going to set the Thames on fire with Gaelic poetry. **1951** JCollier *Fancies* (NY) 255: [He] is the man who's going to set the Thames on fire. **1958** *NYTimes Book Review* 4/27 4: He suddenly set the Thames on fire. 7/13 23: She never set the Seine on fire. **1962** YBridges *Poison* (L) 249: Adelaide Bartlett, whose case had set the Thames on fire. **1963** JLudwig *Confusions* (Greenwich, Conn.) 119: The professor . . . couldn't quite see flames on the Thames from a Ph.D thesis on Reich's use of Thoreau. **1964** JJMarric *Gideon's Lot* (NY) 45: That won't set the Thames on fire. *Oxford* 717. Cf. EAP R93: River. Cf. River *above*; To set the World *below*.

T46 **Thanks** is a poor payment

1934 ERathbone *Brass* (NY) 80: Thanks is a poor payment. Cf. *Oxford* 593: Old thanks. Cf. next entry.

T47 **Thanks** would starve a cat to death

1962 *BangorDN* 8/10 8: Thanks would starve a cat to death. Whiting *NC* 485. Cf. *Oxford* 419: Keep your thanks.

T48 **That** is that

1930 MMPropper *Ticker-Tape* (NY) 234: And that, as the saying is, was that. **1932** AFielding *Wedding-Chest* (NY) 77: And that, as your proverb says, is very much indeed that. **1936** VLoder *Deaf-Mute* (L) 30: That's that. **1940** CSaxby *Death Joins* (NY) 272: So that's that. **1954** THoward *Blood* (NY) 264: I guess that's that. **1956** EMcBain *Pusher* (NY 1959) 330: That was that. **1969** CBush

Deadly (NY) 81: And that, as they say, was that. Webster's New World Dict. (1959) That [*at end*].

T49 To be not all **There**

1960 HSDavies *Papers* (L) 235: He's not quite all there, as the saying goes. Wentworth 358: Not.

T50 Through **Thick** and thin

1908 JCLincoln *Cy Whittaker* (NY) 39: Through thick and thin. **1922** VBridges *Greensea* (NY) 128: Through thick and thin. **1934** RAFreeman *For the Defence* (NY) 24: Swear through thick and thin. **1938** DFrome *Guilt* (L) 120: He's stuck to that family through thick and thin. **1946** MBennett *Time To Change* (NY) 24: Mrs. Carter clung to him through thick, thin and boredom. **1953** *BHerald* 5/4 53: I've worked steadily for 40 years through thick and thin. **1956** PMiller *Raven* (NY) 292: Support him through thick and thin. **1967** COSkinner *Madame* (B) xix: She stuck through the thick and thin of her turbulent life. **1967** WASwanberg *Pulitzer* (NY) 127: To Reid's thick-and-thin *Tribune* all Republicans were paragons. **1973** AWest *Mortal* (NY) 277: Through thick and thin. EAP T38; TW 368.

T51 As thick as **Thieves** (*varied*)

1900 HGarland *Companion on the Trail* (NY 1931) 59: Thicker than thieves. **1924** JSFletcher *Time-Worn* (NY) 94: As thick as thieves, as our local saying goes. **1933** RCurle *Corruption* (I) 92: As thick as thieves. **1935** CGGivens *Rose Petal* (I) 167: They're as close as thieves. **1937** DduMaurier *The duMauriers* (NY) 288: The . . . little cliques that . . . were thicker than the proverbial thieves. **1940** GDHCole *Murder at* (NY) 216: Thick as thieves . . . But thieves may fall out. **1943** EWTeale *Dune Boy* (NY 1957) 158: Th' berries are thicker'n thieves. **1956** *Punch* 11/5 9: Thick as thieves. **1959** GCarr *Swing* (NY) 159: The mist was as thick as thieves up there. **1960** JO'Hara *Ourselves* (NY) 125: You and Calthorp would get along like two thieves. **1965** AGilbert *Voice* (NY) 13: As thick as thieves. **1970** VCClinton-Baddeley *No Case*

(NY) 50: "They've been as thick as—" "'Thieves' is the accepted comparison." TW 368(4); *Oxford* 810.

T52 Set a **Thief** (rogue) to catch a thief (*varied*)

1914 PGWodehouse *Little Nugget* (NY 1929) 290: Set a thief to catch a thief. **1923** HWNevinson *Changes* (NY) 236: A thief set to catch a thief. **1928** GKnevels *Diamond* (NY) 29: Set a rogue to catch a thief, you know. **1932** JHWallis *Capital* (NY) 150: The old saying is that it takes a thief to catch a thief. **1934** JGregory *Emerald* (NY) 136: Set a fox to catch a fox, they say. **1937** NBell *Crocus* (NY) 101: Get a thief, they say, to catch a thief. **1938** HReed *Swing Music* (NY) 248: It takes a crook to catch one, I always said. **1939** HFootner *Murder That* (L) 146: Get a woman to catch a woman. **1939** RForbes *A Unicorn in the Bahamas* (L) 43: On the despairing principle of "set a thief to catch a thief." **1940** DBillany *It Takes a Thief* (NY). **1955** BHitchens *F.O.B.* (NY) 217: It takes a thief to spot a thief. **1955** MO'Brine *Passport* (L) 160: Set a rat to catch a rat. **1957** *BHerald* 1/20 1: There's an old expression: "It takes a rogue to catch a rogue." **1959** JBEthan *Black Gold* (NY DBC) 55: The old maxim: It takes a crook to catch a crook. **1962** EFRussell *Great* (NY) 131: Perhaps we can set a crackpot to catch a crackpot. **1967** JDHoran *Pinkertons* (NY) 26: The slogan "set a thief to catch a thief." **1970** ADean *Dower* (NY) 39: It takes a thief to know one (to paraphrase a proverb from *Bohn's Handbook*). **1974** WSnow *Codline* (Middletown, Conn.) 161: The old adage, "It takes a crow to catch a crow." **1977** PDickinson *Walking* (NY) 107: I set a witch to catch a witch. EAP R123: Rogue, T41; TW 309: Rogue; Brunvand 119: Rogue, 140: Thief (4).

T53 When **Thieves** (rogues) fall out *etc.* (*varied*)

1908 HMSylvester *Olde Pemaquid* (B) 255: In 1688 the rogues fell out. **c1923** ACrowley *Confessions* ed JSymonds (L 1969) 480: When thieves fall out, honest men come to their own. **1927** JMWalsh *Silver* (L) 196: A case of thieves falling out. **1929** CGBowers

Tragic (NY) 362: Here, even when thieves fell out, honest men failed to get their due. **1929** LScott *Living* (NY) 224: When thieves quarrelled, that was when the truth was most likely to spill out. **1931** CJDaly *Third* (NY) 137: When thieves fall out honest men get their due. **1931** ALivingston *In Cold* (I) 151: Thieves sometimes fall out. **1931** LSteffens *Autobiography* (NY) 1.399: When thieves fall out, honest men get their due. **1932** RAFreeman *When Rogues Fall out* (L). **1935** RCWoodthorpe *Shadow* (NY) 100: When rogues fall out, they say honest men come into their own. **1952** MInnes *One-Man* (NY) 70: The answer seems to be in terms of thieves falling out. **1954** AWUpfield *Death* (NY) 152: When thieves fall out honest men like you and me steps in. **1957** *BHerald* 7/9 16: When rogues fall out, the proverb says, honest men come by their own. **1961** MColes *Search* (NY DBC) 81: When thieves fall out . . . the adage is well known. **1975** GBlack *Big Wind* (NY) 162: A case of thieves falling out. EAP R124: Rogues; Brunvand 140(5); *Oxford* 810–11: Thieves.

T54 All good **Things** come to an end (*varied*)

1900 CFPidgin *Quincy A. Sawyer* (B) 251: All such good times come to an end. 259: To all good things an end must come at last. **1925** DVane *Scar* (NY) 242: All good things come to an end. **1930** JRhode *Venner* (L) 7: "All good things come to an end," he said sententiously. **1933** AFTschiffley *Ride* (NY) 208: All good things have to come to an end. **1955** RNathan *Sir Henry* (NY) 142: A good thing must end. **1959** GCarr *Swing* (NY) 69: All good things come to an end. **1966** HTracy *Men* (L) 75: All good things come to an end. **1971** PTabor *Pauline's* (Louisville) 291: All good things eventually come to an end. **1974** DCory *Bit* (NY) 186: All good things must come to an end. TW 120: End(4); Brunvand 141(1). Cf. EAP E54. Cf. All Things . . . end *below*.

T55 All **Things** (*good, bad, or neutral*) come in threes

1927 EWallace *Law* (NY 1931) 261: All events go in threes. **1929** BThomson *Metal*

(L) 78: Death never comes singly—always in threes. **1930** ALivingston *Murder* (I) 227: Things always come in threes. **1930** ATrain *Adventures* (NY) 684: All good things come in threes. **1930** HAdams *Crime* (P) 217: Things do go in threes—good things and bad things. **1930** FWBvonLinsingen *Pressure* (NY) 177: Everything goes in threes. **1931** KTrask *Murder* (NY) 72: They say things like this always come in threes. **1931** HKWebster *Who Is* (I) 127: Things like that always go by threes, don't they? **1931** PGWodehouse *If I Were You* (NY) 169: Things like that are apt to go in threes. **1932** JJFarjeon *Trunk-Call* (NY) 4: Things go in threes. **1933** AChristie *Tuesday* (NY) 173: You know the saying? *Never two without three.* **1934** MBurton *Charabane* (L) 111: They say that luck always goes in threes. **1936** KMKnight *Wheel* (NY) 186: Troubles always come in threes, so they say. **1937** RGDean *Three Lights* (NY) 256: Good things, like bad . . . always come in threes for the superstitious. **1938** CWhitcomb *In the Fine* (NY) 191: Trouble always comes in threes. **1940** EBQuinn *Death Is* (L) 87: She means the old superstition. It [*death*] is supposed to come in threes. **1941** FCrane *Turquoise* (P) 90: Where there is one . . . there will be three. **1941** AWebb *Suicide Club* (L) 171: Things have a tendency to go in threes. **1941** GWYates *If a Body* (NY) 43: Luck runs in threes. **1950** MRHodgkin *Student* (L) 224: The old saying that misfortune travels in threes, an age-old truth. **1952** ECRLorac *Dog* (NY) 123: It's the age-old superstition that things always go by threes. **1956** AChristie *Dead Man's* (L) 99: They do say things go in threes. **1957** *New Yorker* 9/21 45: Never two without three [*said by a Russian*]. **1958** NMacNeil *Death* (Greenwich, Conn.) 71: Someone told me that murders come in threes. **1964** EHuxley *Incident* (NY) 171: There's an old superstition . . . that disasters go in threes. **1967** AMStein *Deadly* (NY) 138: If you've got a superstition that says that these things come in threes, check your count. **1969** AGilbert *Mr. Crook* (NY DBC) 141: Don't they say three's the magical number? **1970** DShannon *Unexpected* (NY) 177: And they do say, never two without three. **1972**

JRoffman *Bad* (NY) 128: Good luck, like bad, comes in threes. **1972** SWoods *They Love* (NY) 149: Mrs. Dibb says troubles never come singly . . . She said they always come in threes. **1973** AGilbert *Nice* (NY) 165: Don't they say things go by threes? **1974** JFleming *How To* (NY) 1: Bad luck always comes in threes. **1975** EXFerrars *Alive* (NY) 147: A nurse . . . who said things always come in threes. **1978** HFleetwood *Roman* (NY) 47: The adage of there never being a second without a third. **1978** CMacLeod *Rest You* (NY) 97: These things [*deaths*] always go in threes, my mother used to say. Cf. Brunvand 37: Dish; Tilley T175. Cf. Misfortunes *above*.

T56 All **Things** come to an end (*varied*)

1904 LFBaum *Marvelous Land of Oz* (NY) 182: Everything has to come to an end, some time. **1911** MLevel *Grip of Fear* (NY) 24: There is an end to all things. **1922** JJoyce *Ulysses* (NY 1934) 517: All things end. **1928** GYoung *Treasure* (NY) 281: All things end. **1930** TCobb *Sark* (L) 134: Everything was bound to come to an end. **1932** EVLucas *Reading* (L) 203: All things, however, come to an end. **1938** JRhode *Invisible* (L) 57: But all things come to an end, as my old mother says. **1955** DGarnett *Flowers* (L) 35: Everything . . . has an end. **1959** DAWollheim *Macabre* (NY) 186: All things end, both good and bad. EAP E54; Whiting T87; *Oxford* 231: Everything.

T57 The best **Things** in life are free

1940 RDarby *Death Conducts* (NY) 129: I never before believed that the best things in life are free. **1955** EWSmith *One Eyed* (NY) 175: The best things in life . . . were free. **1957** WMorris *Love* (NY) 171: The best things in life are free. **1961** HNielsen *Sing Me* (NY DBC) 93: The best things in life are free. **1961** BPeters *Big H* (NY DBC) 39: The best things in life may be free, but not at my age. **1968** SPalmer *Rook* (NY) 104: Luckily for the poor, the best things in life are free.

T58 First **Things** first

1933 GDilnot *Thousandth* (L) 118: It pays to do first things first. **1936** MKennedy *Sic*

Transit (L) 250: First things first. **1945** CBrahms *Six Curtains* (L 1953) 56: First things first. **1949** MGEberhart *House* (NY DBC) 112: First things first. **1953** SRansome *Hear* (NY) 153: First things first. **1958** *CSMonitor* 10/3 3: Putting first things first. **1959** JLatimer *Black* (NY) 151: Last things first. **1960** HLivingston *Climacticon* (NY) 174: But first things first. **1962** FGruber *Brothers* (NY DBC) 133: First things come first. **1967** DTylden-Wright *AFrance* (L) 11: To resist putting second things first. **1968** IPetite *Life* (NY) 20: "First things first" is fine as an adage. **1970** PDickinson *Sinful* (NY) 94: First things first. **1977** JBHilton *Dead-Nettle* (NY) 40: First things first, I always say. NED Suppl. First 4.

T59 Good **Things** come in small packages (*varied*)

1922 JJoyce *Ulysses* (NY 1934) 261: Fine goods in small parcels. **1936** HAdams *Death* (L) 254: Isn't there some proverb about the most precious things being in small parcels? **1961** DLMathews *Very Welcome* (NY DBC) 24: Good things coming in small packages. **1964** DMDisney *Departure* (NY DBC) 5: Good goods come in small packages. **1970** JAiken *Embroidered* (NY) 130: We have a proverb in Turkey: all excellent things are found in small packets. **1971** EPeters *Knocker* (NY) 25: Good stuff lies in small compass. **1975** HBHough *Mostly* (NY) 173: Good things come in small packages. **1981** BSuyker *Death* (NY) 177: Good things come in small packages. **1982** BPronzini *Gun* (NY) 228: Good things, as the saying goes, come in small packages. Whiting *NC* 485(3).

T60 If a **Thing** is worth doing it is worth doing well (*varied*)

1931 WWJacobs *Snug* (NY) 322: Anything that's worth doing at all is worth doing well. **1935** MBeckett *Tea Time* (L) 67: If you're going to do a thing, you may as well do it properly. **1936** KMKnight *Clue* (NY) 37: I always say, "If a thing's worth doin' it's worth doin' well." **1952** MEngel *Length* (NY) 186: A thing worth doing was worth doing well. **1957** *BangorDN* 2/18 18: Anything worth doing is worth doing well. **1957** RArnold *Spring* (NY) 112: If a thing is worth doing at all ... it's worth doing properly. **1960** NBenchley *Sail* (NY) 203: If a thing's worth doing, it's worth doing well. **1970** ACross *Poetic* (NY) 37: If a thing is worth doing, it's worth doing badly. **1977** RRendell *Demon* (NY) 21: If a job's worth doing, it's worth doing well. *Oxford* 921: Worth.

T61 If it isn't one **Thing** it is another

1933 ECRLorac *Murder* (L) 155: If it ain't one thing it's another. **1934** AMerritt *Creep* (NY) 12: If it ain't one thing, it's another. **1959** ASillitoe *Saturday* (NY) 68: If it wasn't one thing, it was another. Cf. Life is one *above*.

T62 If one wants a **Thing** well done he must do it himself (*varied*)

1913 EDBiggers *Seven Keys* (I) 345: If you want a thing done right, do it yourself. **1923** HGartland *Globe* (NY) 36: Julius Caesar was right when he said: "If you want a thing well done, do it yourself." **1924** AChristie *Man* (NY) 3: The maxim, "If you want a thing done safely, do not do it yourself." **1930** CFGregg *Body* (NY) 114: If you want a thing done properly, do it yourself. **1937** GDeJean *Who Killed* (L) 41: The maxim that if you want a thing done well one should do it oneself. **1940** AMcRoyd *Death in Costume* (NY) 199: When I want a thing done right I do it myself. **1951** HE Bates *Colonel* (L) 238: If you want a thing done, do it yourself. **1959** BHerald 5/10 sec. III 3: I'm a firm believer in the adage: "If you want something done have someone else do it." **1968** JTMcIntosh *Take a Pair* (NY) 99: It was true that if you wanted anything well done you had to do it for yourself. **1970** JAiken *Embroidered* (NY) 220: Want something done properly, you have to do it yourself. **1974** MScherf *If You Want a Murder Well Done* (NY). **1975** ELathen *By Hook* (NY) 196: I always say, if you want a thing well done, do it yourself. Whiting *NC* 485(4). Cf. TW 369(5).

T63 Keep a **Thing** long enough and you will find a use for it

1931 EPhillpotts *Found* (L) 265: They say you always find a use for everything if you keep it long enough. Tilley T141.

T64 Little **Things** lead to big (*varied*)

1932 LCharteris *White* (NY) 71: Great things have small beginnings. That is a well-known aphorism, and is therefore unreliable. **1932** CPSnow *Death* (NY) 55: It shows you how little things can have big results. **1952** ECRLorac *Dog* (NY) 185: Little things mount up. **1958** BKendrick *Clear* (NY) 162: It's the little things in life that count. Isn't that the old cliché? **1965** HHarrison *Bill* (NY) 57: From small things do big things grow. EAP T52; Whiting L402: Of little waxes mickle.

T65 Little **Things** please little minds

1931 MAllingham *Police* (NY) 294: Little things may please little minds. **1935** GDilnot *Murder* (L) 149: Little things please little minds. **1969** MFeld *Super* (L) 25: Little things please little minds. *Oxford* 472.

T66 One **Thing** at a time (and that done well) (*varied*)

1926 FWCrofts *Cheyne* (NY) 83: Let's have one thing at a time. **1927** BAtley *Smiler* (NY) 65: One thing at a time and only one. **1930** KCStrahan *Death* (NY) 158: One thing at a time and that done well. **1936** MKennedy *Sic Transit* (L) 250: One thing at a time. **1939** JJones *Murder al Fresco* (NY) 159: One thing at a time and that done well, I always say. **1947** AGilbert *Death in* (L) 25: One thing at a time. **1957** *NYTimes* 5/26 3E: The nursery rime which runs: "One thing at a time—And that done well—Is a very good thing—As many can tell." **1957** DErskine *Pink* (NY) 204: One thing at a time, and that done well. **1972** MKaye *Lively* (NY) 84: One thing at a time. **1978** MHoward *Facts* (B) 3: One thing done and that done well / is a very good thing as many can tell. EAP T53.

T67 One **Thing** (*etc.*) leads to another (*varied*)

1919 JBCabell *Jurgen* (NY 1922) 99: One thing axiomatically leads to another; 101.

1920 JSFletcher *Dead Men's* (NY) 257: One thing leads to another. **1924** RFirbank *Prancing* (Works 5, L 1929) 19: Fo' one t'ing lead sh'o to de nex'. **1928** SMartin *Fifteen* (NY) 150: One step leads to another. **1929** TFPowys *Fables* (NY) 217: One calamity often leads to another. **1929** HMSmith *Jigsaw* (NY) 285: One thing seems to follow another. **1930** HCBailey *Garston* (NY) 27: One dirty trick led to another. **1939** VWilliams *Fox Prowls* (B) 45: You know the way one thing leads to another. **1941** EDaly *Deadly* (NY 1947) 197: One thing leads to another. **1947** ELustgarten *One More* (NY 1959) 100: One thing leads easily to another. **1956** RAHeinlein *Double* (NY 1957) 70: But one thing leads to another. **1958** AHeriot *Zenobia* (L) 69: One thing, as the saying goes, leads to another. **1964** SBecker *Covenant* (NY) 44: One thing leads to another, you know. **1967** MErskine *Case with* (NY) 149: That's the worst of murder. One thing leads to another. **1969** FSwinnerton *Reflections* (L) 188: And one thing, as the song said, leads to another. **1970** GBagby *Killer* (NY) 98: One thing leads to another. **1975** SSchmidt *Newton* (NY) 172: One thing will lead to another. *Oxford* 598: Brings up.

T68 **Things** are not (always) what they seem (*varied*)

1930 WWoodrow *Moonhill* (NY) 135: Things are not always what they seem. **1932** JSFletcher *Man in the Fur Coat* (L) 235: Thou knowest . . . that all things are not what they seem. **1934** BFlynn *Spiked* (P) 17: Things aren't always what they seem. **1940** HCBailey *Mr. Fortune Here* (NY) 32: Things are not what they seem. **1943** EDaly *Evidence* (NY) 26: Things are not what they seem: a cliché. **1959** *NYTimes Book Review* 2/15 1: Things are not what they seem. **1962** AMStein *Home* (NY) 187: Things are not always what they seem. Tilley T199. Cf. Appearances *above*.

T69 Three **Things** (*varied*)

1930 AChristie *Mysterious* (NY) 238: I've heard it said that every man should build a house, plant a tree and have a son. **1931** VWilliams *Masks* (L) 310: You know the saying: "There are three things a man must

do alone—he must be born alone, die alone, and bear witness alone." **1946** JDCarr *He Who Whispers* (NY) 168: The old proverb says that there are two things which will be believed about any man, and one of them is that he has taken to drink. **1956** HCahill *Shadow* (NY) 178: Like the Irishman says, three finest things in the world, a woman just before her time, a ship bellied out with sail, a field of wheat. **1959** AGoodman *Golden* (NY) 205: There's a proverb that you can't really be a man until you have planted a tree, killed a bull and had a son. **1965** HMiller *Quiet Days* (NY) 10: There are only two things you can do on a rainy day, as the saying goes, and the whores never wasted time playing cards. **1970** AEHotchner *Treasure* (NY) 242: There are only three sure things in life—taxes, death and the sanctity of the numbered account [*Swiss banks*]. EAP T51: Four.

T70 To be too much of a good **Thing** (*varied*)

1913 EDBiggers *Seven Keys* (I) 33: Too much of a good thing. **1928** ABerkeley *Silk* (NY) 33: Too much of a good thing. **1933** NBrady *Week-end* (L) 84: This is too much of a good thing. **1934** AWDerleth *Man on All Fours* (NY) 133: Isn't that carrying a good thing too far? **1951** MInnes *Old Hall* (L 1961) 135: Rather too much of a good thing. **1958** *TLS* 5/16 267: Proverbs can and do err; it is unfortunately possible to have too much of a good thing. **1970** JAGraham *Aldeburg* (B) 190: Too much of a good thing. TW 369(15); *Oxford* 831.

T71 To know a **Thing** or two

1951 JCreasey *Puzzle* (L 1962) 131: That man knew a thing or two. **1961** DLoovis *Last* (NY) 291: Mama knows a thing or two. TW 369(12).

T72 To say one **Thing** and think another (*varied*)

1958 HCarmichael *Or Be* (NY) 42: She was saying one thing and thinking another. **1966** JStuart *My Land* (NY) 128: I guess it is all right for a man to think one thing and say another. Whiting T193.

T73 To take **Things** (people) as one finds them (*varied*)

1919 JBCabell *Jurgen* (NY 1922) 333: As I find them, so do I take them. **1929** HFootner *Self-Made* (NY) 115: If you take me as you find me. **1929** BThomson *Metal* (L) 203: I take people as I find them. **1929** CvonHoffman *Jungle* (L) 271: Forced to take things as he found them. **1930** NA Temple-Ellis *Man Who Was There* (NY) 37: People took him as they found him. **1941** DKent *Jason* (NY) 243: You'll have to take me as you find me, and sometimes I'm damned hard to find. **1945** MBurton *Not a Leg* (NY) 23: You must take me as you find me. **1958** ECRLorac *People* (NY) 98: Take us as you find us. **1962** EHuxley *Mottled* (L) 102: I . . . take people as I find them. **1964** DMDisney *Departure* (NY DBC) 79: We have to take people as we find them. EAP T55; *Oxford* 799.

T74 To take **Things** as they come

1912 ERBurroughs *Gods of Mars* (NY 1963) 32: Take things as they come. **1938** MBrucker *Poison* (NY) 134: Nettice took things as they came. **1970** ELathen *Pick* (NY) 63: He'll just have to take things the way they come. EAP T56.

T75 When **Things** are at worst they must amend

1928 MSummers *Vampire* (L) 312: The old adage, that "When things are at worst they must amend." EAP T61.

T76 **Think** before you speak (*varied*)

1964 RMeinertztragen *Diary* (L) xx: I have thought more than I have talked. **1970** RNeely *Walter* (NY) 91: Think before you speak. *Oxford* 263: First think.

T77 **Think** twice—count twenty

1930 JSFletcher *Dressing Room* (L) 176: Think twice!—count twenty, as your Yorkshire saying is. Cf. Amer. Herit. Dict. Think 7: Think twice. Cf. Ten *above*.

T78 To be wishful **Thinking**

1939 LFord *Mr. Cromwell* (L) 102: What they call wishful thinking. **1941** TDowning *Lazy Lawrence* (NY) 40: Wishful thinking. **1948** FWCrofts *Silence* (NY) 179: Our old friend wishful thinking again. **1951** TDubois *Foul* (NY) 137: It was just wishful thinking . . . to use a several-years-stale expression. **1958** VCanning *Dragon* (NY) 176: Lots of damned wishful thinking. **1961** DMDisney *Mrs. Meeker's* (NY) 77: This was wishful thinking. **1967** HStone *Funniest* (NY) 19: "What were you thinking?" "Something wishful." Amer. Herit. Dict. Wishful thinking.

T79 As light as **Thistledown**

1929 LBrock *Murder* (NY) 136: Light on her feet as thistledown. **1929** GGranby *Secret* (NY) 149: Light as thistledown. **1937** NBerrow *One Thrilling* (L) 19: Light as thistledown. **1937** TStevenson *Nudist* (L) 23: She's as light as a thistledown. **1940** CBDawson *Lady Wept* (NY) 125: Crispin looking light as thistledown. **1948** HActon *Memoirs* (L) 81: As light as thistledown. **1957** MLBarnes *Isabel* (P) 53: She was light as thistledown. NED Thistle-down b.

T80 A **Thorn** in the flesh

1904 JCLincoln *Cap'n Eri* (NY) 204: A thorn in the flesh. **1929** LRGribble *Gillespie* (L) 66: A thorn in the fleshy side of the police. **1937** DAllan *Brandon* (L) 26: Distant relatives are a thorn in the flesh. **1938** LAnson *Such Natural* (L) 233: You fellows are a thorn in her flesh. **1941** CWells *Murder . . . Casino* (P) 24: A thorn in the flesh. **1954** OAnderson *Thorn in the Flesh* (L). **1959** PDeVries *Through* (B) 47: A very sweet old thorn in the flesh. **1963** CMackworth *Apollinaire* (NY) 147: A thorn in his flesh. **1966** WTrevor *Love* (L) 38: He's been a thorn in the flesh for seven years. EAP T65; Brunvand 141(2).

T81 A **Thorn** in the side

1920 GBMcCutcheon *Anderson Crow* (NY) 190: A constant thorn in the side. **1932** HFootner *Casual* (L) 135: I've been a thorn in his side. **1941** GDHCole *Counterpoint* (NY) 166: A thorn in the sides of the local police. **1956** FDOmmanney *Isle* (P) 68: A terrible thorn in Rigby's side. **1959** STruss *Man to Match* (NY) 136: A thorn in their political side. **1965** JCleugh *Divine* (L) 59: A thorn in the side of the Vicar of Christ.

1972 TWells *Die* (NY) 127: The thorn in my side. EAP T66; Brunvand 141(3).

T82 To be on Thorns

1931 EPhillpotts *Found* (L) 92: Evidently on thorns for me to depart. **1956** MColes *Birdwatcher's* (NY) 102: Forgan was on thorns. EAP T70; Brunvand 141(4).

T83 As fast as Thought

1967 AWEckert *Wild* (B) 123: As fast as thought. Wilstach 135.

T84 As quick as Thought

1920 AChristie *Mysterious Affair* (NY) 264: Quick as thought. **1932** CDawes *Lawless* (L) 217: Quick as thought. **1935** WSSykes *Harness* (L) 215: Quick as thought. **1946** ESedgwick *Happy* (B) 134: Jim was quick as thought. EAP T72; TW 370(2); Brunvand 141.

T85 As swift as Thought

1934 JGBrandon *One-Minute* (L) 5: As swift as thought. **1969** FLeiber *Swords* (L) 44: Swift as thought. EAP T73; TW 370(4).

T86 First Thoughts are best (*varied*)

1922 JJoyce *Ulysses* (NY 1934) 364: First thoughts are best. **1926** JSFletcher *Massingham* (B) 134: First thoughts are worst. **1929** POldfield *Alchemy* (L) 87: First thoughts are best. *Oxford* 708: Second (quote 1852).

T87 It is the Thought that counts

1936 RLehmann *Weather* (NY) 63: It's the thought that counts. **1949** JBonett *Dead Lion* (L 1953) 155: The theory that it is the thought that counts. **1959** JBonett *No Grave* (NY) 94: After all, it's the thought that counts. **1965** JPorter *Dover Two* (NY 1968) 9: It's the thought that counts. Cf. To take the Will *below*.

T88 Second Thoughts are best (*varied*)

1904 WLewis *Letters* ed WKRose (L 1963) 15: Second thoughts are best. **1918** JBCabell *Letters* ed PColum (NY 1962) 53: I do not . . . find second thoughts to be best. **1933** PMcGuire *Death* (NY) 309: My first thoughts are never to be trusted. My second are invariably better. **1934** AGilbert *An Old Lady* (L) 250: How seldom are second thoughts profitable. **1934** LRGribble *Riddle* (L) 257: Like a wise man, you considered second thoughts best. **1937** FWCrofts *Found* (NY) 273: But as so often happens, second thoughts were less rosy. **1941** HCBailey *Bishop's* (NY) 296: Second thoughts are better. **1958** LSdeCamp *Elephant* (NY) 109: Second thoughts prevailed. **1965** AGilbert *Voice* (NY) 173: Second thoughts are often best. EAP T74.

T89 Thought is free (*varied*)

1937 JMWalsh *White Mask* (L) 38: Thought is free. **1938** RAJWalling *Grimy Glove* (NY) 255: No charge for thinking . . . This is a free country. **1957** THWhite *Master* (L) 249: Thought is free. TW 370(1); Whiting T238; *Oxford* 814–15.

T90 As slender (thin) as a Thread

1936 DWheatley *They Found* (P) 311: Our hopes are slender as a thread. **1969** AChristie *Hallowe'en* (NY) 64: She was thin as a thread. Clark 221: Slender.

T91 To hang by a Thread (hair)

1931 CWells *Horror* (P) 15: Your life hangs by a thread. **1932** FBeeding *Murder* (B) 44: Her life was hanging by a silken thread. **1936** HHolt *There Has Been* (L) 215: His life is hanging by a hair. **1960** JWelcome *Stop* (NY) 154: My life was hanging by a thread. **1969** MGEberhart *Message* (NY) 176: His life hangs by a thread. EAP T77; TW 370(1).

T92 As phony (queer) as a Three-dollar bill

1966 DHitchens *Man Who Cried* (NY) 173: He's as phony as a three-dollar bill. **1967** TWells *Dead by* (NY) 67: That old fink is as queer as a three-dollar bill. Wentworth 542–3.

T93 To eat like a Thresher

1957 RGraves *They Hanged* (NY) 139: I . . . eat like a thresher. Taylor *Prov. Comp.* 82.

T94 Thrift is a proverbial virtue

1919 JBCabell *Jurgen* (NY 1922) 87: Thrift . . . is a proverbial virtue. Cf. *Oxford* 818.

T95   To jump down someone's Throat

1934 VGielgud *Ruse* (NY) 133: I jumped down his throat. **1937** MBurton *Clue* (NY) 103: The doctor would jump down our throats. **1945** MWalsh *Nine Strings* (P) 135: Someone jumped down her throat, as it were. Wentworth 299.

T96   To be all Thumbs

1928 ABerkeley *Silk* (NY) 94: Makes one feel all thumbs. **1932** TThayer *Three Sheet* (NY) 97: He was all thumbs. **1951** HMcCloy *Through a Glass* (L 1961) 25: You're all thumbs these days. **1955** GBagby *Dirty* (NY) 25: Paralyzed with fright . . . All thumbs. **1965** CArmstrong *Turret* (NY) 156: I am all thumbs. DARE i 49: All thumbs; *Oxford* 258: Fingers.

T97   To be an extra (third) Thumb (varied)

1927 JTaine *Quayle's* (NY) 277: [He] stood out as awkwardly as a third thumb. **1933** GYoung *Devil's* (NY) 16: James couldn't need him no more than an extra thumb. **1958** HMasur *Murder* (NY 1959) 156: I feel like an extra thumb. Cf. To be a fifth Wheel *below.*

T98   To be under one's Thumb

1921 IOstrander *Crimson* (NY) 140: Under his thumb. **1933** DGBrowne *Dead* (L) 188: He's right under his wife's thumb. **1940** ELWhite *While She* (NY) 38: His wife is a little under his thumb. **1950** MMurray *Neat* (NY DBC) 113: She does seem pretty much under his thumb. **1959** FLockridge *Murder Is* (P) 188: She's out from under mama's thumb. **1962** JTAppleby *Henry* (NY) 144: He had the Pope under his thumb. **1966** DMDisney *Magic* (NY) 120: Keep his wife under his thumb. EAP T84.

T99   To have a green Thumb (fingers)

1940 HAdams *Chief Witness* (L) 129: Have you the green thumb? **1940** ELWhite *While She* (NY) 16: You must have green fingers. **1952** BMalamud *Natural* (NY) 45: I have that green thumb. **1964** HPentecost *Shape* (NY DBC) 103: She lays claims to a green thumb. **1967** FWeldon *And the Wife* (NY) 145: I haven't got green fingers. **1970** CArmstrong *Protege* (NY DBC) 15: [He] had a very green thumb. **1972** DWalker *Lord's*

(NY) 72: *To Have a Green Thumb* was your granny's saying. Wentworth 230.

T100   To stick (stand) out (up) like a sore Thumb (varied)

1926 MRRinehart *Bat* (NY 1959) 82: Sticks up . . . like a sore thumb. **1931** RSAllen *Washington* (NY) 320: He is as touchy as a sore thumb. **1931** BStarke *Born* (I) 211: A small rattle stuck up like a sore thumb. **1934** TDowning *Cat Screams* (NY) 124: As welcome as a sore thumb. **1937** ATilton *Beginning* (NY) 6: He stood out . . . like the proverbial sore thumb. **1940** AMChase *No Outlet* (NY) 207: He sticks out like a sore thumb. **1940** DHume *Invitation* (L) 38: One fact stands out like the proverbial sore thumb. **1941** GWYates *If a Body* (NY) 188: The battered Buick must have stood out like a thicket of sore thumbs. **1952** MHBradley *Nice* (NY) 76: King sticks out like a sore thumb. **1956** JChristopher *Death* (L) 196: There's one fellow standing out like a sore thumb. **1959** PAnderson *War* (NY) 54: Strangers . . . would stick out like the good old sore thumb. **1961** JWelcome *Beware* (L) 136: My presence stuck out like a sore thumb. **1964** PHighsmith *Two Faces* (L) 90: You'd stand out there like a sore thumb. **1966** AMStein *I Fear* (NY) 18: You'll stand out like the one perfect digit in a double fistful of sore thumbs. **1969** SPalmer *Hildegarde* (NY) 24: Miss Withers . . . stuck out like the proverbial sore thumb. **1970** KGiles *Death* (L) 149: He'll stand out like a sore thumb. **1972** JGores *Dead* (NY) 183: Elkin stuck out like a broken thumb. **1976** JSScott *Poor* (NY) 115: A thousand quid stuck out like a sore thumb. Taylor *Prov. Comp.* 82.

T101   As black as Thunder

1903 EChilders *Riddle* (NY 1940) 170: He was as black as thunder over the prospects. **1922** JJoyce *Ulysses* (NY 1934) 356: Looking as black as thunder. **1931** GDHCole *Dead Man's* (L) 158: Looking as black as thunder. **1936** NMorland *Street* (L) 39: Her face as black as thunder. **1961** MNelson *When the Bed* (L) 206: [A] look as black as thunder. **1967** RRendell *New Lease* (NY) 167: Charles's face as black as thunder. TW

Thunder

371(2); Taylor *Western Folklore* 17(1958) 19; *Oxford* 63.

T102 As unexpected as **Thunder** in winter
1919 JSFletcher *Middle Temple* (NY) 171: Unexpected . . . as a crack of thunder on a fine winter's day. Cf. TW 371(16).

T103 To steal one's **Thunder**
1905 GDEldridge *Millbank Case* (NY) 232: Steal his thunder. **1924** CWells *Furthest* (P) 191: Stealing my thunder. **1932** EQueen *Egyptian* (NY) 303: He's stealing my thunder. **1938** BFlynn *Ebony* (L) 56: Don't steal my thunder. **1940** JDonavan *Plastic Man* (L) 238: Cross had stolen his thunder. **1952** CDickson *Behind* (NY) 155: Not wishing to have anyone steal his own thunder. **1957** CASmart *At Home* (NY) 174: I do not propose to steal his thunder here. **1960** NWilliams *Knaves* (NY) 65: The Bishop having stolen his thunder. **1964** JJMarric *Gideon's Lot* (NY) 154: Stop stealing my thunder. **1972** HCarmichael *Naked* (NY) 172: I don't want to steal your thunder. **1976** JPorter *Package* (NY) 191: Stealing her thunder. NED Suppl. Thunder *sb.* 3d.

T104 To come like a **Thunderbolt**
1934 CBush *100% Alibis* (L) 155: The whole business came as a thunderclap. **1935** ECRLorac *Organ* (L) 239: It came like a thunderbolt out of a clear sky. EAP T91.

T105 As black as a **Thundercloud**
1924 VLWhitechurch *Templeton* (NY) 257: His face was as black as a thunder-cloud. **1928** AChristie *Mystery of the Blue Train* (NY) 220: His face as black as a thundercloud. **1947** AGilbert *Death in* (L) 53: Jack looked as black as a thunder cloud. **1961** ESMadden *Craig's* (NY DBC) 108: [A face] black as a thundercloud. TW 372(1).

T106 As dark as a **Thundercloud**
1930 AGilbert *Mystery* (NY) 7: As dark as a thunder cloud. **1944** BFischer *Hornet's* (NY) 170: His face dark as a thunder cloud. Wilstach 82.

T107 **Tib's** Eve
1957 DDuncan *Occam's* (NY) 117: "Tib's Eve?" "There's no Saint Tib. So there's no

Tib's eve either. It's a time that never was and never will be—or it's a period removed from time altogether." **1958** *New Yorker* 4/5 32: Tib's Eve . . . neither before nor after Christmas. *Oxford* 821; Partridge 881.

T108 As crazy (gloomy) as a **Tick**
1934 MDavis *Hospital* (NY) 218: Crazy as a tick. **1974** GPaley *Enormous* (NY) 180: You're as gloomy as a tick on Sunday. Cf. Bedbug *above*.

T109 As full as a **Tick**
1927 LTracy *Mysterious* (NY) 215: Full as a tick. **1937** WETurpin *These Low* (NY) 135: Gussie was full as a tick with gossip. **1952** CEVulliamy *Don* (L) 8: As full as a tick [*drunk*]. **1956** *Arizona Highways* Oct. 23: Even the dogs were full as ticks. EAP T94.

T110 As tight as a **Tick**
1933 LRGribble *Secret* (L) 161: He's as tight as a tick on a dog's ear [*secretive*]. **1933** DHoldridge *Pindorama* (NY) 33: Tight as ticks. **1936** KCStrahan *Desert* (I) 207: She sat tight as a tick. **1937** GGoodwin *White Farm* (L) 272: Growing as tight and prosperous as ticks. **1938** PHaggard *Death Talks* (NY) 59: Tight as a tick [*in a safe place*]. **1949** RMLaurenson *Six Bullets* (NY) 15: Tighter'n a tick on a dog [*stingy*]. **1952** CDickson *Behind* (NY) 130: I was as tight as a tick [*drunk*]. **1958** PBranch *Murder's* (L 1963) 176: Tight as a tick [*drunk*]. **1970** PAlding *Murder* (NY) 112: He'd been as tight as a tick. **1970** DMacKenzie *Kyle* (B) 156: You're tighter than a tick [*emotionally upset*]. **1972** DLees *Rainbow* (NY) 46: Tight as a tick [*drunk*]. **1974** HCrews *Gypsy's* (NY) 134: I was pumped tight as a tick. Whiting NC 486(3).

T111 In two **Ticks**
1929 HHolt *Mayfair* (L) 120: In two ticks. **1951** JCreasey *Puzzle* (L 1962) 37: It won't take two ticks. Wentworth 544: In a tick; NED Tick *sb.*[3] 4. Cf. Shakes *above*.

T112 To a **Tick**
1937 VMacClure *House* (L) 110: That's the man to a tick [*exactly*]. NED Tick *sb.*[3] 4 (quote 1907). Cf. T *above*.

T113   No **Tickee**, no washee

1942 RBurke *Here Lies* (NY) 107: No tikkee—no shirtee. **1948** ELipsky *Murder One* (NY) 106: No tickee, no washee. **1967** BBaxt *Swing* (NY) 58: No tickee, no washee. Taylor *Proverb* 11.

T114   To be the **Ticket**

1922 JSFletcher *Herapath* (NY) 54: That's the ticket. **1932** JJFarjeon *Z* (NY) 132: That's the ticket! **1957** CWilliams *Big Bite* (L) 120: That's the ticket. **1959** HEBates *Watercress* (L) 62: That's the ticket. TW 372; Brunvand 142.

T115   To write one's own **Ticket**

1940 HSKeeler *Cleopatra's* (L) 13: You can write your own ticket. **1947** WMoore *Greener* (NY 1961) 106: You can write your own ticket. **1949** AAFair *Bedrooms* (NY 1958) 5: She . . . could write her own ticket. Berrey 217.3.

T116   A high **Tide** brings a low ebb

1957 HPBeck *Folklore of Maine* (P) 67: A high tide always brings a low ebb. Whiting E41.

T117   To swim (row) against the **Tide**

1960 CBrossard *Double* (NY) 158: He wasn't swimming against the tide. **1961** HFHutchinson *Hollow* (L) 135: He could not swim against the tide. **1967** DTylden-Wright *AFrance* (L) 124: He was rowing against an adverse tide. **1974** PNobile *Intellectual* (NY) 121: To swim against the tide. EAP T106; Brunvand 142(2).

T118   To be fit to be **Tied**

1922 JJoyce *Ulysses* (NY 1934) 754: I was fit to be tied. **1939** ATilton *Cold Steal* (NY) 173: He was simply fit to be tied. **1954** EQueen *Glass* (B) 121: Mert and Hellie were fit to be tied. **1957** *New Yorker* 12/28 33: [He] is said to have been fit to be tied. **1957** BGill *Day* (NY) 85: She was fit to be tied. **1965** HKane *Midnight* (NY) 161: He was fit to be tied, blowing his wig. **1967** AWEckert *Wild* (B) 119: Molly was fit to be tied. Cole 50. Cf. NED Fit *a.* 5b.

T119   As fierce as a **Tiger**

1932 CDawes *Lawless* (L) 186: Violent and fierce as a tiger. TW 373(1); Taylor *Western Folklore* 17(1958) 19.

T120   As savage as a **Tiger**

1932 RThorndike *Devil* (NY) 49: He went savage as a tiger. Wilstach 335.

T121   He who has a **Tiger** (bear, *etc.*) by the tail dare not let go (*varied*)

1930 ATrain *Adventures* (NY) 161: The position of one having a wildcat by the tail. **1932** MRRinehart *Miss Pinkerton* (NY) 306: He had taken a tiger by the tail, and he didn't dare let go. **1934** WGore *There's Death* (L) 18: [It's] like getting hold of the devil's tail, you can't let go. **1935** GHDoran *Chronicles* (NY) 53: The proverbial man who had a racing bull by the tail. **1935** GDilnot *Murder* (L) 247: Then you had hold of the tiger's tail and it was a question of hanging on or letting go. **1940** WReed *No Sign* (NY) 132: I think you've got a real tiger by the tail. **1947** GGallagher *I Found* (NY DBC) 138: It was the old lion by the tail situation. **1949** FKane *Green* (NY) 26: She had something big by the tail and couldn't let go. **1955** GBagby *Dirty* (NY) 90: He's taken a bear by the tail. **1956** *NYTimes* 12/16 61: I've got a bear by the tail and don't know how to turn it loose. **1957** *BHerald* 2/27 12: We have a lion by the tail and we can't let go. **1957** *Time* 7/1 64: You've got a bull by the tail. **1959** *BGlobe* 3/30 18: China has a bear by the tail in troubled Tibet. **1959** MMillar *Listening* (NY) 228: He had a tiger by the tail. **1961** AAFair *Bachelors* (NY DBC) 149: I've got a bear by the tail and can't let go. **1967** FGruber *Pulp* (LA) 169: I had a bear by the short hairs and I could not let go. **1972** ELathen *Murder* (NY) 30: Sloan . . . might well have a tiger by the tail. **1974** PNobile *Intellectual* (NY) 119: Having gotten the tiger by the tail, he couldn't let go. Cf. next entry. Cf. Wildcat, To hold a Wolf *below*.

T122   He who rides a **Tiger** cannot dismount (*varied*)

1926 EDBiggers *Chinese* (NY) 131: Chinese have saying . . . "He who rides on a tiger cannot dismount." **1927** FLPackard *Devil's* (NY) 78: He who rides a tiger cannot dismount. **1951** LSdeCamp *Hand* (NY 1963) 120: Who rides the tiger cannot dismount. **1959** JWelcome *Run* (NY) 141: Who rides a tiger must never dismount. **1963** NFreeling *Question* (NY 1965) 182: Who rides upon a tiger cannot get down. Champion (Chinese) 379:1153; *Oxford* 677: Rides. Cf. preceding entry.

T123 To fight like a **Tiger**

1922 JJoyce *Ulysses* (NY 1934) 313: The two fought like tigers. **1924** CWells *Furthest* (P) 46: She . . . fought like a tiger; 223. **1932** AGask *Murder* (NY) 38: He fought 'em all like a tiger. **1933** PGWodehouse *Mulliner* (NY) 226: They fought like tigers. **1952** ESHolding *Widow's* (NY DBC) 22: She fought like a tiger. **1963** HPentecost *Only* (NY DBC) 138: You fought like a tiger. **1971** ELinington *Practice* (NY) 38: Fought . . . like a tiger. EAP T111.

T124 To have a **Tile** loose

1930 DDeane *Mystery* (L) 33: Got a tile loose in the upper story. Partridge 886.

T125 To have been out on the **Tiles**

1935 ECRLorac *Organ* (L) 131: Been out on the tiles. **1948** JRhode *Death* (NY) 158: Spent the night on the tiles. **1955** MErskine *Old Mrs.* (NY) 215: My tongue felt as if I'd been on the tiles for a week [*drunk*]. **1962** CWatson *Hopjoy* (NY) 72: I'd been out on the tiles. **1967** LPDavies *Lampton* (NY) 100: I was out on the tiles last night. Partridge 886.

T126 To take to tall **Timber**

1965 ESGardner *Troubled* (NY) 43: He may take to the tall timber. TW 373(1).

T127 As old as **Time**

1931 DLSayers *Suspicious* (NY) 114: Half as old as time. **1938** MECurne *Death* (NY) 136: Horace looked as old as time. **1946** DBHughes *Ride the Pink* (NY 1958) 140: The woman . . . was older than time. **1949** FCrane *Flying* (NY) 96: It's old as time. **1952** EPaul *Black* (NY) 262: She's as old as time. **1956** EMcBain *Mugger* (L 1963) 69:

As old as time. **1966** DMDisney *Magic* (NY) He looked as old as time itself. EAP T112.

T128 As steady as **Time**

1932 AGilbert *Body* (NY) 255: His hands were as steady as Time. Wilstach 387: Old Time.

T129 No **Time** like the present

1924 FWCrofts *Cask* (NY 1936) 176: No time like the present. **1933** FWCrofts *Strange Case* (NY) 224: There was no time like the present. **1940** FWCrofts *Golden Ashes* (NY) 135: No better time than the present. **1953** CHarnett *Nicholas* (NY) 48: There was no time like the present. **1958** ECooper *Tomorrow's* (NY) 44: No time like the present. **1966** DRMason *From Carthage* (NY) 49: There's no time like the present. **1969** ECooper *News* (NY) 106: No time like the present. **1972** WJBurley *Guilt* (NY) 60: No time like the present. **1975** GHousehold *Red* (B) 54: No time like the present. EAP T115.

T130 Not give one the **Time** of day

1951 IChase *New York 22* (NY) 63: He wouldn't give me the time of day. **1954** JPotts *Go* (NY) 12: My mother wouldn't give me the time of day. **1960** TBDewey *Girl* (NY DBC) 96: We didn't even get the time of day. **1961** HReilly *Certain* (NY DBC) 48: She wouldn't give you the time of day, for free. **1970** AAFair *All Grass* (NY DBC) 111: Don't give anyone even the time of day. **1973** ELopez *Seven* (NY) 170: She wouldn't give them the time of day. Wentworth 546.

T131 One is a long **Time** dead

1934 GFairlie *Copper* (L) 241: One is a long time dead. **1935** DMcCleary *Not for Heaven* (NY) 53: You're a long time dead. **1941** MBardon *Murder Does* (NY) 212: You'll be dead a long time. **1956** HEBates *Sugar* (L) 30: We're dead a long time.

T132 Other **Times**, other customs (*varied*)

1919 LThayer *Mystery of the 13th Floor* (NY) 111: Hother times, hother manners. **1930** AChristie *Mysterious* (NY) 3: *Autre temps, autre moeurs.* **1935** EGreenwood *Deadly* (NY) 212: Different times, different customs.

1945 EQueen *Murderer* (NY) 6: Other times, other scandals. **1954** MMcCarthy *Charmed* (NY) 233: Other times, other customs. **1957** PGallico *Thomasina* (NY) 147: Other times, other customs. **1964** RAHeinlein *Farnham's* (NY 1965) 143: I'm aware that other times had other customs. **1969** JMPatterson *Doubly* (NY) 51: Oh well, autre temps, autre tarts. **1970** RDAltick *Victorian* (NY) 69: Autres temps, autres goûts. **1970** GEEvans *Where* (L) 276: Other times, other manners. **1971** EHCohen *Mademoiselle* (B) 104: As the French say, "other times, other manners." **1977** LBlock *Burglars* (NY) 150: Other times, other customs. *Oxford* 600–601. Cf. Other Days *above*.

T133 There is a **Time** and place for everything

1926 OSitwell *Before* (L) 178: There was a time and place for everything. **1938** ME Corne *Death* (NY) 216: The old saying: "There's a time and a place for everything." **1939** GHCoxe *Four Frightened* (NY) 189: There's a time and a place for everything. **1947** LFord *Woman* (NY) 219: There's a time and place for everything. **1950** OAnderson *In for* (NY) 42: There is, to employ a hackneyed phrase, a time and a place for everything. **1958** CLBlackstone *Dewey* (L 1965) 69: There is a time and place for all things. **1962** FLockridge *And Left* (P) 167: Time and place for everything, as they say. **1968** MAllingham *Cargo* (NY) 79: You have the time and the place . . . but not the loved one. **1970** HBlyth *Skittles* (L) 67: There was a time and place for everything. TW 374(7). Cf. A Place for everything *above*; next entry.

T134 There is a **Time** for everything (*varied*)

1911 HHMunro *Chronicles* (L 1927) 49: There is a time for everything. **1929** FBeeding *Pretty* (B) 156: There is a time for all things. **1930** WLewis *Apes* (NY 1932) 21: There is a time for everything. **1935** DHume *Call in* (L) 202: There is a time for all things. **1953** RPostgate *Ledger* (L) 183: There was a time for all things. EAP T116; Brunvand 143(3). Cf. preceding entry.

T135 There is a **Time** for speech and a time for silence

1925 JSFletcher *Secret* (B) 192: There is a time for everything . . . A time for speech and a time for silence. **1971** JCreasey *Murder* (NY) 128: There's a time to talk and a time to keep your mouth shut. EAP T118.

T136 There is always a first **Time** (*varied*)

1924 ADHSmith *Porto* (NY) 220: There's a first time always. **1929** WRBurnett *Little* (NY) 104: There's a first time for everything. **1932** HFootner *Dead Man's* (NY) 279: There has to be a first time for everything. **1938** CKnight *Ginger Lei* (NY) 76: Always a first time. **1947** HCahill *Look* (NY) 189: There's always a first time. **1957** *BangorDN* 4/4 34: There's a first time for everything. **1957** TWicker *Devil* (NY) 62: There's a first time for everything, they say. **1958** WJLederer *Ugly* (NY) 130: There has to be a first time for everything. **1960** JSymons *Progress* (L) 125: There always has to be a first time. **1969** EStewart *Heads* (NY) 86: There's always a first time, ain't there? **1970** HCarmichael *Death* (NY) 46: They say there's always a first time. **1974** LCarter *Valley* (NY) 73: There was a first time for everything. EAP T120.

T137 Third **Time** is a charm

1922 JJoyce *Ulysses* (NY 1934) 428: Third time is the charm. **1930** KCStrahan *Death* (NY) 21: Third time's charm. **1946** LPBaghmann *Kiss of Death* (NY) 4: The third time's the charm. **1968** JCFurnas *Lightfoot* (NY) 183: The third time's the charm. Cf. Charm *above*; next entry.

T138 Third **Time** lucky (*varied*)

1910 EPhillpotts *Tales* (NY) 203: But "third time's luck," he says to himself, and so he tried once more and proved that even proverbs can lie. 210: Third time was lucky with Peter. **1927** OWarner *Secret* (NY) 216: They say the third time is lucky, or unlucky as the case may be. **1932** PGWodehouse *Hot Water* (NY) 305: The third time . . . is always lucky. **1933** BPerowne *Return* (NY) 238: Third time, they say, the luck changes. **1936** LCharteris *Saint Overboard* (NY) 117: Twice is all right, but the third time might be unlucky. **1937** VWilkins *And So—Victoria* (NY) 397: Third time's lucky. **1938** WE Hayes *Black* (NY) 24: The third time might be successful. **1955** CMWills *Death* (L) 59: Third time lucky, you know. **1956** RFoley *Last* (NY DBC) 92: They say the third time is lucky. **1962** ADuggan *Lord* (L) 59: Your third time may be lucky. **1966** BKnox *Devilweed* (NY) 183: Third time lucky. **1973** BKnox *Storm* (NY) 153: Who'd blame you for hoping it would be second time lucky. **1974** NWebster *Burial* (NY) 77: Third time might not be so lucky. **1976** JMcClure *Snake* (NY) 71: He was third-time lucky. EAP T121; Whiting T317; *Oxford* 813.

T139 Third **Time** pays for all (*varied*)

1920 JSFletcher *Dead Men's* (NY) 291: They say the third time pays for all. **1924** EWallace *Green* (B) 346: The third time you're going to pay. **1938** JRRTolkien *Hobbit* (B) 218: "Third time pays for all," as my father used to say. **1955** JRRTolkien *Return* (L) 227: Thrice shall pay for all. **1961** RJWhite *Smartest* (L) 103: Third time pays for all. **1968** MKJoseph *Hole* (NY) 166: Third time pays for all. TW 374(6); *Oxford* 813.

T140 **Time** and tide wait for no man (*varied*)

1910 JCLincoln *Depot Master* (NY) 310: They tell us time and tide wait for no man. **1928** SMartin *Fifteen* (NY) 298: How true it is that time waits for no man. **1930** AE Coppard *Pink* (L) 204: Time and tide wait no one's pleasure. **1930** IWray *Vye* (L) 27: Babies, like the tide, wait for no man. **1938** CDickson *Judas* (L) 82: Time and tide wait for no man. **1940** FGruber *Talking Clock* (NY) 240: Time and tide wait for no man. **1959** *BangorDN* 9/9 25: Time and tide wait for no man. **1959** AHocking *Victim* (NY) 106: Like time and tide they wait for no man and very few women. **1961** NBlake *Worm* (L) 32: Time and tide wait for no man. **1968** CMackenzie *Octave Seven* (L) 55: Trains and trams like time and tide wait for no man. **1975** HCarmichael *Too Late* (NY) 191: Time waits for no man. **1975** TWells *Hark* (NY) 25: Dad, like time and tide, waited for no man. EAP T125; Brunvand 142(1).

T141 **Times** change (and men change with them)

1934 WSharp *Murder* (NY) 48: Times change. **1937** DWhitelaw *Face* (L) 17: Times change . . . and men change with them. **1949** JSStrange *Unquiet* (NY) 94: Well, times change, I guess. *Oxford* 825.

T142 **Time** changes all things

1937 JPMarquand *Late George* (B) 27: Time changes all things. Whiting T320.

T143 **Time** flies (*varied*)

1922 JJoyce *Ulysses* (NY 1934) 165: How time flies. 437: How time flies by! **1924** HCBailey *Mr. Fortune's Practice* (NY) 156: Time runs on, doesn't it? **1925** IOstrander *Neglected* (NY) 6: Tempus *does* fugit. **1932** PMcGuire *Three* (NY) 315: Time, he reflected, is fleeting. **1939** MBurton *Death Leaves* (L) 90: How time flies. **1939** ECRLorac *Black Beadle* (L) 215: Tempus fugit . . . as the classics remind us. **1952** EFBleiler *Imagination* (NY) 114: Time surely does fly. **1956** AWUpfield *Battling* (L 1960) 120: Time flies, as a thousand million people have said before me. **1957** WMorris *Love* (NY) 66: *Tempus* fidgets, as you know. **1961** CBlackstone *House* (L 1965) 143: *Tempus fugit.* **1966** DMDisney *Magic* (NY) 164: Time flies. **1970** TAWaters *Probability* (NY) 65: Time had, to coin a phrase, flown. **1974** SChance *Septimus* (Nashville) 60: How time flies, as the monkey said when it threw the clock at the missionary. **1976** AChristie *Sleeping* (NY) 180: Time flies, as the saying goes. EAP T130; TW 374(10); Brunvand 143(4).

T144 **Time** heals all wounds (*varied*)

1929 DESmalley *Stumbling* (NY) 220: Time heals all wounds. **1933** CBush *April Fools* (L) 32: Time heals all wounds. **1936** VStarrett *Midnight* (NY) 199: Time heals our sorest hurts. **1937** DQBurleigh *Kristiana* (NY) 107: Time heals scars. **1940** AMcRoyd *Death in Costume* (NY) 112: Let time heal the wound. **1941** SFisher *I Wake Up* (NY) 69: There is a coward's philosophy that time heals all wounds. **1942** NMarsh *Enter Murderer* (NY) 99: The tritest of all our tiresome clichés is the one that says that time cures all things. **1946** HHowe *We Happy* (NY) 247: Time wounds all heels. **1951** DWMeredith *Christmas* (NY) 164: Time heals all wounds. **1955** BCarey *Fatal* (NY) 117: Time heals all wounds, you know. **1960** CBeaton *My Royal* (NY) 23: Time heals everything; trite but true. **1962** EMcBain *Like* (NY) 160: Time, as the ancient Arab saying goes, heals all wounds. 161: Another old proverb, an ancient Syrian saying that simply stated, "Time wounds all heels." **1962** CWatson *Hopjoy* (NY) 189: It's simply that time wounds all heels . . . as Marx . . . put it . . . not Karl . . . Groucho. **1963** EVCunningham *Alice* (L 1965) 155: Time eases things. **1967** NWollaston *Jupiter* (L) 86: Time heals everything. **1968** GHellman *Bankers* (NY) 97: Time cures all things, in a way. *Oxford* 823: Time cures.

T145 Time is money (*varied*)

1909 JCLincoln *Keziah* (NY) 369: Time is money. **1921** JCLincoln *Galusha* (NY) 309: If time was money, as they say it is. **1922** JJoyce *Ulysses* (NY 1934) 132: Time is money. **1924** HHBashford *Augustus Carp* (L 1966) 43: Time was money. **1931** AFielding *Upfold* (NY) 172: Time's not money—It's far more valuable. **1938** DHume *Good-bye* (L) 30: Time is money to me. **1954** CBeaton *Glass* (NY) 14: Franklin's notion that time is money. **1957** GMalcolm-Smith *Trouble* (NY) 72: Time is money, money is time. **1958** *New Yorker* 8/2 21: Time means money. **1966** HTracy *Men* (L) 44: Hadn't somebody said that time was money. **1967** JDetre *Happy* (NY) 96: We Americans believe time is money. **1970** MEChaber *Green* (NY) 6: Time was money and all that sort of thing. **1978** BKnox *Witchrock* (NY) 129: Time is money. **1981** ELathen *Going* (NY) 116: Time is money almost everywhere. On Wall Street, the reverse holds true as well. EAP T133; Brunvand 143(6).

T146 Time is of the essence

1941 HReilly *Three Women* (NY) 246: Time was of the essence. **1948** LFord *Devil's* (NY) 56: You know what they say . . . time is of the essence. **1951** SMerwin *House* (NY) 127: "Time is of the proverbial essence." . . . The huge black marshal . . . used the word "proverbial" to soften his cliché. **1957** GMalcolm-Smith *Trouble* (NY) 53: Time, as they say, is of the essence. **1958** SDean *Dishonor* (NY) 130: Time, as the lawyers say, is of the essence. **1961** HPentecost *Deadly* (NY DBC) 58: Time is of the essence. **1969** EPetaja *Nets* (NY) 120: Time is of the essence . . . a cliché. **1975** EMcBain *Where There's Smoke* (NY) 91: Time is of the essence in a homicide investigation. Bartlett 1102a; NED Suppl. Essence 8 (quote 1931).

T147 Time is precious

1910 JCLincoln *Depot Master* (NY) 12: Time was precious. **1922** DLindsay *Haunted Woman* (L 1964) 24: Time was precious. **1934** MBurton *Murder* (NY) 112: My time is precious. **1939** EPhillpotts *Monkshood* (L) 109: Time's precious. **1943** EDaly *Evidence* (NY) 113: "I'm saving you time." . . . "It's precious." **1956** MProcter *Ripper* (NY) 7: Time was precious. **1960** AWUpfield *Mystery* (L) 51: Time was precious. **1961** AMorton *Double* (NY) 124: Waste precious time. **1969** JDrummond *People* (NY) 59: Time's precious. **1970** AAFair *All Grass* (NY DBC) 48: Time may be . . . precious. EAP T134; TW 374(13). Cf. To waste *below*.

T148 Time is the great healer (*varied*)

1933 LGrex *Lonely Inn* (L) 139: Time, we are told, is the great healer. **1938** JTFarrell *No Star* (NY) 457: Time is a great healer. **1958** JBlackburn *Scent* (L) 191: Time is a healer. **1968** ELathen *Stitch* (NY) 12: Time is the only healer. **1972** SWoods *They Love* (NY) 213: Time—as too many people have said before me—is a great healer. *Oxford* 823: Time cures. Cf. Time heals *above*.

T149 Time lost cannot be recovered (*varied*)

1941 VWMason *Rio Casino* (NY) 164: Time . . . once lost could not be recovered. **1957** MBGarrett *Horse* (Univ. Ala.) 157: Lost time is never found. Whiting T307; *Oxford* 824.

T150 Time presses

1929 FBeeding *Pretty* (B) 253: Time presses, as the monkey said when the clock fell on his head. Cf. Whiting T325.

T151 **Time** will tell (*varied*)

1925 JGBrandon *Bond* (L) 92: Time will tell. **1929** FDaingerfield *Linden* (NY) 123: Time will tell; 174. **1934** REast *Murder Rehearsal* (NY) 63: Time will prove. **1934** JGregory *Emerald* (NY) 255: Time telleth all tales. **1938** MECurne *Death* (NY) 222: Time will tell. **1939** EPaul *Mysterious* (NY 1962) 114: Time marches on, and will tell. **1943** ADerleth *Seven* (NY) 132: Time will tell. **1952** FVWMason *Himalayan* (NY 1953) 104: "Time will tell," as the monkey said when he hid the limburger in Grandpa's clock. **1954** JHHodge *Famous Trials, Fourth* (L) 221: Time, despite the popular assurance to the contrary, cannot now be relied upon to tell. **1957** *NYTimes* 6/23 3E: As the old saying is, time will tell. **1957** NBlake *End* (L) 66: Time will show. **1958** *New Yorker* 2/22 28: But time will tell, as the saying goes. **1960** MJones *Forest* (NY) 56: Time settles a heap of things. **1974** RRosenblum *Good* (NY) 89: Time will tell . . . But would it tell the truth? **1977** EXFerrars *Blood* (NY) 8: Time will tell. EAP T141; TW 375(15); Brunvand 143(7): Show.

T152 To have **Time** to kill (*varied*)

1926 JSFletcher *Great* (NY) 126: He had plenty of time to kill. **1941** LThayer *Hallowe'en* (NY) 258: He would have had time to burn. **1954** VWBrooks *Scenes* (NY) 144: Time on his hands to kill. Cf. EAP T146.

T153 To live on borrowed **Time**

1932 MRRinehart *Miss Pinkerton* (NY) 161: I am living on borrowed time. **1967** RFenisong *Villainous* (NY) 149: Your dad's been living on borrowed time, as the saying is. **1969** BCole *Funco* (NY) 28: He's been livin' on borrowed time for years. **1981** SKaminsky *High* (NY) 124: I was living on borrowed time.

T154 To take **Time** (opportunity) by the forelock (*varied*)

1904 SArmitage-Smith *John of Gaunt* (L) 29: Took time by the forelock. **1920** GDilnot *Suspected* (NY) 128: To take time by the forelock. **1928** AEApple *Mr. Chang's* (NY) 208: Seizing opportunity by the forelock.

1930 AGilbert *Mystery* (NY) 94: How true it is that Opportunity has no locks at the back by which she may be restrained. Once she's flown past she's lost forever. **1933** PMcGuire *Death* (NY) 218: Taken fortune by the forelock. **1936** RStout *Rubber* (L) 209: Are you going to grab time by the forelock? **1939** PATaylor *Spring* (L) 251: Kebby was just grippin' opportunity by the horns. **1939** AWebb *Mr. Pendlebury Makes* (L) 66: Taking time by the forelock. **1947** DBowers *Bells* (NY) 132: George took time by the forelock. **1954** AStone *Harvard* (B) 120: Opportunity [had] a hair in front but was bald behind. **1960** EWolf *Rosenbach* (Cleveland) 155: Seizing opportunity by the forelock. Quite soundly the emblematists pictured that fast-fleeing spirit as bald in the back. **1965** JDavey *Killing* (L) 45: A patriot who had taken history by the forelock. **1969** GMFraser *Flashman* (NY) 64: I had taken fortune by the foreskin [*sic*] in my own way. EAP T147; Brunvand 143(8).

T155 To waste (have lost) precious **Time** (*varied*)

1927 FJohns *Victory* (NY) 187: Precious time is lost. **1928** WRoughead *Murderer's* (NY 1968) 108: Wasted much precious time. **1938** CFGregg *Mystery* (L) 264: Why waste precious time? **1956** DDodge *Angel's* (NY 1959) 125: They had lost precious time. **1957** MBryan *Murder* (NY) 102: He had wasted precious time. **1964** CSimmons *Powdered* (NY) 120: I steal their precious time. **1968** ESRussell *She Should* (NY) 180: Wasting twenty precious minutes. **1968** RVanGulik *Poets* (NY) 81: Let's not waste our precious time. **1972** MKaye *Lively* (NY) 82: We wouldn't lose precious time at lunch. **1975** MVonnegut *Eden* (NY) 3: Wasting four years of precious time. Cf. Whiting T307: Time lost, T322: Time is precious. Cf. Time is precious *above*.

T156 Tough **Times** make monkeys eat red peppers

1958 *Time* 11/3 36: An axiom learned during his East Harlem youth: "Tough times make monkeys eat red peppers." Cf. Dainty Dogs *above*.

T157 To be a little **Tin** god (on wheels) (*varied*)

1901 HGarland *Companions* (NY 1931) 76: He had been my little tin-god-on-wheels. **1928** CBarry *Corpse* (NY) 97: You of all men, his little tin god. **1928** CKingston *Guilty* (L) 164: You're a little tin god. **1930** WLewis *Apes* (NY 1932) 515: As if he were a little tin-god. **1936** HHolt *There Has Been* (L) 180: Suzanne looked upon him as a sort of tin god. **1940** CSexby *Death Joins* (NY) 208: We were little tin gods on wheels. **1952** MAllingham *Tiger* (NY) 164: They're little tin gods. **1952** KMKnight *Valse* (NY) 113: He's a tin god on wheels. **1955** DMDisney *Trick* (NY) 34: He had the idea he was a little tin god. **1958** ELacy *Be Careful* (NY) 70: I'm a tin hero. **1966** LPDavies *Paper* (NY) 191: [He] is Harris' little tin god. **1967** EVCunningham *Samantha* (NY) 120: She is a lousey little tin god. **1970** LGraffety-Smith *Bright* (L) 7: In the little tin-god-on-wheels class. Berrey 388.6, 402.2, 421.4.

T158 To put the **Tin** hat on something

1926 LO'Flaherty *Mr. Gilhooley* (L) 39: That puts the tin hat on it. I'll have to go home. **1929** LBrock *Murder* (NY) 156: That put the tin hat on my marrying. **1934** ERPunshon *Information* (B) 131: That puts the hat on it. **1939** LBrock *Four Fingers* (L) 104: [He], to use a favorite cliché . . . put the tin hat on it. Partridge 887.

T159 As dry as **Tinder**

1938 EHuxley *Murder* (NY) 214: It was dry as tinder. **1953** HMyers *O King* (NY) 144: As dry as tinder. **1954** ASeton *Katherine* (B) 368: Dry as tinder [*mouth*]. EAP T151.

T160 To be **Tinder** and flint

1961 MHHood *Drown* (NY) 108: A case of tinder and flint with [them]. Cf. Whiting F182: Fire and tinder.

T161 As fit as a **Tinker's** dog

1974 MKenyon *Sorry* (NY) 64: Fit as a tinker's dog all year. Cf. As fit as a Fiddler *above*.

T162 Not amount to a **Tinker's** dam(n)

1920 GBMcCutcheon *Anderson Crow* (NY) 142: Not amount to a tinker's dam. **1937**

DQBurleigh *Kristiana* (NY) 116: We haven't got evidence . . . to amount to a tinker in a court of law. Cf. Berrey 21.3; NED Tinker *sb.* 1d; Webster's New World Dict. (1959) Tinker's damn.

T163 Not care a **Tinker's** dam(n) (curse)

1908 JCLincoln *Cy Whittaker* (NY) 263: I don't know's I care a tinker's damn. **1909** MRRinehart *Man in Lower Ten* (NY 1947) 315: He didn't care a tinker's damn. **1926** LBrock *Colonel Gore* (NY) 96: Not care a tinker's curse. **1929** CGBowers *Tragic* (NY) 93: Cared not a tinker's dam. **1930** JGBrandon *Death* (L) 57: Cared not a tinker's damn. **1955** MErskine *Old Mrs.* (NY) 111: Not caring a tinker's cuss for his uncle. **1961** RVanGulik *Chinese Nail* (NY) 133: She doesn't care a tinker's curse. **1966** TLang *Darling* (NY) 101: Not to care a tinker's curse. TW 375; Webster's New World Dict. (1959) Tinker's damn. Cf. Not care a Damn *above*.

T164 Not care a **Tinker's** hoot in hell

1934 JGBrandon *One-Minute* (L) 53: I don't care a tinker's hoot in hell. Cf. Not give a Fiddler's fuck *above*.

T165 Not give a **Tinker's** dam(n) (curse)

1915 JLondon *Letters* ed KHendricks (NY 1965) 442: I wouldn't give a tinker's damn. **1931** ELoban *Calloused* (NY) 281: I don't give a tinker's dam. **1938** AGilbert *Treason* (L) 7: He doesn't give a tinker's curse. **1957** *Punch* 2/20 277: People . . . who actually did not give a tinker's dam. **1961** MHHood *Drown* (NY) 12: Not that I give a tinker's dam. **1969** JTrahey *Pecked* (Englewood, NJ) 91: Neither gave a tinker's damn. **1971** PTabor *Pauline's* (Louisville) 226: We don't give a tinker's damn. **1977** BShaw *Wreath* (NY) 17: Nobody'd give a tinker's damn about that. Cf. Berrey 21.3; NED Tinker *sb.* 1d; Webster's New World Dict. (1959) Tinker's damn. Cf. Not give a Damn *above*.

T166 Not have a **Tinker's** chance

1935 KMKnight *Death* (NY) 141: There wasn't a tinker's chance. **1951** PATaylor *Diplomatic* (NY) 58: He . . . wouldn't have a tinker's chance.

T167 Not matter a **Tinker's** curse (cuss, oath, dam(n))

1930 JGBrandon *Death* (L) 8: Don't matter a tinker's cuss. **1930** LBrock *Murder* (NY) 146: Not that it matters a tinker's oath. **1930** LMeynell *Mystery* (P) 111: It doesn't matter a tinker's curse. **1930** BFlynn *Orange* (L) 183: Don't matter a tinker's damn. **1932** LFrost *Murder* (NY) 192: Things no longer mattered a tinker's dam. **1934** JGBrandon *One-Minute* (L) 221: It doesn't matter a tinker's cuss. **1936** EShanks *Dark Green* (I) 170: Doesn't matter a tinker's curse. Webster's New World Dict. (1959) Tinker's damn. Cf. Berrey 21.3; NED Tinker *sb.* 1d. Cf. Not matter a Damn *above*.

T168 Not mean a **Tinker's** curse

1934 CDickson *Plague* (NY) 139: It doesn't mean a tinker's curse. Cf. Berrey 21.3; NED Tinker *sb.* 1d.

T169 Not worth a **Tinker's** dam(n) (cuss)

1908 MDPost *Corrector of Destinies* (NY) 25: Not worth a tinker's dam. **1929** CRJones *King* (NY) 99: My guess ... may not be worth a tinker's. **1930** HSKeeler *Fourth* (NY) 209: Wasn't worth a tinker's damn. **1932** MBurton *Death* (L) 227: Not ... worth a tinker's dam. **1935** VWilliams *Clue* (B) 145: Motive by itself isn't worth a tinker's cuss. **1938** WNMacartney *Fifty Years* (NY) 109: He isn't worth a tinker's dam—which, by the way, is not a cussword at all. **1940** AMorton *Blue Mask* (P) 314: Her evidence wouldn't be worth a tinker's cuss. **1956** *BangorDN* 6/16 11: Minnie Clough of Ellsworth points out that when you say someone "isn't worth a tinker's dam" you aren't swearing. "A tinker's dam" is a lump of clay used to mend tin pans. **1958** *Time* 4/28 6: *Time*, April 7, seeking to cure the curse of triteness in the expression "not worth a tinker's dam," substituted "Tinker's curse." Tinkers of olden times were a sober, industrious lot, little given to damning and cursing things. They repaired pots and pans, making a tiny mud dam about the hole to keep molten metal in place. *Roy E. Roddy*. Cf. Whiting NC 487; Webster's New World Dict. (1959) Tinker's damn. Cf. Not worth a Damn *above*.

T170 Not on your **Tintype**

1939 ATilton *Cold Steal* (NY) 203: Not, as my esteemed mother says, not on your tintype. **1965** SForbes *Relative* (NY) 181: Not on your tintype. **1966** The Gordons *Undercover Cat Prowls* (NY) 27: "You wouldn't believe me." "Not on your tintype." Wentworth 547; DA Tintype b.

T171 **Tit** for tat

1900 CFPidgin *Quincy A. Sawyer* (B) 322: Give tit for tat. **1906** JLondon *Letters* ed KHendricks (NY 1965) 215: It's tit for tat. **1921** JCLincoln *Galusha* (NY) 292: A game of tit-for-tat. **1930** WLewis *Apes* (NY 1932) 208: A preposterous tit-for-tat. **1949** WLewis *Letters* ed WKRose (L 1963) 487: A sort of inverted tit-for-tat. **1953** EBurns *Sex Life* (NY) 110: Tit for tat. **1956** *TLS* 12/7 734: Gives the bishop tit for tat. **1961** MInnes *Silence* (NY) 22: Tit for tat. **1968** JUpdike *Couples* (NY 1969) 382: This is just my tit for your tat. What's sauce for the goose, et cetera. **1975** RStout *Family* (NY) 110: Exchanging tits for tats with [him]. EAP T154; TW 375(1).

T172 As useless as **Tits** on a boar (bull) (*varied*)

1960 JWest *Taste* (NY) 11: That made as much sense to him as tits on a wild boar. **1961** RAKnowlton *Court* (L 1967) 126: About as useful as tits on a boar. **1971** RMStern *Murder* (NY) 84: A handgun was about as utilitarian as tits on a boar. **1982** SFXDean *Such Pretty* (NY) 151: Useless as tits on a bull. Taylor *Prov. Comp.* 84. Cf. Whiting NC 487: Titty(1).

T173 To be tough **Titty**

1957 JWhitehill *Able* (B) 10: You got big tough tit [*hard luck*]. **1962** JWoodford *Autobiography* (NY) 46: It was tough titty for Chicago. **1965** HKane *Midnight* (NY) 20: That's real tough titty. **1969** CMatthews *Dive* (LA) 68: It's tough titty. **1970** DClark *Deadly* (NY) 35: A slice of tough titty. Whiting NC 487(2).

T174 As cold (fat) as a **Toad**

1931 HReilly *Murder* (NY) 97: Fat as a toad. **1949** JDCarr *Below* (NY) 169: Whatever you touched was as cold as a toad. Cf. Wilstach 61: Frog.

T175 To swell (blow up) like a **Toad** (frog)

1957 THWhite *Master* (L) 253: He began to swell like a persecuted toad. **1960** JBWest *Taste* (NY) 119: He was swelling up like the proverbial frog. **1963** JBell *Room* (NY 1964) 23: He was all blown up with suspicion like a toad. TW 376(7); *Oxford* 794.

T176 A **Toad** under a harrow (*varied*)

1906 HNewbolt *Old Country* (L) 282: They would have gone right over us, like a harrow over a toad. **1910** EPhillpotts *Tales* (NY) 313: How do I live? Like a toad under a harrow. **1932** RCWoodthorpe *Public* (L) 17: Defects . . . well known to us poor toads under his harrow. **1934** TMundy *Tros* (NY) 297: He felt himself a toad beneath the harrow of misfortune. **1936** DLSayers *Gaudy* (NY) 337: The toad beneath the harrow knows where every separate toothpoint goes. **1958** PGWodehouse *Cocktail* (L) 83: Another toad beneath the harrow. **1968** GJones *History* (NY) 215: The cry of the toad under the harrow. **1968** WMuir *Belonging* (L) 140: I met it like a toad meeting the teeth of a harrow [*she fought back*]. **1970** LGrafftey-Smith *Bright* (L) 152: The toad beneath the harrow knows. **1974** PGWodehouse *Cat-Nappers* (NY) 118: You see before you a man who is as near to being what is known as a toad in Harrow as a man can be who was educated at Eton. EAP T160; TW 376(8).

T177 As crisp as **Toast**

1956 *TLS* 12/14 751: It is lively, eagerly written, and as crisp as toast. Whiting *NC* 487(1).

T178 As dry as **Toast**

1928 ABCox *Amateur* (NY) 150: Dry and warm as toast. **1958** *New Yorker* 2/8 23: Thus making them dry as toast. Whiting *NC* 487(2).

T179 As warm as (a) **Toast**; Toast-warm

1922 JJoyce *Ulysses* (NY 1934) 642: He would be . . . as warm as a toast on a trivet. **1928** GYoung *Treasure* (NY) 49: We'll leave

him warm as toast. **1934** KTKnoblock *Winter* (NY) 90: As warm as toast. **1937** KPKempton *Monday* (NY) 112: Warm as toast. **1943** EDaly *Nothing Can Rescue* (NY 1963) 16: Warm as toast. **1957** CLandon *Unseen* (NY) 180: As warm as toast. **1959** FPohl *Tomorrow* (NY) 52: A voice as warm as toast. **1965** JGaskell *Atlan* (NY 1968) 266: Warm as toast. **1967** LPDavies *Lampton* (NY) 169: Sound asleep and as warm as toast. **1967** RPeterson *Another View* (NY) 34: As toast-warm an apartment as might be desired. **1972** HTeichmann *Kaufman* (NY) 57: I'm warm as toast. TW 376; *Oxford* 827.

T180 To have (be had) on **Toast**

1913 JSFletcher *Secret* (L 1918) 212: In plain and vulgar language . . . Mrs. Euston had had Campenhaye on toast. **1919** HRHaggard *She and Allan* (NY 1921) 124: Believing that he had me on toast, to use a vulgar phrase. **1933** GDHCole *Lesson* (L) 50: You got him on toast. **1934** EPhillpotts *Mr. Digweed* (L) 88: He has you . . . on a piece of toast. **1938** JSStrange *Silent* (NY) 288: I had the fellow on toast. **1961** RGordon *Doctor on Toast* (NY). **1961** JSStrange *Eye* (NY) 16: The police had them on toast. **1970** EHahn *Times* (NY) 24: Mother had him on toast. Partridge 891.

T181 Here **Today** and gone tomorrow (*varied*)

1909 JCLincoln *Keziah* (NY) 187: He's here today and gone yesterday, as the Scriptur' says. **1909** MRRinehart *Man in Lower Ten* (NY 1947) 326: None of this "here today and gone the next" business. **1922** JJoyce *Ulysses* (NY 1934) 631: The here today and gone tomorrow type. **1929** MRJames *Letters to a Friend* ed GMcBryde (L 1956) 158: Here today and gone tomorrow. **1936** GDHCole *Last Will* (NY) 61: Here today and gone tomorrow, as the Book says. **1937** PATaylor *Figure* (NY) 98: Here, as the saying so cheerily goes, today. Gone tomorrow. **1947** GKersh *Prelude* (NY) 69: Here-today-and-gone-tomorrow easygoingness. **1949** MMuggeridge *Affairs* (L) 170: Here today and gone tomorrow. **1952** PGWodehouse *Angel* (NY) 25: We're here today and gone tomorrow, as the fellow said. **1956** SPalmer

Unhappy (NY 1957) 149: "Here today and gone tomorrow," . . . he quoted. **1958** TSouthern *Flash* (NY) 94: Here today, gone tomorrow. **1960** JLindsay *Writing* (L) 71: Here today and gone tomorrow, as the farmer said when he lost his piebald pig. **1960** RWatters *Murder* (Dublin) 289: Here today, in hell tomorrow. **1964** SRansome *Meet* (NY DBC) 92: Here today and gone tomorrow. **1970** EQueen *Last* (NY) 19: Here today and here tomorrow—maybe. EAP T165; TW 182: Here(1).

T182 Rich **Today**, poor tomorrow (*varied*)

1924 ADHSmith *Porto* (NY) 66: Rich today, poor tomorrow. **1934** KCStrahan *Hobgoblin* (I) 25: Turkey today and feathers tomorrow. You should have saved your money. **1953** AJLiebling *Honest* (NY) 111: Chicken today, feathers tomorrow. EAP T168. Cf. Whiting T351–5.

T183 **Today** mine, tomorrow thine (*varied*)

1928 VWilliams *Crouching* (B) 216: Our German proverb: "Heute mir, morgen Dir"—My turn today, yours tomorrow; 225. **1929** DLSayers *Lord Peter* (NY) 88: My turn tonight, yours tomorrow. **1931** PGWodehouse *Big Money* (NY) 237: You today, me tomorrow. **1934** BFlynn *Spiked* (P) 111: My turn to-day—yours tomorrow. **1954** M Coles *Brief* (NY) 116: "Today to thee, tomorrow to me," as the Spanish say. **1968** CWatson *Charity* (NY) 62: *Hodie mihi, cras tibi.* Whiting T349.

T184 Up **Today**, down tomorrow

1934 AMChase *Murder* (NY) 16: Today you're up; to-morrow you're down. **1952** PGWodehouse *Angel* (NY) 181: You're up today and down tomorrow. EAP T169.

T185 To tread on the **Toes** of someone (*varied*)

1922 ERPunshon *Bittermeads* (NY) 156: I'm treading on sore toes. **1926** HWade *Verdict* (L) 52: A man . . . is liable to tread on a few people's toes. **1945** RLockridge *Death in the Mind* (NY) 20: I am in no danger of treading on anyone's toes. **1951** MColes *Now* (NY) 76: Yeoman had trodden on someone's toes. **1953** HStone *Corpse* (NY) 3: It is wiser to avoid stepping on the toes

of the best people. **1966** RHardwick *Season* (NY) 65: He's stepped on a lot of toes. **1972** WJBurley *Guile* (NY) 10: We must not tread on anybody's toes. TW 376–7(2).

T186 To turn up one's **Toes**

1954 SDeLima *Carnival* (NY) 125: That's the place where Ed Miller turned up his toes. Whiting T360.

T187 As easy as **Toffee**

1930 MKennedy *Death* (L) 223: It was easy as toffee.

T188 Not for **Toffee**

1933 GDHCole *End* (L) 93: I can't bowl for toffee. **1955** CBrand *Tour* (NY) 206: He . . . can't swim for toffee. **1958** HCarmichael *Into* (NY) 46: She can't act for toffee. NED Suppl. Toffee 2; Partridge 893.

T189 To make a **Toil** of pleasure

1953 MNorton *Borrowers* (NY) 94: Make not a Toil of your Pleasure. EAP T170.

T190 **Tom**, Dick, and Harry (*varied*)

1911 CKSteele *Mansion* (NY) 176: Every Tom, Dick and Harry. **1920** EWallace *Three-Oaks* (L) 187: A Tom, or a Jim, or a Harry. **1921** JCLincoln *Galusha* (NY) 181: Every Tom, Dick, and Harry. **1922** JJoyce *Ulysses* (NY 1934) 634: Tom for and Dick and Harry against. **1925** RAFreeman *Red Thumb* (L) 154: Send . . . samples to Thomas, Richard and Henry. **1929** JSFletcher *Ransom* (NY) 3: Every Tom and Dick from Berwick to Penzance. **1930** JSFletcher *Green Rope* (L) 172: Every . . . Tom, Dick, Susan, Betty. **1937** FWCrofts *Found* (NY) 208: At the beck and call of any Tom, Dick or Harry. **1937** ECVivian *Tramp's* (L) 98: Every Tom, Dick, and Nebuchadnezzar. **1941** FWCrofts *Circumstantial* (NY) 44: Any Tom, Dick or Harriet. **1947** JIams *Body* (NY) 207: Every Tom, Dick, and ringtailed Harry. **1951** MInnes *Old Hall* (L 1961) 195: Every Tom, Dick, and Harry. **1955** ELacy *Best* (NY) 27: A Tom, Dick, or Harry Brown. **1957** DJEnright *Heaven* (L) 151: Brother Tom, Brother Dick, or Brother Harry. **1959** *TLS* 4/17 220: Every Tom, Dick and Mrs Harry. **1962** JLindsay *Fanfrolico* (L) 281: Dick and Tom and drunken Harry. **1962** JJMcPhaul *Dead-lines* (NY) 208: He was not going to sell to just any Tom, Dick or Herman. **1962** AM Stein *Home* (NY) 45: Every Tom, Dick and Texan. **1970** EHahn *Times* (NY) 29: Tom, Dick, or Mary. **1970** NMonsarrat *Breaking* (L) 537: "No, no!" said Goldwyn, "Every Tom, Dick and Harry is called Joe!" EAP T172; Brunvand 143. Cf. Brown *above*.

T191 **Tom Tiddler's** ground (*varied*)

1916 NDouglas *London Street Games* (L) 99: I'm on old Tom Tiddler's ground, Picking up gold and silver. **1927** RPertwee *Interference* (NY) 43: It's a kind of Tom Tiddler's ground. **1930** FDBurdett *Odyssey* (L) 185: I called that place Tom Tiddler's ground. **1931** LPowys *Pagan's* (NY) 112: So perilous a game of Tom Tiddler's ground. **1933** JJConnington *Tom Tiddler's Island* (L 1937). **1935** VMacClure *Death* (P) 17: She could think of the stage only as a sort of Tom Tiddler's ground—a field for the picking up of easy money. **1945** ACampbell *With Bated* (NY) 169: She warned you off Tom Tiddler's ground [*a chance for money*]. **1957** NMitford *Voltaire* (L) 25: His perpetual game of Tom Tiddler's ground with the government. **1969** JLunt *Bokhara* (L) 154: A Tom Tiddler's ground for raiding parties. *Oxford* 828–9.

T192 As red as a **Tomato**

1935 Xantippe *Death* (NY) 155: His face was as red as a tomato. **1959** MScherf *Never Turn* (NY) 16: Hugh got as red as a tomato. EAP T174.

T193 As black as a (the) **Tomb**

1958 TBrooke *Under* (NY) 27: Black as a tomb. **1964** LPayne *Deep* (L) 229: The place was as black as the tomb. Cf. Grave *above*.

T194 As cold as a (the) **Tomb**

1941 IAlexander *Revenge* (NY) 97: It was cold as a tomb. **1956** HKubly *Easter* (NY) 109: Each as cold as a tomb. **1959** AGilbert *Death* (NY) 107: [The] place was as cold as a tomb. **1965** EHemingway *Moveable* (NY) 166: As cold as the tomb. **1968** HWAllen *Genesis* (NY 1970) 16: Cold and cheerless as the tomb. Whiting *NC* 487; Taylor *Western Folklore* 17(1958) 19(1). Cf. Grave *above*.

T195 As dark as a (the) **Tomb** (*varied*)

1911 JCLincoln *Woman-Haters* (NY) 330: As dark as a tomb. **1928** AWUpfield *Lure* (NY 1965) 180: As dark as the tomb. **1932** HLandon *Owl's* (L) 98: The house was as dark and silent as a Pharoah's tomb. Cf. Grave *above*.

T196 As dead as the (a) **Tomb**(stone)

1930 JRussell *Cops* (NY) 233: The house was as dead as the tomb. **1935** CMRussell *Murder* (NY) 81: As dead as a tomb. **1952** MColes *Night* (NY) 128: Dead as a tombstone. **1960** RWilson *Thirty Day* (NY) 5: It's dead as a tomb. Cf. Morgue *above*.

T197 As desolate as a (the) **Tomb**

1913 ERBurroughs *Thavia* (NY 1963) 65: As deserted as the tomb. **1941** AAFair *Spill* (NY) 244: The whole place was . . . desolate as a tomb. Wilstach 90.

T198 As gloomy as a **Tomb**

1962 DHonig *No Song* (L) 95: He went on . . . gloomy as a tomb. Cf. Clark 213: Graveyard.

T199 As quiet as the (a) **Tomb**

1911 CKSteele *Mansion* (NY) 24: All was quiet as the tomb. **1933** EBBlack *Ravenelle* (NY) 146: As quiet as a tomb. **1955** FCDavis *Night* (NY) 50: Quiet as a tomb. **1966** TWalsh *Resurrection* (NY) 107: As quiet as the tomb. **1971** ELathen *Longer* (NY) 150: Quiet as a tomb. **1972** SAngus *Arson* (NY) 9: It was quiet as a tomb. Taylor *Western Folklore* 17(1958) 19(3). Cf. Clark 218: Cemetery. Cf. Grave, Morgue *above*.

T200 As safe as the **Tomb**

1930 FRyerson *Seven* (L) 136: He's safe as the tomb [*secretive*]. Cf. Grave *above*.

T201 As silent as a (the, any) **Tomb**; Tomb-silent

1912 ERBurroughs *Gods of Mars* (NY 1963) 85: All was silent as the tomb. **1923** CJDutton *Shadow* (NY) 178: As silent as the proverbial tomb. **1934** SPalmer *Murder* (L) 14: The deserted schoolroom was less silent than the proverbial tomb. **1956** SPalmer *Unhappy* (NY 1957) 72: It was as silent as the proverbial tomb. **1957** *New Yorker* 10/

12 107: Silent as any tomb. **1957** GMal-colm-Smith *Trouble* (NY) 40: Silent as the tomb. **1958** HAlpert *Summer* (L) 247: I'll be silent as a tomb. **1965** PAnderson *Star* (NY) 60: The house was grown tomb silent. **1973** ACClark *Rendezvous* (NY) 22: Rama was silent as a tomb. EAP T175; Brunvand 143(1); Taylor *Western Folklore* 17(1958) 19(4). Cf. Grave *above*.

T202 As soundless as a **Tomb**

1961 MInnes *Silence* (NY) 187: As soundless as the tomb. Wilstach 376.

T203 As still as a (the) **Tomb**

1911 CKSteele *Mansion* (NY) 102: Still as a tomb. **1925** JYBrandon *Bond* (L) 262: A stillness which might well have been called that of the tomb. **1937** AGilbert *Murder* (L) 40: The house was as still as the proverbial tomb. **1970** AHalper *Good-bye* (C) 72: It's as still as a tomb. Brunvand 143(2). Cf. Grave *above*.

T204 Let **Tomorrow** take care of itself

1908 JCLincoln *Cy Whittaker* (NY) 210: There's a proverb . . . about lettin' to-morrow take care of itself. **1927** CBStilson *Seven* (NY) 37: Let tomorrow take care of itself. **1955** STRoy *Half-way* (L) 31: Let tomorrow take care of itself. **1959** RMStern *Bright* (NY) 96: Let tomorrow take care of itself.

T205 Never put off till **Tomorrow** what can be done today (*varied*)

1908 JCLincoln *Cy Whittaker* (NY) 293: Never put off till to-morrow what you can do today. **1922** JJoyce *Ulysses* (NY 1934) 501: Never put on you tomorrow what you can wear today. **1925** FBeeding *Seven* (B) 21: The habit . . . of putting off till tomorrow the things which cannot be done today. **1932** PMacDonald *Rope* (L) 264: Never put off tomorrow . . . what you can do today. **1935** MCRichings *Men Loved* (L) 119: Fools say the morrow—wise men work today. **1936** JBude *Sussex* (L) 119: Never do today what you can put off till tomorrow. **1939** MHealy *Old Munster* (L) 241: Always put off till tomorrow what need not be done today. **1950** CDickson *Night* (NY) 232: Never put off until tomorrow, a stitch in time, and so on. **1952** KFCrossen *Future*

(NY) 105: Never put off to tomorrow what you can do today. **1956** CCockburn *In Time* (L) 219: The axiom that one should never put off till tomorrow what one might possibly be able to do the month after next. **1960** DHayles *Comedy* (L) 56: Never put off till tomorrow what you can do today. **1961** RAHeinlein *6XH* (NY) 137: Never Do Yesterday What Should Be Done Tomorrow. **1965** JTurner *Blue* (L 1967) 34: Mottoes, such as "Put off today what you can do tomorrow." **1977** RRendell *Demon* (NY) 21: Never put off till tomorrow what you can do today. EAP T176; TW 377–8.

T206 **Tomorrow** is another (a new) day (*varied*)

1913 EDBiggers *Seven Keys* (I) 179: Tomorrow is another day. **1922** VBridges *Greensea* (NY) 228: Well, as the Arabs say, "Tomorrow is also a day." **1922** JJoyce *Ulysses* (NY 1934) 398: Tomorrow will be a new day. 504: But tomorrow is a new day will be. **1931** MPlum *Dead Man's* (NY) 150: Tomorrow's another day. **1934** HReilly *McKee* (NY) 256: To-morrow will be a new day. **1936** TDowning *Unconquered Sisters* (NY) 236: The Mexicans have a saying . . . "Tomorrow is another day." **1937** GDilnot *Murder* (L) 242: But there's always a new day. **1938** AGilbert *Treason* (L) 40: Tomorrow is also a day, as they say. **1948** CBush *Curious* (NY) 184: Tomorrow was another day. **1950** SPalmer *Monkey* (NY) 120: Tomorrow is another day. **1956** IShaw *Lucy* (NY) 301: Tomorrow's another day. **1961** CDBurton *Long* (NY) 88: Tomorrow was another day. **1969** RReed *Conversations* (NY) 134: Tomorrow is another day. **1973** DShannon *No Holiday* (NY) 91: Tomorrow is also a day. *Oxford* 829: A new day.

T207 **Tomorrow** never comes

1923 DCScott *Witching* (Toronto) 224: The proverbial tomorrow . . . never came. **1925** EDBiggers *House* (NY) 2: Tomorrow never comes. **1932** VWilliams *Death* (B) 303: Tomorrow never comes. **1940** HReilly *Murder in* (NY) 81: Tomorrow, the day that never came. **1959** RMStern *Bright* (NY) 98: Tomorrow never comes. **1963** HWaugh *Prisoner's* (NY DBC) 14: And, of course, tomorrow never comes. **1972** Bryher *Days* (NY) 170: The wartime saying, "Tomorrow never comes." EAP T177.

T208 To come down on (fall) like a **Ton** of bricks (*varied*)

1908 JCLincoln *Cy Whittaker* (NY) 163: You're down on Phœbe as a thousand of brick. **1910** JCLincoln *Depot Master* (NY) 228: Come down on her like a scow load of brick. **1920** GBMcCutcheon *Anderson Crow* (NY) 155: He . . . set down like ton of bricks. **1928** RHWatkins *Master* (NY) 150: He fell—I believe the phrase is—like a ton of bricks. **1929** PRShore *Bolt* (NY) 117: I fell and made a noise like a ton of bricks. **1930** RWallace *Seven Men* (NY) 196: He's fallen for me like a ton o' brick. **1931** MAllingham *Police* (NY) 27: Julia was down on her like a ton of bricks. **1933** MMPropper *Murder* (L) 124: Coming down on you like a ton of bricks. **1937** ABCaldwell *No Tears* (NY) 120: He had fallen for her like a ton of bricks. **1947** PMcGerr *Pick* (NY) 142: Whipple went down like a ton of bricks. **1948** CBush *Curious* (NY) 213: The girl fell for him like a ton of bricks. **1956** *BHerald* 8/3 2: The sight of the British army at Suez lies like a ton of bricks on the American conscience. **1956** SWTaylor *I Have* (NY) 23: Bring the law down onto them like a ton of bricks. **1959** *NYTimes* 7/26 54: People come down on me like a ton of bricks. **1959** WHMurray *Appointment* (NY) 79: It's falling like a ton of bricks [*barometer*]. **1964** LPayne *Deep* (L) 93: Jameson fell for it . . . like a ton of bricks. **1973** CAird *His Burial* (NY) 39: [He] would have been down on us like a ton of bricks. **1973** ELopez *Seven* (NY) 13: That hit me like a ton of shit. **1977** HDolson *Beauty* (P) 102: She fell like a ton of hot bricks. **1981** WLDeAndrea *Killed* (NY) 106: The kick hit the door to Channel 10 like the proverbial ton of bricks. TW 43: Brick(6); Taylor *Prov. Comp.* 83.

T209 A still **Tongue** makes a wise head (*varied*)

1925 BAtkey *Pyramid* (NY) 71: A still tongue in a cool head. **1931** RAFreeman *Mr Pottermack* (L) 248: A still tongue shows a wise head. **1933** NBrady *Fair Murder* (L) 187: A still tongue makes a wise head. **1933** PMcGuire *Death* (NY) 306: A still tongue in the head is worth a Scottish moor full of birds. **1935** DHume *Murders* (L) 141: A still tongue will save a foolish head. **1935** JVTurner *Death* (L) 93: A still tongue may make a sore head. **1940** JRhode *Murder at* (L) 180: He . . . said something about a still tongue making no enemies. EAP T178: Close.

T210 To have a **Tongue** hung in the middle *etc.* (*varied*)

1900 CFPidgin *Quincy A. Sawyer* (B) 69: With a tongue hung in the middle and running at both ends. **1909** JCLincoln *Keziah* (NY) 187: My tongue was loose at both ends and hung in the middle. **1928** JJConnington *Tragedy* (B) 122: A beggar with a tongue hinged in the middle so that he can talk with both ends at once. **1932** HFootner *Dead Man's* (NY) 7: Your tongue is hung in the middle and wags at both ends. **1938** RMBaker *Death* (NY) 60: She's got a tongue that's hung in the middle and wags at both ends. **1940** GStockwell *Candy* (NY) 181: My tongue just kind of waggles at both ends. **1952** KMKnight *Death Goes* (NY) 74: No wonder his tongue hangs at both ends. **1953** BCClough *Grandma* (Portland, Me.) 50: Jane's tongue was hung in the middle and moved both ways. **1955** DMDisney *Room* (NY) 66: That tongue of yours—hung in the middle and loose on both ends. **1968** EBuckler *Ox Bells* (NY) 163: A tongue that hung in the middle and flapped on both ends. **1968** JCFurnas *Lightfoot* (NY) 135: Tongue hung in the middle and both ends wagging. **1972** TNScortia *Artery* (NY) 12: This smelling pig has a tongue that wags at both ends. EAP T180.

T211 To have one's **Tongue** in his cheek

1922 JJoyce *Ulysses* (NY 1934) 639: With her tongue in her fair cheek. **1924** LSpringfield *Some Piquant* (L) 166: He wrote with his tongue in his cheek. **1932** JHWallis *Capital* (NY) 154: I trust you to keep your tongue in cheek. **1933** ATSheppard *Rosee* (L) 23: Her tongue, as the saying went, in her cheek. **1942** WIrish *Phantom* (NY 1957)

246: Your tongue in your cheek, and my heart in my mouth. **1946** LCores *Let's Kill George* (NY) 110: You can't be a bootlicker with your tongue in your cheek. **1956** CCockburn *In Time* (L) 208: Journalists who wrote with their tongue in their cheek. **1958** WDHassett *Off the Record* (New Brunswick, NJ) 293: He had his tongue in his cheek. **1971** RFDelderfield *For My* (NY) 236: Disraeli . . . never once took his tongue from his cheek. **1972** SBirmingham *Late John* (P) 120: Written mostly with tongue in cheek. Whiting *NC* 488(2).

T212 To speak with a forked **Tongue**
1974 WCAnderson *Damp* (NY) 12: They speak with forked tongue. Brunvand 144(1); DA Forked 2(9).

T213 The **Tongue** returns to the aching tooth
1941 CMRussell *Dreadful* (NY) 35: She went over and over the painful circumstances as a tongue returns to worry and press an aching tooth. **1949** WKrasner *Walk* (NY) 20: The tongue always returns to the sore tooth. **1981** WLDeAndrea *Killed* (NY) 144: After that, I returned like a tongue to an aching tooth, to Studio J. EAP T189.

T214 To play with edged **Tools**
1904 SArmitage-Smith *John of Gaunt* (L) 291: Playing with edged tools. **1927** LTracy *Mysterious* (NY) 248: Playing with edged tools. **1933** AJRees *Aldringham* (NY) 259: Not the first man who, playing with edged tools, had been hurt in consequence. **1963** JIMStewart *Last* (NY) 264: You're playing with edged tools. EAP T190.

T215 In spite of one's **Teeth**
1928 LStrachey *Elizabeth* (L) 200: In spite of her brother's teeth. EAP T194; TW 378(3).

T216 To be armed (dressed) to the **Teeth**
1932 GMitchell *Saltmarsh* (L) 204: Armed to the teeth. **1937** GGoodchild *Operator* (L) 30: Europe is armed to the teeth. **1954** AW Barkley *That Reminds* (NY) 49: I was dressed to the teeth for the event. **1959** PQuentin *Shadow* (NY) 5: She'll be dressed to the teeth. Whiting T407.

T217 To be fed to the (eye, back) **Teeth**
1925 JGBrandon *Bond* (L) 41: He was fed up to the eye-teeth with her. **1930** AChristie *Murder* (NY) 4: Fed to the teeth with him. **1934** GHeyer *Unfinished* (L) 255: I'm fed to the back teeth. **1951** PMcGerr *Death in* (NY) 68: I was fed to the teeth. **1960** AWUpfield *Valley* (NY DBC) 34: I'm fed to the back teeth. **1963** IFleming *On Her* (L) 21: He was fed to the teeth. **1967** RRendell *New Lease* (NY) 104: I am fed to my back teeth. Partridge 269: Fed.

T218 To be like pulling **Teeth** (*varied*)
1931 PATaylor *Cape Cod* (NY 1971) 123: Pullin' teeth is easier than gettin' information out of you. **1934** MKennedy *Corpse* (L) 278: It was like drawing an eye-tooth. **1959** HNielsen *Fifth* (NY DBC) 106: It's like pulling teeth to get anything out of him. **1966** ELinington *Date* (NY) 150: It was a little like pulling teeth [*getting a statement*]. **1970** JAGraham *Something* (B) 173: It was like pulling teeth [*to get information*]. TW 378(1).

T219 To be long in the **Tooth**
1922 JJoyce *Ulysses* (NY 1934) 541: Long in the tooth and superfluous hairs. **1931** PMacDonald *Crime* (NY) 176: She's now beginning to get long in the tooth. **1939** JDCarr *Problem* (B 1948) 149: He said "long in the tooth." **1952** KMKnight *Death Goes* (NY) 10: A bit long in the tooth—too thin—bitchy. **1960** JSymons *Progress* (L) 38: A bit long in the tooth. **1964** WTrevor *Old Boys* (NY) 118: Our own doctor is long in the tooth. **1971** PAlding *Despite* (NY) 146: He must be getting long in the tooth. **1978** DNDurant *Bess* (NY) 46: At twenty-one Ann was comparatively long in the tooth. Partridge 492: Long.

T220 To fight (*etc.*) **Tooth** and nail
1909 JCLincoln *Keziah* (NY) 314: Fight tooth and nail. **1920** GBMcCutcheon *Anderson Crow* (NY) 188: Working tooth and nail for Germany. **1932** EDBiggers *Keeper* (L) 121: Battle him tooth and nail. **1934** EQueen *Adventures* (NY) 32: Fought tooth and nail. **1943** EDaly *Nothing Can Rescue* (NY 1963) 9: She's been at it [*writing a novel*] tooth and nail. **1945** JSymons *Immaterial* (L

1954) 79: He would fight a divorce tooth and nail. **1956** PDeVries *Comfort* (B) 62: I had once fought tooth and nail. **1957** EM Butler *Heine* (NY) 141: Fell on him tooth and nail. **1958** *BHerald* 5/18 V 3: Battling pay television tooth and nail. **1959** HPentecost *Lonely* (NY) 68: He's a tooth-and-nail fighter. **1968** LDurrell *Tunc* (NY) 259: He had to fight tooth and nail. EAP T201; TW 378–9(9).

T221   To have a sweet Tooth (*varied*)
1930 MDalton *Body* (NY) 22: Got a sweet tooth. **1932** JJConnington *Castleford* (B) 56: I had a sweet tooth. **1940** RPenny *Sweet Poison* (L) 28: The old wretch has a sweet tooth. **1960** CBeaton *My Royal* (NY) 16: We were all sweet tooths. **1961** ATCurtis *Poacher's* (L) 36: Like most boys, my tooth was sweet. **1966** MFrome *Strangers* (NY) 258: To satisfy his sweet tooth. **1970** EHahn *Times* (NY) 188: My sweet tooth was gone at last. **1975** AChristie *Curtain* (NY) 232: He has a sweet tooth. EAP T197; TW 378(5).

T222   To have one's back Teeth floating
1934 JO'Hara *Appointment* (NY) 271: Tell you the truth, my back teeth are floating. **1953** EPaul *Waylaid* (NY) 45: So full of Haig and Haig his back teeth would be floating. **1960** CBrossard *Double* (NY) 49: This goddamn stuff is floating my back teeth. DARE i 123: Back teeth; Berrey 124.5. Cf. Partridge 24: Back-teeth, 870: Tipsy.

T223   To lie in (through) one's Teeth
1924 EWallace *Green* (B) 215: You lie in your teeth. **1936** JDCarr *Arabian* (NY) 221: You lie in your teeth. **1952** FVWMason *Himalayan* (NY 1953) 242: You lie in your teeth. **1958** *BHerald* 2/14 1: Schwartz is a g—d—liar. He is lying in his teeth. **1959** LWhite *Meriweather* (NY) 165: Your client has been lying through his teeth. **1962** FCrane *Amber* (NY) 140: [She] was lying through her teeth. **1966** EMcBain *Eighty* (NY) 103: Maria had lied in her teeth. **1968** HWaugh *Con* (NY) 102: She was lying through her teeth. **1972** JDCarr *Hungry* (NY) 54: I lied in my teeth. Whiting T414.

T224   To pay through the Teeth
1929 KCStrahan *Footprints* (NY) 311: Paid through the teeth. **1941** FCrane *Turquoise* (P) 203: Make you pay for it through your teeth. **1960** FCrane *Death-Wish* (NY DBC) 149: Virginia has ... paid through her teeth for years. Cf. To pay through the Nose *above*.

T225   To throw in one's Teeth
1924 JSFletcher *Time-Worn* (NY) 181: If you are going to throw that in my teeth. EAP T195; TW 378(2).

T226   As skinny as a Toothpick
1952 RFenisong *Deadlock* (NY) 41: Skinny as a toothpick. Taylor *Prov. Comp.* 73. Cf. Taylor *Western Folklore* 17(1958) 20: Thin.

T227   From Top to bottom
1930 VLoder *Shop* (L) 79: Discussing him from top to bottom. **1934** NBrady *Ebenezer* (L) 109: I can't make top nor bottom of his behavior. EAP T202. Cf. next entry.

T228   From Top to toe
1930 EFBenson *As We Were* (NY) 153: From top to toe. **1939** CSaxby *Death Cuts* (NY) 146: "You know him?" "Top to toe and inside out." **1945** CEVulliamy *Edwin* (L) 171: From his top to his little toe. **1957** AECoppard *It's Me* (L) 135: A radical from top to toe. **1969** RHarris *Wicked* (NY) 8: A pale fawn-colored child from top to toe. EAP T203; TW 379(1). Cf. Crown *above*.

T229   To be (sit, feel, etc.) on Top of the world
1923 ORCohen *Jim Hanvey* (NY) 50: Sittin' on top of the world. **1933** JVTurner *Amos* (L) 214: Lord Belden is not ... sitting on top of the world. **1939** MMGoldsmith *Detour* (L) 241: We'll be sitting on top of the world. **1948** LFord *Devil's* (NY) 125: On top of the world. **1953** CSWebb *Wanderer* (L) 60: I felt on top of the world. **1957** JYork *Come Here* (NY) 91: She felt on top of the world. **1961** DLMathews *Very Welcome* (NY DBC) 139: I've been on top of the world all day. **1964** JJMarric *Gideon's Lot* (NY) 121: I ought to be feeling on top of the world. **1967** DShannon *Rain* (NY) 161: She was right on top of the world, having a ball.

1968 JRoffman *Grave* (NY) 113: You look on top of the world. **1970** JCreasey *Part* (NY) 115: Richard's on top of the world. **1976** JJMarric *Gideon's Drive* (NY) 6: She was on top of the world. Partridge 900.

T230   To blow one's **Top**

1940 KSteel *Dead of Night* (B) 239: He blew his top at you. **1948** DCDisney *Explosion* (NY DBC) 150: Fisher was about to blow his top. **1951** EQueen *Origin* (B) 147: I predicted he'd blow his top. **1956** SPalmer *Unhappy* (NY 1957) 55: Vonny started to blow his top, as the saying goes. **1960** RMacdonald *Ferguson* (NY) 31: Don't blow your top. **1964** ESGardner *Daring* (NY) 173: She blew her top. **1975** TWells *Hark* (NY) 77: Make him blow his top. Wentworth 46–7.

T231   To talk off the **Top** of one's head

1960 BKendrick *Aluminum* (NY DBC) 108: I'm talking off the top of my head.

T232   To run like a **Top**

1959 DMarkson *Epitaph* (NY) 88: Runs like a top [*a car*]. **1978** WKWren *Nothing's* (NY) 74: She [*an auto*] runs like a top.

T233   To sleep like a **Top**

1911 JCLincoln *Woman-Haters* (NY) 200: Slept like a top. **1922** JJoyce *Ulysses* (NY 1934) 726: Fell asleep as sound as a top. **1924** LTracy *Token* (NY) 236: Slept like a top. **1930** BFlynn *Creeping* (L) 131: I slept like the proverbial old peg, whip or hunting—whichever you like to put your shirt on. **1932** WBMFerguson *Murder* (NY) 235: Sleeping . . . like a hummin' top. **1937** GGoodchild *Operator* (L) 285: Adams slept like a top. **1956** CJay *Brink* (L 1962) 132: She slept like a top. **1962** HEBates *Golden* (L) 109: Slept like a top. **1968** JCFurnas *Lightfoot* (NY) 198: Slept like a top. **1971** GHCoxe *Fenner* (NY) 115: Sleep . . . like a top . . . whatever that means. EAP T205; Brunvand 144.

T234   To spin like a **Top**

1936 LRGribble *Malverne* (L) 32: My head's spinning like a top. TW 379(3).

T235   (Not) out of the **Top drawer**

1930 MMott-Smith *Africa* (NY) 255: As the Irish say . . . Madame may not have come out of the top drawer. **1932** HCBailey *Red Castle* (NY) 37: Prior isn't out of the top drawer. **1932** FBeeding *Take It* (B) 197: Right out of the top drawer. **1932** DLSayers *Have* (NY) 296: Olga . . . is not precisely out of the top-drawer, as my mother would say. **1937** CGordon *Garden* (NY) 167: Whether or not you came, as the Negroes said, "Out of the top drawer." **1943** WLewis *Letters* ed WKRose (L 1963) 345: Not out of the top drawer. **1948** ESherry *Sudden* (NY) 46: [He's] right out of the top drawer. **1951** ESHolding *Too Many* (NY) 71: She's not quite out of the top drawer. **1957** *Punch* 7/24 105: Many of the pictures were not out of the top drawer. **1961** DLMoore *Late Lord* (L) 415: How far they were from being out of the top drawer. **1967** ESalter *Last Years* (L) 36: Not out of the top drawer. **1970** HBlyth *Skittles* (L) 24: She was not out of the top drawer. **1971** PAlding *Despite* (NY) 50: Out of the very top drawer. Partridge 899; Wentworth 551.

T236   As hot as **Tophet**

1931 ALivingston *In Cold* (I) 104: It's hot as tophet. Taylor *Western Folklore* 17(1958) 20.

T237   **Topsy** just growed

1952 AGilbert *Mr. Crook* (NY DBC) 167: She wasn't like Uncle Tom's Topsy, who just growed. **1954** AWBarkley *That Reminds* (NY) 277: So, like Topsey, it just "grew and grew." **1960** COliver *Unearthly* (NY) 42: Like Topsy . . . it just growed. **1971** CAird *Late* (NY) 54: Luston—like Topsy—had just growed. **1975** HPentecost *Time* (NY) 50: Those pickets . . . didn't just grow like Topsy. Taylor *Prov. Comp.* 83.

T238   **Touch** and go

1914 HHMunro *Beasts* (NY 1928) 193: It was touch and go. **1924** LSpringfield *Some* (L) 127: It was touch-and-go. **1930** WLewis *Apes* (NY 1932) 470: That had been touch and go. **1939** GDHCole *Off with* (NY) 15: It'll be touch and go with him. **1953** EQueen *Scarlet* (B) 200: It was touch and go. **1956** NMarsh *Death* (B) 184: Touch and go. **1970** REaston *Max* (Norman, Okla.) 174: It was touch and go. **1970** FSteegmuller *Cocteau* (B) 348: It was touch and go. EAP T211.

T239   A **Touch** (dash, lick) of the tarbrush
1922 VSutphen *In Jeopardy* (NY) 159: The dash of the tar-brush. **1928** AGMacleod *Marloe* (NY) 8: Touch of the tarbrush in some long-gone generation. **1931** MAllingham *Police* (NY) 293: A touch of the tarbrush. **1934** GOrwell *Burmese* (NY) 40: A lick of the tarbrush. **1946** DWilson *Make with the Brains* (NY) 30: She had a touch of the tarbrush. **1964** RAHeinlein *Farnham's* (NY 1965) 229: Not just a touch of the tarbrush but practically the whole tar barrel. **1971** BWAldiss *Soldier* (L) 86: There's a touch of the tarbrush about you. TW 366: Tarbrush.

T240   As near as **Toucher**
1931 JSFletcher *Malvery* (L) 192: It 'ud be nine o'clock, as near as a toucher. Partridge 903.

T241   To throw (chuck, toss) in the **Towel**
1930 GMitchell *Mystery* (NY) 130: Rupert had chucked in the towel [*died*]. **1953** VPJohns *Murder* (NY 1962) 155: She finally threw in the towel. **1955** EJKahn *Merry* (NY) 262: Throw in the towel. **1957** *BHerald* 11/6 5: Spencer tossed in the towel before all of the . . . votes were counted. **1964** HPentecost *Shape* (NY DBC) 109: We might just as well throw in the towel. **1969** JA Graham *Arthur* (NY) 24: She had thrown in the towel. **1973** JPorter *It's Murder* (NY) 147: Dover had already chucked the towel in. Wentworth 543: Throw in. Cf. *Sponge above.*

T242   To paint the **Town** red (*varied*)
1922 JJoyce *Ulysses* (NY 1934) 623: He . . . often painted the town tolerably pink. **c1926** JBaikie *Egyptian Papyri* (L) 282: Set out to paint the town red. **1932** MThynne *Murder* (NY) 230: Painted the town red. **1937** JPMarquand *Late George* (B) 287: To see the town and even paint it red a little. **1941** MBardon *Murder Does* (NY) 75: You paint the town red. **1955** WSloane *Stories*

(L) 370: Liberty to paint the town red. **1962** EFRussell *Great* (NY) 150: Liberty to paint the town red. **1965** MBradbury *Stepping* (L) 56: Paint the town red, as is said. TW 274: Paint(1).

T243   What the whole **Town** is saying cannot be wrong
1940 HFootner *Sinfully* (L) 103: What the whole town is saying can't be wrong. Cf. EAP E80, M82.

T244   To kick over the **Traces**
1931 LHollingworth *Death* (L) 154: To kick over the traces. **1937** JRhode *Death on the Board* (L) 58: Kick over the traces. **1961** RSKnowlton *Court* (L 1967) 54: Kicking over the traces. **1964** HWaugh *Missing* (NY) 132: He doesn't want her to kick over the traces. **1970** AWRaitt *Prosper* (L) 27: To kick over the traces. TW 380; Brunvand 144; *Oxford* 422: Kick.

T245   **Translator,** traitor
1938 VLoder *Wolf* (L) 190: *Traduttore, traditore* . . . The Italian proverb . . . Translator, traitor. *Oxford* 835.

T246   As sharp as a **Trap**
1943 HLMencken *Heathen Days* (NY) 15: He was as sharp as a trap. Wilstach 342: Steel trap.

T247   As tight as a **Trap**
1928 GGardiner *At the House* (NY) 152: Mouth shut tight as a trap. **1972** PDJames *Unsuitable* (NY) 131: Mouth tight as a trap.

T248   To shut up like a **Trap**
1934 VGielgud *Death* (L) 148: Shut up like a trap. **1938** HFootner *Murder* (L) 120: Jule shut up like a trap. **1940** MFitt *Death Starts* (L) 218: Warner's mouth shut like a trap. **1958** HKuttner *Murder* (NY) 138: My mind—it shuts up like a trap. Cf. Steel trap *above.*

T249   **Travel** is broadening (*varied*)
1948 LSdeCamp *Divide* (NY 1964) 14: Travel's broadening, they say. **1952** TClaymore *Reunion* (NY 1955) 186: They say travel broadens the mind. **1958** MKenton *Candy* (NY 1965) 7: They say travel broadens one. **1969** ELathen *When* (NY) 181:

Travel . . . can broaden only so many minds.

T250   Travelers' tales (varied)
1923 ECVivian *City* (NY) 38: Travellers' tales. **1930** HCMcNeile *Guardians* (NY) 137: Those who go down to the sea in ships are proverbially spinners of tall tales. **1930** EWallace *Mr. Reeder* (NY) 15: A myth, a mariner's tale. **1931** RAFreeman *Dr. Thorndyke's* (NY) 212: A mere traveller's tale. **1938** SHorler *Gentleman* (NY) 72: The usual kind of traveller's yarns. **1946** MInnes *Unsuspected* (NY) 301: Always a bit of exaggeration in travellers' tales. **1963** RAHeinlein *Glory* (NY) 128: Most people don't believe travellers' tales. **1964** BWAldiss *Greybeard* (L) 165: The tales of travellers, lies though they generally are. **1969** JLunt *Bokhara* (L) 79: Just another traveller's tale. **1971** CBeaton *My Bolivian* (L) 127: To re-tell her travellers' tales. Cf. EAP T226.

T251   As clear as thick Treacle
1939 AWebb *Mr Pendlebury Makes* (L) 178: It's about as clear as thick treacle. Cf. As clear as Mud *above*.

T252   As easy as taking Treacle from a bear's mouth
1927 GDilnot *Lazy* (B) 25: About as easy as taking treacle from a bear's mouth. Cf. To get Butter *above*.

T253   Where your Treasure is etc.
1932 CBush *Unfortunate* (L) 164: Where your treasure is, you know. **1958** DG Browne *Death* (L) 107: Where your treasure is, there will your heart be also. **1963** RNathan *Devil* (NY) 186: Where your treasure is, there will your heart be also. **1968** HEL Mellersh *FitzRoy* (NY) 164: Where your treasure is, there will your heart be also. **1971** PMHubbard *Dancing* (NY) 16: Where your treasure is there shall your heart be also. EAP T230; TW 381.

T254   As dumb as a Tree
1957 MProcter *Midnight* (NY) 55: As dumb as trees. Wilstach 106.

T255   As still as a Tree
1936 NBlake *Thou Shell of* (L) 236: Still as a tree [*a girl*]. Wilstach 389: The stump of a tree.

T256   As straight as a Tree
1931 AAbbot *Night Club Lady* (NY) 228: Straight as a tree. Wilstach 393: The palm tree.

T257   Go climb a Tree
1933 JWVandercook *Murder* (NY) 297: Go climb a tree. **1935** CRawson *Footprints* (L) 99: If he didn't like it he could go climb a tree. **1940** JPPhilips *Murder in Marble* (NY) 160: You can go climb a tree for it. **1952** KMKnight *Valse* (NY) 165: Hugo told him to go climb a tree.

T258   Not grow on Trees (etc.) (varied)
1925 JGBrandon *Cork* (L) 24: Wibleys [*a name*] don't grow on every bush. **1930** CBarry *Boat* (L) 18: I found out that jobs don't grow in trees. **1930** EDTorgerson *Murderer* (NY) 268: You talk . . . as though money grew upon trees. **1930** GVenner *Next To Die* (L) 192: They [*diamonds*] don't grow on gooseberry bushes. **1934** JJFarjeon *Mystery* (NY) 55: Good-looking guests do not grow on every gooseberry. **1934** AHalper *Foundry* (NY) 39: Nice young widows don't grow on trees. **1937** CGordon *Garden* (NY) 202: Mrs. Camp thought money grew on trees. **1939** VBridges *Seven Stars* (L) 24: Professorships . . . don't grow on blackberry bushes. **1940** GPatten *Autobiography* ed HHinsdale (Norman, Okla. 1964) 78: Spending money as if it grew on trees. **1946** AEMartin *Death in the Limelight* (NY) 107: Money! Do you think it grows on bushes? **1948** TKyd *Blood* (P) 123: Money isn't growing on trees. **1949** MGilbert *He Didn't* (NY DBC) 134: Good cooks don't grow on gooseberry bushes. **1952** KMKnight *Valse* (NY) 55: Tossed away as if money grew on bushes. **1953** VPJohns *Murder* (NY 1962) 19: Jobs don't grow on trees. **1957** *BangorDN* 1/26 21: New hats don't grow on trees. **1958** JSStrange *Night* (NY) 200: He said money doesn't grow on trees. **1959** DAngus *Ivy* (I) 12: Do you think toilet paper grows on trees? **1959** ADean *Something*

(NY) 145: You'd think money grew on trees. **1966** MMcShane *Night's* (NY) 30: Money doesn't grow on trees. **1968** GBagby *Another* (NY) 43: Secretaries like Miss Pierson don't grow on bushes. **1971** WHWalling *No One* (NY) 43: Assassins do not grow on every tree and bush. **1973** FFelton *Peacock* (L) 94: Money was not growing on trees. **1973** CAird *His Burial* (NY) 18: Cars like Mr. Tindell's don't grow on trees. TW 48: Bush(1), 248: Money(8).

T259 To bark up the wrong **Tree** (gumtree) (*varied*)

1915 JBuchan *Thirty-Nine* (NY) 210: I had been barking up the wrong tree. **1924** A Christie *Man* (NY) 169: Barking up the wrong tree. **1931** ELoban *Calloused* (NY) 162: You're barking up a lemon tree. **1931** SFWright *Bell Street* (NY) 168: I've been barking under the wrong tree. **1933** CFitzsimmons *Red Rhapsody* (NY) 182: You're barking up the same tree with Wiggins. **1936** HWade *Bury Him* (L) 100: I expect I'm barking up a gum-tree, or whatever the expression is. **1938** NMorland *Rope* (L) 31: Barking, metaphorically, up the wrong tree. **1940** GBagby *Corpse Wore* (NY) 38: Barking up the wrong tree. **1940** CFGregg *Fatal Error* (L) 42: I'm barking up a gumtree. **1943** NMarsh *Colour Scheme* (L 1960) 164: I've been barking up the wrong tree. **1945** HQMasur *Bury Me* (NY 1948) 201: You're whistling up the wrong tree. **1949** JSymons *Bland* (L) 122: We may be altogether up the wrong tree. **1957** MProcter *Midnight* (NY) 144: You might be barking up the wrong tree. **1958** *New Yorker* 7/19 32: You are barking up the wrong tree. **1958** JByrom *Or Be* (L 1964) 29: A . . . genealogist barking up the wrong family-tree. **1962** ESGardner *Mischievous* (NY DBC) 84: You're barking up the wrong tree, running off on a false scent, chasing a red herring. **1962** RLockridge *First* (P) 17: We've been barking down the wrong well. **1964** LCharteris *Vendetta* (NY) 49: You are—as the Americans say—woofing up the wrong tree. **1968** JPorter *Dover Goes* (NY) 104: You were barking up a gum tree. **1971** KLaumer *Deadfall* (NY) 131: You're sniffing up the wrong tree. **1973** ARoudybush

Gastronomic (NY) 108: You're barking up the wrong tree. **1977** CAlverson *Not Sleeping* (B) 90: You're barking down the wrong hole. EAP T236; Brunvand 145(3). Cf. Brunvand 136: Stump(1).

T260 To fall (go down) like a **Tree**

1938 EHuxley *Murder* (NY) 119: He . . . fell like a tree. **1940** MAllingham *Black Plumes* (L) 146: He went down like a tree. Whiting T467.

T261 To whistle up a hollow **Tree**

1930 FIAnderson *Book* (NY) 2: He left his heirs whistling up a hollow tree. Cf. NED Whistle *v.* 9. Cf. Rain barrel *above*.

T262 A **Tree** is judged (known) by its fruit

1928 DHLawrence *Lady* ("Allemagne") 40: Ye shall know the tree by its fruit. **1952** AWilson *Hemlock* (L) 170: I judge trees by their fruit. **1955** SNGhose *Flame* (L) 15: A tree should be judged by its fruit. EAP T237; TW 381(2); Brunvand 145(2).

T263 In a **Trice**

1928 EHamilton *Four* (L) 6: In a trice. **1937** GDilnot *Murder* (L) 109: In a trice. **1971** EHCohen *Mademoiselle* (B) 196: In a trice. EAP T240.

T264 There are **Tricks** in every trade (*varied*)

1913 TDreiser *Traveler* (NY 1923) 87: There are tricks in every trade. **1928** GGardiner *At the House* (NY) 177: Every trade has its ways. **1928** ESnell *Kontrol* (P) 96: Every profession has its tricks. **1929** BFlynn *Billiard* (P) 63: Tricks in every trade. **1932** JRhode *Dead Men* (L) 71: There are tricks in every trade. **1937** WDickinson *Dead Man* (P) 41: There are tricks in all trades. **1939** JDonavan *Coloured Wind* (L) 83: Every trade has its secret. **1939** GGoodchild *We Shot* (L) 154: There's tricks in every trade. **1941** MColes *Drink* (NY) 192: Every trade has its hall-mark, you know. **1943** PATaylor *Going* (NY) 17: She knows every trick to the trade. **1953** EPaul *Waylaid* (NY) 199: There's tricks to every trade. **1957** *New Yorker* 12/21 55: There are tricks in every trade. **1960** AWUpfield *Valley* (NY DBC) 47: There are tricks and knacks in every trade.

1966 HLCory *Sword* (NY) 157: Each profession has its secrets. **1968** DBagley *Vivero* (NY) 125: There are tricks to every trade. TW 380(2).

T265   To know a **Trick** or two

1939 VWilliams *Fox Prowls* (B) 236: Your old man still knows a trick or two.

T266   To know a **Trick** worth two of that

1931 TFPowys *Unclay* (L) 82: Dawe knew a trick worth two of that. **1933** JCMasterman *Oxford* (L) 169: We know a trick worth two of that. **1959** EGrierson *Storm* (L) 196: Georgina had a trick worth two of that. **1959** JWyndham *Outward* (NY) 98: The smile of a man who knows a trick worth two of that. EAP T245.

T267   To be quick on the **Trigger**

1931 MJFreeman *Murder* (NY) 93: He's pretty quick on the trigger. **1934** RStout *Fer-de-lance* (NY 1958) 184: You certainly are quick on the trigger. **1936** NMorland *Clue* (L) 276: He was quick on the trigger. **1940** PATaylor *Criminal* (NY) 147: Quick on the trigger. EAP T246.

T268   As bright (fit, gay, square) as a **Trivet**

1928 HCMcNeile *Female* (NY) 45: As fit as a trivet. **1937** VWilkins *And So—Victoria* (NY) 9: As square as a trivet. **1938** AGilbert *Treason* (L) 56: Bright as a trivet. **1971** PMoyes *Season* (NY) 71: Giselle, gay as a trivet, made a great joke.

T269   As right as a **Trivet**

1905 FMWhite *Crimson Blind* (NY) 274: Right . . . as a trivet. **1925** GKnevels *Octagon* (NY) 296: Right as a trivet. **1937** GDHCole *Missing* (L) 21: She'll soon be as right as a trivet. **1939** MInnes *Stop Press* (L) 226: "He's as right as a rivet." . . . "Isn't it *trivet*?" **1957** JBrooks *Water* (L) 244: Right as a trivet [*true*]. **1961** HReilly *Certain* (NY DBC) 56: Right as a trivet. **1966** NMonsarrat *Life(I)* (L) 321: Right as a trivet . . . whatever a trivet may be. TW 382(1); *Oxford* 677.

T270   To (act) like a **Trojan**

1930 ALivingston *Murder* (I) 72: "How is she taking it?" "Like a Trojan." **1930** AMuir *Silent* (I) 178: You've stuck to it like a Trojan. **1931** TThayer *Greek* (NY) 9: He stuck to it "like a Trojan," as we say. **1933** GDilnot *Thousandth* (L) 288: He lied to me like a Trojan. **1961** RFoley *It's Murder* (NY DBC) 61: Like the little Trojan she is, she is coping with the telephone. TW 382; NED Trojan 2; Partridge 911.

T271   To eat like a **Trojan**

1958 HWaugh *Girl* (NY) 37: Patty always eats like a Trojan. EAP T248. Cf. Navvy *above*.

T272   To fight like a **Trojan**

1929 LHousman *Duke* (L) 166: He fought like a Trojan. **1958** JPlayfair *Pursued* (L) 63: They fought like Trojans to keep you alive. Whiting *NC* 489(2).

T273   To work (slave) like a **Trojan**

1900 CFPidgin *Quincy A. Sawyer* (B) 430: You've worked like a Trojan. **1925** EMillay *Letters* ed ARMacdougall (NY 1952) 194: Working like Trojans. **1935** TAPlummer *Creaking* (L) 23: Slaved like a trojan. **1941** GBagby *Red Is* (NY) 38: He worked like a trojan. **1948** DCDisney *Explosion* (NY DBC) 57: Worked like Trojans. **1972** TWells *Die* (NY) 45: Working like Trojans. **1973** DHart-Davis *Ascension* (NY) 228: In spite of Trojan work. **1979** CDexter *Service* (NY) 107: He worked like a Trojan—although exactly why the Trojans are proverbially accredited with a reputation for industriousness has always been a mystery to me. TW 382; Taylor *Western Folklore* 17(1958) 19: Slave(2). Cf. Navvy *above*.

T274   To be off one's **Trolley** (*varied*)

1941 AAFair *Spill* (NY) 249: If the shock hadn't thrown her off her trolley. **1949** GHHall *End* (NY) 27: More than a little off her trolley. **1950** BSpicer *Blues* (NY) 242: Thrown him off his trolley. **1959** CMKornbluth *Marching* (NY) 77: Benson was slipping his trolley. Wentworth 554.

T275   To curse like a **Trooper**

1933 TSmith *Turnabout* (NY) 136: She was cursing and damning like a trooper. **1941** BHalliday *Bodies* (NY 1959) 134: She . . . started cursing like a trooper. **1961** EPeters

Death (NY) 31: Cursing like a trooper. EAP T249. Cf. Navvy *above*.

T276   To lie like a Trooper

1927 FEverton *Dalehouse* (NY) 41: Lie like troopers; 105. **1931** FFFoster *Something* (L) 94: Even if I have to lie like a trooper— sorry, Hawkenbridge, I mean like a sailor. **1934** AGilbert *Man in Button* (L) 183: Circumstantial evidence can lie like the proverbial trooper. **1938** DCDisney *Strawstack* (NY) 99: She's lying like a trooper. **1952** HCecil *Ways* (L) 65: He'd been lying like a trooper. **1956** ESGardner *Terrified* (NY) 76: I lied like a trooper. **1961** MHHood *Drown* (NY) 219: Lying like troopers. **1968** GWagner *Elegy* (L) 59: Lie like a trooper. **1972** PRReynolds *Middle* (NY) 46: I decided to lie like a trooper. Taylor *Western Folklore* 17(1958) 20; NED Trooper 1b (quote 1854). Cf. Partridge 911.

T277   To swear like a Trooper

1903 ADMcFaul *Ike Glidden* (B) 136: He'll swear like a trooper. **1924** TMundy *Om* (NY) 9: Swore like a trooper. **1940** JDonavan *Plastic Man* (L) 71: He swore like a trooper. **1957** APowell *At Lady* (L) 33: They swear like troopers. **1959** FSmith *Harry* (B) 117: Swearing like Irish troopers. **1964** CMackenzie *Life III* (L) 266: Swearing like a trooper. **1965** MJones *Set* (L) 221: "She'd lie like a trooper." . . . "Swear like a trooper, dear." "What? Oh, for God's sake, don't pick me up like that." **1971** EHCohen *Mademoiselle* (B) 161: She swore like one of her own troopers. EAP T249. Cf. Marine *above*.

T278   To sweat like a Trooper

1967 MWilkins *Last* (Englewood Cliffs, NJ) 137: I . . . was sweating like a trooper. Cf. Partridge 911: Trooper, like a.

T279   To work like a Trooper

1931 LEpply *Murder* (NY) 99: Working like troopers. **1974** SKrim *You* (NY) 305: Worked like a trooper. Cf. Navvy, Trojan *above*.

T280   Never trouble Trouble till trouble troubles you (*varied*)

1931 LEppley *Murder* (NY) 218: Stay away from trouble till it troubles you is my motto.

1933 FHShaw *Atlantic* (NY) 20: Why trouble trouble till trouble comes along? **1938** PWentworth *Run!* (L) 49: Our old nurse used to say: "If you don't trouble trouble, trouble won't trouble you." **1948** WMiller *Fatal* (NY) 22: Don't trouble trouble and it won't trouble you. **1950** ECRLorac *Accident* (NY DBC) 20: I never trouble trouble till trouble troubles me. **1959** RCFrazer *Mark* (NY) 66: His policy of never troubling trouble unless trouble troubled him. **1967** VSPritchett *Cab* (NY) 24: Dinna trouble trouble till trouble troubles you. Whiting *NC* 489(4).

T281   To borrow Trouble

1908 LFBaum *Dorothy and the Wizard of Oz* (I) 29: It's foolish to borrow trouble. **1931** CWells *Umbrella* (NY) 267: Don't borrow trouble. **1934** JHWallis *Murder Mansions* (NY) 138: Don't borrow trouble. **1969** IWallace *Deathstar* (NY) 68: We may be merely borrowing trouble. **1970** RFoley *Calculated* (NY) 140: We aren't going to borrow trouble. **1976** LEgan *Scenes* (NY) 13: Don't borrow trouble. EAP T252; Brunvand 145.

T282   To look (ask) for Trouble

1930 HAdams *Crime* (P) 236: He never looked for trouble. **1940** HReilly *Murder in* (NY) 274: There's enough trouble in the world without going to look for it. **1948** RFoley *No Tears* (NY DBC) 90: There's trouble enough without asking for it. **1962** EF Russell *Great* (NY) 44: One can find trouble enough without going looking for it. **1970** WMasterson *Death* (NY) 37: You don't have to go looking for trouble. **1973** WMasterson *Undertaker* (NY) 93: He didn't just meet trouble, he went looking for it. Whiting *NC* 489(2); DA Trouble 2b.

T283   To meet Trouble half-way (*varied*)

1923 TFPowys *Black Bryony* (L) 96: No need to meet trouble half-way. **1927** LBamburg *Beads* (NY) 19: It's no use meeting difficulties halfway; 137. **1927** MRJames *Letters to a Friend* ed GMcBryde (L 1956) 142: I was never one to meet trouble halfway. **1936** GHeyer *Behold* (NY) 62: You're too fond of meeting troubles half way. **1938** FWCrofts

End (L) 17: It was silly to meet trouble half-way. **1940** JBentley *Mr. Marlow Stops* (B) 111: No use meeting trouble halfway. **1941** CRice *Right Murder* (NY) 213: Man is born to be the spark that flies upward to meet trouble halfway. **1952** KFuller *Silken* (L) 172: What's the good of meeting trouble half-way? As my father used to say: Don't worry, it may never happen. **1957** *Punch* 7/10 33: Meet trouble more than half-way. **1962** PDJames *Cover* (NY 1976) 22: To meet trouble half-way. *Oxford* 523: Meet. Cf. Do not greet the Devil *above.*

T284 A **Trouble** (burden, sorrow) shared is a trouble halved (*varied*)

1931 DLSayers *Suspicious* (NY) 109: Trouble shared is trouble halved. **1933** MKennedy et al. *Ask* (L) 205: A trouble shared, they say, is a trouble halved. **1939** JCreasey *Toff Goes on* (L) 125: A burden shared is a burden halved. **1956** MProcter *Ripper* (NY) 200: A trouble shared, you know. **1957** GAshe *Wait* (NY 1972) 154: "Don't you know that a trouble shared was a trouble halved?" . . . "Old adage." **1975** JvandeWetering *Outsider* (B) 113: The proverb that says shared sorrow is half sorrow. Cf. Pleasure *above.*

T285 As smooth as a **Trout**

1903 ADMcFaul *Ike Glidden* (B) 69: He is as smooth as a trout. **1958** TBrooke *Under* (NY) 141: The satin . . . sleek and smooth as a trout. Cf. Smelt *above.*

T286 To rise like a **Trout** to a fly (*varied*)

1928 CJDutton *Clutching* (NY) 193: Like a trout rising to a fly. **1947** TKyd *Blood* (P) 31: He rose like a trout. **1952** HFMPrescott *Man on* (NY) 124: Gib went to the books, like a fish to a may-fly. **1954** SJepson *Black* (NY) 209: He was on it like a trout at a fly. NED Rise *v.* 14b; Berrey 165.5, 314.10: Rise to the fly.

T287 To lay it on with a **Trowel** (*varied*)

1925 EBChancellor *Hell Fire* (L) 216: Flattery laid on with a trowel. **1929** RJCasey *Secret* (I) 74: He had spread his flattery with so wide a trowel. **1929** RKing *Murder* (NY) 231: He unearthed a trowel, and laid it [*flattery*] on pretty thick. **1936** RKing *Con-*

stant God (NY) 113: Amateurs will lay it on with a trowel. **1939** HReilly *All Concerned* (NY) 246: [His] joviality was laid on with a trowel. **1941** HLMencken *Newspaper Days, 1899–1906* (NY) 273: I laid it on, as they used to say in those days, with a shovel. **1942** WIrish *Phantom* (NY 1957) 169: He said, laying it on with a shovel. **1946** ESedgwick *Happy* (B) 41: My father . . . laid it on with a trowel. **1948** JTey *Franchise* (NY 1955) 42: You could lay it on with a trowel. **1952** GBagby *Corpse* (NY) 91: Alexander laid on the charm with a trowel. **1969** DClark *Nobody's* (NY) 156: Green has been laying it on with a trowel [*giving an unfriendly report*]. EAP T256.

T288 To blow one's own **Trumpet**

1928 GGardiner *At the House* (NY) 18: A man to blow his own trumpet. **1932** RCWoodthorpe *Public* (L) 127: He can be trusted to blow his own trumpet. **1939** FGerard *Red Rope* (NY) 264: Don't think I'm blowing my own trumpet. **1945** AChristie *Remembered* (NY) 202: It will be a shameless blowing of my own trumpet. **1954** GKerr *Under* (P) 13: The sort of man who believes in blowing his own trumpet. **1957** *Punch* 7/10 52: His blowing of his own trumpet. **1963** AHBrodrick *Abbé Breuil* (L) 101: Not averse from blowing his own trumpet. EAP T258. Cf. To blow one's own Horn *above.*

T289 Put your **Trust** in God and keep your powder dry

1956 AChristie *Dead Man's* (L) 44: An older [slogan] in this country [*England*] . . . "Put your trust in God and keep your powder dry." **1965** MStewart *Airs* (NY 1966) 211: Keep our powder dry. **1970** JAGraham *Something* (B) 130: Keep your powder dry. *Oxford* 842.

T290 To **Trust** no further than one can see (or throw something heavy, or do any of a variety of things that suggest a short distance)

1911 JCLincoln *Woman-Haters* (NY) 8: I wouldn't trust you as fur as I could see you. **1922** JJoyce *Ulysses* (NY 1934) 344: She wouldn't trust those washerwomen as far as she'd see them. **1924** HCBailey *Mr. Fortune's Practice* (NY) 23: I wouldn't trust him round the corner. **1924** JSFletcher *Time-Worn* (NY) 59: Wouldn't trust him any further than I could throw his big carcase. **1928** AGilbert *Mrs. Davenport* (NY) 221: He didn't trust these foreigners the length of their foxy noses. **1928** JRhode *Tragedy* (NY) 293: I didn't trust him any further than I could see him. **1928** HKWebster *Clock* (NY) 196: I wouldn't trust Charles much further than I can see into a brick wall. **1930** CBarry *Boat* (L) 64: A [I] wouldn't trust her as far as A could throw her and that is not far. **1930** LThayer *They Tell* (NY) 165: I wouldn't trust Mr. Cranston farther than I could hurl a church. **1931** MJFreeman *Murder* (NY) 102: I wouldn't trust him farther than I could throw an elephant by the tail. **1931** VWMason *Vesper* (NY) 82: He's a type I wouldn't trust as far as I could throw a bull by the tail. **1932** BGQuin *Murder* (NY) 279: I don't trust you farther than I can see you. **1935** SVestal *Wise Room* (B) 269: I wouldn't trust any of them as far as I could throw a feather. **1937** VWilliams *Mr Treadgold* (L) 199: I wouldn't have trusted him farther than you could toss a biscuit, as the saying goes. **1939** WTarg *Mr. Cassidy* (NY) 114: I wouldn't trust him as far as I could toss a piano. **1940** KMKnight *Death Came* (NY) 28: Don't trust each other any further than you can spit. **1941** AAFair *Double* (NY) 174: I wouldn't trust that man as far as I could throw an elephant by the tail. **1942** PGWodehouse *Money* (NY) 152: He trusted neither of them as far as he could spit, and he was a poor spitter. **1943** PATaylor *Going* (NY) 107: That boy can't be trusted as far as you can shake a stick. **1948** RFoley *No Tears* (NY DBC) 7: I'd trust him . . . as far as I could swing a cat. **1955** PGWodehouse *French* (L) 52: I wouldn't trust a French Markee as far as I could throw an elephant. **1957** *New Yorker* 4/27 26: That's why I always say I wouldn't trust one [*a foreigner*] as far as I could fling him. **1957** LBeam *Maine* (NY) 203: I wouldn't trust him any further than I can see through a sifter. **1959** RCFrazer *Mark* (NY) 126: I wouldn't trust a single one of them . . . not as far as I can see them. **1960** FHer-

bert *Dragon* (L) 137: I wouldn't trust you as far as I could see you. **1961** SDean *Credit* (NY) 124: Wouldn't trust him as far as I can spit. **1966** DMDisney *At Some* (NY) 183: Not that I'd trust you any farther than I could throw a horse by his tail. **1970** JA Graham *Aldeburg* (B) 33: I wouldn't trust that man farther than I could throw a rhinoceros. **1973** JFleming *Alas* (NY) 30: He wouldn't trust him any farther than he could kick him. EAP T262; *Oxford* 842, 843; Tilley T556, 557.

T291 **Trust** and be trusted (*varied*)

1930 HAdams *Golden* (L) 72: Trust and be trusted, I always say. **1939** TStevenson *Silver Arrow* (L) 89: A man w'at trusts nobody isn't t' be trusted hisself. **1958** JByrom *Or Be* (L 1964) 92: One trust deserves another.

T292 The greater the **Truth** the greater the libel

1950 ECrispin *Sudden* (NY DBC) 87: "The greater the truth, the greater the libel" . . . this forensic saw had been scarcely tactful. *Oxford* 336.

T293 Tell (speak) the **Truth** and shame the devil (*varied*)

1929 RGraves *Good-bye* (L) 55: Speak the truth and shame the devil. **1930** DLSayers *Documents* (NY) 219: Do right and shame the devil is my motto. **1933** GDilnot *Thousandth* (L) 58: Speak the truth and shame the devil, that's my motto. **1934** LO'Flaherty *Shame the Devil* (L). **1942** FLockridge *Hanged* (NY) 165: Tell the truth and shame the devil. **1958** *New Yorker* 3/1 31: Tell the truth and shame the Devil. **1958** *NYTimes* 3/2 21X: Tell the truth and shame the devil. **1960** DShannon *Case* (NY) 163: Tell the truth—shame the devil, like her. EAP T264.

T294 Tell the **Truth** to your lawyer and doctor (*varied*)

1933 ESGardner *Sulky Girl* (NY) 56: You've got to tell your lawyer and your doctor the whole truth. **1953** BCarey *Their Nearest* (NY) 115: They say there are two people you should always tell the truth to: Your doctor and your lawyer. *Oxford* 371: Hide nothing.

Truth

T295 To be more Truth than poetry

1931 CWells *Horror* (P) 195: There's more truth than poetry in that. **1938** RTorrey *42 Days* (NY) 41: I figured my crack was probably more truth than poetry. **1957** *BHerald* 4/7 18A: There was more truth than poetry to the councillor's comment. **1958** *NYTimes* 9/21 21X: There is more truth than poetry in saying that John A. Lomax heard America singing. **1966** TWells *Matter* (NY) 53: There was more truth than poetry in that sentence. **1972** DShannon *Murder* (NY) 99: More truth than poetry. TW 383(1).

T296 Truth harms (hurts) no man (varied)

1934 CBush *Dead Shepherd* (L) 90: The truth never harmed no man. **1934** CFGregg *Execution* (L) 67: The truth hurts no one. **1938** MECorne *Death* (NY) 163: The truth never harmed anyone. **1941** PWilde *Design* (NY) 22: The truth never hurts, they say, but if it does, just grin and bear it. **1956** SWTaylor *I Have* (NY) 36: It's the truth that hurts. Oxford *DQ* (2nd ed) 91.24 [*RBrowning*].

T297 Truth is a naked lady

1969 JBrunner *Jagged* (NY) 124: They say "truth is a naked lady." Oxford 845: Truth shows best.

T298 The Truth is not to be spoken at all times

1941 CWells *Murder . . . Casino* (P) 159: The truth is not to be spoken at all times. EAP T267; TW 383(3).

T299 Truth (fact, life) is stranger (stronger) than fiction (varied)

1900 CFPidgin *Quincy A. Sawyer* (B) v: Truth is stranger than fiction. **1920** JSFletcher *Dead Men's* (NY) 170: Fact's been a lot stranger than fiction. **1922** JJoyce *Ulysses* (NY 1934) 659: Truth stranger than fiction. **1927** OWarner *Secret* (NY) 168: They speak of fact being stranger than fiction. **1929** ABCox *Poisoned* (NY) 49: Life is certainly stranger than fiction. **1932** VLoder *Red Stain* (NY) 260: That . . . is where life is much less strange than fiction. **1933** EE Cummings *Eimi* (NY) 112: Truth is after all stranger than fiction. **1938** FBeeding *Big Fish* (L) 54: Truth, I know, is often stranger

than fiction. **1947** RKing *Lethal* (NY DBC) 28: She was a sitting duck for clichés, and thoroughly believed that truth was so much stranger than fiction. **1947** EWallace *Stronger than Fiction* (NY). **1957** *NYTimes Book Review* 11/10 28: The truth-is-stranger-than-fiction dictum. **1957** AECoppard *It's Me* (L) 232: Truth is by no means stranger than fiction, it *is* fiction, and familiarity with it breeds contempt. **1957** RStandish *Prince* (L) 90: It is proverbial that truth is stranger than fiction. **1959** JBonett *No Grave* (NY) 111: My truth should prove to be as strange as your fiction. **1959** E Sherry *Defense* (NY) 171: Spare me the "stranger than fiction" cliché. **1961** RVanGulik *Nail* (NY) viii: Fact is indeed stranger than fiction. **1964** LCohen *New York* (P) 70: Truth was stronger than *Graphic* fiction. **1966** GKanin *Remembering* (NY) 161: In this case truth may be stranger than fiction, but fiction is better. **1966** JPearson *Ian Fleming* (NY) 245: One more reminder that fiction is stranger and infinitely more satisfactory than truth. **1967** RDavies *Marchbank's* (Toronto) 53: Truth, alas, is sometimes even uglier than fiction. **1972** JCreasey *First* (NY) 140: It was a revelation . . . to her that truth could sound so much more plausible than fiction. **1973** EJBurford *Queen* (L) 11: It is often said that fact is stranger than fiction. **1973** HDolson *Dying* (P) 147: Truth was a damn sight stranger than mystery fiction. **1975** MKWren *Multitude* (NY) 63: Truth is stranger than fiction, so they say. **1976** RBDominic *Murder* (NY) 105: And they say that truth isn't stranger than fiction. TW 384(5); Oxford 844.

T300 Truth lies at the bottom of a well (varied)

1926 JSFletcher *Sea Fog* (B) 210: There's an old saying . . . truth lies at the bottom of a well. **1932** MTurnbull *Return* (P) 167: Truth's at the bottom of the well. **1936** NBlake *Thou Shell* (L) 97: The lady who sits at the bottom of the well was totally invisible. **1937** VLoder *Choose* (L) 241: "You know what one expects to find at the bottom of wells." "The truth—well watered down." **1939** CBClason *Dragon's* (NY) 109:

Truth lies at the bottom of a well, as Democritus informs us. **1941** CEVulliamy *Ghost History* (NY) 225: Truth is better left in the well. **1951** MGilbert *Death Has* (NY) 238: Truth had come up from the bottom of a well. **1957** *Arizona Highways* May 36: Black as the well / Where Truth is said to dwell. **1964** HBourne *In the Event* (NY) 100: Truth lies at the bottom of a well. **1973** MInnes *Appleby's Answer* (NY) 123: Truth lies at the bottom of the well? . . . A foolish proverb—but most proverbs are thoroughly foolish. Folk-wisdom is almost always fatuous. One doesn't come at truth—or at any truth worth finding by peering down into dark places. EAP T268.

T301 **Truth** pays (is) best (*varied*)

1928 GDHCole *Man* (NY) 230: Truth pays best in the long run. **1934** EBBlack *Crime* (NY) 143: The truth is always best. **1937** GBarnett *I Knew* (L) 305: They say the truth pays. **1959** NBlake *Widow's* (L) 47: The truth always wins in the end. Whiting T501. Cf. Honesty *above*.

T302 The **Truth**, the whole truth *etc.*

1903 ADMcFaul *Ike Glidden* (B) 52: The truth, the whole truth, and nothin' but the truth. **1925** FWCrofts *Groote* (NY) 145: As the legal phrase puts it, you must tell me the truth, the whole truth, and nothing but the truth. **1935** GDilnot *Murder* (L) 257: Tell the truth, the whole truth, and nothing but the truth. **1941** TChanslor *Our Second* (NY) 246: Just tell the truth, the whole truth, and nothing but the truth. **1949** MGilbert *He Didn't* (NY DBC) 61: The truth, the whole truth, and nothing but the truth. **1952** MVHeberden *Tragic* (NY) 61: You'll tell him the truth, all the truth, and nothing but the truth. **1959** NFitzgerald *Midsummer* (NY) 144: Tell the truth, the whole truth and nothing but the truth. **1960** JDCarr *In Spite* (NY) 32: The truth and the whole truth and nothing but the truth. **1961** HReilly *Certain* (NY DBC) 47: The truth, the sole truth and nothing but the truth. **1972** JBonett *No Time* (NY) 116: The truth, the whole truth and nothing but the truth. **1973** RStout *Please* (NY) 71: There is no sillier formula than the old legal phrase,

"the truth, the whole truth, and nothing but the truth." EAP T273.

T303 The **Truth** will out (*varied*)

1913 JSFletcher *Secret* (L 1918) 143: The truth will out. **1928** RTGould *Oddities* (L) 220: So true it is that Truth will out. **1933** JSFletcher *Burma* (NY) 98: Truth, like murder, will out. **1936** MMPropper *Murder* (L) 201: Truth will out. **1940** RPenny *Sweet Poison* (L) 234: They say truth will out. **1950** MRHodgkin *Student* (L) 124: Truth will out. **1957** EMButler *Heine* (NY) 269: Truth like murder (which it strongly resembles) will out. **1963** MGEberhart *Run* (NY) 13: The truth always comes out. **1965** CGaskin *File* (NY) 156: *Veritas Prævalet* . . . Truth will out—or something like that. **1970** LGraffey-Smith *Bright* (L) 48: Truth must out. **1974** GWheeler *Easy* (NY) 33: I always say the truth will out. EAP T274. Cf. Murder will out *above*.

T304 As fat as a **Tub**

1965 ASeyton *Avalon* (NY 1966) 271: [She] had grown fat as a tub. Taylor *Prov. Comp.* 40: Fat [*of lard*]; Clark 211.

T305 As round as a **Tub**

1928 SHuddleston *Paris Salons* (NY) 234: Round like a tub. **1954** JSymons *Narrowing* (NY) 151: He's round as a tub. Cf. Cole 61: Barrel.

T306 Every **Tub** (barrel) must stand on its own bottom

1933 HAdams *Golf House* (P) 78: Every tub must stand on its own bottom. **1972** JRipley *Davis* (NY) 35: Every barrel has to stand on its own bottom. EAP T276.

T307 To throw a **Tub** to amuse a whale

1940 JJConnington *Four Defences* (B) 114: Throwing out a tub to amuse a whale, as Dean Swift advises. EAP T277.

T308 As mad as **Tucker**

1952 JKnox *Little* (P) 173: All of them madder'n Tucker at each other. TW 384.

T309 There is many a good **Tune** played on an old fiddle (*varied*)

1926 LO'Flaherty *Mr. Gilhooley* (L) 178: There's more ways than one for playing a tune on an old fiddle. **1933** QPatrick *S.S.Murder* (NY) 162: There's many a good tune played on an old fiddle. **1956** AGilbert *Riddle* (NY) 184: You know what they say— there's many a good tune played on an old fiddle. **1957** RGraves *They Hanged* (NY) 36: Many's the good tune played on an old fiddle. **1960** AGilbert *Out for* (NY 1965) 112: Many a good tune played on an old fiddle. **1964** ABurgess *Eve* (L) 22: There's many an old fiddle plays a good tune, as the saving goes. **1972** RRendell *Murder* (NY) 90: There's many a good tune played on an old fiddle. *Oxford* 325: Good tune.

T310   To change (alter) one's **Tune**

1904 JCLincoln *Cap'n Eri* (NY) 137–8: He's sort of changed his tune. **1931** MKennedy *Death to the Rescue* (L) 31: She would soon alter her tune. **1931** EQueen *Dutch* (NY) 192: You've changed your tune. **1936** LRGribble *Riley* (L) 169: To alter his tune. **1938** PATaylor *Banbury* (NY 1964) 140: He'll change his tune. **1952** EQueen *King* (B) 66: What . . . made the owner change his tune. **1956** RStout *Eat* (NY) 122: His wife changed her tune with a vengeance. **1970** RBernard *Deadly* (NY) 176: He changed his tune. **1970** ELathen *Pick* (NY) 159: You changed your tune. EAP T280.

T311   To sing (whistle) a different (another, new) **Tune**

1900 CFPidgin *Quincy A. Sawyer* (B) 55: He'll whistle another tune. **1928** RKing *Fatal* (NY) 162: The poor kid sang a different tune. **1931** LEppley *Murder* (NY) 307: You may laugh to a different tune. **1933** RRobins *Murder* (NY) 149: Sing another tune. **1937** HWade *High Sheriff* (L) 3: They'd sing a different tune. **1940** MArmstrong *Man with* (NY) 7: I bet he sings a different song now. **1953** KMKnight *Three* (NY) 36: You're singing a new tune. **1957** *BHerald* 4/7 19A: Now he is singing a different tune. **1961** JRChild *Casanova* (L) 88: Critics began to sing another tune. **1971** RFDelderfield *For My* (NY) 81: He would have sung a very different tune. EAP T281; TW 385(3,4).

T312   As hot as **Tunket**

1954 EForbes *Rainbow* (B) 116: He had a hot as Tunket little forge shop. **1961** MHHood *Drown* (NY) 56: It's hotter'n tunket in here. DA Tunket.

T313   The more you stir a **Turd** the worse it stinks (*varied*)

1929 TCobb *Crime* (L) 161: The more we stir the worse it stinks. **1956** SWTaylor *I Have* (NY) 174: To her, this was a mess which only smelled worse if you stirred it. **1971** HVanDyke *Dead* (NY) 100: But like my mama always used to say, "The more you stir shit, the more it stinks." *Oxford* 775: Stir it.

T314   To stick out like a **Turd** in a punch bowl (*varied*)

1960 JBWest *Taste* (NY) 26: Betsey [*a revolver*] stuck out of his mitt like a turd in a punch bowl. **1977** CAlverton *Not Sleeping* (B) 75: Talk about the impact of the legendary turd in the punch bowl. Cf. Whore *below*.

T315   **Turd** calls to turd

1936 AHuxley *Eyeless* (NY) 239: Turd calls to turd.

T316   As jealous as a **Turk**

1936 AFielding *Mystery* (L) 149: He's as jealous as a Turk. Cf. Turkey cock *below*.

T317   To work like a **Turk**

1969 RNye *Tales* (L) 123: I worked like a Turk. **1971** TCatledge *My Life* (NY) 59: He was working like a Turk. EAP T292. Cf. Trojan *above*.

T318   To talk **Turkey**

1924 HSKeeler *Voice* (NY) 22: You're talking turkey. **1937** ABCaldwell *No Tears* (NY) 178: To talk turkey. **1941** RStout *Alphabet* (NY) 256: I'm ready to talk turkey. **1950** FO'Malley *Best* (NY) 55: Let's talk turkey. **1952** AGilbert *Mr. Crook* (NY DBC) 61: The gentleman was not talking turkey [*nonsense*]. **1959** WHaggard *Venetian* (NY DBC) 163: I was talking turkey. **1964** ELathen *Accounting* (NY) 62: We'll just have to talk turkey to him. Whiting *NC* 490(5); Wentworth 536: Talk. Cf. DA Turkey 9(1a).

T319 As jealous as **Turkey cocks**

1933 AWynne *Death* (P) 246: Jealous as turkey-cocks. Cf. Turk *above*.

T320 As proud (vain) as a **Turkey cock**

1936 GVerner *Hangman* (NY) 107: As vain as turkey cocks. **1948** HActon *Memoirs* (L) 36: Proud as turkeycocks. **1961** HEBates *Now Sleeps* (L) 77: Proud as a turkey cock. TW 385(4,5).

T321 As red as a **Turkey cock** (*varied*)

1928 HWade *Missing* (NY) 109: He was as red as the proverbial turkey-cock. **1933** MKennedy *Murderer* (NY) 53: Red as a turkey-cock. **1941** CEVulliamy *Short History* (L) 113: The old man went as red as a turkey. **1943** CEVulliamy *Polderoy* (L) 25: He went as red as a gobbler. **1947** PWentworth *Wicked* (NY) 124: As red as a turkey cock. **1949** JSymons *Bland* (L) 37: Went red as a turkey. **1966** JStuart *My Land* (NY) 223: His face was as red as a turkey snout. TW 385(6); *Oxford* 668.

T322 One good **Turn** deserves another (*varied*)

1915 JBuchan *Thirty-Nine* (NY) 156: Ae guid turn deservin' anither. **1922** JJoyce *Ulysses* (NY 1934) 229: One good turn deserves another. **1923** JSClouston *Lunatic* (NY) 26: One good turn deserves another. **1930** FDGrierson *Mysterious* (L) 120: One good turning deserves the other one. **1936** DHume *Bring 'Em Back* (NY) 195: One good turn deserves another. **1940** JBentley *Mr. Marlow Stops* (B) 163: One good turn deserves another. As the dog said, chasing his tail. **1947** HWade *New Graves* (L) 190: One good turn deserves another. **1952** RVickers *Kynsard* (L 1965) 115: One good turn deserves another. **1955** JRRTolkien *Return* (L) 298: One ill turn deserves another. **1956** *BangorDN* 9/10 1: One good term deserves another. **1961** MClingerman *Cupful* (NY) 114: One good marriage deserves another. **1964** HMHyde *Norman* (L) 108: The old adage that one good turn deserves another. **1968** WGRogers *Ladies*

(L) 89: The theory that one good turn deserved a bad one. **1975** ARoudybush *Suddenly* (NY) 74: One good turn deserves another. EAP T294; TW 386(1); Brunvand 146(2).

T323 **Turn** about is fair play (*varied*)

1910 JCLincoln *Depot Master* (NY) 47: Turn about's fair play. **1922** JJoyce *Ulysses* (NY 1934) 530: Turn about. Sauce for one goose, my gander. **1927** EHBall *Scarlet* (NY) 181: Turn about is the first rule of the game. **1930** JJConnington *Two Tickets* (L) 262: Turn and turn about's fair play. **1937** EGreenwood *Under the Fig* (NY) 295: It was turn and turn about. **1938** CCMunz *Land* (NY) 311: Turn about is fair play. **1945** JTRogers *Red Right* (NY 1957) 99: Turn-about is fair play. **1957** KGBallard *Coast* (NY) 66: Turnabout is fair play. **1959** TWalsh *Dangerous* (B DBC) 52: Turn about . . . fair play. **1964** WTrevor *Old Boys* (NY) 184: Turn and turn about, you know. **1973** WMasterson *Undertaker* (NY) 88: Turnabout's fair play. EAP T295.

T324 As bald as a **Turnip**

1937 JDCarr *Four False* (NY) 75: He was as bald as a turnip. Cole 45.

T325 As plain as a **Turnpike**

1929 RAJWalling *Murder* (NY) 287: Plain as a turnpike. Cf. As plain as the Way *below*.

T326 As close as **Turtledoves**

1939 AMorton *Alias Blue* (P) 199: They've been as close as turtle doves.

T327 As happy as two **Turtledoves**

1934 MKing-Hall *Gay* (NY) 261: Happy as two turtledoves. TW 387.

T328 As innocent as **Turtledoves**

1934 MThomas *Inspector Wilkins* (L) 68: As innocent as a couple of turtle-doves. Lean II ii 844: Dove; Wilstach 216: Dove. Cf. As innocent as Doves *above*.

T329 **Tweedledum and Tweedledee** (*varied*)

1936 MBurton *Murder* (L) 6: Arnold . . . thought of Tweedledum and Tweedledee. **1937** BCobb *Fatal* (L) 34: Playing Tweedledee to his Tweedledum. **1940** RAHeinlein *Puppet* (NY 1965) 150: Tweedledum becomes exactly like Tweedledee. **1956** *New Yorker* 11/10 60: Two young men as alike as Tweedledum and Tweedledee. **1964** EHuxley *Forks* (L) 246: Freedom is like Tweedledum and Tweedledee. **1964** JBPriestley *Sir Michael* (L) 228: Like Tweedledum and Tweedledee. **1970** LKronenberger *No Whippings* (B) 90: They were virtually Tweedledum and Tweedledee. **1971** RFDelderfield *For My* (NY) 236: Tweedledum and Tweedledee. **1973** CAird *His Burial* (NY) 30: [They] went together as inevitably as Tweedledum and Tweedledee. EAP T297.

T330   Twenty-three skidoo

1934 JBCarr *Man with Bated Breath* (NY) 209: Twenty-three skidoo for you. **1962** MCarleton *Dread* (NY) 143: My grandmother was always saying "twenty-three skidoo." **1967** EVCunningham *Samantha* (NY) 181: That has gone the way of 23 skiddoo. Wentworth 558.

T331   As the Twig is bent so grows the tree (*varied*)

1956 IShaw *Lucy* (NY) 201: Though, as the tree is bent . . . **1959** *BGlobe* 5/2 6: As the twig is bent so grows the tree, the proverb . . . **1961** ENowell *T.Wolfe* (NY) 32: As the twig was bent, the tree would grow. **1965** HHowe *Gentle* (NY) 287: One might have guessed the way the tree would incline, considering how the young twig had been bent. **1966** LEGoss *Afterglow* (Portland, Me.) 95: As the twig is bent so doth the tree incline. **1969** JBoyd *Rakehells* (NY 1971) 71: As the twig is bent, so grows the tree. EAP T300; Brunvand 146.

T332   To hop the Twig

1925 JGBrandon *Bond* (L) 51: Hopped the twig [*vanished*]. **1937** GDilnot *Murder* (L) 169: Eloped—hopped the twig. TW 387(3,4); *Oxford* 383.

T333   In two Twinks

1932 EWallace *Frightened* (L) 195: In two twinks. NED Twink *sb.*[1] 1.

T334   In a Twinkle

1934 FBeeding *One Sane* (B) 171: Out of my depth in a twinkle. **1952** FVWMason *Himalayan* (NY 1953) 70: Done so in a twinkle. TW 387; *Oxford* 849: Twinkling.

T335   In the Twinkle of an eye

1929 VLWhitechurch *Robbery* (NY) 250: In the twinkle of an eye. **1953** CMRussell *Market* (NY) 49: In the twinkle of an eye. Whiting T547.

T336   In a Twinkling

1903 ADMcFaul *Ike Glidden* (B) 17: In a twinkling. **1919** KHoward *Peculiar* (NY) 176: In a twinkling. **1932** JJFarjeon *Z* (NY) 90: In a twinkling. **1957** *Punch* 8/28 233: Enough to empty the streets of the suburb in what is known as a twinkling. **1973** AM Stein *Finger* (NY) 159: In a twinkling. EAP T302.

T337   In the Twinkling (winking) of an eye (hand)

1913 MPShiel *Dragon* (L) 25: In the twinkling of an eye. **1931** RAFreeman *Dr. Thorndyke's* (NY) 146: In the twinkling of an eye; 240. **1936** MAllingham *Flowers* (NY) 153: In the twinkling of a hand. **1940** HSKeeler *Cleopatra's* (L) 136: In the twinkling of an eye, so to speak. **1956** JBarlow *Protagonists* (L) 5: In the twinkling of an eye. **1962** JLeCarré *Murder* (NY 1964) 7: In the twinkling of an eye. **1970** GSmith *Shattered* (NY) 233: In the winking of an eye. **1974** PThomas *Seven* (NY) 227: In the twinkling of an eye. EAP T305.

T338   If Two ride on a horse one must ride behind

1929 RGraves *Good-bye* (L) 51: If two ride together one must ride behind. **1930** CBush *Dead Man* (NY) 178: If two men ride on a horse, one has to go behind. *Oxford* 851–2.

T339   In two Twos

1922 JJoyce *Ulysses* (NY 1934) 357: In two twos. **1929** VLoder *Between* (NY) 261: Get you something in two twos. **1939** MStuart *Dead Men* (L) 119: All over the place in two two's. **1959** ECRLorac *Last* (NY) 155: The cops'll get you in two twos. **1962** LDavidson

Rose (NY) 308: They'll have you out of here in two two's. TW 388(1).

T340   It takes **Two** to make a bargain (*etc.*) (*varied*)

1908 JCLincoln *Cy Whittaker* (NY) 200: A bargain's a bargain, but it takes two to keep it. **1919** EWallace *Secret House* (NY) 8: There are two parties to every bargain. **1930** JSFletcher *Heaven-sent* (NY) 117: It takes two parties to make a bargain. **1932** TThayer *Three Sheet* (NY) 279: It takes two to make a bargain. **1934** WGore *There's Death* (L) 113: Takes two to make a wedding. **1940** AMorton *Blue Mask* (P) 154: It takes two to make a bargain. **1952** AGilbert *Mr. Crook* (NY DBC) 33: It took two to keep a bargain. **1952** HCecil *No Bail* (NY) 12: It takes two to make love. **1953** EQueen *Scarlet* (B) 74: It takes two to build a love nest. **1957** PJFarmer *Green* (NY) 51: It takes two to make a bargain. **1958** *BHerald* 7/8 25: It takes two to start something. **1958** EXFerrars *Depart* (NY) 55: Doesn't it take two to make a friendship? **1959** PFrank *Alas* (NY 1964) 208: It takes two to make a peace but only one to make a war. **1962** HCarmichael *Of Unsound* (NY) 58: It always takes two to make a bargain. **1965** GMaxwell *House* (NY) 165: It takes two to make a rendez-vous. **1966** MGEberhart *Witness* (NY) 124: It takes two to make a bargain. **1971** PTabor *Pauline's* (Louisville) 266: It takes two to tango and men . . . are equally to blame. *Oxford* 852.

T341   It takes **Two** to make a quarrel (*varied*)

1912 JCLincoln *Postmaster* (NY) 257: It takes two to make a row. **1928** CDane *Enter* (L) 216: It takes two to make a quarrel. **1941** IAlexander *Revenge* (NY) 127: A quarrel takes two. **1941** ESGardner *Empty Tin* (NY 1958) 243: It takes two to make an argument. **1956** EDillon *Death* (L) 131: It takes two to play that game. **1957** *Punch* 1/16 118: It takes two to make a mischief. **1958** ADuggan *Three's* (L) 283: It takes two to make a quarrel. **1958** JPlayfair *Pursued* (L) 33: It took two to make a failure. **1962** LEgan *Against* (NY DBC) 116: Takes two to make a fight, they say. **1962** JLudwig *Con-*

fusions (Greenwich, Conn.) 212: It takes two to make frigidity. **1964** RMacdonald *Chill* (NY) 67: It takes two to make a quarrel. **1965** PAnderson *Star* (NY) 105: It only takes one to make a quarrel. **1970** HCarmichael *Death* (NY) 203: It takes two to make a quarrel but only one to do a killing. **1974** SForbes *Some* (NY) 137: It takes two to fight. EAP T306.

T342   To put **Two** and two together

1900 CFPidgin *Quincy A. Sawyer* (B) 361: Put two and two together. **1922** JJoyce *Ulysses* (NY 1934) 630: Putting two and two together. **1926** AFielding *Footsteps* (L) 93: Haviland could add two and two together as quickly as any man. **1927** SWilliams *Drury* (NY) 192: Putting the famous "two and two" together. **1930** EDTorgerson *Murderer* (NY) 17: Adding two to the proverbial two. **1937** RPenny *Policeman in* (L) 124: You put the proverbial two and two together. **1939** JDonavan *Coloured Wind* (L) 230: He had an unhappy knack of putting two and two together. **1950** TFuller *Keep Cool* (B) 110: People are going to put two and two together. **1958** JYork *My Brother's* (NY DBC) 77: They might put two and two together. **1971** ELinington *Practice* (NY) 97: We can add two and two. **1974** AMorice *Killing* (NY) 153: I put two and two together. NED Two *sb.* II 1; Whiting *NC* 491(2).

T343   **Two** and two make four (*varied*)

1926 LThayer *Poison* (NY) 169: Two added to two will make four. **1928** RThorndike *Slype* (NY) 83: Two and two did not quite make four. **1930** WWoodrow *Moonhill* (NY) 216: Two and two don't always make four. **1931** DFrome *Strange* (NY) 304: She put two and two together and got five or six. **1933** MPlum *Murder* (NY) 249: Put two and two together to make a dangerous four. **1934** MKennedy *Corpse* (L) 212: They put two and two together and made the answer five. **1940** HAdams *Chief Witness* (L) 202: I put two and two together and made five of it. **1940** CFGregg *Fatal Error* (L) 60: Put two and two together and make twenty-two. **1941** CLittle *Black Paw* (NY) 176: He'll put two and two together and get five out of it—like always. **1950** AWUpfield *Widows* (NY) 141: Two added to two make four. **1952** ESGardner *Grinning* (NY) 45: You're always putting two and two together and making six. **1957** MSharp *Eye* (L) 154: He put two and two together and made not four but a dozen. **1959** ADuggan *Children* (NY) 219: He knew that two and two make four, that what goes up must come down, and that in the end every man will die. **1961** GHCoxe *Last* (NY) 149: You put two and two together and get five. **1964** HRFKeating *Perfect* (NY 1966) 157: Putting two and two together and making five. **1969** RDavies *Print* (L) 62: Putting two and two together . . . leads to error. **1975** DRussell *Tamarisk* (NY) 49: Put two and two together to make five. EAP T307.

T344 Two are stronger than one (*varied*)

1913 JCLincoln *Mr. Pratt's Patients* (NY) 84: Two to one's a big majority. **1941** DBHughes *Bamboo* (NY) 234: Two are stronger than one. Whiting T548. Cf. EAP T312.

T345 Two can keep a secret if one of them is dead

1969 ELeComte *Notorious* (L) 82: Ben Franklin opined that two may keep a secret if one of them is dead. **1981** CMacleod *Palace* (NY) 56: Like they say, two people can keep a secret if one of them's dead. Cf. *Oxford* 708. Cf. Secret *above*.

T346 Two can live as cheaply as one (*varied*)

1921 RLardner *Big Town* (NY 1925) 31: They say two can live cheap as one. **1939** HFootner *Murder That* (L) 111: The old hooey about two could live as cheap as one. **1953** EBurns *Sex Life* (NY) 64: The theory that "two can live as cheaply as one." **1959** DTaylor *Joy* (NY) 211: Two can't live as cheaply as one. **1967** JSymons *Man Who* (L) 38: The untruth of the old saying that two can live as cheaply as one.

T347 Two can play at that game (*varied*)

1924 TMundy *Om* (NY) 177: Two could play at that game. **1928** ABCox *Amateur* (NY) 176: Three can play at that game as well as two. **1931** JJFarjeon *House* (NY) 169:

Two can play at that game. **1939** SFowler *Wills* (L) 173: Two can play at that game. **1940** AAFair *Turn on* (NY) 233: It's a game two can play. **1941** KMKnight *Exit a Star* (NY) 163: Two could play at this cat-and-mouse game. **1950** DAWollheim *Flight* (NY) 247: Two can play at the same game. **1957** JCheever *Wapshot* (NY) 80: Two can play at this game as well as one. **1960** LHale *Blood* (L) 28: Two can play that game. **1964** CSimmons *Powdered* (NY) 39: Two can play this game. **1970** JAtkins *Sex* (L) 265: It is a game that two can and must play. **1974** ROllard *Pepys* (NY) 160: A game that two could play. EAP T309.

T348 Two is company and three is a crowd (none) (*varied*)

1900 CFPidgin *Quincy A. Sawyer* (B) 171: Swiss seemed to recognize that two was company. **1904** JCLincoln *Cap'n Eri* (NY) 234: Two's company and three's a crowd, you know. **1922** JJoyce *Ulysses* (NY 1934) 438: Under the mistletoe two is company. **1922** ERPunshon *Bittermeads* (NY) 115: Am I being the third that's proverbially no company? **1928** JJConnington *Tragedy* (B) 21: A case of two's company and three's none. **1928** BAWilliams *Dreadful* (NY) 51: I know three's a crowd. **1932** GDyer *Five* (B) 126: A case of two's company and three's a crowd. **1933** TSmith *Turnabout* (NY) 311: Two's company, three's a crowd, and four makes a vice squad. **1934** AChristie *Patriotic* (NY) 187: Alas, the proverb is true. When you are courting, two is company, is it not, three is none? **1937** JDonovan *Case* (L) 100: You know the old gag: "Two's company, three's a crowd." **1941** DBHughes *Bamboo* (NY) 251: Three's proverbial [*a crowd*]. **1952** FKane *Bare* (NY 1960) 90: Haven't you heard three's a crowd—especially in a motel. **1954** EWChase *Always* (NY) 28: Three was not only a crowd but a controversy. **1957** *BHerald* 11/8 55: Like I always say, two's company, three's a crowd. **1958** CLBlackstone *All Men* (NY) 110: It's a case of two's company . . . I don't like playing gooseberry. **1958** ADuggan *Three's Company* (L). **1960** AGilbert *Out for* (NY 1965) 31: You know the one about three being a crowd. **1961** JMaclaren-Ross *Doomsday* (L)

46: Two's company, three's none, as the saying goes. **1963** HWaugh *Death* (NY) 59: Four's company, three's a crowd. **1969** ELeComte *Notorious* (L) 43: Maybe she thought three's company, four a crowd. **1969** SPalmer *Hildegarde* (NY) 181: The principle that two's company and five's a mob. **1971** DMDisney *Three's a Crowd* (NY). **1973** JDMacDonald *Turquoise* (P) 56: Four was company, three was a crowd. TW 388–9(8); *Oxford* 851.

T349 Two of a trade never agree (*varied*)

1914 HHMunro *Beasts* (NY 1928) 74: The old saying that two of a trade never agree. **1930** GMitchell *Mystery* (NY) 297: It was a case of two of a trade. **1945** PWentworth *She Came* (NY) 17: I didn't think two of a trade would agree. EAP T311.

T350 Not care Twopence

1924 JSFletcher *Time-Worn* (NY) 169: I don't care twopence. **1932** FWCrofts *Double* (NY) 132: I don't believe . . . Brenda cared tuppence. NED Twopence 3.

T351 Not matter (worth) Twopence

1929 CBush *Perfect* (NY) 228: It's not worth tuppence. **1930** JSFletcher *Matheson* (L) 306: It doesn't matter twopence. NED Twopence 3. Cf. Apperson 458(41): Three halfpence.

T352 A Twopenny-ha'penny chap (*etc.*)

1928 GDHCole *Man* (NY) 46: A little tupenny-ha'penny chap. **1949** MAllingham *More Work* (NY) 104: The whole tupenny-ha'penny outfit. **1956** JFStraker *Ginger* (L) 126: This isn't a tupenny ha'penny theft. NED Twopenny B 3.

U

U1 Better be **Unborn** than untaught

1931 PBaron *Round* (NY) 294: It is better to be unborn than untaught. *Oxford* 56–7.

U2 Like **Uncle**, like nephew (niece)

1933 EPhillpotts *Captain's* (NY) 47: Like uncle, like nephew. **1956** SDean *Marked* (NY) 188: Like uncle, like niece. **1957** FLockridge *Tangled* (P) 183: He said that he had never heard that it was like uncle like nephew. Cf. Like Father, Like Mother *above*.

U3 To cry (*etc.*) **Uncle**

1935 CGFinney *Circus* (NY) 100: He was ready to cry uncle. **1937** ATilton *Beginning* (NY) 236: Do you cry uncle? **1947** FCDavis *Thursday's* (NY) 218: To make you call uncle. **1955** JEGill *House* (NY) 107: You'd know enough to cry uncle. **1957** RFenisong *Schemers* (NY) 68: She'll be glad to say "uncle." **1960** MClifton *Eight* (NY) 54: I'm not saying uncle yet. **1963** FGruber *Bridge* (NY DBC) 1: Shall I make him holler uncle? Wentworth 445: Say.

U4 Leave it to your **Uncle Dudley**

1933 VWilliams *Clock* (L) 138: You can leave her to your Uncle. 254: Trust your Uncle. **1939** EQueen *Dragon's* (NY) 133: Leave it to your Uncle Dudley. Berrey 379.3; Wentworth 560.

U5 It is the **Unexpected** that always happens (*varied*)

1911 HHMunro *Chronicles* (L 1927) 220: The old saying that in politics it's the unexpected that always happens. **1925** JGBrandon *Bond* (L) 55: They say it's the unexpected that happens. **1925** JSFletcher *Wrychester* (L) 201: It's the least expected that happens. **1932** BFlynn *Crime* (NY) 156: The unlooked for is always happening. **1936** RHull *Keep It Quiet* (NY) 18: It's the unexpected that always happens. *Oxford* 854: Unforeseen.

U6 In **Union** (unity) is strength

1933 HAdams *Strange Murder* (P) 279: Union is strength. **1935** ECRLorac *Death* (L) 224: The old adage that unity is strength. **1940** ARLong *Corpse* (NY) 48: The old adage that in unity there is strength. **1947** HWade *New Graves* (L) 275: But union is strength. **1957** *BHerald* 12/7 5: They say in unity is strength. **1966** ELathen *Murder* (NY) 159: In union there is strength. **1968** HWaugh *Con* (NY) 47: In unity there is strength. EAP U3; Brunvand 147.

U7 **United** we stand, divided we fall

1962 EFRussell *Great* (NY) 16: United we stand, divided we fall. **1968** PSBeagle *Last Unicorn* (NY) 57: United we stand, divided we fall. EAP U4.

U8 To be on one's **Uppers**

1933 GDilnot *Thousandth* (L) 221: Pretty nearly on my uppers. **1938** HAustin *Lilies* (NY) 78: You were on your uppers. **1940** FWBronson *Nice People* (NY) 7: She's on her uppers. **1947** PWentworth *Wicked* (NY) 6: You're . . . on your uppers. **1956** RMacdonald *Barbarous* (NY) 13: She was on her uppers. **1958** GHolden *Something's* (NY)

86: [She] might be on her uppers. **1974** LKronenberger *Wilkes* (NY) 67: Wilkes on his uppers. Partridge 928.

U9 Ups and downs

1930 JSFletcher *Behind* (NY) 67: You must take its ups and downs. **1938** SCallaway *Conquistador* (NY) 96: We'd had our ups and downs. **1940** MCharlton *Death of* (L) 79: I have me ups and downs like the rest of us. **1958** BNichols *Rich* (NY) 87: One has his ups and downs. **1968** CDSimak *Goblin* (NY) 40: We had our ups and downs. **1969** JBurke *Firefly* (L) 77: Every morning has its ups and downs. **1970** MStocks *My Commonplace* (L) 197: My own family life had its ups and downs. **1975** MErskine *Harriet* (NY) 4: A life of ups and downs. EAP U7; Brunvand 147.

V

V1 Variety is the spice of life (love)

1908 JCLincoln *Cy Whittaker* (NY) 40–1: Variety . . . is the spice of life. **1927** RKing *Mystery* (NY) 162: They do say that variety is the spice of life. **1934** JTFarrell *Young Manhood* (NY 1935) 292: Variety is the spice of life. **1938** JJConnington *For Murder* (L) 27: Variety was the very spice of life to him. **1957** *New Yorker* 4/6 24: Variety is the spice of the Handy system. **1958** *New Yorker* 5/3 32: Is variety the spice of life? **1960** JSymons *Progress* (L) 237: Variety . . . It's the spice of life. **1969** SPalmer *Hildegarde* (NY) 40: Variety is the spice of life. **1971** EHCohen *Mademoiselle* (B) 174: Variety . . . is the spice of love. TW 391. Cf. EAP V8.

V2 As safe as a Vault

1934 SPalmer *Silver Persian* (NY) 152: Safe as a vault. Cf. Bank *above*.

V3 As smooth as Velvet

1931 MGEberhart *From This* (NY) 230: Her low voice was as smooth as velvet. **1954** RStout *Black* (NY) 75: Guido's oars were as smooth as velvet [*rowing at night*]. **1965** RDrexler *I Am* (NY) 142: He also said my vagina was smooth as velvet. **1969** HPentecost *Girl Watcher* (NY) 156: His manner became smooth as velvet. Whiting *NC* 491(2); Taylor *Prov. Comp.* 75.

V4 As soft as Velvet

1929 CReeve *Ginger* (NY) 12: A voice . . . soft as velvet. TW 391; Taylor *Western Folklore* 17(1958) 20.

V5 To be on Velvet

1929 BFlynn *Billiard* (P) 255: I should be on velvet. **1937** JJConnington *Minor* (L) 71: I'm on velvet, after all. EAP V11.

V6 Empty Vessels make most noise (*varied*)

1922 JJoyce *Ulysses* (NY 1934) 278: Empty vessels make most noise. **1936** KSteel *Murder Goes* (I) 283: The more hollow the vessel, the louder the sound. TW 391. Cf. EAP V12. Cf. Wagon *below*.

V7 The Vicar of Bray

1962 ABurgess *Wanting* (L) 232: Derek . . . would have power, in his trimmer's Vicar of Bray way, whatever party reigned. **1970** DMDevine *Illegal* (NY) 129: He'll be on the winning side . . . Like the Vicar of Bray. EAP V13.

V8 As sour as Vinegar

1975 MErskine *Harriet* (NY) 121: Looking as sour as vinegar. EAP V22.

V9 Vinegar is the wife of wine

1971 ADavidson *Peregrine* (NY) 12: *Vinegar was the wife of wine.* EAP V23: Son.

V10 Violence begets violence

1930 WLivingston *Mystery* (NY) 142: Violence begets violence. **1936** NBlake *Thou Shell* (L) 96: Violence, they say, begets violence. **1952** KMKnight *Valse* (NY) 91: Violence begets violence.

V11 As modest as a Violet (*varied*)

1938 HHolt *Wanted* (L) 68: I'm a modest shrinking violet. **1938** VLoder *Kill* (L) 10:

Modest as a violet. **1945** MColes *Green Hazard* (NY) 116: The proverbial violet is a peony compared to me [*modest*]. Wilstach 264. Cf. Brunvand 149: Pure; Taylor *Prov. Comp.* 72: Shy.

V12 A **Viper** (snake, serpent) in one's bosom

1926 LThayer *Poison* (NY) 277: We've been warming a viper in our bosoms. **1930** CClausen *Gloyne* (NY) 193: A nice rattlesnake to be harboring in one's bosom. **1934** EQueen *Adventures* (NY) 342: We're nursing a viper at our bosoms. **1935** PGWodehouse *Blandings* (NY) 47: You're a serpent in the bosom. I mean a snake in the grass. **1940** CBDawson *Lady Wept* (NY) 152: You are a snake in me bosom. **1947** LFord *Woman* (NY) 24: Dorothy had taken a viper to her bosom. **1952** TClaymore *Reunion* (NY 1955) 47: Snake . . . viper in my bosom. **1966** DHitchens *Man Who Cried* (NY) 141: Cannon had, as the saying goes, taken a snake to his bosom. **1968** NFleming *Counter* (NY) 123: Quite the little snake in the bosom. **1970** JPorter *Dover Strikes* (NY) 148: Talk about nursing a viper in your bosom! **1975** HDolson (P) 193: I don't mean that [he] could have nursed a viper of revenge in his bosom—do men have bosoms? EAP V24. Cf. Brunvand 149(2).

V13 To make a **Virtue** of necessity (*varied*)

1928 WRoughead *Malice* (L) 202: Make a merit of necessity. **1929** EDBiggers *Black* (I) 236: Making a virtue of necessity. **1929** JSFletcher *Ransom* (NY) 17: Make a virtue of necessity. **1930** HWade *Dying* (L) 180: Necessity was best treated as a virtue. **1947** HCahill *Look* (NY) 11: A new wrinkle on the virtue of necessity. **1948** WLewis *Letters* ed WKRose (L 1963) 432: Of that necessity he typically makes a virtue. **1957** *BangorDN* 6/24 12: Mao Tze-tung makes virtue out of urgent necessity. **1958** *Portland Press Herald* 7/21 8: Maine must make a virtue of necessity. **1959** *NYTimes* 12/20 24: Adenauer has made a virtue of a necessity. **1964** RO'Connor *Jack* (B) 72: It was more a matter of necessity than virtue. **1969** JLunt *Bokhara* (L) 126: Making a virtue of necessity. **1971** EHCohen *Mademoiselle* (B) 103:

She . . . of necessity made a virtue out of virtue. EAP V27; TW 392(1).

V14 **Virtue** is its own reward (*varied*)

1906 JCLincoln *Mr. Pratt* (NY) 227: Virtue must be its own reward. **c1923** ACrowley *Confessions* ed JSymonds (L 1969) 468: Virtue brings its own reward. **1929** JSStrange *Clue* (NY) 257: Virtue is its own reward. **1933** RBCGraham *Portrait* (L) 253: The futility of the old saw, "virtue is its own reward." **1936** FWCrofts *Man Overboard!* (NY) 344: He had frequently been assured that virtue was its own reward. **1952** HCecil *Ways* (L) 266: Virtue must be its own reward. **1960** RRMathison *Faiths* (I) 47: Virtue, as the old saw goes, is its own reward. **1960** JSymons *Progress* (L) 202: The old phrase, virtue is its own reward. **1966** NMonsarrat *Life* (L) 21: Virtue is its own reward, the primmest of all the proverbs. **1974** HCarmichael *Most* (NY) 224: Who says virtue is its own reward? **1976** JPorter *Package* (NY) 90: Virtue, they say, is its own reward. EAP xxix, V29; Brunvand 149.

V15 As tight as a **Vise**

1930 JSFletcher *Green Rope* (L) 36: Held their tongues as tight as a vice. **1943** AAbbott *Shudders* (NY) 122: Holding that audience tight as a vise.

V16 The **Voice** of the people is the voice of God (*varied*)

1930 RGBrowne *By Way* (NY) 51: Vox populi, vox Dei. **1935** SWilliams *Murder* (NY) 80: A case of "Vox Roosevelt, vox Dei." **1937** HCBailey *Black Land* (NY) 147: Voice of the people, voice of God. Sometimes. **1937** RWWinston *It's a Far Cry* (NY) 169: The voice of the people is the voice of God. **1944** VWBrooks *Washington Irving* (NY 1946) 327: As if the voice of the majority were the voice of God. **1948** ELipsky *Murder One* (NY) 105: Vox populi, vox Dei. The People's voice is the voice of God. **1950** VSReid *New Day* (L) 103: The people's voice which is the voice o' God. **1955** RDavies *Heaven* (L) 10: The voice of the people, no editor is ever permitted to forget, is the voice of God. **1956** FSwinnerton *Background* (L) 180: The voice of the people would indeed prove to be the voice of God. **1961** CJenkins *Message* (L) 71: *Vox populi . . . vox dei.* **1964** MColes *Knife* (NY DBC) 149: The Voice of the People . . . is the Voice of God. **1964** RDuncan *All Men* (L) 209: Voice of God . . . Vox Populi. **1974** WBridges *Gathering* (NY) 117: The doctrine of *vox populi, vox Dei.* EAP V31; TW 392.

W

W1   As thin as a **Wafer**

1953 ECrandall *White* (B) 47: One hand, thin as a wafer. **1963** MErskine *No. 9* (NY) 76: It was thin as a wafer and sharp as a razor. **1973** BPronzini *Undercurrent* (NY) 11: A body thin as a wafer. EAP W1.

W2   As cute as a little red **Wagon**

1952 PGWodehouse *Angel* (NY) 116: You're as cute as a little red wagon. Taylor *Prov. Comp.* 31.

W3   Empty **Wagons** make the most noise

1931 JTully *Blood* (NY) 70: Empty wagons make the most noise. **1957** *BangorDN* 4/13 12: The old saying that "an empty wagon makes the most noise." Whiting *NC* 491(2). Cf. Vessels *above*.

W4   To fix (stop) one's **Wagon** (wheel, bucket)

1936 EQueen *Door* (Cleveland 1946) 293: I'll fix her wagon. **1940** EHealy *Mr. Sandeman* (NY) 73: I'll see that your wagon is fixed for you. **1947** VSiller *Curtain* (NY) 153: He might have fixed my bucket [*killed*]. **1947** HCahill *Look* (NY) 145: That would stop their wagons. **1951** HRigsby *Murder for* (NY 1952) 5: Somebody's trying to fix my wagon. **1952** DBOlsen *Enrollment* (NY) 96: I'm going to fix his little red wagon. **1959** BClifton *Murder* (NY) 147: All he needed was a little time, and he'd fix Petersen's wheel. **1964** AMStein *Blood* (NY) 18: It don't mean I can't still fix your wagon. **1971** ADavidson *Peregrine* (NY) 8: Chuck would soon fix the old lady's wagon.

1982 BPronzini *Scattershot* (NY) 24: I'm going to fix his wagon [*get him in trouble*]. Wentworth 187: Fix.

W5   To hitch one's **Wagon** to a star (*varied*)

1935 BFlynn *Edge* (L) 136: Bathurst hitched his wagon to my star. **1936** AM Chase *Twenty Minutes* (NY) 129: Hitch your wagon to a star. **1945** GBellairs *Calamity* (NY) 206: Hitched his wagon to a shooting star. **1948** HActon *Memoirs* (L) 198: He had hitched his wagon to some unattainable star. **1956** BCClough *More* (Portland, Me.) 162: Hitching his wagon to a star. **1958** SBarr *Purely* (NY) 122: She had believed in his star and she had hitched her wagon to it. **1964** BKaufman *Up the Down* (NY 1966) 63: Hitch your wagon to a star. **1968** BBlack *Passionate* (NY) 153: Moira's wagon was hitched directly to Jonathan's shooting star. **1974** JKaplan *LSteffens* (NY) 104: Hitching their wagons to the star of reform. *Oxford* 375.

W6   **Wait** and see

1928 JArnold *Surrey* (L) 53: Wait and see. **1935** ECRLorac *Affair* (L) 204: Wait and see's a very good motto. **1940** ECRLorac *Tryst* (L) 234: Wait and see's a good motto. **1958** ECRLorac *People* (NY) 190: Emma's motto was wait and see. EAP W4.

W7   To get (give, be given) one's **Walking** ticket (papers)

1900 CFPidgin *Quincy A. Sawyer* (B) 361: She'll git her walkin' ticket. **1911** JCLincoln *Woman-Haters* (NY) 49: Given his walking papers. **1939** TPolsky *Curtains* (NY) 306: I got my walking papers. **1952** EPaul *Black* (NY) 121: You'll get your walking ticket. **1960** RWatters *Murder* (Dublin) 304: I was to give him his walking papers. **1965** HBevington *Charley* (NY) 41: She had given him his walking papers. TW 393; Brunvand 150: Papers.

W8   As blank as a (stone) **Wall**

1927 JSFletcher *Lynne* (L) 220: [His] face was blank as a stone wall. **1954** MAllingham *No Love* (NY) 87: His face blank as a wall. **1962** RMacdonald *Zebra* (NY) 153: Her face was blank as a wall.

W9   As well talk to a stone (brick) **Wall** (*varied*)

1928 GDHCole *Man* (NY) 61: You might as well have talked to a stone wall. **1930** JCournos *Grandmother* (NY) 108: You might as well talk to a stone wall. **1934** JSStrange *Chinese Jar* (L) 249: You might as well argue with a stone wall. **1937** HAshbrook *Murder* (NY) 84: It was like talking to the proverbial stone wall. **1941** JJConnington *Twenty-one* (B) 8: One might as well talk to a stone wall. **1960** TFurlong *Time* (NY) 91: I might as well talk to the wall. **1965** JTurner *Blue* (L 1967) 84: It's like talking to a brick wall. Cf. Whiting W26.

W10   To be driven to the **Wall**

1935 TAPlummer *Creaking* (L) 233: Driven to the wall. **1971** TMcLaughlin *Dirt* (NY) 120: Most of the others were driven to the wall. EAP W11; Whiting W21; Tilley W15.

W11   To be up against a brick (*etc.*) **Wall**

1920 N&JOakley *Clevedon* (P) 162: I have run up against a brick wall. **1923** JSFletcher *Lost Mr. Linthwaite* (NY) 139: Running against a dead wall. **1924** JSFletcher *Safety* (NY) 131: Up against a brick wall. **1930** The Aresbys *Murder* (NY) 39: He was up against a blank wall. **1932** JSFletcher *Squire's Pew* (NY) 225: Chaney was up against a brick wall. **1933** HAshbrook *Murder* (NY) 160: Absolutely stymied, up against a stone wall. **1940** HAshbrook *Murder Comes* (NY) 137: Stymied. Up against a stone wall. Checkmated. **1958**

NFitzgerald *Suffer* (L) 207: We're up against the same blank wall. EAP W11; Tilley W15.

W12   To drive (be driven) up the **Wall(s)**

1959 KBulmer *Changeling* (NY) 15: It'd drive me up the wall. **1962** STruss *Time* (NY) 16: Driving her up the wall with boredom. **1965** EMcBain *Doll* (NY) 185: I was ready to climb the walls. **1969** DClark *Nobody's* (NY) 49: He really does drive us up the wall. **1971** JLymington *Nowhere* (NY) 138: He's up the wall yelling from the top.

W13   To go to the **Wall**

1933 JVTurner *Amos* (L) 120: I had to go to the wall. **1938** ECRLorac *Slippery* (L) 110: Other loyalties must go to the wall. EAP W11; Tilley W15.

W14   To see through a brick (*etc.*) **Wall** (*varied*)

1923 JSFletcher *Markenmore* (NY) 255: "I can't see through a brick wall." "Tis a true saying, that!" **1925** GHGerould *Midsummer* (NY) 126: If Edge can see through the stone wall we seem to be facing. **1928** RAJWalling *That Dinner* (NY) 134: You can see as far as anybody through a wall. **1929** HAdams *Oddways* (P) 275: We squabbled as to who could see furthest through a brick wall. **1930** JSFletcher *Investigators* (NY) 98: I'm a woman; I can see through a wall where you can't see through a window. **1933** DGBrowne *Cotfold* (L) 138: Ashlyn . . . could see as far through a brick wall as any one. **1936** RAFreeman *Penrose* (NY) 103: I understood . . . you could see through a brick wall. **1953** JRhode *Mysterious* (NY DBC) 93: I can see as far through a brick wall as most people. **1957** RChurch *Golden* (NY) 87: A wise person who could see further through a brick wall than most people. **1962** ALOwen *Famous* (Oxford) 119: [He] could see farther into a stone wall than most. **1971** DClark *Sick* (NY) 47: I can see as far through a brick wall as the next person. **1972** HPentecost *Champagne* (NY) 82: He can see through brick walls. NED Wall *sb.* 18; Berrey 171.2: Millstone. Cf. Grindstone *above*.

W15 Walls have ears (*varied*)

1905 FMWhite *Crimson Blind* (NY) 212: Stone walls have ears. **1922** DFox *Ethel* (NY) 44: An old saying . . . that walls are sometimes provided with ears. **1922** JJoyce *Ulysses* (NY 1934) 435: Walls have ears. **1929** JJFarjeon *Person* (NY) 11: Walls have ears and eyes. **1930** DOgburn *Ra-ta-plan!* (B) 212: The very trees have ears. **1933** RAJWalling *Prove It* (NY) 101: If walls have ears the woods have eyes. **1937** JPMarquand *Late George* (B) 108: The walls have no ears to speak of. **1938** MECorne *Death* (NY) 207: Walls have ears and they have eyes. **1946** VKelsey *Whisper Murder* (NY) 16: Over a drink where walls don't have eyes and ears. **1947** AGilbert *Death in* (L) 109: He expected the walls to part and reveal a listening ear. **1950** ECRLorac *And Then* (NY) 221: Though they say walls have ears, they don't talk. **1958** *NYTimes Magazine* 11/2 28: The ears have walls. **1959** M Millar *Listening Walls* (NY). **1960** JO'Hara *Ourselves* (NY) 174: The walls have ears, they say. **1964** EHuxley *Incident* (NY) 128: The old saying, walls have ears. **1970** HActon *Memoirs* (NY) 57: Even walls have ears. **1970** JJMarric *Gideon's Sport* (NY) 52: Walls have ears, in these electronic days. **1974** EMcBain *Bread* (NY) 69: Walls have ears these days. EAP W12; Brunvand 150(1). Cf. Brunvand 145: Tree(1).

W16 To be a Wallflower

1922 JJoyce *Ulysses* (NY 1924) 727: Not liking to see her a wallflower. **1927** EHBall *Scarlet* (NY) 71: You'll be one of the wall flowers. **1940** DWheelock *Murder at Montauk* (NY) 253: She was sick and tired of being a wall-flower. EAP W14.

W17 To snore like a Walrus

1961 RFoley *It's Murder* (NY DBC) 104: "Snoring like a walrus." "Do they snore?" Cf. Grampus *above*.

W18 As thin as a Wand

1957 MLBarnes *Isabel* (P) 270: Thin as a wand. **1963** ABurgess *Vision* (L) 116: Thin as a wand. **1971** RFDelderfield *For My* (NY) 349: A young man, thin as a wand.

Cf. Whiting W31: Small; *Oxford* 744: Small.

W19 For Want of a nail *etc.*

1957 *Time* 12/30 16: Battles that were lost for want of a nail. EAP W16.

W20 To be War to the knife

1941 PWilde *Design* (NY) 243: It was war to the knife between us. **1960** EXFerrars *Fear* (NY) 144: It's war to the knife between us. **1964** RBlythe *Age* (B) 25: It was war to the knife. TW 394(1); *Oxford* 867.

W21 To carry the War into the enemy's country (camp, Africa)

1926 HAdams *Crooked* (L) 173: He carried the war into the enemy's country. **1931** AChristie *Sittaford* (L) 111: She always carried the war into the enemy's country. **1931** MAHamilton *Murder* (L) 19: Carrying the war right into the enemy's camp. **1938** DCDisney *Strawstack* (NY) 169: To carry the offensive into the enemy's country. **1938** HMcCloy *Dance* (NY) 237: He carried the war into Africa. **1956** JFStraker *Ginger* (L) 69: To lead the war into the enemy's camp before it was taken into his. **1964** DCecil *Max* (L) 80: Carry the war into the enemy's country. **1971** EMannin *Young* (L) 79: Take the war into the enemy camp. EAP W23; Brunvand 150: Africa.

W22 War with all the world but not with England

1935 RGarnett *Death* (L) 48: You may war with all the world . . . but not with England—*Con todo el mundo guerra, y paz con Inglaterra!* *Oxford* 867.

W23 To be getting Warm, as the children say (*varied*)

1929 HFootner *Doctor* (L) 101: I was becoming "warm" as the children say. **1929** EJMillward *Copper* (NY) 163: You were hot then, as the kids say. **1930** CBush *Dead Man* (NY) 292: Wharton, in the words of the children's game, was getting very warm. **1935** BFlynn *Case* (L) 197: Now you're getting warm, as the children say in their game. **1937** WSMasterman *Border* (NY) 106: We are getting warm, as children say in hunt the thimble. **1940** CRawson *Headless* (NY) 112: You suppose wrong ... though you're warm. **1954** AWUpfield *Sinister* (NY) 134: As the children say, I'm getting warm. **1963** AWUpfield *Body* (NY) 143: I may be getting warm, as the children say. NED Warm *adj.* 6.

W24 As plain as a **Wart** on the nose (face)
1933 REssex *Slade* (NY) 151: That's as plain as a wart on the nose. **1938** SKing *If I Die* (NY) 56: You can see plain as the wart on my face. Wilstach 294: As a nose.

W25 To come out in the **Wash**
1925 JGBrandon *Bond* (L) 208: It all comes out in the wash. **1936** EQueen *Door* (Cleveland 1946) 221: It'll all come out in the wash. **1938** FDGrierson *Acrefield* (L) 127: It'll all come out in the wash. **1941** DVanDeusen *Garden Club* (I) 182: Come out in the wash. **1951** ECRLorac *I Could* (NY) 167: They'll all come out in the wash, as the saying is. **1954** MMcCarthy *Charmed* (NY) 304: What is the expression? It will all come out in the wash. **1961** NBlake *Worm* (L) 121: It'll all come out in the wash. **1962** AWUpfield *Will* (NY) 96: Everything will come out in the wash. **1975** RStout *Family* (NY) 112: It will all come out in the wash. *Oxford* 135: Come.

W26 Not to **Wash**
1928 JArnold *Surrey* (L) 309: It won't wash. **1937** CDickson *Ten Teacups* (L) 123: That wouldn't wash. **1945** ADerleth *In Re* (Sauk City, Wisc.) 56: That will not wash. **1953** CLittle *Black* (NY) 185: That one won't wash. Partridge 939; NED Wash *v.* 2j.

W27 **Wash** and wipe together, live in peace forever
1957 HPBeck *Folklore of Maine* (P) 79: Wash and wipe together, live and fight forever.

W28 As dizzy (wicked) as a **Wasp**
1954 RKLeavitt *Chip* (P) 139: He's wicked as a wasp. **1957** COLocke *Hell Bent* (NY) 204: I was dizzy as a wasp. Cf. Whiting *NC* 492(1): Ill. Cf. Hornet *above*.

W29 As mad as a **Wasp**
1953 EPaul *Waylaid* (NY) 153: Madder than wasps. Cf. Hornet *above*.

W30 Wilful **Waste** makes woeful want
1946 RFinnegan *Lying* (NY) 44: Wilful waste makes woeful want. **1958** RLDuffus *Williamstown* (NY) 165: We used to say that wilful waste makes woeful want. EAP W27.

W31 **Waste** not, want not (*varied*)
1923 Anonymous *Horn Book* (L) 93: Waste not, want not. **1932** TSmith *Topper Takes* (NY) 237: Waste not, want not. **1933** NBell *Lord* (B) 233: Waste not want not, as my old Mum used to say. **1954** MColes *Brief* (NY) 16: "Waste not, want not," is a good saying. **1957** *Punch* 4/17 493: A meticulous man, wasting not, and thus hoping not to want. **1962** ABurgess *Wanting* (L) 172: Waste not, want not. **1968** JTStory *I Sit* (L) 158: Waste not want not. **1970** EHahn *Times* (NY) 98: Waste not, want not. **1973** AMorice *Death* (NY) 13: Waste not, want not is my motto. *Oxford* 869.

W32 To keep **Watch** and ward
1931 CWells *Umbrella* (NY) 266: To keep watch and ward. EAP W28.

W33 As clear as **Water** (*varied*)
1933 PMacDonald *Mystery* (NY 1958) 143: Isn't it clear as water? **1942** VCaspary *Laura* (NY 1957) 119: It was clear as water out of the old oaken bucket. **1947** DBowers *Bells* (NY) 44: Her eyes clear as water. **1953** RChandler *Long* (L) 184: Her eyes were as clear as water. Whiting W61 (quote 1387).

W34 As free as **Water**
1937 GGVanDeusen *Henry Clay* (B) 154: Loans were as free as water. Whiting *NC* 492(1).

W35 As sure as **Water's** wet
1940 RStout *Where There's* (NY) 179: As sure as water's wet. Taylor *Prov. Comp.* 86: As wet as water.

W36 As unstable (slippery) as **Water** (*varied*)
1930 The Aresbys *Murder* (NY) 247: Reuben, unstable as water. **1939** HFootner *Murder That* (L) 98: Unstable as water.

1940 HFootner *Sinfully* (L) 193: Amy's emotions were as unstable as water. **1953** JFleming *Good* (L) 57: Her morals were as unstable as water. **1961** LFielden *Natural* (P) 57: I was unstable as water. **1965** CArmstrong *Turret* (NY) 40: The old lady was slippery as water. **1970** MGEberhart *El Rancho* (NY DBC) 97: She's no more stable than water. EAP W29.

W37 As weak as (rain) **Water**

1925 FBeeding *Seven* (B) 188: I was . . . weak as water. **1927** WDSteele *Man Who* (NY) 213: Weak as water. **1933** AE Housman *Letters* ed HMaas (Cambridge, Mass. 1971) 346: Leaves one as weak as water. **1939** FGerard *Red Rope* (NY) 45: Vernon was always weak as water. **1947** VWMason *Saigon* (NY) 193: The fellow was as weak as rain water. **1956** ACLewis *Jenny* (NY) 281: A man weak as water. **1957** *NYTimes Book Review* 12/1 57: Inconstant, weak as water. **1963** AChristie *Clocks* (NY) 98: Weak as water. **1971** PTabor *Pauline's* (Louisville) 49: My knees were as weak as water. EAP W30; Brunvand 150(1).

W38 Like **Water** off (on) a duck's back (*varied*)

1920 AChristie *Mysterious Affair* (NY) 24: Probably water off a duck's back. **1925** JSFletcher *False* (NY) 193: It all goes off me . . . like rain off a fat duck's back. **1932** AGilbert *Body* (NY) 210: Ordinary punishments were like water on a duck's back. **1934** PATaylor *Sandbar* (NY) 194: It was all rolling off Asey like the proverbial water off a duck's back. **1937** NBell *Crocus* (NY) 153: Allowing the few jests . . . to slip off him like the proverbial water off a duck's back. **1937** SPalmer *Blue Banderilla* (NY) 256: An intended sarcasm which passed like water from the back of the proverbial duck. **1938** ESGardner *Shoplifter's Shoe* (NY) 102: It would run off your back like water off a duck's stomach. **1938** WLewis *Letters* ed WKRose (L 1963) 255: Denunciations . . . will just roll like water off the back of the proverbial duck. **1940** GPatten *Autobiography* ed HHinsdale (Norman, Okla. 1964) 186: Flattery . . . rolls off me like rain off a duck's back. **1952** HHun-

ter *Bengal* (NY) 67: It runs off you like water off a duck. **1953** EBGarside *Man from* (NY) 14: Rolled off her like water from an eider's back. **1956** *Cambridge Chronicle Sun* 10/4 2: He said such complaints rolled off him like water off a duck. **1956** FAllen *Much* (B) 267: It is like pouring water on a duck's back—in one ear and out the other. **1962** JWoodford *Autobiography* (NY) 209: It rolls off, to coin a phrase, like water off a duck's back. **1966** COgburn *Winter* (NY) 62: Maine [would] prove as impervious [*to outsiders*] as the proverbial duck's back off which water flows. **1966** ACarter *Honeybuzzard* (NY) 34: Relationships ran off him like water off the proverbial duck's back. **1968** JPorter *Dover Goes* (NY) 69: [It] is like water off a dead duck's back. **1972** PRReynolds *Middle* (NY) 206: My words were water off a duck's back. **1977** PDickinson *Walking* (NY) 255: Water off a duck's back. TW 395(15); Oxford 871.

W39 Much **Water** has run under the bridge since then (*very varied*)

1917 WLewis *Letters* ed WKRose (L 1963) 91: Much water must have flown under that bridge. **1923** HWNevinson *Changes* (NY) 218: A good deal of water has passed under the bridge since then. **1927** HE Wortham *Victorian Eton* (L 1956) 143: A good deal of water has flowed beneath Windsor Bridge since then. **1930** SBHustvedt *Ballad Books* (Cambridge, Mass.) 3: Much water has flowed beneath the bridges of criticism since that time. **1930** RVDMagoffin *Romance* (L) 154: Much water will yet run under the mill before that. **1931** MJFreeman *Murder* (NY) 131: Much water has flowed down the Seine since then. **1931** CWells *Skeleton* (NY) 69: Much water will flow over the Hudson Tunnel before we find out the truth. **1935** CCranston *Murder* (P) 50: A lot of water has run under the ship since. **1936** JDosPassos *Big Money* (NY) 540: A lot of water's run under the bridge since then. **1938** JCLenehan *Guilty* (L) 185: You can't bring back water that's flowed under the bridge. **1948** HReilly *Staircase* (NY) 122: Water under the bridge, over the dam.

1952 AChristie *Mrs. McGinty* (NY) 239: A lot of water under the bridge since then. **1959** *BHerald* 1/11 5: A lot of water has gone under the bridge, as the old fellow said, since the Republicans lost the last election. **1964** PBecker *Rule* (L) xvi: Since those far-off days much of the proverbial water has passed beneath the bridges of time. **1964** MWiddemer *Golden* (NY) 52: Much water had flowed under the bridge. **1970** RFenisong *Drop* (NY) 188: It was all water under the bridge. **1974** JFlaherty *Chez* (NY) 227: [It] is, to coin a phrase, water under the bridge. **1975** HLawrenson *Stranger* (NY) 158: A lot of girls had gone under Bernie's bridge by then. **1982** SAllen *Talk* (NY) 41: A lot of water had passed under the bridge since then, eroding away a great many rough edges. *Oxford* 870.

W40 Not to hold **Water**

1918 JWatson&AJRees *Mystery of the Downs* (NY) 91: Your story won't hold water. **1922** JJoyce *Ulysses* (NY 1934) 641: Some of which wouldn't exactly hold water. **1924** MDPost *Walker* (NY) 236: So it'll hold water. **1933** ABCox *Jumping* (L) 173: Your case . . . won't hold water. **1940** CKnight *Death Valley* (NY) 258: The thing doesn't hold water. It's like a sieve. **1951** RJHealey *New Tales* (NY) 40: That just doesn't hold water. **1961** JSStrange *Eye* (NY) 65: That argument didn't hold water. **1966** ELathen *Murder* (NY) 114: It held no water. **1973** WMasterson *Undertaker* (NY) 157: It won't hold water. EAP W36.

W41 Not to miss the **Water** till the well runs dry

1958 *BangorDN* 6/12 25: You never miss the water till the well runs dry. **1970** EHahn *Times* (NY) 98: You never miss the water till the well runs dry. *Oxford* 435: Know.

W42 Still **Waters** run deep (*varied*)

1915 RFirbank *Vainglory* (Works 1, L 1929) 67: Still waters run deep. **1928** HWade *Missing* (NY) 17: Still waters run deep. **1928** EBYoung *Murder* (P) 156: Still waters run deep. **1932** JVTurner *Who Spoke* (L) 233: If still waters don't run deep now how many rolling stones can you buy for a shilling? **1933** JSFletcher *Who Killed* (L) 65: There's a saying, you know, that still waters run deep. **1934** JTFarrell *Young Lonigan* (NY 1935) 396: A case of still waters running deep. **1940** TChanslor *Our First* (NY) 170: Still waters run deep I always say. **1941** CWells *Murder . . . Casino* (P) 115: Still waters run deep. **1950** PMcGerr *Fellow* (NY) 98: Still water, eh? . . . how deep, I wonder. **1959** EMButler *Paper* (L) 29: The stiller waters which run so deep. **1962** AGarve *Prisoner's* (NY DBC) 53: She's a case of still waters. **1968** DMDisney *Voice* (NY) 164: Still waters run deep, they say. **1969** AGilbert *Mr. Crook* (NY DBC) 44: Still waters run deep—no one ever said a truer word. **1972** JRipley *Davis* (NY) 135: Tha's a deep 'un. Talk about still waters. **1973** RRendell *Some* (NY) 149: They are still waters which not only run deep but which have turbulent undercurrents. EAP W38; TW 394(10).

W43 Stolen **Waters** are sweet *etc.* (*varied*)

1925 DVane *Scar* (NY) 20: Stolen waters are sweet and bread eaten in secret is pleasant. **1930** IWray *Vye* (L) 92: I discovered long ago that those proverbs about stolen things being the sweetest are all wrong. **1934** HAdams *Knife* (L) 23: Solomon tells us stolen joy is the sweetest. **1959** GMitchell *Man Who* (L) 32: There are no pleasures like forbidden pleasures. EAP W39.

W44 There is aye **Water** where the stirkie is drowned

1931 AWynne *Blue* (P) 132: We have a proverb in Scotland that says: "There's aye water where the stirkie's drowned." *Oxford* 871; Apperson 669(7).

W45 To be in deep **Water(s)** (*varied*)

1930 EBarker *Redman* (NY) 84: In pretty deep water. **1933** FDGrierson *Mystery* (L) 134: He felt that he was swimming in deep water. **1939** CFGregg *Danger* (L) 187: You've got into mighty deep waters. **1958** GHolden *Something's* (NY) 115: He might have meant the old saying about getting into deep water. Wentworth 569.

W46 To be in (get into) hot **Water**

1922 JJoyce *Ulysses* (NY 1934) 630: He got landed into hot water. **1925** EMPoate *Pledged* (NY) 291: You ain't outa hot water yet. **1932** RAFreeman *When Rogues* (L) 216: Always in hot water. **1953** EBigland *Indomitable* (L) 39: Fanny's tongue got her into hot water. **1962** FBrown *Five-Day* (NY DBC) 89: Got myself into hot water. **1972** DDevine *Three* (NY) 18: He was in hot water again. EAP W42.

W47 To be **Water** over (under) the dam (*varied*)

1921 JBCabell *Figures* (NY 1925) 77: All water that is past the dam must go its way. **1928** DCSeitz *Also Rans* (NY) 106: Much water had gone over the dam since 1848. **1929** JLeonard *Back to Stay* (NY) 84: Lots of water runnin' under the dam. **1936** CGBowers *Jefferson in Power* (B) 320: In the meantime much water had passed under the dam. **1939** HReilly *All Concerned* (NY) 206: A lot of water had gone over the dam since 1923. **1942** FLockridge *Hanged* (NY) 78: [Water] "under the dam" . . . "the bridge." . . . "Of course, *over* the dam." **1953** BBloch *Mrs. Hulett* (NY) 278: And that's water over the dam. **1957** *BHerald* 10/20 3A: As the old fellow said, a lot of water is going over the dam before then. **1966** DMDisney *At Some* (NY) 169: That was all water over the dam. **1967** TWells *Dead by* (NY) 61: It's too much water under the dam. **1970** MGEberhart *El Rancho* (NY DBC) 27: That is all water over the dam. **1970** RMungo *Famous* (B) 185: It was all blood under the dam. **1974** SForbes *Some* (NY) 93: A lot of water had gone under the dam. EAP W49.

W48 To carry **Water** on both shoulders

1930 MMott-Smith *Africa* (NY) 220: The African is quite capable of carrying water on both shoulders. **1931** DFrome *Strange* (NY) 214: She was trying to carry water on both shoulders. **1951** IChase *New York 22* (NY) 307: She would in some subtle man-

ner be able to carry water on both shoulders. **1958** WDHassett *Off the Record* (New Brunswick, NJ) 276: Baruch . . . who always carries water on both shoulders. **1968** LSdeCamp *Great Monkey* (NY) 102: Managed to carry water on both shoulders. **1974** EPHoyt *Horatio's* (Radnor, Penn.) 248: [He] was carrying water on both shoulders.

W49 To fish in troubled (muddy, *etc.*) **Waters** (*varied*)

1904 SArmitage-Smith *John of Gaunt* (L) 352: Bent on fishing . . . in troubled waters. **1919** JSClouston *Simon* (NY) 184: Fishing in very deep waters. **1929** JJConnington *Case* (B) 276: We may be able to fish something out of the disturbed waters. **1931** MDalton *Night* (NY) 163: I think that he fished in very muddy waters. **1934** MKennedy *Corpse* (L) 81: I believe in fishing in troubled waters. **1936** PFleming *News* (NY) 253: It is profitless to fish for history in such troubled waters. **1938** FDGrierson *Acrefield* (L) 95: He's fishing in damn deep waters. **1940** CEVulliamy *Calico Pie* (L) 219: Our traditional policy of angling in muddy waters to see if we could hook a stray advantage. **1948** CRBoxer *Fidalgos* (Oxford 1968) 252: To fish in troubled waters. **1952** JSherwood *Ambush* (NY) 145: He was . . . trying to stir up trouble in exceedingly muddy political waters. **1958** *BHerald* 5/2 38: They enjoy fishing in muddy waters. **1959** HCarmichael *Marked* (NY) 102: The superintendant was fishing in the same dirty water. **1961** WHLewis *Scandalous* (NY) 122: [He] was fishing in troubled waters. **1967** ANL Munby *Portrait* (L) 194: Panizzi . . . had no distaste for fishing in troubled waters. **1970** MGrant *Ancient* (NY) 291: Fishing skillfully in troubled waters. **1972** MInnes *Open* (NY) 43: [He] fished in some deuced muddy waters. **1978** DNDurant *Bess* (NY) 119: Mary . . . would have been happy to fish in these very troubled waters. EAP W41.

W50 To get **Water** out of a bone

1910 JCLincoln *Depot Master* (NY) 179: Not even a lawyer could get water out of a bone. Cf. *Oxford* 869–70: Water from a stone. Cf. You cannot get Blood *above*.

W51   To hold one's **Water**

1958 SDean *Dishonor* (NY) 117: Hold your water. NED Water 18.

W52   To pour **Water** into a sieve

1952 GBullett *Trouble* (L) 88: Giving money to Andrew was like pouring water into a sieve. **1956** RFoley *Last* (NY DBC) 42: It would be pouring water into a sieve. **1957** *NYTimes* 2/17 10E: Ministering to the people's needs is like pouring water into a sieve—it never gets filled. **1959** PMoyes *Dead Men* (L) 249: That . . . holds about as much water as a broken sieve. Whiting W86; *Oxford* 870.

W53   To take (back) **Water**

1903 ADMcFaul *Ike Glidden* (B) 69: I will not take back water [*retreat*]. **1935** HFootner *Whip-poor-will* (NY) 317: I dared myself to do it. I couldn't take water on that! EAP W44; TW 395(18).

W54   To throw away dirty **Water** *etc.*

1922 VBridges *Greensea* (NY) 122: It's no good throwing away dirty water until you get clean. *Oxford* 106: Cast not out.

W55   To throw cold **Water**

1929 ABCox *Layton* (NY) 94: Throw cold water upon everything. **1936** MBurton *Death* (L) 181: You threw cold water upon every suggestion. **1937** ASoutar *One Page* (L) 94: I cannot dash cold water on her hopes. **1952** AAFair *Top* (NY) 68: Don't throw cold water. EAP W45; Brunvand 150(2).

W56   **Water** finds (*etc.*) its own level (*varied*)

1930 CFitzsimmons *Manville* (NY) 194: The old idea of water seeking its own level. **1952** EHahn *Love* (NY) 254: I am water finding its own level. **1955** DParry *Sea* (L) 128: People find their own level. **1959** JWebb *Deadly* (NY) 54: Water . . . returns to its own level. **1973** EJKahn *Fraud* (NY) 138: Greed, like water, usually finds its own level. EAP W50.

W57   **Water** that has passed cannot make the mill go

1952 GKersh *Brazen* (L) 212: But Thomas Draxe is right: the water that has passed cannot make the mill go. *Oxford* 531: Mill cannot grind.

W58   To meet one's **Waterloo** (*varied*)

1922 JJoyce *Ulysses* (NY 1934) 446: You do get your Waterloo sometimes. **1925** IOstrander *Neglected* (NY) 111: [He'd] met his Waterloo. **1936** PQuentin *Puzzle* (NY) 283: I had met my Waterloo. **1938** NMarsh *Death* (NY) 39: He met his Waterloo. **1943** PATaylor *Going* (NY) 149: That was our Waterloo. **1948** ECrispin *Buried* (L 1958) 173: Old Samuel's met his Waterloo. **1959** JBonnett *No Grave* (NY) 152: Just my Waterloo. **1963** AChristie *Clocks* (NY) 53: Everybody meets his Waterloo in the end. **1968** MSteen *Pier* (L) 17: Her Waterloo came over the word "evacuees." **1970** CDrummond *Stab* (NY) 39: It had been Waterloo for [him]. NED Waterloo *a*.

W59   To be on (off) the **Water wagon**

1939 HMiller *Capricorn* (NY) 156: Went on the water wagon. **1941** LThayer *Hallowe'en* (NY) 50: He's fallen off the wagon. Wentworth 566: Off, on.

W60   As close as **Wax**

1925 HHext *Monster* (NY) 72: Keep it to yourself—close as wax. **1927** FDGrierson *Smiling* (NY) 255: [He's] as close as wax. Tilley W134.

W61   As neat as **Wax**

1912 JCLincoln *Postmaster* (NY) 114: The house is as neat as wax. **1934** RCAshby *Out Went* (NY) 211: Neat as wax. EAP W55.

W62   As tight as **Wax**

1931 DOgburn *Death* (B) 78: He may keep his mouth shet tight as wax. TW 395(3).

W63   As white (pale) as **Wax**; Wax-white

1922 JJoyce *Ulysses* (NY 1934) 83: Skin . . . white like wax. **1932** HFootner *Dead Man's* (NY) 290: His face was as pale as wax. **1933** DFrome *Eel Pie* (NY) 102: She was as white as wax. **1943** AAbbott *Shudders* (NY) 59: [His] wax-white visage. **1963** WMankowitz

Cockatrice (L) 10: Girl . . . pale as wax. **1966** SRansome *Hidden* (NY) 207: [He] had gone pale as wax. Wilstach 471.

W64 As yellow as **Wax**

1905 HRHaggard *Ayesha* (NY) 83: Features . . . yellow as wax. Whiting W101.

W65 To be as **Wax** in someone's hands

1923 HGartland *Globe* (NY) 227: The fellow's brain was as wax in Capwell's hands. **1928** ABCox *Amateur* (NY) 5: They became as wax in his hands. **1932** PMacDonald *Mystery* (NY) 186: Thérèse would be wax in his hands. **1937** ECRLorac *Bats* (L) 78: He was as wax in her hands. **1941** CWells *Murder . . . Casino* (P) 9: Andrew . . . was in that deplorable condition known as "wax in her hands." **1954** NBlake *Whisper* (L) 60: She was wax in Bert's hands. **1958** CCockburn *Crossing* (NY) 126: He would be as wax in your hands. **1965** PGWodehouse *Galahad* (L) 29: [He] was as wax in her hands. TW 395(5); *Oxford* 634: Pliable. Cf. Clay, Putty *above*.

W66 To melt like **Wax**

1922 JSFletcher *Ravensdene* (NY) 150: To melt like wax in a fire. EAP W58; Wilstach 258. Cf. Brunvand 150.

W67 To stick (cling) like **Wax**

1933 FHShaw *Atlantic* (NY) 114: He stuck like wax to his story. **1937** ECVivian *38 Automatic* (L) 236: He clung on to Oliver like wax. EAP W59.

W68 As motionless (still) as a **Waxwork**

1919 LMerrick *Chair* (L) 348: The young man remained . . . as motionless as a waxwork. **1940** HFootner *Sinfully* (L) 99: Cumming's face grew as still as a waxwork. **1944** MVenning *Jethro* (NY) 26: Face as still as wax. **1946** MInnes *Unsuspected* (NY) 262: Standing as stock still as waxworks. Cf. TW 396(2): Onmovable; Wilstach 265: A woman of wax.

W69 As plain as the **Way** to parish church

1926 FBeeding *Little White* (L) 71: That's as plain as the way to parish church. Wilstach 294. Cf. EAP W61: Market. Cf. Turnpike *above*.

W70 The longest **Way** round is the shortest way home (*varied*)

1920 N&JOakley *Clevedon* (P) 20: The longest way round is the quickest way home. Is that a proverb? It sounds like one. **1922** JJoyce *Ulysses* (NY 1934) 370: Longest way round is the shortest way home. **1931** JMWalsh *Company* (NY) 36: The longest way round is the sweetest way home. **1936** JO'Neill *Day* (L) 147: It would be a longer way round but a shorter way home. **1938** NBerrow *Terror* (L) 44: The longest way round is the sweetest way home. **1946** HRCampbell *Crime in Crystal* (NY) 135: He says the long way round is the short way home, and it's a long lane that has no turning. **1957** *Time* 4/29 106: The longest way round is the shortest way home. **1962** AGilbert *Uncertain* (NY DBC) 63: They had decided to take a short cut, which, as so often happens, proved the longest way home. EAP W62.

W71 One (you) cannot have it both (two) **Ways**

1927 HEWortham *Victorian Eton* (L 1956) 91: One cannot have it both ways. **1941** RStout *Broken Vase* (NY 1965) 28: You can't have it both ways. **1956** RBloomfield *When* (NY) 98: You can't have it two ways. **1956** JFStraker *Ginger* (L) 86: You can't have it both ways. **1970** CArmstrong *Protege* (NY DBC) 49: You . . . assume you can have it both ways. **1972** KCConstantine *Vicksburg* (NY) 79: He couldn't have it both ways. Cf. NED Way 28.

W72 Six (*etc.*) **Ways** from the ace (from breakfast, Sunday) (*varied*)

1923 ORCohen *Jim Hanvey* (NY) 112: She was there seven ways from the ace [*pretty*]. **1927** JTully *Circus* (NY) 178: You sure got it on Marie five ways from Sunday. **1932** LFord *Murder* (NY) 176: Got 'em beat six ways for Sunday. **1933** BRoss *Tragedy of Z* (NY) 95: Fawcett was framin' . . . Dow both ways to the ace. **1935** JTFarrell *Judgment* (NY) 28: The lad was the kind to knock a girl's heart six ways from Sunday. **1936** GMilburn *Catalogue* (NY) 61: Beat four ways to Sunday fer good looks. **1940** ECameron *Malice* (NY) 76: She's got my boardin' house beat four ways from Sunday. **1950** MCarleton *Bride* (NY) 113: You got five ways to Sunday to run in case of fire. **1951** ADerleth *Outer* (NY) 34: I had that checked every way from Sunday. **1952** CDickson *Cavalier's* (NY) 165: I am with you four ways from the ace. **1952** RMarshall *Jane* (NY) 82: I turned all ways to Sunday. **1953** FCDavis *Drag* (NY) 178: Right six ways from breakfast. **1953** SRansome *Shroud* (NY) 63: She . . . could count on my friendship forty ways from breakfast. **1955** SRansome *Frazer* (NY) 74: Bender checked sixty ways from breakfast. **1956** *BTraveler* 11/5 29: The Democrats are split five ways from Sunday. **1957** SDean *Murder* (NY) 99: You have to cut it six ways from Sunday [*divide a salary*]. **1959** EMcBain *'Til Death* (L 1964) 101: It beats television six ways from the middle. **1961** LDelRay *And Some* (NY) 70: You've got the ice packs beat three ways from Sunday. **1962** PDennis *Genius* (NY) 289: Comfort beats excitement six ways from Sunday. **1963** NBenchley *Catch* (NY) 219: You've got it made six ways to Sunday. **1968** KLaumer *Retief* (NY) 98: He outranks you forty ways from Sunday. **1968** HWaugh *"30"* (NY) 171: He'd seen her six ways to Sunday [*clothed and naked*]. **1974** SKrim *You* (NY) 170: They'll put you down from five ways to Sunday. **1980** PDeVries *Consenting* (B) 125: Did they fantasize about us twenty ways to Sunday. TW 397(15); Brunvand 151(2).

W73 There are more **Ways** than one into the woods

1929 KCStrahan *Footprints* (NY) 14: There's more than one way into the woods—and out of them. EAP W66.

W74 There are more **Ways** than one of killing (to skin) a cat (*very varied*)

1911 HHMunro *Chronicles* (L 1927) 49: There are more ways of killing a cat than by choking it with cream. **1923** JGollomb *Girl* (NY) 80: There's more'n one way to skin a cat. **1927** GDilnot *Lazy* (B) 120: There are more ways of killing a cat than one. **1929** RKing *Murder* (NY) 52: There were so many more ways than one of

frying an eel. **1931** JTully *Blood* (NY) 246: There's more'n one way to skin a cat. **1933** CBarry *Wrong Murder* (NY) 160: Have ye ever heard the old saying that there's more ways of killing a cow than choking it with butter? **1933** WBlair *Mike Fink* (NY) 101: There's mor'n one way of gettin' out of a skunk hole. **1936** PATaylor *Out of Order* (NY) 242: There were . . . more ways of killing a cat than choking it to death with sour cream. **1937** DFrome *Black Envelope* (NY) 252: An old country saying . . . There are more ways of killing a horse than choking him to death with butter. **1937** WETurpin *These Low* (NY) 322: There are more ways of picking a chicken than scalding it. **1938** HAustin *Lilies* (NY) 273: There's more than one way to skin a cat. **1938** CFGregg *Mystery* (L) 218: There's more ways of killing a cat than biting the head off. **1940** CMWills *REPipe* (L) 198: There are more ways of killing a cat than one. **1945** ABarber *Noose* (NY) 53: There are many ways of skinning a cat. **1952** JKnox *Little* (P) 125: There's more than one way to skin a rabbit. **1952** RFenisong *Deadlock* (NY) 160: There are more ways of killing a cow than slitting its throat. **1952** JWKrutch *Desert* (NY) 29: Though there are more ways to kill a cat than by stuffing him with cream that is, nevertheless, one way. **1952** SSmith *Crooked* (NY) 59: There are more ways of killing a cat than choking it to death with whiskey. **1954** EQueen *Glass* (B) 125: I know a dozen ways to skin a balky calf. **1955** EFrankland *Murders* (L) 36: There are more ways of killing a dog than hanging it. **1955** RFenisong *Widows* (NY) 116: It reminded her of an adage . . . There are more ways of killing a cow than slitting its throat. **1956** *PMLA* 71.1: There is more than one way to skin a sheep. **1956** MLSettle *O Beulah* (NY) 300: They's more ways to kill a dawg than choke hit to death with butter. **1957** *BHerald* 2/10 7A: There's more than one way to skin a political cat. **1959** FPohl *Tomorrow* (NY) 78: There were more ways than one to open a cat's eyes. **1959** *BGlobe* 7/27 6: There's more than one way to skin a cat. **1961** WMasterson *Evil* (NY) 171: There's more than one way to skin a cat. **1963** RAHeinlein *Podkayne* (NY)

138: There are more ways of killing a cat than buttering it with parsnips. **1969** JMasters *Casanova* (L) 207: There are more ways of killing a cat than by drowning it in cream, but it's probably the best. **1970** RCowper *Twilight* (NY) 190: There's more ways round a brick wall than kicking a hole in it. **1970** JPorter *Dover Strikes* (NY) 194: There's more ways of killing a cat than skinning it. **1972** SCloete *Victorian* (L) 167: One of the first sayings of my father's that I can remember was that there were more ways of killing a cat than by choking it with butter. **1972** JGreenway *Down* (B) 86: There is more than one way to skin a dingo. **1975** SJPerelman *Vinegar* (NY) 51: The hoary precept that there is more than one way to skin a cat. TW 396–7(12); Brunvand 151(1); *Oxford* 872.

W75 There are no two **Ways** about it

1922 JSFletcher *Rayner-Slade* (NY) 158: There's no two ways about it. **1969** AGilbert *Missing* (NY) 43: There are no two ways about it. **1972** MKaye *Lively* (NY) 151: There are no two ways about it. TW 397(16).

W76 There is aye a **Way**

1933 JJConnington *Tom* (L 1937) 123: There's aye a way, as they say. Cf. *Oxford* 594: Once a way.

W77 To cut both **Ways**

1903 EChilders *Riddle* (NY 1940) 138: It cuts both ways. **1930** FDGrierson *Blue Bucket* (NY) 62: The old argument . . . is one that cuts both ways. **1937** NBlake *There's Trouble* (L) 208: This cuts both ways. **1958** DGBrown *Death* (L) 150: But it cuts both ways. **1973** KAmis *Riverside* (NY) 209: That can cut two ways. EAP W67.

W78 To fight one's **Way** out of a paper bag (*varied*)

1931 HSimpson *Prime* (NY) 4: Couldn't fight his way out of a paper bag. **1947** NMailer *Naked* (NY) 99: Too weak to punch my way out of a paper bag. **1950** RMacdonald *Drowning* (NY 1951) 114: He couldn't fight his way out of a wet paper bag. **1951** DSDavis *Gentle* (NY 1959) 176: You couldn't find your way out of a flour-

sack. **1954** EPangborn *Mirror* (NY 1958) 77: I can battle my way out of a damp paper bag. **1957** JCheever *Wapshot* (NY) 239: I couldn't punch a hole in a paper bag. **1958** EQueen *Finishing* (NY) 168: Lewis couldn't write his way out of a paper bag. **1959** AGoodman *Golden* (NY) 121: He couldn't screw his way out of a paper bag. **1961** FLockridge *Murder* (P) 41: The two-bit phony couldn't punch his way out of a paper bag. **1961** MMillar *How Like* (NY DBC) 40: He couldn't think his way out of a wet paper bag. **1963** GHCoxe *Hidden* (NY) 176: I couldn't fight my way out of a wet paper bag. **1968** JMills *Prosecutor* (NY) 65: That son of a bitch couldn't fight his way out of a paper bag. **1974** ELathen *Sweet* (NY) 12: [He] couldn't fight his way out of a paper bag. Partridge 274.

W79 To go the **Way** of all flesh

1926 FBeeding *Little White* (L) 190: Go way of all flesh. **1933** FWCrofts *Hog's Back* (L) 127: Miriam goes the way of all flesh. **1937** CDickson *Judas* (L) 219: Mary went the way of all flesh [*was seduced*]. **1953** RDuncan *Where* (L) 95: Gone the way of all flesh. **1959** ESherry *Defense* (NY) 49: Gray went the way of all flesh. **1972** HPentecost *Champagne* (NY) 20: Went the way of all flesh [*drunk*]. EAP W69.

W80 To know one's **Way** around

1940 IMontgomery *Golden* (NY) 35: She knew her way around. **1948** PCheyney *Dance* (NY DBC) 29: He knew his way about. Partridge 463: Know.

W81 To know which **Way** is up (*varied*)

1954 HStone *Man Who* (NY 1957) 96: Before I knew which way was up. **1971** ELathen *Longer* (NY) 130: He doesn't know which way is up. **1972** KCConstantine *Vicksburg* (NY) 81: It'll be a miracle if she tells me which way is up. Cf. Berrey 201.4: Which end up?

W82 To see which **Way** the cat jumps (*varied*)

1908 JCLincoln *Cy Whittaker* (NY) 165: Whichever way the cat jumps. **1911** JSHay *Amazing Emperor* (L) 150: Which way the . . . cat was going to jump. **1922** JJoyce

Ulysses (NY 1934) 625: If . . . that turned out to be how the cat jumped. **1927** AGilbert *Tragedy* (NY) 134: To see which way the cat would jump. **1932** WMartyn *Trent* (NY) 132: There is an old proverb to the effect that any fool can put a cat on a well, but only God can tell which side it is going to jump down. **1938** DHume *Corpses* (L) 131: We'll see which way the proverbial cat jumps. **1939** DHume *Make Way* (L) 102: Unless you know which way the proverbial cat is going to jump. **1951** CArmstrong *Black-eyed* (NY) 212: Waiting to see which way the cat jumps. **1952** CRand *Hongkong* (NY) 35: Nobody was sure how the cat would jump. **1956** *BHerald* 9/2 31: You often can tell which way the rabbit will jump. 10/18 26: His uncanny ability to move which way the cat jumps. **1962** L Egan *Borrowed* (NY DBC) 97: Hoping to find out which way the cat would jump. **1968** ABridge *Facts* (NY) 54: Waiting to see which way the cat would eventually jump. **1970** MStewart *Crystal* (NY) 265: I told him which way the wolf would jump. **1973** JBrooks *Go-Go* (NY) 17: To guess which way the cat would jump. *Oxford* 108: Cat.

W83 To see which **Way** the wind is blowing (*varied*)

1928 AGMacleod *Marloe* (NY) 89: So that was the way the wind blew. **1928** HRMayes *Alger* (NY) 61: He senses which way the wind blows. **1930** WLewis *Apes* (NY 1932) 303: On realizing the way the wind was blowing. **1939** GGoodchild *McLean Excels* (L) 273: Clever enough to see which way the wind was blowing. **1940** KMKnight *Death Came* (NY) 15: So that's how the wind blows! **1952** CLittle *Black* (NY) 103: Let Lewis see which way the wind blew. **1957** *New Yorker* 5/11 42: She could see the way the wind was blowing. **1959** MGEberhart *Melora* (NY DBC) 136: Emma soon saw the way the wind was blowing. **1967** RGarrett *Too Many* (NY) 39: That's the way the wind blows, is it? **1968** RSDominic *Murder* (NY) 44: To see which way the wind was blowing. **1970** RRendell *Guilty* (NY) 110: So that's the way the wind's blowing, is it?

1976 RBDominic *Murder* (NY) 138: Until he sees which way the wind is blowing. EAP W211: Wind; TW 404: Wind(18); Brunvand 153: Wind(7).

W84 The **Way** of the world

1927 BAtkey *Smiler* (NY) 95: That's the way of the world. **1929** CWells *Tapestry* (P) 147: The way of the world. **1935** AWDerleth *Sign* (NY) 178: The way of the world. **1946** HCBailey *Life Sentence* (NY) 166: The way of the world. **1958** WHCanaway *Ringgivers* (L) 198: That is the way of the world. **1959** MMillar *Listening* (NY) 175: Such is the way of the world. **1968** SPalmer *Rook* (NY) 87: That was the way of the world. **1972** JGreenway *Done* (B) 236: The way of the world. **1977** RRendell *Judgment* (NY) 21: It's the way of the world. EAP W74; TW 396(11).

W85 The **Way** the ball bounces (rolls)

1959 JWebb *Deadly* (NY) 62: That's the way the ball rolls. **1960** JBWest *Taste* (NY) 135: That's how the ball bounces. **1966** BHDeal *Fancy's* (NY) 87: It was the way the ball bounced. **1968** RMStern *Merry* (NY) 24: That was the way the cookie bounced. **1971** MCollins *Walk* (NY) 114: That's the way the ball bounces. Cf. next entry.

W86 The **Way** the cookie crumbles

1958 HPentecost *Obituary* (NY 1960) 139: It's the way the cookie crumbles. **1959** AGoodman *Golden* (NY) 154: That's the way the cookie crumbles. **1970** JPorter *Dover Strikes* (NY) 202: That's the way the cookie crumbles. **1974** MScherf *If You Want* (NY) 40: That's the way the cookie crumbles.

W87 The **Way** the world wags

1905 JBCabell *Line* (NY 1926) 132: The world wags. **1930** JSFletcher *Heaven-sent* (NY) 176: The world was wagging in pretty much the usual way. **1931** AC Edington *Monk's Hood* (NY) 272: That's the way the world wags. EAP W344.

W88 The **Way** to a man's heart is through his stomach (*varied*)

1913 HTFinck *Food* (NY) 153: The old adage that the way to a man's heart is through his stomach. **1921** RLardner *Big Town* (NY 1925) 20: The way to a man's heart is through his stomach. **1941** GMitchell *Hangman's* (L) 59: The way to a gentleman's heart is through his stomach. **1958** BHerald 5/1 39: The way to a man's heart is through his stomach. **1959** BHerald 5/29 14: The way to a man's heart is through his stomach. **1960** CBeaton *My Royal* (NY) 54: The old adage that the best way to reach a man's heart is through his stomach. **1967** RDavies *Marchbank's* (Toronto) 13: The road to a nation's pocketbook is through its stomach. **1974** AMenen *Fonthill* (NY) 104: The way to a man's heart is through his belly. *Oxford* 871–2.

W89 The **Way** to heaven is never easy

1956 EGann *Twilight* (NY) 148: I told them the way to heaven is never easy. Cf. EAP W76; Tilley W172.

W90 The **Way** (road) to hell is paved with good intentions (*varied*)

1913 JSFletcher *Secret* (L 1918) 109: If it is really true that the infernal regions are actually paved with good intentions. **1936** VMcHugh *Caleb* (NY) 107: The streets of hell was paved with good intentions. **1938** KMKnight *Acts* (NY) 264: As it is, they're naming a four-lane highway in hell for me—it's paved with my good intentions. **1940** JCLincoln *Out of the Fog* (NY) 124: The saying is that a certain place is paved with good intentions. **1957** RFenisong *Schemers* (NY) 48: The adage about hell and good intentions. **1959** ECooper *Seed* (NY) 39: The way to hell is paved with good intentions. **1959** AGilbert *Prelude* (NY DBC) 92: The road to hell is paved with good intentions. **1964** EHuxley *Forks* (L) 40: Good intentions paving the way to a new hell. **1966** GKanin *Remembering* (NY) 288: Good intentions—we all know what road is paved with them, don't we? **1966** HBlyth *Pocket* (L) 61: The way to hell, it has been said, is paved with good inten-

tions. **1971** JBlake *Joint* (NY) 184: The road to hell is paved with good intentions. EAP H192: Hell; *Oxford* 367: Hell.

W91 The **Way** to the daughter is through the mother

1975 GHousehold *Red* (B) 170: It's an old saying that the way to the daughter is through the mother. *Oxford* 168–9. Cf. Calf *above*.

W92 Where there is a **Way** in, there is a way out

1955 AChristie *So Many* (NY) 153: But as I say, where there's a way in, there's a way out. Whiting *NC* 493(3): See your way out, etc. Cf. EAP G67: What goes in.

W93 The **Weakest** (weak, weaker) goes to the wall (*varied*)

1914 PGWodehouse *Little Nugget* (NY 1929) 173: The weaker goes to the wall. **1928** TCobb *Who Opened* (L) 46: The weakest would go to the wall. **1934** LCharteris *Saint Intervenes* (NY) 90: In his philosophy, the weakest went to the wall. **1939** AWebb *Thank You* (L) 176: The old saying that the weakest go to the wall. **1960** LPHartley *Facial* (L) 32: The weakest went—not to the wall, for there were no walls. **1961** FSinclair *But the Patient* (NY) 26: The weak go to the wall. **1965** AGilbert *Voice* (NY) 186: The weaker goes to the wall. EAP W77; Brunvand 150: Wall(2).

W94 **Wealth** begets wealth

1928 CJDaly *Man* (NY) 12: The proverb that wealth begets wealth. Cf. Money attracts *above*.

W95 To fight (beat) one with his own **Weapons**

1932 FDGrierson *Murder* (L) 88: Fight him with his own weapons; 107. **1936** ECR Lorac *Crime* (L) 113: You've got to beat them with their own weapons. EAP W84. Cf. Game *above*.

W96 Better to **Wear** out than to rust out

1938 SHorler *Gentleman* (NY) 147: The old adage that it is better to work out than to rust out. **1950** REGould *Yankee* (NY) 199:

Weasel

An old maxim said that, "It is better to wear out than to rust out." **1967** CAird *Most Contagious* (NY) 16: Better to wear out than to rust out. **1971** MErskine *Brood* (NY) 24: I would rather wear out than rust out. **1979** JCrowe *Close* (NY) 90: I decided I wanted to wear out not rust out. EAP W85.

W97   As cunning (artful) as a **Weasel**

1925 FBeeding *Seven* (B) 202: They're . . . cunning as weasels and absolutely ruthless. **1933** NGordon *Shakespeare* (NY) 125: She's as artful as a sack of weasels. **1933** DLSayers *Murder* (NY) 155: They're as cunning as weasels. **1944** LAGStrong *All Fall* (NY) 209: [He] would be cunning as a weasel. NED Weasel 1b.

W98   As sharp as a **Weasel**

1930 AGilbert *Night* (NY) 216: The man was sharp as a weasel. **1938** FWCrofts *End* (L) 222: Sharp as a weasel [*alert*].

W99   As sly as a **Weasel**

1930 CTalbott *Droll* (NY) 19: Sly as a weasel. **1941** EPhillpotts *Ghostwater* (NY) 36: Sly as a weasel. TW 397(6).

W100   To catch a **Weasel** asleep (*varied*)

1911 RAFreeman *Eye of Osiris* (NY 1929) 300: There is an old saying as to catching a weasel asleep. **1923** FPitt *Shetland* (L) 152: The proverb about catching a weasel asleep. 155: I do not suppose any one has ever caught a wild weasel asleep. **1935** JJConnington *In Whose* (L) 126: Catching weasels asleep. **1960** MProcter *Devil's* (NY DBC) 146: When you catch a weasel asleep, whistle in his ear. TW 397(8); DARE i 562; *Oxford* 110: Catch.

W101   Nice **Weather** (*etc.*) for ducks

1904 JCLincoln *Cap'n Eri* (NY) 350: Nice mornin' for ducks. **1931** VStarrett *Dead Man* (NY) 49: Good weather for ducks. **1933** RRobins *Murder* (NY) 10: The old Maryland saying, "a fine day for ducks." **1936** PATaylor *Crimson* (L) 167: Nice weather for ducks. NED Duck *sb.*[1] 2: Duck's weather.

W102   To be under the **Weather**

1925 IOstrander *Neglected* (NY) 120: A bit under the weather. **1928** RHWatkins *Master* (NY) 243: A bit under the weather [*drunk*]. **1932** MRRinehart *Miss Pinkerton* (NY) 41: A little under the weather . . . from drinking. **1934** ACampbell *Desire* (NY) 107: A bit under the weather from that drug. **1939** AChristie *Sad Cypress* (NY 1958) 23: A bit under the weather [*cross*]. **1941** LThayer *Hallowe'en* (NY) 123: Slightly under the weather [*drunk*]. **1950** ECrispin *Sudden* (NY DBC) 61: I was a bit under the weather [*drunk*]. **1959** EAllen *Man Who* (L 1967) 70: A little under the weather [*hit on head*]. **1959** GMalcolm-Smith *If a Body* (NY) 102: "A bit under the weather." "Drunk is the word." **1964** D Bagley *Golden* (NY) 91: A little under the weather . . . but not too drunk. **1969** HWaugh *Run* (NY) 236: The count is a little under the weather [*ill and drunk*]. **1970** RRendell *Best Man* (NY) 154: Bit under the weather [*ill*]. EAP W90.

W103   To be a **Weather-breeder**

1941 MGEberhart *With This Ring* (NY) 44: A weather breeder. **1957** MPHood *In the Dark* (NY) 27: Like a weather breeder before a storm. **1974** CMSmith *Reverend* (NY) 224: It's a weather breeder. EAP W92; NED Weather-breeder; Partridge 942.

W104   As changeable as a **Weathercock**

1934 EBBlack *Crime* (NY) 153: She is changeable as a weather-cock. **1940** MBurton *Murder in* (L) 160: You're as changeable as a weather-cock. **1975** JBland *Death* (NY) 117: I'm as changeable as a weathercock. Cf. EAP W93: To turn (etc.) like a weathercock.

W105   To be slewed (blown) about like a **Weathercock**

1931 JSFletcher *Malvery* (L) 196: He was the veriest weathercock that ever slewed about with every wind. **1944** MFitt *Clues* (NY) 32: [She is] blown about like a weathercock. Cf. EAP W93.

W106   To keep a **Weather eye** out (open, *etc.*) (*varied*)

1913 JCLincoln *Mr. Pratt's Patients* (NY) 57: Keep his weather-eye out for squalls.

1922 JJoyce *Ulysses* (NY 1934) 280: Want to keep your weathereye open. **1923** JSClouston *Lunatic* (NY) 29: Keep our weather eye open. **1928** RAFreeman *As a Thief* (L) 172: I have to keep my weather eyelid lifting, as the mariners express it. **1933** GCollins *Dead Walk* 191: Keep your weather eye skinned. **1934** GHeyer *Why Shoot* (L) 301: He had . . . been keeping a weather-eye cocked in my direction. **1939** NBlake *Smiler* (L) 265: I must keep my weather eye lifting for him. **1951** DBOlsen *Cat* (NY) 38: Keep a weather-eye out. **1952** KMKnight *Death Goes* (NY) 139: Keep a weather eye out. **1959** ESherry *Defense* (NY) 15: He didn't even keep a weather eye on Bellair. **1961** RKirk *Old House* (NY DBC) 65: To keep a weather eye on him. **1965** AGilbert *Voice* (NY) 125: Keep a weather eye open. **1972** MKramer *Mother* (NY) 18: I had a weather eye out for it. TW 398; *Oxford* 419: Keep.

W107 As cranky (variable) as a **Weather vane**

1910 EPhillpotts *Tales* (NY) 23: So cranky as a weather-vane. **1939** TScudder *JWCarlyle* (NY) 66: Variable as a weather vane. Cf. Whiting W161: Be like.

W108 One **Wedding** leads to another

1926 AFielding *Footsteps* (L) 167: I don't know about weddings, but one funeral is sure to lead to another. **1937** DduMaurier *The duMauriers* (NY) 53: One wedding always leads to another, so they say. EAP W96.

W109 As merry (*etc.*) as a **Wedding** (marriage) **bell** (*varied*)

1928 AGMacleod *Marloe* (NY) 233: Happy as wedding bells we was. **1929** MAllingham *Crime* (L 1950) 75: All would have been merry as a wedding bell. **1931** MJFreeman *Murder* (NY) 267: All would have been as merry as a marriage bell. **1937** RWWinston *It's a Far Cry* (NY) 81: All went merry as a marriage bell. **1952** PGosse *Dr. Viper* (L) 190: Everything went like a wedding bell. **1954** EForbes *Rainbow* (B) 103: And all had gone . . . happy as wedding bells. **1957** NMitford *Voltaire* (L) 56: All was merry as a wedding bell. **1959** PCurtis *No Question* (NY) 44: All went merry as the proverbial wedding bell. **1967** COSkinner *Madame* (B) 15: Things went as merry as the sound of wedding bells. **1970** KGiles *Death* (L) 86: It'll go as sweetly as a wedding bell. EAP M107: Marriage; Brunvand 9: Bell(1); Taylor *Western Folklore* 17(1958) 20. Cf. TW 398(1).

W110 As cold as a **Wedge**

1908 MDPost *Corrector of Destinies* (NY) 35: Cold as a wedge. **1933** ISCobb *Murder* (I) 19: Stiff and cold as an iron wedge. TW 398(1).

W111 An opening (entering) **Wedge**

1939 MGEberhart *Chiffon* (NY) 294: It must have been the opening wedge. **1949** AMStein *Days* (NY) 130: What might be called an entering wedge. EAP W97.

W112 **Wedlock** is padlock

1950 CEVulliamy *Henry* (L) 211: Wedlock is a padlock, says our proverb. *Oxford* 876.

W113 **Wednesday** fortnight always comes

1965 HSLatham *My Life* (NY) 183: "Wednesday fortnight always comes," as the old English adage has it—the appointed weekend arrived.

W114 To grow like a **Weed** (*varied*)

1930 JWilliamson *American Hotel* (NY) 150: With Buffalo growing like a weed. **1936** VMcHugh *Caleb* (NY) 40: Growing like a weed. **1942** WABarber *Murder Enters* (NY) 13: He's grown like a weed. **1957** *NYTimes* 11/10 3: Spreading like a weed. **1959** ECooper *Dees* (NY) 38: They grow like weeds. **1970** TWells *Dinky* (NY) 25: Tim is growing like the proverbial weed. **1973** TWells *Brenda's* (NY) 93: Growing like a weed. **1973** TZinkin *Weeds Grow Fast* (L). TW 398; Brunvand 151.

W115 To be worth one's **Weight** in gold (*etc.*)

1910 EPhillpotts *Tales* (NY) 276: Worth her own weight in gold. **1922** JJoyce *Ulysses* (NY 1934) 349: A little heart worth its weight in gold. **1930** JGBrandon *McCarthy* (L) 221: He'll be worth his weight in diamonds. **1934** HVines *This Green* (B) 306: She's not worth her weight in piss ants. **1938** FDGrierson *Covenant* (L) 18: She was worth her weight in gold. **1939** GBagby *Bird* (NY) 71: She was worth her weight in ebony. **1942** JBell *Death . . . Medical Board* (NY) 58: They are worth their weight in gold. **1947** HLawrence *Death of* (NY) 290: Clara, like the Aga Khan, is worth her considerable weight in gold. **1953** ECRLorac *Speak* (NY) 165: Hannah's worth her weight in gold. **1958** BNichols *Rich* (NY) 219: Cold cream . . . worth its weight in gold. **1960** AGilbert *Out for* (NY 1965) 97: That space . . . is worth its weight in gold. **1966** ARRandell *Sixty* (L) 62: Jack was worth his weight in gold. **1970** JLeasor *They Don't* (NY) 7: There's an old lie about people being worth their weight in gold. **1971** SMilligan *Adolf* (L) 71: It was worth its weight in gold [*a large chamber pot*]. EAP W102; TW 398(1); Brunvand 151.

W116 To lick (whip, fight) one's **Weight** in wildcats

1925 GBeasley *My First* (Paris) 202: She can fight her way [*sic*] in wild-cat. **1932** HFootner *Dead Man's* (NY) 148: I can lick my weight in wildcats. **1933** RRobins *Murder* (NY) 8: To use the argot of the day, he . . . could lick his weight in wild cats. **1940** AAFair *Gold Comes* (NY) 27: I am capable of whipping my weight in wildcats. **1950** RMacdonald *Drowning* (NY 1951) 2: Can you whip your weight in wildcats? **1959** JWebb *Deadly* (NY) 211: The . . . waitress who looked as if she could lick her weight in wildcats. **1966** JDosPassos *Best* (NY) 188: Ready to lick our weight in wildcats. **1976** HPentecost *Fourteenth* (NY) 22: A little man who can lick twice his weight in wildcats if he has to. TW 398–9(2).

W117 To pull (carry) one's (own) **Weight**

1929 GDHCole *Poison* (NY) 130: He's not pulling his weight. **1929** GMWhite *Square* (L) 128: I don't feel that I've been pulling my weight. **1933** WADarlington *Mr Cronk's* (L) 18: The little man pulled a good deal more than his weight. **1942** JBell *Death . . . Medical Board* (NY) 101: She pulls all her own weight and some of the other maids'

as well. **1955** DMDisney *Trick* (NY) 19: She couldn't even carry her own weight. **1958** MUnderwood *Lawful* (NY) 176: We all pull our weight. **1969** RAirth *Snatch* (NY) 29: Everyone has to pull his weight. NED Weight *sb.*[1] 10c.

W118 To throw one's **Weight** around (about)

1929 LBrock *Murder* (NY) 43: Liable to throw his weight about. **1937** DInce *In Those* (L) 45: She doesn't waste time throwing her weight about. **1940** AChristie *Patriotic* (NY) 169: Why don't you throw your weight about a bit? **1949** FKane *Green* (NY) 183: Mike threw his weight around. **1953** SBellow *Adventures* (NY) 234: He threw his weight around. **1957** CWilliams *Big Bite* (L) 161: She starts throwing her weight around. **1960** CErwin *Orderly* (NY) 205: But don't start throwing any weight around. **1965** RBissell *Still* (NY) 133: You don't throw your weight around much. **1976** SWoods *My Life* (NY) 174: Graham had to throw his weight about. Partridge 944.

W119 To wear out (outstay) one's **Welcome**

1960 RMacdonald *Ferguson* (NY) 244: I don't want to wear out my welcome. **1967** GHousehold *Courtesy* (NY) 41: I did not want to outstay my welcome. Amer. Herit. Dict. Wear *v.*: Wear out 2.

W120 As deep as a (draw) **Well**

1922 JJoyce *Ulysses* (NY 1934) 544: Deep as a drawwell. **1923** JSFletcher *Markenmore* (NY) 251: So deep as my well. **1930** VLoder *Essex* (L) 135: Brews is as deep as a draw-well [*astute*]. **1932** VWilliams *Death* (B) 132: She's as deep as a well. **1939** HFootner *Murder That* (L) 119: I'm as deep as a well [*secretive*]. **1949** FCrane *Flying* (NY) 14: Easy on the surface. Deep as a well inside. **1966** LBeers *Wild* (NY) 96: Deep as a well, he is. **1973** CAird *His Burial* (NY) 60: Not so deep as a well, not so wide as a church door. TW 399; *Oxford* 175: Deep.

W121 To let (leave) **Well** (bad) enough alone (*varied*)

1913 EDBiggers *Seven Keys* (I) 142: Letting well enough alone. **1924** LTracy *Token*

(NY) 156: Couldn't leave well enough alone. **1928** CKingston *Guilty* (L) 283: It would have been better if I'd let well alone. **1928** AWynne *Red* (P) 10: Let well, or ill, alone. **1929** NBMavity *Tule* (NY) 253: He wisely decided to let bad enough alone. **1932** LFord *Murder* (NY) 79: Let well enough alone. **1934** GFowler *Father Goose* (NY) 106: We should let bad enough alone. **1940** GHCoxe *Glass Triangle* (NY) 89: He had better let well enough alone. **1941** CCoffin *Mare's Nest* (NY) 27: I let bad enough alone. **1951** IChase *New York 22* (NY) 86: Why the devil couldn't she let well enough alone? **1953** BBloch *Mrs. Hulett* (NY) 64: She couldn't let bad enough alone. **1957** DMDisney *My Neighbour's* (NY) 96: Why can't you let well enough alone? **1957** *NYTimes* 3/31 70: Leave well alone. **1961** RAKnowlton *Court* (L 1967) 143: Why can't they ever let good enough alone? **1962** DAlexander *Tempering* (NY) 280: Play the leave-well-enough-alone game. **1969** NHale *Life* (B) 81: Never being able to leave well enough alone. **1970** RMungo *Famous* (B) 162: To leave bad enough alone. **1972** PKruger *Cold* (NY) 167: Better let well enough alone. EAP W104.

W122 As cold as a **Well digger's** (gravedigger's) butt (*etc.*) (*varied*)

1952 FVWMason *Himalayan* (NY 1953) 146: It's colder than a well digger's butt out here. **1953** RFMirvish *Eternal* (NY) 30: You look as blue as a well digger's butt in Labrador. **1953** JSanford *Land* (NY) 188: You're colder than a grave-digger's ass. **1956** *BangorDN* 6/23 15: Spinning is a form of angling that leaves him colder than a well-digger's toes. **1960** JBWest *Taste* (NY) 38: It was as cold as a well-digger's ass in the Klondike. **1967** JFDobie *Some Part* (B) 134: He was as cold as a well-digger's rump toward some of the preachers. Taylor *Prov. Comp.* 28–9: Cold. Cf. Partridge 349. Cf. Eskimo, Polar bear *above.*

W123 As white as **Whalebone**

1973 JCashman *Gentleman* (NY) 5: As white as whalebone. Whiting W203; *Oxford* 884; NED Whalebone 1.

W124 As low as **Whale shit**

1954 GScott *Sound* (NY) 178: As low as whale shit, sir. And that is at the bottom of the ocean. Whiting *NC* 494(2): Whale manure. Cf. As low as Shit *above.*

W125 To know (*etc.*) **What's** what (*varied*)

1915 JFerguson *Stealthy* (L 1935) 12: He little kens what's what. **1931** HCBailey *Fortune Speaking* (NY) 226: She knows what's what. **1939** HCBailey *Great Game* (L) 221: Knew what was what. **1940** CDickson *And so to Murder* (NY) 31: Show her what's what. **1941** CRice *Right Murder* (NY) 35: We'll . . . see what's what. **1953** BCarey *Their Nearest* (NY) 81: I'll tell him what's what. **1954** ECRLorac *Shroud* (NY) 79: To find out what's what. **1957** MSharp *Eye* (L) 267: He knew what was what. **1959** CElliott *Unkind* (L) 68: He knows what's what. **1965** ESGardner *Troubled* (NY) 169: You seem to know what's what. **1965** HMiller *Quiet Days* (NY) 74: We tumbled her over and gave her what's what. **1971** PAlding *Despite* (NY) 5: I know what's what. **1975** HCarmichael *Too Late* (NY) 69: I like to know who's who and what's what. EAP W109; TW 399.

W126 As good as **Wheat**

1931 WMorton *Mystery* (NY) 150: That will's as good as wheat. TW 399(1); Brunvand 151. Cf. As good as Bread *above.*

W127 To separate (*etc.*) the **Wheat** from the chaff (*varied*)

1920 GBMcCutcheon *Anderson Crow* (NY) 241: They separated the wheat from the chaff. **1925** JSFletcher *Wolves* (NY) 294: Amongst all the chaff . . . some grain of wheat. **1930** AFlexner *Universities* (NY) 128: Separate wheat from chaff. **1930** VLoder *Essex* (L) 80: You collected a lot of chaff, but you saw a grain of corn. **1936** CFGregg *Tragedy* (L) 163: Any wheat in the chaff? **1939** JRWarren *Murder from* (NY) 109: You have to sift a stack of chaff to eat a grain of wheat. **1940** RKing *Holiday* (NY) 37: The wheat is infrequent and there is a good deal of chaff. **1945** HLawrence *Time to Die* (NY) 230: He sifts the wheat from the chaff. **1950** MScherf *Cu-*

rious (NY) 64: You manage to separate the wheat from the chaff. **1958** FLockridge *Long* (P) 109: An afternoon of chaff and very little wheat. **1959** HLoeb *Way* (NY) 6: I could separate the wheat from the chaff. **1962** GBrooks *Boston* (NY) 141: Select the wheat from the chaff. **1963** HPentecost *Tarnished* (NY DBC) 89: You could separate the wheat from the chaff. **1966** HRDaniels *House* (NY) 48: Sifting the wheat from the chaff. **1969** DARandall *Dukedome* (NY) 34: [He] knew wheat from chaff. **1970** JJMarric *Gideon's Sport* (NY) 14: To sort the wheat from the chaff. **1978** JLangton *Memorial* (NY) 102: He didn't know the wheat from the chaff. EAP W110; TW 399(3,4). Cf. Grain, To separate the Sheep *above*.

W128 The squeaky **Wheel** (axle, gate) gets the grease (*varied*)

1952 RMarshall *Jane* (NY) 12: 'Tis the squeaky hinge that gets the oil. **1956** *BangorDN* 6/28 39: It's the squeaking axle wot gets the grease. **1958** *BHerald* 7/10 1: It was "the creaky wheel that got the grease." **1959** *BangorDN* 8/1 15: The squeaking wheel gets the oil. **1961** MMillar *How Like* (NY DBC) 114: It's the squeaky wheel that gets the grease. **1978** HLawrenson *Whistling Girl* (NY) 60: So true is the maxim "The squeaky wheel gets the grease." Bartlett 685a [*Josh Billings (HWShaw)*].

W129 To be a fifth **Wheel** (*varied*)

1929 BThomson *Metal* (L) 161: I don't like being a fifth wheel to the coach, as you might say. **1935** TThayer *Cluck* (NY) 210: I am really a—a ninth wheel! **1936** HHolt *There Has Been* (L) 93: I may be as useless as the fifth wheel of a coach. **1939** JJones *Murder al Fresco* (NY) 107: I have always been one of those fifth wheel women. **1940** HReilly *Death Demands* (NY) 185: Kent seemed a bit embarassed at having been a fifth wheel to the intimacy of the exchange between the man and the woman. **1945** MBurton *Not a Leg* (NY) 107: You can't drag a fifth wheel on a coach indefinitely. **1954** AWBarkley *That Reminds* (NY) 206: A sort of fifth wheel to the executive branch. **1957** *BHerald* 12/8 2A: The move-

ment to abolish this fifth wheel in the government. **1960** HLivingston *Climacticon* (NY) 55: I'd only be a fifth wheel. **1964** DForbes-Robertson *My Aunt* (NY) 188: At best beauty is only a fifth wheel. **1967** JPurdy *Eustace* (NY) 125: You'll be the fifth leg on a fine old chair. **1969** MGilbert *Etruscan* (L) 209: A fifth wheel to the chariot. **1975** EGundy *Naked* (NY) 6: Now I'm a fifth wheel. **1975** TWells *Hark* (NY) 91: I've been feeling like a fifth wheel. EAP W111; TW 399–400(1); Brunvand 151(1). Cf. Thumb *above*.

W130 To grease (oil) the **Wheels**

1930 FDGrierson *Blue Bucket* (NY) 225: Grease the official wheels a bit. **1936** SFowler *Was Murder Done?* (L) 153: It isn't a case we can defend unless he's ready to grease the wheels. **1939** VBridges *Seven Stars* (L) 240: It will oil the wheels considerably. EAP W112.

W131 The weakest **Wheel** creaks loudest

1919 JBCabell *Jurgen* (NY 1922) 323: It is notorious that the weakest wheel of every cart creaks loudest. EAP W115: Worst.

W132 The **Wheel** comes (turns) full circle (*varied*)

1925 JSFletcher *Wrychester* (L) 214: Mind the wheel doesn't come full circle. **1934** ERPunshon *Crossword* (L) 205: The wheel had come full circle again. **1938** SLeslie *Film* (L) 260: The wheel had come full circle. **1942** ESHolding *Kill Joy* (NY) 131: Now the wheel has turned, and here I am myself. **1958** WDHassett *Off the Record* (New Brunswick, NJ) 281: The wheel has come full circle. **1961** LAGStrong *Green* (L) 129: The wheel has turned full circle. NED Circle *sb.* 17c.

W133 **Wheels** within wheels

1911 MLevel *Grip of Fear* (NY) 97: All the wheels-within-wheels of police action. **1923** JSFletcher *Charing Cross* (NY) 197: Many wheels within wheels. **1933** EPhillpotts *Captain's* (NY) 221: There are wheels within wheels, as they say. **1938** RCroft-Cooke *Escape* (NY) 265: He saw again the wheels within wheels. **1940** NBlake *Malice* (L) 133: Wheels within wheels. **1949**

FLockridge *Spin* (P) 48: Wheels within wheels. **1950** ERPunshon *So Many* (NY) 172: Wheels within wheels. **1952** M O'Brine *Corpse* (L) 215: Wheels within wheels and palm-oil to make them turn. **1956** *Punch* 12/5 681: Wheels within wheels within wheels. **1959** RMStern *Bright* (NY) 117: Wheels within wheels. That's the traditional statement. **1965** MAllingham *Mind* (NY) 65: We may have stumbled upon Catherine wheels within Catherine wheels. **1966** JBell *Death* (NY) 140: "Wheels within wheels." "Pardon?" "A saying, Shirley. Too old fashioned for you." **1974** AMorice *Killing* (NY) 74: Wheels within wheels. **1976** MRReno *Final* (NY) 106: Wheels within wheels. EAP W114.

W134   As blue as a **Whetstone**

1906 JCLincoln *Mr. Pratt* (NY) 249: He was blue as a whetstone [*depressed*]. **1912** JCLincoln *Postmaster* (NY) 204: Blue as a whetstone; 267. **1968** EBuckler *Ox Bells* (NY) 164: The low-spirited were "blue as a whetstone." DARE i 296–7: Blue. Cf. EAP W119.

W135   Not know **Which** from t'other

1965 VRandolph *Hot Springs* (Hatboro, Penn.) 115: He was so drunk he didn't know which from t'other. Berrey 150.4.

W136   As bright as a **Whip**

1936 *New Yorker* 7/4 9: Bright as a whip, she was. **1937** LFord *Ill Met* (NY) 218: Clara is as bright as a whip. **1956** HKubly *Easter* (NY) 44: Bright as a whip. Taylor *Prov. Comp.* 21.

W137   As keen as a **Whip**

1937 HFootner *Dark Ships* (L) 143: Keen as a whip. **1954** MMcCarthy *Charmed* (NY) 173: She was . . . keen as a whip. Clark 215.

W138   As quick as a **Whip**

1964 LCharteris *Vendetta* (NY) 95: [He] was as quick as a whip [*mentally*]. **1966** PO'Donnell *Sabre-Tooth* (L) 18: Quick as a bloody whip. Whiting *NC* 495(1).

W139   As sharp as a **Whip**

1906 JCLincoln *Mr. Pratt* (NY) 195: Sharp as a whip [*a person*]. **1929** SMartin *Only Seven* (NY) 19: His voice . . . as sharp as a whip. Taylor *Prov. Comp.* 72.

W140   As smart as a **Whip** (*varied*)

1929 KCStrahan *Footprints* (NY) 44: Smart as a whip; 246. **1933** VMacClure *Clue* (L) 105: Smart as the snap of a whip. **1936** ISCobb *Judge Priest* (I) 312: Smart ez a whip. **1936** VRath *Murder* (NY) 257: She was smart as a whip. **1940** EDean *Murder Is* (NY) 83: Sally was . . . smart as a whip. **1946** JTShaw *Hard-Boiled* (NY) 448: Smart as a buggy whip. **1951** JSStrange *Reasonable* (NY) 157: Jane was as smart as a whip. **1956** *BangorDN* 7/17 5: Smart as a whip. **1964** LWhite *Ransomed* (NY DBC) 112: He's smart as a whip. **1970** NMilford *Zelda* (NY) 8: Smart as a whip [*a girl*]. **1974** DCavett *Cavett* (NY) 317: Maddox is smart as a whip, or should I say knout? **1975** HBlack *My Father* (NY) 129: She is beautiful—smart as a whip too. Whiting *NC* 495(2).

W141   As tough as **Whipcord**

1935 AGilbert *Man* (L) 97: Fingers as tough as whipcord. **1976** MGilbert *Night* (NY) 131: She's as tough as whipcord. NED Whipcord 1a (quote 1861).

W142   As bright (keen, quick) as a **Whippet**

1940 EQueen *New Adventures* (NY) 125: He's keen as a whippet [*mentally alert*]. **1958** RKing *Malice* (NY) 123: You are quick as a whippet. **1968** ELathen *Stitch* (NY) 185: The . . . boy . . . is bright as a whippet.

W143   As thin as a **Whippet**

1954 FCDavis *Another* (NY) 17: Speare is as thin as a whippet. **1955** ECDavis *Night* (NY) 19: A young man thin as a whippet.

W144   As poor as a **Whippoorwill**

1960 BCClark *Long* (NY) 207: You were as poor as a whippoorwill. Whiting *NC* 495(1).

W145   As mean as a **Whiskey** fart *etc.*

1976 JFoxx *Freebooty* (I) 162: Damned strong woman, and mean as a whiskey fart in Sunday church.

W146 As clean (bare) as a **Whistle**

1906 JCLincoln *Mr. Pratt* (NY) 187: Clean as a whistle [*washed*]. **1919** KHoward *Peculiar* (NY) 258: As clean as a whistle. **1920** ACrabb *Samuel* (NY) 339: The bridge and the piers . . . were as clean as a penny whistle. **1928** RThorndike *Slype* (NY) 152: It's gone, clean as a whistle. 201: Taken away as clean as a whistle pipe. **1930** GDHCole *Berkshire* (NY) 206: As bare as a whistle. **1932** AWynne *White Arrow* (P) 253: The room's as bare as a whistle. **1932** SHPage *Resurrection* (NY) 11: He disappeared as clean as a whistle. **1936** EQueen *Halfway* (NY) 37: The fireplace is clean as the proverbial whistle. **1940** KRoos *Made Up* (NY) 13: I'll come clean as a whistle [*confess all*]. **1949** KMKnight *Bass* (NY) 122: Broke that rail plumb off, clean as a whistle. **1952** EGCarey *Jumping* (NY) 196: A modest little business, neat and clean as a whistle. **1956** *BHerald* 10/15 5: He's an honest man, clean as a whistle. **1958** WGraham *Wreck* (NY) 147: Clean as a baby's whistle. **1963** WMankowitz *Cockatrice* (L) 124: Clean as a witch-doctor's whistle. **1963** NMarsh *Dead* (B 1964) 13: Clean as a whistle [*a decent story*]. **1969** RDavies *Print* (L) 132: Clean as a whistle, a daily sea-bather. **1972** NMarsh *Tied* (B) 52: As clean as a whistle and as neat as a new pin, aren't I? **1976** MButterworth *Remains* (NY) 5: Never stuck his nose into politics. Clean as a whistle. **1976** JJMarric *Gideon's Drive* (NY) 9: Clean as a whistle [*morally*]. EAP W131.

W147 As clear as a **Whistle**; Whistle-clear

1929 NSLincoln *Fifth* (NY) 230: The palmprint's as clear as a whistle; 256. **1935** HLDavis *Honey* (NY) 232: Come as clear as a whistle. **1972** JLHensley *Legislative* (NY) 16: The day was cold and whistle clear. EAP W132.

W148 As neat as a **Whistle**

1937 KMKnight *Seven* (NY) 126: It's turned down neat as a whistle. **1941** DBHughes *Bamboo* (NY) 39: Neat as a whistle. **1965** MAllingham *Mind* (NY) 235: Neat as a whistle. **1970** PAlding *Murder* (NY) 142: Everything wrapped up as neat as a whistle. **1971** BWAldiss *Soldier* (L) 152:

Cut his foreskin off as neat as a whistle. **1971** VKing *Candy* (L) 48: He showed his mandible as neat as a whistle.

W149 As slick as a **Whistle**

1926 Anonymous *Great American Ass* (NY) 130: Slick as a whistle. **1934** ORCohen *Scrambled* (NY) 67: Slick as a whistle. **1934** HSKeeler *Riddle* (NY) 20: The fifth key turned in the lock as slick as the proverbial whistle. **1940** EDean *Murder Is* (NY) 296: The window goes up slick as a whistle. **1943** AAFair *Bats Fly* (NY) 6: Worked things slick as a whistle. **1955** ESGardner *Sun* (NY) 42: It's cleaned out slick as a whistle. **1961** BJames *Night* (NY DBC) 116: Slick as a whistle. TW 400(3).

W150 Not care two **Whistles**

1953 CDickson *Cavalier's* (NY) 244: You . . . don't care two whistles about money. Cf. Whiting W223–4.

W151 Not give a **Whistle** (in hell)

1945 HQMasur *Bury Me* (NY 1948) 187: You didn't give one whistle in hell about it. **1956** JBlish *They Shall* (L) 173: I didn't give a whistle about your spy. Cf. Whiting W223–4.

W152 To blow the **Whistle** on someone (something)

1954 GFowler *Minutes* (NY) 56: Someone had blown the whistle on me [*betrayed*]. **1958** GHCoxe *Impetuous* (NY) 148: You're the one that blew the whistle on me. **1972** JGores *Dead* (NY) 116: Odum . . . was kiting checks . . . and somebody blew the whistle. **1976** RBDominic *Murder* (NY) 166: I'm blowing the whistle. Wentworth 46: Blow.

W153 To pay too much for one's **Whistle**

1947 DTrumbo *Additional* (NY 1970) 45: When a man realizes he has paid too much for his whistle. EAP W133; Whiting *NC* 495(5).

W154 To wet one's **Whistle**

1900 CFPidgin *Quincy A. Sawyer* (B) 29: I shall have to wet my whistle. **1922** JJoyce *Ulysses* (NY 1934) 325: And he ups with his pint to wet his whistle. **1932** DLSayers

Have (NY) 351: You'll be wanting a wet to your whistle. **1936** VMcHugh *Caleb* (NY) 248: A jolt of *tequila* to wet his whistle. **1941** ABCunningham *Strange Death* (NY) 172: Somethin' to wet my whistle. **1950** MRHodgkin *Student* (L) 197: Nothing that would wet your whistle. **1959** PDeVries *Through* (B) 85: He wet his whistle from the tumbler of water. **1966** HTracy *Men* (L) 193: She now proposed that they wet their whistles. **1975** RO'Connor *HBroun* (NY) 72: To wet their whistles. EAP W134; TW 401(5); Brunvand 152.

W155 To **Whistle** for one's money (rent)
1921 JCLincoln *Galusha* (NY) 406: He can whistle for his money. **1958** MProcter *Three* (NY) 87: She told me I could whistle for my money. **1968** KHConnell *Irish* (Oxford) 115: Letting the landlord whistle for his rent. EAP W135; TW 401.

W156 Not care a **Whit**
1944 PATaylor *Dead Ernest* (NY) 192: I didn't care a whit. **1968** LSdeCamp *Great Monkey* (NY) 60: Caring not a whit. **1970** FDorn *Forbidden* (NY) 122: They cared not a whit. **1971** MRugoff *Prudery* (NY) 348: Cares not a whit. Cf. Whiting W228: Set not.

W157 To be **White-livered** (*varied*)
1903 EChilders *Riddle* (NY 1940) 128: A white-livered cur. **1923** JSFletcher *Exterior* (NY) 259: Ye damned white-livered rat. **1959** MMillar *Listening* (NY) 215: I feel my liver turning ... white like snow. EAP W138.

W158 Not a **Whoop** and a holler from wherever
1967 EVCunningham *Samantha* (NY) 11: As they say, no more than a whoop and a holler from the Pacific Ocean. Berrey 1.3 [*time*], 40.3 [*distance*].

W159 Not care a **Whoop** (*varied*)
1908 JLondon *Letters* ed KHendricks (NY 1965) 268: I don't care a whoop in high water. **1927** SWilliams *Drury* (NY) 93: Not that I care a whoop. **1932** GDyer *Five* (B) 96: He don't care a whoop in hell. Berrey 21.3.

W160 Not give a **Whoop** (whoopee) (*varied*)
1904 JLondon *Letters* ed KHendricks (NY 1965) 160: I don't give a whoop. **1909** MRRinehart *Man in Lower Ten* (NY 1947) 252: I wouldn't give a whoop. **1927** CBStilson *Seven* (NY) 76: I don't give a whoop. **1930** LTracy *Manning* (NY) 74: I don't give a whoop in Hades for him. **1931** LEppley *Murder* (NY) 7: I don't give a whoopee; 173. **1931** HSKeeler *Matilda* (NY) 351: I don't give two whoops in hell. **1940** FGruber *Talking Clock* (NY) 242: Eric didn't give a whoop and a holler about clocks. **1953** BCarey *Their Nearest* (NY) 39: I don't give a whoop in Hades. **1960** JBarry *Malignant* (NY) 157: I won't give a whoop in a hurricane what it says. Berrey 21.3.

W161 Not trust two **Whoops** in hell
1931 EABlake *Jade* (NY) 83: Not one of us trusts the others two whoops in hell. Berrey 21.3. Cf. Hurrahs *above*.

W162 Out of all **Whooping**
1918 JBCabell *Letters* ed PColum (NY 1962) 96: He ... considers the indecency out of all whooping. *Oxford* 601: Out.

W163 As cold as a **Whore's** heart (*varied*)
1959 FSmith *Harry* (B) 106: It is as cold as a hoor's heart on a Saturday night. **1975** HLawrenson *Stranger* (NY) 182: His cell ... was as cold as a black whore's heart. **1977** HPentecost *Murder* (NY) 91: "It's colder than a whore's heart out there." She waited for a laugh. Taylor *Prov. Comp.* 28.

W164 As long as a **Whore's** dream
1969 MDorman *King* (NY) 164: A list of them as long as a whore's dream. Cf. Taylor *Prov. Comp.* 28: Cold as a whore's dream.

W165 As soft as a **Whore**-lady's heart
1937 CRCooper *Here's to Crime* (B) 245: There is a saying in the underworld: "As soft as a whore-lady's heart." Cf. To have a Heart of gold *above*.

W166 Like a **Whore** at a christening (*varied*)

1960 BMcKnight *Running* (NY) 56: I was as nervous as a whore in church. **1969** SMays *Fall Out* (L) 56: Don't sit there like a whore at a christenin', do somethin! **1969** FLeiber *Swords* (L) 7: Stands out like a whore in church. **1974** WSnow *Codline* (Middletown, Conn.) 27: As polite as a whore at a christening. EAP W141: Solemn. Cf. Pig in a parlor, Skunk, Turd *above*.

W167 The **Why(s)** and wherefore(s)

1910 JCLincoln *Depot Master* (NY) 69: Explainin' whys and wherefores. **1920** EWallace *Three-Oaks* (L) 193: To explain the why and wherefore of it. **1922** JJoyce *Ulysses* (NY 1934) 299: Bloom comes out about the why and the wherefore. **1932** GKChesterton et al. *Floating* (NY) 77: She could not understand the whys and wherefores. **1936** LRGribble *Malverne* (L) 213: Must I explain every little why and wherefore? **1938** NMorland *Case Without* (L) 195: There's a why and wherefore in that. **1940** HAshbrook *Murder Comes* (NY) 255: I know the whys and the hows and the wherefores. **1950** LAGStrong *Which I* (L) 185: You see the whys and wherefores. **1956** RFenisong *Bite* (NY) 94: He'll want to know the whys and wherefores. **1958** AMacKinnon *Summons* (NY) 103: The why and wherefores of the case. **1962** AWUpfield *Death* (NY) 77: The whys and wherefores of this latest death. **1973** AMStein *Finger* (NY) 33: The whys and wherefores. EAP W143; TW 401.

W168 A grass **Widow** (widower) (*varied*)

1922 JJoyce *Ulysses* (NY 1934) 131: "Is he a widower?" . . . "Ay, a grass one." 608: There she sits, a grass widow. . . . Believes me dead. 642: The grasswidower in question. **1927** NMartin *Mosaic* (NY) 4: A grass widow. **1931** CBrooks *Ghost* (NY) 261: A little wanton of a grass widow. **1936** CMRussell *Death* (NY) 5: A widow, whether grass or sod. **1946** CBush *Second Chance* (L) 26: [He] was a grass widower. **1955** MErskine *Old Mrs.* (NY) 150: She was a widow . . . Trouble is to know whether it was grass or sod. **1964** HWaugh *Missing* (NY) 138: I've heard of grass widows and golf widows. **1965** JGaskell *Atlan* (NY 1968) 236: She's no screwed-up grass widow. **1968** JCFurnas *Lightfoot* (NY) 53: Grass bachelors. NED Grass widow 2, Suppl. *sv.* 2; Partridge 349; Wentworth 227.

W169 Old **Wives'** tales (*varied*)

1927 CDiehl *Byzantine* (NY) 47: Old wives' tales. **1933** JDCarr *Hag's Nook* (NY) 29: These old woman's tales. **1933** PMcGuire *Death* (NY) 99: These old wives' tales. **1944** HTalbot *Rim* (NY 1965) 43: Old wives' tales. **1947** FCDavis *Thursday's* (NY) 210: That's an old wives' tale. **1952** PPiper *Corpse* (NY) 48: Old wives' tales. **1957** *Time* 11/25 75: Old wives' tales. **1962** MInnes *Connoisseur's* (L) 34: Some legend or old wives' tale. **1969** HEBates *Vanished* (L) 5: If old wives' tales are to be believed. **1971** PRubenstein *Groupsex* (NY) 84: The old wives' tale about a black person's . . . overpowering sexuality. **1976** JPorter *Package* (NY) 112: Old wives' tales. EAP W152; TW 402(2).

W170 A **Wife** should be a lady in the parlor *etc.*

1966 MMcShane *Crimson* (NY) 111: And if it was true that a wife should be a lady in the parlour, a mother in the kitchen and a whore in the bed, she was not a wife. Cf. Tilley W702.

W171 There will be **Wigs** on the green

1922 JJoyce *Ulysses* (NY 1934) 346: There'd be wigs on the green. **1928** RA Freeman *A Certain* (NY) 300: There would be wigs on the green presently. *Oxford* 889.

W172 To keep one's **Wig** on

1964 SRansome *One-Man* (NY DBC) 100: Keep your wig on. **1969** AGilbert *Missing* (NY) 182: Keep your wig on and remember that enough is enough. Cf. To keep one's Hair on, Pants, Shirt *above*.

W173 As easy as letting go of a **Wildcat**

1970 RRood *Wild* (NY) 65: I know now what the pioneers meant when they said something was "as easy as letting go of a wildcat." Cf. Tiger *above*; To hold a Wolf *below*.

W174 As savage as a **Wildcat**

1930 JRhode *Dr. Priestly* (NY) 210: He could be as savage as a wildcat. Cf. TW 402(1): Fierce.

W175 To fight like a **Wildcat** (*varied*)

1932 AGilbert *Body* (NY) 103: People fight like wildcats. **1933** GDilnot *Thousandth* (L) 266: He fought like a wildcat. **1952** TClaymore *Reunion* (NY 1955) 62: As full of fight as a bag of wild cats. **1953** CLittle *Black Iris* (NY) 109: They all fought like wildcats. **1965** CArmstrong *Turret* (NY) 24: I'm fighting like a wildcat. Whiting *NC* 496.

W176 To go like **Wildfire**

1957 GAshe *Wait* (NY 1972) 5: He goes at it like wildfire. EAP W159.

W177 To run like **Wildfire**

1924 LSpringfield *Some* (L) 61: The story . . . ran like wildfire. **1925** HHext *Monster* (NY) 163: The news will run like fire. **1943** WMcCully *Doctors* (NY) 100: The news ran through the hall like wildfire. **1956** HTreece *Great* (NY) 208: The news ran like wildfire. EAP W161; TW 402; Brunvand 152.

W178 To sell like **Wildfire**

1935 AChristie *Death* (L) 158: It ought to sell like wildfire. **1960** FWarburg *Occupation* (B) 110: *Daedalus* began to sell like wildfire. EAP W162.

W179 To spread like **Wildfire**

1911 CKSteele *Mansion* (NY) 12: The news spread like wildfire. **1933** LCharteris *Brighter* (NY) 249: [It] spread like wildfire. **1939** MStuart *Dead Men* (L) 49: The news spread like wildfire. **1947** HWade *New Graves* (L) 226: News . . . spread . . . like wildfire. **1957** FHoyle *Black* (L) 20: The story would spread like wildfire. **1970**

AKarmey *My Revolution* (NY) 40: The news spread through Paris like wildfire. EAP W163; TW 402. Cf. Brushfire *above*.

W180 To take the **Will** for the deed (*varied*)

1903 HGarland *Companions on the Trail* (NY 1931) 189: She took the will for the deed. **1922** VBridges *Greensea* (NY) 236: Take the will for the deed. **1922** JJoyce *Ulysses* (NY 1934) 145: You must take the will for the deed. **1935** DOgburn *The Will and the Deed* (NY). **1936** HAdams *Death* (L) 213: You might be wise to take the will for the deed. **1936** JRhode *In Face* (L) 66: The intention is as good as the deed. **1957** NBlake *End* (L) 226: My parents took the will for the deed, as they say. **1961** NBlake *Worm* (L) 204: Shall we take the will for the deed? **1965** JPorter *Dover Two* (NY 1968) 7: Take the thought for the deed. **1967** RLockridge *Murder* (P) 129: The will for the deed. EAP W164; TW 402(1); Whiting W267; Brunvand 152(1). Cf. It is the Thought *above*.

W181 Where there's a **Will** there's a way (*varied*)

1925 GBeasley *My First* (Paris) 109: Where there was a will there was a way. **1929** RAJWalling *Murder* (NY) 156: Where there's a girl there's a way. **1933** ESGardner *Sulky Girl* (NY) 7: The old saying that where there's a will there's a way. **1939** FWCrofts *Fatal* (L 1959) 82: Where there's a will there's a way. **1940** WLewis *Letters* ed WKRose (L 1963) 283: Where there's a will there's a way. **1940** RStout *Where There's a Will* (NY). **1947** MBurton *A Will in the Way* (NY). **1950** ECRLorac *Accident* (NY DBC) 7: Where there's a will there's a way. **1958** HWeenolsen *To Keep* (NY) 483: And the will to find a way. **1961** OHesky *Purple* (L) 105: Where there's a will there's a way. **1961** ESherry *Call* (NY DBC) 22: Where there's a will, there's an estate. **1967** DBloodworth *Chinese* (NY) 159: For them there was a will and so, of course, a way. **1970** MMcGrady *Stranger* (NY) 4: Young people with the will but not the way. **1975** ELathen *By Hook* (NY) 198: Where there's a will . . . TW 402(2); Brunvand 152(2); *Oxford* 891.

W182   He who **Will** not when he may, when he will he shall have nay (*varied*)

1930 TCobb *Sark* (L) 18: She who will not when she may! **1934** JCameron *Body* (L) 149: He that will not when he may, when he will he shall have but nay. **1939** LBlack *Mr Preed* (L) 289: Those who will not when they may, when they would they shall have nay. **1948** CRBoxer *Fidalgos* (Oxford 1968) 211: He who will not when he may, when he will he shall have nay. **1971** PAlding *Despite* (NY) 132: As my mother used to say, what you didn't do then, can't be done now. Whiting W275; *Oxford* 890–1.

W183   What **Will** be, will be (*che será será*) (*varied*)

1928 VWilliams *Crouching* (B) 11: What will be, will be. **1930** EDBiggers *Charlie* (NY 1943) 242: What is to be, will be. **1932** MTurnbull *Return* (P) 99: What will be, will be. **1948** LSdeCamp *Divide* (NY 1964) 140: What would be would be. **1951** DWMeredith *Christmas* (NY) 45: What will be, must be. **1957** AAmos *Fatal* (NY) 26: *Que será, será.* **1958** MUnderwood *Lawful* (NY) 180: "What will be, will be." . . . The words of a popular song. **1959** AGoodman *Golden* (NY) 232: *Que sera sera*, whatever will be, will be. **1961** RJWhite *Smartest* (L) 45: But what will be, will be. **1966** DGilman *Unexpected* (NY) 71: *Che sera, sera*, as they say. Cf. Whiting G254. Cf. What Must be *above.*

W184   **Willy-nilly** (*varied*)

1906 JLondon *Letters* ed KHendricks (NY 1965) 216: Willy-nilly. **1921** JBCabell *Figures* (NY 1925) 328: Willy-nilly. **1928** DHLawrence *Lady* ("Allemagne") 9: Willynilly. **1932** Anonymous *Hot-cha* (L) 21: It should be "Nolens Volens." **1935** TFPowys *Captain Patch* (L) 21: Willy-nilly. **1940** HSKeeler *Crimson Boy* (L) 233: Willy-nilly. **1955** RStout *Before* (NY) 57: Willy-nilly. **1957** RFenisong *Schemers* (NY) 57: The dishes, stacked willy-nilly, clattered in her hands. **1958** PDWestbrook *Biography* (NY) 214: Willy-nilly. **1960** EPetajs *Nets* (NY) 84:

Don might . . . be a willy-nilly tool. **1967** IReed *Free-lance* (NY) A bunch of willy-nilly nervous Nellie champs. **1972** AFriedman *Hermaphrodeity* (NY) 30: She called me Willy-Nilly. EAP W166; TW 403: Will vb.; Whiting W277.

W185   As jimp as a **Willy-wand**

1939 LBrock *Riddle* (L) 15: [She was] as jimp about the middle as ay willy wand. Cf. Whiting *Scots* II 149: Wand(3); NED Jimp 1.

W186   All **Wind** and piss like a tanyard cat (*varied*)

1922 JJoyce *Ulysses* (NY 1934) 322: All wind and piss like a tanyard cat. **1950** OAnderson *In for* (NY) 115: They're nowt but wind and water like the barber's cat. **1975** SJPerelman *Vinegar* (NY) 33: They were as full of wind as a barber's cat [*SJP ascribes this to Joyce*]. Spears 301: Piss and wind. Cf. To be full of Piss *above.*

W187   As changeable as the **Wind** (*varied*)

1939 DDean *Emerald* (NY) 242: A woman changeable as a March wind. **1939** DHume *Heads* (L) 141: He was as changeable as the wind. Whiting W289; Brunvand 152(1). Cf. As variable *below.*

W188   As fast as the **Wind**

1947 HWade *New Graves* (L) 97: Fast as the wind. **1954** SJepson *Black* (NY) 157: I should be off faster than the wind. **1970** DStuart *Very* (NY) 54: She drove back home as fast as the wind. EAP W173.

W189   As fickle as the **Wind**

1956 HTreece *Great* (NY) 86: You are as fickle as the winds. EAP W174.

W190   As fleet as the **Wind**

1922 ERPunshon *Bittermeads* (NY) 223: Fleet as the wind. **1951** ADerleth *Outer* (NY) 282: Fleet as the wind. EAP W175.

W191   As free as the **Wind**

1929 HHolt *Mayfair* (L) 85: Free as the four winds of heaven. **1937** CGGivens *All Cats* (I) 28: As free as the wind. **1947** VSiller *Curtain* (NY) 91: You'll be as free as the wind. **1954** NBlake *Whisper* (L) 17:

Free as the wind. **1956** GMason *Golden* (NY) 109: As free as the wind. **1965** NFreeling *Criminal* (L) 192: Free as the wind. **1973** CJackson *Kicked* (NY) 94: It's free as the wind. EAP W176; Taylor *Western Folklore* 17(1958) 20(1). Cf. As free as the Breeze *above*.

W192   As inconstant as the **Wind**
1968 SMorrow *Dancing* (NY) 43: Inconstant as the wind. EAP W177.

W193   As swift as the **Wind**
1908 LFBaum *American Fairy Tales* (I) 136: Swift as the wind he strode. **1922** ERPunshon *Bittermeads* (NY) 220: Swift as the wind. **1936** GDHCole *Last Will* (NY) 35: Rupert rode away as swift as the wind. Whiting W294.

W194   As variable as the **Wind**
1929 OGray *Bagshot* (NY) 11: As variable as the wind. EAP W181. Cf. As changeable *above*.

W195   As wild as the **Wind**
1937 JDCarr *To Wake* (L) 285: My idea was as wild as wind. **1961** JDCarr *Witch* (L) 126: It's as wild as wind [*detective fiction*]. **1964** EPangborn *Davy* (NY) 100: They go wild as the wind. EAP W184: Winds.

W196   Between **Wind** and water
1906 JCLincoln *Mr. Pratt* (NY) 12: Hit me betwixt wind and water. **1929** CSLewis *Letters* ed WHLewis (NY 1966) 138: Got me between wind and water. **1932** THWhite *Darkness* (L) 202: It [*dying in one's sleep*] would catch you between wind and water. **1952** HFMPrescott *Man on* (NY) 309: [He] was taken between wind and water. **1953** LThompson *Time* (L) 69: Her eye . . . took them between wind and water. **1960** MProcter *Devil's* (NY DBC) 55: You're goin' to get on between wind an' water. **1966** GWBrace *Between Wind and Water* (NY). **1966** PMHubbard *Holm* (NY DBC) 18: It was the . . . casual intimacy of the gesture that hit us between wind and water. **1972** CARobertson *Oneida* (Syracuse, NY) 13: [It] left her, at the end, between wind and water, as the saying goes, bereft of all sup-

port. **1974** FWatson *Year* (NY) 87: [It] had smitten Lord Campbell between wind and water. EAP W185.

W197   It is an ill **Wind** that blows nobody good (*varied*)
1903 EChilders *Riddle* (NY 1940) 240: It is an ill wind that blows nobody good. **1924** CWells *Furthest* (P) 293: It's an ill wind that blows nobody good. **1926** HAdams *Sloane* (NY) 15: It's an ill wind that doesn't blow apples into someone's garden. **1927** SHorler *Black* (L 1935) 72: It's an ill wind that blows the saxophone. **1928** EKRand *Founders* (Cambridge, Mass.) 157: It is an ill wind that blows nobody good luck. **1929** WKSmith *Bowery* (NY) 24: It's an ill wind that brings strange bed fellows, or something to that effect. **1929** PGWodehouse *Fish* (NY) 86: It's an ill wind that has no turning. **1930** HAdams *Golden* (L) 132: Ill winds proverbially bring unexpected blessings. **1932** CAndrews *Butterfly* (NY) 249: It's an ill wind—and all that sort of rot. **1935** CBarry *Death* (NY) 257: It's an ill wind that blows no man down. **1945** HCBailey *Wrong Man* (NY) 66: It's a mighty good wind that blows nobody ill. **1945** CEVulliamy *Edwin* (L) 80: It's an ill wind that gathers no moss. **1947** HWade *New Graves* (L) 151: Perhaps this is the ill wind that'll blow you a bit of good. **1954** IFleming *Live* (NY 1959) 57: The clarinet—"an ill woodwind that nobody blows good." **1956** *Punch* 7/4 20: It is an ill wind that blows no one any good. **1957** *BangorDN* 9/17 9: Hurricane Carrie was an ill wind that blew somebody some good today. **1958** *BHerald* 6/26 2: It's an ill wind that blows no good. **1960** JBWest *Taste* (NY) 23: An oboe [is] an ill wind that nobody blows good. **1961** PDennis *Little* (NY) 213: It is indeed an ill wind that blows no one good (to paraphrase the late Thomas Tucker). **1961** MMillar *How Like* (NY DBC) 34: He was the ill wind that blew the wolf away from my door. **1962** AGilbert *Uncertain* (NY DBC) 15: It's an ill wind that blows no one any good. **1966** CMBowra *Memories* (L) 74: In this case a very ill wind might bring us a bit of good. **1970** WMasterson

Death (NY) 158: It was an ill wind that blew no one good. **1976** SBrett *So Much* (NY) 11: It's an ill wind, they say, and it's certainly blown some good the way of . . . Anna. **1977** LBlock *Burglars* (NY) 104: An ill wind that blows no good. EAP W191; TW 403(3); Brunvand 153(3).

W198 Sits the **Wind** in that corner? (*varied*)
1924 ADHSmith *Porto* (NY) 249: Sets the wind in that quarter? **1932** RAJWalling *Fatal* (NY) 150: That's where the wind sits. **1936** DWheatley *They Found* (P) 38: Sits the wind in that quarter? **1955** RGraves *Homer's* (NY) 94: Is the wind at that door? **1956** MStewart *Wildfire* (NY) 139: Sits the wind in that quarter? **1972** NMarsh *Tied* (B) 18: Sits the wind in that quarter? TW 404(11); *Oxford* 893: Door, corner. Cf. Brunvand 153(3): Quarter.

W199 To be in the **Wind** (*varied*)
1924 TFPowys *Mark Only* (L) 42: Matters . . . in the wind. **1931** MBurton *Menace* (L) 53: What's in the wind now? 232: When he sees what's in the wind. **1933** CBarry *Death* (NY) 281: There was something in the wind. **1954** JTey *Shilling* (NY) 25: What's in the wind? **1960** SRaven *Doctors* (L) 133: Something in the wind that didn't smell quite right. EAP W195; TW 403(6); Brunvand 153(5).

W200 To cast to the **Winds**
1928 EHamilton *Four* (L) 139: Cast my salary to the winds. TW 405(25): Throw.

W201 To drive like the **Wind**
1961 EWilliams *George* (NY) 305: He drove like the wind. Taylor *Prov. Comp.* 88.

W202 To fight the **Wind**
1924 JSFletcher *Time-Worn* (NY) 185: A man who fights the wind. *Oxford* 255: Fight. Cf. To talk *below.*

W203 To fly like the **Wind**
1927 RAFreeman *Magic* (NY) 32: They flew like the wind. EAP W198.

W204 To get the **Wind** up (*varied*)
1924 DMackail *Majestic* (NY) 104: Once you get the wind up them; 152. **1929** CBarry *Clue* (NY) 160: The old man has

got the wind-up about this business. **1936** LBrock *Stoat* (L) 115: I've got the wind up. **1937** ERPunshon *Mystery* (NY) 88: He had got the wind up and meant to do a bunk. **1940** MCharlton *Death of* (L) 252: His pals got the wind up. **1941** ELFetta *Dressed* (NY) 119: Manchester, as the English say, had got the wind up about something. **1954** MHastings *Cork* (NY) 222: [He's] got the wind up. **1961** HKlinger *Wanton* (NY) 162: She really got the wind up. **1966** LLafore *Nine* (NY) 143: Everybody else concerned must—in the peculiar British phrase—have got the wind up. **1973** SWoods *Yet She* (NY) 75: I really did get the wind up. Partridge 960.

W205 To get **Wind** of something
1911 JSHay *Amazing Emperor* (L) 43: Got wind of what had been done. **1922** JSFletcher *Ravensdene* (NY) 241: Got wind of something. EAP W199.

W206 To go like the **Wind**
1936 LWMeynell *On the Night* (NY) 165: Went like the wind. **1958** JBlackburn *Scent* (L) 195: [The auto] went like the wind. EAP W202; Brunvand 153(10).

W207 To piss (spit) against the **Wind** (*varied*)
1953 SBellow *Adventures* (NY) 434: I can see you pissing against the wind. **1954** JSymons *Narrowing* (NY) 40: It's no use fighting the police, just pissing against the wind. **1958** *TLS* 7/18 409: To call it trivial . . . is to spit into the wind. **1964** EPangborn *Davy* (NY) 9: Anyone who seriously entertained that upsydown mahoola would almost certainly piss to windward. **1971** MUnderwood *Trout* (NY) 129: A plea for mitigation . . . was like spitting in a gale. **1973** JCashman *Gentleman* (NY) 264: They'll be spitting in the wind. TW 405(23): Spit; *Oxford* 766–7: Spit.

W208 To put the **Wind** up someone
1930 MAllingham *Mystery* (NY) 51: It puts the wind up me. **1936** AChristie *Murder* (L) 170: Putting the wind up her—to put it vulgarly. **1936** JWVandercook *Murder in Fiji* (NY) 222: We had at any rate, as they say, put the wind up. **1967** JSymons *Man*

Who (L) 144: I only did it to put the wind up him. **1970** MStewart *Crystal* (NY) 324: You've put the wind up there. Partridge 960.

W209   To raise the **Wind**

1915 JLondon *Letters* ed KHendricks (NY 1965) 443: An attempt to raise the wind. **1922** JJoyce *Ulysses* (NY 1934) 145: If I could raise the wind anyhow. 628: Raise the wind on false pretences. **1933** GCollins *Dead Walk* (L) 254: Something had to be done to raise the wind. **1957** PGWodehouse *Butler* (NY) 113: A handy way of raising the wind. **1959** PMoyes *Dead Men* (L) 209: A pretty good way of raising the wind. **1970** MInnes *Death* (L) 60: How to raise the wind. EAP W207.

W210   To run like the **Wind**

1915 JFerguson *Stealthy* (L 1935) 17: Ran like the wind. **1916** SRohmer *Tales* (NY 1922) 208: Ran like the wind. **1935** ECRLorac *Organ* (L) 129: Running like the wind. **1956** HTreece *Golden* (L) 21: Running like the wind. **1965** LHWhitten *Progeny* (NY) 189: The man ran like the wind. Whiting W333.

W211   To sail near (close to) the **Wind**

1925 EPhillpotts *Voice* (NY) 91: Mighty near the wind he sails. **1926** FWCrofts *Cheyne* (NY) 199: Sailing rather close to the wind. **1937** MBurton *Clue* (NY) 63: You begin to sail too near the wind to suit me. **1941** EDaly *Deadly* (NY 1947) 114: It was sailing too close to the wind. **1951** SRattray *Knight* (NY 1966) 72: He had sailed too near the wind. **1962** AChristie *Pale* (NY DBC) 101: She sailed as near the wind as she could. **1973** AWest *Mortal* (NY) 125: To see how close to the wind they could go. **1973** RRendell *Some* (NY) 91: He likes sailing near the wind. EAP W208.

W212   To sow the **Wind** and reap the whirlwind (*varied*)

1922 JJoyce *Ulysses* (NY 1934) 124: Reaping the whirlwind. **1940** PMcGuire *Spanish* (L) 227: You may reap the whirlwind. **1970** EQueen *Last* (NY) 43: Johnny's gone with the wind he sowed. TW 404(14); Brunvand 153(8); *Oxford* 757: Sow.

W213   To take the **Wind** out of one's sails (*varied*)

1915 JFerguson *Stealthy* (L 1935) 33: That took the wind out of his sails. **1931** MDalton *Night* (NY) 176: The answer had taken the wind out of his sails. **1938** JDonovan *Beckoning Dead* (L) 157: That took the wind right out of my sails. **1940** CRawson *Headless* (NY) 189: Takes some of the wind out of my sails. **1949** MAllingham *More Work* (NY) 53: Taking any wind there might be right out of his sails. **1954** MAllingham *No Love* (NY) 35: I had the wind taken out of my sails. **1957** *BangorDN* 3/27 14: Wilson took the wind completely out of my sails. **1969** LPDavies *Stranger* (NY) 159: A matter . . . of taking the wind out of sails. **1976** JPorter *Package* (NY) 74: Took the wind out of the Hon. Con's sails. TW 405(24); *Oxford* 801: Take.

W214   To talk (speak) to (argue with, whistle at) the **Wind**

1931 WMorton *Mystery* (NY) 111: You might as well argue with the wind. **1934** HVines *This Green* (B) 135: He might as well talk to the wind. **1939** DBOlson *Cat Saw* (NY) 38: She might as well be talking to the wind. **1941** ADerleth *Mr. George* (NY 1964) 47: I might as well have talked to the wind. **1953** KMKnight *Akin* (NY) 18: I might as well have whistled at the west wind. **1966** MWorthington *Strange* (NY) 228: I might as well have talked to the wind. **1967** SBlanc *Rose* (NY) 149: It's like speaking to the wind. EAP W215. Cf. To fight *above*.

W215   To whistle up a **Wind** (rain) (*varied*)

1922 JJoyce *Ulysses* (NY 1934) 369: Whistle brings rain they say. **1934** SPalmer *Murder* (NY) 67: The way sailors are supposed to whistle up a wind when they want one. **1956** EGann *Twilight* (NY) 103: Whistling for wind only brought bad weather. **1959** MPHood *Bell* (NY) 73: Whistlin' up a gale's been known to flounder the ship. TW 405(26); *Oxford* 884: Whistle.

W216   What (good) **Wind** blew you wherever

1924 FWCrofts *Cask* (NY 1936) 15: What good wind blows you this way? **1932**

JTFarrell *Young Lonigan* (NY 1935) 50: Look what the wind blew in. **1933** MBurton *Death* (L) 174: What fair wind has blown you here? **1950** HReilly *Murder* (NY) 121: What good wind blows you to Eastwalk? **1957** *New Yorker* 9/14 45: What wind blew you in from California? TW 404(16); *Oxford* 893.

W217 When the **Wind** is in the East *etc.*

1930 AWynne *Room* (P) 226: When the wind is in the East . . . 'Tis neither good for man nor beast. *Oxford* 893.

W218 To tilt at **Windmills** (*varied*)

1943 HAdams *Victory* (L) 38: Edward was no Quixote to tilt at windmills. **1949** JDCarr *Conan Doyle* (NY) 157: Was he tilting at windmills? **1953** ECRLorac *Speak* (NY) 30: Don't go tilting at windmills. **1956** UCurtiss *Widow's* (NY) 25: Seeking windmills to tilt at. **1960** TPowell *Man-Killer* (NY) 61: You're hell bent on tilting against the windmills. **1968** RTruax *Doctors* (B) 255: Tilting at windmills. **1972** TWells *Die* (NY) 151: I was too beat to joust at windmills. EAP W217.

W219 To live on **Wind pudding**

1934 RPTCoffin *Lost Paradise* (NY) 143: Live on wind-pudding. Partridge 960.

W220 Good **Wine** needs no bush (*varied*)

1926 AMarshall *Mote* (NY) 52: Good wine needs no bush. **1936** VMcHugh *Caleb* (NY) 25: Good wine needs no bush. **1939** LFord *Mr Cromwell* (L) 221: His colonel's word needed no bush [*was good*]. **1959** *TLS* 7/24 429: He held that frames should be no more to pictures than a good bush to a good wine. **1964** JBlish *Doctor* (L) 45: Good wine needs no bush. **1966** SCRoberts *Adventures* (Cambridge, Eng.) 139: Frank's good wine needed no bush. **1975** DRussell *Tamarisk* (NY) 194: Good wine needs no bush. **1978** NFreeling *Night Lords* (NY) 13: If the wine is really good, it needs no bush. EAP W219.

W221 In **Wine** is truth (*varied*)

1905 HRHaggard *Ayesha* (NY) 205: Out of trouble comes truth, as out of wine. **1926** BNiles *Black Haiti* (NY) 162: Nor do I believe in all that *veritas* that's supposed to lurk in *vino*. **1927** GTNathan *Land* (NY) 189: *Veritas in Vino*. One of the greatest morsels of balderdash that has come down the ages in proverb form is to the effect that in wine there is truth. **1927** TFPowys *Mr Weston's* (L) 45: You know the saying, that there is truth in wine. **1928** CWood *Shadow* (NY) 165: In drink, the truth. **1929** HFootner *Self-Made* (NY) 115: When a man's drunk, the truth generally comes out. **1929** WMartyn *Recluse* (NY) 258: Truth, you know, lives under a cork. **1930** EMarjoribanks *EMHall* (L) 316: There is a maxim . . . that drunken people tell the truth. **1931** VLWhitechurch *Murder* (NY) 318: The old proverb *In vino veritas*. **1938** NJones *Hanging Lady* (NY) 203: A practical case of where in *vino* there would be *veritas*. **1941** GBagby *Red Is* (NY) 166: That old "In vino veritas" saw. **1942** EXFerrars *Murder of a Suicide* (NY) 146: There's a certain well-known proverb, isn't there, about wine and truth? **1950** LordDunsany *Strange* (L) 15: I have found in life that all the old proverbs are true, discovering it as one comes across them one by one; and none truer than that which the wisdom of Rome discovered, *in vino veritas*. **1950** RVickers *Murdering* (L 1955) 171: You know that gag "in vino veritas." **1953** MLowndes *Monsoon* (L) 200: "Truth in wine" is a stupid thing to say. **1954** RKLeavitt *Chip* (P) 7: The truth being proverbially in wine. **1955** ELustgarten *Woman* (NY) 40: Did truth, obedient to the Latin tag, spill from her drunken tongue? **1958** ECRLorac *People* (NY) 155: There's an old saying, "In vino veritas," meaning, as I see it, that a man sees things plainer when he's drunk. **1964** RMacdonald *Chill* (NY) 167: In wine was truth. **1972** GBlack *Bitter* (NY) 3: Wine tells the truth. **1973** JDMacDonald *Turquoise* (P) 65: In vino was veritas. EAP W221.

W222 When the **Wine** is in, the wit is out (*varied*)

1935 BGraeme *Body* (L) 173: To paraphrase an old tag . . . "When the wine is in, the wit is out." **1937** AGilbert *Murder* (L) 215: *When the beer goes in, the wit goes* *out*—Old Proverb. **1937** VWilkins *And So—Victoria* (NY) 51: With wine in, wits go out. **1946** GBellairs *Death in the Night* (NY) 41: When wine's in, wit's out, they say. **1970** CDrummond *Stab* (NY) 93: An old fool, drink in, brains out. EAP W223; TW 406(3).

W223 To be under someone's Wing

1929 LRGribble *Gillespie* (NY) 36: Offering to take me under his wing. **1933** GRichards *Memoirs* (NY) 252: Paris had taken him under her wing. **1939** EQueen *Dragon's* (NY) 38: Vi took me under her wing ... Just like a hen. **1963** MPHood *Sin* (NY) 129: This girl, been under my wing, manner of speakin'. **1968** HSwann *Home* (L) 91: To have us back under their wing. EAP W226; Brunvand 153.

W224 To have one's Wings clipped

1920 AChristie *Mysterious Affair* (NY) 234: His wings were ... clipped. **1968** SEdwards *Barbary* (Englewood, NJ) 205: Trying to clip his wings. EAP W227.

W225 As quick as a Wink (*varied*)

1908 LFBaum *Dorothy and the Wizard of Oz* (I) 117: Quick as a wink. **1913** JCLincoln *Mr. Pratt's Patients* (NY) 220: Quick as a wink. **1954** EWalter *Untidy* (P) 127: She's quick as a wink. **1956** MPHood *Scarlet* (NY) 159: She's quick as a wink. **1960** BKendrick *Aluminum* (NY DBC) 137: He'd leave her quick as wink of an eye. **1965** VRandolph *Hot Springs* (Hatboro, Penn.) 31: Quick as a wink. EAP W228; Brunvand 154(1). Cf. Blink *above*; Winking *below*.

W226 In the Wink of an eye

1928 VWilliams *Crouching* (B) 239: Guess the truth in the wink of an eye. **1934** HMiller *Tropic of Cancer* (NY 1962) 192: To toss it off in the wink of an eye. **1940** MBoniface *Murder As* (NY) 30: In the wink of an eye. **1966** TWalsh *Resurrection* (NY) 161: In the wink of an eye. TW 406(2, 3, 4). Cf. Blink *above*.

W227 To get (*etc.*) forty Winks

1921 IOstrander *Crimson* (NY) 120: Going to get forty winks. **1933** NGordon *Shakespeare* (NY) 234: Forty winks save one, as the Bible says. **1933** ECRLorac *Murder* (L) 149: I'll have forty winks. **1940** CWorth *Trail* (NY) 146: Catching forty winks. **1957** MCRoberts *Little* (NY 1963) 178: He could get forty winks. **1960** JJMarric *Gideon's Risk* (NY) 89: Don't spoil your forty winks. **1965** ESGardner *Troubled* (NY) 71: To take forty winks. TW 406(10).

W228 As easy as Winking (wink)

1924 JSFletcher *Time-Worn* (NY) 167: Easy as winking. **1928** DHLawrence *Lady* ("Allemagne") 325: It'll be as easy as wink. **1933** CBush *April Fools* (L) 119: Easy as winking. **1936** LBruce *Case* (L) 283: As easy as wink. **1938** JJConnington *For Murder* (L) 139: Suicide's easier than winking, nowadays. **1939** AMuir *Death Comes* (L) 86: Easy as wink. **1947** ELustgarten *One More* (NY 1959) 77: As easy as wink. **1948** CDickson *Skeleton* (NY 1967) 87: As easy as winking. **1952** JDCarr *Nine Wrong* (NY) 115: As easy as winking. **1970** GEEvans *Where* (L) 256: As easy as winking. **1975** PDickinson *Lively* (NY) 79: They'd rub her out, easy as winking. NED Winking *vbl. sb.*[1] 4; Partridge 961; Wilstach 108. Cf. Wink-me-eye *below*.

W229 As quick as Winking

1924 WBMFerguson *Black* (NY) 299: Quicker'n winking. **1940** ACampbell *They Hunted* (NY) 238: Quick as winking. TW 406(1). Cf. Blink, Wink *above*.

W230 As easy as Wink-me-eye

1926 MLewis *Island* (L) 285: As easy as wink-me-eye. Cf. Wink *above*.

W231 As cruel as Winter

1910 EPhillpotts *Tales* (NY) 77: Cruel as winter. Wilstach 76. Cf. Taylor *Prov. Comp.* 71: Sharp.

W232 Winter fills the ponds before it freezes them (*varied*)

1975 AHOlmstead *Threshold* (NY) 51: The adage is that winter fills its ponds before it freezes them. Cf. Brunvand 154; Dunwoody 91.

W233 **Winter** never rots in the sky

1959 *BHerald* 3/13 42: Winter never rots in the sky, says the old proverb. EAP W232 *Oxford* 897; Tilley W512.

W234 To **Winter** and summer (with) one (*varied*)

1953 OAtkinson *Golden* (I) 158: I've wintered with her and I've summered with her and never had any notion that she was aught but a drudge. **1955** MColes *Man in* (NY) 166: Man and boy, they wintered him and summered him. **1967** MWilkins *Last* (Englewood Cliffs, NJ) v: An old Maine saying: "you don't know your neighbors until you've summer'd 'em and winter'd 'em." **1969** RBlythe *Akenfield* (NY) 69: You'll have to winter us and summer us [*get to know*]. EAP W236; Whiting *NC* 442(33). Cf. Know me *above*.

W235 As taut (tight) as a **Wire**

1963 WHaggard *High* (NY DBC) 162: Walking up ... taut as a wire. **1964** JWCampbell *Analog II* (NY) 2: Her husband was as tight as a wire. **1972** SBrooke *Queen* (NY) 163: The atmosphere was as taut as wire.

W236 As tough as (steel) **Wire**

1928 CBarry *Corpse* (NY) 187: Those London lads are as tough as wire. **1935** AMuir *Raphael* (L) 140: Looked as tough as steel. **1939** WMartyn *Noonday* (L) 105: She's as tough as wire. TW 407(1).

W237 It is **Wisdom** sometimes to seem a fool

1921 P&MThorne *Sheridan* (NY) 270: What is the proverb—"'Tis wisdom sometimes to seem a fool." Whiting W378.

W238 There is no **Wisdom** (below the girdle)

1945 RLHine *Confessions* (L) 90: The *obiter dictum* of ... Sir Matthew Hale (1609–76): "There is no wisdom *sub cingulo*." Tilley W520.

W239 If **Wishes** were fishes we'd all cast nets

1965 FHerbert *Dune* (NY) 44: If wishes were fishes we'd all cast nets. Cf. Apperson 698–9; *Oxford* 903.

W240 If **Wishes** were horses, beggars would ride (*varied*)

1930 DOgburn *Ra-ta-plan!* (B) 285: If wishes were horses, beggars would ride. **1932** TCobb *Who Closed* (L) 90: If wishes were horses, darling! **1958** *TLS* 4/11 viii: If wishes were horses. **1959** NFitzgerald *Midsummer* (NY) 75: If wishes were horses ... **1960** NFitzgerald *Candles* (L) 59: If wishes were horses, think how cheap horses would be. **1966** DMDisney *Magic* (NY) 35: If wishes were horses, beggars could ride. *Oxford* 903.

W241 The **Wish** is father (parent) to the thought

1914 JLondon *Letters* ed KHendricks (NY 1965) 425: The wish is parent to the thought. **1925** HAdams *By Order* (L) 35: The wish was father to the thought. **1929** CWells *Tapestry* (P) 64: There is an old proverb ... about the wish being father to the thought. **1937** DFrome *Black Envelope* (NY) 296: The old business of the wish being father to the thought. **1938** MTeagle *Murders* (NY) 108: A woman's wish is almost invariably father to the thought. **1943** FScully *Rogues* (Hollywood) 188: The wish being father to the thought. **1953** DMDisney *Prescription* (NY) 36: The wish is father to the thought. **1956** *BangorDN* 7/30 18: The wish was father to the thought. **1970** RCowper *Twilight* (NY) 64: The wish was father to the thought. EAP W240.

W242 Bought **Wit** is best

1969 APHannum *Look* (NY) 156: Bought wit is best, if you don't pay too dear for it. EAP W242, 246.

W243 One's **Wits** are woolgathering (*varied*)

1922 JJoyce *Ulysses* (NY 1934) 614: [He] fell to woolgathering. **1928** VLWhitechurch *Shot* (NY) 33: My wits be a woolgathering. **1930** AChristie *Murder* (NY) 291: Your wits must have all gone woolgathering. **1932** VLoder *Red Stain* (NY) 50: My wits have gone woolgathering. **1936** JCLenehan *Deadly* (L) 270: His wits would go wool-gathering. **1956** MPHood *Scarlet* (NY) 167: My wits have gone wool-gathering. **1960** DShannon *Case* (NY 1964) 91: I'm a wool-gathering, silly old woman. **1963** LEgan *Run* (NY DBC) 123: I've just been woolgathering. **1964** FLockridge *Quest* (P) 125: Woolgathering. He'd gathered a lot of wool. **1969** APHannum *Look* (NY) 170: Afore I knowed it, I was wool-gatherin'—all the wool in the fields, by gollies [*drunk*]. TW 412: Wool(7); *Oxford* 905.

W244 To be at one's **Wits'** (wit's) end

1900 CFPidgin *Quincy A. Sawyer* (B) 348: At her wits' end. **1924** TMundy *Om* (NY) 71: At my wits end. **1935** WSSykes *Harness* (L) 78: At my wit's end. **1940** HBest *Twenty-fifth* (NY) 118: Ann was at her wits' end. **1953** EBigland *Indomitable* (L) 32: At her wits' end. **1967** JGribble *That Had* (NY) 83: The German police were at their wits' end. **1975** LSdeCamp *Lovecraft* (NY) 433: Ay his wit's end. **1981** AKOffit *Night* (NY) 226: One woman patient was at her wit's end. EAP W245.

W245 To live on one's **Wits**

1927 VWilliams *Eye* (B) 72: He was living on his wits, as the saying goes. EAP W247.

W246 As cold as a **Witch's** tit (kiss); Witch-tit cold

1951 WBrebner *Second* (NY) 90: Cold as a witch's tit. **1951** JDSalinger *Catcher* (B) 7: It was cold as a witch's teat. **1959** MRuss *Half Moon* (NY) 115: Cold as a witch's tit. **1963** KAmis *Spectrum* (L) 258: Cold as a witch's kiss. **1963** FWTolman *Mosquitobush* (Peterborough, NH) 24: Colder'n a wet witch's tit. **1968** KTopkins *Passing* (B) 21: It was witch tit cold. **1969** SFisher *Saxon's* (LA) 138: Cold as a witch's tit in here. Taylor *Prov. Comp.* 28.

W247 As cross as a **Witch**

1961 UCurtiss *Hours* (NY) 47: You'll be as cross as a witch in the morning. EAP W249.

W248 As nervous (flight, jumpy) as a **Witch**

1923 HGartland *Globe* (NY) 285: I'm as nervous as a witch. **1930** MGEberhart *While* (NY) 292: I was as nervous as a witch. **1935** FErskine *Naked* (L) 93: She's as flighty as a witch. **1935** TWilder *Heaven's*

(NY) 127: They're nervous as witches. **1943** EDaly *Nothing Can Rescue* (NY 1963) 32: Louise is as nervous as a witch. **1962** PDennis *Genius* (NY) 211: I'm nervous as a witch. **1962** LEgan *Borrowed* (NY DBC) 118: She was as nervous as a witch. (Why as a witch?) **1963** UCurtiss *Wasp* (NY DBC) 46: You're as jumpy as a witch. TW 407(1).

W249 **Woe** to the land where the king is a child

1974 MGAVale *Charles VII* (Berkeley) 15: Woe to the land where the king is a child. EAP W255.

W250 As black (dark) as a **Wolf's** (dog's) mouth

1925 HHext *Monster* (NY) 56: The place is dark as a wolf's mouth. **1931** JSFletcher *Malvery* (L) 43: 'Twas so dark as a dog's mouth. **1936** NGayle *Murder* (L) 105: Black as a wolf's mouth. **1959** *NYTimes* 1/11 1: "Black as a wolf's mouth," an old Cumberland Mountains saying. TW 408(2,5); *Oxford* 167-8: Dark.

W251 As hungry as a (bitch) **Wolf**

1910 JCLincoln *Depot Master* (NY) 36: Hungry as a wolf. **1930** VWMason *Seeds* (NY) 89: I'm as hungry as a wolf. **1934** HMiller *Tropic of Cancer* (NY 1962) 140: Hungry as a wolf. **1940** AGaines *While the Wind* (NY) 112: I'm hungry as a wolf. **1943** FMcDermid *Ghost Wanted* (NY 1945) 33: Hungry as a wolf. **1958** JAHoward *Murder* (NY 1959) 7: I was hungry as a bitch wolf. **1960** JBWest *Taste* (NY) 37: I was as hungry as a bitch wolf with a half-grown litter of pups. **1961** RFoley *It's Murder* (NY DBC) 68: I'm hungry as a wolf. **1965** JMitchell *Joe Gould* (NY) 10: I was as hungry as a bitch wolf. **1968** EQueen *House* (NY) 133: I'm hungry as a wolf. EAP W256; Brunvand 154(2).

W252 The lean **Wolf** runs the faster

1958 *BHerald* 8/14 17: The lean wolf runs the faster. Cf. A lean Horse *above*.

W253 To be a **Wolf** in sheep's clothing (*varied*)

1922 JJoyce *Ulysses* (NY 1934) 332: A wolf in sheep's clothing. **1925** RAFreeman *Red*

Thumb (L) 5: A mere sheep in wolf's clothing. **1928** ABCox *Amateur* (NY) 54: If not a wolf, at any rate a fox in sheep's clothing. **1929** DFrome *Murder* (L) 42: You're a wolf in sheep's clothing. **1932** FBeeding *Take It* (B) 274: A viper in sheep's clothing . . . a peacock in wren's feathers. **1932** PMacDonald *Rope* (L) 254: Shrouding a wolf in lambskin. **1935** KSteel *Murder* (I) 18: You're a viper, a snake in sheep's clothing. **1939** JRonald *This Way Out* (P) 201: A wolf in sheep's clothing. **1940** AChristie *Patriotic* (NY) 171: He is no longer the wolf . . . No, he has put on the sheep's clothing. **1946** LAllen *Murder . . . Rough* (NY) 49: You're a wolf in sheep's eye clothing. **1955** SNGhose *Flame* (L) 167: He is a wolf in sheep's clothing. **1956** *BHerald* 6/3 54: Don't trust Wolves in Sheepskin. **1959** JA Brussel *Just* (NY) 176: He was the wolf in sheep's clothing. **1960** HLivingston *Climacticon* (NY) 164: Talk about wolves in sheep's clothing. **1961** GMSutton *Iceland* (Norman, Okla.) 84: A sort of wolf in lamb's clothing. **1963** BWAldiss *Male* (L 1966) 148: A sheep in wolf's clothing. **1968** DSkirrow *I Was* (NY) 184: Two wolves in monk's clothing. **1970** RFoley *Calculated* (NY) 75: I can see the wolf behind the sheep's clothing. **1970** JRoss *Deadest* (NY) 93: A wily wolf wearing a sheepskin jacket. **1973** EJKahn *Fraud* (NY) 216: They are wolves who top off their sheeps' clothing with clerical collars. **1975** EGundy *Naked* (NY) 161: Lester is the sheep in the clothes of the wolf. EAP W264; TW 407–8(1); Brunvand 154(1).

W254 To cry **Wolf** (*varied*)

1913 MRRinehart *Jennie Brice* (NY 1947) 373: There's no shouting "Wolf" yet. **1926** MRRinehart *Bat* (NY 1959) 57: She had cried "Wolf!" too often. **1932** CDawes *Lawless* (L) 137: Who was she to cry "wolf"? **1939** ADemarest *Murder on* (NY) 156: She had cried wolf so often. **1941** TChanslor *Our Second* (NY) 299: I'd been crying "Wolf!" and you'd never trust me again. **1947** JDCarr *Sleeping* (NY) 244: She had cried "Wolf!" too often. **1954** HRAngeli *Pre-Raphaelite* (L) 105: He had cried wolf too often. **1957** *Time* 5/13 94: The crape-

hangers are crying wolf in the marketplace. **1958** HWaugh *The Girl Who Cried Wolf* (NY). **1960** PJFarmer *Stranger* (NY) 40: Don't cry "wolf." **1967** TWells *Dead by* (NY) 15: [She] wasn't crying wolf this time. She's been killed. **1970** RCowper *Twilight* (NY) 96: The familiar cry of "Wolf! Wolf!" **1976** EXFerrars *Cup* (NY) 13: You're crying "wolf." EAP W259.

W255 To eat like a **Wolf**

1913 MRRinehart *Jennie Brice* (NY 1947) 403: He ate like a wolf. **1924** AOFriel *Mountains* (NY) 382: The . . . men ate like wolves. **1957** BHitchens *End* (NY) 40: He ate like a wolf. EAP W260.

W256 To hold a **Wolf** by the ears

1932 JCollier *Full Circle* (NY) 262: Holding it, as one holds a wolf by the ears. **1960** JLindsay *Writing* (L) 1: It's like holding a wolf by the ears. EAP W261. Cf. Tiger *above*.

W257 To keep the **Wolf** from the door (*varied*)

1915 PGWodehouse *Something Fresh* (L 1935) 78: The wolf was glued to the door like a postage stamp. **1917** JCLincoln *Extricating* (NY) 225: Keep the wolf from the door. **1917** GRSims *My Life* (L) 190: The wolf was at the door. **1931** MAllingham *Gyrth* (NY) 97: To keep the wolf from the door. **1932** MStDennis *Death Kiss* (NY) 153: There's no wolf at the door. **1933** HHolt *Gallows* (L) 179: Enough money . . . to keep the wolf at bay. **1937** DAllan *Brandon* (L) 26: That'll bring you enough to keep the wolf away. **1941** HAshbrook *Purple Onion* (NY) 147: She . . . shooed the wolf from the door. **1948** CBush *Curious* (NY) 109: I'm keeping the wolf from the door. **1950** ECBentley *Chill* (NY) 155: We can keep the wolf from the door, as you say. **1957** *Time* 4/29 72: One way to keep the wolf from the door is to act like one. **1957** RStandish *Prince* (L) 107: The wolf was not actually snapping at the door. **1957** PGWodehouse *Over* (L) 18: The wolf was not actually whining at the door. **1958** *BHerald* 6/20 20: Goes about crying wolf-at-the-door. **1958** DThorp *Only* (B) 185:

The wolf is not yet at the door, but I can hear his howls getting plainer. **1961** ESeeman *In the Arms* (NY) 201: When the proverbial wolf comes to our door. **1963** JIM Stewart *Last* (NY) 27: Kept the wolf from the family door. **1973** AGilbert *Nice* (NY) 83: Keeping a hungry wolf from the door. 141: Sniffing at the door like the famous wolf. EAP W262; TW 408(12,13); Brunvand 154(3).

W258 To throw to the **Wolves** (lions)

1935 LThayer *Dead* (NY) 129: The police are going to throw somebody to the lions. **1938** TDubois *Death Wears* (B) 69: I don't want to throw anybody to the wolves. **1940** JCLincoln *Out of the Fog* (NY) 222: Throw Harvey to the wolves. **1941** RStout *Alphabet* (NY) 266: Throwing out the baby to appease the wolves. **1953** BCarey *Their Nearest* (NY) 158: Throwing someone else to the wolves to save our skins. **1956** EX Ferrars *Kill* (NY) 170: You'd be quite glad to throw me to the wolves. **1958** RFenisong *Death* (NY) 41: I've got to throw you to the lions. **1961** LThayer *And One* (NY DBC) 89: I ought to throw him to the lions. **1962** RLockridge *First* (P) 158: Throwing the girl to the wolves. **1963** JNHarris *Weird* (NY DBC) 120: You are throwing Wes to the wolves. Cole 66: Thrown.

W259 **Wolf** should not eat wolf

1935 PMcGuire *Murder* (NY) 147: Wolf should not eat wolf. *Oxford* 353: Hard winter. Cf. Crow should not, Dog does not *above*.

W260 Find (look for) the **Woman** (*cherchez la femme*) (*varied*)

1905 FMWhite *Crimson Blind* (NY) 80: *Cherchez la femme.* **1922** JJoyce *Ulysses* (NY 1934) 165: *Cherchez la femme.* **1927** HCNewton *Crime* (NY) 92: The old proverb, "*Cherchez la femme.*" **1928** ARMartin *Cassiodore* (NY) 162: You know the maxim: *Cherchez la femme.* **1928** PThorne *Spiderweb* (P) 65: The age-old maxim of the police that back of every human entanglement you will find a woman. **1928** RAJWalling *That Dinner* (NY) 138: Look for the woman, as the Frenchmen say. **1929** A

Fredericks *Mark* (NY) 31: There's generally a woman back of these things, as the French say. **1930** CFitzsimmons *Bainbridge* (NY) 54: Another case of "find the woman." **1930** IWray *Vye* (L) 146: There is something in the French proverb "Cherchez la femme." **1931** JMWalsh *Company* (NY) 266: "*Cherchez la femme.*" "What is that?" ... "It means ... where there's a woman there's trouble." **1932** RAJWalling *Fatal* (NY) 156: You know the saw: look for the woman. **1933** CJDutton *Circle* (NY) 59: The old saying, "look for a woman," won't apply here. **1938** AWebb *Mr Pendlebury's Hat* (L) 134: When Talleyrand first coined the phrase, *Cherchez la femme* may well have sounded like an epigram. Constant repetition had made it the dreariest of platitudes. **1940** RStout *Double for Death* (L) 26: I'm not saying tritely find the woman. **1957** *New Yorker* 7/6 64: The rule of *cherchez la femme*. **1958** MKenton *Candy* (NY 1965) 180: Cherchez la tight-pussy femme, as Colette used to say. **1962** DMDisney *Find the Woman* (NY DBC). **1966** HTravers *Madame* (NY) 145: The time-honored phrase, "cherchez la femme." **1975** HDolson *Please* (P) 113: When a man dies, *cherchez la* wife. **1976** SBrett *So Much* (NY) 126: *Cherchez la femme*, that's what they always say in detective stories. Oxford *DQ* (2nd ed) 194. 32 [ADumas].

W261 New **Woman**, fresh courage (fresh cunt, fresh courage)

1941 RGDean *Murder in Mink* (NY) 12: And a new woman, as the saying goes, gave him fresh courage. Cf. *DARE* i 803: Courage.

W262 Two **Women** in one house *etc.* (*varied*)

1943 MCarpenter *Experiment* (NY) 119: Two women in one house, and all that. **1953** BCClough *Grandma* (Portland, Me.) 73: How true is the saying that no kitchen is big enough for two women to work in at the same time. **1956** SPalmer *Unhappy* (NY 1957) 24: The orientals have a proverb that no house is big enough for two women. **1959** *Portland Sunday Telegram* 6/

14 2B: Two women cannot live in one house. EAP W274.

W263 A **Woman**, a spaniel and a walnut tree *etc.* (*varied*)

1928 ACampbell *Juggernaut* (NY) 67: A woman, a spaniel, and a walnut tree—. **1930** HAdams *Golden* (L) 17: The adage about the dog, the woman, and the walnut tree. **1933** JBCarr *Death* (NY) 268: A spaniel, a woman, and a walnut tree ... the more they be beaten, the better they be. **1938** VLoder *Kill* (L) 6: He would be as much improved as a walnut tree by a good beating. **1955** LCochran *Hallelujah* (NY) 156: A woman, a dog and a walnut tree; the more you beat them, the better they be. **1956** *Punch* 5/30 659: Women will have to be whipped a little more since walnut trees are becoming so scarce. **1960** VWilliams *Walk* (NY) 41: A woman, a dog, and a pecan tree, the more you beat them, the better they be. **1970** HBlyth *Skittles* (L) 129: The ancient doggrel ... declares that "A woman, a dog, and a walnut tree, the more you beat them the better they be." TW 408–9(1); *Oxford* 758: Spaniel.

W264 A **Woman** can throw out more with a spoon *etc.* (*varied*)

1957 *BangorDN* 3/8 3: A woman can throw out more with a spoon than a man can bring in with a shovel. **1961** ESeeman *In the Arms* (NY) 58: She could throw more money out the back door with a teaspoon than her man could bring in the front door with a shovel. TW 409(7); Whiting *NC* 498(2).

W265 A **Woman** cannot keep a secret

1926 JTully *Beggars* (NY) 24: I often smile when I hear people say that a woman cannot keep a secret. **1936** ECRLorac *Death* (L) 26: We know that no woman can keep a secret, for men have told us so. Whiting W534. Cf. *Oxford* 908: Woman conceals.

W266 A **Woman** has her way

1935 AFielding *Tragedy* (L) 51: A wilful woman maun hae her way. EAP W292.

W267 A **Woman** has the last word

1913 HHMunro *When William* (L 1929) 126: The last word belongs by immemorial right to the sex which Miss Muttelford adores. **1928** HWade *Missing* (NY) 162: [A woman] accustomed to linger and have the last word—and generally the last laugh. **1930** HReilly *Thirty-first* (NY) 19: The last word—the very last—and *not* a woman's? **1930** HMSmith *Inspector Frost in the City* (NY) 122: It is the privilege of woman to have the last word. **1941** MTYates *Midway* (NY) 23: I got in my woman's last word. **1957** MColes *Death* (NY) 146: But the ladies, you know, have the last word. **1961** ESherry *Call* (NY DBC) 120: The Prosecutor, like the proverbial woman, had the last word. **1965** AGilbert *Voice* (NY) 189: The lady always gets the last word. EAP W291.

W268 A **Woman** may change her mind (*varied*)

1912 ERBurroughs *Princess of Mars* (NY) 125: The prerogative of woman to change her mind. **1917** GRSims *My Life* (L) 306: The lady exercised the privilege of her sex and changed her mind. **1929** HFootner *Self-Made* (NY) 265: I [a woman] exercised the privilege of changing my mind. **1930** LMeynell *Mystery* (P) 67: You novelists tell us that ladies have the privilege of changing their minds. **1933** QPatrick *S.S.Murder* (NY) 23: It's a woman's privilege to change her mind and her drinks. **1937** GGoodchild *Having No* (L) 14: I've changed my mind—a woman's prerogative, as they say in the classics. **1938** WNMacartney *Fifty Years* (NY) 303: I exercise the privilege accorded women and doctors—I changed my mind. **1942** FGruber *Buffalo Box* (NY) 137: I've exercised a woman's prerogative. I've changed my mind. **1967** ESGardner *Queenly* (NY) 101: A woman has a right to change her mind. **1969** LPDavies *Stranger* (NY) 39: A woman's privilege is to change her mind. TW 410(20).

W269 The **Woman** pays

1930 GDHCole *Berkshire* (NY) 179: There's a tag which says the woman pays. **1936** SWilliams *Aconite* (NY) 143: The good old saw . . . "The woman pays." **1937** EGreenwood *Under the Fig* (NY) 235: The woman always pays. **1959** LColeman *Sam* (NY) 59: It's not always the woman who pays.

W270   A **Woman's** place is in the home

1936 RAJWalling *Dirty Face* (L) 108: Woman's place is in the home. **1941** MTYates *Midway* (NY) 16: I wish woman's place weren't the home. **1953** RBloomfield *Stranger* (NY) 137: After all, women's place is in the home. **1959** *NYTimes Magazine* 5/10 4: The old saying that "woman's place is in the home." TW 409(9).

W271   A **Woman's** wit is a help

1940 HFootner *Murderer's* (NY) 215: They say sometimes a woman's wit is a help. EAP W270; Whiting W536; *Oxford* 903–4, 909.

W272   **Women** are kittle (queer) cattle (*varied*)

1927 GDilnot *Lazy* (B) 101: Women are queer cattle. **1930** JSFletcher *Heaven-sent* (NY) 109: Women were queer cattle to deal with. **1934** RAFreeman *For the Defense* (NY) 162: Women . . . are kittle cattle. **1934** VLoder *Murder* (L) 10: Kittle cattle, some of 'em [*hard to get along with*]. **1937** ERPunshon *Mystery* (NY) 169: Dukes are kittle cattle. **1938** CWells *Missing* (P) 32: Women are kittle cattle. **1946** HCBailey *Life Sentence* (NY) 55: Girls are kittle cattle. **1952** ECRLorac *Dog* (NY) 33: Married women are queer kittle-cattle. **1955** MissRead *Village* (L 1960) 43: Moffat thought . . . what kittle-cattle women were. **1963** MPHood *Sin* (NY) 137: People are kittle cattle. **1969** EBagnold *Autobiography* (B) 99: Women on the whole were kittle-cattle to him. **1971** PNapier *Sword* (NY) 4: The young . . . are kittle cattle.

W273   **Women** are weathercocks

1933 AWilliams *Death* (NY) 39: You know us women . . . uncertain weathercocks in the wind. *Oxford* 908.

W274   **Women** be forgetful *etc.*

1945 RLHine *Confessions* (L) 46: The old rhyme: "Women be forgetful, Children be

unkind, Executors are covetous and take what they can find." Tilley W700.

W275   A nine (*etc.*) days' **Wonder** (*varied*)

1910 EPhillpotts *Tales* (NY) 196: A nine days wonder. **1924** JSFletcher *King* (NY) 135: Nine days' sensations are quickly forgotten. **1924** JSFletcher *Time-Worn* (NY) 36: A nine days' wonder. 117: Curiosity . . . was lasting well over the proverbial nine days. **1925** FWCrofts *Groote* (NY) 294: A theme for animated discussion during more than the allotted nine days. **1928** ABerkeley *Silk* (NY) 37: A three days' wonder. **1930** GBaxter *Ainceworth* (NY) 239: A six days' wonder. **1930** CFitzsimmons *Bainbridge* (NY) 253: Made a three-day wonder of it. **1930** TThayer *Thirteen Men* (NY) 318: He was a nine minutes wonder. **1934** GHolt *Trafalgar* (L) 164: The wonder would scarcely last the proverbial nine days. **1936** MAllingham *Flowers* (NY) 2: A wonder may degenerate into a funny thing after the proverbial nine days. **1936** EH Fonseca *Death Blow* (NY) 219: He'll be the seven days' wonder along the waterfront. **1940** RPenny *Sweet Poison* (L) 126: The occurrence . . . provided a topic of conversation for several days . . . almost for the proverbial nine. **1945** HLawrence *Time to Die* (NY) 176: The seven-day wonder. **1947** WMoore *Greener* (NY 1961) 28: You're a ninety day wonder. **1948** EQueen *Ten Days' Wonder* (B). **1952** AWilson *Hemlock* (L) 115: Peter out as a five-day wonder. **1955** BCarey *Fatal* (NY) 51: As if it were a seven-day wonder. **1955** IWallace *Fabulous* (NY) 175: The mystery of Mary Rogers was a nine-week wonder. **1955** JTrench *Dishonoured* (NY) 52: Nine days up for that wonder, and it doesn't look like dyin', not by a long way. **1956** *Punch* 12/12 718: The Crusade subsided to a nine day's commonplace. **1957** *Punch* 9/18 311: A well-run nine-days' wonder. **1959** *TLS* 2/2 6: The nine days' wonder. **1959** JWebb *Deadly* (NY) 126: You were a ninety-day wonder. **1960** *TLS* 9/2 562: The nine days' wonder. **1960** RWilson *Thirty Day Wonder* (NY). **1964** EHuxley *Incident* (NY) 57: A three days' wonder. **1965** EQueen *Queens* (NY)

45: It was a one-day wonder. **1968** RGSherriff *No Leading* (L) 219: A deflated seven days' wonder. **1969** MGilbert *Etruscan* (L) 253: He had been a nine-day wonder and this was the tenth day. **1974** JPHennessy *Stevenson* (NY) 67: A nine days' wonder. **1977** CWatson *Fourth* (B) 12: A nine-day scandal. EAP W294; TW 410(1); Brunvand 155.

W276 **Wonders** (miracles) will never cease (*varied*)

1909 JCLincoln *Keziah* (NY) 254: Miracles 'll never cease. **1910** EPhillpotts (NY) 268: Wonders never cease. **1921** JCLincoln *Galusha* (NY) 371: Wonders 'll never cease. **1930** CBush *Dead Man* (NY) 160: The age of miracles is not yet over. **1932** AMizener *Many* (NY) 130: Wonders will never cease. **1934** CRyland *Murder* (L) 45: Miracles do happen. **1936** HWade *Bury Him* (L) 36: Wonders would never cease. **1939** FBeeding *Ten Holy* (NY) 328: Miracles happen sometimes, you know. **1940** NBlake *Malice* (L) 63: Wonders never cease. **1955** AHocking *Poison* (NY) 45: Wonders will never cease. **1955** PWentworth *Gazebo* (L 1965) 113: Oh, well, miracles happen. **1959** EMcBain *'Til Death* (L 1964) 67: Miracles will never cease. **1960** ASinclair *Project* (L) 74: Miracles . . . never cease. **1966** JGaskell *City* (NY 1968) 175: Wonders never cease. **1970** LWolfe *Journey* (NY) 93: Will wonders never cease? **1973** WMasterson *Undertaker* (NY) 79: Miracles sometimes occur. **1974** GMcDonald *Fletch* (I) 13: Will wonders never cease. EAP M187: Miracles; TW 410: Wonder(2).

W277 To knock on (touch) **Wood** (*varied*)

1925 FBeeding *Seven* (B) 101: Touch wood, Tom. The story isn't finished yet. **1933** JVTurner *Amos* (L) 28: You had better touch wood after saying that. **1939** MMGoldsmith *Detour* (L) 241: A good sign. Knock wood. **1941** GWYates *If a Body* (NY) 63: Knock on wood. **1945** MWalsh *Nine Strings* (P) 124: I touch every piece of wood I see. **1951** JCollier *Fancies* (NY) 128: Still, touching wood, let's hope it won't. **1956** GBagby *Cop* (NY) 88: I never had no accident myself, not once, knock on wood.

1961 WMasterson *Evil* (NY) 9: Vecchio looked about for wood to knock on. **1964** EHemingway *Moveable* (NY) 38: "We're always lucky," I said and like a fool I did not knock on wood. **1968** HWaugh *"30"* (NY) 7: You ought to knock on wood . . . That's the kind of talk that makes the roof fall in. **1969** JDrummond *People* (NY) 92: Who answers when you knock on wood? **1970** JLeasor *They Don't* (NY) 148: But they haven't yet, touch wood. *Oxford* 833: Touch.

W278 To saw **Wood**

1932 PATaylor *Death* (I) 294: I'd of sat tight an' sawed wood. DA Saw *v.*(3). Cf. DARE i 651: Chop wood.

W279 **Wood** warms you twice (*varied*)

1947 RDavies *Diary* (Toronto) 84: There is a saying, attributed to Lincoln, that "he who splits his own wood, warms himself twice." **1948** JRhode *Death* (NY) 67: As they say in these parts, wood's the best fuel for it warms you twice. Once while you're cutting it up, and again when you're burning it. **1966** GWBrace *Between Wind* (NY) 22: Every able-bodied man spent the good days of winter "chopping"—warming himself three times, as the old saying had it. Once cutting, once loading and hauling, once burning.

W280 Do not halloo till you are out of the **Woods** (*varied*)

1906 JCLincoln *Mr. Pratt* (NY) 297: I ought to have known better than to crow afore we was out of the woods. **1930** SFowler *King* (L) 99: We mustn't halloo till we're out of the wood. **1936** ECRLorac *Crime* (L) 18: Don't hallo till you're out of the wood. Whiting *NC* 499(1); Brunvand 155.

W281 Not to be out of the **Wood(s)** (*varied*)

1919 JSClouston *Simon* (NY) 223: We're out of that wood. **1924** JJFarjeon *Master* (NY) 124: We're not out of the wood. **1932** MThynne *Murder* (NY) 252: You're not out of the wood yet. **1937** MWGlidden *Long Island* (NY) 225: West isn't out of the woods by a long shot. **1940** SMSchley *Who'd Shoot* (NY) 199: Adams wasn't out of the woods yet by a long shot. **1952**

DGBrowne *Scalpel* (NY) 151: Martin . . . was not out of the wood yet. **1957** JCreasey *Model* (L 1961) 68: He wasn't right out of the wood yet, but at least he could see the trees at the edge. **1958** *Time* 5/26 19: But reciprocal trade is still a long way from being out of the wood. **1964** ESGardner *Daring* (NY) 210: We're probably out of the woods. **1969** SPalmer *Hildegarde* (NY) 134: As the old saying goes, you are not out of the woods yet. **1971** MUnderwood *Trout* (NY) 163: He's certainly not out of the wood. **1977** KClark *Other* (NY) xi: The old-fashioned proverbial saying "We're not out of the wood yet." EAP W302.

W282 Not to see the **Wood** (forest) for the trees (*reversed and otherwise varied*)

1921 CTorr *Small Talk Second Series* (Cambridge, Eng.) 105: Cannot see the wood for the trees. **1928** JChancellor *Dark* (NY) 149: There's so much wood that you can't see the trees. **1928** AGMacleod *Marloe* (NY) 151: The legendary gentleman who was unable to see the wood for the trees. **1930** AWynne *Room* (P) 268: Isn't that losing the forest for looking too closely at the trees? **1934** DFrome *Mr. Pinkerton Finds* (NY) 54: Inclined to overlook the trees for the wood. **1935** CBush *Chinese Song* (NY) 292: They're the trees that keep one from seeing the wood. **1940** JLBonney *Death by* (NY) 261: We saw a tree—a motive—so we ignored the forest. **1949** NMarsh *Wreath* (NY) 221: Unable to see the factual woods for the emotional trees. **1950** REGould *Yankee* (NY) 206: The curse of the old-time Yankees has always been an inability to see the trees for the woods. **1955** DParry *Sea* (L) 16: We must learn to know the wood before we can recognize the trees. **1956** *NYTimes Book Review* 10/7 32: At times we cannot see the wood for the trees. **1956** *TLS* 11/9 669: To avoid making it hard to see the wood for the trees. **1957** *BHerald* 2/10 6A: Citizens . . . who see the tree rather than the forest. 11/13 44: The problem of education is to make the pupil see the wood by means of the trees. **1957** *BangorDN* 5/9 16: One of those who can't see the forest for the trees. **1958** *NYTimes Book Review* 6/8 22: We are still in the thick of all these trees, and the shape of the wood is hard to make out. **1958** RFraser *Jupiter* (L) 165: There is danger of losing sight of the wood for the trees. **1959** *BHerald* 3/24 14: To object . . . is to let the trees obscure the wood. **1960** HHarrison *Death World* (NY) 50: You know the old business of not being able to see the forest for the trees in the way. **1962** KAmis *Spectrum(1)* (L) 64: We were too close to the forest to see the trees. **1964** RDuncan *All Men* (L) 9: We . . . can't see the trees for the wood. **1965** GMaxwell *House* (NY) 103: I was too scared of the wood to examine many of the trees. **1967** RBrett-Smith *Berlin* (NY) 173: As someone aptly remarked, one could not see the trees for the wood of the cutover Tiergarten. **1972** SCloete *Victorian* (L) 15: He can at last see the wood without being confused by the trees. **1973** EMc Bain *Hail* (NY) 158: I don't want you to lose sight of the forest for the trees. **1977** CRLarson *Academia* (NY) 7: [We] no longer see the forest for the trees. **1982** NDelbanco *Group* (NY) 58: Biographers can sometimes lose the forest for the trees. EAP W303.

W283 To go through the **Woods** and (then) pick a crooked stick

1937 CGordon *Garden* (NY) 92: You the kind'll go through the woods and pick up a crooked stick. DARE i 857: Crooked stick. Cf. To Go farther *above*.

W284 Happy is the **Wooing** that is not long doing

1930 AChristie *Mysterious* (NY) 55: The old saying . . . "Happy the wooing that's not long doing." **1957** DJEnright *Heaven* (L) 109: Blessed is the wooing, that is not long a-doing. EAP W306.

W285 All **Wool** and a yard wide (*varied*)

1900 CFPidgin *Quincy A. Sawyer* (B) 255: He's all wool and a yard wide. **1927** NMartin *Mosaic* (NY) 4: All wool and a yard wide. **1933** PMacDonald *Menace* (NY) 191: All wool and a mile wide. **1937** DFrome *Black Envelope* (NY) 312: You're all wool and a yard wide. **1941** ESGardner *Haunted Husband* (NY) 34: She's all wool . . . and her friend's a yard wide. **1949** KMKnight *Bass* (NY) 58: She's all wool and a yard wide. **1954** CIsherwood *World* (L) 128: All ghoul and a yard wide. **1956** PDeVries *Comfort* (B) 277: All wool and a yard wide. **1959** JPhilips *Killer* (NY) 49: All ham and a yard wide. **1961** GGFickling *Blood* (NY) 95: Pepper . . . is all woman and a yard wide. **1965** PDeVries *Let Me* (NY 1966) 209: All wool and a yard wide. **1968** PDeVries *Witch's* (B) 232: All wool and a yard wide. **1973** AGilbert *Nice* (NY) 42: An alibi all wool and a yard wide. Whiting *NC* 499(1); Brunvand 155(1); DARE i 50: All wool.

W286 As soft as **Wool**

1970 RPowell *Whom the Gods* (NY) 370: It will feel as soft as wool. Whiting *NC* 499(2).

W287 As white as **Wool**

1957 THWhite *Master* (L) 30: His . . . hair was nearly as white as wool. EAP W307; TW 411(1).

W288 A dyed-in-the-**Wool** this or that

1922 VBridges *Greensea* (NY) 102: A dyed in the wool happy . . . home. **1936** RCWoodthorpe *Silence* (L) 45: A dyed-in-the-wool, pigheaded Englishman. **1948** PCheyney *Dance* (NY DBC) 88: A dyed-in-the-wool damned fool. **1951** MHead *Congo* (NY) 21: A pure, unadulterated dyed-in-the-wool yard-wide son of a bitch. **1957** *Harvard Library Bulletin* 11.288: He was a dyed-in-the-wool Tory. **1957** VHHGreen *Oxford* (L) 47: A dyed-in-the-wool conservative. **1960** AMoorehead *White Nile* (NY) 58: He was a dyed-in-the-wool slave driver. **1966** MWorthington *Strange* (NY) 6: Willie . . . was a dyed-in-the-wool Republican. **1971** BWAldiss *Soldier* (L) 35: A dyed-in-the-wool Communist. TW 411–12(2).

W289 To get **Wool** off a goat

1926 LO'Flaherty *Tent* (L) 136: Ye can't get wool off a goat. TW 154: Goat(1); *Oxford* 307: Go to a goat. Cf. Feathers from a toad *above*.

W290 To go out for **Wool** and come home shorn

1928 JAFerguson *Man in the Dark* (NY) 229: You will know the story we in Scot-land tell about the woman who went out for wool and came home shorn. TW 412(6); *Oxford* 913–4.

W291 To keep one's **Wool** on (lose one's wool)

1928 CBarry *Corpse* (NY) 145: Keep your wool on! **1934** LRGribble *Riddle* (L) 34: Keep your wool on. **1935** ECRLorac *Death* (L) 221: I don't often lose my wool [*get angry*]. **1958** ECRLorac *People* (NY) 107: It's no use losing your wool with me [*getting angry*]. Partridge 964: Keep. Cf. To keep one's Hair, Shirt, Wig *above*.

W292 To pull **Wool** over someone's eyes (*varied*)

1911 CKSteele *Mansion* (NY) 223: She pulled the wool over the doctor's eyes. **1919** JBCabell *Jurgen* (NY 1922) 355: There is no pulling wool over my eyes any longer. **1927** CBStilson *Seven* (NY) 122: I'm getting the wool out of my eyes. **1928** EO'Neill *Strange* (NY) 70: Trying to pull the wool over my eyes. **1936** LRGribble *Malverne* (L) 98: She hasn't been pulling any wool over my eyes. **1936** VStarrett *Midnight* (NY) 131: Let her pull the wool over your eyes. **1940** CDickson *And So to Murder* (NY) 263: To pull the wool over the old man's eyes. **1940** BHalliday *Uncomplaining* (NY) 130: He pulled the wool over your eyes. **1952** PPiper *Corpse* (NY) 60: Pull the wool over the eyes of the audience. **1956** DWheatley *Ka* (L) 97: No pulling of wool over the eyes of experts. **1958** DGoodman *Crime* (L) 36: She knew how to pull the wool over his eyes. **1964** FSwann *Brass* (NY) 41: I've finally pulled the wool from over my own eyes. **1968** MMackay *Violent* (NY) 62: Pull the wool over Mrs. Stevenson's gentle eyes. **1976** JJMarric *Gideon's Drive* (NY) 100: They're pulling the wool over our eyes. TW 412(5); Brunvand 155(3); *Oxford* 914.

W293 Fine (*etc.*) **Words** butter no parsnips (*varied*)

1917 JBCabell *Letters* ed PColum (NY 1962) 14: Our pecuniary parsnips remain unbuttered. **1931** RScarlett *Cat's* (NY) 59: Fine words butter no parsnips. **1932** JC

Lenehan *Mansfield* (L) 205: Kind words are better than—than buttered parsnips. **1935** DOgburn *Will* (NY) 26: That doesn't butter any parsnips. **1937** CBClason *Blind* (NY) 33: You're always sorry, but that doesn't butter any parsnips. **1939** MStuart *Dead Men* (L) 271: Meaning that fine words—and headlines—butter no parsnips. **1957** JCheever *Wapshot* (NY) 250: Pancras . . . began to butter Coverly's parsnips [*flatter him*]. **1958** MHastings *Cork* (NY) 73: It won't butter any parsnips hanging about here. **1961** MErskine *Woman* (NY) 88: Soft words butter no parsnips. **1965** HPearson *By Himself* (L) 82: One person's butter ain't another person's parsnip. **1973** THeald *Unbecoming* (NY) 55: Education on its own never buttered any parsnips. **1974** LKronenberger *Wilkes* (NY) 23: While buttering his own parsnips. TW 413(6); *Oxford* 241: Fair.

W294   From the **Word** "go"

1930 BFlynn *Creeping* (L) 152: Right from the word "Go." **1936** LRobinson *General* (NY) 143: It was doomed to failure from the word "go." **1940** NBlake *Malice* (L) 132: It had been queer from the word go. **1943** GHCoxe *Murder for Two* (NY) 99: She's out for Rosalind from the word go. **1953** JMFox *Code* (B) 112: It was a freak deal from the word go. **1976** SWoods *My Life* (NY) 91: From the word go. **1981** JBHilton *Playground* (NY) 102: He knew from the word go that it wasn't going to make an atom of difference. Brunvand 155(2).

W295   Hard **Words** break no bones (*varied*)

1929 EWallace *Dark Eyes* (NY) 26: "Hard words never killed anybody," he said sententiously. **1933** EPhillpotts *Captain's* (NY) 179: Hard words break no bones. **1935** RGarnett *Starr* (L) 63: Hard words break no bones: an old saying, but a true one. **1935** ECRLorac *Organ* (L) 101: Hard words cut no bones. **1938** ECVivian *Rainbow* (L) 18: Ugly threats . . . which break no bones. **1950** CEVulliamy *Henry* (L) 74: Hard words break no bones. **1959** JWelcome *Run* (NY) 80: Hard words break no

bones. EAP W312. Cf. Looks, Sticks and stones, Talking *above*.

W296   A kind **Word** is never lost

1965 FHerbert *Dune* (NY) 22: A kind act is never lost. TW 412(1).

W297   Many a true **Word** is spoken in jest (*varied*)

1922 JJoyce *Ulysses* (NY 1934) 332: There's many a true word spoken in jest; 428, 744. **1927** JHawk *Serpent* (NY) 256: Many a truth is spoken in jest. **1930** ABCox *Vane* (L) 130: There's many an untrue word spoken in jest. **1930** KCStrahan *Death* (NY) 206: Many a true word spoken in jest. **1933** LRobinson *Manuscript* (L) 87: There's many a true word spoken in execrable verse. **1937** LFord *Simple Way* (NY) 149: A fine old adage . . . "Many's the true word spoke in jest." **1938** MSaltmarsh *Clouded* (NY) 162: There's many a true word spoken in verse. **1952** HHunter *Bengal* (NY) 314: Many a true word spoken in jest, as they say. **1960** HLivingston *Climacticon* (NY) 49: Many a true word is said in jest. **1964** DCecil *Max* (L) 136: Some of Max's true words spoken in jest. **1968** CHaldane *Queen* (I) 90: Never were truer words spoken in jest. EAP W315.

W298   One's **Word** is his bond (*varied*)

1916 MGibbon *Inglorious* (L 1968) 130: An Englishman's word is his bond. **1931** EPhillpotts *Found* (L) 135: My word is my bond. **1935** WIrwin *Julius* (NY) 254: My word's as good as my bond. **1939** CBClason *Dragon's* (NY) 253: Your word is as good as your bond. **1949** MGEberhart *House* (NY DBC) 171: His word was as good as a bond. **1953** PChadburn *Treble* (L) 60: A gentleman's word was as good as his oath. **1957** *Punch* 8/7 165: An Englishman's bond is as good as his word. **1957** YBridges *How Charles* (L) 102: An Englishman's word was proverbially as good as his bond. **1967** SForbes *Encounter* (NY) 130: His word was his bond. **1968** PMoyes *Death* (NY) 193: A gentleman's word is his bond. **1968** RGSherriff *No Leading* (L) 165: A man's word is his bond. **1974** AMorice *Kill-*

ing (NY) 137: A man whose word was his bond. EAP W319.

W299   There is no such **Word** as "can't" (in the dictionary)

1936 ESdePuy *Long Knife* (NY) 164: There isn't any such word as "can't." **1938** PMacDonald *Warrant* (NY 1957) 59: It's time somebody's old governers joined this party to tell us there's no such word as "can't" in the dictionary. **1960** DHolman-Hunt *My Grandmothers* (L) 18: There are no such words as "can't" and "don't."

W300   To be as good as one's **Word**

1900 CFPidgin *Quincy A. Sawyer* (B) 486: She was as good as her word. **1924** FWCrofts *Cask* (NY 1936) 277: As good as his word. **1933** GBegbie *Sudden* (L) 49: [He] was as good as his word. **1937** BThomson *Milliner's* (L) 28: The foreman had been as good as his word. **1941** MVHaberden *Lobster Pick* (L) 142: [He] was as good as his word. **1956** ACLewis *Jenny* (NY) 203: Gould was as good as his word. **1958** GHCoxe *Impetuous* (NY) 213: Elinor was as good as her word. **1960** GSAlbee *By the Sea* (NY) 116: He was as good as his word. **1964** LLafore *Devil's* (NY) 41: He was almost as good as his word. **1970** LKronenberger *No Whippings* (B) 255: He was, as they used to say in the Alger books, as good as his word. **1974** EPHoyt *Horatio's* (Radnor, Penn.) 27: Adam was as good as his word. EAP W322.

W301   To eat one's **Words**

1929 STruss *Living* (NY) 119: Rosenblum tried to eat his words. **1932** FWCrofts *Sudden* (NY) 229: And each time to eat our words! **1936** WMartyn *House* (L) 65: To have to eat his words. **1940** KSteel *Dead of Night* (B) 167: I'd rather eat my own words myself than have 'em fed to me. **1949** JReach *Late* (NY) 66: I'll make them eat their words. **1952** HPearson *Whistler* (NY) 212: The critics had to eat their words. **1960** NWilliams *Knaves* (NY) 137: Making the two witnesses eat their words. **1968** KMartin *Editor* (L) 214: The *Observer* had

to eat its words. **1976** CHigham *CLaughton* (NY) 52: He was forced to eat his words. EAP W323.

W302   To get a **Word** in edgeways (edgewise)

1908 JCLincoln *Cy Whittaker* (NY) 79: Nobody else . . . could get a word in edgeways. **1929** JMWalsh *Mystery* (L) 158: I could hardly get a word in edgeways. **1930** RScarlett *Beacon Hill* (NY) 182: He wouldn't let James get a word in edgewise. **1931** DLSayers *Suspicious* (NY) 393: The moment he could get a word in edgewise. **1932** RThorndike *Devil* (NY) 47: The fellow never lets you get a word in edgewise. **1938** LBarret *Though Young* (NY) 99: Um got a word in edgewise. **1940** ABCunningham *Murder at* (NY) 169: You can't get a word in edgeways. **1944** LAGStrong *All Fall* (NY) 5: You wouldn't get a word in edgeways. **1946** RFinnegan *Lying* (NY) 14: If you'll let me get a word in edgewise. **1955** PDennis *Auntie* (NY) 256: I couldn't have gotten a word in edgewise. **1955** CJay *Yellow* (NY) 35: I cannot get a small little word in edgeways. **1956** *Punch* 11/14 580: Let me get a word in edgeways. **1958** *BHerald* 4/20 sec. I 4: I can't get a word in edgewise. **1960** FWarburg *Occupation* (B) 246: Impossible to get a word in edgeways. **1962** PDennis *Genius* (NY) 111: You can't get a word in edgewise. **1964** RDuncan *All Men* (L) 160: When I could get a word in edgeways. **1966** EPangborn *Judgment* (NY) 145: It was still ten minutes before he could get three consecutive words in by the thin edge. **1967** AJToynbee *Acquaintances* (L) 257: I could not get a word in edgewise. **1970** RCrawshay-Williams *Russell* (L) 37: Unable to get a word in edgeways. **1972** JMcClure *Caterpillar* (NY) 201: The boy failed to get a word in edgewise. EAP W318; Brunvand 155(3).

W303   To say two **Words** for oneself and one for another

1930 WWoodrow *Moonhill* (NY) 122: She was saying one word for Miss Mae and two for herself. EAP W325.

W304 To take the **Words** out of one's mouth

1922 JJoyce *Ulysses* (NY 1934) 627: You just took the words out of my mouth. **1939** JDonavan *Coloured Wind* (L) 63: You take the words out of my own mouth. Cole 65.

W305 A **Word** and a blow (*varied*)

1922 JJoyce *Ulysses* (NY 1934) 388: He was indeed but a word and a blow on any the least colour. **1929** BDuff *Central* (NY) 159: His method was the time-honoured word-and-blow affair, with the blow invariably coming first. **1931** DLSayers *Suspicious* (NY) 70: A harum-scarum, word-and-a-blow fellow. **1959** AHocking *Victim* (NY) 147: A word-and-a-blow type of behavior. **1960** JSymons *Progress* (L) 42: Quick's the word and sharp's the action, that's my motto. EAP W327.

W306 **Word(s)** and (or) deed(s) (*varied*)

1924 TMundy *Om* (NY) 115: A man's word and his deed should be one. **1929** JCameron *Seven* (L) 155: The time for words had passed and for deeds had come. **1934** HWade *Constable* (L) 77: It would be by deeds and not by words. **1965** KAmis *SpectrumIV* (L) 40: They abandoned words for deeds. **1965** JLindsay *Thunder* (L) 57: Words need deeds and deeds need words. **1968** LPDavies *Grave* (NY) 100: I've got to rely on words, not actions. **1969** RPearsall *Worm* (NY) 188: Words were more important than deeds. EAP W333; Whiting W642; Tilley W820. Cf. Deeds, Talk, Talker *above*.

W307 A **Word** to the wise (is sufficient) (*varied*)

1923 DFox *Doom* (NY) 80: A word to the wise. **1924** JSFletcher *Mazaroff* (NY) 7: *Verbum sapienti.* **1927** WDSteele *Man Who* (NY) 224: A word to the wise is sufficient. **1932** TThayer *Three Sheet* (NY) 170: A word to the wise. **1937** IIFootner *Dark Ships* (L) 134: They say a word to the wise is sufficient. **1941** PStrong *Other Worlds* (NY) 103: A word to the wise, as it were. **1950** IAsimov *Pebble* (NY) 37: A word to the wise. **1953** JRMacDonald *Meet* (NY) 202: I

dropped a word to the wise. **1956** *BangorDN* 7/16 4: A word to the wise should be enough. **1956** *New Yorker* 8/11 19: A word to the wise is not sufficient if it doesn't make any sense. **1959** *BangorDN* 8/24 9: A word to the wise is sufficient. **1962** ALOwen *Famous* (Oxford) 72: A word to the wise no longer carried conviction. **1967** MDolbier *Benjy* (NY) 118: A word to the wise. **1974** GPaley *Enormous* (NY) 180: A word to the wise. EAP W329; TW 412(3); Brunvand 155(1).

W308 A **Word** too much cannot be recalled

1932 JJFarjeon *Trunk-Call* (NY) 103: The word too much cannot be recalled. EAP W328; Whiting W605; *Oxford* 914, 916.

W309 All **Work** and no play *etc.* (*varied*)

1926 EDBiggers *Chinese* (NY) 258: Too many puzzles make Jack a dull boy. **1928** ACBrown *Dr. Glazebrook* (NY) 32: A case of all work and no play. **1929** JRhode *Murder* (NY) 250: All work and no play—you know the proverb. **1932** PMcGuire *Three* (NY) 227: All work and no play make Jill a dull—. **1940** DBurnham *Last Act* (NY) 154: All work and no play . . . makes Jack. **1952** MInnes *One-Man* (NY) 144: All work and no play makes Jack a dull boy. **1956** *BangorDN* 6/13 24: You know the old saw—"All work and no play"—"Yeah—and all play and no work, and we both wind up in the bread line." **1957** *TLS* 5/17 301: The maxim that "All work and no play make Jack a dull boy." **1958** *BHerald* 3/23 16IV: All work and no play . . . makes Jack. At least we hope it will. **1959** JCreasy *Hit* (NY DBC) 123: All work and no play makes Jack a dull boy. **1961** HCromwell *Dirty* (LA) 226: After all, I thought, all work and no play makes Helen a dull lay. **1962** DGillon *Unsleep* (NY) 16: All play and no work makes Jack a dull jerk. **1962** ESherry *Girl* (NY DBC) 8: All play and no work makes Jack a drug on the market. **1964** BWAldiss *Greybeard* (L) 136: All play and no work makes Jack a dull boy. **1964** AMStein *Blood* (NY) 159: All crime and no play makes Jack a dull goon. **1964** LWoolf *Beginning* (L) 233: One of the great truths

I learned from her [*his nurse*] was that all work and no play did irreparable harm to all humanity whom she and I recognized in a boy called Jack. **1971** JAiken *World* (NY) 159: There is an old saying of your race . . . all work and no play makes a dullard. **1971** TCatledge *My Life* (NY) 50: Our voyage had not been all work and no play. **1983** RJeffries *Deadly Petard* (NY) 27: But you know what they say? All work and no play, how the hell can you stay gay? EAP W334.

W310 Dirty **Work** at the crossroads

1914 HCBailey *Mr. Fortune's Practice* (NY) 149: Dirty work at the crossroads. **1928** EJepson *Emerald* (NY) 224: Dirty work at the cross-roads tonight. **1935** NBlake *Question* (L) 78: Dirty work at the cross-roads. **1938** RAJWalling *Grimy Glove* (NY) 30: A dirty-work-at-the-cross-roads look. **1950** SPalmer *Green* (NY) 154: There is dirty work at the crossroads. **1958** MHastings *Cork* (NY) 158: Dark deeds at the crossroads. **1964** GJenkins *River* (NY) 121: Dirty work at the crossroads. **1969** LPDavies *Stranger* (NY) 142: Dirty work at the crossroads. **1974** PGWodehouse *Cat-Nappers* (NY) 96: Dirty work at the crossroads. **1976** SWoods *My Life* (NY) 81: Dirty work at the crossroads. Partridge 223.

W311 Hard **Work** never killed (hurt) anyone (*varied*)

1936 JRhode *Death at* (NY) 12: Hard work had never killed anybody yet. **1946** MColes *Fifth Man* (NY) 49: Honest work never hurt any man. **1957** PGWodehouse *Over* (L) 168: Hard work never hurt anyone. **1958** CLBlackstone *Dewey* (L 1965) 201: Work doesn't kill anyone, so they say. **1963** RNathan *Devil* (NY) 38: Work never hurt anybody. **1968** JDHicks *My Life* (Lincoln, Neb.) 75: Hard work never killed anybody. **1970** PAlding *Guilt* (NY) 176: Hard work never killed anyone.

W312 Nice **Work** if one can get it (*varied*)

1933 VWilliams *Clock* (L) 24: As the lady said, "Nice work if you can get it." **1936** HWeiner *Crime on the Cuff* (NY) 143: Good work if you can get it. **1938** VSwain *Hollow*

Skin (NY) 245: It's nice work—if you can get paid for it. **1939** LBrock *Fourfingers* (L) Love's nice work, if you can get it. **1940** HAshbrook *Murder Comes* (NY) 240: Nice work if you can get it [*blackmail*]. **1953** AA Fair *Some Women* (NY DBC) 163: Nice business if you can get it. **1960** AGilbert *Out for* (NY 1965) 55: Nice work if you can get it. **1962** ESGardner *Blonde* (NY DBC) 15: To quote a famous phrase . . . "it's nice work if you can get it." **1963** EFerber *Kind* (NY) 184: To quote a bawdy phrase, nice work if you can get it. **1972** HPentecost *Champagne* (NY) 147: Nice work if you can get it [*blackmail*].

W313 To gum (up) the **Works**

1938 WMartyn *Marrowby* (L) 207: He might gum up the works. **1938** PATaylor *Banbury* (NY 1964) 43: Someone was gumming up the works. **1941** LThayer *Hallowe'en* (NY) 30: Be careful not to gum the works. **1959** SDean *Merchant* (NY) 29: She might gum the works. **1960** JO'Hara *Girl* (NY) 80: You know the old saying, "Don't buck the system or you're liable to gum the works." Whiting *NC* 500(2); Berrey 35.5, 254.2; Wentworth 235.

W314 To shoot the **Works**

1960 CErwin *Orderly* (NY) 13: Ready to shoot the works. Whiting *NC* 500(5).

W315 **Work** is work (and play is play)

1924 HCBailey *Mr. Fortune's Practice* (NY) 112: Work's work. **1931** WMorton *Mystery* (NY) 96: Work is work and play is play. Cf. Bradley 98: Work while you work and play while you play. Cf. Business *above*.

W316 If one does not **Work** he shall not eat (*varied*)

1970 NMonsarrat *Breaking In* (L) 446: A healthy if-you-don't-work-you-don't-eat look. **1972** JGreenway *Down* (B) 331: No bloody work, no bloody eat. EAP W341; TW 414(1).

W317 A **Workman** is as good as his tools

1947 RDavies *Diary* (Toronto) 85: A workman is as good as his tools. Cf. Whiting W653; *Oxford* 917.

W318 All the **World** and his wife (*varied*)

1925 JGBrandon *Bond* (L) 52: All the world and his wife. **1932** CAndrews *Butterfly* (NY) 5: The world and his wife came. **1937** GDilnot *Murder* (L) 26: All the world and his wife. **1938** EQueen *Four* (NY) 182: All the world and his wife and children knew. **1940** VRath *Death of a Lucky* (NY) 95: The world and his wife could tell you that. **1948** HActon *Memoirs* (L) 131: All the world and his wife. **1953** HCozens-Hardy *Glorious* (L) 55: The world and his wife. **1961** LPayne *Nose* (NY) 102: Everybody and his wife were out shopping. **1965** JSUntermeyer *Private* (NY) 71: The small crowd turned out to be the world and his wife. **1969** RVanGulik *Haunted* (NY) 143: You shouldn't rope in all the world and his wife. **1970** JBlackburn *Bury* (NY) 61: The world and his wife had turned up. **1973** KAmis *Riverside* (NY) 174: Wait till we're shot of the world and his wife. EAP W354. Cf. Everybody *above*.

W319 All the **World** loves a lover

1927 HCNewton *Crime* (NY) 138: Doubtless it is true that "all the world loves a lover." **1953** BCClough *Grandma* (Portland, Me.) 195: All the world loves a lover. **1966** HBlyth *Pocket* (L) 112: All the world loves a lover. Oxford *DQ* 200.24 [*RWEmerson*]; Bartlett 606b.

W320 As sure as the **World**

1933 WMarsh *Company K* (NY) 77: He'll shoot me sure as the world. **1939** IJones *Hungry Corpse* (NY) 211: You'll kill me as sure as the world. TW 414(2); Brunvand 156(1).

W321 At (to) the **World's** end

1944 RAJWalling *Corpse Without* (NY) 91: It was at the end of the world. **1948** JTey *Franchise* (NY 1955) 34: Follow you to the world's end. EAP W353.

W322 It's a funny (half-arsed) **World** (*varied*)

1933 FDGrierson *Mystery* (L) 92: It's a funny world. **1934** ABinns *Lightship* (NY) 321: What a half-arsed world! Cf. next entry.

W323 It's a mad **World** (my masters)

1944 LAGStrong *All Fall* (NY) 175: It's a mad world we live in. **1960** AWUpfield *Mystery* (L) 175: Yes, Jack, it's a mad world. **1968** MAllingham *Cargo* (NY) 181: A mad world, my masters. *Oxford* 498: Mad.

W324 It's a small **World** (*varied*)

1905 MLPeabody *To Be Young* (B 1967) 310: The world is small. **1919** LMerrick *Chair* (L) 105: The world is small. **1921** JSFletcher *Orange-Yellow* (NY) 186: What a small world this is, after all. **1927** JSFletcher *Lynne* (L) 42: [He] reflected . . . on the extreme smallness of the world. **1932** VWilliams *Mystery* (B) 174: It's a small world, as the saying goes. **1935** BGraeme *Disappearance* (L) 226: If I wished to be trite I should say, the world is a small place. **1938** NMarsh *Death* (NY) 247: Everybody exclaims tiresomely at the smallness of the world. **1946** MGEberhart *Five Passengers* (NY) 64: The good old business of a it's a small world doesn't seem to fit in this case. **1947** AGilbert *Death in* (L) 40: There's a saying about it's being a small world. **1953** JTrench *Docken* (L 1960) 64: It's a small world, I always say. **1958** *BHerald* 3/1 20: To say that the world is small nowadays is trite. **1958** JSymons *Pipe* (NY) 125: It's a small world, as they say. **1959** *BangorDN* 9/14 22: Whoever said "It's a small world" sure had a point. **1961** JBPriestley *Thirty-first* (L) 47: It just shows what a damned small world we live in. **1965** SGray *Simple* (L) 128: That cliché about it's being a small world. **1968** JRoffman *Grave* (NY) 53: Pardon me if I remark that the world is a very small place. **1973** EXFerrars *The Small World of Murder* (NY). **1975** PMoyes *Black* (NY) 141: It's a small world, isn't it? Whiting *NC* 501(7); *Oxford* 918: Little.

W325 It's a wicked **World**

1931 AChristie *Murder* (NY) 74: It's a wicked world. **1932** RAJWalling *Fatal* (NY) 193: It's a wicked world. **1936** VStarrett *Midnight* (NY) 214: It's a wicked world. **1956** AChristie *Dead Man's* (L) 59: It's a very wicked world. **1969** AGilbert *Mr. Crook* (NY DBC) 132: It's a wicked world. EAP W346.

W326   To be quite out of this **World**

1925 JSFletcher *False* (NY) 14: Villages that are quite out of the world. **1956** A Christie *Dead Man's* (L) 57: Quite, as the saying goes, out of this world. **1960** MColes *Concrete* (NY) 21: Quite out of this world, as they say. EAP W347.

W327   To have the **World** (bull) by the tail *etc.* (*varied*)

1933 DHoldridge *Pindorama* (NY) 200: He had the world by the tail. **1937** SPalmer *No Flowers* (L) 63: It looks like I got the world by the tail with a downhill drag. **1941** ELFetta *Dressed* (NY) 158: She had the world too much by the tail. **1951** MHead *Congo* (NY) 122: She thought she had her own mean little world by the tail. **1954** EMarriner *Kennebec* (Waterville, Me.) 299: He had the world by the horns on a downhill haul. **1956** JHoward *Blow* (Toronto) 73: He's got the bull by the tail on a downhill pull. **1957** ESGardner *Screaming* (NY) 146: He'd have the world by the tail on a downhill pull. **1959** DMDisney *No Next* (NY) 161: He'd have the world by the tail. **1959** FPohl *Tomorrow* (NY) 16: We had the world by the tail. **1963** RAHeinlein *Glory* (NY) 12: They had the world by the tail. **1967** ESGardner *Queenly* (NY) 87: She had the world by the tail on a downhill pull. **1969** JGould *Jonesport* (NY) 57: We have the world by the tail on a downhill cant. Whiting *NC* 501(4). Cf. EAP W349.

W328   To set the **World** (town) on fire

1925 IOstrander *Neglected* (NY) 39: Set the world on fire. **1932** WMartyn *Trent* (NY) 6: I didn't set the world on fire. **1936** SWilliams *Aconite* (NY) 27: He never would have set the world on fire. **1938** JDonovan *Beckoning Dead* (L) 18: He doesn't seem to have set the town on fire. **1957** AWilson *Bit* (L) 161: He'll never set the world on fire. **1958** FLockridge *Long* (P) 99: The one who was going to set the world on fire. **1960** MGEberhart *Jury* (NY DBC) 31: Nothing to set the world on fire. **1965** JPotts *Only Good* (NY) 55: He's never going to set the world on fire. **1972** FFarmer *Will There* (NY) 49: You're not setting the world on fire. **1972** BLillie *Every* (NY) 178: [Not]

anything to set the world on fire. EAP W350. Cf. River, Thames *above*.

W329   To take the **World** as one finds it

1932 PMcGuire *Three* (NY) 217: I was always one what took the world as I found it. **1937** HWade *High Sheriff* (L) 57: One had to take the world as one found it. EAP W352.

W330   What's all the **World** to a man when his wife's a widow (*varied*)

1961 RKirk *Old House* (NY DBC) 62: "What's all the world to a man," the Irish say, "when his wife's a widdy?" **1976** CDexter *Last Seen* (NY) 22: A man is little use when his wife's a widow [*Scottish proverb*].

W331   The **World** is one's oyster

1929 CBush *Perfect* (NY) 3: The world was thenceforth their oyster. **1937** RAJWalling *Bury Him* (L) 57: The world was our oyster. **1940** LMacNeice *Strings* (L 1965) 173: The world is his oyster. **1957** *Punch* 7/31 134: An avuncular schoolmaster to whom the world is his oyster. **1958** RKing *Malice* (NY) 80: The world is my oyster. **1959** RMacdonald *Galton* (NY) 139: A world-is-my-oyster grin. **1967** ESGardner *Queenly* (NY) 17: The world was her oyster. **1972** SCloete *Victorian* (L) 178: The world was my oyster. Shakespeare *Merry Wives* II ii.

W332   The **World** owes one a living

1946 PQuentin *Puzzle for Fools* (NY) 158: The world owed me a living. **1952** PLoraine *Dublin* (L) 142: The world . . . had always owed Stephen . . . a living. **1960** BWAldiss *Bow Down* (NY) 9: The world owed me a living. **1969** PMcGerr *For Richer* (NY) 42: The world owes me a living.

W333   The **World**, the flesh, and the devil

1933 BReynolds *Very Private* (NY) 13: A bit too much of the world, the flesh, and the devil. **1964** CRSumner *Withdraw* (NY) 61: The ways of the world, not to mention the flesh and the devil. *Oxford* 919.

W334   The **World** with a fence around it (*varied*)

1931 JTully *Blood* (NY) 53: All the world I'd give, with a silver fence around it. **1952**

KMKnight *False* (NY) 178: You promised Christy the world with a diamond fence around it. Whiting *NC* 501(3). Cf. The Moon with a little *above*.

W335 As naked as a (fish-) **Worm**

1933 GYoung *Devil's* (NY) 7: Stripped Gregg naked as a fish-worm. **1954** T Howard *Blood* (NY) 225: As naked as worms. **1958** MRenault *King* (NY 1960) 92: A babe as naked as a worm. *Oxford* 553: Naked.

W336 Even a **Worm** will turn (*very varied*)

1926 AFielding *Footsteps* (L) 149: The worm turned. **1927** NMartin *Mosaic* (NY) 108: The turning of the worm. **1930** AB Cox *Vane* (L) 206: Even a mouse will turn, you know. **1930** ABCox *Second* (NY) 176: The tapeworm turning with a vengeance. **1930** VStarrett *Blue Door* (NY) 294: It's a long worm, you know, that gathers no moss, and he who laughs last is worth two in the bush. **1934** AThorne *Delay* (NY) 170: Would the worm turn and bite the hand that fed it? **1935** NBlake *Question* (L) 119: I wonder does a worm turn, in actual fact. **1938** HHolt *Wanted* (L) 100: It's a long worm that has no turning. **1939** CSaxby *Death Cuts* (NY) 224: It's a long worm that has no turning. **1941** KMKnight *Exit a Star* (NY) 268: Even the worm will turn—to coin a phrase. **1947** FCrane *Murder on* (NY) 237: The worm finally turned. **1950** SPalmer *Monkey* (NY) 83: It's a long worm . . . that has no turning. **1953** JSanford *Land* (NY) 144: Up to where the worm turned and ate the bird. **1953** AWUpfield *Murder Must* (NY) 57: Could be that the worm will turn and bump her off. **1959** MErskine *Graveyard* (NY) 78: There must always be . . . something rather disconcerting in the turning of the worm. **1959** AGilbert *Prelude* (NY DBC) 143: Fred turns. The proverbial worm. **1970** JPorter *Dover Strikes* (NY) 155: MacGregor wasn't exactly a worm but even he had his turning point. **1975** JPearson *Edward* (NY) 112: This most accommodating of human worms actually turned. **1981** AAndrews *Pig* (NY) 98: Worms turn. EAP W366; TW 414–5(2).

W337 To be **Worm's** meat

1941 RAldington *Life* (NY) 271: They have made worm's meat of the world. **1966** HTreece *Green* (L) 204: When this little Arthur is worm's meat and gone. EAP W365; Whiting W675.

W338 As bitter as **Wormwood**

1955 LCochran *Hallelujah* (NY) 101: [He] could be as bitter as wormwood and as hard as flint. **1959** EMarshall *Pagan* (NY) 326: More bitter than wormwood. EAP W367.

W339 To be the **Worse** for wear

1926 JArnold *Murder!* (L) 28: You looked a little the worse for wear [*sick*]. **1928** VMarkham *Death* (NY) 51: I'm rather the worse for wear [*tired and torn*]. **1932** GHeyer *Footsteps* (L) 19: The worse for wear [*drunk*]. **1936** LRGribble *Malverne* (L) 156: He was definitely the worse for wear. Liquid wear. **1940** EHealy *Mr. Sandeman* (NY) 262: You look a little the worse for wear [*slightly drunk*]. **1940** PWentworth *Rolling* (P) 115: A good deal the worse for wear [*a corpse*]. **1947** RHichens *Yesterday* (L) 336: Feeling decidedly the worse for wear [*had lost money*]. **1952** HCecil *Ways* (L) 46: A little the worse for wear [*drunk*]. **1957** LHanson *Verlaine* (NY) 336: Slightly the worse for wear [*drunk*]. **1962** MGEberhart *Enemy* (NY) 174: Something the worse for wear [*drunk*]. **1963** NMarsh *Dead* (B 1964) 85: Looking . . . the worse for wear [*hangover*]. **1970** MCollis *Journey* (L) 132: I looked much the worse for wear [*not well dressed*]. **1971** PMHubbard *Dancing* (NY) 63: I awoke a little the worse for wear [*nervous*]. **1975** NGuild *Lost* (NY) 30: He was a little the worse for wear [*drunk*]. EAP W368.

W340 Expect the **Worst**, hope for the best

1961 NBogner *In Spells* (L) 102: An old adage . . . "expect the worst, hope for the best." Cf. EAP W369; *Oxford* 250: Fear.

W341 It is ill to open an old **Wound**

1905 JBCabell *Line* (NY 1926) 206: It is ill to open an old wound. EAP W371.

W342   To go to **Wrack** and ruin

1960 EXFerrars *Fear* (NY) 19: The place has gone to wrack and ruin. NED Wrack *sb.*[1] 2b(*b*).

W343   To keep under **Wraps**

1947 FCDavis *Thursday's* (NY) 101: Something Hester was keeping under wraps. **1958** RFenisong *Death* (NY) 171: I want the . . . business kept under wraps. **1959** HNielsen *Fifth* (NY DBC) 82: We can't keep the nurse under wraps much longer. Berrey 222.3.

W344   To look like the **Wrath** of God (*varied*)

1932 VWilliams *Mystery* (B) 187: She looked like the wrath of God. **1938** NMarsh *Artists* (L 1941) 21: She behaves like the wrath of God. **1938** HWSandberg *Crazy* (NY) 51: I look like the wrath of hell. **1939** TPolsky *Curtains* (NY) 109: Looking, to coin a phrase, like the wrath of God. **1950** MLong *Louisville* (NY) 101: Looking like the wrath of God. **1951** MHead *Congo* (NY) 104: You look like the wrath of God. **1963** RLPike *Mute* (NY DBC) 117: You look like the wrath of God. **1965** DoctorX *Intern* (NY) 291: I felt like the wrath of God. **1970** PAlding *Murder* (NY) 100: Rowena, looking like the wrath of God. Taylor *Prov. Comp.* 89; Cole 56.

W345   To be put through a (the) **Wringer**

1931 RScarlett *Cat's* (NY) 53: You look as if someone had put you through a wringer. **1947** VSiller *Curtain* (NY) 206: They both looked . . . as though they had been through the wringer. **1955** JPotts *Death* (NY) 139: Looked like she'd been put through a wringer. **1959** HStone *Man Who* (NY) 22: He had been through the wringer. Wentworth 589.

W346   The (hand) **Writing** on the wall

1922 DFox *Ethel* (NY) 156: The writing on the wall. **1928** HAsbury *Gangs* (NY) 295: Had seen the handwriting on the wall. **1958** HCarmichael *Into* (NY) 46: She must have seen the writing on the wall. **1960** JLindsay *The Writing on the Wall* (L). **1974** MInnes *Appleby's Other* (NY) 174: Here was the writing on the wall. *Oxford* 923.

W347   Two **Wrongs** do not make a right

1922 JJoyce *Ulysses* (NY 1934) 718: As two wrongs did not make one right. **1929** CGBowers *Tragic* (NY) 318: Two wrongs cannot make a right. **1935** VWilliams *Clue* (B) 112: Two wrongs never make a right. **1949** KMKnight *Bass* (NY) 10: Two wrongs never did make a right. **1958** *BHerald* 2/16 5A: "Two wrongs don't make a right," said Vernon J. Veritas, the old truth-teller. **1961** BKnox *In at* (NY) 46: Two wrongs don't make a right. **1967** FSwinnerton *Sanctuary* (NY) 43: Two wrongs don't make a right. **1975** ARoudybush *Suddenly* (NY) 119: Two wrongs never made a right yet. EAP W373. Cf. Two Blacks *above*.

Y

Y1 A **Yankee** answers one question with another (*varied*)

1934 EBBlack *Crime* (NY) 59: The Yankee trick of answering one question with another. **1956** RILee *Happy* (B) 139: Before I ventured to answer the question, like a sound Yankee I asked *him* a question. EAP N57: New Englander. Cf. *Oxford* 405: Irishman.

Y2 To a stick out a **Yard**

1932 VLoder *Death* (L) 136: It sticks out a yard. **1933** ACLord *Edgware* (L) 140: He's got a motive sticking out a yard. **1944** RAJWalling *Corpse Without* (NY) 153: It sticks out a yard. Cf. Mile *above*.

Y3 The first hundred **Years** are the hardest (*varied*)

1928 LThomas *Raiders* (NY) 279: The first hundred years are the hardest. **1956** *NY Times Book Review* 8/26 29: The first hundred years were the hardest. **1965** A Sharp *Green Tree* (NY 1966) 60: It's the first fifty years is the worse. **1965** VPurcell *Memoirs* (L) 31: The popular cliché that the first seven years are the worst. Berrey 256.15, 299.6.

Y4 It will all be the same in a hundred **Years** (*varied*)

1938 SLeslie *Film* (L) 9: An excellent Irish proverb ... it will all be the same in a hundred of years. **1952** MHBradley *Nice* (NY) 31: It will be all the same a thousand years from now. **1954** NCunard *Grand* (L) 16: It'll be all the same in a hundred years.

1956 ABurgess *Time* (L) 8: It'll all be the same in a hundred bloody years. **1963** EFerber *Kind* (NY) 15: The hackneyed old philosophy of "It'll all be the same a hundred years from now." ... The fruity senseless old saying. EAP Y6. Cf. We shall all be dead *below*.

Y5 Seven **Years**

1922 JJoyce *Ulysses* (NY 1934) 608: My own true wife I haven't seen for seven years now. **1929** EBarker *C.I.D.* (NY) 85: A seven-year interval. **1931** AAbbot *Clergyman's Mistress* (NY) 212: In seven long years. **1931** MMagill *Murder* (P) 14: Seven years' bad luck [*mirror broken*]. **1931** RA Freeman *Dr. Thorndyke's* (NY) 21: A matter of seven years. **1939** GBarnett *There's Money* (L) 195: 'Bout seven years. **1945** MWalsh *Nine Strings* (P) 83: For at least seven years. **1956** EDillon *Death* (L) 132: After about seven years. **1972** JDMacDonald *Long* (P) 85: About seven years ago. EAP Y7; TW 416(3).

Y6 To scare (be scared) out of a **Year's** growth (*varied*)

1929 VLoder *Between* (NY) 182: Frighten him out of a year's growth. **1931** WMorton *Mystery* (NY) 173: You scared me out of a year's growth. **1938** HWSandberg *Crazy* (NY) 237: To scare me out of a year's growth. **1941** EDaly *Murders* (NY) 228: He's scared out of a year's growth. **1950** MScherf *Curious* (NY) 206: Something to scare you out of seven years' growth. **1955** KMKnight *Robineau* (NY) 144: You sure scared me out of a year's growth. **1958** HPentecost *Obituary* (NY 1960) 52: "You were scared." "Out of ten years growth." TW 416(2); Brunvand 62: Growth.

Y7 We shall all be dead in a hundred **Years**

1930 WSMaugham *Cakes* (L 1948) 153: We shall all be dead in a hundred years. **1932** JJFarjeon *Z* (NY) 200: We'll all be dead in a 'undred years. **1936** FDGrierson *Heart* (L) 198: We'll all be dead in a hundred years. **1944** FLockridge *Killing* (P) 186: He'd have been dead anyway in a hundred years. Cf. It will all be the same *above*.

Y8 Not born **Yesterday**

1912 JCLincoln *Postmaster* (NY) 152: Jacobs ... wasn't born yesterday. **1928** RHFuller *Jubilee* (NY) 154: I wasn't born yesterday. **1937** HCBeck *Murder* (NY) 168: You weren't born yesterday. **1938** NMorland *Rope* (L) 183: Think I was born yesterday? **1940** HFootner *Sinfully* (L) 219: I wasn't born yesterday. **1955** DParry *Sea* (L) 11: I wasn't born yesterday. **1959** EHNisot *Sleepless* (NY) 14: I wasn't born yesterday. **1960** JWyndham *Trouble* (NY) 157: I was not, as they say, born yesterday. **1967** GBaxt *Swing* (NY) 19: I wasn't born yesterday. **1974** MButterworth *Villa* (NY) 111: If ... you don't know why ... either you were born yesterday, or you must think I was born yesterday. **1977** JThomson *Death* (NY) 158: I wasn't born yesterday. EAP Y8; TW 417.

Y9 One is only **Young** once

1929 DAGPearson *Golden* (L) 79: We're only young once. **1930** WLewis *Apes* (NY 1932) 147: We're only young once. **1935** JTFarrell *Judgment* (NY) 85: You're only young once. **1944** ECrispin *Gilded Fly* (NY 1970) 59: One's only young once, as the dreary cliché has it. **1947** PWentworth *Wicked* (NY) 78: You're only young once. **1955** AChristie *Hickory* (NY) 35: One's only

young once. **1958** HReilly *Ding* (NY DBC) 73: You're old a long time—and young only once. **1963** LEgan *Run* (NY DBC) 45: We're only young once. **1966** AAHomans *Education* (B) 100: You were only young once and had better make hay while the sun shone. **1970** SKilpatrick *Wake* (NY) 68: You're only young once.

Y10 What is **Yours** is mine and what is mine is my own

1922 JJoyce *Ulysses* (NY 1934) 541: What's yours is mine and what's mine is my own. **1964** MColes *Knife* (NY DBC) 10: We [*English*] have a saying ... "What's yours is mine, and what's mine's my own." EAP Y11; TW 245: Mine.

Y11 **Youth** will (must) be served

1930 FDGrierson *Mysterious* (L) 27: Youth will be served. **1932** RCWoodthorpe *Public* (L) 93: Youth must be served. **1957** *Time* 7/1 19: Youth will be served, the saying goes. **1957** NBlake *End* (L) 48: Youth will be served, as they say. **1958** *BHerald* 1/13 16: This prized AP award both refutes and sustains a proverb. Youth was not served. Justice did prevail. **1971** ELathen *Longer* (NY) 194: Youth must be served. *Oxford* 929.

Y12 **Youth** will have its fling (way)

1921 APHerbert *House* (NY) 83: Youth'll 'ave its fling, they say. **1928** MChideckel *Strictly* (NY) 3: Damn the fling, if youth must have it. **1932** ERPunshon *Cottage* (B) 101: Youth must have its way. **1934** AChristie *Three Acts* (NY) 37: Youth must have its fling. **1939** FBeeding *Ten Holy* (NY) 255: Youth must have its way. *Oxford* 929: Course, swing.

Y13 **Youth** will (calls) to youth

1929 GDHCole *Poison* (NY) 46: Youth will to youth, you know. **1959** RVickers *Girl* (NY DBC) 5: Youth calls to youth. **1968** ELustgarten *Business* (NY) 135: Youth calls to youth. Whiting Y37.

Z

Z1 The **Zeal** of the convert (*varied*)

1919 AEHousman *Letters* ed HMaas (Cambridge, Mass. 1971) 167: The intemperate zeal of the convert. **1934** DGBrowne *Plan XVI* (NY) 37: The zeal of the convert. **1954** VWBrooks *Scenes* (NY) 236: I was to be accused in time of the convert's zeal. **1957** LHanson *Verlaine* (NY) 223: Like all converts he rushed to extremes. **1962** JLeCarré *Murder* (NY 1964) 77: With the fury of the convert. **1967** EHayn *Romantic* (B) 75: A convert's proverbial fervor. **1969** DClark *Nobody's* (NY) 4: Converts are more fanatical than those born to it. EAP Z1.

This book was shepherded through the early stages of the production process by John Walsh, Production Manager of Harvard University Press, who took personal responsibility for the safety of the author's shoe boxes and their irreplaceable contents and for overseeing their transformation into a printed book. The entire volume was keyboarded from handwritten entry slips by Lillian Johnson of the DEKR Corporation; throughout fifteen months of uncommonly exacting work her patience, care, and vigilance never flagged.